CREATIVE HOMEOWNER®

ULTIMATE GUIDE TO

Outdoor Projects

CREATIVE
HOMEOWNER®

Outdoor Projects

STEP-BY-STEP PROJECTS ▪ BUILDING TIPS ▪ DESIGN GUIDES

CREATIVE HOMEOWNER®, Upper Saddle River, New Jersey

COPYRIGHT © 2009

CREATIVE
HOMEOWNER®

A Division of Federal Marketing Corp.
Upper Saddle River, NJ

ULTIMATE GUIDE TO OUTDOOR PROJECTS

MANAGING EDITOR Fran Donegan
SENIOR GRAPHIC DESIGNER Glee Barre
TECHNICAL EDITOR Steve Willson
PHOTO COORDINATOR Mary Dolan
JUNIOR EDITORS Jennifer Calvert, Angela Hanson
PROOFREADER Sara Markowitz
DIGITAL IMAGING SPECIALIST Frank Dyer
INDEXER Schroeder Indexing Services
COVER DESIGN David Geer

CREATIVE HOMEOWNER

VICE PRESIDENT AND PUBLISHER Timothy O. Bakke
ART DIRECTOR David Geer
MANAGING EDITOR Fran J. Donegan
PRODUCTION COORDINATOR Sara Markowitz

Current Printing (last digit)
10 9 8 7 6 5 4 3 2 1

Ultimate Guide to Outdoor Projects, First Edition
Library of Congress Control Number: 2009921971
ISBN-10: 1-58011-465-2
ISBN-13: 978-1-58011-465-3

CREATIVE HOMEOWNER®
A Division of Federal Marketing Corp.
24 Park Way
Upper Saddle River, NJ 07458
www.creativehomeowner.com

Planet Friendly Publishing
✔ Made in the United States
✔ Printed on Recycled Paper
Text: 10%   Cover: 10%
Learn more: www.greenedition.org

GREEN EDITION

At Creative Homeowner we're committed to producing books in an earth-friendly manner and to helping our customers make greener choices.

Manufacturing books in the United States ensures compliance with strict environmental laws and eliminates the need for international freight shipping, a major contributor to global air pollution.

And printing on recycled paper helps minimize our consumption of trees, water, and fossil fuels. *Ultimate Guide to Outdoor Projects* was printed on paper made with 10% post-consumer waste. According to Environmental Defense's Paper Calculator, by using this innovative paper instead of conventional papers, we achieved the following environmental benefits:

Trees Saved: 60

Water Saved: 27,364 gallons

Solid Waste Eliminated: 1,661 pounds

Air Emissions Eliminated: 5,682 pounds

For more information on our environmental practices, please visit us online at www.creativehomeowner.com/green

safety

Although the methods in this book have been reviewed for safety, it is not possible to overstate the importance of using the safest methods you can. What follows are reminders—some do's and don'ts of work safety—to use along with your common sense.

▌ Always use caution, care, and good judgment when following the procedures described in this book.

▌ Always be sure that the electrical setup is safe, that no circuit is overloaded, and that all power tools and outlets are properly grounded. Do not use power tools in wet locations.

▌ Always read container labels on paints, solvents, and other products; provide ventilation; and observe all other warnings.

▌ Always read the manufacturer's instructions for using a tool, especially the warnings.

▌ Use hold-downs and push sticks whenever possible when working on a table saw. Avoid working short pieces if you can.

▌ Always remove the key from any drill chuck (portable or press) before starting the drill.

▌ Always pay deliberate attention to how a tool works so that you can avoid being injured.

▌ Always know the limitations of your tools. Do not try to force them to do what they were not designed to do.

▌ Always make sure that any adjustment is locked before proceeding. For example, always check the rip fence on a table saw or the bevel adjustment on a portable saw before starting to work.

▌ Always clamp small pieces to a bench or other work surface when using a power tool.

▌ Always wear the appropriate rubber gloves or work gloves when handling chemicals, moving or stacking lumber, working with concrete, or doing heavy construction.

▌ Always wear a disposable face mask when you create dust by sawing or sanding. Use a special filtering respirator when working with toxic substances and solvents.

▌ Always wear eye protection, especially when using power tools or striking metal on metal or concrete; a chip can fly off, for example, when chiseling concrete.

▌ Never work while wearing loose clothing, open cuffs, or jewelry; tie back long hair.

▌ Always be aware that there is seldom enough time for your body's reflexes to save you from injury from a power tool in a dangerous situation; everything happens too fast. Be alert!

▌ Always keep your hands away from the business ends of blades, cutters, and bits.

▌ Always hold a circular saw firmly, usually with both hands.

▌ Always use a drill with an auxiliary handle to control the torque when using large-size bits.

▌ Always check your local building codes when planning new construction. The codes are intended to protect public safety and should be observed to the letter.

▌ Never work with power tools when you are tired or under the influence of alcohol or drugs.

▌ Never cut tiny pieces of wood or pipe using a power saw. When you need a small piece, saw it from a securely clamped longer piece.

▌ Never change a saw blade or a drill or router bit unless the power cord is unplugged. Do not depend on the switch being off. You might accidentally hit it.

▌ Never work in insufficient lighting.

▌ Never work with dull tools. Have them sharpened, or learn how to sharpen them yourself.

▌ Never use a power tool on a workpiece—large or small—that is not firmly supported.

▌ Never saw a workpiece that spans a large distance between horses without close support on each side of the cut; the piece can bend, closing on and jamming the blade, causing saw kickback.

▌ When sawing, never support a workpiece from underneath with your leg or other part of your body.

▌ Never carry sharp or pointed tools, such as utility knives, awls, or chisels, in your pocket. If you want to carry any of these tools, use a special-purpose tool belt that has leather pockets and holders.

contents

introduction

Think of your yard as a blank canvas. You can add any type of amenity you wish to make the outdoor part of your home more enjoyable, more attractive, or just plain nicer—a place where you can gather with family and friends, get away from it all by yourself, or a little of both. What would it take? That's the question that launched the *Ultimate Guide to Outdoor Projects*. It contains dozens of projects to help you transform your yard. Do you want a homey picket fence or a new swimming pool? Do you want a patio for family parties or a garden shed to hold tools? Looking for a serene patch of green lawn or a showcase perennial garden? The *Ultimate Guide to Outdoor Projects* has them all—and much more.

GUIDE TO SKILL LEVEL

 Easy. Made for beginners.

Challenging. Can be done by beginners who have the patience and willingness to learn.

Difficult. Can be handled by most experienced do-it-yourselfers who have mastered basic construction skills. Consider consulting a specialist.

NAVIGATE THROUGH THE LANDSCAPE by adding a simple, winding walkway made of stone or concrete pavers.

Don't know where to start? *Ultimate Guide to Outdoor Projects* helps you by first going through the process of assessing your property. You'll learn to observe sun and wind patterns, study drainage, and evaluate the condition of your property. From there you can fix the problem areas and draw up a plan that includes everything you want in your yard.

The second section of the book, "Backyard Structures," covers the hardscape options available. Here you can delve into plans, ideas, and instructions for building a wide-range of projects. You'll find everything from wood and vinyl fences to enclose your property to rustic stone walls to contain a garden or serve as a retaining wall. Need walkways to navigate around your yard or to connect one planting bed to another? You'll find step-by-step instruction for walkways made of pavers set in mortar and as well as pavers set in sand. You will find the type of

CREATE A PATIO HIDEAWAY using pavers set in an interesting pattern, as shown above. Complement the patio with planted gardens and container-grown plants.

RETAINING WALLS can serve a number of purposes. At left, this wall provides a foundation for plantings.

walk and material that best suits your yard. Want a place from which to enjoy the great outdoors or to hold barbecues? Do you prefer a masonry, ground-level patio or an elevated, wood deck? The *Ultimate Guide to Outdoor Projects* contains both. Build a garden shed to store your lawn and landscape tools, serve as potting shed, or use as a personal workshop. The chapter contains information on selecting the best site for your new shed as well as material on building codes and zoning laws. For adding a decorative or ornamental structure to your yard, there is a chapter on trellises, arbors, and gazebos. These structures make attractive focal points, and trellises and arbors are great for climbing plants.

All of the these chapters provide you with design ideas and the know-how to do the work yourself. Each project contains a list of materials you will need. Some of the more complicated projects also include a cutting list to help you make the most of your resources. Then step-by-step photographs or illustrations take you through every phase of the project. If you are not sure if you are up to tackling a specific project, the "Skill Level Guide," described on page 8 will help you decide.

A DRAMATIC STONE WALL, above, encloses a stone patio. Note how one side of the patio is open to the landscape beyond.

ADD A VERTICAL DESIGN ELEMENT by including an arbor, right, or a trellis. This structure serves as the entrance to a garden and as a base for climbing plants.

ADD A SMALL STRUCTURE to create a landscape focal point.

In "Gardening and Landscaping," the third section of *Ultimate Guide to Outdoor Projects,* you'll find how to add plants, lawns, and trees to your property. Healthy, thriving plants are essential for a successful landscape and go hand in hand with the structures shown in the other parts of this book. In this section, you'll learn how to choose plants that are suitable for your particular landscape and how to keep them flourishing. The book is rich with plant lists. Every growing environment on the continent is represented in one form or another.

You'll also find labor-saving techniques and tips on how to maintain healthy soil, minimize weeds, and reduce the need for watering. Find out about companion planting to create pretty combinations as well as to increase the vigor of the paired plants. The emphasis here is on practical organic care so that you can keep your plants thriving with a minimum of poisons and synthetic materials.

In this section, you'll get ideas for improving the structure of any landscape by adding trees and shrubs. You'll find instructions for selecting the right tree or shrub for your yard and for planting it to ensure that it will thrive. If an existing plant has become overgrown over the years, you can bring it back into scale with careful pruning, which is also explained.

Lawns are a major feature of most gardens in North America. You'll find detailed instructions for planting, caring for, and renovating lawns, as well as suggestions for low-maintenance alternatives to turf.

Flowers, herbs, ornamental grasses, and vegetables get full attention, with plenty of beautiful pictures to inspire you to combine plants with hardscapes to create memorable outdoor living areas.

In his book, *A Love of Flowers,* H.E. Bates wrote, "A garden that is finished is dead. A garden should be in a constant state of fluid change, expansion, experiment, adventure; above all it should be an inquisitive, loving but self-critical journey on the part of its owner. It should in fact reflect its owner." Use this book to guide you on your adventure of creating a personal landscape.

DECK RAILINGS are usually a building code-mandated element, and they add design interest.

CONCRETE IS A VERSATILE MATERIAL to use on patios and entryways.

HARDINESS

Plants thrive in an environment that approximates their native habitat. For many years, plants have been labeled with their USDA (United States Department of Agriculture) hardiness zone rating, which indicates their tolerance to cold. All of the plants listed in this book are labeled with their USDA Hardiness Zone rating.

Although the USDA ratings are a good starting point, several factors can affect their accuracy. For example, city temperatures tend to be 5° to 10°F warmer than those of the surrounding countryside, raising the hardiness rating of a city garden by a full zone.

Every garden has microclimates that may be warmer or cooler or drier or more humid. The longer you garden in one location, the more familiar you will become with its microclimates. A hardiness rating of "Zones 4 or 5–7 or 8," suggests that the plant may survive the winter cold with protection in the warmer parts of Zone 4, but is safer in Zone 5. That same plant may need shade to protect it from the sun's heat in Zone 8, but it is more likely to thrive in Zone 7. A plant that is surviving, but not thriving, is under stress and therefore more vulnerable to pests and diseases. Don't be dissuaded from growing a plant at the extremes of its stated cold tolerance. But be prepared to give that plant more attention.

Average Annual Minimum Temperature

Temp. (°C)	Zone	Temp. (°F)
–45.6 & below	1	below –50
–42.8 to –45.5	2a	–45 to –50
–40.0 to –42.7	2b	–40 to –45
–37.3 to –40.0	3a	–35 to –40
–34.5 to –37.2	3b	–30 to –35
–31.7 to –34.4	4a	–25 to –30
–28.9 to –31.6	4b	–20 to –25
–26.2 to –28.8	5a	–15 to –20
–23.4 to –26.1	5b	–10 to –15
–20.6 to –23.3	6a	–5 to –10
–17.8 to –20.5	6b	0 to –5
–15.0 to –17.7	7a	5 to 0
–12.3 to –15.0	7b	10 to 5
–9.5 to –12.2	8a	15 to 10
–6.7 to –9.4	8b	20 to 15
–3.9 to –6.6	9a	25 to 20
–1.2 to –3.6	9b	30 to 25
1.6 to –1.1	10a	35 to 30
4.4 to 1.7	10b	40 to 35
4.5 & above	11	40 & above

THE USDA HARDINESS MAP divides North America into 11 zones according to average minimum winter temperatures. Hardiness zones are used to identify regions to which plants are suited based on their cold tolerance, which is what "hardiness" means. Many factors, such as elevation and moisture level, come into play when determining whether a plant is suitable for your region. Local climates may vary from what is shown on this map. Contact your local Cooperative Extension Service for recommendations for your area.

CANADA'S PLANT HARDINESS ZONE MAP outlines the different zones in Canada where various types of trees, shrubs, and flowers will most likely survive. It is based on the average climatic conditions of each area. The hardiness map is divided into nine major zones: the harshest is 0 and the mildest is 8. Relatively few plants are suited to zone 0. Subzones (e.g., 4a or 4b, 5a or 5b) are also noted in the map legend. These subzones are most familiar to Canadian gardeners. Some significant local factors, such as micro-topography, amount of shelter, and subtle local variations in snow cover, are too small to be captured on the map. Year-to-year variations in weather and gardening techniques can also have a significant impact on plant survival in any particular location.

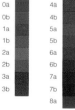

Plant Hardiness Zones

0a	4a
0b	4b
1a	5a
1b	5b
2a	6a
2b	6b
3a	7a
3b	7b
	8a

HEAT TOLERANCE

Researchers have recently discovered that plants begin to suffer cellular damage at temperatures over 86°F (30°C). The American Horticultural Society's Heat-Zone Map divides the country into 12 zones, based on the average number of days each year that a given region experiences "heat days," or temperatures over 86°F. The zones range from Zone 1 (no heat days) to Zone 12 (210 heat days).

In the near future, plants will be labeled with four numbers to indicate cold hardiness and heat tolerance. For example, a tulip may be 3–8, 8–1. If you live in USDA Zone 7 and AHS Zone 7, this label indicates that you can leave tulips outside in your garden all year.

It will take several years for most garden plants to be labeled reliably for heat tolerance. Unusual seasons with fewer or more hot days than normal will invariably affect results. The AHS Heat-Zone ratings assume that adequate water is supplied to the roots of the plant at all times. The accuracy of the coding can be substantially distorted by a lack of water, even for a brief period in the life of the plant.

Both the Cold-Hardiness Zone Map and the Heat-Zone Map are tools to help you get started on creating gardens and landscapes. After growing plants in one place for several years, you will become the expert and come to know what plants you can and cannot successfully grow.

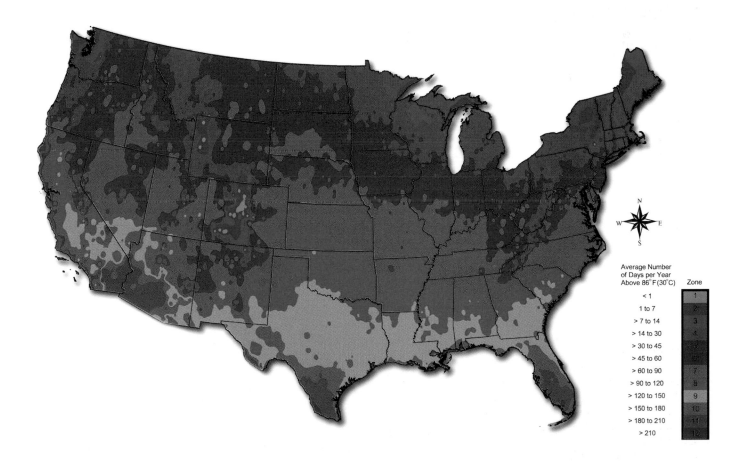

Average Number of Days per Year Above 86°F (30°C) — Zone

Average Number of Days per Year Above 86°F (30°C)	Zone
< 1	1
1 to 7	2
> 7 to 14	3
> 14 to 30	4
> 30 to 45	5
> 45 to 60	6
> 60 to 90	7
> 90 to 120	8
> 120 to 150	9
> 150 to 180	10
> 180 to 210	11
> 210	12

THE AMERICAN HORTICULTURAL SOCIETY HEAT-ZONE MAP divides the United States into 12 zones based on the average annual number of days a region's temperatures climb above 86°F (30°C), the temperature at which the cellular proteins of plants begin to experience injury. Introduced in 1998, the AHS Heat-Zone Map holds significance, especially for gardeners in southern and transitional zones. Nurseries, growers, and other plant sources will gradually begin listing both cold hardiness and heat tolerance zones for plants, including grass plants. Using the USDA Plant Hardiness map, which can help determine a plant's cold tolerance, and the AHS Heat-Zone Map, gardeners will be able to safely choose plants that tolerate their region's lowest and highest temperatures.

PART I
getting started

1 planning projects

A master plan will serve as the blueprint for your project. This plan is essentially an overhead map of your property that shows all of its features. These will include your house and other structures such as gazebos, fences, walls, hedges, swing sets, lawns, gardens, patios, terraces, decks, ponds, and pools—anything you are not going to move. Because knowing the light intensity in different locations on your property is extremely important when choosing plants, you will also want to record the patterns of sun and shade that occur throughout the day and, ideally, throughout the year. Whether you wish to landscape your property all at once or will be working on one section at a time as budget and schedule allow, it is a good idea to create this detailed master plan.

CREATE A BASE MAP

YOU CAN CREATE A BASE MAP from a copy of your plat (or property survey) prepared by surveyors, which most homeowners receive when they purchase their house. A plat typically shows several individual properties and may or may not show structures, including houses. If you don't have a plat, request one from your tax assessor's office; copies are usually available at no cost or for a nominal fee.

In addition to showing locations of property lines, a footprint of the house, and any other significant structures, the plat should show easements and the location of overhead and underground utility lines owned by the county or city. It should also have a legend indicating its drawing scale, which is typically 1:20, meaning that every inch on the paper is equivalent to 20 feet on your property. If the scale isn't shown, you can calculate it by measuring a distance on the plat in inches, and then correlating that with the same actual distance on your property.

Make Several Enlarged Copies. Property surveys and plats are usually a standard size, which is tiny considering all the information you want to record. Take your plat or property survey to a copy shop or blueprint company to get an enlargement. While you're there, you might as well have them make four or five copies, one for your site analysis, one for drawing your design, and extras for updates and changes over the years. If you can, have the blueprint company enlarge the original scale to at least 1:12. This will give you more room to draw garden features.

Even if your map shows the primary dimensions of your property, you'll need to take other measurements. This task will be easier if you use a fiberglass, nylon-clad steel, or chrome-steel measuring tape on a reel. These tapes, noted here in order from least to most expensive, come in longer lengths than the retractable type and are more suited to measuring larger spaces.

EXAMINE YOUR PROPERTY

The first step before drawing the plan is to make a site analysis of your property. This is simply an inventory of all features that relate to the current landscape. Record this information on a base map, drawn to scale. The map should show your property boundaries, as well as your house and any other structures. Even if you opt to employ a professional designer for the landscape plan, you'd be wise to record information yourself on the site analysis.

Besides all the structures on the property, the site analysis should include major trees and specimen plants, utility easements, equipment such as air-conditioner units, and the topography of the lot—significant slopes, dips, and hills. A really thorough analysis will also record any aesthetic factors, including attractive or unsightly views, and information on conditions that affect plant growth.

Most homeowners can record the necessary information in a couple of hours. However, if you are new to the property and it is already planted, you may want to record changes throughout a whole year in order to get a true sense of your property.

Kinds of Information to Gather. The following pages outline the kinds of information you should gather. Although the list is long and comprehensive, don't feel overwhelmed. A site analysis will greatly help you in

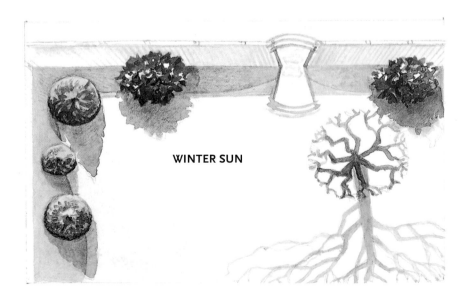

WINTER SUN

TYPICAL PLAT MAP

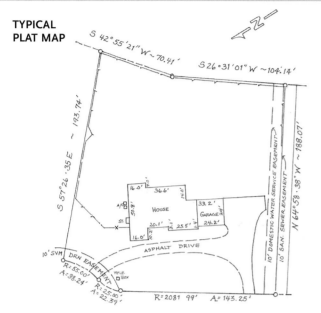

A PLAT MAP shows the precise boundaries, the measurements of the lot, and the position of the house, garage, and existing easements. Get one from the tax assessor's office.

CUSTOM BASE MAP

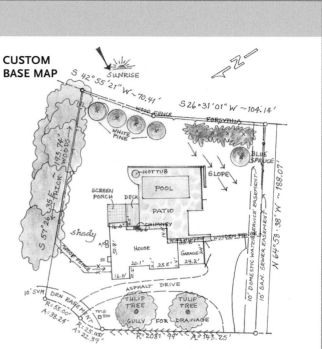

COMPLETING A BASE MAP is an important first step in landscaping. Here the owner has indicated extensive information about his property and plans.

making informed design decisions, and will save you time and effort over the long haul. Use the information here as a guide, disregarding items that do not apply to your project. Remember, though, that an accurate site analysis now can help you prevent expensive design errors later.

Place Lot Boundaries

If you're starting with an official drawing of your lot, it will accurately show property boundaries. You can then measure and write down other distances that aren't recorded on the plat. For example, you will want to know the length of the front walk, the size of an existing patio, the distance from the patio to the back of the lot, and so on. If the surveyors' pipes or markers are no longer in place, be sure you find and indicate the exact locations of property corners and edges. (You may need the help of a surveyor.) An error of even a few inches beyond your property line can lead to a dispute with the affected neighbor, especially if you build a fence or plant a hedge. If you don't have an existing plat to work from, measure the property carefully, and draw the boundaries to scale on graph paper. With your boundaries correctly drawn, you'll have a bird's-eye view of your property.

SUMMER SUN

SHADE PATTERNS change over the course of the year. In the winter, the shadows cast by deciduous trees and shrubs are longer than those cast in the summer sun—important information if you want a shady area on a patio.

IS THE LIGHT RIGHT?

WHEN YOU PLAN YOUR LANDSCAPE, consider the availability and intensity of light throughout the year. Most plants tolerate a range of light but have specific conditions in which they perform at their best. To determine optimal light conditions for particular trees, shrubs, and plants, look up the plants or ask your supplier. The following definitions will help you determine which conditions you have on your property.

- **Full Sun**—a daily minimum of six hours of direct, unobstructed sun.
- **Semisunny or partial shade**—a daily minimum of four to six hours of direct sun.
- **Light shade or dappled shade**—sunlight under tall trees and under trees with sparse foliage.
- **Shade or full shade**—no direct sun; this occurs on the north side of structures and under dense leaf canopies.
- **Dense shade**—shade so deep that no shadows are cast; this occurs between tall buildings and in woods with a dense canopy.

SHADE LOG

Date _____

Property Section _____

Hour	Full Sun	Partial Sun	Full Shade
6:00 AM			
8:00 AM			
10:00 AM			
12:00 NOON			
2:00 PM			
4:00 PM			
6:00 PM			
8:00 PM			

TO CREATE A SUN/SHADE LOG for various parts of your property, make photocopies of this chart. Then, monthly during the growing season, check off the hours of full sun.

Underground Utilities

Again, you need to know the location of underground utilities such as electric cables, water pipes, and sewer pipes or a septic system in case you plan to dig anywhere near them. In addition, you need to know about any easements on your land that are subject to public use. If this information isn't provided on your plat, call your utility company and municipal jurisdiction to determine exact locations and depths. Buried cables and pipes generally aren't an issue if you're putting in shallow-rooted plants, but utilities could pose hazards if you dig deep holes for trees, pools, and ponds, or if you excavate for foundations or terracing. Also record any overhead wires and their approximate height so you can choose trees that will comfortably fit. Too many lovely trees eventually need to be heavily pruned to keep their branches away from overhead power lines.

In addition to belowground utilities, remember to indicate locations of utility meters and air-conditioning units. Consider planting shrubs or building a trellis to screen these from view. Also, try to avoid placing a patio too close to a noisy air conditioner.

NOTICE HOW THE SUN PATTERNS change through the day. In the scene above, the large tree casts a shadow across the lawn in the afternoon. However, earlier in the day the space receives more light and smaller shadows.

INDICATE SLOPES on a site plan using angled arrows. The slope in the front garden shown above presents an attractive view to the neighborhood. It is landscaped with drought-tolerant grasses, small shrubs, and a dry stream bed.

Drainage

Use angled arrows to indicate slopes and any other changes in elevation. On a lot with abrupt changes in elevation, you'll need to decide whether to work around the natural topography or do major grading or terracing.

Study your land during and after heavy rains to understand how runoff flows. Look to low-lying spots where water accumulates, and note how long they remain wet. Prolonged wetness may indicate poor grading or clay soil that doesn't allow water to be absorbed readily. If your property doesn't handle water well, you may need to install drainage trenches. Also note runoff routes and evidence of erosion. If runoff hasn't already been channeled away from your house by foundation perimeter drains, you may need to build a berm (mounded earth) or find another way to redirect the flow.

Draw in the locations of house and outbuilding downspouts on your site map, and show any buried pipes that lead the water away. After heavy rains, check to ensure the drains are open and functioning properly.

Wind and Climate Patterns

Most properties have pockets where temperatures and wind patterns vary from the prevailing climate. For example, a south-facing wall will catch the sun and radiate heat and light, warming that section of the garden early in the spring and helping to maintain the warmth late into autumn. A west-facing deck or patio will receive afternoon sun, which may be uncomfortable in some areas. Windchill can lower temperatures significantly in exposed areas of the garden. Try to keep all of these factors in mind as you map your site and develop your landscape and building plans.

If your property is windy, you may want to install windbreaks. These can consist of trees or shrubs, open board or latticework fencing or walls, or a glass wall that preserves your view. If you garden in coastal conditions, be mindful that the salt content of sea winds can damage some plants. In that case, be sure to choose plants that will tolerate the salty air. Local nurseries can usually provide advice. In general, plants with silver, gray, or fuzzy leaves do well near the shore.

COLD AIR tends to settle into low-lying pockets, creating a frigid microclimate. Notice air patterns in your garden, and mark spots on your site plan that are noticeably hotter or colder than the norm.

MARK EXISTING LIGHT FIXTURES on your site plan; if possible, include where the power lines run. Low-voltage lights can be easily moved around, but 120-volt systems are more permanent.

Existing Elements

It is possible that you will want to conserve existing structures and plants in your new design. Record their locations on your base map. Draw the shapes of beds to scale, and indicate what is growing in them. Represent decks, patios, walkways, and sheds by drawing them to scale. Do the same with trees and shrubs. If you know plant names, label them, and note the general health of these plants.

Because deciduous trees lose their leaves in winter, they can be a boon for temperature control. If they are planted near the house, they provide desired shade in the summer and allow the sun to warm the house in winter. However, too many trees can make your house feel like a dark cave. Consider whether the house needs any shade trees to provide protection from the hot summer sun. Also consider whether trees that now provide shade need to be thinned or removed.

If you have a spectacular tree, you will probably want to keep it and plan your landscape around it. However, you may have valuable shrubs planted where you don't want them. Right plants in the wrong places can potentially save you a lot of money. When handled properly, most shrubs and small trees can be successfully transplanted. On the other hand, you may not need to move them, as a little pruning can transform many overgrown plants and give them a new look and a new life.

Views, Noise, and Odors

Indicate any attractive views that you would like to emphasize, as well as unsightly scenes that you would like to hide or disguise. A good view doesn't need to be a vast panorama of mountain ridges or ocean. It might be as simple as a tall, beautiful tree on your neighbor's property or a tiny slice of a view of the surrounding countryside.

Mark trees or shrubs that need to be removed to open up scenic vistas. For ideas on how to be creative with good views and bad ones, see "Accentuate the Positive," on page 27.

Our world is full of ambient noise. Some of it, such as bird song, is pleasant to the ear, but there are other sounds we would rather not hear. Make a note of the source of unpleasant noise, such as traffic sounds. You might be able to reduce the noise with a dense planting of shrubbery, or with a fence or wall. Another possibility is to mask the unpleasant noise with a splashing fountain. A third technique is to practice avoidance—keep outdoor seating areas away from noisy air conditioners, for instance.

Also, when you locate your patio, keep potential odors in mind. You could do a marvelous job of screening your trash bin from view, only to have your nose be reminded of its proximity on hot summer days.

Lights and Sprinklers

If your property has outdoor lighting, mark the locations of the fixtures, and if possible, indicate where the wiring is buried. Also draw in weatherproofed outdoor outlets. If you wish to install outdoor lighting for patios, decks, or pools, or as accent lighting, now is the time to plan for it. Especially if you opt for a traditional 120-volt system, which requires digging trenches to bury wires that are encased in waterproof conduits. You won't want to do such disruptive digging after you've planted or installed a new patio. As an alternative, you might consider low-voltage lighting, because its wires do not need to be buried.

Draw in the locations of sprinkler heads on your base map, along with their water lines and spigots. Make plans for any underground watering system in the early stages of your design. For an easier option, consider drip irrigation systems, which deliver water directly to the root system at a slow rate. Drip systems soak in deeply without watering the leaf surfaces. Drip-irrigation lines can be moved as your needs evolve. For more on drip irrigation systems, see Chapter 11.

DEVELOPING A LANDSCAPE DESIGN

An ancient Roman maxim states, "It is a bad plan that admits of no modifications," and a plan for a landscape design illustrates this point perfectly. A good landscape design is the foundation upon which you will build for years to come. You'll likely make adjustments as time passes, but the basic structure of a well-designed landscape will guide you.

Local Restrictions

Rules and regulations on issues such as fence height, pools, spotlights, decks, and other construction projects vary from community to community. Before you embark on any hardscape project, check with your local building authorities to learn whether permits are required and whether any restrictions will apply.

If your property has any public rights-of-way or setbacks (areas along property boundaries where construction is prohibited), be sure you know their exact locations. Be aware that your property may not extend all the way to the public road. In many communities, the town or county may own as much as 20 feet of what may look like your property.

Ways to Visualize Your Plans

While a landscape map can give a good, two-dimensional top view of your property design, it doesn't give you the perspective that you have on foot. For this, you need what architects call a frontal elevation. It's a simple matter to create this view using a photograph.

Find a vantage point that gives you a good overview of your property. If your property is too wide to fit into one frame, shoot several photo prints and tape them together, or borrow a camera with a wide-angle lens. Request 4 x 6-inch prints or larger; then have a copy center make enlarged copies up to 11 x 17 inches.

A black-and-white photograph or a photocopy is an excellent means of assessing the strengths and weaknesses of an existing design. Without the distraction of color, you can better analyze the design in terms of its basic forms and textures.

ENLARGE A PHOTOGRAPH of your property that provides good perspective to help you visualize a landscape design. Cover the enlargement with a clear sheet of plastic, and use water-based markers to draw proposed garden features.

For evaluating color schemes or coordinating with house colors, you'll need color prints. A photograph, whether in black and white or color, is uncompromising in capturing a landscape as it really is, whereas your eye tends to overlook design flaws in the same way that your ears screen out unwanted background noise.

Add New Features. Place a clear sheet of plastic over the photograph and draw on it using water-based markers. Plastic makes the use of different colored pens easier, giving a sense of form and color in your design. And it lets you easily erase.

As an alternative to plastic, tape a piece of tracing paper over the enlarged photocopy, and draw in the existing plantings and features you plan to keep. Then draw in the new outdoor projects you have in mind. It's not necessary to give an artistically accurate rendering of the plants and structures. Simply capture the basic shapes, and draw them as close to scale as possible. Be sure to draw the plants at their mature size so that you can see how the design will look when it has grown. If you don't like the design, no problem: just try again with a new piece of tracing paper.

To give you a better sense of scale, it may help to position reference markers before you take the photograph. Place several 6-foot vertical stakes at different points on your property to serve as guides to height. When you draw in your plants, 3-foot plants will be half the height of the pole.

More Design Help

Today there's a wide selection of computer programs that help you design decks. Others allow you to experiment with plant combinations and move plants around easily without the effort of drawing and redrawing on paper. Some of the programs include information on each plant's growing requirements. In others, you can input plants when they are young and small and then push a button to see how much they will grow in five years. The programs include predrawn mapping symbols for trees, shrubs, annuals, and perennials. There are even shapes and symbols that represent hardscape elements such as decks, stone walls, fences, and pools, and different textures to represent paving materials such as gravel, mulch, and brick.

If you'd prefer to arrange landscaping symbols using your hands rather than draw them or manipulate them on a computer, consider the various garden design books and drafting kits available. Many of these include grid paper and reusable, movable flower and plant images. The better versions feature step-by-step directions, plant lists with cultivation information, as well as how and when to shop for plants and valuable information and advice on regional differences. Some of these kits will also indicate how the plants will relate to one another by color, height, and bloom time, as well as by shape, texture of flower and leaf, and seasonal color.

FOR A MORE HANDS-ON APPROACH, you can position stick-on trees, shrubs, and flowers with kits such as the one shown above. The "plants" come in different sizes and are scaled to fit the grids to which they adhere.

COMPUTER-GENERATED landscape design programs allow you to move plants around and try different designs almost effortlessly. The programs help you to visualize how a proposed design will actually look.

ACCENTUATE THE POSITIVE

"Accentuate the positive, eliminate the negative." So goes an old song by Johnny Mercer and Harold Arlen. The same philosophy applies to landscaping. Try to showcase the positive features of your property, such as a beautiful view, established trees and shrubs, large windows in your home that look onto the garden, or cooling summer breezes. Work to create designs that emphasize and enhance these good features.

If your land is evenly rectangular, you may want to make it appear more interesting by breaking up the space so that the entire back or front garden can't be seen at once. A screen of plants, a trellis, or a wall can divide a property, creating separate garden rooms.

An unevenly dimensioned lot offers both a challenge and an opportunity. For example, on a triangular lot, you can partition the narrow end from the rest of the lot by means of a hedge or fence. Include a narrow gate or doorway to give access to a secret retreat.

You can draw attention to a pretty view by framing it with a pair of trees, an arbor, or a pair of statues. Preserve panoramic views by keeping the plantings low so that the vista isn't obscured. If a distant view is just visible through a gap in the trees or between two buildings, use paths or other landscape elements to draw attention to the distant scene. Above all, if you have a good view, create a comfortable place where you can sit and enjoy it. This viewing place can be a patio or deck, or simply a couple of chairs placed where the outlook is best.

Large windows give you a wonderful opportunity to enjoy your yard from indoors as well as outside. To improve this view, you can design a vignette (a small, room-like garden) centered on the window, or design plantings around a focal point, such as a pond or attractive patio, that invites viewers to look outside. Connect these elements with paths and walkways throughout the yard. For evening viewing, you can install garden lights. Place plants with sweet-smelling foliage or flowers near the windows so you can enjoy their fragrance when the windows are open. Good choices for fragrance include gardenia, apothecary rose, Oriental lilies, flowering tobacco, daphne, honeysuckle, star magnolia, and many others.

AN AWKWARD triangle-shape lot is divided into two garden rooms, transforming a challenging space into a delightful and functional asset. The front garden has a more usefully proportioned shape, and the hidden, pointed garden beyond is a gem.

27

Working with Prevailing Breezes

Because a cooling summer breeze is a major asset in hot climates, try to locate seating areas in the path of cool moving air. Where summers are cool, look instead for a sheltered, sunny spot, and furnish it with comfortable chairs. Also consider planting fragrant shrubs and herbs in the path of the breeze.

Maintain Established Trees. Beautiful, established trees and shrubs are a landscape treasure, giving a sense of permanence and history. Their value will be increased if you take care of them. Keep them pruned so that they stay in good health and maintain an attractive form and scale. You may want to feature a rare or special specimen plant as the central focal point of a garden.

Wyatt and Dorothy Williams were dismayed when water from a newly built pond seeped underneath the pond and collected at the far end, drowning the oldest and largest tree on their property in Virginia. The Williamses turned that tragedy into a triumph when they built a gazebo where the tree had been. The gazebo adds architectural interest to the garden and provides a pleasant place from which to view the pond.

Hiding Bad Views

A property's negative features are generally more challenging than its assets, but with skill and creativity, you can turn a problem into an advantage. Unsightly views and lack of privacy are common problems facing homeowners today. While the neighbor's house may be attractive, most people nonetheless want their yards to be a private retreat, out of sight of the neighbors' houses and yards. Many communities have restrictions on the

CHANGE A GARDEN PROBLEM into an attractive solution. This family built a gazebo on the spot where a large and ancient tree died due to water seeping from a new pond.

height of fences and walls, so be sure to check with the building department before adding these types of structures. You can create screens using trees, shrubs, and hedges.

If you already have a chain-link fence, you can mask it with a dense-growing evergreen vine. In just a few years, the fencing will disappear under the thick vine. In restricted spaces where a tall wall or fence would take up too much room, consider building a trellis. It can become an effective screen without overwhelming the space. Turn the trellis into a stunning vertical element by covering it with flowering vines. You can add to your privacy by topping existing fences or walls with lattice or trellis.

Managing Slopes

Many people address the mowing problem and reduce erosion on steep slopes by planting masses of low-maintenance shrubs or ground covers. While that solution is functional, it sometimes misses an opportunity to create a really special place.

Terraces for a Hillside. Consider terracing a slope or turning it into a strolling garden with stepping-stone paths that zigzag across the face. A hillside is an excellent place for a rock garden because the slope presents the garden, making small plants readily visible. Consider building a retaining wall at the bottom of the slope, filling the space behind the wall with soil to create a planter, and incorporating cascading plants. (See Chapter 6, "Landscape Walls.") For a more ambitious design, create a series of waterfalls that run down the slope into a pond at the bottom.

Sunny Areas

In hot climates, a shady retreat is especially welcome. But shade trees take many years to grow. Nevertheless, they are an investment worth making. In our society, statistics show that people, on average, live in one house for only five years. With prospects of a possible move, you might find it tempting to go for instant results rather than long-term benefits. Instant gratification makes sense to a point, but it is often carried too far. Gardens throughout North America are being planted with fast-growing trees and shrubs that may be past their prime and dying in just 15 to 20 years. Even if you don't plan to be around to see a slow-growing sapling mature to a tree, prospective buyers of your home will appreciate your foresight, perhaps by being willing to pay a better price.

ONE WAY TO MANAGE A SLOPE is to create a cozy sitting nook. Here, a flagstone bench that appears to be carved out of the hillside encourages visitors to pause to reflect on the pond tucked under the stone walkway.

THIS CLEVER LANDSCAPE DESIGN makes the most of the sloping backyard. The rustic stone and brick retaining wall hugs the hillside, then spirals down to encircle a small pond. Flowers and shrubs thrive in this multilevel planting.

PART II
backyard structures

2 tools and materials

There are four things you need to consider when building a fence, arbor, stone wall, patio, or one of the other outdoor projects detailed in this book. You'll start by choosing a location for the new structure. Then you will have to decide whether you will be doing the work yourself or hiring a professional. The third and fourth decisions deal with the materials and tools you will use—the subjects of this chapter. The tools and materials available are as varied as the number of outdoor projects you'll find on these pages. While this chapter doesn't attempt to cover every available tool or material, it does highlight the most common ones. For specifics, see the lists that accompany each project. They'll tell you everything you'll need for your outdoor project.

LAYOUT AND EXCAVATION

A basic collection of rulers, squares, and levels should be sufficient for a typical outdoor project. Note that it always helps to follow the adage "Measure twice and cut once," particularly when it can save an extra trip to the lumberyard for more wood.

For measuring, you can use a classic carpenter's fold-out ruler or a measuring tape. The fold-out variety takes a little time to open and close, but some models have a handy pull-out extension that makes it easy to take accurate inside dimensions.

To square up measurements for cutting, use a combination square on smaller boards and a framing square on sheet materials. But you can also check for square by measuring the diagonals between posts. They should be equal if the posts are square.

Another trick that's good for corners is to use the proportions of a 3-4-5 triangle. If one leg is 3 feet long, another is 4 feet long, and the hypotenuse is 5 feet long, the angle between the two legs will be 90 degrees. The 3-4-5 system works at any scale.

MARKING BOARDS

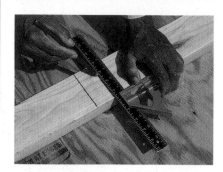

COMBINATION SQUARES mark straight, square lines.

SLIDING T-BEVELS mark and transfer odd angles.

LAYOUT TOOLS

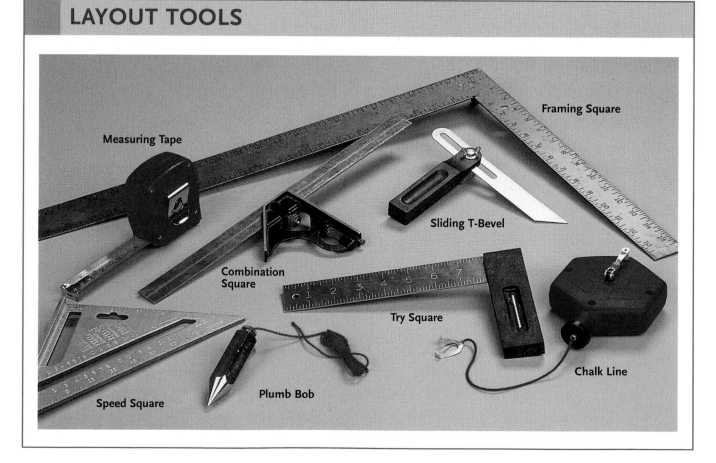

Measuring Tape

Framing Square

Combination Square

Sliding T-Bevel

Try Square

Speed Square

Plumb Bob

Chalk Line

EXCAVATION TOOLS

Wheelbarrow

Posthole Digger

Rake

Hoe

Trowels

Shovels

DIGGING OPTIONS

USING A SHOVEL is the most basic way to dig piers. But you'll wind up moving more dirt than you need to.

A POSTHOLE DIGGER has a scissor action to cut and scoop out dirt. It makes a neater, smaller hole.

YOU CAN RENT a one- or two-person power auger. They churn through dirt but are a handful to operate.

CONSTRUCTION TOOLS

Many do-it-yourselfers already own the basic hand tools required for building fences, arbors, and other outdoor projects. Unless you plan a special application, such as a fence with boards and gates with highly detailed gingerbread trim, you won't need any specialized tools.

But if you are in the process of accumulating tools, consider these general buying guidelines. The selection that's right for you depends not only on the work you want to do, but also on how often you'll use the tools, how expert you are at handling them, and how much you want to spend.

■ **Durability.** Buy better quality in tools you'll use often, such as a hammer and saw, that are basic requirements for building anything. It's worth a little extra to have a set of chisels with steel-capped heads that stand up better than plastic heads. But don't pay top dollar for heavy-duty contractor tools you'll use only occasionally. Many have features you don't need. And the truth is that inexperienced do-it-yourselfers don't get professional results just by using top-notch tools. For the most part, skill is in the hand that holds them, not in the tools themselves.

■ **Precision.** Stick with basic tools designed to do one job well, and avoid multipurpose gimmick tools that are loaded with bells and whistles. That nine-in-one wrench may be handy in the car glove compartment but not so much on home-improvement projects.

■ **Strength.** Look for hammers, wrenches, pry bars, and other mainly metal tools that are drop-forged instead of cast metal. Casting can trap air bubbles in molten metal, creating weak spots that could cause the metal to fracture under stress. Drop-forging removes more bubbles and makes the metal stronger and safer to use. In general, when manufacturers take the time and money to drop-forge a tool and machine-grind its surface, they leave the fine-grained metal in plain view. Sometimes inferior cast tools are disguised with a coat of paint.

■ **Price**. If in doubt, avoid the most and least expensive models and aim instead for the middle ground. The top end can have more capacity than you need, and the bottom end often has flaws that make work difficult—especially for a novice. There are some exceptions, of course. For example, a throw-away brush is fine for slapping some stain on a rough fence post. You don't need a high-quality and high-priced sash paintbrush for the job.

Finally, be sure to wield the tool in the store, checking the feel and comfort, to see whether it seems controllable, too heavy, or too light. If you shop in a large outlet store where there are several brands of the same tool, compare one against another.

It can be difficult to compare tools you can't normally test on the spot, such as power saws. But some tools you *can* test. Before you buy a level, for example, check three or four on the store floor or counter, and stack them on top of each other to see whether one has a bubble that is out of line with the others. In the end, of course, careful measurements and layouts will do more than top-notch tools to make your project both good-looking and long lasting.

smart tip

MARKING THE SITE FOR UTILITIES
BEFORE YOU START DIGGING HOLES FOR SUPPORT POSTS, CHECK INTO THE LOCATION OF UNDERGROUND UTILITY LINES, SUCH AS A NATURAL GAS MAIN OR A SEWER PIPE. ON A BIG PROJECT WHERE YOU'RE USING A CONTRACTOR TO DO THE DIGGING, YOU SHOULD MARK THE LOCATIONS OF THESE LINES AHEAD OF TIME TO AVOID AN ACCIDENT. EVEN IF YOU ARE RENTING A PORTABLE POWER AUGER AND DIGGING THE HOLES YOURSELF, YOU CAN'T AFFORD TO ACCIDENTALLY PUNCTURE A GAS LINE OR SHORT OUT UNDERGROUND ELECTRICAL CABLES. LOCAL UTILITY COMPANIES HAVE A RECORD OF THE LOCATIONS, AND IN MANY REGIONS, A UTILITY COMPANY REPRESENTATIVE WILL COME TO THE SITE AND HELP YOU LOCATE UNDERGROUND LINES SO YOU CAN MARK THEM WITH FLAGS.

HAND TOOLS

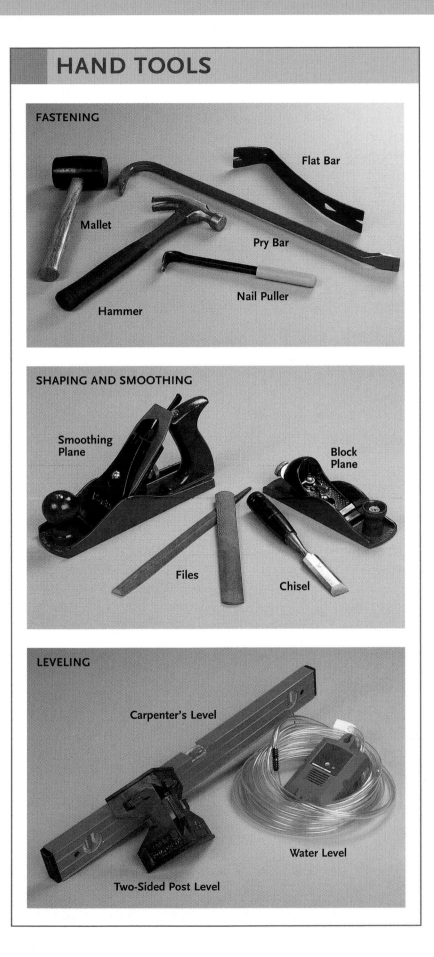

FASTENING

Mallet

Hammer

Flat Bar

Pry Bar

Nail Puller

SHAPING AND SMOOTHING

Smoothing Plane

Block Plane

Files

Chisel

LEVELING

Carpenter's Level

Water Level

Two-Sided Post Level

TRIMMING BOARDS

YOU DON'T NEED TO DO MUCH trimming and finishing on a rustic project made of rough-sawn boards. But you may need to clean up a few edges on picket styles and other types of decorative fencing. A basic smoothing plane (top) works well on most wood, but to increase your production you can use a power planer (middle). A belt sander (bottom) makes quick work of rough spots and blemishes.

POWER TOOLS AND SAFETY EQUIPMENT

A set of basic power tools will carry you through a typical outdoor project. With a lot of wood to cut, including posts, rails, and boards, you'll probably need a circular saw. The most practical is a standard corded model with a 7½-inch blade.

In remote locations, battery-powered saws (and other tools) will save you the trouble and tangle of extension cords. But on large projects you're likely to deplete the battery fairly quickly by cutting through thick posts. Even the latest battery-powered saws can't handle continuous pro-

duction cutting as well as a corded saw can. To cut large posts you'll have to get the knack of making two passes from opposing sides because most saws don't have the blade diameter to cut completely through the wood.

To make a neat, nearly seamless combination of cuts, it helps to transfer the cut lines around the post with a combination square. Another option is to bury any rough cuts you make by eye in the ground and set the cleaner, factory-cut ends up.

Whenever possible, it's wise to make repetitive cuts ahead of time. You'll find that it's most economical to shape pickets, post tops, and such in a shop. Make cuts such as angled joints on mating boards in the field.

POWER TOOLS

Circular Saw

Drill-Driver

Saber Saw

Reciprocating Saw

PNEUMATIC NAIL GUN

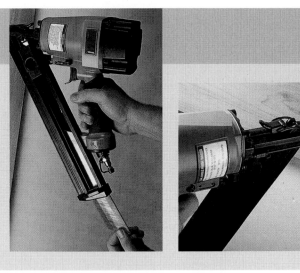

WITH AIR-POWERED NAILERS you can load many nails in one clip (near right). Then position the tool and squeeze the trigger to drive them (far right). Once you get a feel for the tool, you'll be able to drive nails quickly and accurately, which is handy on a large fence project. And the tools are safe if handled properly. Check into the safety-head feature, which forces you to set the head firmly against the work before the trigger will fire a fastener.

SAFETY EQUIPMENT

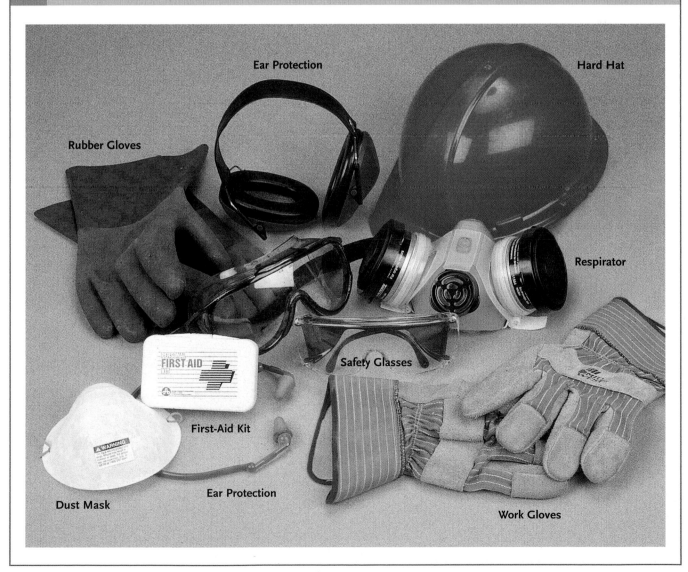

Ear Protection

Hard Hat

Rubber Gloves

Respirator

Safety Glasses

First-Aid Kit

Dust Mask

Ear Protection

Work Gloves

TOOLS FOR MASONRY PROJECTS

A clean wheelbarrow makes a handy mixer for mortar and modest amounts of concrete. And unlike a mixing tub or trough, it's easy to move around the work site. But bear in mind that a 40-pound bag of concrete makes only about 1/3 cubic foot, and a 60-pound bag only about 1/2 cubic foot. On larger jobs you can rent a portable mixer to save time. On big projects such as a patio slab, order concrete from a ready-mix company.

To cut block, brick, and other masonry, the most important tools are a short-handled 2-lb. hammer and a cold chisel or brick set. These hardened tools are tough enough to score and break block and brick. Another option is to use a standard circular saw with a special masonry cutting blade. This operation produces a lot of debris, so wear a dust mask in addition to the standard protection of gloves and safety glasses.

The most commonly used tool is a mason's trowel, available in several sizes that you can match to the scale of your project. Use it for placing mortar, forming furrows, buttering the ends of block and brick, and trimming mortar flush at joints. You'll also need one or more floats to handle surfacing work, and special trowels to cut control joints and form edges on concrete jobs.

MIXING TOOLS

WHEELBARROW   **HOE AND TROUGH**   **SPINNER MIXER**   **PORTABLE MIXER**

CUTTING TOOLS

CIRCULAR SAW AND MASONRY BLADE   **2-LB. HAMMER AND CHISEL**   **MASON'S HAMMER**   **BRICK SET**

SETTING AND FINISHING TOOLS

METAL FLOAT

DARBY WOOD FLOAT

BULL FLOAT

TROWEL

EDGER

JOINTER

GROUT BAG

STRIKING TOOL

RUBBER MALLET

FASTENERS

Besides common nails, which are the easiest to drive, you can use spiral or rink-shank nails on fence boards for more holding power. Although screws take more time to drive, they have the most holding power by far. A screw's number indicates the diameter of its shank. Common sizes are #6, #8, and #10. Of course, the length for any of these screws can vary. A #8 screw, for example, can be nearly any length up to about 3½ inches. The heavier the gauge, the more likely you are to find it in longer lengths.

You also may want to use large lag screws for making heavy-duty wood-to-wood attachments. Lag screws are heavy-duty screws that you drive using a socket wrench.

Lags are sized according to the diameter of their shanks, usually ⁵⁄₁₆, ³⁄₈, or ½ inch.

You can also use through bolts, mainly carriage bolts, which have unslotted oval heads, for attaching structural lumber face to face, such as large rails to posts. Carriage bolts have a square shoulder just beneath the head that digs into the wood as you tighten the bolt to prevent slipping. They are sized according to the diameter of their shanks as well as their length. You can also secure major joints between rails and posts using framing hardware, such as a U-shaped bracket that can support a heavy rail between posts. To prevent corrosion, hardware should be galvanized. Always check with the manufacturer for the proper fasteners to use with pressure-treated lumber.

FASTENERS

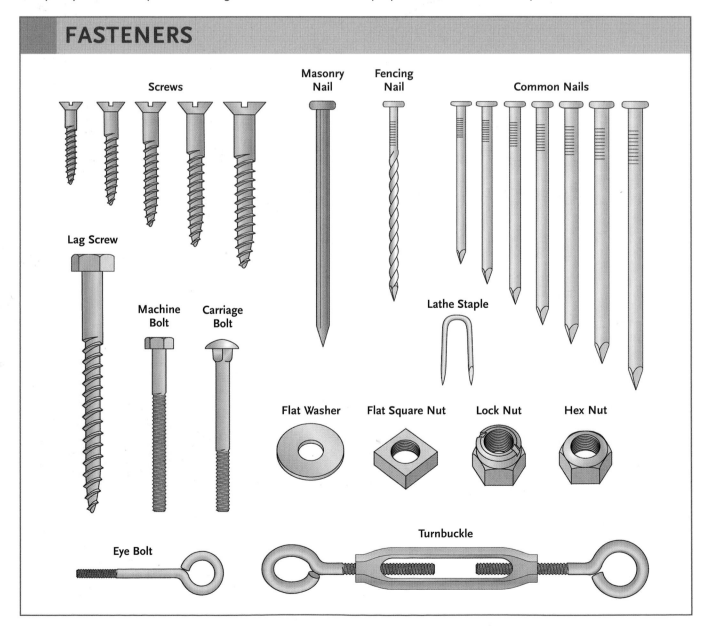

Screws · Masonry Nail · Fencing Nail · Common Nails · Lag Screw · Machine Bolt · Carriage Bolt · Lathe Staple · Flat Washer · Flat Square Nut · Lock Nut · Hex Nut · Eye Bolt · Turnbuckle

POSTS

Many lumberyards stock several types of posts, including round posts and square timbers, generally sized 4x4 or 6x6. The selection may include redwood and cedar but often is limited to rough grades of fir and pressure-treated (PT) wood. PT wood is the most durable because it is infused under pressure with an insecticide and a fungicide to ward off pests and decay. Be sure to observe the warnings of the manufacturer.

4x4 Cedar

4x4 PT

4x4 Fir

6x6 PT

PT Round Post

TRIM POSTS

LARGE POSTS often are beyond the one-cut capacity of do-it-yourself circular saws and may be too thick for standard drill bits. But there are other options. One is to use a chain saw (observing manufacturer's cautions) or a reciprocating saw with a long wood-cutting blade. But most DIYers get by with squaring the cut line around the post and making two passes that meet in the middle (near right). You can follow the same process when drilling holes, or use longer spade-point bits (far right).

BOARD OPTIONS

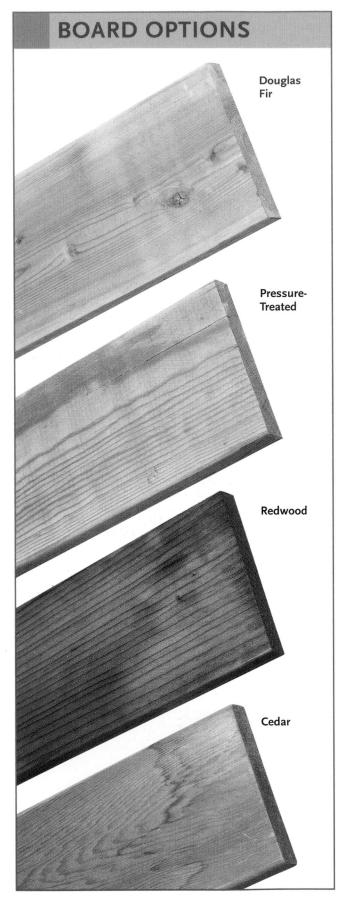

Douglas Fir

Pressure-Treated

Redwood

Cedar

LUMBER

As with any organic material that gains and loses water, wood swells when it is moist and shrinks as it dries. This can lead to warping, checking, bowing, twisting, and cupping. Softwoods such as pine, Douglas fir, and cedar are particularly vulnerable. But most of these problems can be avoided by fastening boards securely and supporting them with posts, rails, and braces over their spans.

When it comes to ordering posts, rails, and boards, bear in mind that a piece of lumber has two sizes: nominal and actual. A 2x4 rail may start out at 2x4 inches (its nominal size) when it is cut from a raw log, but it soon

DECAY-RESISTANCE

REDWOOD AND CEDAR are viable but pricey options to PT wood. Both combine good rot and insect resistance with an elegant appearance and are available in several grades. Less expensive grades with a rougher, saw-textured surface are generally used for fencing.

Redwood

- **Clear All Heart**
  Finest grade heartwood
- **Heart B**
  Limited knots
- **Clear (Sapwood)**
  Some defects
- **B Grade**
  Limited knots

Cedar

- **Clear Heart**
  Exposed wood
- **Grade A Clear**
  Shingles
- **Grade B Clear**
  Fencing
- **Knotty Grades**
  Closets

Redwood Clear

Cedar Clear

Redwood B Grade

Cedar Grade B

shrinks when it is dried. Then it becomes even smaller when it is planed. A 2x4 soon becomes 1½ x 3½ inches—the lumber's actual size. For wood lengths, the nominal and actual lengths are almost always the same. When you buy a 10-foot 2x4, it is usually 10 feet long and sometimes a bit longer.

Some lumberyards charge for lumber by the board foot, though increasingly yards are charging by the individual stick, or piece of lumber. If your lumberyard charges you by the board foot, here's how to figure it: take the nominal thickness, multiply it by the nominal width and the length, and divide by 12. A 10-foot 2x6 (usually written 2x6x10' in the industry) would be 10 board feet.

smart tip

FASTENERS FOR TREATED WOOD
THERE IS EVIDENCE THAT SOME OF THE NEWER WOOD-TREATMENT CHEMICALS ARE MORE CORROSIVE FOR FASTENERS THAN THE ORIGINAL TREATMENTS FOR PRESSURE-TREATED WOOD. CHECK PRODUCT INFORMATION SHEETS FOR SPECIFIC FASTENER REQUIREMENTS. SOME MANUFACTURERS ARE RECOMMENDING STAINLESS-STEEL NAILS OR SCREWS FOR TREATED LUMBER.

BASIC LUMBER GRADES

 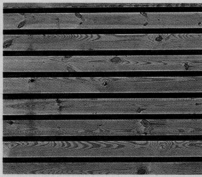 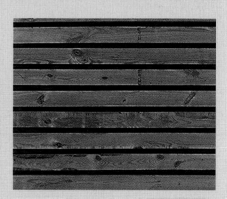

NUMBER 1 GRADE has few knots. It's not normally stocked at lumberyards.

NUMBER 2 GRADE, the most common lumber, has more knots and defects.

NUMBER 3 GRADE of most lumber species has knots and edge defects.

COMMON LUMBER DEFECTS

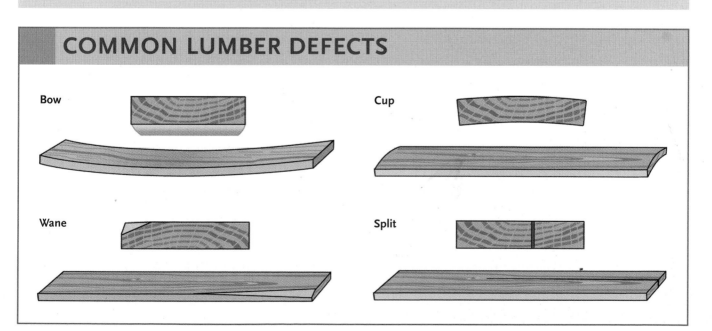

Bow

Cup

Wane

Split

3 patios

A well-designed patio may add more to the value of your home than it costs to build. Patios can be anything from a small pad outside the back door to a large expanse wrapping around a corner of your home. Typically, however, a patio is about one-third the size of the house—larger perhaps than any interior room. Site your patio to protect it from the hottest sun and the coldest wind. Also consider the terrain. Place your patio in an area that is well drained, and make sure you're not blocking or disrupting existing drainage. To prevent flooding, a patio is usually built an inch or so above ground level. You should also construct your patio to slope away from the house to keep rain and melting snow from leaking inside.

FLAGSTONE PATIO AND STEPS

FLAGSTONE is a traditional and proven material for patios and walkways. It is sold in several thicknesses (generally from 1 to 2 inches) and in muted colors with subtle shadings that help your installation blend with the landscape. There are many ways to lay a flagstone patio and build steps, which is often the most complicated part of the job. The most durable method is to pour a concrete slab and embed the stones in its sur-face. More often, flagstones are laid in sand on a bed of fine compacted gravel or a mixture of compacted dirt and sand. Sand is useful for screeding to a pitch of about 1 percent for drainage. Using random shapes is the most challenging approach and creates the greatest waste. You can also use square-cut flagstones designed to fit together in several modular patterns that reduce cutting time.

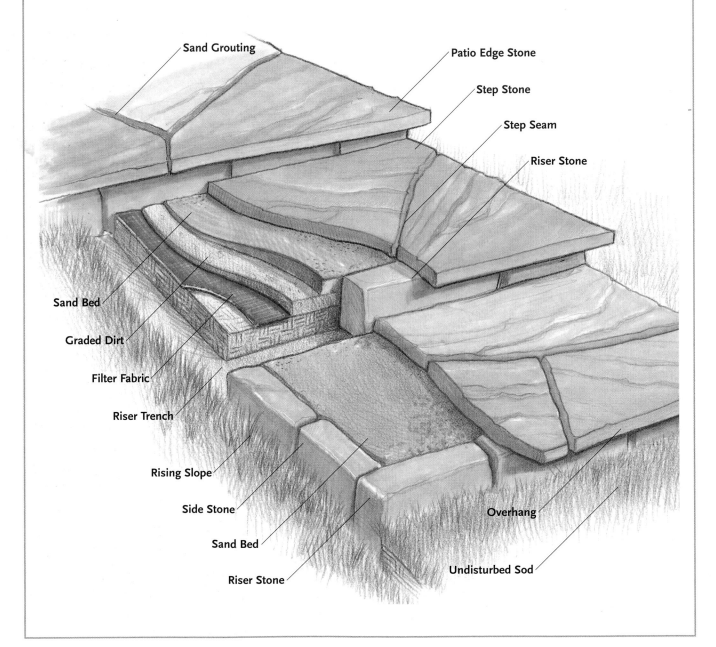

FLAGSTONE PATIO AND STEP INSTALLATION

project

TOOLS & MATERIALS

▌Work gloves ▌Shovel and tamper
▌Spirit level and measuring tape ▌Clamps
▌Mortar mixing box ▌Mixing hoe
▌Hammer ▌Garden hose with spray head
▌Rubber mallet and cold chisel
▌Push broom ▌Stone ▌Gravel base
▌Filter fabric ▌Screeding sand
▌Mortar mix ▌Stakes and layout string

SMART TIP

TO INCREASE THE DURABILITY OF GROUTED SEAMS, ADD CEMENT TO THE SAND BEFORE BRUSHING IT INTO CRACKS. WITH SAND ONLY, YOU'LL HAVE TO COME BACK AFTER A DAY OR TWO TO REFILL THE JOINTS THAT SETTLE AFTER WETTING. ANOTHER APPROACH IS TO LEAVE LARGER GAPS; FILL WITH TOPSOIL; AND SOW GRASS SEED IN THE SEAMS.

1 Use stakes and strings to lay out the patio. When the diagonals are equal, the patio is square.

2 Dig a shallow trench to embed the edging support stones below the graded patio level.

3 Use a hand tamper or the end of a 2x4 to compact the dirt in the bottom of the trench.

4 Set the edge stones in the trench so that the tops will be level with the screeded sand of the patio.

(continued on page 50) **49**

(continued from page 49)

PLANNING FLAGSTONE TREADS AND RISERS

THE MOST RELIABLE WAY to establish the sizes of treads and risers is to stake a long, straight, and level board along the edge of the slope. This allows you to try several combinations. For example, you can extend the treads 18 inches or more to reach a comfortable maximum of 6- or 7-inch risers, or reduce them to achieve a comfortable minimum of about 4-inch risers.

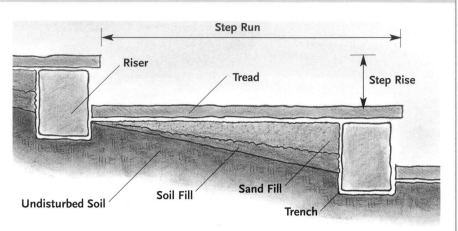

Step Run

Riser

Tread

Step Rise

Undisturbed Soil

Soil Fill

Sand Fill

Trench

5 Spreading a layer of filter fabric or black plastic can suppress weed growth through patio joints.

6 Cover the excavation with at least 2 in. of sand, and use a straight board to screed the surface.

9 Set up a level board to gauge the slope, and lay out the treads and risers of the steps.

10 Measure down from the level board at the edge of the tread to establish the step rise.

MOVING STONE

THE KEY to working with heavy stones is leverage. You'll want to move stones with pry bars and dollies instead of with your back, arms, and legs. For clearing and moving large rocks of any kind, consider investing in an oversize pry par, generally called a wrecking bar. A dolly is very handy, considering that a delivered pallet of flagstones weighs about 3,000 pounds.

WRECKING BARS are long pry bars that apply exceptional leverage.

A DOLLY is handy for transporting stones around the work site.

7 Set the perimeter flagstones in the screeded sand, laying the straightest edges to the outside.

8 Embed flagstones using a rubber mallet. Check the surface using a straightedge and/or level.

11 Set up stakes and strings to mark the treads and guide excavation work on the slope.

12 Dig a shallow trench at the outer edge of each tread so that you can embed riser stones.

(continued on page 52) **51**

(continued from page 51)

PLANNING LAYOUT PATTERNS

A TYPICAL DELIVERY of rough flagstones contains many shapes and sizes that are graded by color and width. You can also order cut stones that fit together neatly. With rough material you need to carefully plan the intricate joints on patios and steps. Narrow, sand-filled seams generally require some trimming, while wider seams make greater use of existing shapes.

CONSISTENTLY NARROW JOINTS filled with sand require a puzzle-like fit.

WIDER, GRASS-FILLED JOINTS are easier to plan and create less waste.

13 Set and level the riser stones for the steps. You'll need to remove the sod before screeding.

14 Compact the area behind the risers; add sand; screed the bed; and check for level.

17 Embed flagstones in the sand to form the steps. It's wise to work out the patterns in advance.

18 You can grout the flagstone joints with sand or a mix of 4 parts sand and 1 part dry mortar.

SHIMMING A STEP

EVEN WITHIN THE STANDARD SIZE categories of 1- and 2-inch flagstone, it's common to find variations of ¼ inch either way. That means one step stone could be up to ½ inch thicker than the next one. Compensate by shimming with flakes of stone. To keep a shim from shifting and the step from sinking, embed the shim in a small mound of mortar.

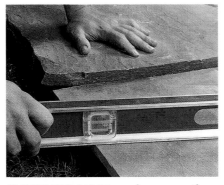

CHECK FOR LEVEL, and measure the thickness of the required shim.

KEEP THE SHIM STONE from shifting by embedding it in mortar.

15 Follow the same procedures as you work down the slope, maintaining the tread and riser sizes.

16 Check the riser stones by leveling from step to step with scraps of flagstone in place.

19 Push the sand mix back and forth across the patio and steps with a broom, filling the joints.

20 Spray the sand with water, and refill and respray the joints after the first layer settles.

PATIO PAVERS ON A SAND BASE

CONCRETE PAVERS, available at home-improvement centers, can be used to make a simple, attractive patio. Pavers may include a tab system that helps you space the blocks accurately without measuring. Concrete pavers are available in a variety of patterns, and instal-lation will vary slightly from brand to brand and pattern to pattern. All concrete paving blocks, however, can be laid over a sand-and-gravel bed. The basic principles for building a paver patio are provided here, but be sure to follow the manufacturer's directions as well.

INSTALLING PATIO PAVERS

Lay Out the Patio. Use wood 1x2 stakes and string lines to outline your patio. Begin by driving two stakes near the house wall at the patio edges. Set up batter boards at the outer corners. Stretch mason's twine along what will be the perimeter of your patio. Level the twine by hanging a line level at midspan.

Check to make sure the layout is square using the 3-4-5 triangle method. Measure from one stake 3 feet along the house, then 4 feet along the line. The corner is square if the diagonal between the two points measures 5 feet. If the corner is not square, slide the string along the batter boards until it is, and mark the location of the string on the board. For large areas, increase the measurements proportionally. For example, increase the measurements to 6, 8, and 10 feet.

Square the second line that meets the house; then square the remaining side of the patio. When all the sides are placed properly, make a saw cut where each string line crosses its batter board.

Plot the Slope. To drain well, the patio should slope away from the house $\frac{1}{4}$ inch per foot. Adjust your level string lines to reflect this. If, for example, the patio is 12 feet wide, the edge nearest the house needs to be 3 inches higher than the far end. Compute the slope for your patio, and mark the new location with a saw cut. Slide the string up into the cut. Sprinkle sand over the strings to transfer

PAVER INSTALLATION

project

TOOLS & MATERIALS

▌Work gloves ▌Safety glasses ▌String
▌Line level ▌4-ft. level ▌Tamper
▌1½-in.-diameter pipe ▌Mallet
▌Screed board ▌Stiff-bristled broom
▌Gravel ▌Sand ▌Pavers
▌Edging material

1 Excavate the area to the desired depth. Tamp down and level the soil.

2 Add a 4- to 6-in. layer of gravel. Tamp the gravel using a hand or mechanical tamper.

3 Spread landscape fabric over the gravel. Overlap seams by at least 6 in.

(continued on page 56)

(continued from page 55)

the layout to the ground. Where the strings cross to mark the corner of the patio, suspend a plumb bob from the line, and mark the corner using a nail struck through a piece of paper into the ground.

Determine Depth. Begin by digging out all organic material. Then dig deep enough to allow for the depth of the pavers, plus a 1½-inch sand subbase, plus 4 to 6 inches of gravel. To determine the depth of the excavation, first figure out the total thickness of the finished patio. If the pavers sit on 1½ inches of sand, for example, and the required gravel subbase is 4 inches, the combined thickness is 7 inches ($1\frac{1}{2}+1\frac{1}{2}+4=7$). If you wanted to have the surface 1 inch above grade, the depth of the excavation at the end farthest from the house would be 6 inches—

7 inches for the patio thickness minus 1 inch for the elevation. In this case, you dig a hole 6 inches deep at the batter boards. To slope the bed, measure from the bottom of the string to the bottom of the hole. Keep the bottom of the excavation roughly this distance from the string. Compact the soil by tamping and leveling it.

Lay the Gravel Base. Lay a 4- to 6-inch layer of gravel as required by code. Spread the gravel about 1 foot beyond the edges of the patio on all sides. Tamp the gravel down. Roll landscape fabric out over the tamped gravel.

Place the Edging. Dig a deeper trench around the perimeter of the excavation, as needed, to hold the edging. Measure down from the layout lines periodically to make sure the trench will put your edging at the desired

4 Install the edging. This system uses a plastic edging, but bricks set on edge is an option.

5 Shovel the sand over the landscape fabric. Try to get the sand as smooth as possible.

8 To trim small pavers, clamp the paver to a worktable and cut with a masonry blade.

9 Go back over the patio with a mallet and 2x4 to make sure the pavers are seated properly.

height—at or just below the finished elevation of the pavers. Install edging on two sides—one of which should be the house wall. Set the edging flush with or slightly below what will be the surface of the patio.

Spread a thin layer of fine sand over the gravel base. Then spread a coarse concrete sand over the gravel to create a layer 1½ inches deep. To level the bed, place pipes with a 1½-inch outer diameter along the edges of the patio. Push the pipes down into the sand until the top of the pipe is at the proper grade, as measured from the strings. Level the sand by laying a 2x4 across the pipes and sliding it along the pipes. Remove pipes.

Lay the Pavers. Starting in a corner, begin laying pavers on the smooth sand. Tap each one several times with a

rubber mallet to set it firmly on the sand.

Most block pavers have built-in spacers to create a minimum joint width. If you're working with ones that don't, space them to create 1/16- to 1/8-inch joints. Continue setting the rest of the pavers.

Complete the Edging. If you're working with rectangular pavers, install the outer edging snugly against the pavers. If the units are irregular, install the edging with space to spare; then cut the units to fill the spaces.

Fill the Joints. Sweep fine, dry mortar sand into the joints between the units and around the edges. Spray the surface with a hose to wet the units. You may need to repeat the sweeping and wetting process until the joints in order to completely fill the joints.

6 Embed 1½-in. pipes in the sand to use as a guide for your 2x4 screed board.

7 Begin placing the pavers. Seat each paver with a tap of a rubber mallet; check for level.

10 Brush dry sand into the joints between pavers. Brush in all directions for even coverage.

11 Wet down the sand using a fine mist from a garden hose. Don't dislodge the sand.

CONCRETE SLAB

A CONCRETE SLAB is one of the most basic types of masonry construction and is employed in various locations. Using the same basic procedures you'll find in this project, you can build a slab to stand alone as a walkway or patio. Slabs are also used on basement floors and to support small sheds and other outbuildings. Although many houses are built on slabs, they require a perimeter footing. Building a slab is not difficult, but mixing the concrete can be, particularly on a large project. For large projects you should order by the cubic yard from a ready-mix company that will deliver the mix ready to pour. If you plan to mix your own concrete for a small project, remember that one wheelbarrow-sized batch generally makes less than 3 cubic feet. You would need approximately nine wheelbarrow batches to make just 1 cubic yard.

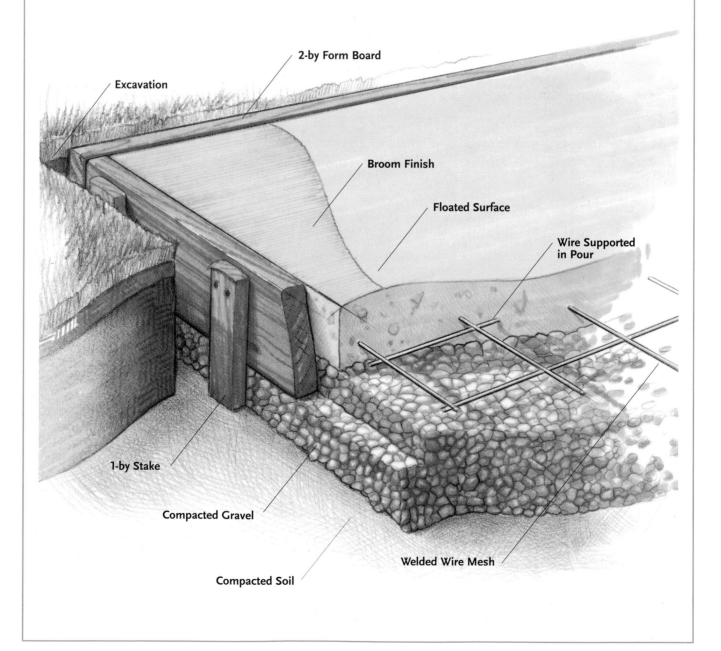

Excavation

2-by Form Board

Broom Finish

Floated Surface

Wire Supported in Pour

1-by Stake

Compacted Gravel

Welded Wire Mesh

Compacted Soil

CONCRETE SLAB INSTALLATION

project

TOOLS & MATERIALS

▌Work gloves ▌Vibrating power tamper
▌Line level and pencil ▌Pry bar
▌Broom and rake ▌Spirit level
▌Wheelbarrow ▌Power drill-driver
▌Bull float and hose ▌Edging and
jointing trowels ▌Mason's string
▌Welded-wire mesh ▌Gravel
▌Concrete mix ▌Burlap ▌Lumber for
forms, screeding boards, and stakes

SMART TIP

ALTHOUGH A REINFORCED-CONCRETE SLAB SEEMS NEARLY INDESTRUCTIBLE, IT CAN CRACK UNLESS YOU BUILD IT OVER SOLID, COMPACTED SOIL. FOR BEST RESULTS, RENT A VIBRATING POWER TAMPER THAT CONSOLIDATES SOIL. USE IT ON THE DIRT SUBBASE AND THEN ON THE GRAVEL BASE BEFORE POURING THE CONCRETE.

1 Mark outside the perimeter of the slab with spray paint. Then cut and roll up the sod to reuse.

2 Excavate below the frost line, and drive stakes to mark the outside line of the form boards.

3 Use a line level strung between corner stakes to establish the level (and drain slope) of the slab.

4 Use a large steel pry bar to remove any large rocks that would interfere with the concrete.

(continued on page 60) **59**

(continued from page 59)

FORMING SLABS ON A SLOPE

YOU CAN REGRADE the work area to create a level excavation for a slab. But in many cases it's more practical to accommodate a gentle slope by increasing the depth in a small area of the pour. Where the ground falls away, drive longer form stakes and maintain level with the main form board. Then add an angled filler board below to contain the gravel and concrete.

RUN THE TOP FORM BOARDS to a pair of long stakes at the low corner.

FILL IN THE SLOPE with angled boards attached with extra stakes.

5 Fill any large depressions in the excavation with gravel to save on concrete.

6 Use a mechanical tamper to compact gravel recesses and the dirt floor of the excavation.

9 If you need to butt form boards on a long run, join them using screws over an extra-wide stake.

10 Screed the gravel bed so that it is roughly even with the bottom edges of the form boards.

USING WELDED WIRE

EVEN ON A SMALL SLAB or narrow walkway, you should reinforce the pour with welded wire. On larger projects you can overlap sheets by at least one grid and join the sections using wire ties (near right). Ideally, the mesh should rest in the lower third of the slab. On large jobs you can rest the wire on supports. On small jobs, simply lift the mesh (far right) as you pour.

OVERLAP WELDED WIRE on large slabs, and tie the sheets together.

ON SMALL JOBS, lift the wire off the gravel as you pour the concrete.

7 Rake out a 4- to 6-in. bed of gravel. Reset your string guides, if needed, to judge the thickness.

8 Install and level the form boards to the string guides you set between your corner stakes.

11 Use a mechanical tamper to consolidate and compact the gravel base for the pour.

12 Cut welded-wire reinforcing mesh to fit inside the forms. Then roll it into place over the gravel.

(continued on page 62)

(continued from page 61)

SLOPING SLABS FOR DRAINAGE

LARGE EXPOSED SLABS should slope up to ¼ inch per foot to encourage drainage and eliminate puddling. One option is to slope the entire slab in one direction—for example, from the house toward the yard. Another is to crown the slab by creating curved screed boards as shown at right. Even a ½-inch crown over a 10-foot slab or driveway will encourage water flow.

TACK A ½-IN. SPACER in the center, and fasten a 1x2 over it.

FOLLOW THE CURVED SCREED to create a drainage slope in the pour.

13 Fill the forms with concrete. The wire mesh can rest on supports, or you can raise it by hand.

14 Work a straight 2x4 in a back-and-forth motion across the forms to smooth and level the mix.

17 Use a jointing trowel against a straightedge to cut control joints about every 10 ft.

18 Run an edging trowel around the perimeter to provide a clean, crack-resistant edge.

SETTING PERMANENT FORMS

IN LARGE EXPOSED SLABS that are difficult to level and finish, you can install permanent intermediate forms that divide the pour into smaller, more manageable sections. To attach the intermediate boards, make square cuts and fasten the boards to the perimeter forms using screws. Brace the boards with stakes, but recess them so that they will not interfere with screeding.

SET INTERMEDIATE FORMS flush with the permanent perimeter forms.

BRACE INTERMEDIATE FORMS with stakes set below the top edges.

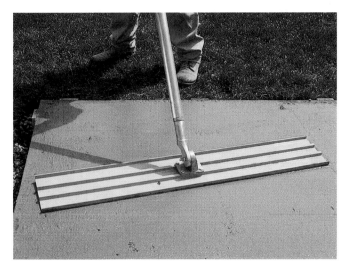

15 Rent a bull float with a long handle to create a smooth finish on the surface of the slab.

16 Lightly sweep the concrete with a broom to create a rougher, more slip-resistant surface.

19 Cover the wet slab with burlap (or plastic) to contain moisture. Or you can use a curing agent.

20 Periodically spray water on the burlap over the next several days to help the concrete cure.

CONCRETE LANDING AND STEPS

WHEN DOORS are anywhere from several inches to several feet off the ground, you need a landing and steps to make safe and smooth transitions in and out of the house. (Check local codes for minimum landing sizes at entries, and for riser and tread regulations.) On new homes, concrete landings and steps sometimes are included as part of the foundation, and poured at the same time. This can prevent the chronic problem of cracking where the house foundation meets the steps. But in this add-on installation you'll see how to build sturdy steps that won't shift, and how to join the structure to the house with an isolation joint. You can minimize the concrete needed on a project like this by stacking masonry rubble inside the forms. But keep the pile at least 6 inches away from all exterior surfaces to avoid weakening the pour.

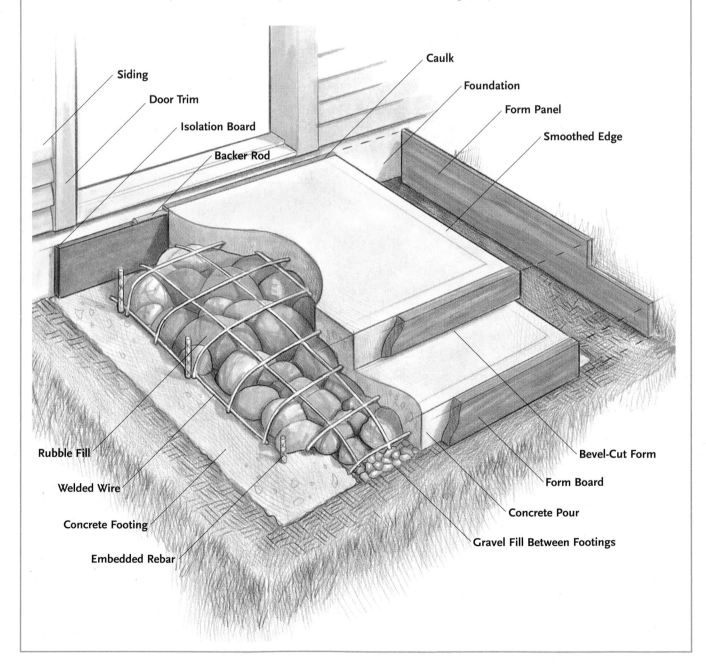

Siding
Door Trim
Isolation Board
Backer Rod
Caulk
Foundation
Form Panel
Smoothed Edge
Rubble Fill
Welded Wire
Concrete Footing
Embedded Rebar
Bevel-Cut Form
Form Board
Concrete Pour
Gravel Fill Between Footings

CONCRETE LANDING AND STEPS INSTALLATION

project

TOOLS & MATERIALS

▮ Stakes and layout string ▮ Shovel or spade and tamper ▮ Square, measuring tape, pencil ▮ Circular saw ▮ Hammer and level ▮ Power drill-driver ▮ Caulking gun ▮ Edging trowel ▮ Roller (for curing sealer) ▮ Rebar ▮ Concrete ▮ Wire lath ▮ ³/₄-in. exterior-grade plywood ▮ Isolation board ▮ 2x2 and 1x4 braces ▮ 1x6 riser form boards ▮ Curing sealer (or plastic)

SMART TIP

STRENGTHEN THE STRUCTURE BY ADDING BOTH RE-INFORCING WIRE AND REBAR. REBAR SET INTO THE FOOTINGS HELPS TO ANCHOR THE POUR. A BLAN-KET OF WELDED WIRE WILL HELP HOLD THE RUBBLE CORE IN PLACE AS YOU POUR. SETTING ADDITIONAL REBAR INTO THE RUBBLE CORE HELPS TO TIE THE TWO MASONRY COMPONENTS TOGETHER.

1 Set up stakes and strings to level out from the house, and then measure the rise and run of the steps.

2 Dig two footing trenches (below the frost line) along the sides of the landing and steps.

3 Set rebar into the footings, but keep them a few inches below the final concrete surface.

4 Fill in the remaining area with gravel, and compact it to keep the concrete from settling.

(continued on page 66) **65**

(continued from page 65)

BUILT-IN DRAINS FOR LARGE LANDINGS

DRAINS are normally set underground to carry off water. But concrete surfaces, particularly large landings, may need drainage as well. To give rainwater a place to go, form a channel in the surface concrete and insert segmented drain fittings. Water enters through a grille and drains to an outlet pipe. You'll need to include a pipe outlet in the form before pouring.

SET PREFAB SURFACE DRAINS in a channel formed in the concrete.

CONNECT DRAINPIPES to a collar at the end of the drainage channel.

5 Transfer tread and riser dimensions to the two side forms made of ¾-in. exterior-grade plywood.

6 Use a circular saw to cut out the side forms. On most jobs you'll get all the forms from one sheet.

9 With this setup, two braces hold the form at the nailer, and a third holds the step section.

10 Bevel the bottom edge of the riser form board so that you can work concrete across the step.

SLIP-RESISTANT FINISHES FOR LANDINGS AND STAIRS

CONCRETE is normally floated to a smooth finish. This looks good, of course, but on a landing and steps a smooth surface can be dangerous, particularly in northern climates. You can create a rougher surface by embedding aggregate in the concrete before it cures or simply by brushing the surface with a stiff broom to create a striated, more slip-resistant finish.

ADD EXPOSED AGGREGATE to the concrete before it hardens.

BROOM A TEXTURED SURFACE into the floated concrete.

7 Tack 2x2 nailers against the foundation ¾ in. outside the location of the side forms.

8 Add 2x2 nailers to the outsides of the forms, and screw them into place with angled braces.

11 Secure the riser forms with the bevels down. Without a bevel, the form would block the tread.

12 Add vertical nailers (left long) to the riser forms, and secure them to a stake with an angled 1x4.

(continued on page 68) **67**

(continued from page 67)

SHARP VS. ROUNDED EDGES

EDGING A LANDING AND STEPS can save you repair work later on. Using a round-over edging trowel actually helps in two ways. (See step 18.) First, it allows for a clean release of the form boards. Second, it creates stronger edges that resist cracking and chipping. Sharp corners are weaker because there is less concrete for support the closer you move to the edge.

SHARP, RIGHT-ANGLE EDGES can easily chip, particularly on steps.

ROUNDED-OVER EDGES have more strength to resist chipping.

13 Use adhesive to fasten a piece of ½-in. isolation board against the house foundation wall.

14 Conserve concrete and mixing time by piling clean masonry rubble in the center of the forms.

17 Use a long, straight 2x4 to screed the surface, working the board back and forth on the forms.

18 Strengthen and finish edges of the landing and steps by running an edger just inside the forms.

BUILDING AN ISOLATION JOINT

THIS JOINT ISOLATES THE LANDING from the house foundation, acts as a buffer, and prevents one from moving against and cracking the other. Mount asphalt-impregnated isolation board against the foundation, recessing the top edge down about an inch. Fill this gap with a spacer board to keep out concrete. Finish the gap with backer rod and exterior-grade caulk.

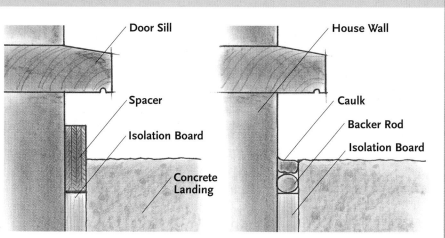

Door Sill
Spacer
Isolation Board
Concrete Landing

House Wall
Caulk
Backer Rod
Isolation Board

15 Cover the masonry rubble with welded wire reinforcement folded down and around the pile.

16 Mix enough concrete (or order ready-mix) to fill the forms at least 6 in. deep around the core.

19 The easiest way to hold in moisture required for curing is to spray or roll on a curing sealer.

20 Wait several days before stripping the forms. Backing out screws is easier than pulling nails.

PATIO ENTRY

A PLAIN CONCRETE SLAB may serve well enough as a landing or small patio to keep you up off the grass and soil as you enter and leave the house. But it's not very attractive. This project builds on an existing slab, adding a decorative and sturdy layer of tile. You could also use pavers or other masonry units rated for exterior installation. If your slab is sound, you can jump into this project at Step 10, where you start laying tile. If your slab is only a few inches thick, cracked, or sunken, start from scratch. Here you'll see how to form around the existing concrete and pour a secondary slab reinforced with wire mesh. One concern is the joint against the house wall. To prevent cracking and still make the seam weatherproof, you need to pack foam backer rod into the joint and finish the surface with flexible, exterior-grade caulk.

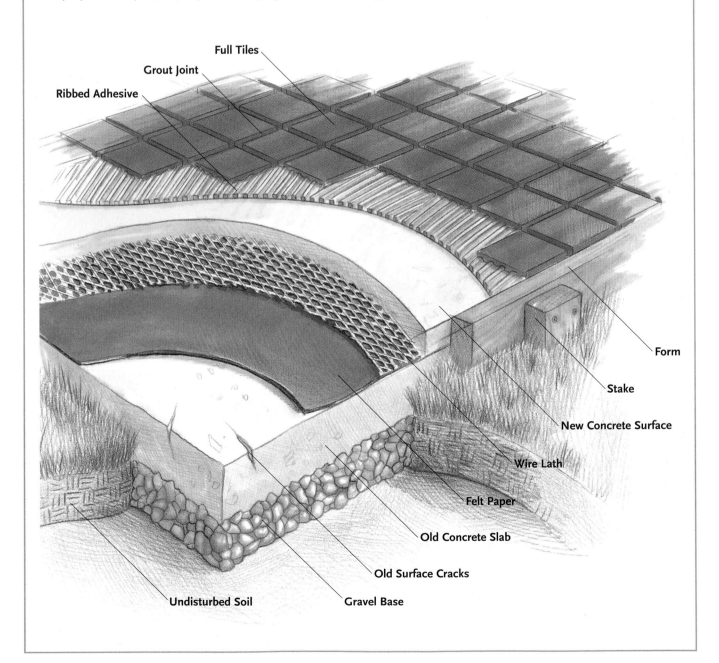

Full Tiles

Grout Joint

Ribbed Adhesive

Form

Stake

New Concrete Surface

Wire Lath

Felt Paper

Old Concrete Slab

Old Surface Cracks

Undisturbed Soil

Gravel Base

PATIO ENTRY INSTALLATION

TOOLS & MATERIALS

▮ Power drill and caulking gun ▮ Mortar hoe and metal float ▮ Sponge and bucket ▮ Chalk-line box ▮ Snap cutter ▮ Notched trowel ▮ Grout float ▮ Sponge mop ▮ Rubber mallet ▮ Putty knife ▮ Screws ▮ Builder's felt paper ▮ Wire lath ▮ Lumber for form and screeds ▮ Concrete ▮ Tile, adhesive, and spacers ▮ Grout, caulk, and sealer ▮ Plastic sheeting ▮ Foam backer rod

SMART TIP

To create a slight slope that encourages surface runoff, simply set a piece of gravel under the midpoint of the center screed board. As you pour and screed the upper slab, this will build a gradual and basically unnoticeable slope into the patio surface.

1 Verify the condition of your existing slab. If necessary, build a form to contain a new surface pour.

2 Cover the old surface with 30-lb. felt paper to prevent cracks from continuing into the new pour.

3 Roll sheets of wire lath onto the builder's felt. This will reinforce the new concrete pour.

4 Screw intermediate screeds to the form on large slabs where forms can't support all screeding.

(continued on page 72) **71**

(continued from page 71)

PIPE SCREEDS

SOME SLABS ARE TOO LARGE or shaped too irregularly to screed with a single board. In this case you can install intermediate screeds to control surfacing. One option is to use wood screeds (shown in step 6 below). Another is to use lengths of pipe supported on stakes. After you screed the surface you need to remove the pipes; then fill and smooth the narrow troughs.

DRIVE STAKES into the gravel to support the temporary screed pipes.

DRIVE PAIRS OF NAILS to hold the pipes in place on the stakes.

5 Pour concrete into the form; spread it into the corners; and add more to reach the tops of the forms.

6 Screed excess concrete off the pour by moving a straight 2x4 back and forth along the screeds.

9 Add concrete to fill the recesses left by the screed boards, and finish with a float.

10 Snap lines to lay out the tile after the slab has cured. Always make a dry layout first.

CONCRETE SURFACE PROBLEMS

SPALLING can leave an older slab looking chipped and pitted. In some cases the surface may be missing large chunks that need to be filled before you can lay tile. To prevent spalling in a new pour, be sure to mix dry ingredients thoroughly before adding water. When finishing, do not overfloat the surface. That can leave a thin, watery layer of cement.

SPALLING leaves a concrete surface looking chipped and pitted.

7 Finish the surface of the slab using a metal float, moving it side to side across the surface.

8 Unfasten the intermediate screeds, and carefully lift them from the surface of the pour.

11 Spread adhesive up to layout lines in a small area of the field using a notched trowel.

12 Embed the field tiles; check the surface for flatness; and insert plastic spacers in the seams.

(continued on page 74) **73**

(continued from page 73)

CUTTING TILE

TO USE A SNAP CUTTER, position the tile against the stop at the head of the tool, and draw the scoring wheel across the surface. After making the scoring stroke, press down to split the tile along the score line. To use a wet saw, hold the tile on the cutting table, and feed the work into the blade. A circulating system feeds water onto the cutting area to lubricate the blade.

A SNAP CUTTER makes a square score line and snaps the tile.

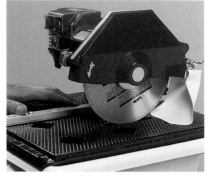

A POWER WET SAW cuts tile using a water-lubricated masonry blade.

13 Measure the sizes of the edge pieces, and trim full tiles to size using a snap cutter.

14 Place the edge tiles, and continue installing field tiles. A rubber mallet can help to level them.

17 Cover the backer rod with exterior-grade caulk to prevent cracking between dissimilar materials.

18 Grout the tile by working the mix on the diagonal to the seams using a rubber float or squeegee.

SPACING TILE

TO MAINTAIN EVEN SPACES that result in uniform grout lines, the surest approach is to insert small plastic spacers between tiles. (You can also use a story pole marked for tiles and grout lines.) Suppliers sell several different sizes of spacers. You usually remove them before grouting. But check with the tile manufacturer because some spacers can be left under grout.

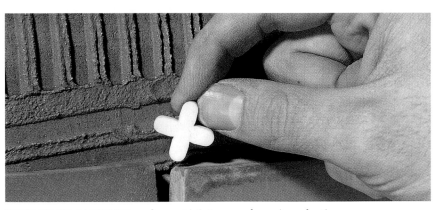

KEEP TILES ALIGNED and grout joints even by using plastic spacers.

15 Cover the tile with plastic sheeting to protect the installation and help the adhesive cure.

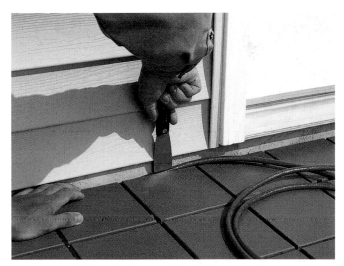

16 Push foam backer rod into the seam between the slab and the house and any control joints.

19 Remove the grout haze using a damp sponge. Clean the sponge regularly in a bucket of water.

20 Finish by applying a clear tile sealer to the entire surface with a sponge mop.

4 decks

A backyard deck can enhance your life in several ways. It makes entertaining easy and provides a pleasant outdoor space that you and your friends can enjoy together. To get ready, just give the deck a quick sweep, prepare some cool drinks, and fire up the grill as your guests gather round. For more private times, it offers a retreat where you can lounge during the day and catch up on your reading or take a quiet nap. It's also a great place to toast the sunset as night starts to fall, savoring the outdoor air without venturing far from the amenities of civilization. A good deck improves the appearance and usefulness of your home by providing a smooth transition between the house and your surrounding yard. If the costs worry you, keep in mind that a high-quality deck is bound to increase your home's resale value.

BUILDING BY THE NUMBERS

These two pages show how a typical backyard deck is constructed. The photo sequence shows a simple design to make sure the basics can be seen clearly. Of course, if you plan to build something more complicated, with multiple levels, a curved perimeter, or something that is elevated high above the ground, your job will look a lot different from this one, and it will take a lot longer. But it will still have a lot in common with this structure. These

eight sequential photos show how a typical deck evolves.

First is site preparation, which includes removing the existing sod and installing concrete piers below the frost line depth in your area. This measurement is available from your local building inspector.

Attach a joist ledger to the side of the house, and install pressure-treated posts on top of all the concrete piers. The ledger is usually placed so the decking falls just below the doorsill on the back door.

The posts are cut to the proper height so the top of the

TYPICAL DECK CONSTRUCTION SEQUENCE

1 Remove the sod; install the concrete piers.

2 Attach the ledger to house; attach the posts to the piers.

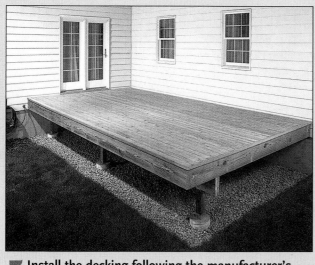

5 Install the decking following the manufacturer's directions.

6 Frame the stair landing; add the stringers.

girder that spans them will be at the same height as the top edge of the ledger that is installed on the house.

The deck joists are nailed to the top of the girder and the side of the ledger. The ledger is outfitted with galvanized joist hangers that provide pockets for the ends of the joists. When installed properly, the top of the joists should be flush with the top of the ledger. Also, install solid blocking between the joists at the mid-point of their span to keep the joists straight.

Install the deck boards perpendicular to the direction of the joists. Maintain uniform spacing between the boards of about $\frac{1}{4}$ inch to create the best appearance and aid in drainage.

In most cases, just a couple of steps are all the stairs you will need. You may need to install separate piers and concrete pavers for the bottom of the stair stringers.

Finish up by adding a railing on the deck and the open side of the stairs. Specific stair and railing designs often depend on local regulations. Check with your building inspector before proceeding.

3 Attach the girder to the tops of the posts.

4 Attach the joists to the ledger and girder; add the end joist.

7 Install the stair treads. Some stairs also have risers.

8 Install the deck railing system.

LAYING OUT AND PREPARING THE SITE

Your first job is to accurately lay out the footings of your deck. Begin by marking the ends of the ledger on your house. (See also pages 85 and 86.) Account for the outside joists and the fascia board, if there will be any. If you will be applying one-by fascia, for example, your ledger board will need to be 2 ¼ inches shorter than the finished deck on each end (1 ½ inches for the framing lumber plus ¾ inch for the fascia). Once you have marked the

ends of the ledger, use a level or a plumb bob to bring the line down to a place on the house a foot or so off the ground. Attach a screw or nail to this spot, so that you can tie a string line to it and lay out the deck.

Assemble Batter Boards. For each outside deck corner, construct two batter boards. Make these by attaching a 36- or 48-inch-long crosspiece squarely across two stakes. You can buy premade stakes or cut pieces of 1x4 to a point on one end. Although they are temporary, the batter boards must be sturdy—they will probably get bumped around.

Once the sod is removed from your deck location, cover the soil with black plastic and gravel. This will prevent plant growth and give the finished job a neat, professional look. You can also omit both the sod removal and gravel base steps.

3 Measure up one leg 3 ft.; measure up the other 4 ft.; in a square corner, the connected points equal 5 ft.

4 You could also measure the diagonals. If they are equal, the corners are square.

7 Lift the plant and roots free of the hole, and place the root ball on a piece of burlap.

8 Tie the burlap with string to protect the root area, particularly if the new planting site is not ready.

1 Construct batter boards from the 1x4 lumber. Make pointy ends to drive the boards into the ground.

2 Tie lines to the house, and set the batter boards in pairs a few feet outside the actual construction zone.

5 Use a plumb bob or level at the intersection of your lines to determine the location of the corner pier.

6 Use a shovel to dig under the root of the shrub. Mature plant roots can be difficult to remove.

9 Following a guideline about 1 ft. outside the layout line, score 16-in.-wide strips of sod using the shovel.

10 Sod rolls can get heavy, so work with sections that you can easily manage.

(continued on page 82) **81**

(continued from page 81)

11 Clear away rocks, roots, and other debris. The ground should slope away from the house.

12 Roll out the plastic. Overlap the edges by 6 in. shingle-style so that water runs away from the house.

13 Dump the gravel in several piles around the site. Rake it out to create an even surface.

TYPES OF FOOTINGS

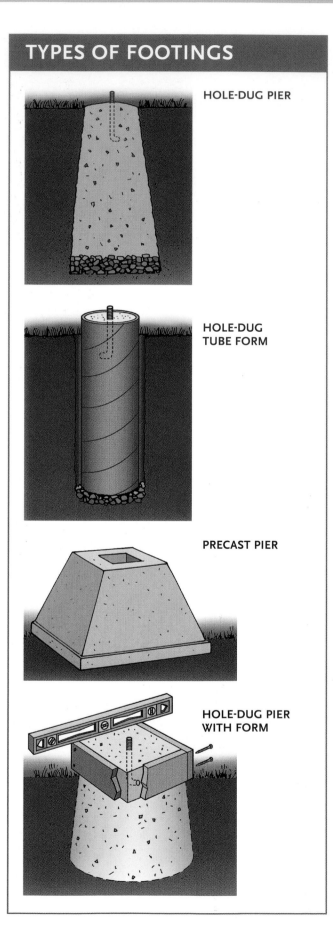

HOLE-DUG PIER

HOLE-DUG TUBE FORM

PRECAST PIER

HOLE-DUG PIER WITH FORM

DIGGING & MIX-ING CONCRETE

project

Digging pier holes can be done with a shovel, which is difficult, a posthole digger, which is easier, or a rented gas-powered auger, which is the easiest option of all. Premixed bags are the most convenient type of concrete for small jobs.

1 Using a shovel is the basic and back-breaking way to dig piers.

2 A posthole digger makes a neat hole with a small diameter.

3 The power auger is a tool you can rent. There are one- and two-person models that churn through the dirt.

4 Whether you use premixed ingredients or combine them yourself, do the mixing in a wheelbarrow.

5 Mix the dry ingredients using a hoe. Create a crater in the center of the pile.

6 Pour in the water slowly, following the directions on the bag. Too much water ruins the mixture.

83

BUILDING PIERS

project

Round fiberboard forms are the default choice for concrete piers. They come in different diameters (we used 8-inch-diameter tubes) and can be easily cut to length using a circular saw. Keep in mind that the bottom of the pier hole should be excavated to a depth just below the frost line in your area. Once the form is in place, fill it with concrete and add the post connector hardware.

1 Place a cut tube in the hole. The top of the tube should project 6 in. above grade.

2 Level the tube, and backfill to hold the tube steady. Check for level while backfilling.

3 Pour concrete into the form. Insert the J-bolt that comes with the hardware into the center of the form.

4 After the concrete cures, attach the rest of the post anchor hardware.

POST HARDWARE

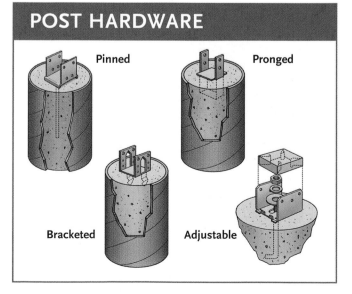

Pinned

Pronged

Bracketed

Adjustable

REMOVING SIDING

project

A ledger board is the best way to attach the deck joists to the house. These boards are usually made of 2x8 or 2x10 stock with joist hangers nailed to one side. To be attached securely, ledgers must be bolted flat against the house wall. And to accomplish this, the siding has to be removed. Work carefully when doing this job to prevent damaging the siding that will remain in place.

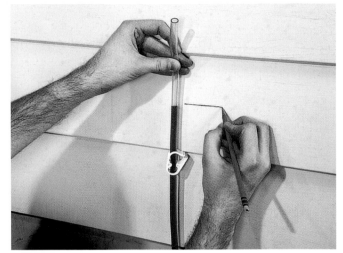

1 Establish the ends of your ledger; then find level points using a water level and snap a chalk line.

2 Set your saw to cut through the siding but not the sheathing. Make cuts at each end of the ledger.

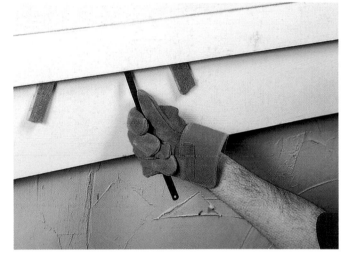

3 Pry the siding up, and insert wedges to hold it up. Use a metal blade to cut nails.

4 Make the horizontal cut with your saw. Set the blade to siding depth to avoid cutting the sheathing.

5 The siding should come out easily. If it does not, use a pry bar and hammer to ease it out.

INSTALLING LEDGERS ON WOOD

The ledger and the rim joist that covers the outside ends of the deck joists are made of the same size lumber and should be laid out at the same time. Clamp the two boards together so their edges are flush; then mark both with a square and a heavy pencil. Once the layout is done, transfer the marks from the top to the sides of the boards and install the ledger as shown below.

1 Transfer the layout marks for the joists from the ledger to the end joist.

2 Predrill and countersink holes for fasteners. This will guarantee clearance for joist hangers later.

smart tip

FLOATING DECKS

SOME DECKS DON'T HAVE A LEDGER AND AREN'T CONNECTED TO THE HOUSE, ALTHOUGH THEY MIGHT LOOK AS THOUGH THEY ARE. AN ISLAND DECK, BUILT RIGHT NEXT TO THE HOUSE, GIVES THE ILLUSION OF A STANDARD DECK BUT SKIPS THE LEDGER WORK AND ADDS AN EXTRA GIRDER NEAR THE HOUSE. BE SURE TO CHECK LOCAL CODES ABOUT FLOATING DECKS.

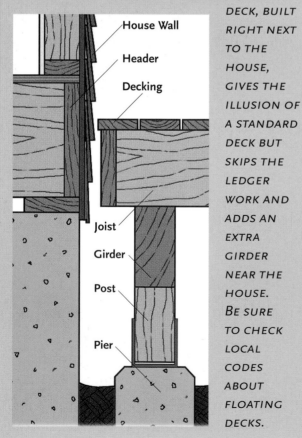

House Wall
Header
Decking
Joist
Girder
Post
Pier

3 Prop the ledger into position, and drive lag screws with a ratchet, or install carriage bolts if possible.

PLACING RAISED-DECK POSTS

project

A raised deck is built just like a low-to-the-ground deck except the posts are higher. And if your local building department approves, these posts can be buried directly in the ground instead of resting on top of concrete piers, which makes the job much easier. Just be sure to use pressure-treated posts that are rated for ground contact, and install them as shown below.

1 To locate the posts, start from a reference point on the house and plumb down.

2 Extend layout strings from plumb marks to batter boards. Mark the hole locations.

3 Remove the strings, and start digging the hole. Dig below the frost line.

4 The type of footing that supports the post will be determined by the local building code.

5 Brace the post in two directions. Plumb the post, and fill the hole with concrete to secure the post.

ANCHORING POSTS

If you install concrete piers, the last step is to place a post connector in the top of the pier before the concrete dries. If your site layout was accurate, these connectors should fall in the middle of the pier. Before attaching each post to the connector, make sure the bottom is square and flat. If it isn't, cut the end of the post so it is. Then join the post to the connector using galvanized nails.

1 Square off the bottom of the posts so that it seats securely in the post anchor.

2 Set the post in the anchor. Adjustable hardware provides some play in the anchor position.

3 Close the anchor around the post, and drive nails through the anchor into the post.

smart tip

BRACING

EVEN SHORT 4x4 POSTS FOR A DECK GIRDER NEAR GROUND LEVEL NEED TO BE BRACED SECURELY IN TWO DIRECTIONS. DRIVE POINTED STAKES INTO THE GROUND ABOUT 2 FEET AWAY FROM THE POST AS SHOWN. ATTACH A 2x4 TO EACH STAKE AND TO THE SIDES OF THE POST AT A 45-DEGREE ANGLE.

ESTABLISHING POST HEIGHT

project

Cutting the posts to finished height after they are attached to the piers (and braced in a plumb position) is the best way to get the correct height. To accomplish this, select a straight 2x4 that is long enough to span from the ledger to the posts. Hold it so its top edge is flush with the top of the ledger and it's against the side of each post. Move it so it's level; then mark the posts at the top of the 2x4.

1 Use a straight 2x4 and level to mark the elevation of the ledger on the posts.

2 Use a section of joist stock to measure down from the mark to find the bottom edge of the joist.

3 Using girder stock, measure down to find the bottom of the girder. This will be the top of the posts.

4 Mark a cutline with a square. Use a circular saw to cut the posts. You will need to make two passes.

5 Install the post caps to each post, and secure using screws or nails. Predrill nailholes.

89

MAKING AND SETTING A BUILT-UP GIRDER

project

The deck joists are supported on both ends. On the house side, the joist hangers (that are mounted on the ledger) support the joists. On the other end, the joists rest on top of a girder. This member is usually made of two 2x10s that are nailed together securely. In some cases, it may need to be made of 2x12s. Check with your local building department for the specification in your area.

1 Sight down the stock and locate the crown. Place the crowns side by side.

2 Screw or nail the boards together; use groups of 3 fasteners 12 in. on center.

3 Put the girder in the post caps crown side up. You may need a helper in some cases.

4 Plumb the girder. Braces help keep the posts from shifting.

5 Secure the girder using a series of braces. Drive screws through the post caps into the girder.

MAKING SPACED GIRDERS

If you are working alone, a spaced girder (like the one shown here) may be easier to build. It's made of two boards, like a built-up girder, but these are installed one at a time so it's easier to lift them in place. Also, this approach lets you attach the girder boards before you need to cut the posts to height. This reduces the chance of making a measuring error and cutting the posts too short.

1 Start with plumb posts. Use braces and a level to make sure the posts are plumb.

2 Use props and clamps to hold the girder stock in position, as shown. Level the boards.

3 Drill pilot holes through the girder stock and the posts about 1 in. from each edge.

4 Insert carriage bolts. (Check with building department for bolt diameter.) Use washers under nut and bolt.

5 Use a handsaw to trim the posts. The top of the post should be flush with the girder.

SETTING THE INNER JOIST

project

To install the first joist next to the house, often called the inner joist, check it for a crown and put the crowned edge up. Push it toward the house until there's a space about 1 inch wide between the side of the joist and the house wall. Attach the joist to the ledger using a corner bracket, and toenail it to the top edge of the girder using two 16d spikes, or a twist fastener like the one shown in photo 5, below.

1 When you set the first joist in place, sight down its length to find the crown. Install it crown side up.

2 Tack the edge of the joist to the ledger by toenailing the two together.

3 Make sure the corner is square. There should be about 1 in. of space between the joist and house.

4 Because you won't be able to reach both sides of the joist, secure it in place using a corner bracket.

5 To provide added strength, nail on a twist fastener where the joist crosses the main girder.

SETTING THE OUTER JOIST

project

Attach the outer joist to the ledger and the girder as you installed the inner joist. Then mark its overall length on the side, and use this mark to check that the deck is square. Compare opposite diagonal measurements; if both are the same, the deck is square. If the deck is less than ½ inch out of square, don't worry about it. But if it's more, move the outer joist as necessary to make it square.

1 Measure out from the girder to determine the amount of overhang.

2 Use a framing square to draw a cut line on the joist. Leave girder and post braces in place.

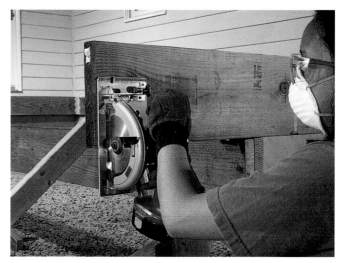

3 Cut the outer joist using a circular saw. This is usually a prominent area, so make a clean cut.

4 Before nailing, make sure the deck frame is square and the two outside joists are equal.

5 Drive a toenail through the joist into the girder. Reinforce this using a twist fastener.

93

SETTING JOISTS

project

Installing the interior joists is an easy, if repetitive, job. Start by making a square cut on the ledger end of each joist. Then nail a scrap strip to the top so it extends about ³/₄ inch beyond the end of the joist. Lower this assembly onto the ledger, and make sure the joist falls next to its layout line. Then install a joist hanger on the ledger and a twist connector on the girder for each joist.

1 Make a square cut on the ledger end of the joists. Allow the other end to run long for now.

2 To help support the joist, nail a strip of wood with a small overhang to the joist.

3 Slip the joist hanger around the joist. Check for level, and drive nails through the joist hanger.

4 For added stability, add a twist fastener where the joist crosses the girder.

5 Copy ledger layout lines to a brace. Tack to joist at midspan, bringing joists to your marks.

SETTING THE HEADER JOIST

project

Once the interior joists are nailed in place, enclose the open end of the deck by installing a header joist. Start by marking the proper joist locations on the side of the header using your original layout as a guide. Then lift the header in place; line up each joist with its mark; and nail the boards together. You can make holding the header easier by clamping scrap blocks to the bottom edge of a few joists.

1 The header, or belt, holds the ends of the joists in place and helps maintain proper spacing.

2 Create a temporary shelf for the header by clamping strips of wood to the bottom of three or four joists.

3 Making sure the top edge of the header and the tops of the joists are flush, nail the header in place.

4 Install corner framing hardware where the header meets the end joists.

5 To reinforce the deck framing, install a joist hanger where the joists meet the header.

95

INSTALLING BRIDGING

Solid bridging boards, like the blocks shown here, are installed between joists to keep the joists straight. They are cut to fit the space between the joists, which is usually 14½ inches if you have placed your joists on uniform 16-inch centers. Installing these blocks is time-consuming. But they make for a much stronger deck, with very little joist deflection when you walk over the surface.

1 Find the centerpoint of the two outer joists. Snap a chalk line between them.

2 Transfer the marks to the sides of the joist. Use a square that will reach the bottom of the joists.

3 Each joist bay will get a section of solid blocking, but you will need to offset them for nailing.

4 Cut bridging from joist stock, and install between joists. The brace helps maintain proper spacing.

5 Drive two nails into each edge of the bridging. Remove the brace when bridging is installed.

LAYING OUT DECK BOARDS

project

For the best finished appearance, plan the placement of the deck boards before you start installing them. You don't want to begin with a full-width board against the house, followed by the rest of the boards on the deck, only to discover that the last board is only 1 or 2 inches wide. Make sure that the last board is at least half its standard width and that it overhangs the header joist by at least ½ inch.

1 Set a ½-in. strip of plywood against the house, and set the first board in place. String a chalk line.

2 Use a scrap piece of decking to make sure that there will be a gap between the first board and the house.

3 A common nail makes a good spacer for kiln-dried lumber. Position the board, and remove the nail.

4 String a chalk line from one end of the deck to the other. Check for bulges and depressions.

5 Set out the boards and spacers if necessary. The end board should overhang the framing.

INSTALLING DECKING

Nailing decking boards in place is easy if you are using straight stock. But if you are not, then you need a standard to determine if a board is OK. Here's a good rule of thumb: If a board is bowed more than 1 inch in 16 feet, discard it; if it is bowed ³/₄ in. in 16 feet, cut it in half; if it is bowed ½ in. or less in 16 feet, then use it as is and just pry it into a straight line as you nail it in place.

1 The decking should overhang the outer joist plus any fascia or skirting by 1 to 2 in.

2 Set the first board on the chalk line drawn earlier. Maintain the gap between the board and house.

3 For professional results, keep nails spaced evenly. Use the shank to locate each nail from the edge.

4 Drive nails an inch from each edge. Protect the deck with scrap wood when pulling bent nails.

5 Lay out 10 to 12 rows as you work. This will help you keep butt joints several rows apart.

EDGE TRIMMING

project

When you install deck boards let them overhang the open end slightly. This allows you to cut off all the boards at once, which yields a neat edge. You can dress up these edges with a simple trim board (see below) or you can just leave them exposed. If you don't use the trim board, then sand the ends using a belt sander to remove any cut marks left over from the circular saw.

1 The overhang should cover the end joist and the fascia by about 1 in.

2 Snap a chalk line from one end of the deck to the other. This will be your cut line.

3 Run the circular saw along the cut line with the saw's shoe resting on the deck.

4 Install the trim to the edges of the deck board using finishing nails.

5 Because some deck boards may be higher than others, trim the surface using a belt sander.

STAIR STRINGER LAYOUT

project

Local codes usually require stairs from the ground to the deck if the difference in elevation is greater than 12 inches. Your building department will tell you what the local standards are. On this deck, we built a small landing at the top of the stairs. (See page 78.) If you want to do the same thing, build the landing like you built the deck; then calculate your stair length as shown here.

1 Extend a level 2x4 from the platform, and measure the distance down to a level landing area.

2 Set stops on a framing square where numbers on opposite sides match your rise and unit run.

3 Mark the top of the stringer. Slide the stops along the stringer to repeat tread layout lines.

STRINGER MARKUP

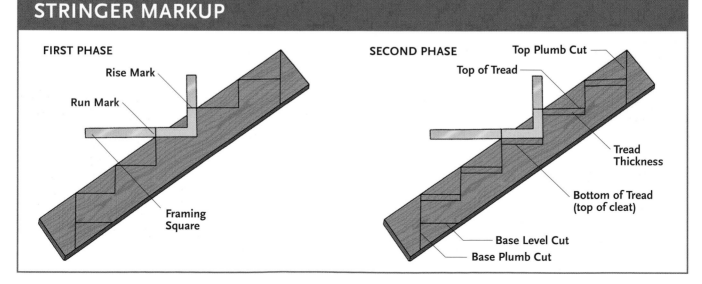

FIRST PHASE

Rise Mark

Run Mark

Framing Square

SECOND PHASE

Top Plumb Cut

Top of Tread

Tread Thickness

Bottom of Tread (top of cleat)

Base Level Cut

Base Plumb Cut

INSTALLING SOLID STRINGERS

project

There are several ways to build outdoor stairs. Our choice was to use galvanized steel tread brackets to support the steps, which is easier than the alternatives. To make sure the stairs are stable and feel solid when you walk on them, you need a good landing pad. Precast concrete pavers, like those which we used, are a good choice. Just install them so they are level from side to side and front to back.

1 Make sure the landing pad is level before installing the stringers.

2 Mark the location of each stringer on the platform or deck. The edges of the stringer must be straight.

3 Attach the top edges of the stringers to the platform using corner brackets.

4 Screw galvanized tread brackets to the stringer, following the layout lines.

5 Attach a galvanized clip to the pad.

101

SETTING CARRIAGES

If you have a level deck and landing pad, then installing the stair parts it a simple matter. Attach the side stringers, and locate the center carriage midway between the two. Once all three are in place, cut the tread boards to length and nail them to the stringers and carriage. On this deck our treads ran between the stringers, but you can build stairs with open treads, as shown on the next page.

1 Tack the center carriage in place, checking for level at each tread location.

2 Use the access space from inside the platform framing to drive lag screws into the top of the carriage.

3 Reinforce the carriage attachment by installing corner brackets.

4 Measure the stair opening, and center the middle carriage.

5 Tack a brace across the bottom of the stringers. This secures them as you add fasteners and treads.

TREAD OPTIONS

ON SOLID STRINGERS, do not rely on nails driven into the treads through the stringers to support the step. This weak detail can cause splits and accidents.

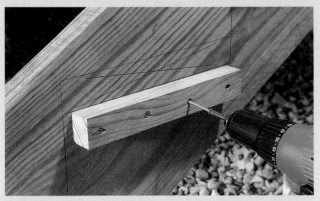

A BETTER WAY to support treads is to attach a nailing block, or cleat, to the stringer, and nail or screw the tread to the cleat. However, with time the wood may decay.

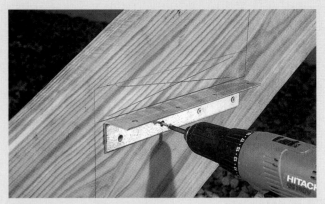

GALVANIZED BRACKETS provide durable support for treads. Fasten treads by screwing through the flange into the bracket.

ON SAWTOOTH STRINGERS, the sawtooth pattern creates a ready-made support for the treads

IF TREADS EXTEND BEYOND THE STRINGERS, finish treads with curved corners and beveled edges.

smart tip

BOX STEPS

IF YOUR DECK IS ONLY A STEP UP FROM THE YARD, YOU MIGHT AVOID STRINGERS ALTOGETHER AND BUILD BOX STEPS. THESE ARE EASY-TO-BUILD REC-TANGULAR FRAMES, USUALLY MADE OF 2x6 TREATED LUMBER AND COVERED WITH DECK TREADS. FOR TWO OR MORE STEPS, BUILD A LARGE BOX, PLACING PROGRESSIVELY SMALLER ONES ON TOP.

project

HOW TO MAKE RAILING POSTS

There must be almost as many railing designs as there are deck builders. But generally all types fall to two basic categories: railings that are supported by posts that seem to rest on the deck (but actually go through the deck), and railings with posts that are attached to the side of the deck. The second type is easier to build and it's the approach used on this deck.

1 Use a circular saw to make a 45-deg. angled cut at the top end of the posts.

2 Make a series of closely spaced cuts on the opposite side of the posts to create a recess for the top rail.

3 Make another set of cuts for the bottom rail. Clean the recess using a chisel.

4 Notch the deck overhang so that the post lies flat against the joist.

5 Attach the post using lag screws and washers. Check for level, and adjust as necessary.

HOW TO INSTALL RAILS

project

Careful preparation and assembly are the keys to installing rail boards. If the notches that were cut in the posts for the horizontal rails and the side of the deck were done accurately, then attaching the rails should be an easier job. Once they're in place, both rails should be level and parallel with the deck surface. Any seams made in these rails should be formed with 45-degree scarf joints.

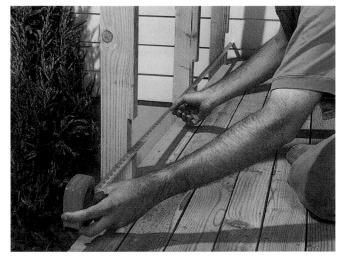

1 On long runs that require more than one piece of lumber, create a scarf joint that falls on a post.

2 To make a scarf joint, cut 45-deg. angles in opposing ends of the rails that meet at the post.

3 Tap the rails into the post notches, and drill pilot holes for the screws. Install two screws per joint.

4 This top rail projects past posts on opposite sides of a corner. Cut 45-deg. angles in the rails.

5 Apply adhesive to the mitered ends; clamp in place; and drive screws to secure the joint.

project

HOW TO INSTALL BALUSTERS

If you have a lot of balusters to make, it's hard to get good results using any tool but a table saw. If you don't have one, rent one, or borrow one from a friend. These saws make a better cut than circular saws in a fraction of the time. Be sure to keep all the guards in place when you are working. Photo 1 shows the blade guard removed so that you can see how the stock is cut.

1 Mark a sound 2x4 for cutting, and rip the balusters using a table saw.

2 Using the T-bevel, copy the angle on the support posts and transfer it to the balusters.

3 Clamp a group of balusters together, and remove imperfections using a belt sander.

4 Drill pilot holes for the screws in the balusters to avoid splitting the wood.

5 Work your way around the perimeter of the deck, fastening the balusters with screws.

FINISHING THE SURFACE

THE SAME DECK BOARDS can look dramatically different depending on the type of protection you apply. Most decks require some protection from the elements. So a final waterproof sealer is always in order. The sealer, even a clear sealer, will alter the look of the lumber, but you can make more drastic changes by applying a stain or paint. The most practical finishes are clear sealers and semi-transparent stains. They do not crack or chip like paint and some heavy-bodied stains. These pictures show different coatings on the same kind of Douglas fir. Before you select a finish, test it on scrap deck lumber.

SEMITRANSPARENT STAINS allow some grain to show but add tone to the decking. They come in water-based or oil-based solutions.

SOLID-BODY STAINS cover the wood grain completely. They can also unify deck boards that have different hues and grain patterns.

PAINT provides the most opaque finish, but it lies on the surface rather than penetrating into the wood's fibers.

OIL-BASED CLEAR SEALERS are the easiest to apply because they are thin and flow readily. You may need more than one coat.

LATEX-BASED CLEAR SEALERS feature easy cleanup, but the finish may not be as durable as a comparable oil-based finish.

5 walkways

"Paths are more or less essential ... [to a garden], a pathless garden being not only a contradiction in terms but highly inconvenient, as anybody will agree who has ever had to hop across a cabbage patch in order to inspect a pedigree lobelia." So wrote Heath Robinson and K. R. G. Browne in their book, *How to Make Your Garden Grow*, published in 1938.

As these experts suggested, paths and steps are a practical as well as an aesthetic component of a landscape. Superficially, paths lead comfortably from point A to point B, keeping the feet clean and dry. However, walking in a yard is a type of journey with different experiences available along the way. The sort of path you create will help determine the nature of that journey. You can use paths to choreograph the way visitors move through your landscape.

MORTAR-LAID WALK

TO BUILD A SLAB for a small walkway, you may want to mix by hand, always stirring the dry mix before adding any water. But bear in mind that one wheelbarrow-sized batch generally makes less than 3 cubic feet. You would need about nine batches to make just 1 cubic yard. To strengthen the slab, it's important to add a layer of welded wire reinforcement. The wire should run in the center area of the slab. Wires should not protrude from the pour. Accomplish this by rolling out the wire onto half bricks or special mounting hardware called chairs. To estimate the amount of concrete you'll need, total up the volume inside the forms in feet, and divide by 27 to convert into the conventional ordering standard of cubic yards. It's wise to play it safe and build in an excess of about 8 percent by changing the conversion factor from 27 to 25.

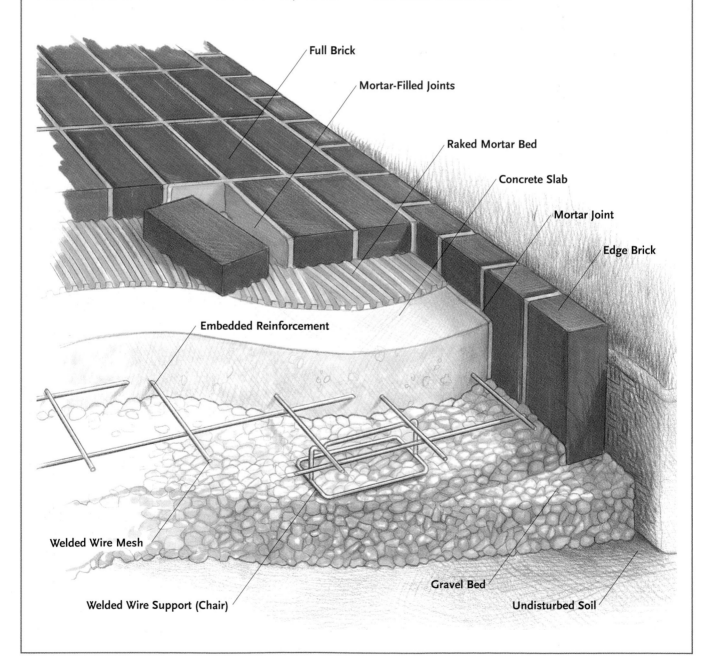

Full Brick

Mortar-Filled Joints

Raked Mortar Bed

Concrete Slab

Mortar Joint

Edge Brick

Embedded Reinforcement

Welded Wire Mesh

Welded Wire Support (Chair)

Gravel Bed

Undisturbed Soil

MORTAR-LAID WALK INSTALLATION

project

TOOLS & MATERIALS

- Wheelbarrow ▪ Measuring tape
- Work gloves and safety glasses
- Hammer ▪ Rake ▪ Mason's and notched trowels ▪ Grout bag ▪ Striking tool
- String and line level ▪ Exterior-grade paving bricks ▪ Reinforcing welded wire
- Gravel ▪ Lumber for forms and stakes
- Mortar mix ▪ Concrete mix

SMART TIP

EVEN A CONCRETE SLAB REINFORCED WITH WELDED WIRE CAN CRACK IF THE GRAVEL AND GROUND BENEATH THE SLAB GIVE WAY. PREVENT THIS BY COMPACTING THE BOTTOM OF THE EXCAVATION AND THE GRAVEL. IF THE WALK AREA IS IN A LOW SPOT, ADD A HIGH-SIDE PERFORATED PIPE IN GRAVEL TO DIVERT WATER.

1 Measure down from a level line on stakes to check the level of the excavation at several points.

2 Rake gravel over the compacted base of the excavation, creating a base about 4 in. thick.

3 Build forms to contain the concrete. Support the boards with stakes driven outside the form.

4 Lay welded wire to reinforce the concrete. Support it on wire chairs, as shown, or half bricks.

(continued on page 112)

111

(continued from page 111)

EASY-FILL MORTAR JOINTS

FILLING JOINTS with wet mortar can be time consuming if you want to keep the brick surface clean and avoid a lot of cleanup work. A faster approach is to sweep dry mix into the joints and then add water. You need to sweep back and forth to thoroughly fill the seams. Then use a fine spray to soak the surface. Too strong a spray can wash out the mortar mix.

SWEEP the dry mortar mix into the joints between bricks.

LIGHTLY SPRAY water over the surface, and cover to cure the mortar.

5 Mix your concrete by hand in a wheelbarrow or in a rented mixer, or have ready-mix delivered.

6 Mortar soldier bricks against the sides of the slab to edge and contain the field bricks.

9 Set the bricks in the mortar, using a guide string to keep the courses square and aligned.

10 Use a grout bag to force mortar fully into the joints. This device leaves the surface clean.

PROTECTING YOUR YARD

RUNNING HEAVY WHEELBARROWS full of concrete to your excavation can chop up your lawn and require reseeding. To protect the grass and grounds around the work site, you can mix your concrete on a tarp laid in the driveway, and lay a series of planks and plywood sheets along the supply route from your driveway mixing station to the excavation.

LAY BOARDS as a track for heavy wheelbarrows to preserve the grass.

7 Make a dry layout with the field bricks, placing them in the pattern you have chosen.

8 Trowel out a layer of mortar in an area you can work before it dries. Rake it with a notched trowel.

11 Smooth and compact the mortar between bricks by drawing a striking tool over the joints.

12 Clean any mortar that is forced onto the brick surfaces. Use a mason's trowel.

DRY-LAID PAVER WALK

THE KEY PART OF ANY DRY-LAID WALK is its base. If you skimp on gravel and sand or skip the crucial compacting steps, whatever you lay on the base will shift. To reduce future maintenance and keep your walkway looking good, remove the sod and dig to undisturbed soil. If you need to remove some large rocks, fill those holes and compact your fill. For small projects and tight spaces, you can use a hand tamper. (See Step 2.) On larger areas you'll need to rent a gasoline-powered tamper. (See Step 9.) If your walkway is in the path of natural groundwater runoff, it's wise to divert the water. One way to do this is to build a gravel collection trench on the high side of the walkway and run a pipe from it to carry water under the walkway. This extra step can prevent groundwater from gradually eroding the base and undermining the pavers or bricks.

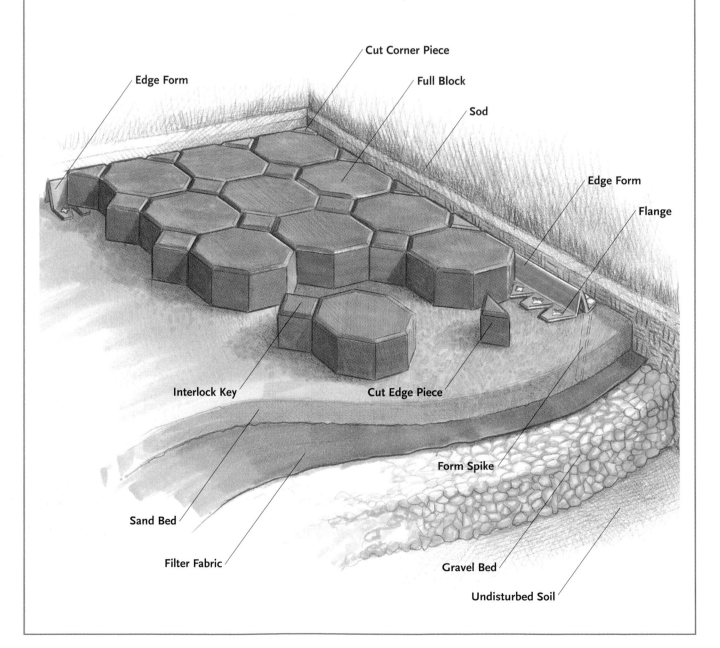

DRY-LAID PAVER WALK INSTALLATION

project

TOOLS & MATERIALS

▪ Work gloves and safety goggles ▪ Spade
▪ Rake or hoe ▪ Hand or mechanical
tamper ▪ Mallet and bedding board
▪ Broom ▪ Water hose ▪ Ruler and pencil
▪ Brick set and 2-lb. hammer
▪ Landscape sheeting ▪ Sand ▪ Gravel
▪ Shims or wedges ▪ Edging material
▪ Edging spikes ▪ Exterior-grade pavers
▪ Lumber for screed board

SMART TIP

*YOU CAN USE REDWOOD, CEDAR, OR PRESSURE-
TREATED WOOD TO KEEP BRICKS OR PAVERS FROM
SHIFTING. BUT THIS KIND OF EDGING REQUIRES
STAKES AND CAN DETERIORATE IN TIME. PLASTIC
EDGING IS LONGER LASTING, EASIER TO INSTALL,
AND AVAILABLE IN SEGMENTED LENGTHS THAT YOU
CAN BEND ALONG THE EDGES OF CURVING WALKS.*

1 Remove the sod, and rake out the area to form a uniform base. If you remove large rocks, fill their holes.

2 After raking out gravel to form a base of 4 in. minimum, compact it over the entire excavation.

3 Roll out a layer of landscape sheeting to suppress weeds and contain the embedding layer of sand.

4 Spread 1 to 2 in. of sand over the sheeting, and rake it out to form a roughly uniform base.

(continued on page 116) **115**

(continued from page 115)

CURVING CORNERS

PLASTIC EDGING is flexible, but continuous strips are more prone to kink in tight turns than the segmented type (near right), which is flexible enough to edge a serpentine walk. Bear in mind that bricks and pavers have square corners. If you lay out a sharp bend, you'll need to do a lot of cutting. With gradual bends (far right) you can taper the joints and thus need to make fewer cuts.

DRIVE GALVANIZED SPIKES to secure flexible edging in a gentle curve.

GRADUAL CURVES allow a fan pattern with tapered joints.

5 Level the sand base using a screed board. You can set up guides for the screed beside the walkway.

6 Lay edging along the walkway, and secure it using long spikes driven through the perforations.

9 Finish seating the pavers or bricks by running a power tamper over the surface.

10 If a paver is still slightly raised, lay a board on the surface and pound it down using a mallet.

TRIMMING BRICKS

TO CUT BRICKS and pavers by hand, mark your cut line, allowing for joint space (near right), and score the line with several taps on a brick set (far right) before delivering a heavy blow to make the cut. You can also use a masonry blade on a circular saw for scoring (wearing eye protection), or rent a wet saw to make many complicated cuts on a large project.

MARK your cut line, allowing for the joint space between units.

SCORE the full line with taps on a brick set before breaking the brick.

7 Set the edging to accommodate your pattern, and start embedding the bricks or pavers.

8 Work out from the corner, interlocking pavers and setting them into the sand using a mallet.

11 Spread fine sand over the surface, and sweep back and forth to force it into the joints.

12 Spray the surface with water to settle the sand, and repeat the last two steps to finish the job.

STONE WALK INSTALLATION

project

On walkways and patios, setting stone in a bed of sand is the most practical approach. You do need to compact the base, but you don't need to pour a concrete slab. The drawback is that a sand base will shift over time. Generally, use a 2- to 3-inch bed for stones of the same thickness but a thicker bed for stones of varying thickness.

Screed a sand bed using a straight 2x4 with the ends riding on guides to keep the sand surface uniform. The guides can be forms built around the work area and secured with stakes once they are level with each other. You can also embed pipes in the sand, use them as screeds, and fill in the shallow troughs with more sand after you remove them.

Embed stones in the sand bed with firm taps of a rubber mallet. Finish by sweeping sand between the joints with a stiff broom, working a 5- or 6-foot section at a time. A light spray of water will pack down the sand and wash it off the surface. Allow the surface to dry, and repeat the process until all the joints are filled and compacted. You'll probably need to replenish the sand periodically, usually once a year.

TOOLS & MATERIALS
▮ Shovel, rake, and tamper
▮ Layout string and level
▮ Hammer and cold chisel
▮ Broom and garden hose
▮ Plastic sheeting
▮ Sand and gravel
▮ Pavers
▮ Screed boards or pipes

1 Embedded pipes serve as screeds for a straight board that you pull along to level the sand base.

3 Check the surface with a level; run a straightedge across the seams to find and correct high spots.

5 Spray the surface with water, and brush on another layer of sand until the joints are full.

2 Use string guides to layout the stones. Set them firmly in the sand using a rubber mallet.

4 Brush sand across the surface, working your broom back and forth to fill the joints.

smart tip

MOVING STONE

To move heavy stones, rely on an oversized pry bar or a dolly instead of your back, arms, and legs.

CUTTING STONE

FOR CUTTING AND SHAPING STONE, you'll need a small sledgehammer that is tempered to strike metal tools safely. You can cut relatively thin stone with a circular saw fitted with a masonry blade. Another option is to score the stone with a blade cut before finishing the cut by hand. This can help you get a clean edge. To cut by hand, mark your cut line across the stone and score it with a stone chisel and hammer, working back and forth. With the score line etched into the surface, place a board or pipe under the stone for leverage and use heavier hammer blows to break the stone.

THE PIPE provides a fulcrum that helps the stone break cleanly when you strike it.

THE STONE CHISEL scores the surface, and heavier blows with a 2-lb. hammer break the stone.

6 landscape walls

Landscape designs greatly benefit from a strong vertical element, such as a freestanding or retaining wall. While there are numerous materials, shapes, and construction methods from which to choose, all types help to define boundaries, enclose special spaces, and provide a foundation for a variety of plants. Perhaps the easiest materials for the do-it-yourselfer are mortarless interlocking concrete blocks, designed especially for retaining walls. Building a mortared stone wall requires more time and effort than constructing a dry-laid wall, but the mortared wall is sturdier and has a more formal appearance. No matter which material you choose, check with your local building department to find out whether you will require a building permit.

DRY-LAID STONE WALL

DRY-LAID STONE WALLS generally rest on undisturbed or compacted soil instead of on concrete footings. But you should remove the sod to avoid major settling. If the ground has been graded recently, rent a vibrating compactor to make sure the base is solid. It's also wise to use the largest, flattest stones for the base course and save smaller, more irregular stones for higher courses. To plan the job, you need to lay out your raw materials ahead of time. This time-consuming task will pay off as you gain experience with the stonemason's art of picking the right stone for each location. Although dry-laid walls are meant to look rustic, you will likely need to cut some stone. A hammer and a cold chisel or brick set should serve well enough, although you can score corner stones using a special masonry blade to get straighter cuts.

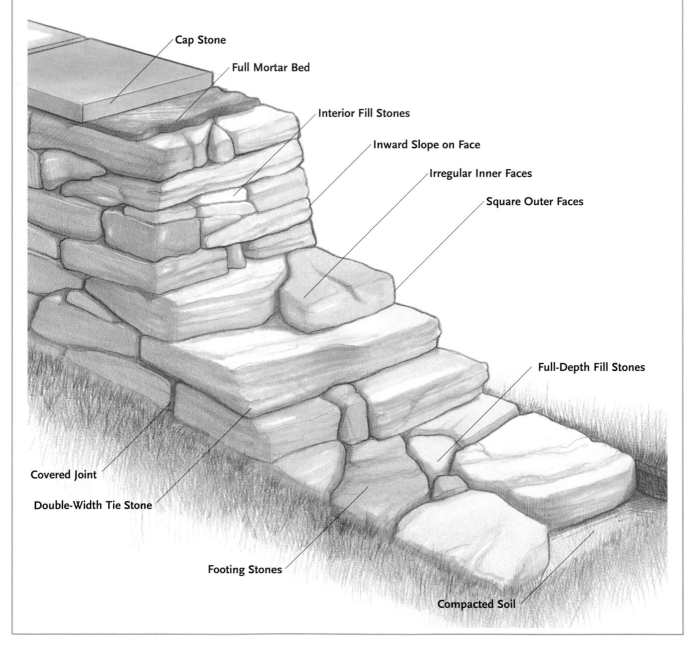

Cap Stone

Full Mortar Bed

Interior Fill Stones

Inward Slope on Face

Irregular Inner Faces

Square Outer Faces

Full-Depth Fill Stones

Covered Joint

Double-Width Tie Stone

Footing Stones

Compacted Soil

DRY-LAID STONE WALL INSTALLATION

project

TOOLS & MATERIALS

- Work gloves ■ Mason's trowel ■ Shovel
- Spirit level ■ Hawk ■ Mortar box
- Hammer ■ Slope gauge (optional)
- Stones ■ Shims or wedges
- Mortar mix ■ Cap stones
- Stakes and string

SMART TIP

Stones can be very heavy. Be sure to lift them carefully, keeping your back straight and using your legs to raise the weight. A special back brace or lifting belt will also help to prevent injury during a long day of stonework.

1 Group your stones by size and shape, putting aside the largest, flattest stones for the base course.

2 Mark the wall location using string and stakes. Then cut along the edges, and roll up the sod.

3 Dig into the soil base, if necessary, to nest irregular projections on bottoms of base stones.

4 Use a flat, double-width stone to head off both rows in the first course at the end of the wall.

(continued on page 124) **123**

(continued from page 123)

USING A SLOPE GAUGE

STONE WALLS SHOULD SLOPE inward from bottom to top. The rule of thumb is to factor in about 1 inch of slope per 2 feet of height. You can estimate the slope using a level (Step 9) or make a slope gauge from scrap lumber. This gauge consists of two 1x2s joined at one end and spread apart at the other. With the gauge against the wall, wide end up, the level should read plumb.

BUILD THE GAUGE using 1x2s with a spread equal to the wall's slope.

THE LEVEL reads plumb when the slope gauge rests against the wall.

5 Fill the interior gaps between the larger stones with smaller stones and rubble.

6 Lay the stones to a guide along the outsides of the wall, with irregular edges facing inward.

9 Dry-laid stone walls should slope slightly inward. (See "Using a Slope Gauge," above.)

10 Use small stones as wedges to prop up and level larger stones in the course above.

SPECIAL MASONRY BLADES

A HAMMER AND COLD CHISEL can handle most of the cuts on rustic, dry-laid walls. But if you need to make very accurate corner cuts on end stones, for example, you can score the stone using a solid carborundum disk or with a special diamond-carbide tipped blade. Not all of these masonry blades are rated for stone, so you need to check the labels.

WOOD BLADE (left) compared to diamond masonry blade (right).

NEW CARBORUNDUM BLADES (left) wear down quickly (right).

7 Use occasional double-wide stones in the courses that follow to help tie the wall together.

8 In alternate courses at the end of the wall, you should install a square-edged cross stone.

11 Trowel a layer of mortar over the top course of stones to level and embed the cap stones.

12 You can use cut stones with a slight overhang on each side to finish the wall.

MORTAR-LAID STONE WALL

TO SUPPORT A MORTARED WALL you need a solid footing. As a guide, pour a footing that's as deep and about twice as wide as the wall is thick. (For sloped walls, take the average thickness.) Stake the forms to keep their boards from being forced apart by the concrete. Also reinforce the footing with at least two continuous lengths of rebar set in the lower third of the form, several inches in from each side. If the footing turns a corner, bend the rebar to suit, and use wire ties at connections, which should be overlapped by about a foot. If the wall will be wide, with a rubble center, you also can set vertical rebar every few feet. On narrower walls this isn't possible because the rebar will keep you from setting and adjusting at least some of the stones. Sort your stones ahead of time by thickness, and set aside double-width stones.

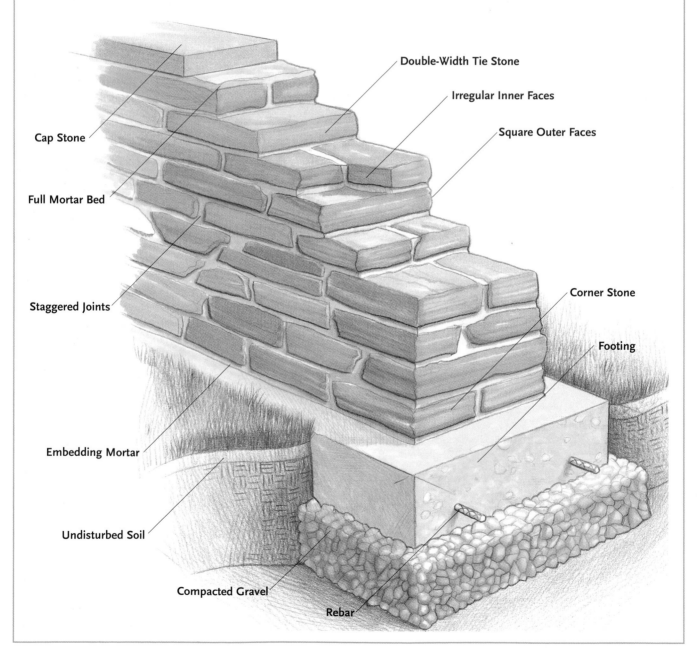

Double-Width Tie Stone

Irregular Inner Faces

Square Outer Faces

Cap Stone

Full Mortar Bed

Staggered Joints

Corner Stone

Footing

Embedding Mortar

Undisturbed Soil

Compacted Gravel

Rebar

MORTAR-LAID STONE WALL INSTALLATION

project

TOOLS & MATERIALS

- Chalk-line box
- Work gloves
- Trowels
- String and line level
- Whisk broom
- Striking tool
- Mallet
- Level
- Ruler and pencil
- Hose and adjustable spray head
- Prepared footing
- Stone
- Mortar mix
- Shims or wedges
- 1x2 stakes

SMART TIP

BECAUSE MORTARED WALLS ARE EXTREMELY HEAVY, YOU SHOULD POUR A CONCRETE FOOTING ON UNDISTURBED SOIL. IF YOU EXCAVATE AFTER REMOVING SOD AND LOOSE TOPSOIL, ON A SLOPE FOR EXAMPLE, TAKE THE TIME TO COMPACT THE BASE BEFORE ADDING GRAVEL AND FORMS FOR THE POUR.

1 Snap chalk lines along each side of the footing to help you align the course of base stones.

2 Make a dry layout to determine an economical fit, keeping the straightest edges to the outside.

3 Trowel a liberal layer of mortar up to the guidelines, and embed the first course of stones.

4 Use small stones or trimmed scrap to fill in the core of the wall between large stones.

(continued on page 128)

(continued from page 127)

WEDGING-UP IRREGULAR STONES

SOME STONES have surfaces that are too irregular to seat properly on the course below. The solution is to temporarily prop them into a level position with one or two small wooden wedges. Wet the wedges (so they will be easier to remove later); insert them; and mortar the joint. When the mortar is firm, you can pull out the wedges and fill in the small holes.

INSERT wet wooden wedges to temporarily support irregular stones.

PULL the wedges when the mortar firms up. Then fill in the holes.

5 Drive 1x2 stakes at each end of the wall, and attach a string and line level to guide the courses.

6 Build up the corners using full-width stones in every other course to tie the wall together.

9 Use a striking tool to smooth and compact the joints into a rain-shedding concave shape.

10 Spread a full mortar bed over the top course of full stones and fillers, and then embed the caps.

USING A GROUT BAG

PASTRY CHEFS use bags to ice cakes, and you can use a larger, heavy-duty version to grout stone walls. This approach helps keep the edges of the stones free of mortar, which reduces cleanup time. Masonry supply outlets sell bags with a variety of nozzles that control the flow. Simply fill the bag with a slightly soupy mix; close the end; and squeeze to apply.

MIX THE MORTAR slightly wet, and trowel it into the bag.

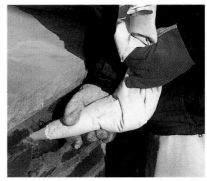

USE THE BAG like a caulking gun, moving the nozzle as you squeeze.

7 As your materials permit, also lay double-wide stones in a staggered pattern throughout the wall.

8 When the mortar begins to set up, use a whisk broom to sweep away excess mortar.

11 Long bluestone caps on this wall are being tapped level using a rubber mallet.

12 Wash the wall with muriatic acid and water (1 to 10 parts), and rinse with a garden hose.

BLOCK RETAINING WALL

THE TWO KEYS to building a sound retaining wall are the strength of its basic construction and the wall's ability to release groundwater, which is the biggest cause of deterioration and tipover. Of the many possible designs and materials, the strongest is solid masonry—either poured concrete or the block construction shown in this project. The blocks rest on a poured foundation and are reinforced with vertical rebars embedded in the concrete. There are two systems for reducing the amount of hydrostatic pressure on a wall. One is a water-collection trench filled with gravel on the high side of the wall. This employs a drainpipe near the base to carry the water to a release point at the end of the wall. The other system is a series of weep holes that allow any water reaching the wall to flow through.

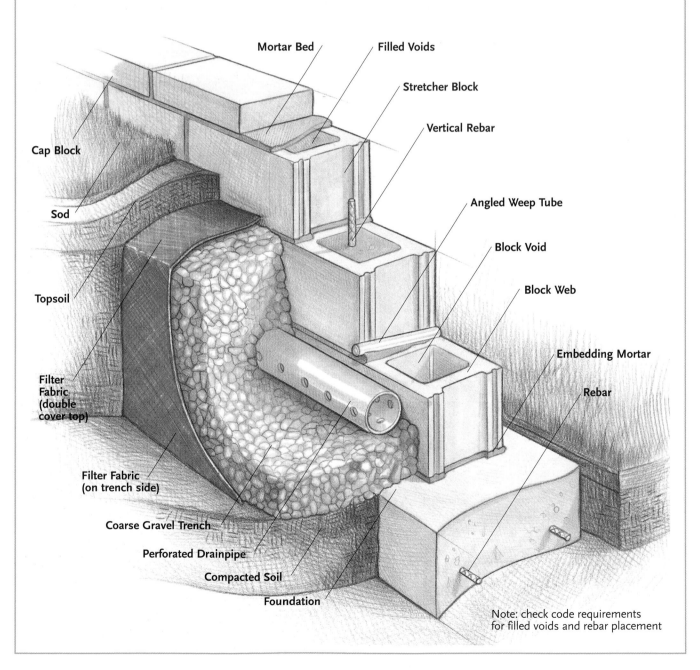

Mortar Bed

Filled Voids

Stretcher Block

Vertical Rebar

Cap Block

Angled Weep Tube

Sod

Block Void

Block Web

Topsoil

Filter Fabric (double cover top)

Embedding Mortar

Rebar

Filter Fabric (on trench side)

Coarse Gravel Trench

Perforated Drainpipe

Compacted Soil

Foundation

Note: check code requirements for filled voids and rebar placement

BLOCK RETAINING WALL INSTALLATION

project

TOOLS & MATERIALS
- Work gloves and safety glasses
- Shovel ▪ Hammer ▪ Tamper
- Hoe ▪ Wheelbarrow and bucket
- Mason's trowel ▪ Chalk line or string guide ▪ Measuring tape and pencil
- Wooden forms ▪ Concrete
- Rebar ▪ Mortar ▪ Concrete block
- Galvanized pipe ▪ Gravel
- Perforated drainpipe ▪ Filter fabric

SMART TIP
WITH A DRAINAGE TRENCH AND PIPE TO CARRY WATER AWAY FROM THE WALL, YOU NEED ONLY SMALL-DIAMETER WEEP HOLES SET OVER THE FIRST COURSE ABOUT EVERY TWO OR THREE BLOCKS. THE SMALL DIAMETER MINIMIZES TRIMMING AT BLOCK CORNERS. WITHOUT A DRAINAGE TRENCH, AND WHERE WATER FLOW IS GREAT, USE LARGER PIPES.

1 Dig a trench to accommodate the poured concrete footing you will use to support the wall.

2 Construct a form twice as wide as the block, and brace it with stakes driven outside the form.

3 Mix concrete for the footing in a wheelbarrow, and screed across the form to level the pour.

4 Before the concrete hardens, set lengths of rebar aligned with the block voids.

(continued on page 132) **131**

(continued from page 131)

GUARDING WEEP HOLES

THE MAIN PROBLEM with weep holes is clogging, which lets water build up pressure on the high side of the wall. A gravel trench backed and topped with filter fabric will help keep out dirt. In addition, cover the pipe inlets with galvanized wire mesh. Shape it to create a hollow area around the pipe. Then pour in gravel carefully so you don't dislodge the mesh.

CUT GALVANIZED MESH, and form it into a basket to cover the pipe.

A WIRE BASKET keeps the uphill end of the pipe from clogging.

5 Set the block with buttered ends into a layer of mortar. Use a string to check alignment.

6 Form sloped weep holes with a ¾-in. galvanized or PVC pipe set into the joint at every third block.

9 Set solid cap blocks on the wall, tapping them into position, and checking alignment and level.

10 Add about 6 in. of gravel on the high side of the wall. Note the screened weep-hole pipe.

LAYING LANDSCAPE FILTER FABRIC

FILTER FABRIC is a tightly woven material that lets water through but filters out fine dirt that can eventually clog weep holes and the entire drainage trench. You can spread fabric over the gravel on the high side of the gravel trench behind the wall and over the filled trench, as well. The fabric cover allows you to replace topsoil and sod, and conceal the gravel.

FILTER FABRIC lets water into the gravel but keeps out most dirt.

YOU CAN COVER the filter fabric with mulch or topsoil and sod.

7 Use a trowel to remove excess mortar that squeezes out of the joints.

8 For maximum strength, fill the voids between the block webs. Note the rebar.

11 Lay perforated pipe, holes down, with a slight slope to drain water toward the end of the wall.

12 Bury the pipe, and fill the trench with gravel. You can apply filter fabric and sod at the top.

INTERLOCKING BLOCK WALL

IF MORTARING A MASONRY GARDEN WALL seems like too much work, or just too complicated, try one of the interlocking designs. Available in many sizes and finishes, these manufactured blocks are built to stack without mortar. Some have a lip to create an offset so that the wall can slope back into a hill. Others, like the units in this project, have slots to help you offset the blocks or align them in a vertical wall. Because these blocks have no mortar joints, the structure is porous, so they can serve either in a retaining wall laid into a bank or as a freestanding garden wall. Typical interlocking systems use rigid plastic pins set both horizontally and vertically in preformed slots to keep the blocks aligned. To stagger joints, you will need to cut a few blocks. Aside from that, the job involves heavy but very simple stacking.

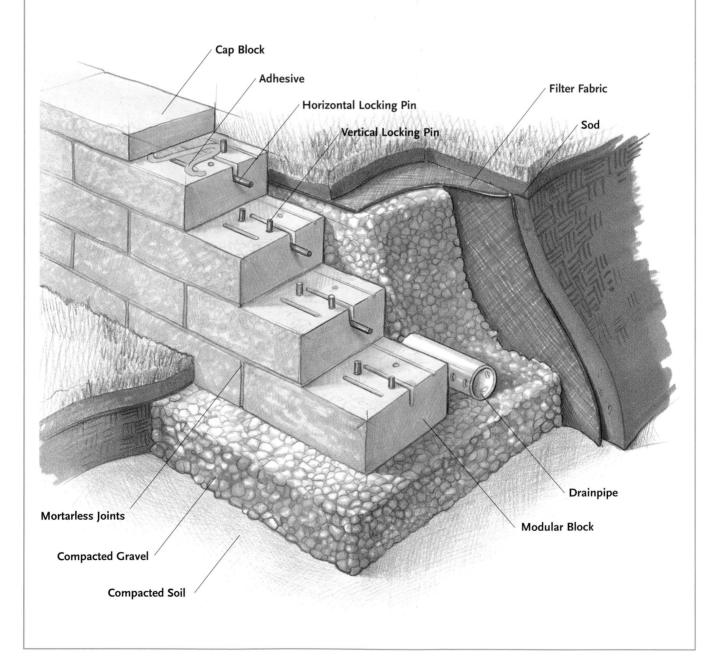

Cap Block

Adhesive

Horizontal Locking Pin

Vertical Locking Pin

Filter Fabric

Sod

Drainpipe

Modular Block

Mortarless Joints

Compacted Gravel

Compacted Soil

INTERLOCKING BLOCK RETAINING WALL INSTALLATION

project

TOOLS & MATERIALS

▪ Shovel and wheelbarrow
▪ 4x4 for tamping soil ▪ Caulking gun
▪ Spirit level ▪ Hammer and brick set
▪ Work gloves and safety glasses
▪ String and mason's blocks
▪ Retaining wall block ▪ Block connectors
▪ Perforated pipe ▪ Gravel
▪ Adhesive for cap block

SMART TIP

GENERALLY, YOU CAN LAY A SHORT WALL OF INTER-LOCKED BLOCKS ON COMPACTED OR UNDISTURBED SOIL COVERED WITH ABOUT 6 INCHES OF GRAVEL. BE SURE THAT THE BASE COURSE IS LEVEL. CHECK MANUFACTURER'S RECOMMENDATIONS ABOUT HEIGHT LIMITS AND REQUIREMENTS FOR FOOTINGS UNDER HIGHER AND HEAVIER WALLS.

1 Dig a trench for the retaining wall, leaving enough room on the high side for gravel and a drainpipe.

2 Compact the soil at the bottom of the shallow trench using a 4x4 or hand tamper.

3 Fill the trench with about 4 in. of gravel to provide a firm base for the interlocking blocks.

4 Place the first few blocks on the gravel bed, aligning the faces and checking the tops for level.

(continued on page 136) **135**

(continued from page 135)

IMPROVING DRAINAGE

EVEN A POROUS BLOCK RETAIN-ING WALL may need supplemental drainage. Although a porous, un-mortared wall doesn't need the extra drainage to resist cracking or tipover, it might need drainage to prevent muddy streams of water from washing through it. The best bet is a gravel trench with perforated pipe at the base, sloped slightly to carry water away from the wall.

PERFORATED PIPE sections fit into one another behind long walls.

A WRAP of filter fabric keeps out silt that can clog the pipe.

5 Install perforated drain piping, holes down, on gravel behind the wall after laying the first course.

6 Set mason's blocks at each end of the wall with a string to check the face as you insert connectors.

9 Insert plastic pegs in preformed holes to align the courses. Some systems allow setback positioning.

10 Also install connectors horizontally in preformed slots between mating blocks.

TERRACING SLOPING YARDS

RETAINING WALLS ARE CRUCIAL on sloping sites where you want to terrace part of the yard to make it flat. One key to terracing is to equalize cut and fill. That means planning the retaining wall location and height so that the amount of dirt you remove, or cut, from the high side of the slope equals the amount you need to fill on the low side to make a level yard.

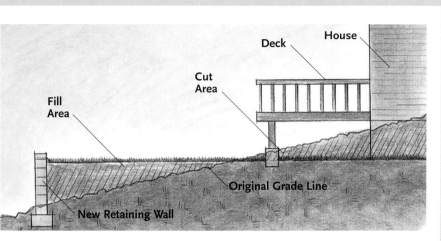

Deck · House · Cut Area · Fill Area · Original Grade Line · New Retaining Wall

7 Cover the perforated drainpipe with gravel up to the height of the first course.

8 Use a hammer and brick set to cut half blocks for the ends so that you can stagger the block joints.

11 Check for plumb regularly as you work. Some types of block step back a bit in each course.

12 Attach cap blocks using a caulking gun and construction adhesive as specified.

7 fences

Erecting a fence is the quickest and generally easiest way to define the boundaries of your property. To be a successful part of a landscape design, however, a fence should be planned to complement the architecture of your house. You might design your fence to echo the color and materials used in your home's exterior. Also bear in mind the character of your neighborhood and region. While your fence may be beautiful in its own right, make sure that it fits well within the overall look of the yards and properties in your area. In addition to style, other considerations for making a fence harmonious with its surroundings include its height, construction, and the materials used.

INSTALLING POSTS

project

The hardest part of installing a wood post is digging the hole. If you have soft, sandy soil, then a posthole digger will handle the job. For many posts, a rented power auger will cut the job down to size. But rocky soil is another matter. Using a posthole digger and a 6-foot steel bar to loosen rocks will dig most rocky holes. But it's a lot easier to hire a contractor with a small auger on the back of a tractor to dig these holes.

TOOLS & MATERIALS
▌Posthole digger ▌Hoe ▌Tape measure
▌Trowel ▌Shovel ▌Hammer
▌Level ▌Drill-driver ▌Wood stakes
▌String ▌Braces ▌Concrete
▌Wood posts ▌Gravel ▌Spray paint

1 Install layout strings that match the final location of the fence sections. If you want a square corner, make sure that the strings intersect at a 90-deg. angle. Drive a stake at the intersection point to indicate where the corner post should be.

4 Check with your local building department to learn the frost-line depth in your area. Then make sure to excavate 6 in. below this point. If you don't do this, frost heave will move the post up and either distort or break apart the finished fence.

5 Pour about 6 in. of gravel into the bottom of each posthole to create a stable base for the post and to provide some drainage for water that enters the hole.

2 Determine where the posts will fall along all sides of the fence; then mark these spots with a spray paint or chalk "X." When the marking is done, remove the string.

3 A hand-operated posthole digger works well in soft, sandy soil. But in rocky or clay-filled soil it makes more sense to rent a power auger. Or hire a contractor to dig the postholes using a tractor-mounted auger.

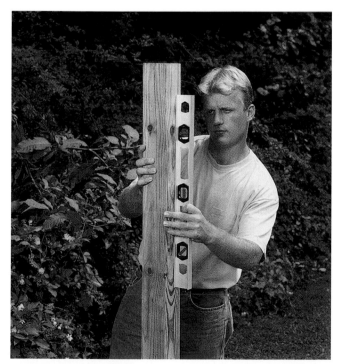

6 Cut the post about 12 in. longer than finished length so it can be trimmed exactly after the fence is complete. Slide the post into the hole, and use it to tamp down and compact the gravel at the bottom of the hole. Check for plumb.

7 Replace the layout string so you know exactly where to place the post. Then support the post with wood braces attached to stakes on adjacent sides of the post. Use a level to check for plumb in both directions.

(continued on page 142)

(continued from page 141)

8 For the strongest installation, fill around each post with concrete. Use premixed dry concrete sold in bags at home centers and lumberyards. Just mix it with water in a tub or a wheelbarrow using a garden hoe. For 10 or more posts, rent a concrete mixer.

9 Pour the mixed concrete into the hole around the post using a shovel. Work carefully to avoid dislodging any loose soil from the sides of the hole. When mixed in with the concrete, the soil weakens the mix.

10 Once the hole is filled with concrete, use a long stick or the shovel handle to remove any air bubbles from the mix. Use an up-and-down plunging motion to break apart these air pockets.

11 To encourage water to drain away from the post, create a beveled cap in the top of the concrete using a small trowel or wide putty knife. When the concrete dries, fill the gap between it and the post with silicone caulk.

NOTCHING POSTS

project

Most fences are built with rails nailed to the surfaces of supporting posts. But on some fences, particularly designs with only a few widely spaced rails, you may want to dress up the installation by recessing the horizontal boards into the posts. Here's how to create those notches.

TOOLS & MATERIALS
- Circular saw ▪ Posts
- Sawhorses ▪ Line level
- Hammer ▪ Tape measure
- Chisel ▪ Safety glasses ▪
Combination square

1 Set the depth of the circular saw blade to match the thickness of the rail. Mark the post and make repeated saw kerfs between layout lines, approximately ¼ in. apart.

2 Start the kerfs by carefully making square cuts down the middle of both layout lines. If you have trouble making square cuts, you can use a speed square as a guide.

3 Once all the kerfs are cut, break them out of the notch by striking them from the side with a hammer. Once the wood pieces are removed, smooth the bottom of the notch using a hammer and sharp chisel (inset). Test fit a rail in the notch.

4 Once all the notches are cut, lower the posts into their holes, and check for alignment with the notches in other posts, using a mason's string and a line level. When you're satisfied with the alignment, brace the posts in a plumb position.

project

INSTALLING A PICKET FENCE

There are many ways to build a basic frame for a picket fence. One of the best is to notch the posts for the rails so they sit flush, and make any rail joints in the centerline of the post notches. Just make sure to drill nail pilot holes in the ends of the rails so you don't split them when they are attached. Then nail the pickets to the top and bottom rails. Space them according to your own taste, though a common rule of thumb is to use a space that's the same width as one of the pickets.

TOOLS & MATERIALS
▌ Drill-driver ▌ Plumb bob ▌ Saw
▌ Hammer ▌ Line level or 4-ft. level
▌ Tape measure ▌ 1x4s for pickets
▌ 2x4s for rails ▌ 4x4 posts
▌ Scrap for spacers ▌ Mason's string

1 Once the posts are notched and installed, begin installing the rails. The easiest way to attach these boards is to clamp them in place, drill pilot holes, and drive galvanized screws or nails through them into the posts.

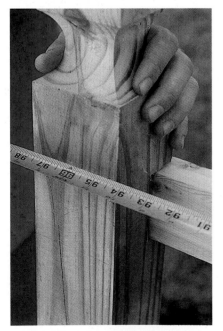

2 To determine the finished picket spacing, first measure the distance between the posts. Then divide this by the width of a picket and of a single space. If you don't come up with a whole number, adjust the width of the spaces.

3 One way to keep the pickets level as you attach them to the fence rails is to install a guide string between the posts, usually at the bottom of the pickets.

4 Once you establish the proper spacing between pickets, cut a scrap wood spacer to match this dimension. Then use the spacer to align each successive picket. Use galvanized screws to prevent corrosion.

POST TOP VARIATIONS

THERE ARE SEVERAL WAYS to top a post aside from the basic square cut. Some of the best options combine decorative details with the ability to shed water, which can shorten post life by causing rot where it collects on the porous end grain. The easiest approach is to make an angled cut. Chamfering the top edges helps, as well. Adding a full cap rail, either chamfered or angled, also reinforces the fence.

Angle Cut

Chamfered Edges

Angled Cap

Flat Cap with Chamfers

RAIL CONNECTORS

Nailed Butt Joint

Nailed On Edge

Screwed Hardware

Recessed

INSTALLING A RUSTIC FENCE

Rustic fences define space without blocking the view. And they are relatively easy to build, so you can cover a lot of ground with less effort and fewer materials than most other designs. While these fences do have some built-in adjustability—the rails can slide a couple of inches in either direction—it's still important to lay out the fence carefully. Usually the post spacing is 6 or 8 feet to match the typical length of stock rails. Different spacing is possible, as long as you modify the rails to fit.

TOOLS & MATERIALS
▌ Drill and bits ▌ Hammer ▌ Saw
▌ Shovel ▌ Tape measure ▌ 4-ft. level
▌ Chisel ▌ Safety glasses ▌ Posts and rails
▌ 2x4 braces ▌ 1x2 stakes ▌ Concrete mix
▌ Galvanized nails

1 If you use posts that aren't pre-mortised, you'll have to cut the mortises yourself. Start by laying out the hole from both sides of the post. Then bore overlapping holes through the posts to remove most of the wood stock. Use a Forstner or a spade bit.

2 Clean up the sides of the mortise with a hammer and a sharp chisel. Work to the layout lines, and try to make the sides square to the surface of the post.

3 When the mortises are complete, dig the posthole, and lower the post into it. Make sure the mortises are at the correct height and pointing in the right direction.

4 Check the post for plumb, and attach two braces (at a 90-deg. angle to each other) to keep it properly aligned when you backfill most of the hole with gravel.

● ALTERNATE RUSTIC RAILS

RUSTIC-STYLE post-and-rail fences are generally available with posts already notched and rails already tapered. But you can also use rough lumber and make those cuts yourself. Another low-cost option is to use 2x4s for the rails in place of stock rails with tapered ends. Instead of making a typical side-by-side rustic joint, simply cut a half-lap so that the boards join inside the post notch. With the 2x4s on edge, the lap itself is concealed inside the post. Pressure-treated 2x4s are the best choice for economy rails. But you may want to apply two coats of preservative and penetrating stain to get a color match between the posts and rails.

5 Slide mating rails into each mortise, and pin them using a single galvanized nail driven through both rails and into the post. The nail is not required structurally. It just helps keep the rails from accidentally sliding out of their mortises.

6 Once all the rails are installed, finish backfilling the postholes. You can use soil for this job and just plant some grass seed on top. Or you can pour a concrete collar on top of the gravel. This will stiffen the posts and make the whole fence stronger.

147

INSTALLING A VINYL FENCE

On most vinyl fences, you need to assemble stock pieces that are designed to fit into slots in the posts and tracks in the rails without cutting. (Of course, you can cut as needed to modify the stock sizes. Manufacturers explain how to do this for their products.) Although basic assembly procedures do vary, generally you fit the rails into mortises in the hollow posts, and attach them using screws, clips, or special rings that vary with the specific fence design. Usually the rails are also hollow and are made with built-in channels to hold fence boards or pickets.

Keep in mind, using vinyl won't make installing the posts any easier. You still have to dig postholes, which is usually the hardest part of any fence installation. Start with a careful layout and use a posthole digger or rented power auger. Because the components are already formed, and the slots or mortises for the rails are already cut, you must install all the posts at the same height. This means you must add (or remove) fill under posts as needed to make sure the rails will fit properly. Once you firm up the posts, you can add the rails, or you can assemble subcomponents, such as rails and boards, and join them as units to the posts. In most cases, the components simply fit together under hand pressure. But when screws are used, small decorative caps are provided to hide the screw heads.

TOOLS & MATERIALS
- Shovel ▌Mason's trowel
- Hammer ▌Drill-driver
- Tape measure
- 2-ft. level
- Mason's string
- Concrete mix
- 1x2s for stakes
- 2x4s for braces
- Mixing tub ▌Screws

1 Accurate layout is the crucial first step in any fence project. Begin by driving stakes into the ground past the corner points. Then stretch mason's string between the stakes. Make sure the strings cross at a 90-deg. angle to ensure a square corner.

3 Pour 4 to 6 in. of crushed stone or gravel in the bottom of the hole; then set the post on top of this stone. Raise or lower the posts (so the rail mortises on adjacent posts align with each other) by removing or adding crushed stone to the hole.

2 Lay out the position of all the posts along the strings. Then remove the strings and start digging the postholes. Use a shovel for shallow holes like this. But for deeper holes, where the local frost line is more than 12 in., use a posthole digger or a rental auger.

● ASSEMBLY JIG

HANDLING MANY FENCE PARTS at the same time can be difficult. Just when you have several boards or pickets coming together in a subassembly, they can fall out of position. A simple assembly jig (or a pair of them) helps. The base is a 2x4 or 2x6 a few feet long for stability. Two short pieces serve as holding blocks. Screw them to the base, allowing just enough room for the base rail between. The jig will hold the section upright as you assemble the pieces.

4 Brace the post in the plumb position from two directions that are 90 deg. apart. Attach the bottom end of the braces to stakes driven into the ground. Attach the top of the braces to the post using clamps.

5 Double-check the post for plumb using a 2- or 4-ft. level. Inspect adjacent sides, and adjust the clamps as necessary to keep the post plumb.

(continued on page 150)

149

(continued from page 149)

6 With the post securely braced in a plumb position, use a plastic tub and a shovel to mix dry concrete and water into a stiff consistency. Pour this concrete around the post, and taper the top surface so water will run off.

7 Once the concrete has set on the first post, slide the rails (or any rail-and-fencing subassembly) into their post mortises. Then add a post on the other ends of the rails, and plumb and brace this second post in its hole.

10 Once the panels are resting in the bottom rail groove, cover the top edges with either a top rail or—in this case—a mid rail. Spread the top of the second post slightly so the rail can fit into the mortise. After the rail is in place, the post will move back.

11 In some cases, like the one shown here, a mid rail needs to be outfitted with a channel to hold the decorative lattice at the top of the fence. It is attached using either galvanized or stainless-steel screws.

8 After installing the second post, check the rails for level using a 2- or 4-ft. level. If the ground has a gentle slope (1 to 2 in. per 10 ft. of run), and you want to follow it, then push the top and bottom rails up or down slightly to conform to this slope.

9 Some fence panel sections are joined together with splines that slide into edge groves on adjacent pieces. To make the job go faster, preassemble several panels before installing them in the fence rails.

12 Cut the lattice panel to size using a circular saw with a fine-tooth blade. Slide the lattice into the mid-rail channel and push it against the post. Then hold it in place by installing the top fence rail.

13 Once all the fence sections are installed, finish up the job by installing a decorative cap on the top of each post. Generally, these caps just slide over the top of the posts. No fasteners are required.

151

8 trellises, arbors, and gazebos

Trellises, arbors, and gazebos can lend an air of magic and romance to a garden. Generally we think of trellises in terms of the prefabricated sheets of diamond- or square-grid lattice and the fan-shaped supports for training climbers, both of which are readily available at home and garden centers in both wood and plastic. Lacking a pattern book, most gardeners are unaware of the incredible variety of designs, patterns, and optical illusions that can be created with trellises. Today's landscapes feature arbors to frame a walkway or serve as the entrance to a garden. The one we show provides a bit of shade on a hot day. And while gazebos may seem like a throwback to an earlier time, new versions serve as focal points in many modern landscapes.

BUILDING A MODULAR CORNER TRELLIS

project

Cut all the parts that make up the two frames to size on a table saw and a miter saw or chop saw. (See "Top and Side Views," page 156.) Next, cut the lattice strips to size on a table saw. (See "Cutting List," below.) After cutting the first one, make sure it fits in all the frame grooves before cutting the rest. Cut one extra strip, and rip it to 3/8 inch. This is the strip gauge.

From the half-sheet of 1/4-inch hardboard, cut three strips 6 inches wide. Crosscut two into 16-inch-long pieces, for a total of six, and the third into a 16-inch- and a 32-inch-long piece. These are the latticework gauges. Once the lattice panels are complete, join the frame parts and these panels as shown in steps 7 to 9.

Cut and install the decorative brackets. Finish up by installing the trellis posts in postholes with 6 or more inches of gravel at the bottom.

CUTTING LIST

Part	Qty.	Thickness	Width	Length	Stock
Frame tops/bottoms	4	3/4"	2 1/4"	27 3/4"	1x6 white oak
Frame sides	4	3/4"	2 1/4"	39 1/4"	1x6 white oak
Vertical lattice strips	6	1/2"	1/2"	39 1/2"	1x6 white oak
Long filler strips	4	1/2"	1/2"	39 1/2"	1x6 white oak
Horizontal lattice strips	20	1/2"	1/2"	26 3/4"	1x6 white oak
Short filler strips	16	1/2"	1/2"	6"	1x6 white oak
Corner post	1	3 1/2"	3 1/2"	96"	4x4 8' red cedar
End posts	2	3 1/2"	3 1/2"	72"	4x4 12' red cedar
Bottom/top rails	4	1"	3 1/8"	27 3/4"	5/4x4 12' red cedar
Brackets	2	1 1/2"	5 7/8"	24 3/16"	2x8 8' red cedar
Post trim	12	1 1/16"	1 1/2"	4 7/8"	1x6 8' red cedar

LUMBER
- Half sheet of 1/4-in. hardboard
- 4 pcs. 1x6 8-ft. white oak
- 1 pc. 4x4 12-ft. western red cedar
- 1 pc. 4x4 8-ft. western red cedar
- 1 pc. 5/4x4 12-ft. western red cedar
- 1 pc. 2x8 8-ft. western red cedar
- 1 pc. 1x6 8-ft. western red cedar

TOOLS & MATERIALS
- Table saw ▌Circular saw
- Saber saw ▌Miter box or chop saw ▌Router with bits
- Bar clamps ▌Power drill with bits ▌Pipe clamps
- Spring clamps
- Stainless-steel screws, #8 x1 5/8 in.
- Stainless-steel screws, #8 x 2 in.
- 2 stainless-steel screws, #10 x 3 in.
- 17-gauge, 3/4 in., 1 in., and 1 1/4 in. stainless-steel brads
- Waterproof glue

1 Cut the frame parts to size, and cut a ½-in.-wide by ⅛-in.-deep groove down the middle of each using a router with an edge guide. Clamp the frame piece to a worktable, and move the clamps as necessary to allow the router to move along the board.

2 Clamp a side frame board to the edge of a worktable, and position the horizontal lattice strips and the six latticework gauges against it. Apply clamps to key parts of the assembly to keep them from shifting.

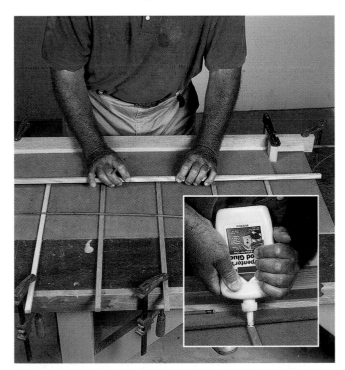

3 Set the ⅜-in. strip gauge against the frame board, over the horizontal lattice strips, and abut a 6 x 32-in. latticework gauge to it. Align the centers of a vertical lattice strip and the middle horizontal strip. Apply a dab of glue at each intersection point (inset).

4 Reposition the vertical strip, and drill pilot holes for the brads (inset). Use ¾-in.-long stainless-steel brads to join the strips. Carefully drive them with light strokes. If you have a 13-oz. hammer, use it. It's easier to use for delicate work. Repeat for the rest of the vertical strips.

(continued on page 156) **155**

(continued from page 155)

TOP AND SIDE VIEWS

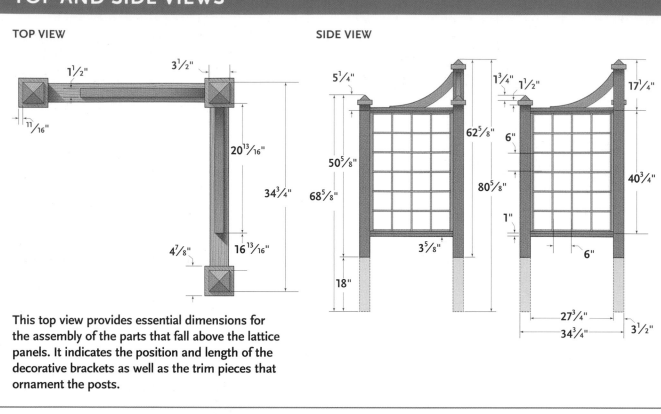

TOP VIEW

SIDE VIEW

This top view provides essential dimensions for the assembly of the parts that fall above the lattice panels. It indicates the position and length of the decorative brackets as well as the trim pieces that ornament the posts.

PANEL ASSEMBLY

Vertical Lattice Strip

Frame Top

Short Filler Strip

Long Filler Strip

Frame Side

Horizontal Lattice Strip

Frame Bottom

7 Glue a long filler strip into the side piece. Remove the brace, and place the frame on top of your worktable. Slide the lattice panel into the frame so the vertical strips slide in the grooves in the top and bottom frame pieces and the filler strip fits between the horizontal strips.

5 Install the second layer of horizontal strips so they align exactly with the first layer of horizontal strips. Glue and nail them to the vertical strips.

6 Once the lattice panel is complete, join one frame side to a bottom and a top frame piece to form a U-shaped assembly. Use a pipe clamp to hold the other side piece between the bottom and top frames to help hold the angle at the corner.

8 Fit the second side frame board into the lattice panel and against the top and bottom frame pieces. Hold this assembly tight with clamps as necessary. Then join the corners of the frame boards using stainless-steel screws.

9 Fill the grooves between the vertical strips on the top and bottom frame boards with the short filler strips, which are the same width and thickness as the other filler strips. Glue and clamp them in place using one spring clamp per filler.

(continued on page 158) **157**

(continued from page 157)

10 The top of each trellis post must be shaped to a point. To do this, cut a 45-deg. bevel at the top of all four sides of each post. Clamp the post to a worktable to keep it from moving when you make these cuts.

11 Lay out the decorative brackets that appear on the top of both lattice frames using the drawing on the facing page as a guide. Draw the curves with a trammel arm and the straight sections with a framing square.

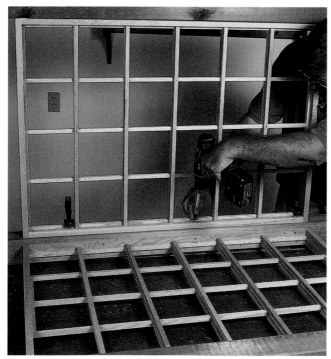

14 Once the first lattice panel is attached to one side post and the corner post, lay this assembly on the worktable and lift the second panel, with side post attached, onto the corner post. Clamp it in place, and attach it using screws driven through the side frame.

15 Attach the brackets to the top rails and then to the top of the lattice frames and to the sides of the corner posts. Use two screws to join each bracket to its rail and frame and a single 3-in. screw, driven at an angle, to join the top of the bracket to the corner post.

12 Cut the bracket arcs using a router attached to a plywood trammel. Bolt one end of the trammel to the router base. Screw the other end to the same spots where the trammel arm used for drawing the arcs was attached.

13 Cut the posts to size, and lay out the sides of all three posts for the proper location of the lattice panels. Then lift each panel in place and attach it with stainless-steel screws.

16 Cut miters on the ends of the trim pieces that decorate the post tops. Make sure these pieces fit properly; apply waterproof glue; and nail them in place with stainless-steel brads. Finish by installing the trellis posts in postholes with gravel at the bottom.

BRACKET LAYOUT

This pattern shows the shape of the two brackets that sit on top of the lattice panels. The red "X's" indicate the sections that abut the trellis parts.

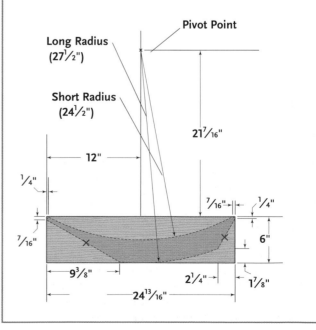

Pivot Point

Long Radius
($27\frac{1}{2}$")

Short Radius
($24\frac{1}{2}$")

$21\frac{7}{16}$"

12"

$\frac{1}{4}$"

$\frac{7}{16}$" $\frac{1}{4}$"

$\frac{7}{16}$"

6"

$9\frac{3}{8}$"

$2\frac{1}{4}$"

$1\frac{7}{8}$"

$24\frac{13}{16}$"

project

BUILDING A GRAPE ARBOR

Begin by laying out your lawn for the location of the postholes. Then determine how deep the holes should be excavated to prevent frost damage.

Dig the holes accordingly, and place the posts in the holes. (See "Setting Posts," on page 163) When all the posts are aligned and braced, backfill the postholes with concrete mixed in a wheelbarrow.

Join the top of the posts in pairs with the arbor rafters. These are attached to the sides of the posts with galvanized carriage bolts. Make sure that they are installed level from side to side. Then cut and install lattice strips on the top of these rafters, followed by attaching lattice strips to the sides of the arbor. Keep in mind that this structure was designed as a module so that you can easily adjust the measurements.

CUTTING LIST

Part	Quantity	Thickness	Width	Length	SYP Stock
Posts	8	$3\frac{1}{2}$"	$3\frac{1}{2}$"	144"	4x4 12'
Rafters	4	$1\frac{1}{2}$"	$5\frac{1}{2}$"	67"	2x6 12'
Nailers	4	$\frac{3}{4}$"	$1\frac{1}{2}$"	4"	1x2 8'
Roof interior strips	6	$\frac{3}{4}$"	$1\frac{1}{2}$"	$42\frac{1}{2}$"*	1x2 8'
Roof cross strips	12	$\frac{3}{4}$"	$1\frac{1}{2}$"	55"*	1x2 8'
Roof long strips	7	$\frac{3}{4}$"	$1\frac{1}{2}$"	$59\frac{1}{8}$" **	1x2 8'
Roof long strips	7	$\frac{3}{4}$"	$1\frac{1}{2}$"	$85\frac{3}{8}$" **	1x2 8'
Side horizontal strips	16	$\frac{3}{4}$"	$1\frac{1}{2}$"	$47\frac{3}{4}$" **	1x2 8'
Side horizontal strips	16	$\frac{3}{4}$"	$1\frac{1}{2}$"	$93\frac{3}{4}$" **	1x2 8'
Side vertical strips	24	$\frac{3}{4}$"	$1\frac{1}{2}$"	77"*	1x2 8'

*Approximate finished lengths

**Approximate finished lengths. Sets of strips will be butted and then trimmed to produce strips to equal length of arbor.

LUMBER
- 8 pcs. 4x4 12-ft. treated southern yellow pine
- 2 pcs. 2x6 12-ft. treated southern yellow pine
- 75 pcs. 1x2 8-ft. treated southern yellow pine

TOOLS & MATERIALS
- Tape measure ▮ Line level
- Mason's string ▮ Shovel and hoe
- Clamshell posthole digger
- Level ▮ Wheelbarrow ▮ Trowel
- Chop saw ▮ Power drill with bits
- Framing square ▮ Hammer
- Bar and spring clamps
- 16 galvanized carriage bolts, nuts, and washers, $\frac{1}{4}$ x 5 in.
- $1\frac{5}{8}$-in. deck screws
- 1-in. deck screws
- $1\frac{1}{4}$-in. stainless-steel brads
- Concrete as needed

LAYING OUT POSTHOLES

This diagram shows the location of the postholes for the grape arbor project. To make sure the holes line up on the sides and are square at the corners, set up batter boards and string as shown. The red numbers indicate the pairs of batter boards that support a single string: 1 and 2, 3 and 4, 5 and 6, and 7 and 8.

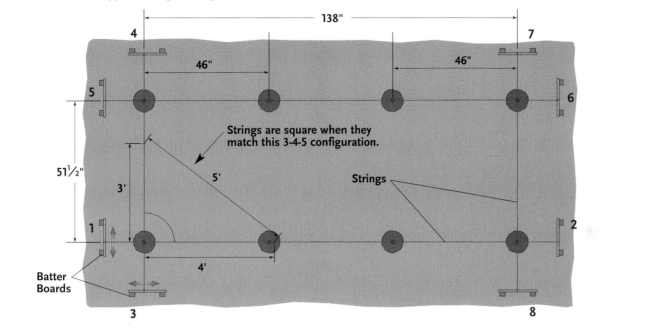

1 For the posthole locations, set up one batter board with a level crosspiece. For the opposite batter board, add a line level to a string, and attach the string to the first crosspiece. Use the string to level the second crosspiece. When level, attach the crosspiece to the stakes.

2 Set up the adjacent batter boards, and make sure the intersecting strings are square using the 3-4-5 method. (See drawing.) To find the center of the corner posts, drop a plumb bob below the intersection point of the end and side strings. Drive a stake at this point.

(continued on page 162) **161**

(continued from page 161)

3 Once the holes are excavated, lower the posts into the holes and attach braces to adjacent sides. Drive stakes in the ground so the braces can reach from post to stake. Then plumb each post with a level, and attach the braces to the stakes so the post doesn't move.

4 Once the corner posts are done, continue to install the rest of the posts in a similar fashion. Plumb and brace each post in place, and make sure that the distance between the posts on one side of the arbor and those on the other side is 42½ in. using a spacer (on the ground).

5 When all the posts are installed and braced in a plumb position, mix some concrete in a wheelbarrow and pour it around each post to backfill the holes. Smooth and taper the top of the concrete (so water will run off) using a mason's trowel.

6 Mark the finished post height on one of the corner posts. Then stretch a string with a line level in place between this post and others in the arbor. Mark a level line on each; then use a square to draw a cutline through the level line. Cut off the waste using a circular saw.

SETTING POSTS

After the postholes are excavated and the posts are lowered into the holes, reattach the layout strings to the batter boards to establish the exact locations of the posts. These strings have to move $1\frac{3}{4}$ inches out from their original location at the centerline of the posts. Now the reference line is on the outside surface of the posts.

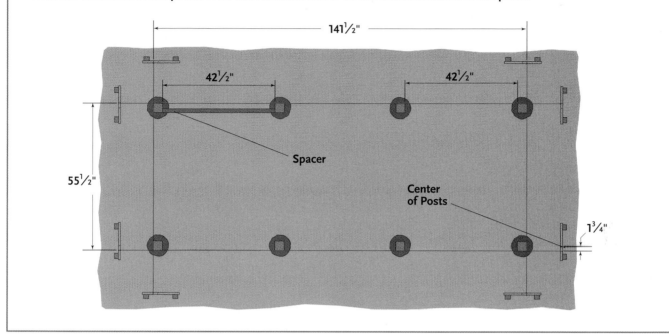

RAFTER LAYOUT

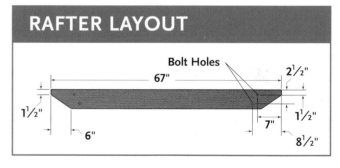

7 Lay out the size and shape of the arbor rafters using a framing square and tape measure. Place the rafters on sawhorses or a worktable, and make the cuts using a circular saw.

8 Clamp each rafter to the sides of the posts. Then lay out and drill $\frac{1}{4}$-in. carriage bolt holes through both. Use a $\frac{7}{8}$-in. spade bit to create $\frac{1}{2}$-in.-deep counterbores for washers and nuts. Slide the galvanized bolts into these holes, and tighten them in place.

(continued on page 164)

(continued from page 163)

9 Install the nailer blocks on the side of the rafters to receive the interior roof strips. Then attach these strips between the rafters with galvanized screws. Be sure to drill pilot holes to avoid the risk of splitting the thin strip.

10 Cut the cross strips for the arbor roof lattice to size, and install them over the interior roof strips. Space these strips evenly using blocks made of scrap wood. Nail the strips together using stainless-steel brads.

TOP VIEW

This top view shows how the lattice strips fit on top of the arbor. First, the interior roof strips are installed between the rafters. Then the short roof strips are nailed to the interior strips, followed by the long roof strips that are joined to the short strips underneath with stainless-steel screws.

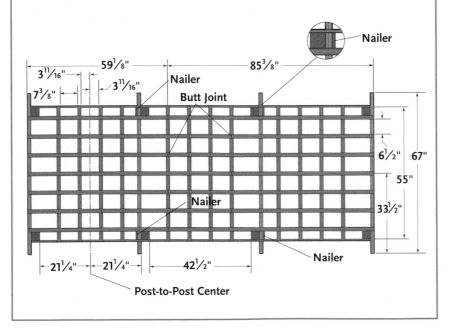

VERTICAL LATTICE

Once the lattice is done on the top of the arbor, install the strips on the side. Attach the horizontal ones to the outside of the posts and the verticals to the inside of the horizontals. Use stainless-steel screws to attach them, and make sure all the strips are spaced evenly.

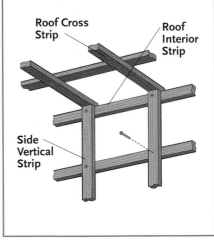

11 Once all of the roof cross strips are installed, lay the long roof strips over them. Attach the long strips with 1⅝-in. deck screws and to cross strips with 1-in. screws. Use scrap blocks as spacers between the long strips, and be sure to drill pilot holes to prevent splitting.

12 Install the horizontal strips on the sides of the arbor posts using 1⅝-in. deck screws. To maintain even spacing, clamp uniform scrap blocks to the posts before sliding the next strip in place.

13 You will need to attach the side vertical strips to the inside surface of the horizontal strips. Clamp each vertical strip in place so it aligns with the roof cross strip above. Then plumb the strip so its bottom aligns with where the top is clamped.

14 Attach the vertical strips to the horizontal ones underneath using 1-in. deck screws. Drill pilot holes for these screws, and check for uniform spacing from side to side and top to bottom as you go along.

BUILDING A HIP-ROOF GAZEBO

project

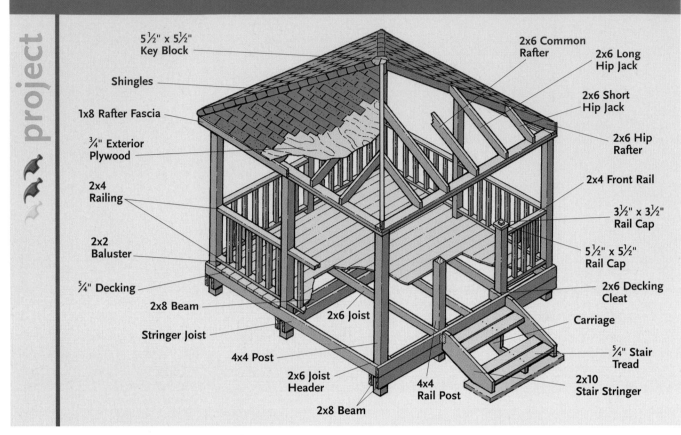

- 5½" x 5½" Key Block
- Shingles
- 1x8 Rafter Fascia
- ¾" Exterior Plywood
- 2x4 Railing
- 2x2 Baluster
- ⁵⁄₄" Decking
- 2x8 Beam
- Stringer Joist
- 4x4 Post
- 2x6 Joist Header
- 2x8 Beam
- 2x6 Common Rafter
- 2x6 Long Hip Jack
- 2x6 Short Hip Jack
- 2x6 Hip Rafter
- 2x4 Front Rail
- 3½" x 3½" Rail Cap
- 5½" x 5½" Rail Cap
- 2x6 Decking Cleat
- Carriage
- ⁵⁄₄" Stair Tread
- 2x10 Stair Stringer
- 4x4 Rail Post
- 2x6 Joist

CONSTRUCT THE DECK

THE BASIC STRUCTURAL COMPONENTS of this gazebo deck include 4x4 posts that support the deck beams and roof headers; 2x8 beams that bolt to the posts and support the floor joists; and 2x6 joists, stringer joists, and joist headers that fasten to the beams and support the 1-inch-thick decking. Decking of this dimension is known as ⁵⁄₄ (pronounced "five-quarter") stock. The gazebo must be square, level, and built to exact dimensions. All sides of the deck should measure 8 feet. The corner posts are located 1½ inches inside the outside corners of the layout so that standard 8-foot lumber can be used for beams, joists, and decking. Accurate post placement is critical.

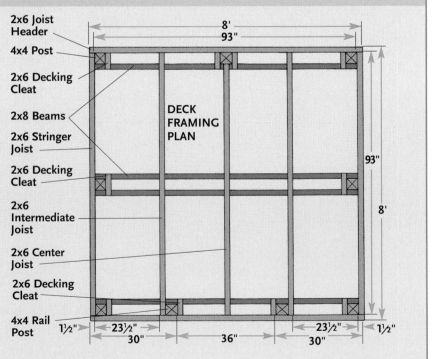

- 2x6 Joist Header
- 4x4 Post
- 2x6 Decking Cleat
- 2x8 Beams
- 2x6 Stringer Joist
- 2x6 Decking Cleat
- 2x6 Intermediate Joist
- 2x6 Center Joist
- 2x6 Decking Cleat
- 4x4 Rail Post

DECK FRAMING PLAN

8'
93"
93"
8'
1½"   23½"   36"   23½"   1½"
30"   30"

MATERIALS / CUTTING LIST

NAME	QTY.	SIZE
Gazebo Deck Framing		
Posts (Roof Support)	7	4x4 8'
Posts (Rail)	2	4x4 54"
Beams	6	2x8 8'
Stringer and Intermediate Joists	4	2x6 93"
Header Joists	2	2x6 8'
Center Joist	1	2x6 89$\frac{1}{2}$"
Decking Cleats	8	2x6 5"
Decking Cleats (Middle)	2	2x6 6$\frac{1}{2}$"
Stair Stringers	3	2x10 30"
Stair Treads	4	$\frac{5}{4}$x6 33"
Decking	18	$\frac{5}{4}$x6 10'
Roof Framing		
Top and Cap Plates	8	2x4 89$\frac{1}{2}$"
Key Block	1	5$\frac{1}{2}$" x 5$\frac{1}{2}$" x 8"
Common Rafters	4	2x6 59"
Hip Rafters	4	2x6 74$\frac{1}{4}$"
Long Hip Jacks	8	2x6 39$\frac{3}{4}$"
Short Hip Jacks	8	2x6 20$\frac{1}{2}$"
Rafter Fascia	4	1x8 94$\frac{1}{2}$"
A/C Exterior-Grade Plywood Sheathing	4	$\frac{3}{4}$" x 4' x 8'
15-lb. Roofing Felt		100 sq. ft.
Metal Drip Edge	4	8' lengths
Composite Shingles		100 sq. ft.
Composite Hip and Ridge Shingles		Needed to cover approximately 26'

NAME	QTY.	SIZE
Railing		
Rails	12	2x4 41$\frac{1}{4}$"
Front Rails	4	2x4 20$\frac{1}{2}$"
Rail Cap Pieces	2	1$\frac{1}{2}$" x 5$\frac{1}{2}$" x 5$\frac{1}{2}$"
	2	1$\frac{1}{2}$" x 3$\frac{1}{2}$" x 3$\frac{1}{2}$"
Balusters	48	2x2 30"
Nail and Fasteners		
Carriage Bolts	18	$\frac{3}{8}$" x 8"
Nails		
16d Common		
12d Common		
10d Common		
8d Common		
10d Finishing		
Roofing		
Post Anchors	9	
Stair Angles	4	
Framing Angles	2	for stair stringers
Premixed Concrete		As required to set post and step footings below frost line

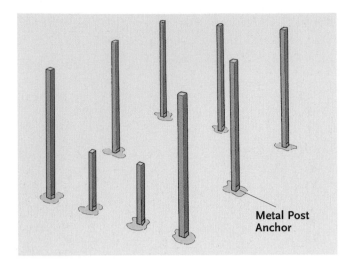

Metal Post
Anchor

1 To install the posts, first cut the posts to the sizes listed in the materials list. Pour footings to the depth required by the building department, and install anchors. Adjust the post length as needed. Make sure you position the footings so the outside edges of the corner posts will be no more than 93 in. apart.

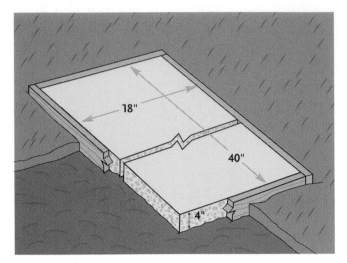

18"

40"

4"

2 Next, you'll need to place the step footing. Pour a 4-in.-thick concrete slab where the gazebo stairs will meet the ground. Make the slab 18 x 40 in., with the front edge 26 in. out from the edge of the deck.

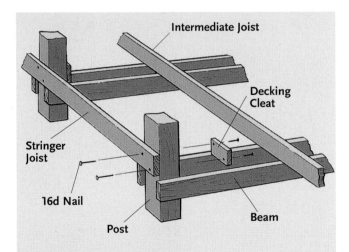

Intermediate Joist

Decking
Cleat

Stringer
Joist

16d Nail

Post

Beam

5 Rest two joists, called stringer joists, across the beams against the outside posts. Nail them to the posts with two 16d nails. Face-nail two more joists, called intermediate joists, to the front posts and toenail them to the beams. Cut the center joist to length. Toenail each side of the joist to the back center post. Cut cleats for the ends of the decking, which is unsupported whenever it meets the post. Nail the cleats to posts as shown to provide the necessary support.

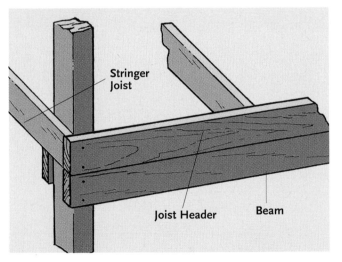

Stringer
Joist

Joist Header

Beam

6 Nail joist headers to the exposed ends of the joists you've installed and to the ends of the cleats and to the posts.

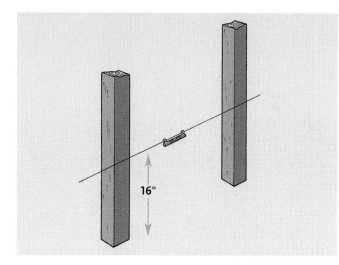

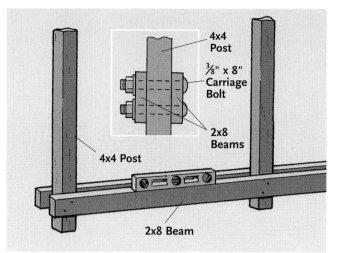

3 The finished deck is 16 in. above grade. Mark the 16-in. height on one of the posts, and transfer this dimension to all other posts using a level or line level. Once the deck height is marked, measure down 1 in. and draw a line marking the top of each joist. Measure down an additional 5½ in. to locate the top of the beams.

4 The beams are 2x8s attached to the sides of the posts. Temporarily clamp a 2x8 to one of the posts at the marks you drew. Level it, and nail it temporarily in place. Temporarily attach the rest of the beams, leveling them with the first beam. Lay a straight 2x4 diagonally across the beams; check for level; and make any necessary adjustments. Drill ⅜-in.-dia. holes all the way through the beams at each post, and bolt them in place with 8-in.-long, ⅜-in.-dia. hex-head bolts, with nuts and washers.

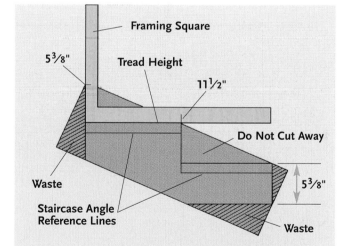

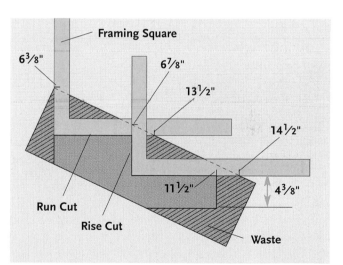

7 Cut the end stringers from two 30-in.-long 2 x 10s. Place a framing square on a stringer as shown so that the 5⅜-in. mark on the outside of the square's tongue and the 11½-in. measurement on the outside of the square's blade both align with the top edge of the stringer, and trace along the square. Extend the rise line to the bottom of the stringer. Lay out the lower step the same way; then measure down 1¼ in. from each of the treads and draw layout lines for the stair angles. Make cuts at the back, front, and bottom of the stringer. Do not cut notches for the stairs.

8 You will need a middle stringer, called a carriage, to support the stair tread. Start by marking out the top step with the outside edge of the tongue of the square at 6⅜ in. and the blade at 13½ in. For the second step, put the tongue at 6⅜ in. and the blade at 14½ in. Make a mark at 11½ in., too, and draw a 4⅜-in. line as shown to lay out the front of the carriage. Cut the back, front, and bottom, as in Step 7. Cut along each rise and each run using a circular saw to cut notches for the stairs. Finish using a handsaw.

(continued on page 170) **169**

(continued from page 169)

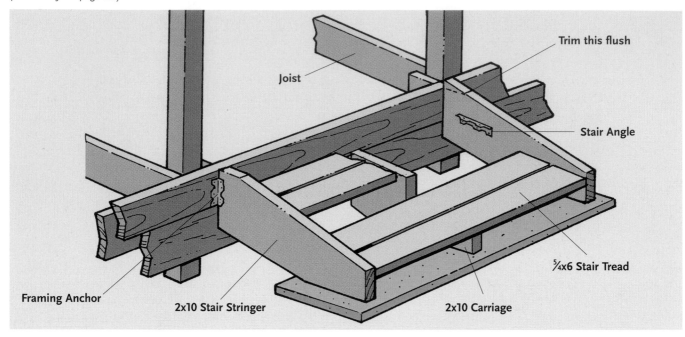

Joist

Trim this flush

Stair Angle

⁵⁄₄x6 Stair Tread

Framing Anchor

2x10 Stair Stringer

2x10 Carriage

9 Nail the stair angles to the stringers with heavy-duty joist-hanger nails. Attach the stringers to the joist header using framing anchors, spacing them 33 in. apart and equidistant from the rail posts. Nail the carriage to the front beam, centering it between the two outer stringers. When the bottoms of the stringers sit flat on the concrete slab, the top points of the stringers will extend about 1 in. higher than the header joist and will get in the way later on. Cut the top of the stringers flush with the header using a handsaw. Cut the treads 33 in. long. Attach the front tread pieces flush with the front of the stringers. Leave ½ in. of space between the front and back treads for drainage.

10 Install the decking boards perpendicular to the floor joists, starting at the front of the gazebo and working toward the rear. Let the boards overhang the stringer joists. You'll trim them to length later. Align the first board so it overhangs the header by ½ in., and notch the deck boards as needed to fit around the posts. When cutting the notches, leave about ⅛ in. of clearance around the post. Nail the decking to each joist with two 8d nails driven at a slight angle. Put a 10d nail between kiln-dried boards to space them properly. Decking that is not kiln-dried can be butted. After every three or four boards, measure to make sure the boards are running parallel with the back joist header. As you near the opposite end of the deck, lay the last few deck boards in place before nailing them. If the last board doesn't overhang the back header by about ½ in., adjust the spacing so that it will. Snap chalk lines across the ends of the deck boards ½ in. from the outside faces of the stringer joists. Tack a board to the deck as a guide for the saw, and make the cuts. Make the cuts by hand where the posts get in the way.

FRAME THE ROOF

THIS SQUARE HIP ROOF has four types of rafters, all made of 2x6 stock. As shown in the "Roof Framing Plan," there are four common rafters, four hip rafters, eight short hip jacks, and eight long hip jacks. The rafters don't have bird's-mouth cuts or tails that overhang the cap plate. Instead, they have a seat cut and a tail plumb cut.

ROOF FRAMING PLAN

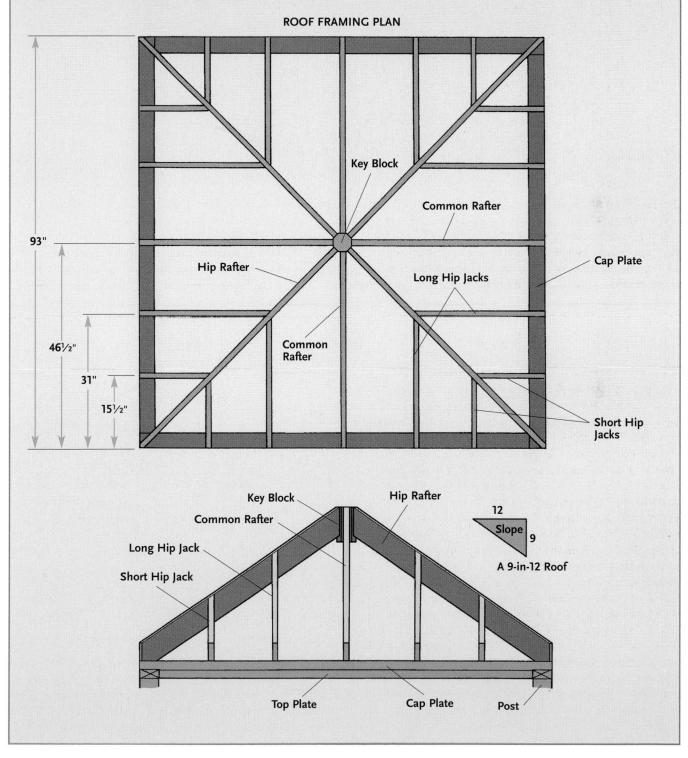

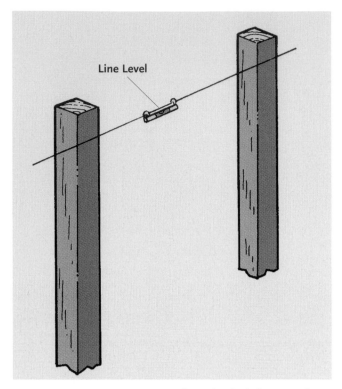

1 Measure up one post 78 in. from the deck floor. Mark this height, and then use a line level to transfer this to the other posts. Cut the posts at the marks.

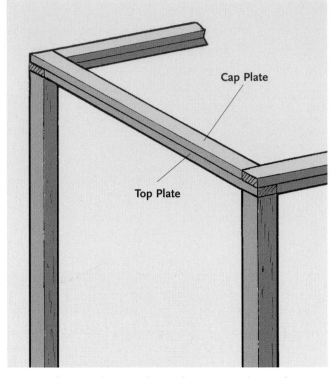

2 Cut the top plates and cap plates to overlap at the corners as shown. Nail cap plates to top plates with 8d nails. Nail one of these assemblies atop the front posts and another atop the back posts with 12d nails. Install the remaining two assemblies.

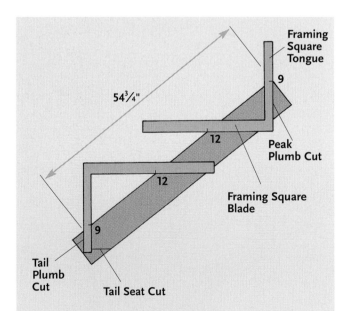

4 The common rafters and the hip jack rafters have a rise of 9 in. per 12 in. of run. If the corner posts are all 93 in. apart, as planned, cut your rafters to the lengths given in the materials list. Use a framing square to lay out the tail plumb cut, the seat cut, and the peak cut as shown.

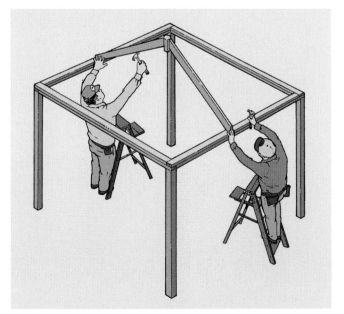

5 To install the common rafters, toenail two opposing common rafters to the key block with two 8d nails on each side of each rafter. Position the rafters to land exactly on the middle of opposing cap plates. With a helper, lift the two-rafter assembly onto the gazebo. Toenail it to the cap plates with 8d nails. Install the two remaining common rafters.

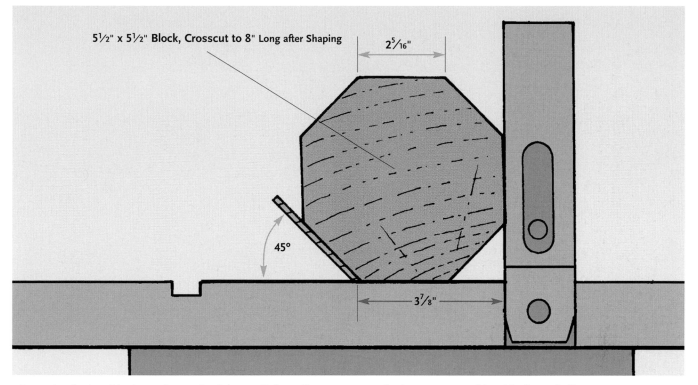

5½" x 5½" Block, Crosscut to 8" Long after Shaping

2⁵⁄₁₆"

45°

3⁷⁄₈"

3 Make the key block. At the peak of the roof, the rafters meet an 8-in.-long octagonal key block made from a 6x6. For safety, cut the block on a table saw from a piece about 20 in. long. Set the table saw rip fence 3⅞ in. from the blade. Set the blade at 2¾ in. high, and tilt it 45 deg. Remove the four corners.

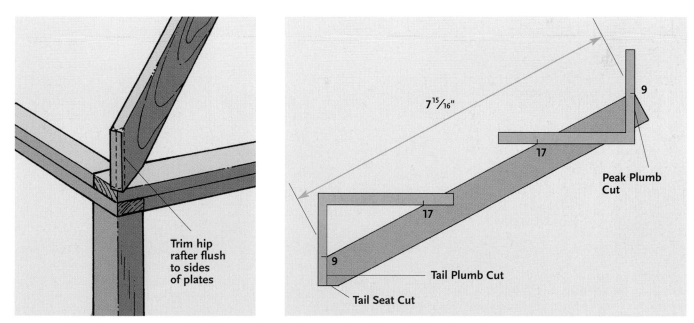

Trim hip rafter flush to sides of plates

7¹⁵⁄₁₆"

9

17

Peak Plumb Cut

17

9

Tail Plumb Cut

Tail Seat Cut

6 A gazebo whose common rafters have a rise of 9 in. per 12 in. of run will have hip rafters with a rise of 9 in. per 17 in. of run. Use the 9- and 17-in. marks on the framing square blade, as shown in the drawing. Put the hip rafters in place, toenailing them to the plates and the key block. The rafters will overlap the corners of the cap plates slightly as shown. After you have installed the rafters, use a handsaw to cut them off flush with the sides of the plates.

(continued on page 174) **173**

(continued from page 173)

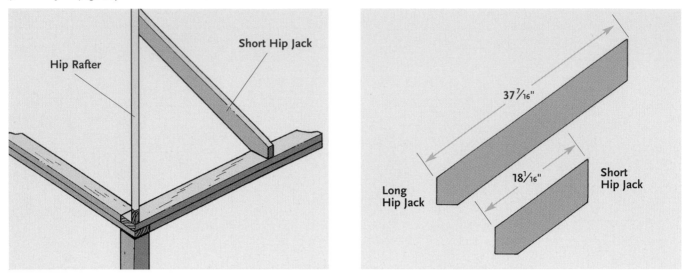

7 The hip jacks have the same 9-in-12 slope as the common rafters. Measure between the plates and hip rafters before cutting to make sure the lengths are right. Lay out the plumb and seat cuts in the same way you did for the common rafters. Make the tail plumb cut and the seat plumb cut just as you did for the common rafters. To make the peak plumb cut, set your saw blade to 45 deg. to cut the correct bevel. Note that four long hip jacks and four short hip jacks are beveled to the left, while the rest are beveled to the right. Toenail the hip jacks to the cap plate with 8d nails, and nail them through the bevel into the hip rafters with 10d nails.

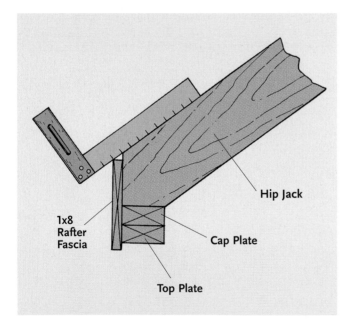

8 The 1x8 roof fascia covers the ends of the rafters. Measure between the ends of the hip rafters and cut the fascia to fit, mitering the ends. Attach the fascia to the ends of the rafters with 8d nails. Use a square as shown to keep the fascia boards low enough so the plywood roof sheathing can go over it.

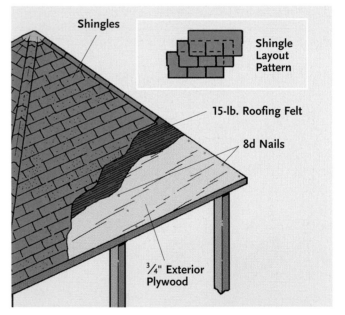

9 The roof is sheathed with ¾-in. exterior-grade plywood. Each roof side requires two pieces of plywood—a trapezoid below a triangle. Cut the plywood to size, and nail it to the rafters with 8d nails every 8 in. Put the better side of the plywood facing down, where it will be seen as the gazebo ceiling. Cover the sheathing with 15-lb. roofing felt. Install an aluminum drip edge, and then install the shingles. Starting at the bottom. (See page 190.)

INSTALL THE RAILINGS

CUT THE RAIL SUPPORT POSTS to their final height of 35 inches.

Build and install the railing using 2x4 top and bottom rails with equally spaced 2x2 balusters. Space the balusters as shown. Lay out the top of the upper rail at 33 inches above the deck. Measure and cut each top and bottom rail section separately to ensure a snug fit between the posts, but don't install them yet. Cut the balusters to 27 inches long. Lay out the baluster positions on the rails, spacing them as shown. Attach the balusters to the rails using 8d nails. Nail through the bottom rail into the balusters, but carefully toenail the top of the baluster to the top rail from below so there are no exposed nailheads on the top rail. Attach the assembled section to the post using railing hangers or by toenailing with 10d nails.

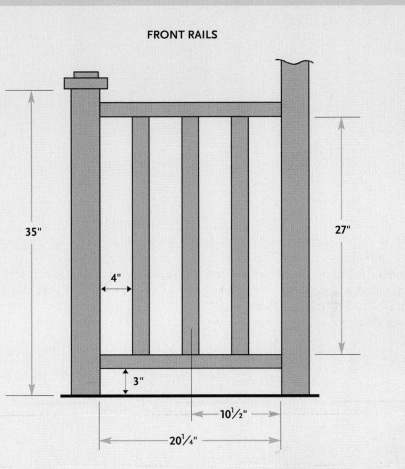

FRONT RAILS

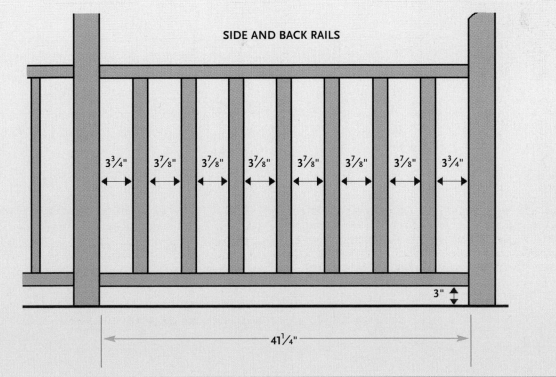

SIDE AND BACK RAILS

9 garden sheds

Everyone could use a little more storage and living space. If you are like most homeowners, your garage and basement are filled to the brim with tools, shovels, the snowblower and mower, lawn care products, sports equipment, and the other paraphernalia you need to keep your home and your life smoothly functioning. Some of these items are used only a few times per year; others you may reach for on a regular basis. A shed is an inexpensive storage alternative that is relatively easy to design and build, and it can improve the look and value of your property. Depending upon its size, you can also use one of these structures as an office, guest quarters, or as a secluded spot away from your house to escape for a little bit of rest and relaxation.

CHOOSING A SHED SIZE

The term "shed" has come to include a number of different types of buildings. While most people think of a shed as a place to store tools and equipment, a shed can also be used for potting plants, or as a hobby area, a workshop, a playhouse, or even a private place for relaxation. The first step in building a shed is to decide how you will use the building. Determining its intended use will help you pick the right size structure for your needs and for the limitations of your property.

The Right Size. With proper shelving, a shed that is 6 x 5 x 8 feet can store your power mower, a trimmer, and a number of hand tools and garden supplies. But you may have to remove some of those items to reach the tool you want. When planning, consider the actual floor space each item will occupy along with enough room to navigate around the building. A rule of thumb is to leave a 12-inch buffer zone around equipment. If the shed will double as a work area, you'll need 36 inches or more between workspaces. For example, allow 8 feet on either end of a table saw. (See "Shed Plans," below.)

The Right Proportions. The size of the shed should also be in harmony with the other structures on your property. Though a small shed won't draw much attention, a shed that is grossly oversized compared with nearby structures will appear out of place. Scale drawings that compare existing structures with planned buildings

SHED PLANS

TYPICAL POTTING SHED

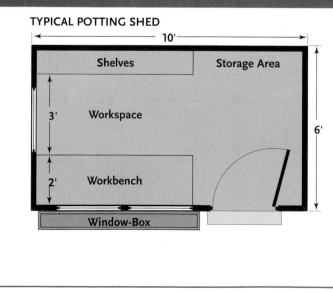

10'

Shelves

Storage Area

3' — Workspace

6'

2' — Workbench

Window-Box

TYPICAL EQUIPMENT SHED

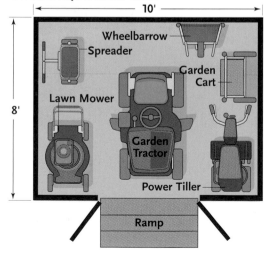

10'

Wheelbarrow
Spreader

Garden Cart

Lawn Mower

8'

Garden Tractor

Power Tiller

Ramp

RURAL AREAS usually do not have stringent building codes or restrictions on sheds. The structure shown here is a focal point and a destination in a large garden.

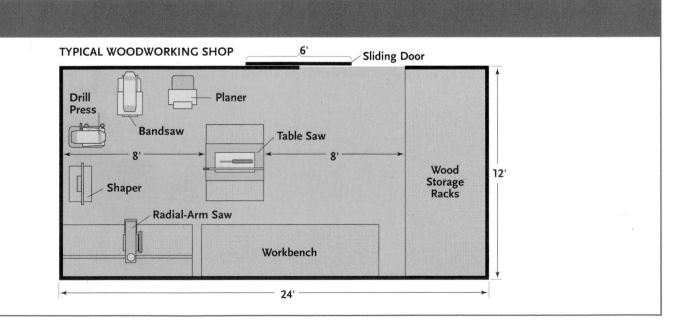

TYPICAL WOODWORKING SHOP

6'
Sliding Door

Drill Press

Planer

Bandsaw

8'

Table Saw

8'

Shaper

Wood Storage Racks

12'

Radial-Arm Saw

Workbench

24'

give you an indication of relative size. Simple sheds rarely require detailed drawings unless specified by your local building department.

THE RIGHT SITE

The siting of the shed—where it is positioned on your property—will influence its size. For any location, there must be enough room to accommodate the foundation "footprint" of the shed with a border of clear ground around the perimeter, as the eaves will extend beyond the foundation by 12 to 18 inches. Moreover, the ground must be level, or it must be modified through excavation to be made level. The type of foundation you choose can also level the shed. So your dream location may not be the ideal spot to place your shed, once you consider the structural and space requirements that will inevitably come into play during the design and building processes.

Setbacks. For most suburban locations, you will likely need to comply with setback requirements. A setback is

THIS VICTORIAN-STYLE STRUCTURE is outfitted with all the comforts of home.

the minimum allowable distance between the structure you want to build and some other landmark, such as another building, the property line, the street, a wetland, even an easement that is identified only on a deed. Setbacks can range up to 100 feet or more. Adhering to setbacks is no small matter. Violation of a setback is grounds for dismantling or moving your shed, so call your local building department to determine applicable setbacks for your property.

If your plans don't comply with local zoning laws, you can apply for a variance. Your application will be considered by the local zoning board or the building inspector. Inquire at the building department for zoning variance procedures.

Covenants. These are rules set by local communities, neighborhoods, or homeowner associations that can hold sway over aspects of your shed that might surprise you. There may be restrictive covenants that apply to the type of siding or color paint you can use. Check with your homeowner association to see what rules, if any, apply to garden-shed construction. In addition to your local building permit authority, a homeowner association's architectural review board may want building plans and elevations (scale sketches of the shed as seen from the side) to review before approval can be granted to build a shed.

Zoning. These requirements may cover shed construction and what you can keep in it. Zoning can regulate everything from roof types—wood shake and shingle roofs are illegal in some fire-prone areas—to live animals. Goats or chickens may seem like a great idea, until you learn that your town bars you from keeping them. You may not even be allowed to have an "outbuilding," as sheds are called. So, early on in the planning stages, check with your town or city's building department for applicable codes and ordinances, and check with your homeowners association for any required architectural review.

Building Codes. In rural locations, building codes, as well as covenants and zoning regulations, may be less restrictive than those found in towns and cities. If you are building a shed on a 5- or 10-acre lot, local building codes and zoning may not impact your design at all. However, it is important to remember that building codes are good guidance for "best-practices" and minimum design standards when building any structure. Your municipality or building code authority—the city or town department that issues the building permit—will tell you the code to which you must adhere. Increasingly the International Building Code (IBO) is the standard that applies, but some counties, especially in hurricane- or tornado-prone areas, can demand that structures be beefed up beyond IBO requirements.

Building Permits and Inspections. Building permits are usually required for building any structure on your property. If a building permit is required and you don't have one, you may be asked to remove the shed, even long after it is built. However, for small structures you can usually obtain a building permit after the structure is erected and simply pay a fine or extra fee.

The requirements for building permits vary widely. Some towns and cities exempt structures that are built on non-permanent foundations, such as concrete blocks or wood skids resting on gravel. If you must obtain a building permit, apply for one at your municipality's building department. The type of permit and fee you pay is usually related to the proposed square footage or cost of the shed.

You may need to provide rudimentary building plans and know your square footage. It may take a few days or a week for permit approval, and if you are asking for a zoning variance, your permit may take even longer and be subject to public notice and hearings. Investigate the building permit process early in your planning.

If you require a building permit, your shed will be subject to building inspections. Even though your shed may be a small structure, the building inspector may be called in to approve the foundation, electrical, and framing. You will also be required to get a final inspection once you complete the building. You may also get a "pass with condition," which requests that you make a fix that the inspector doesn't have to reinspect.

smart tip

CODE REQUIREMENTS
BE PRESENT DURING THE BUILDING INSPECTIONS SO THAT THE INSPECTOR CAN TELL YOU WHAT NEEDS TO BE DONE TO GET A "PASS." SOMETIMES YOU CAN FIX A PROBLEM WHILE THE INSPECTOR IS THERE.

● BUILDING A SHED

IF YOU ARE GOING TO BUILD A SHED FROM SCRATCH, it should not look like a prefabricated shed that you bought and had delivered, all assembled, to your site. A shed you build yourself can differ markedly from a prefab in appearance, spaciousness, and construction. And it will probably last longer.

The shed shown here measures 12 x 16 feet with a traditional saltbox-style roofline. It contains two open-ings for yard and garden equipment. The material presented here is meant to be a general guide to shed building, not specific directions for building this shed. You should adjust the measurements to suit the requirements of your yard. As you will see, shed building requires standard residential construction practices. If you have experience with carpentry, you should be able to build a typical garden shed.

Building the Foundation

The saltbox shed is built on a perimeter foundation composed of 6x6 pressure-treated timbers spiked together with 10-inch galvanized nails. It's a practical, easy-to-construct foundation that even a lone builder can complete, though it sure is nice to have some help hefting the timbers.

It's important to extend the foundation down below the frost line and to promote drainage away from the foundation. You can hire an excavator to dig the foundation trenches and to strip the sod from the interior area using a backhoe.

1 Use two tape measures and the 3-4-5 method to lay out the foundation corners.

2 Drive rebar pins through pilot holes in the first-course timbers to tie them to the ground.

3 Build up the foundation with the timbers alternating at the corners. Spike the new one to the one below.

4 Backfill the trenches as soon as you can. Shovel a layer of soil into the gap, and then tamp it.

5 Have fine gravel dumped directly into the foundation, and tamp it in place.

Building the Back Wall

Because of the saltbox roofline, the roof is framed after the front and back walls are up but before the side walls are framed. The side-wall studs extend from the sill to the rafters, and they are cut and fastened one at a time.

In general, you frame a wall by cutting the parts, laying them out on a flat surface, and nailing them together. You nail the sheathing to the frame while it's still lying flat, primarily because it's easier to do it this way. Also, it enables you to square the wall assembly before erecting it.

1 Lay out the top and soleplates for the back wall together. Measure and mark the stud locations.

2 Line up the plates and studs, and drive nails through the plate into the end of each stud.

3 Take the diagonal measurements to ensure the frame is square. Shift the alignment (if necessary).

4 Nail the plywood sheathing to the frame once it is square. The job is easier with the frame lying flat.

5 Set up the frame, and brace it. The job requires at least two: one at the level, the other at the brace.

Building the Front Wall

Although the front and back walls on this shed are the same length, they differ in height and construction. The front wall is taller to create the characteristic saltbox shape and to allow enough head room for the two front doors. To support the roof structure above these two openings, you have to install a beefy header for each. We used 2x8 lumber for this job, with a spacer of ½-inch-thick plywood sandwiched between the sides, giving you a header that is the thickness of a 2x4 wall. A good nailing pattern is a vertical pair of nails every 12 inches from both sides.

1 Build up a header by face-nailing two 2x8s together, with a ½-in. plywood spacer between them.

2 Line up the wall parts on the appropriate layout lines, and nail through the plates into the ends of the studs.

3 Sheathe the wall frame after squaring it. After the wall is sheathed, snap cut lines and cut out the doorways.

4 Raise the wall into position. It is heavy; you'll need a strong helper or two to tip it up.

5 Install temporary bracing to hold the wall erect. Nail 2x4s to the corner posts and to the foundation.

Framing the Roof

The biggest challenge in building a saltbox shed is framing the roof, and there are a couple of reasons for this. In this example, the ridge beam is longer than any standard board, so you'll have to join two pieces end to end. Because the shed is saltbox style, the front rafters are a different length than the back rafters. Of course, you can adjust the measurements so that you don't need to splice together a ridge beam, and you can avoid the different length rafters by building a standard gable roof.

For the saltbox design, install some temporary braces to hold the ridge boards in place. Then place the ridge boards on these braces, and nail the ridge together. Then lay out and cut the rafters as shown in the drawings below. The front rafters are 8 feet long and the back rafters are 12 feet long.

The end rafters also require notches for the outriggers that hold the overhangs in place.

LAYING OUT FRONT RAFTERS

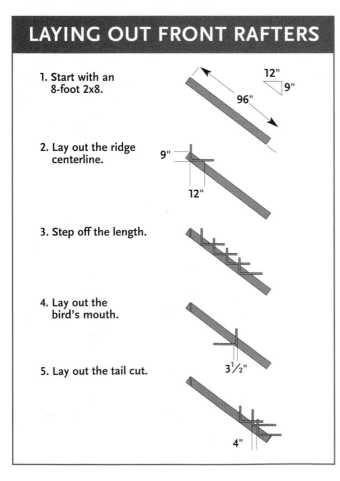

1. Start with an 8-foot 2x8.

12"
9"
96"

2. Lay out the ridge centerline.

9"
12"

3. Step off the length.

4. Lay out the bird's mouth.

3½"

5. Lay out the tail cut.

4"

1 Mark the ridge centerline, then offset to locate the ridge cut line. Then step off the length of the rafter.

4 Mark off the rafter locations on the ridge. Measure from the scarf-joint on both of the 2x8 ridge sections.

8 With the collar tie resting on the front top plate, level it; then face-nail it to the side of the back rafter.

2 For the seat cut, align the tongue on the building line and the 4-in. mark on the blade with the rafter edge.

3 Use the first rafter cut that fits properly as a pattern for laying out the others.

5 Drive three nails through the ridge into the end of the rafter.

6 Toenail each rafter to the top plate using 16d nails.

7 Close in the spaces between rafters with blocking.

9 Cut the overhang outrigger notches in both rafters at the same time. Use a circular saw and chisel.

10 Fit the outriggers into the notches; pull their ends tight to the adjacent rafter; and nail.

Framing the End Walls

With careful measuring, the end walls can be built on the shed floor and lifted into place. But anyone who has done this job knows how easily little variations can cause big problems. The better approach is to install the studs, one at a time, between the sole plate and the bottom of the rafters.

Start by laying out the studs on the sole plate. Then stand up a 2x4 so it abuts a layout line on the bottom and rests against the side of the rafter. Make sure the 2x4 is plumb; then mark the underside of the rafter against the side of the stud for the notch.

1 One by one, stand the end-wall studs on the soleplate markings, and mark along the underside of the rafter.

2 Cut the notch using your circular saw. Cut an angled shoulder cut across the stud's edge.

3 For openings, stand the cripples one by one on the plate, and face-nail through the sill into their ends.

4 The header, made up of two 2x8s and ½-in. plywood, rests on trimmers that extend up from the rough sill.

5 More cripples extend from the header to the rafters. Mark and notch these, and nail them in place.

Applying the Sheathing

We used ½-inch-thick CDX plywood for this shed. But, you may be able to save some money by using OSB (oriented strand board) for this job. To make handling these large sheets easier, nail temporary ledger boards to the side of the foundation timbers to hold the sheets before moving them into their final position. The joints should be made over a stud.

On the roof, start at the lowest side. Tack-nail the first sheet, making sure it is flush with the edges before nailing the entire panel.

1 Temporarily nail a ledger to the foundation, and set a sheet of plywood on the ledger.

2 From inside the shed, mark the window rough openings. Then saw on the lines to remove the sheathing.

3 The barge rafter is beyond the side wall and is nailed in place on the ends of the outriggers.

4 Nail the fascia board to the ends of the rafters. Join the fascia boards on the end of a rafter.

5 Begin sheathing the roof at the back. After the first sheets are nailed, add a 2x4 to provide footing.

189

Applying Roofing

The roofing system for this shed is pretty simple. All you need is some roofing felt to use as a base, drip edge for the eaves and rakes, and 3-tab shingles for the finish roofing. Several options are available. The traditional asphalt shingles are the least expensive, and good ones have warranties of 20 years.

Galvanized roofing nails are considered the standard fastener. Their length depends on the thickness of the sheathing. Add ⅛ inch to the thickness of the plywood to get the minimum length of the nail.

1 Staple builder's felt to the roof. Cut the strips to span the full width of the roof.

2 Install drip edge under the felt on the eaves and over the felt on the gables.

3 Begin shingling with a starter course. Cut the tabs off shingles; invert these strips; and nail in place.

4 Lay the first full course of shingles with the tabs overlaying the starter course.

5 Begin the next several courses. The notches between tabs must be staggered from course to course.

Siding the Shed

A lot of different siding materials are available. Beveled-wood siding is especially attractive and durable. However, the siding itself is more expensive than most other sidings, and it can be time-consuming to install. If you are building the shed yourself and you enjoy doing the work, time shouldn't be a major consideration.

Western red cedar siding is delivered in random lengths, ranging in 1-foot increments from 4 feet up to 16 feet. Cedar splits easily, so drill a pilot hole for every fastener you drive.

1 Begin by nailing a starter strip at the bottom of a wall. Align it with the bottom of the corner boards.

2 Install the first strip of siding over the starter strip. Cut it to fit tight between the cornerboards.

3 A power miter saw makes fast crosscuts, but a jigsaw is useful for notching strips as well as crosscutting.

4 Deep notches can be difficult to maneuver into position without breaking.

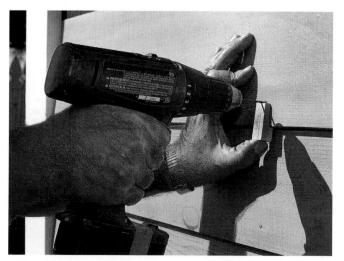

5 Drill a pilot hole for every nail you drive through the siding. A simple gauge aligns the bit to the edge.

191

10 pools and spas

While it is possible to select the type of pool or spa that best suits your needs entirely on your own, it's probably better to consult with several pool installers before you make your final decision. That way, you will know what questions to ask, and you will be in a better position to judge quality when it is time to hire a contractor. An educated consumer is more likely to get a good pool at a fair price than a homeowner who relies totally on the contractor to make all of the decisions. In this chapter, you'll see examples of above- and in-ground pools, and the different types of materials used to build them—concrete, vinyl, and fiberglass. There's also information you'll find useful regarding the various kinds of spas, swim spas, and hot tubs that are on the market today, and the installation considerations that pertain to them.

IN-GROUND POOLS

As the name implies, an in-ground pool is set into the ground. A hole is dug and is finished, usually with concrete, vinyl, or fiberglass. Each material has its own benefits and uses. A variety of shapes is possible with an in-ground pool.

Concrete

When most people think of an in-ground pool, they think of a concrete one. This is supported by numbers from The Association of Pool and Spa Professionals (APSP),

a trade group for the industry, which estimates that about 65 to 70 percent of the pools built each year are made of concrete. Those numbers come from a survey of the group's members, and although they may be not reflect the entire industry (not all pool companies are members), there is little doubt that concrete is a popular material for pools.

Advances in concrete materials and the techniques for applying them have helped concrete retain its popularity. Few, if any, professionally installed pools are poured or built with concrete block anymore. Pouring refers to building wooden forms that establish the shape of the

pool, pouring wet concrete into the forms, and removing the wood after the concrete hardens. Today, installers build concrete pools by spraying either gunite or shotcrete onto a steel-reinforced form.

Both gunite and shotcrete are cement-like materials. Although gunite is the more widely used of the two, both are considered equal in strength. It's only the mixing process that differentiates gunite from shotcrete. When applying gunite, the installer uses a hose that mixes the material with water. Shotcrete is delivered to the site already wet; then it is mixed with air during application. For the sake of clarity, we will use the term gunite to refer to both materials.

To build a gunite pool, the contractor installs steel bars, called rebar, around the sides and bottom of the excavation to create a mold for the pool's shape and to reinforce the concrete. That means the contractor can create just about any shape of pool you want. In cold climates, the walls and floor of a gunite pool should be about 9 inches thick. The top of the sides of the pool is called the bond beam because it bonds to the ground-level deck. It should be about 12 inches thick and will extend down about 18 inches. There isn't as much freezing and thawing of the soil around pools in warm climates, and there-fore less stress on the gunite, so the shells of these pools should be no less than 6 inches thick.

Once the gunite cures, the installer will apply plaster over it. Plaster is similar in makeup to gunite, so the materials bond easily. Plasters are available in a variety of colors. Another option is a textured surface made of aggregate and epoxy. Perhaps the most popular choice is a plaster floor and walls topped by a few rows of ceramic tile.

A gunite pool takes approximately two to three weeks to build. Most contractors will stipulate 30 dry working days for the project.

smart tip

CHOOSING A COLOR
DISCUSS THE OPTIONS WITH YOUR POOL BUILDER, AND BE SURE TO ASK HOW THE FINISH COLOR AND TEXTURE WILL AFFECT THE POOL WHEN IT IS FILLED WITH WATER. FOR EXAMPLE, PLAIN WHITE PLASTER MAKES THE WATER IN A POOL TAKE ON A BLUISH CAST.

ACCENTUATE A CONCRETE POOL, opposite, with tile, and a distinctive patio, such as the one shown here.

A FREE-FORM IN-GROUND POOL, right, makes the most of this natural setting.

A FIBERGLASS POOL, left, comes as a one-piece shell, but you can add accessories, such as a diving board.

A VINYL POOL, opposite, can come in one of many liner designs and colors.

Vinyl

When people talk about a vinyl in-ground pool they are referring to the liner material. Products vary from one pool manufacturer to another, but basically a vinyl pool consists of the liner and wall panels, which can be constructed of aluminum, galvanized steel, plastic, or pressure-treated plywood. Each company has its own method for anchoring the walls. To support the liner on the floor of the pool, some contractors pour a thin concrete pad while others use a sand base.

These pools are packaged systems. The manufacturer has probably honed and refined the design over the years. And if the installer has worked in the past with the product you select, there should not be any problem with the installation. For most vinyl in-ground pools, the installer does need to backfill the area behind the panels while the pool is filling with water so that the pressure on both sides of the panel remains equal. An experienced crew should be able to install a vinyl pool in about one week.

Vinyl pools used to be an inexpensive alternative to gunite pools. But because vinyl is a petroleum-based product, an increase in the cost of petroleum may signal an increase in the cost of vinyl pool liners.

Unlike gunite pools, vinyl pools come in a finite number of shapes—but there are dozens available. And what they lack in choice of shapes they certainly make up for in liner designs. The number of liner patterns is endless; most companies offer dozens. You can find everything from solid colors to designs resembling ceramic tile or round river rock. If you desire, you can even have your initials printed on the liner. The liners themselves are usually 20 to 27 millimeters thick and will last up to 15 years.

Fiberglass

A fiberglass pool arrives at your house in one monolithic shell—sort of like a big tub on a flatbed truck. This is the complete pool shell, including cutouts for the drain, skimmer, and returns. While this does limit your choice of sizes and shapes, you will still find plenty fiberglass pools from which to choose. One manufacturer offers over 40 different pools, including some that have deep sections for diving.

Actually, fiberglass is the reinforcing material used in this type of pool. The inside surface of the pool is a gel coat to which the fiberglass has been laminated. A fiberglass pool costs about 10 percent more than a comparable gunite pool, and shipping costs can drive the price up even more. In addition, it may not be available in some areas. But the typical $1/2$- to $3/8$-inch walls are slick and smooth and discourage algae growth, thereby cutting down on maintenance and saving on the use of pool chemicals. Once the pool is on site, a crew can install it in about one week.

Hybrid System. At least one manufacturer offers what it calls a Uniwall system. Here fiberglass panel walls are rolled into the excavation. The panels are only about 4 feet tall, however, so the lower walls of pools that are more than 4 feet deep are made of concrete.

ABOVEGROUND POOLS

When it comes to aboveground, or on-ground, pools, there are a variety of products from which to choose, including rectangular, round, and oval shapes; small, shallow, child-size pools; large pools that are usually 48 to 52 inches deep; and even custom-sized models. The pools consist of vinyl liners supported by steel, aluminum, or resin walls. In general, prices range from about $1,500 to close to $20,000.

Aboveground pools offer numerous advantages, the most obvious of which is the speed of installation. You can get the notion to buy a pool on a Monday and host a pool party by the weekend. Some preparation work should be performed before installing this type of pool, but it is minimal compared with what's involved with any of the in-ground installations.

The higher-end aboveground pools are those that have attached decking systems. These systems range from a small platform at one end of the pool to decks that totally surround the swimming area with space at one end for chaise lounges and dining tables. Some pools come with decking systems, or you can add your own. Adding decks, fencing, and landscaping turns the pool into a complete recreation area that can also be an attractive focal point in the yard.

Although aboveground pools should be installed on a level spot, the condition of the soil itself usually isn't a concern. The same is true if there's a high water table or poor subsurface drainage. As long as there is a firm base below the pool, it should be fine.

While nothing takes the place of full-time adult supervision of children using a pool, it is possible to make a case in favor of an aboveground pool based on safety. Aboveground pools are usually 4 or 4½ feet deep—a good depth for pool games but not so deep that an adult or even an older child couldn't reach a small child in trouble quickly and easily.

Finally, because the pool sits on the ground, the chances of a small child accidentally falling into the water are reduced dramatically. For enhanced security, you can greatly limit access to a pool that is surrounded by a deck by installing a gate that locks at the bottom of the stairway leading up to the swimming area.

SPAS AND HOT TUBS

When compared with full-size swimming pools, spas and hot tubs seem to come in an endless variety of sizes and designs. For the sake of clarity, we will use the term "hot tub" to refer to the classic, aboveground, round wooden tub that is outfitted with benches and may or may not have jets for stirring up the water. Here, "spas" will refer to any in-ground or aboveground vessel that has built-in benches for seating and jets to agitate the water and relax and soothe tired muscles.

In-Ground Spas

Many in-ground spas are installed at the same time as an in-ground swimming pool. Pool dealers who sell concrete pools may even include a matching spa as part of the installation. In most cases, these spas are located within easy reach of the main pool, usually right next to it. Other options include acrylic, thermoplastic, stainless-steel, and fiberglass in-ground spas. Finishes range from the smooth coatings on acrylic spas to ceramic tiles on steel or fiberglass shells.

As with swimming pools, the spa's circulation system is usually located away from the spa itself. That is one of the reasons in-ground spas are often part of a larger swimming-pool project. It is less expensive and easier on the homeowner to dig up the yard just once in order to bury the necessary piping.

In-ground spas have a low-profile look that many people prefer. If the new spa is part of the pool project, make sure that the circulation system can handle the requirements

AN ABOVEGROUND POOL with a deck, opposite, makes the most of a limited backyard area.

A FIBERGLASS SPA, above right, can be combined with a large pool.

TILE DECKING, right, looks terrific surrounding a custom-built spa and pool.

199

of both a pool and a spa. Often the pool and spa share a common filtration system and heater. Spas have different sanitation, water movement, and heat requirements than pools. A circulation system dedicated to the pool—and another one for the spa—will ensure the proper water quality for both.. If you are putting in a spa without a pool, consider an in-ground model carefully. These spas require excavation and trenching while aboveground models don't, although the latter do have some installation requirements of their own.

Aboveground Spas

Also called portable spas, the typical aboveground model includes an acrylic, fiberglass, or thermoplastic shell and skirting to surround the shell. Between the tub itself and the exterior cladding are all the piping, filters, heaters, and controls.

Size. Portable spas range in size from models that can hold two people to those that can seat up to eight. A large model can easily measure 7 x 9 feet, but because it is only about 3 feet high, delivery people can turn the spa on its side to get it through most doorways and openings.

The larger the size of the spa, the more expensive it is. A bigger spa means more jets, more plumbing, and bigger heaters and filters to service a larger amount of water. An empty 7- x 9-foot spa can weigh up to 1,000 pounds. Fill it, and it could easily weigh 5,500 pounds.

Jets. Premium spas might contain 20, 30, or over 40 jets, depending on the size of the shell. Better companies provide a number of different types of jets. They all mix air with water under pressure, but the size and type of jet can create different effects. Some jets are specially designed and located for back muscles, others provide a vigorous foot massage, and so on. Look for adjustable jets where they will do you the most good. Sit in a spa to see how it feels before you buy it.

Finish. Acrylic shells are the most common. Look for a smooth, even finish. Some of the new plastics are solid color all the way through the material.

Pumps and Filters. Buying a portable spa means that there is no worrying about sizing pumps and filters. Better spas have multiple pumps—one dedicated to the filtration system and one, sometimes two, dedicated to the jets. Portable spas usually have cartridge-type filters the size of which will vary with the size of the spa. With spa filters, bigger is better. Consider filter area when comparing one model against another.

Insulation. Energy-efficient spas are built with foam insulation around the shell. Most of the cost of running a spa can be attributed to the spa's heater, so insulation is an important consideration in many parts of the country. All spas should have covers.

Controls. Most controls are mounted right on the top of the shell. One advantage of controls that are covered when the spa's cover is in place is that they cannot be turned on accidentally. Top-of-the-line models have electronic programmable controls.

A PORTABLE SPA in a sunroom, left, allows you to enjoy it every season of the year.

A CIRCULAR ABOVE-GROUND SPA, right, can be installed indoors or outdoors.

A SECLUDED BACKYARD, below, is a great setting for an outdoor spa on a deck.

smart tip

IN ADDITION TO SAVING MONEY IN ENERGY, INSULATED SPAS TEND TO BE LESS NOISY THAN UNINSULATED MODELS.

SKIMMERS, DRAINS, AND INLETS

Skimmers, drains, and inlets are the beginning and end points of the pool's circulation system. Skimmers and the main drain work together to get water from the pool to the pump and filtration system, which are discussed later in this chapter. Inlets are the re-entry points for the water after it has been filtered and, in some cases, heated.

Skimmers are usually built into the side of in-ground pools just below the coping. Aboveground pools may have skimmers that hang over the side of the pool.

Skimmers consist of a basket, a floating gatelike device called a weir, and plumbing that connects the skimmer to the pool's pump. As the name states, they are designed to skim the surface of any floating debris. As the pool's

THE POOL AND SPA CIRCULATION SYSTEM

THE POOL AND SPA CIRCULATION SYSTEM begins at the skimmers and main drain. The pump, which is the heart of the circulation system, pulls water from these areas and then pushes it to the filter's heater (if there is one), and any other equipment in the system. The clean water then returns to the pool or spa through the inlets.

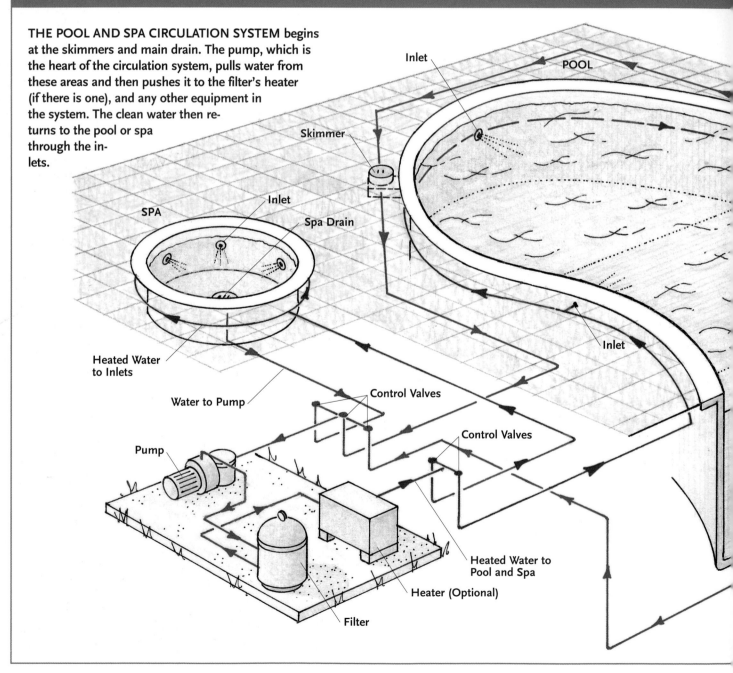

pump pulls water through the system, the weir drops to let in anything floating on the surface of the water. When the pump is switched off, the weir returns to a vertical position so as not to release anything that is in the skimmer cavity. The basket keeps material from going to the pump and filter. You can reach it through an access hatch in the pool deck. Debris that blocks the flow of water makes the pump work harder, so clean the basket daily.

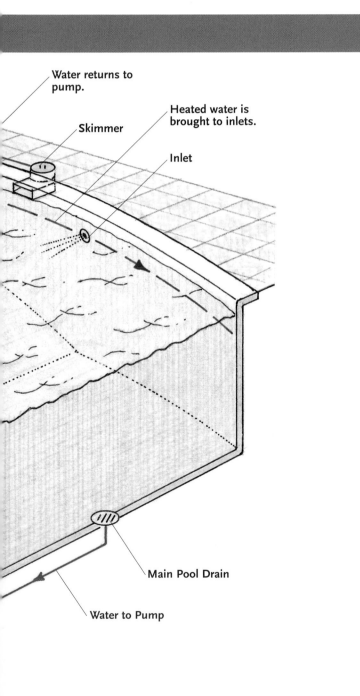

Water returns to pump.

Skimmer

Heated water is brought to inlets.

Inlet

Main Pool Drain

Water to Pump

A SKIMMER BASKET, located within the pool deck, above, is easy to reach under the cover.

AN IN-GROUND SKIMMER, below, is located in the side of the pool and catches leaves and other debris.

THE HYDROSTATIC VALVE

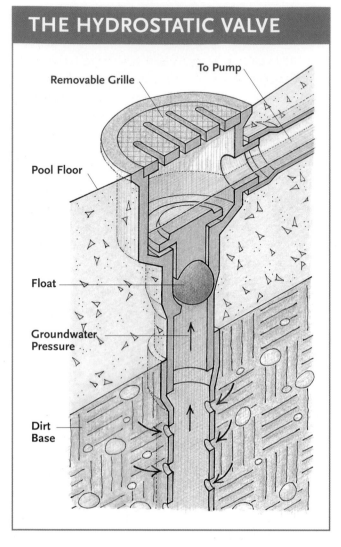

Removable Grille

To Pump

Pool Floor

Float

Groundwater Pressure

Dirt Base

The plumbing for some skimmers is connected to the plumbing from the main drain. A diverter valve allows you to adjust the suction for each. Another type has an equalizer line, which is a 12- to 18-inch section of pipe that connects the bottom of the skimmer to an opening in the side of the pool well below normal water level. The reason for both is that if the pool's water level should drop below the skimmer, the pump can still pull water to prevent air from entering the system.

Plan on installing one skimmer for every 500 square feet of pool surface. Skimmers also provide a connection for pool vacuums.

Main Drain

The main drain at the bottom of the pool is connected to the pump. The grate on many drains conceals a port that runs to the pump, and also a hydrostatic or pressure-relief valve. This valve is designed to relieve pressure created by ground water under the pool.

For safety, main drain lines should contain a Safety Vacuum Release System. This system automatically cuts power should a swimmer or wader become stuck to a drain due to its suction. Discuss this option with your pool builder.

Inlets. Inlets direct water back into the pool. Some inlets are adjustable. This is important because inlets aid the distribution of any chemicals added to pool water through the circulation system.

AN ADJUSTABLE INLET next to the stairs allows you to change the direction of the water flowing into your pool.

PUMPS

Pools require centrifugal pumps to keep the water moving through the system. Pool water enters through the inlet—pool installers call it an influent line. The water first flows into a strainer basket that catches any large debris, such as leaves or grass clippings. The basket should remove anything that might clog or damage the pump. The heart of the pump is the impeller, which is a circular disk with raised vanes that spins to create centrifugal force. The spinning of the impeller, along with the design of the chamber, called the volute, that houses the impeller, creates the pulling or sucking action of the pump. From the volute, the impeller directs the water up through the top of the pump housing to an effluent line and on to the pool's filter. The pump always comes before the pool's filtration system.

There are two impeller designs used in pools pumps: closed-face and semi-open-face impellers.

Closed-Face Impeller. This device has two plates with vanes in between them. Water is forced in through a hole in the center and then thrown out at the end of each vane. Closed-face models are very efficient at moving water. But any material that gets past the strainer basket can clog up the impeller.

Semi-Open-Face Impeller. This type of impeller has a flat plate with slots. It will pulverize any debris and tends to be easier to maintain than the closed-face version.

Modern pool and spa pumps are self-priming, meaning they automatically expel air from the system when the pump is turned on. If the pump on your pool wasn't self-priming and you didn't remove the air from the system, the pump would not be able to pull the water and the motor could be damaged. Pool pumps range in power from 0.5 to up to 3 horsepower. They are also rated for continuous duty, which means the pump is designed to run 24 hours a day.

There are single-speed and two-speed pumps. Two-speed pumps are becoming more popular because their motors run at a low speed—about 1,750 revolutions per minute (rpm)—for routine pumping but then increase to high speed—about 3,450 rpm—when a lot of people are using the pool at the same time. Most spas have two-speed pumps. The lower speed pulls the water through the filtration system, and the higher speed operates the jets.

Sizing the Pump

Your pool dealer will recommend a certain pump for your pool and circulation system. He will base his decision on the capacity of your pool in gallons of water and the desired flow rate, or the amount of water that should flow through the pump to help keep the pool water clean. To find it, you will have to determine the turnover time, which is how often all of the water in the pool should be circulated through the system. Recommended turnover times vary, but eight hours is about average. So if you want the pool water to go through the circulation system every eight hours, divide the pool's capacity by 8 to find the flow rate in gallons per hour (capacity/turnover rate in hours = flow rate per hour).

For example, in a pool that holds 16,875 gallons of water, the equation would be:

16,875/8 = 2,109 (approximately)

To find the flow rate in gallons per minute, divide that number by 60. For example:

2,109/60 = 35.15 gallons per minute

The next step involves determining the amount of resistance in the circulation system. This is called total dynamic head or head loss. Everything in the circulation system resists the flow of water and makes the pump work harder. Even the smooth inside surfaces of the PVC

smart tip

IT DOESN'T ADD UP

ONE WAY TO CALCULATE HEAD LOSS IS TO CONVERT THE RESISTANCE OFFERED BY VALVES AND FITTINGS TO AN EQUIVALENT LENGTH OF STRAIGHT PIPE. BUT THERE'S A LITTLE QUIRK IN MEASURING RESISTANCE.

A 90-DEGREE ELBOW ON A 2-INCH PIPE EQUALS THE RESISTANCE OF 8.6 FEET OF STRAIGHT 2-INCH PIPE. A 45-DEGREE ELBOW ON A 2-INCH PIPE EQUALS THE RESISTANCE OF 2.8 FEET OF STRAIGHT 2-INCH PIPE. THE 90-DEGREE ELBOW HAS OVER THREE TIMES THE RESISTANCE OF A 45-DEGREE ELBOW, RATHER THAN TWO TIMES THE RESISTANCE THAT LOGIC WOULD INDICATE. THERE MAY BE TIMES WHEN USING TWO 45-DEGREE ELBOWS MAKES BETTER SENSE.

pipe offers some resistance to the flow of water. Your contractor will make this calculation. A good contractor will try to come up with ways to limit head loss. (See the Smart Tip on page 205.)

Pump manufacturers print pump curves (see the illustration, "Pump Performance Curves," right) for their products so that you and your contractor can match the right pump to your needs. To use the curve, find the head loss on the vertical axis, and draw a horizontal line. Then find the flow rate in gallons per minute on the horizontal axis, and draw a vertical line up through the chart. The intersection of the two lines indicates the pump that is best for you. When the line falls between two curves, choose the higher, more powerful pump. You will compensate for any errors made in calculating head loss, and the cost difference between pumps is minimal, about $100 between a 1- and 2-horsepower pump.

As the homeowner, there are a few other things to consider in pump selection. For one, the strainer basket needs to be cleaned on a regular basis. A pump with a clear plastic cover over the basket allows you to check the condition of the basket at a glance. The lid itself should be easy to remove and replace.

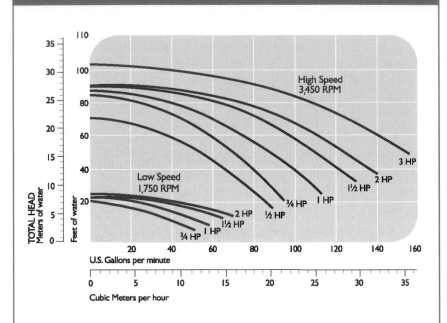

PUMP PERFORMANCE CURVES

A PUMP CURVE CHART is used by the manufacturer to help homeowners buy the right pump for their individual and specific pool needs.

smart tip

THERE MAY BE SMALL DIFFERENCES IN COST FOR FILTERS, BUT IT PAYS TO COMPARE BECAUSE MANUFACTURERS OFTEN OFFER SPECIALS. YOUR POOL DEALER OR CONTRACTOR WILL DEFINITELY HAVE AN OPINION ON WHICH TYPE OF FILTER TO INSTALL. BUT THEY ALL WORK DIFFERENTLY AND HAVE DIFFERENT MAINTENANCE REQUIREMENTS OF WHICH YOU SHOULD BE AWARE BEFORE YOU MAKE A FINAL DECISION.

FILTERS

If you review the illustration on page 202, you'll see that the pool's filter is located downstream of the pump. The filter's job is to remove dirt from the pool water. Actually, the cleaning process starts at the strainer basket that is attached to the pump. But the basket catches only large items such as leaves or branches. For the stuff that makes water cloudy, much of which you can't even see with the naked eye, you need a pool filter.

It's important to remember that a filter is only one-half of the cleaning system. No filter is fine enough to catch and remove bacteria from the water. For that you need to

sanitize the water using chlorine or some other chemical.

There are three types of filters that are used in residential pools: cartridge filters, diatomaceous earth filters, and sand filters. They all do a good job of removing impurities from water.

BE SURE TO MAINTAIN your pool's cleaning system on a regular basis so that the water is clean and refreshing for the entire swimming season, opposite.

Cartridge Filters

Cartridge filters have been around for some time, but they seem to be gaining in popularity in many parts of the country. They consist of a tank that houses three or four cylindrical filtering elements. The filters are actually made of polyester or some other material that can provide a superfine filtering surface. The fabric catches and holds the impurities until you clean or replace the filter.

The cartridges can filter out anything down to about 5 to 10 microns in size. A grain of table salt is about 90 microns; anything below about 35 microns is invisible to the naked eye. It is important to remember that with any filter, a small amount of dirt actually aids the filtering process. In other words, a filter becomes more efficient the longer it operates. However, there is a point at which the filter is holding onto too much dirt and must be replaced.

In most areas, cartridge filters are less expensive than diatomaceous earth filters but cost more than sand filters. However, cartridge filters are popular because of the minimal maintenance involved. Some families will find it sufficient to simply hose off the cartridges a few times during the swimming season to keep them working properly. Others may need to soak the filters in detergent or replace them. In any case, maintenance takes only a few minutes to keep the filtration system in top shape. Most portable spas contain cartridge filters and require the same type of maintenance.

POOL FILTER ANATOMY

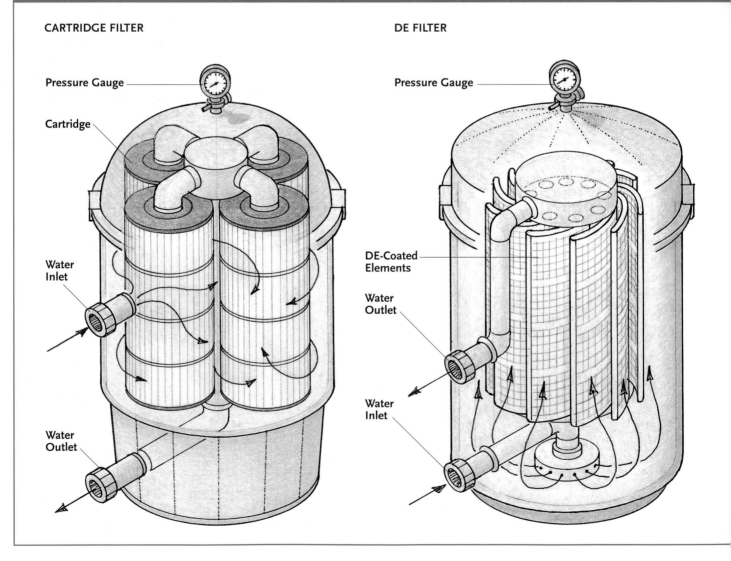

CARTRIDGE FILTER

Pressure Gauge

Cartridge

Water Inlet

Water Outlet

DE FILTER

Pressure Gauge

DE-Coated Elements

Water Outlet

Water Inlet

Diatomaceous Earth Filters

Called DE filters, these products can filter out dirt as small as 3 to 5 microns. If you opened the tank of a DE filter it would look somewhat similar to a cartridge filter. But the grids are packed with diatomaceous earth, a powder made up of billions of fossilized plankton skeletons. It is this powder that actually catches and holds the dirt.

DE filters are usually the most expensive type, and they get the water cleaner than the other filters. But the necessary maintenance can be a drawback for some homeowners. Most manufacturers call for backwashing to clean the filter. In backwashing, the system reverses the flow of water. The clean water cleanses the filter. The dirty water is then drained from the system.

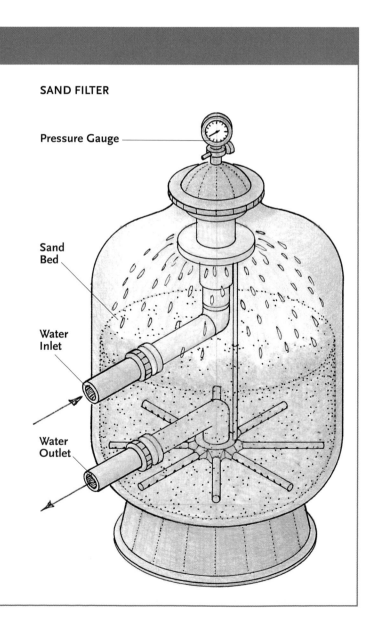

SAND FILTER

Pressure Gauge

Sand
Bed

Water
Inlet

Water
Outlet

However, you'll find many pool service technicians who say that backwashing alone usually isn't sufficient for DE filters. Water takes the path of least resistance, so if there is a channel or hole in the DE pack on the grids, the water will flow through openings in the filter cake and leave the rest of the filter dirty. To really clean a DE filter, you must remove the grids and clean off the spent DE. This presents the problem of what to do with the old DE. Many towns will not allow you to simply dump it down the sewer. Some places classify it as a hazardous waste that requires special handling. Be sure to check local ordinances before deciding on a DE filter.

Sand Filters

These filters use—you guessed it—sand as the filtering medium. Sand filters look like large balls and they can hold hundreds of pounds of pool-grade sand. Basically, water flows into the top of the filer housing and makes its way down through the sand bed where the sharp edges of the sand catch the dirt. On a micron-to-micron comparison, sand filters remove the least amount of dirt—particles as small as about 20 to 25 microns. But again, for a time, the dirt left behind contributes to the filtering process. Sand filters certainly are efficient enough to keep just about any pool clean.

To keep a sand filter working, you must clean it as often as once a week during swimming season. Maintenance means backwashing where the flow of clean water is reversed back into the filter. The problem with this, however, is that the backwashed water is simply wasted. A typical backwashing session can waste a few hundred gallons of water—water that must be replaced in the pool. Sand filters may not be a good idea in areas that are often under water restrictions.

Sizing Filters

As with sizing a pump, you will need to know the capacity of the pool, a two-step process that involves multiplying the pools's volume by the number of gallons of water it holds.

You will also have to calculate the flow rate. This is a measurement of the amount of water that should flow through the filter. To find it, you or your pool dealer will need to determine how often all of the water in the pool should be circulated. This exercise is the same as the one explained in "Sizing the Pump," on page 205.

Let's assume that you want all of the water in the pool to be circulated through the filter system in eight hours, an average circulation rate. Divide the pool's capacity by 8 to find the flow rate in gallons per hour (capacity/turn-over rate in hours = flow rate per hour). For example, for a pool that holds 16,875 gallons of water, the equation would be:

16,875/8 = 2,109 (approximately)

That is the number of gallons that should flow through the filter per hour. Divide that number by 60 to find the flow rate in gallons per minute.

2,109/60 = 35.15 gallons per minute

Once you have the flow rate that you need to keep the pool clean, in this case 35.15 gallons per minute, you can look for a filter that meets those requirements. To determine a filter's flow rate, multiply the square footage of filtering area by filter rate, which is the number of gallons that flow through 1 square foot of filter area per minute. This isn't as confusing as it sounds. Both numbers are available through the filter manufacturer. They are listed

WATERFALLS, TREES, AND ROCKS serve as the perfect disguise for your pool circulation system.

POOL FILTERS AT A GLANCE

DIATOMACEOUS EARTH
Cost: Most Expensive
Remarks: Although they provide the best filtration at start up, these filters must be backwashed once a week. They should be disassembled and cleaned at least two times a year. This is a messy process, and there may be local restrictions on disposing of spent DE earth.

CARTRIDGE
Cost: Midrange
Remarks: Good for installing a large filter area in a tight spot. Cartridges require cleaning about three times per year. Cartridges should be replaced about every five years.

SAND
Cost: Least Expensive
Remarks: Good choice for a homeowner who plans on maintaining his or her own pool. Filters require backwashing (which wastes water) about once a week, but multiport valves make this an easy process that takes about five minutes.

DE FILTER

CARTRIDGE FILTER

SAND FILTER

Multiport Valve

on the product's fact sheets and in some cases you can even find them on the manufacturer's Web site. So suppose you are looking for a sand filter. Manufacturer X offers one model with 1.8 square feet of filter area (that is the actual filtering medium, not the size of the tank) with a filter rate of 20 gallons per minute per square foot.

1.8 x 20 = 36 gallons per minute

That is pretty close to our requirement of 35.15 gallons per minute flow rate. But unfortunately, even though Brand X meets the requirements, it is too close for comfort. Common wisdom in the industry calls for oversizing filters. Remember, once the filter begins catching impurities it actually does a better job of filtering out debris. But the debris also lowers the filter's rate of flow. To compensate for this, the filter should be a little larger than indicated by the calculations. How much larger? A lot of that will depend on the swim load and how often the pool is used. Your pool dealer will be able to help you.

You can either buy a filter with a faster filter rate or one with a larger filtering area. Say you went up to a filter with 2.5 square feet of area:

2.5 x 20 = 50 gallons per minute

This is a better filter for the pool. You could also find one with a faster filter rate, but the faster water flows through the filtering medium, the fewer impurities it leaves behind. It is best to chose a filter with a larger filtering area.

When making your final selection, remember that filters will require maintenance. If you are considering a DE or sand filter, you or your pool service will have to backwash it. Most newer filters are equipped with multiport valves that make backwashing as simple as turning a dial on the valve, about as close to automatic as possible. You should also make sure that it is easy to open the tank to get at cartridge filters. You will need to replace the cartridges about every 5 years.

PART III

gardening
and landscaping

11 soil and water

Whether you are creating a new landscape or improving an existing one, think of plants as temperamental stars who won't deliver their full potential unless the stage is set just right. Soil and water are as important to your plants as temperature or sunlight. Drainage can affect plant health as much as any other factor. If the pore spaces are large, water and air easily move through the soil, ensuring good drainage. And drainage improves dramatically over a period of just a year or two as you add compost and other organic matter to the soil. This chapter can help you through the mundane, but necessary, process of preparing your garden. If you take the time now to create the optimal soil, water, and drainage conditions, your landscape plantings will perform at their peak for many years to come.

THOROUGH PREPARATION allows you to create the landscape that best suits your needs.

SOIL AND WATER BASICS

Although most successful landscape designs incorporate a number of elements, such as plantings, hardscapes, lighting, and such, there are two fundamental aspects that are *essential* to the success of any landscape: the soil (and drainage) and irrigation. While few people find preparation of the soil and irrigation infrastructure as visually and emotionally satisfying as planting, these tasks are as important to a landscape as utilities are to a house.

Soil and Drainage. Good soil is essential for your plants to grow properly. For a garden to flourish with healthy plants that are strong enough to resist pests and diseases, you must first invest in improving the soil. Unless your property drains sufficiently so that rain water doesn't cause flooding or erosion, you may need to improve the drainage.

Irrigation. An irrigation system may be seen as a seldom-needed convenience in regions that only occasionally experience extended dry periods. However, as droughts become more widespread, an irrigation system is almost essential unless you have lots of time to move the garden hose about. Often when a garden is hand-watered, some areas get more than enough water while other parts are slighted.

Examine the Soil

Unless you purchase a home where the previous owners were avid gardeners and worked the soil for some time, the odds are high that the quality of soil on your property is poor. Once you commit to improving the soil, have it analyzed to find out its pH level and nutrient content.

Soil is a living organism, and as with most organisms, it changes constantly. To keep abreast of any changes in pH and nutrient balance, you should test your soil every three to four years. The trouble and expense are small costs for the advantage of knowing exactly what nutrients or soil amendments your plants need to perform at their best.

Soil Analysis

Cooperative Extension agents get many calls from people whose plants are ailing. Agent Patricia McAleer in Fairfax County, Virginia, says, "The first question they ask me is what spray should they use. Instead they should be asking if there is something wrong with the soil."

The basis of a healthy garden is its soil. Pests may annoy and diseases may intrude, but in most cases if the plants are growing in good soil, they will be resilient enough to overcome these travails. On the other hand, if the soil is missing a key nutrient or if the pH is off for a particular plant, the plant will begin to fail and will then be vulnerable to a host of pests and diseases.

pH Levels. The pH level is a measure of how much hydrogen is in the soil, which in turn affects how available nutrients are to your plants. Most ornamental plants, vegetables, and herbs do best in soil with a pH between 5 and 7. Woodland plants, including rhododendrons, azaleas, ferns, and astilbes do best in slightly acidic, or "sour," soil (below 5), while plants such as clematis prefer alkaline, or "sweet," soil with a pH of 8 or higher. Turf grass does best with a pH of 5.8 to 6.6. Soil pH figures are always given in a range. But be aware that pH figures change exponentially. If your soil is at the extreme ends of the range or outside the suggested figure, you will most likely need to add amendments.

Most garden centers sell pH test kits with which you can test your own soil. However, for a nominal fee, the Cooperative Extension will measure the pH, and more importantly, give you a report indicating what, if anything, should be added to the soil and in what amounts. The Extension agent will determine whether the soil is sandy, clay, loam, or some combination of the three. This is important information because it affects the amounts and types of amendments needed.

FROM PROPERLY PREPARED SOIL, healthy seedlings emerge and grow strong.

pH EFFECT ON PLANTS

Acid ← → Alkaline

.0 4.5 5.0 5.5 6.0 6.5 7.0 7.5 8.0 8.5 9.

Nitrogen

Phosphorus

Potassium

Sulfur

Calcium

Magnesium

Iron

Manganese

Boron

Copper

Zinc

Molybdenum

THIS CHART SUGGESTS THE IMPORTANCE of conducting a soil test before planting new trees or shrubs or attempting to chemically amend existing problems. For most plants, the ideal soil pH ranges from moderately acidic (5.5) to neutral (7.0). A low pH number (4.5 or lower) indicates high soil acidity; a high pH number (10.0 or higher) indicates high soil alkalinity. Relative acidity greatly affects the availability of nutrients to the plants.

The bar widths in this chart approximate the availability of essential nutrients at various pH levels; the narrower the bar width, the less available the nutrients. The first six elements are needed in larger amounts. Based on USDA charts showing the availability of nutrients in various kinds of soil, the chart represents only an approximation of nutrient availability in hypothetical "general" garden soil.

Acidic and Alkaline Soil. Parts of the country that receive plenty of rain, such as the eastern third of the United States and Canada, have acidic soil. Dry regions, such as the southwestern United States, usually have alkaline soil. However, don't assume that the soil on your property matches what is typical for the region. Parts of your property could have significantly different pH levels if the soil was heavily fertilized, if it's located at the end of a flood runoff, or if mineral substances ever leached into the soil. If you are new to the property, it's a good idea to bring in several samples from different parts of the property for analysis to obtain a complete picture of your soil.

Nutrient Analysis. A nutrient analysis requires serious chemistry. It's usually best to pay the fee for a soil analy-

sis from your Cooperative Extension Service or from a commercial laboratory that includes information on soil pH as well as a breakdown of the soil's nutrients. The report will include recommendations on the amounts and types of amendments and fertilizers needed. Nitrogen is the one basic nutrient that usually isn't included because nitrogen levels in soil fluctuate daily, making that measurement meaningless.

Testing and Treating Lawns. Because lawns cover a large proportion of most properties, they are particularly important areas for soil testing. Although many people regularly lime their lawns, frequent applications of limestone may be unnecessary or even harmful to your grass. Save money by applying lime only when a soil test shows your

TAKING A SOIL SAMPLE

THE DIRECTIONS ARE THE SAME whether you are measuring the pH or nutrient content. Indicate what you plan to grow because lawns, vegetables, and perennials have different pH requirements. Collect samples from several spots for an average reading. Mix the samples in a jar or plastic bag; allow the soil to thoroughly air-dry before testing it.

STEP 1: DIG DOWN 8 INCHES. Bag the soil. Remove soil from several spots and mix it together.

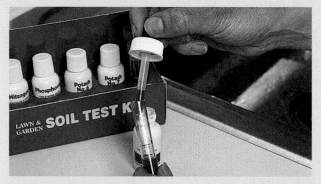

STEP 2: TEST THE SOIL WITH A KIT. Add the appropriate solution to a measured amount of the soil .

STEP 3: SHAKE THE SOLUTION. Cap and shake the tube until the contents are thoroughly blended.

STEP 4: READ THE RESULTS. Match the color of the resulting solution with the chart to determine the pH.

SOIL SQUEEZE TEST

ALL GARDENERS ARE ANXIOUS to get into the garden in spring, but digging while the ground is still half frozen or wet can break down soil structure and cause compaction. To tell if your soil is ready to work in spring, scoop up a handful of dirt and squeeze it into a ball inside your palm. Then open your fingers. If the soil ball sticks together when you poke it gently, the ground is still too wet to work. But if the ball crumbles easily when you poke it, you can start digging. If it's really powdery, run a sprinkler on the area and wait a few hours so you won't be working in a cloud of dust.

SOIL TOO MOIST holds a fingerprint.

SOIL TOO DRY won't hold together.

SOIL JUST RIGHT holds together...

...THEN CRUMBLES at a touch.

lawn needs it. Grass needs a different balance of primary nutrients (nitrogen, phosphate, and potassium) than ornamental plants, so be sure to specify that the tested soil will be used for a lawn. Excessive use of fertilizer is not only a waste of money, it disturbs the natural balance of microorganisms and makes lawns more prone to disease and thatch build-up. Plus the excess fertilizer may wash into water sources and pollute them. If you have a complete soil analysis done on your lawn every few years, you will know how much fertilizer to buy and whether the soil needs any additional lime. As a result, you will be able to make informed and environmentally responsible decisions on nutrients.

Understanding Soil Texture

In addition to having an appropriate pH and blend of nutrients, your soil should have a good structure, with spaces for air and water. Structure can be improved, although the texture—clay, sand, or loam—will not change.

Clay Soil. To determine the soil texture, squeeze a handful in your palm. Heavy clay soil will form a tight ball. Clay is composed of extremely fine particles that pack together closely, so water drains slowly. Clay soil contains very little oxygen. Because it is dense, roots have a hard time pushing through.

Sandy Soil. Sandy soil, by contrast, will not hold together. Its loose, coarse particles allow space for lots of oxygen and easy root growth. Water can drain easily, but it can also leach out essential nutrients. Another disadvantage of sandy soil is that it dries out quickly.

Silty Soil. Silty soil feels silky or even soapy. Silt is sedimentary material that is coarser than clay but still comprised of fine particles. It compacts easily.

Loam. The ideal soil is a rich loam balanced in its composition of clay, silt, and sand particles, and containing plenty of organic material such as humus or manure. When you squeeze loam in your hand, it will form a shape, but then crumble easily. Loam retains enough water for plant roots, but it still drains freely and is well aerated.

SAND (left) is composed of large particles. CLAY (right) is made of smaller particles. LOAM (center) contains sand and clay and is ideal.

219

You can't change the texture of your soil, but by improving soil structure you can make any soil behave more like ideal loam. The easiest way to improve the structure of any soil is to add organic matter.

Organic matter lightens up heavy clay soil, improving drainage by creating more spaces for air and water. It also improves the structure of sandy soil by acting as a sponge to help hold water and nutrients so they aren't so easily washed away.

Amending any soil with organic materials brings its structure as close as possible to the ideal for growing plants, and at the same time enriches it with microorganisms that increase the soil's (and therefore your plants') health.

SOIL IMPROVEMENTS

Soil Amendments

"Put a five-dollar plant into a ten-dollar hole" is common advice. If you've invested money in a plant, you'd better invest even more in creating an environment where it can grow and be healthy.

Soil scientists have identified about 4,000 species of beneficial microorganisms. These unseen creatures perform a host of valuable functions. Some convert nitrogen from the air into water-soluble compounds, making the nutrient available to plants. Others promote the decay process, which transforms garden waste into nutrient-rich humus. There are microbes that feed on harmful plant pathogens and others that interact with plant roots to help them absorb mineral nutrients. Another group works to bind together the mineral particles in soil with the organic additions. Soil without these beneficial microorganisms is literally dead.

Once you've committed to amending the soil in at least a small area, the next step is to check the moisture content. Slightly moist soil is easiest to dig. If a handful feels moist and crumbles easily, you're ready to go. If soil feels dry, water the ground thoroughly and wait a couple of days. If the handful feels wet or leaves mud on your hands, wait a few days and retest. Soil structure can be severely damaged if you try to work wet soil.

COMPOSTING

Compost is the result of a marvelous alchemy that transforms garden and kitchen waste into garden gold. When piled together for a period of time, everyday garden ingredients, including fallen leaves, garden trimmings, weeds, grass clippings, and kitchen scraps, decompose into a crumbly black, organic material rich in earthworms and healthy soil bacteria.

This free garden resource, often referred to as "black

ORGANIC AMENDMENTS FOR SOIL

Amendment	Significant Source of Organic Matter	Nutrients/Minerals Provided
Alfalfa Meal	Yes	Trace Minerals
Crab Meal		Nitrogen
Greensand		Potash, 32 Trace Minerals
Kelp Meal		Potash, Trace Minerals
Peat Moss	Yes	
Rock Phosphate		Phosphate, Calcium, Silicas, 11 Trace Minerals
Sul-Po-Mag		Potash, Magnesium
Manure	Yes	Many Nutrients
Worm Castings	Yes	11 Trace Minerals

HEALTHY SOIL is alive with beneficial organisms. In addition to worms, which till the soil and add nutrients in the form of their castings, loam is rich in microscopic life that makes nitrogen available and feeds on plant pathogens.

gold," is ideal for amending soil, topdressing lawns and beds instead of using chemical fertilizers, mulching beds, improving the texture and moisture-retentive properties of soil, and even using straight as a planting medium.

Use Compost to Improve Soil Texture. Compost loosens clay soil, improving its structure and tilth (workability) so that the soil is easy to cultivate and holds moisture well. In sandy soil, compost acts like a sponge to hold nutrients and water. In any soil, compost supplies nutrients and beneficial microorganisms. Compost also brings the pH closer to neutral. Don't worry about overdosing the soil with organic amendments. You never can have too much.

Compost happens naturally. Walk through an old-growth forest and notice the spongy, rich soil under the trees, which is the result of centuries of decomposing leaves breaking down into humus. However, you can speed up the natural process. To work most efficiently, the microorganisms that cause composting need a balanced diet of carbon and nitrogen as well as air and moisture.

Composting is easy. Anyone can create their own black gold regardless of the size of their garden. No fancy equipment or special expertise is needed. At the end of the season, you'll reap the rewards of finished compost, knowing that you made it all by yourself.

Containers for Composting

There are more than 100 composting bins currently on the market, as well as a lot of do-it-yourself designs such as suggestions for creating compartments with stacked cinder blocks or wire cages supported with stakes. While a specially designed bin may be useful, it is not essential. Don't let the lack of a container keep you from composting. Many gardeners successfully make wheelbarrow-loads of compost simply by piling all the material directly on the ground.

Compost: The Best Soil Amendment

Composting is simply creating the optimal conditions for very fast microbial decomposition of organic matter. You can build your own compost bin using plywood in a few hours. (See instructions on pages 222-223.)

To create compost, begin by building a pile that includes about 6 inches of dry plant material, such as old cornstalks or shredded autumn leaves. Then add a 2- to 4-inch layer of moist green material.

COMPOST BREAKS DOWN FASTEST if you layer the "brown" and "green" material. The other ingredients for successful compost are air and water. Here the wire cage allows for ample air. Water your compost heap during periods of drought.

CREATE DISPOSABLE COMPOST BINS using bales of straw. The straw will decompose along with the other garden waste, eventually contributing to the compost supply. These bins are based on a design by organic gardening specialist Elliot Coleman.

ONE POUND OF WORMS will turn a pound of kitchen waste into compost every day under average conditions. An outdoor wormery should be in a sheltered spot where temperatures do not fluctuate greatly. Worms thrive in temperatures ranging from 60° to 70°F.

221

Sprinkle on a half-inch layer of good garden soil before you begin again with the dry material. If you have manure, add it with the green layer. Manure adds nitrogen and microorganisms. Another way to supply microbes is to substitute compost from a previous batch for the garden soil. Or buy a canister of compost-activator (which is full of

BUILDING A WOODEN COMPOST BIN

A FEW HOURS OF SIMPLE CARPENTRY is all it takes to build a sturdy compost bin that will serve you for many years. You can build a single bin, as shown below, or a row of bins, as shown to the right.

Forego the temptation to use pressure-treated wood; the chemicals used to treat it may kill many of the beneficial organisms that transform garden waste products and kitchen scraps into life-supporting compost.

1 Side panels of a compost bin can be made by attaching 1x6 boards to 4-ft. long 2x2 wooden stakes set 2 in. apart so they form a channel.

2 After cutting off the excess length of the stakes, pound them into the soil using a mallet. Protect them from splitting with a piece of scrap wood.

3 Make certain that the panels are plumb before you finish driving the stakes into the soil. Get help if you need it to make them plumb.

4 After setting both side panels in place, attach the first of the back boards. Make certain it is level before going on to add the remaining boards.

5 Slide the boards for the front of the bin into place in the channel formed by the two 2x2 wooden stakes on the side panels.

6 Begin filling your compost bin. As you add materials, you can add boards to the front. When you want to turn the pile, remove boards.

microorganisms) and sprinkle it between the green and dry layers. This proportion of dry to green materials gives the decomposing microorganisms the optimal blend of

ADDING A COVER

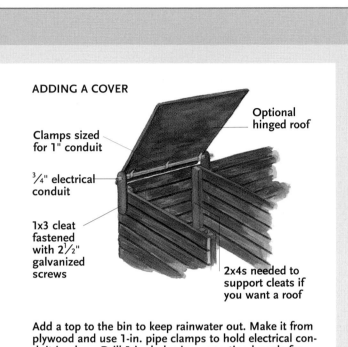

Optional hinged roof

Clamps sized for 1" conduit

¾" electrical conduit

1x3 cleat fastened with 2½" galvanized screws

2x4s needed to support cleats if you want a roof

Add a top to the bin to keep rainwater out. Make it from plywood and use 1-in. pipe clamps to hold electrical conduit in place. Drill 1-in. holes in supporting boards for the conduit.

THREE-BIN COMPOSTER

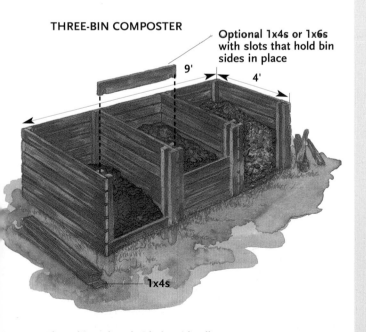

Optional 1x4s or 1x6s with slots that hold bin sides in place

9'

4'

1x4s

Three bins placed side by side allow you to turn compost into a new area as it decomposes. To hold the front boards in place, cut slots into a 1x4 where the top boards can fit.

carbon (dry stuff) to nitrogen (green stuff), roughly 25 to 40 times as much carbon as nitrogen. To start, try to make the pile at least 3 feet tall. If the materials are very dry, sprinkle them with water until they glisten in the sunlight. Properly moist compost should be damp, never wet, about the consistency of a wrung-out sponge. As the materials begin to decompose, the interior of the pile will get hot, simply from the microorganisms working. Oxygen on the inside of the pile will be depleted; soil organisms consume oxygen (O^2) and give off carbon dioxide (CO^2), just as we do. To keep them active, introduce more air by turning or poking holes in the pile. For the very best final product, turn the pile so that you reverse the outside and inside portions. That way, disease-causing fungi and bacteria, as well as most weed seeds, will be exposed to temperatures hot enough to kill them. A hayfork (a pitchfork with curved tines), is an excellent tool with which to turn compost in a pile. To be on the safe side, avoid adding diseased plants or weeds with seeds to the compost pile; that way you won't have to worry whether all parts of the pile got hot enough to kill them. Compost is considered "finished" when it no longer heats up after it is turned and most materials are decomposed. Look at the finished product closely; if you can still recognize some of the plant materials, it's likely that the microorganisms need more nitrogen to finish the job.

Wait for Compost to Cure. While it is decomposing, compost can produce compounds that are phytotoxic, or poisonous to plants. Also, instead of supplying plants with nutrients, unfinished compost can actually cause a deficiency. This is because soil microorganisms attack the undecomposed bits as soon as you put the compost within reach. But these organisms need nitrogen to complete the job, and they take it from the surrounding soil. Plants growing in the area may suffer from a temporary nitrogen deficiency until the composting is complete. Finished compost, on the other hand, slowly releases nitrogen to plants. Consequently, you're wise to let your compost cure awhile before you apply it to be certain that decomposition is really finished.

To cure compost, pile it in an out-of-the-way spot; cover it with a tarp to keep the rain or snow off; and let it sit—undisturbed—for one to three months. If you plan to use it in a vegetable garden in the spring, you can also cure the compost by spreading it over the bare soil in late fall after the crops are finished; the compost will cure in place over the winter and be ready for spring planting.

COMPOST RECIPES

THE IDEAL COMPOST HEAP should be 3 feet wide x 3 feet deep x 3 feet tall. It quickly will shrink by as much as 50 percent. That's a good sign that the material is breaking down. Another way of checking if everything is working is to reach inside. It should feel warm.

A compost pile should be contained so it attains a minimum height of three feet. A simple three-sided wire mesh fence on posts or a specially created wire bin works fine. If you are starting your first compost pile, dig a shallow hole and build on top of that. This will help introduce earthworms to your pile and bring in the microorganisms. If you are using a pre-made container with a closed bottom, put a shovel-full of dirt into the bottom.

Alternate 4- to 6-inch-thick layers of brown material (dry leaves, straw, and wood shavings) that are high in carbon and green matter such as grass clippings, manure, and kitchen scraps (except meat and dairy products), and garden scraps which are high in nitrogen. Sprinkle a little water and garden soil between each layer to help things along. Or apply a compost inoculant to boost the microbial activity of the heap.

About once a week, turn the pile using a pitchfork. Turning adds oxygen, which stokes the stove and helps the compost to cook faster. Keep the pile watered. The compost is properly moist when it feels like a wrung-out sponge, neither soggy nor bone dry. Using this technique, it takes about six weeks to produce finished compost.

The microorganisms working busily in your compost need about three times as much carbon as nitrogen. Heavy doses of carbon also speed up the process. But most home gardeners usually end up with all nitrogen-rich material in the spring and summer, and only carbon (dried leaves) in the fall. An easy solution is to stockpile leaves collected in the fall and add them a layer at a time.

You'll never have enough compost. The more you make, the more uses you will find for compost.

Compost Ingredients

Browns (carbon)
Need 2–3 times as much Browns as Greens (nitrogen)
- Dry leaves
- Brown plant wastes
- Shredded newspapers, cardboard
- Wood chips, sawdust
- Corn stalks
- Used potting soil

Greens (nitrogen)
- Manure
- Grass clippings
- Garden waste
- Kitchen waste
- Kelp meal
- Blood meal
- Alfalfa
- Human hair

How Compost Happens

COMBINE ORGANIC MATTER. An apple core, banana peel, lemon rind, egg shell, and garden clippings are the raw materials.

DECOMPOSITION HAS BEGUN. The ingredients have started to turn crumbly and brown, but are still recognizable.

FINISHED COMPOST OR HUMUS. The humus has a rich, earthy smell. This "black gold" is found at the bottom of the pile.

OTHER SOIL AMENDMENTS

Rotted Manure. Rotted manure from cows, chickens, horses, or rabbits provides key nutrients as well as organic matter. It is especially good for sandy and heavy clay soils. Make sure the manure is properly rotted (6 to 10 weeks) to prevent the risk of burning plants. You also can buy composted and bagged manure. Spread at least 1 to 2 inches over the ground.

Leaves. Leaves are an inexpensive soil amendment. In autumn, pile leaves on the plot you plan to amend and leave them to rot during the winter. If the leaves are large, such as those of oaks or maples, shred them before spreading them on the garden, or use a lawn mower. In communities that collect fallen leaves, you usually can arrange for a truckload delivery of leaves for free or for a nominal charge. Come spring, you should either dig or till the rotted leaves into the soil.

Commercial/Organic Amendments. There are many organic soil amendments on the market. Depending on where you live, you can find products such as kelp meal, alfalfa meal, or rotted manure bagged and ready to use.

Working in Amendments

The size of your plot will influence whether you rototill or dig in amendments. If you are working a large area, a gas-powered tiller is a great labor saver, although even the large machines cannot penetrate the soil as deeply as you can if you dig by hand. To get the best results with a tiller, use a rear-tined machine with blades that can penetrate up to 10 inches.

Single and Double Digging. There are essentially two options for systematic hand digging soil: single digging, which turns the soil to a depth of 8 to 12 inches, and double digging, which loosens the soil to twice that depth. (See "Aerating a Garden Bed: Single and Double Digging," below.) Double digging is worth the effort if you have heavy clay soil, level soil that doesn't drain well, or a garden that has never before been cultivated.

The next step is to check the moisture content; slightly moist soil is the easiest to dig. If a handful feels moist and crumbles easily, you're ready to dig. If the soil feels dry, water the ground thoroughly and wait a few days. If the handful feels wet or muddy, wait a few days; working very wet soil may damage the soil's structure.

AERATING A GARDEN BED: SINGLE AND DOUBLE DIGGING

DOUBLE DIGGING is a process used to aerate a bed to double the depth of a shovel or spading fork—approximately 20 inches. To single dig a bed, follow the directions below, but do not use the spading fork to loosen the ground at the bottom of the trench.

STEP 1: Dig Out the First Trench. Divide the bed into sections, and dig out a 12-inch layer of earth from the first trench, setting aside the removed soil for the final section.

STEP 2: Add Soil Amendments. Spread amendments into the bottom of the trench. Use a spading fork to loosen the soil on the bottom of the trench another 10 inches. (Single diggers can skip the spading fork step and proceed to Step 3.)

STEP 3: Dig Out the Second Trench to 12 Inches. Move the soil dug from the second trench into the first trench. Repeat Step 2 in the second trench.

STEP 4: Continue to Dig Trenches. Add the soil dug from the last trench into the adjacent newly dug trench.

Approx. 8"–12"

BUILDING WOODEN RETAINING WALLS

WOODEN RETAINING WALLS are generally the easiest and least expensive way to tame a slope; they usually look less formal than terraces walled with stone or brick. Wood tends to survive longer in drier climates than wet ones and on well-drained slopes. On a large slope, where the wall must support tons of earth, you must use heavy lumber such as landscape timbers. To delay rotting, choose either pressure-treated lumber or wood that is resistant to decay such as redwood, cedar, or cypress. If you want to avoid digging deep holes for support posts, you can use deadman braces to give structural strength to a timber retaining wall. Deadmen should be installed along your wall in the second or third course from the bottom and in the second course from the top.

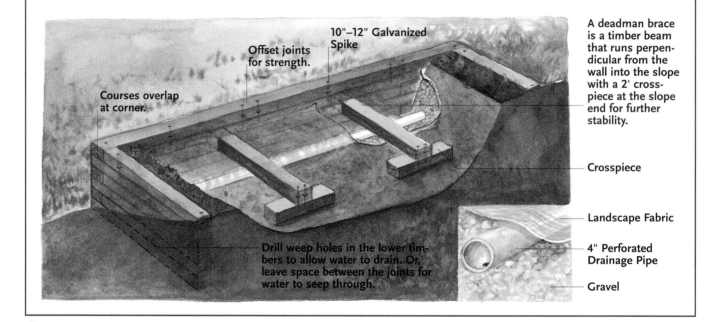

Courses overlap at corner.

Offset joints for strength.

10"–12" Galvanized Spike

A deadman brace is a timber beam that runs perpendicular from the wall into the slope with a 2' crosspiece at the slope end for further stability.

Crosspiece

Landscape Fabric

4" Perforated Drainage Pipe

Gravel

Drill weep holes in the lower timbers to allow water to drain. Or, leave space between the joints for water to seep through.

CREATING TERRACES

Terracing a steep hillside is a time-honored way to transform unused land into broad level "steps" for garden beds or paved areas. If you want several terraces to traverse a slope, connect them with steps made of stone, pavers, or wood, depending on which material would look best in your overall design.

Some communities have regulations against homeowners building retaining walls more than 4 feet high. If your embankment requires a taller wall, either build a series of terraces with shorter retaining walls, or hire a professional engineer to design your wall and a contractor to build it. Many communities require landscape construction permits for walls 3 feet or taller, so be sure to check with your local building inspector before you begin building.

Even well-packed soil is not completely stable on a slope. If you need to do extensive grading to create your terraces, contact a soil engineer or landscape architect to ensure that the final terracing will be structurally sound. If you plan to attack the project without professional help, begin at the bottom, just below the slope. Build a retaining wall on ground that is already level. Use the soil from the low end of the slope near the wall to backfill the gap between the wall and the slope until you have created a level terrace. Continue until you have created the number of terraces you want. It is essential to provide drainage for a retaining wall so water doesn't build up behind it. Either build weep holes in the wall, or run perforated drain pipe behind the wall before you backfill with soil.

Materials for Retaining Walls Include Wood, Stone, Precast Blocks, and Concrete. Choose a building material that is suitable for the site, and that creates the overall effect you want. Details for constructing wooden retaining walls are given with the illustration above. (See Chapter 6 for information about brick and stone retaining walls.)

PROVIDING IRRIGATION

Although hand watering can be a relaxing, therapeutic occupation, it is time consuming. Except for plants growing in containers, it's almost impossible to give plants the thorough soaking they need with just a watering can. Portable sprinklers do a better job and take less hands-on time, but they require that you remember to move them at regular intervals.

To save hours of hand watering and dragging hoses, consider installing systems that drip water directly into the soil, or sprinkle water through the air. If you include automatic timers with your system, you can ensure that your plants consistently receive the amount of water they need.

Installing your own irrigation system is a great do-it-yourself project, challenging enough to give a sense of accomplishment when the job is done but not so complicated that it takes a professional to do it right. In addition, the savings are significant. You can save 50 percent or more from the cost of a professional installation, and the time you spend on the project is minimal compared to the time you'd otherwise spend watering by hand over the years.

Drip Irrigation Systems

Drip irrigation is more versatile and flexible than sprinklers for most situations, other than lawns and ground covers. Drip irrigation delivers water at a slow rate directly to root systems. The long, slow delivery ensures that plants are deeply watered, even in clay soil where water absorption is slow.

With drip irrigation, there is no waste due to runoff and evaporation, and the deep watering encourages plants to grow deeper roots, making them more drought-tolerant. Because drip irrigation doesn't wet the foliage, plants are less likely to suffer from diseases resulting from damp foliage (which encourages some fungi), or from pathogens carried from upper leaves to lower ones in descending water droplets. Drip irrigation also reduces the need for pesticides, because damp leaves harbor some pests. Because the water is applied exactly where it is needed through custom-made emitters (holes) located only where water is needed, weed plants have a harder time getting their share. In addition, drip lines do not need to be buried. Thus you can move the lines around easily and adapt your system to any changes you make in your garden design. It is easy to add new lines, remove old ones, or plug the holes for old feeder lines that are no longer required.

Planning Drip Systems. Starting with a base map of your property that shows the location of buildings, walkways, patios, water sources, and a layout of your garden beds and plants, divide your garden into zones based on the types of plants and their watering needs. For example, plants growing in shade would be one zone, trees and shrubs in another, the vegetable garden a third zone, and containers and hanging baskets in yet another zone. Annuals, which require frequent shallow watering, should be in a different zone from trees and shrubs which require infrequent but deep watering. Ideally each zone should have a separate drip watering circuit that is connected to its own valve.

The kind of soil you have will be a factor in determining the rate of flow you want from each emitter (water delivery device), and how many emitters you will need. Because heavy clay soil absorbs water slowly, you will want long, slow water delivery and therefore fewer emitters. Because sandy soil soaks up water quickly, allowing water to drain straight down rather than spreading, you'll need more emitters spaced closely.

A DRIP IRRIGATION SYSTEM is ideal for vegetable beds because the layout can be revised and amended as needed with each new crop. Set out the lines when the plants are young, and in a few weeks they will be completely hidden by the growing produce.

Materials. Supplies you will need for drip systems include ½-inch polyethylene hose (sufficient length to complete your design), hose fittings, an anti-siphon control valve for each watering zone, a pressure regulator, a filter to keep pipe debris from clogging the emitters, Y-filters to enable you to fertilize as you water, end caps, transfer barbs for extending lateral lines, polyethylene microtubing (the spaghetti-like lines that take the water from the main hose to the plants), and emitters.

Although not essential, an automatic timer is a real asset. Drip systems run for hours at a time, making it easy to forget that the water is running. With a timer, you don't have to remember to shut off the water. In the case of a large fruit or ornamental tree with a canopy spread of 15 feet in diameter, you should plan for six emitters. Smaller trees and shrubs require one emitter for every 2½ feet of canopy diameter.

Make a shopping list of all the supplies you will need to complete the system. Use the parts lists available from the manufacturers as a guide.

WATERING TABLE

Type of Plant	Water Needed Gallons/Week	Watering Frequency per Week		
		Moderate	Hot	Cool
Vines & Shrubs (2–3')	7	2	3	1–2
Trees & Shrubs (3–6')	10–15	2	3	1–2
Trees & Shrubs (6–10')	30–40	2	3	1–2
Trees & Shrubs (10–20')	100–140	2	3	1–2
Mature Trees (Over 20')	160–240	2	3	1–2
Flowers, Plants, Vegetables	3	2	3	1–2
Potted Plants	¾	2	3	1–2
Rows of Flowers or Vegetables	6	2	3	1–2

PLAN YOUR DRIP IRRIGATION SYSTEM by dividing your plants into groups or zones based on their water requirements. Here large trees that require deep, infrequent watering are on one line, the vegetable garden is a zone of its own, the flower beds are grouped together, and the containers have a separate system with drip lines running to each pot. Such a map is also useful for underground sprinklers with which you can water all of these plants plus lawns, but not containers. Also separate out plants growing in full sun, which will dry out faster than plants growing in shady areas.

DRIP WATERING ZONES
—— Trees & Shrubs
—— Vegetable Gardens
—— Container Plants
—— Flower Beds & Ground Covers

Installing Drip Systems. You can either bury the lines—being careful to keep the ends of the microtubing aboveground—cover them with mulch, or leave them above the ground. In annual and vegetable beds, the growing plants will soon hide most, if not all, of the aboveground tubing. (See page 230.)

Maintenance. Sediment present in your tap water will accumulate in the irrigation lines and clog them. Every four to six months, flush out the lines by opening the end caps and allowing water to run freely through the system for a few minutes. Also flush out the lines if they haven't been used for several months.

Filters should be checked monthly. Wash them under running water, checking for tears or other damage; replace any that are damaged. Y-filters need less regular maintenance. They handle up to 720 gallons per hour (gph) through a screen.

Every few months, check the emitters to make sure they are working properly. Also check an emitter if you notice that a nearby plant is wilting, or an unusual wetting pattern. Clean any emitters that have become clogged, and replace damaged ones.

If a line is damaged, repair it with a slip-on coupling. In areas with winter freezes, drain the lines and shut off the system before the first major frost. You also should protect the control head from freezing. The best way to do this is to install the control head with a union on either side of it. When the weather turns cold, just unbolt the control head and store it indoors until spring.

Underground Sprinkler Systems

These irrigation systems involve buried pipes with sprinkler heads placed at regular intervals. Sprinklers spray water over the plants, wetting them the same way that rain does, at a rate as high as 9 gallons per minute. Sprinkler systems tend to work better for lawns and ground covers than for garden beds.

Planning Your Underground Sprinkler System. Excellent brochures by the major sprinkler companies give detailed step-by-step instructions for designing and installing their own sprinkler systems. In addition, some of the larger companies will create a custom design for your property free of charge. Call their hotlines if you need help or have questions.

Use a copy of the landscape base map you created earlier to work out and draw your sprinkler system's design. If you haven't yet created a base map of your property, draw your property to scale on a piece of graph paper. (See Chapter 1 for how to make a base map.) Then indicate the location of your water meter and the location and length of the service line to your house. If your water supply comes from a well, show where the well and pump are located.

SPRINKLER VALVES

THIS GROUP OF VALVES, called a manifold, shows a 3-circuit system. Anti-siphon valves (which are available with built-in backflow prevention) are always installed aboveground. In-line valves (which require separate backflow prevention) are installed below ground, usually in protective boxes. PVC pipe is shown in this illustration. In areas where freezing occurs, poly pipe may be used instead of PVC downstream of valves. Check local codes for pipe recommendations and before installing backflow protection devices.

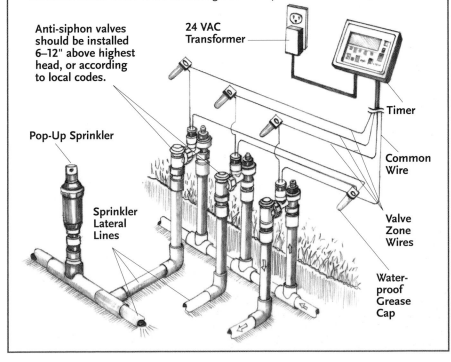

Anti-siphon valves should be installed 6–12" above highest head, or according to local codes.

24 VAC Transformer

Pop-Up Sprinkler

Sprinkler Lateral Lines

Timer

Common Wire

Valve Zone Wires

Waterproof Grease Cap

DRIP IRRIGATION INSTALLATION

DRIP SYSTEMS are fun to design and easy to install. You don't need wrenches, saws, or glue, and if you make a mistake, it is simple and inexpensive to remedy. Drip lines can be installed aboveground or belowground, and the design can be expanded or relocated as your needs evolve.

Companies that manufacture drip irrigation supplies provide free brochures that give detailed instructions for designing and installing the systems. You can purchase kits with complete instructions for specific applications such as containers, vegetable gardens, and general landscape areas. Following is a brief summary of the usual steps.

1 MEASURE THE TUBING. Lay out the line, measure carefully, and cut it to the proper length. This system is designed to water containers. The tubing becomes round when it is filled with water.

2 CONNECT THE TUBING AT T-JOINTS. These joints connect several lines to a single water source. Punch holes where you want the emitters. These holes can be plugged and new ones punched later.

3 ATTACH A FILTER TO THE WATER SOURCE. Filters vary in size from very fine mesh to trap tiny particles to larger mesh openings. The sediment content of your water supply will dictate the type of filtering system necessary.

4 SET A TIMER. The easiest way to run a drip irrigation system is to put everything on an automatic timer, which will turn the water on and off at custom intervals. The duration of each watering can also be programmed.

Divide Sprinklers into Circuits. You will not have enough water pressure to water the entire garden at once. Instead you need to divide the sprinklers into separate groups called circuits. Each circuit will be an independent sprinkler line. Group the sprinklers into sections or circuits, being careful not to mix areas with different watering requirements on the same circuit (keep lawns separate from flower beds). In general, plants with different water requirements will have different types of sprinkler heads (rotating, spray, bubbler), so you can usually organize circuits by the type of sprinkler head. The number of heads you can have in any section will depend on the gallons per minute your water system produces. Sprinkler manufacturers provide excellent guidelines to calculate the gpm. Once you've grouped your sprinklers into different circuits for valve control, draw the piping system on your map, connecting each sprinkler group to a separate control valve.

Sprinkler Heads for Different Jobs. Sprinkler heads come in varied designs, each meant for a different job. Among the many options are bubblers for watering individual plants, such as roses; pop-up heads designed to spray in a full circle, half circle, quarter circle, or square; and shrubbery spray sprinklers, which are mounted on a riser pipe high enough to spray over shrubs. Each product brochure lists all available sprinkler heads and describes the purpose of each. For full coverage, you need to space sprinkler heads so their spray slightly overlaps. Sketch the position of the sprinkler heads on your site map, using arced lines (circles or portions of circles) to indicate the spray pattern.

(continued on page 234)

OVERVIEW OF SPRINKLER HEADS

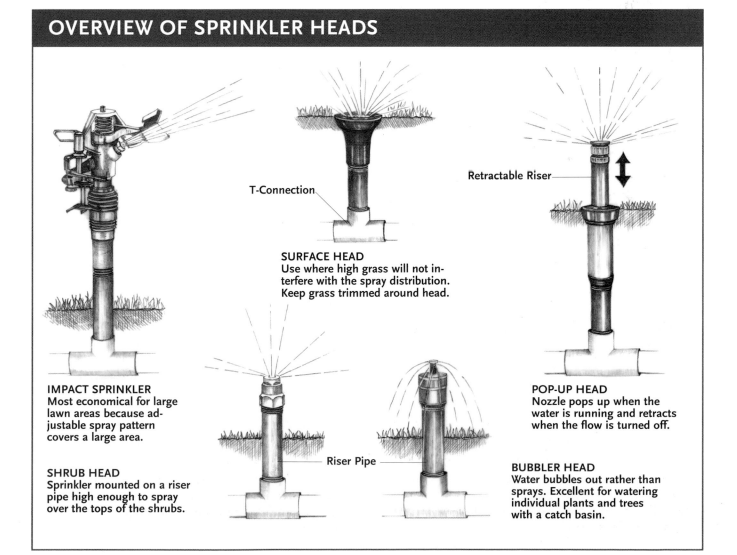

T-Connection

SURFACE HEAD
Use where high grass will not interfere with the spray distribution. Keep grass trimmed around head.

Retractable Riser

IMPACT SPRINKLER
Most economical for large lawn areas because adjustable spray pattern covers a large area.

SHRUB HEAD
Sprinkler mounted on a riser pipe high enough to spray over the tops of the shrubs.

Riser Pipe

POP-UP HEAD
Nozzle pops up when the water is running and retracts when the flow is turned off.

BUBBLER HEAD
Water bubbles out rather than sprays. Excellent for watering individual plants and trees with a catch basin.

SPRINKLER SYSTEM INSTALLATION

AS YOU PLAN HOW TO TAP INTO YOUR SERVICE LINE, it is also important to determine your water meter size, the diameter of your water service line, and the water pressure. This information is important because it tells you how many sprinkler heads you can attach to one watering line and the rate in gallons per minute (gpm) of water delivery. The sprinkler manufacturer will specify a minimum rate of water flow for its system to work. If your water pressure is low, you will need more pipelines (known as circuits), with fewer sprinkler heads on each. The more sprinkler heads you have, the more water pressure you need to supply enough water fast enough to feed them.

In regions where pipes freeze in cold winters, you'll need a shutoff valve and drain to empty the system before

1 MAP THE SYSTEM. On the base map, mark the water source and the circuits you will be watering. Dig the trenches 8 inches deep (or below the frost line in cold regions). Line the trench with sand or gravel.

2 APPLY PVC CEMENT. Measure and cut the pipe. Connect the risers. Brush PVC cement around the end of the pipe and inside the fitting. Quickly connect the two pieces.

5 CONNECT WATER SHUTOFF VALVE AND DRAIN. Every line must have its own shutoff. Locate the drain at the lowest point in each circuit line. Drain the system before the first frost.

6 INSTALL THE ANTI-SIPHON VALVE. Close to the main water supply, attach the anti-siphon valve, which prevents water from flowing backward out of the irrigation system into the main water supply.

the first freeze. This drain must be installed horizontally at the lowest point in each circuit line, and every pipe must run slightly downhill to it so that all the water will drain out. In cold regions, you will also have to dig the trenches below the frost line. The depth of the frost line varies; check with local authorities for specifics. As an added precaution, you can opt for an automatic drain valve that opens automatically to drain the pipes every time the water is turned off. With this device there is never any water standing in the pipes at any time. If you are concerned that your system isn't draining all of the water out of the pipes, there are garden maintenance companies that will come in autumn and blow out the lines with compressed air.

3 ATTACH THE SPRINKLER HEAD TO RISER. After you've determined the type of head needed, attach it to the appropriate riser. For complete coverage, you will need to space the heads so their spray overlaps.

4 TEST THE RISER HEIGHT. Shrub heads should be mounted high enough to spray over the tops of shrubs; surface heads should be at ground level, where they won't be damaged by the lawn mower.

7 FLUSH THE SPRINKLER VALVES. Wait four hours to ensure that the cement is fully dry. Then run the water to clear any debris in the pipes. Check for leaks, and go back and re-cement any leaky joints

8 PROGRAM THE CONTROLLER. The controller (or timer) is the brains of the sprinkler system. It will turn the water on and off at intervals you determine, and will control how long each circuit stays on.

(continued from page 231)

Materials. Once you've drawn a satisfactory plan, create a shopping list of all the materials you'll need. Also ask local building authorities whether you'll need a permit and if so, what codes apply. Some communities require a backflow preventor to stop water in the irrigation pipes from flowing back into the household drinking water.

Consider any accessories you may want. For example, it is very helpful to have a timer that turns the various sprinkler lines on and off automatically according to a preprogrammed schedule. With timers the garden continues to be watered even when you're away on a trip. Another possible accessory is a rain meter, which measures the rainfall and turns off the watering system after a predetermined amount of rain. Rain meters are particularly useful for sprinkler systems. Still another useful device is a soil moisture sensor, which activates the sprinkler system when the soil becomes too dry. Both of these last two accessories are good ways to conserve water.

Be aware that sprinkler pipe is made from several materials. Two commonly available types are PVC (short for polyvinyl chloride) and "poly," (short for polyethylene). PVC is semirigid, and poly is flexible. Poly pipe is easier to install because you can bend it around corners, saving time on joints. However, PVC is generally preferred because it is less expensive than poly and holds up better under high water pressure. PVC pipe is stamped with a pressure rating on the side of the pipe. Use PVC rated with a lower pressure rating for regular sprinkler lines. Always use PVC schedule-40 rated pipe to connect the pipe between the service line and the control valves because of surge pressure.

MAKING CONNECTIONS IN PVC AND POLY PIPE

POLY PIPES are quicker to install than PVC pipes because they bend around corners. Never use poly pipe to connect between the service line and the control valves where the surge pressure can be high. PVC pipe is less expensive than poly, and although you'll need to cut and join pipes more often, connecting pipes is easy.

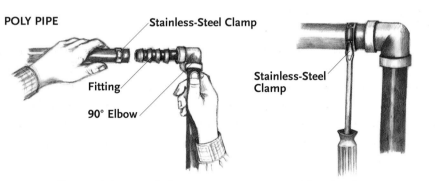

POLY PIPE — **Stainless-Steel Clamp** — **Fitting** — **90° Elbow** — **Stainless-Steel Clamp**

STEP 1: Slip a stainless-steel clamp over the cut pipe, and then insert the fitting into the pipe.

STEP 2: Position the clamp over the inserted fitting ridges and tighten with a screw driver.

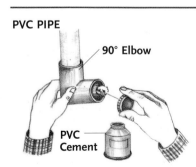

PVC PIPE — **90° Elbow** — **PVC Cement**

STEP 1: Clean off any burrs from the cut pipe, and then brush the cement evenly on the outside end of the pipe and inside the fitting.

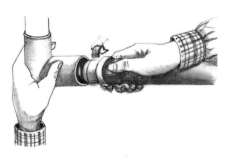

STEP 2: Quickly slide pipe into the fitting as far as it will go, twist to ensure a complete seal, and then hold for 10 to 15 seconds while the cement sets.

STEP 3: Use a rag or paper towel to wipe any excess cement off the outside of the pipe.

Test the System. Once you have connected all the lines, wait four hours to ensure that all the joints have set completely. Then run the water to flush out the pipes and remove any dirt that may have collected while you were working. At the same time, check for leaks. If you find a leak, apply more cement to the joint. If that doesn't solve the problem, you need to cut out the leaky joint and connect new pipe. Also measure to see how far the risers are above the ground. For lawns, you want the sprinkler heads flush with the ground. Trim any risers that are too tall, then attach the sprinkler heads. Finally, bury the lines, using the soil you removed from the trenches. Be careful not to bury the sprinkler heads. If you saved your sod, replace it. Otherwise, you'll need to reseed.

Water will spray with more force from sprinkler heads closest to the water supply. To get a relatively even flow from all the heads on each line, adjust the main circuit valve so that the flow is greatest from the heads nearest the water source. Then put on your bathing suit, and beginning nearest the water supply, adjust each head (there's a screw you turn) while the water is running until each sprays about the same amount.

Irrigation Map. Keep the final map of your sprinkler design, showing the location of all pipes. You'll be grateful for the information if you need to dig for other projects or make repairs in your system. You can bequeath the map to the next owner of your house. The map will remain a valuable piece of information.

Other Systems

Additional options for irrigation include soaker hoses and mist irrigation. Soaker hoses are porous hoses that weep water at a slow rate. They are the easiest form of irrigation to use. Laid on top of the soil, they are excellent for watering a row of flowers or vegetables that are planted close together. Soaker hoses can be installed in shrub borders and perennial beds for an entire season, hidden from sight under a layer of mulch. Use quick-release attachments to connect them to the ordinary garden hose that delivers water from the spigot.

In mist irrigation systems, the water is delivered as a fine mist through specially designed heads. If you have a greenhouse, you should also investigate mist irrigation systems.

SPRINKLER HEAD HEIGHT

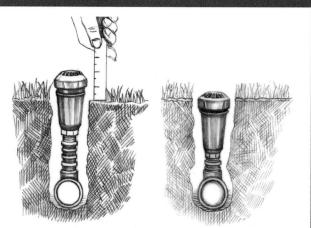

The head shown on the left is too high; the one on the right is flush with ground level and is correct. Measure and mark the pipe. Cut the riser if necessary, and cement the pipe.

EFFICIENT WATERING

- Water early in the morning so wet leaves can dry off before the sun becomes too strong. The second-best time is early evening. Less water is lost to evaporation at these times, so more will reach plants.
- Avoid watering in the heat of the day, especially in bright sunlight, because water droplets on the leaves act like magnifying glasses in the sun, causing leaf burn.
- Avoid getting water on the leaves, especially after dark, because wet leaves are prone to fungal diseases.
- Allow the water to run slowly so it penetrates deeply. Plants will be much healthier and more drought-tolerant if you water thoroughly and less often than if you lightly splash them frequently.
- Avoid using sprinklers when it's windy. The wind will blow the water droplets away from where they're meant to fall, and the wind increases water loss through evaporation.
- Water newly planted trees and shrubs and young seedlings frequently until their root systems develop.
- Mulch plants to reduce evaporation and minimize the amount of watering you need to do.

12 landscape tools

Landscape tools fall into two basic categories: hand tools and power tools. Generally speaking, the hand tools are cheap and the power tools are expensive. For example, you can get a good hand weeder for $10 but may spend several hundred to get a good mulching mower. When buying tools, a couple rules-of-thumb pertain: you usually get what you pay for, and most tools will last a lifetime if you take good care of them. One good approach is to buy less, but buy better. The specialty tool that looks like such a good idea in the store may be used once or twice and then consigned to the far corner of the garage. And don't forget that power tools need yearly maintenance to perform well and long. Always use fresh gas; replace the fuel filter and spark plug annually; and clean the air filter at least twice a year.

MOWERS, SPREADERS, AND SPRAYERS

The tools and machines in this group are essential to a good lawn-care program.

Mowers

Choose a lawn mower according to the size of your lawn, the terrain, your energy level, and your own feelings about noise and air quality.

Gasoline-Powered Rotary Mower. This lawn mower is currently the most popular. The single horizontal blade can cut through the toughest grass, and the four wheels allow you to mow a bumpy lawn without scalping it. Available in walk-behind, riding, or tractor designs, with op-

tions such as self-propulsion, grass catchers, and electric starters, these new mowers also produce less pollution than they did in former years, thanks to EPA standards. Gas engine emissions standards have required manufacturers to phase in cleaner-burning engines. These machines are reliable unless you commit the cardinal sin of leaving gas in the tank during the off-season. If you don't drain the gasoline prior to long-term storage, gumlike varnish deposits may form and cause starting problems or poor engine operation.

Gasoline-Powered Mulching Mower. This machine is similar to the rotary mower. Its specially shaped mower housing and blade work together to suspend clippings long enough for several passes with the blade, making the clippings fine enough to leave where they fall.

MOWERS

Gasoline-Powered Mulching Mower (walk-behind)

Manual Reel Mower

Cordless Electric Mower

Gasoline-Powered Tractor Mower

SPREADERS AND SPRAYERS

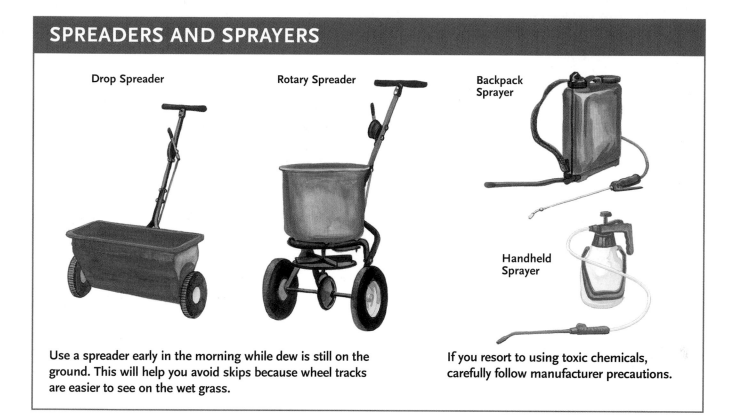

Drop Spreader   Rotary Spreader   Backpack Sprayer

Handheld Sprayer

Use a spreader early in the morning while dew is still on the ground. This will help you avoid skips because wheel tracks are easier to see on the wet grass.

If you resort to using toxic chemicals, carefully follow manufacturer precautions.

Reel Mower. Available in manual or gasoline-powered models, reel mowers have five or more horizontal blades that rotate in a cylindrical path, pressing grass against a cutting bar and making a scissorlike cut. Reel mowers give a cleaner cut than rotary mowers, and their blades stay sharp longer. But reel mowers are more susceptible to jamming from twigs and wet, heavy grass than rotary mowers are, and they are not well suited to tough-bladed grasses or to lawns with frequent dips and rises. Reel mowers generally have limited height adjustment, to a maximum of $1\frac{1}{2}$ or 2 inches, making it impossible to cut grass at a greater height, and the blades must be sharpened by a professional. Also, the design of this machine does not allow the blades to reach to the outside width of the wheels, as the blades on most rotary mowers do, so reel mowers won't trim close along most lawn edges.

Electric Mower. These mowers come in corded or cordless models. Corded mowers are lightweight, but you need to drag a heavy power cord around as you mow. They are fine for small lawns with few obstacles. Cordless electrics free you from extension cords, thanks to improved battery technology. One charge in a cordless mower with a 36-volt battery will run for well over three hours doing light mowing or for about two hours doing heavier mowing. Compared with gas-powered models,

electrics tend to have narrower cutting widths, which add to mowing time, but they make less noise, emit no noxious fumes, and require no engine maintenance, such as annual oil and spark-plug changes.

Spreaders

Today's spreaders are usually made of lightweight plastic and are easy to operate. Precision of application is the main difference between the two types.

Drop Spreader. Drop spreaders distribute seed, fertilizer, and other amendments, such as lime, in swaths the width of the spreader. Settings allow you to control the amount distributed. This type of spreader is ideal for distributing its payload along edges, flower beds, and paths.

Rotary Spreader. A rotary spreader flings seed or amendments over a wide area, thereby covering ground faster than drop spreaders. However, it is not well suited for use on windy days or with small, irregularly shaped lawns.

Sprayers

You will need a sprayer for dispensing insecticidal soap or oil solutions. Sprayers are typically available in canister or backpack styles with 2- to 4-gallon polyethylene tanks and interchangeable nozzles for varying application patterns and rates.

239

HAND TOOLS

Spade. Often mistakenly called shovels, spades have flat or gently curved blades and are used for planting or transplanting and for edging.

Round-Point shovel. These are designed to move large quantities of fine-textured material, such as sand, soil, or nonfibrous mulches, from one place to another. But they can serve quite well digging soil too.

Garden Rake. The steel-headed type is useful for preparing small areas of soil for the planting of seeds.

Lawn-and-Leaf Rake. Those rakes with an extra-wide head make the work go faster but require more muscle. Bamboo rakes are usually the lightest, but steel rakes and the modern plastics are durable.

Landscape Rake. This has a wide, 36-inch aluminum head mounted on an aluminum or wood shaft. Use it to remove debris from prepared soil and to level the soil prior to planting a new lawn.

Thatching Rake. The thatching, or dethatching, rake is made primarily for removing thatch from your lawn without damaging the structure of the turf.

Pruning Tools. Keep several types on hand for various situations. Use a sharp pruning knife or one-hand prun-

HAND TOOLS

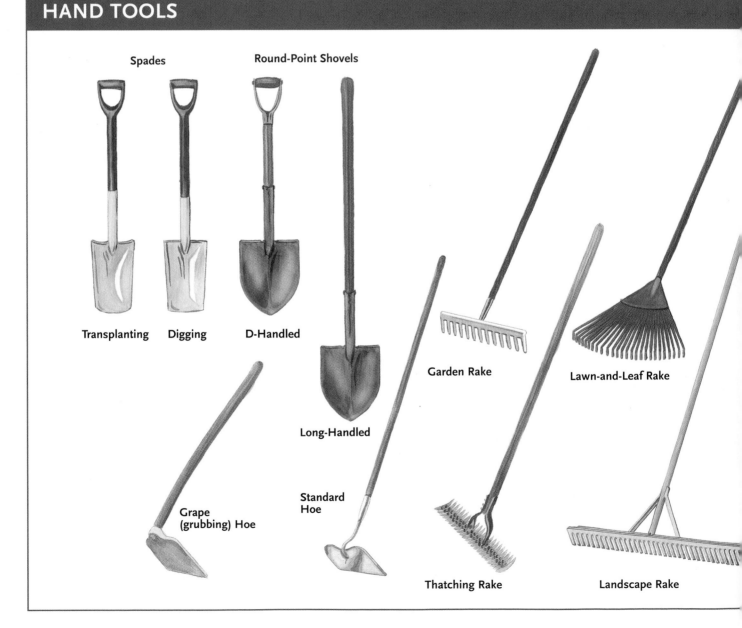

Spades

Round-Point Shovels

Transplanting

Digging

D-Handled

Long-Handled

Grape (grubbing) Hoe

Standard Hoe

Garden Rake

Lawn-and-Leaf Rake

Thatching Rake

Landscape Rake

ing shears for twigs and branches up to ½ inch; lopping shears for ½- to 1½-inch branches; pruning saws for woody branches up to 3 inches in diameter; and a bow saw or chain saw for larger branches.

Grape (Grubbing) Hoe. This wide, heavy-bladed hoe offers a low-tech but surprisingly efficient way to remove turf you no longer want. A standard hoe is great for loosening soil, planting seeds, and mixing concrete in a wheelbarrow.

Grass Shears. Shears provide a time-honored means of clipping grass along the edge of a garden bed.

Weeders. Standing weeders, hand weeders, and a hand cultivator make short work of removing weeds from planting beds.

Turf Edger. A half-moon-shaped steel cutting head is mounted to a hardwood handle. Use it to keep lawn edges neat or to trim away excess when laying sod along irregular lawn edges.

Garden Carts and Wheelbarrows. These indispensable aids haul everything from lawn tools and fertilizer to weeds and prunings. (See page 242.)

Planting Tools. A spading fork and a hand trowel break up compacted soil to prepare for planting. A bulb planter is used for flower bulbs.

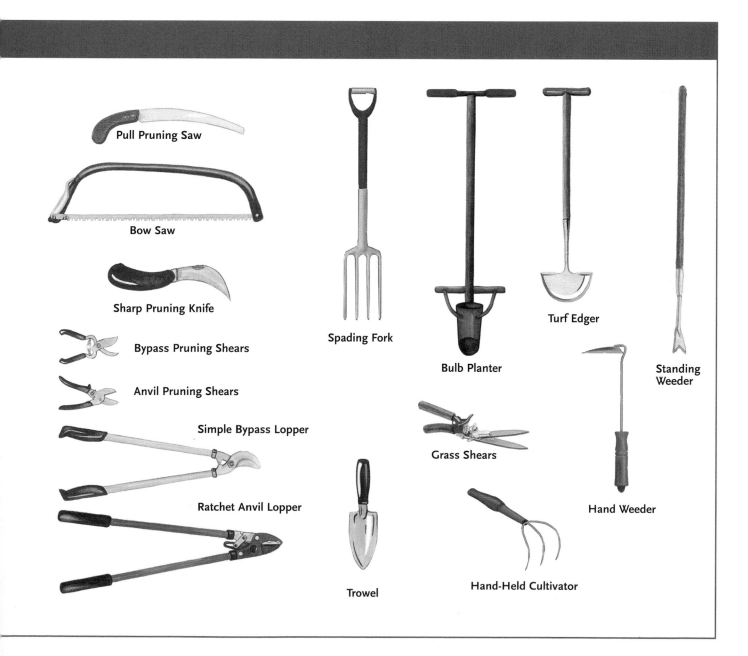

Pull Pruning Saw

Bow Saw

Sharp Pruning Knife

Bypass Pruning Shears

Anvil Pruning Shears

Simple Bypass Lopper

Ratchet Anvil Lopper

Spading Fork

Bulb Planter

Turf Edger

Standing Weeder

Grass Shears

Hand Weeder

Trowel

Hand-Held Cultivator

Garden Carts and Wheelbarrows. These devices are indispensable for just about every gardening and landscaping job. The most common, and least expensive, is the traditional wheelbarrow that has a steel or plastic tub mounted on two handles that are connected to a single front wheel. An improvement on the single-wheel design features two front wheels, like the model we show below. It's much more stable and can usually carry much more weight. The top-of-the-line carrier is the bicycle-wheel garden cart. It features two large wheels with pneumatic tires that make pushing the cart very easy. The tub is usually made of plastic, but traditional models are made with exterior grade plywood panels.

Watering Can. Many inexperienced gardeners think this tool is a bit old-fashioned. They would rather just set the spray nozzle on their hose to a gentle setting and do their watering that way. This makes sense as long as you don't mind dragging the hose around. But if you want to conveniently water in remote locations, a watering can can't be beat. It's also a great container for premixing fertilizers and dispensing nutrients for an individual plant.

Manual Aerator. This foot-powered tool is pushed into the soil, then rocked back and forth to open up compacted areas. It works great for small areas of less that 100 sq.ft. But for larger sections, consider using a rented gas-powered aerator.

MORE HAND TOOLS

Watering Can

Manual Aerator

Garden Cart

Two-Wheeled Wheelbarrow

Garden Cart

SPECIALTY TOOLS

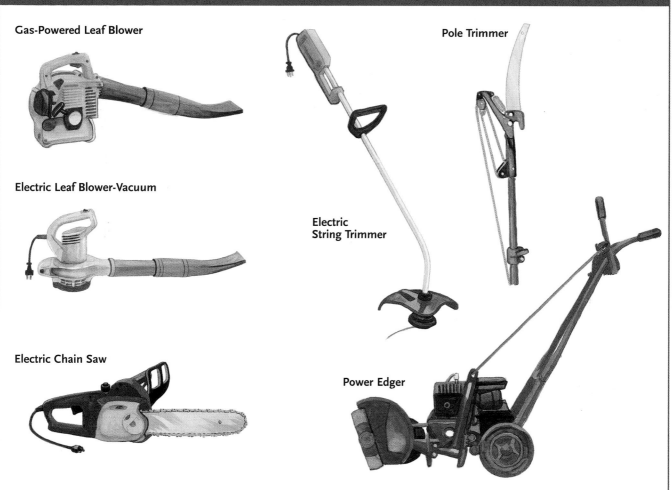

Gas-Powered Leaf Blower

Electric Leaf Blower-Vacuum

Electric Chain Saw

Pole Trimmer

Electric
String Trimmer

Power Edger

SPECIALTY TOOLS

The following tools are convenient to own.

Power Edger. This is a gasoline-powered tool with a short blade that you can use horizontally to trim grass at lawn edges or vertically to create and maintain edges.

String Trimmer. There are gas-, electric-, and battery-powered models. Plastic line at the cutting end rotates at high speed to trim grass or weeds along lawn edges and near fixtures such as lampposts and fences. The better-balanced and easier-to-use models have the power unit at the top end of a long shaft and an adjustable handle in the middle. As the line wears or breaks, you feed more line by tapping the cutting head on the ground. Excess line is sheared off by a small blade built into the debris guard. Cutting swaths range from 6 to 10 inches for cordless units, 8 to 10 inches for corded electric models, and 15 to 18 inches for larger, heavier, gas-powered units.

Pole Trimmer. This is a pruning saw at the end of a 12-foot telescoping pole. It's great for homeowners who like to do high pruning with their feet firmly planted on the earth; it's also available with lopping shears.

Blower. Powered by gas or electricity, this machine blows leaves into piles for easier collection. Blowers are available in either hand-held, wheeled, or backpack styles, the last two types leaving you less tired on big jobs. Even if you like raking leaves on the lawn, you'll appreciate a blower's help in moving leaves out from under shrubs. Drawbacks include noise, noxious emissions of gas-powered units, and difficulty of use on windy days.

Chain Saw. For the cutting of tree limbs and trunks larger than a few inches in diameter, an electric saw can be a smarter buy than a gas-powered saw. If you can keep all your cutting within 100 feet or so of an outdoor outlet protected by a ground-fault circuit interrupter, this is the only saw you'll need, even for cutting firewood.

13 improving your landscape

A landscape is a living thing and thus is constantly changing. What was once a beautiful design, perfectly in scale, eventually may overgrow its bounds. When mature trees and shrubs crowd each other, create dense shade, or encroach upon pathways, they need to be taken in hand. Short-lived trees and shrubs eventually need to be replaced. Whatever the reason for making major changes to your landscape design, remember that your existing plants are rich assets. Before you uproot and remove your old plantings, take time to decide whether each plant is worth saving. You'll save hundreds of dollars if you can incorporate existing plants into your new landscape design.

PRUNING

How you prune will determine the future growth patterns of your trees and shrubs. If you want a full and bushy shrub (or perennial, for that matter), give it that message by shearing or pinching. Botanists have found that there is a concentration of growth hormone in the tips (*apexes* or *apices*) of growing plants. They've dubbed this phenomenon *apical dominance*. The net result is that when you pinch back a plant or shear it, you redirect the growth hormone to the growing buds below the cut. Every time you cut or pinch off the end of a branch, the plant sends out two shoots from each bud. The result is that every pinched or sheared branch will develop two or three new lateral branches, ultimately doubling the plant's fullness.

You can pinch back just about any plant, but not all tolerate shearing. For example, you would seriously damage a rhododendron if you sheared it, although there is no problem with shearing azaleas. Forsythia, with its lovely, loose shape, is a good example of a shrub that is spoiled by shearing. Generally shearing should be reserved for hedges and to shape formal evergreens.

Pruning for Fullness

When you are pruning to make a plant bushier, always cut back to a growth bud. To find the buds, look for a swelling or projection along the stem or branch. The large, easily visible buds are actively waiting to grow. In addition, there are smaller, dormant buds that will sprout if you cut off the branch just above them. Make the cut at a 45-degree angle with the low end of the cut opposite the bud and even with it. If you cut too sharp an angle, or too high above the bud, the cut tip will die back rather than stimulate fresh growth. If you cut too close to the bud, you'll damage it. Cut to a bud that faces the outside of the stem or plant to encourage the shrub to grow in an open shape. Branches that grow inward, crisscrossing over and under each other, make a less attractive shrub and reduce the air circulation inside the plant.

PRUNING TECHNIQUES

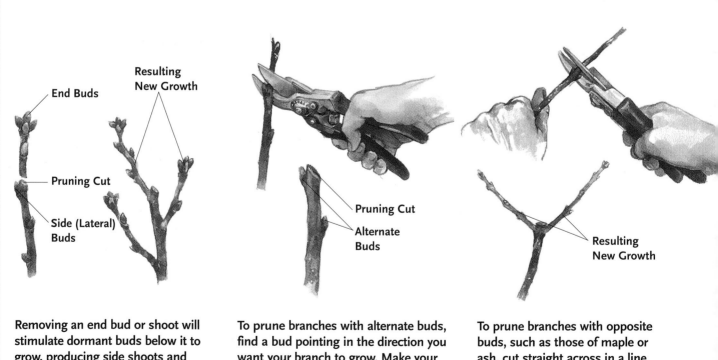

Removing an end bud or shoot will stimulate dormant buds below it to grow, producing side shoots and creating a bushier plant. If you allow end buds to remain, they will inhibit the growth of side buds, and the stem will grow mainly from the tip.

To prune branches with alternate buds, find a bud pointing in the direction you want your branch to grow. Make your cut about ¼ inch above the bud and on an angle parallel with that bud. There is no need to apply tree-wound dressing to cuts, whether large or small.

To prune branches with opposite buds, such as those of maple or ash, cut straight across in a line that just clears the bud tips. This will result in fairly uniform growth of both buds.

Prune Summer-Flowering Shrubs in Late Winter. Summer-flowering shrubs such as glossy abelia (*Abelia* x *grandiflora*), broom (*Cytisus* species), butterfly bush (*Buddleia* species except for *B. alternifolia*), rose of Sharon (*Hibiscus syriacus*), peegee hydrangea (*Hydrangea paniculata* 'Grandiflora'), and shrubby cinquefoil (*Potentilla fruticosa*) bloom on new growth. You can create a bushier plant and increase the number of flowers if you prune these shrubs in late winter or early spring before the plant has started to actively grow. Cut each branch back to a growth bud. Every branch you prune should produce at least two new shoots, doubling the shrub's blossom potential. Because you prune these shrubs before the buds emerge, there is no danger you will cut off a flower bud.

THE SUMMER-BLOOMING BUTTERFLY BUSH (*Buddleia davidii*) will produce more flowers if you trim the bush back in early spring. Cut the shrub back to a framework of permanent branches, cutting at strong buds or where vigorous shoots are developing.

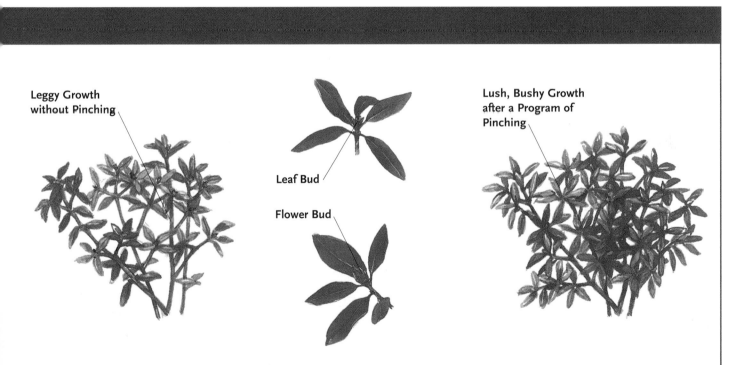

Leggy Growth
without Pinching

Leaf Bud

Flower Bud

Lush, Bushy Growth
after a Program of
Pinching

When pinching back broad-leaved evergreens on plants, such as rhododendrons, you can avoid leggy growth (shown at left), stimulate lush branching growth (shown at right), and control plant size by pinching back end buds of new branches. In a phenomenon known as apical dominance, these end buds control hormonal flow and inhibit growth of dormant side buds. Pinching (removal) of end buds sends chemical signals that stimulate the growth of side buds. CAUTION: avoid mistakenly pinching off the bigger, fatter flower buds.

Wait Until Flowers Finish for Spring Bloomers. Wait to prune spring-blooming shrubs such as lilacs until they are flowering (use the cuttings for flower arrangements indoors) or until after the blooms are spent. Most of these shrubs set flower buds on year-old wood, so an early spring trimming will cut off this year's blossoms. The pruning you do in early summer on spring-flowering shrubs will stimulate more flowers the following spring. *To avoid the risk of cutting off next year's buds just as they are being set, prune within a month after the shrub stops flowering.*

Prune Nonflowering Plants Any Time. Nonflowering trees and shrubs can be pruned at any time, but again you have an opportunity to communicate a definite message to the plant by when you prune.

■ *To improve health, prune in the winter.* To increase the plant's vigor, prune when the plant is dormant.

■ *To slow down growth, prune in the active growth season.* If you want to slow growth on a tree or shrub, cut it back when it is actively growing.

■ *To open up a tree's form, remove the inside branches.* In cases where branches cross over each other or are too dense, you may wish to open up the form of a tree or shrub by removing inside lateral branches. Instead of cutting from the tip back to a growth bud, remove the branch at its growing source, either the tree trunk or the primary branch. The message you deliver to the plant is clear: don't send out extra shoots, there are enough here already. This type of pruning can enhance the form of a tree as well as improve the tree's health, as it lets light and air into the interior of the plant.

■ *When pruning to a growing source, do not cut it flush with the trunk.* If you do, you'll create a wound larger than necessary and increase the risk of disease. Instead, make the cut on the branch side of the slight swelling where the branch meets the trunk, but as close to the swelling, also known as the collar or saddle, as possible.

THE THINNED CANOPY of this pine tree makes a pretty, lacy pattern against the sky. The extra space, or portholes, between branches also allows the wind to blow through unobstructed—a useful attribute in this ocean-facing west-coast garden.

Yearly Maintenance Pruning

Not all trees and shrubs need pruning every year. However, you should inspect your woody ornamentals once a year to see whether they need to be pruned.

Remove Dead or Diseased Wood. Look for dead and diseased wood, and remove any you find. In addition to being unsightly, the problem that killed a branch could spread to the rest of the plant if you don't cut it out. To prevent the spread of infectious diseases through your pruning tools, disinfect the tools by dipping them between each cut in rubbing alcohol. In the spring, prune away any branches or wood killed over the winter.

Regular Pruning Keeps the Job Manageable. It's much easier to keep a tree or shrub at a maintainable size if you prune it back once a year rather than once every five years or so. In addition to the job being less work, you'll make life much easier on the plant if you remove just a little foliage every year rather than a large amount all at once. In addition, you can more easily influence the shape of the tree or shrub if you prune annually. If you see a garden full of beautifully shaped trees and shrubs, the odds are they are pruned at least once a year.

MAINTAINING TREES AND SHRUBS

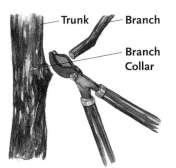

Trunk — Branch

Branch Collar

When removing an entire branch, cut just outside the slightly thickened area, called the branch collar, where the branch grows from the trunk.

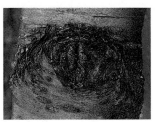

Proper pruning cuts just beyond the collar on this kwanzan cherry resulted in the nicely healing wound shown at left and the almost completely healed wound on another branch, shown above.

Improper pruning results are shown in both pictures. Left: Careless lopping left a small, protruding chunk of wood, which won't heal as quickly as the surrounding edges. Right: A single top-to-bottom cut resulted in torn bark that gives diseases and pests access to the tree.

These rubbing limbs will eventually abrade the bark on one or both limbs, leaving exposed wood open to pests and diseases. Remove the weaker limb or the one facing inward.

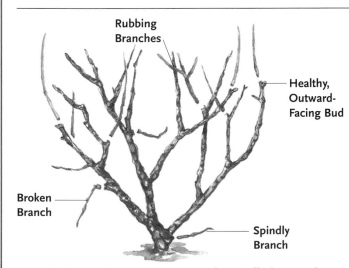

Rubbing Branches

Healthy, Outward-Facing Bud

Broken Branch

Spindly Branch

SELECTIVE PRUNING. Remove weak, spindly, bent, or broken shoots (red). Where two branches rub on each other, remove the weaker or the one that's pointing inward (orange). Cut back long shoots to a healthy, outward-facing bud (blue).

SEVERE PRUNING. In late winter or early spring, before new growth starts, cut all the stems of the shrub back close to the ground.

REVIVING SHRUBS

Unless the plant has reached the end of its natural life span, most old but healthy shrubs can be made new again or at least brought back into scale with the rest of the garden. However, shrub renovation is not for the faint of heart. It requires severe pruning, in some cases cutting the plant right back to the ground or to a few bare stubs. It also requires patience. It can take several years to restore a tired, overgrown old shrub to a youthful thing of beauty. When successful, however, the risk is well worth the patience and effort. You'll enjoy the benefit of having a beautiful, well-established shrub.

Propagate Shrubs before Pruning

Just as there are risks when a doctor performs major surgery on a human, there is the possibility that the shrub you try to renovate will not survive. If you plan to work on an unusual or hard-to-replace specimen, propagate new plants as a precaution. To improve the chances of renovated shrubs making a good recovery, feed and water them well during the following growing season. Ideally, flowering shrubs should be fed twice a year—in the spring and autumn.

Take Softwood Cuttings in Spring. Softwood cuttings are taken in late spring before the new growth has fully hardened. Softwood is pliable because lignan, the substance that stiffens woody stems, has not yet developed. Cut off the new growth tips of branches, cutting pieces a minimum of 3 to 4 inches long. If the parent plant is large or if you are pruning away large sections, the cuttings can be as long as 2 feet. Remove the lower leaves from each cutting to expose a length of bare stem. Bury the stems of short cuttings 1 to 2 inches deep in a mix of perlite and vermiculite. Insert taller cuttings deeper into the pot so they stand on their own.

Trees and shrubs that root well from softwood cuttings taken in late spring include barberry, butterfly bush, flowering quince, deutzia, forsythia, and bush honeysuckle.

Summer is the Time for Semiripe Cuttings. Semiripe cuttings are taken a few weeks later in early summer. They should be rooted using the same procedure as for softwood cuttings. Good candidates for semiripe cuttings are camellia, cotoneaster, daphne, hydrangea, mahonia, privet, pyracantha, spirea, and weigela.

Take Hardwood Cuttings in Autumn. Hardwood cuttings are taken at the end of the growing season when the wood has developed lignan and is no longer flexible. In parts of the country where the ground freezes, take the cuttings in early winter, and store them buried in slightly damp sand, wood shavings, or vermiculite. They should be kept moist and between 32° to 40°F. After the ground has thawed, you can place the stored cuttings directly into the ground or into pots or beds with prepared soil. In warm climates you can take hardwood cuttings in autumn. Hardwood cuttings should be pencil-thick and 5 to 8 inches long.

IF YOU SEVERELY PRUNE BACK old, tired-looking shrubs, they will generate fresh new growth, giving them a new lease on life. *Spirea japonica* 'Little Princess' (shown here) will rebloom if the spent flowers are sheared off the plant.

STARTING PLANTS WITH SOFTWOOD CUTTINGS

PROPAGATING NEW PLANTS by rooting cuttings is strongly recommended before you transplant or severely prune a mature tree or shrub that may not survive the process. Growing new plants from softwood and semiripe cuttings is an inexpensive way of reproducing shrubs, especially if you want many plants for a hedge or to fill a large space.

STEP 1: Cut off the new growth tips. Softwood cuttings are taken in late spring; semiripe cuttings in early summer. Each cutting should be 3 to 4 inches long. Remove the lower leaves, keeping just a few at the tip of the cutting.

STEP 2: Dip the cutting in rooting hormone. To keep the powder in the storage container fresh, pour out a small amount of powder; use what you need; and throw away the leftover.

STEP 3: Plant the cutting. Bury the stem of each cutting in the premoistened medium, with just the leafy top section sticking out. At this stage, the cuttings do not need a lot of growing room; you can fit several into one pot. Water well, making sure the soil or rooting medium is saturated.

STEP 4: Keep the cutting moist and warm. To ensure consistent moisture, cover the pot with a clear plastic bag. The cuttings will root more successfully if you keep the soil mix evenly moist and warm. Look for a place, such as the top of the refrigerator or dryer, where the cuttings will remain warm and get plenty of light.

STARTING PLANTS WITH HARDWOOD CUTTINGS

THE PROCESS OF TAKING HARDWOOD CUTTINGS is another way to propagate woody plants. It is quite similar to taking softwood or semi-ripe cuttings. The difference between the methods is when the cuttings are taken. Hardwood is older; cuttings are taken at the end of the growing season, after lignan has developed in the wood.

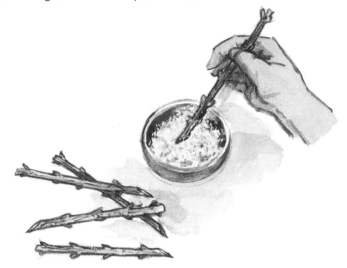

STEP 1: Make the cut. Cut the section at an angle just below a leaf node. Roots develop out of the cut, and the angle provides more surface area for more roots. Make sure there are at least three leaf nodes along the stem of the cutting. Remove all the leaves.

STEP 2: Dip the bottom end in rooting hormone. Rooting hormone powder will boost your rate of success. To remember which is the top end and which is the bottom, cut the bottom at an angle, the top straight across.

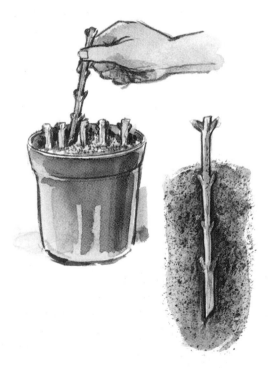

STEP 3: Plant the cuttings. Several cuttings can fit into one pot. Be sure to put the bottom end (cut at an angle) into the rooting medium. Bury most of the cutting; roots will develop from each growing node.

STEP 4: Check whether the cutting has grown roots. Signs of successful rooting include new leaves sprouting on the stem and resistance if you tug gently on the cutting. Do not disturb the roots by pulling too hard.

Rejuvenating Old Deciduous Flowering Shrubs

You can increase the production of blooms and improve the form of shrubs by pruning. The best time to prune flowering shrubs varies with the type of plant. If you don't know when to work on a specific shrub, contact the local Cooperative Extension Service. Most plants respond best to severe pruning in late winter.

Prune Deciduous Shrubs over Three Years. Some plants can be cut completely down to the ground all at once. However, cutting one third of the branches down to the ground or the main stem the first year, another third the second year, and the final third the last year is a safer method. Remove the oldest and least desirable stems first, but also try to remove stems from all sides of the shrub so that you maintain a balanced form. In the second and third years, also remove new growth that is weak or that will spoil the shrub's form and balance.

To reduce the size of an overgrown shrub, cut the oldest stems right down to the ground, and remove all dead branches. Be sure to leave enough stems to provide energy to the plant. No tree or shrub will be able to survive without enough stems to produce chlorophyl. Then trim back the remaining stems to just below the ideal height you have in mind. Once the pruning wounds are healed, establish a maintenance pruning routine.

If shrubs such as flowering quince (*Chaenomeles* species) and shrub roses grow leggy, with branches arching to the ground, cut back the branches from their tips, at the same time thinning out the older, thick, woody ones.

Prune Shrubs Gradually in Colder Regions. In northern climates or for plants you don't want to put at any risk, rejuvenate the shrub by cutting back one-third of the branches at a time, spreading the operation over three years. Choose the longest, most unproductive branches first, and cut them back to their source.

MAKING OVERGROWN SHRUBS LOOK LIKE TREES

OVERGROWN SHRUBS can also be renovated by arborizing them, or pruning them to look like trees. This technique is especially effective with single-stemmed shrubs such as camellias and multi-stemmed shrubs with a prominent major stem, such as hollies. To arborize, choose a large and healthy stem as the primary trunk, removing smaller vertical stems and cutting back the lower horizontal branches to the main trunk. These shrubs are especially effective in small gardens where a full-size tree would take up too much space. To cover the newly exposed bare earth, underplant the pruned shrub with a shade-loving ground cover or with shallow-rooted annuals.

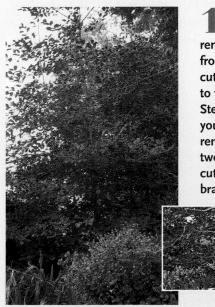

1 **Prune the lower branches. Start** removing branches from the bottom, cutting them back to the main trunk. Step back to check your work after removing a row or two, so you don't cut off too many branches.

2 **Complete the arborization.** Continue cutting until the plant is the shape you want. Instead of a large shrub, the holly now resembles a small tree. There is now plenty of room to grow shallow-rooted plants underneath that appreciate the shade the holly provides.

253

IMPROVING BROAD-LEAVED EVERGREEN SHRUBS

Radical Pruning is Recommended in Warm Climates

In warm southern climates, shrubs such as rhododendrons, azaleas, and mountain laurels can be renewed by cutting them back to the ground. Old boxwood, which can live for hundreds of years, also has a good chance of surviving when pruned in this drastic fashion.

■ *Heavy Feeding Prior to Surgery Lessens Stress.* The plant's chances for survival are improved if you feed it with a heavy dose of cottonseed meal and manure (or a high-nitrogen fertilizer formulated for acid-loving plants) at least a year before the radical surgery.

■ *Prune in Early Spring for Best Results.* Whether you cut the plant down to the ground or remove the old growth in stages, do the job in late winter or early spring when the plant is bursting to send out new shoots.

Renovating Formal Hedges

Some of the best hedging plants include boxwood, holly, hornbeam, privet, and yew because they grow slowly and are long-lived. If you have an overgrown hedge comprising any of these plants, it is well worth your time and trouble to restore it. Although the hedge will look odd for several years while the restoration is going on, you'll have an attractive hedge much sooner than if you start over with young plants.

■ *Late Winter: Cut Down to the Desired Height.* Begin in late winter by cutting the top back to the height you want. Don't be afraid to cut back to bare branches. Any of the above-mentioned plants will send out new shoots, even from thick, bare branches.

■ *Prune One Side of the Hedge to the Main Stem.* Next, severely prune just one side of the hedge, cutting it back to the main stem or stems. Leave the other side untouched. (See page 255, bottom right.) Feed the pruned plant with a balanced fertilizer, and top-dress with compost or aged manure that will slowly release additional nutrients into the soil. Severe pruning makes the shrub more susceptible to drought stress. Water the hedge deeply if the weather gets dry, and add a thick layer of mulch to help maintain even moisture.

■ *After One Side Has Recovered, Cut the Other Side.* Wait until the pruned side of the hedge is showing vigorous growth before you cut back the other side. You may need to wait two or three years to ensure that the plant is strong enough to take another shock. Once you think the hedge is ready, cut back the second side, following the same procedure as you did for the first.

When the hedge is in shape, prune it so that the sides flare out slightly at the bottom. That way the entire surface will be exposed to light, ensuring a healthier, leafier hedge. When hedges are pruned in a wedge shape with the top wider than the bottom, the upper branches shade the lower portion of the hedge, preventing the foliage from growing properly.

THIS NEATLY TRIMMED formal boxwood hedge makes a beautiful frame to the perennials growing inside and provides a pleasing structure to the garden as a whole. Overgrown boxwood hedges can be brought back into scale with severe pruning.

MAINTAINING A HEDGE

FAST-GROWING SHRUBS, such as the Euonymus 'Manhattan' shown here, will need pruning three or four times a year. Slower-growing plant materials, such as boxwood or yew, take longer to establish themselves as hedges, but they subsequently need pruning much less often.

1 PRUNE THE SIDES. Trim hedge sides slightly wider at the bottom than the top to allow light to reach the entire surface. Use an even, sweeping motion with the power clippers to cut a level top surface.

2 FINISH SHAPING THE HEDGE. To achieve a crisp, clean finish on a shaggy hedge and to maintain the desired size, don't be afraid to cut back the new growth by several inches—or even a foot or more.

Maintenance Pruning

SET UP A PRUNING GUIDE. For accurate pruning on a formal hedge, it is helpful to tie string guides that have been set and leveled at the desired final height and width. Be sure to keep the electrical cord away from the blades of the hedge clipper.

Renewing an Old Hedge

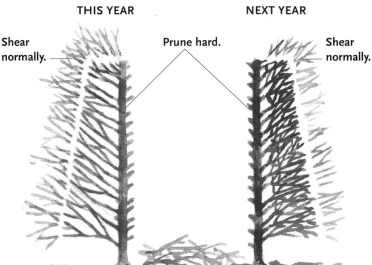

THIS YEAR   NEXT YEAR

Shear normally.   Prune hard.   Shear normally.

PRUNE ONE SIDE PER YEAR. To avoid shocking a severely-pruned hedge to death, trim back one side the first year, and wait a year or two until the pruned side has started growing properly again before you cut back the opposite side.

255

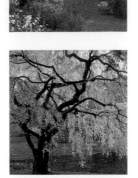

14 trees and shrubs

A beautiful landscape, like a lovely face, requires good bone structure. One of the major components of a garden's bones are trees and shrubs. If you are starting from scratch, you should select your trees, hedges, and other large plantings before you think about smaller details such as perennials and ground covers. Determine which plants will do well in your climate, making sure to consider the specific soil, water, and light conditions on your property. Choose trees and shrubs that help define your garden spaces, provide shade, or serve as a foil for other plantings. And don't overlook the importance of a bold statement. A spectacular specimen tree, such as a weeping cherry, or one that grows in a striking form, such as the pagoda dogwood (*Cornus alternifolia*), can provide the focal point for your entire landscape.

ALL-SEASON DESIGN

Create a View or a Border, or Both. Plant an avenue of trees to create a vista in your garden. Line your driveway with flowering trees such as crab apples for a spectacular "welcome home" in spring when the blossoms are open and a cool, shady drive in the summer. Add interest to an expanse of lawn with a grove of trees. Place a bench among the trees, and you'll have a special shaded seat.

Trees and shrubs are excellent for providing mass in your landscape. Include shrubs and even small trees in flower borders to provide interest in winter and to anchor the design. Border a bed with a low-growing shrub such as dwarf boxwood or *Santolina* to frame and give definition to the plantings. Line a path with scented shrubs such as lavender or plant a bulky shrub at the curve of a winding path to obscure the view around a corner.

Obscure Eyesores, and Save Energy. Trees can be useful to screen an unattractive view, lower noise levels, cut the wind, and provide shade. A deciduous tree planted near the house, especially on the south side, can save heating and cooling costs. Likewise, a row of trees planted in the path of prevailing winds can deflect the icy gusts, thus helping to cut down on heating costs.

Design for the Seasons

Plant trees and shrubs for seasonal interest such as spectacular autumn color, spring or summer flowers, or a compelling silhouette in winter. Choose a shrub for its fragrant flowers or foliage. Place a sweet-smelling shrub under a window, or beside a patio or outdoor seating area so you can enjoy the scent. Some trees, such as the crab apple or dogwood, shine in more than one season.

Viburnum is another delightful plant that gives good value for the space it uses. This is a large plant family with species such as V. lentago that is hardy down to Zone 2, to more tender specimen that need Zone 8 or warmer. Among the excellent choices for the home garden is the doublefile viburnun (*V. plicatum f. tomentosum*). In spring it is covered in white, lacecap-like flowers. The crinkled leaves (the Latin name *plicatum* refers to the leaf's pleated look) are a joy throughout the summer, and then in autumn, bright red fruit lights up the shrub.

For tight spaces, consider *Viburnum dilatatum* 'Catskill', a compact shrub that takes at least 15 years to reach a height of 5 feet with an 8-foot spread. The dark green foliage takes on shades of red and yellow in fall. Abundant dark red fruit persists until midwinter. Viburnum 'Conoy' grows about as big as 'Catskill.' Its glossy, evergreen foliage is the perfect backdrop to the creamy white flowers in the spring and the brilliant red berries in autumn.

THE TREES IN THIS LANDSCAPE screen the view of the house beyond. Although the shrubs in front of the tree stand are not fully grown, they will grow into a continuous line and provide an understory for the larger trees.

THE BRIGHT ORANGE JAPANESE MAPLE TREE in the distance is the focal point of this path. Notice how the yellow flowering tree frames the path and points the way to the exclamation point in the distance.

THE GARDEN IN WINTER

WINTER IS THE BEST SEASON to evaluate your landscape. In spring and summer, lush foliage and lavish floral displays can disguise many design problems. But once the foliage falls and the flowers fade, the true structure of the garden is clearly visible.

Evergreen trees are an obvious choice for maintaining color and interest in the fall and winter garden. The Colorado blue spruce (*Picea pungens* 'Glauca') is a wonderful choice both for its almost-perfect Christmas tree form and its silvery blue color. The golden yellow foliage of *Chamaecyparis lawsoniana* 'Lutea', brings a sense of sunshine into even the drabbest winter day. Evergreen hedges are real assets in the winter garden.

Deciduous Trees with Strong Silhouettes. Good possibilities include Japanese maple (*Acer palmatum*), with its marvelous twisting branches, and Harry Lauder's walking stick (*Corylus avellana* 'Contorta'). Another twisted wonder is the willow *Salix matsudana* 'Tortuosa'.

Berry-Bearing Plants. Berry-bearing shrubs and trees are a delight in a winter landscape. Hollies, *Nandina, Cotoneaster,* and *Pyracantha* all hold their berries into winter. Also look for *Viburnum dilatatum* 'Erie'. In addition to their visual appeal, berry-laden trees and shrubs attract birds.

Colorful Bark. Many deciduous trees and shrubs have colorful bark that stands out dramatically in a winter landscape. One excellent choice for beautiful bark is the red twig dogwood (*Cornus alba*), a small, multi-stemmed shrub with striking red twigs. Another interesting dogwood member is the golden-twig dogwood (*Cornus stolonifera* 'Flaviramea'), which has bright yellow winter shoots.

Birch trees are lovely in the winter landscape. There is a choice of bark colors from dark gray to silvery gold to the classic white. Some varieties of crape myrtle (*Lagerstroemia indica*) have beautiful bark streaked with green, gold, and pink. Moosewood or striped maple (*Acer pensylvanicum*) has green- and white-striped bark; *A. pensylvanicum* 'Erythrocladum' has coral red bark striped with silvery white.

Peeling Bark. Trees with peeling bark are another interesting phenomenon. Look for the paperbark maple (*A. griseum*), which grows 20 to 30 feet tall and peels off thin flakes of cinnamon to reddish-brown bark, and Heritage river birch (*Betula nigra* 'Heritage'), which exfoliates at an early age and peels off beautiful flakes of salmon white and orange brown bark.

Chamaecyparis 'Aurea nana' (Japanese false cypress)

Nandina (heavenly bamboo)

Bark of *Betula papyrifera* (birch)

DISTINCTIVE TREES AND SHRUBS

TOO OFTEN A YOUNG TREE OR SHRUB is planted close to a building or fence with no allowance made for its growth over time. The ultimate size of a tree depends on many variables, including the quality of the soil, average temperatures, and the potential of each individual specimen. Some of the plants listed here may technically be shrubs, but because of their mature height, they are listed as trees.

Small Trees (up to 30 feet tall)

Acer japonicum (Japanese maple), Zones 6–9
   A. tataricum ssp. *ginnala* (Amur maple), Zones 3–7
Amelanchier laevis (Allegheny serviceberry), Zones 4–9
Arbutus unedo (strawberry tree), Zones 7–9
Cercis canadensis (eastern redbud), Zones 4–9
Chionanthus retusus (Chinese fringe tree), Zones 6–8
Cornus florida (flowering dogwood), Zones 5–9
Franklinia alatamaha (Franklin tree), Zones 5–8 or 9
Magnolia x soulangiana (saucer magnolia), Zones 5–9
Magnolia stellata (star magnolia), Zones 4–8
Malus sp. (flowering crab apple), zones vary with species
Oxydendrum arboreum (sourwood), Zones 5–9
Prunus x blireana (flowering plum), Zones 5–8
Styrax japonicum (Japanese snowbell), Zones 5–9

Medium to Large Trees (30 feet and taller)

Acer rubrum (red maple), Zones 3–9
Acer saccharinum (silver maple), Zones 3–9
Albizia julibrissin (silk tree or mimosa), Zones 6–10
Cercidiphyllum japonicum (Katsura tree), Zones 4–8
Fraxinus pennsylvanica (green ash), Zones 3–9
Ginkgo biloba (ginkgo, maidenhair tree), Zones 4–9
Gleditsia triacanthos (honey locust), Zones 4–9
Gymnocladus dioica (Kentucky coffee tree), Zones 4–9
Halesia tetraptera (Carolina silver bell), Zones 5–9
Koelreuteria paniculata (varnish tree), Zones 5–9
Lagerstroemia indica (crape myrtle), Zones 7–9
Nyssa sylvatica (sour gum), Zones 4–9
Parrotia persica (Persian ironwood), Zones 5–8
Sophora japonica (pagoda tree), Zones 4–9
Stewartia pseudocamellia, Zones 5–8
Tilia cordata (littleleaf linden), Zones 4–7
Zelkova serrata (Japanese zelkova), Zones 5–9

Malus sylvestris (flowering crab apple)

Acer japonicum (Japanese maple)

Lagerstroemia indica (crape myrtle) with Spanish moss

Shrubs with Attractive Flowers

Camellia japonica, and *C. sasanqua,* Zones 7–10

Chaenomeles (flowering quince), Zones 5–9

Cytisus x *praecox* (Warminster broom), Zones 7–9

Daphne cneorum (garland flower), Zones 4–9

Deutzia gracilis, Zones 4–9

Hamamelis x *intermedia* (witch hazel), Zones 5–9

Hydrangea macrophylla, Zones 6–10

Hypericum sp. (St.-John's-wort), zones vary with
    species

Kalmia latifolia (mountain laurel), Zones 4–9

Kerria japonica (Japanese rose or kerria), Zones 4–9

Lagerstroemia indica (crape myrtle), Zones 7–9

Philadelphus species and cultivars (sweet mock
    orange), Zones 4–8

Pieris japonica (Japanese andromeda), Zones 6–8

Potentilla fruticosa (shrubby cinquefoil), Zones 2–7

Prunus triloba (flowering almond), Zones 3–8

Spiraea japonica (Japanese spirea), Zones 4–8

Viburnum species (viburnum), zones vary with species

Weigela florida (weigela), Zones 5–9

Shrubs with Attractive Berries

Berberis darwinii, Zones 8–10

Berberis wilsoniae (Wilson barberry), Zones 7–10

Callicarpa americana (beautyberry), Zones 7–10

Callicarpa bodinieri (beautyberry), Zones 6–8, good to
    Zone 10 in West

Cotoneaster lucidus (hedge cotoneaster), Zones 4–7

Cotoneaster salicifolius (willowleaf cotoneaster),
    Zones 6–8 in the East; 6–10 in the West.

Euonymus alata (burning bush), Zones 4–9

Ilex species (holly), zones vary with species

Mahonia aquifolium (Oregon grape), Zones 5–9

Mahonia bealei, Zones 7–9

Nandina domestica (heavenly bamboo), Zones 7–10

Photinia serratifolia (Chinese photinia), Zones 7–9 in
    the East; 7–10 in the West

Pyracantha coccinea (scarlet firethorn), Zones 6–9

Rhus typhina (staghorn sumac), Zones 4–8

Viburnum species (viburnum), zones vary with species

Chaenomeles (flowering quince)

Hypericum in summer

Cotoneaster lacteus (cotoneaster) in fall

Pyracantha (firethorn)

ADDING HEDGES

Hedges are invaluable in the landscape to screen unwanted views or high winds, to define garden spaces, to frame vistas, and to serve as a backdrop to borders or decorative elements such as sculpture. Traditionally we think of a hedge as a neatly pruned row of one species of plant. While that approach creates a tidy, uniform look that is ideal for informal settings, there is no rule against combining different shrubs with a variety of leaf colors and textures to create a hedge with a tapestry effect. You can either shear the plants for a tailored look or allow the shrubs to billow in their natural form for a soft, informal backdrop.

Plants That Live Longer

The natural inclination when choosing a tree or shrub for a hedge is to choose a plant that will grow as fast as possible. While the quick results are gratifying, the downside is that faster growing plants tend to be shorter-lived. Slow-growing yew and boxwood, which can survive for hundreds of years, are the traditional shrubs used for hedges because they live so long. For this reason, boxwoods need only occasional pruning to keep them within bounds. As you consider all the wonderful plants available for creating hedges, weigh the pros and cons of the faster-growing hedging plants versus slower-growing plants with greater longevity.

A "WILD" HEDGE, above, of mixed plantings is a garden in itself. Some of the shrubs shown here include roses, forsythia, andromeda, peony, and yew.

THIS LOW-MAINTENANCE HEDGE, left, is also long-lived, thanks to the classic combination of slow-growing boxwood (*Buxus*) interplanted with columnar yew (*Taxus*).

Hedgerows: Underused

Another option for a living wall that is too seldom exercised in American gardens is a hedgerow. These are the mixed plantings of trees and shrubs that line the country roads and divide the fields in rural England and parts of Europe. In addition to being a fascinating combination of plants, hedgerows are wonderful habitats for a variety of birds, small animals, and other wildlife; they provide food, shelter, and protected travel routes.

There are two approaches to planting a hedgerow. The first is to select the trees, shrubs, and vines you want and plant them in a random mixture. Space them half the distance recommended by the supplier. Once the plants have reached the height and width you want, shear them periodically to maintain the shape. Don't be shy about cutting back the trees. They will adapt and grow appropriately for a hedge.

Planting a Hedge or Hedgerow

Planting a hedge or hedgerow takes a little more care than simply putting in one or two plants at random because you want the plants to follow the line of the hedge and to be spaced properly.

To work out the number of plants you need, first find out the expected mature width of the shrub. In theory you should then simply divide the length of the hedge by the projected width of each plant to find out how many plants to buy.

HEDGES MADE OF CONIFERS

WITH REGULAR PRUNING, some of these plants can be kept the size of medium to large shrubs.

Cephalotaxus fortunei (Chinese plum yew), Zones 7–9, slow growing

Chamaecyparis lawsoniana (Lawson false cypress or Port Orford cedar), Zones 5–9, medium growth rate
C. x *Cupressocyparis leylandii* (Leyland cypress), Zones 6–10, very fast growing

Cupressus macrocarpa (Monterey cypress), Zones 7–9, growth rate varies with cultivars

Juniperus chinensis (Chinese juniper), Zones 4–10, slow to medium growth rate

Juniperus scopulorum (Rocky Mountain juniper), Zones 4–10, slow-growing

Podocarpus macrophylla (southern yew), Zones 7–10, slow growing

Pseudotsuga menziesii (Douglas fir), Zones 4–7, medium growth rate

Taxus baccata (English yew), Zones 5–8 in the East; 5–10 in the West, slow growing

Thuja plicata (western red cedar), Zones 6–7, growth varies with cultivars

Tsuga canadensis (Canada hemlock), Zones 4–7, medium growth rate

Podocarpus macrophyllus (Southern yew)

Chamaecyparis (false cedar), center

However, you can't count on a plant ever growing to its optimal size. If soil, light, or moisture conditions are not ideal, the shrub may take years to fulfill its potential—or it may never reach it. Because you definitely want the plants to touch and even overlap to make an unbroken hedge, reduce the average expected width of each plant by about one third, and then do the division. For example, Japanese holly (*Ilex crenata*) is listed as having a spread of 10 feet at maturity. Figure on planting a maximum of 7 feet apart—and closer if you want a fully closed-in hedge more quickly. Divide the length of the hedge by 7 to get the number of plants needed. If your holly hedge will be 100 feet long, then you would need 14 or 15 plants. Because holly is such a slow growing plant, you might want to add another 3 to 5 plants to shorten the gaps. In that case, plant 20 hollies 5 feet apart. Commercial landscapers typically plant shrubs much closer together than necessary to get a filled-in hedge more quickly. As a homeowner, you probably want to compromise between using a minimum number of plants and jamming them in tightly for an instant effect.

Leave Planting to the Birds: Plow and Perch. The second technique of planting a hedgerow is rather fun because it leaves a lot to chance and nature. Called the plow-and-perch method, you create conditions that encourage the birds to "plant" the hedgerow for you. In summer or early autumn, till the line where you want your hedgerow to grow, making the soil receptive to seeds. Rent or borrow a large, heavy-duty rototiller that can cut through sod with ease. Mount posts at 15 foot intervals along the line, and attach a double row of strong string or wire between the posts. Seed- and fruit-eating birds will perch along the line, distributing plant seeds with their droppings. There are several advantages to the plow-perch method of planting a hedgerow:

■ *Less work.* It requires less trouble and less expense than seeking out and purchasing plants suitable for a hedgerow.

■ *Birds will do the job.* The seeds sown are of plants definitely favored by local birds.

■ *Plants will thrive in local conditions.* The plants are native, and so are well suited to the area where they will be growing.

■ *Transplant shock eliminated.* These seed-grown species should mature as quickly as those planted from rootstocks because they won't undergo transplant shock.

A WINDSCREEN OF MATURE LILACS separate a field from the road. When allowed to grow without pruning, these shrubs eventually reach the height of small trees.

PLANTING A HEDGE

FIRST MARK OUT THE LINE where you want the hedge. If you are making a curved hedge, use a hose to mark out the line you want, and leave it in place until you are ready to dig. Once you have your plants, position them along the line, making the spaces between each as even as possible. Remember to allow growing space for the plants at each end; set these half the spacing distance in from the desired end of your hedge. Follow the appropriate directions for bare-root, balled-and-burlapped, or container-grown plants. (See pages 267–269.) Mulch along the row with an organic material such as straw, shredded bark, or shredded leaves. The mulch should be 4 to 6 inches deep to be the most effective in minimizing evaporation and smothering weeds.

1 MARK THE HEDGE LINE. Run string between stakes along the hedge line. Dig a trench beneath the string or position the plants using a tape measure. Dig a hole for each plant, putting the soil on a tarp.

2 PLANT EACH SHRUB. Break up the root ball with your fingers. Position the plant straight in the hole, and backfill until the crown of the plant is at the same depth as it was growing in the pot.

3 WATER AND MULCH. Water each plant thoroughly as you dig it in. Allow the water to disperse in the hole, and water again. Apply an organic mulch around each plant and between plants along the row.

4 FINISH THE PLANTING. Check again that the plants are in a straight line. Dig new holes if nec- essary, and replant any shrubs that are out of line. Pull up the stakes and string, and fold up the tarp.

PURCHASING TIPS

Once you've decided on the trees or shrubs that will best suit your purpose in the garden, it's time to make the purchase. Contrary to what instinct may tell you, the largest plant is not necessarily the best. The larger the specimen, the more transplant shock it will experience. In the case of big trees and shrubs, it can take two or three years from the time of planting before the plant will begin to grow vigorously. A small tree or shrub will usually adapt in one season. The result is that in just a few years, a smaller, less expensive tree will catch up in size to a larger one. Save money by purchasing small plants, and give yourself the pleasure of watching your garden grow.

Unless you want to nurse a sick plant back to health, pass by any plant that isn't thriving. Trees and shrubs are major investments, so it is worth paying a little extra to get top-quality plants. Shop only from the most reputable nurseries and mail-order catalogs, and check for a guarantee.

Avoid Trees with Injured Bark. Inspect the bark of trees for signs of injury or mistreatment. A strong tree should be able to stand on its own without staking. If you see sunburn damage—indicated by split, flattened, or unusually dull-colored bark—find a different tree. Also look for signs of pests and diseases. In addition to getting a weakened plant, you risk introducing the problem into your own garden.

CAREFULLY INSPECT PLANTS

BEFORE YOU PURCHASE A WOODY PLANT, take the time to closely examine the condition of its root system or rootball. Container and balled-and-burlapped plants should show evidence of regular watering. Bare-root plants should be kept damp. If you are considering a container-grown plant, slide the plant out of its pot. Look for symmetrical roots that are white and plump, not dried out. Cut away the twine, basket wire, and burlap on balled-and-burlapped plants after placing the plant in the hole.

CONTAINER

GOOD — Symmetrical, Well-Established Root System

BAD — Excessive, Encircling "Potbound" Roots, Some Perhaps Emerging from Base of Container

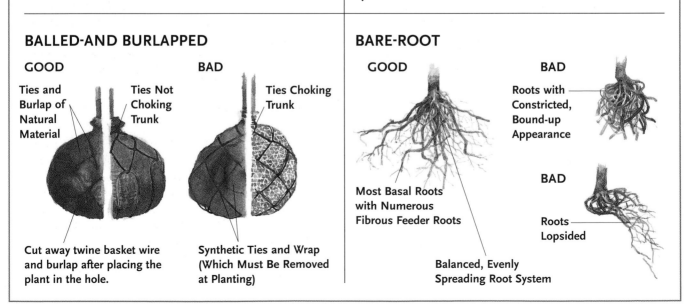

BALLED-AND BURLAPPED

GOOD

Ties and Burlap of Natural Material

Ties Not Choking Trunk

Cut away twine basket wire and burlap after placing the plant in the hole.

BAD

Ties Choking Trunk

Synthetic Ties and Wrap (Which Must Be Removed at Planting)

BARE-ROOT

GOOD

Most Basal Roots with Numerous Fibrous Feeder Roots

Balanced, Evenly Spreading Root System

BAD

Roots with Constricted, Bound-up Appearance

BAD

Roots Lopsided

PLANTING BASICS

The rules for planting trees and shrubs have changed. Today, instead of recommending a planting hole twice the width and depth of the rootball, experts suggest digging a hole just big enough to hold the plant. That way the soil won't settle.

Evidence suggests that trees and shrubs grow better if they are planted directly into the native soil rather than into amended soil. Ultimately you want the tree's roots to extend well beyond the original hole. If the soil in the hole is much richer than the surrounding native soil, the roots will avoid growing beyond that luxurious environment. The result is that they become rootbound in their own hole. These facts make it all the more important to choose trees and shrubs that are suited to the native soil. You'll experience nothing but frustration if you select a tree or shrub that prefers sandy soil and plant it in clay, or plant a shrub that needs acidic soil (a low pH) in alkaline soil. If your soil is heavy, plant trees and shrubs about 2 inches above the level it grew in the nursery field. Look for the soil-line stain on the trunk for a guide.

Don't Prune at Planting Time

Conventional wisdom has called for pruning trees at planting time to create a balance between roots and foliage. Recent evidence shows that the extra foliage produces hormones that encourage root regeneration. Remove any broken branches, but leave the rest alone.

HOW TO PLANT BARE-ROOT STOCK

MANY DECIDUOUS TREES AND SHRUBS are available in early spring as bare-root stock. This is an economical way to buy plants because they are lighter and less bulky for nurseries to ship. If you don't have time to plant them in their proper place, plant them temporarily in a shady, wind-protected location with the trunk tilted on a sharp diagonal to discourage rooting. (This technique is called heeling in.) Bare-root trees and shrubs are still dormant. Until they start sprouting, water only if the soil becomes dry. Once the active growing season begins, water as you would any new plant. (See page 265 for information on watering.)

Root Flare at or Slightly above Ground Level

STEP 1: Check the depth. Place the roots on a cone of undisturbed soil. Lay a shovel across the hole, and make sure the crown is at or slightly above ground level.

STEP 2: Fill the hole. After removing any broken roots, use your hands to pack soil in and around the roots, firming the soil as you go to eliminate air pockets.

STEP 3: Finish planting. When the hole is half full of soil, water well. After the water seeps down, add the remaining soil and create a moat. Tamp the soil down with your foot. Apply several inches of mulch around the tree or shrub, keeping it about 2 inches from the trunk.

HOW TO PLANT BALLED-AND-BURLAPPED STOCK

NURSERY-GROWN TREES are often balled and burlapped after they are dug from the ground. This means that the roots are enclosed in a ball of original soil that is wrapped in burlap and tied together. Like any newly planted tree or shrub, balled-and-burlapped plants need extra care their first year. Be especially careful with watering. Many balled-and-burlapped plants are field-grown in heavy clay soil, which absorbs water slowly. If your native soil is lighter, it will take in water much more quickly. Make sure the rootball gets properly saturated. To know if you have watered enough, gently insert a dry wooden stick into the soil. Pull it out after an hour or so. If the soil is moist enough, the stick will be damp and will have become slightly darker.

1 DIG THE HOLE. Remove enough soil to make a hole about the same depth as the rootball and twice as wide. Put the soil on the tarp. The bottom of the hole should be covered with firm, undisturbed soil.

2 CHECK THE HOLE. Hold the plant at the trunk's base, and place it in the hole to check the depth, making sure the crown is slightly above ground level. Add water until it pools in the bottom of the hole.

3 REMOVE THE BURLAP. Untie the wrapping, or cut the cage off, and remove the burlap. Fill the hole with soil from the tarp, and tamp it down with your foot to eliminate air holes and stabilize the plant.

4 WATER AND MULCH. Build a shallow moat around the trunk. Fill the moat with water, and let it dissipate. Put several inches of mulch around the trunk, but do not pack it right up against the trunk.

HOW TO PLANT CONTAINER-GROWN STOCK

TO GET THE PLANT OFF TO A GOOD START, loosen up its roots when you take it out of the container. Untangle any roots that are growing in circles around the bottom of the pot. Dig the planting hole to accommodate the roots stretched out to their full length. (You can dig special trenches to accommodate one or two extra long roots.) Place the soil from the hole on a tarp. Don't be shy about pruning, tearing, and cutting the roots. This seemingly rough handling will stimulate the plant to grow important new feeder roots.

1 REMOVE THE PLANT. Water the plant; then lay the pot on its side and slide the plant out. If the plant doesn't come out easily, tap the sides of the container or cut open the pot.

Note: This potbound plant needs emergency surgery. The goal is to break up the rootball as shown in the next photo.

2 BREAK UP THE ROOTBALL. Make several vertical cuts deep into the soil mass, and firmly tease the roots outward by hand. Thick, heavily tangled roots require more and deeper cuts.

3 CHECK THE DEPTH. Lay a shovel across the hole. With the roots on undisturbed soil, the crown should be slightly above ground level. If necessary, build up the soil under the root mass.

4 PLANT THE SHRUB. Return half of the soil on the tarp to the hole, and gently tamp it down with your foot to stabilize the plant and eliminate air holes in the soil.

5 WATER. Pour enough water into the half-filled hole so that it pools. Wait for the water to dissipate; then fill the hole with the remainder of the soil.

6 CREATE A MOAT. Using the shovel, build a shallow, moat-like depression around the trunk. Add more water, and let that settle. Note that the trunk's crown remains above ground level.

15 lawn care

If trees and shrubs are the bones of a landscape, then lawns and ground covers are the foundation. Sweeping oceans of lawn give a sense of spaciousness to a property. Ground covers add richness and a sense of depth. Ornamental grasses are another diverse family of plants that can perform a host of landscape functions. There are tiny grasses for bordering a pathway or bed, and large varieties that work well as dramatic specimens.

This chapter is full of design ideas to get the most out of lawns, ground covers, and ornamental grasses in your garden. In addition, you'll find valuable information on caring for your plantings and preventing pests and diseases. With care and planning, your garden floor can be an outstanding feature, laying the foundation for the rest of the landscape.

PLANNING A LAWN

In many home landscapes, the lawn is the default solution for covering bare ground, rather than a deliberately designed landscape feature. To really make the most of your lawn, put some thought into its design so that it becomes an emerald jewel in your garden. You might, for example, surround a small lawn with beds of flowers and shrubs to create an intimate, fragrant spot. You can use a lawn to provide horizontal relief in a garden with lots of vertical elements, or as a link between different parts of the garden. When you are planning your landscape, think of the role you want the lawn to play in its overall look.

The Best Grass for You?

The ideal lawn grass is fine-textured and a deep, rich green. It should grow in a dense mat to keep out weeds. It should also send its roots deep into the soil to grow vigorously and to withstand drought. However, there is no one all-purpose grass that does well throughout the country and meets every need. You should research the best grasses for your area just as you would study which

BARE SPOTS in the patch of sparse grass shown to the left have been worn by heavy foot traffic. Dense turf crowds out weeds and withstands traffic better.

BUFFALOGRASS (left) thrives in hot, dry climates and only occassionally needs watering or mowing. **BERMUDA-GRASS** (right) also tolerates sun, heat, and drought. However, it is invasive and needs frequent edging.

trees, shrubs, and perennials are the best to plant.

Grasses for Cool and Warm Seasons. There are more than 40 different kinds of grass for home gardens. They are divided into two main categories: cool-season and warm-season. Cool-season grasses are appropriate for regions where temperatures drop below freezing during the winter months. They grow best in spring and fall, going dormant in winter and during spells of hot, dry summer weather. Warm-season grasses are ideal for the mild climates of the southern third of the country; they require less water than most cool-season grasses. They go dormant and turn brown in winter. When selecting, consider the amount of sun the area gets, foot traffic, the soil quality, and the amount of water available.

Sun-Loving Plants. In the wild, grass grows in open meadows where sunlight is plentiful. There are a few varieties bred to grow in some shade, but even these require at least a few hours of daily sunlight and do even better if the shade is relatively bright. (See opposite.) To reduce the amount of shade for lawns, you can prune lower tree branches to allow more light to reach the ground.

Heavy Foot Traffic. If you have children who will be running and playing on the lawn, select a sturdy variety such as perennial rye, tall fescue, Bermudagrass, Bahiagrass, or zoysia. Lawns growing in seaside gardens need to be salt tolerant. In northern climates, the cool-season fescues tolerate salty air; try St. Augustinegrass in southern regions.

Difficult Soil Conditions

Other grasses are well suited to difficult soil conditions. Bahiagrass is adapted to southern coastal areas and will grow in sandy, infertile soil. Buffalograss is suited to the heavy clay soils found in western Louisiana, north-central Texas, eastern Colorado, western Kansas, Nebraska, and Oklahoma. In addition, it is extremely drought tolerant, surviving on as little as 12 inches of rain a year. It also requires minimal mowing because its natural height is only 3 to 4 inches. For acidic soil, plant Canada bluegrass, chewings fescue, or hard fescue. Perennial ryegrass, wheatgrass, and Bermudagrass all adapt to alkaline soil conditions.

Some of the grasses, such as Bermudagrass, are invasive, spreading horizontally in an aggressive manner. If you have flower beds or a shrub border next to a lawn that includes Bermudagrass, plan to use a sturdy metal or plastic edging to help keep the spreading grass in the lawn and out of the beds.

GRASSES THAT GROW IN THE SHADE

FOLLOWING is a list of cool- and warm-season grasses that tolerate shade. Recommended cultivars are listed after the hardiness zones.

Cool-Season Turf Grasses

Fine fescue (*Chewings, Festuca rubra* commutata; creeping red, *F. rubra rubra*; and Hard fescue, *F. longifolia*), Zones 1–6, 'Aurora', 'Jamestown II', 'Reliant', 'Scaldis', 'SR3100', 'SR5000', SR5100'

Kentucky bluegrass (*Poa pratensis*), Zones 1–6, 'A34', 'Georgetown', 'Glade'

Perennial ryegrass (*Lolium perenne*), Zones 4–6, 'Advent', 'APM', 'Express', 'Fiesta II', 'Manhattan II', 'Palmer II', 'SR4000', 'SR4100', 'SR4200'

Tall fescue (*Festuca elatior*), Zones 5–7, 'Apache', 'Arid', 'Bonanza II', 'Duster', 'Mustang', 'Pixie', 'Rebel Jr.', 'SR8200', 'Tomahawk'

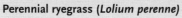

Kentucky bluegrass (*Poa pratensis*)   Perennial ryegrass (*Lolium perenne*)   Tall fescue (*Festuca elatior*)

Warm-Season Turf Grasses

Bahiagrass (*Paspalum notatum*), Zones 9–11, 'Argentine', 'Pensacola'

Centipedegrass (*Eremochloa ophiuroides*), Zones 8–9, common, 'Oaklawn', 'Tennessee Hardy', Centennial'

St. Augustinegrass (*Stenotaphrum secundatum*), Zones 9–11, common, 'Bitterblue', 'Floralawn', 'Floratine', 'Raleigh'

Zoysia (*Zoysia species*), Zones 8–9, 'Belair'

Bahiagrass (*Paspalum notatum*)   Centipedegrass (*Eremochloa ophiuroides*)   Zoysiagrass (*Zoysia*)

BUYING SEED

PACKETS OF INEXPENSIVE OR BUDGET-PRICED SEED are likely to have a low germination rate and contain a high proportion of weed seeds and inert matter or filler. Because these "cheap" packages contain so little that will actually grow, the real cost per pound often is higher than more expensive seed.

Read the package label carefully. Be sure that the seed is dated for the current year, and look for a guarantee of at least 85 percent germination and no more than 0.5 percent weed seeds. Make sure the label specifically states no noxious weed seed. Also look for a low percentage of annual grasses—no more than 3 to 5 percent. While annual rye is useful for overseeding warm-season lawns for winter green, it is not appropriate in a permanent lawn mixture because it dies after one season.

Today's grass has been bred for better long-term performance, disease resistance, deeper roots, and general attractive appearance. Look for trade or variety names rather than the generic name, such as Kentucky bluegrass. Don't buy the seed labeled VNS, which means Variety Not Stated. For cool-season grasses, look for a mixture that has been blended

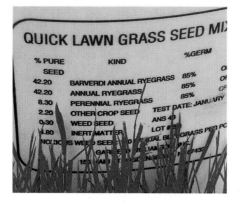

Chinch bug

Sod webworm

Japanese beetle grub

GRASS SEED PACKAGE LABELS are required by law to provide information about seed content including germination rates, the date the seeds were tested, and percentage of different types of seed in the blend.

to meet specific growing requirements such as sun or shade, wet or dry, rich or poor soil, heavy or light traffic. According to The Lawn Institute (Marietta, Georgia), warm-season grasses should not be mixed. Most spread by stolons, and therefore instead of blending into a pleasing whole, they tend to form patches of distinct varieties. The Lawn Institute recommends choosing one particular turf grass among the warm-season grasses, one that will best adapt to your geographic area and particular lawn conditions.

If you are planting fescue or perennial rye, choose a seed mixture that contains at least 50 percent endophyte-enhanced seed. This seed is treated with fungi that kill many insects, including chinch bugs, billbugs, armyworms, aphids, and sod webworms. Unfortunately, endophytes do not attack grubs or Japanese beetles. The fungi survive only about 9 months, so be sure the seed is fresh.

HOW MUCH SEED TO USE FOR NEW LAWNS

Seed Type	Kentucky Bluegrass	Tall Fescue	Perennial Ryegrass	Fine Fescue
Pounds per 1,000 square feet	2–3	5–7	4–6	4

Note: Setter spreadings may vary with type and model of spreader. Consult your owner's manual for exact settings.

Apply 50 percent more seed if you are attempting to sow a new lawn in the spring.

HOW TO PREPARE THE SOIL

BEFORE PLANTING A NEW LAWN, send soil samples to a laboratory for an analysis of its components. The results will tell you whether you need to add any fertilizer, lime, gypsum, or sulfur to the soil before you plant. While you are waiting for the results, clean up the area, removing any debris, stones, stumps, or leftover building materials.

Amend the Soil. Using the results of your soil analysis as a guide, add whatever amendments are necessary to make the soil a suitable host for the grass seed. If you are committed to using a minimum of chemicals to keep your lawn robust and free of weeds, spend time and money now building the soil before you plant. Grass growing in deep, rich soil will be less vulnerable to pests and diseases, and less likely to need chemical treatments to solve those problems. It will grow vigorously, choking out weeds before they get a foothold, thus eliminating the need for chemical weed killers. Top-quality soil is the foundation of organic gardening; it will also make nonorganic lawns grow better and look better.

When you amend the soil, add a fertilizer high in phosphorus (such as 15-30-15) at a rate of 2 to 3 pounds per 1,000 square feet to help the new lawn establish a good root system. Till the soil to a depth of 4 to 6 inches to incorporate the amendments you have added and to make it easier for the new roots to penetrate.

Eliminate the Weeds. After you've prepared the soil, you should eliminate the weeds and weed seed already present in the soil. A month before you plan to sow the grass seed, water the area regularly to encourage any seeds present to sprout. When they begin to grow, dislodge them with gentle tilling. Don't till too deeply, or you'll bring new weed seeds to the surface. While this step delays getting the lawn started by four weeks, it will make a major difference in successfully establishing a weed-free lawn. You can skip this step if you are laying sod; weed seeds won't sprout under the thick mats.

Grade the Site. If necessary, grade the site to create as level an area as possible. Mowing steep slopes is difficult. In hilly situations where you don't want to grade, consider planting a low-maintenance ground cover over the slope rather than grass. Small dips and hummocks are also hard to mow; level these before planting to minimize scalping bumps with the lawn mower. Rake the area to smooth the soil and to remove any extra rocks and debris that were unearthed by the tiller. At the same time, fill in any low spots where water might pool, and create a pleasing, smooth surface. Finally, broadcast the seed, lay the sod, or plant the sprigs or plugs.

STEP 1: Work in amendments. Till fertilizer, lime, and organic matter or other soil amendments into the soil. Follow the recommendations from the soil test for amounts and types of amendments needed.

STEP 2: Water the area. Mist the area to be planted with a fine spray, and look for where puddles form. After the ground dries, fill any areas that puddled with soil taken from high spots.

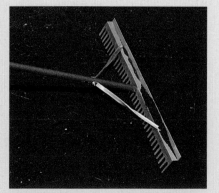

STEP 3: Make minor grade adjustments. A wide metal landscape rake is the ideal tool to level the surface and remove any loose stones. A smooth lawn is easier to maintain than one with bumps.

HOW TO SOW SEED

IN ADDITION TO BEING LESS EXPENSIVE than sod or even plugs and sprigs, seed provides a better choice of new high-quality cultivars. You can choose the grass type that will do best in your specific garden. However, it takes about a month for a newly seeded lawn to fill in, and several months for it to be durable enough for heavy use. In the meantime, there is a risk that the seed will wash away or be eaten by birds and that weeds will grow along with the grass.

Warm-season grasses germinate best when the soil is warm, between 70° and 90°F. To ensure a speedy and high rate of germination, wait to sow grass seed until late spring or early summer. Don't wait too long, however, or you'll risk giving the newly sown grass too short a growing season.

Late summer or early autumn, when the weather is cooling, is ideal for sowing (or overseeding) cool-season lawns. Cooler temperatures stimulate the germination process, and the autumn rains will relieve you of some of the watering chores. In northern climates, some people overseed their cool-season lawns in spring to fill in bare or thin patches and to improve the overall vigor of the lawn. Although possible, success is harder to achieve at that time of year. You must water faithfully until the grass is well-rooted and hope that the weather stays cool long enough so that summer heat doesn't damage young, tender roots.

Scatter the grass seed evenly over the soil. If you spread by hand, walk in one direction first, then walk perpendicular across the lawn to ensure full coverage. If you use a spreader, set it to release the grass seed at the rate recommended on the package label.

Once the seed is spread, rake lightly over the surface to scratch it into the soil, but don't bury it too deeply. All you really want to do is make good contact between the seed and the soil. Then lightly spread organic mulch, such as compost or straw, over the area to help keep the seed moist. Use a fine water spray to thoroughly moisten both grass seed and ground. Grass seed must continually be kept moist until it has germinated. If the weather is hot and dry the first week, you may need to water as frequently as three times a day. Once the roots start growing, you can back off to daily watering until the lawn looks strong.

Rope off the seeded area to discourage foot traffic. If seed-eating birds are a problem, try tying strips of cloth on the rope at regular intervals; these will frighten the birds when they flap in the wind. Don't mow a newly seeded lawn for at least four to six weeks to prevent tearing up the shallow-rooted grass plants.

STEP 1: Spread the seed. Aim for coverage of between 15 to 20 seeds per square inch after you've crossed the lawn twice with the spreader.

STEP 2: Rake the seeded surface. Rake lightly to mix the seed into the top $\frac{1}{8}$ in. of soil. The raking can also disperse seed that was spread too thickly.

STEP 3: Nurture the young plants. Keep newly sprouted grass moist, watering twice a day if there is no rain. Maintain this level of moisture until the plants are 2 in. tall.

HOW TO OVERSEED A BARE PATCH

LAWNS OCCASIONALLY DEVELOP BARE PATCHES, which should be repaired so that they do not detract from the look of the rest of the lawn. Bare spots can easily be fixed by overseeding, a process similar to seeding, except in a smaller area. In the North, the best time to overseed is in late summer and ealy fall; in the South the recommended time is spring or early summer. Before you begin, choose an appropriate seed, as discussed on pages 268–269. First, roughen the surface using the rake. Then spread the seed using your hand or a spreader.

STEP 1: Loosen the soil. To repair a bare patch of lawn, use a pitchfork to loosen the soil in the bare spot to a depth of 6 to 8 in.

STEP 2: Level the soil. Drag the flat end of a landscape rake over the patch to level the planting surface and remove all debris.

STEP 3: Spread the seed. With your hand, evenly spread a mixture of seed, fertilizer, and soil over the affected area.

STEP 4: Tamp the seeds down. Use the flat end of the rake to tamp the seeds into the soil, or roll with a one-third full roller.

HOW TO LAY SOD

SOD IS STRIPS OF GROWING LAWN that has been cut out of the ground. Although more expensive than seed or plugs, sod provides instant coverage. When you order sod, have it delivered when it can be laid immediately. Even a few hours in the sun can damage the grass.

First, moisten the ground where you plan to put the sod. Then lay the sod, butting ends of adjoining strips together but not overlapping them. Work from the sodded area to the open soil. To protect the already-laid sod from excess foot traffic, place a plywood sheet over the surface while you are working.

Tamp down the soil to ensure that the roots make good contact with the soil, and then water thoroughly. The traditional way to tamp sod is to roll a water-filled roller over it.

Water within 30 minutes of laying the sod. Irrigate daily for the first ten days; then back off to every second or third

1 Cut the sod into pieces. Use a sharp trowel to cut sod to fit at butt joints (shown above) or when cutting against a straightedge. You may also use the trowel to level any irregularities in the soil.

2 Lay the sod. It's important to have full strips at the perimeter; narrow strips dry out faster than wide ones. As you lay the sod, keep all joints as tight as possible, but avoid overlapping or stretching the sod.

4 Cut the last piece to fit. After you have laid sod to the opposite side of the area you're working in, cut the next-to-last piece to fit. Before cutting, roll out the sod for a test fit.

5 Roll the new sod lawn. If necessary, use an edger to trim between the edge of the sod and the bed. Then use a water-filled roller to eliminate air pockets and ensure that the roots make good contact with the soil.

day until the new roots are well developed. It should take from two to four weeks for the sod to become properly established. After that, water slowly and deeply so that the water penetrates at least 6 inches into the soil. This method will encourage a deep root system that is more drought-tolerant than shallow-rooted grass. (See "Deep Watering" on page 284 to determine how long to water for best results.)

3 Fit sections together. When fitting two pieces of sod at an odd angle, lay one piece over the other, and cut through both at once. Then lift the top piece, and remove the waste underneath.

6 Clean up remaining soil. Fill the joints between strips with fine soil. Use a small rake to work any excess soil into the cracks between sod pieces. Always stand on the board to protect planted areas.

GRASS SPRIGS should be planted so that the top one-quarter of each plant is exposed. Grass sprigs can be broadcast at a rate of 5 to 10 bushels per 1,000 sq. ft. or planted in furrows 1 to 2 in. deep.

How to Plant Plugs and Sprigs

An inexpensive alternative to sod is sprigs or plugs of grass. Warm-season grasses that spread readily— Bermuda, centipede, St. Augustine, and zoysia—are available as sprigs and plugs. Plugs are small strips or cubes of sod. Sprigs are individual grass plants or runners. Generally the plugs are sold in trays or flats of 12 or 24. Sprigs are usually sold by the bushel. In most cases you should plan for 4 to 5 bushels of grass sprigs per 1,000 square feet of lawn.

Plant the plugs or sprigs as you would any small plant, spacing them at recommended intervals. Bermudagrass plugs should be put in 4 to 12 inches apart. Centipedegrass, St. Augustinegrass, and zoysiagrass plugs all can be planted 6 to 12 inches apart. To save money, put them a little farther apart; for quicker coverage, put them closer together.

GRASS PLUGS can be planted in furrows 6 to 12 in. apart or in individual holes. You can make your own plugs from unwanted areas of turf. Use a golf-green cup cutter for circular plugs or a sharp knife to cut square plugs.

HOW TO DETHATCH A LAWN

THATCH is an accumulation of grass stems, stolons, rhizomes, roots, and leaves in the lawn that have not decomposed. It is more common in lawns with grasses that have stoloniferous roots running above ground such as bent grass, Bermudagrass, St. Augustinegrass, and zoysiagrass. Overfertilized grasses (especially those treated with concentrated, fast-acting synthetic fertilizers) are also more prone to develop thatch. Proper mowing (cutting off no more than one-third of the grass at one time) and fertilizing (not giving the lawn too much nitrogen, or using a slow-release formula) will help reduce the likelihood of thatch buildup. Also, aerate the lawn at least once a year. (See next page.) For lawns that develop thick thatch no matter what you do, experts recommend dethatching every three to five years. Topdressing with organic matter (ideally compost, which supplies organisms that break down thatch) is the best way to reduce thatch in the long run. Dethatching doesn't do anything to improve the soil or prevent future thatch buildup.

You may want to rent a power rake to remove the thatch and weeds. Set the blades to penetrate the thatch layer plus the top ¼ inch of soil. Run the machine back and forth in rows going in one direction, and then repeat the process, covering the ground from another angle. Water the lawn throughly to stimulate fresh growth. If you are seeding, keep the grass seed moist until it sprouts.

STEP 1: Analyze the severity of the problem. Dig up some lawn. Short roots, such as these, can result from excess thatch buildup.

STEP 2: Measure the thatch. Roll back the grass. Thatch of more than ½ in. thick hinders water and amendments from reaching roots.

STEP 3: Power rake the lawn. Some grasses naturally produce more thatch. A healthy population of earthworms breaks down thatch.

RENOVATING A LAWN

Over the years a lawn may begin to look ragged, especially if it isn't cared for properly. If more than half your lawn is full of weeds, has large worn-out or bare spots, or is rough and bumpy, consider replanting the entire area. Strip off the existing grass using a spade, working the blade in horizontal thrusts to cut through the roots. If the lawn is extensive, it may be more efficient to rent a sod-cutting machine. When the old grass is removed, prepare the soil as described on page 275, and replant.

In most cases you can renovate an existing lawn, rather than starting over. The best time of year to renovate a lawn is autumn or spring.

The first step is to determine the source of the problem. Patchy, yellowed lawns are frequently the result of thatch buildup or soil compaction. Thatch is a light brown layer of grass debris that builds up just above the soil surface. Eventually it forms a dense mat that stops water and fertilizer from penetrating the soil. As a result, the lawn languishes. Compacted soil, caused from heavy traffic (especially when the soil is very wet) also keeps water and oxygen from penetrating the soil, starving and suffocating the grass roots. Cut out a 3-inch section of lawn, and study the cross section. If the thatch is more than ½ inch thick or the soil is compacted, take remedial action. Both dethatching and aerating are best done before you spread any seed, fertilizer, or amendments.

A MANUAL AERATOR does the job well, but slowly. Step down on the aerator every few inches as you walk across the lawn. Special aerating shoes with prongs are easier to use.

Aerate

There are special forks and shoes with prongs designed to penetrate the ground to aerate the grass. While wearing the shoes, walk around the lawn, punching holes as you step. The forks and shoes that remove plugs are fine for a small lawn, but the most efficient and effective way to do the job on a large lawn is to use an aerating machine. Look for the kind that actually lifts out the cores of soil. These machines are available at outdoor equipment rental stores. Crisscross over the lawn in different directions to thoroughly work the space. Lawns growing in heavy clay soil will need aerating more often than those growing in sandy soil or loam. Aerating lawns growing in clay soils when they're wet will cause compaction rather than improvement.

Replant

Begin by mowing the lawn as close to the ground as possible. Then use a dethatching machine or power rake (available from equipment rental stores) to break up the grass. Run the machine back and forth in rows going in one direction; then repeat, covering the same territory from a different angle. Continue passing over the area until the grass is well broken up and the soil surface is exposed between the remaining grass plants. Rake off the excess debris.

If a soil test recommends lime or sulfur to adjust soil pH, spread it over the lawn now. If you aren't using lime, you can fertilize now. Don't spread fertilizer at the same time that you spread lime, or a chemical reaction will cause the nitrogen to evaporate. It is best to wait a few weeks before adding fertilizer. Wait until after you seed to spread topdressings of compost or aged manure.

Select a blend or mixture of named, improved varieties of lawn seed. Look for ones that match your growing conditions (sun, shade, or high-traffic). Insect and disease resistance, stress tolerances, and sufficient vigor to crowd out weeds are other factors to consider. Because you are going to all this trouble, you want to be sure to plant a seed variety that you know is an improvement over the common older varieties. Sow the seed using a drop or broadcast spreader. You can plug grasses that spread with runners (St. Augustine, zoysia, Bermuda, and buffalo) directly into the renovated lawn. Water the newly seeded lawn frequently to keep the seed moist but not overly wet until it sprouts.

If you are overseeding a warm-season lawn with annual rye for a green winter lawn, simply mow the existing lawn as short as possible, rake off clippings and thatch, spread the seed, and water to keep the seed continuously moist until it sprouts. This technique also works for areas of lawn that are a bit thin but not too weedy.

AN AERATING MACHINE (below) is the best way to do the job. Long, slim corers (top left) scoop out plugs of the soil's top layer (top right) and deposit them on the surface, where they eventually break down to feed the grass.

TYPES OF NITROGEN FERTILIZERS

SLOW-RELEASE	Advantages	Disadvantages
Sulfur-coated urea Bone meal Dried poultry waste Soybean meal Composted manure Alfalfa meal	Nitrogen released gradually; low incidence of burning; fewer applications used; lasts longer	Higher initial costs; dependent on warm weather for release; takes longer for turf grass response
FAST-RELEASE	**Advantages**	**Disadvantages**
Ammonium nitrate Calcium nitrate Ammonium phosphate Ammonium sulfate Urea	Immediate nitrogen availability; generally costs less; better known release rate; releases even in cold weather	More apt to leach; more apt to burn foliage; more frequent applications required; may acidify soil; may make plants vulnerable to disease; requires more frequent watering

MAINTENANCE GUIDE

Grass is probably the highest-maintenance plant in a garden. It requires weekly mowing during the growing season, edging, trimming, fertilizing, and watering. Nevertheless, by following a few basic principles for a care regimen, you can grow a healthy, beautiful lawn.

Feed and Weed

Poor soil leaves a lawn looking thin and weedy. Too much fertilizer also causes problems, making the lawn prone to thatch buildup as well as insects and disease. The ideal for the health of your lawn and your budget is to use the minimum amount of fertilizer necessary to keep the grass looking healthy and green.

Your goal is to provide enough nutrients to encourage a strong root system that will support healthy top growth. The best way to fertilize a lawn is to use slow-release nitrogen. Homeowners who spread quick-release nitrogen in large quantities on their lawn for an instant rich, green effect do more damage than good. The lush leaf growth will occur at the expense of the roots, creating thatch and weakening the overall plant. Also, those lawns will need much more frequent mowing.

The quick-fix nitrogen fertilizers most commonly used are ammonium nitrate and ammonium sulfate. They are less expensive than the slower-acting fertilizers, making them attractive to budget-conscious gardeners. However, they can be more costly in the long run. Quick-release nitrogen is designed to dissolve easily, but that means a heavy downpour may wash much of it out of the soil and off your lawn. Slow-release forms of nitrogen include sulfur-coated urea, resin-coated urea, urea formaldehyde, and organic fertilizers such as Milorganite. While these are more expensive, they do not have to be applied as often. As a rule, lawns fed with a slow-release form of nitrogen have better color and thickness and reduced leaf growth than lawns treated with quick-release nitrogen.

Organic Fertilizers. More and more gardeners are opting for organic fertilizers that boost the lawn without damaging the environment. You'll need to use the organics in larger quantities than chemical fertilizers. However, with organic fertilizers, you are incorporating organic material into the soil in addition to feeding. This builds the quality of the soil and provides longer-term benefits than are provided by quick-acting, concentrated fertilizers.

Other Lawn Boosters. In addition to fertilizers, substances called biostimulants have recently become available. These compounds increase the grasses' ability to absorb important nutrients from the soil, thus improving growth and increasing resistance to pests and diseases. One product called Mycor contains mycorrhizal fungi. It works to create a favorable environment for nitrogen-fixing bacteria in the soil and improves the grasses' ability to take in nutrients through their roots. Another product, BioPro, contains peat derivatives and micronutrients. It provides three benefits to lawns: improvement of the structure, increase in the plant's ability to use available nitrogen, and introduction of organic material to the soil. Compost and seaweed products are also sources of biostimulants. Talk to an experienced nurseryman to find out what organic options are available in your community.

An easy way to add extra nutrients to your lawn is to leave the clippings in place when you mow. Contrary to popular wisdom, these clippings do not build up a layer of thatch. If you mow before the grass gets too long so the clippings aren't left in large clumps that block light to the grass, the clippings will quickly decompose, adding organic matter to the soil as well as nutrients. A mulching mower is a great asset because it chops up the grass into little pieces that can decompose quickly. Decomposing grass clippings also encourage earthworms, which aerate the soil and add to the nutrient content with their castings. Instead of throwing your clippings away, leave them on the lawn. The clippings can reduce the need for fertilization by as much as 25 percent, helping your lawn and the environment.

Weed Control. A healthy lawn will grow dense enough to crowd out weedy plants. Control any annual weeds that intrude simply by mowing. You'll remove the seed head before it matures, and the plant will die at the end of its growth cycle. Perennial weeds are more of a problem. If you have them in small quantities, hand-weed the lawn before they set seed, and work to remove each weed's entire root system. It's easiest to weed by hand when the soil is moist and soft. An easy way to remove weeds is to pour boiling water on them. This is especially effective when trying to remove weeds from between the cracks of a patio or on the edge of the lawn. Another option is to use a fertilizer in early spring that is mixed with a pre-emergent weed killer. Be aware, however, that this is a nonselective herbicide. It will kill grass seed as well as weed seeds.

WHEN TO FERTILIZE

The best time to fertilize a lawn is when it is actively growing.

- Cool-season grasses grow best in spring and fall, so fertilize cool-season grasses at the beginning of the growing season in spring or as cooler temperatures return in fall.
- If you plan to fertilize at regular intervals over a period of months in spring, stop as soon as the weather gets hotter. If you like, you can feed once more in autumn after the first frost to set up the lawn for next spring's growth.
- Feed warm-season grasses in late spring and again in August.
- If you are using a slow-release form of nitrogen, feed smaller doses every six to ten weeks until about eight weeks before the first frost date.
- If the lawn has good color and is growing well, delay additional feedings by a week or two.
- Overfeeding a lawn is wasteful and damaging to the environment. Excess fertilizer may be leached out by watering and carried into underground water systems.

POISON IVY grows in recently disturbed soil, such as in new lawns. The three red leaves are distinctive, but be aware that the leaves turn green as they mature.

CRABGRASS is the bane of homeowners. Mowing high, removing seed heads, and maintaining dense turf are essential to control this common lawn weed.

PURSLANE is a warm-season annual that thrives in hot, dry weather. Its fibrous roots are easy to pull, but new roots develop from stem fragments.

GILL-OVER-THE-GROUND, also called ground ivy, spreads by aboveground stolons, shown here, and by underground rhizomes.

Deep Watering

Lawns grow best when they are watered deeply and infrequently. The deep water penetration encourages roots to grow down, rather than sideways, improving the root structure and drought tolerance of the grass. If your soil is dense clay, water slowly so that the water can soak in rather than run off. The average lawn needs about 1 inch of water on a weekly basis. If your soil is a heavy clay, it can take as long as 5 hours for 1 inch of water to penetrate properly. At the other extreme, sandy soil will absorb 1 inch of water in approximately 10 minutes. To determine how much water you are delivering, space shallow cans at regular intervals along your lawn and time how long it takes them to fill. One inch of water will penetrate about 12 inches in sandy soil, 7 inches in loam, and 4 to 5 inches in clay. If you have clay soil and want to water the lawn to a depth of 6 inches, you would need to leave the sprinkler on until there is 1½ inches of water in each test container. Ideally, a lawn should be watered to a depth of 6 to 12 inches.

Water lawns early in the morning or late in the afternoon. It is generally less windy at those times of day, so the water won't blow into the air. The cooler temperatures and lack of wind also will minimize evaporation.

Proper Mowing

Many lawn problems are a result of cutting grass too short. Grass that is shorn too close is more likely to succumb to stresses caused by drought, insect injury, foot traffic, or inadequate sun. Ideally, you should never remove more than one-third of the leaf surface each time you mow. See the table on the following page for guidelines on ideal heights for different grasses. The lawn's rate of growth—and therefore how often you need to mow—will depend on how warm the weather is, how much water the lawn has received, and whether you fertilized. Those factors will vary throughout the season, although most people find that a schedule of weekly mowing works well.

At least once a year you should sharpen your lawn mower blades. Blunt mower blades can ruin a lawn by tearing the leaves. Each torn blade will die back ⅛ to ¼ inch, giving the lawn a brown tinge. The ragged edge on each blade of grass also makes the lawn more susceptible to disease.

LAWNS MOWED TO THE PROPER HEIGHT are typically healthier and better able to resist disease than grass cropped short. Keep the mower blades sharp, and follow the recommended mowing heights given on the next page.

THE BEST MOWING HEIGHTS

Grass Type	Finished Height
Bluegrass	2 inches
Perennial ryegrass	2 inches
Tall fescue	2 inches
Fine fescue	2 inches
St. Augustinegrass	2 inches
Buffalograss	2 inches
Bermudagrass	1½ inches
Zoysiagrass	1½ inches
Centipedegrass	1½ inches

Source: The Lawn Institute (Marietta, Georgia)

ADJUST THE CUTTING HEIGHT of the mower. By setting the mower to cut higher, you will reduce weed growth and slow the frequency of mowing. Short grass does not shade out weeds like taller grass, and its crown is exposed.

TYPES OF LAWN MOWERS

LAWNS MOWED TO THE PROPER HEIGHT are typically healthier and better able to resist disease than grass cropped short. Keep the mower blades sharp, and follow the recommended mowing heights given above.

REEL MOWER. The reel mower is the type with a cylinder of blades. Most have five blades, although for a finer cut (as on golf courses) there are seven- and nine-blade machines. There are gas-powered reel-style mowers, but most homeowners who select this option stick with the hand-push models. A reel-type hand mower is excellent for a small, level and even lawn. It is compact to store, quiet to use, doesn't pollute, and in a small space takes no more time to do the job than a motorized version.

ELECTRIC MOWER. If you prefer a motorized mowing machine, the electric ones are ideal for small properties. They run quietly and are nearly maintenance-free. You can choose a cordless one that runs for an hour or more on a rechargeable battery, or opt for one with a long cord. In that case, take care that you don't run over the cord, cutting it along with the grass.

GAS-POWERED MOWER. Gas engines are often more powerful than electric motors, and they do not limit you by the length of the cord. There is a great range of gas mowers, including hand-propelled and self-propelled walk-behind designs as well as ride-on models for large properties. You can buy them with detachable bags for collecting the clippings and with mulchers that chop up the grass finely and spray it back onto the lawn. You will have a choice of horsepower, safety features, and starting features; you can choose a two-cycle engine, in which the oil is mixed with the gasoline, or a four-cycle engine, which runs on regular gasoline with a separate place for pouring in the oil. Gas-powered mowers need regular maintenance to run properly.

BRIGHT GROUND COVER ADDS LIGHT. *Lamium maculatum* 'White Nancy' sparkles under the shade of a large conifer. Even when out of bloom, the silver leaves margined with green brighten the otherwise dark spot.

FOLIAGE CREATES COVER. *Phlox divaricata*, hosta, foamflower, ajuga, and sweet woodruff foliage intermingle compatibly on this shady slope. In due course, their foliage will mask the dying daffodil leaves.

ADDING GROUND COVERS

Ground covers are marvelous alternatives to lawns in garden areas that aren't subject to foot traffic. Ground covers add color and texture to the garden, and most don't require mowing or raking. Use them instead of grass around trees and shrubs to eliminate trimming, and in difficult areas where grass won't grow or mowing would be difficult.

Once established, most ground covers will block out weeds. Use ground covers to control erosion on steep slopes or to fill in space in beds until the slower growing plants mature.

Ground Covers Galore

Although many people think of ground covers as plants that hug the ground, almost any low-growing plant with a spreading habit is suitable for a ground cover. This includes small shrubs and conifers such as rockspray cotoneaster (*Cotoneaster horizontalis*) and creeping juniper (*Juniper horizontalis*). These shrubs grow as tall as 3 feet but cover the ground admirably. Rockspray cotoneaster provides three-season interest with small pink flowers in spring, glossy green foliage in summer, and red berries and foliage in autumn. Creeping juniper is a hardy plant that will grow in difficult situations where other plants won't survive, including steep slopes. It is an excellent choice for erosion control.

Vigorous clumping perennials such as daylilies also work well as ground covers; they are particularly useful on a steep slope because they require little care. Other perennials that cover the ground effectively if they are planted close together include lady's mantle (*Alchemilla mollis*), beach wormwood (*Artemisia stelleriana*), and showy sundrops (*Oenothera speciosa*). In addition to its silvery gray-green foliage, which catches water droplets and displays them like shiny jewels on velvet, lady's mantle produces pretty chartreuse blooms that combine well with blue flowers. Plant lady's mantle with catmint to create a mixed ground cover that resembles a tapestry. As its name suggests, beach wormwood does well by the seaside in sandy soil. It grows up to 2 feet tall with a 3-foot spread. Showy sundrops, which tolerate drought, will grow happily in full sun or partial shade. Harsh, difficult conditions are a good way to keep them under control; in moist, fertile soil they will invade. They are easy to grow and reward gardeners with a pretty display of cup-shaped soft pink flowers in early summer.

Ferns that spread with underground runners are a lovely ground cover in shady areas, and fringed bleeding heart (*Dicentra eximia*) blooms in partial shade through-out most of the summer. Plant hostas close together as a ground cover in shady areas, both for their ornamental foliage and pretty flowers that grow on tall stalks in summer. Most hostas will tolerate both wet and dry conditions, adding to their usefulness.

Problem-Solving Ground Covers

Within the plant kingdom there are ground covers that will grow in almost any difficult spot in the garden. In a hot, dry garden, consider planting pussytoes (*Antennaria dioica*) or hardy iceplant (*Delosperma cooperi*). Choose crown vetch (*Coronilla varia*) or creeping juniper (*Juniperus horizontalis*) on steep, sunny slopes where mowing is difficult. If sandy soil and salt spray are a problem, look into growing rugosa rose, mondo grass (*Ophiopogon japonicus*), bearberry (*Arctostaphylos uva-ursi*), or creeping lilyturf (*Liriope spicata*).

Ivy will grow in deep, dry shade and in areas where there is little root room. Snow-in-summer (*Cerastium tomentosum*) will tolerate clay soil and loves a hot, sunny bank; if the soil is too good, however, the plant can become invasive. Pachysandra is happy competing with tree roots and makes a pretty, tailored green collar when planted around trees.

Grow an evergreen ground cover such as periwinkle (*Vinca minor*) over spring-flowering bulbs. The dark green periwinkle leaves make a pretty backdrop when the bulbs are in bloom; later they help disguise the dying leaves. Also, you won't disturb the bulbs by digging about in the bed later in the season. Choose bulbs such as Narcissus varieties, whose flowers are tall enough to be visible above the vinca.

The obvious approach to ground covers is to mass-plant one species for uniform coverage. Another alternative is to intermingle different creeping plants with a variety of leaf and flower colors and textures for a dazzling tapestry effect. For best success, mix plants that require similar growing conditions. For example, mix different varieties of creeping thyme, such as caraway-scented thyme (*Thymus Herba-barona*), with its dark green leaves and matting growth, golden lemon thyme (*T.* x *citriodorus* 'Aurea'), with its green and yellow variegated leaves, and silver thyme (*T. vulgaris* 'Argenteus'), with silver and green variegated leaves.

When selecting ground covers, choose ones that are suited to the soil and climate conditions in your garden.

MANY GROUND COVERS offer a ready-made solution for shady areas as well as sloping sites. You have the option of mass planting one variety or mixing varieties to add a truly unique look to your landscape.

A WEED BARRIER, *Liriope muscari* 'Big Blue' grows in a dense mass, so weeds cannot invade. In autumn, violet blue flower spikes brighten the display. The evergreen grass grows 10 to 18 in. tall.

GROUND COVERS FOR SHADY AREAS

Asarum caudatum (British Columbia wild ginger), Zones 6–8, partial shade

Ceratostigma plumbaginoides (leadwort), Zones 5–9, full sun to partial shade

Chrysogonum virginianum (green and gold), Zones 5–8, partial shade in North, full shade in South

Convallaria majalis (lily-of-the-valley), Zones 3–8, partial to full shade

Cornus canadensis (bunchberry), Zones 2–7, partial shade

Epimedium **spp.,** (bishop's hat), Zones 5–8, light to heavy shade

Euphorbia amygdaloides **var.** *robbiae* (spurge), Zones 7–9, partial shade

Galium odoratum (sweet woodruff), Zones 3–8, full shade

Gaultheria procumbens (wintergreen), Zones 4–8, light to full shade

Hosta species and cultivars (plantain lily), zones vary with variety, light to full shade

Lamium **spp.,** Zones 4–9, partial to full shade

Lysimachia nummularia (creeping Jenny), Zones 3–8, full sun in North, full shade in South

Mazus reptans, Zones 5–8, full sun to partial shade

Paxistima canbyi (paxistima), Zones 3–8, partial shade

Phlox divaricata (wild sweet William), Zones 3–8, partial shade

Saxifraga **x** *urbium* (London pride), Zones 5–8, partial shade

Tiarella cordifolia (foamflower), Zones 4–9, partial shade

Vinca minor (periwinkle), Zones 4–8, light to moderately heavy shade

GROUND COVERS FOR SUNNY AREAS

Achillea tomentosa (woolly yarrow), Zones 3–7

Arabis caucasica (wall rock cress), Zones 4–8

Aurinia saxatilis (basket-of-gold), Zones 3–7

Cerastium tomentosum (snow-in-summer), Zones 2–7

Chamaemelum nobile (Roman chamomile), Zones 3–8

Cotoneaster horizontalis (rockspray cotoneaster), Zones 5–8

Euphorbia polychroma (cushion spurge), Zones 4–9

Geranium sanguineum (bloodred cranesbill), Zones 4–8

Iberis sempervirens (perennial candytuft), Zones 4–9

Juniperus communis 'Prostrata' (common juniper), Zones 3–9

Juniperus horizontalis (creeping juniper), Zones 4–10

Juniperus procumbens (Japanese garden juniper), Zones 5–9

Lithodora diffusa, Zones 7–9

Nepeta **x** *faassenii mussinii* (Persian catmint), Zones 4–8

Osteospermum fruticosum (freeway daisy), Zones 8–10

Phlox subulata (moss pink), Zones 3–9

Stachys byzantina (lamb's ears), Zones 4–9

Thymus **spp.** (low-growing varieties), zones vary with species

Veronica prostrata (prostrate speedwell), Zones 4–8

GRASSES THAT SOLVE PROBLEMS

THE TOUGH, TENACIOUS CHARACTER that enables these plants to survive in difficult situations also makes some of them invasive. Keep a barrier, such as a wide strip of lawn, between these and flower beds.

Dry, Sunny Spots

Achillea tomentosa (woolly yarrow), Zones 3–7
Aegopodium podagraria 'Variegatum' (variegated bishop's weed), Zones 3–9 (grows in sun or shade)
Antennaria dioica (pussytoes), Zones 4–7
Cerastium tomentosum (snow-in-summer), Zones 2–10
Ceratostigma plumbaginoides (leadwort), Zones 5–9
Helianthemum nummularium (sun rose), Zones 6–8
Oenothera speciosa (showy sundrops), Zones 3–8
Rosa rugosa (rugosa or saltspray rose), Zones 2–9
Saponaria ocymoides (soapwort), Zones 4–10
Sempervivum tectorum (hen and chickens), Zones 5–9

Erosion Control

Coronilla varia (crown vetch), Zones 3–9
Euonymus fortunei (winter creeper), Zones 5–9
Hedera helix (English ivy), Zones 5–9
Hypericum calycinum (Aaron's beard/ St. John's Wort), Zones 6–8
Juniperus horizontalis (creeping juniper), Zones 4–10

Poor Soil

Aegopodium podagraria 'Variegata' (variegated bishop's weed), Zones 3–9
Antennaria dioica (pussytoes), Zones 4–7, dry, sandy soil
Arctostaphylos uva-ursi (bearberry), Zones 2–7, dry, sandy soil
Artemisia stelleriana (beach wormwood), Zones 3–8, dry, sandy soil
Calluna vulgaris (Scotch heather), Zones 5–7, sandy, acidic soil
Cerastium tomentosum (snow-in-summer), Zones 2–10, needs good drainage
Ceratostigma plumbaginoides (leadwort), Zones 5–9
Chamaemelum nobile (Roman chamomile), Zones 3–8, poor, sandy soil
Hedera helix (English ivy), Zones 5–9
Juniperus horizontalis (creeping juniper), Zones 4–10
Opuntia compressa (prickly pear), Zones 5–9, dry, sandy soil
Santolina chamaecyparissus (lavender cotton), Zones 6–9, poor, but well drained
Sedum spurium (stonecrop), Zones 3–8, average to poor soil, needs good drainage

Juniperus horizontalis (creeping juniper)

Sempervivum (hen and chicks)

Saponaria ocymoides (soapwort)

INVASIVE GROUND COVERS

THE FOLLOWING GROUND COVERS can become invasive. They are easier to control if you grow them in less-than-ideal conditions. Don't plant them next to delicate perennials.

Aegopodium podagraria (bishop's weed), Zones 3–9
Cerastium tomentosum (snow-in-summer), Zones 2–10
Chamaemelum nobile (Roman chamomile), Zones 3–8,
    self sows
Coronilla varia (crown vetch), Zones 3–9
Hedera helix (English ivy), Zones 5–9
Hypericum calycinum (Aaron's beard/St. John's Wort),
    Zones 6–8
Houttuynia cordata 'Chameleon' (chameleon plant),
    Zones 5–9
Lamium galeobdolon (yellow archangel), Zones 4–9
Lamium maculatum (spotted lamium, deadnettle),
    Zones 3–8
Lysimachia nummularia (creeping Jenny), Zones 3–8
Mazus reptans, Zones 5–8
Oenothera speciosa (showy sundrops), Zones 3–8
Opuntia compressa (formerly *Opuntia humifusa*)
    (prickly pear), Zones 5–9, in South where birds sow

**Lamium maculatum 'Beacons silver'
(spotted nettle)**

Cerastium tomentosum (snow-in-summer)

USING ORNAMENTAL GRASSES

Ornamental grasses have grown remarkably in popularity in the past decade or so, as people appreciate their many positive qualities. The grass family is vast, with plants ranging in size from petite clumps suitable for edging a border or working as a ground cover, to monumental specimens that are excellent for using as screens or as a garden focal point. In addition to the diverse sizes, ornamental grasses come in many colors. As its nickname suggests, blood grass (*Imperata cylindrica* 'Red Baron') is a distinctive blood red, while blue oat grass (*Helictotrichon sempervirens*) has spiky, luminous blue leaves. Blue fescue (*Festuca ovina* 'Glauca') is particularly appealing,

A BACKDROP of billowing fountain grass (*Pennisetum lopecuroides*) and eulalia grass (*Miscanthus sinensis*) backs the narrow lap pool. Many grasses are well suited to wet areas.

with its evergreen tufts of silvery blue foliage. There are variegated grass forms with silver or yellow stripes running the length of the leaves, as well as the amazing porcupine grass (*Miscanthus sinensis* 'Strictus'), with golden stripes running horizontally along each blade. Depending on the grass, the flower plumes (inflorescences) also come in a great range of colors, from burgundy red and soft pink to cream, ivory, and tawny shades of beige.

Landscapes and Ornamental Grasses

In a landscape, ornamental grasses add a special quality. Many of them are in almost constant motion, swaying gently in the slightest breeze to add a dynamic element to the garden. As the leaves brush against each other, they rustle pleasingly, soothing the ear. Silhouetted by backlighting, ornamental grasses glow and take on a magical quality.

There are ornamental grasses that work well in myriad garden applications. Some, such as the giant reed (*Arundo donax*), grow well along the edge of ponds or in bog gardens. Small, mounding grasses such as the fescues (*Festuca* species) keep tidy forms and make fascinating ground covers when massed. These small ornamental grasses adapt well to many garden situations. Generally, the large specimens such as eulalia grass (*Miscanthus* species) and the fall-blooming reed grass (*Calamagrostis brachytricha*) work better on a large property with a modern, informal garden. Grasses also can look at home in country-style and naturalistic gardens.

Ornamental grasses are touted for their year-round interest in the garden. Grasses such as maiden grass (*Miscanthus sinensis* 'Gracillimus') and fountain grass (*Pennisetum alopecuroides*) begin the growing season with fresh, green sprouts that develop into arching mounds. As the summer progresses, flower plumes wave from the tops of the plants; in winter the grass turns a tawny color that persists through the snowy season in many gardens (except in areas with winds or heavy snowfall). They are cut down in late winter to make room for the new growth in spring, and the cycle begins again.

FOLIAGE AND FLOWER PANICLES glow in the golden light when ornamental grasses are backlit. This creates a particularly dramatic look.

AN AUTUMN FLOWERING GRASS, the diffuse flower panicles of *Panicum virgatum* 'Haense Herms' contrast pleasingly with the upright, narrow inflorescences of the feather reed grass (*Calamagrostis* x *actiflora*) at right. Striped ribbon grass (*Phalaris arundinacea*) fills the foreground.

THE HORIZONTAL STRIPES on zebra grass (*Miscanthus sinensis* 'Zebrinus') make this ornamental grass a striking landscape accent.

A single, tall-growing ornamental grass makes a striking focal point or specimen plant in the garden. Pampas grass (*Cortaderia selloana*), with feathery plumes that stand tall among its saw-toothed grassy leaves in late summer, is a dramatic grass. Hardy from Zones 7–10, it will grow in wet or dry soil and acid or alkaline pH, and it tolerates dry desert winds, coastal fogs, and high humidity. (Avoid planting it in coastal areas of California, where it has become a nuisance weed.) In northern gardens silverfeather grass (*Miscanthus sinensis* 'Silberfeder'), giant Chinese silver grass (*Miscanthus floridulus*), or ravenna grass (*Erianthus ravennae*) are excellent large specimens.

Use one of the smaller fountain grasses, such as *Pennisetum setaceum*, as a centerpiece in a bed of lowgrowing annuals. Its green, grassy leaves provide a pleasing contrast to red begonia flowers. Later in the summer, the red begonias are echoed in the fountain grass's pink or mauve flower panicles.

More Suggestions for Landscape Accents. Generally pestfree and easy to grow, ornamental grasses are great low-maintenance plants for hard-to-reach parts of the garden. Combine them with other plants to create an unexpected contrast of textures or colors. Plant them around the edge of a pond to make a soft transition between the hard edge and the water. Blur the edge of a path with mounds of blue fescue. Tall varieties make outstanding background plants in perennial borders. Plant a collection of grasses in a separate bed to enjoy the great variety available. Some grasses, such as *Miscanthus*, are tolerant of the salt and humidity prevalent in coastal areas and make great screens or buffers. They are useful to create a protected microclimate for less-tolerant plants.

DESIGNING FOR ALL SEASONS

ORNAMENTAL GRASSES provide interest in the landscape every season. Below, *Pennisetum alopecuroides* (fountain grass) is shown in the same garden throughout the year.

EARLY SPRING: The daffodils are up and the grass has been cut.

EARLY SUMMER: Grasses hide the bare stalks of Allium aflatunense.

MID SUMMER: Fountain grass underplanted with lilies (*Lillium*).

LATE SUMMER: Grass mixes with black-eyed Susans (*Rudbeckia*).

FALL: Grass with seed heads takes on tawny fall colors.

WINTER: Fountain grass pokes through deep snow.

TRIMMING WITH THE SEASONS

ALTHOUGH IT ISN'T NECESSARY for the plant's health, many ornamental grasses look better in spring if the old, dead growth is cut back in late winter before the new growth begins to show. Warm-season grasses, such as reed grass (*Calamagrostis arundinacea*) and pampas grass, should be cut to 3 or 4 inches above the ground; trim cool-season grasses, including large blue hairgrass (*Koeleria glauca*), at about two-thirds their height. Check the list on page 295 for trimming information for each specific plant.

PREPARE FOR SPRING by cutting grass down to about 8 inches in late winter. Within a few weeks this *Miscanthus 'Giganteum'* is already beginning to show signs of new growth.

A GRASS THAT WAS NOT CUT BACK. The new leaves have grown up among the dead leaves, causing the grass clump to open up in the middle and flop.

Smart Selection of Grasses

Consult the local Cooperative Extension Service or a reliable nearby nursery for recommendations on grasses suited to your area. A few grasses are invasive in some parts of the country. For example, feathertop grass (*Pennisetum villosum*) grows too aggressively in the Southwest, and the giant reed (*Phragmites australis*) is harming water birds by overtaking wetlands in the East. Pampas grass (*Cortaderia selloana*) is invasive in parts of the West, spreading rapidly by reseeding. Those same grasses are well behaved in other parts of the country. If possible, visit a nursery with a display garden that features ornamental grasses or a local botanical garden, park, or arboretum. You'll make better choices if you can see the grasses in their mature size in landscape situations. It's also helpful to observe how they perform throughout the year. Depending on where you live, some grasses that are touted for their year-round beauty actually get quite scruffy or look sickly in winter.

Care and Maintenance

Ornamental grasses are generally low maintenance and disease free. If you plant them in a spot that is well suited to their growing requirements, they'll reward you with almost carefree beauty. Like any newly planted specimen, ornamental grasses should be watered their first year in the ground. After that, their water requirements are minimal. They also need little or no supplemental fertilizer. In fact, adding high-nitrogen fertilizer can slow down flowering and cause the foliage to grow unattractively floppy. An annual dose of compost will supply a slow-release dose of all the necessary nutrients.

As with most plants, the care of ornamental grasses depends on where you live and the specific grass. A large number of the plants benefit from an annual cutting. You may find that a chain saw or hedge trimmer is the best tool to cut back large clumps of ornamental grass. Cut the grass to a few inches above the ground, being careful not to damage the crown. Wear gloves when handling ornamental grass; the term blade of grass is well-deserved.

If an ornamental grass clump grows too big, you will need to divide it. You can unearth the entire plant and then pull or cut it apart into smaller portions and replant the new bits. Another option is to insert your spade firmly into the middle of the clump, cutting it in half while it is in the ground. (You might need a sharp ax to cut through the roots). Then dig out one half, leaving the rest in place. Put fresh soil or a mix of half soil, half compost into the hole left by the plant half that's being removed; then replant the divided piece in another location.

HOW TO TRANSPLANT AND DIVIDE *MISCANTHUS* GRASS

ORNAMENTAL GRASSES occasionally need to be divided if they have outgrown their space or grown old and floppy in the middle. This task is similar to the process of dividing perennials shown in Chapter 16 on page 306 except that a pruning saw is the best tool to cleanly cut through the tough clumps of grass. Divide ornamental grasses in the early spring after they have been cut back. Dig the new holes before you lift the divisions to minimize the time the plants spend exposed to the drying air.

STEP 1: Dig Out the Grass. Use a shovel to cut the soil around and under the grass clump. Pry the clump up, and lift the grass out of the ground. The grass shown here is *Miscanthus*.

STEP 2: Determine Where You Will Divide. The shallow-rooted *Miscanthus* is out of the ground and ready for division. Choose a section that has a good balance of top growth and roots.

STEP 3: Make the Divisions. After identifying where to divide, use a pruning saw to make a clean cut through the clump of roots. One clump of ornamental grass can easily yield several new divisions (shown in the inset).

STEP 4: Plant the Division. The new divisions should be planted at the same depth at which they were originally growing. Fill the hole, and water. Add more soil if necessary. Tamp the soil down with your foot.

WHEN TO TRIM ORNAMENTAL GRASSES

THE TIMING FOR TRIMMING BACK ORNAMENTAL GRASSES depends in part on your own style of gardening and the region where you live. In cold climates, you can remove the brown leaves in autumn or leave them on to enjoy through the winter and then cut them back very early in spring. In warm climates, a fall trim will stimulate new growth immediately, so that you can have new green foliage by winter. It is particularly important to remove dried foliage in places where risk of fire is severe.

Andropogon gerardii (big bluestem), Zones 4–9, cut back to 6 inches in early winter

Arrhenatherum elatius subspecies bulbosum (bulbous oat grass), Zones 4–9, cut back whenever it turns brown

Arundo donax (giant reed), Zones 7–10, cut dead stems to ground in winter

Bouteloua spp. (grama grass), zones vary with species,

Briza media (quaking grass), Zones 4–10, cut back old foliage in midsummer, cut back again in late fall

Calamagrostis spp. Zones 4–9, cut back in late winter

Chasmanthium latifolium (northern sea oats), Zones 5–9, cut back dead foliage in spring or fall

Cortaderia selloana (pampas grass), Zones 7–10, cut back every year or two in early spring

Erianthus ravennae (Ravenna grass), Zones 5–10, cut back dead leaves in late winter

Festuca glauca (blue fescue), Zones 4–9, cut back in early spring or fall for new growth

Helictotrichon sempervirens (blue oat grass), Zones 4–8, cut back to 3 inches in early spring

Miscanthus spp., zones vary with variety, cut back in late winter

Molinia caerulea (purple moor grass), Zones 5–8, cut back foliage in winter

Panicum virgatum and cultivars (switch grass), Zones 4–9, cut back in early spring

Pennisetum spp. (fountain grass), Zones 5–9, cut off seed heads to prevent selfsowing, cut back leaves in early spring

Phalaris arundinacea 'Picta' (ribbon grass), Zones 3–9, cut back in summer for new growth and in early spring

Schizachyrium scoparium (little bluestem), Zones 3–19, cut back in early spring

Sorghastrum nutans (Indian grass), Zones 4–9, cut back in early spring

Spodiopogon sibiricus (silver spikegrass), Zones 5–9, cut back in winter

Sporobolus spp. (dropseed), Zones 3–9, cut back in winter

Calamagrostis x acutiflora (feather reed grass)

Pennisetum alopecuroides 'Little Bunny' (dwarf fountain grass)

Cortaderia selloana (pampas grass)

16 flowers

Flowers are as important to your landscape as any architectural element, with the added benefit of being far less permanent. You can redesign flower beds over the years, experimenting with color, placement, and variety until you achieve the look that suits your current preference.

The right flowers will attract birds, bees, and butterflies to your yard, and even a small flower bed can provide blossoms to cut throughout the season.

Flowering plants can also prevent erosion while creating a trouble-free area. For example, flowering ground cover planted on a steep, rocky bank will hold the soil in place and requires minimal annual maintenance. But one of the best things about a flower garden is the endless fascination it gives as a succession of flowering plants comes into bloom throughout the season.

A BRIGHT SPOT of color can serve as a focal point. Here, the yellow hues of the Heliopsis and Coreopsis emphasize the vivid orange tones of 'Enchantment' and foxtail lilies.

PLANNING FLOWER BEDS

Planning a flower garden can be as involved as designing a house or as simple as opening a can of soup for supper. The very best advice you'll ever hear—to start small—is also the hardest to follow. It's natural to want to put in gardens all over the property. But think twice before you give in to this desire; major plantings require major commitments. It is more sensible to begin with one portion of a yard at a time, eliminating weeds before planting and learning how to deal with problems as they arise before expanding your garden.

By the time you sit down to plan your individual flower gardens, you should be well along in the visualization process. The garden you see in your mind's eye will have a color scheme and general style, formal or informal. Now is the time to translate the vision into reality.

From Vision to Reality

Begin by focusing on the aspect that is most important to you, whether it's color, season of bloom, or style. If color or season of bloom is what matters most to you, make a list of plants, like the table on page 300, that have the appropriate hues or that bloom at the right time. If a particular style is what you are after, begin by sketching a plant placement map, indicating simple plant shapes without necessarily identifying the plants.

As you go through this process, remember that all gardens do not have to bloom all the time or include all the colors of the rainbow. A bed of nothing but red tulips and white anemones makes an effective spring planting, for example. After such a bed is finished blooming, you can mulch it for the remainder of the season or transplant some quickly blooming annuals into it for summer color.

Plant a Moon Garden Near the Patio. Near a patio, you might want to create an evening garden by planting only white and pale pastel flowers so that they will reflect moonlight and starlight. To add another dimension to this garden, include some plants that release their fragrance in the evening. 'Only the Lonely' flowering tobacco (*Nicotiana alata*), white and yellow four o'clocks (*Mirabilis jalapa*), moonflower vine (*Ipomoea alba*), and 'Colvin's White' sand phlox (*Phlox bifida*) are all good choices for an evening garden. You'll also want to note some practical things about each plant that you are considering. Make columns in your list of plants for height and width, soil requirements, exposure preferences, and general cultural needs. For example, it may be that you can only spend an hour or so each week tending the flower bed. In that case, you will want to concentrate on low-maintenance species.

Now that you have a list of possible plants to include in your garden, it's time to get out the graph paper again and start sketching their placement on the map. This part of the design process can be mystifying until you understand that, even in a seemingly random planting, most flower beds are built around at least one focal point.

Find a Focal Point. A focal point is usually a plant or a plant grouping to which the eye is drawn, but it can also be a structural element such as a birdbath. A prominent size or color generally makes something a focal point, although a common design trick can also create one. Say that you have decided to make a group of yellow Asiatic lilies the focal point of a summer garden. They are certainly bright enough to draw the eye, but you can emphasize them even more by planting them with a group of daylilies in the same or a complementary color, such as yellow 'Hyperion'. The daylilies can completely surround the lilies, flank them, or be planted as a background. The daylilies will effectively frame the Asiatic lilies, making them even more prominent.

smart tip

PLANT POSITION DEFINES GARDEN STYLE

PLACEMENT OF YOUR "FRAME PLANTS" HELPS TO DEFINE THE GARDEN'S STYLE. IF YOU PLANT THEM AROUND THE FOCAL POINT IN A SYMMETRICAL PATTERN, YOU ARE CREATING A FORMAL STYLE. BUT IF YOU GROUP THEM IN AN IRREGULARLY SHAPED DRIFT, THE PLANTING WILL APPEAR INFORMAL.

THE WHITE PETUNIAS AND FEVERFEW, above, that surround these steps glow at night with reflected moonlight as they lead visitors to the home's entrance.

START SMALL, left, when developing your garden. Here, a corner of the lawn has been transformed. Although it makes a big statement, it's small enough to care for easily.

DAFFODILS naturalize easily in the right location. Here, they thrive in the bright springtime light under deciduous trees.

BULBS

Most of the plants we call bulbs are extremely easy to grow. They bloom reliably, are rarely bothered by pests or diseases, require very little maintenance, and—with the exception of most tulips—multiply quickly.

Bulbs provide the very first signs of spring throughout most of North America. Shortly after the days have begun to lengthen, the first snowdrops (*Galanthus nivalis*) and winter aconites (*Eranthis*) peek through the melting snow cover. Once these plants bloom, gardeners know that spring is on the way.

Although most people strongly associate bulbs with spring flowers, many bulbs bloom in summer, autumn, and even late winter.

Plan for Multi-Season Interest. With just a little planning, you can feature color-coordinated bulbs or even bulbs of the same color from early spring to fall. Siberian squill, glory-of-the-snow, species crocus, and species tulips come first, followed by hybrid crocus, hyacinths, and a succession of daffodils, narcissus, and hybrid tulips.

FLOWER GARDEN PLANNER

USE THE TABLE BELOW as a guideline for listing flowering plants that are appropriate to your garden design. You can photocopy and enlarge this table or use it as a model to create your own. As you consider new plants, add them to your chart, filling in all the columns. You'll have a quick reference to use whenever you want to add to your plantings.

Flower Name	Color	Height	Blooming Season	Notes
Dahlia	All but blue	1' to 6'	Summer to frost	Tender, lift in fall
Perennials *Astilbe*	Pink, red	1' to 2'	Spring to summer	Divide every 3 to 4 years
Annuals *Centaurea*	Pink, red rose, blue	1' to 3'	Summer	Deadhead for continual bloom
Biennials *Alcea rosea*	All but blue	4' to 8'	Midsummer to fall	Easy in the correct location

TRUE BULBS AND OTHER BULB-LIKE STRUCTURES

DESPITE WHAT WE CALL THEM, not all of these plants are true bulbs. Instead, many fit into the categories of corms, tubers, tuberous roots, or rhizomes. But all of them share an important characteristic. They evolved in places where the climate was hospitable for only a few months of the year, so they developed the capacity to go dormant for long periods of time and survive harsh conditions. All bulbs grow quickly and store enough nutrients in swollen underground structures to see them through months of high temperatures, droughts, snow, and frozen soil. Where environments roughly match the native locations of bulbs, these plants are among the most dependable you can grow in the home garden.

CORMS. Crocus and gladiolus grow from corms. Although small buds grow on the top of a corm and roots grow from its base, corms are primarily food storage organs, rather than a means of reproduction for the plant. Each year, a new corm forms above the old one. When you dig gladiolus in the fall, discard the old, shrunken corm and keep the new, firm one.

TUBERS AND TUBEROUS ROOTS. Winter aconite grows from a tuber, an enlarged part of the stem that stores food and contains a bud. Dahlias and tuberous begonias are called tubers, but they grow from tuberous roots.

RHIZOMES. Both bearded iris and calla lilies grow from rhizomes. Like tubers, rhizomes are food-storing parts of the stem. But, rhizomes are long, slender, and branched, while tubers are rounded and unbranched. Divide plants with rhizomes by cutting or breaking the rhizome into smaller pieces, each with some leaves and roots growing from it.

You will most appreciate seeing these harbingers of spring when the calendar says it's still winter. You can guarantee this by planting the very earliest bulbs in a warm, sheltered spot, such as tucked between a porch and a wall on the south side of the house.

The weather will still be chilly, so you'll appreciate early bulbs more if you plant them where you can see them from a window. Even though the bulbs are tiny, crocus and species tulips make a huge color impact when massed under deciduous shrubs or in the front of a flower border.

Summer Bulbs Extend the Show. Summer bulbs include both those that are hardy, such as alliums and lilies, as well as tender species such as gladiolus and dahlias. The flowers of summer bulbs are so spectacular that they easily become the focal points in a planting.

When you choose summer bulbs, pay attention to blooming time as well as size and color. Gladiolus bloom eight to ten weeks after you've planted them, so it's possible to keep them blooming from midsummer until frost.

Autumn Bulbs Are a Bonus. In addition to the last of the gladiolus, planted at midsummer, late lilies, dahlias, colchicums (*Colchicum autumnale, Colchicum speciosum*), autumn crocus (*Crocus sativus, C. speciosus*), snowflake (*Leucojum autumnale*),and winter daffodils (*Sternbergia lutea*) all bloom when days get short and temperatures cool. Like spring bulbs, these are best planted in spots where they can be seen and appreciated from a window or as you pass in and out of the house.

GROWING BULBS

Hardy bulbs are planted in the fall. They need time to grow roots and become established before the ground freezes but not enough time, or warmth, to send up shoots. In general, gardeners in Zones 2 and 3 plant in mid-September; Zones 4 and 5, late September to early October; Zones 6 and 7, mid-October to early November; Zone 8, mid-November to early December; and Zone 9, early to mid-December. If in doubt about when to plant, use a soil thermometer. Soil temperature should be 60°F or lower when you plant bulbs.

Planting Depth Is Important for Bulbs. Individual requirements for planting bulbs may vary, so consult the package before planting. As a general guideline, however, the proper planting depth for bulbs is two to three times the bulb's length from tip to base. For example, a bulb that measures 3 inches should be planted 6 to 9 inches deep. If you have sandy soil, plant the bulb the full three-times depth, but if you have heavy soil, use the two-times rule. Many bulbs grow well when they are planted more shallowly than recommended, especially if they are well mulched over the winter months. However, burrowing rodents are less likely to damage bulbs that are more deeply buried. So try to keep to the recommended planting depths. Bulbs should be planted with the base down and the tip up. But bulbs such as windflower (*Anemone*) that don't have an indentifiable top or bottom will sprout no matter how they are positioned in the planting hole.

Soil Requirements. Bulbs tolerate a great range of soil types and fertility levels, as long as the soil is well drained. If you want to plant bulbs where the soil remains soggy, dig in ample amounts of compost or, if that isn't adequate, some sand. If water still puddles, make a raised bed, and fill it with a light soil mix such as potting soil.

Despite not needing high fertility, bulbs do best in soils with moderate levels of organic matter and high calcium content. Spread about ½ inch of compost over the bulb bed, and dig it in. For the calcium, add 2 to 4 tablespoons of gypsum to each planting hole. In subsequent

PROTECTING BULBS FROM PESTS

THIS CAGE of ½-inch galvanized wire mesh should prevent tunneling rodents from getting to the bulbs. If you don't have a problem with rodents, skip the cage. But it's a good idea to protect shallow bulbs by covering them with a piece of mesh.

1 Add soil with plenty of organic matter to promote drainage. If your soil is sandy or contains a lot of clay, dig in extra leaf mold or compost.

2 After leveling the soil, set a wire-mesh cage in the excavated area. Bulb-loving rodents will not be able to chew through this cage. Then add an inch of soil.

3 Place bulbs at the depth recommended on the packaging (usually twice as deep as they are long) or as listed in the bulb directory.

4 After placing your bulbs, cover them with soil. For more protection from animals, place a lid of wire mesh over the area before mulching for winter.

FLOWERS FOR FRAGRANCE

Botanical Name	Common Name
Dianthus plumarius	Cottage pinks (perennial)
Erysimum cheiri, formerly	Wallflower (biennial)
Cheiranthus cheiri Lillium 'Stargazer'	Lily (bulb)
Heliotropium arborescens	Heliotrope (annual)
Hyacinthus orientalis	Hyacinth (bulb)
Narcissus poeticus 'Plenus'	Daffodil (bulb)
Nicotiana alata	Flowering tobacco (annual)
Paeonia lactiflora	Peony (perennial)
Petunia x hybrida	Petunia (annual)
Phlox paniculata	Garden phlox (perennial)
Reseda species	Mignonette (annual)

FRAGRANCE GARDENS are delightful additions to outdoor lounging and entertaining areas. Choose from plants such as those listed here.

years, dust the bed lightly with gypsum, and then cover the soil with ½ inch of finished compost in the very early spring.

Digging and Dividing Bulbs. If the leaves begin to look crowded and blooms diminish in size or number, the plants are probably running out of space. The best times to dig and divide bulbs are either right after the leaves have died back or in autumn; the timing for this depends on the other plantings in the bed. If you are concerned that your other plants will be disturbed by early summer digging, mark the location of the crowded bulbs, and wait until the fall when the other plants are dying back.

smart tip

SEEKING INSPIRATION

LOOKING AT OTHER PEOPLE'S GARDENS IS ONE OF THE BEST WAYS TO GET IDEAS FOR YOUR OWN. VISIT PUBLIC GARDENS, TOO, AND ANALYZE THE COLOR SCHEMES AND PLANT GROUPINGS. ALTHOUGH THE PLANTINGS AT PUBLIC GARDENS ARE ON A GRAND SCALE, YOU CAN STILL COME AWAY WITH IDEAS FOR PLANT GROUPINGS AND COLOR COMBINATIONS.

DAHLIAS are excellent companions for these lilies. The dahlias keep the lily bulbs and roots cool, and the plants look good together.

PERENNIALS such as the yellow Coreopsis combine well with annuals such as cleome and salvia.

ROSES thrive in soils rich in organic matter. Sidedress them with compost or aged manure each year to keep supplies high.

PERENNIALS

Most flowering perennials are tough, sturdy plants that tolerate a wide range of environmental conditions, are resistant to pests and diseases, and require very little coddling. Along with beauty, these are the qualities that people considered when they began to select and breed the wild flowers that have become our favorite ornamentals. The easier a plant was to care for, the more likely it was to become popular. And aside from the often troublesome rose, you can usually be certain that the more "old-fashioned" a plant is, the more reliable and trouble-free it is, particularly if it was widely grown in colonial America.

Soil Preparation

Perennials do not require the same high levels of nutrients as fruits and vegetables, but inasmuch as they will remain in the same spot with the same soil for many years, it's best to take the time to prepare the bed well.

Good drainage is the most important characteristic of soil for perennials. Soggy soil promotes root diseases, and it can contribute to winter damage. The wetter soil is, the more it expands and contracts with freezing and thawing. This continual movement heaves plant roots out of the soil, where they lie exposed to the cold and drying winds. Soil heaving can also tear the roots. Improve drainage by adding compost to soils with a high percent

of sand or clay, and make raised beds in really problematic areas.

Most perennials are deep-rooted and prefer to grow in loose, fertile topsoil a foot deep. Soil that is worked to a depth of 18 inches gives plants an even better start.

Fertilizing

Perennials do not tend to be heavy feeders. Most will thrive in soils of average fertility if you add an inch-deep layer of compost to the bed each spring, just as growth is beginning. But there are some exceptions to this rule. Delphiniums and peonies are both heavy feeders that profit from a second compost application just before midsummer.

If your compost supply is short, you can also use a liquid or bagged fertilizer. A mix of liquid seaweed and fish emulsion is an excellent choice because it generally contains ample phosphorus, the nutrient most needed by flowering plants. Apply this combination once the soil temperature reaches 55° to 60°F and again at midsummer if soil tests indicate that phosphorus levels are low.

Watering

Perennials require less water than fruits or vegetables. However, in dry periods or areas where the soil drains exceptionally quickly, it's often necessary to water perennials. Water perennial plants deeply but infrequently. This

STAKING

MANY FLOWERING PLANTS look better if they are staked. Choose stakes to complement the looks of the plant you are supporting.

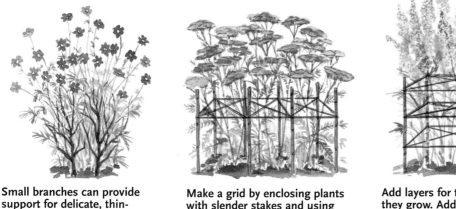

Small branches can provide support for delicate, thin-stemmed plants such as these cosmos.

Make a grid by enclosing plants with slender stakes and using twine to create the supporting structure.

Add layers for tall plants as they grow. Add each layer just before plants reach that height.

Use stakes to support single stems such as this lily.

guarantees that roots at lower depths have enough water to survive and saves you time and trouble. Set up a rain gauge to measure natural rainfall. If you get less than an inch during an eight- or nine-day period and your soil is average—neither very sandy nor clayey—it's time to water. You'll want to add at least an inch of water, or slightly over 2 gallons for every square foot of garden area. If using a sprinkler, take advantage of your rain gauge by setting it up to measure how much water you add to the soil.

Staking

Staking plants can make an enormous difference to the appearance of the garden. It seems like a lot of extra work and something that couldn't possibly be worth the trouble, but staking is important. First of all, you can do it in the blink of an eye and second, it will prevent enough fungal problems to be well worth this tiny expenditure of time.

The need to stake plants with very large or heavy flowers, such as peonies, delphiniums, and lilies, is obvious. But surprisingly, plants with smaller flowers, such as tickseed, ballonflower, and speedwell, may also look better if you stake them.

Set Stakes Early In the Season. Staking is best done in early to midspring, before plants have grown to their full size. Ideally, the stakes should be about two-thirds as tall

as the mature plant will be, so they won't be conspicuous. Thick green wire supports and green bamboo stakes are both good choices for tall plants such as delphiniums and peonies. Use green gardener's twine to secure the plants to their supports. Smaller, bushy plants such as tickseed often look best when they are grown against twiggy tree branches. The plants can be tied to the branches or just left to grow through them as they will. Beyond preventing fungal diseases, staking can also improve the look of the plant.

smart tip

CHEAT pH NEEDS BY PLANTING IN CONTAINERS

MOST PERENNIALS GROW WELL IN SOIL WITH A pH BETWEEN 6.3 AND 6.8—BUT SOME TOLERATE MORE ACID OR ALKALINE CONDITIONS. (CHECK THE DIRECTORY LISTINGS FOR pH REQUIREMENTS.) IF THE PERENNIALS YOU WANT TO GROW HAVE SPECIAL pH NEEDS, CONSIDER GROWING THEM IN A CONTAINER OR DISCRETE SECTION OF A BED SO THAT YOU CAN DO SOME SPOT pH ADJUSTMENTS.

PINCH OFF all but one or two flower buds to stimulate development of exhibition-size blooms.

Deadheading and Trimming

Some species flower for a longer period of time if they are consistently deadheaded before seeds start to form, while others are just lovelier to look at if you remove spent flowers. When you deadhead, you can just snap or cut off the flower at the top of its stem, or you can remove the whole stem. The choice depends on the growth habit of the plant.

Most of the perennials you will be planting are herbaceous, meaning that their stems die back to the ground each fall and regrow each spring. Consequently, they don't need the kind of heavy pruning that woody trees, shrubs, and some vines require. But judicious pinching and trimming of some species can promote bushiness and increase flowering. Asters, chrysanthemums, phlox, and salvias all respond well to having the tips of their stems pinched back in early to mid-spring.

Dividing and Renovating

Perennials vary in the frequency with which they need to be divided. Some, such as peonies, are so slow growing that they almost never need to be divided. But others will die unless they are dug up and divided every few years. In most cases, a little observation will tell you if plants need division. The first sign is that the plant is running out of space. In some species, the center of the plant begins to die back while the growth toward the outside of the clump is still vital, and in others, stems and flowers grow smaller than normal.

Bed Renovation. Whole beds of perennials require major renovation every six to eight years. In a big bed, it's best to split the area into sections that you work on in sequential seasons. The best time to renovate a bed is in the fall, but early enough so plants can establish new roots before winter. In areas north of Zone 5, renovate in the spring as soon as the soil is workable.

No matter where you live, the first step of bed renovation happens in the spring, when bulbs bloom. Mark their locations, colors, and any other information you want to retain on small plastic or metal tags that you insert beside the plant. If possible, make the stake location consistent, always to the front, rear, or the right or left side of the plant so that it will be easier to know where to dig later on without damaging any bulbs.

When you renovate, dig up the bulbs and each plant in the bed. Take as large a root ball as possible. Dig around plants that resent transplanting, such as peonies and bleeding heart. Place dug out plants on a tarp in the shade and cover any exposed roots with layers of wet newspaper.

Apply a 3- to 4-inch layer of finished compost or aged manure to the bed and till or fork it into the top few inches of soil. Then begin replacing your plants, dividing those that need it.

smart tip

WHEN TO DIVIDE PERENNIALS

PLANTS ARE EASIER TO DIVIDE SUCCESSFULLY AT CERTAIN POINTS IN THEIR GROWTH CYCLE. DIVIDE SPRING-BLOOMING PERENNIALS A MONTH BEFORE THE GROUND FREEZES IN AUTUMN OR IN VERY EARLY SPRING, BEFORE NEW GROWTH HAS BEGUN. DIVIDE FALL-BLOOMING PERENNIALS IN SPRING.

DIVIDE HOSTAS in early spring when they first appear. Use a shovel to simply dig down and split a plant into sections.

SEASONAL CARE

EACH SEASON brings its own routine into the perennial garden. As you gain experience you'll naturally fall into these rhythms. Greet the spring by taking frequent trips to the garden to see what's sprouted, how large it is, and what, if anything, needs to be divided or replaced. As the weather warms, remove the winter mulch from plant crowns because it can promote fungal diseases by retaining too much moisture. If frost is still a possibility, just pull the mulch to the side so that you can easily replace it to protect against a cold night.

Spring. Once the weather has settled and the soil is dry enough to work without compacting it, it's time to add new plants to the garden. You'll also want to cultivate around established plants to get rid of weeds and add needed oxygen to the soil. Compost or other sources of nutrients should be applied as the soil warms to about 50°F.

Mid to late spring is the best time to lay new mulch. Try to wait until the worst of the spring rains have finished, but apply the mulch before the soil begins to get summer-dry.

Summer. Adjust the mulch as necessary to retain soil moisture around the roots, but don't let it touch the stems for fear of encouraging fungal diseases. Staking, trimming, and deadheading are the other chores of summer, with some weeding and watering when necessary. Monitoring for pests and diseases is also a routine job.

Autumn. Autumn is the time for garden clean up. Some plants will need to be divided, and you may want to make some new plantings. If you have been keeping up with deadheading and removing spent flower stalks through the summer, you won't have to do much trimming now. However, as the leaves and stems of herbaceous perennials die back, you may want to move them into the compost pile. Don't add diseased or infested plant material to the compost pile for fear of spreading the problem.

Winter. Winter mulches protect plant roots from damage from freezing/thawing fluctuations; their purpose is to keep the soil consistently frozen. If possible, spread a winter mulch after the top inch or so of the soil surface has frozen. In years when this is impossible, choose the coldest morning you can and apply the mulch before the sun has had a chance to warm the soil surface.

ANNUALS

Annual plants complete their entire life cycle, from germination to seed formation, in a single season. This speed makes them ideal for many garden situations, especially if you want an instant garden. Annuals can also help to fill out a perennial flower bed, giving you color and bloom while you are waiting for the perennials to grow large. You can use annuals to experiment with color and form, too; by planting an annual that is similar in form and color to a perennial you are thinking of buying, you can see if the design choice will work.

Annuals have other advantages as well. Most of them produce scores of flowers over a very long season. They can keep the garden colorful between bursts of bloom from perennials. Annuals make some of the best cut flowers you can grow. Though some annuals look better if you stake them, most get by with almost no care aside from planting and deadheading. Pests and diseases tend to be problems only if you've sited your plants in unsuitable environments.

The diversity of annual flowering plants is astounding. No matter what your design needs or growing environment, you can probably find an annual to suit it. And lastly, these plants are so easy to grow from seed that both the seeds and started plants are inexpensive enough for anyone's budget.

Types of Annuals

Annuals are often categorized as tender, hardy, or half-hardy, and some books and catalogs describe them as "warm-weather" or "cool-weather" plants. For example, Mexican sunflower (*Tithonia rotundifolia*) simply doesn't grow or flower well in temperatures less than 75° to 80°F, while bachelor's buttons (*Centaurea cyanus*) and blue-eyed African daisies (*Arctotis venusta*) stop blooming in hot weather. The catalog descriptions tell you what the plants can tolerate as well as the conditions that will favor their best development.

Protect Tender Annuals from Frost. Tender annuals cannot tolerate temperatures close to freezing. Plant them out after the frost-free date and either dig them out

CUTTING GARDENS are usually composed of rows of selected annuals such as zinnias and marigolds.

YELLOW AND ORANGE MARIGOLDS contrast beautifully with purple heliotrope in this garden. Both provide a long bloom season.

or be prepared to lose them at the first fall frost. Zinnias, nasturtiums, and impatiens are all in this group.

Hardy Annuals Survive Light Frost. Hardy annuals can take some frost. However, frost can sometimes damage seedlings of hardy annuals if they were started indoors, even if you've hardened them off. Try to wait until the danger of hard frost (temperatures of 28°F and below) has passed before setting out these plants, and keep plastic or row cover material handy for covering them on frosty nights.

Hardy annuals have two advantages over their tender cousins. First, direct-seeded and volunteer seedlings of hardy plants will withstand far cooler temperatures than transplants, so they can be planted outside very early in the season, as soon as the soil can be worked. In Zones 7 and warmer, gardeners can plant them for winter bloom. Second, hardy annuals live through the first fall frosts unless it is particularly cold. Take advantage of these qualities by planting annuals such as larkspur, calendula, and bachelor's buttons in the fall if you live in Zone 6 and southward. In Zone 5 and northward, wait until early spring to plant and be certain to add some later plantings to the garden to prolong the bloom season.

Half-hardy annuals succumb to cold before hardies. However they tolerate a few degrees of frost. Petunias and cosmos both fall into this category. If you are transplanting these plants, wait until after the frost-free date to set them out, but you needn't worry that night temperatures in the high 30s will stunt their development. Again, the primary advantage comes in fall, when they can live through temperatures that kill the tender annuals.

MEXICAN SUNFLOWER provides brilliant color and a strong presence in any area where it grows.

LEAVE ROOM for annuals so they can fill the spaces between the perennials and add color when the perennials aren't in bloom.

Perennials and Biennials Grown as Annuals. Some of the plants grown as annuals are actually perennials or biennials that will bloom the first year. The perennials tend to be "warm-weather" plants that will not overwinter outside of their tropical homes. These include geraniums (*Pelargonium* species), impatiens (*Impatiens* species), flowering tobacco (*Nicotiana* species), wax begonias (*Begonia* Semperflorens Cultorum Hybrids), and snapdragons (*Antirrhinum majus*). Biennials that bloom the first season if started early indoors, and are usually used as annuals include forget-me-nots (*Myosotis* species), larkspur (Consolida ambigua), and pansies (*Viola* x *wittrockiana*). These are "cool-weather" plants because they perform best in cool temperatures.

Cultural Requirements

Annuals are so diverse that it's impossible to define only one set of cultural requirements for all of them. However, there are some very strong common preferences, even between plants that evolved on different continents.

Soil Conditions. Well-drained soil is almost always required. The plants that like bogs and swamps tend to be perennials, not annuals. Pay attention to the drainage qualities of your soil when you first lay out the beds, and improve it if necessary.

Most annuals require slightly acidic soil pH. When in doubt, always assume that a pH of 6.5 is appropriate for your annual flowers and amend your soil accordingly. A few annuals, such as impatiens and wax begonias, do best in partial or light shade. But most thrive in full sun. Site gardens where the annuals will receive at least six full hours of sunlight daily.

Keep Annuals Deadheaded. The whole point of being an annual, from the plant's point of view, is to flower and set seed. Once this is accomplished, it's time to die. The gardener's only way around this lamentable habit is to prevent the plants from forming seeds. Even if you don't cut them for bouquets, pick annual flowers as soon as they begin to wilt, making certain to pluck off the whole flower, not just the petals. If annuals are deprived of the chance to set seeds, they will keep producing flowers.

Most annuals branch well without any help from you, but some really benefit from a judicious pinch or two. If you start your own seedlings, pinch the terminal bud on snapdragons, cosmos, petunias, and gaillardia when the seedling is about 4 to 6 inches tall. The resulting branches will carry flower buds and the plant will bloom for a longer period than it would have without pinching.

Give Plants Room. Correct spacing is important for most plants. If you space them too far apart, for example, you are providing bare ground in which windborne weed seeds can take root. If you grow annuals too close together, you are setting the stage for pest and disease troubles. Most annuals are remarkably resistant to pests and diseases, in the right conditions. But if they suffer from the nutrient deficiencies or high relative humidity levels that are brought on by crowding, pest and disease problems are inevitable.

It's easy to remember to space plants well when you are transplanting. Even if you are setting out tiny plants, it's possible to imagine them as mature specimens and give them enough room to grow. However, when you plant seeds in the soil or have the luxury of a self-seeded crop, it's easy to put off thinning. Do your best to tend to this job as soon as the seedlings have two sets of true leaves. If it is too hard for you to get rid of the tiny extra plants, transplant them to another area of the yard or put them into pots to give away. But thin them to the correct spacing if you want healthy plants that bloom to their full potential.

Clean Beds When Annuals Finish. End-of-the-season work is particularly important with annuals. In mixed beds, where both perennials and annuals have been growing, pull out the annual plants as soon as they begin to die back. In the case of tender annuals, this will be right after frost, though hardy annuals, such as calendula, will keep going until late into the year. But no matter when they die back, remove annuals from the bed and put them in a compost pile that stays at 160°F for at least three days. Throw diseased or insect-ridden material in the trash rather than a compost pile.

Flower beds composed of only annual plants should be cleared of all plant debris before winter. Work any small debris left on the bed surface into the top inch or so of the soil so that the beneficial organisms will be able to prey on the pathogens or pest eggs.

Choosing Annual Species

The selection of annual species and cultivars at local garden centers and nurseries is often quite limited. However, if you are just beginning to garden, it is probably easier to buy established plants until you gain more experience.

Mail Order Offers Variety. For a greater selection of unusual plants, consult mail-order seed catalogs. Seed companies specialize in plants that are rarely found at local nurseries. The seeds are easy to grow and will perform just as well as any of the more common species. Read plant descriptions carefully. Expand your gardening horizons, and choose one or two new annuals to try every year.

Write or Call for Catalogs in Early January. Then sit back, with budget and garden maps by your side, and choose annuals that seem appropriate to your plans. After all, with annuals you can afford to experiment.

smart tip

MULCH BEDS FOR WEED CONTROL

ANNUAL FLOWER BEDS CAN BE IDEAL PLACES FOR WEEDS TO GROW IF THE SOIL IS BARE, AND THUS RECEPTIVE, EARLY OR LATE IN THE SEASON. MULCH ANNUAL BEDS TO KEEP WEEDS FROM SPROUTING. YOU'LL AVOID INJURING PLANTS WITH DEEP CULTIVATION AND SAVE YOURSELF SOME WORK AS WELL. HOWEVER, IF YOU LIVE IN A RAINY CLIMATE WHERE SLUGS THRIVE, DON'T LAY THE MULCH TOO CLOSE TO PLANT STEMS. INSTEAD, HAND-PULL ANY WEEDS THAT SPROUT AND SPRINKLE A SLUG DETERRENT SUCH AS DRIED, CRUSHED EGGSHELLS OR DIATOMACEOUS EARTH AROUND THE PLANTS.

BIENNIALS

Biennial plants complete their life cycle in two years. They grow leaves, generally in the form of a rosette or mound, during the first season. These leaves overwinter, then early in the following spring, the plant sends up a flower stalk and dies. If the overwintering leaves die, the roots usually die as well. Consequently, the most important thing to learn about growing any biennial is how to overwinter it successfully. (Many biennials can be forced into bloom in Zones 5b and warmer if they are started indoors early and transplanted to the garden).

Overwintering

Keeping biennials alive over the winter is relatively easy in most areas. However, in the North or in spots with a great deal of freezing and thawing action over the winter months, you'll have to pay particular attention to most of the biennials.

Plants that are transplanted in early fall must have time for their roots to take hold in the new spot before the ground freezes. So be sure to get them into the ground early enough. After the soil is frozen, cover the entire plant with a 6-inch layer of loose straw.

In spring, draw the mulch back from the crown as soon as the ground thaws.

Biennials Reward Your Efforts. Biennial plants are well worth the care you'll give them. The tall spikes of large biennials such as hollyhock (*Alcea rosea*) and foxglove (*Digitalis purpurea*) can provide a necessary focal point in a flower bed or give color and grace to a planting meant to screen an area. Small biennials such as English daisies (*Bellis perennis*) and forget-me-nots (*Myosotis sylvatica*) add color and contrast to beds of early-blooming bulbs such as tulips and daffodils. The seed pods of honesty plants (*Lunaria annua*) are unique and lovely additions to dried arrangements, Johnny-jump-ups (*Viola tricolor*) are as decorative in salads and on cakes as they are in the garden, sweet Williams (*Dianthus barbatus*) add wonderful fragrance to fresh bouquets, and the dramatic spikes of mullein (*Verbascum* species) and Canterbury bells (*Campanula medium*) can define a yard.

Biennials also give you the opportunity to completely transform the look of your garden during the season. For example, once a border of English daisies has stopped blooming, you can remove the plants and transplant a low-growing annual, already in bloom, into the space where the daisies grew. Similarly, you can move Canterbury bells or foxglove into a garden bed shortly before they are to bloom, let them flower, and dig them out in time to put in fall-blooming chrysanthemums or calendula. This flexibility, along with their stunning and sometimes dramatic appearance, is what endears biennials to flower gardeners.

BLOOMING BIENNIALS, such as these hollyhocks, can add a vertical dimension to a planting.

SET BIENNIALS, such as these Canterbury bells, in place in late summer.

Starting Biennials

One-year-old potted biennials are sometimes available at nurseries and garden supply stores in early spring. Buying them at this age practically guarantees success inasmuch as they have already survived the winter. And, one-year old biennials will bloom the year you plant them. However, you'll find that the selection of started biennials is quite limited. If you want a particular color or cultivar, you'll probably have to start your own from seed.

June is the perfect time to start most biennials in Zones 5 and warmer. This schedule allows you time to care for them adequately and also gives them time to grow large enough to live through the winter and respond to spring by forming flowers.

But in Zones 3 and 4, start biennials in early spring, along with the annuals and perennials. Move them to larger containers when they outgrow their starting areas, and put them in an appropriate overwintering site in late summer or early fall.

If you have a seed starting area set up indoors, take advantage of it for the biennials. Germination is always higher in a controlled, indoor spot far away from the insects and animals that prey on seeds outdoors.

Nursery Beds

No matter where you start your biennials, you'll need a place to grow them during the first year. Some biennials, such as felty mullein, have such lovely leaves that they add an ornamental touch to flower beds all through their lives. These plants also decline after disturbance so much that you have to leave them in place after their first transplanting. But other biennials are easily moved around and have such unremarkable leaves that you'll want to grow them in an out-of-the-way spot for the first summer.

Many gardeners develop "nursery beds" where they can grow first-year biennials, young perennials, and plants that they want to move into place late in the season.

Choose the site for a nursery bed carefully. Most biennials, for example, require full sun to develop adequately, so the nursery bed must have excellent exposure. Humus-rich, moderately fertile, rock-free soils that drain well are a second requirement for a place to coddle young plants. If your property does not have the sort of nooks and crannies that will allow hiding this area, set aside a bed or two in the vegetable garden for it.

Plants that are transplanted to garden locations in spring must develop substantial roots quickly. Help them along by transplanting them with as large a root ball as possible when moving them from nursery beds or by growing them in big pots if you have overwintered them in a cold frame.

smart tip

OVERWINTER BIENNIALS IN A COLD FRAME

IF YOU DON'T HAVE A GOOD INDOOR SEED-STARTING SPACE, CONSIDER INVESTING IN A SMALL COLD FRAME. YOU CAN MAKE ONE YOUR-SELF OR BUY ONE AT A GARDEN CENTER. IT WILL PROTECT NEWLY SEEDED FLATS AND ALSO PRO-VIDE A GOOD ENVIRONMENT FOR THE BIENNI-ALS THAT NEED WINTER PROTECTION.

17 vegetable gardens

No matter how great the produce section at your local supermarket may look, homegrown vegetables are still a wonderful option. In fact, surveys show that more than half of American families grow some of their own produce. It's likely that this number is on the rise, thanks to the explosion of interest in all things organic and affordable. Besides, vegetable gardening is just plain fun. You can try crazy new crops and cultivars and innovative planting schemes. Or you can create vegetable gardens that are like tapestries in time and space, with new crops and colors coming up throughout the growing season. And if you don't like something you've planted, you can always deal with it in a very practical way. After all, in the vegetable garden, most of your mistakes will taste just as good as your successes.

PLANNING YOUR VEGETABLE GARDEN

Planning is imperative in all types of gardening, but nowhere is it more important than in the vegetable garden. Without some advance preparation, it's entirely possible to end up with 20 heads of cauliflower ready to harvest in the same week, followed by 20 heads of broccoli the next week, dump-truck loads of zucchini for a month, and bitter, inedible lettuces from July onward. That first burst of enthusiasm about vegetable gardening can also lead to plans that are so ambitious that they'd wear you to a frazzle if you actually carried them out.

Scale

Small gardens tend to be neat gardens. Weeds are pulled when they are tiny, and crops are harvested when they are ripe. If a disease or insect threatens a plant, it's easy to notice and control. If you build the soil with compost, mulch to keep down the weeds, and plant intensively, vegetable gardens take less time on a per-square-foot basis than flower gardens. It's impractical to plant so much that you can't keep up with it, but it's perfectly reasonable to plan a garden that's large enough to grow a significant amount of food.

If you are a beginning vegetable gardener, start with a garden that ranges between 15 x 20 feet and 20 x 30 feet. A 15- x 20-foot garden is large enough to grow fresh vegetables to feed a family of four as well as a few extras for preserving or storing for winter use. In a 20- x 30-foot garden, you can fit some of the space "hogs" such as sweet corn and pumpkins, plus summer veg-

SMALL VEGETABLE PLOTS are easy to maintain. As you gain experience, add space for more plants.

etables and a few crops for preserving. As you gain familiarity with each crop's needs, build your soil, and prevent or avoid pest and disease problems, you will attain the experience you need to increase the size of your garden.

Deciding What to Grow

Some people hate brussels sprouts; others would plant a whole garden of them. Growing your own vegetables allows you to be as choosy and idiosyncratic as you want to be—within reason. If you grow exactly the same thing in the same spot every year, certain weeds, pests, and diseases will build up in that area. So if you want to grow nothing but brussels sprouts (or sweet corn), you'll need to find four different places to grow them so that you can "rotate," or change the location, each year for four years. But if you grow a more varied assortment of crops, you can set up a rotation system that puts each crop in a different part of the garden over a four-year cycle.

Begin choosing what to grow by making a list of the vegetables that your family eats most frequently and the approximate number of heads or pounds that you use each week. The table "How Much Should You Plant?" (on page 318) lists approximate amounts of each veg-

etable that the "average" adult eats each year and the space required to produce that quantity, figured on both a row-foot and a bed-foot basis.

CHOOSING CROPS, above, can be one of the most challenging tasks of vegetable gardening.

HEIRLOOM VEGETABLES and edible flowers, below, can enchant even the youngest gardeners.

HOW MUCH SHOULD YOU PLANT?

CROP	YIELD LBS. PER ROW FOOT	LBS. NEEDED PER ADULT	ROW FEET PER ADULT	ROWS PER 4' BED	BED FEET PER ADULT
Asparagus	0.33–0.25	7	20	1	20
Beans, bush, snap	0.8	8	6.4	2	3.2
Beans, pole	1.5	10	15	2	7.5
Beet, greens	0.4	4	1.6	4	0.4
Beets	1	10	10	4	2.5
Broccoli	0.75	15	11.25	3	3.75
Brussels sprout	0.6	5	3	3	1
Cabbage	1.5	12	18	3	6
Cantaloupe	1	10	10	1	10
Carrot	1	20	20	4	5
Cauliflower	0.9	10	9	3	3
Chard	0.75	6	4.5	3	1.5
Collard	0.75	6	4.5	3	1.5
Corn	0.96	30	28.8	2	14.4
Cucumber	1.2	10	12	1	12
Eggplant	0.75	10	7.5	2	3.75
Kale	0.75	5	3.75	3	1.25
Leek	1.5	6	9	3	3
Lettuce	0.5	30	15	4	3.75
Onion	1	20	20	4	5
Parsnip	0.75	10	7.5	4	1.88
Pea, English or shell	0.2	5	1	2	0.50
Pea, snow	2	6	12	2	6
Pepper	0.5	10	5	2	2.5
Potato	5	50	250	2	125
Rhubarb	0.8–1.2	8–12	10	1	10
Rutabaga	1.5	5	7.5	3	2.5
Salad greens, misc.	0.5	25	12.5	4	3.13
Spinach	0.75	8	6	4	1.5
Squash, summer	2	8	16	1	16
Squash, winter	2	20	40	1	40
Strawberry	1–3	30 qts	10–20	1 (3)	10–20
Tomato	1.5	20	30	2	15
Turnip	1	8	8	4	2

TIME YOUR PLANTINGS so that new crops are maturing as you harvest those planted earlier.

smart tip

MAPPING THE GARDEN

MAPPING THE VEGETABLE GARDEN IS SIMILAR TO MAPPING THE FLOWER GARDEN, EXCEPT THAT THE DATES IN THE VEGETABLE GARDEN TEND TO BE MORE COMPLICATED AND THE LAYOUT TENDS TO BE MUCH SIMPLER.

PLACE PLANTS THAT ARE GOOD COMPANIONS ADJACENT TO EACH OTHER, AND KEEP POOR COMPANIONS FAR APART FROM EACH OTHER. CONSIDER SUCCESSIVE PLANTINGS OF EACH CROP SO THAT YOU'LL HAVE ENOUGH SPACE IN THE RIGHT PLACE WHEN YOU NEED IT.

CHANGE, OR ROTATE, CROP LOCATIONS EVERY YEAR FOR AT LEAST FOUR YEARS.

The wonderful world of seed catalogs is the next step in your planning process. Request several, including at least two that are located in your region. Read catalog descriptions carefully, noting such things as disease resistance and seasonal or cultural recommendations. Try to steer clear of cultivars that are said to "ripen uniformly." This means that the crop has been bred for the convenience of commercial growers; it may taste good, but the flavor is secondary to the harvest characteristics.

You'll soon discover the joys of growing many varieties of the same vegetable. For example, different lettuces and broccoli grow, mature, and taste different, depending on the time that they grow. Similarly, some root vegetable cultivars store well while others don't, and some cultivars of greens stand up better than others under the first frosts and snows of the year. Good seed catalogs guide you by letting you know what cultivars perform best in your area and in the different parts of the season.

After you've made a list of the seeds you want—on a sheet of paper, never directly on the order form—go back through to cross off the nonessentials. Even though you can keep the seeds of most crops for a couple of years if you store them in cool, dark, dry conditions, it's best to try to keep your seed purchases to a reasonable quantity. This will make it easier to maintain a planting plan and harvesting schedule.

Companion Planting. Plants exert strong influences over each other. They release chemical compounds from their roots and aboveground tissues that affect other

EVEN IF you never read directions, pay attention to the information given in catalogs and seed packets.

plants as well as insects and microorganisms. Some of these effects are directly beneficial, as in the case of a root *exudant* (liquid that is released from the plant) that stimulates the growth or flavor of a nearby plant. Other companion planting effects are indirectly beneficial, as in the case of a flower that serves as a nectar source for an insect that preys on the pest insects of neighboring plants. Still other companion plant effects are negative, as in the case of a root exudant that inhibits the growth or flavor of another plant. Generations of gardeners have been noting these reactions. Although not all of these effects have been proved by scientists, gardeners generally find that they work. The table "Companion Plant Influences," on page 321, lists the effects of combining vegetables with each other as well as some weeds, herbs, and flowering plants.

Succession Planting. It's important to plan where successive plantings will go right from the beginning. Otherwise, you can find yourself without a good spot to plant fall broccoli or lettuce. Although this extensive planning may seem mind-boggling at first, here are a few tips to make it easier.

Short-season crops, such as lettuce, can follow other short-season crops. If the soil is very fertile, you can get away with simply replanting the area. However, few soils are that rich, especially when you first start to garden. So it's best to apply at least ½ inch of compost, a light dusting of alfalfa or soybean meal, or a balanced organic bagged fertilizer for the second crop. Work the compost or fertilizer into the top couple of inches of soil a week or so before direct-seeding or a few days before transplanting.

CROP DIVERSITY confuses those pests that depend on odor or appearance to find their hosts.

319

If you have lots of space, you can grow a green manure in a planting area until it is time to plant the crop. Green manure is a type of cover crop grown primarily to add nutrients and organic matter to the soil. Typically, a green manure crop is grown for a specific period, and then plowed under and incorporated into the soil. Green manure crops planted in the early spring include frost-tolerant annual grasses, grains, or legumes such as oats or fava beans. If you are planting later in the summer, use a tender crop such as buckwheat or forage soybeans.

Two weeks before you plan to direct-seed or transplant your vegetable crop, till or pull up the green manure, and let it decompose on the soil surface. Water the area lightly if it's dry to promote decomposition. This system not only adds nutrients to the soil, it also prevents weeds from establishing themselves in the garden.

People usually think of crop rotations in terms of where plants grow in successive years. However, if you are double-cropping an area by growing two different crops on it in the same year, that counts as a rotation, too. Refer to the table "Companion Plant Influences," opposite, to avoid planting a crop where an adversary previously grew.

Crop Rotation

There is no doubt that plants affect one another over time (the reason behind rotations) as much as they do through space (the reason for companion planting). Certain crops deplete or replenish particular nutrients in the soil, and some pests and diseases are drawn to soils where their favorite hosts have recently grown. Consequently, gardeners rotate their crops to vary the soil nutrient requirements as well as minimize pests and diseases. Use the following guidelines to develop your own rotation system:

- Leave at least four years between planting members of the same plant family in the same spot.
- Follow heavy feeders, such as corn and squash, with light feeders, such as beets, beans, or peas.
- Follow deep-rooted crops, such as broccoli, with shallow-rooted crops such as onion.

A Specialized Vegetable Rotation. Researchers at the University of Rhode Island conducted a 30-year study of crop rotations. Eliot Coleman, an innovative market grower and author, has worked with and fine-tuned this system for more than a decade. After much refining, he has settled on the following rotation as being the most beneficial—and others who have tried it agree. As you make your garden map, try to follow this system:

- Potatoes follow sweet corn,
- Sweet corn follows the cabbage family,
- Cabbage family crops, undersown with legumes, follow peas,
- Peas follow tomatoes,
- Tomatoes, undersown with a non-hardy green oat manure, follow beans,
- Beans follow root crops,
- Root crops follow squash or potatoes,
- Squashes follow potatoes.

SUCCESSION PLANTING for continuous harvests is as easy to do in a small garden bed as in a whole garden.

COMPANION PLANT INFLUENCES

SPECIES	ATTRACTS	REPELS/INHIBITS	COMMON COMPANION CROPS
Allium		Aphids, peas	Roses, daffodils, tulips, aphid hosts in vegetable garden
Beans, bush		Inhibits onions	Carrots, cauliflower, beets, cucumbers, cabbage
Borage		Tomato worm	Strawberry, tomato
Broccoli/cabbage		Tomato	Dill, celery, chamomile, sage, beets, onions, potatoes
Carrots		Dill	Onions, leeks, herbs, lettuce, peas
Catnip	Small beneficials		Catnip tea repels flea beetles
Celery			Leeks, tomatoes, cauliflower, cabbage, bush beans
Chamomile	Small beneficials		Onions, cabbage family
Dill	Small beneficials	Inhibits carrot	Cabbage, beets, lettuce, onion
Eggplant	Potato bugs		Potatoes
Fennel		Inhibits many species	Plant by itself
Garlic		Aphids, Japanese beetles, mites, deer, rabbits	Roses and many vegetables
Hyssop	Bees	Cabbage moth, radish	Grapes, cabbage
Kohlrabi		Potatoes, beans	Onions, beets, cukes, cabbage family crops
Marigold		Nematodes, Mexican bean beetles	Tomatoes, beans, potatoes
Nasturtium	Aphids	Squash bugs	Trap crop with cabbage family
Nicotiana	Potato bugs		Potatoes
Orach		Inhibits potato	
Parsley	Small beneficials		Interplant with carrot, rose
Petunia		Mexican bean beetles	Beans
Potato		Repels Mexican bean beetles/Inhibits tomato, squash, sunflower, raspberry	Beans, corn, cabbage, eggplant, horseradish, marigold
Rue		Japanese beetle	Inhibits many plants
Sage		Cabbage moth, carrot flies	Cabbage family, carrots
Sunflowers		Inhibits nitrogen-fixing bacteria, potatoes	Corn, cukes
Stinging Nettle	Small beneficials		Almost all plants benefit
Summer Savory		Mexican bean beetles	Beans
Thornapple		Deters Japanese beetles	Near grapes, roses, pumpkin
Tidytips	Small beneficials		With aphid hosts
Tomato		Asparagus beetle	Asparagus, gooseberries, roses

4-YEAR VEGETABLE ROTATION

TAKE ADVANTAGE of the work that crop researchers and farmers have already done to develop the best rotation possible. Although this scheme may seem complicated before you implement it, ultimately it simplifies your garden

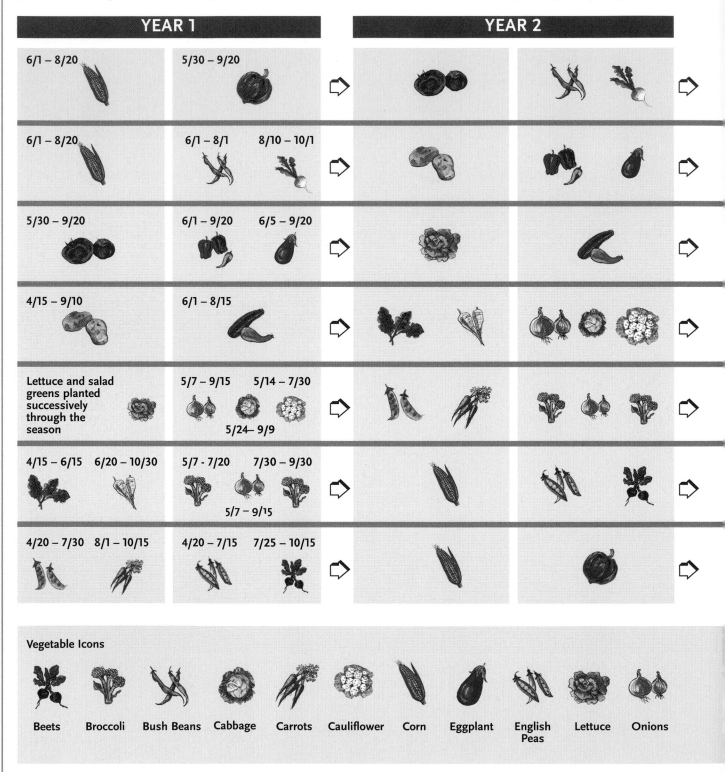

| YEAR 1 | | YEAR 2 | |

Vegetable Icons

Beets   Broccoli   Bush Beans   Cabbage   Carrots   Cauliflower   Corn   Eggplant   English Peas   Lettuce   Onions

planning. This rotation can also contribute to the health and vitality of your plants, making them more resistant to many pests and diseases.

YEAR 3				YEAR 4	

Parsnips · **Peppers** · **Potatoes** · **Scallions** · **Snap Peas** · **Spinach** · **Summer Squash** · **Tomatoes** · **Turnips** · **Winter Squash**

Timing

If you plant all of your lettuce in the first week of April, it will all mature between the end of May and the end of June, even if your cultivars have different "Days to Maturity." Good timing solves this problem. Rather than plant everything at once, experienced gardeners plant small amounts of each of the short-season crops all through the season. Most people take a few years to develop a "starting schedule" appropriate to their climate and chosen cultivars.

Using the list of vegetables you'd like to grow, make a chart with the same columns as shown in the table "Typical Starting Schedule—Zone 5," page 326. To customize it for your own use, begin by filling in the "Days to Maturity" (DTM) column. For example, if the crop is one that you direct-seed outdoors, fill in a date when it is safe to plant the seed according to its temperature requirements. Remember not to plant frost-sensitive plants until after the frost-free date in your area. Days to Maturity are listed in the catalog or on the seed packet. Add the Days to Maturity to the planting date to learn approximately when the harvest will begin.

Begin by filling in the date that it is safe to transplant to the garden, and then count backward, using the information in the vegetable directory, to learn the date you'll need to plant the seeds indoors. Then count forward, again from the transplanting date, to learn when to expect a harvest. For example, if you know that it's safe to plant cool-loving cauliflower with a DTM of 54 in the garden on May 7th, count backward six weeks to March 26 to learn when to plant the seeds. It ought to be ready by June 30th.

DTM numbers can be confusing if you don't know whether the catalog is referring to days from direct-seeding the crop in the garden or transplanting seedlings. The table below tells you the usual way of counting for each crop.

Adjust the DTM for Transplants. When you transplant a crop with a DTM date that is counted from direct seeding, (seeds that are planted directly into the ground where they will grow), you'll have to adjust your figures. As a general rule, subtract 10 to 14 days from the DTM. (Even though the plant has been growing for 4 to 6 weeks inside, transplanting sets the crop back, so you only gain 10 to 14 days.) If you find yourself direct-seeding a crop that is counted from the transplant date, such as broccoli, add between 14 and 20 days to the DTM. (By direct seeding, you gain 14 to 20 days.)

With experience, you'll learn how long each crop will stand in the garden without losing quality. For example, the earliest spring lettuces and greens stay good for a week or two. But in midsummer, they become tough and bitter very quickly; they will also taste best if picked when slightly young and undersized. Until you know your climate and cultivars, plan so that salad crops slightly overlap each other. If you overplant, you can always give some salad away or add it to the compost pile.

DATES TO MATURITY CHART

From Direct-Seeding Date	From Transplanting Date
Beans	Broccoli
Beets	Brussels sprouts
Carrots	Cabbage
Corn	Cauliflower
Cucumbers	Celeriac
Fennel, bulbing	Celery
Greens, salad or cooking	Eggplant
Kohlrabi	Leeks
Lettuce	Melons
Okra	Peppers
Onions	Tomatoes
Parsnips	
Peas	
Pumpkins	
Radishes	
Squashes	
Turnips and rutabagas	

USE THE DAYS TO MATURITY on the seed pack to calculate when to plant crops for harvest throughout the season.

PLANTING LETTUCE IN BEDS

BROADCAST PLANTED SPINACH

DIRECT-SEEDED MESCLUN

RAISED-BED PLANTING

PLANTING TIPS AND TECHNIQUES

Planting the vegetable garden is always fun. And the more sophisticated you become as a vegetable gardener, the more planting you will do. Not only will you plant successive crops throughout the summer, you'll also be taking advantage of season-extension technologies to plant earlier and later than normal.

Vegetable gardens were once planted the way farm fields were—in single rows spaced far apart from each other. This system is useful for crops planted in hills, such as potatoes and corn, but many gardeners and small farmers have abandoned it in favor of more practical beds that make use of limited space..

There are several advantages to planting vegetables in beds rather than in rows:

- Compost and soil amendments can be concentrated where plants are growing, rather than being wasted on the pathways.
- You can build up the height of the bed, increasing aeration, drainage, and spring heating.
- Plants can be spaced so that they shade out weeds when they are nearly mature, decreasing weeding time.
- Plants grow more quickly and vigorously because their soil has not been compacted by being trod upon. (continued on page 328)

TYPICAL STARTING SCHEDULE: ZONE 5

USE THIS TABLE as a guide to create your own starting schedule. Although this table covers much of the season, you'll notice that you would have to add some crops or plantings, particularly lettuce and salad greens, to be assured of having each type of vegetable at all the possible times during the season. Remember to adjust timing to take into account the low light and cool temperatures in fall.

	Days to Maturity	Starting Method	Seeding Date	Transplant Date	Harvest Date	Notes
Beans, Snap						
Provider	50	DS*	5/27		7/10	
Rattlesnake (Pole bean)	70	DS*	6/24		9/2	
Jade	56	DS*	7/8		8/7	
Beets						
Early Wonder Tall Top	48	DS*	5/5		6/22	
Lutz Green Leaf	60	DS*	7/22		9/16	
Broccoli						
Green King	65	Inside	4/9	5/19	7/23	Each planting yields for 2–3 weeks
Saga	56	Inside	6/27	8/6	10/1	
Genji	59	Inside	7/22	8/31	10/15	
Brussels Sprouts						
Prince Marvel	110	Inside	4/24	6/3	9/21	Harvest all fall
Cabbage						
Hermes	62	Inside	4/5	5/15	7/16	
Storage No. 4	95	Inside	6/9	7/19	10/22	
Carrot						
Kinko	55	DS*	4/23		6/17	Each planting gives 3–4 harvests
Nantes Fancy	68	DS*	6/17		8/24	
Canada Gold	73	DS*	7/14		9/25	
Cauliflower						
Rushmore	54	Inside	3/29	5/8/	7/1	
Snow Crown	50	Inside	6/12	7/22	9/10	
Cucumber						
Lemon	51	Inside	5/14	6/11	8/1	
Marketmore 76	44	Inside	5/16	6/13	7/27	
Eggplant						
All Cultivars	55–68	Inside	3/30	6/6	7/25 on	Harvest until frost
Kale						
Wild Garden Kale Mix	55	DS*	7/16		9/9	
Leeks						
King Richard	75	Inside	4/19	6/28	9/11	

	Days to Maturity	Starting Method	Seeding Date	Transplant Date	Harvest Date	Notes
Lettuce						
Buttercrunch Bibb	40	Inside	3/22	5/1	6/10	DTM is from transplanting and reflects seasonal changes
Crispino	44	Inside	4/10	5/20	7/3	
Cerise	48	Inside	5/11	6/20	8/7	
Parris Island Cos	48	Inside	6/8	7/18	9/4	
Carmona	64	Inside	6/13	7/23	9/25	
Onions						
Ailsa Craig	110	Inside	3/15	5/24	9/1	
Redman	101	Inside	3/11	5/20	8/29	
Parsnip						
Andover	120	DS*	6/10		10/8	
Peas						
All cultivars	56–70	DS*	4/20		6/14–7/10	
Peppers, Sweet						
All Cultivars	59–75	Inside	4/2	6/3	8/5 on	
Pepper, Hot						
All cultivars	55–75	Inside	3/31	6/6	8/12 on	
Potatoes						
All cultivars		DS*	4/16		8/1 on	
Radish						
Cherry Belle	28	DS*	5/7		6/4	
Daikon	50	DS*	7/22		9/21	
Miyashige	50	DS*	7/23		9/1	
Rutabaga						
Pike	100	DS*	6/12		9/20	
Scallions						
Evergreen White Hardy	65	DS*	5/10		7/14	
Spinach						
Denali	36	DS*	4/22		5/28	
Denali	36	DS*	8/6		9/11	
Squash, Summer						
Condor	48	Inside	5/12	6/2	7/20	
Seneca Prolific	51	DS*	6/11		8/1	
Squash, Winter						
All Winter Cultivars	85–110	Inside	5/5	5/26	8/18 on	
Tomatoes						
All Cultivars	60–80	Inside	4/26	6/4	8/2	
Turnip						
Purple Top Globe White	50	DS*	8/11		9/30	

*DS-Direct Seed

(continued from page 325)

STAKES AND STRINGS

PREPARE SOME STAKES and strings by wrapping slightly more string than the length of your bed around one stake and tying it to another. Set up the stakes and strings each time you plant, measuring at both ends of the bed. Make your furrows directly under each string. Planting in straight rows saves time in the long run. You'll be able to hoe and cultivate between the rows very quickly if you don't have to adjust for inconsistencies.

do some hand-weeding in the row, of course, but the major part of the job can be done in only a few minutes. However, rows are not the only way to plant in beds.

Broadcast Seeding. Small crops like carrots and baby lettuce can be broadcast-seeded in a bed. A broadcast pattern is scattershot. You plant by holding the seed loosely in your hand and releasing small amounts as you flick your wrist over the area. After the plants are up and have their second set of leaves, thin them to the recommended in-row spacing.

The advantage to a broadcast planting is that the plant density and yields per square foot are much greater than they are in a row system. But to work well, the soil must be largely free of weeds. If it isn't, you'll have to do so much hand-weeding that the crop will end up costing you lots of extra time, or you'll abandon it and turn it all under. Once your garden is well established and weeds are under control, it's certainly worth experimenting with broadcast seeding to see how you like it. Carrots, beets, scallions, radishes, salad greens, baby turnips, and spinach are appropriate for broadcast seeding.

Planting Designs

Many gardeners make their beds 4 feet wide. This width allows you to grow four rows of a small crop such as lettuce, three rows of a larger crop such as Chinese cabbage, two rows of big crops such as corn or tomatoes, and a single row for members of the space-hogging squash family in a single bed. If you look back to the table "How Much Should You Plant?" on page 318, you'll see a column giving the numbers of rows per 4-foot bed for every vegetable listed. These figures assume that the soil is adequately supplied with both nutrients and moisture for the particular crop. If the fertility is still a little lean, plant two rows of either broccoli, cabbage, or cauliflower instead of three.

Row Planting. Planting in rows makes weeding quick and efficient. You can simply move a hoe down the bed between the rows to uproot the weeds. You will have to

Planting Techniques

Whether you are planting in single rows or rows in a bed, begin by marking the row locations. You may feel that the stake and twine system (shown above) is overly complicated, but this technique saves time and trouble by making weeding easier and assuring that plants have adequate growing space. Make shallow furrows just under the strings—no deeper than three times the width of the seed.

In drought conditions, it's sometimes best to plant in deep furrows. This works best if the soil along the sides of the furrow will not fall in and bury the seed too deeply. To make the most of this technique, create a deeper-than-normal furrow, and water it well. Then plant in the bottom as usual. Cover the seed with an appropriately thin layer of soil, and water again, using a misting nozzle or water-breaker on your hose to avoid displacing the soil.

Proper Seed Practices. Space seeds carefully. Most seed packets list a spacing distance, but in many cases this recommendation will require that you thin the plants once they start growing. There are usually directions for thinning on the seed packet as well. The goal is to remove some small plants so that the others will have the proper spacing that will allow them to thrive.

It's easy to handle large seeds such as beets, peas, and corn. Even the smaller broccoli and cabbage seeds won't cause you problems. But tiny seeds, such as carrot, can be hard to space well. If you have difficulty getting a sparse enough seeding, use an old trick. Mix the carrot seed with equal portions of dry sand. Take up pinches of this mixture, and sprinkle them along the furrow. The tiny seed should be spaced well with this method.

Seeds must be consistently moist to germinate. In the spring, when the soil is wet and rains are frequent, this is rarely a problem. Water just after you plant, using a fine misting nozzle or hose. Check the soil each morning and evening until the seeds germinate to see whether you need to water again. But if you're planting seeds in hot weather or in a drought, you'll have to cover the soil with something that will hold moisture. See the smart tip, right, for details.

Seeds that require light to germinate often dry out if you leave them on the soil surface. Avoid this problem by making the furrow as described on page 328 and filling it with vermiculite. Plant the seeds on the surface of the vermiculite and then water with a misting nozzle or fine hose. The water will work the seeds into niches in the vermiculite so that they will remain wet, but enough light will penetrate the vermiculite so that they can germinate.

Transplanting

Many vegetable seedlings are transplanted directly into the garden. Transplant seedlings late in the day or when it is overcast. This decreases transplant shock because the plants lose less water from their leaves. Most vegetables are set into the soil at the same depth they grew in their starting containers, but there are exceptions. Large portions of the stems of tomato plants are routinely buried. Roots will grow from the stem, further stabilizing the plant and increasing its ability to obtain food and water.

Seedlings that have grown top-heavy and tall as a consequence of low light levels can be planted deeper as long as they grow from the top, as broccoli does. However, deep planting will kill plants such as lettuce, which grow from the crown.

Vegetable seedlings require immediately available supplies of phosphorous, especially in cold soil. Soak the flats or root balls in a solution of liquid seaweed and fish emulsion, diluted as recommended on the bottle, for at least 15 minutes before planting. Later in the season, when the soil is warm, this root drench will keep the root ball wet while the plant adjusts to its new environment.

smart tip

KEEPING SEEDS MOIST

Keeping the soil moist in summer or during periods of drought can be a challenge. You can either plant in a deep furrow, as described in "Planting Techniques," opposite, or plant in a furrow of normal depth and cover your rows with row-cover material or untreated burlap. Saturate the covering with water several times a day. If the seeds germinate in the dark, you can even cover them with a layer of wet newspapers, as long as you check for germination every morning and evening.

PLANT LETTUCE so that the crown is just level with the soil surface. If you bury the crown, or leave the roots exposed, the plant will die.

FLOATING ROW COVER **SQUARE CAGE** **GLASS CLOCHE**

COLD FRAME **POLY ROW COVER**

EXTENDING THE SEASONS

Season extenders enable you to grow plants outside earlier and later in the season than normal, and they also give a certain amount of security against sudden cold snaps. Unless you live in a frost free area, it's well worth investing in a roll of row-cover material at the very least. As your vegetable gardening horizons expand, you'll probably want to add other season extenders to your tool kit.

Although a number of devices are classified as "season extenders," they vary tremendously in both effectiveness and cost. Some are most useful for covering large areas when a light frost threatens, while others can actually protect plants from temperatures in the low 20s.

Most experienced vegetable gardeners have several extenders to use for whatever situation arises.

Once you get used to using season-extension devices, you can plan your spring gardening schedule around them. In the fall, most gardeners depend on floating row covers to keep their plants producing through the first frosts. Row covers can be put up quickly and, because they "breathe," do not have to be removed unless the succeeding days are bright and hot. Use two layers of row cover material whenever temperatures threaten to fall below 28°F. You'll be getting at least 6°F and possibly as much as 8°F of protection, meaning that your plants will not only survive, they will also suffer less than those that just make it through the low temperatures.

KEEPING SOIL AND PLANTS HEALTHY

Healthy soils make healthy gardens. But knowing that your soil should be healthy and knowing how to help it become that way are two different things.

Basic soil science is covered in Chapter 11, "Soil and Water," pages 214 to 235. That information is essential for all kinds of gardening, from roses to tomatoes. But you'll need to add to that fundamental information to grow many other vegetables.

Feed the Soil

Vegetables absorb huge amounts of nutrients from the soil. Some, like corn and spinach, are nitrogen hogs, while others, such as onions and peppers, use and store more phosphorus, potassium, and minor nutrients such as magnesium. But no matter what the vegetable, you can be sure that you will need to replenish the nutrients frequently.

Compost Is the Best Way to Maintain Soil Health. Compost is the first line of defense, of course. Vegetable gardens need an average application of ½ to 2 inches each spring. The ½-inch application simply replenishes what the crop has removed from the soil during the past growing season, while a 2-inch application helps build up soil that is deficient in organic matter and/or nutrients.

Getting Vines off the Ground

Training tomatoes up a trellis instead of letting them sprawl has a huge impact on the plant's health. Trellising improves air circulation, keeps animal and soil-dwelling pests away from the crops, and decreases soil-borne diseases.

Tomatoes can be "determinate," meaning that they are bred to grow to a certain height, or "indeterminate," meaning that they will continue to grow for as long as they are alive. Catalogs indicate which is which.

Knowing how a tomato plant grows is important. Determinate tomatoes form fruit on the branches (or suckers) that grow between the main stem and first branches. If you remove these suckers, you will be removing the fruit-production sites.

In contrast, removing suckers is a good way to prune indeterminate plants. Because the plants continue to grow from the top of the stem, they continue to produce blossom- and fruit-bearing branches. This pruning technique is referred to as "suckering."

BEAN TEPEES are easy to make and lots of fun. You can pick the beans from inside or outside.

GOURDS, like other cucurbit crops, are healthier when the vines are supported and off the ground.

331

HEIRLOOM cultivars such as these 'Clear Pink' tomatoes and the assortment (left), tend to have superior flavor.

HYBRIDS such as these 'Black Bell' eggplants are uniform in appearance and may have disease resistance.

SAVING YOUR OWN SEED

Until the 1940s all gardeners and farmers saved their own seeds. People often had specialties that they shared with friends and relatives. Certain families became known for their superior varieties of this tomato or that bean.

All of these seeds were open-pollinated (OP) varieties or cultivars, meaning that the parents of the seed were genetically similar, but not identical, to each other. The plants that grew from these seeds were similar to their parents, and the seeds they produced were "true to type" because they carried the characteristic traits of their parents. These plants are called *heirlooms*.

Hybrid seeds result from crossing two or more plants of the same species that are quite different genetically. A hybrid seed produces a plant that is different from each of its parents but almost identical to every other plant grown from the same cross. If you grow a hybrid crop and save seed from it, the resulting plants will not come "true to type." Instead, they can resemble any plant, or combination of plants, in their heritage. Examples of OP tomatoes include 'Arkansas Traveler' and 'Brandywine', while hybrids include cultivars such as 'Celebrity' and 'Big Beef'.

Ironically, open-pollinated plants of the same variety or cultivar usually have more genetic diversity between individual plants than do hybrids. This makes qualities such as their days to maturity, size, color, and pest- and disease-resistance variable but also provides a certain security for the gardener. If a disease strikes an open-pollinated crop, for example, it is likely that some of the plants will be resistant to it, and the gardener can then save and propagate seeds from these plants.

But hybrids make life much more convenient. Knowing that all the broccoli heads will mature within a few days of each other makes it possible to schedule the harvest as well as streamline freezing operations.

Benefits of Hybrids vs. Open-Pollinated Plants

Most of the seeds you find in catalogs are hybrids that have been bred for certain characteristics. In some cases, these plants are superior to any open-pollinated crop you can grow, but in others, delicacy and flavor have been inadvertently bred out of the plant while hybridizers were working on good shipping or processing qualities. Many hybrids used by commercial farmers have another limitation. Seeds are being bred that will not grow unless they are treated with specific fertilizers and pesticides.

Shrinking Gene Pool Creates Problems. Gardeners and small farmers all over the continent have become concerned by the shrinking gene pool of our most common crops. Not only are thousands of wonderful varieties being lost in favor of the hybrids that are replacing them, the genetic similarity of many crops is making them more vulnerable to catastrophe. In 1970, for example, more than half of the U.S. corn crop in the South was stricken with a fungal disease; overall, more than a billion bushels were lost. All of the affected corn shared parentage, even though they had different cultivar names. This disaster, as well as the loss of 40 percent of the Soviet wheat crop in 1971, which was also due to genetic uniformity, alerted farmers and gardeners alike to these serious problems.

In response, people all over this continent began to save seeds, just as their grandparents and great grandparents once did. Seed-saving groups are now selling open-pollinated seeds as well as trading them between members. The Seed Starters Association, based in Decorah, IA, is the pioneering group.

Getting Started with Seed Saving

You'll discover how exciting it is to carefully protect a plant from crossing with other members of the species, save its seed, and then grow it out again for the seed. Before too many years have passed, you'll see some tangible benefits, too. Crops for which you save seed will become healthier and stronger as they become more and more adapted to the conditions in your backyard.

Some plants are easier to save

seed from than others. Many people begin with tomatoes, partially because the seeds are easy to save and because some of the old-fashioned open-pollinated varieties are more flavorful than the new hybrids. But hybrid tomato cultivars are often more resistant to diseases than open-pollinated tomatoes. So even if you are totally committed to saving seed, grow a few hybrids along with the heirloom types until you learn how the open-pollinated cultivars respond to the diseases in your environment.

Pepper and lettuce are also good choices for beginning seed savers. But no matter what crop you begin with, start by buying open-pollinated seed. Seed catalogs indicate whether a plant is a hybrid by describing it that way or putting a small F1 or F2 beside the cultivar name. Without such a designation, you can be pretty sure it's open-pollinated.

How Pollination Works. Seeds are formed when the ovule at the base of the flower is fertilized by pollen from the same or another flower. "Perfect" flowers are those that contain both pollen and ovules. Many of these flowers can fertilize themselves if the wind or an insect pushes the pollen from the anthers to the stigma. Tomatoes, peppers, beans, and peas are all self-pollinating.

A few perfect flowers are "self-incompatible," meaning that they contain all the parts but can only be fertilized by pollen from another flower. Wind rarely achieves the necessary transfer, so these plants are dependent on insects for pollination. Radishes, broccoli, and cabbage all fit into this category.

smart tip

MALE AND FEMALE PLANTS

Spinach is one of the few vegetables with male and female flowers on different plants. You can't tell the difference before the plants flower, so it is best to enclose an entire bed with row-cover material and let the wind pollinate them.

Male plant

Female plant

Ovule

Other plants have flowers that are either "male," producing only pollen, or "female," with ovules. Usually, insects move the pollen from one to another bloom, but sometimes, as in the case of corn, wind accomplishes the task. In some cases, such as squash and corn, male and female flowers grow on the same plant, but in others, such as spinach, entire plants are either male or female.

Commercial breeders keep lines pure by "isolating" plants, or growing them miles away from any others in the same species. In the home garden, this degree of isolation is virtually impossible. Even if you were to grow only one type of squash, for example, foraging bees traveling from neighboring gardens could fertilize the squash growing in your garden with pollen from a different type of squash.

Instead, gardeners can use barriers to protect flowers from this sort of stray crossing. Flower clusters may be bagged with floating row-cover material, (Photos 2 and 3 below), or plants may be grown in cages covered with row-cover material or fine-mesh screening or kept under row covers for the season.

Effecting Pollination. To pollinate flowers that are normally wind-pollinated, such as tomatoes, enclose the flower clusters before the blooms open. Check them daily after the morning dew has dried. Once they do open, jiggle the stem gently to release the pollen from the male flower to the female flower. Remove the floating row cover pouch after the petals from all the flowers have dropped or dried up. Then mark the branch by tying a piece of string or ribbon on it to show that the fruits should be saved for seed rather than eaten.

Insect-pollinated flowers, such as squashes, must also be protected. The normal procedure is to check plants every evening for both male and female flowers that will open the following day. Tape the tips of male and female flowers closed with masking tape. In the morning, remove the tape from a male flower, cut it off the plant with a few inches of its petiole, and pull off the petals. Now gently remove the tape from the female flower and rub pollen from the male into each section of the stigma on the female plant. Success will be best guaranteed if you use several male flowers for each female flower.

SAVING TOMATO SEEDS

TOMATOES are one of the many plants that have perfect flowers that contain both male and female organs and fertilize themselves.

1 Tomatoes often fertilize themselves before they open, but you can still protect them from cross-fertilization.

2 Cover the unopened flower clusters with a square of floating row-cover material.

3 Leave the row-cover material in place until all the petals in the cluster drop

4 Tie a ribbon around the stem of the flower cluster so that you remember to save the seed.

HAND POLLINATING SQUASH

SUMMER SQUASH, like all cucurbits, bears male and female flowers on the same plant. You can identify the female flowers by the fruit behind them.

1 Check your plants nightly so you can identify the female flowers that are going to open the next day. Tape them shut to keep them closed.

2 Tape the male flowers shut too. Even though they can't be fertilized, an insect could transfer pollen from another cultivar onto them.

3 Remove petals from the male flower, and rub it against the inside of the female flower.

4 To ensure plant vigor, use several male flowers to pollinate each female flower.

5 Retape the female flower closed so that insects don't add new pollen to the flower.

After pollinating a female flower, tape it shut again to exclude insects. Tie a plastic strap around the flower stem so that you'll know which ones have been hand-pollinated.

To breed for a particular characteristic of a plant, choose male and female flowers only from that plant, but to ensure genetic vigor, choose flowers from several different plants. If possible, work with the first and second batches of flowers that form on the plant because later blooms may be aborted if the plant is under any stress.

Melon and cucumber flowers, which are much smaller than squash blossoms, are sometimes hard to retape closed. Instead, just enclose the bloom in a sack of row-cover material after you have fertilized it and leave the material in place until the fruit starts to grow.

Even if seed-saving seems complicated to you, experiment with the technique by saving the seed of only one or two vegetables, such as a favorite pepper or tomato. (See "Saving Tomato Seeds," opposite.) It won't take long before you discover that seed-saving can be a simple, effective, and cost-saving way to increase your gardening pleasure.

335

VARYING FOLIAGE COLORS of herbs give this formal garden a distinct look.

DESIGNING HERB GARDENS

Say the words "herb garden," and many people conjure up a picture of a formal, stylized design, such as a knot garden or a geometrically patterned bed. Most herbs are ideal subjects for formal designs because all it takes is a little pruning every year to coax them into the tidy forms that make up the structure of formal gardens. And the wide range of green tones displayed by herbs makes it easy to create a garden built around a subtle tapestry of hues.

Herb gardens certainly do not have to be formal. Increasingly, gardeners are creating informal designs or using herbs as elements in other gardens. In a formal design, simply for appearances' sake, you usually have to grow much more of particular herbs than you may plan to use. Sometimes this will spur your creativity, and you'll be inspired to dry a collection of thymes for everyone on

INFORMAL HERB GARDENS can be planned according to the herbs you'll actually use and the quantities you'll need rather than the amount required in the design of a formal herb garden.

your gift list. But if you don't react this way to overwhelming abundance, you may want to consider creating an informal herb garden where you can grow only as much as you need of each species.

Guidelines for Design

Formal gardens are generally based on geometric shapes. For example, the perimeter of the garden may be a square or rectangle, while the interior space is divided into smaller rectangles, squares, or triangles. Circular designs are also common, with either pie-shaped or curved divisions inside the outline. In some cases, the pathways of the garden form the structure of the design, while in others, the herbs themselves create it. In either case, for the best results, keep the lines simple. Formal gardens look good only if they are well maintained. You'll have to keep up with weeding, pruning, and edging if you want the garden to continue to look its best. Fortunately, these gardens are often easier to maintain than informal ones because the spaces are so clearly delineated, but again, routine maintenance is always easiest if the lines of the design are simple.

KITCHEN HERB GARDENS needn't be all work and no play. Here, marigolds liven up a collection of culinary herbs.

You can build informal herb gardens in any shape that is convenient. Although they are designed more for function than for aesthetics, you'll probably enjoy informal herb gardens more and take better care of them if you give careful thought to the design.

Kitchen Herb Gardens. Whether you live in a city apartment or a house with a yard, you'll want to grow the herbs you use most frequently. It's a treat to have parsley (*Petroselinum crispum*), dill (*Anethum graveolens*), basil (*Ocimum basilicum*), tarragon (*Artemisia dracunculus*), and chervil (*Anthriscus cereifolium*) just outside the door. So whether it's a container garden, or a bed in the ground, be sure to plant some kitchen herbs to use in your cooking.

Kitchen herb gardens are ideal places to mix perennial and annual plants. It's usually best to site the perennial herbs first, leaving ample space between them so that

you can tuck in annuals during the season. Tarragon (*Artemisia dracunculus*), oregano (*Origanum vulgare*), some of the thymes (*Thymus* spp.), mints (*Mentha* spp.), chives, and sage (*Salvia officinalis*) usually form the perennial backbone of the kitchen garden. Oregano and the thymes make good edging plants, while sage, chives, and tarragon grow large enough to be used in the middle or back of the bed. As always, confine mints to pots or a garden all their own.

Successive plantings are the best way to maintain steady supplies of many annual herbs. Chervil and coriander (*Coriandrum sativum*), for example, can be picked for only a few weeks to a month before they flower and die. Midseason plantings of chervil will only thrive in a cool, shady spot, generally under a taller plant such as bee balm (*Monarda didyma*). However, the last chervil planting of the year, which usually matures a week or so before the first frost, can tolerate brighter conditions. In contrast, cilantro and basil grow well in summer heat and full sun. But unlike basil, which is easy to transplant into the

337

garden and generally gives good yields from only two plantings per year, cilantro must be direct-seeded or carefully transplanted every month to provide continuous harvests.

Tea Gardens. Herbal teas have become a mainstay in most homes. Many of us routinely buy colorful boxes of exotic combinations with wonderful names. Many basic tea ingredients—the mints, chamomile (*Matricaria recutita*), rosehips, and berry leaves—are easy to grow and dry at home. And even though you might not harvest hibiscus flowers or citrus peel, you can buy these ingredients and mix them into your homegrown tea combinations.

Many of the best tea ingredients are members of the invasive mint family, so it's wise to give the tea garden several beds of its own, far away from the ornamental flowers or vegetables.

Or you can simply plant mint in pots. You can sink them in the soil or not, depending on the look you want, but if you sink them, you'll have to keep stems from taking root in the surrounding soil.

Chamomile is another ingredient often used in herbal tea. The first planting usually blooms in early to midsummer and dies shortly after you harvest its flowers. To keep the garden looking tidy, pull out the dead plants, and mulch the area or transplant a second crop in its place. If you don't want a second crop of chamomile, try an edible flower such as dwarf nasturtium (*Tropaeolum minus*), Johnny-jump-ups (*Viola tricolor*), or sweet alyssum (*Lobularia maritima*), which feeds beneficial insects.

smart tip

MANAGING INVASIVE MINT PLANTS

DIVIDE THE AREA INTO SQUARES THAT MEASURE AT LEAST 2 FEET ON EACH SIDE. PLANT ONE MINT IN THE CENTER OF EACH OF THESE AREAS, AND MULCH THE SPACE WITH STRAW OR ANOTHER NON-WEEDY MATERIAL. AT MONTHLY INTERVALS DURING THE SUMMER, PULL BACK THE MULCH, AND USE A SHARP SPADE TO CUT INTO THE SOIL AT THE DIVISIONS OF THE SQUARES. BY THE SECOND YEAR, YOU'LL HAVE TO PRUNE OFF TRAVELING STEMS, WHICH, ALONG WITH UNDERGROUND RHIZOMES, WILL BE TRYING TO MOVE INTO THEIR NEIGHBORS' AREAS.

MANY HERBS are so versatile that they can be used in teas and cooking as well as in medicines and cosmetics.

A WINDOW BOX of fresh herbs is delightful outside a kitchen window where it can be tended regularly.

CONTAINERS make an ideal growing environment for many herbs and offer more flexibility because they can be moved.

CONTAINER GARDENING

Herbs are wonderful container plants. The qualities that make container gardening a bit more demanding than growing in the soil are often inconsequential or even beneficial for many herbs. For example, the soil in containers dries out quite quickly. Depending on conditions, many pots must be watered at least once, if not twice, a day. Fast-growing annual herbs, such as basil and chervil, require as much water as vegetable plants. But the heat-loving Mediterranean herbs—oregano, thyme, and rosemary—all welcome a bit of drying between watering.

Vegetables in containers normally require fertilization every week to ten days. Again, this will be true for some of the fast-growing annual herbs, but perennials such as tarragon, rosemary, thyme, oregano, and sage are less demanding. They require supplemental feeding, but less frequently. Use a mixture of liquid seaweed and fish emulsion once a month. If the leaves begin to yellow, fertilize container-grown herbs once every two weeks.

Containers have the virtue of being adaptable, too. You can move them to areas where they are needed most or where the environment suits them best. For example,

when you're serving iced tea, set a pot of lemon verbena (*Aloysia triphylla*) on the table to use as a garnish, or set out a pot of basil when you have a pizza party.

smart tip

USE SMALL CONTAINERS TO CONTROL GROWTH

SMALL CONTAINERS CAN STUNT PLANTS. WHEN PLANTS BECOME ROOTBOUND, THEY SLOW THEIR TOP GROWTH ACCORDINGLY. IN THE CASE OF VEGETABLES OR FLOWERS, THIS IS RARELY DESIRABLE. HOWEVER, GIVEN THAT A ROSEMARY (ROSMARINUS OFFICINALIS) CAN GROW INTO A SHRUB WITHIN TWO OR THREE YEARS, A SINGLE SPRIG OF LEMON GRASS (CYMBOPOGON CITRATUS) CAN BECOME A 3-FOOT-WIDE THICKET IN A SINGLE SUMMER, AND OREGANO AND THYME CAN TAKE OVER AN AREA SEVERAL FEET IN ALL DIRECTIONS, SOME DWARFING ISN'T ALL BAD.

HERBAL VINEGARS, honeys, and jams make wonderful gifts from your garden that friends will treasure.

For maximum flexibility, site this garden where part of it will receive full sun and part of it will receive several hours of shade or filtered sun a day; the soil should be well drained. If you don't have such a spot, split the herb garden into two areas: one in full sun and one with shade or filtered sun. As in the kitchen herb garden, use the perennials to form the backbone structure of the garden, and leave enough space between them to plant annuals.

Drying and Freezing Herbs

Once you start growing herbs successfully, you may want to preserve some for winter use. With a broad enough selection, you can make numerous combinations of both dried and frozen herbs. But begin by simply preserving the herbs you use most frequently.

smart tip

HARVESTING HERBS FOR PRESERVING

IN MOST CASES, IT'S BEST TO HARVEST HERBS FOR PRESERVING IN THE MORNING, AFTER THE DEW HAS DRIED. RINSE THEM QUICKLY AND SHAKE OFF THE EXTRA WATER. IF YOU INTEND TO DRY THEM, TRY NOT TO BRUISE OR BEND THE LEAVES. LAY THE HERBS ON ABSORBENT CLOTH OR PAPER TOWELS TO SOAK UP ADDITIONAL MOISTURE. WHEN THEIR SURFACES ARE DRY, YOU CAN CONTINUE WITH THE PRESERVING PROCESS.

A GARDEN OF TREASURES

Herbal products are another luxury that herb growers can give themselves, as well as to their friends and family. In the following pages, you'll learn how to make some of the most basic items such as potpourris, infusions (very strong teas covered while steeped), and skin lotions. But the first step is growing as many ingredients as possible.

Begin your "Treasures Garden" by listing all of the herbs you'll want to use in various preparations. You'll quickly see that most herbs can play several roles. Mint and chamomile, for example, are as important as tea herbs as they are for beauty preparations. Calendula flowers are as useful in a salad or fresh bouquet as in a skin salve, and lavender can be used in everything from baked goods to teas, dried arrangements, potpourris, and antiseptic skin lotions.

340

Drying Herbs. Drying is the easiest way to preserve herbs. Most herbs are dried the same way as flowers, hung upside down in a dark dry area with good air circulation. If dust can get into the drying area, drape cheese-cloth or floating row cover material over the herbs to keep them clean during the drying process. When you are drying plants for their seeds, en-close the ripe flower heads in small paper bags before you hang them. As the seeds dry, they'll drop into the bag.

Delicate herbs such as chamomile dry best on screens. As shown in the drawing below, it's important to allow for good air circulation under as well as over the screens. If you are using old window screens, keep your herbs clean by covering the screening with cheesecloth or row cover material. Use upturned glasses to hold a second layer of material above the herbs. This layer protects against dust and stray insects.

Making herbal products seems like a big undertaking until you actually do it. But once you get into the habit of routinely drying and preserving various herbs and flowers

smart tip

FREEZING HERB STEMS

FREEZING RETAINS EVEN MORE FLAVOR AND COLOR AND IS THE ONLY WAY TO MAINTAIN THE QUALITY OF DELICATE HERBS SUCH AS CORIANDER AND CHERVIL. IF YOU ARE FREEZING WHOLE STEMS OF PLANTS SUCH AS PARSLEY, SIMPLY LAY THEM ON COOKIE SHEETS IN THE FREEZER. WHEN THEY HAVE FROZEN, PACK THEM INTO REUSABLE PLASTIC BAGS OR TUBS, LABEL AND STORE UNTIL YOU NEED TO REMOVE A STEM OR TWO.

when they are at their peak, you'll discover how easy it is to put a few gifts together on a rainy fall day.

Dried arrangements are lovely mementos of the previous summer. Dry flowers for them, of course, but don't neglect the herb garden when you are looking for materials for these bouquets. Bee balm (*Monarda didyma*), lavender cotton (*Santolina chamaecyparissus*), lavender, rue (*Ruta graveolens*), sage (*Salvia officinalis*), and tansy (*Tanacetum vulgare* var. *crispum*) all make wonderful additions to winter bouquets.

DRYING CHAMOMILE

USE SCREENS to dry your most delicate herbs, such as chamomile. Use coated or nylon screening rather than aluminum, which could give an off flavor to the herbs. Rinse it after every use with a 10 percent bleach solution; then with clear water. If insects fly under the top covering, cut it so that it is large enough to fold under the boards used as feet.

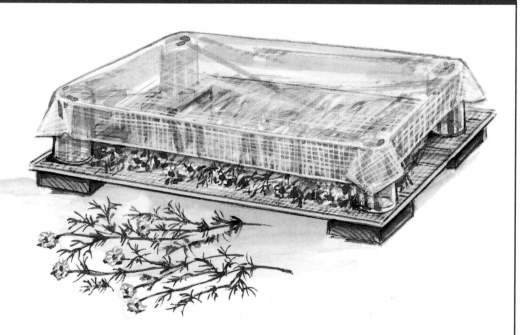

18 fruit trees

Growing fruit adds new dimensions to your gardening. You'll be required to learn some new skills, but the visual and edible benefits make it well worth the effort. Most fruiting plants make ideal focal points for the landscape. A pair of apple trees can mark the entryway to the backyard; a neatly trellised row of raspberries can define one side of the vegetable garden; blueberries can make a double-duty foundation planting; and kiwi vines can add interest to a garage wall. Good planning ensures both blooms and fruit for a long stretch, and, as you'll quickly discover, yields of fruiting plants are generally high. All the attention you give to fruiting plants reaps great rewards. But the only way to discover this is to take courage in hand and get started.

CITRUS TREES are easy to grow in the right climate but can be disappointing in areas that occasionally get frost.

SELECTING FRUIT TREES

The flavor of homegrown fruit is a revelation for many people. Even experienced vegetable gardeners who expect to taste the difference between store-bought winter tomatoes and their homegrown summer bounty are surprised to find that the difference in fruit can be just as dramatic.

Homegrown fruit is picked when it is naturally ripe, and as with vegetables, home gardeners can choose cultivars for flavor rather than shipping characteristics.

When you think of growing fruit, you may visualize a bowl of strawberries covered with a dollop of sweet whipped cream, or jars of brandied peaches, apple pies, or blueberry muffins. But whatever your tastes, your first task as a fruit grower is to learn whether the fruits you want to grow will thrive in your area, and if so, which cultivars are the best choice to plant.

Environmental Considerations

Climate determines whether or not you can grow a particular fruit. For example, though few Vermonters expect to be able to grow oranges or bananas in their backyards, they are usually surprised to learn that sweet cherries are beyond their climatic reach. Similarly, it is a rare apple

that can survive and produce in Zones 8b, 9, and 10. Two factors are responsible for plants' climatic preferences—their tolerance to temperature extremes and their requirements for certain numbers of "chilling" or "heating" hours. (See "Heating and Chilling Hours," opposite.)

Trees and shrubs are similar to other plants in their ability to stand extreme cold or heat. A prolonged period of below-freezing temperatures is as certain to kill a lemon tree as it is to kill a tomato plant. But just as some tomato cultivars can stand cooler temperatures than others, certain fruit cultivars are bred to tolerate warmer or colder conditions where January thaws are common.

Hardiness Ratings Do Not Tell the Full Story. Fruit cultivars are given hardiness ratings, just as other perennials. However, the hardiness rating doesn't tell the whole story. No matter where you live, try to buy plants that have been raised in your region. This is particularly important in Zones 3, 4, and 5a, because conditions within these zones can vary so much as a consequence of location. In the Northeast, temperatures fluctuate widely during the winter and early spring, but in the Midwest and prairie provinces of Canada, they are much more stable. Because alternating thaws and freezes are much harder on plants than a period of steady cold, trees grown in the Midwest sometimes have difficulty adjusting to New England conditions. In Massachusetts for example, January thaws are common, but they're rare in northern Michigan.

Pollinators

The flowers of most apples, pears, blueberries, and sweet cherry cultivars are "self-infertile," meaning that they cannot pollinate themselves. Instead, insects and other pollinators must fertilize them with pollen from an entirely different cultivar. To make this even more complicated, certain cultivars can pollinate one another, but others can't.

Check for Compatibility. When you buy fruit plants, check with the nursery or mail-order distributor to learn which plants and trees to pair with which, and be sure to buy those pollenizers at the same time. Some growers also graft, or attach, selected scion (or top growth) branches of different cultivars to the top of their trees. However, grafting is not always reliable, and it is difficult to obtain predictable results. For inexperienced fruit growers, it is usually recommended to begin by growing compatible trees, then move on to grafted trees.

HEATING AND CHILLING HOURS

FRUITING PLANTS require sustained cold or warm temperatures. "Heating hours" are the number of hours above 65°F to which a plant is exposed. If the heating requirements are not met, the plant will decline, and in some cases, fruit will not develop or mature.

"Chilling hours" are the number of hours below 45°F that a plant experiences. If a plant is not exposed to adequate chilling hours, it will not be able to break dormancy in the spring. Because the plant cannot leaf out, it dies. The lack of an appropriate number of chilling hours is usually the culprit when a proven northern cultivar fails to grow in a southern location.

You may find that various cultivars of the same species have different chilling-hour requirements. When you buy a plant, ask how many chilling hours the cultivar requires. If the nursery lists them as low, moderate, or high, translate these terms to mean 300 to 400 hours for a low, 400 to 700 for moderate, and 700 to 1,000 for a high requirement. For the average chilling hours in your area, check with the Cooperative Extension Service or local horticultural societies.

CHOOSE A DWARF or semidwarf tree if working on a ladder bothers you. Harvesting safety will never be a concern.

Maintenance Requirements

Some tree species are harder to successfully grow than others. In Zone 5, for example, many peaches are prone to frost damage at either end of the season. If you choose to grow peaches in Zone 5 anyway, plan from the beginning to take the steps necessary to protect them from frost.

Similarly, some apple cultivars are relatively pest- and disease-free while others are more susceptible. If you know the characteristics of a cultivar before you buy, you can choose to prepare well for potential problems or sidestep them by selecting a more resistant plant.

Research your choices before you purchase any fruiting plant. Begin this process by searching out other fruit growers through local gardeners' associations. Growers in your own area will be able to tell you specifics about the performance of various trees in your climate.

Other Considerations. Ripe soft fruits such as peaches and nectarines attract yellow jackets, so try to pick up all of the fallen fruit as soon as possible. You may also want to plant the trees in a remote part of the yard so that children will be less likely to play in the area and risk getting stung. Even if you have to stretch your imagination, try to think of all the possible annoyances your fruit can give you; then develop strategies to avoid these problems.

Big or Small?

Think carefully about the mature size of the trees you select. In most parts of the country, you can choose between dwarf, semidwarf, and standard trees. This choice will not only affect the design of your yard, it will also affect the number of years before the tree bears fruit, and in many cases, the type and amount of care it requires.

Tree sizes can vary naturally, without any help from breeders. The smallest naturally growing fruit trees, which are called "genetic dwarfs," grow only 10 to 15 feet high, making them easy to maintain. However, the flavor of their fruit usually leaves much to be desired, and they tend to be quite susceptible to diseases.

In the early 1900s, horticulturists at the East Malling Research Station in England discovered that when they grafted top growth from a standard tree (with good flavor) onto the roots of a genetic dwarf, the fruit remained the same size, but the tree grew only as large as the dwarf. In some cases, resistance to diseases increased too. Since then, breeders have developed several different dwarf rootstocks and have worked with combinations of rootstocks and scions. Each combination produces a different result, but growers can tell you what to expect.

Dwarf trees have several advantages. Because they are so small, it is easy to give them adequate attention. Their yields per tree are lower, but a well-tended orchard of dwarf trees gives as much or more fruit per square foot as an orchard of standard trees. Picking is easier and safer too. With a small stepladder, you can reach the fruit on every branch.

But there are some disadvantages to dwarf trees. Most dwarf trees have a shorter life expectancy than standards of the same cultivar, and almost all of them are shallow

rooted. Consequently, they don't survive harsh winters well. Their roots are also brittle; a strong windstorm can knock over a mature dwarf tree. To counteract this, commercial orchardists support their dwarf trees with post-and-cable-trellises.

Growers have simply adapted to the shorter life span by planting new orchards more frequently. And in the North, where dwarfs really don't survive well, gardeners and orchardists use semidwarf rootstocks or work with dwarfing interstems. To create a tree with a dwarfing interstem, breeders begin by growing a standard, long-lived, hardy rootstock. They graft a genetic dwarf scion onto this rootstock and let it grow for a year or two. The next step is to prune off all of the branches and the top of the genetic dwarf and graft a scion of the selected cultivar onto the top of the interstem. The resulting tree is usually the size of a semidwarf.

While dwarf trees typically grow anywhere from 20 to 60 percent the size of a standard of the same cultivar, semi-dwarf trees usually grow to about 75 percent of that size. If you live in Zones 3 to 5a, the extra size is worth it when compared with losing a tree to bad weather.

Trees in Containers

Many dwarf fruit trees grow well in containers. Ask your nursery or supplier for cultivar and rootstock combinations that thrive with a restricted root space.

Both plastic and wooden containers are appropriate choices. Because container soils dry so quickly, look for

THESE 'RED PIXIE' apples are one of the many cultivars that grow well in containers and give a small yield.

containers with the thickest walls possible. Most dwarf trees will grow in a pot that is 2 feet wide by 3 feet deep, although more room never hurts. Because fruit-bearing trees can be top-heavy, the best containers are wide enough at the bottom that they won't tip over in the wind.

Soil drainage is essential. If you are planting in an old barrel or other container, drill several $\frac{3}{4}$-inch holes in the bottom. Add a layer of nylon window screening, and then fill the container with a nutrient-rich and quickly draining soil mix.

THE VERSATILITY of dwarf trees, shown from left to right, training an apple tree on a dwarf rootstock; a tabletop apple tree, 'Red Grieve'; and a stepover apple tree, 'Pixie'.

smart tip

PROTECT CONTAINER-GROWN PLANTS FROM FROST

You can protect the roots of your trees over the winter if temperatures go below freezing in your area. The best solution is to sink the pots in soil during the late fall. Or you can move the container to a garage or shed once the plant is dormant. If neither option is possible, move the container to a somewhat protected niche and pile plastic bags filled with dead leaves all around the container. Tie a strong plastic tarp around this construction to hold it in place. In spring, wait until heavy frosts have subsided to bring the container out in the open.

PLANTING

Choosing where your fruit trees will grow is the first step in planting them. Although this might seem straightforward, determining the location of a tree is as important as deciding what species and cultivars to grow. If possible, take a year to make this decision. During that time, you'll be able to observe various locations closely. You will know where frost comes first and last, where puddles form in heavy rainstorms, and where winds are strong, moderated, or stagnant. In cases where you simply do not have this much time to learn about the site, try to take the following characteristics into consideration.

Exposure. Most fruiting plants require full sun to bear well. But the topic certainly doesn't end there. Full sun on a southern slope is far different than full sun on a northern one, and your plants will respond accordingly. If you live in an area with late spring frosts, which can damage the blooms of a tree, plant on a northern slope if at all possible. Because it is cooler there than on a southern slope or on level ground, trees will be a little later in

CHOOSE LOCATIONS for each of your fruit trees carefully to minimize the chance of environmental damage.

blooming. As a result, there will be fewer years when you need to protect the trees from late spring frosts.

Space. Adequate space is essential for fruiting plants. Plan to space trees as far apart from each other as they will be tall when they are mature. If trees of different heights are planted next to each other, use the taller one as your guide.

Soil Characteristics. Fruit trees grow in the same location, with the same soil, for anywhere from 15 to 50 years. You won't be able to do much to improve the soil once the trees are planted, so choose the site with the best possible soil in the beginning.

Look for soil that has good drainage, a pH of 6.0 to 6.8, and moderate to high fertility levels with a high concentration of organic matter content. Because so few garden soils are totally ideal, you'll probably have to do some soil improvement before planting. (See Chapter 11, "Soil and Water," beginning on page 212.) Only two circumstances should prevent you from planting fruit in an area: one is a pH that is more than one point away from ideal, and the other is extremely poor drainage. Both of these problems will be so difficult to manage over the long term that they may seem like a losing battle not worth waging.

Air Drainage. Many fungal diseases become more troublesome on plants growing where the air is stagnant. Fruit trees are especially susceptible to fungi, so try to site them where the prevailing breeze will rustle through their leaves each day.

Planting Considerations. For decades, common knowledge asserted that the best way to plant a tree was to dig a big hole with straight sides and then amend the soil

AIR DRAINAGE

COLD AIR always sinks to the lowest possible level, so the placement of your fruit plants can either protect them or make them more vulnerable to frost damage. Plants sited at the bottom of a slope are likely to suffer from light frosts, while those sited midway down the slope may be protected.

The wise use of windbreaks such as buildings or other plants can also moderate temperatures.

from the hole with compost, peat moss, or sand before using it to backfill around the roots. Today, however, researchers report that many trees planted this way may have difficulty establishing themselves because their roots tend to stay in the area where the soil has been modified. Because there is plenty of nourishment right there, the roots do not spread out in search of food and water. As a result, the best contemporary advice contradicts the old knowledge.

Do not dig the hole too deep, and remember that trees often sink a bit after they are planted. Try to plant your

trees at the same depth that they were growing at the nursery. This level will be easy to determine if the tree is balled and burlapped or in a container. Even if it is bareroot, you should be able to see the soil mark on the trunk. Proper planting depth is particularly important in the case of grafts and interstems.

Always plant so that the graft union is 2 to 3 inches above the soil, and never cover the graft with mulch. Ask the nursery how deep to plant the rootstock because it can vary depending on cultivar, interstem, and rootstock.

THE HEDGE EFFECT

HEDGES make excellent windbreaks because they trap some of the air coming through them but, unlike walls, do not create a turbulent area on the far side.

Plant your fruits far enough away from the hedge so they still get good light exposure.

smart tip

HOW TO PLANT FRUIT TREES

Make a hole with sloping sides, as deep as the depth of the root ball and twice that width at the top. To help the roots penetrate the surrounding soil, use a handheld claw to roughen up the sides of the hole. After the tree is in position, backfill with the soil from the hole without amending it in any way. Form a mound of soil 12 to 18 inches from the trunk to create a 6-inch deep basin for watering. As always, water deeply when the hole is half to three-quarters filled and again when the backfilling is complete.

PRUNING

Pruning intimidates most new gardeners, primarily because it seems so irrevocable. Many people worry that they will cut off a necessary branch, leaving their tree without a proper framework. But the fearful should take heart. If you pay attention to what you are doing, it is unlikely that you will cut off an important branch—even if you did, trees have the capacity to grow more than one limb in roughly the same area. Remember, too, that if pruning required the IQ of a genius or a sixth sense about plants, there would be far fewer apples in the world. Pruning, despite its importance to the tree, is not difficult to learn to do successfully. But pruning does require some

thought. Before you begin, think about the purposes of your pruning task, the ways that the tree will react to various cuts, and the best timing for your pruning operation.

Purposes of Pruning. Good pruning strengthens the tree and makes it more productive. When the tree is young, you prune to give it a strong framework of scaffold branches that are positioned to allow both light and air into the center of the tree.

As the tree matures, you prune to keep the tree from growing too large; to maintain a balance between shoot and fruit production; to remove weak, damaged, or diseased growth; to allow air and light to reach all parts of the tree; and to stimulate new growth where you want it.

The Consequences of Pruning. Plant growth is regulated by chemical compounds called auxins. They promote growth at the tip of the stem but inhibit the development of buds lower down on that stem. This effect, known as apical dominance, is what prevents a tree from growing a new limb at every bud. When you prune off the tip of a stem, you remove the site where the auxin is produced and stimulate once-dormant buds to develop. By choosing how much of a branch to remove, you can direct the plant's response. For example, pinching off the very tip of the branch encourages branching just

TREE ANATOMY

PRUNING is much easier once you can identify the various parts of a tree. Though each tree is different, you'll see many of these structures on your own tree.

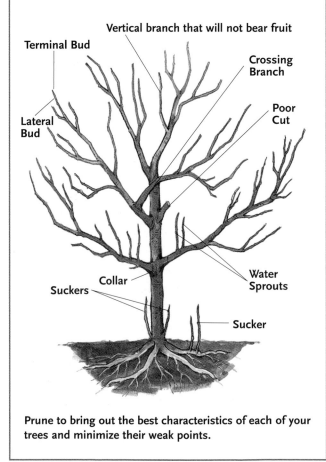

Terminal Bud

Vertical branch that will not bear fruit

Crossing Branch

Poor Cut

Lateral Bud

Water Sprouts

Collar

Suckers

Sucker

Prune to bring out the best characteristics of each of your trees and minimize their weak points.

WINTER is the perfect time to study the form of your trees and decide how best to prune them.

TREE SHAPES

THE SHAPE OF YOUR TREE will be determined in large part by the type of tree it is. In general, dwarf and semidwarf trees are best pruned as vase or modified central leader trees, while standard trees can be pruned as central leader or modified central leader trees.

Central leader pruning depends on well-placed scaffold branches to allow light into the center.

Modified central leader pruning requires you to cut out the central leader after the fourth or fifth scaffold branch grows.

Vase, or open, pruning is done by cutting back the leader to form a completely open center.

below the pinched area. When you shorten a stem by cutting back by a third, several of the buds just below the cut will begin to grow. To promote even more vigorous growth of a bud very low on the branch, prune off two-thirds of the stem. In general, the buds nearest the cut make the most vigorous upright growth, while those that grow lower down on the stem make wider angles. The bud that develops nearest the tip of the stem will eventually become a dominant branch and produce auxins to inhibit the growth of buds below it. All pruning cuts used to cut back stems are referred to as heading cuts.

Thinning cuts are those that totally remove growth. Use thinning cuts to prune off weak or poorly positioned branches, water sprouts, and sprouts from the rootstock. When you remove a branch along a stem, the tip of the stem grows even more vigorously and latent buds are

less likely to develop. If you want the stem to form a branch in a different spot than the branch that you pruned, remove the site of auxin production by heading back the stem an appropriate distance, as discussed at left.

Fruit seeds also produce auxins that affect subsequent growth. If too many auxins are present, such as when the tree has produced a large crop, far fewer flower buds will sprout for the next year's crop. This is why some trees bear heavily only in alternate years.

Thinning, or pruning off, the developing fruit not only evens out production from one year to the next, but it also increases the size of the remaining fruit. It is best to thin the fruit twice, once just after the blossoms have dropped and again just after the June fruit drop. As a general rule, allow a space two to three times the size of the mature fruit between the fruit you leave on the tree.

BEFORE PRUNING. The branches of this peach tree are too closely spaced and prevent light from reaching the center of the tree.

AFTER PRUNING. The same peach tree has been opened up so light can reach the center, eliminating weak or misplaced growth.

smart tip

PRUNING WHIPS

IF YOUR TREE IS A "WHIP" (ALL OF THE BRANCHES HAVE ALREADY BEEN PRUNED OFF), PLANT IT AND THEN HEAD BACK THE STEM TO ABOUT TWO TO THREE FEET ABOVE THE SOIL SURFACE. BY HEADING BACK THE CENTRAL STEM, YOU WILL ENCOURAGE THE GROWTH OF BUDS LOWER DOWN. THE TOPMOST BUD THAT DEVELOPS WILL EVENTUALLY BECOME THE CENTRAL LEADER AND EXERT APICAL DOMINANCE OVER LOWER BUDS. HOWEVER, THE TREE WILL DEVELOP BRANCHES THAT CAN BECOME SCAFFOLD LIMBS BEFORE THE TOP BUD EXERTS APICAL DOMINANCE OVER THE LOWER BUDS.

Timing. Most heading-cut pruning on apples, pears, and quinces is done in late winter or very early spring, while the plant is still dormant. When the tree comes out of dormancy, the lack of auxin production at the headed-back stem tips causes lateral buds to grow vigorously.

In contrast, very little to no dormant pruning is done on peaches and nectarines because it promotes early blooming. The first defense against frost damage to these trees is to wait until the tree is already in bloom to make heading cuts. If done at this time, the tree still responds by producing new growth along branches that have been headed back.

Pruning in summer reduces rather than stimulates regrowth. You can use this to your advantage when you are making thinning cuts to bring light into the center of the tree or to remove unwanted growth. Heading cuts done in midsummer can have the effect of stimulating the formation of flower buds rather than those that will grow into shoots. Growers use this method to promote maximum fruiting on espalier-trained trees.

Preparing for Pruning. Before taking so much as the first cut on your tree, learn about its natural growth habits and the shape that most growers give it. As illustrated on page 351, the three most common ways to prune and train fruit trees are central leader, modified central leader, and vase, or open, shape. In general, dwarf and semi-dwarf trees are pruned to a vase or modified central leader, while standards are frequently pruned to a modified central leader or central leader.

In the past, gardeners were advised to prune off all the branches of a young tree when they planted it to allow roots to grow before leaves did. However, current knowledge about plant growth means that growers now give very different instructions.

If the tree is "feathered," meaning that it already has some branches, plant it, and then look carefully at it. Your goal is to retain any well-positioned branches. Pruning, even if done when the tree is dormant, stimulates growth near the cuts but sets back the tree's overall growth. Ideally, the bottom branch will be about 2 feet above the soil surface and will be growing at an angle of at least 40 degrees from the trunk. If as many as two other branches are spaced 6 to 8 inches apart on the trunk, grow or can be trained to grow at a 40-degree or greater angle, and are positioned in a neat spiral around the trunk, you'll want to retain them too. Head back each of the retained branches to a few inches, always cutting just above an outward-facing bud unless the tree is a dwarf that you are growing in a trellised system. Thin branches that are growing too closely to a desired branch, that do not help to form a spiral around the trunk, or grow at such a strong angle that they cannot be trained to a more horizontal position. Head back the central leader to about 3 feet from the soil surface.

In the second year, pruning is dictated by the tree's form. If you are growing a central-leader tree, head back the leader again so that a new tier of scaffold branches will develop; thin out undesirable growth; and head back the branches. Cut back about a third of the previous year's growth from the central leader.

With a modified central-leader tree, cut back the central leader to just above the fourth scaffold branch. If the tree lacks this branch, head back the central leader. By the third season, there will be enough branches for you to cut back the central leader. Head back the branches you have decided to keep, and then thin out any undesirable growth.

With trees with open centers, the central leader is usually removed during the second year. By this time, the trees usually have grown the three branches that form the vase shape. Thin undesirable growth.

You can widen branch angles in several ways. Insert a wooden toothpick between a developing branch and the leader to force the branch into a more horizontal form, or weight the branch with wooden clothespins. You can hang weights from larger branches or tie these branches to weights on the ground.

Pruning Mature Trees. Trees require pruning at all growth stages. Good pruning helps to maintain the health of the tree, keeps it a manageable size, and promotes top-quality fruit every year. Make it a habit to cut out diseased branches while the tree is dormant, unless it is a peach or nectarine (these should be pruned when the trees are actively growing.) As the tree ages, you'll make most of your thinning cuts, many of which can be done in summer, toward the top of the tree and most of the heading cuts toward the bottom.

USE A SMALL PRUNING SAW to cut branches that are no thicker than ½ in. thick.

DORMANT PRUNING on a warm winter day can be a highlight of the gardening season.

353

This list of manufacturers and associations is meant to be a general guide to additional industry and product-related sources. It is not intended as a listing of products and manufacturers represented by the photographs in this book.

Decks

AGI Group, Inc.
800-823-6677
www.shuttertime.com
Offers a varied selection of patio umbrellas and retractable awnings.

Arch Wood Protection, Inc.
770-801-6600
www.wolmanizedwood.com
Manufactures pressure-treated wood for decks, landscaping, walkways, gazebos, fences, and picnic tables.

AridDek
877-270-9387
www.ariddek.com
Manufactures aluminum decking and railings.

CableRail/Feeney Architectural Products
800-888-2418
www.cablerail.com
Manufactures a line of standard and custom cable stainless-steel cable assemblies.

California Redwood Association
888-225-7339
www.calredwood.org
A nonprofit trade organization that offers extensive technical information about redwood. The association also has design and how-to help for a variety of outdoor structures.

DekBrands
800-664-2705
www.deckplans.com
Manufactures easy-to-do deck systems, including the award-winning Floating Foundation Deck System.

Deckmaster
800-869-1375
www.deckmaster.com
Manufactures the Hidden Deck Bracket System, its patented deck board fastening system. Its Web site offers additional information about the system, as well as testimonials and reviews.

Dry-B-Lo
800-437-9256
www.dry-b-lo.com
Manufactures aluminum deck drainage systems that keep the space below decks dry.

Procell Decking Systems
251-943-2916
www.procelldeck.com
Manufactures synthetic decking from PVC that's stain- and scratch-resistant.

TAMKO Building Products, Inc.
EverGrain Composite Decking
Elements Decking
800-641-4691
www.tamko.com
www.evergrain.com
www.elementsdecking.com
Manufactures composite decking products using compression molding for a real wood look. Visit the Web site for a photo gallery and distributors in your area.

Trex Company, Inc.
800-289-8739
www.trex.com
Specializes in alternate lumber made from recycled plastic and waste wood.

Wolman Wood Care Products, a div. of Zinsser Co., Inc.
800-556-7737
www.wolman.com
Makes products used to restore, beautify, and protect decks and other exterior wood structures.

Fences, Arbors & Trellises

Carolina Vinyl Products
252-524-5000
www.carolinavp.com

Manufactures a line of PVC products, including fences and fence materials.

CertainTeed Corporation
800-233-8990
www.certainteed.com
Sells numerous types of building materials, including Bufftech fences.

Chain Link Manufacturers Institute
301-596-2583
www.chainlinkinfo.org
Offers a list of approved chain-link retailers and chain-link information.

Elyria Fence Inc.
800-779-7581
www.elyriafence.com
Provides custom fences, trellises, arbors, and decks.

FenceLink
www.fencelink.com
A directory of fence manufacturers, distributors, and associations for all types and parts of fences.

The Flood Company
800-321-3444
www.floodco.com
Makes a variety of paint-related products, including penetrating stains, sealers, wood renewers, and cleansers.

Heritage Vinyl Products
800-736-5143 ext. 2944
www.heritagevinyl.com
Maufactures fencing made from polyvinyl chloride.

Hoover Fence
330-358-2624
www.hooverfence.com
Sells metal, vinyl, chain-link, and specialty fences.

Kroy Building Products
800-933-5769
www.kroybp.com
Manufactures vinyl fencing and deck materials and offers free technical advice.

Southern Pine Council
504-443-4464
www.southernpine.com

A nonprofit trade organization that offers construction tips, complete project plans, and other helpful information on pine and its uses.

Stanco Incorporated
800-443-7826
www.stanco-inc.com
Offers a full line of fences, including privacy, decorative, and ranch.

Landscaping

American Nursery and Landscape Association (ANLA)
202-789-2900
www.anla.org
Offers educational seminars and other services to its members. The Web site offers a way to locate garden centers and landscape designers.

Garden Supplies Guide
www.gardeningsuppliesguide.com
Online guide to a variety of suppliers of garden-tool manufacturers.

Garden Web
www.gardenweb.com
Boasts that it is home to the Internet's garden community. Its Web site offers seed and plant exchanges, plant reference guides, and links to shopping sites.

Gardens Alive!
513-354-1482
www.gardensalive.com
A mail-order company that offers environmentally responsible products for lawns and gardens.

Home, Garden, and Patio Outlet
913-422-7792.
www.homegardenandpatio.com
Retail source for home, garden, and patio furniture and decor, as well as landscaping tools and products.

Hunter Industries
760-744-5240
www.hunterindustries.com
Manufactures irrigation and sprinkler systems. Its Web site offers a product list and installation instructions.

Landscape USA
www.landscapeusa.com
800-966-1033
Sells landscaping, irrigation, and gardening supplies.

Park Seed Company
www.parkseed.com
Offers a catalog of herb and plant seeds, bulbs, and gardening supplies. All of their products are backed by an expansive guarantee.

Peaceful Valley Farm & Garden Supply
530-272-4769
www.groworganic.com
Offers tools and supplies for organic farming and gardening, including in-ground irrigation supplies, pest-control products, and soil test kits.

The Scotts Company
www.scotts.com
Offers a wide array of do-it-yourself lawn and garden consumer products.

Seeds of Change
888-762-7333
www.seedsofchange.com
*Offers everything from seeds to garden-
ing tools and strives to help preserve
biodiversity and promote sustainable,
organic agriculture.*

The Toro Company
888-384-9939
www.toro.com
*Manufactures outdoor power equip-
ment, including mowers, lawn tractors,
zero-turn-radius mowers, and irrigation
products.*

Woodstream Corporation
800-800-1819
www.woodstream.com
*Manufactures a variety of natural and
organic Safer® Brand products for lawn
care, gardening, and pest control.*

Masonry

Buechel Stone Corp.
800-236-4473
www.buechelstone.com
*Provides natural, quarried stone from
select areas of the United States. Its
product line includes patio stone, accent
boulders, and custom-cut stones for
steps.*

Cast Stone Institute
717-272-3744
www.caststone.org
*A non-profit trade organization that
aims to improve the quality of cast
stone.*

The Colonial Stoneyard
978-448-3329
www.colonialstoneyard.com
*Specializes in natural stone and stone
products for landscaping projects. The
company claims that it has the right
stone to match anyone's style or budget.*

Cooley Stone
570-278-2355
www.cooleystone.net
*Offers landscaping options with stone from
quarries in northeastern Pennsylvania.*

High Plains Stone
303-791-1862
www.highplainsstone.com
*Provides builders with a selection of
building, masonry, and landscape stone
from across America. The company's
Web site includes a how-to section.*

Ideal Concrete Block Company, Inc.
800-444-7287
www.idealconcreteblock.com
*Offers an assortment of concrete pavers
and landscape retaining walls.*

Learning Stone
www.aboutstone.org
*Offers a number of links to various stone
resources. Its Web site also features a
stone message board where visitors can
read and write posts on the subject of
stonework.*

Lemke Stone, Inc.
262-502-1579
www.lemkestone.com
*Specializes in cobblestone, boulders,
Lannon stone, and Bedford stone. The
company supplies DIY homeowners as
well as professional landscapers, ma-
sons, and contractors.*

Little Meadows Stone Company
866-305-3250
www.littlemeadowsstone.com
*Offers a variety of natural stone for any
landscaping project. The company's
Web site offers a photo gallery of its
products.*

Luck Stone Corporation
800-898-5825
www.luckstone.com
*Manufactures a number of construction
aggregates and architectural stone. The
company's Web site features a product
listing and location guide.*

Marshalltown Company
800-888-0127
www.marshalltown.com
*Sells a variety of quality tools to home-
owners and masonry professionals.*

The Masonry Advisory Council
847-297-6704
www.maconline.org
*Provides the public with general and
technical information about masonry
design and detail. Its Web site contains
articles and a guide to brick selection.*

**National Stone, Sand,
and Gravel Association (NSSGA)**
703-525-8788
www.nssga.org
*Represents the aggregate industries. Its
member companies produce more than*

90 percent of the crushed stone used annually in the United States. Visit the association's Web site for workshop and conference information.

Pools

Anthony & Sylvan
877-891-7946
www.anthonysylvan.com
Provides new pool and spa installations, modernizations of existing pools, equipment, service, supplies, and other backyard extras. Its Web site will direct you to a sales and design center in your area.

Association of Pool and Spa Professionals (APSP)
703-838-0083
www.nspi.org
An international trade association that promotes the safety and proper maintenance of pools and spas. APSP also offers free consumer information on building and maintaining pools and spas.

Cascade Pools
503-620-6174
www.cascadepoolsandspas.com
Manufactures residential in-ground pools in a wide variety of styles.

Comfort Line
888-997-6366
www.comfortlineproducts.com
Manufactures portable spas, saunas, and accessories for indoor or outdoor use.

Custom Pools
www.custompools.com
Designs and builds pools and spas. The company's Web site offers information on residential swimming pools.

Frontgate
888-263-9850
www.frontgate.com
Sells and manufacturers products such as pool and spa accessories, outdoor furniture, and electronics.

Hayward
www.haywardnet.com
Sells a variety of pool purification and circulation equipment including filters, valves, heaters, pumps, cleaners, and Goldline salt chlorinators.

Intermatic, Inc.
815-675-7000
www.intermatic.com
Manufactures a variety of control systems and timers for pools and spas, as well as a line of low-voltage lighting products.

Lombardo Swimming Pool Co.
Phone: 704-847-4648
www.lombardopools.com
Builds in-ground pools that are designed to fit the landscape.

National Swim School Association
www.nationalswimschools.com
A trade organization. Its Web site can direct you to qualified swim schools in your area.

Pacific Pools
716-636-1480
www.pacificpools.com
Manufactures pools with a lifetime warranty.

Sharkline
631-951-9800
www.sharkline.com
An aboveground swimming pool company that manufactures pools, liners, decking systems, and accessories.

Splash Superpools
501-945-4999
www.splashpools.com
Manufactures and sells portable, aboveground pools that are supported by steel for extra durability.

SR Smith
800-824-4387
www.srsmith.com
Manufactures pool accessories such as slides, diving boards, ladders, and rails for residential and commercial pools.

Zodiac Pools, Inc.
www.zodiacpools.com
Offers a variety of automatic pool cleaners, chlorinators, and purifiers. The company also manufacturers a line of aboveground pools available in a variety of sizes and shapes.

Tools

Bosch Power Tools
800-267-2499
www.boschtools.com
Manufactures tools and accessories for a number of trades.

DeWalt Industrial Tools Company
800-433-9258
www.dewalt.com
Sells a wide selection of power tools.

Hitachi Power Tools U.S.A.
3950 Steve Reynolds Blvd.
Norcross, GA 30093
800-829-4752
www.hitachi.com/powertools
Carries an extensive line of heavy-duty electric tools.

Jepson Power Tools, a div. of Ko-shin Electric and Machinery Company
800-456-8665
www.jepsonpowertools.com
Manufactures electric drills, saws, and other tools.

Porter-Cable Corp.
888-848-5175
www.porter-cable.com
Manufactures compressors, electric drills, and other professional power tools.

Ryobi North America
800-525-2579
www.ryobitools.com
Produces portable and bench-top power tools for contractors and DIYers.

The Stanley Works
860-225-5111
www.stanleyworks.com
Manufactures an extensive line of hand and power tools.

Acidic A pH measure less than 7 (neutral), indicating a low level of hydrogen. Woodland plants, including rhododendrons, azaleas, and ferns, do best in slightly acidic soil with a pH between 5 and 7. The pH of acidic soils can be raised by adding lime products.

Aggregate Crushed stone, gravel, or other material added to cement to make concrete or mortar. Gravel and crushed stone are considered coarse aggregate; sand is considered fine aggregate.

Alkaline A pH measure above 7 (neutral), indicating a high level of hydrogen. The pH of alkaline soils can be reduced by adding acidic materials, such as leaf mold or pine needles.

Apex (plural: apices) The tip (tips) of branches or the end buds of a growing plant.

Apical dominance Concentration of growth hormone in the tips of branches.

Arbor An arched, open structure that spans a doorway or provides shelter for a seat. Often covered with vines and used as a garden focal point.

Backfill To fill in an area, such as a planting hole, trench, or around a foundation, using soil or gravel.

Backwash The process of running water through a filter opposite the normal direction of flow in order to flush out contaminants.

Balusters The vertical pieces, generally made of 2x2s, that fill the spaces between rails and posts to create a guardrail.

Balustrade A guardrail, often used around the perimeter of a deck, consisting of balusters, posts, and top and bottom rails.

Base map A drawing or survey that details the location of all property boundaries, structures, slopes, significant plantings, and location of sunrise and sunset. An important first step in landscaping.

Bed joint Horizontal masonry joint, as opposed to a vertical masonry joint (called a head joint). Also called beds.

Berm A mound of earth that directs or retains water. A 6-inch berm built around the drip line of a tree or shrub will create a basin, ensuring that water reaches the plant's roots.

Blind fasteners Clips, brackets, or biscuits used to fasten decking to joists in such a way as to be hidden from view.

Bond stones Support stones that extend through the full thickness of a wall. They are staggered and placed every few feet along the length of the wall for extra strength.

Check valve A valve that permits the flow of water or air in only one direction through a pipe.

Collar The slight swelling that occurs where a branch of a tree or shrub meets the trunk. (see Saddle)

Compost Decomposed organic materials, such as grass clippings, fallen leaves, plant trimmings, and kitchen scraps. The crumbly, black product holds and slowly releases nutrients and water. Rich in earthworms and healthy soil bacteria, it is ideal for amending soil, top-dressing lawns, and mulching beds.

Concrete bonder A material applied to concrete block to help stucco adhere to the surface.

Coping The top, flat layer of a masonry structure. Often ornamental, it also keeps out water, thus preventing the expansion and contraction caused by freezing and thawing of water caught in the seams.

Course A horizontal row of bricks or stones.

Cultivar Short for cultivated variety. A plant variety developed in cultivation, rather than occurring naturally in the wild.

Diatomaceous earth A mineral created from the fossilized remains of ancient marine creatures. Its abrasive quality makes it an excellent control for soft-bodied pests, such as slugs and snails. Use only horticultural grade diatomaceous earth, not the type sold for swimming pools.

Drip irrigation A system that delivers water at a slow rate directly to plant roots, thus ensuring that plants are thoroughly watered, even in clay soils that absorb water at a slow rate. Little or no water is wasted from run-off or evaporation.

Drip line An imaginary line in the soil around a tree or shrub that mirrors the circumference of the canopy above.

Dry wall A stone wall that does not contain mortar.

Emitter Water delivery device on a drip irrigation system.

Erosion feeder A device that allows water to slowly dissolve a sanitizing tablet. Some feeders are connected directly to the circulation system; others simply float on the surface of the pool.

Float A steel, aluminum, or wood object used to smooth the surface of poured concrete by driving large aggregate below the surface.

Footing The concrete base that supports a masonry wall or other structure. It is built below the local frost line to prevent heaving.

Footprint The perimeter of a house or other significant structures, shown on a property survey.

Genus (plural: genera) A closely related group of species sharing similar characteristics and probably evolved from the same ancestors.

Grade The finished level of the ground surrounding a landscaping or construction project.

Green manure A cover crop grown and turned or plowed under the soil to improve its texture and nutrient content.

Gunite A mixture of water, sand, and cement that is applied with a sprayer to form a pool or spa shell.

Hardiness A plant's ability to survive winter cold or summer heat without protection.

Hardscape Parts of a landscape constructed from materials other than plants, such as walks, walls, and trellises, made of wood, stone, or other materials.

Headers Bricks turned horizontal to the stretcher courses.

Humus Decayed organic material rich with nutrients. Its spongy texture holds moisture.

Hydrostatic valve A valve located under the main drain that relieves the buildup of ground water under the pool. Also known as a pressure-release valve.

IPM (Integrated Pest Management) An approach to pest control that utilizes regular monitoring of pests to determine if and when control is needed.

Landscape fabric A synthetic fabric, sometimes water-permeable, spread under paths or mulch to serve as a weed barrier.

Lateral branch A side branch that connects to the trunk or primary branch of a tree or shrub.

Ledger An important structural component used to attach a deck to the side of a house.

Limbing up Pruning a tree's lower branches as high as 30 to 40 feet to allow more light to reach lawn and plants.

Organic matter Plant and animal debris such as leaves, garden trimmings, and manure, in various stages of decomposition.

Pergola A tunnel-like walkway or seating area with columns or posts to support an open "roof" of beams or trelliswork; usually covered with vines.

pH The measure of hydrogen content on a scale of 0 to 14, with 7 considered neutral. A pH above 7 is considered al-kaline, while a pH below 7 is considered acidic. Soil pH affects the availability of nutrients to plants.

Pinching Removing the growing tips of branches or shoots to encourage lush, bushy growth. Removing the end buds sends chemical signals that stimulate the growth of side buds.

Polyethylene A material used as a lining for temporary pools. Extended exposure in sunlight causes it to crack or tear within two to three years.

Potbound Excessive roots encircle the inside of the pot and sometimes emerge from its drainage holes.

Pressure gauge A device that measures air or water pressure.

Pressure-treated lumber Wood that has had preservative forced into it under pressure to make it decay- and insect-resistant.

PVC (Polyvinyl Chloride) Material used for irrigation pipes; also used to make flexible pond liners.

Reinforcing rod Steel bar inside the concrete foundation of a wall, used for extra support.

Riser Vertical boards sometimes placed between stringers and under treads on stairs.

Run wild To allow decking boards to overhang the edges of the deck during construction. When all boards are installed, the ends are then cut off in a straight line.

Saddle The slight swelling where the branch of a tree or shrub meets the trunk. (see Collar)

Setback The legally required distance of a structure or some other feature (a well or a septic system, for example) from the property line.

Softscape The palette of plants used in a landscape, as opposed to the hardscape, which refers to nonliving landscape objects, such as paths, stones, patios, and walls.

Species Among plants, a group that shares many characteristics, including essential flower types, and that can interbreed freely.

Stringer A wide, angled board that supports stair treads and risers.

Weep holes Holes that allow water to seep through a retaining wall so that it does not build up behind the wall.

Weir The barrier in a skimmer over which water flows. A floating weir raises and lowers its level to match the water level in a pool or spa.

359

index

Metric Equivalents

Length

1 inch	25.4mm
1 foot	0.3048m
1 yard	0.9144m
1 mile	1.61km

Area

1 square inch	645mm^2
1 square foot	0.0929m^2
1 square yard	0.8361m^2
1 acre	4046.86m^2
1 square mile	2.59km^2

Volume

1 cubic inch	16.3870cm^3
1 cubic foot	0.03m^3
1 cubic yard	0.77m^3

Common Lumber Equivalents

Sizes: Metric cross sections are so close to their U.S. sizes, as noted below, that for most purposes they may be considered equivalents.

Dimensional lumber	1 x 2	19 x 38mm
	1 x 4	19 x 89mm
	2 x 2	38 x 38mm
	2 x 4	38 x 89mm
	2 x 6	38 x 140mm
	2 x 8	38 x 184mm
	2 x 10	38 x 235mm
	2 x 12	38 x 286mm
Sheet sizes	4 x 8 ft.	1200 x 2400mm
	4 x 10 ft.	1200 x 3000mm
Sheet thicknesses	¼ in.	6mm
	⅜ in.	9mm
	½ in.	12mm
	¾ in.	19mm
Stud/joist spacing	16 in. o.c.	400mm o.c.
	24 in. o.c.	600mm o.c.

Capacity

1 fluid ounce	29.57mL
1 pint	473.18mL
1 quart	0.95L
1 gallon	3.79L

Weight

1 ounce	28.35g
1 pound	0.45kg

Temperature

Fahrenheit = Celsius x 1.8 + 32
Celsius = Fahrenheit - 32 x ⁵/₉

Nail Size and Length

Penny Size	Nail Length
2d	1"
3d	1¼"
4d	1½"
5d	1¾"
6d	2"
7d	2¼"
8d	2½"
9d	2¾"
10d	3"
12d	3¼"
16d	3½"

All how-to and tool shots by Brian C. Nieves/CH, John Parsekian/CH, & Freeze Frame Studio/CH.

Front Cover: *(top left)* Donna Chiarelli; *(vertical insets top to bottom)* Carl Weese & Joe Provey; Jerry Pavia; Donna Chiarelli; desk design: Clemens Jellema; *(horizontal insets right to left);* Brian C. Nieves/CH; Michael S. Thompson; Freeze Frame Studios/CH; John Glover; John Parsekian/CH

Back Cover: *(top to bottom)* Bill Rothschild; John Parsekian/CH; Catriona Tudor Erler; John Parsekian/CH; Brian C. Nieves/CH

page 1: Jerry Pavia **page 2:** Harpur Garden Images, design: Connie Cross **page 3:** Harpur Garden Images, design: David Stevens **page 7:** Derek Fell **page 8:** Jessie Walker **page 9:** Walter Chandoha **pages 10–11:** *top center* Harpur Garden Images, design: Steve Martino; *bottom right* Jessie Walker; *bottom center* Jerry Pavia; *bottom left* Jerry Howard/Positive Images **page 12:** Jerry Pavia **page 13:** *both* Tony Giammarino/Giammarino & Dworkin, left design: Cheryl Palmore **pages 16–17:** Mark Lohman **pages 18–19:** *all* Catriona Tudor Erler **page 22:** Catriona Tudor Erler **page 23:** Mark Lohman **page 24:** Catriona Tudor Erler **page 25:** James Walsh Erler **pages 26–29:** Catriona Tudor Erler **pages 30–31:** Richard Felber **page 33:** Brian Vanden Brink **page 40:** *top right* courtesy of ineedparts.com **page 44:** *top & bottom right*

Stephen E. Munz; *top & bottom center* courtesy of California Redwood Association **page 45:** courtesy of California Redwood Association **page 47:** Harpur Garden Images, design: Jacqueline van der Kloet **page 54:** Jessie Walker **page 76:** *top* davidduncanlivingston.com; *center* courtesy of TimberTech; courtesy of California Redwood Association **page 77:** Brad Simmons Photography **page 109:** Mark Lohman **page 120:** *top & center* Catriona Tudor Erler; *bottom* Crandall & Crandall **page 121:** Mark Lohman **page 138:** *top* courtesy of Stanco; *center* Mark Lohman; *bottom* Brad Simmons Photography **page 139:** Jerry Pavia **page 152:** *top* David Goldberg; *center* Donna Chiarelli/CH; *bottom* courtesy of Lancaster County Barns **page 153:** Brian Vanden Brink, architect: Dominic Mercadante **pages 154–165:** *all* Donna Chiarelli/CH **page 176:** *top & bottom* Andrew Kline/CH; *center* Ed Reeve/Redcover.com **page 177:** Jessie Walker **pages 178–179:** Eric Roth **page 180:** Harpur Garden Images, design: Ulf Nordfjell **pages 182–191:** Donna Chiarelli/CH **page 192:** *top* courtesy of National Pools & Spa Institute; *center* Brian Vanden Brink; *bottom* Steven Wooster/The Garden Picture Library/Photolibrary.com

page 193: Brian Vanden Brink **page 194:** Beth Singer **page 195:** Mark Samu **page 196:** courtesy of National Pools & Spa Institute **page 197:** Randall Perry **page 198:** courtesy of National Pools & Spa Institute **page 199:** *top* Steven Wooster/The Garden

Picture Library/Photolibrary.com; *bottom* Tim Griffith/The Garden Picture Library/Photolibrary.com **pages 200–201:** *left* Brian Vanden Brink; *top right* carolynbates.com; *bottom right* Brad Simmons Photography, design: Barry Wehrman/architect: Greg Staley **page 203:** *top* Richard Felber; *bottom* Gay Bumgarner/Positive Images **page 204:** Bill Rothschild **page 207:** Brian Vanden Brink **page 210:** Bill Rothschild **page 211:** *all* courtesy of Hayward **pages 212–213:** Catriona Tudor Erler **page 214:** *top* Catriona Tudor Erler; *center* Carl Weese/Joe Provey; *bottom* Crandall & Crandall **page 215:** David Cavagnaro **page 216:** Michael S. Thompson **page 217:** John Glover **page 218:** *top left* Neil Soderstrom; *sequence* Carl Weese/Joe Provey **page 219:** *top sequence* Neil Soderstrom; *bottom* Lee Foster/Bruce Coleman/Photoshot **page 220:** Catriona Tudor Erler **page 221:** *top & center* Neil Soderstrom; *bottom* Derek Fell **page 222:** *all* Carl Weese/Joe Provey **page 224:** Neil Soderstrom **page 227:** James Walsh Erler **pages 230–233:** *all* Crandall & Crandall **page 236:** *top & bottom* Neil Soderstrom; *center* Carl Weese/Joe Provey **page 237:** Harpur Garden Images **page 244:** *all* John Glover **page 245:** Derek Fell **page 247:** Richard Shield/Dembinsky Photo Associates **page 248:** Catriona Tudor Erler **page 249:** *all* Neil Soderstrom **pages 250–253:** *all* Catriona Tudor Erler **page 254:** Rick Mastelli **page 255:** *all* Catriona Tudor Erler **page 256:** *top* Brigitte Thomas/The Garden Picture Library/Photolibrary.com; *center & bottom* Derek Fell **page 257:** Walter Chandoha **page 258:** *left* Jerry Howard/Postive Images; *right* Joy Sporr/Bruce Coleman/Photoshot **page 259:** *left* Pam Spaulding/Positive Images; *center* Catriona Tudor Erler; *right* David Cavagnaro **page 260:** *left* David Cavagnaro; *center* Robert Isaacs/Photo Researchers; Robert Falls/Bruce Coleman/Photoshot **page 261:** *top to bottom* John Glover; Lamontagne/The Garden Picture Library/Photolibrary.com; Howard Rice/The Garden Picture Library/Photolibrary.com; Phillip Minnis/Dreamstime.com **page 262:** *left* Eric Crichton/The Garden Picture Library/Photolibrary.com; *right* John Glover **page 263:** *top* Michael Dirr; *bottom* John Glover **page 264:** Patricia Bruno/Positive Images **pages 265–268:** *all* Catriona Tudor Erler **page 269:** *all* Neil

Soderstrom **page 270:** *top* Derek Fell; *center* Renee Lynn/Photo Researchers; *bottom* Crandall & Crandall **page 271:** Harpur Garden Images, design: Jack Lenor Larsen **page 272:** *top* Joe Provey; *bottom right* Karen Williams; *bottom left* Steve Wiest/Jack Fry **page 273:** *top sequence* Dr. Peter Landschoot; *bottom sequence* Dr. Shirley Anderson **page 274:** *top to bottom* Neil Soderstrom; Alexander Kuzovlev/Dreamstime.com; R.J. Erwin/Photo Researchers; Sergey Goruppa/Dreamstime.com **page 275:** *all* Carl Weese/Joe Provey **page 276:** *left & center* Carl Weese/Joe Provey; Nikolay Petkov/Dreamstime.com **pages 277–278:** *all* Carl Weese/Joe Provey **page 279:** *left* Carl Weese/Joe Provey; *right* Karen Williams **pages 280–281:** *all* Carl Weese/Joe Provey **page 283:** *top* Neil Soderstrom; *bottom* Dennis Oblander/Dreamstime.com **page 284:** *top both* Carl Weese/Joe Provey; *bottom* Dallaseventsinc/Dreamstime.com **page 285:** Carl Weese/Joe Provey **page 286:** *left* Charles Mann; *right* Pam Spaulding/Positive Images **page 287:** *top* Jeremy Swinborne/Dreamstime.com; *bottom* Catriona Tudor Erler **page 289:** *left & right* Charles Mann; *center* Morozova Tatiana/Dreamstime.com **page 290:** *top & bottom* Catriona Tudor Erler; *center right* Charles Mann **page 291:** *top & center* Alan & Linda Detrick/Photo Researchers; *bottom* David Goldberg **pages 292–295:** *all* Carole Ottensen **page 296:** *top* Roger Harvey/Photo Horticultural/Garden World; *center* Walter Chandoha; *bottom* Michael Germann/Dreamstime.com **page 297:** Robert Scoverski/Dreamstime.com **page 298:** Walter Chandoha **page 299:** *top* John Glover; *bottom* Jerry Howard/Positive Images **page 300:** *top* Walter Chandoha; *bottom* Jerry Howard/Positive Images **page 301:** *left & center* Photos Horticultural/Photoshot; *right* Phillipe Bonduel/The Garden Picture Library/Photo- library.com **page 302:** *all* Neil Soderstrom **page 303:** *top* John Glover; *bottom* Photos Horticultural/Photoshot.com **page 304:** *left* Walter Chandoha; *right* PhotosHorticultural/Photoshot **page 306:** *top* Neil Soderstrom; *bottom* Walter Chandoha **page 307:** *all* Walter Chandoha **page 308:** Derek Fell **page 309:** *top* Photos Horticultural/Photoshot.com; *bottom* Alan & Linda Detrick/Photo Researchers **page 310:** Walter Chandoha

page 311: Michael S. Thompson **page 312:** Roger Harvey/Photo Horticultural/Garden World **page 313:** *top* Photos Horticultural/Photoshot.com; *bottom* David Cavagnaro **page 314:** *top* David Cavagnaro; *center* Walter Chandoha; *bottom* Derek Fell **page 315:** Walter Chandoha **page 316:** John Glover **page 317:** *top* Carole Ottensen; *bottom* David Cavagnaro **pages 318–319:** Walter Chandoha **page 320:** Derek Fell **page 324:** David Cavagnaro **page 325:** *top left* David Cavagnaro; *top right* Walter Chandoha; *bottom both* Derek Fell **page 329:** Neil Soderstrom **page 330:** *top left* Walter Chandoha; *top center* Neil Soderstrom; *top right* John Glover; *bottom right* Derek Fell; *bottom left* Walter Chandoha **page 331:** *top* David Cavagnaro; *bottom* Marianne Majerus/The Garden Picture Library/Photolibrary.com **page 332:** *left & top right* David Cavagnaro; *bottom right* Derek Fell **page 333:** David Cavagnaro **pages 334–335:** *all* Neil Soderstrom **page 336:** *top* J.S. Sira/The Garden Picture Library/Photolibrary.com; *bottom* John Glover/The Garden Picture Library/Photolibrary.com **page 337:** Walter Chandoha **page 338:** Photos Horticultural/Photoshot.com **page 339:** *left* John Glover; *right* Lynne Brotchie/ The

Garden Picture Library/Photolibrary **page 340:** *top left* Photos Horticultural/Photoshot.com; *bottom right* Derek Fell **page 341:** John Glover **page 342:** *top & bottom* John Glover; *center* Crandall & Crandall **page 343:** Mayer/Le Scanff/The Garden Picture Library/Photolibrary.com **page 344:** John Glover **page 345:** Walter Chandoha **pages 346–347:** *top left* Crandall & Crandall; *top right, bottom right & center* John Glover; *bottom left* Photo Horticultural/Photoshot.com **page 348:** John Glover **pages 350–352:** *all* Walter Chandoha **page 353:** *left* Photo Horticultural/Photoshot.com; *right* Walter Chandoha **page 355:** Jerry Pavia **page 356:** Catriona Tudor Erler **page 366:** Jerry Pavia **page 367:** Harpur Garden Images

Illustrations by:

Vincent Alessi, Vincent Babak, Clarke Barre, Glee Barre, Steve Buchanan, Ron Carboni, Bob Crimi, Warren Cutler, Rick Daskam, Tony Davis, Michele Angle Farrar, Todd Ferris, Craig Franklin, Michael Gellatly, Wendy Smith Griswold, Nancy Hull, Robert LaPointe, Frank Rohrbach, Kathleen Rushton, Paul M. Schumm, Mavis Augustine Torke, Ian Warpole

Have a home improvement, decorating, or gardening project? Look for these and other fine Creative Homeowner books wherever books are sold.

Offers the latest deck designs from four premier deck builders. Over 480 photographs and illustrations. 240 pp. 8½" × 10⅞"
BOOK #: 277382

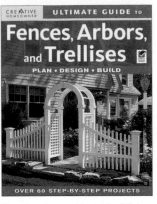

Step-by-step guide to building fences, arbors, and trellises. Over 825 color photos and illustrations. 288 pp.; 8½" × 10⅞"
BOOK #: 277990

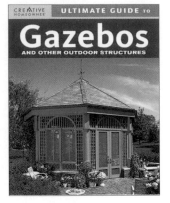

Design and build a gazebo, garden arbor, or pavillion. Over 450 photographs and illustrations. 208 pp.; 8½" × 10⅞"
BOOK #: 277142

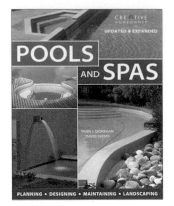

Ideas and advice on the process of planning, building, and maintaining a pool/spa. Over 300 photographs. 240 pp. 8½" × 10⅞"
BOOK #: 277860

Building guides for 10 durable, attractive, and safe play structures; Over 450 illustrations and photos. 192 pp. 8½" × 10⅞"
BOOK #: 277321

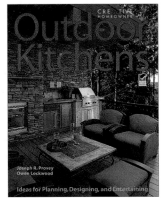

Planning and design advice and easy how-to projects from top designers. Over 335 photographs. 224 pp. 8½" × 10⅞"
BOOK #: 277571

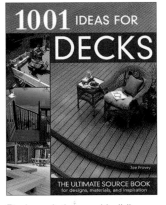

Design solutions and building techniques for decks. Over 450 photographs and illustrations. 287 pp. 8½" × 10⅞"
BOOK #: 277194

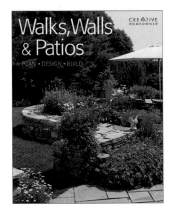

Build landscape structures from concrete, brick, stone. 500 photos and illustrations. 240 pp.; 8½"×10⅞"
BOOK #: 277997

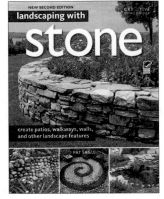

Ideas for incorporating stone into the landscape. Over 335 color photos. 224 pp.; 8½"×10⅞"
BOOK #: 274179

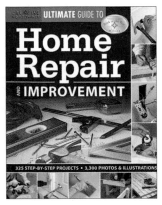

The ultimate home-improvement reference. Over 300 step-by-step projects. 608 pp.; 8½"×10⅞"
BOOK #: 267870

An impressive guide to garden design and plant selection. 950 color photos and illustrations. 384 pp.; 9" × 10"
BOOK #: 274610

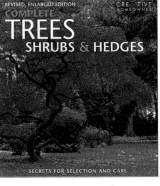

How to select and care for landscaping plants. More than 700 photos. 240 pp.; 9" × 10"
BOOK #: 274222

For more information and to order direct, visit our Web site at **www.creativehomeowner.com**

Sustaining the Earth
An Integrated Approach

G. TYLER MILLER, JR.

Adjunct Professor of Human Ecology
St. Andrews Presbyterian College

Wadsworth Publishing Company
Belmont, California
A Division of Wadsworth, Inc.

Biology and Environmental Science Publisher: Jack Carey
Editorial Assistant: Kristin Milotich
Development Editor: Mary Arbogast
Production Editors: Karen Garrison and Catherine Linberg
Managing Designer: Andrew H. Ogus
Print Buyer: Barbara Britton
Art Editor: Donna Kalal
Permissions Editor: Peggy Meehan
Text Designers: James Chadwick, Andrew H. Ogus, Cynthia Schultz
Copy Editor: George Dyke
Technical Illustrators: Darwin and Vally Hennings; Tasa Graphic Arts, Inc.; Susan Breitbard; Teresa Roberts; Carlyn Iverson; Cindie Wooley; Jill Turney; Craig Hanson; and Jeff Tucker
Box Logo Designs: The Weller Institute
Electronic Composition: Brandon Carson, Wadsworth Digital Productions
Cover Design: Andrew H. Ogus
Printer: Malloy Lithographing, Inc.
Cover Photograph: Proxy Falls, Oregon. © David Muench, 1993.

Thanks to the Center for Plant Conservation for providing source material for the illustration of the Knowlton cactus on p. 161.

Books in the Wadsworth Biology Series

Environment: Problems and Solutions, Miller

Environmental Science, 4th, Miller

Living in the Environment, 8th, Miller

Resource Conservation and Management, Miller

Sustaining the Earth, Miller

Biology: Concepts and Applications, 2nd, Starr

Biology: The Unity and Diversity of Life, 6th, Starr and Taggart

Biology of the Cell, 2nd, Wolfe

Dimensions of Cancer, Kupchella

Evolution: Process and Product, 3rd, Dodson and Dodson

Molecular and Cellular Biology, Wolfe

Introduction to Cell Biology, Wolfe

Biology: The Foundations, 2nd, Wolfe

Oceanography: An Introduction, 4th, Ingmanson and Wallace

Oceanography: An Invitation to Marine Science, Garrison

Plant Physiology, 4th, Devlin and Witham

Exercises in Plant Physiology, Witham et al.

Plant Physiology, 4th, Salisbury and Ross

Plant Physiology Laboratory Manual, Ross

Plants: An Evolutionary Survey, 2nd, Scagel et al.

Psychobiology: The Neuron and Behavior, Hoyenga and Hoyenga

Sex, Evolution, and Behavior, 2nd, Daly and Wilson

This book is printed on acid-free recycled paper.

Two trees have been planted in a tropical rain forest for every tree used to make this book, courtesy of G. Tyler Miller, Jr., and Wadsworth Publishing Company. The author also sees that 50 trees are planted to compensate for the paper he uses and that several hectares of tropical rain forest are protected.

I(T)P™

International Thomson Publishing
The trademark ITP is used under license.

Printed in the United States of America
2 3 4 5 6 7 8 9 10—98 97 96 95 94

Library of Congress Cataloging-in-Publication Data
Miller, G. Tyler (George Tyler)
    Sustaining the Earth : an integrated approach / G. Tyler Miller, Jr.
      p.   cm.
    Includes bibliographical references and index.
    ISBN 0-534-21432-0
    1. Environmental sciences. 2. Environmental protection.
  I. Title.
GE105.M558 1994
363.7—dc20   93-33112

HOW I BECAME INVOLVED In 1966 I heard a scientist give a lecture on the problems of overpopulation and environmental abuse. Afterward I went to him and said, "If even a fraction of what you have said is true, I will feel ethically obligated to give up my research on the corrosion of metals and devote the rest of my life to environmental issues. Frankly, I don't want to believe a word you have said, and I'm going into the literature to try to prove that your statements are either untrue or grossly distorted."

After six months of study I was convinced of the seriousness of these problems. Since then I have been studying, teaching, and writing about them. I have also attempted to live my life in an environmentally sound way—with varying degrees of success—by treading as lightly as possible on the earth. This book summarizes what I have learned in almost three decades of trying to understand environmental principles, problems, connections, and solutions. I agree with the late Norman Cousin's statement: "The first aim of education should not be to prepare young people for careers, but to enable them to develop a respect for life."

CONCEPTS, PROBLEMS, CONNECTIONS, AND SOLUTIONS This book treats environmental science as an *interdisciplinary* study, combining ideas and information from natural sciences (such as biology, chemistry, and geology), along with social sciences (such as economics, politics, and ethics). The overall goal is to present a general idea of what we know about how nature works and how things are interconnected. This study of connections in nature examines how the environment is being used and abused, and what individuals can do to protect and improve it for themselves, for future generations, and for other living things. My aim is to provide a readable and accurate introduction to environmental science without the use of mathematics or complex scientific information.

In this book I use basic scientific laws, principles, and concepts (presented in Chapter 2) to help us understand environmental and resource problems, possible solutions to these problems, and how these concepts, problems, and solutions are connected. I have introduced only the concepts and principles necessary to understanding material in this book, and I have tried to present them simply but accurately.

To help make sure the material is accurate and up to date, I have consulted more than 10,000 research sources in the professional literature. In writing this book I have also profited from the more than 200 experts and teachers who have provided detailed reviews of the various editions of my other three books in this field.

After Chapters 1 and 2 are covered, the rest of the book can be used in almost any order. In addition, many sections within chapters can be moved around or omitted to accommodate courses with different lengths and emphases.

I also relate the information in the book to the real world and to our individual lives, both in the main text and in various kinds of boxes sprinkled throughout the book. The *Spotlights* (16) highlight and give further insights into environmental and resource problems. The *Case Studies* (13) give in-depth information about key issues, and they apply concepts. The *Pro/Con* discussions (3) outline both sides of controversial environmental and resource issues. The *Connections* (14) show how various environmental concepts, problems, and solutions are related. The *Solutions* (18) summarize possible solutions to environmental problems or describe what individuals have done, while *Individuals Matter* (14) give examples of what we as individuals can do to help sustain the earth.

The book's 211 illustrations are designed to present complex ideas in understandable ways and to relate learning to the real world. To save space and improve clarity, I have converted important ideas to detailed drawings instead of using photographs.

To reduce student costs this book is printed in black and white and has a soft cover. It is also printed on acid-free recycled paper with the maximum content of post-consumer waste currently available at an affordable cost.

AN INTEGRATED APPROACH This is the first environmental science textbook designed to fully integrate environmental concepts, problems, connections, and solutions. This book is integrated in several ways:

- The first chapter provides an overview of the problems of population, pollution, and resource use and how they are connected.

- Key scientific concepts are discussed and integrated into one chapter (Chapter 2) and then used as needed throughout the book.

- Major topics are discussed and integrated within a single chapter, except for the keystone concept of biodiversity, which is discussed in three chapters—Chapter 5 (Biodiversity in Ecosystems), Chapter 6 (Biodiversity of Species), and Chapter 7 (Biodiversity in Soils and Food Producing Systems). Problems and solutions to human population growth are integrated and discussed in Chapter 3, energy in Chapter 4, health and risk in Chapter 8, air (including atmosphere, weather, climate, global warming, ozone depletion, and indoor and outdoor pollution) in Chapter 9, water (including use of water resources and water pollution) in Chapter 10, wastes and resource conservation (including solid waste, hazardous waste, recycling, reuse, waste reduction, and pollution prevention) in Chapter 11, and the social science aspects of environmental problems and solutions (economics, politics, and worldviews) in Chapter 12.

- In addition to vertical integration within chapters, horizontal integration is achieved by using several major themes as connecting threads woven throughout the book. These integrating themes are *exponential growth, ecological concepts (developed in Chapter 2), population, energy and energy efficiency, biodiversity and Earth capital, pollution prevention and waste reduction, uncertainty and controversy, economics, politics, sustainability, solutions, and individual action.*

- Throughout the book material is connected through extensive cross-references.

WELCOME TO UNCERTAINTY, CONTROVERSY, AND CHALLENGE There are no easy or simple answers to the environmental problems and challenges we face. We will never have scientific certainty or agreement about what we should do, because science provides us with probabilities not certainties, and it advances through continuous controversy. What is important is not what scientists disagree on (which represents the frontiers of knowledge still being developed and argued about) but what they generally agree on—the scientific consensus on concepts, problems, and possible solutions. Despite considerable research, we still know relatively little about how nature works at a time when our numbers and lifestyles are altering nature at an accelerating pace. This uncertainty and the complexity of these issues and their importance to our lives and to present and future generations of humans and other species make them highly controversial.

Intense controversy also arises because environmental science is a dynamic blend of natural and social sciences that sometimes questions the ways we view and act in the world around us. This interdisciplinary attempt to mirror reality asks us to evaluate our worldviews, values, and lifestyles and our economic and political systems. This can often be a threatening process.

Many environmental books and articles overwhelm us with the problems we face without suggesting ways we might deal with these problems. This book is loaded with solutions to environmental problems at global, national, local, and individual levels that have been proposed by scientists, environmental activists, and analysts with a wide range of viewpoints and expertise.

Don't take the numerous possible solutions given in this book as gospel. They are given to encourage you to think critically and to make up your own mind. In deciding how to walk more gently on the earth, don't feel guilty about all of the things you are not doing to help sustain the earth. No one can even come close to doing all of these things and you may disagree with some of the actions suggested by a diverse array of environmentalists. Pick out the things you are willing to do or agree with and then try to expand your efforts.

People with widely different worldviews, political persuasions, and ideas can and need to work together to help sustain the earth. We are all in this together, and we need to respect our differences and work together to find a rainbow of solutions to the problems and challenges we face.

Rosy optimism and gloom-and-doom pessimism are traps that usually lead to denial, indifference, and inaction. I have tried to avoid these two extremes and give a realistic—and yet hopeful—view of the future. My reading of history reveals that hope converted into action has been the driving force of our species. This book is filled with stories of individuals who have acted to help sustain the earth for us and all life and whose actions inspire us to do better.

I wish everything were more certain, but it isn't. Making difficult choices without ever having enough information is what being human is all about. It's an exciting time to be alive as we struggle to enter into a new relationship with the planet that is our only home.

INTERACT WITH AND HELP ME IMPROVE THIS BOOK I urge you to interact with this book as a way to make learning more interesting and effective. When I read books and articles I mark key sentences and paragraphs with a highlighter or pen. I put an asterisk in the margin next to something I think is important and double asterisks next to something that I think is especially important. I write comments in the margins, such as *Beautiful, Confusing, Bull, Wrong,* and so on. I fold down the top corner of pages with highlighted passages and the top and bottom corners of especially important pages. This way, I can flip through a book and quickly review the key passages. I urge you to interact in such ways with this book.

Tell me how you think this book can be improved, and if you find any errors, please let me know about them. Most errors can be corrected in subsequent printings of this edition, rather than waiting for a new edition. Send any errors you find and your suggestions for improvement to Jack Carey, Biology and Environmental Science Publisher, Wadsworth Publishing Company, 10 Davis Drive, Belmont, CA 94002. He will send them on to me.

If you value what you have learned from this book, I urge you to keep it as a part of your personal library for future reference on how we can work together to help sustain the earth.

STUDY AIDS   When a new term is introduced and defined, it is printed in **boldface type**. There is also a glossary of all key terms at the end of the book.

Factual recall questions (with answers) are listed at the bottom of most pages. You might cover the answer (on the right-hand page) with a piece of paper and then try to answer the question on the left-hand page. These questions are not necessarily related to the chapter in which they are found.

Each chapter ends with a set of questions designed to encourage you to think critically and apply what you have learned to your life. Some ask you to take sides on controversial issues and to back up your conclusions and beliefs.

Readers who become especially interested in a particular topic can consult the brief list of suggested readings for each chapter, given in the back of the book. For the most complete list of such readings consult my largest book, *Living in the Environment*. The Appendix contains a list of publications to help keep up to date on the book's material and a list of some key environmental organizations.

SUPPLEMENTS   The following supplements are available:

- *Instructor's Manual* (with test items), by Jane Heinze-Fry (Ph.D. in Science and Environmental Education). For each chapter, it has goals and objectives; key terms; teaching suggestions; multiple-choice test questions with answers; projects, field trips, and experiments; term-paper and report topics; and audiovisual materials and computer software.

- *Green Lives-Green Campuses: An Activities Workbook,* by Jane Heinze-Fry, is designed to help students apply environmental concepts by inves-

tigating their lifestyles and by making an environmental audit of their campus.

- *Laboratory Manual,* by C. Lee Rockett (Bowling Green State University) and Kenneth J. Van Dellen (Macomb Community College).

- A set of 50 color acetates and 387 black and white transparency masters, for making overhead transparencies or slides of line art, is available to adopters.

- A special version of STELLA II software, a tool for developing critical thinking, is available, together with an accompanying workbook.

ACKNOWLEDGMENTS   I wish to thank the many students and teachers who responded so favorably to the eight editions of *Living in the Environment,* the four editions of *Environmental Science,* and the first edition of *Resource Conservation and Management* and who offered many helpful suggestions for improvement.

I am also deeply indebted to the reviewers who pointed out errors and suggested many important improvements to these books, which have in turn benefited this book. Any errors and deficiencies left are mine.

The members of Wadsworth's talented production team, listed on the copyright page, have also made important contributions. My thanks also go to Wadsworth's dedicated sales staff, to Jane Heinze-Fry for her outstanding work on the instructor's manual and the *Green Lives-Green Campuses* supplement, and to C. Lee Rockett and Kenneth J. Van Dellen for developing a laboratory manual to accompany this book.

Special thanks go to Jack Carey, Biology and Environmental Science Publisher at Wadsworth, for his encouragement, help, friendship, and superb reviewing system. It helps immensely to work with the best and most experienced editor in college textbook publishing.

I also wish to thank Peggy Sue O'Neal, my spouse and best friend, for her love and support of me and the earth. I dedicate this book to her and to the earth that sustains us all.

G. Tyler Miller, Jr.

Brief Contents

Detailed Contents

1 Environmental Problems and Their Causes

1-1 Living in an Exponential Age

EXPONENTIAL GROWTH Once there were two kings who enjoyed playing chess, with the winner claiming a prize from the loser. After their match was over the winning king asked the loser to place one grain of wheat on the first square of the chessboard, two on the second, four on the third, and so on. The number of grains was to double each time until all 64 squares were filled.

The losing king, thinking he was getting off easy, agreed with delight. It was the biggest mistake he ever made. He bankrupted his kingdom and still could not produce the 2^{64} grains of wheat he had promised. In fact, it's probably more than all the wheat that has ever been harvested! This is an example of **exponential growth**, in which a quantity increases by a fixed percentage of the whole in a given time. As the loser learned, exponential growth is deceptive. It starts off slowly, but after only a few doublings it rises to enormous numbers, because each doubling is more than the total of all earlier growth.

Here is another example. Fold a piece of paper in half to double its thickness. If you could manage to do this 42 times, the stack would tower from Earth to the moon, 386,400 kilometers (240,000 miles) away. If you could double it 50 times, the folded paper would almost reach the sun, 149 million kilometers (93 million miles) away!

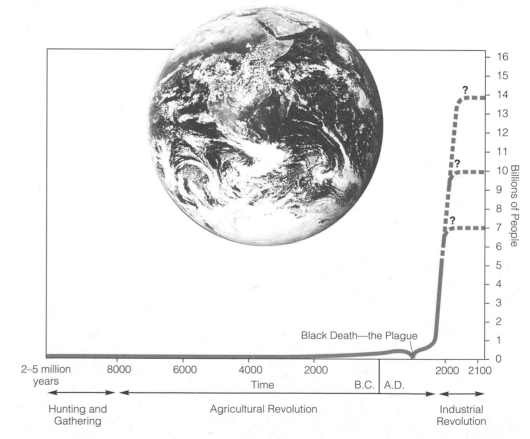

Figure 1-1 The J-shaped curve of past exponential world population growth with projections to 2100. Notice that exponential growth starts off slowly, but as time passes the curve becomes steeper and steeper. (Data from World Bank and United Nations)

Q: How many people are there in the world?

The environmental problems we face—population growth, excessive and wasteful resource use, wildlife extinction, and pollution—are interconnected and growing exponentially. For example, world population has more than doubled in only 43 years, from 2.5 billion in 1950 to 5.5 billion in 1993. Unless death rates rise sharply or birth rates drop sharply, it may reach 11 billion by 2045 and 14 billion by 2100 (Figure 1-1).

Exponential growth in population and resource use has drastically changed the face of the planet. Each year more forests, grasslands, and wetlands disappear, and some deserts grow larger. Vital topsoil, washed or blown away from farmland and cleared forests, clogs streams, lakes, and reservoirs with sediment. Underground water is pumped from wells faster than it can be replenished. Oceans are poisoned with our wastes. Every hour, we drive as many as four wildlife species to extinction.

Burning fossil fuels and cutting down and burning forests raise the concentrations of carbon dioxide and other heat-trapping gases in the lower atmosphere. Within the next 40 to 50 years, Earth's climate may become warm enough to disrupt agricultural productivity, alter water distribution, and drive countless species to extinction.

Extracting and burning fossil fuels pollute the air and water and disrupt land. Other chemicals we add to the air drift into the upper atmosphere and deplete ozone gas, which now filters out much of the sun's harmful ultraviolet radiation. Toxic wastes from factories and homes poison the air, water, and soil. Agricultural pesticides contaminate some of our drinking water and food.

Sooner or later there is a limit to exponentially growing resource use and the capacity of Earth's life-support systems to absorb, dilute, and degrade the resulting waste and pollution. Environmentalists and a number of the world's leading scientists warn that we are depleting and degrading Earth capital for us and other species and thus coming close to or exceeding the limits to human population growth and resource use (Spotlight, p. 15).

LIVING SUSTAINABLY Our existence, lifestyles, and economies depend totally on the sun and the

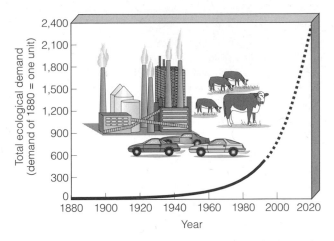

Figure 1-2 J-shaped curve of exponential growth in the total demand on Earth's resources from agriculture, mining, and industry between 1890 and 1993. Projections to 2020 assume that resource use will continue to grow at the current rate of 5.5% per year. At that rate our total ecological demand on Earth's resources doubles every 13 years. If global economic output grew by only 3% a year, this would still double resource consumption every 23 years. (Data from United Nations, World Resources Institute, and Carrol Wilson, *Man's Impact on the Global Environment*, Cambridge, Mass.: MIT Press, 1970)

earth. We can think of energy from the sun as **solar capital**, and we can think of the planet's air, water, fertile soil, forests, grasslands, wildlife, minerals, and natural purification and recycling processes as **Earth capital**.

The basic problem we face is that we are depleting and degrading Earth's natural capital at an accelerating rate (Figure 1-2). To environmentalists, such behavior is unsustainable. Thus, they believe that we must learn to live sustainably (Solutions, p. 5).

The bad news is the problems we face and their root causes, as outlined in this chapter. The good news is that it's not too late to replace our Earth-degrading actions with Earth-sustaining ones, as discussed throughout the rest of this book. The key is *Earth wisdom*—learning how Earth sustains itself—and integrating such lessons from nature into the ways we think and act.

A: Approximately 5.5 billion in mid-1993 (0.1 billion added per year)

1-2   Population Growth and the Wealth Gap

THE J-SHAPED CURVE OF HUMAN POPULATION GROWTH   Fossil evidence suggests that the current form of our species, *Homo sapiens sapiens*, has walked

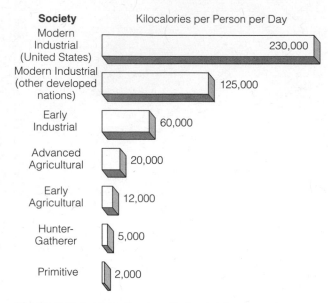

Figure 1-3 Average direct and indirect daily energy use per person at various stages of human cultural development. A *calorie* is the amount of energy needed to raise the temperature of 1 gram of water 1°C (1.8°F). A *kilocalorie* is 1,000 calories. Food calories or calories expended during exercise are kilocalories (sometimes represented by spelling *Calories* with a capital *C*).

the earth for only about 40,000 years, an instant in the planet's estimated 4.6-billion-year existence. During the first 30,000 years we survived as mostly nomadic hunter-gatherers. Since then there have been two major cultural shifts: the *Agricultural Revolution*, which began 10,000–12,000 years ago, and the *Industrial Revolution*, which began about 275 years ago.

These cultural revolutions have given us much more energy (Figure 1-3) and new technologies with which to alter and control more of the planet to meet our basic needs and increasing wants. By expanding food supplies, lengthening average life spans, and raising average living standards, each shift increased the human population (Figure 1-4).

The increasing size of the human population provides an example of exponential growth. As the population base grows, the number of people on Earth soars. The population growth curve rounds a bend and heads almost straight up, creating a J-shaped curve (Figure 1-1).

It took 2 million years to reach a billion people; 130 years to add the second billion; 30 years for the third; 15 years for the fourth; and only 12 years for the fifth billion. At present growth rates the sixth billion will be added during the 11-year period between 1987 and 1998, and the seventh only 10 years later, in 2008. The relentless ticking of this population clock means that in 1993 the world's population of 5.5 billion people grew by about 90 million—an average increase of 247,000 people a day, or 10,300 an hour. At this 1.63% annual rate of exponential growth, it takes about

- 5 days to add the number of people equal to the number of Americans killed in all U.S. wars

Figure 1-4 Expansion of Earth's carrying capacity for our species. Technological innovation has led to major cultural changes, and we have displaced and depleted numerous species that compete with us for—and provide us with—resources. Dashed lines represent three alternative futures: **(1)** uninhibited human population growth; **(2)** population stabilization; and **(3)** growth followed by a crash and stabilization at a much lower level.

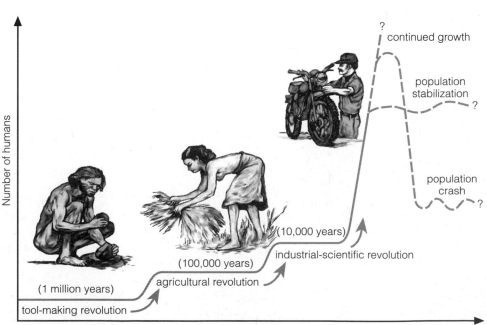

4

Q: How many people are added to the world's population each day?

Imagine you inherit $1 million. If you invest this capital at 10% interest, you will have a sustainable annual income of $100,000. That is, you can spend up to $100,000 a year without touching your capital.

But suppose you develop a taste for diamonds or a yacht—or all your relatives move in with you. Spend $200,000 a year, and your million will be gone early in the seventh year. Even if you spend just $110,000 a year, you will be bankrupt early in the eighteenth year.

The lesson here is a very old one: Don't kill the goose that lays the golden eggs. Deplete your capital, and you move from a sustainable to an unsustainable lifestyle. Get too greedy and you'll soon be needy.

The same lesson applies to Earth capital. With the help of solar energy, natural processes developed over billions of years can renew topsoil, water, air, forests, grasslands, and wildlife that we and other species depend on—as long as we

don't use these resources faster than they are renewed. Some of our wastes can also be diluted, decomposed, and recycled by natural processes as long as these processes are not overloaded.

Likewise, most of Earth's nonrenewable minerals such as aluminum and glass can be recycled or reused if we don't contaminate them or mix them in landfills so that recycling and reuse are too costly. History also shows that we can often find substitutes as certain nonrenewable minerals become scarce.

Conserving energy and relying on virtually inexhaustible solar energy in the form of heat, wind, flowing water, and renewable wood are a sustainable lifestyle. The brief "fossil-fuel age" we now live in is unsustainable because it depletes Earth's natural energy capital. By wasting less energy we could make these fuels last longer, reduce their massive environmental impact, and make an easier transition to a new, renewable-energy age.

A **sustainable society** is one that manages its economy and population size without doing irreparable environmental harm. It satisfies the needs of its people without depleting Earth capital and thus jeopardizing the prospects of future generations of humans or other species. This is done **(1)** by regulating population growth, **(2)** by taking no more potentially renewable resources from the natural world than can be replenished naturally, **(3)** by not overloading the capacity of the environment to cleanse and renew itself by natural processes, **(4)** by encouraging Earth-sustaining rather than Earth-degrading forms of economic development, and **(5)** by minimizing poverty and human misery. We can help sustain Earth for human beings and other species indefinitely by learning how to live off Earth income instead of Earth capital.

- 10 months to add 75 million people—the number killed by the bubonic plague (the Black Death) in the fourteenth century

- 1.8 years to add 165 million people—the number of people killed in all wars fought during the past 200 years

This should give you some idea of what it means to go around the bend of the J curve of exponential growth.

RICH AND POOR COUNTRIES: THE WEALTH GAP
Virtually all countries seek **economic growth**: increasing their capacity to provide goods and services for final use. Such growth is usually measured by an increase in a country's **gross national product (GNP)**: the market value in current dollars of all goods and services produced by an economy for final use during a year. To show one person's slice of the economic pie, economists often calculate the **GNP per capita** (per person): the GNP divided by the total population.

The United Nations broadly classifies the world's countries as more developed or less developed. The **more developed countries (MDCs)**, or *developed countries*, are highly industrialized, and most have high average GNPs per capita. They include the United States, Canada, Japan, the former USSR, Australia, New Zealand, and the western European countries. These countries, with 1.2 billion people (22% of the world's population), command about 85% of the world's wealth and income, use 88% of its natural resources and 73% of its energy, and generate most of its pollution and wastes.

All other nations are classified as **less developed countries (LDCs)**, or *developing countries*, with low to moderate industrialization and GNPs per capita. Most are in Africa, Asia, and Latin America. Their 4.3 billion people, or 78% of the world's population, have only about 15% of the wealth and income, and they use only about 12% of the natural resources and 27% of the energy. The "less developed" label, invented by

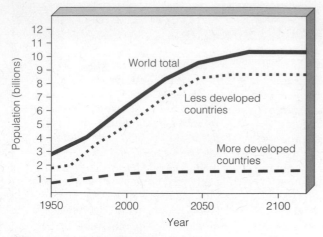

Figure 1-5 Past and projected population size for MDCs, LDCs, and the world, 1950–2120. (Data from United Nations)

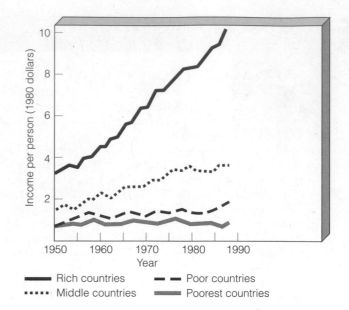

Figure 1-6 The wealth gap. Changes in the distribution of global income per person in four types of countries, 1950–1990. Instead of trickling down, most of the income from economic growth has flowed up, with the situation worsening since 1980. (Data from United Nations)

MDC political scientists and economists, is in some ways a misnomer because LDCs are highly developed culturally and in other ways. It also assumes that Western-style industrialization is the best model for all countries.

Most of the projected increase in world population will take place in LDCs, where 1 million people are added every 4 days (Figure 1-5). By 2010 the combined populations of Asia and Africa are projected to be 5.3 billion—almost as many as now live on the entire planet.

The growing gap since 1960 between rich and poor in GNP per capita has widened further since 1980 (Figure 1-6). The rich have grown much richer, while the poor have stayed poor or grown even poorer. Today, one in five people lives in luxury and the next three get by, while the fifth struggles to survive on less than $1 a day (Spotlight, p. 7).

 **Pollution**

WHAT IS POLLUTION? Any addition to air, water, soil, or food that threatens the health, survival capability, or activities of humans or other living organisms is called **pollution**. Most pollutants are solid, liquid, or gaseous by-products or wastes produced when a resource is extracted, processed, made into products, or used. Pollution can also take the form of unwanted energy emissions, such as excessive heat, noise, or radiation.

A major problem is that people differ on whether something is a pollutant and on acceptable levels of pollution, especially if they have to choose between pollution control and their jobs. As the philosopher Georg Hegel pointed out, tragedy is not the conflict between right and wrong, but the conflict between right and right.

SOURCES Pollutants can enter the environment naturally (for example, from volcanic eruptions) or through human activities (for example, from burning coal). Most natural pollution is dispersed over a large area and diluted or broken down to harmless levels by natural processes. By contrast, most serious pollution from human activities occurs in or near urban and industrial areas, where pollutants are concentrated in small volumes of air, water, and soil. Industrialized agriculture is also a major source of pollution.

Some pollutants contaminate the areas where they are produced. Others are carried by winds or flowing water to other areas. Pollution does not respect state or national boundaries.

Some pollutants come from single, identifiable sources, such as the smokestack of a power plant, the drainpipe of a meat-packing plant, the chimney of a house, or the exhaust pipe of an automobile. These are called **point sources**. Other pollutants enter the air, water, or soil from dispersed, and often hard-to-identify, **nonpoint sources**. Examples are the runoff of fertilizers and pesticides (from farmlands and suburban

6

Q: Where does everything that supports your life come from?

lawns and gardens) into streams and lakes, and pesticides sprayed into the air or blown by the wind into the atmosphere. It is much easier and cheaper to identify and control pollution from point sources than from widely dispersed nonpoint sources.

EFFECTS   Unwanted effects of pollutants are **(1)** disruption of life-support systems for us and other species; **(2)** damage to wildlife; **(3)** damage to human health; **(4)** damage to property; and **(5)** nuisance effects such as noise and unpleasant smells, tastes, and sights.

Three factors determine how severe the effects of a pollutant will be. One is its *chemical nature*—how active and harmful it is to living organisms. Another is its **concentration**—the amount per volume unit of air, water, soil, or body weight. One way to lower the concentration of a pollutant is to dilute it in a large volume of air or water. Until we started overwhelming the air and waterways with pollutants, dilution was the solution to pollution. Now it is only a partial solution.

A third factor is a pollutant's *persistence*—how long it stays in the air, water, soil, or body. **Degradable**, or **nonpersistent**, **pollutants** are broken down completely or reduced to acceptable levels by natural physical, chemical, and biological processes. Those broken down by living organisms (usually by specialized bacteria) are called **biodegradable pollutants**. Human sewage in a river, for example, is biodegraded fairly quickly by bacteria if it is not added faster than it can be broken down.

Unfortunately, many of the substances we introduce into the environment take decades or longer to degrade. Examples of these **slowly degradable** or **persistent pollutants** include the insecticide DDT, most plastics, aluminum cans, and chlorofluorocarbons (CFCs)—these latter used as coolants in refrigerators and air conditioners, as spray propellants (in some countries), and as foaming agents for making some plastics.

Nondegradable pollutants cannot be broken down by natural processes. Examples include the toxic elements lead and mercury. The best ways to deal with nondegradable pollutants (and slowly degradable hazardous pollutants) are to not release them into the environment, to recycle them, or to remove them from contaminated air, water, or soil (an expensive process).

We know little about the possible harmful effects of 80% of the 70,000 synthetic chemicals now in commercial use. Our knowledge about the effects of the other 20% of these chemicals is limited, mostly because it is quite difficult, time-consuming, and expensive to get this knowledge.

DEALING WITH POLLUTION: PREVENTION AND CLEANUP   Pollution prevention, or **input pollution control**, reduces or eliminates the input of pollutants

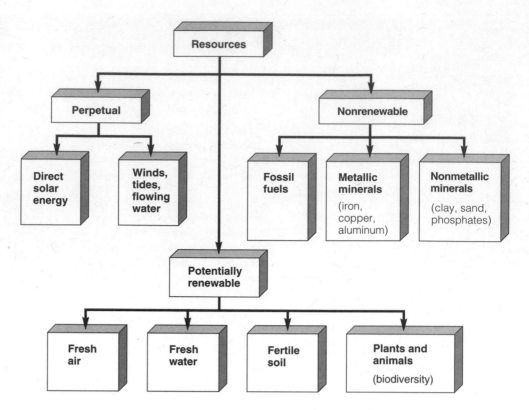

Figure 1-7 Major types of material resources. This scheme isn't fixed; potentially renewable resources can become nonrenewable resources if used for a prolonged time at a faster rate than they are renewed by natural processes.

and wastes into the environment. This approach is summarized in biologist Barry Commoner's **principle of pollution prevention**: If you don't put something into the environment, it isn't there. Pollution can be prevented, or at least reduced, by the three R's of resource use: *Reduce, Reuse, Recycle.*

Pollution cleanup, or **output pollution control**, deals with pollutants after they have been produced. Relying mostly on pollution cleanup causes several problems. One is that, as long as population and consumption levels continue to grow, cleanup is only a temporary bandage. For example, adding catalytic converters to cars has reduced air pollution. However, increases in the number of cars and the total distance they travel have made this cleanup approach less effective.

Another problem is that cleanup often removes a pollutant from one part of the environment only to cause pollution in another part. We can collect garbage, but the garbage must be burned (perhaps causing air pollution and leaving a toxic ash that must be put somewhere), dumped into streams, lakes, and oceans (perhaps causing water pollution), buried (perhaps causing soil and groundwater pollution), recycled, or reused.

Both pollution prevention and pollution cleanup are needed, but environmentalists urge us to emphasize prevention because it works better and is cheaper

than cleanup or repair. As Benjamin Franklin reminded us long ago, "An ounce of prevention is worth a pound of cure."

An increasing number of businesses have found that *pollution prevention pays.* It saves them money and at the same time helps the earth—a win-win strategy. So far, however, about 99% of environmental spending in the United States is devoted to pollution cleanup and only 1% to pollution prevention—a situation that environmentalists believe must be reversed as soon as possible.

1-4 Resources

TYPES OF RESOURCES   A **resource** is anything we get from the living or nonliving environment to meet our needs and wants. We usually define resources in terms of humans, but resources are needed by all forms of life for their survival and good health. Some resources, such as solar energy, fresh air, fresh surface water, fertile soil, and wild edible plants, are directly available for use. Most human resources, such as petroleum (oil), iron, groundwater (water occurring

Q: How long does it take to add people equal to all those killed in all wars fought during the past 200 years?

underground), and modern crops, aren't directly available, and their supplies are limited. They become resources only with some effort and technological ingenuity.

Petroleum, for example, was a mysterious fluid until we learned how to find it, extract it, and refine it into gasoline, heating oil, and other products at affordable prices. On our short human time scale we classify resources as renewable, potentially renewable, and nonrenewable (Figure 1-7).

NONRENEWABLE RESOURCES Nonrenewable, or **exhaustible**, **resources** exist in fixed quantities in the earth's crust. They include *energy resources* (coal, oil, natural gas, uranium, geothermal energy), *metallic mineral resources* (iron, copper, aluminum), and *nonmetallic mineral resources* (salt, gypsum, clay, sand, phosphates, water, and soil) (Figure 1-7). We know how to find and extract more than 100 nonrenewable minerals from the earth's crust. We convert these raw materials into many everyday items we use and then discard, reuse, or recycle them.

We never completely run out of any nonrenewable mineral. But a mineral becomes *economically depleted* when finding, extracting, transporting, and processing the remaining deposits cost more than the results are worth. At that point we have five choices: recycle or reuse existing supplies, waste less, use less, find a substitute, or do without and wait millions of years for more to be produced.

Some nonrenewable material resources, such as copper and aluminum, can be recycled or reused to extend supplies. **Recycling** involves collecting and reprocessing a resource into new products. For example, aluminum cans can be collected, melted, and made into new beverage cans or other aluminum products. And glass bottles can be crushed and melted to make new bottles or other glass items. **Reuse** involves using a resource over and over in the same form. For example, glass bottles can be collected, washed, and refilled many times.

Other nonrenewable fuel resources—such as coal, oil, and natural gas—can't be recycled or reused. Once burned, the useful energy in these fossil fuels is gone, leaving behind only waste heat and polluting exhaust gases. Most of the economic growth per person shown in Figure 1-6 has been fueled by nonrenewable oil, which is expected to be economically depleted within 40 to 80 years.

Most published supply estimates for a given nonrenewable resource refer to **reserves**: known deposits from which a usable mineral can be extracted profitably at current prices. Reserves can be increased when new deposits are found or when price rises

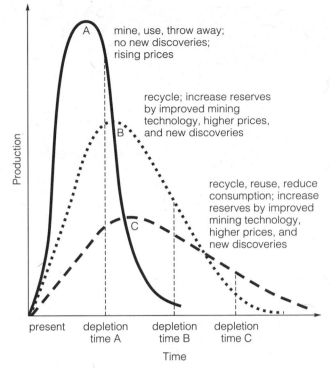

Figure 1-8 Depletion curves for a nonrenewable resource, such as aluminum or copper, using three sets of assumptions. Dashed vertical lines show when 80% depletion occurs.

make it profitable to extract identified deposits that were previously too expensive to exploit.

Depletion time is the time it takes to use a certain portion—usually 80%—of the reserves of a mineral at a given rate of use (Figure 1-8). The shortest depletion time assumes no recycling or reuse and no increase in reserves (curve A, Figure 1-8). A longer depletion time assumes that recycling will stretch existing reserves and that better mining technology, higher prices, and new discoveries will, say, double the reserves (curve B, Figure 1-8). An even longer depletion time assumes that new discoveries will expand reserves, say, five- or tenfold, and that recycling, reuse, and reduced consumption will extend supplies (curve C, Figure 1-8). Finding a substitute for a resource dictates a whole new set of depletion curves for the new resource.

The greatest danger from high levels of resource consumption may not be the exhaustion of resources but the damage that their extraction and processing do to the environment. The mining, processing, and use of mineral resources require enormous amounts of energy and often cause land disturbance, erosion, and pollution of air and water (Figure 1-9).

RENEWABLE RESOURCES Solar energy is called a **renewable resource** because on a human time

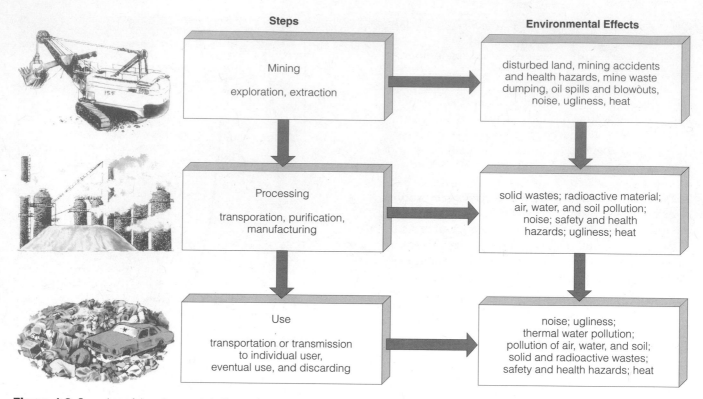

Steps		Environmental Effects
Mining exploration, extraction	→	disturbed land, mining accidents and health hazards, mine waste dumping, oil spills and blowouts, noise, ugliness, heat
Processing transporation, purification, manufacturing	→	solid wastes; radioactive material; air, water, and soil pollution; noise; safety and health hazards; ugliness; heat
Use transportation or transmission to individual user, eventual use, and discarding	→	noise; ugliness; thermal water pollution; pollution of air, water, and soil; solid and radioactive wastes; safety and health hazards; heat

Figure 1-9 Some harmful environmental effects of resource extraction, processing, and use. The energy used to carry out each step causes further pollution and environmental degradation.

scale it is essentially inexhaustible. It is expected to last at least 4 billion years while the sun completes its life cycle.

A **potentially renewable resource*** can be renewed fairly rapidly through natural processes. Examples of such resources include forest trees, grassland grasses, wild animals, fresh lake and stream water, groundwater, fresh air, and fertile soil. One important potentially renewable resource for us and other species is **biological diversity**, or **biodiversity**. It consists of all of Earth's living organisms, classified into groups of organisms called *species*, which resemble one another in appearance, behavior, and chemical and genetic makeup.

But potentially renewable resources can be depleted. The highest rate at which a potentially renewable resource can be used without reducing its available supply is called its **sustainable yield**. If this natural replacement rate is exceeded, the available supply begins to shrink—a process known as **environmental degradation**.

---

*Most sources use the term *renewable resource*. I have added the word *potentially* to emphasize that these resources can be depleted if we use them faster than natural processes renew them.

Several types of environmental degradation can change potentially renewable resources into nonrenewable or unusable resources (Connections, p. 11):

- *Covering productive land with water, concrete, asphalt, or buildings so that plant growth declines and wildlife habitats are lost.*

- *Cultivating land without proper soil management, causing soil erosion and depletion of plant nutrients.* Topsoil is now eroding faster than it forms on about 33% of the world's cropland—a loss of about 23 billion metric tons (25 billion tons) per year.

- *Irrigating cropland without good drainage, causing salinization or waterlogging.* Salt buildup has cut yields on one-fourth of all irrigated cropland, and waterlogging has reduced productivity on at least one-tenth.

- *Taking fresh water from underground sources (aquifers) and from streams and lakes faster than it is replaced by natural processes.* In the United States, one-fourth of the groundwater withdrawn each year is not replenished.

- *Destroying wetlands and coral reefs.* Between 25% and 50% of the world's wetlands have been

Q: What percentage of the world's resources are used by people in more developed countries?

One cause of environmental degradation is the overuse of **common-property resources**, which are owned by none and available to all. Most are potentially renewable. Examples include clean air, fish in the open ocean, migratory birds, Antarctica, gases of the lower atmosphere, and the ozone content of the upper atmosphere.

In 1968, biologist Garrett Hardin called this the **tragedy of the commons**. It happens because each user reasons, "If I don't use this resource,

someone else will. The little bit I use or pollute is not enough to matter." With few users, this logic works. However, the cumulative effect of many people trying to exploit a common-property resource eventually exhausts or ruins it. Then no one can benefit from it. Therein lies the tragedy.

The obvious solution is to use common-property resources at rates below their sustainable yields or overload limits by reducing population, regulating access, or both. Unfortunately, it is difficult to determine the sustainable yield of a

forest, a grassland, or an animal population, partly because yields vary with weather, climate, and unpredictable biological factors. These uncertainties mean that *it is best to use a potentially renewable resource at a rate well below its estimated sustainable yield*. This is a *prevention or precautionary approach* designed to reduce the risk of environmental degradation. However, this approach is rarely used because it conflicts with the drive for short-term profit regardless of the future consequences.

---

drained, built upon, or seriously polluted. The United States has lost 55% of its wetlands and loses another 150,000 hectares (371,000 acres) each year. Coral reefs are being destroyed or damaged in 93 of the 109 significant locations.

- *Cutting trees from large areas without adequate replanting (deforestation).* If current deforestation rates continue, within 30–50 years there may be little of these forests left. In MDCs many of the remaining diverse, old-growth forests are being cleared and replaced with single-species tree farms or often much less diverse second-growth forests. This reduces wildlife habitats and forms of wildlife that make up the planet's biodiversity.

- *Overgrazing of grassland by livestock, which converts productive grasslands into unproductive land or deserts (desertification).* Each year almost 60,000 square kilometers (23,000 square miles) of new desert are formed, mostly from overgrazing.

- *Eliminating or decimating wild species (biodiversity) through destruction of habitats, commercial hunting, pest control, and pollution.* Each year thousands of wildlife species become extinct, mostly because of human activities. If habitat destruction continues at present rates, as many as 1.5 million species could disappear over the next 25 years—a drastic loss in vital Earth capital.

- *Polluting renewable air, water, and soil so that they are unusable.*

1-5 Unsustainability: Problems and Causes

KEY PROBLEMS A number of interconnected environmental and resource problems make up the overall *crisis of unsustainability* many of the world's leading scientists believe we face (Spotlight, p. 15). Four of these problems—possible climate change from global warming, acid rain, depletion of stratospheric ozone, and urban air pollution—result from the chemicals we have put into the atmosphere (mostly from burning fossil fuels). A fifth problem, the continued poisoning of the soil and water by pesticides and numerous other toxic wastes, is the result of not relying on pollution prevention. Another six problems—depletion of nonrenewable minerals (especially oil), depletion and contamination of groundwater, deforestation, soil erosion, conversion of productive cropland and grazing land to desert (desertification), and species loss (biodiversity depletion)—result from exponentially growing depletion and degradation of Earth capital.

Population growth (more consumers) and environmentally harmful forms of economic growth (more resource depletion, pollution, and environmental degradation) can intensify these problems. Poverty can also increase environmental degradation by causing poor people to destroy potentially renewable

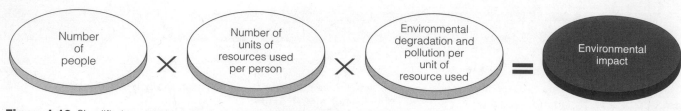

Figure 1-10 Simplified model of how three factors—population (P), affluence (A), and technology (T)—affect the environmental impact (I) (environmental degradation and pollution) of population.

resources such as soil, forests, and wildlife for short-term survival.

ROOT CAUSES Once we have identified key environmental problems, the next step is to identify their underlying causes. They include:

- *Overpopulation.*
- *Overconsumption of resources, especially by the affluent.*
- *Poverty.*
- *Resource waste.*
- *Widespread use of environmentally damaging fossil fuels (especially oil and coal).*
- *Loss of biodiversity through oversimplification of Earth's life-support systems.*
- *Failure to encourage Earth-sustaining forms of economic development and discourage Earth-degrading forms of economic growth.*
- *Failure to have market prices represent the overall environmental cost of an economic good or service. This promotes inefficiency and depletion of Earth capital for short-term profit by concealing the harmful effects of the products we buy.*
- *Our urge to dominate and control nature for our use.*

CONNECTIONS BETWEEN ROOT CAUSES AND PROBLEMS Once we have identified the causes of our problems, the next step is to understand how they are connected to one another. The three-factor model in Figure 1-10 is a good starting point.

According to this model, total environmental degradation and pollution—that is, the environmental impact of population—in a given area depends on three factors: **(1)** the number of people (population size, P), **(2)** the average number of units of resources each person uses (consumption per capita or affluence, A), and **(3)** the amount of environmental degradation

and pollution produced for each unit of resource used (the environmental destructiveness of the technologies used to provide and use resources, T). This model, developed in the early 1970s by biologist Paul Ehrlich and physicist John Holdren, can be summarized in simplified form as Impact = Population × Affluence × Technology, or $I = P \times A \times T$.

Overpopulation occurs when too many people deplete the resources that support life and economies, and when they introduce more wastes than the environment can handle. It happens when people exceed the **carrying capacity** of an area: the number of people an area can support given its resource base and the way those resources are used. The three factors in Figure 1-10 can interact to produce two types of overpopulation (Figure 1-11).

People overpopulation exists where there are more people than the available supplies of food, water, and other important resources can support at a minimal level. Here, population size and the resulting degradation of potentially renewable resources, as the poor struggle to stay alive, tend to be the key factors determining total environmental impact. In the world's poorest LDCs people overpopulation and the wealth gap cause premature death for 40 million people each year and absolute poverty for 1.2 billion.

Consumption overpopulation, or **overconsumption**, exists in industrialized countries, where only one-fifth of the world's people use resources at such a high rate that significant pollution, environmental degradation, and resource depletion occur. With this type of overpopulation, high rates of resource use per person (and the resulting high levels of pollution and environmental degradation per person) are the key factors determining overall environmental impact.

For example, the average U.S. citizen consumes 50 times as much as the average citizen of India (and 100 times as much as the average person in some LDCs). If we take the average Indian's consumption as the norm, the environmental impact of 258 million Americans is equal to that of 12.9 billion Indians—more than

Q: What royalties do companies and individuals removing hard-rock minerals from federal public lands pay the federal government?

People Overpopulation

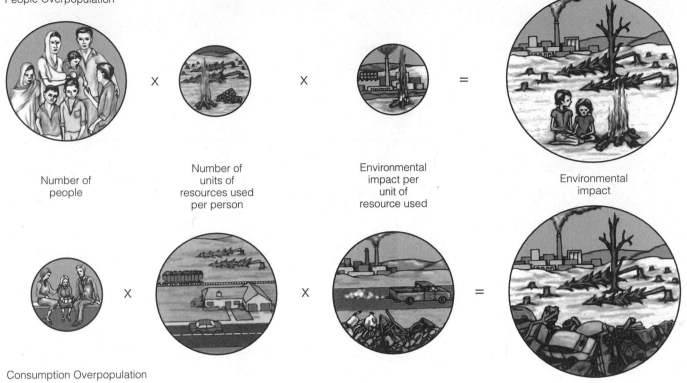

| Number of people | Number of units of resources used per person | Environmental impact per unit of resource used | Environmental impact |

Consumption Overpopulation

Figure 1-11 Two types of overpopulation, based on the relative importance of the factors in the model shown in Figure 1-10. Circle size shows relative importance of each factor. People overpopulation is caused mostly by growing numbers of people. Consumption overpopulation, or overconsumption, is caused mostly by growing affluence (resource consumption).

twice the world's population. *This means that poor parents in an LDC would need 100–200 children to have the same environmental impact as 2 children in a typical family in the United States.*

We know from studying other species that when a population exceeds or *overshoots* the carrying capacity of its environment, it suffers a *dieback* that reduces its population to a sustainable size. How long will we be able to continue our exponential growth in population and resource use without suffering overshoot and dieback? No one knows, but warning signals from the Earth are forcing us to consider the question seriously (Spotlight, p. 15).

The three-factor model in Figure 1-10 is useful in understanding how key environmental problems and some of their causes are connected. However, the interconnected environmental, resource, and social problems we face are much more complex and involve a number of poorly understood interactions among a number of factors (Figure 1-12).

WORKING WITH THE EARTH   This chapter has presented you with an overview of the serious problems we face and their root causes. Some analysts (mostly economists) contend that the world is not overpopulated and that more people are our most important resource as consumers to fuel continued growth and as sources of technological ingenuity. They believe that technological advances will allow us to clean up pollution to acceptable levels and find substitutes for resources that become scarce. To these analysts, there is no actual or potential crisis of unsustainability, and they accuse environmentalists of overstating the seriousness of the problems we face. The rest of this book presents a more detailed analysis of these problems, along with solutions proposed by various scientists and environmentalists. There are also encouraging examples of things individuals and groups are doing to help sustain the earth, as well as a number of "Individuals Matter" boxes that suggest what you can do to work with the earth.

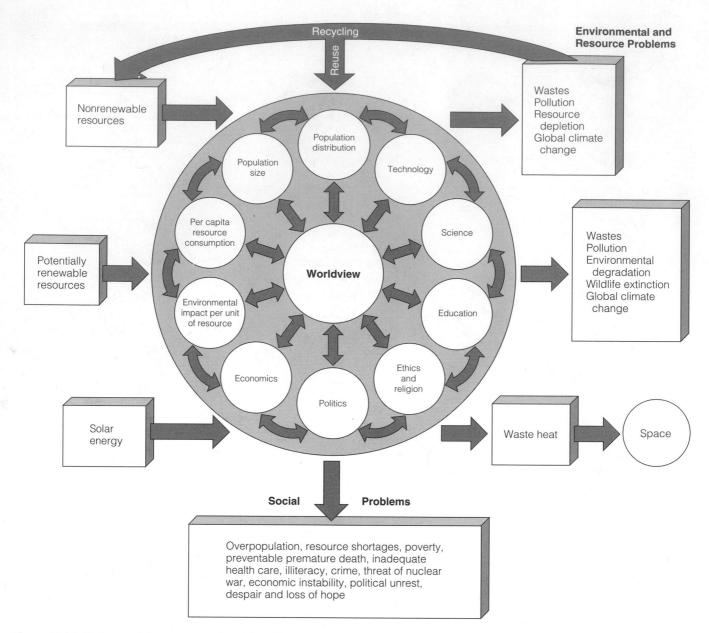

Figure 1-12 Environmental, resource, and social problems are caused by a complex, poorly understood mix of interacting factors, as illustrated by this simplified model.

The key to dealing with the problems we face is recognizing that *individuals matter*. Anthropologist Margaret Mead has summarized our potential for change: "Never doubt that a small group of thoughtful, committed citizens can change the world. Indeed it is the only thing that ever has."

What's the use of a house if you don't have a decent planet to put it on?

HENRY DAVID THOREAU

CRITICAL THINKING

1. Is the world overpopulated? Explain. Is the United States suffering from consumption overpopulation? Explain.

2. Do you favor instituting policies designed to reduce population growth and stabilize
    a. the size of the world's population as soon as possible and
    b. the size of the U.S. population as soon as possible?

Q: How many children under age 5 die each day in poor countries of causes that could be prevented?

The following urgent warning to humanity was issued on November 18, 1992 and sent to government leaders of all nations. It was signed by over 1,600 scientists from 70 countries, including 102 out of the 196 living scientists who are Nobel laureates.

INTRODUCTION. The environment is suffering critical stress:

The Atmosphere. Stratospheric ozone depletion threatens us with enhanced ultraviolet radiation at the earth's surface, which can be damaging or lethal to many forms of life. Air pollution near ground level, and acid deposition, are already causing widespread injury to humans, forests, and crops.

Water Resources. Heedless exploitation of depletable groundwater supplies endangers food production and other essential human systems. Heavy demands on the world's surface waters have resulted in serious shortages in some 80 countries, containing 40% of the world's population. Pollution of rivers, lakes, and groundwater further limits the supply.

Oceans. Destructive pressure on the oceans is severe, particularly on coastal regions which produce most of the world's food fish. The total marine catch is now at or above the estimated maximum sustainable yield. Some fisheries have already shown signs of collapse. Rivers carrying heavy burdens of eroded soil into the seas carry industrial, municipal, agricultural, and livestock waste—some of it toxic.

*Used by permission from Union of Concerned Scientists, Cambridge, MA 02238.

Soil. Loss of soil productivity, which is causing extensive land abandonment, is a widespread by-product of current practices in agriculture and animal husbandry. Since 1945, 11% of the earth's vegetated surface has been degraded—an area larger than India and China combined—and per capita food production in many parts of the world is decreasing.

Forests. Tropical rain forests, as well as tropical and temperate dry forests, are being destroyed rapidly. At present rates, some critical forest types will be gone in a few years, and most of the tropical rain forests will be gone before the end of the next century. With them will go large numbers of plant and animal species.

Living Species. The irreversible loss of species, which by 2100 may reach one-third of all species now living, is especially serious. We are losing the potential they hold for providing medicinal and other benefits, and the contribution that genetic diversity of life forms gives to the robustness of the world's biological systems and to the astonishing beauty of the earth itself.

Much of this damage is irreversible on a scale of centuries or permanent. Other processes appear to pose additional threats. Increasing levels of gases in the atmosphere from human activities, including carbon dioxide released from fossil fuel burning and from deforestation, may alter climate on a global scale. Predictions of global warming are still uncertain—with projected effects ranging from tolerable to very severe—but the potential risks are very great.

Our massive tampering with the world's interdependent web of life—coupled with the environmental damage inflicted by deforestation, species loss, and climate change—could trigger widespread adverse effects, including unpredictable collapses of critical biological systems whose interactions and dynamics we only imperfectly understand. Uncertainty over the extent of these effects cannot excuse complacency or delay in facing the threats.

POPULATION. The earth is finite. Its ability to absorb wastes and destructive effluent is finite. Its ability to provide food and energy is finite. Its ability to provide for growing numbers of people is finite. And we are fast approaching many of the earth's limits. Current economic practices which damage the environment, in both developed and undeveloped nations, cannot be continued without the risk that vital global systems will be damaged beyond repair.

Pressures resulting from unrestrained population growth put demands on the natural world that can overwhelm any efforts to achieve a sustainable future. If we are to halt destruction of our environment, we must accept limits to that growth. A World Bank estimate indicates that world population will stabilize at 12.4 billion, while the United Nations concluded that the eventual total could reach 14 billion, a near tripling of today's 5.4 billion. But, even at this moment, one person in five lives in absolute poverty without enough to eat, and one in ten suffers serious malnutrition.

No more than one or a few decades remain before the chance to avert the threats we now confront will be lost and the prospects for humanity immeasurably diminished.

WARNING. We the undersigned, senior members of the world's scientific community, hereby warn all humanity of what lies ahead. A great change in the stewardship of

(continued)

the earth and the life on it, is required, if vast human misery is to be avoided and our global home on this planet is not to be irretrievably mutilated.

WHAT WE MUST DO. Five inextricably linked areas must be addressed simultaneously:

1. **We must bring environmentally damaging activities under control to restore and protect the integrity of the earth's systems we depend on**. We must, for example, move away from fossil fuels to more benign, inexhaustible energy sources to cut greenhouse emissions and the pollution of our air and water. Priority must be given to the development of energy sources matched to third world needs—small scale and relatively easy to implement. We must half deforestation, injury and loss of agricultural land, and the loss of terrestrial and marine plant and animal species.

2. **We must manage resources crucial to human welfare more effectively**. We must give high priority to efficient use of energy, water, and other materials, including expansion of conservation and recycling.

3. **We must stabilize population.** This will be possible only if all nations recognize that it requires improved social and economic conditions, and the adoption of effective, voluntary family planning.

4. **We must reduce and eventually eliminate poverty**.

5. **We must ensure sexual equality, and guarantee women control over their own reproductive decisions**.

The developed nations are the largest polluters in the world today.

They must greatly reduce their overconsumption, if we are to reduce pressures on resources and the global environment. The developed nations have the obligation to provide aid and support to developing nations, because only the developed nations have the financial resources and technical skills for these tasks.

Acting on this recognition is not altruism, but enlightened self-interest: whether industrialized or not, we all have but one lifeboat. No nation can escape injury when global biological systems are damaged. No nations can escape from conflicts over increasingly scarce resources. In addition, environmental and economic instabilities will cause mass migrations with incalculable consequences for developed and undeveloped nations alike.

Developing nations must realize that environmental damage is one of the gravest threats they face, and that attempts to blunt it will be overwhelmed if their populations go unchecked. The greatest peril is to become trapped in spirals of environmental decline, poverty, and unrest, leading to social, economic, and environmental collapse.

Success in this global endeavor will require a great reduction in violence and war. Resources now devoted to the preparation and conduct of war—amounting to over $1 trillion annually—will be badly needed in the new tasks and should be diverted to the new challenge.

A new ethic is required—a new responsibility for caring for ourselves and for the earth. We must recognize the earth's limited capacity to provide for us. We must recognize its fragility. We must no longer allow it to be ravaged. This ethic must motivate a great movement, convincing reluctant leaders and reluctant governments and reluctant peoples themselves to effect the needed changes.

The scientists issuing this warning hope that our message will reach and affect people everywhere. We need the help of many.

We require the help of the world community of scientists—natural, social, economic, political;

We require the help of the world's business and industrial leaders;

We require the help of the world's religious leaders; and

We require the help of the world's people.

We call on all to join us in this task.

Q: What percentage of environmental spending in the United States is devoted to preventing pollution?

Explain. What policies do you believe should be implemented?

3. Explain why you agree or disagree with the following propositions:
   a. High levels of resource use by the United States and other MDCs are beneficial.
   b. MDCs stimulate the economic growth of LDCs by buying their raw materials.
   c. High levels of resource use also stimulate economic growth in MDCs.
   d. Economic growth provides money for more financial aid to LDCs and for reducing pollution, environmental degradation, and poverty.

4. Explain why you agree or disagree with the following proposition: The world will never run out of resources because technological innovations will produce substitutes or allow use of lower grades of scarce resources.

*5. Make a list of the resources you truly need. Then make another list of the resources that you use each day only because you want them. Then make a third list of resources you want and hope to use in the future.

---

*Questions preceded by an asterisk are laboratory exercises or individual or class projects.

2 Matter, Energy, and Ecology: Connections in Nature

2-1 Science and Environmental Science

WHAT IS SCIENCE? **Science** is an attempt to discover order in nature and then use that knowledge to make predictions or projections about what will happen in nature. Scientists collect **scientific data**, or facts, by making observations and taking measurements, but this is not the main purpose of science. As French scientist Henri Poincaré put it, "Science is built up of facts, but a collection of facts is no more science than a heap of stones is a house."

Scientists try to describe what is happening in nature by organizing data into a generalization or scientific law. Thus scientific data are stepping-stones to a **scientific law**, a description of the orderly behavior observed in nature—a summary of what we find happening in nature over and over in the same way. For example, after making thousands of measurements involving changes in matter, chemists concluded that in any physical change (such as converting liquid water to water vapor) or any chemical change (such as burning coal) no matter is created or destroyed. This summary of what we always observe in nature is called the *law of conservation of matter*.

Scientists then try to explain how or why things happen the way a scientific law describes. To answer such questions, investigators develop a **scientific hypothesis**, an educated guess that explains a scientific law or certain scientific facts. More than 2,400 years ago Greek philosophers proposed that all matter is composed of tiny particles called atoms, but they had no experimental evidence to back up their *atomic hypothesis*. Scientists also develop and use various types of **models** to simulate complex processes and systems.

If many experiments by different scientists support a hypothesis or model, it becomes a **scientific theory**—a well-tested and widely accepted scientific hypothesis. During the last two centuries scientists have done experiments that elevated the atomic hypothesis to the *atomic theory of matter*. This theory, in turn, explains the law of conservation of matter with the idea that in any physical or chemical change no atoms can be created or destroyed. Establishing a scientific law or converting a scientific hypothesis to a widely accepted theory is an arduous and rigorous undertaking, and such laws and theories should not be taken lightly.

SCIENTIFIC METHODS The ways scientists gather data and formulate and test scientific hypotheses, laws, and theories are called **scientific methods**. A scientific method is a set of questions with no particular rules for answering them. The major questions a scientist attempts to answer are these:

- What questions about nature should I try to answer?

- What relevant facts are already known, and what new data should I collect?

- How should I collect these data?

- How can I organize and analyze the data I have collected to develop a pattern of order or scientific law?

- How can I come up with a hypothesis to explain the law and use it to predict some new facts?

- Is this the simplest and only reasonable hypothesis?

- What new experiments should I run to test the hypothesis (and modify it if necessary) so it can become a scientific theory?

New discoveries happen in many ways. Some follow a data $\longrightarrow$ law $\longrightarrow$ hypothesis $\longrightarrow$ theory sequence. Other times scientists simply follow a hunch or a bias and then do experiments to test it. Some discoveries occur when an experiment gives totally unexpected results and the scientist insists on finding out what happened. So, in reality, there are many methods of science rather than one scientific method. Trying to discover order in nature requires logical reasoning, but it also requires imagination and intuition. As Albert Einstein once said, "Imagination is more important than knowledge, and there is no completely logical way to a new scientific idea." Intuition and creativity are as important in science as they

Q: How much of the world's population is in the United States?

> *When we try to pick out anything by itself, we find it hitched to everything else in the universe.*
>
> JOHN MUIR

are in poetry, art, music, and other great adventures of the human spirit that awaken us to the wonder, mystery, and beauty of the universe, the earth, and life.

ENVIRONMENTAL SCIENCE Environmental science is the study of how we and other species interact with one another and with the nonliving environment of matter and energy. It is a *physical and social science* that uses and integrates knowledge from physics, chemistry, biology (especially ecology), geology, geography, resource technology and engineering, resource conservation and management, demography (the study of population dynamics), economics, politics, and ethics. In other words, it is a study of how everything works and interacts—a study of *connections* in the common home of all living things. This is an incredibly complex, uncertain, and controversial task.

LIMITATIONS AND MISUSE OF SCIENCE Some people misunderstand the nature and limitations of science, and others may deliberately misuse it. Those who say that something has or has not been "scientifically proven" imply falsely that science yields absolute proof or certainty. *Scientists can disprove things, but they can never establish absolute proof or truth.*

Instead of certainty, science gives us information in the following form: If we do so-and-so (say, add certain chemicals to the atmosphere at particular rates), there is a certain chance (high, moderate, or low) that we will cause various effects (such as change the climate or deplete ozone in the stratosphere). The more complex the system or problem being studied, the less certain the hypotheses, models, and theories used to explain it.

Science advances by debate, argument, speculation, and controversy. Disputes among scientists over the validity of data, hypotheses, and models (tentative ideas still being rigorously evaluated and tested) are what the media usually report. Such disagreements make juicier stories, but what's really important is the *consensus* among scientists about various scientific laws, theories, and issues (Spotlight, p. 15). This substantial agreement—the real knowledge of science—rarely gets reported, which gives the public a false idea of the nature of science and of scientific knowledge.

Most environmental problems involve such complex mixtures of data, lack of data, hypotheses, and theories in the physical and social sciences that we don't have enough information to understand them very well. This allows advocates of any proposed action or inaction on an environmental problem to support their beliefs, and it can lead to *scientific overkill*. It can also lead to the *paralysis-by-analysis* trap, which insists that we fully understand a problem before taking any action—an impossible dream because of the inherent limitations of science and the complexities of environmental problems.

Since environmental problems won't go away, at some point we have to evaluate available information and make a political or economic decision about what to do (or not do), often based primarily on gut feelings, intuition, common sense (which each side claims it is using), and values. This is why differing worldviews and values are at the heart of most environmental controversies (Section 12-7). People with different worldviews and values can take the same information, come to completely different conclusions, and still be logically consistent. There are no easy answers.

2-2 Matter and Energy

NATURE'S BUILDING BLOCKS Matter is anything that has mass (the amount of material in an object) and takes up space. It includes the solids, liquids, and gases around you and within your body. Scientists classify matter as existing in various levels of organization (Figure 2-1).

Matter is found in three *chemical forms*: **elements** (the distinctive building blocks of matter that make up every material substance), **compounds** (two or more different elements held together in fixed proportions by attractive forces called *chemical bonds*), and **mixtures** (combinations of elements, compounds, or both). All matter is built from the 109 known chemical elements. To simplify things, chemists represent each element by a one- or two-letter symbol, for example,

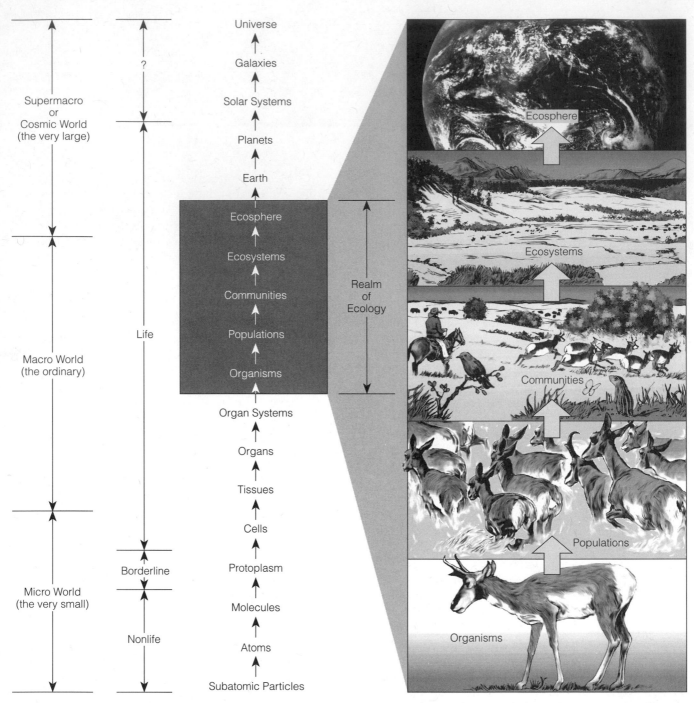

Figure 2-1 Levels of organization of matter according to size and function. This is one way scientists classify patterns of matter found in nature.

hydrogen (H), carbon (C), oxygen (O), nitrogen (N), phosphorus (P), sulfur (S), chlorine (Cl), fluorine (F), bromine (Br), sodium (Na), calcium (Ca), and uranium (U).

If you had a supermicroscope to look at elements and compounds, you would discover that they are made up of three types of building blocks: **atoms** (the smallest unit of matter that is unique to a particular element), **ions** (electrically charged atoms), and **mole-**

cules (combinations of atoms of the same or different elements held together by chemical bonds). Since ions and molecules are formed from atoms, atoms are the ultimate building blocks for all matter.

If you increased the magnification of your supermicroscope, you would find that each different type of atom is composed of a certain number of *subatomic particles*. The main building blocks of an atom are positively charged **protons** (represented by the symbol *p*),

Q: In terms of resource use and environmental impact, what is the most overpopulated country in the world?

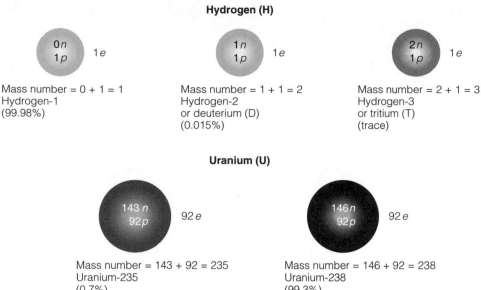

Hydrogen (H)

Mass number = 0 + 1 = 1
Hydrogen-1
(99.98%)

Mass number = 1 + 1 = 2
Hydrogen-2
or deuterium (D)
(0.015%)

Mass number = 2 + 1 = 3
Hydrogen-3
or tritium (T)
(trace)

Uranium (U)

Mass number = 143 + 92 = 235
Uranium-235
(0.7%)

Mass number = 146 + 92 = 238
Uranium-238
(99.3%)

Figure 2-2 Isotopes of hydrogen and uranium. All isotopes of hydrogen have an atomic number of 1 because each has 1 proton in its nucleus; similarly, all uranium isotopes have an atomic number of 92. However, each isotope of these elements has a different mass number because its nucleus contains a different number of neutrons. Figures in parentheses show the percentage abundance by weight of each isotope in a natural sample of the element.

uncharged **neutrons** (*n*), and negatively charged **electrons** (*e*).

Each atom consists of a relatively small center, or **nucleus**, containing protons and neutrons, and one or more electrons in rapid motion somewhere around the nucleus.

The distinguishing feature of an atom of any given element is the number of protons in its nucleus, called its **atomic number**. The simplest element, hydrogen (H), has only 1 proton in its nucleus; its atomic number is 1. Carbon (C), with 6 protons, has an atomic number of 6, while uranium (U), a much larger atom, has 92 protons and an atomic number of 92.

Because electrons have so little mass, most of an atom's mass is concentrated in its nucleus. We describe the mass of an atom in terms of its **mass number**: the number of neutrons plus the number of protons in its nucleus. Although all atoms of an element have the same number of protons in their nuclei, they may have different numbers of uncharged neutrons in their nuclei and thus different mass numbers. These different forms of an element with the same atomic number but a different mass number are called **isotopes** of that element. Isotopes are identified by attaching their mass numbers to the name or symbol of the element. Hydrogen, for example, has three isotopes: hydrogen-1, or H-1; hydrogen-2, or H-2 (common name, deuterium); and hydrogen-3, or H-3 (common name, tritium). A natural sample of an element contains a mixture of its isotopes in a fixed proportion or percent abundance by weight (Figure 2-2).

Most matter exists as *compounds*. Chemists use a shorthand **chemical formula** to show the number of atoms (or ions) of each type found in the basic structural unit of a compound. The formula contains the symbols for each of the elements present and uses subscripts to show the number of atoms (or ions) of each element in the compound's basic structural unit. Each molecule of water, for example, consists of two hydrogen atoms chemically bonded to an oxygen atom, giving H_2O (read as "H-two-O") molecules. The subscript after the symbol of the element gives the number of atoms of that element in a molecule. Other examples you will encounter in this book are O_2 (oxygen), O_3 (ozone), N_2 (nitrogen), nitrous oxide (N_2O), nitric oxide (NO), carbon monoxide (CO), carbon dioxide (CO_2), nitrogen dioxide (NO_2), sulfur dioxide (SO_2), ammonia (NH_3), sulfuric acid (H_2SO_4), nitric acid (HNO_3), methane (CH_4), and glucose ($C_6H_{12}O_6$).

MATTER QUALITY **Matter quality** is a measure of how useful a matter resource is, based on its availability and concentration. **High-quality matter** is organized and concentrated, and it is usually found near the earth's surface. It has great potential for use as a matter resource. **Low-quality matter** is disorganized, dilute, or dispersed, and it is often found deep underground or dispersed in the ocean or in the atmosphere. It usually has little potential for use as a matter resource (Figure 2-3).

An aluminum can is a more concentrated, higher-quality form of aluminum than aluminum ore with the same amount of aluminum. That's why it takes less energy, water, and money to recycle an aluminum can than to make a new can from aluminum ore.

Matter is also found in three *physical states*: solid, liquid, and gas. Water, for example, exists as ice, liquid water, and water vapor, depending on its temperature and pressure. The differences among the three physical states of a sample of matter are in the relative

High Quality   **Low Quality**

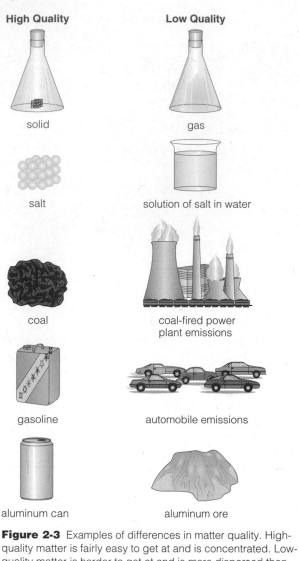

solid

salt

coal

gasoline

aluminum can

gas

solution of salt in water

coal-fired power
plant emissions

automobile emissions

aluminum ore

Figure 2-3 Examples of differences in matter quality. High-quality matter is fairly easy to get at and is concentrated. Low-quality matter is harder to get at and is more dispersed than high-quality matter.

orderliness of its atoms, ions, or molecules, with solids having the most orderly arrangement and gases the least orderly.

ENERGY   Energy is the capacity to do work. You cannot pick up or touch energy, but you can use it to do work. You do work when you move matter, such as your arm or this book. Work, or matter movement, also is needed to boil liquid water and change it into steam—or to burn natural gas to heat a house or cook food. Energy is also the heat that flows automatically from a hot object to a cold object. Touch a hot stove and you experience this energy flow in a painful way.

Energy comes in many forms: light; heat; electricity; chemical energy stored in the chemical bonds in coal, sugar, and other materials; moving matter such as water, wind (air masses), and joggers; and nuclear energy emitted from the nuclei of certain isotopes.

Scientists classify energy as either kinetic or potential. **Kinetic energy** is the energy that matter has because of its motion and mass. Wind (a moving mass of air), flowing streams, falling rocks, heat, electricity (flowing charged particles), and moving cars have kinetic energy. Radio waves, TV waves, microwaves, infrared radiation, visible light, ultraviolet radiation, X rays, gamma rays, and cosmic rays are also forms of kinetic energy traveling as waves and known as **electromagnetic radiation** (Figure 2-4).

Potential energy is stored energy that is potentially available for use. A rock held in your hand, still water behind a dam, nuclear energy stored in the nuclei of atoms, and chemical energy stored in molecules in gasoline and in food all have potential energy because of their position or the position of their parts. When you drop a rock held in your hand its potential energy changes into kinetic energy. When you burn

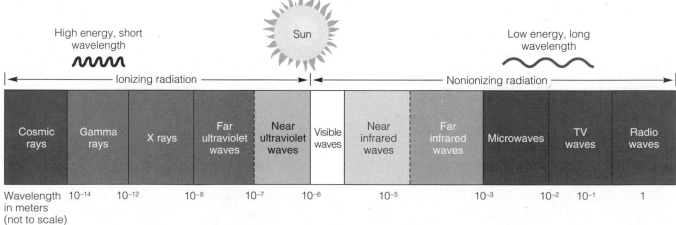

High energy, short
wavelength

Sun

Low energy, long
wavelength

|←――――――――――――― Ionizing radiation ―――――――――――――→|←――――――――――― Nonionizing radiation ―――――――――――→|

Cosmic rays	Gamma rays	X rays	Far ultraviolet waves	Near ultraviolet waves	Visible waves	Near infrared waves	Far infrared waves	Microwaves	TV waves	Radio waves

Wavelength 10^{-14} 10^{-12} 10^{-8} 10^{-7} 10^{-6} 10^{-5} 10^{-3} 10^{-2} 10^{-1} 1
in meters
(not to scale)

Figure 2-4 The electromagnetic spectrum: the range of electromagnetic waves, which differ in wavelength (distance between successive peaks or troughs) and energy content. *Ionizing radiation* has enough energy to knock electrons from atoms and ions and change them to positively charged ions. The resulting highly reactive electrons and ions can alter organic compounds in living cells, interfere with bodily processes, and cause illness, including various cancers.

Q: Do scientists establish absolute proof or truth?

gasoline in a car engine, the potential energy stored in the chemical bonds of its molecules changes into heat, light, and mechanical (kinetic) energy that propels the car.

ENERGY QUALITY   Energy varies in its ability to do useful work. **Energy quality** is a measure of usefulness (Figure 2-5). **High-quality energy** is organized or concentrated and has great ability to perform useful work. Examples of these useful sources of energy are electricity, coal, gasoline, concentrated sunlight, nuclei of uranium-235, and heat concentrated in fairly small amounts of matter so that its temperature is high.

By contrast, **low-quality energy** is disorganized or dispersed and has little ability to do useful work. An example is heat dispersed in the moving molecules of a large amount of matter, such as the atmosphere or a large body of water, so that its temperature is relatively low. For instance, the total amount of heat stored in the Atlantic Ocean is greater than the amount of high-quality chemical energy stored in all the oil deposits of Saudi Arabia. However, the ocean's heat is so widely dispersed that it can't be used to move things or to heat things to high temperatures.

We use energy to accomplish certain tasks, each requiring a certain minimum energy quality (Figure 2-5). Electrical energy, which is very high-quality energy, is needed to run lights, electric motors, and electronic devices. We need high-quality mechanical energy to move a car, but we need only low-temperature air (less than 100°C) to heat homes and other buildings. It makes sense to match the quality of an energy source to the quality of energy needed to perform a particular task (Figure 2-5)—this saves energy and usually money.

PHYSICAL AND CHEMICAL CHANGES   A physical change is one that involves no change in chemical composition. For example, cutting a piece of aluminum foil into small pieces is a physical change—each cut piece is still aluminum. Changing a substance from one physical state to another is also a physical change. For example, when solid water, or ice, is melted or liquid water is boiled, none of the H_2O molecules involved are altered; instead, the molecules are organized in different spatial patterns.

In a **chemical change**, or **chemical reaction**, there is a change in the chemical composition of the

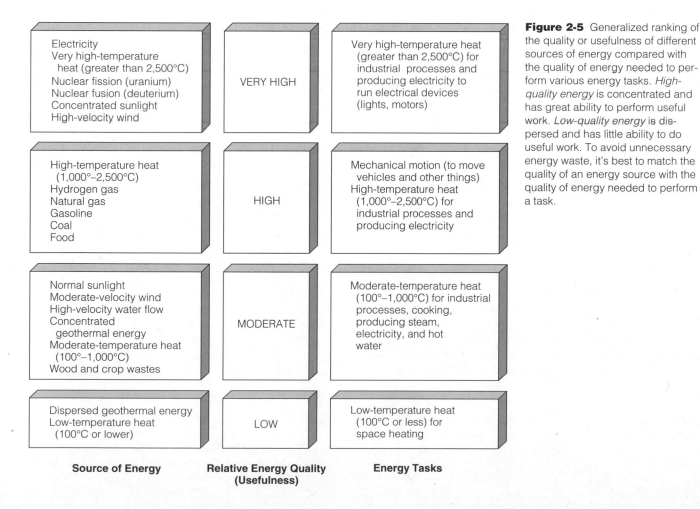

Figure 2-5 Generalized ranking of the quality or usefulness of different sources of energy compared with the quality of energy needed to perform various energy tasks. *High-quality energy* is concentrated and has great ability to perform useful work. *Low-quality energy* is dispersed and has little ability to do useful work. To avoid unnecessary energy waste, it's best to match the quality of an energy source with the quality of energy needed to perform a task.

Source of Energy	Relative Energy Quality (Usefulness)	Energy Tasks
Electricity Very high-temperature heat (greater than 2,500°C) Nuclear fission (uranium) Nuclear fusion (deuterium) Concentrated sunlight High-velocity wind	VERY HIGH	Very high-temperature heat (greater than 2,500°C) for industrial processes and producing electricity to run electrical devices (lights, motors)
High-temperature heat (1,000°–2,500°C) Hydrogen gas Natural gas Gasoline Coal Food	HIGH	Mechanical motion (to move vehicles and other things) High-temperature heat (1,000°–2,500°C) for industrial processes and producing electricity
Normal sunlight Moderate-velocity wind High-velocity water flow Concentrated geothermal energy Moderate-temperature heat (100°–1,000°C) Wood and crop wastes	MODERATE	Moderate-temperature heat (100°–1,000°C) for industrial processes, cooking, producing steam, electricity, and hot water
Dispersed geothermal energy Low-temperature heat (100°C or lower)	LOW	Low-temperature heat (100°C or less) for space heating

elements or compounds involved. For example, when coal burns completely, the solid carbon (C) it contains combines with oxygen gas (O_2) from the atmosphere to form the gaseous compound carbon dioxide (CO_2). We can represent this chemical reaction in shorthand form as $C + O_2 \longrightarrow CO_2 + energy$.

Energy is given off in this reaction, making coal a useful fuel. The reaction also shows how the burning of coal or any carbon-containing compounds, such as those in wood, natural gas, oil, and gasoline, adds carbon dioxide gas to the atmosphere.

THE LAW OF CONSERVATION OF MATTER: THERE IS NO "AWAY"

You, like most people, probably talk about consuming or using up material resources, but the truth is that we don't consume matter. We only use some of Earth's resources for a while. We take materials from the earth, carry them to another part of the globe, and process them into products. These products are used and then discarded, reused, or recycled.

We may change various elements and compounds from one physical or chemical form to another, but in all physical and chemical changes we can't create or destroy any of the atoms involved. All we can do is rearrange them into different spatial patterns (physical changes) or different combinations (chemical changes). This fact, based on many thousands of measurements of matter undergoing physical and chemical changes, is known as the **law of conservation of matter**.

The law of conservation of matter means that there is no away to throw things to. *Everything we think we have thrown away is still here with us in one form or another.*

The law of conservation of matter means that we will always be faced with the problem of what to do with some quantity of chemical wastes. By placing much greater emphasis on pollution prevention and waste reduction, however, we can greatly reduce the amount of chemical wastes we add to the environment.

FIRST LAW OF ENERGY: YOU CAN'T GET SOMETHING FOR NOTHING

Scientists have observed energy being changed from one form to another in physical and chemical changes, but they have never been able to detect any energy being created or destroyed. This summary of what happens in nature is called the **law of conservation of energy**, also known as the **first law of energy** or **first law of thermodynamics**. This law means that when one form of energy is converted to another form in any physical or chemical change *energy input always equals energy output: We can't get something for nothing in terms of energy quantity.*

SECOND LAW OF ENERGY: YOU CAN'T BREAK EVEN

Because the first law of energy states that energy can be neither created nor destroyed, you might think that there will always be enough energy; yet, if you fill a car's tank with gasoline and drive around, or if you use a flashlight battery until it is dead, you have lost something. If it isn't energy, what is it? The answer is energy quality (Figure 2-5).

Countless experiments have shown that in any conversion of energy from one form to another, there is always a decrease in energy quality (the amount of useful energy). These findings are expressed in the **second law of energy**, or the **second law of thermodynamics**: When energy is changed from one form to another, some of the useful energy is always degraded to lower-quality, more-dispersed, less-useful energy. This degraded energy is usually in the form of heat, which flows into the environment and is dispersed by the random motion of air or water molecules.

In other words, *we can't break even in terms of energy quality because energy always goes from a more useful to a less useful form*. No one has ever found a violation of this fundamental scientific law.

Consider three examples of the second energy law in action. First, when a car is driven, only about 10% of the high-quality chemical energy available in its gasoline fuel is converted into mechanical energy to propel the vehicle and into electrical energy to run its electrical systems. The remaining 90% is degraded heat that is released into the environment and eventually lost into space. Second, when electrical energy flows through filament wires in an incandescent light bulb, it is changed into about 5% useful light and 95% low-quality heat that flows into the environment. What we call a light bulb is really a heat bulb. A third example of the degradation of energy quality in living systems is illustrated in Figure 2-6.

The second energy law also means that *we can never recycle or reuse high-quality energy to perform useful work*. Once the concentrated energy in a piece of food, a tank of gasoline, a lump of coal, or a chunk of uranium is released, it is degraded to low-quality heat that becomes dispersed in the environment. We can heat air or water at a low temperature and upgrade it to high-quality energy, but the second energy law tells us that it will take more high-quality energy to do this than we get in return.

2-3 Earth's Life-Support Systems: From Organisms to the Ecosphere

EARTH'S MAJOR COMPONENTS We can think of Earth as being made up of layers or spheres (Figure 2-7):

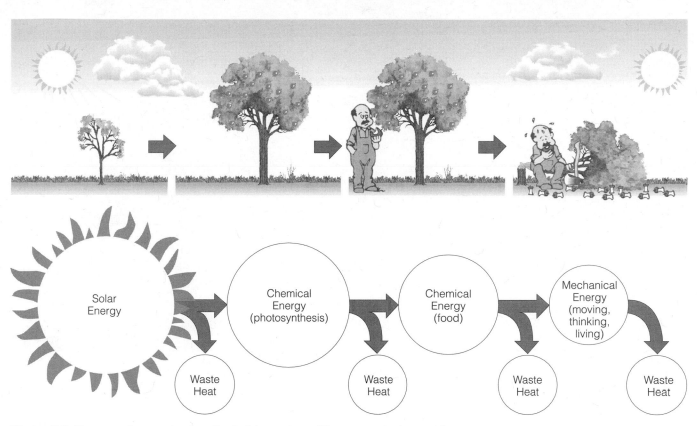

Figure 2-6 The second energy law in action in living systems. When energy is changed from one form to another, some of the initial input of high-quality energy is degraded, usually to low-quality heat, which disperses in the environment.

- The **atmosphere**—a thin, gaseous envelope of air around the planet. Its inner layer, the **troposphere**, extends only about 17 kilometers (11 miles) above sea level but contains most of the planet's air—mostly nitrogen (78%) and oxygen (21%). The next layer, stretching 17–48 kilometers (11–30 miles) above Earth's surface, is called the **stratosphere**. Its lower portion contains enough ozone (O_3) to filter out most of the sun's harmful ultraviolet radiation, thus allowing life on land to exist.

- The **hydrosphere**—liquid water (both surface and underground), frozen water (polar ice, icebergs, permafrost in soil), and water vapor in the atmosphere.

- The **lithosphere**—Earth's crust and upper mantle. It contains the fossil fuels and minerals we use and the soil chemicals (nutrients) needed to support plant life.

- The **ecosphere** or **biosphere**—the portion of the earth where living (biotic) organisms are found and interact with one another and with their nonliving (abiotic) environment. This zone reaches from the deepest ocean floor 20 kilometers (12

miles) upward to the tops of the highest mountains. If Earth were an apple, the ecosphere would be no thicker than the apple's skin, a haven for life between Earth's molten interior and the lifeless cold of space. *The goal of ecology is to learn how this thin global skin of air, water, soil, and organisms works.*

CONNECTIONS: ENERGY FLOW, MATTER CYCLING, AND GRAVITY Life on Earth depends on three connected factors (Figure 2-8):

- The *one-way flow of high-quality (usable) energy* from the sun, through materials and living things on or near the earth's surface, then into the environment as low-quality energy (mostly heat dispersed into air or water molecules at a low temperature), and eventually back into space as infrared radiation (Figure 2-9)

- The *cycling of matter* required by living organisms through parts of the ecosphere

- *Gravity*, caused mostly by the attraction between the sun and the earth, allows the planet to hold onto its atmosphere and causes the downward movement of chemicals in the matter cycles

Figure 2-7 Our life-support system: the general structure of the earth.

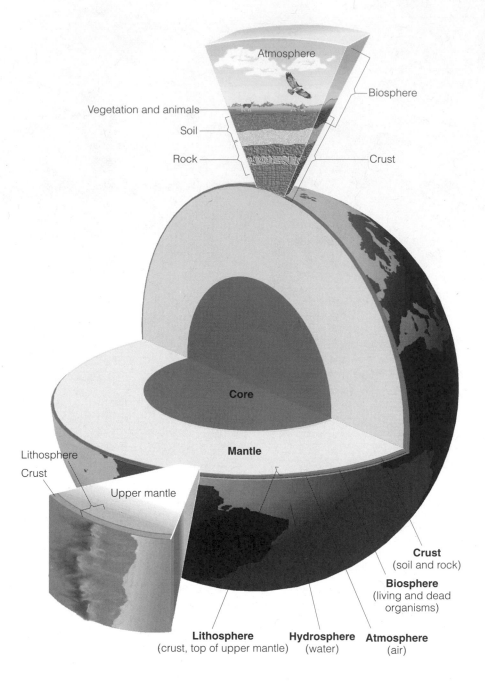

Atmosphere

Biosphere

Vegetation and animals

Soil

Rock

Crust

Core

Mantle

Lithosphere

Crust

Upper mantle

Crust
(soil and rock)

Biosphere
(living and dead organisms)

Lithosphere
(crust, top of upper mantle)

Hydrosphere
(water)

Atmosphere
(air)

THE REALM OF ECOLOGY Ecology, from the Greek *oikos* ("house" or "place to live") and *logos* ("study of"), is the study of how organisms interact with one another and with their physical and chemical environment. Ecology deals mainly with interactions among organisms, populations, communities, ecosystems, and the ecosphere (Figure 2-1). It is a study of connections in nature.

An **organism** is any form of life. Organisms can be classified into **species**, groups of organisms that resemble one another in appearance, behavior, chemistry, and genetic structure. Most organisms reproduce sexually and are classified in the same species if

they can breed with one another and produce fertile offspring under natural conditions.

We don't have the foggiest notion how many species exist on Earth. Estimates range from 5 million to 100 million, most of them insects, microscopic organisms, and tiny sea creatures. So far biologists have identified and named only about 1.4 million species. They know a fair amount about roughly one-third of these species and the detailed roles and interactions of only a few.

A **population** is a group of individuals of the same species occupying a given area at the same time. Examples are all sunfish in a pond, white oak trees in

Q: Worldwide, how much of the water withdrawn is unnecessarily wasted?

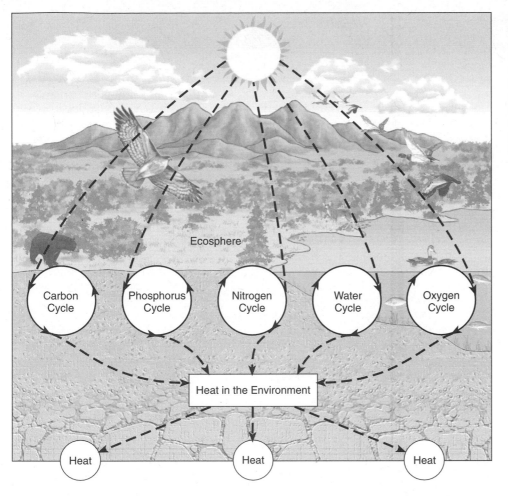

Figure 2-8 Earth's life depends on the *one-way flow of energy* (dashed lines) from the sun through the ecosphere, the *cycling of critical elements* (solid lines around circles), and *gravity,* which keeps atmospheric gases from escaping into space and draws chemicals downward in the matter cycles. This simplified overview shows only a few of the many cycling elements.

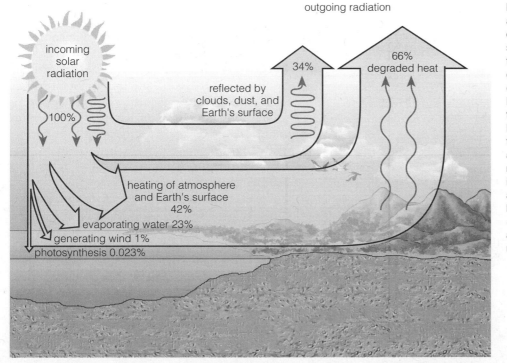

Figure 2-9 The flow of energy to and from Earth. The ultimate source of energy in most ecosystems is sunlight. Solar energy also powers the cycling of matter and drives the climate and weather systems that distribute heat and fresh water over Earth's surface. How fast this heat flows through the atmosphere and back into space is affected by heat-trapping (greenhouse) gases, such as water vapor, carbon dioxide, methane, nitrous oxide, and ozone, in the troposphere. Without this atmospheric thermal "blanket," known as the *natural greenhouse effect,* Earth would be nearly as cold as Mars, and life as we know it could not exist.

Earth: The Just-Right, Resilient Planet

Like Goldilocks tasting porridge at the house of the three bears, life as we know it is picky about temperature. Venus is much too hot, Mars is much too cold, and Earth is just right. Otherwise, you wouldn't be reading these words.

Life as we know it also depends on water. Again, temperature is crucial. Earthly life needs average temperatures between the freezing and boiling points of water—between 0°C and 100°C (32°F and 212°F)—at Earth's atmospheric pressures.

Earth's orbit is the right distance from the sun to have these conditions. If it were much closer, it would be too hot—like Venus—for

water vapor to condense to form rain. If it were much farther, its surface would be so cold—like Mars—that its water would have existed only as ice. Earth also spins. Otherwise, the side facing the sun would be too hot (and the other side too cold) for water-based life to exist. So far, the temperature has been, like Baby Bear's porridge, just right.

Earth is also the right size. That is, it has enough gravitational mass to keep its iron-nickel core molten and to keep its atmosphere around it. The slow transfer of this heat (geothermal energy) to the surface helps keep the planet at the right temperature for life. A much smaller Earth would not have enough gravitational mass to hold onto an

atmosphere consisting of light molecules such as N_2, O_2, CO_2, and H_2O. And thanks to the development of photosynthesizing bacteria over 2 billion years ago, an ozone sunscreen protects us from an overdose of ultraviolet light.

On a time scale of millions of years, Earth is also enormously resilient and adaptive. Earth's average temperatures have remained between the freezing and boiling points of water even though the sun's energy output has increased by about 30% over the 3.6 billion years since life arose. Earth in short is just right for life as we know it to have arisen.

---

a forest, and people in a country. All members of the same population have certain structural, functional, and behavioral traits in common. In most natural populations individuals vary slightly in their genetic makeup so that they don't all look or behave exactly alike—something called **genetic diversity**.

The place where a population (or an individual organism) normally lives is its **habitat**. Populations of all the different species occupying a particular place make up a **community** or **biological community**.

An **ecosystem** is a community of different species interacting with one another and with their nonliving environment of matter and energy. The size of an ecosystem is arbitrary and is defined by the system we wish to study. All of Earth's ecosystems together make up the *biosphere* or *ecosphere*.

BIODIVERSITY   As environmental conditions have changed over billions of years, many species have become extinct and new ones have formed. The result of these changes is **biological diversity**, or **biodiversity**. It consists of the forms of life that can best survive the variety of conditions currently found on Earth and includes **(1) genetic diversity** (variability in the genetic makeup among individuals within a single species), **(2) species diversity** (the variety of species on Earth and in different habitats of the planet), and **(3) ecolog-**

ical diversity (the variety of forests, deserts, grasslands, streams, lakes, oceans, and other biological communities that interact with one another and with their nonliving environments).

We are utterly dependent on this mostly unknown "bio-capital." This rich variety of genes, species, and ecosystems gives us food, wood, fibers, energy, raw materials, industrial chemicals, and medicines, and it pours hundreds of billions of dollars yearly into the world economy.

Earth's vast library of life forms and ecosystems also provides free recycling and purification services and natural pest control. Every species here today contains stored genetic information representing thousands to millions of years of adaptation to Earth's changing environmental conditions, and that is the raw material for future adaptations. Biodiversity is nature's "insurance policy" against disasters.

Some also include *human cultural diversity* as part of Earth's biodiversity. The variety of human cultures on the planet represent our "solutions" to survival and can help us adapt to changing conditions.

How did life on Earth evolve to its present system of diverse species living in an interlocking network of matter cycles, energy flow, and species interactions? We don't know the full answers to these questions, but a large body of evidence indicates that through chemical and physical changes taking place over billions of years the right conditions for life as we know it to exist

Q: How many people don't have a safe supply of drinking water?

Insects play vital and largely unrecognized roles. A large fraction of Earth's plant species depend on insects for pollination and reproduction. Plants also owe their lives to the insects that help turn the soil around their roots and decompose dead tissue into nutrients the plants need. In turn, we and other land-dwelling animals depend on plants for food, either by eating them or by consuming plant-eating animals.

Indeed, if all insects were to disappear, we and most of Earth's amphibians, reptiles, birds, and other mammals would become extinct within a year because of the disappearance of most plant life. Earth would be covered with dead and rotting vegetation and animal carcasses being decomposed by unimaginable hordes of bacteria and fungi. The land would be largely devoid of animal life and covered by mats of wind-pollinated vegetation and clumps of small trees and bushes here and there.

This, however, is not a realistic scenario. Insects, which originated on land nearly 400 million years ago, are so diverse, abundant, and adaptable that they are virtually invincible. Some have asked whether insects will take over if the human race extinguishes itself. This is the wrong question. The roughly billion billion (10^{18}) insects alive at any given time around the world have been in charge for millions of years. Insects can thrive without newcomers such as us, but we and most other land organisms would quickly perish without them.

---

on Earth developed (Connections, p. 28). This body of evidence suggests that life on Earth developed in two phases: **(1)** *chemical evolution* of the molecules needed for Earth's primitive cells (about 1 billion years) and **(2)** *biological evolution* of primitive cells into a diversity of organisms (about 3.6–3.8 billion years).

TYPES OF ORGANISMS Earth's diverse organisms are classified as eukaryotic or prokaryotic on the basis of their cell structure. All organisms except bacteria are **eukaryotic**: The cells of such organisms have a *nucleus* (genetic material surrounded by a membrane) and several other internal parts surrounded by membranes. Bacterial cells are **prokaryotic**: They have no distinct nucleus or other internal parts enclosed by membranes. Although most of the organisms we see are eukaryotic, they could not exist without hordes of microscopic prokaryotic organisms (bacteria) toiling away unseen.

In this book Earth's organisms are classified into five kingdoms (Figure 2-10):

- **Monera (bacteria and cyanobacteria)** are single-celled, microscopic prokaryotic organisms.

- **Protista (protists)** are mostly single-celled eukaryotic organisms such as diatoms, amoebas, golden brown and yellow-green algae, protozoans, and slime molds.

- **Fungi** are mostly many-celled organisms (some microscopic), and eukaryotic organisms such as mushrooms, molds, and yeasts.

- **Plantae (plants)** are mostly many-celled, eukaryotic organisms such as red, brown, and green algae; mosses, ferns, and conifers (cone-bearing trees such as pine, juniper, redwood, and yew); and flowering plants (cacti, grasses, beans, roses, bromeliads, and maple trees). **Evergreens** like ferns, magnolias, pines, spruces, and sequoias keep some leaves or needles all year. This allows them to carry out photosynthesis year-round in tropical climates or take maximum advantage of a short growing season in colder climates. **Deciduous plants**, such as oak and maple trees, survive drought and cold by shedding their leaves during such periods. **Succulent plants**, such as desert cacti, survive in dry climates by having no leaves, thus conserving scarce water. **Epiphytes**, or "air plants," grow on tree branches rather than in soil. Examples are some species of mosses, ferns, lichens, and orchids in tropical forests.

- **Animalia (animals)** are many-celled, eukaryotic organisms. Most, called **invertebrates**, have no backbones. They include sponges, jellyfish, worms, arthropods (insects, shrimp, spiders), mollusks (snails, clams, octopuses), and echinoderms (sea stars, sea urchins). The **vertebrates**, animals with backbones, include fish (sharks, tuna), amphibians (frogs, salamanders), reptiles (turtles, crocodiles, snakes), birds (eagles, penguins, robins, ducks), and mammals (kangaroos, moles, bats, cats, rabbits, elephants, whales, seals, rhinos, humans). Insects and other arthropods such as spiders are vital to our existence (Connections, above).

COMPONENTS OF ECOSYSTEMS Figures 2-11 and 2-12 are greatly simplified diagrams showing a few of

---

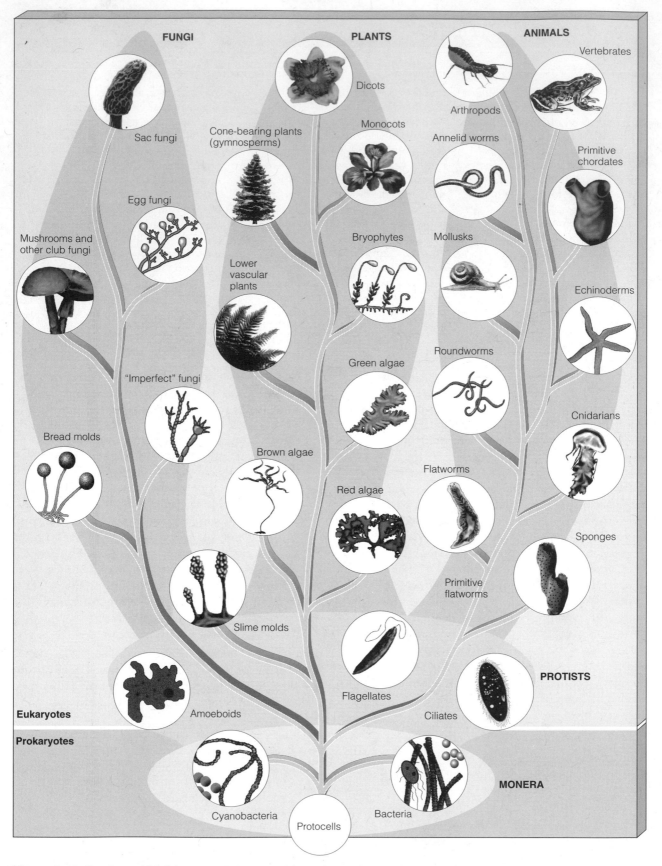

Figure 2-10 Kingdoms of the living world. This is one of several ways that biologists classify Earth's diverse species into major groups. Most biologists believe that protocells gave rise to single-celled prokaryotes and that these in turn evolved into more complex protists, fungi, plants, and animals that make up the planet's stunning biodiversity.

Q: How much of the available high-quality energy is transferred from one trophic level to another in a food chain or food web?

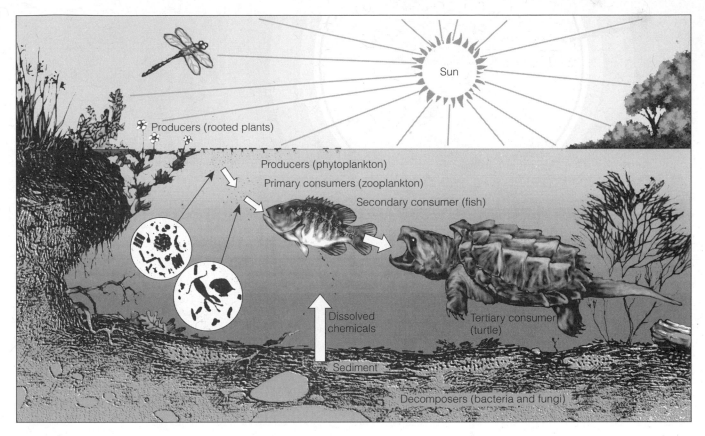

Figure 2-11 Major components of a freshwater pond ecosystem.

the components of ecosystems in a freshwater pond and in a field. Living organisms in ecosystems are usually classified as either *producers* or *consumers*, based on how they get food. **Producers**—sometimes called **autotrophs** (self-feeders)—can make the nutrients they need to survive from compounds in their environment. In most land ecosystems green plants are the producers. In aquatic ecosystems most of the producers are *phytoplankton*, floating and drifting bacteria and protists, mostly microscopic.

Most producers use sunlight to make complex nutrient compounds (such as the carbohydrate glucose) by **photosynthesis**. Although hundreds of chemical changes take place in sequence during photosynthesis, the overall net change can be summarized as follows:

carbon dioxide + water + **solar energy** $\longrightarrow$ glucose + oxygen

Although plants do most of the planet's photosynthesis today, bacteria "invented" this process. Photosynthetic bacteria still exist, including the highly successful cyanobacteria (once called blue-green algae).

A few producers, mostly specialized bacteria, can convert simple compounds from their environment into more complex nutrient compounds without sunlight—a process called **chemosynthesis**. In this case, the source of energy is heat generated by the decay of radioactive elements deep in the earth's core and released at hot-water vents in the ocean's depths. In the pitch-darkness around such vents, specialized producer bacteria use the heat to convert dissolved hydrogen sulfide (H_2S) and carbon dioxide into more complex nutrient molecules.

All other organisms in ecosystems are **consumers**, or **heterotrophs** (other-feeders), which get most of their nutrients by feeding on the tissues of producers or other consumers. There are several classes of consumers, depending on their food sources.

- **Herbivores** (plant-eaters) are called **primary consumers** because they feed directly on other producers.

- **Carnivores** (meat-eaters) feed on other consumers. Those called **secondary consumers** feed only on primary consumers. Most secondary consumers are animals, but a few such as the Venus flytrap trap and digest insects. **Tertiary (higher-level) consumers** feed only on other carnivores.

- **Omnivores** eat both plants and animals. Examples are pigs, rats, foxes, cockroaches, and humans.

Figure 2-12 Major components of an ecosystem in a field.

■ **Detritivores** (decomposers and detritus feeders) live off **detritus**, parts of dead organisms and cast-off fragments and wastes of living organisms (Figure 2-13).

Decomposers digest the complex molecules in detritus into simpler compounds and absorb the soluble nutrients. These decomposers—mostly bacteria and fungi—(Figure 2-13) are an important source of food for worms and insects in the soil and water. **Detritus feeders**, such as crabs, carpenter ants, termites, and earthworms, extract nutrients from partly decomposed matter.

Both producers and consumers use the chemical energy stored in glucose and other nutrients to drive their life processes. This energy is released by the process of **aerobic respiration** (not the same as the breathing process called respiration), which uses oxygen to convert nutrients such as glucose back into carbon dioxide and water. The net effect of the hundreds of changes in this complex process is

glucose + oxygen $\longrightarrow$ carbon dioxide + water + **energy**

Thus, although the detailed steps differ, the net chemical change for aerobic respiration is the opposite of that for photosynthesis.

The survival of any individual organism depends on the *flow of matter* and *energy* through its body. However, the community of organisms in an ecosystem survives primarily by a combination of *matter recycling* and *one-way energy flow* (Figure 2-14). Decomposers complete the cycle of matter by breaking detritus into nutrients usable by producers. Without decomposers the entire world would soon be knee-deep in plant litter, dead animal bodies, animal wastes, and garbage.

TOLERANCE RANGES OF SPECIES Each population in an ecosystem has a **range of tolerance** to variations in its physical and chemical environment (Figure 2-15). Individuals within a population may have slightly different tolerance ranges for temperature, for example, because of small differences in their genetic makeup, health, and age. Thus, although a trout population may do best at one narrow band of temperatures (optimum level), a few individuals can survive both above and below that band. But, as Figure 2-15 shows, tolerance has its limits. Beyond them, none of the trout will survive.

These observations are summarized in the **law of tolerance**: *The existence, abundance, and distribution of a species in an ecosystem are determined by whether the levels*

Q: What are the three most productive types of ecosystems?

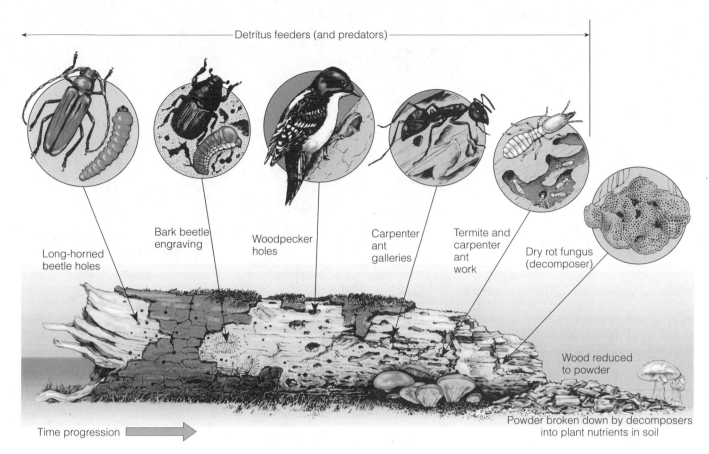

Long-horned beetle holes

Bark beetle engraving

Woodpecker holes

Carpenter ant galleries

Termite and carpenter ant work

Dry rot fungus (decomposer)

Wood reduced to powder

Powder broken down by decomposers into plant nutrients in soil

Time progression

Figure 2-13 Some detritivores, called *detritus feeders*, directly consume fragments of this log. Other detritivores, called *decomposers* (mostly fungi and bacteria), digest complex chemicals in fragments of the log into simpler nutrient compounds. If these nutrients are not washed away or otherwise removed from the system, they can be used again by producers. The woodpecker shown in this diagram is not a detritivore. In its search for insects, it pecks out fragments of matter that are consumed by detritivores.

Figure 2-14 The main structural components (energy, chemicals, and organisms) of an ecosystem are linked by energy flow and matter recycling.

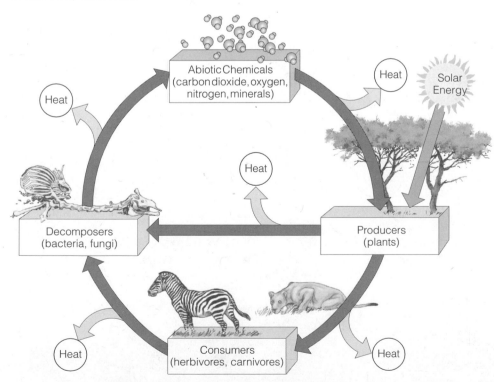

Abiotic Chemicals (carbon dioxide, oxygen, nitrogen, minerals)

Heat

Solar Energy

Heat

Heat

Decomposers (bacteria, fungi)

Producers (plants)

Heat

Heat

Consumers (herbivores, carnivores)

Heat

A: Estuaries, swamps and marshes, and tropical rain forests

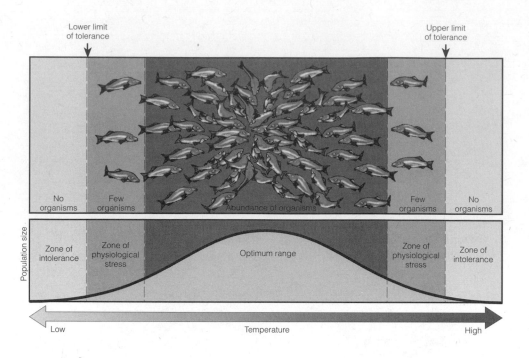

Figure 2-15 Range of tolerance for a population of organisms of the same species to an abiotic environmental factor—in this case, temperature.

of one or more physical or chemical factors fall within the range tolerated by the species.

A species may have a wide range of tolerance to some factors and a narrow range of tolerance to others. Most organisms are least tolerant during juvenile or reproductive stages of the life cycle. Highly tolerant species can live in a range of habitats with different conditions.

Some species can adjust their tolerance to physical factors such as temperature if change is gradual, just as you can tolerate a hotter bath by slowly adding hotter and hotter water. This adjustment to slowly changing new conditions, or **acclimation**, is a useful protective device. However, acclimation has limits. At each step the species comes closer to its absolute limit. Suddenly, without warning, the next small change triggers a **threshold effect**, a harmful or even fatal reaction as the tolerance limit is exceeded—like adding that proverbial single straw that breaks the already heavily loaded camel's back.

The threshold effect explains why many environmental problems seem to arise suddenly. For example, spruce trees suddenly begin dying in droves, but the cause may be exposure to numerous air pollutants for decades. The threshold effect also explains why we must prevent pollution to keep thresholds from being exceeded.

LIMITING FACTORS IN ECOSYSTEMS An ecological principle related to the law of tolerance is the **limiting factor principle**: *Too much or too little of any abiotic factor can limit or prevent growth of a population even if all other factors are at or near the optimum range of tolerance.* Such a factor is called a **limiting factor**.

Limiting factors in land ecosystems include temperature, water, light, and soil nutrients. For example, suppose a farmer plants corn in phosphorus-poor soil. Even if water, nitrogen, potassium, and other nutrients are at optimum levels, the corn will stop growing when it uses up the available phosphorus. Here, phosphorus determines how much corn will grow in the field. Growth can also be limited by too much of an abiotic factor. For example, plants can be killed by too much water or too much fertilizer.

In aquatic ecosystems **salinity** (the amounts of various salts dissolved in a given volume of water) is a limiting factor. It determines the species found in both marine (oceans) and freshwater ecosystems. Aquatic ecosystems can also be divided into surface, middle, and bottom layers or life zones. Important limiting factors for these layers are temperature, sunlight, **dissolved oxygen content** (the amount of oxygen gas dissolved in a given volume of water at a particular temperature and pressure), and availability of nutrients.

2-4 Roles of Species in Ecosystems

TYPES OF SPECIES IN ECOSYSTEMS One way to look at an ecosystem's species from a human standpoint is to divide them into four types:

■ **Native species**, which normally live and thrive in a particular ecosystem.

Q: How much of the world's net primary productivity on land is used by the world's 5.5 billion people?

The American Alligator: A Keystone Species

CONNECTIONS

The American alligator, North America's largest reptile, has no natural predators except people. Hunters once killed large numbers of these animals for their exotic meat and for the supple belly skin used to make items such as shoes, belts, and pocketbooks. People also considered alligators to be useless, dangerous vermin and hunted them for sport or out of hatred. Between 1950 and 1960 hunters wiped out 90% of the alligators in Louisiana, and by the 1960s the alligator population in the Florida Everglades was also near extinction.

People who say "So what?" are overlooking the alligator's keystone role in subtropical wetland ecosystems such as Florida's Everglades. Alligators dig deep depressions, or "gator holes," which collect fresh water during dry spells. These holes are refuges for aquatic life and supply fresh water and food for birds and other animals. Large alligator nesting mounds also serve as nest sites for herons and egrets. As alligators move from gator holes to nesting mounds, they help keep areas of open water free of invading vegetation. Alligators also eat large numbers of predatory gar fish and thus help maintain populations of game fish such as bass and bream.

In 1967, the U.S. government placed the American alligator on the endangered species list. Protected from hunters, the alligator population had made a strong comeback in many areas by 1975—too strong, according to people who find alligators in their backyards and swimming pools.

The problem is that people are invading the alligator's natural habitats. And while the gator's diet consists mainly of snails, apples, sick fish, ducks, raccoons, and turtles, a pet or a person who falls into or swims in a canal, a pond, or some other area where a gator lives is subject to attack.

In 1977, the U.S. Fish and Wildlife Service reclassified the American alligator from *endangered* to *threatened* in Florida, Louisiana, and Texas, where 90% of the animals live. In 1987, this reclassification was extended to seven other states. It is illegal to kill alligators as a threatened species, but limited hunting by licensed professional game wardens is allowed in some areas to control the population. The comeback of the American alligator is an important success story in wildlife conservation.

- **Immigrant**, or **alien species**, which migrate into an ecosystem or which are deliberately or accidentally introduced into an ecosystem by humans. Some of these species are beneficial to humans, while others can take over and eliminate many native species.

- **Indicator species**, which serve as early warnings that a community or an ecosystem is being damaged. For example, the present decline of migratory, insect-eating songbirds in North America indicates that their summer habitats there and their winter habitats in the tropical forests of Latin America and the Caribbean are rapidly disappearing.

- **Keystone species** affect many other organisms in an ecosystem.* For example, in tropical forests, various species of bees, bats, ants, and hummingbirds play keystone roles in pollinating flowering plants, dispersing seed, or both. Some keystone species, such as the alligator (Connections, above),

the wolf, the leopard, the lion, the giant anteater, and the giant armadillo, are top predators that exert a stabilizing effect on their ecosystems by feeding on and regulating the populations of certain species. The loss of a keystone species can lead to population crashes and extinctions of other species that depend on it for certain services—a ripple or domino effect that spreads throughout an ecosystem. According to biologist E. O. Wilson, "The loss of a keystone species is like a drill accidentally striking a power line. It causes lights to go out all over."

A given species may be more than one of these types in a particular ecosystem.

NICHE The **ecological niche**, or simply **niche** (pronounced *nitch*), of a species is its total way of life or its role in an ecosystem. It includes all the physical, chemical, and biological conditions a species needs to live and reproduce in an ecosystem.

Species can be broadly classified as specialists or generalists, according to their niches. **Specialist species** have narrow niches. They may be able to live in only one type of habitat, tolerate only a narrow range of climatic and other environmental conditions, or use only one or a few types of food. Examples of

---

*All species play some role in their ecosystem and thus are important. Some scientists consider all species equally important, but others consider certain species to be keystone species, more important than others, at least in helping maintain the ecosystems of which they are a part.

Figure 2-16 Stratification of specialized plant and animal niches in various layers of a tropical rain forest. These specialized niches allow species to avoid or minimize competition for resources with other species; they lead to the coexistence of a great diversity of species. Niche specialization is promoted by the adaptation of plants to the different levels of light available in the forest's layers and by hundreds of thousands of years of evolution in a fairly constant climate.

specialists are tiger salamanders, which can breed only in fishless ponds so their larvae won't be eaten; red-cockaded woodpeckers, which carve nest-holes almost exclusively in longleaf pines at least 75 years old; and the endangered giant panda (about 800 left in the wild in China), which gets 99% of its food from bamboo. In a tropical rain forest an incredibly diverse array of species survives by occupying specialized ecological niches in distinct layers of the forest's vegetation (Figure 2-16). The widespread clearing and degradation of such forests is dooming millions of such specialized species to extinction.

Generalist species have broad niches. They can live in many different places, eat a variety of foods, and tolerate a wide range of environmental conditions. Flies, cockroaches, mice, rats, white-tail deer, raccoons, and human beings are all generalist species.

CONNECTIONS: WAYS SPECIES INTERACT

When any two species in an ecosystem have some activities or requirements in common, they may interact to some degree. The principal types of species interactions are *interspecific competition*, *predation*, *parasitism*, *mutualism*, and *commensalism*.

As long as commonly used resources are abundant, different species can share them. This allows each species to come closer to occupying its **fundamental niche**: the full potential range of physical, chemical, and biological factors it could use if there were no competition from other species.

In most ecosystems each species faces competition from one or more other species for one or more of the same limited resources (such as food, sunlight, water, soil nutrients, or space) it needs. Because of such **interspecific competition**, parts of the fundamental niches

Q: What are the three major types of biomes?

Why We Need Sharks

The world's 350 species of sharks range in size from the dwarf dog shark—about the size of a large goldfish—to the whale shark—the world's largest fish at 18 meters (60 feet) long. Various shark species are the key predators in the world's oceans, helping control the numbers of many other ocean predators. By feeding at the top of food webs, these shark species cull injured and sick animals from the ocean, thus keeping these species stronger and healthier.

Influenced by movies and popular novels, most people think of sharks as people-eating monsters. This is far from the truth. Every year a few species of shark—mostly great white, bull, bronze whale, tiger, gray reef, blue, and oceanic whitetip—injure about 100 people worldwide and kill between 5 and 10. If you are a typical ocean-goer, you are 150 times more likely to be killed by lightning and thousands of times more likely to be killed when you drive a car than to be killed by a shark.

For every shark that injures a person, we kill 1 million sharks—a total of more than 100 million sharks each year. Sharks are killed mostly for their fins (widely used in Asia as a soup ingredient—at around $50 a bowl in some restaurants—and as a pharmaceutical cure-all), livers, meat (especially mako and thresher), and jaws (especially great whites), or because we fear them. Some sharks (especially blue, mako, and oceanic whitetip) die when they are trapped in nets meant for swordfish, tuna, shrimp, and other commercially important species.

Why should we care how many sharks are killed? Because they perform valuable services for us and other species. Sharks save human lives by helping us learn how to fight cancer, bacteria, and viruses, because sharks seem to be free of almost all diseases (including most cancers and eye cataracts) and are not affected by most toxic chemicals. Understanding why can help us improve human health.

Chemicals extracted from shark cartilage have killed cancerous tumors in laboratory animals and may someday be the basis of cancer-treating drugs. Another chemical extracted from shark cartilage is being used as an artificial skin for burn victims. Sharks' highly effective immune system allows wounds to heal quickly without becoming infected, and it is being studied for protection against AIDS. And shark corneas have been transplanted into human eyes.

With more than 400 million years of evolution behind them, sharks have had a long time to get things right. We could undo most of this evolutionary "wisdom" in a few decades. Preventing this from happening begins with the recognition that sharks don't need us, but we and other species need them.

---

of different species overlap significantly. When the fundamental niches of two competing species do overlap, one species may occupy more of its fundamental niche than the other species through competitive interactions.

Another process that reduces the degree of fundamental niche overlap is **resource partitioning**, the dividing up of scarce resources so that species with similar requirements use them at different times, in different ways, or in different places (Figure 2-16). In effect, they "share the wealth," with each competing species occupying a **realized niche**, the portion of the fundamental niche that a species actually occupies. For example, hawks and owls feed on similar prey, but hawks hunt during the day and owls hunt at night. Where lions and leopards live in the same area, lions take mostly larger animals as prey and leopards take smaller ones. Some species of birds, such as warblers and tanagers, avoid competition by hunting for insects in different parts of the same coniferous trees.

Experiments have shown that no two species can occupy exactly the same fundamental niche indefinitely in a habitat where there is not enough of a particular resource to meet the needs of both species. This is called the **competitive exclusion principle**. As a result, one of the competing species must migrate to another area (if possible), shift its feeding habits or behavior, suffer a sharp population decline, or become extinct.

The most obvious form of species interaction is **predation**. Members of a **predator** species feed on parts or all of an organism of a **prey** species, but they do not live on or in the prey. Together, the two kinds of organisms, such as lions and zebras, are said to have a **predator–prey relationship**. Examples of predators and their preys are shown in Figures 2-11 and 2-12. Many shark species are key predators in the world's oceans (Case Study, above).

Another type of predator-prey interaction is parasitism. A **parasite** is a predator that preys on another organism—its **host**—by living on or in the host for all or most of the host's life. The parasite is smaller than its host and draws nourishment from and gradually weakens the host, sometimes killing it. Tapeworms, disease-causing organisms (pathogens), and other parasites live inside their hosts. Lice, ticks, mosquitoes,

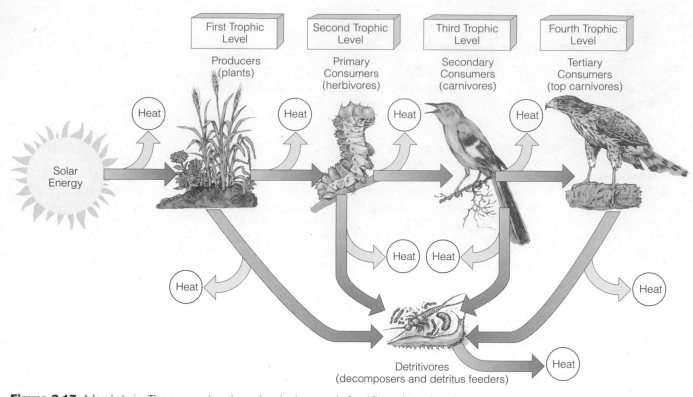

First Trophic Level
Producers (plants)

Second Trophic Level
Primary Consumers (herbivores)

Third Trophic Level
Secondary Consumers (carnivores)

Fourth Trophic Level
Tertiary Consumers (top carnivores)

Solar Energy

Heat

Detritivores
(decomposers and detritus feeders)

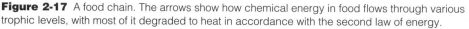

Figure 2-17 A food chain. The arrows show how chemical energy in food flows through various trophic levels, with most of it degraded to heat in accordance with the second law of energy.

mistletoe plants, and lampreys attach themselves to the outside of their hosts.

Mutualism is a type of species interaction in which both participating species generally benefit. The honeybee and certain flowers have a mutualistic relationship. The honeybee feeds on a flower's nectar and in the process picks up pollen, pollinating female flowers when it feeds on them. Other important mutualistic relationships exist between animals and the vast armies of bacteria in their stomachs or intestines that break down (digest) their food. The bacteria gain a safe home with a steady food supply; the animal gains access to a large source of energy.

In another type of species interaction, called **commensalism**, one species benefits while the other is neither helped nor harmed to any great degree. An example is the relationship between various species of clownfish and sea anemones, marine animals with stinging tentacles that paralyze most fish that touch them. The clownfish gain protection by living unharmed among the deadly tentacles and feed on the detritus left from the meals of the host anemone. The sea anemones seem to neither benefit nor suffer harm from this relationship.

On land there are commensalistic relationships between trees and epiphytes or "air plants" that attach themselves to tree branches. The epiphytes benefit by obtaining water and nutrients from air or bark surfaces without penetrating or harming their hosts.

2-5 Energy Flow in Ecosystems

FOOD CHAINS AND FOOD WEBS All organisms, dead or alive, are potential sources of food for other organisms. A caterpillar eats a leaf; a robin eats the caterpillar; a hawk eats the robin. When plant, caterpillar, robin, and hawk all die, they in turn are consumed by decomposers.

The sequence of who eats or decomposes whom in an ecosystem is called a **food chain** (Figure 2-17). It determines how energy moves from one organism to another through the ecosystem. Ecologists assign every organism in an ecosystem to a *feeding level*, or **trophic level** (from the Greek *trophos*, "nourishment"), depending on whether it is a producer or a consumer and on what it eats or decomposes. Producers belong to the first trophic level, primary consumers to the second trophic level, secondary consumers to the third trophic level, and so on. Detritivores process detritus from all trophic levels.

Real ecosystems are more complex than this. Most consumers eat—and are eaten by—two or more types of organisms. Some animals feed at several trophic levels. Thus, the organisms in most ecosystems form a complex network of feeding relationships called a **food web**. Figure 2-18 shows a simplified Antarctic

Q: How much of Earth's surface is covered by oceans?

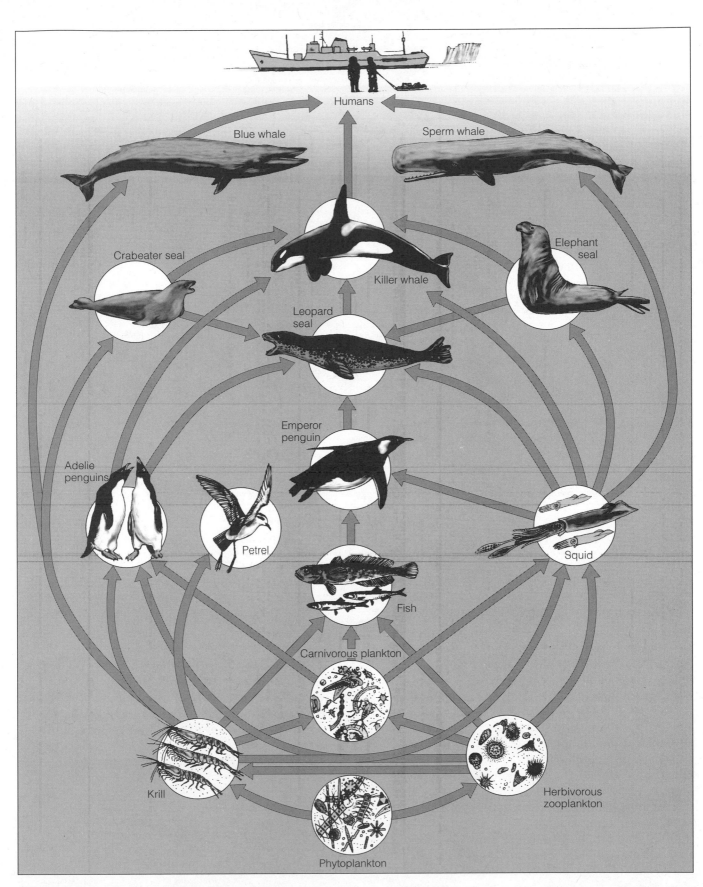

Figure 2-18 Greatly simplified food web in the Antarctic. There are many more participants, including an array of decomposer organisms.

Figure 2-19 Generalized pyramid of energy flow, showing the decrease in usable energy available at each succeeding trophic level in a food chain or web. This diagram shows a 90% loss in usable energy with each transfer from one trophic level to another. In nature such losses vary from 80% to 95%.

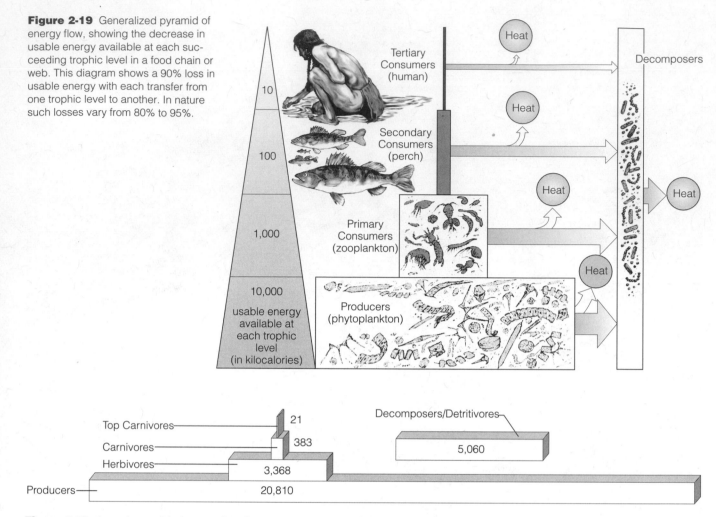

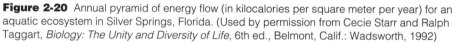

Figure 2-20 Annual pyramid of energy flow (in kilocalories per square meter per year) for an aquatic ecosystem in Silver Springs, Florida. (Used by permission from Cecie Starr and Ralph Taggart, *Biology: The Unity and Diversity of Life*, 6th ed., Belmont, Calif.: Wadsworth, 1992)

food web. Trophic levels can be assigned in food webs just as in food chains.

The percentage of usable energy transferred from one trophic level to the next varies from 5% to 20% (that is, a loss of 80–95%), depending on the types of species and the ecosystem involved. The pyramid in Figure 2-19 illustrates this energy loss for a simple food chain, assuming a 90% energy loss with each transfer. This **pyramid of energy flow** shows that the more trophic levels or steps in a food chain or web, the greater the cumulative loss of usable energy. Figure 2-20 shows the actual pyramid and details of energy flow during one year for an aquatic ecosystem in Silver Springs, Florida.

The energy flow pyramid explains why Earth can support more people if they eat at lower trophic levels by consuming grains directly (for example, rice ⟶ human) rather than eating grain-eaters (grain ⟶ steer ⟶ human). The large energy loss in going to each consecutive trophic level explains why food

chains and webs rarely have more than four consecutive links or energy transfers.

PRODUCTIVITY OF PRODUCERS The *rate* at which an ecosystem's producers capture and store chemical energy as *biomass* (nutrient matter produced by photosynthesis) is the ecosystem's **gross primary productivity**. However, since the producers must use some of this biomass to stay alive, what we need to know is an ecosystem's **net primary productivity**.

net primary productivity	=	rate at which producers produce chemical energy stored in biomass through photosynthesis	−	rate at which producers use chemical energy stored in biomass through aerobic respiration

Net primary productivity, usually reported as the energy output of a specified area of producers over a

Q: How much of Earth's wetlands have been destroyed or polluted?

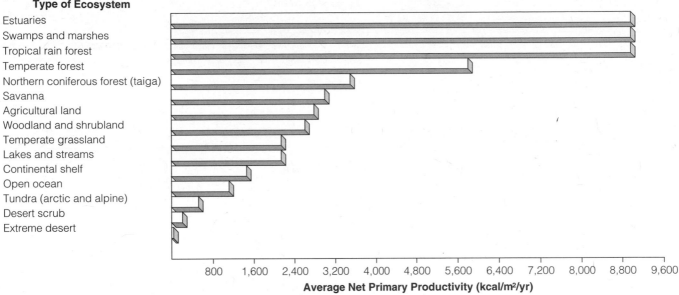

Type of Ecosystem

Estuaries
Swamps and marshes
Tropical rain forest
Temperate forest
Northern coniferous forest (taiga)
Savanna
Agricultural land
Woodland and shrubland
Temperate grassland
Lakes and streams
Continental shelf
Open ocean
Tundra (arctic and alpine)
Desert scrub
Extreme desert

800   1,600   2,400   3,200   4,000   4,800   5,600   6,400   7,200   8,000   8,800   9,600

Average Net Primary Productivity (kcal/m²/yr)

Figure 2-21 Estimated average net primary productivity in major life zones and ecosystems. Values are given in kilocalories of energy produced per square meter per year.

given time (typically as kilocalories per square meter per year), is the basic food source or "income" for an ecosystem's consumers. It is the rate at which energy is stored in new biomass—cells, leaves, roots, stems— available for use by consumers. Figure 2-21 shows how this productivity varies in different parts of Earth.

Estuaries, swamps and marshes, and tropical rain forests are highly productive; open ocean, tundra (arctic grasslands), and desert are the least productive (Figure 2-21). You might conclude that we should harvest plants in estuaries, swamps, and marshes to feed our hungry millions—or clear tropical forests and plant crops. Wrong. The grasses in estuaries, swamps, and marshes cannot be eaten by people, but they are vital food sources (and spawning areas) for fish, shrimp, and other aquatic life that provide us and other consumers with protein. Thus we should protect, not harvest or destroy, these plants.

In tropical forests (Figure 2-16) most nutrients are stored in vegetation rather than in the soil. When the trees are cleared, the nutrient-poor soils are rapidly depleted of their nutrients by frequent rains and by growing crops. Thus food crops can be grown only for a short time without massive applications of commercial fertilizers. Again, as with estuaries, swamps, and marshes, we should protect, not clear, these forests.

It is estimated that humans now use or waste about 27% of the world's potential net primary productivity (40% for land systems). To do this our species has crowded out or eliminated other species. The resulting biodiversity impoverishment crisis is reducing Earth's carrying capacity for *all* species, including ourselves.

When earlier civilizations failed because they exceeded the carrying capacity of the land, people could expand into new areas. If we take over (or try to take over) 80% of the planet's primary land productivity as our population doubles over the next 40 years, most biologists believe we will exceed the carrying capacity in vast areas. There will be no place to expand to and no place to hide from the consequences of such biological impoverishment (Spotlight, p. 15).

 2-6 **Matter Cycling in Ecosystems**

NUTRIENT CYCLES Any chemical element or compound an organism must take in to live, grow, or reproduce is called a **nutrient**. Some elements such as carbon, oxygen, hydrogen, nitrogen, and phosphorus are needed in fairly large amounts. Others such as iron, copper, chlorine, and iodine are needed in small, or trace, amounts.

These nutrient elements and their compounds are continuously cycled from the nonliving environment (air, water, soil) to living organisms and then back to the nonliving environment in what are called **nutrient cycles**, or **biogeochemical cycles** (literally, "life-earth-chemical" cycles). These cycles, driven directly or indirectly by incoming solar energy and gravity, include the carbon, oxygen, nitrogen, phosphorus, and hydrologic (water) cycles (Figure 2-8).

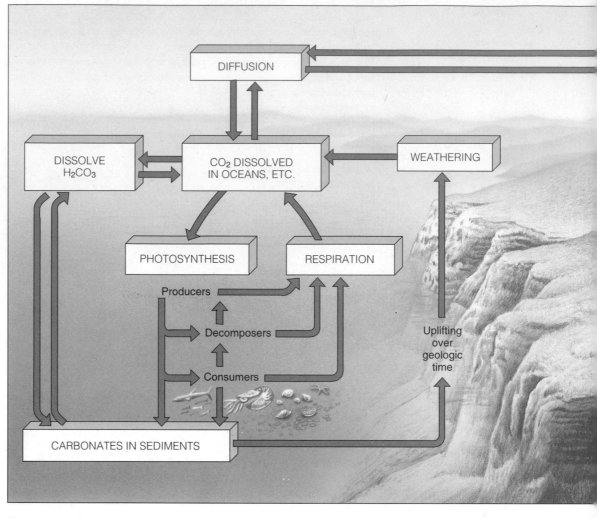

Figure 2-22 Simplified diagram of the global carbon cycle. The left portion shows the movement of carbon through marine ecosystems, and the right portion shows its movement through terrestrial ecosystems. (Used by permission from Cecie Starr and Ralph Taggart, *Biology: The Unity and Diversity of Life*, 6th ed., Belmont, Calif.: Wadsworth, 1992)

Earth's chemical cycles connect past, present, and future forms of life. Thus, some of the carbon atoms in the skin of your right hand may once have been part of a leaf, a dinosaur's skin, or a layer of limestone rock. And some of the oxygen molecules you just inhaled may have been inhaled by your grandmother, by Plato, or by a hunter-gatherer who lived 25,000 years ago.

CARBON CYCLE The **carbon cycle** is based on carbon dioxide gas, which makes up almost 0.036% by volume of the troposphere and is also dissolved in water. Producers remove CO_2 from the atmosphere (terrestrial producers) or water (aquatic producers) and use photosynthesis to convert it into complex carbohydrates such as glucose ($C_6H_{12}O_6$). Then the cells in oxygen-consuming producers and consumers carry out aerobic respiration, which breaks down glucose and other complex nutrient compounds and converts

the carbon back to CO_2 in the atmosphere or water for reuse by producers. This linkage between photosynthesis in producers and aerobic respiration in producers and consumers circulates carbon in the ecosphere and is a major part of the global carbon cycle (Figure 2-22). Oxygen and hydrogen, the other elements in carbohydrates, cycle almost in step with carbon.

Especially since 1950, as world population and resource use have soared, we have disturbed the carbon cycle in two ways that add more carbon dioxide to the atmosphere than oceans and plants can remove:

- Forest and brush clearing, leaving less vegetation to absorb CO_2

- Burning fossil fuels and wood, which produces CO_2 that flows into the atmosphere

Q: How many species are there on the earth?

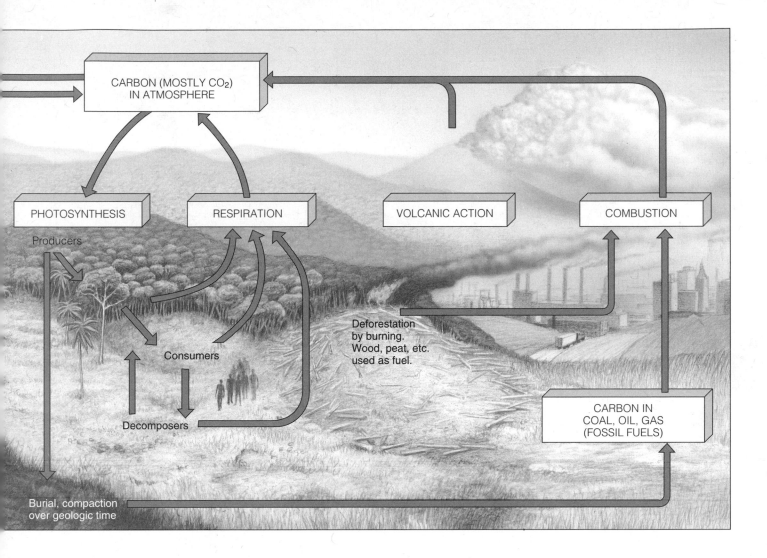

CARBON (MOSTLY CO₂) IN ATMOSPHERE

PHOTOSYNTHESIS

Producers

RESPIRATION

VOLCANIC ACTION

COMBUSTION

Consumers

Decomposers

Deforestation by burning. Wood, peat, etc. used as fuel.

CARBON IN COAL, OIL, GAS (FOSSIL FUELS)

Burial, compaction over geologic time

NITROGEN CYCLE: BACTERIA IN ACTION The nitrogen gas (N_2) that makes up 78% of the volume of the troposphere cannot be used directly as a nutrient by multicellular plants or animals. Fortunately, bacteria convert nitrogen gas into water-soluble compounds containing nitrogen, which are taken up by plant roots as part of the **nitrogen cycle** (Figure 2-23).

The conversion of atmospheric nitrogen gas into other chemical forms useful to plants is called **nitrogen fixation**. It is done mostly by cyanobacteria in soil and water and by *Rhizobium* bacteria living in small nodules (swellings) on the roots of alfalfa, clover, peas, beans, and other legumes.

After nitrogen has served its purpose in living organisms, armies of specialized decomposer bacteria convert the complex, nitrogen-rich compounds, wastes, cast-off particles, and dead bodies of organisms into simpler nitrogen-containing compounds.

Other specialized bacteria then convert these forms of nitrogen back into nitrogen gas, which is released to the atmosphere to begin the cycle again.

We intervene in the nitrogen cycle in several ways:

- Emitting large quantities of nitric oxide (NO) into the atmosphere when any fuel is burned. (Most of this NO is produced when nitrogen and oxygen molecules in the air combine at high temperatures.) This nitric oxide combines with oxygen to form nitrogen dioxide (NO_2) gas, which can react with water vapor to form nitric acid (HNO_3). This acid is a component of acid deposition (commonly called acid rain), which can damage trees and upset aquatic ecosystems.

- Emitting heat-trapping nitrous oxide (N_2O) gas into the atmosphere by the bacteria on livestock

A: We don't know. Estimates range from 5 to 100 million

CHAPTER 2   **43**

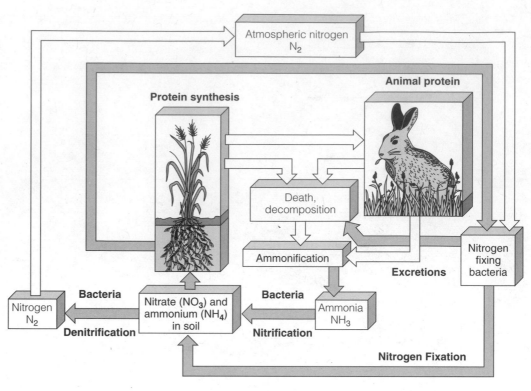

Figure 2-23 Simplified diagram of the nitrogen cycle in a terrestrial ecosystem. (Adapted with permission from Carolina Biological Supply)

wastes and commercial inorganic fertilizers applied to the soil.

- Mining nitrogen-containing mineral deposits for fertilizers.

- Depleting nitrogen from soil by harvesting nitrogen-rich crops.

- Adding excess nitrogen compounds to aquatic ecosystems in agricultural runoff and discharge of municipal sewage. This excess of plant nutrients stimulates rapid growth of cyanobacteria, algae, and aquatic plants. The subsequent breakdown of dead algae by aerobic decomposers depletes the water of dissolved oxygen gas and can disrupt aquatic ecosystems.

PHOSPHORUS CYCLE Phosphorus moves through water, Earth's crust, and living organisms in the **phosphorus cycle** (Figure 2-24). In this cycle phosphorus moves slowly from phosphate deposits on land and shallow ocean sediments to living organisms, and then back to the land and ocean. Bacteria are less important here than in the nitrogen cycle. Phosphorus does not circulate in the atmosphere.

We intervene in the phosphorus cycle chiefly in two ways:

- Mining phosphate rock to produce commercial inorganic fertilizers and detergents.

- Adding excess phosphorus to aquatic ecosystems in runoff of animal wastes from livestock feed-

lots, runoff of commercial phosphate fertilizers from cropland, and discharge of municipal sewage. Too much of this nutrient causes explosive growth of cyanobacteria, algae, and aquatic plants, disrupting life in aquatic ecosystems.

HYDROLOGIC CYCLE The **hydrologic cycle** or **water cycle**, which collects, purifies, and distributes Earth's fixed supply of water, is shown in simplified form in Figure 2-25. The main processes in this water recycling and purifying cycle are *evaporation* (conversion of water into water vapor), *transpiration* (evaporation of water extracted by roots and transported upward from leaves or other parts of plants), *condensation* (conversion of water vapor into droplets of liquid water), *precipitation* (dew, rain, sleet, hail, snow), *infiltration* (movement of water into soil), *percolation* (downward flow of water through soil and permeable rock formations to groundwater storage areas), and *runoff* downslope back to the sea to begin the cycle again. At different phases of the cycle water is stored for varying amounts of time on the planet's surface (oceans, streams, reservoirs, glaciers) or in the ground.

We intervene in the water cycle in two main ways:

- Withdrawing large quantities of fresh water from streams, lakes, and underground sources. In heavily populated or heavily irrigated areas, withdrawals have led to groundwater depletion or intrusion of ocean salt water into underground water supplies.

Q: How many of Earth's species have been identified?

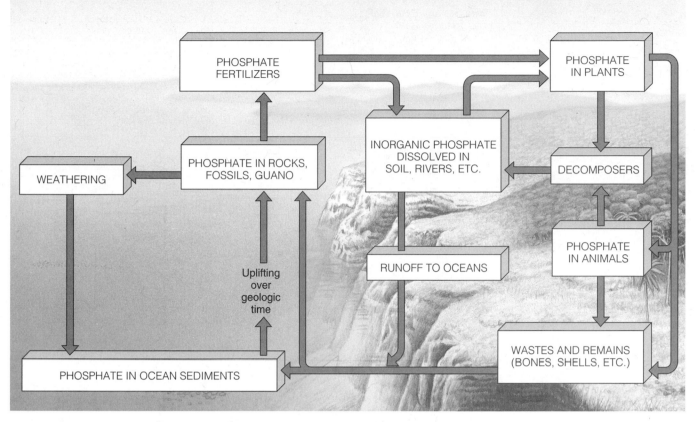

Figure 2-24 Simplified diagram of the phosphorus cycle. (Used by permission from Cecie Starr and Ralph Taggart, *Biology: The Unity and Diversity of Life*, 6th ed., Belmont, Calif.: Wadsworth, 1992)

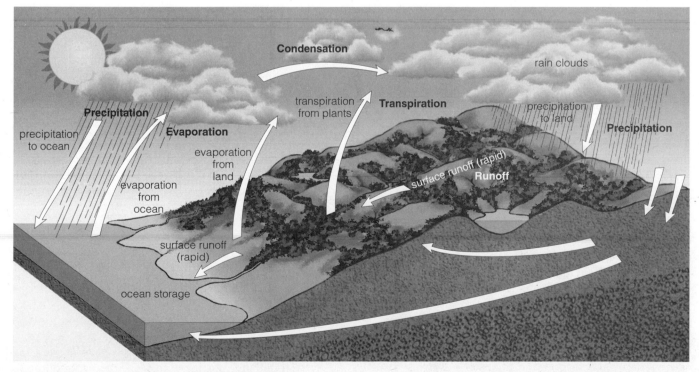

Figure 2-25 Simplified diagram of the hydrologic cycle.

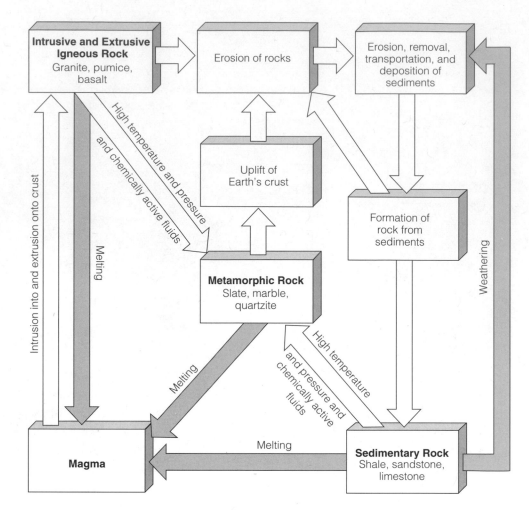

Figure 2-26 The rock cycle, the slowest of Earth's cyclic processes. Earth's materials are recycled over millions of years by three processes: melting, erosion, and metamorphism. These processes produce igneous, sedimentary, and metamorphic rocks. Rock of any of the three classes can be converted to rock of either of the other two classes or can even be recycled within its own class.

Within the diagram:

- Intrusive and Extrusive Igneous Rock: Granite, pumice, basalt
- Erosion of rocks
- Erosion, removal, transportation, and deposition of sediments
- Uplift of Earth's crust
- Formation of rock from sediments
- Metamorphic Rock: Slate, marble, quartzite
- Magma
- Sedimentary Rock: Shale, sandstone, limestone
- Intrusion into and extrusion onto crust
- High temperature and pressure and chemically active fluids
- Melting
- Weathering
- Melting
- High temperature and pressure and chemically active fluids
- Melting

■ Clearing vegetation from land for agriculture, mining, roads, construction, and other activities. This reduces seepage, which recharges groundwater supplies. This reduction also increases the risk of flooding and speeds surface runoff, producing more soil erosion and landslides.

THE ROCK CYCLE Geologic processes redistribute the chemical elements within and at the surface of the earth. Based on the way it forms, rock is placed in three broad classes: igneous, sedimentary, or metamorphic. **Igneous rock** forms when molten rock material (magma) wells up from Earth's upper mantle or deep crust, cools, and hardens into rock. Examples are granite (formed underground) and lava rock (formed above ground when molten lava cools and hardens).

Sedimentary rock forms from the accumulated products of erosion of preexisting rock and, in some cases, from the compacted shells, skeletons, and other remains of dead organisms. As these deposited layers become buried and compacted, the resulting pressure causes their particles to bond together to form sedimentary rocks such as shale, limestone, and lignite and bituminous coal.

Metamorphic rock is produced when a preexisting rock is subjected to high temperatures (which may cause it to melt partially), high pressures, chemically active fluids, or a combination of those agents. Examples are anthracite (a form of coal), slate, and marble.

Rocks are constantly being exposed to various physical and chemical conditions that over time can change them. The interaction of processes that change rocks from one type to another is called the **rock cycle** (Figure 2-26). Recycling material over millions of years, this slowest of Earth's cyclic processes is responsible for concentrating mineral resources on which humans depend (Figure 1-7).

 2-7

Life on Land and in Water Environments

BIOMES: LIFE ON LAND Biologists have divided the terrestrial (land) portion of the ecosphere into **biomes**, large regions such as forests, deserts, and grasslands characterized by certain climatic conditions and inhab-

Q: What percentage of all species that have ever lived have become extinct?

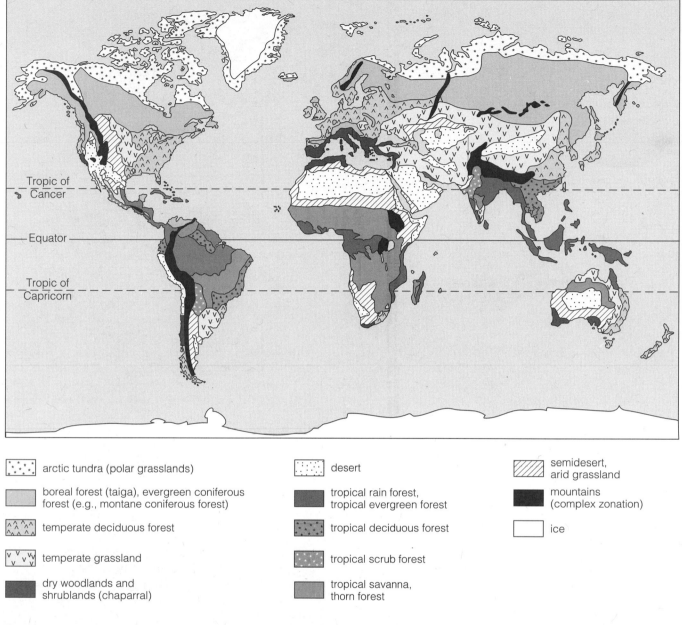

arctic tundra (polar grasslands)

boreal forest (taiga), evergreen coniferous forest (e.g., montane coniferous forest)

temperate deciduous forest

temperate grassland

dry woodlands and shrublands (chaparral)

desert

tropical rain forest, tropical evergreen forest

tropical deciduous forest

tropical scrub forest

tropical savanna, thorn forest

semidesert, arid grassland

mountains (complex zonation)

ice

Figure 2-27 Earth's major biomes. This map indicates the main types of natural vegetation we would expect to find in different undisturbed land areas, mostly because of differences in climate. Each biome contains many ecosystems whose communities have adapted to smaller differences in climate, soil, and other environmental factors within the biome. In reality, people have removed or altered much of this natural vegetation for farming, livestock grazing, lumber and fuelwood, mining, water transfer, villages, and cities, thereby altering the biomes.

ited by certain types of life, especially vegetation. Each biome consists of many ecosystems whose communities have adapted to small differences in climate, soil, and other environmental factors.

Why is one area of Earth's land surface a desert, another a grassland, and another a forest? Why are there different types of deserts, grasslands, and forests? The general answer to these questions is differences in *climate* (long-term weather)—specifically, differences in average temperature and average precipitation. Figure 2-27 shows the global distribution of

13 biomes. Figure 2-28 shows the effect of climate on biomes across a portion of the United States.

For plants, *precipitation is generally the limiting factor that determines whether a land area is desert, grassland, or forest*. A **desert** is an area where evaporation exceeds precipitation and the average amount of precipitation is less than 25 centimeters (10 inches) a year. Such areas have little vegetation or have widely spaced, mostly low vegetation.

Grasslands are regions where the average annual precipitation is great enough to allow grass, and in

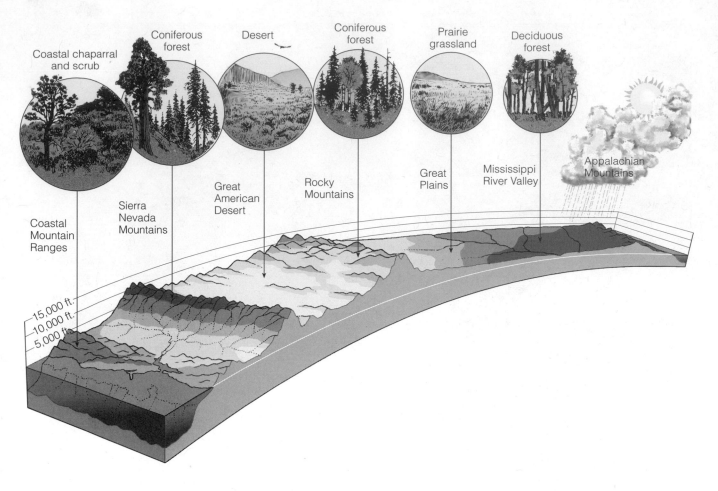

Coastal chaparral and scrub

Coniferous forest

Desert

Coniferous forest

Prairie grassland

Deciduous forest

Coastal Mountain Ranges

Sierra Nevada Mountains

Great American Desert

Rocky Mountains

Great Plains

Mississippi River Valley

Appalachian Mountains

15,000 ft.
10,000 ft.
5,000 ft.

Figure 2-28 Major biomes found along the 39th parallel crossing the United States. The differences mostly reflect changes in climate, mainly differences in average annual temperature and precipitation.

some areas a few trees, to prosper. Yet the precipitation is so erratic that drought and fire prevent large stands of trees from growing. Grasses in these biomes are renewable resources if not overgrazed. They grow out from the bottom instead of at the top, and their stems can grow again after being nibbled off by grazing animals. Undisturbed areas with moderate to high average annual precipitation tend to be covered with **forest**, containing various species of trees and smaller forms of vegetation.

Average annual precipitation and temperature, along with soil type, are the most important factors determining the type of desert, grassland, or forest in a particular area. Acting together, these factors lead to tropical, temperate, and polar deserts, grasslands, and forests (Figure 2-29).

Climate and vegetation both vary with **latitude** (distance from the equator) and **altitude** (height above sea level). If you travel from the equator toward either pole, you will encounter ever colder and wetter climates and zones of vegetation adapted to each (Figure 2-30). Similarly, as elevation or height above sea level

increases, the climate becomes colder and is often wetter. Thus, if you climb a tall mountain from its base to its summit, you will find changes in plant life similar to those you would find in traveling from equator to poles (Figure 2-30).

OCEANS   A more accurate name for Earth would be Ocean, because oceans cover about 71% of its surface (Figure 2-31). By serving as a gigantic reservoir for carbon dioxide (Figure 2-22), oceans help regulate the temperature of the troposphere. Oceans provide habitats for about 250,000 species of marine plants and animals, which are food for many organisms, including human beings. They also serve as a source of iron, sand, gravel, phosphates, magnesium, oil, natural gas, and many other valuable resources. Because of their size and currents, the oceans mix and dilute many human-produced wastes flowing or dumped into them to less harmful or even harmless levels, as long as they are not overloaded.

Oceans have two major life zones: the coastal zone and the open sea (Figure 2-32). Although it makes up

48

Q: What is the *first law of human ecology?*

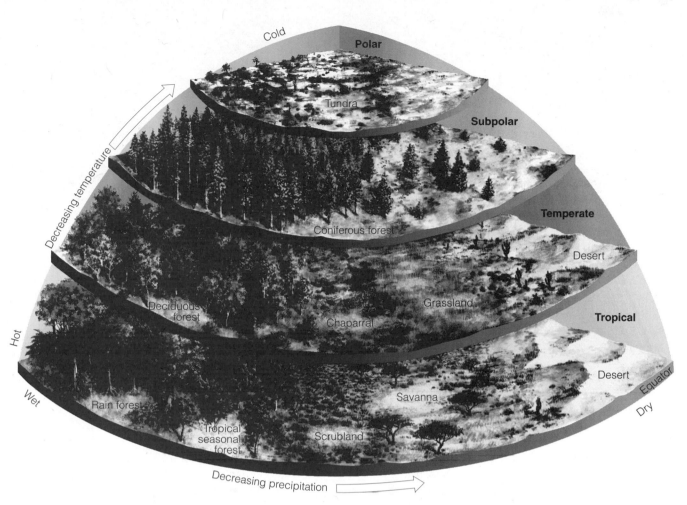

Figure 2-29 Average precipitation and average temperature, acting together over a period of 30 or more years as limiting factors, determine the type of desert, grassland, or forest biome in a particular area. Although the actual situation is much more complex, this simplified diagram gives you a general idea of how climate determines the types and amounts of natural vegetation you would expect to find in an undisturbed area. (Used by permission of Macmillan Publishing Company from Derek Elsom, *Earth*, New York: Macmillan, 1992. Copyright ©1992 by Marshall Editions Developments Limited.)

less than 10% of the ocean's area, the **coastal zone** contains 90% of all marine species and is the site of most of the large commercial marine fisheries. Because of ample sunlight and nutrients deposited from land and stirred up by wind and ocean currents, this coastal zone has a very high net primary productivity per unit of area (Figure 2-21). Examples of highly productive ecosystems in the coastal zone include:

- **Coral reefs** often found in warm tropical and subtropical oceans. They are formed by massive colonies containing billions of tiny coral animals, called polyps. They provide habitats for a diversity of aquatic life and help protect 15% of the world's coastlines from storms by reducing the energy of incoming waves. These ecosystems grow slowly and are easily disrupted.

- **Estuaries**—partially enclosed coastal areas at the mouths of rivers, whose fresh water, carrying fertile silt and runoff from the land, mixes with salty seawater.

- **Coastal wetlands**—land in a coastal area covered all or part of the year with salt water. They are breeding grounds and habitats for waterfowl and other wildlife and dilute and filter out large amounts of nutrients and waterborne pollutants. In temperate areas these wetlands usually consist of a mix of bays, lagoons, salt flats, mud flats, and salt marshes where grasses are the dominant vegetation. In warm tropical climates we find highly productive mangrove swamps dominated by mangrove trees, any of about 55 species of trees and shrubs that can live partly submerged in the relatively salty environment of coastal swamps.

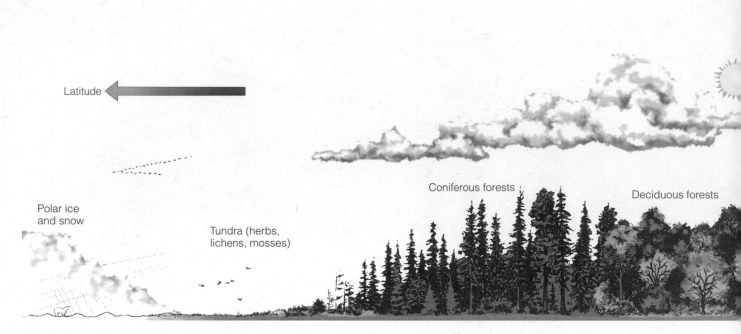

Latitude

Polar ice
and snow

Tundra (herbs,
lichens, mosses)

Coniferous forests

Deciduous forests

Figure 2-30 Generalized effects of latitude and altitude on climate and biomes. Parallel changes in types of vegetation occur when we travel from equator to poles or from plain to mountaintop.

- **Barrier islands**—long, thin, low, offshore islands of sediment that generally run parallel to the shore along some coasts (such as most of North America's Atlantic and Gulf coasts). These islands help protect the mainland, estuaries, lagoons, and coastal wetlands by dispersing the energy of approaching storm waves.

Despite their ecological importance these coastal ecosystems are under severe stress from human activities. Coastal zones are among our most densely populated and most intensely used—and polluted—ecosystems.

The **open sea** is divided into three vertical zones—euphotic, bathyl, and abyssal—based primarily on the penetration of sunlight (Figure 2-32). This vast volume contains only about 10% of all ocean species. Except at an occasional equatorial upwelling of nutrients from the ocean bottom, average net primary productivity per unit of area in the open sea is quite low (Figure 2-21). This is because sunlight cannot penetrate the lower layers and because the surface layer normally has fairly low levels of nutrients for phytoplankton, which are the main photosynthetic producers of the open ocean.

FRESHWATER LAKES Lakes are large natural bodies of standing fresh water formed when precipitation, land runoff, or groundwater flowing from underground springs fills depressions in the earth. Lakes

normally consist of four distinct zones (Figure 2-33), providing habitats and niches for different species.

A lake with a large or excessive supply of nutrients (mostly nitrates and phosphates) needed by producers is called a **eutrophic** (well-nourished) **lake** (Figure 2-34). A lake with a small supply of nutrients is called an **oligotrophic** (poorly nourished) **lake** (Figure 2-34). Many lakes fall somewhere between the two extremes of nutrient enrichment and are called **mesotrophic lakes**.

FRESHWATER STREAMS Precipitation that doesn't sink into the ground or evaporate is **surface water.** This water becomes **runoff**, which flows into streams and eventually to the oceans to continue circulating in the hydrologic cycle (Figure 2-25). The entire land area that delivers water, sediment, and dissolved substances via small streams to a major stream (river), and ultimately to the sea, is called a **watershed**, or a **drainage basin**.

The downward flow of water from mountain highlands to the sea takes place in three phases in a *river system* (Figure 2-35). Because of different environmental conditions in each phase, a river system is a series of different ecosystems.

As streams flow downhill, they become powerful shapers of land. Over millions of years the friction of moving water levels mountains and cuts deep canyons. The rock and soil the water removes are deposited as sediment in low-lying areas.

Q: At what rate is the world's population growing?

Altitude

Mountain ice and snow

Tundra (herbs, lichens, mosses)

Coniferous forests

Deciduous forests

Tropical forests

Tropical forests

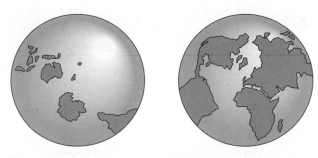

Figure 2-31 The ocean planet. The oceans cover about 71% of Earth's surface. About 97% of Earth's water is in the interconnected oceans, which cover 90% of the planet's mostly ocean hemisphere (left) and 50% of its land-ocean hemisphere (right). The average depth of the world's oceans is 3.8 kilometers (2.4 miles).

Figure 2-32 Major zones of life in an ocean. Actual depths of zones may vary.

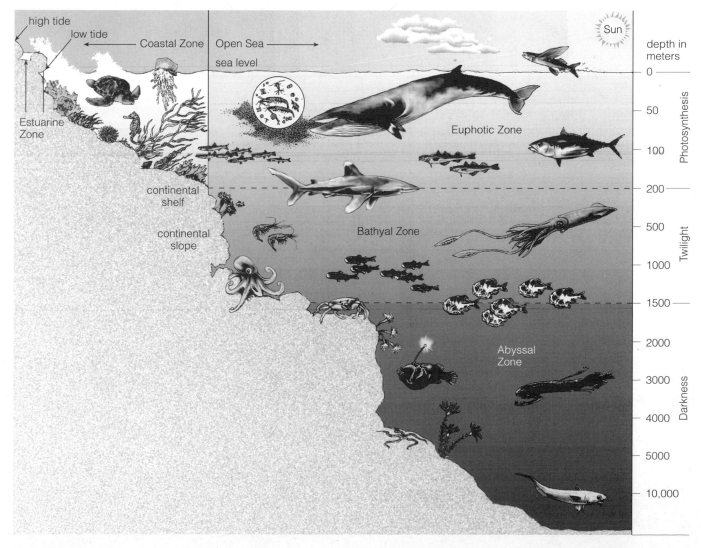

high tide
low tide
Coastal Zone
Open Sea
sea level
Sun
depth in meters

Estuarine Zone

Euphotic Zone

Photosynthesis

continental shelf

continental slope

Bathyal Zone

Twilight

Abyssal Zone

Darkness

0
50
100
200
500
1000
1500
2000
3000
4000
5000
10,000

A: 1.63% per year

CHAPTER 2   51

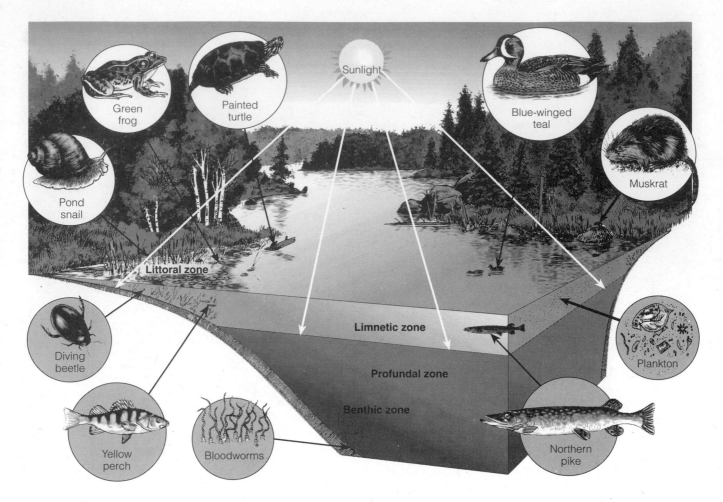

Figure 2-33 The four distinct zones of life in a lake in the eastern United States.

INLAND WETLANDS Lands covered with fresh water at least part of the year (excluding lakes, reservoirs, and streams) and located away from coastal areas are called **inland wetlands**. They include bogs, marshes, prairie potholes, swamps, mud flats, floodplains, bogs, fens, wet meadows, and the wet arctic tundra in summer.

Some wetlands are covered with water year-round. Others, such as prairie potholes, floodplain wetlands, and bottomland hardwood swamps are *seasonal wetlands* that are underwater or soggy for only a short time.

Inland wetlands provide habitats for fish, waterfowl, and other wildlife, and they improve water quality by filtering, diluting, and degrading sediments and pollutants as water flows through. Floodplain wetlands near rivers help regulate stream flow by storing water during periods of heavy rainfall and releasing it slowly, which reduces riverbank erosion and flood damage. By storing water, many seasonal and year-round wetlands allow increased infiltration, thus helping recharge groundwater supplies.

Despite the ecological importance of year-round and seasonal inland wetlands, they are under attack. Each year some 1,200 square kilometers (470 square miles) of inland wetland in the United States are lost, about 80% to agriculture and the rest to mining, forestry, oil and gas extraction, highways, and urban development. Other countries have suffered similar losses.

 **2-8** **Responses to Environmental Stress**

CHANGE: THE DRIVING FORCE OF NATURE There is no such thing as "natural balance" or "balance of nature." The key thing going on in nature is constant change caused by natural and human-related forces and adjustments to such environmental stresses. Populations, communities, and ecosystems constantly change and have always done so.

Q: What two countries have the world's largest populations?

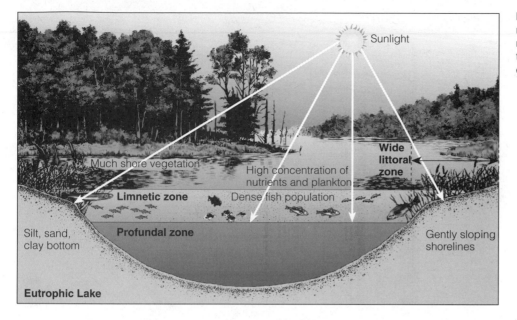

Figure 2-34 Eutrophic, or nutrient-rich, lake (top) and oligotrophic, or nutrient-poor, lake (bottom). Mesotrophic lakes fall between these two extremes of nutrient enrichment.

Sunlight

Much shore vegetation

High concentration of nutrients and plankton

Wide littoral zone

Limnetic zone

Dense fish population

Profundal zone

Silt, sand, clay bottom

Gently sloping shorelines

Eutrophic Lake

Sunlight

Little shore vegetation

Low concentration of nutrients and plankton

Narrow littoral zone

Limnetic zone

Sparse fish population

Steeply sloping shorelines

Sand, gravel, rock bottom

Oligotrophic Lake

Sustainability does not imply a static situation. Instead, it includes the capacity of populations, communities, ecosystems, and human economic, political, and social systems to adapt to new conditions.

CHANGES IN POPULATION SIZE Four variables—births, deaths, immigration, and emigration—govern changes in population size. A population gains individuals by birth and immigration and loses them by death and emigration:

$$\text{population change rate} = \text{births} + \text{immigration} - \text{deaths} + \text{emigration}$$

These variables in turn depend on changes in resource availability or other environmental changes.

Populations vary in their capacity for growth. The **biotic potential** of a population is the *maximum* rate (r_{max}) at which it can increase when there are no limits on its growth. Animal species have different biotic potentials because of variations in **(1)** when reproduction starts and stops (reproductive span), **(2)** how often reproduction occurs, **(3)** how many live offspring are born each time (litter size), and **(4)** how many offspring survive to reproductive age.

No population can grow exponentially indefinitely. In the real world an exploding population reaches some size limit imposed by a shortage of one or more

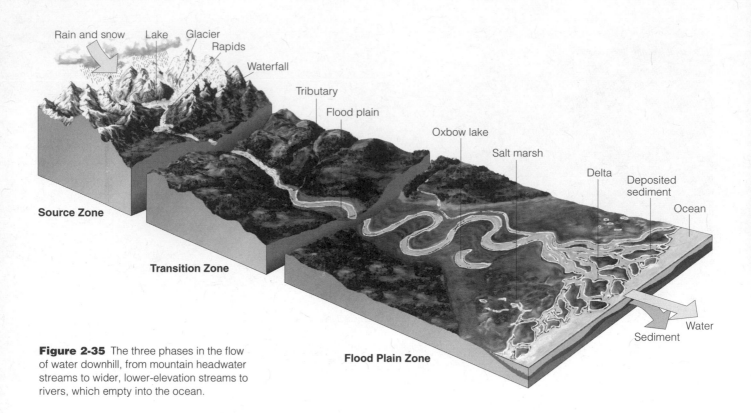

Figure 2-35 The three phases in the flow of water downhill, from mountain headwater streams to wider, lower-elevation streams to rivers, which empty into the ocean.

Labels in figure: Rain and snow, Lake, Glacier, Rapids, Waterfall, Tributary, Flood plain, Oxbow lake, Salt marsh, Delta, Deposited sediment, Ocean, Water, Sediment

Source Zone

Transition Zone

Flood Plain Zone

limiting factors, such as light, water, space, and nutrients. *There are always limits to growth in nature.*

Environmental resistance consists of all the factors acting jointly to limit the growth of a population. They determine the **carrying capacity (K)**, the number of individuals of a given species that can be sustained indefinitely in a given area. Carrying capacity is determined by many factors, including predation, competition among species, migration, and climate. The carrying capacity for a population can vary with seasonal or abnormal changes in the weather or supplies of food, water, nesting sites, or other crucial environmental resources.

Because of environmental resistance, any population growing exponentially starts out slowly, goes through a rapid growth phase, and then levels off once the carrying capacity of the area is reached. In most cases the size of such a population fluctuates slightly above and below the carrying capacity. A plot of this type of growth yields an *S-shaped curve* (Figure 2-36a). Sometimes, however, a population temporarily overshoots the carrying capacity (Figure 2-36b). This happens because of a *reproductive time lag*, the time required for the birth rate to fall and the death rate to rise in response to resource limits. Unless large numbers of individuals can move to an area with more favorable conditions, the population will suffer a *dieback* or *crash*, falling back to a lower level that typically fluctuates around the area's carrying capacity. An area's carrying capacity can also be lowered

because of resource destruction and degradation during the overshoot period.

Humans are not exempt from this phenomenon. Ireland, for example, experienced a population crash after a fungus infection destroyed the potato crop in 1845. About 1 million people died, and 3 million people emigrated to other countries.

Technological, social, and other cultural changes have extended Earth's carrying capacity for the human species (Figure 1-4). We have increased food production, controlled many diseases, and used energy and matter resources at a rapid rate to make normally uninhabitable areas of Earth habitable. A crucial question is how long we will be able to keep doing this on a planet with finite size and resources.

The idealized S-shaped and crash or dieback curves of population growth shown in Figure 2-36 can be observed in laboratory experiments. In nature, however, we find three general types of population change curves: relatively stable, irruptive, and cyclic (Figure 2-37).

A species whose population size fluctuates slightly above and below its carrying capacity (as long as that capacity doesn't change significantly) has a relatively stable population size. Such stability is characteristic of many species found in habitats of undisturbed tropical rain forests (Figure 2-16), where there is little variation in average temperature and rainfall.

Some species, such as the raccoon, normally have a fairly stable population. However, the population

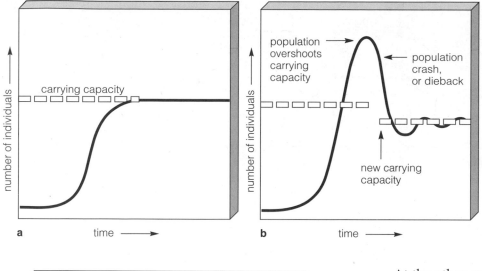

Figure 2-36 (a) Idealized S-shaped curve of population growth. **(b)** Population curve crash or dieback occurs. These idealized curves only approximate what goes on in nature.

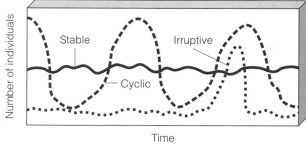

Figure 2-37 General types of idealized population change curves found in nature.

may occasionally explode, or *irrupt*, to a high peak and then crash to a relatively stable lower level. The population explosion is due to some factor that temporarily increases carrying capacity for the population. Examples are better weather, more food, or fewer predators, including human hunters and trappers.

Some species undergo sharp increases in their numbers followed by seemingly periodic crashes. Predators are sometimes blamed, but the actual causes of such "boom–bust" cycles are poorly understood.

Each species has a characteristic mode of reproduction. At one extreme are species that produce hordes of offspring early in their life cycle. The offspring, usually small and short-lived, mature rapidly with little or no parental care. Typically, many of them die before they can reproduce, but others survive. Algae, bacteria, rodents, annual plants, many fish, and most insects are examples. Such species tend to be *opportunists*, reproducing rapidly when conditions are favorable or when a new habitat or niche becomes available—a cleared forest or a newly plowed field, for example. Unfavorable environmental conditions, however, can cause such populations to crash. Hence, such species tend to go through "boom–bust" cycles.

At the other extreme are species that produce a few, often fairly large offspring and often look after them for a long time to ensure that most reach reproductive age. Living in fairly stable environments and tending to maintain their population size near their habitat's carrying capacity, their populations typically follow an S-shaped growth curve (Figure 2-36a). Examples are sharks, most large mammals—including humans, elephants, rhinoceroses, and whales—birds of prey, and large, long-lived plants. The reproductive strategies of most species fall somewhere between these two extremes.

EVOLUTION, ADAPTATION, AND NATURAL SELECTION The major driving force of adaptation to environmental change is **biological evolution**, or **evolution**, the change in the genetic makeup of a population of a species in successive generations. Note that populations—not individuals—evolve. According to the **theory of evolution** all life forms developed from earlier life forms. Although this theory conflicts with the creation stories of most religions, it is the way biologists explain how life has changed over the past 3.6–3.8 billion years (Figure 2-38) and why it is so diverse today.

Evolutionary change occurs as a result of the interplay of genetic variation and changes in environmental conditions. The first step in evolution is the development of *genetic variability* in a population. Genetic information in *chromosomes* is contained in various sequences of chemical units (called nucleotides) in DNA molecules. Distinctive DNA segments that are found in chromosomes impart certain inheritable traits and are called **genes**.

A population's **gene pool** is the sum total of all genes possessed by the individuals of the population. Individuals of a population of a particular species, however, don't have exactly the same genes. The source of this genetic variability is **mutations**—random

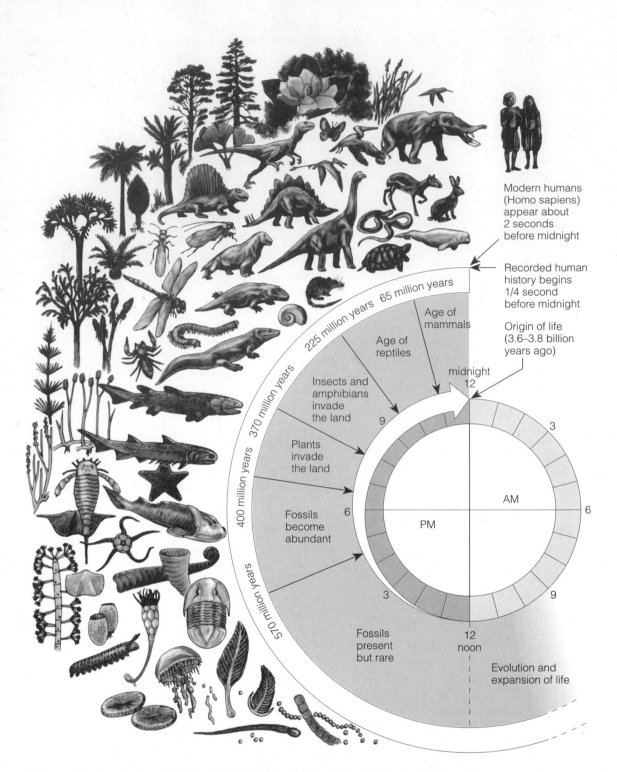

Figure 2-38 Greatly simplified history of biological evolution of life on Earth, which was preceded by about 1 billion years of chemical evolution. The early span of biological evolution on Earth, between 3.8 billion and about 570 million years ago, was dominated by microorganisms (mostly bacteria and later protists). Plants and animals evolved only about 570 million years ago, and we arrived on the scene only a short time ago. If we compress Earth's roughly 3.8-billion-year history of life to a 24-hour time scale, our closest human ancestors (*Homo sapiens*) appeared about 2 seconds before midnight, and our species (*Homo sapiens sapiens*) appeared less than 1 second before midnight. Agriculture began only 1/4 second before midnight, and the Industrial Revolution has been around for only seven thousandths of a second. Despite our brief time on Earth, humans may be hastening the extinction of more species in a shorter time than ever before in Earth's long history. (Adapted from George Gaylord Simpson and William S. Beck, *Life: An Introduction to Biology*, 2d ed., New York: Harcourt Brace Jovanovich, 1965)

Q: Worldwide, what is the average number of children per woman?

changes in DNA molecules making up genes that can yield changes in anatomy, physiology, or behavior in offspring. Such mutations, or random changes in genetic makeup, can occur and be transmitted to offspring in several ways:

- When DNA molecules are copied every time a cell divides.

- During *sexual reproduction*, when offspring are produced by the union of a male sperm and a female ovum (egg). For example, when a human sperm and egg unite there are over 70 billion potentially different chromosomal combinations.

- During the *production of ova (eggs) or sperm cells*, known as *gametes*. When gametes are formed, the genetic deck is "reshuffled," and the number of chromosomes in each cell is reduced by half.

- *By crossing over*. This occurs when pieces of chromosomes break off and become attached to other chromosomes during the production of germ cells (which make sperm in males and ova in females).

- *By exposure to an external agent*. Examples are chemicals (called mutagens) and high-energy electromagnetic radiation such as ultraviolet light, cosmic rays, X rays, and radioactivity (Figure 2-4).

The net result of millions of such random and unpredictable changes in the DNA molecules of individuals in a population is genetic variability.

Most mutations are harmful, but some result in new genetic traits that give its bearer and most of its offspring better chances for survival and reproduction. Any genetically controlled structural, physiological, or behavioral characteristic that enhances the chance for members of a population to survive and reproduce in its environment is called an **adaptation**.

Structural adaptations include *coloration* (allowing more individuals to hide from predators or to sneak up on prey), *mimicry* (looking like a poisonous or dangerous species), *protective cover* (shell, thick skin, bark, thorns), and *gripping mechanisms* (hands with opposable thumbs). *Physiological adaptations* include the ability to hibernate during cold weather, to poison predators, and to give off chemicals that repel prey. The ability to fly to a warmer climate during winter is an example of *behavioral adaptation*. So are resource partitioning (Figure 2-16) and species interactions such as parasitism, mutualism, and commensalism.

Individuals with one or more adaptations that allow them to survive under changed environmental conditions are more likely to reproduce, and they will leave behind more offspring with the same favorable adaptations than individuals without such adaptations. This phenomenon is known as **differential reproduction**.

The process by which a particular beneficial gene or set of beneficial genes is reproduced more than others through adaptation and differential reproduction is called **natural selection**. Natural selection is the major (but not necessarily the only) mechanism leading to evolution through a combination of mutation-caused genetic variability and changes in environmental conditions.

LIMITS TO ADAPTATION Shouldn't adaptations to new environmental conditions allow our skin to be able to become more resistant to the harmful effects of ultraviolet radiation, our lungs better able to cope with air pollutants, and our liver more capable of detoxifying pollutants we are exposed to? The answer is *no*, because there are limits to adaptations in nature:

- A change in environmental conditions can lead to adaptation only for traits already present in the gene pool of a population.

- Even if a beneficial heritable trait is present in a population, its ability to adapt can be limited by its reproductive capacity. If members of a population can't reproduce fast enough to adapt to a particular environmental change (or group of environmental changes), all of its members can die. For example, species of weeds, mosquitoes, rats, or bacteria that can produce hordes of offspring early in their life cycle can adapt to a change in environmental conditions through natural selection in a short time. By contrast, populations of species such as elephants, tigers, sharks, and humans cannot produce large numbers of offspring rapidly, and they take long periods of time (typically thousands or even millions of years) to adapt through natural selection.

- Even if a favorable genetic trait is present, most members of the population would have to die or become sterile so that individuals with the trait could dominate and pass the trait on—hardly a desirable solution to the environmental problems humans face.

SPECIATION AND EXTINCTION Earth's 5–100 million species are believed to be the result of two processes over the past 3.6–3.8 billion years. One is **speciation**: the formation of two or more species from one as a result of divergent natural selection in response to changes in environmental conditions.

A common speciation mechanism is *geographic isolation*, the situation in which populations of a species become separated in areas with different environmental conditions for fairly long periods, as when part of the group migrates in search of food and doesn't return (Figure 2-39). Populations may also become separated by a physical barrier or change such as a

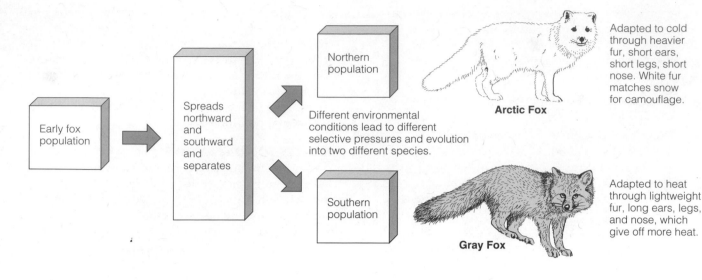

Figure 2-39 Geographic isolation leading to reproductive isolation and speciation.

highway or volcanic eruption or when a few individuals are carried to a new area by wind, water, or humans.

After long geographic separation during which the two groups don't interbreed, they may begin to diverge in their genetic makeup because of different selection pressures. If this *reproductive isolation* continues long enough, members of the separated populations may become so different that they can't interbreed and produce fertile offspring. Then one species has become two (Figure 2-39).

The second process affecting the various species on Earth is **extinction**: A species ceases to exist because it cannot genetically adapt and successfully reproduce under new environmental conditions. Extinction is nothing new on Earth. Biologists estimate that 99% of all the species that have lived are now extinct. Some species inevitably disappear as local conditions change. This is *background extinction*. In contrast, a **mass extinction** is an abrupt rise in extinction rates above the background level. It is a catastrophic, widespread—often global—event in which not just one species but major groups of species are wiped out simultaneously. Fossil and geological evidence indicates that Earth's species have experienced five great mass extinctions—at roughly 26-million-year intervals—with smaller ones in between.

A crisis for one species, however, is an opportunity for another. The fact that 5–100 million species exist today means that speciation, on average, has kept ahead of extinction. Evidence shows that Earth's mass extinctions have been followed by periods of recovery and **adaptive radiations**, in which numerous new species evolved to fill new or vacant ecological niches in changed environments.

Speciation minus extinction equals *biodiversity*, one of the planet's most important resources.

ECOLOGICAL SUCCESSION One characteristic of most communities and ecosystems is that the types of species in a given area are usually changing. This gradual process of change in the composition and function of communities and ecosystems is called **ecological succession**, or **community development**.

Succession is a normal process in nature. It reflects the results of the continuing struggle among species with different adaptations for food, light, space, nutrients, and other survival resources. Ecological succession can result in a progression from immature, rapidly changing, unstable communities to more mature, self-sustaining communities when this process is not disrupted by large-scale natural events or human actions. Immature communities or ecosystems at an early stage of succession and mature ones at a later stage have strikingly different characteristics (Table 2-1).

Ecologists recognize two types of ecological succession, primary and secondary, depending on the conditions at a particular site at the beginning of the process. **Primary succession** involves the development of biotic communities in a barren habitat with no or very little topsoil. Examples of such areas include the rock or mud exposed by a retreating glacier (Figure 2-40) or a mudslide, newly cooled lava, a new sandbar deposited by a shift in ocean currents, and surface-mined areas from which all topsoil has been removed.

After such a large-scale disturbance, life usually returns first with a few hardy **pioneer species**—microbes, mosses, and lichens. They are usually species with the ability to establish large populations quickly in a new area—species that Edward O. Wilson calls "nature's sprinters."

The more common type of succession is **secondary succession**, which begins in an area where the natural vegetation has been removed or destroyed but

Q: What is the population of the United States?

Table 2-1 Ecosystem Characteristics at Immature and Mature Stages of Ecological Succession

Characteristic	Immature Ecosystem	Mature Ecosystem
Ecosystem Structure		
Plant size	Small	Large
Species diversity	Low	High
Trophic structure	Mostly producers, few decomposers	Mixture of producers, consumers, and decomposers
Ecological niches	Few, mostly generalized	Many, mostly specialized
Community organization (number of interconnecting links)	Low	High
Ecosystem Function		
Food chains and webs	Simple, mostly plant → herbivore with few decomposers	Complex, dominated by decomposers
Efficiency of nutrient recycling	Low	High
Efficiency of energy use	Low	High

Figure 2-40 Primary succession of plant communities over more than 100 years on bare rock exposed by a retreating glacier in the Glacier Bay region of Alaska.

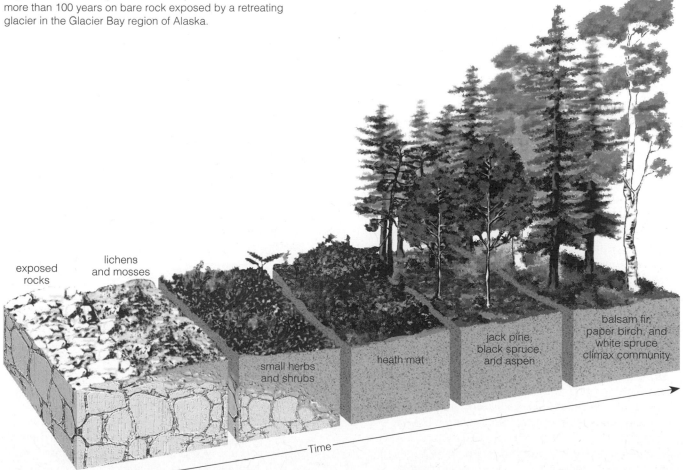

exposed rocks

lichens and mosses

small herbs and shrubs

heath mat

jack pine, black spruce, and aspen

balsam fir, paper birch, and white spruce climax community

Time

Figure 2-41 Secondary ecological succession of plant communities on an abandoned farm field in North Carolina. After the farmland was abandoned it took about 150 years for the area to be covered once again with a mature oak and hickory forest.

annual weeds

perennial weeds and grasses

shrubs

young pine forest

mature oak–hickory forest

Time

where the soil or bottom sediment has not been covered or removed. Examples of candidates for secondary succession include abandoned farmlands, burned or cut forests, heavily polluted streams, and land that has been dammed or flooded to produce a reservoir or pond. Because some soil or sediment is present, new vegetation can usually sprout within only a few weeks. In the central (Piedmont) region of North Carolina, for example, European settlers cleared the mature forests of native oak and hickory, and replanted the land with crops. Later some of the land was abandoned. Figure 2-41 shows how such abandoned farmland, covered with a thick layer of soil, has undergone secondary succession until, after about 150 years, the area again supports a mature oak and hickory forest.

It is tempting to conclude that ecological succession is an orderly sequence, with each successional stage leading predictably to the next, more stable stage until an area is occupied by a *mature or climax community*, dominated by plant species. Research has shown, however, that this does not necessarily happen. The exact sequence of species and community types that appear during primary or secondary succession can be highly variable. We cannot predict the course of a given succession or view it as some preordained progress toward an ideally adapted climax community.

2-9   Human Impacts

SIMPLIFYING ECOSYSTEMS   In modifying natural ecosystems for our use, we usually simplify them: We plow grasslands, clear forests, and fill in wetlands. Then we replace their thousands of interrelated plant and animal species with one crop or one kind of tree, called **monocultures**—or with buildings, highways, and parking lots.

We spend a lot of time, energy, and money trying to protect such monocultures from continual invasion by pioneer species, which we call *weeds* if they are plants (because weeds and annual crop plants typically occupy the same niches), *pests* if they are insects or

Q: What is the average number of children per woman in the United States?

other animals, and *pathogens* if they are fungi, viruses, or disease-causing bacteria. Weeds, pests, or pathogens can wipe out an entire monoculture crop unless it is protected by pesticides or by some form of biological control.

When fast-breeding insect species begin to undergo natural selection and develop genetic resistance to pesticides, the salespeople encourage farmers to use stronger doses or switch to a new pesticide. As a result natural selection in the pests increases to the point that these chemicals eventually become ineffective.

This process illustrates two important ideas. One is what biologist Garrett Hardin calls the **first law of human ecology**: We can never do merely one thing. The other is the **principle of connectedness**: *Everything is connected to and intermingled with everything else; we are all in it together.* Because of these principles any human intrusion into nature has multiple effects, many (perhaps most) of them unpredictable. They are unpredictable because of our limited understanding of how nature works and which connections are the strongest and most important in the sustainability and adaptability of ecosystems (Connections, at right).

Cultivation is not the only way people simplify ecosystems. Ranchers, who don't want bison or prairie dogs competing with sheep for grass, eradicate those species, as well as wolves, coyotes, eagles, and other predators that occasionally kill sheep. In addition, far too often, ranchers and nomadic herders allow livestock to overgraze grasslands until erosion converts these ecosystems to simpler and less productive deserts. The cutting of vast areas of diverse tropical rain forests also destroys part of Earth's biodiversity. And people tend to overfish and overhunt some species to extinction or near extinction, another way of simplifying ecosystems. Finally, the burning of fossil fuels in industrial plants, homes, and vehicles creates air pollutants that simplify forest ecosystems by killing or weakening trees and that simplify aquatic ecosystems by killing fish.

The challenge is to maintain a balance between simplified, human ecosystems and the neighboring, more complex (mature) natural ecosystems, on which our simplified systems and other forms of life depend—and to slow down the rates at which we are altering nature for our purposes. If we alter and simplify too much of the planet to meet our needs and wants, what's at risk is not the earth—which will eventually evolve new forms of life—but our current social systems and our own species. According to biodiversity expert E. O. Wilson, "If this planet were under surveillance by biologists from another world, I think they would look at us and say, 'Here is a species in the mid-stages of self-destruction.'" The evolutionary lesson to be learned from nature is that no species can get too big for its britches, at least not for long.

The Day the Roof Fell In

CONNECTIONS

Malaria once infected 9 out of 10 people in North Borneo, now known as Brunei. In 1955, the World Health Organization (WHO) began spraying the island with dieldrin (a DDT relative) to kill malaria-carrying mosquitoes. The program was so successful that the dread disease was virtually eliminated.

Other, unexpected things began to happen, however. The dieldrin killed other insects, including flies and cockroaches living in houses. At first the islanders applauded this turn of events, but then small lizards that also lived in the houses died after gorging themselves on dead insects. Next, cats began dying after feeding on the dead lizards.

Then, without cats, rats flourished and overran the villages. Now people were threatened by sylvatic plague carried by the rat fleas. WHO then parachuted healthy cats onto the island to help control the rats.

Then the villagers' roofs began to fall in. The dieldrin had killed wasps and other insects that fed on a type of caterpillar that either avoided or was not affected by the insecticide. With most of its predators eliminated, the caterpillar population exploded. The larvae munched their way through one of their favorite foods, the leaves used in thatched roofs.

Ultimately, the Borneo episode ended happily: Both malaria and the unexpected effects of the spraying program were brought under control. However, the chain of unforeseen events shows the unpredictability of interfering in an ecosystem.

SOLUTIONS: WORKING WITH NATURE

The brief discussion of principles in this chapter reveals that living systems have six key features: *interdependence, diversity, resilience, adaptability, unpredictability,* and *limits.* This suggests that the best way for us to live sustainably is to understand and mimic how nature is perpetuated based primarily on the scientific laws, concepts, and principles discussed in this chapter. This begins by recognizing three things: **(1)** We are part of—not apart from—Earth's dynamic web of life; **(2)** our survival, lifestyles, and economies are totally dependent on the sun and Earth; and **(3)** everything is connected to everything, but some connections are stronger and more important than others.

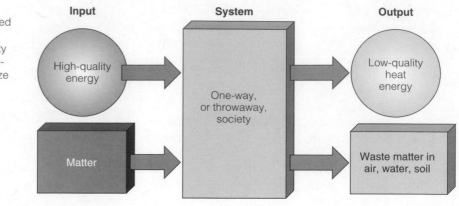

Figure 2-42 The throwaway or high-waste society of most industrialized countries is based on maximizing the rates of energy and matter flow, rapidly converting the world's high-quality matter and energy resources into waste, pollution, and low-quality heat—in order to maximize short-term economic gain.

DEVELOPING SUSTAINABLE SOCIETIES Because of the law of conservation of matter and the second law of energy, resource use by each of us automatically adds some waste heat and waste matter to the environment. Most of today's advanced industrialized countries are largely **throwaway societies** or **high-waste societies**, sustaining ever-increasing economic growth by increasing the flow or *throughput* of planetary *sources* of materials and energy. These resources flow through the economy to planetary *sinks* (air, water, soil, organisms) where pollutants and wastes end up (Figure 2-42). There is an important lesson to be learned from the scientific laws of matter and energy and the ecological concepts discussed in this chapter. They tell us that if more and more people continue to use and waste more and more energy and matter resources at an increasing rate, sooner or later the capacity of the local, regional, and global environments to dilute and degrade waste matter and absorb waste heat will be exceeded.

A stopgap solution to this problem is to convert from a throwaway society to a **matter-recycling society**. The goal of such a shift would be to allow economic growth to continue without depleting matter resources and without producing excessive pollution and environmental degradation. However, the two laws of energy tell us that *recycling matter resources always requires high-quality energy, which cannot be recycled*. In the long run a matter-recycling society based on continuing economic growth must have an inexhaustible supply of affordable high-quality energy. The environment must also have an infinite capacity to absorb and disperse waste heat and to dilute and degrade waste matter. Thus, *shifting from a throwaway society to a matter-recycling society is only a temporary solution to our problems*. Nevertheless, making such a shift is necessary to give us more time to convert to a sustainable-Earth or low-waste society.

We can use the scientific principles discussed in this chapter to understand that the best long-term solution to our environmental and resource problems is to shift from a society based on maximizing matter and energy flow (throughput) to a **sustainable-Earth**, or **low-waste, society** (Figure 2-43). Such a society would:

- Reduce the throughput of matter and energy resources to prevent excessive depletion and degradation of planetary sources and overload of planetary sinks

- Use energy more efficiently and not use high-quality energy for tasks that require only moderate-quality energy (Figure 2-5)

- Shift from exhaustible and potentially polluting fossil and nuclear fuels to less harmful renewable energy obtained from the sun and from Earth's natural cycles and flows

- Not waste potentially renewable resources, and use them no faster than the rate at which they are regenerated

- Not waste nonrenewable resources, and use them no faster than the rate at which a renewable resource, used sustainably, can be substituted for it

- Recycle and reuse at least 60% of the matter we now discard as trash

- Reduce use and waste of matter resources by making things that last longer and are easier to recycle, reuse, and repair

- Add wastes and pollutants to environmental sinks no faster than the rate at which they can be recycled, reused, absorbed, or rendered harmless to us and other species by natural or human-designed processes

- Emphasize pollution prevention and waste reduction instead of pollution cleanup and waste management

- Slow (and eventually halt) human population growth to help reduce stress on global life-support systems

- Greatly reduce poverty, which degrades humans and the environment by causing people to use resources unsustainably to stay alive

Q: What percentage of the world's population is under age 15?

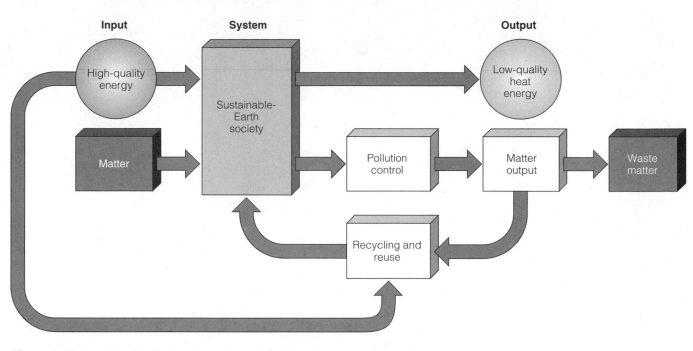

Figure 2-43 A sustainable-Earth or low-waste society—based on energy flow and matter recycling—reuses and recycles nonrenewable matter resources; uses potentially renewable resources no faster than they are replenished; uses matter and energy resources efficiently; reduces unnecessary consumption; emphasizes pollution prevention and waste reduction; and controls population growth.

The scientific laws and principles discussed in this chapter reveal that we are all in it together and that we must learn how to work with—not against—the rest of nature.

If we love our children, we must love the earth with tender care and pass it on, diverse and beautiful, so that on a warm spring day 10,000 years hence they can feel peace in a sea of grass, can watch a bee visit a flower, can hear a sandpiper call in the sky, and can find joy in being alive.

HUGH H. ILTIS

CRITICAL THINKING

1. If there is no "away," why isn't the world filled with waste matter?

2. Use the second energy law to explain why a barrel of oil can be used only once as a fuel.

3. **a**. A bumper sticker asks, "Have you thanked a green plant today?" Give two reasons for appreciating a green plant.
   b. Trace the sources of the materials that make up the bumper sticker and see whether the sticker itself is a sound application of the slogan.

4. Using the second law of energy, explain why there is such a sharp decrease in usable energy as energy flows through a food chain or web. Doesn't an energy loss at each step violate the first law of energy?

Explain.

5. Using the second law of energy, explain why many poor people in LDCs are primarily vegetarians.

6. Since the deep oceans are vast and are located far away from human habitats, why not use them as the depository for our radioactive and other hazardous wastes? Give your reasons for agreeing or disagreeing with this proposal.

7. Why are coastal and inland wetlands and coral reefs such important ecosystems? Why have so many of these vital ecosystems been destroyed by human activities?

8. Someone tells you not to worry about air pollution because through natural selection the human species will develop lungs that can detoxify pollutants. How would you reply?

9. Explain why a simplified ecosystem such as a cornfield is much more vulnerable to harm from insects, plant diseases, and fungi than a more complex, natural ecosystem such as a grassland. Why are natural ecosystems less vulnerable?

10. **a**. Use the law of conservation of matter to explain why a matter-recycling society will sooner or later be necessary.
    b. Use the first and second laws of energy and the ecological concepts discussed in this chapter to explain why, in the long run, a sustainable-Earth or low-waste society, not just a matter-recycling society, will be necessary.

3 The Human Population: Growth, Urbanization, and Regulation

Factors Affecting Human Population Size

BIRTH RATES AND DEATH RATES Populations grow or decline through the interplay of three factors: births, deaths, and migration. The **birth rate**, or **crude birth rate**, is the number of live births per 1,000 persons in a population in a given year. The **death rate**, or **crude death rate**, is the number of deaths per 1,000 persons in a population in a given year. Figure 3-1 shows the crude birth and death rates for various groups of countries in 1993. Worldwide, there are more births than deaths; every time your heart beats three more babies are added to the world's population—amounting to roughly 247,000 more people each day.

When the death rate equals the crude birth rate and migration is not a factor, population size remains stable, a condition known as **zero population growth (ZPG)**.

The annual rate at which the size of a population changes (excluding migration) is called the **annual rate of natural population change**.

$$\begin{aligned}
\text{annual rate of population change (\%)} &= \frac{\text{birth rate} - \text{death rate}}{1{,}000 \text{ persons}} \times 100 \\
&= \frac{\text{birth rate} - \text{death rate}}{10}
\end{aligned}$$

The world's annual rate of population growth dropped 18% between 1965 and 1993, from 2% to 1.63%. This is good news, but the population base rose by 72% from 3.2 billion to 5.5 billion during the same period. This 18% drop in the growth rate of population is akin to learning that a truck heading straight at you has slowed from 100 kilometers per hour to 82 kilometers per hour while its weight has increased by almost three-fourths. The current annual growth rate of 1.63% adds 90 million people per year—the equivalent of adding the population of Mexico each year and that of the United States about every three years.

In terms of sheer numbers of people, China and India dwarf all other countries, making up 38% of the world's population (Figure 3-2). One person in five is

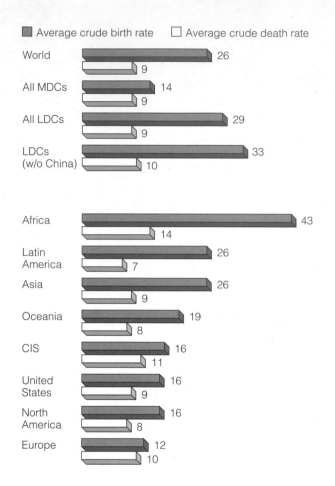

Figure 3-1 Average crude birth and death rates for various groups of countries in 1993. (Data from Population Reference Bureau)

Chinese, and 60% of the world's population is Asian. Figure 3-3 shows how the population in various regions is projected to grow between 1993 and 2025.

FERTILITY RATES Two types of fertility rates affect a country's population size and growth rate. **Replacement-level fertility** is the number of children a couple must bear to replace themselves. The actual average replacement-level fertility rate is slightly higher than two children per couple (2.1 in MDCs and as high as 2.5 in some LDCs), mostly because some female children die before reaching their reproductive years.

Q: How many legal immigrants are admitted to the United States each year?

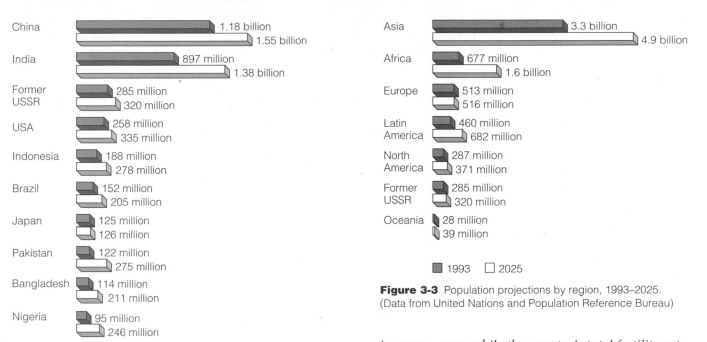

Figure 3-2 The world's 10 most populous countries in 1993, with projections of their population size in 2025. (Data from World Bank)

Figure 3-3 Population projections by region, 1993–2025. (Data from United Nations and Population Reference Bureau)

The most useful measure for projecting future population change is the **total fertility rate (TFR)**: an estimate of the average number of children a woman will have during her childbearing years.

In 1993 the average total fertility rate was 3.3 children per woman for the world as a whole, 1.8 in MDCs (down from 2.5 in 1950), and 3.7 in LDCs (down from 6.5 in 1950). If the world's total fertility rate remains at 3.3, its population will reach 694 billion by 2150—391 times the current population! Clearly this is not possible, but it does illustrate the enormous power of exponential population growth. Population experts expect TFRs in MDCs to remain around 1.8 and those in LDCs to drop to around 2.3 by 2025—the basis of the projections in Figure 3-3. That is good news, but it will still lead to a projected world population of around 9 billion by 2025, with most of this growth taking place in LDCs (Figure 1-5).

The population of the United States has grown from 4 million in 1790 to 258 million in 1993—a 64-fold

increase—even while the country's total fertility rate has oscillated wildly (Figure 3-4). At the peak of the post-World War II baby boom (1946–64) in 1957, the TFR reached 3.7 children per woman. Since then it has generally declined, remaining at or below replacement level since 1972. Various factors contributed to this decline in TFR:

- Widespread use of effective birth control methods (Figure 3-5).
- Availability of legal abortions.
- Social attitudes favoring smaller families.
- Greater social acceptance of childless couples.
- Increasing cost of raising a family. It will cost $86,000–$168,000 to raise a child born in 1992 to age 18.
- Rise in the average age at marriage between 1958 and 1991 from 20 to 24 for women and from 23 to 26 for men.
- More women working outside the home. In 1993 75% of American women ages 25 to 54 worked outside the home; their childbearing rate was one-third that of women not in the paid labor force.

A: About 1 million

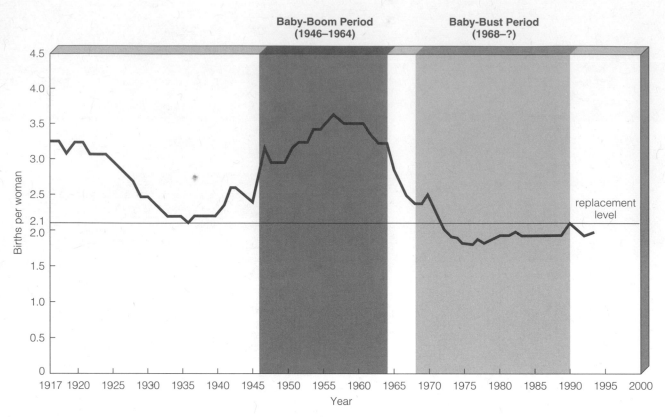

Figure 3-4 Total fertility rate for the United States between 1917 and 1993. (Data from Population Reference Bureau and U.S. Census Bureau)

The drop in the total fertility rate has led to a decline in the annual rate of population growth in the United States, but the country has not reached zero population growth (ZPG), nor is it even close. The main reasons for this are:

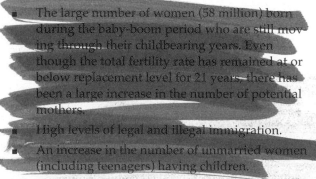

- The large number of women (58 million) born during the baby-boom period who are still moving through their childbearing years. Even though the total fertility rate has remained at or below replacement level for 21 years, there has been a large increase in the number of potential mothers.

- High levels of legal and illegal immigration.

- An increase in the number of unmarried women (including teenagers) having children.

In 1993 the U.S. population of 258 million grew by 1.2%—faster than that of any other industrialized country. This added 3.1 million people: 2.0 million more births than deaths, 900,000 legal immigrants, and 200,000–500,000 illegal immigrants. This is equivalent to adding another California every 10 years.

CONNECTIONS: FACTORS AFFECTING BIRTH RATES AND FERTILITY RATES　The most significant and interrelated factors affecting a country's average birth rate and total fertility rate are:

- *Average level of education and affluence*. Rates are usually lower in MDCs, where levels of both education and affluence are higher than in LDCs.

- *Importance of children as a part of the family labor force*. Rates tend to be lower in MDCs and higher in LDCs (especially in rural areas).

- *Urbanization*. People living in urban areas usually have better access to family planning services and tend to have fewer children than those living in rural areas, where children are needed to help grow food, collect firewood and water, and perform other essential tasks.

- *Cost of raising and educating children*. Rates tend to be lower in MDCs, where raising children is much more costly because most children don't enter the labor force until their late teens or early twenties.

- *Educational and employment opportunities for women*. Rates tend to be low when women have access to education and to paid employment outside the home.

- *Infant mortality rate*. In areas with low infant mortality rates, people tend to have fewer children because more of their children survive to help them out.

Q: How many illegal immigrants enter the United States each year?

- *Average marriage age* (or more precisely, the average age at which women give birth to their first child). People tend to have fewer children when the average marriage age of women is 25 or older.
- *Availability of private and public pension systems.* Pensions eliminate the need for parents to have many children to support them in old age.
- *Availability of reliable methods of birth control.* Widespread availability tends to reduce birth and fertility rates (Figure 3-5).
- *Religious beliefs, traditions, and cultural norms that influence the number of children couples want to have.* In many LDCs these factors favor large families.

CONNECTIONS: FACTORS AFFECTING DEATH RATES

The rapid growth of the world's population over the past 100 years was not caused by a rise in crude birth rates. Rather, it is due largely to a decline in crude death rates, especially in the less developed countries (Figure 3-6).

The principal interrelated reasons for this general drop in death rates are:

- *Better nutrition* because of greater food production and better distribution
- *Fewer infant deaths and longer average life expectancy* because of improved personal hygiene, sanitation, and water supplies, which have curtailed the spread of many infectious diseases
- *Improvements in medical and public health technology*, including antibiotics, immunizations, and insecticides

Two useful indicators of overall health in a country or region are **life expectancy**—the average number of years a newborn infant can be expected to live—and the **infant mortality rate**—the number of babies out of every 1,000 born each year that die before their first birthday (Figure 3-7). In most cases a low life expectancy in an area is the result of high infant mortality.

It is encouraging that life expectancy has increased since 1965 and averaged 74 in MDCs and 63 in LDCs in 1993. But in the world's 41 poorest countries, mainly in Asia and Africa, average life expectancy is only 47 years.

Between 1900 and 1993 average life expectancy at birth rose sharply in the United States from 47 to 75 (79 for females and 72 for males); yet, in 1993, the average life expectancy at birth for people in 25 countries was higher than that for people in the United States. Japan has the highest life expectancy (79), followed by Sweden (78).

Because it reflects the general level of nutrition and health care, infant mortality is probably the single most

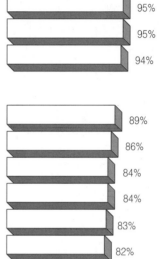

Extremely Effective

Total abstinence	100%
Abortion	100%
Sterilization	99.6%
Hormonal implant (Norplant)	99%

Highly Effective

IUD with slow-release hormones	98%
IUD plus spermicide	98%
Vaginal pouch ("female condom")	97%
IUD	95%
Condom (good brand) plus spermicide	95%
Oral contraceptive	94%

Effective

Cervical cap	89%
Condom (good brand)	86%
Diaphragm plus spermicide	84%
Rhythm method (Billings, Sympto-Thermal)	84%
Vaginal sponge impregnated with spermicide	83%
Spermicide (foam)	82%

Moderately Effective

Spermicide (creams, jellies, suppositories)	75%
Rhythm method (daily temperature readings)	74%
Withdrawal	74%
Condom (cheap brand)	70%

Unreliable

Douche	40%
Chance (no method)	10%

Figure 3-5 Typical effectiveness of birth control methods in the United States. Percentages are based on the number of undesired pregnancies per 100 couples using a specific method as their sole form of birth control for a year. For example, a 94% effectiveness rating for oral contraceptives means that for every 100 women using the pill regularly for one year, 6 will get pregnant. Effectiveness rates tend to be lower in LDCs because of human error and lack of education. (Data from Alan Guttmacher Institute)

important measure of a society's quality of life. A high infant mortality rate usually indicates insufficient food (undernutrition), poor nutrition (malnutrition), and a high incidence of infectious disease (usually from contaminated drinking water). Between 1965 and 1993, the world's infant mortality rate dropped 31% in MDCs and 35% in LDCs. This is an impressive achievement, but it still means that at least 12 million infants die each year of preventable causes.

Although the U.S. infant mortality rate of 8.6 per 1,000 in 1993 was low by world standards, 23 other countries had lower rates. Several factors keep it higher than it could be, including:

- Inadequate health care for poor women during pregnancy and for their babies after birth

- Drug addiction among pregnant women

- The high birth rate among teenage women. The United States has the highest teenage pregnancy rate of any industrialized country. Among U.S. teenage women there are about 406,000 abortions and 490,000 births per year (68% to unmarried mothers—up from 48% in 1980). Babies born to teenagers are more likely to have a low birth weight—the most important factor in infant deaths.

MIGRATION The rate of population change for a specific geographic area is also affected by movement of people into (immigration) and out of (emigration) that area:

$$\text{population change} = \begin{pmatrix} \text{births} \\ + \\ \text{immigration} \end{pmatrix} - \begin{pmatrix} \text{deaths} \\ + \\ \text{emigration} \end{pmatrix}$$

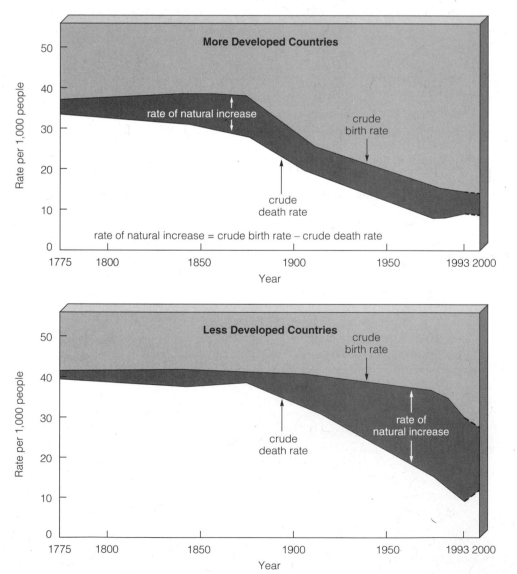

Figure 3-6 Changes in crude birth and death rates for MDCs and LDCs between 1775 and 1993, and projected rates (dashed lines) to 2000. (Data from Population Reference Bureau and United Nations)

Q: How many of the world's people live in urban areas?

Most countries control their rates of population growth to some extent by restricting immigration. Only a few countries accept large numbers of immigrants or refugees. Thus population change for most countries is determined mainly by the difference between their birth rates and death rates.

Migration within countries, especially from rural to urban areas, plays an important role in the population dynamics of cities, towns, and rural areas, as discussed in Section 3-3.

3-2 Population Age Structure

AGE STRUCTURE DIAGRAMS   Even if the replacement-level fertility rate of 2.1 were magically achieved globally by tomorrow, the world's population would keep on growing for at least another 60 years! Why? The answer lies in an understanding of the **age structure**, or age distribution, of a population: the percentage of the population (or the number of people of each sex) at each age level.

Demographers construct a population age structure diagram by plotting the percentages or numbers of males and females in the total population in three age categories: *prereproductive* (ages 0–14), *reproductive* (ages 15–44), and *postreproductive* (ages 45–85+). Figure 3-8 shows the age structure diagrams for countries with rapid, slow, zero, and negative growth rates.

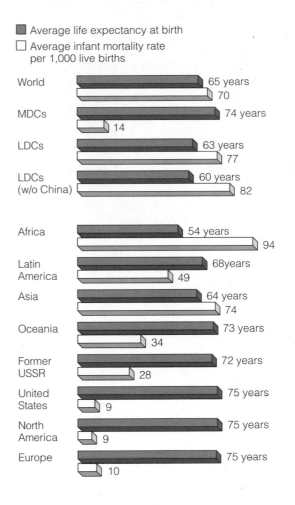

■ Average life expectancy at birth
□ Average infant mortality rate per 1,000 live births

World — 65 years / 70
MDCs — 74 years / 14
LDCs — 63 years / 77
LDCs (w/o China) — 60 years / 82

Africa — 54 years / 94
Latin America — 68 years / 49
Asia — 64 years / 74
Oceania — 73 years / 34
Former USSR — 72 years / 28
United States — 75 years / 9
North America — 75 years / 9
Europe — 75 years / 10

Figure 3-7 Average life expectancy at birth and average infant mortality rate for various groups of countries in 1993. (Data from Population Reference Bureau)

Rapid Growth
Kenya
Nigeria
Saudi Arabia

Slow Growth
United States
Australia
Canada

Zero Growth
Denmark
Austria
Italy

Negative Growth
Germany
Bulgaria
Hungary

☐ Ages 0 – 14   ▨ Ages 15 – 44   ■ Ages 45 – 85+

Figure 3-8 Population age structure diagrams for countries with rapid, slow, zero, and negative population growth rates. Bottom portions represent prereproductive years (ages 0–14), middle portions represent reproductive years (ages 15–44), and top portions represent postreproductive years (ages 45–85+). (Data from Population Reference Bureau)

A: 42% (72% in MDCs, 34% in LDCs, 75% in the U.S.) in 1993

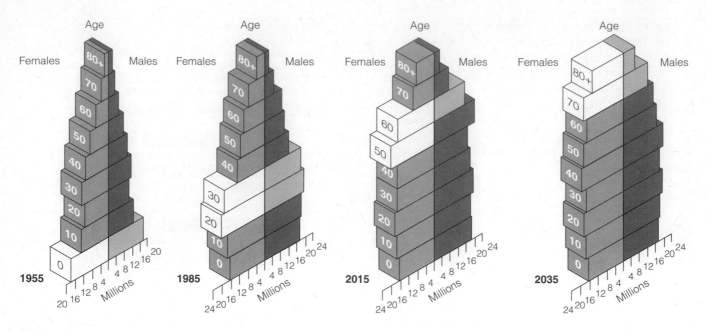

Figure 3-9 Tracking the baby-boom generation in the United States. (Data from Population Reference Bureau and U.S. Census Bureau)

CONNECTIONS: AGE STRUCTURE AND POPULATION GROWTH MOMENTUM Any country with many people below age 15 (represented by a wide base in Figure 3-8) has a powerful built-in momentum to increase its population size unless death rates rise sharply. The number of births rises even if women have only one or two children, because of the large number of women moving into their reproductive years.

Today half of the world's 2.6 billion women are in the reproductive ages of 15–44, and one-third of the people on this planet are under 15 years old and are poised to move into their prime reproductive years. In LDCs the number is even higher—36% compared with 21% in MDCs. Even if each female in LDCs has only two children, world population will still grow for 60 years unless the death rate rises sharply. And women in LDCs now average 3.7 children, well above the replacement level. This powerful force for continued population growth, mostly in LDCs, will be slowed only by an effective program to reduce birth rates or by a catastrophic rise in death rates.

CONNECTIONS: MAKING PROJECTIONS FROM AGE STRUCTURE DIAGRAMS A baby boom took place in the United States between 1946 and 1964 (Figure 3-4). This 80-million-person bulge, known as the *baby-boom generation*, will move upward through the country's age structure during the 94-year period between 1946 and 2040 as baby boomers leave young adulthood behind and enter their middle and then old age (Figure 3-9).

Today baby boomers make up nearly half of all adult Americans. They dominate the population's demand for goods and services and play an increasingly important role in deciding who gets elected and what laws are passed. In 1993, for example, baby boomers made up about 60% of registered voters.

The economic burden of helping support so many retired baby boomers will be on the *baby-bust generation*, the much smaller group of 47 million people born between 1970 and 1985, when total fertility rates fell sharply (Figure 3-4). Retired baby boomers may use their political clout to force members of the baby-bust generation to pay higher income, health care, and Social Security taxes.

In other respects the baby-bust generation should have an easier time than the baby-boom generation. Fewer people will be competing for education, jobs, and services, and labor shortages may drive up their wages, at least for jobs requiring education or technical training beyond high school. On the other hand, the baby-bust group may find it hard to get job promotions as they reach middle age because most upper-level positions will be occupied by the much larger baby-boom group. And many baby boomers may delay retirement because of improved health and the need to build up adequate retirement funds.

From these few projections we see that any baby-boom bulge or baby-bust indentation in the age structure of a population creates social and economic changes that ripple through a society for decades (Case Study, p. 71).

Q: What percentage of the cars carrying people to and from work in the United States have only one passenger?

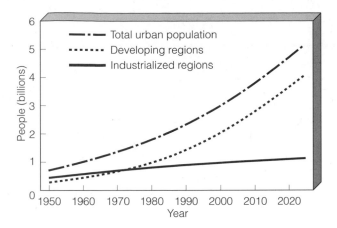

Figure 3-10 Urban population growth in MDCs and LDCs, 1950–2025. In 1993, 72% of the people in MDCs and 34% of those in LDCs lived in urban areas. (Data from United Nations and Population Reference Bureau)

3-3 Population Distribution: Urbanization and Urban Problems

THE FUTURE IS URBAN Today about 42% of the world's population lives in urban areas, and by 2025 this figure is expected to increase to 61% (Figure 3-10).

People are pulled to urban areas in search of jobs and a better life. They may also be pushed into urban areas by modern mechanized agriculture, which uses less farm labor and allows large landowners to buy out subsistence farmers who cannot afford to modernize. Without jobs or land, these people are forced to move to cities. The poor fortunate enough to get a job usually must work long hours for low wages. These jobs may expose them to dust, hazardous chemicals, excessive noise, and dangerous machinery.

The number of large cities is mushrooming. Today 1 of every 10 persons lives in a city with a million or more inhabitants, and many of these live in *megacities* with 10 million or more people. The United Nations projects that by 2000 there will be 26 megacities, more than two-thirds of them in LDCs.

As they grow outward, some urban areas merge with other urban areas to form *megalopolises*. For example, the remaining open space between Boston and Washington, D.C., is rapidly urbanizing and merging. This sprawling, 800-kilometer-long (500-mile) urban area, sometimes called *Bowash*, has almost 60 million people—more than twice Canada's entire population (Figure 3-11).

Poverty is urbanizing as more poor people migrate from rural to urban areas, especially in Latin America (Case Study, p. 72). At least 1 billion

The Graying of Japan

In only seven years, between 1949 and 1956, Japan cut its birth rate, total fertility rate, and population growth rate in half, mostly because of a liberal abortion law and access to family planning implemented by the post–World War II U.S. occupation forces and the Japanese government. Since 1956 these rates have declined further. In 1949 Japan's total fertility rate was 4.5. In 1993, it was 1.5—one of the world's lowest—and is projected to fall to 1.35 in 1996.

Average life expectancy at birth is 79 years—the highest in the world. Japan also has one of the world's lowest death rates for infants under 1 year of age. Japan's population of 125 million in 1993 is growing very slowly and is projected to be only 126 million in 2025. Its population could shrink to 65–96 million by 2090, depending on the fertility rate and immigration rate (which is currently negligible).

As Japan approaches zero population growth, it is beginning to face some of the problems of an aging population. Between 1993 and 2010 Japan's population age 65 or older is expected to increase from 13% to 21%, and by 2045 reach 27%.

Japan's universal health insurance and pension systems used about 41% of Japan's national income in 1993. This economic burden is projected to rise to 60% or higher in 2020, with at least two-thirds of the expenditures for pensions and the virtually free health care provided to the elderly. Economists worry that the steep taxes needed to fund these services could discourage economic growth.

Since 1980 Japan has been feeling the effects of a declining work force. This is one reason it has invested heavily in automation and has encouraged women to work outside the home. How Japan deals with these problems will provide ideas for the United States and other countries as they make the transition to zero population growth and, eventually, to population decline.

people—18% of the world's population—live in the crowded slums of central cities and in the vast, mostly illegal squatter settlements or shantytowns that ring the outskirts of most cities in LDCs.

THE U.S. SITUATION In 1800 only 5% of Americans lived in cities. Since then three major internal population shifts have taken place in the United States.

Mexico City, Mexico

In 1993 the population of Mexico City was 16.2 million—the world's fourth most populous city. Every day an additional 1,000 poverty-stricken rural peasants pour into the city, hoping to find a better life.

The city suffers from severe air pollution, high unemployment (close to 50%), deafening noise, congestion, and a soaring crime rate. One-third of the city's people live in crowded slums (called barrios) or squatter settlements, without running water or electricity. And at least 8 million people—as many as live in New York City—have no sewer facilities, which means huge amounts of human waste are left in gutters and vacant lots every day. When the winds pick up dried excrement, a "fecal snow" often falls on parts of the city—leading to widespread salmonella and hepatitis infections, especially among children. About half of the city's garbage is left in the open to rot, attracting armies of rats and swarms of flies.

Some 3.5 million motor vehicles and 30,000 factories spew pollutants into the atmosphere. Air pollution is intensified because the city lies in a basin surrounded by mountains, and frequent thermal inversions trap pollutants at ground level. Since 1982 the amount of contamination in the city's smog-choked air has more than tripled. Breathing the air is like smoking two packs of cigarettes a day.

The city's air and water pollution cause an estimated 100,000 premature deaths a year. Some doctors have advised parents to take their children and leave the city—permanently. These problems, already at crisis levels, will become even worse if the city grows as projected to 25.8 million people by the end of this century.

The Mexican government is industrializing other parts of the country in an attempt to slow migration to Mexico City. In 1991, the government closed the city's huge state-run oil refinery and ordered many of the industrial plants in the basin to go elsewhere by 1994. Cars have also been banned from a 50-block central zone. Taxis built before 1985 have been taken off the streets, and trucks can run only on liquefied petroleum gas (LPG). The government began phasing in unleaded gasoline in 1991, but it will be years before millions of older lead-burning vehicles are eliminated. If you were in charge of Mexico City, what would you do?

Figure 3-11 Bowash—an example of urban sprawl and coalescence leading to a megalopolis between Boston and Washington, D.C.—and Chipitts, extending from Chicago to Pittsburgh.

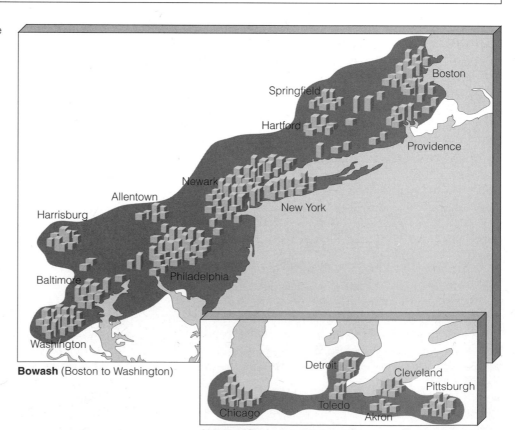

Bowash (Boston to Washington)

Chipitts (Chicago to Pittsburgh)

Q: What percentage of Americans use public transportation to get to and from work?

- *Migration to large central cities.* Currently about 75% of Americans live in the nation's 350 *metropolitan areas*—cities and towns with at least 50,000 people. Nearly half of the country's population lives in large metropolitan areas with 1 million or more residents (Figures 3-11 and 3-12). By 1995 83% of the U.S. population will probably live in urban areas.

- *Migration from large central cities to suburbs and smaller cities.* Since 1970 this type of migration has followed new jobs to such areas. Today about 41% of the country's urban dwellers live in central cities, and 59% in suburbs.

- *Migration from the North and East to the South and West.* Since 1980 about 80% of the U.S. population increase has occurred in the South and West, particularly near the coasts. This shift is expected to continue.

The biggest problems facing numerous cities in the United States and other industrialized countries are deteriorating services, aging infrastructures (housing, streets, schools, bridges, sewers), budget crunches from lost tax revenues and rising costs (as businesses and more affluent people move out), and increased crime.

CONNECTIONS: TRANSPORTATION AND URBAN DEVELOPMENT

If a city cannot spread outward it grows upward and downward below ground, occupying a relatively small area with a high population density. Many people living in such compact cities walk, ride bicycles, or use energy-efficient mass transit. Residents often live in multistory apartment buildings; with few outside walls, heating and cooling costs are reduced. Many European cities and urban areas such as Hong Kong and Tokyo are compact and tend to be more energy-efficient than the dispersed cities of the United States, Canada, and Australia, where there is often ample land for outward expansion.

A combination of cheap gasoline, plentiful land, and a network of highways leads to dispersed, car-culture cities with a low population density—often called *urban sprawl.* Most people living in such urban areas rely on cars for transportation and live in single-family houses, with unshared walls that lose and gain heat rapidly unless they are well insulated and airtight. Urban sprawl also gobbles up unspoiled natural habitat and paves over fertile farmland.

THE AUTOMOBILE

With only 4.7% of the planet's people, the United States has 35% of the world's cars and trucks (190 million vehicles). In the United States the car is used for 86% of all trips (compared to about 45% in most western European countries), 98% of all urban transportation, and 86% of travel to work. Almost 75% of commuting cars carry only one person, and only 13% of commuters use car pools. Only about 5% of Americans use public transportation, and only 7% walk or use a bicycle to get to and from work. Each year Americans drive as far as the rest of the world combined. No wonder British author J. B. Priestley remarked, "In America, the cars have become the people." In LDCs most people cannot afford a car; they travel mostly by foot, bicycle, or motor scooter but hope someday to own a car.

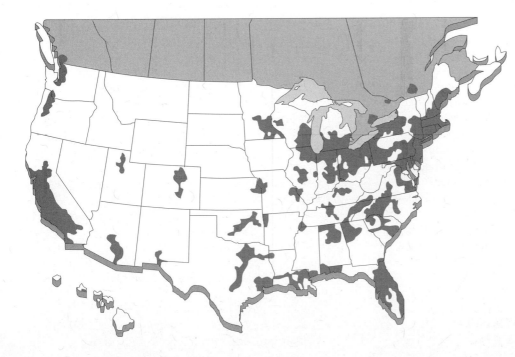

Figure 3-12 Major urban regions in the United States and Canada by 2000. Nearly half (48%) of Americans live in *consolidated metropolitan areas* with 1 million or more people. (Data from U.S. Census Bureau and Statistics Canada)

The automobile does provide convenience and undreamed-of mobility. To many people cars are also symbols of power, sex, excitement, and success.

Moreover, much of the world's economy is built on producing motor vehicles and supplying roads, services, and repairs for them. In the United States one of every six dollars spent and one of every six nonfarm jobs are connected to the automobile. In spite of their benefits, motor vehicles have many destructive effects on human lives and on air, water, land, and wildlife resources.

Since 1885, when Karl Benz built the first automobile, almost 18 million people have been killed by motor vehicles. This death toll increases by about 250,000 people per year (40,000 in the United States), and each year about 10 million people are injured or permanently disabled. More Americans have been killed by cars than were killed in all the country's wars.

Motor vehicles are also the largest source of air pollution, laying a haze of smog over the world's cities. In the United States they produce at least 50% of the air pollution, even though emission standards are as strict as any in the world. Gains in fuel efficiency and emission reductions have been largely offset by the increase in cars and a doubling of the distance Americans traveled by car between 1970 and 1990.

By making long commutes and distant shopping possible, automobiles and highways have helped create urban sprawl and reduced use of mass transit, bicycling, and walking. Worldwide, at least a third of urban land is devoted to roads, parking lots, gasoline stations, and other automobile-related uses. Half the land in an average American city is used for cars, prompting urban expert Lewis Mumford to suggest that the U.S. national flower should be the concrete cloverleaf.

In 1907, the average speed of horse-drawn vehicles through the borough of Manhattan was 18.5 kilometers (11.5 miles) per hour. Today cars and trucks with the potential power of 100–300 horses creep along Manhattan streets at 8 kilometers (5 miles) per hour. In Paris and Tokyo average auto speeds are even lower. If present trends continue, U.S. motorists will spend an average of two years of their lifetimes in traffic jams. The U.S. economy loses at least $100 billion a year because of time lost in traffic delays. Building more roads is not the answer, because as economist Robert Samuelson put it, "Cars expand to fill available concrete."

One way to break this cycle is to make drivers pay directly for most of the true costs of auto use. Federal, state, and local government auto subsidies in the United States amount to at least $300 billion a year (almost 5% of the country's GNP)—an average of $1,600 per vehicle. Taxpayers (drivers and nondrivers) foot this bill mostly without knowing this is part of their car-use bill. If drivers had to pay these hidden costs direct-

ly as a gasoline tax, the tax on each gallon would be about $5. They're paying this anyway but don't associate these hidden costs with driving.

By failing to make transportation strategy the basis of land-use planning, many of the world's cities have allowed the automobile to shape and dominate them. Now they are learning that the costs can outweigh the benefits.

ALTERNATIVES TO THE CAR   Cars are an important form of transportation, but some countries are encouraging alternatives. One alternative is the *bicycle*. It is an inexpensive form of transportation, burns no fossil fuels, produces no pollution, takes few resources to make, and is the most energy-efficient form of transportation (including walking).

In urban traffic cars and bicycles move at about the same average speed. Using separate bike paths or lanes running along roads, bicycle riders can make most trips shorter than 8 kilometers (5 miles) faster than a car.

Chinese cities often provide exclusive pedestrian and bicycle lanes and bridges for the country's 300 million cyclists. In the Netherlands bicycle travel makes up 30% of all urban trips, and in Japan 15% of all commuters ride bicycles to work or to commuter-rail stations.

Another alternative is *mass transit*. Rapid-rail, suburban train, and trolley systems can transport large numbers of people at high speed, but they are efficient only where many people live along a narrow corridor and can easily reach properly spaced stations. However, high-speed trains between cities can greatly reduce the need for travel by car and plane (Solutions, p. 75).

Bus systems are more flexible than rail systems. They can be routed throughout sprawling cities and rerouted overnight if transportation patterns change. Bus systems also require less capital and have lower operating costs than rail systems. However, because they must offer low fares to attract riders, bus systems often cost more to operate than they bring in. Because buses are cost-effective only when full, they are sometimes supplemented by car pools, van pools, and jitneys (small vans or minibuses traveling along regular routes).

CONNECTIONS: URBAN RESOURCE AND ENVIRONMENTAL PROBLEMS   Most of today's cities aren't sustainable. They have become dependent on distant sources for their food, water, energy, and materials. Their massive use of resources damages nearby and distant air, water, soil, and wildlife (Figure 3-14).

Major urban resource and environmental problems are:

- *Scarcity of trees, shrubs, and other natural vegetation.* Plants absorb air pollutants, give off oxygen, help

Q: How many people die every year from preventable waterborne diseases?

SOLUTIONS

In western Europe and Japan "bullet" or supertrains travel on new or upgraded existing tracks at speeds up to 320 kilometers (200 miles) per hour. They are ideal for trips of intermediate length—240–480 kilometers (150–300 miles). Journeys between major cities within a region on these trains are smoother and cheaper than an airplane. However, such systems are expensive to run and maintain, and they must operate along heavily used transportation routes to be profitable.

A future alternative to the automobile and the airplane for medium-distance travel of 970 kilometers (600 miles) or less between cities is the magnetic-levitation (MAGLEV) train, which uses powerful superconducting electromagnets to suspend the train on a cushion of air a few centimeters above a guiding rail. Such trains zoom along without rail friction at speeds up to 500 kilometers (310 miles) per hour. Germany and Japan have prototypes in operation.

Because these trains never touch the track, they make little noise, require little maintenance, and can be elevated over existing median strips or other rights-of-way along highways, avoiding costly and disruptive land acquisitions. MAGLEV and bullet trains reduce energy consumption as well as greenhouse and other air emissions.

A U.S. MAGLEV network could replace airplanes, buses, and private cars for most medium-distance travel between major American cities (Figure 3-13). Such systems could use the airport of a major metropolitan area as a hub to provide rapid transportation to cities.

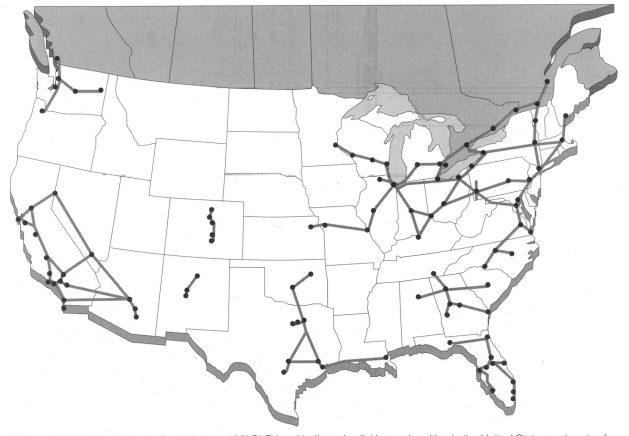

Figure 3-13 Potential routes for high-speed MAGLEV and bullet trains linking major cities in the United States and parts of Canada. Such a system would allow rapid, comfortable, safe, and affordable travel between major cities in a region, and it would squash dependence on cars, buses, and airplanes. (Data from High Speed Rail/MAGLEV Association)

A: At least 5 million (mostly children under age 5)

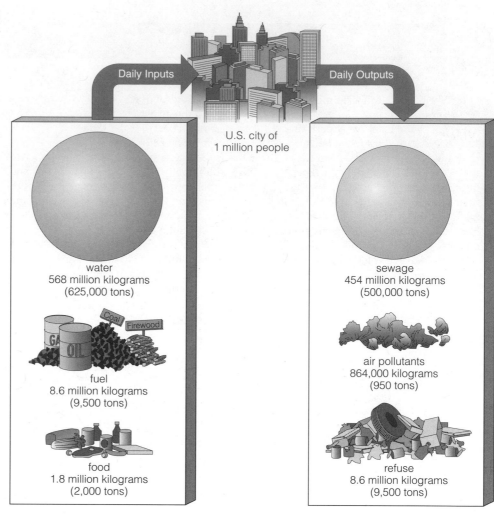

Figure 3-14 Typical daily input and output of matter and energy for a U.S. city of 1 million people.

Daily Inputs

U.S. city of 1 million people

Daily Outputs

water
568 million kilograms
(625,000 tons)

fuel
8.6 million kilograms
(9,500 tons)

food
1.8 million kilograms
(2,000 tons)

sewage
454 million kilograms
(500,000 tons)

air pollutants
864,000 kilograms
(950 tons)

refuse
8.6 million kilograms
(9,500 tons)

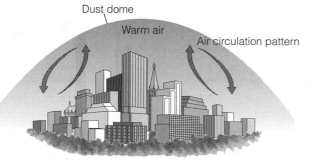

Dust dome

Warm air

Air circulation pattern

Figure 3-15 An urban heat island causes patterns of air circulation that create a dust dome over the city. Winds elongate the dome toward downwind areas. A strong cold front can blow the dome away and lower urban pollution levels.

cool the air as water evaporates from their leaves, muffle noise, provide wildlife habitats, and give aesthetic pleasure. As one observer remarked, "Most cities are places where they cut down the trees and then name the streets after them." According to the American Forestry Association

(AFA) one city tree provides over $57,000 worth of air conditioning, erosion and storm-water control, wildlife shelter, and air pollution control over a 50-year lifetime.

- *Alteration of local and, sometimes, regional climate.* Generally cities are warmer, rainier, foggier, and cloudier than suburbs and nearby rural areas. The enormous amounts of heat generated by cars, factories, furnaces, lights, air conditioners, and people in cities create an **urban heat island** surrounded by cooler suburban and rural areas. The dome of heat also traps pollutants, especially tiny solid particles (suspended particulate matter), creating a **dust dome** above urban areas (Figure 3-15). If wind speeds increase, the dust dome elongates downwind to form a **dust plume**, which can spread the city's pollutants for hundreds of kilometers. As cities grow and merge (Figure 3-11), individual heat islands also merge. This can affect the climate of a large area and keep polluted air from being adequately diluted and cleansed.

Q: What percentage of Americans walk or use a bicycle to get to and from work?

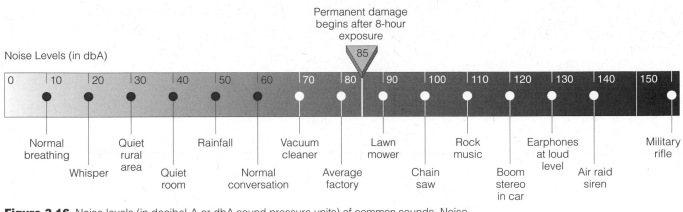

Permanent damage begins after 8-hour exposure

85

Noise Levels (in dbA)

0 10 20 30 40 50 60 70 80 90 100 110 120 130 140 150

Normal breathing

Whisper

Quiet rural area

Quiet room

Rainfall

Normal conversation

Vacuum cleaner

Average factory

Lawn mower

Chain saw

Rock music

Boom stereo in car

Earphones at loud level

Air raid siren

Military rifle

Figure 3-16 Noise levels (in decibel-A or dbA sound pressure units) of common sounds. Noise pollution can be reduced by **(1)** modifying noisy activities and devices, **(2)** shielding noisy devices or processes, **(3)** shielding workers from noise, and **(4)** using antinoise—a new technology that cancels out one noise with another. The control of noise pollution in the United States has lagged behind that in the former Soviet Union and many western European and Scandinavian countries.

- *Lack of water.* This requires expensive reservoirs, canals, and deep wells.

- *Rapid runoff of water from asphalt and concrete.* This can overload sewers and storm drains, contributing to water pollution and flooding in cities and downstream areas.

- *Production of large quantities of air pollution (Chapter 9), water pollution (Chapter 10), and garbage and other solid waste (Chapter 11).*

- *Excessive noise* (Figure 3-16). Every day, one of every nine Americans (28 million people) lives, works, or plays around noise of sufficient duration and intensity to cause some permanent hearing loss, and that number is rising rapidly.

- *Loss of rural land, fertile soil, and wildlife habitats as cities expand.*

MAKING URBAN AREAS MORE LIVABLE AND SUSTAINABLE An important goal in coming decades should be to make urban areas more self-reliant, sustainable, and enjoyable places to live (Solutions, p. 79).

3-4 Solutions: Influencing Population Size

CONTROLLING MIGRATION A society can influence the size and rate of growth or decline of its population by encouraging a change in any of the three basic demographic variables: births, deaths, and migration. Only a few countries, chiefly Canada, Australia, and the United States, allow large annual increases in population from immigration, and some countries encourage emigration to reduce population pressures.

Between 1820 and 1993, the United States admitted almost twice as many immigrants and refugees as all other countries combined. However, the number of legal immigrants has varied during different periods because of changes in immigration laws and rates of economic growth (Figure 3-17). Between 1820 and 1960 most legal immigrants came from Europe. Since then most have come from Asia and Latin America.

Between 1960 and 1993, the number of legal immigrants per year rose from 265,000 to about 1 million (1.8 million in 1991)—twice as many legal immigrants as all other countries combined. Each year 200,000–500,000 more people enter illegally, most from Mexico and other Latin American countries. This means that in 1993, legal and illegal immigration accounted for 37%–43% of the country's population growth. These figures do not include refugees, who are admitted under other regulations. Soon, immigration is expected to be the primary factor increasing the population of the United States (Figure 3-18).

Some demographers and environmentalists call for an annual ceiling of no more than 450,000 people for all categories of legal immigration, including refugees. They argue that this will allow the United States to reach ZPG sooner and reduce the country's enormous environmental impact from consumption overpopulation (Figure 1-11). Others oppose such limits, arguing that it would diminish the historical role of the United States as a place of opportunity for the world's poor and oppressed.

A: 2%

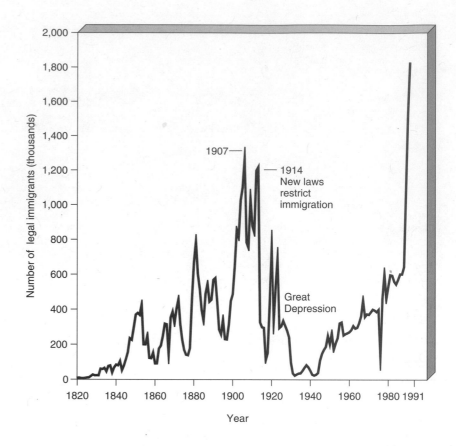

Figure 3-17 Legal immigration to the United States, 1820–1993. The much higher rates since 1989 represent a combination of normal immigration levels, of around 700,000 per year, plus illegal immigrants who had been living in the country for years and were granted legal status under the Immigration Reform and Control Act of 1986. This explains the large increase in immigration in 1991, when this new policy was implemented. (Data from U.S. Immigration and Naturalization Service)

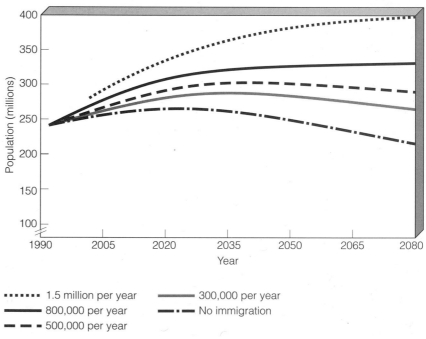

Figure 3-18 Immigration and projected population growth of the United States, 1990–2080. These projections assume that fertility levels will remain around 1.9 children per woman during this period. These projections may be too low, because traditionally most immigrants have tended to have large families. (Data from U.S. Bureau of the Census and Population Reference Bureau)

REDUCING BIRTHS: A CONTROVERSIAL ISSUE

Because raising the death rate is not ethically acceptable, lowering the birth rate is the focus of most efforts to slow population growth. Today about 93% of the world's population and 91% of the people in LDCs live in countries with fertility reduction programs. Three general approaches to decreasing birth rates are economic development, family planning, and socioeconomic changes.

The funding for and effectiveness of these programs vary widely from country to country. Few governments spend more than 1% of the national budget on them.

Q: How many people have been killed by motor vehicles since the first automobile was built in 1885?

SOLUTIONS

In a sustainable and ecologically healthy city—called an *ecocity* or *green city*—matter and energy resources are used efficiently, and far less pollution and waste are produced than in conventional cities. Emphasis is on pollution prevention, reuse, recycling, and efficient use of energy and matter resources. Per capita solid waste is greatly reduced, and 60%–80% of what is produced is recycled, composted, or reused. An ecocity takes advantage of locally available energy sources and requires that all buildings, vehicles, and appliances meet high energy-efficiency standards.

Trees and plants adapted to the local climate and soils are left or are planted throughout the ecocity to provide shade and beauty, to reduce pollution and noise, and to supply habitats for wildlife. Abandoned lots and polluted creeks are cleaned up and restored. Nearby forests, grasslands, wetlands, and farms are preserved instead of being devoured by urban sprawl. Much of the ecocity's food comes from nearby organic farms, solar greenhouses, community gardens, and small gardens on rooftops and in yards and window boxes.

An ecocity is a people-oriented city—not a car-oriented city. Its residents are able to walk or bike to most places, including work, and to take low-polluting mass transit. It is designed, retrofitted, and managed to provide a sense of community built around cooperative and vibrant neighborhoods.

The ecocity concept is not a futuristic dream. The citizens and elected officials of Davis, California—a city of about 40,000 people northeast of San Francisco—committed themselves in the early 1970s to making it an ecologically sustainable city.

City building codes encourage the use of solar energy for water and space heating. All new homes must meet high standards of energy efficiency. When an existing home changes hands the buyer must bring it up to the energy conservation standards for new homes. In Davis's Village Homes—America's first solar neighborhood—houses are heated by solar energy. They face into a common open space reserved for people and bicycles; cars are not allowed in the interior area. The neighborhood also has orchards, vineyards, and a large community garden. Since 1975 the city has cut its use of energy for heating and cooling in half.

Davis has a solar power plant, with some of the electricity it produces sold to the regional utility company. Eventually the city plans to generate all of its own electricity.

The city discourages the use of automobiles and encourages the use of bicycles by closing some streets to automobiles and by building bicycle paths and lanes. Any new housing tract must have a separate bicycle lane, and some city employees are given bikes. As a result, 28,000 bikes account for 40% of all in-city transportation, and less land is needed for parking spaces. This heavy dependence on the bicycle is aided by the city's warm climate and flat terrain.

Davis limits the type and rate of its growth, and it maintains a mix of homes for people with low, medium, and high incomes. Development of the fertile farmland surrounding the city for residential or commercial use is restricted.

Davis and other cities—San Jose, California; Arcosanti, Arizona; Cerro Gordo, Oregon; Osage, Iowa (p. 96); Horsen, Denmark; and Tapiola, Finland, for example—are blazing the trail by developing Earth-sustaining neighborhoods that involve people in making their city a better place to live. What is being done to make the earth where you live more sustainable?

There is also intense controversy over whether the earth is overpopulated and over what measures, if any, should be used to reduce population growth. To some the planet is already overpopulated (Figure 1-11), but others disagree. Some analysts—mostly economists—believe we should encourage population growth.

Critics of the view that Earth is overpopulated point out that the world now supports 5.5 billion people whose average life span is longer than at any time in the past. Things are getting better, not worse, for many of the world's people. These critics say that talk of a population crash is alarmist, that the world can support billions more people, and that people are the world's most valuable resource for solving the problems we face. More people increase economic productivity by creating and applying new knowledge, and they stimulate economic growth by becoming consumers.

Some view population regulation as a violation of their deep religious beliefs, while others see it as an intrusion into their personal privacy and freedom. And minorities sometimes regard it as a form of genocide to keep their numbers and power from rising.

Proponents of slowing and eventually stopping population growth point out that we currently are not providing adequate basic necessities for one out of five

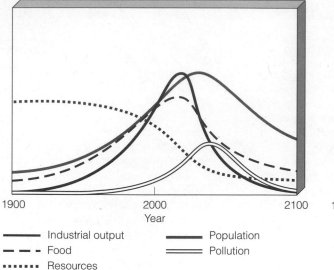

State of the World

1900   2000   2100
            Year

━━━━━ Industrial output ━━━━━ Population
━ ━ ━ Food ═════ Pollution
•••••• Resources

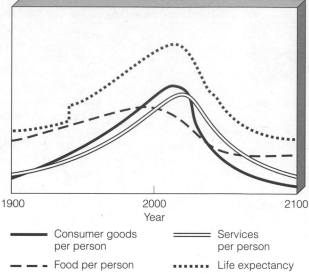

Material Standard of Living

1900   2000   2100
            Year

━━━━━ Consumer goods ═════ Services
        per person   per person
━ ━ ━ Food per person •••••• Life expectancy

Figure 3-19 Computer-model scenario projecting what might happen if the world's population and economy continue growing exponentially at 1990 levels, assuming no major policy changes or technological innovations. This scenario projects that the world has already overshot some of its limits and that if current trends continue unchanged, we face global economic and environmental collapse sometime in the next century. (Used by permission from Donella Meadows et al., *Beyond the Limits: Confronting Global Collapse, Envisioning a Sustainable Future.* Post Mills, Vt.: Chelsea Green Publishing Co., 1992)

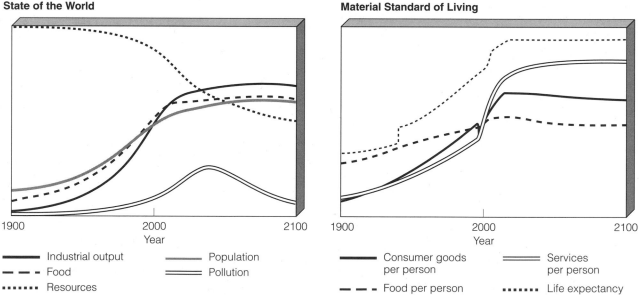

State of the World

1900   2000   2100
            Year

━━━━━ Industrial output ━━━━━ Population
━ ━ ━ Food ═════ Pollution
•••••• Resources

Material Standard of Living

1900   2000   2100
            Year

━━━━━ Consumer goods ═════ Services
        per person   per person
━ ━ ━ Food per person •••••• Life expectancy

Figure 3-20 Computer-model scenario projecting how we can avoid overshoot and collapse and make a fairly smooth transition to a sustainable future. This scenario assumes that **(1)** technology allows us to double supplies of nonrenewable resources, double crop and timber yields, cut soil erosion in half, and double the efficiency of resource use within 20 years; **(2)** 100% effective birth control is made available to everyone by 1995; **(3)** no couple has more than two children beginning in 1995; and **(4)** industrial output per capita is stabilized at 1990 levels. Another computer scenario projects that waiting until 2015 to implement these changes would lead to collapse and overshoot sometime around 2075, followed by a transition to sustainability by 2100. (Used by permission from Donella Meadows et al., *Beyond the Limits: Confronting Global Collapse, Envisioning a Sustainable Future.* Post Mills, Vt.: Chelsea Green Publishing Co., 1992)

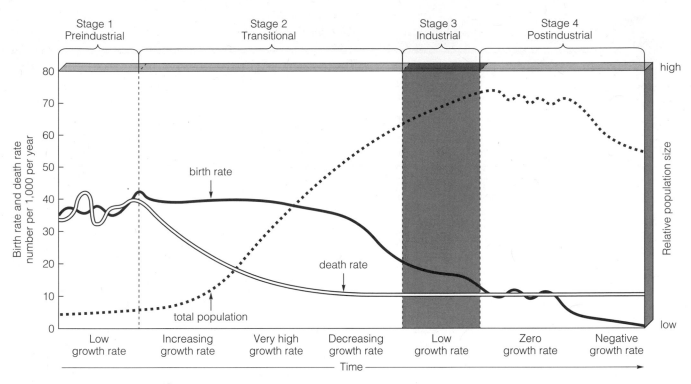

Stage 1
Preindustrial

Stage 2
Transitional

Stage 3
Industrial

Stage 4
Postindustrial

Figure 3-21 Generalized model of the demographic transition.

people on Earth. They see people overpopulation in LDCs and consumption overpopulation in MDCs (Figure 1-11) as threats to Earth's life-support systems. They contend that if we don't sharply lower birth rates and resource consumption, we are deciding by default to raise death rates and face global and environmental collapse sometime in the next century (Figure 3-19).

These analysts recognize that population growth is not the only cause of our numerous environmental and resource problems. They believe, however, that adding several hundred million more people in MDCs and several billion more in LDCs will intensify many environmental and social problems by increasing resource use and waste, increasing environmental degradation and pollution, causing rapid climate change, and reducing biodiversity. They call for drastic changes to prevent accelerating environmental decline (Figure 3-20).

Proponents of population regulation believe that the United States and other MDCs, rather than encouraging births, should establish an official goal of stabilizing their populations by 2025 and then begin a gradual population decline. This would help reduce their severe environmental impact on the ecosphere. Proponents also believe that MDCs have a better chance of influencing LDCs to reduce their population growth more rapidly if the more affluent countries officially recognize the need to stabilize their own populations.

These analysts believe that people should have the freedom to produce as many children as they want

only so long as this does not reduce the quality of other people's lives now and in the future by impairing the ability of Earth to sustain life. Limiting an individual's freedom to protect the freedom of other individuals is the basis of most laws in modern societies.

REDUCING BIRTHS THROUGH ECONOMIC DEVELOPMENT Demographers have examined the birth and death rates of western European countries that industrialized during the nineteenth century. From these data they developed a hypothesis of population change known as the **demographic transition**: As countries become industrialized, first their death rates and then their birth rates decline.

This transition takes place in four distinct phases (Figure 3-21). In the *preindustrial stage* harsh living conditions lead to a high birth rate (to compensate for high infant mortality) and a high death rate. Thus there is little population growth.

In the *transitional stage* industrialization begins, food production rises, and health care improves. Death rates drop, but birth rates remain high, so the population grows rapidly (typically 2.5%–3% a year).

In the *industrial stage* industrialization is widespread. The birth rate drops and eventually approaches the death rate. Reasons for this include better access to birth control, drops in the infant mortality rate, more job opportunities for women, and the high costs of raising children—most of whom don't enter the

Cops and Rubbers Day in Thailand

In 1960 the population of Thailand was growing rapidly at 3.2% per year, and the average Thai family had 6.4 children. Today its population is growing at a rate of 1.4%, and the average number of children per family is 2.4. And since 1960 the country's average per capita income has doubled.

There are several reasons for this impressive feat: the creativity of the government-supported family-planning program; the openness of the Thai people to new ideas; the willingness of the government to work with the private, nonprofit Population and Community Development Association (PCDA); and support of family planning by the country's Buddhist religious leaders (95% of

Thais are Buddhist). Buddhist scripture teaches that "many children make you poor."

This remarkable transition was catalyzed by the charismatic leadership of Mechai Viravidaiya, a former government economist and public relations genius, who launched the PCDA. Anywhere there was a crowd, PCDA workers handed out condoms—at festivals, movie theaters, even traffic jams. Schoolchildren held condom-blowing championships. Mechai showed how a condom—now commonly called "mechais"—could be used as a tourniquet for deep cuts and snakebites and as a coin or beverage container. Humorous songs were written about condom use and the reasons to have no more than two children.

Mechai also persuaded traffic police to hand out condoms on New Year's Eve, now known as "Cops and Rubbers Day." On the Thai king's birthday the PCDA offers free vasectomies; sterilization is now the most widely used form of birth control in the country.

All is not completely rosy. While Thailand has done well in slowing population growth, it has been less successful in improving public health, especially maternal health and control of AIDS and other sexually transmitted diseases. And the capital, Bangkok, remains one of the world's most polluted and congested cities.

workforce until after high school or college. Population growth continues, but at a slower and perhaps fluctuating rate, depending on economic conditions. Most MDCs are now in this third phase.

In the *postindustrial stage* the birth rate declines even further to equal the death rate, thus reaching zero population growth. Then the birth rate falls below the death rate, and total population size slowly decreases. Emphasis shifts from unsustainable to sustainable forms of economic development.

In most LDCs today death rates have fallen much more than birth rates (Figure 3-6). In other words, these LDCs, mostly in Southeast Asia, Africa, and Latin America, are still in the transitional stage, halfway up the economic ladder, with high population growth rates. Some economists believe that LDCs will make the demographic transition over the next few decades without increased family-planning efforts. But many population analysts fear that the rapid population growth in many LDCs will outstrip economic growth and overwhelm local life-support systems—causing many of these countries to be caught in a *demographic trap*.

Furthermore, some of the conditions that allowed the MDCs to develop are not available to today's LDCs. Even with large and growing populations, many LDCs do not have enough skilled workers to

produce the high-technology products needed to compete in today's economic environment. Most low- and middle-income LDCs also lack the capital and resources needed for rapid economic development. Also, the amount of money being given or loaned to LDCs—struggling under tremendous debt burdens—has been decreasing since 1980. Indeed, since the mid-1980s the LDCs have paid MDCs about $50 billion a year more (mostly in debt interest) than they have received from these countries.

REDUCING BIRTHS THROUGH FAMILY PLANNING Family planning programs provide educational and clinical services that help couples choose how many children to have and when to have them. It has been an important factor in increasing the percentage of married women in LDCs using contraception from 10% in the 1960s to 54% today and in the drop in TFRs (total fertility rates) in LDCs from 6 in 1960 to 3.7 in 1993. Family planning saves a government money by reducing the need for various social services. It also has health benefits. In LDCs, for example, about 1 million women per year die from pregnancy-related causes. Half of these deaths could be prevented by effective family-planning and health care programs.

The effectiveness of family planning has varied depending on program design and funding. It has

Q: What is the largest source of water pollution in the United States?

been a significant factor in reducing birth and fertility rates in populous countries such as China, Indonesia, and Brazil. Family planning has also played a major role in reducing population growth in Japan (Case Study, p. 71), Thailand (Case Study, at left), Mexico, and several other countries with moderate-to-small populations. These successful programs based on committed leadership, local implementation, and wide availability of contraceptives show that population rates can be decreased significantly within two to three decades.

Family planning, however, has had moderate-to-poor results in more populous LDCs such as India, Egypt, Pakistan, and Nigeria. Results have also been poor in 79 less populous LDCs—especially in Africa and Latin America—where population growth rates are usually very high.

Family planning could be provided in LDCs to all couples who want it for about $10 billion a year—less than four days' worth of world military spending. Currently only about $4.5 billion is being spent.

REDUCING BIRTHS THROUGH ECONOMIC REWARDS AND PENALTIES Some population experts argue that family planning, even coupled with economic development, cannot lower birth and fertility rates fast enough to avoid a sharp rise in death rates in many LDCs. The main reason for this is that most couples in LDCs want 3 or 4 children—well above the 2.1 fertility rate needed to halt population growth.

These experts call for increased emphasis on bringing about socioeconomic change to help regulate population size. The key is improving the quality of life, especially in rural areas of LDCs, so that people don't feel that they must have large families to assure that enough children survive to support elderly family members. They call for better basic health care and education, expanded women's rights, increased equity in land ownership, and fair prices for agricultural products.

About 20 countries offer small payments to individuals who agree to use contraceptives or to be sterilized. They also pay doctors and family-planning workers for each sterilization they perform and each IUD they insert. In India, for example, a person receives about $15 for being sterilized, the equivalent of about two weeks' pay for an agricultural worker. Such payments are most likely to attract people who already have all the children they want, however.

Some countries, such as China (Section 3-5), penalize couples who have more than a certain number of children—usually one or two—by raising their taxes, charging other fees, or not allowing income tax deductions for a couple's third child (as in Singapore, Hong Kong, Ghana, and Malaysia). Families who have more children than the prescribed limit may also lose health care benefits, food allotments, and job choice.

Experience has shown that economic rewards and penalties designed to reduce fertility work best if they:

- Nudge rather than push people to have fewer children
- Reinforce existing customs and trends toward smaller families
- Do not penalize people who produced large families before the programs were established
- Increase a poor family's income or land

Once population growth is out of control, a country may be forced to use coercive methods to prevent mass starvation and hardship. This is what China has had to do (Section 3-5).

REDUCING BIRTHS BY EMPOWERING WOMEN Research has shown that women tend to have fewer children when they have access to education and to paying jobs outside the home, and when they live in societies where their individual rights are not suppressed. Today women do almost all of the world's domestic work and child care and provide more health care with little or no pay than all the world's organized health services put together. They also do more than half the work associated with growing food, gathering fuelwood, and hauling water. As one Brazilian woman put it, "For poor women the only holiday is when you are asleep."

Despite their vital economic and social contributions, most women in LDCs don't have a legal right to own land or to borrow money to increase agricultural productivity. Although women work two-thirds of all hours worked in the world, they get only one-tenth of the world's income and own a mere 1% of the world's land. In some LDCs, where male children are strongly favored, young girls are sometimes sold as work slaves or sex slaves, or are even killed.

Giving women everywhere full legal rights and the opportunity to become educated and to work at paid jobs outside the home will require some major social changes. However, this will be difficult to bring about in male-dominated societies.

3-5 ## Case Studies: Population Control in India and China

INDIA India started the world's first national family-planning program in 1952, when its population was nearly 400 million. In 1993, after 41 years of population control efforts, India was the world's second most populous country, with a population of 897 million.

In 1952 India was adding 5 million people to its population each year. In 1993 it added 18 million—49,300 more mouths to feed each day. Future population growth is fueled by the 36% of India's population under age 15. India's population is projected to reach 1.4 billion by 2025, and possibly 1.9 billion before leveling off early in the twenty-second century.

India's people are among the poorest in the world. The average income per person is about $330 a year, and for at least one-third of the population it is less than $100 a year—27¢ a day. To add to the problem, nearly half of India's labor force is unemployed or can find only occasional work. Almost one-third of the present population goes hungry. Life expectancy is only 59 years, and the infant mortality rate is 91 deaths per 1,000 live births.

Some analysts fear that India's already serious hunger and malnutrition problems will increase as its population continues to grow rapidly. About 40% of India's cropland is degraded as a result of soil erosion, waterlogging, salinization, overgrazing, and deforestation; and roughly 80% of the country's land is subject to repeated droughts—often lasting two to five years.

Without its long-standing family-planning program, India's numbers would be growing even faster. However, the results of the program have been disappointing. Factors contributing to this failure have been poor planning, bureaucratic inefficiency, the low status of women (despite constitutional guarantees of equality), extreme poverty, and a lack of administrative and financial support.

For years the government has provided information about the advantages of small families; yet, Indian women still have an average of 3.9 children because most couples believe they need many children as a source of cheap labor and old-age survival insurance. Almost one-third of Indian children die before age 5, reinforcing that belief. And although 90% of Indian couples know of at least one method of birth control, only 45% actually use one. Finally, many social and cultural norms favor large families—as does the strong preference for male children, which means that some couples will keep having children until they produce one or more boys.

CHINA Since 1970, China has made impressive efforts to feed its people and bring its population growth under control. Between 1972 and 1993 China achieved a remarkable drop in its crude birth rate, from 32 to 18 per 1,000 people; and its total fertility rate dropped from 5.7 to 1.9 children per woman. Since 1985 China's infant mortality rate has been al-most one-half the rate in India. Life expectancy in China is 70 years—11 years higher than in India. China's average per capita income of $370 is similar to that in India.

To achieve a sharp drop in fertility, China has established the most extensive, intrusive, and strict population control program in the world. Couples are strongly urged to postpone the age at which they marry and to have no more than one child. Married couples have ready access to free sterilization, contraceptives, and abortion. Paramedics and mobile units ensure access even in rural areas.

Couples who pledge not to have more than one child are given extra food, larger pensions, better housing, free medical care, and salary bonuses; their child will be provided with free school tuition and with preferential treatment in employment when he or she enters the job market. Those who break the pledge lose all the benefits. All leaders are expected to set an example by limiting their own family size. The result is that 83% of married women in China are using contraception, compared to only 42% in other LDCs.

These are drastic measures, but government officials realized in the 1960s that the only alternative to strict population control was mass starvation. China is a dictatorship and, unlike India, has been able to impose a unified population policy from the top down. Moreover, Chinese society is fairly homogeneous and has a widespread common written language. India, by contrast, has over 1,600 languages and dialects and numerous religions, which make it more difficult to educate people about family planning and to institute population regulation policies.

Most countries do not want to use the coercive elements of China's program. Coercion is not only incompatible with democratic values and notions of basic human rights but ineffective in the long run because sooner or later people resist being coerced. Other parts of this program, however, could be used in many LDCs. Especially useful is the practice of localizing the program, rather than asking the people to go to distant centers. Perhaps the best lesson that other countries can learn from China's experience is not to wait to curb population growth until the choice is between mass starvation and coercive measures that severely restrict human freedom.

CUTTING GLOBAL POPULATION GROWTH

Birth rates and death rates are coming down, but death rates have fallen more, especially in LDCs (Figure 3-6). If this trend continues, one of two things will probably happen during your lifetime: (1) the number of people on Earth will at least double and perhaps almost triple (Figure 1-1), or (2) the world will experience an unprecedented population crash, with hun-

Q: How much of the commercial energy used in the world comes from nonrenewable resources?

dreds of millions of people—perhaps billions—dying prematurely.

Lester Brown, president of the Worldwatch Institute, urges the leaders of countries to adopt a goal of cutting world population growth in half during the 1990s by reducing the average global birth rate from 26 to 18 per 1,000 people. The experience of countries such as Japan (Case Study, p. 71), Thailand (Case Study, p. 82), and China indicates that this could be achieved.

We need the size of population in which human beings can fulfill their potentialities; in my opinion we are already overpopulated from that point of view; not just in places like India and China and Puerto Rico, but also in the United States and Western Europe.

GEORGE WALD
(NOBEL LAUREATE, BIOLOGY)

CRITICAL THINKING

1. Why is it rational for a poor couple in India to have six or seven children? What changes might induce such a couple to think of their behavior as irrational?

2. What conditions, if any, would encourage you to rely less on the automobile? Would you regularly travel to school or work by bicycle or motor scooter, on foot, by mass transit, or by a car pool or van pool? Explain.

3. Do you believe there are physical limits to population growth on Earth (Figure 3-19)? Explain.

4. Do you believe that all U.S. high schools and colleges should have health clinics that make contraceptives available to students and provide prenatal care for pregnant teenage women? Explain. Should such services be available at the junior-high-school level, when many teenagers first become sexually active? Explain.

5. a. Should the number of legal immigrants and refugees allowed into the United States each year be sharply reduced? Explain.
   b. Should illegal immigration into the United States be sharply decreased? Explain. If so, how would you go about achieving this?

6. Should families in the United States be given financial incentives and be persuaded to have more children to prevent population decline? Explain.

7. Should the United States adopt an official policy to stabilize its population and reduce unnecessary resource waste and consumption as rapidly as possible? Explain.

8. Why has China been more successful than India in reducing its rate of population growth? Do you agree with China's present population control policies? Explain. What alternatives, if any, would you suggest?

4 Energy

4-1 What Energy Resources Are Available?

ENERGY RESOURCES USED TODAY Energy is the thread sustaining and integrating all life and supporting all economies. *Some 99% of the energy used to heat Earth, and all our buildings, comes directly from the sun* (Figure 2-9). Without this direct input of renewable solar energy, Earth's average temperature would be −240°C (−400°F), and life as we know it would not have arisen. Solar energy also helps recycle the chemicals we and other organisms need to stay alive and healthy (Figure 2-8).

Broadly defined, **solar energy** includes both direct energy from the sun and several forms of energy produced indirectly by the sun's energy. These include wind, falling and flowing water (hydropower), and biomass (solar energy converted to chemical energy stored in the chemical bonds of organic compounds in trees and other plants).

The remaining 1% of the energy we use, the portion we generate to supplement the solar input, is *commercial energy* sold in the marketplace and *noncommercial energy* used by people who gather fuelwood, dung, and crop wastes for their own use. Most commercial energy comes from extracting and burning mineral resources in the earth's crust, primarily nonrenewable fossil fuels (Figure 4-1).

MDCs and LDCs differ greatly in their sources of energy (Figure 4-2), the total amount used, and average energy use per person. The most important supplemental source of energy for LDCs is biomass—mostly fuelwood—burned for heating and cooking. Within a few decades one-fourth of the world's population in MDCs may face an oil shortage, but half the world's population in LDCs already faces a fuelwood shortage.

The United States is the world's largest user of energy. With only 4.7% of the population, it uses 25% of the commercial energy, mostly by burning nonrenewable fossil fuels (Figure 4-2). In contrast, India, with almost 16% of the world's people, uses only

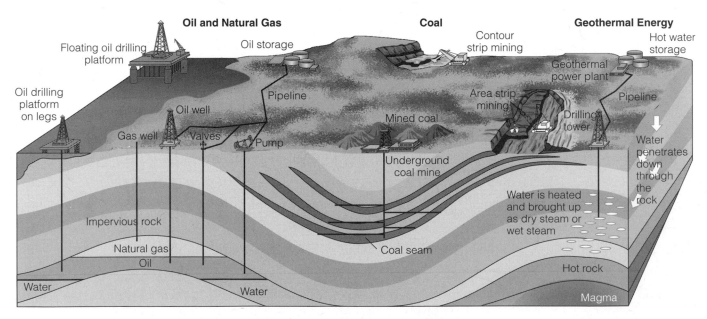

Figure 4-1 Important energy resources from Earth's crust are geothermal energy, coal, oil, and natural gas. Uranium ore is also extracted from the crust and then processed to increase its concentration of uranium-235 (Figure 2-2), which can be used as a fuel in nuclear reactors used to produce electricity.

Q: How much of the commercial energy used in the United States comes from nonrenewable resources?

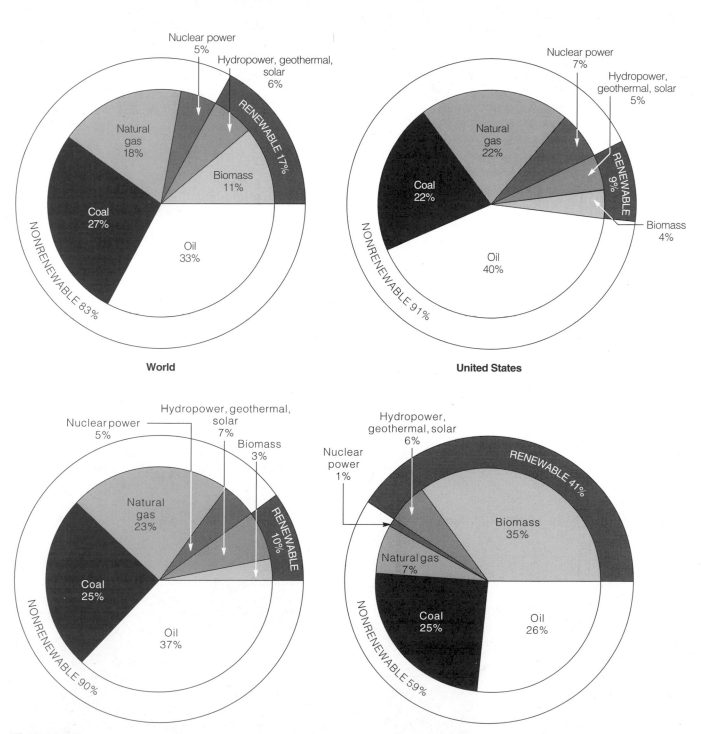

Figure 4-2 Commercial energy use by source in 1991 for the world, the United States, MDCs, and LDCs. This amounts to only 1% of the energy used in the world. The other 99% of the energy used to heat Earth comes from the sun and is not sold in the marketplace. (Data from U.S. Department of Energy, British Petroleum, and Worldwatch Institute)

A: 91% (84% from fossil fuels and 7% from nuclear power)

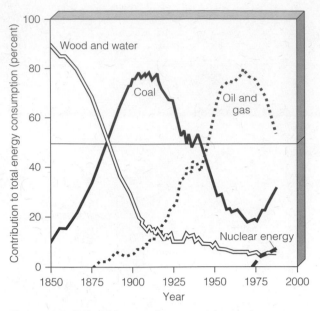

Figure 4-3 Shifts in the use of commercial energy resources in the United States since 1850. Shifts from wood to coal and then from coal to oil and natural gas have each taken about 50 years. Affordable oil is running out, and burning fossil fuels is the primary cause of air pollution and projected warming of the atmosphere. For these reasons most analysts believe we must make a new shift in energy resources over the next 50 years. (Data from U.S. Department of Energy)

about 3% of the commercial energy. In 1993, 258 million Americans used more electricity for air conditioning alone than 1.2 billion Chinese used for all purposes.

EVALUATING ENERGY RESOURCES The types of energy we use and how we use them are the major factors determining our quality of life and how much we abuse the earth's life-support system. Our current dependence on nonrenewable fossil fuels is the primary cause of air and water pollution, land disruption, and projected global warming—and affordable oil will probably be depleted within 40–80 years.

What is our best option for reducing dependence on oil and other fossil fuels? Cut out unnecessary energy waste by improving energy efficiency. What is our next best energy option? There is disagreement about that.

Some say we should get much more of the energy we need from the sun, wind, flowing water, biomass, heat stored in Earth's interior (geothermal energy), and hydrogen gas by making the transition to a new *solar age*.

Others say we should burn more coal and synthetic liquid and gaseous fuels made from coal. Some believe natural gas is the answer, at least as a transition fuel to a new solar age built around improved energy efficiency and renewable energy. Others think nuclear power is the answer.

Past experience shows that it takes at least 50 years and huge investments to phase in new energy alternatives (Figure 4-3). Thus, we have to plan for and begin the shift to a new mix of energy resources now. This involves answering the following questions for each energy alternative:

- How much will be available during the short (1995 to 2005), intermediate (2005 to 2015), and long term (2015 to 2045)?

- What is the net useful energy yield for each alternative (Spotlight, p. 89)?

- How much will it cost to develop, phase in, and use?

- How will extracting, transporting, and using it affect the environment (Figure 1-9)?

- Which energy choices will do the most to sustain the earth for us, for future generations, and for the other species living on this planet?

4-2 Improving Energy Efficiency

DOING MORE WITH LESS You may be surprised to learn that *84% of all commercial energy used in the United States is wasted* (Figure 4-5). About 41% of this energy is wasted automatically because of the degradation of energy quality imposed by the second energy law (Section 2-2). However, about 43% is wasted unnecessarily, mostly by using fuel-wasting motor vehicles, furnaces, and other devices—and by living and working in leaky, poorly insulated buildings. The United States unnecessarily wastes as much energy as two-thirds of the world's population consumes.

The easiest, fastest, and cheapest way to get more energy with the least environmental impact is to cut much of this energy waste. One way to do this is to reduce energy consumption. Examples include walking or biking for short trips, using mass transit, putting on a sweater instead of turning up the thermostat, and turning off unneeded lights.

Another way is to increase the efficiency of the energy conversion devices we use. **Energy efficiency** is the percentage of total energy input that does useful work and is not converted to low-quality, essentially useless heat in an energy conversion system. The energy conversion devices we use vary considerably in their energy efficiencies (Figure 4-6). We can save energy and money by buying the most energy-efficient home heating systems, water heaters, cars, air conditioners, refrigerators, and other household appliances available. The energy-efficient models may cost

Q: How much of the commercial energy used in the United States is wasted?

SPOTLIGHT

It takes energy to get energy. For example, oil must be found, pumped up from beneath the ground, transported to a refinery and converted to useful fuels (such as gasoline, diesel fuel, and heating oil), transported to users, and then burned before it is useful to us. All of these steps use energy, and the second law of energy (Section 2-2) tells us that each time we use energy to perform a task some of it is always wasted and degraded to low-quality energy.

The usable amount of energy (Figure 2-5) from a given quantity of an energy resource is its **net useful energy**. It is the total useful energy available from the resource over its lifetime minus the amount of energy used (the first energy law), automatically wasted (the second energy law), and unnecessarily wasted in finding, processing, concentrating,

and transporting it to users. For example, if 9 units of fossil fuel energy are needed to supply 10 units of nuclear, solar, or additional fossil fuel energy (perhaps from a deep well at sea), the net useful energy gain is only 1 unit of energy.

We can express this relationship as the ratio of useful energy produced to the useful energy used to produce it. In the example just given, the net energy ratio would be 10/9, or approximately 1.1. Thus, the higher the ratio or the equivalent real number, the greater the net useful energy yield. When the ratio is less than 1, there is a net energy loss over the lifetime of the system.

Figure 4-4 lists estimated net useful energy ratios for various systems of space heating, high-temperature heat for industrial processes, and vehicle fuels. Currently, oil has a relatively high net useful energy ratio because much of it comes from

large, accessible deposits such as those in Saudi Arabia and other parts of the Middle East. When those sources are depleted, however, the net useful energy ratio of oil will decline and prices will rise. Then more money and more high-quality fossil fuel will be needed to find, process, and deliver new oil from widely dispersed small deposits and deposits buried deep in the earth's crust or located in remote areas like Alaska, the Arctic, and the North Sea.

Conventional nuclear energy has a low net energy ratio because large amounts of energy are required to extract and process uranium ore, to convert it into a usable nuclear fuel, and to build and operate power plants. Energy is also needed to dismantle the plants after their 25–30 years of useful life and to store the resulting highly radioactive wastes for thousands of years.

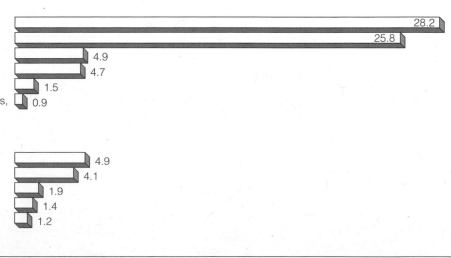

Space Heating

Passive solar	5.8
Natural gas	4.9
Oil	4.5
Active solar	1.9
Coal gasification	1.5
Electric resistance heating (coal-fired plant)	0.4
Electric resistance heating (natural-gas-fired plant)	0.4
Electric resistance heating (nuclear plant)	0.3

High-Temperature Industrial Heat

Surface-mined coal	28.2
Underground-mined coal	25.8
Natural gas	4.9
Oil	4.7
Coal gasification	1.5
Direct solar (highly concentrated by mirrors, heliostats, or other devices)	0.9

Transportation

Natural gas	4.9
Gasoline (refined crude oil)	4.1
Biofuel (ethyl alcohol)	1.9
Coal liquefaction	1.4
Oil shale	1.2

Figure 4-4 Net useful energy ratios for various energy systems over their estimated lifetimes. (Data from Colorado Energy Research Institute, *Net Energy Analysis*, 1976; and Howard T. Odum and Elisabeth C. Odum, *Energy Basis for Man and Nature*, 3d ed., New York: McGraw-Hill, 1981)

A: 84% (43% of this energy is unnecessarily wasted)

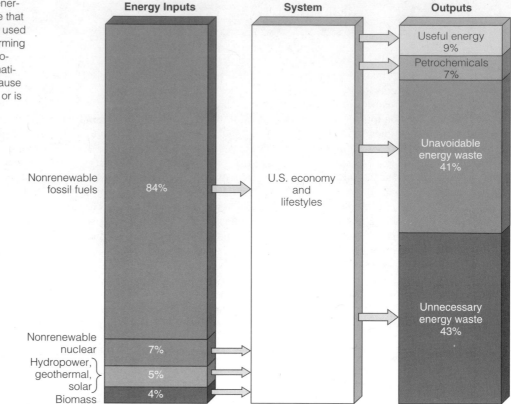

Figure 4-5 Flow of commercial energy through the U.S. economy. Note that only 16% of all commercial energy used in the United States ends up performing useful tasks or is converted to petrochemicals. The rest either is automatically and unavoidably wasted because of the second law of energy (41%) or is wasted unnecessarily (43%).

Energy Inputs

Nonrenewable fossil fuels — 84%

Nonrenewable nuclear — 7%

Hydropower, geothermal, solar — 5%

Biomass — 4%

System

U.S. economy and lifestyles

Outputs

Useful energy 9%

Petrochemicals 7%

Unavoidable energy waste 41%

Unnecessary energy waste 43%

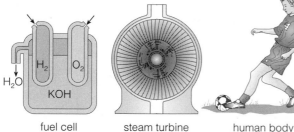

fuel cell
60%

steam turbine
45%

human body
20 to25%

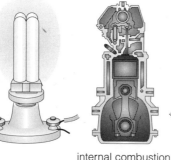

fluorescent light
22%

internal combustion engine (gasoline) 10%

incandescent light
5%

Figure 4-6 Energy efficiency of some common energy conversion devices.

more, but in the long run they usually save money by having a lower **life-cycle cost**: initial cost plus lifetime operating costs.

The net efficiency of the entire energy delivery process for a space heater, water heater, or car is determined by finding the efficiency of each step in the energy-conversion process. For example, the sequence of energy-using and energy-wasting steps involved in using electricity produced from fossil or nuclear fuels is:

extraction → transportation → processing → transportation to power plant → electric generation → transmision → end use

Figure 4-7 shows how net energy efficiency is determined for heating a well-insulated home **(1)** with electricity produced at a nuclear power plant, transported by wire to the home, and converted to heat (electric resistance heating); and **(2)** passively with an input of direct solar energy through windows facing the sun, with heat stored in rocks or water for slow release. This analysis shows that the process of converting the high-quality energy in nuclear fuel to high-quality heat at several thousand degrees, converting this heat to high-quality electricity, and then using the electricity to provide low-quality heat for warming a house to only about 20°C (68°F), is extremely wasteful of high-quality energy. Burning coal, or any fossil fuel,

Q: How much of the energy input of an incandescent light bulb is converted to light?

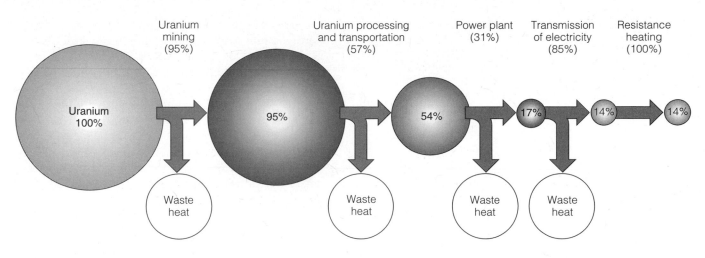

Electricity from Nuclear Power Plant

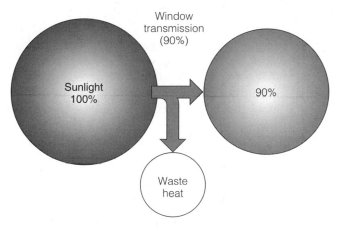

Passive Solar

Figure 4-7 Comparison of net energy efficiency for two types of space heating. The cumulative net efficiency is obtained by multiplying the percentage shown inside the circle for each step by the energy efficiency for that step (shown in parentheses). Usually, the greater the number of steps in an energy conversion process, the lower its net energy efficiency. About 86% of the energy used to provide space heating by electricity produced at a nuclear power plant is wasted. By contrast, with passive solar heating, only about 10% of incoming solar energy is wasted.

at a power plant to supply electricity for space heating is also inefficient. By contrast, it is much less wasteful to collect solar energy from the environment, store the resulting heat in stone or water, and—if necessary—raise its temperature slightly to provide space heating or household hot water.

Using high-quality electrical energy to provide low-quality heating for living space or household water is like using a chain saw to cut butter or a sledgehammer to kill a fly. As a general rule, we should *match energy quality to energy tasks*: Don't use high-quality energy to do a job that can be done with lower-quality energy (Figure 2-5). This is illustrated by looking at the prices for providing heat using various fuels. In 1991, the average price of obtaining 250,000 kilocalories (1 million Btus) for heating space or water in the United States was $6.05 using natural gas, $7.56 using kerosene, $9.30 using oil, $9.74 using propane, and $24.15 using electricity. As these numbers suggest, if you like to throw away hard-earned dollars, then use electricity to heat your house and bath water.

REDUCING WASTE: AN ECONOMIC AND ENVIRONMENTAL OFFER WE DARE NOT REFUSE Reducing energy waste is one of the planet's best and most important bargains. It would:

- *Make nonrenewable fossil fuels last longer.*
- *Buy time to phase in renewable energy resources.*

- *Decrease dependence on oil imports* (almost 50% in the United States).

- *Lessen the need for military intervention in the oil-rich but potentially unstable Middle East.*

- *Reduce environmental damage* because less of each energy resource would provide the same amount of useful energy (Figure 1-9).

- *Be the cheapest and quickest way to slow projected global warming* (Section 9-2).

- *Save money, provide more jobs, and promote more economic growth per unit of energy than other alternatives.* According to energy expert Amory Lovins, if the world really got serious about improving energy efficiency, we could save $1 trillion per year—about 5% of the gross global product. A 1993 study by economists estimated that a full-fledged energy-efficiency program could produce 1.3 million jobs in the United States by 2010.

- *Improve competitiveness in the international market-place.* Currently, the United States spends about 11% of its GNP on energy, while Japan spends only 5%. That gives Japanese goods an automatic 6% cost advantage.

Energy analysts and the Office of Technology Assessment estimate that fully implementing existing energy-efficiency technologies could save the United States

- Four times as much electricity as all U.S. nuclear power plants now produce, at about a seventh the cost of just running them, even if it cost nothing to build them

- More than 40 times as much oil as *might* be under Alaska's Arctic National Wildlife Refuge, at roughly one-tenth the cost of drilling for it

Despite the numerous environmental and long-term economic advantages of improving energy efficiency, the United States is not vigorously pursuing the energy option. Major reasons for this include emphasis on short-term profits regardless of the long-term economic and environmental consequences, a glut of low-cost fossil fuels, and relatively little federal support since 1980 for improvements in energy efficiency.

USING WASTE HEAT   Could we save energy by recycling energy? No. The second law of energy tells us that we cannot recycle energy, but we can slow the rate at which waste heat flows into the environment when high-quality energy is degraded. For a house, the best way to do this is to heavily insulate it, eliminate air leaks, and equip it with an air-to-air heat exchanger to prevent buildup of indoor air pollutants. Many homes in the United States are so full of leaks that their heat loss in cold weather and heat gain in hot weather are equivalent to having a large hole the size of a typical window in the wall of the house.

In office buildings and stores, waste heat from lights, computers, and other machines can be collected and distributed to reduce heating bills during cold weather; during hot weather, this heat can be collected and vented outdoors to reduce cooling bills. Waste heat from industrial plants and electrical power plants can be distributed through insulated pipes and used to heat nearby buildings, greenhouses, and fish ponds, as is done in some parts of Europe.

SAVING ENERGY IN INDUSTRY   Here are some ways to save energy and money in industry:

- *Cogeneration, the production of two useful forms of energy such as steam and electricity from the same fuel source.* Waste heat from coal-fired and other industrial boilers can be used to produce steam that spins turbines and generates electricity at half the cost of buying it from a utility company. The electricity can be used by the plant or sold to the local power company for general use, saving energy and money. Cogeneration is widely used in western Europe. If this option is pursued, within eight years cogeneration could produce more electricity than all U.S. nuclear power plants—and do it much more cheaply. If all large industrial boilers in the United States used cogeneration, there would be no need to build any electric power plants through the year 2020. New micro-cogeneration units that run on natural gas or liquefied petroleum gas (LPG) and that can supply heat and electricity for a restaurant or apartment building are now being produced in Germany. They may soon be available for homes.

- *Replace energy-wasting electric motors.* About 60–70% of the electricity used in U.S. industry drives electric motors. Most of them are run at full speed with their output "throttled" to match their task—somewhat like driving with the gas pedal to the floor and using the brake to slow the car down. According to Amory Lovins it would be cost-effective to scrap virtually all such motors and replace them with adjustable-speed drives. Within a year the costs would be paid back.

- *Switch to high-efficiency lighting.*

- *Use computer-controlled energy management systems to turn off lighting and equipment in nonproduction areas and to make adjustments during periods of low production.*

Q: How much of the energy input of a screw-in fluorescent light bulb produces light?

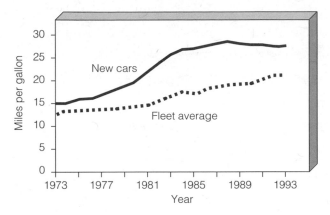

Figure 4-8 Average fuel efficiency of new cars and all cars in the United States between 1973 and 1993. (Data from U.S. Department of Energy and Environmental Protection Agency)

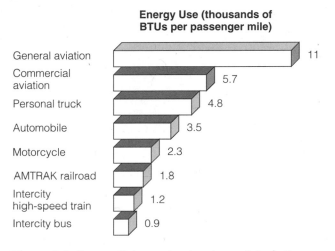

Energy Use (thousands of BTUs per passenger mile)

General aviation	11
Commercial aviation	5.7
Personal truck	4.8
Automobile	3.5
Motorcycle	2.3
AMTRAK railroad	1.8
Intercity high-speed train	1.2
Intercity bus	0.9

Figure 4-9 Energy efficiency of various types of domestic passenger transportation.

- *Increase recycling and reuse and make products that last longer and are easy to repair and recycle.*

SAVING ENERGY IN TRANSPORTATION Important ways to save energy (especially oil) and money in transportation and to reduce pollution are:

- *Increase the fuel efficiency of motor vehicles.* Between 1973 and 1985 the average fuel efficiency doubled for new American cars and rose 54% for all cars on the road, but it has risen only slightly since then (Figure 4-8). According to the U.S. Office of Technology Assessment, however, existing technology could be used to raise the fuel efficiency of the entire U.S. automotive fleet to 15 kilometers per liter (35 miles per gallon) by 2010, eliminate oil imports, and save more than $50 billion per year in fuel costs. Buyers of gas-miser cars would get back any extra purchase costs—probably about $500 per car—in fuel savings in about a year (Solutions, p. 95).

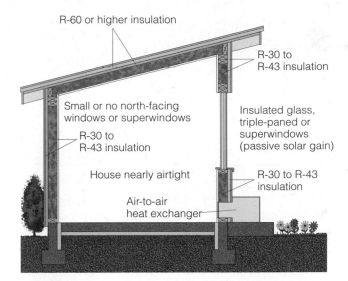

Figure 4-10 Major features of a superinsulated house. Such a house is heavily insulated and nearly airtight. Heat from direct solar gain, appliances, and human bodies warms the house, which requires little or no auxiliary heating. An air-to-air heat exchanger prevents buildup of indoor air pollution.

- Shift more freight from trucks and planes to trains and ships (Figure 4-9).
- Raise the fuel efficiency of new transport trucks 50% with improved aerodynamic design, turbocharged diesel engines, and radial tires.

SAVING ENERGY IN BUILDINGS Here are some ways to improve the energy efficiency of buildings:

- *Build more superinsulated houses* (Figure 4-10). Such a house typically costs 5% more to build than a conventional house of the same size. However, this extra cost is paid back by energy savings within five years and can save a home owner $50,000–$100,000 over a 40-year period.
- *Improve the energy efficiency of existing houses by adding insulation, plugging leaks, and installing energy-saving windows.* One-third of the heat in U.S. homes and buildings escapes through closed windows—equal to the energy in all the oil flowing through the Alaskan pipeline every year. During hot weather these windows also let heat in, increasing the use of air conditioning. A double-pane window has an insulating value of only R-2. (The R value is a measure of resistance to heat flow.) Windows with R values as high as R-8 are now available and even better ones are being developed. They pay for themselves in lower fuel bills within two to five years and then save money every year thereafter.
- *Use the most energy-efficient ways to heat houses* (Figure 4-11). The most energy-efficient way to

A: 22% (over 4 times as much as an incandescent bulb)

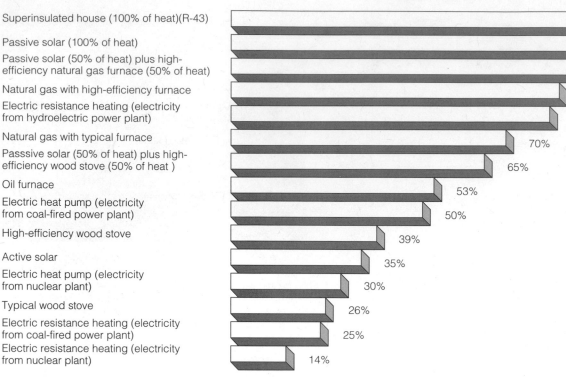

Net Energy Efficiency

Superinsulated house (100% of heat)(R-43)	98%
Passive solar (100% of heat)	90%
Passive solar (50% of heat) plus high-efficiency natural gas furnace (50% of heat)	87%
Natural gas with high-efficiency furnace	84%
Electric resistance heating (electricity from hydroelectric power plant)	82%
Natural gas with typical furnace	70%
Passsive solar (50% of heat) plus high-efficiency wood stove (50% of heat)	65%
Oil furnace	53%
Electric heat pump (electricity from coal-fired power plant)	50%
High-efficiency wood stove	39%
Active solar	35%
Electric heat pump (electricity from nuclear plant)	30%
Typical wood stove	26%
Electric resistance heating (electricity from coal-fired power plant)	25%
Electric resistance heating (electricity from nuclear plant)	14%

Figure 4-11 Net energy efficiencies for various ways to heat an enclosed space such as a house.

heat space is to build a superinsulated house (Figure 4-10), followed by passive solar and high-efficiency natural gas furnaces. The most wasteful and expensive way is to use electric resistance heating with the electricity produced by a nuclear or a coal-fired power plant. Some utilities push heat pumps as a more efficient alternative to electric resistance heating. Heat pumps can save energy and money for space heating in warm climates (where they aren't needed much), but not in cold climates because at low temperatures they switch to wasteful, costly electric resistance heating. Also, most heat pumps in their air-conditioning mode are less efficient than many available stand-alone air-conditioning units. Most heat pumps are noisy, don't produce hot enough air, and also require expensive repair every few years.

■ *Use the most energy-efficient ways to heat household water.* The most efficient method is to use tankless instant water heaters (about the size of bookcase loudspeakers) fired by natural gas or liquefied petroleum gas (LPG). They heat the water instantly as it flows through a small burner chamber, and they provide hot water only when, and as long as, it is needed. Tankless heaters are widely used in many parts of Europe and are slowly beginning to appear in the United States.

A well-insulated, conventional natural gas or LPG water heater is also fairly efficient (although all conventional natural gas and electric resistance heaters keep a large tank of water hot all day and night—and can run out after a long shower or two). The least efficient and most expensive way to heat water for washing and bathing is to use electricity produced by any type of power plant.

■ *Set higher energy-efficiency standards for buildings.* Building codes could be changed to require that all new houses use 80% less energy than conventional houses of the same size, as has been done in Davis, California (Solutions, p. 79). Because of tough energy-efficiency standards, the average Swedish home consumes about one-third as much energy as an average American home of the same size.

■ *Buy the most energy-efficient appliances and lights* (Figure 4-12).* If the most energy-efficient lights

---

*Each year the American Council for an Energy-Efficient Economy (ACEEE) publishes a list of the most energy-efficient major appliances mass-produced for the U.S. market. To obtain a copy, send $3 to the council at 1001 Connecticut Ave. N.W., Suite 530, Washington, DC 20036. Each year they also publish *A Consumer Guide to Home Energy Savings,* available in bookstores or from the ACEEE for $8.95.

Q: How much of the energy in gasoline is used to move a motor vehicle powered by an internal combustion engine?

Fuel-efficient cars will take decades to develop and will be sluggish, small, and unsafe. Wrong! Since 1985 at least 10 companies have had nimble and peppy prototype cars that meet or exceed current safety and pollution standards, with fuel efficiencies of 29–59 kilometers per liter (67–138 miles per gallon). If they were mass-produced, their slightly higher costs would be more than offset by their fuel savings.

One such ecocar is Volvo's LCP 2000 prototype, which would be in production today if consumer demand in the United States—the world's largest car market—were there. Its supercharged diesel engine averages 35 kpl (81 mpg) on the highway and 27 kpl (62 mpg) in the city. It can run on various fuels, including diesel, a diesel-gasoline mixture, and vegetable oil—which means the driver could carry a bottle of vegetable oil along as an emergency source of fuel. Using better design and lighter but stronger

materials (magnesium, aluminum, and plastics), it exceeds U.S. crash standards. It carries four passengers in comfort, is quiet, resists corrosion better than most of today's cars, and has better than average acceleration. This car also meets California's air pollution emission standards—the tightest in the world. It is also designed for easy assembly and for recycling of its materials when it is taken off the road.

We can have roomy, peppy, safe gas sippers, but only if consumers begin demanding them and buying them and insisting that the government enact higher fuel-efficiency standards and greatly increase gasoline taxes. All of these actions will eventually save the country and consumers large amounts of money. In 1992 there were more than 25 car models on the market with fuel efficiencies of at least 17 kpl (40 mpg), but they made up only 5% of U.S. car sales.

Electric cars might also help reduce dependence on oil, especially for urban commuting and short

trips. All major U.S. car companies have prototype electric cars and minivans, some available by 1995. They are extremely quiet, need little maintenance, and produce no air pollution, except indirectly from the generation of electricity needed to recharge their batteries. If solar cells could be used for recharging, this environmental impact would be eliminated.

On the negative side the batteries in current electric cars have to be replaced about every 40,000 kilometers (25,000 miles) at a cost of about $1,500. This requirement and the electricity costs for daily recharging mean double the operating cost of gasoline-powered cars. If longer-lasting batteries that hold a higher charge density and last at least 160,000 kilometers (100,000 miles) can be developed, operating costs would be reduced and performance would increase.

$16.40 $17.76 $65.80 $87.50

E-lamp   Compact fluorescent   Standard   Traditional long-life

Figure 4-12 Light up your life, help the earth, and save money by using energy-efficient bulbs. Cost of electricity for comparable light bulbs used for 10,000 hours. Since conventional incandescent bulbs are only 5% efficient (Figure 4-6) and last only 750–1,500 hours, they waste enormous amounts of energy and money, and they add to the heat load of houses during hot weather. (Data from Electric Power Research Institute)

Saving Energy, Money, and Jobs in Osage, Iowa

Osage, Iowa (population about 4,000), has become the energy-efficiency capital of the United States. It began in 1974 when easy-going Wes Birdsall started going door-to-door preaching energy conservation to help his community deal with the energy crisis of 1973. As general manager of Osage Municipal Gas and Electric Company, he wanted the townspeople to save energy and reduce their natural gas and electric bills. The utility would save money, too, by not having to add new electrical generating facilities.

Wes started his crusade by telling home owners about the importance of insulating walls and ceilings and plugging leaky windows and doors. These repairs provided jobs for people selling and installing insulation, caulking, and energy-efficient windows.

He also advised people to replace their incandescent light bulbs with more efficient fluorescent bulbs (Figure 4-12) and to turn down the temperature on water heaters and wrap

them with insulation—an economic boon to the local hardware and lighting stores. The utility company even gave away free water-heater blankets. Wes also suggested saving water and fuel by installing low-flow shower heads.

As people saw how much money they could save, Wes stepped up his campaign. He offered to give every building in town a free thermogram—an infrared scan that shows where heat escapes. When people could see the energy (and money) hemorrhaging out of their buildings, they took action to plug these leaks—again helping the local economy. Teacher Ken Swenson and his family, who live in a large 865-square-meter (9,634-square-foot) house, can testify to the program's success. Their heating bill is about $50 a year.

Wes then went even further: He announced that no new houses could be hooked up to the company's natural gas line unless they met minimum energy-efficiency standards.

Since 1974 the town has cut its natural gas consumption by 45%;

no mean feat in a place where winter temperatures can plummet to −103°C (−80°F). In addition, the utility company saved enough money to prepay all its debt, accumulate a cash surplus, and cut inflation-adjusted electricity rates by a third (which attracted two new factories). Furthermore, each household saves more than $1,000 per year. This money supports jobs, and most of it circulates in the local economy. Before the energy-efficiency revolution, about $1.2 million a year went out of town, usually out of state—to buy energy. The town's lower fossil-fuel use also eases local and regional air pollution and the threat of global warming.

Osage's success in making energy efficiency a way of life earned the town a National Environmental Achievement Award in 1991. What are your local utility and community doing to improve energy efficiency and stimulate the local economy?

and appliances now available were installed in all U.S. homes over the next 20 years, the savings in energy would equal the estimated energy content of Alaska's entire North Slope oil fields—and U.S. consumers would save $5–8 billion per year. Replacing a standard fluorescent bulb with an energy-efficient compact fluorescent or E-lamp bulb saves about $50—or $1,250 for a typical house with 25 light bulbs. Energy-efficient lighting could save U.S. businesses $15–20 billion per year in electricity bills.

■ *Give rebates or tax credits for building energy-efficient buildings, improving the energy efficiency of existing buildings, and for buying high-efficiency appliances and equipment.*

Japan and many western European countries are leading the world in the *energy-efficiency revolution*. A few places in the United States, such as Davis, Califor-

nia (Solutions, p. 79) and Osage, Iowa (Solutions, above), are leading the way in the United States.

4-3 Renewable Solar Energy

THE SOLAR AGE: BUILDING A SOLAR ECONOMY

About 92% of the known reserves and potentially available energy resources in the United States are renewable energy from the sun, wind, flowing water, biomass, and Earth's internal heat. The other 8% of potentially available domestic energy resources are nonrenewable coal (5%), oil (2.5%), and uranium (0.5%). Developing the mostly untapped renewable energy resources could meet 50–80% of projected U.S. energy needs by 2030 or sooner, and it could meet vir-

Q: What is the most inefficient and costly way to produce electricity for heating an interior space or water?

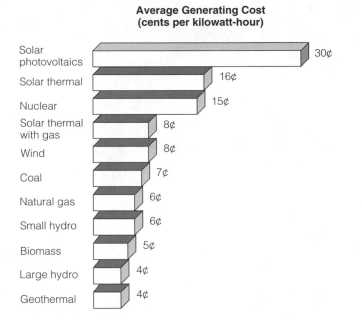

Average Generating Cost (cents per kilowatt-hour)

Solar photovoltaics	30¢
Solar thermal	16¢
Nuclear	15¢
Solar thermal with gas	8¢
Wind	8¢
Coal	7¢
Natural gas	6¢
Small hydro	6¢
Biomass	5¢
Large hydro	4¢
Geothermal	4¢

Figure 4-13 Generating costs of electricity per kilowatt-hour by various technologies in 1989. By 2000 costs per kilowatt-hour for wind are expected to fall to 4–5¢, solar thermal with gas assistance to 6¢, and solar photovoltaic to 10¢. Costs for other technologies are projected to remain about the same. (Data from U.S. Department of Energy, Council for Renewable Energy Education, and Investor Responsibility Research Center)

tually all energy needs if coupled with improvements in energy efficiency.

Developing these resources would save money, create jobs, eliminate the need for oil imports, cause less pollution and environmental damage per unit of energy used, and increase economic, environmental, and military security. According to the Minnesota Department of Energy, each dollar spent on renewable energy generates $2.33–$2.92 of local economic activity, versus only $0.64 for imported oil. In the United States geothermal power plants, wood-fired (biomass) power plants, hydropower plants, wind farms, and solar thermal power plants can already produce electricity more cheaply than can new nuclear power plants, and with far fewer federal subsidies (Figure 4-13).

HEATING HOUSES AND WATER   Buildings and water can be heated by solar energy using two methods: passive and active (Figure 4-14). A **passive solar heating system** captures sunlight directly within a structure and converts it into low-temperature heat for space heating (Figures 4-14 and 4-15). With available and developing technologies, passive solar designs can provide at least 80% of a building's heating needs and at least 60% of its cooling needs (Solutions, p. 100).

Roof-mounted passive solar water heaters can supply all or most of the hot water for a typical house.

In hot weather, passive cooling can be provided by blocking the high summer sun with deciduous trees, window overhangs, or awnings (Figure 4-15). *Earth tubes* can also be used for cooling (Figure 4-15). At a depth of 3–6 meters (10–20 feet), the soil temperature stays at about 5–13°C (41–55°F) all year long in cold northern climates and about 19°C (67°F) in warm southern climates. Several earth tubes—simple plastic (PVC) plumbing pipes with a diameter of 10–15 centimeters (4–6 inches)—buried about 0.6 meter (2 feet) apart at this depth can pipe cool and partially dehumidified air into an energy-efficient house at a cost of a few dollars per summer. For a large space, two or three of these geothermal cooling fields running in different directions from the house can be installed. When heat degrades the cooling effect from one field, home owners can switch to another. During cold months these geothermal cooling fields are renewed naturally for use during the summer. Initial construction costs (mostly for digging) are high, but operating and maintenance costs are extremely low. People allergic to pollen and molds should add an air purification system, but they would also need to do that with a conventional cooling system.

In an **active solar heating system** specially designed collectors absorb solar energy, with a fan or a pump used to supply part of a building's space-heating or water-heating needs (Figure 4-14). Several connected collectors are usually mounted on a roof with an unobstructed exposure to the sun. Active solar collectors can also supply hot water.

Solar energy for low-temperature heating of buildings is free and is naturally available on sunny days; the net useful energy yield is moderate (active) to high (passive). Both active and passive technology are well developed and can be installed quickly. No carbon dioxide is added to the atmosphere, and environmental impacts from air and water pollution are low. Land disturbance is also minimal because passive systems are built into structures and active solar collectors are usually placed on rooftops.

On a life-cycle cost basis good passive-solar and superinsulated design is the cheapest way to heat a home or a small building in regions where full sunlight is available more than 60% of daylight hours. Such a system usually adds 5–10% to the construction cost, but the life-cycle cost of operating such a house is 30–40% lower.

Active systems cost more than passive systems over their lifetime because they use more materials to build, need more maintenance, and eventually deteriorate and must be replaced. However, retrofitting existing buildings is often easier with an active solar

A: Nuclear power (only 14% efficient), Figures 4-7 and 4-11

Figure 4-14 Passive and active solar heating for a home.

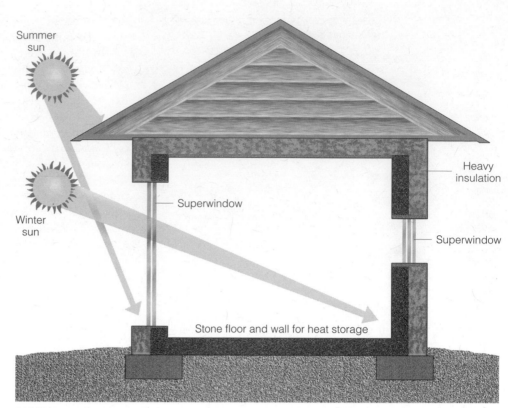

Summer sun

Winter sun

Superwindow

Heavy insulation

Superwindow

Stone floor and wall for heat storage

PASSIVE

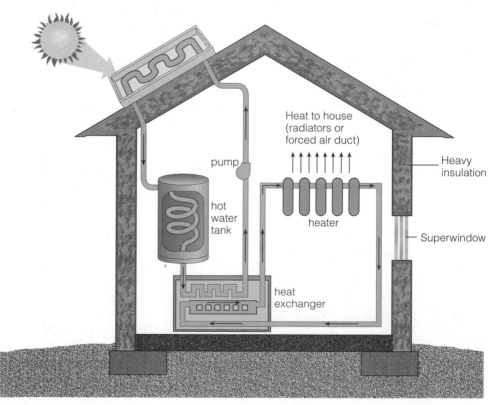

Heat to house (radiators or forced air duct)

pump

hot water tank

heater

heat exchanger

Heavy insulation

Superwindow

ACTIVE

Q: What are the two most energy-efficient ways to heat interior space?

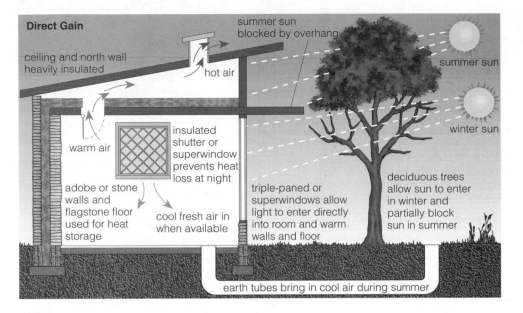

Direct Gain

ceiling and north wall heavily insulated

summer sun blocked by overhang

hot air

warm air

insulated shutter or superwindow prevents heat loss at night

adobe or stone walls and flagstone floor used for heat storage

cool fresh air in when available

triple-paned or superwindows allow light to enter directly into room and warm walls and floor

summer sun

winter sun

deciduous trees allow sun to enter in winter and partially block sun in summer

earth tubes bring in cool air during summer

Figure 4-15 Three examples of passive solar design.

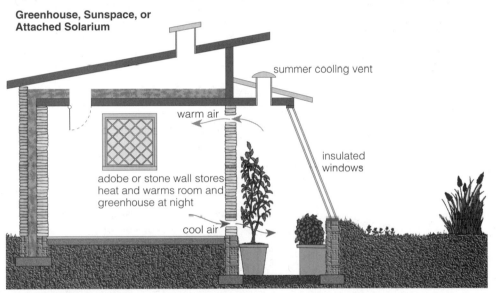

Greenhouse, Sunspace, or Attached Solarium

summer cooling vent

warm air

insulated windows

adobe or stone wall stores heat and warms room and greenhouse at night

cool air

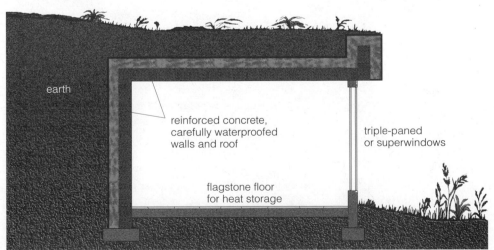

Earth Sheltered

earth

reinforced concrete, carefully waterproofed walls and roof

triple-paned or superwindows

flagstone floor for heat storage

A: Passive solar and natural gas

Engineer and builder Michael Sykes has designed a solar envelope house that is heated and cooled passively by solar energy and the slow storage and release of energy by massive timbers and the earth beneath the house (Figure 4-16). The front and back sides of this house are double walls of heavy timber impregnated with salt to increase the ability of the wood to store heat. The space between these two walls, plus the basement, forms a convection loop or envelope around the inner shell of the house.

Solar energy enters through windows or a greenhouse on the side of the house facing the sun, circulates around the loop, is stored in the heavy timber, and is released slowly during the day and at night. In summer, roof vents release heated air from the convection loop throughout the day. At night these roof vents, with the aid of a fan, draw air into the loop, which passively cools the house.

The interior temperature of the house typically stays within 2° of 21°C (70°F) year-round, without any conventional cooling or heating system. In cold or cloudy climates a small wood stove or vented natural gas heater in the basement can be used as a backup to heat the air in the convection loop.

He sells these houses in kits with all timber precut, which enables quick assembly. Buyers can save money by erecting the inner and outer shells themselves, which requires little experience and few tools. And Michael plants 50 trees for each one used in providing builders with his timber kits.

For his Enertia design he has received both the Department of Energy's Innovation Award and the North Carolina Governor's Energy Achievement Award.

Figure 4-16 Solar envelope house that is heated and cooled passively by solar energy and Earth's thermal energy. This patented Enertia design needs no conventional heating or cooling system in most areas. It comes in a precut kit engineered and tailored to the buyer's design goals.

© 1989 Enertia® Building Systems, Inc.   U.S. Patent No. 4,621,614

Enertia Building Systems, Rt. 1, Box 67, Wake Forest, NC 27587

system. Existing and emerging technologies are expected to make solar heating increasingly attractive.

There are disadvantages, however. Higher initial costs discourage buyers who are not used to considering life-cycle costs or who move every few years. With present technology active solar systems usually cost too much for heating most homes and small buildings, but improved designs and mass-production techniques could change that. Some people also consider active solar collectors sitting on rooftops or in yards ugly. Most passive solar systems require that windows and shades be opened and closed to regulate heat flow and distribution, but this can be done by inexpensive microprocessors. Owners of passive and active solar systems also need "solar rights" laws against building structures that block their access to sunlight.

SOLAR THERMAL: HIGH-TEMPERATURE HEAT AND ELECTRICITY   Several systems are in operation that draw on solar energy to generate electricity and

Q: What is the most energy-efficient fuel for powering a motor vehicle?

high-temperature heat (Figure 4-17). In one such system, huge arrays of computer-controlled mirrors, called heliostats, track the sun and focus sunlight on a central heat-collection tower (Figure 4-17c) or on oil-filled pipes running through the middle of curved solar collectors (Figure 4-17b). This concentrated sunlight can generate temperatures high enough for industrial processes or for producing steam to run turbines and generate electricity. Molten salt stores solar heat to produce electricity at night or on cloudy days.

The most promising approach to intensifying solar energy is *nonimaging optics*, which has been under development since 1965 by American and Israeli scientists. With this technology, the sun's rays are allowed to scramble instead of being focused on a particular point (Figure 14-17d). Experiments show that a nonimaging parabolic concentrator can intensify sunlight striking the earth 80,000-fold—producing the highest intensity of sunlight anywhere in the solar system, including that in the sun's surface.

Because of its high efficiency and ability to generate extremely high temperatures, nonimaging concentrators may make solar energy practical for widespread industrial and commercial use within a decade. Soon rows of glass nonimaging optic cylinders on the rooftops of factories, schools, and businesses may provide the electricity, space heating, and high temperatures needed for industrial processes. Giant arrays of these concentrators at solar power plants may power turbines to generate electricity, to produce hydrogen gas for fuel (Section 4-4), and to convert some hazardous wastes into less harmful substances. Inexpensive solar cookers can also be used to focus and concentrate sunlight and cook food, especially in rural villages in sunny LDCs (Figure 4-17e).

The impact of solar power plants on air and water is low. They can be built in 1–2 years, compared to 5–15 years for coal-fired and nuclear power plants. Thus builders would save millions in interest on construction loans. Solar thermal power plants produce electricity almost as cheaply as a new nuclear power plant, and with small turbines burning natural gas as backup, they can produce electricity at almost half the cost of nuclear power plants (Figure 4-13). Solar thermal power plants, however, need large collection areas. Even so, they use one-third less land area than coal-burning plants (when the land used to extract coal is included) and 95% less land per kilowatt-hour than most hydropower projects.

ELECTRICITY FROM SOLAR CELLS   Solar energy can be converted directly into electrical energy by **photovoltaic cells**, commonly called **solar cells** (Figure 4-18)—an entirely different technology from active solar collectors, which yield heat, not electricity.

Because a single solar cell produces a tiny amount of electricity, many cells are wired together in a panel providing 30–100 watts. Several panels, in turn wired together and mounted on a roof or on a rack that tracks the sun, produce electricity for a home or a building. The DC electricity produced can be stored in batteries and used directly or converted to conventional AC electricity.

Solar cells are reliable and quiet, have no moving parts, and should last 30 years or more if encased in glass or plastic. They can be installed quickly and easily. Maintenance consists of occasional washing to keep dirt from blocking the sun's rays. Small or large solar-cell packages can be built, and they can be easily expanded or moved as needed. Solar cells can be located in deserts and marginal lands, alongside interstate highways, in yards, and on rooftops.

Solar cells produce no carbon dioxide during use. Air and water pollution during operation is extremely low, air pollution from manufacture is low, and land disturbance is very low for roof-mounted systems. The net useful energy yield is fairly high and rising with new designs. By 2030, electricity produced by solar energy could drop to 4¢ per kilowatt-hour, making it fully cost-competitive. With an aggressive program starting now, solar cells could supply 17% of the world's electricity by 2010—as much as nuclear power does today—at a lower cost and much lower risk. By 2050, that figure could reach 30% (50% in the United States).

There are some drawbacks. The present costs of solar-cell systems are high (Figure 4-13) but should become competitive in 5–15 years and are already cost-competitive in some situations. In 1991 Texas Instruments and Southern California Edison developed new low-cost solar-cell roof panels that look like metallic sandpaper and should cut the current cost of solar electricity (Figure 4-13) in half. Moderate levels of water pollution from chemical wastes introduced through the manufacturing process could be a problem without effective pollution controls. Also, some people find racks of solar cells on rooftops or in yards unsightly. Unless federal and private research efforts on photovoltaics are increased sharply, the United States will lose out on a huge global market (at least $5 billion per year by 2010) and may have to import photovoltaic cells from Japan, Germany, Italy, and other countries that have been investing heavily in this promising technology since 1980.

ELECTRICITY FROM FLOWING WATER   Hydroelectric power, or hydropower, supplies about 20% of the world's electricity and 5% of its total commercial energy (Figure 4-2). Hydropower supplies Norway with essentially all its electricity, Switzerland with 74%, Austria with 67%, and LDCs with 50%.

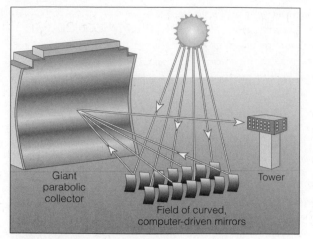

a. Solar Furnace

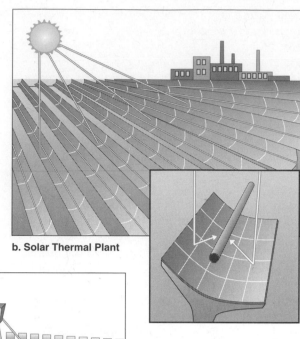

b. Solar Thermal Plant

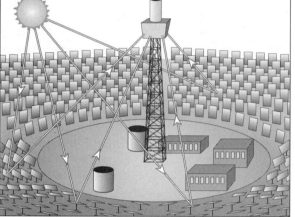

c. Solar Power Tower

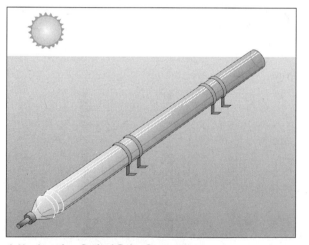

d. Nonimaging Optical Solar Concentrator

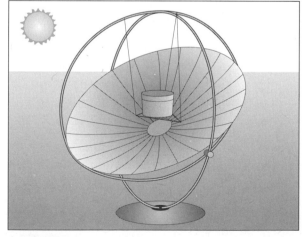

e. Solar Cooker

Figure 4-17 Several ways are being used to collect and concentrate solar energy to produce high-temperature heat and electricity. Today such plants are used mainly to supply reserve power for daytime peak electricity loads, especially in sunny areas with a large demand for air conditioning. Backed up by small natural gas turbines, solar thermal plants occupying less than 1% of the Mojave Desert could probably supply Los Angeles with electricity. With an even economic playing field these plants could produce electricity more cheaply than a coal-burning or nuclear power plant.

Q: What is the best way to save oil, slow ozone depletion and global warming, and reduce air pollution?

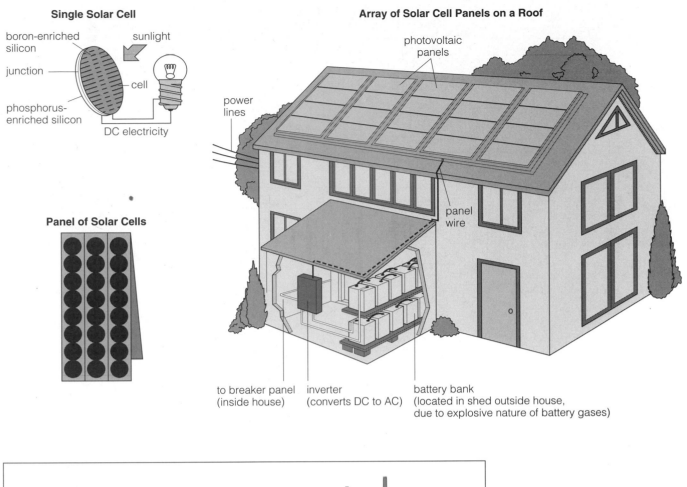

Single Solar Cell

boron-enriched silicon

junction

phosphorus-enriched silicon

sunlight

cell

DC electricity

Panel of Solar Cells

Array of Solar Cell Panels on a Roof

photovoltaic panels

power lines

panel wire

to breaker panel (inside house)

inverter (converts DC to AC)

battery bank (located in shed outside house, due to explosive nature of battery gases)

34 feet

Figure 4-18 Use of photovoltaic (solar) cells to provide electricity. Small and easily expandable arrays of such cells can provide electricity for urban villages throughout the world without the need for building large power plants and power lines. Massive banks of such cells can also produce electricity at a small power plant. Today at least two dozen U.S. utility companies are using photovoltaic cells in their operations. As the price of such electricity drops, usage will increase dramatically.

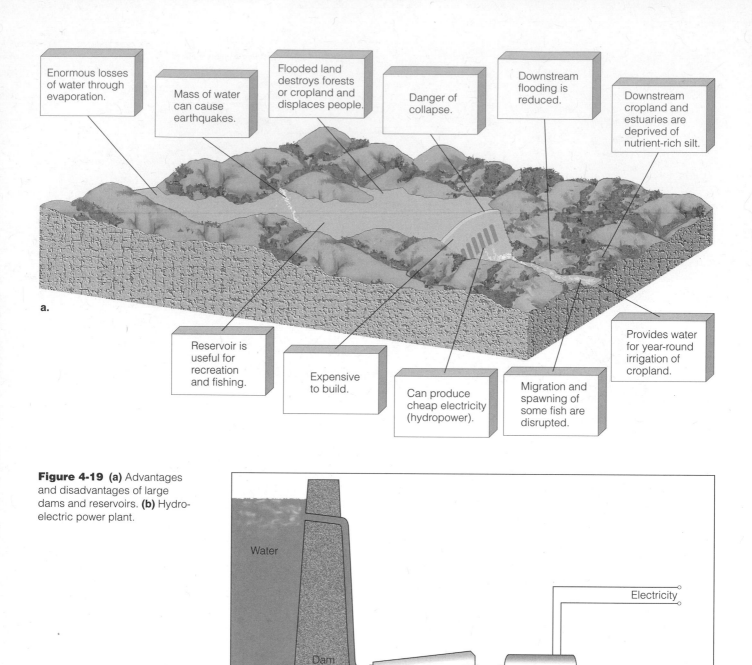

Figure 4-19 **(a)** Advantages and disadvantages of large dams and reservoirs. **(b)** Hydro-electric power plant.

Boxes in figure:

Enormous losses of water through evaporation.

Mass of water can cause earthquakes.

Flooded land destroys forests or cropland and displaces people.

Danger of collapse.

Downstream flooding is reduced.

Downstream cropland and estuaries are deprived of nutrient-rich silt.

Reservoir is useful for recreation and fishing.

Expensive to build.

Can produce cheap electricity (hydropower).

Migration and spawning of some fish are disrupted.

Provides water for year-round irrigation of cropland.

Labels in diagram b: Water, Dam, Turbine, Generator, Electricity, To stream

Hydroelectric Power Plant

In *large-scale hydropower projects* high dams are built across large rivers to create large reservoirs (Figure 4-19a). The stored water then flows through huge pipes at controlled rates, spinning turbines and producing electricity. In *small-scale hydropower projects* a low dam with no reservoir, or only a small one, is built across a small stream. Since natural water flow generates the electricity, output can vary with seasonal changes in stream flow.

Hydropower has a moderate to high net useful energy yield and fairly low operating and mainte-

nance costs. Hydroelectric plants rarely need to be shut down, and they emit no carbon dioxide or other air pollutants during operation. They have life spans 2–10 times those of coal and nuclear plants. Large dams also help control flooding and supply a regulated flow of irrigation water to areas below the dam (Figure 4-19a). However, hydropower also has adverse effects on the environment (Figure 4-19a).

Currently, the United States is the world's largest producer of hydroelectricity, which supplies 10% of its electricity and 3–5% of all commercial energy.

Q: How much money could be saved if the United States got serious about improving energy efficiency?

However, the era of large dams is ending in the United States because construction costs are high, few suitable sites are left, and environmentalists oppose many of the proposed projects due to their harmful effects (Figure 4-19a). Any new large supplies of hydroelectric power in the United States will be imported from Canada, which gets more than 70% of its electricity from hydropower. Large-scale development of hydropower is planned in many LDCs such as China, India, and Brazil.

ELECTRICITY FROM TIDES AND WAVES Twice a day water that flows into and out of coastal bays and estuaries in high and low tides can be used to spin turbines to produce electricity (Figure 4-20). However, most analysts expect tidal power to make only a tiny contribution to world electricity supplies. There are few suitable sites, construction costs are high, and the output of electricity varies daily with tidal flows, which means there must be a backup system.

The kinetic energy in ocean waves, created primarily by wind, is another potential source of electricity (Figure 4-20). Most analysts expect wave power to make little contribution to world electricity production, except in a few coastal areas with the right conditions. Construction costs are moderate to high, and the net useful energy yield is moderate. Also, equipment could be damaged or destroyed by saltwater corrosion and severe storms.

ELECTRICITY FROM HEAT STORED IN TROPICAL OCEANS Ocean water stores huge amounts of heat from the sun, especially in tropical waters. Japan and the United States have been evaluating the use of the large temperature differences between the cold, deep waters and the sun-warmed surface waters of tropical oceans to produce electricity. If economically feasible, this would be done in *ocean thermal energy conversion* (OTEC) plants anchored to the bottom of tropical oceans in suitable sites (Figure 4-20).

The energy source for OTEC is limitless at suitable sites; no costly energy storage and backup system is needed; and the floating power plant requires no land area. Nutrients brought up when water is pumped from the ocean bottom might nourish schools of fish and shellfish. However, most energy analysts believe that the large-scale extraction of energy from ocean thermal gradients may never compete economically with other energy alternatives. Despite 50 years of work, the technology is still in the research and development stage.

ELECTRICITY AND HEAT FROM SOLAR PONDS *Saline solar ponds*—usually located near inland saline seas or lakes in areas with ample sunlight—can be used to produce electricity. Heat accumulated during the daytime in the bottom layer can be used to produce steam that spins turbines, generating electricity (Figure 4-20). An experimental saline solar-pond power plant on the Israeli side of the Dead Sea has been operating successfully for several years.

Freshwater solar ponds can be used for water and space heating (Figure 4-20). A shallow hole is dug and lined with concrete. A number of large, black plastic bags, each filled with several centimeters of water, are placed in the hole and then covered with fiberglass insulation panels. The top of the pond is then covered with the panels, which let sunlight in and keep most of the heat stored in the water during the daytime from being lost to the atmosphere. When the water in the bags has reached its peak temperature in the afternoon, a computer turns on pumps to transfer hot water from the bags to large, insulated tanks for distribution.

Both saline and freshwater solar ponds require no energy storage and backup systems, emit no air pollution, and have a moderate net useful energy yield. Freshwater solar ponds can be built in almost any sunny area and have moderate construction and operating costs. With adequate research and development support, proponents believe that solar ponds could supply 3–4% of U.S. energy needs within 10 years.

ELECTRICITY FROM WIND Worldwide, by 1993, there were over 20,000 wind turbines, most grouped in clusters called *wind farms* (Figure 4-21), producing 2,700 megawatts of electricity. Most are in California (17,000 machines, which produce enough electricity to meet the residential needs of a city as large as San Francisco) and Denmark (which gets 2–3% of its electricity from wind turbines). Most are located in windy mountain passes and ridges and along coastlines, which generally have strong and steady winds. If wind farms were built on favorable sites in North Dakota, that state alone could supply more than one-third of all the electricity used in the continental United States.

Wind power is virtually an unlimited source of energy at favorable sites, and wind farms can be built in 6–12 months and then easily expanded as needed. With a moderate to fairly high net useful energy yield, these systems emit no carbon dioxide or other air pollutants during operation; they need no water for cooling; making them produces little air and water pollution; and they operate 95–98% of the time. The land under wind turbines can be used for grazing cattle and other purposes, while the leases to use the land for wind turbines can provide extra income for farmers and ranchers. Wind power (with much lower subsidies) also has a significant cost advantage over nuclear

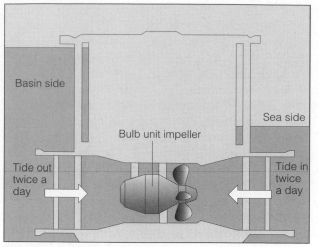

Tidal Power Plant

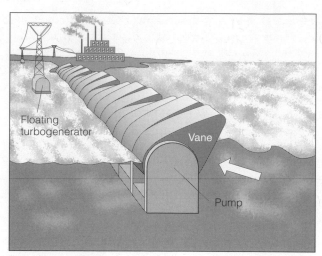

Wave Power Plant

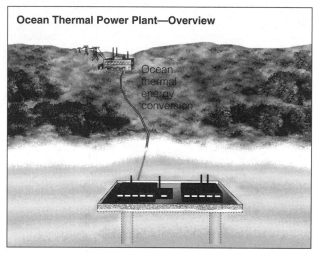

Ocean Thermal Electric Plant

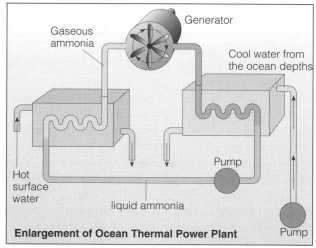

Enlargement of Ocean Thermal Power Plant

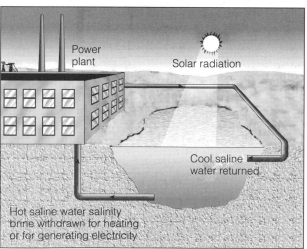

Saline Water Solar Pond

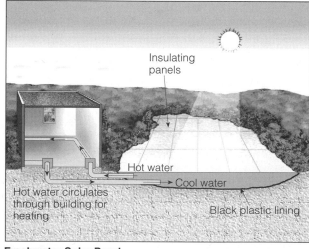

Freshwater Solar Pond

Figure 4-20 Ways to produce electricity from moving water and to tap into solar energy stored in water as heat. None of these is expected to be a significant source of energy in the near future.

Q: What is the largest untapped energy source in the United States?

Wind Turbine   **Wind Farm**

Figure 4-21 Using wind to produce electricity. Wind turbines can be used individually or in clusters (wind farms).

power (Figure 4-13) and should become competitive with coal in many areas before 2000.

However, wind power is economical only in areas with steady winds. When the wind dies down, backup electricity from a utility company or from an energy storage system becomes necessary. Backup power could also be provided by linking wind farms with a solar-cell or hydropower system or with efficient natural gas turbines. Other drawbacks to wind farms include visual pollution and noise, although these can be overcome with improved design and location in isolated areas. Large wind farms might also interfere with the flight patterns of migratory birds in certain areas, as well as with large birds of prey (especially hawks, falcons, and eagles) that prefer to hunt along the same ridge lines that are ideal for wind turbines.

Wind power experts project that by the middle of the next century wind power could supply more than 10% of the world's electricity and 10–25% of the electricity used in the United States. Danish companies, with tax incentives and low-interest loans from their government, have taken over the lion's share of the global market for manufacturing wind turbines. European governments are currently spending 10 times more for wind energy research and development than the U.S. government. With 25 wind-turbine manufacturers, the European Community plans to produce almost twice as much electricity from wind by 2000 as the United States.

BIOMASS: A VERSATILE FUEL   Biomass is organic matter produced directly or indirectly by solar energy through photosynthesis. It includes wood, agricultur-

al wastes (including animal manure), and some components of garbage. Some of this plant matter can be burned as solid fuel or converted into more convenient gaseous or liquid *biofuels* (Figure 4-22). Biomass, mostly from the burning of wood and manure to heat buildings and cook food, supplies about 15% of the world's energy (4–5% in Canada and the United States) and about half of the energy used in LDCs.

Various types of biomass fuels can be used for heating space and water, producing electricity, and propelling vehicles. Biomass is a renewable energy resource as long as trees and plants are not harvested faster than they grow back—a requirement that is not being met in many places (Section 5-4). Also, no net increase in atmospheric levels of carbon dioxide occurs as long as the rate of removal and burning of trees and plants—and the rate of loss of below-ground organic matter—do not exceed the rate of replenishment. Burning biomass fuels adds much less sulfur dioxide and nitric oxide to the atmosphere per unit of energy produced than does the uncontrolled burning of coal, and thus it requires fewer pollution controls.

However, it takes a lot of land to grow biomass fuel—about 10 times as much land as solar cells need to provide the same amount of electricity. Without effective land-use controls and replanting, widespread removal of trees and plants can deplete soil nutrients and cause excessive soil erosion, water pollution, flooding, and loss of wildlife habitat. Biomass resources also have a high moisture content (15–95%), which lowers their net useful energy. The added weight of the moisture makes collecting and hauling wood and other plant material fairly expensive and reduces the net useful energy yield.

A: Renewable energy (92%), compared with coal (5%), oil (2.5%), and uranium (0.5%)

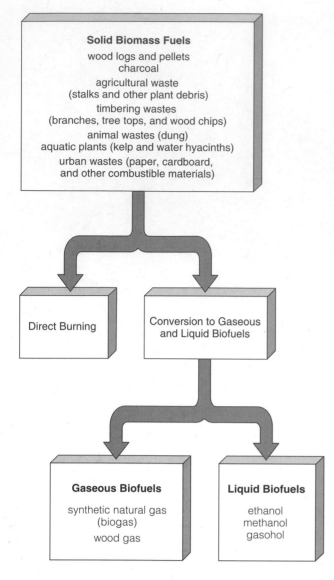

Solid Biomass Fuels

wood logs and pellets
charcoal
agricultural waste
(stalks and other plant debris)
timbering wastes
(branches, tree tops, and wood chips)
animal wastes (dung)
aquatic plants (kelp and water hyacinths)
urban wastes (paper, cardboard,
and other combustible materials)

Direct Burning

Conversion to Gaseous
and Liquid Biofuels

Gaseous Biofuels

synthetic natural gas
(biogas)
wood gas

Liquid Biofuels

ethanol
methanol
gasohol

Figure 4-22 Principal types of biomass fuel.

Biomass sources of energy include:

- *Biomass plantations.* Plant large numbers of fast-growing trees, shrubs, and water hyacinths. After being harvested, these "BTU bushes" can be burned directly, converted into burnable gas, or fermented into fuel alcohol. The plantations can be located on semiarid land not needed to grow crops (although lack of water can limit productivity), and they can be planted to reduce soil erosion and help restore degraded lands. However, this industrialized approach to biomass production usually requires large areas of land (as well as heavy use of pesticides and fertilizers, which can pollute drinking water supplies and harm wildlife), and in some areas the plantations might compete with food crops for prime farmland.

Conversion of large forested areas into monoculture energy plantations also reduces biodiversity.

- *Burning wood and wood wastes.* Almost 70% of the people living in LDCs heat their dwellings and cook their food by burning wood or charcoal. However, at least 1.1 billion people in LDCs cannot find, or are too poor to buy, enough fuelwood to meet their needs, and that number may increase to 2.5 billion by 2000. Wood has a moderate to high net useful energy yield when collected and burned directly and efficiently near its source. However, in urban areas where wood must be hauled from long distances, it can cost home owners more per unit of energy produced than oil or electricity. Harvesting wood can cause accidents (mostly from chain saws), and burning wood in poorly maintained or operated wood stoves can cause house fires. According to the EPA, air pollution from wood burning also causes as many as 820 cancer deaths a year in the United States. Since 1990 the EPA has required all new wood stoves sold in the United States to emit at least 70% less particulate matter than earlier models.

- *Using agricultural wastes.* In agricultural areas crop residues and animal manure can be collected and burned or converted into biofuels. The ash from biomass power plants can sometimes be used as fertilizer. This approach makes sense when residues are burned in small power plants located near areas where the residues are produced. Otherwise, it takes too much energy to collect, dry, and transport the residues to power plants. Some ecologists argue that it makes more sense to use animal manure as a fertilizer and to use crop residues to feed livestock, retard soil erosion, and fertilize the soil.

- *Burning urban wastes.* An increasing number of cities in Japan, western Europe, and the United States have built incinerators that burn trash and use the energy released to produce electricity or to heat nearby buildings. However, this approach has been limited by opposition from citizens concerned about emissions of toxic gases and disposal of toxic ash. Some analysts argue that more energy is saved by composting or recycling paper and other organic wastes than by burning them, as discussed in Section 11-2.

- *Converting biomass into gaseous fuel.* In China, anaerobic bacteria in more than 6 million *biogas digesters* (500,000 of them improved models built in the 1980s) convert organic plant and animal wastes into methane fuel for heating and cooking. After the biogas has been separated, the solid residue is used as fertilizer on food crops or, if

Q: How much of U.S. and world energy needs could be provided by renewable energy resources by 2030 or sooner?

Table 4-1 Evaluation of Alternatives to Gasoline

Advantages	Disadvantages
Compressed Natural Gas	
Fairly abundant domestic and global supplies	Cumbersome fuel tank required
Low emissions of hydrocarbons, CO, and CO_2	Expensive engine modification required ($2,000)
Currently inexpensive	One-fourth the range
Vehicle development advanced	New filling stations required
Reduced engine maintenance	Nonrenewable resource
Well suited for fleet vehicles	
Electricity	
Renewable if not generated from fossil fuels or nuclear power	Limited range and power
Zero vehicle emissions	Batteries expensive
Electric grid in place	Slow refueling (6–8 hours)
Efficient and quiet	Power-plant emissions if generated from coal or oil
Reformulated Gasoline (Oxygenated Fuel)	
No new filling stations required	Nonrenewable resource
Low to moderate reduction of CO emissions	Dependence on imported oil perpetuated
No engine modification required	Possible high cost to modify refineries
	No reduction of CO_2 emissions
	Higher cost
	Water resources contaminated by leakage and spills
Methanol	
High octane	Large fuel tank required
Reduction of CO_2 emissions (total amount depends on method of production)	One-half the range
	Corrosive to metal, rubber, plastic
Reduced total air pollution (30–40%)	Increased emissions of potentially carcinogenic formaldehyde
	High CO_2 emissions if generated by coal
	High capital cost to produce
	Difficult to start in cold weather
Ethanol	
High octane	Large fuel tank required
Emission reduction of CO_2 (total amount depends on distillation process and efficiency of crop growing)	Much higher cost
	Corn supply limited
Reduction of CO emissions	Competition with food growing for cropland
Potentially renewable	Less range
	Smog formation possible
	Corrosive
	Difficult to start in cold weather
Solar-Hydrogen	
Renewable if produced using solar energy	Nonrenewable if generated by fossil fuels or nuclear power
Lower flammability	Large fuel tank required
Virtually emission-free	No distribution system in place
Zero emissions of CO_2	Engine redesign required
Nontoxic	Currently expensive

contaminated, on trees. When they work, biogas digesters are very efficient. However, they are slow and unpredictable—a problem that could be corrected with development of more reliable models. Methane gas can also be produced by anaerobic digestion of manure from animal feedlots and sludge from sewage treatment plants.

■ *Converting biomass into liquid fuel*. Some analysts believe that liquid ethanol and methanol could replace gasoline and diesel fuel when oil becomes too scarce and expensive. Table 4-1 gives the advantages and disadvantages of using ethanol, methanol, and several other fuels as alternatives to gasoline.

A: 50-80%

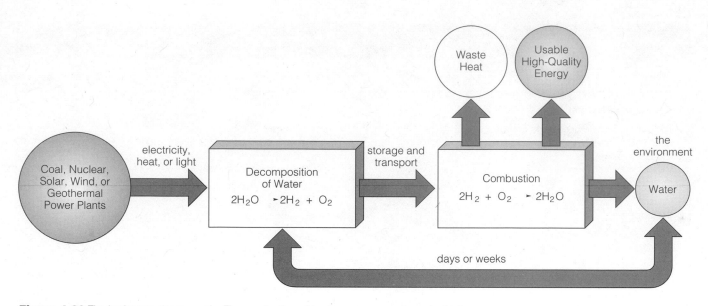

Figure 4-23 The hydrogen energy cycle. The production of hydrogen gas requires electricity, heat, or solar energy to decompose water, thus leading to a negative net useful energy yield. However, hydrogen is a clean-burning fuel that can be used to replace oil and other fossil fuels and nuclear energy. Using solar energy to produce hydrogen from water could also eliminate most air pollution and greatly reduce the threat of global warming.

4-4 The Solar-Hydrogen Revolution

GOOD-BYE OIL AND SMOG, HELLO HYDROGEN

When oil is gone or what's left costs too much to use, what will fuel our vehicles, our industry, and our buildings? Some scientists say the fuel of the future is hydrogen gas (H_2).

There is very little hydrogen gas around, but we can get it from something we have plenty of: water, split by electricity into gaseous hydrogen and oxygen (Figure 4-23). If we can make the transition to an energy-efficient solar-hydrogen age, we could say good-bye to smog, oil spills, acid deposition, and nuclear energy, and perhaps to the threat of global warming. The reason is simple. When hydrogen burns in air it reacts with oxygen gas to produce water vapor (Figure 4-23)—not a bad thing to have coming out of our tail pipes, chimneys, and smokestacks.

WHAT'S THE CATCH?
Hydrogen sounds too good to be true, doesn't it? You're right. We must solve several problems to make hydrogen one of our primary energy resources, but we're making rapid progress in doing this.

One problem is that it takes energy to get this marvelous fuel. The electricity to split water might come from coal-burning and nuclear power plants, but this subjects us to the harmful environmental effects asso-

ciated with using these fuels, and it costs more than the hydrogen fuel is worth.

Most proponents of hydrogen believe that the energy to produce hydrogen from water must come from the sun. This means we have to develop solar-cell technology (Figure 4-18) or solar energy concentrators (Figure 4-17) to the point where the energy they produce can decompose water at an affordable cost.

If we can learn how to use sunlight to decompose water cheaply enough, we will set in motion a *solar-hydrogen revolution* over the next 50 years that will change the world as much as—if not more than—the Agricultural and Industrial Revolutions did. Scientists—especially in Japan, Germany, and the United States—are hard at work trying to bring about this revolution.

Hydrogen gas is much easier to store than electricity. It can be stored in a pressurized tank or in metal powders that absorb gaseous hydrogen and release it when heated for use as a fuel in a car. If metal powder storage turns out to be economical, instead of pumping gas you'll drive up to a fuel station, pull out a metal rack, replace it with a new one charged with metallic hydrogen, and zoom away. Unlike gasoline, solid metallic hydrogen compounds will not explode or burn if a vehicle's tank is ruptured in an accident. The problem is that it's difficult to store enough hydrogen gas in a car as a compressed gas or as a metal powder for it to run very far—the same problem current electric cars face. Scientists and engineers are hard at work trying to solve this problem.

Q: What can be done when groundwater becomes contaminated?

Another possibility is to power a car with a *fuel cell* in which hydrogen and oxygen gas combine to produce electrical current. Fuel cells have high energy efficiencies of up to 60% (Figure 4-6)—several times the efficiency of conventional gasoline-powered engines and electric cars. Hydrogen-powered fuel cells may also be the best way to meet the heating and electricity needs of homes. Currently fuel cells are expensive, but this could change with more research and mass production.

WHAT'S HOLDING UP THE SOLAR-HYDROGEN REVOLUTION? Designing the technology for hydrogen-fueled cars, factories, home furnaces, and appliances is the easy part. The biggest problem is economic and political. It involves figuring out how to replace an economy based largely on oil with entirely new production and distribution facilities and jobs. It means convincing investors and energy companies with strong vested interests in fossil and nuclear fuels that they should risk lots of capital on hydrogen. It also means convincing governments to put up some of the money for developing hydrogen energy, as they have done for decades for fossil fuels and nuclear energy.

In the United States, large-scale government funding of hydrogen research is generally opposed by powerful U.S. oil companies, electric utilities, and automobile manufacturers, because a solar-hydrogen revolution represents a serious threat to their short-term economic well-being.

By contrast, the Japanese and German governments have been spending 7–8 times more on hydrogen research and development than the United States. Germany and Saudi Arabia have each built a large solar-hydrogen plant, and Germany and the former Soviet Union have entered into an agreement for the joint development of hydrogen propulsion technology for commercial aircraft. Hydrogen has about 2.5 times the energy by weight of gasoline, making it an especially attractive aviation fuel. Without greatly increased government and private research and development, Americans will be buying solar-hydrogen equipment and fuel cells from Germany and Japan and lose out on a huge global market and source of domestic jobs.

The solar-hydrogen revolution has already started. Sometime in the 1990s a German firm plans to market solar-hydrogen systems that would meet all the heating, cooling, cooking, refrigeration, and electrical needs of a home, as well as providing hydrogen fuel for one or more cars.

We don't need to invent hydrogen-powered vehicles. Mercedes, BMW, and Mazda already have prototypes being tested on the roads. A fleet of 20 Mercedes-Benz hydrogen-powered test cars have logged more

than 800,000 kilometers (500,000 miles) powered by electricity from fuel cells. And in Japan, in 1992 Mazda unveiled a prototype car that runs on hydrogen released slowly from metal hydrides heated by the car's radiator coolant. By 2000, hydrogen cars could be cost-competitive with gasoline cars in the United States if gasoline prices rise to about 53¢ per liter ($2 per gallon)—half the current price in some European countries.

Hydrogen-powered submarines cruised the deep as early as 1988, and Mercedes hydrogen-powered buses could be on the streets of Hamburg, Germany, by 1997. A large jet airplane in the former Soviet Union has been running on hydrogen fuel for several years.

4-5 Geothermal Energy

TAPPING EARTH'S INTERNAL HEAT Heat contained in underground rocks and fluids is an important source of energy. Over millions of years this **geothermal energy** from the earth's mantle (Figure 2-7) is transferred to underground concentrations of *dry steam* (steam with no water droplets), *wet steam* (a mixture of steam and water droplets), and *hot water* trapped in fractured or porous rock at various places in the earth's crust (Figure 4-1).

If geothermal sites are close to the surface, wells can be drilled to extract the dry steam, wet steam (Figure 4-24), or hot water. This thermal energy can be used for space heating and to produce electricity or high-temperature heat for industrial processes.

Geothermal reservoirs can be depleted if heat is removed faster than it is renewed by natural processes. Thus geothermal resources are nonrenewable on a human time scale, but the potential supply is so vast that it is often classified as a potentially renewable energy resource. Easily accessible concentrations of geothermal energy, however, are fairly scarce.

Currently, about 20 countries are extracting energy from geothermal sites and supplying enough heat to meet the needs of over 2 million homes in a cold climate and enough electricity for over 1.5 million homes. The United States accounts for 44% of the geothermal electricity generated worldwide, with most of the favorable sites in the West, especially in California and the Rocky Mountain states. Iceland, Japan, New Zealand, and Indonesia are among the countries with the greatest potential for tapping geothermal energy.

PROS AND CONS The biggest advantages of geothermal energy include a vast and sometimes renew-

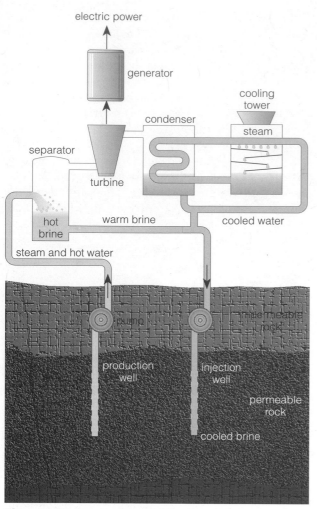

Figure 4-24 Tapping the earth's heat or geothermal energy in the form of wet steam to produce electricity.

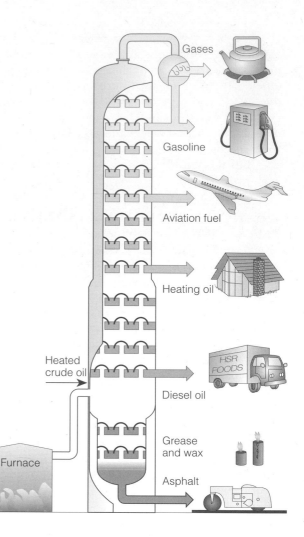

Figure 4-25 Refining of crude oil. Components are removed at various levels, depending on their boiling points, in a giant distillation column.

able supply of energy, for areas near geothermal sites; moderate net useful energy yields, for large and easily accessible reservoir sites; far less carbon dioxide emission per unit of energy than fossil fuels; and competitive cost of producing electricity (Figure 4-13).

A serious limitation of geothermal energy is the scarcity of easily accessible reservoir sites. Geothermal reservoirs must also be carefully managed, or they can be depleted within a few decades. Furthermore, geothermal development in some areas can destroy or degrade forests or other ecosystems. Without pollution control, geothermal energy production causes moderate to high air and water pollution. Noise, odor, and local climate changes can also be problems. With proper controls, however, most experts consider the environmental effects of geothermal energy to be less, or no greater, than those of fossil-fuel and nuclear power plants.

4-6   **Nonrenewable Fossil Fuels**

CONVENTIONAL CRUDE OIL   Petroleum, or **crude oil**, is a gooey liquid consisting mostly of hydrocarbon compounds with small amounts of oxygen, sulfur, and nitrogen compounds. Crude oil and natural gas are often trapped together deep within Earth's crust (Figure 4-1). The crude oil is dispersed in pores and cracks in rock formations. A well can be drilled, and the crude oil that flows by gravity into the bottom of the well can be pumped out. Most crude oil travels by pipeline to a refinery. There it is heated and distilled to separate it into gasoline, heating oil, diesel oil, asphalt, and other components (Figure 4-25). Some of the resulting products, called **petrochemicals**, are used as raw materials in industrial chemicals, fertiliz-

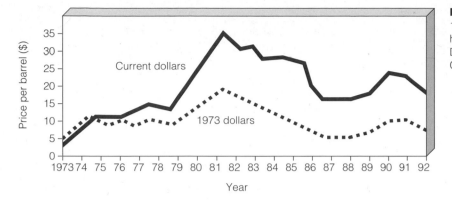

Figure 4-26 Average world crude oil prices, 1973–93. When price is adjusted for inflation, oil has been cheap since 1950. (Data from Department of Energy and Department of Commerce)

ers, pesticides, plastics, synthetic fibers, paints, medicines, and many other products (Figure 4-5).

Oil is the lifeblood of the global economy (Figure 4-2). Oil is still cheap (Figure 4-26), easily transported within and between countries, and from some deposits has a high net useful energy yield (Figure 4-4). Oil's low price has encouraged MDCs and LDCs to become heavily dependent on—indeed, addicted to—this important resource. Low prices have also encouraged waste of oil and discouraged both the switch to other sources of energy and improvements in energy efficiency.

Oil's fatal flaw is that affordable supplies may be depleted within 35–80 years (Spotlight, p. 116). In addition, burning it releases carbon dioxide, which could alter the global climate, and other air pollutants such as sulfur oxides and nitrogen oxides, which damage people, crops, trees, fish, and other species. Oil spills and leakage of toxic drilling muds pollute water, and the brine solution injected into oil wells can contaminate groundwater. Indeed, if all the harmful environmental effects of using oil (Figure 1-9) were included in its market price, and if current government subsidies were removed, oil would be too expensive to use and would be replaced by a variety of less harmful and cheaper renewable energy resources.

HEAVY OIL FROM OIL SHALE AND TAR SAND

Oil shale is a fine-grained rock that contains a solid, waxy mixture of hydrocarbon compounds called **kerogen**. After being removed by surface or subsurface mining, the shale is crushed and heated to vaporize the kerogen (Figure 4-27). The kerogen vapor is condensed, forming heavy, slow-flowing, dark-brown **shale oil**.

The shale oil potentially recoverable from U.S. deposits—mostly on federal lands in Colorado, Utah, and Wyoming—could probably meet the country's crude oil demand for 41 years at current use levels. Canada, China, and the former USSR also have big oil-shale deposits.

There are problems with shale oil. It has a lower net useful energy yield than that of conventional oil

because it takes the energy from almost half a barrel of conventional oil to extract, process, and upgrade one barrel of shale oil (Figure 4-4). Processing the oil requires lots of water, which is scarce in the semiarid locales of the richest deposits. Aboveground mining of shale oil tears up the land, leaving mountains of shale rock (which expands somewhat like popcorn when heated). In addition, salts, cancer-causing substances, and toxic metal compounds can be leached from the processed shale rock into nearby water supplies. Some of these problems can be reduced by extracting shale oil underground (Figure 4-27). However, this method is too expensive with present technology and produces more sulfur dioxide air pollution than does surface processing.

Tar sand (or oil sand) is a mixture of clay, sand, water, and **bitumen**, a gooey, black, high-sulfur heavy oil. Tar sand is usually removed by surface mining and heated with pressurized steam until the bitumen fluid softens and floats to the top. The bitumen is purified and chemically upgraded into a synthetic crude oil suitable for refining (Figure 4-28).

The world's largest known deposits of tar sands—the Athabasca Tar Sands—lie in northern Alberta, Canada. Economically recoverable deposits there can supply all of Canada's projected oil needs for about 33 years at today's consumption rate, but they would last the world only about two years.

Producing synthetic crude oil from tar sands has several disadvantages. The net useful energy yield is low because it takes the energy in almost one-half a barrel of conventional oil to extract and process one barrel of bitumen and upgrade it to synthetic crude oil. Also, large quantities of water are needed for processing, and upgrading bitumen to synthetic crude oil releases large quantities of air pollutants. The plants also create huge waste disposal ponds.

NATURAL GAS In its underground gaseous state **natural gas** is a mixture of 50–90% by volume of methane (CH_4) and smaller amounts of heavier gaseous hydrocarbons such as propane (C_3H_8) and butane

(C_4H_{10}). *Conventional natural gas* lies above most reservoirs of crude oil (Figure 4-1). *Unconventional natural gas* is found by itself in other underground sources, including coal seams, Devonian shale rock, deep underground deposits of tight sands, and deep geopressurized zones that contain natural gas dissolved in hot water. It is not yet economically feasible to get natural gas from unconventional sources, but the extraction technology is being developed rapidly.

When a natural gas field is tapped, propane and butane gases are liquefied and removed as **liquefied petroleum gas (LPG)**. LPG is stored in pressurized tanks for use mostly in rural areas not served by natural gas pipelines. The rest of the gas (mostly methane) is dried to remove water vapor, cleaned of hydrogen sulfide and other impurities, and pumped into pressurized pipelines for distribution. At a very low temperature of −184°C (−300°F), natural gas can be

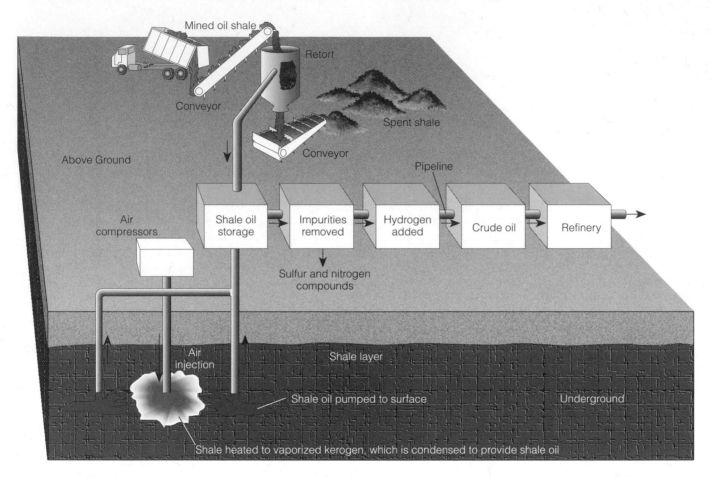

Figure 4-27 Aboveground and underground (*in situ*) methods for producing synthetic crude oil from oil shale.

Figure 4-28 Generalized summary of how synthetic crude oil is produced from tar sand.

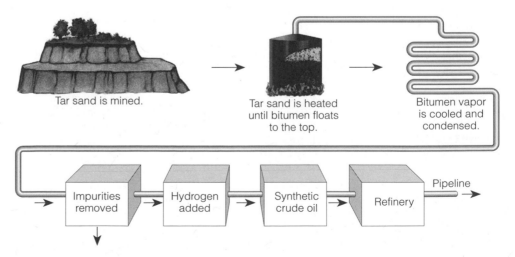

Q: What is the most promising fuel for replacing oil and other fossil fuels?

converted to **liquefied natural gas (LNG)**. This highly flammable liquid can then be shipped to other countries in refrigerated tanker ships.

The countries making up the former Soviet Union, with 40% of the world's natural gas reserves, are the world's largest extractors of natural gas. Other countries with large proven natural gas reserves are Iran (14%), the United States (5%), Qatar (4%), Algeria (4%), Saudi Arabia (3%), and Nigeria (3%). Geologists expect to find more natural gas, especially in LDCs. Most U.S. natural gas reserves are located in the same areas as crude oil.

So far natural gas has been less expensive than oil. Known reserves and undiscovered, economically recoverable deposits of conventional natural gas in the United States are projected to last 60 years and world supplies at least 80 years, at present consumption rates. It is estimated that conventional supplies of natural gas, as well as unconventional supplies available at higher prices, will last about 200 years at the current

rate, and 80 years if usage rates rise 2% per year. Natural gas can be transported easily over land by pipeline, has a high net useful energy yield, and burns hotter and produces less air pollution than any other fossil fuel. Burning natural gas produces only half as much carbon dioxide, per unit of energy produced, as coal and two-thirds that of oil (Figure 4-29). And extracting natural gas damages the environment much less than extracting coal or uranium ore for use in nuclear reactors.

Because of its advantages over oil and coal, some analysts see natural gas as the best fuel to help us make the transition to improved energy efficiency and renewable energy over the next 50 years. Also, hydrogen gas produced from water by solar-generated electricity (Figures 4-18 and 4-23) could be blended gradually with natural gas to smooth the transition to a solar-hydrogen economy (Section 4-4).

COAL Coal is a solid formed in several stages as plant remains are subjected to intense heat and pressure over millions of years (Figure 4-30). It is used to generate 44% of the world's electricity (56% in the United States) and make 75% of its steel. About 68% of the world's proven coal reserves and 85% of the estimated undiscovered coal deposits are located in the United States, the former USSR, and China (which gets 76% of its commercial energy from coal).

Coal is the most abundant conventional fossil fuel in the world and in the United States. Identified world reserves of coal should last about 220 years at current usage rates and 65 years if usage rises 2% per year. The world's unidentified coal reserves are projected to last about 900 years at the current rate and 149 years if the usage rate increases 2% per year. Identified U.S. coal

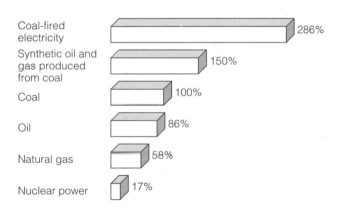

Figure 4-29 Carbon dioxide emissions per unit of energy produced by various fossil fuels as percentages of those produced by coal.

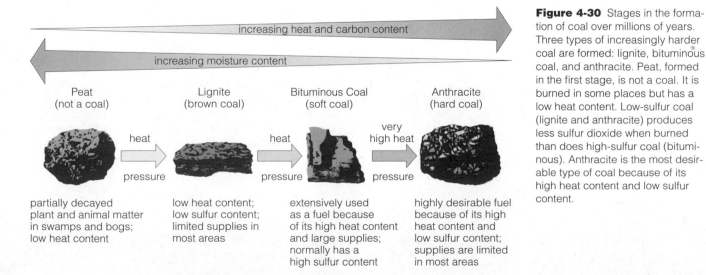

Figure 4-30 Stages in the formation of coal over millions of years. Three types of increasingly harder coal are formed: lignite, bituminous coal, and anthracite. Peat, formed in the first stage, is not a coal. It is burned in some places but has a low heat content. Low-sulfur coal (lignite and anthracite) produces less sulfur dioxide when burned than does high-sulfur coal (bituminous). Anthracite is the most desirable type of coal because of its high heat content and low sulfur content.

A: Hydrogen gas produced from water by using solar energy

Oil *reserves* are identified deposits from which oil can be extracted profitably at present prices with current technology. The 13 countries that make up the Organization of Petroleum Exporting Countries (OPEC)* have 67% of these reserves. Saudi Arabia, with 25%, has the largest known crude oil reserves. Geologists believe that the politically volatile Middle East also contains most of the world's undiscovered oil. Therefore, OPEC is expected to have long-term control over world oil supplies and prices.

With only 4% of the world's oil reserves, the United States uses nearly 30% of the oil extracted worldwide each year, 63% of it for transportation. Despite an upsurge in exploration and test drilling, U.S. oil extraction has declined since 1985. As a result, the United States

*OPEC was formed in 1960 so that LDCs with much of the world's known and projected oil supplies could get a higher price for this resource. Today its 13 members are Algeria, Ecuador, Gabon, Indonesia, Iran, Iraq, Kuwait, Libya, Nigeria, Qatar, Saudi Arabia, United Arab Emirates, and Venezuela.

imports almost half of the oil it uses (Figure 4-31). By 2010 the United States could depend on imports for 70% of its oil supply. This dependence and the likelihood of much higher oil prices could drain the United States (and other major oil-importing nations) of vast amounts of money, leading to severe inflation and widespread economic recession, perhaps even a major depression.

When Iraq invaded Kuwait during the summer of 1990, the United States and other MDCs went to war, mostly to protect their access to oil in the Middle East, especially from Saudi Arabia, which has the world's largest oil reserves. As Christopher Flavin and Nicholas Lenssen put it, "Not only is the world addicted to cheap oil, but the largest liquor store is in a very dangerous neighborhood."

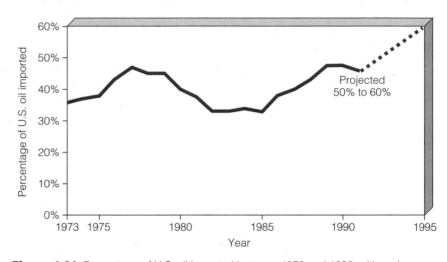

Figure 4-31 Percentage of U.S. oil imported between 1973 and 1993, with projections to 1995. (Data from U.S. Department of Energy and Spears and Associates, Tulsa, Oklahoma)

reserves should last about 300 years at the current consumption rate; and unidentified U.S. coal resources could extend those supplies for perhaps 100 years, at a much higher average cost. Coal also has a high net useful energy yield (Figure 4-4).

But coal has a number of drawbacks. Coal mining is dangerous because of accidents and black lung disease, a form of emphysema caused by prolonged breathing of coal dust and other particulate matter. Underground mining causes subsidence when a mine shaft collapses during or after mining. Surface mining causes severe land disturbance and soil erosion. Most surface-mined coal is removed by area strip mining or contour strip mining, depending on the terrain (Figure 4-1). In arid and semiarid areas the land cannot be fully restored. Surface and subsurface coal mining also

can severely pollute nearby streams and groundwater from acids and toxic metal compounds. Furthermore, once coal is mined it is expensive to move from one place to another; and it cannot be used in solid form as a fuel for cars and trucks.

Because coal produces more carbon dioxide per unit of energy than do other fossil fuels (Figure 4-29), burning more coal accelerates projected global warming (Section 9-2). Without expensive air-pollution control devices, burning coal also produces more air pollution per unit of energy than any other fossil fuel. Each year air pollutants from coal burning kill thousands of people (with estimates ranging from 5,000 to 200,000) and cause at least 50,000 cases of respiratory disease and several billion dollars in property damage in the United States alone. However, new methods,

Q: What percentage of Earth's proven reserves of oil are in OPEC countries?

At the current rate of consumption, known world oil reserves will last for 42 years. Undiscovered oil that is thought to exist might last another 20–40 years (Figure 4-32). U.S. reserves will be depleted by 2018 at today's consumption rate and by 2010 if usage rises 2% per year.

Some analysts argue that rising oil prices will stimulate exploration and that the earth's crust may contain 100 times more oil than is generally thought. Most geologists, however, do not believe this oil exists.

Other analysts argue that such optimistic projections about future oil supplies ignore the consequences of exponentially increasing use of oil. Just to keep on using oil at the current rate and not run out, we must discover the equivalent of a new Saudi Arabian supply *every* *10 years.* The estimated reserves under Alaska's North Slope—the largest ever found in North America—would meet current world demand for only 6 months or U.S. demand for 3 years. Moreover, if the economies of LDCs grow, the rate of oil use will probably exceed current rates and deplete supplies even faster.

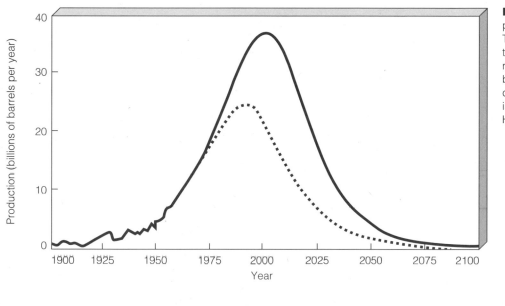

Figure 4-32 The end of the petroleum age is in sight. These two curves show that the world's known petroleum reserves will be 80% depleted between 2025 and 2035, depending on how fast this oil is used. (Data from M. King Hubbert)

such as *fluidized-bed combustion,* have been developed to burn coal more cleanly and efficiently.

If all of coal's harmful environmental costs (Figure 1-9) were included in its market price, and if government subsidies were removed, coal would become so expensive that it would likely be replaced by cheaper and less environmentally harmful renewable energy resources.

CONVERTING SOLID COAL INTO SYNFUELS

Coal can also be converted into **synthetic natural gas (SNG)** by *coal gasification* or into a liquid fuel such as methanol or synthetic gasoline by *coal liquefaction* (Table 4-1). These synfuels can be transported by pipeline. They produce much less air pollution than solid coal and can be burned to produce high-temper-ature heat and electricity, heat houses and water, and propel vehicles.

However, coal gasification has a low net useful energy yield (Figure 4-4), as does coal liquefaction. A synfuel plant costs much more to build and run than an equivalent coal-fired power plant fully equipped with air pollution control devices. In addition, the widespread use of synfuels would accelerate the depletion of world coal supplies because 30–40% of the energy content of coal is lost in the conversion process. It would also lead to greater land disruption from surface mining because producing a unit of energy from synfuels uses more coal than does burning solid coal. Producing synfuels requires huge amounts of water. Burning synfuels releases larger amounts of carbon dioxide per unit of energy than does burning

A: 67% (25% in Saudi Arabia), compared to only 4% in the U.S.

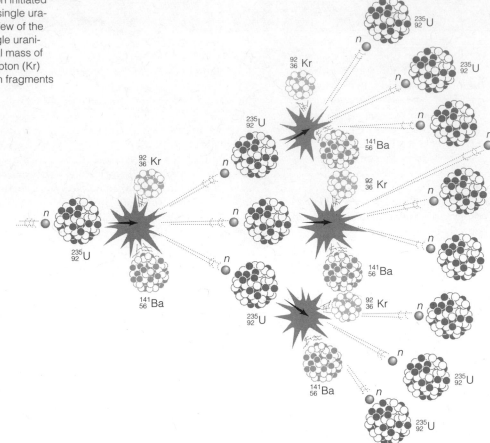

Figure 4-33 A nuclear chain reaction initiated by one neutron triggering fission in a single uranium-235 nucleus. This shows only a few of the trillions of fissions caused when a single uranium-235 nucleus is split within a critical mass of uranium-235 nuclei. The elements krypton (Kr) and barium (Ba) shown here as fission fragments are only two of many possibilities.

coal (Figure 4-29). Because of these problems, most analysts expect synfuels to play only a minor role as an energy resource in the next 30–50 years.

4-7 **Nonrenewable Nuclear Energy**

NUCLEAR FISSION: A FADING DREAM   In the 1950s, researchers predicted that by the end of the century 1,800 nuclear power plants would supply 21% of the world's commercial energy and 25% of that used in the United States. By 1993, after 45 years of development and enormous government subsidies, about 420 commercial nuclear reactors in 25 countries were producing only 17% of the world's electricity and less than 5% of its commercial energy.

In western Europe plans to build more new nuclear power plants have come to a halt, except in France, where the government builds standardized plants and has allowed little public criticism of nuclear power. No new nuclear power plants have been ordered in the United States since 1978, and 119 previous orders have been canceled. In 1993, the 108 licensed commercial nuclear power plants in the United States generated about 20% of the country's electricity, a percentage that is expected to fall over the next two decades when many of the current reactors reach the end of their useful life.

What happened to nuclear power? The answer is billion-dollar construction cost overruns, high operating costs, frequent malfunctions, false assurances and cover-ups by government and industry officials, overforecasts of electricity use, poor management, and public concerns about safety, costs, and radioactive waste disposal. To evaluate nuclear power we need to know how a nuclear power plant works.

NUCLEAR FISSION AND RADIOACTIVITY The source of energy for nuclear power is **nuclear fission**: a nuclear change in which nuclei of certain isotopes with large mass numbers (such as uranium-235; Figure 2-2) are split apart into lighter nuclei when struck

Q: How much of the oil used in the United States is imported?

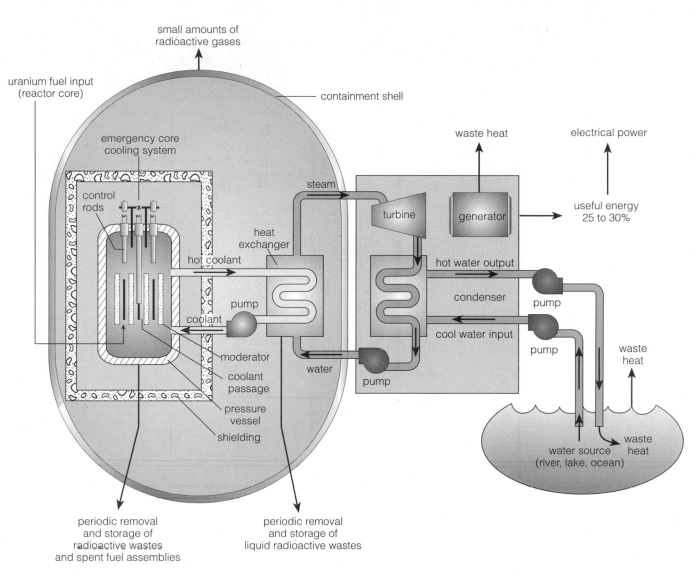

small amounts of
radioactive gases

uranium fuel input
(reactor core)

containment shell

emergency core
cooling system

control
rods

steam

waste heat

electrical power

turbine

generator

useful energy
25 to 30%

heat
exchanger

hot coolant

hot water output

pump

condenser

pump

coolant

cool water input

pump

moderator

water

waste
heat

coolant
passage

pump

pressure
vessel

shielding

water source
(river, lake, ocean)

waste
heat

periodic removal
and storage of
radioactive wastes
and spent fuel assemblies

periodic removal
and storage of
liquid radioactive wastes

Figure 4-34 Light-water-moderated-and-cooled nuclear power plant with a pressurized water reactor.

by neutrons; each fission releases two or three more neutrons and energy. Multiple fissions within a critical mass of the uranium-235 form a **chain reaction**, which releases an enormous amount of energy (Figure 4-33). The rate at which this happens can be controlled in the nuclear fission reactor of a nuclear power plant, and the heat generated can be used to spin a turbine and produce electricity.

Nuclear fission produces radioactive fission fragments containing isotopes that spontaneously shoot out fast-moving particles, high-energy radiation, or both at a fixed rate. The unstable isotopes are called **radioactive isotopes**, or **radioisotopes**. This spontaneous process is called *radioactive decay*. The most common form of ionizing energy released from radioisotopes is **gamma rays**, a form of high-energy electromagnetic radiation (Figure 2-4). High-speed particles emitted from unstable nuclei are a different form of ionizing radiation. The two most common

types of ionizing particles emitted by radioactive isotopes are **alpha particles** (fast-moving, positively charged chunks of matter that consist of two protons and two neutrons) and **beta particles** (high-speed electrons).

The alpha, beta, and gamma ionizing radiation and the high-speed neutrons emitted in nuclear fission (Figure 4-33) can harm cells in two ways. One is harmful mutations of DNA molecules in genes and chromosomes; these mutations can cause genetic defects in immediate offspring or several generations later. The other is tissue damage that causes harm—such as burns, miscarriages, eye cataracts, and cancers (bone, thyroid, breast, skin, and lung)—during the victim's lifetime.

HOW DOES A NUCLEAR FISSION REACTOR WORK? *Light-water reactors (LWRs)* like the one shown in Figure 4-34 generate about 85% of the

Figure 4-35 The nuclear fuel cycle.

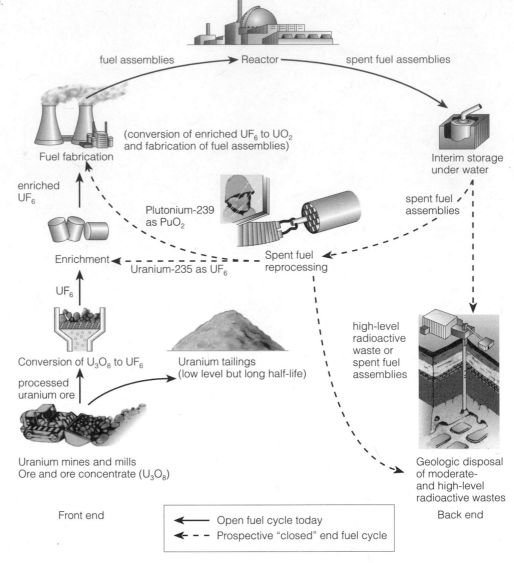

fuel assemblies → Reactor — spent fuel assemblies

(conversion of enriched UF_6 to UO_2 and fabrication of fuel assemblies)

Fuel fabrication

Interim storage under water

enriched UF_6

Plutonium-239 as PuO_2

spent fuel assemblies

Enrichment

Uranium-235 as UF_6

Spent fuel reprocessing

UF_6

high-level radioactive waste or spent fuel assemblies

Conversion of U_3O_8 to UF_6

Uranium tailings (low level but long half-life)

processed uranium ore

Uranium mines and mills
Ore and ore concentrate (U_3O_8)

Geologic disposal of moderate- and high-level radioactive wastes

Front end

Back end

← Open fuel cycle today
← - - Prospective "closed" end fuel cycle

---

world's electricity (100% in the United States) produced by nuclear power plants. Key parts of an LWR are the

- *Core.* This typically contains 35,000–40,000 long, thin fuel rods bundled in 180 fuel assemblies of around 200 rods each. Each fuel rod is packed with pellets of uranium oxide fuel the size of a pencil eraser. The fissionable uranium-235 in each fuel rod produces energy equal to that in three railroad carloads of coal over its lifetime of about three to four years.

- *Control rods.* These are made of materials that absorb neutrons. They are moved in and out of the reactor core to regulate the rate of fission and thus the amount of power the reactor produces.

- *Moderator.* This is a material, such as liquid water or solid graphite, used to slow down the neutrons

emitted by the fission process so that the chain reaction can be kept going (Figure 4-34).

- *Coolant.* This material, usually water, is circulated through the reactor's core to remove heat to keep fuel rods and other materials from melting and to produce steam for generating electricity.

Nuclear power plants, each with one or more reactors, are only one part of the nuclear fuel cycle (Figure 4-35). In evaluating the safety and economy of nuclear power, we need to look at the entire cycle, not just the nuclear plant itself.

Nuclear power has some important advantages. As long as they are operating properly, nuclear plants don't emit air pollutants into the atmosphere, as do coal-fired plants. The entire fuel cycle needed to mine uranium ore, convert it to nuclear fuel, run nuclear plants, and deal with nuclear wastes adds about one-

Q: Will the United States ever again be self-sufficient in oil?

sixth as much heat-trapping carbon dioxide per unit of electricity as does using coal (Figure 4-29), thus making it more attractive than fossil fuels for reducing possible global warming. Also, water pollution and disruption of land are low to moderate if the entire nuclear fuel cycle operates normally. Moreover, multiple safety systems greatly decrease the likelihood of a catastrophic accident releasing deadly radioactive material into the environment.

HOW SAFE ARE NUCLEAR POWER PLANTS? To greatly reduce the chances of a meltdown or other serious reactor accident, commercial reactors in the United States (and most countries) have many safety features:

- Thick walls and concrete-and-steel shields surrounding the reactor vessel

- A system for automatically inserting control rods into the core to stop fission under emergency conditions

- A steel-reinforced concrete containment building to keep radioactive gases and materials from reaching the atmosphere after an accident

- Large filter systems and chemical sprayers inside the containment building to remove radioactive dust from the air and further reduce chances of radioactivity reaching the environment

- Systems to condense steam released from a ruptured reactor vessel and prevent pressure from rising beyond the holding power of containment building walls

- An emergency core-cooling system to flood the core automatically with huge amounts of water within one minute to prevent meltdown of the reactor core

- Two separate power lines servicing the plant and several diesel generators to supply backup power for the huge pumps in the emergency core-cooling system

- An automatic backup system to replace each major part of the safety system in the event of a failure

Such elaborate safety systems make a complete reactor core meltdown very unlikely. However, a partial or complete meltdown or explosion is possible, as Chernobyl (Connections, p. 122) and Three Mile Island have taught us. On March 29, 1979, one of the two reactors at the Three Mile Island (TMI) nuclear plant near Harrisburg, Pennsylvania, lost its coolant water because of a series of mechanical failures and human operator errors not anticipated in safety studies, and the reactor's core became partially uncovered. At least

70% of the core was damaged, and about 50% of it melted and fell to the bottom of the reactor. Unknown amounts of radioactive materials escaped into the atmosphere, 50,000 people were evacuated, and another 50,000 fled the area on their own. Investigators discovered that if a valve had stayed stuck open for another 30–60 minutes, there would have been a complete meltdown.

No one can be shown to have died because of the accident. Cleanup of the damaged TMI reactor has cost $1.2 billion, more than the $700 million construction cost. Opponents of nuclear power point to the Three Mile Island accident as a reason to be concerned about the safety of nuclear power. Supporters of nuclear power, however, point to it as an example that built-in safety systems did work, although they could be (and have been) improved as a result of the accident.

Scientists in Germany and Sweden project that worldwide there is a 70% chance of another serious core-damaging accident within the next 5.4 years. Especially risky are 13 nuclear reactors in Russia, Lithuania, and Belarus with a Chernobyl-type design (Figure 4-36). Environmentalists urge that these and 10 other poorly designed and poorly operated nuclear plants in eastern Europe be shut down.

A 1982 study by the Sandia National Laboratory estimated that a possible, but highly unlikely, *worst-case accident* in a reactor near a large U.S. city might cause 50,000–100,000 immediate deaths, 10,000–40,000 subsequent deaths from cancer, and $100–$150 billion in damages. Most citizens and businesses suffering injuries or property damage from a major nuclear accident would get little if any financial reimbursement because combined government-nuclear industry insurance covers only 7% of the estimated damage from such a worst-case accident. Nuclear power critics also contend that plans for dealing with major nuclear accidents in the United States are inadequate.

Since 1986, government studies and once-secret documents have revealed that most of the nuclear weapons production facilities supervised by the Department of Energy (DOE) have been operated with gross disregard for the safety of their workers and people in nearby areas. Since 1957, these facilities have released huge quantities of radioactive particles into the air and dumped tons of radioactive waste and toxic substances into flowing creeks and leaking pits without telling local residents. Senator John Glenn of Ohio summed up the situation: "We are poisoning our own people in the name of national security."

RADIOACTIVE WASTES Each part of the nuclear fuel cycle (Figure 4-35) produces solid, liquid, and gaseous radioactive wastes. Those classified as *low-level radioactive wastes* give off small amounts of ionizing

CONNECTIONS

Chernobyl is a chilling word recognized around the globe as the site of the worst nuclear disaster ever. On April 25, 1986, a series of explosions in a nuclear power plant in the then Soviet Union blew the massive roof off the reactor building and flung radioactive debris high into the atmosphere. Over the next several days winds carried some of those radioactive materials over parts of the then Soviet Union and much of eastern and western Europe as far as 2,000 kilometers (1,250 miles) from the plant.

The accident happened when engineers turned off most of the reactor's automatic safety and warning systems to keep them from interfering with an unauthorized safety experiment (Figure 4-36). The consequences of the Chernobyl disaster include:

- 31 people died shortly after the accident from massive radiation exposure, and 259 people were hospitalized with acute radiation sickness. Some put the death toll at more than 8,000.
- 135,000 people were evacuated within a few days; 125,000 more were evacuated in 1991; 2.2 million more may need to be moved.
- 576,000 people were exposed to dangerous radioactivity, and some may suffer from cancers, thyroid tumors, and eye cataracts.
- 4 million people, mostly in the Ukraine, Belarus, and northern Europe, may suffer health effects.
- Government officials say that the total cost of the accident is expected to reach at least $358 billion.

People evacuated from the region around Chernobyl had to leave their possessions behind and say good-bye, with little or no notice, to lush green wheat fields and blossoming apple trees, to land their families had farmed for generations, to cows and goats that would be shot because the grass they ate was radioactive, and to their radioactive cats and dogs. They will not be able to return.

World-famous gymnast Olga Korbut reported in 1991:

I was…in Minsk when Chernobyl happened, and they didn't tell us for three or four days….We were all outdoors, because it was close to the May 1 celebration, and we were planting gardens and enjoying the spring. If they had told us Chernobyl had happened, we would have stayed inside…It has been five years…, but people are still very frightened…and very angry. Our food and water supply is contaminated, and we suffer sicknesses from radiation.

When I went into the schools in Byelorussia, I learned that the first-graders have never been in the forest…because the trees were so contaminated…When children want to see what nature used to be like, they go into a little courtyard inside the building, and the teacher says, 'This is a bird and this is a tree,' and they are plastic. Isn't that sad?

Others must speak for the penguins of Antarctica, where radioactive snow fell 20 months after Chernobyl; for the reindeer of Lapland, whose food was so contaminated with radioactive cesium-137 that thousands had to be destroyed; or for the sheep of the English Lake District, where as late as 1990 some lambs were too radioactive to be sold. The primary lesson of Chernobyl is that *a major nuclear accident anywhere is a nuclear accident everywhere.*

radiation, usually for a long time. From the 1940s to 1970 most low-level radioactive waste produced in the United States (and most other countries) was dumped into the ocean in steel drums; Great Britain and Pakistan still dispose of their low-level wastes in this way. Since 1970 low-level radioactive wastes from U.S. military activities have been buried in government-run landfills.

Today low-level waste materials from commercial nuclear power plants, hospitals, universities, industries, and other producers are put in steel drums and shipped to regional landfills run by federal and state governments. Such landfills are strongly opposed by local citizens and environmental groups. Since all landfills eventually leak, some environmentalists believe that low-level radioactive waste should be stored in carefully designed above-ground buildings. All such buildings would be located at nuclear power plant sites, which produce most of these wastes (60–80%, depending on the state) and have the expertise and equipment to manage them.

High-level radioactive wastes give off large amounts of ionizing radiation for a short time and small amounts for a long time. Most high-level radioactive wastes are spent fuel rods from commercial nuclear power plants and an assortment of wastes from nuclear weapons plants. Currently most spent fuel rods in the United States are being stored at reactor sites in specially designed cooling ponds, but some plants are running out of storage space.

After 38 years of research and debate scientists still don't agree on a safe method of storing these

Q: Adjusting for inflation, how does the price of gasoline in the United States in 1993 compare with its price in 1950? In 1973?

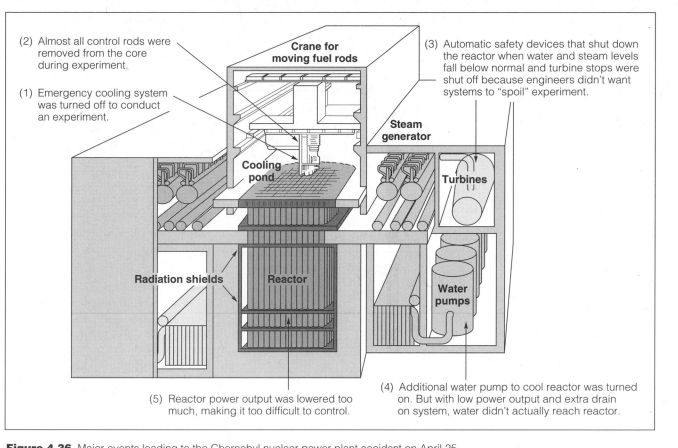

(2) Almost all control rods were removed from the core during experiment.

(1) Emergency cooling system was turned off to conduct an experiment.

Crane for moving fuel rods

(3) Automatic safety devices that shut down the reactor when water and steam levels fall below normal and turbine stops were shut off because engineers didn't want systems to "spoil" experiment.

Steam generator

Cooling pond

Turbines

Radiation shields

Reactor

Water pumps

(5) Reactor power output was lowered too much, making it too difficult to control.

(4) Additional water pump to cool reactor was turned on. But with low power output and extra drain on system, water didn't actually reach reactor.

Figure 4-36 Major events leading to the Chernobyl nuclear power plant accident on April 25, 1986, in the then Soviet Union.

wastes (Case Study, p. 124). Regardless of the storage method, most citizens strongly oppose the location of a low-level or high-level nuclear waste disposal facility anywhere near them.

In 1992 the EPA estimated there may be as many as 45,000 sites in the United States contaminated with radioactive materials, 20,000 of these sites belonging to the DOE and the Department of Defense. The General Accounting Office and the DOE estimate that it will cost taxpayers at least $270 billion over 30 years to get these facilities cleaned up. Some doubt that the cleanup funds will be provided by Congress.

This tragic situation in the United States pales in comparison to the legacy of nuclear waste and contamination in the former Soviet Union. Mayak, a plutonium production facility in southern Russia, has spewed

out 2½ times as much radiation as Chernobyl into the atmosphere and into the nearby Techa River and into Lake Karachay. Today the lake is so radioactive that standing on its shores for about an hour would be fatal. Around the shores of Novaya Zemyla off the coast of Russia, 8 contaminated nuclear-powered submarines have been dumped (at least three of them loaded with nuclear fuel), along with as many as 17,000 containers of radioactive waste. If released by corrosion, radioactivity from these submarines and containers threatens people in the area as well as many along the northern shores of Finland, Sweden, and Norway.

WHAT CAN WE DO WITH WORN-OUT NUCLEAR PLANTS? The useful operating life of today's nuclear power plants is supposed to be 40 years, but

Some scientists believe that the long-term safe storage or disposal of high-level radioactive wastes is technically possible. Others disagree, pointing out that it is impossible to show that any method will work for the 10,000–240,000 years of fail-safe storage needed for such wastes. Here are some of the proposed methods and their possible drawbacks:

■ *Bury it deep underground.* This favored strategy is under study by all countries producing nuclear waste. Spent fuel rods would be reprocessed to remove very long-lived radioactive isotopes. The remainder would be fused with glass or a ceramic material and sealed in metal canisters for burial in a deep underground salt, granite, or other stable geological formation that is earthquake-resistant and waterproof (Figure 4-37). However, according to a 1990 report by the National Academy of Sciences, "Use of geological information— to pretend to be able to make very accurate predictions of long-term site behavior—is scientifically unsound."

■ *Shoot it into space or into the sun.* Costs would be very high, and a launch accident, such as the explosion of the space shuttle *Challenger*, could disperse high-level radioactive wastes over large areas of the earth's surface. This strategy has been abandoned, for now.

■ *Bury it under the Antarctic ice sheet or the Greenland ice cap.* The long-term stability of the ice sheets is not known. They could be destabilized by heat from the wastes, and retrieval of the wastes would be difficult or impossible if the method failed. This strategy has also been abandoned, for now.

■ *Dump it into descending subduction zones in the deep ocean.* Again, our geological knowledge is incomplete; wastes might eventually be spewed out somewhere else by volcanic activity. Also, waste containers might leak and contaminate the ocean before being carried downward, and retrieval would be impossible if the method did not work. This method is under active study by a consortium of 10 countries.

■ *Change it into harmless, or less harmful, isotopes.* Currently there is no way to do this. Even if a method were developed, costs would probably be extremely high; and resulting toxic materials and low-level, but very long-lived, radioactive wastes would still have to be disposed of safely for thousands of years.

In 1985 the U.S. Department of Energy announced plans to build the first repository for underground storage of high-level radioactive wastes from commercial nuclear reactors (Figure 4-37) on federal land in the Yucca Mountain desert region, 160 kilometers (100 miles) northwest of Las Vegas, Nevada. The facility was scheduled to open by 2003, but in 1990 it was postponed to at least 2010. There is a

many plants are wearing out and becoming dangerous faster than anticipated. Because so many of its parts become radioactive, a nuclear plant cannot be abandoned or demolished by a wrecking ball the way a worn-out coal-fired power plant can.

Decommissioning nuclear power plants and nuclear weapons plants is the last step in the nuclear fuel cycle. Three methods have been proposed: **(1)** *immediate dismantling,* **(2)** *mothballing* for 30–100 years before dismantling by putting up a barrier and setting up a 24-hour security system, and **(3)** *entombment* by covering the reactor with reinforced concrete and putting up a barrier to keep out intruders. Each method involves shutting down the plant, removing the spent fuel from the reactor core, draining all liquids, flushing all pipes, and sending all radioactive materials to an approved waste storage site yet to be built (Figure 4-37).

Worldwide more than 25 commercial reactors (10 in the United States) have been retired and await decommissioning. Another 228 large commercial reactors (20 in the United States) are scheduled for retirement between 2000 and 2012. By 2030 all U.S. reactors will have to be retired based on the life of their operating licenses. Many reactors may be retired early because of mysterious cracks or because they can't be run profitably.

Utility company officials currently estimate that dismantling a typical large reactor should cost about $170 million, and mothballing $225 million, but most analysts place the cost at around $1 billion per reactor. So far U.S. utilities have only $3.5 billion set aside for decommissioning more than 100 reactors. The balance of the cost could be passed along to ratepayers and taxpayers, adding to the already high cost of electricity produced by nuclear fission (Figure 4-13).

Q: How long will the world's oil reserves last at the current consumption rate?

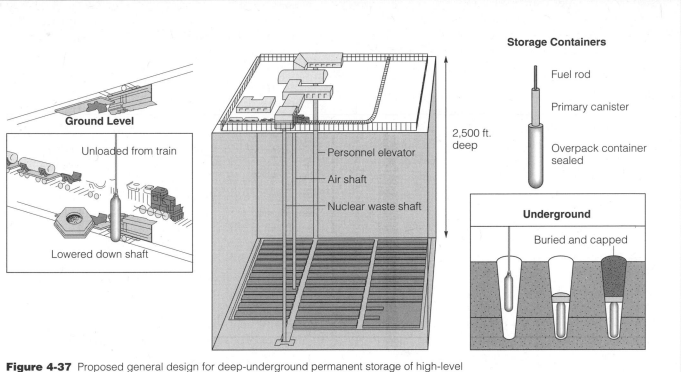

Figure 4-37 Proposed general design for deep-underground permanent storage of high-level radioactive wastes from commercial nuclear power plants in the United States.

strong possibility that the site may never open. A young, active volcano is only 11 kilometers (7 miles) away, and, according to the DOE's own data, there are 32 active earthquake faults on the site itself. Yucca Mountain's many rock fractures also suggest that water flowing through the site could leach out radioactive wastes and carry them 5 kilometers (3.1 miles) or more from the site in 400–500 years.

CONNECTIONS: REACTORS AND THE SPREAD OF NUCLEAR WEAPONS Since 1958 the United States has been giving away and selling to other countries various forms of nuclear technology, mostly in the form of nuclear power plants and research reactors. Today at least 14 other countries sell nuclear technology in the international marketplace.

For decades the U.S. government denied that the information, components, and materials used in the nuclear fuel cycle could be used to make nuclear weapons. In 1981, however, a Los Alamos National Laboratory report admitted that "there is no technical demarcation between the military and civilian reactor and there never was one."

We live in a world with enough nuclear weapons to kill everyone on Earth 60 times—20 times if current nuclear arms reduction proposals are carried out. By the end of this century 60 countries will have either nuclear weapons or the ability to build them. Dismantlement of thousands of Russian and American nuclear warheads can increase this threat, given the huge amounts of bomb-grade plutonium that must be safeguarded.

The best ways to slow down the spread of bomb-grade material are to abandon civilian reprocessing of power-plant fuel in the nuclear fuel cycle, develop substitutes for bomb-grade uranium in research reactors, and tighten international safeguards.

CAN WE AFFORD NUCLEAR POWER? Despite massive subsidies, the latest nuclear power plants built in the United States produce electricity at an average of about 13¢ per kilowatt-hour—the equivalent of burning oil costing well over $100 per barrel to produce electricity. All methods of producing electricity in the United States except solar photovoltaic and solar thermal plants have average costs below those of new nuclear power plants (Figure 4-13). By 2000 even these methods (with relatively few subsidies) are expected to be cheaper than nuclear power.

Banks and other lending institutions have become leery of financing new U.S. nuclear power plants. The Three Mile Island accident showed that utility companies could lose $1 billion worth of equipment in an hour and at least $1 billion more in cleanup costs, even without any established harmful effects on public health. Abandoned reactor projects have cost U.S. utility investors over $100 billion since the mid-1970s. *Forbes* magazine has called the failure of the U.S. nuclear power program "the largest managerial disaster in U.S. business history." In fact, no U.S. utility company is planning to build any new nuclear power plants because they are no longer a cost-effective or wise investment even with massive government subsidies.

Despite massive economic and public relations setbacks, the nuclear power industry hopes for a comeback. Since the Three Mile Island accident the U.S. nuclear industry and utility companies have financed a $21-million-a-year public relations campaign by the U.S. Council for Energy Awareness. Its goals are to improve the industry's image, resell nuclear power to the American public, and downgrade the importance of solar energy, energy efficiency, geothermal energy, wind, and hydropower as important sources of energy.

Most ads use the argument that the United States needs more nuclear power to reduce dependence on imported oil and improve national security. The truth is that since 1979 only about 5% (3% in 1991) of the electricity in the United States has been produced by burning oil, and 95% of that is residual oil that can't be used for other purposes. Even if all electricity in the United States came from nuclear power—which would require about 500 nuclear plants—this would reduce U.S. oil consumption by less than 5%. The nuclear industry also does not point out that half of the uranium used for nuclear fuel in the United States is imported (most from Canada).

Using nuclear power instead of coal does reduce carbon dioxide emissions. However, to offset just 5% of current global CO_2 emissions would require nearly doubling the world's nuclear power capacity at a cost of more than $1 trillion. According to energy expert Amory Lovins, if we hope to reduce CO_2 emissions using the least-cost methods, then investing in energy efficiency and renewable energy resources are at the top of the list and nuclear power is at the bottom.

The U.S. nuclear industry also hopes to persuade governments and utility companies to build hundreds of new "second-generation" plants using standardized designs with passive "fail-safe" features. Supposedly they are safer and can be built more quickly (3 to 5 years). However, according to *Nucleonics Week*, an important nuclear industry publication, "experts are flatly unconvinced that safety has been achieved—or even substantially increased—by the new designs."

Furthermore, none of the new designs solves the problem of what to do with nuclear waste and the problem of using nuclear technology and fuel to build nuclear weapons. Indeed, these problems would become more serious if the number of nuclear plants increased from a few hundred to several thousand.

BREEDER NUCLEAR FISSION There are some nuclear power proponents who urge the development and widespread use of **breeder nuclear fission reactors**, which generate more nuclear fuel than they consume by converting nonfissionable uranium-238 into fissionable plutonium-239. Since breeders would use over 99% of the uranium in ore deposits, the world's known uranium reserves would last for at least 1,000 years, and perhaps several thousand years.

However, if the safety system of a breeder reactor should fail, the reactor could lose some of its liquid sodium coolant. This could cause a runaway fission chain reaction and perhaps a small nuclear explosion powerful enough to blast open the containment building and release a cloud of highly radioactive gases and particulate matter. Leaks of flammable liquid sodium can also cause fires, as has happened with all experimental breeder reactors built so far.

Since 1966 small experimental breeder reactors have been built in the United Kingdom, the former Soviet Union, Germany, Japan, and France. In December 1986 France opened a $3-billion commercial-size breeder reactor. Not only did it cost three times the original estimate to build, but the little electricity it has produced was twice as expensive as that generated by France's conventional fission reactors. In 1987, shortly after the reactor began operating at full power, it began leaking liquid sodium coolant and was shut down. Repairs may be so expensive that the reactor will never be put back into operation.

Tentative plans to build full-size commercial breeders in Germany, the former Soviet Union, the United Kingdom, and Japan have been abandoned because of the French experience and an excess of electric generating capacity. Also, the experimental breeders already built produce only about one-fourth of the plutonium-239 needed to replace their own fissionable material. If this problem is not solved, it would take 100–200 years for breeders to produce enough plutonium to fuel a significant number of other breeders.

NUCLEAR FUSION: FORCING NUCLEI TO COMBINE **Nuclear fusion** is a nuclear change in which two isotopes of light elements, such as hydrogen (Figure 2-2), are forced together at extremely high temperatures until they fuse to form a heavier nucleus, releasing

Q: How much new oil must be discovered and developed to continue using oil at the current rate?

energy in the process (Figure 4-38). Temperatures of at least 100 million°C are needed to force the positively charged nuclei (which strongly repel one another) to join together.

After World War II the principle of *uncontrolled nuclear fusion* was used to develop extremely powerful hydrogen, or thermonuclear, weapons. These weapons use the deuterium-tritium (D-T) fusion reaction (Figure 4-38). Scientists have also tried to develop *controlled nuclear fusion*, in which the D-T reaction is used to produce heat that can be converted into electricity.

Despite almost 50 years of research, however, controlled nuclear fusion is still at the laboratory stage. Deuterium and tritium atoms have been forced together using electromagnetic reactors the size of 12 locomotives, 120-trillion-watt laser beams, and bombardment with high-speed particles. So far, none of these approaches has produced more energy than it uses. In 1989 two chemists claimed to have achieved deuterium-deuterium (D-D) nuclear fusion (Figure 4-38) at room temperature using a simple apparatus, but subsequent experiments could not substantiate their claims.

If researchers eventually can get more energy out than they put in, the next step would be to build a small fusion reactor and then scale it up to commercial size—one of the most difficult engineering problems ever undertaken. Also, the estimated cost of a commercial fusion reactor is several times that of a comparable conventional fission reactor.

If things go right, a commercial nuclear fusion power plant might be built by 2030. Even if everything goes right, however, energy experts don't expect nuclear fusion to be a significant energy source until 2100, if then. Meanwhile, we can produce more electricity than we need using several other quicker, cheaper, and safer methods.

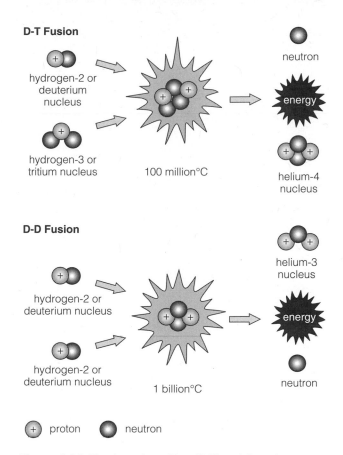

Fuel ⟹ Reaction Conditions ⟹ Products

Figure 4-38 The deuterium-tritium (D-T) and deuterium-deuterium (D-D) nuclear fusion reactions, which take place at extremely high temperatures.

4-8 A Sustainable-Earth Energy Strategy

OVERALL EVALUATION OF ENERGY ALTERNATIVES Table 4-2 summarizes the major advantages and disadvantages of the energy alternatives discussed in this chapter, with emphasis on their potential in the United States. Energy experts argue over these and other projections, and new data and innovations may affect the status of certain alternatives, but the table does provide a useful framework for making decisions based on currently available information. Three conclusions can be drawn:

- The best short-term, intermediate, and long-term alternatives are a combination of improved energy efficiency and greatly increased use of locally available renewable energy resources.

- Future energy alternatives will probably have low-to-moderate net useful energy yields and moderate-to-high development costs. Since there is not enough financial capital to develop all energy alternatives, projects must be chosen carefully.

- We cannot and should not depend mostly on a single nonrenewable energy resource such as oil, coal, natural gas, or nuclear power.

ECONOMICS Cost is the biggest factor determining which commercial energy resources are widely used by consumers. Governments throughout the world use three basic economic and political strategies to

Table 4-2 Evaluation of Energy Alternatives for the United States (boxes indicate favorable conditions)

Energy Resources	Estimated Availability			Estimated Net Useful Energy of Entire System	Projected Cost of Entire System	Actual or Potential Overall Environmental Impact of Entire System
	Short Term (1995–2005)	Intermediate Term (2005–2015)	Long Term (2015–2045)			
Nonrenewable Resources						
Fossil fuels						
Petroleum	High (with imports)	Moderate (with imports)	Low	High but decreasing	High for new domestic supplies	Moderate
Natural gas	High (with imports)	Moderate (with imports)	Moderate (with imports)	High but decreasing	High for new domestic supplies	Low
Coal	High	High	High	High but decreasing	Moderate but increasing	Very high
Oil shale	Low	Low to moderate	Low to moderate	Low to moderate	Very high	High
Tar sands	Low	Fair? (imports only)	Poor to fair (imports only)	Low	Very high	Moderate to high
Synthetic natural gas (SNG) from coal	Low	Low to moderate	Low to moderate	Low to moderate	High	High (increases use of coal)
Synthetic oil and alcohols from coal	Low	Moderate	High	Low to moderate	High	High (increases use of coal)
Nuclear energy						
Conventional fission (uranium)	Low to moderate	Low to moderate	Low to moderate	Low to moderate	Very high	Very high
Breeder fission (uranium and thorium)	None	None to low (if developed)	Moderate	Unknown, but probably moderate	Very high	Very high
Fusion (deuterium and tritium)	None	None	None to low (if developed)	Unknown, but may be high	Very high	Unknown (probably moderate to high)
Geothermal energy (some are renewable)	Low	Low	Moderate	Moderate	Moderate to high	Moderate to high
Renewable Resources						
Improving energy efficiency	High	High	High	Very high	Low	Decreases impact of other sources
Hydroelectric						
New large-scale dams and plants	Low	Low	Very low	Moderate to high	Moderate to very high	Low to moderate

Q: What would happen if the harmful effects of using oil were included in its market price and government subsidies were removed?

Renewable Resources (continued)

Hydroelectric (continued)

Energy Resources	Estimated Availability			Estimated Net Useful Energy of Entire System	Projected Cost of Entire System	Actual or Potential Overall Environmental Impact of Entire System
	Short Term (1995–2005)	Intermediate Term (2005–2015)	Long Term (2015–2045)			
Reopening abandoned small-scale plants	Moderate	Moderate	Low	Moderate	Moderate	Low to moderate
Tidal energy	Very low	Very low	Very low	Moderate	High	Low to moderate
Ocean thermal gradients	None	Low	Low to moderate (if developed)	Unknown (probably low to moderate)	High	Unknown (probably moderate to high)
Solar energy						
Low-temperature heating (for homes and water)	High	High	High	Moderate to high	Moderate	Low
High-temperature heating	Low	Moderate	Moderate to high	Moderate	High initially, but probably declining fairly rapidly	Low to moderate
Photovoltaic production of electricity	Low to moderate	Moderate	High	Fairly high	High initially but declining fairly rapidly	Low
Wind energy	Low	Moderate	Moderate to high	Fairly high	Moderate	Low
Geothermal energy (low heat flow)	Very low	Very low	Low to moderate	Low to moderate	Moderate to high	Moderate to high
Biomass (burning of wood and agricultural wastes)	Moderate	Moderate	Moderate to high	Moderate	Moderate	Moderate to high
Biomass (urban wastes for incineration)	Low	Moderate	Moderate	Low to fairly high	High	Moderate to high
Biofuels (alcohols and biogas from organic wastes)	Low to moderate	Moderate	Moderate to high	Low to fairly high	Moderate to high	Moderate to high
Hydrogen gas (from coal or water)	Very low	Low to moderate	Moderate to high	Variable but probably low	Variable	Variable, but low if produced with solar energy

A: It would be too expensive to use and would be phased out

How to Save Energy and Money

INDIVIDUALS MATTER

- *Don't use electricity to heat space or water (unless it is provided by affordable solar cells or hydrogen).*

- *Insulate new or existing houses heavily, caulk and weather-strip to reduce air infiltration and heat loss, and use energy-efficient windows. Add an air-to-air heat exchanger to minimize indoor air pollution.*

- *Obtain as much heat and cooling as possible from natural sources—especially sun, wind, geothermal energy, and trees (windbreaks and natural shading).*

- *Buy the most energy-efficient homes, lights, cars, and appliances available, and evaluate them only in terms of lifetime cost.*

- *Consider walking or riding a bicycle for short trips—and using buses or trains for long trips.*

- *During cold weather dress more warmly indoors, humidify air, and use fans to distribute heat so that the thermostat setting can be lowered.*

- *Turn down the thermostat on water heaters to 43–49°C (110–120°F) and insulate hot-water pipes.*

- *Lower the cooling load on an air conditioner by increasing the thermostat setting, installing energy-efficient lighting, using floor and ceiling fans, and using whole-house window or attic fans to bring in outside air (especially at night when temperatures are cooler).*

- *Turn off lights and appliances when not in use.*

stimulate or dampen the short-term and long-term use of a particular energy resource:

1. *Not attempting to control the price.* Use of a resource depends on open, free-market competition (assuming all other alternatives also compete in the same way). This is not politically feasible, however, because of well-entrenched government intervention into the marketplace in the form of subsidies, taxes, and regulations. Also, the free-market approach, with its emphasis on short-term gain, inhibits long-term development of new energy resources, which can rarely compete in their development stages without government support.

2. *Keeping prices artificially low.* This encourages use and development of a resource. In the United States (and most other countries) the energy marketplace is greatly distorted by huge government subsidies and tax breaks (such as depletion write-offs for fossil fuels) that make the prices of fossil fuels and nuclear power artificially low. At the same time, improving energy efficiency and solar alternatives receive much lower subsidies and tax breaks, creating an uneven economic playing field. Keeping prices low is popular with consumers, and often helps leaders in democratic societies get reelected. However, artificially low prices encourage waste and rapid depletion of an energy resource (such as oil) and discourage the development of those energy alternatives not getting at least the same level of subsidies and price control. And once an energy industry gets government subsidies, it usually has enough clout to maintain that support long after it becomes unproductive.

3. *Keeping prices artificially high.* Governments can raise the price of an energy resource artificially high by withdrawing existing tax breaks and other subsidies, or by adding taxes on its use. This provides increased government revenues, encourages improvements in energy efficiency, reduces dependence on imported energy, and decreases use of an energy resource (like oil) that has a limited future supply. Raising energy prices can stimulate employment because building solar collectors, adding insulation, and carrying out most forms of improving energy efficiency are labor-intensive activities. Increasing taxes on energy use, however, can dampen economic growth and put a heavy economic burden on the poor and lower middle class, unless some of the energy tax revenues are used to help offset their increased energy costs.

SOLUTIONS: A SUSTAINABLE-EARTH ENERGY FUTURE FOR THE UNITED STATES Communities, such as Davis, California (Solutions, p. 79), and Osage, Iowa (Solutions, p. 96), and individuals are taking energy matters into their own hands (Individuals Matter, at left). At the same time, environmentalists urge citizens to exert pressure from the bottom up on elected officials to develop national energy policies based on much greater improvements in energy efficiency and a more rapid transition to a mix of renewable energy resources.

A few countries and states are leading the way in making the transition from the age of oil to the age of energy efficiency and renewable energy. Brazil and Norway get more than half their energy from renew-

Q: How long will proven reserves of natural gas last at current consumption rates?

able hydropower, wood, and alcohol fuel. Israel, Japan, the Philippines, and Sweden plan to rely on renewable sources for most of their energy. California has become the world's showcase for solar and wind power. What are you, your local community, and your state doing to save energy?

In the long run, humanity has no choice but to rely on renewable energy. No matter how abundant they seem today, eventually coal and uranium will run out.

DANIEL DEUDNEY AND CHRISTOPHER FLAVIN

CRITICAL THINKING

1. Explain why most energy analysts urge that the basis of any individual, corporate, or national energy plan should be improved energy efficiency. Is it an important part of your personal energy plan or lifestyle? Why or why not?

2. **a.** Should air pollution emission standards for *all* new and existing coal-burning plants be tightened significantly? Explain.
   b. Do you favor a U.S. energy strategy based on greatly increased use of coal-burning plants to produce electricity? Explain. What are the alternatives?

3. Explain why you agree or disagree with the following proposals by various analysts:
   a. The United States should cut average per capita energy use by at least 50% over the next 20 years.
   b. To solve world and U.S. energy supply problems, all we need do is recycle some or most of the energy we use.
   c. To solve present and future U.S. energy problems, all we need to do is find and develop more

domestic supplies of oil, natural gas, and coal—and increase dependence on nuclear power.
   d. The United States should institute a crash program to develop solar photovoltaic cells and solar-produced hydrogen fuel.
   e. Federal subsidies for all energy alternatives should be eliminated so that all energy choices can compete in a true free-market system.
   f. All government tax breaks and other subsidies for conventional fuels (oil, natural gas, coal), synthetic natural gas and oil, and nuclear power should be removed and replaced with subsidies and tax breaks for improving energy efficiency and developing solar, wind, geothermal, biomass, and hydrogen energy alternatives.
   g. Development of solar energy alternatives should be left to private enterprise with little or no help from the federal government, but nuclear energy and fossil fuels should continue to receive large federal subsidies.
   h. A heavy federal tax should be placed on gasoline and imported oil used in the United States.
   i. Between 2000 and 2020 the United States should phase out all nuclear power plants.
   j. The licensing time for new nuclear power plants in the United States should be halved (from an average of 12 years) so they can be built at lower cost and can compete more effectively with coal-burning and other energy-producing facilities or technologies.
   k. A large number of new, better-designed nuclear fission power plants should be built in the United States to reduce dependence on imported oil and slow down projected global warming.

5 Biodiversity: Sustaining Ecosystems

5-1 The Importance of Ecological Diversity

Forests, grasslands, deserts, wetlands, coral reefs, and other ecosystems throughout the world are coming under increasing stress from population growth and economic development. In Chapter 2 you learned that there are three components of the planet's biodiversity: **(1)** *genetic diversity* (variability in the genetic make-up among individuals within a single species), **(2)** *species diversity* (the variety of species on Earth and in different habitats of the planet), and **(3)** *ecological diversity* (the variety of forests, deserts, grasslands, streams, lakes, oceans, and other biological communities that interact with one another and with their nonliving environments).

The planet's variety of genes, species, and ecosystems gives us food, wood, fibers, energy, raw materials, industrial chemicals, and medicines, and it helps support the world economy. These life forms and ecosystems also provide free recycling and purification services and natural pest control.

Because biodiversity is a vital part of the Earth capital that sustains all life, preserving the planet's genes, species, and ecosystems should be one of our most important priorities. One way to do this is to protect species from sharp population declines and extinction, as discussed in the next chapter.

However, the best way to protect species diversity is to sustain and protect the earth's ecosystems that serve as habitats for them, as discussed in this chapter. Protecting these vital oases of biodiversity from damage, using them sustainably by learning how nature does so, and helping to heal those we have damaged are important challenges.

This scientific approach recognizes that saving wildlife means saving the places where they live. It is also based on Aldo Leopold's ethical principle that something is right when it tends to maintain Earth's life-support systems for us and other species, and wrong when it doesn't.

5-2 Forest Management and Conservation

TYPES OF FORESTS   There are three general types of forests, depending primarily on climate: tropical, temperate, and polar (Figure 2-29). Since agriculture began about 10,000 years ago, human activities have reduced Earth's forest cover by at least one-third, to about 34% of the world's land area (Figure 2-27). Forests are disappearing almost everywhere, although losses in Europe and North America have been partially offset by new forest growth.

Old-growth forests are virgin (uncut) forests and old second-growth forests that have not been seriously disturbed for several hundred years. They contain massive trees hundreds or even thousands of years old and provide ecological niches for a variety of wildlife (Figure 2-16). These forests also have large numbers of standing dead trees (snags) and fallen logs (boles), which are habitats for a variety of plants, animals, and microorganisms. Their decay returns nutrients to the soil.

Second-growth forests are stands of trees resulting from secondary ecological succession after cutting (Figure 2-41). Most forests in the United States and other temperate areas are second-growth forests that grew back after virgin forests were logged or farms were abandoned. Some of these second-growth stands have remained undisturbed and become old-growth forests, but many are **tree farms**—intensively managed tracts of even-aged trees of one species. About 40% of tropical forests are second-growth forests.

COMMERCIAL AND ECOLOGICAL IMPORTANCE
Forests give us lumber for housing, biomass for fuelwood, pulp for paper, medicines, and many other products worth more than $300 billion a year. Many forestlands are also used for mining, grazing livestock, and recreation. Three countries—the United States, the former Soviet Union, and Canada—supply 53% of the world's commercial timber.

Q: How long will the world's proven reserves of coal last at current consumption rates?

Forested watersheds act as giant sponges, slowing down runoff and absorbing and holding water that recharges springs, streams, and groundwater. Thus they regulate the flow of water from mountain highlands to croplands and urban areas, and they help control soil erosion, moderate flooding, and reduce the amount of sediment washing into streams, lakes, and reservoirs.

Forests also influence local, regional, and global climates. For example, 50–80% of the moisture in the air above tropical forests comes from trees by transpiration and evaporation. If large areas of these lush forests are cleared, average annual precipitation drops; the region's climate gets hotter and drier; and its soils are depleted of already-scarce nutrients, baked, and washed away.

Forests are also vital to the global carbon cycle (Figure 2-22), and they provide habitats for more wildlife species than any other biome, making them the planet's major reservoir of biodiversity. They also buffer us against noise, absorb air pollutants, and nourish the human spirit.

TYPES OF FOREST MANAGEMENT   The volume of wood produced by a forest varies as it goes through different stages of growth and ecological succession (Figure 5-1). If the goal is to produce the most fuelwood or fiber for paper production in the shortest time, the forest is usually harvested on a short rotation cycle, before the growth rate peaks (point A of Figure 5-1). Harvesting at the peak growth rate gives the maximum yield of wood per unit of time (point B of Figure 5-1). If the goal is high-quality wood for fine furniture or veneer, forest managers use longer rotations to develop larger, older-growth trees (point C of Figure 5-1).

There are two basic forest management systems: even-aged management and uneven-aged. With **even-aged management**, trees in a given stand are maintained at about the same age and size. Even-aged management begins with the cutting of all or most trees from an area. Then the site is replanted all at once.

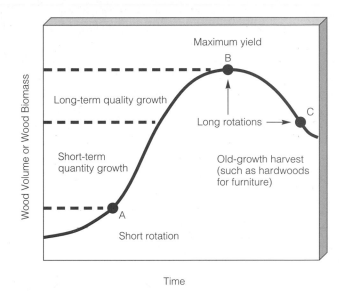

Figure 5-1 Rotation cycle of forest management.

Many important tree species that need ample sunlight to grow can only be grown in even-age stands. Most even-age stands in the United States are of mixed tree species and frequently are managed to produce high-quality trees on long rotation. Indeed, the majority of second-growth forests in the United States are even-aged and contain a mixture of species.

With even-age tree plantations, growers often emphasize single species (monocultures) of fast-growing softwoods to get the best return on their investment in the shortest time. Crossbreeding and genetic engineering can improve both the quality and the quantity of tree-farm wood. Once the trees in such a tree farm reach maturity, the entire stand is harvested and the area is replanted.

With **uneven-aged management**, trees in a given stand are maintained at many ages and sizes to foster natural regeneration. Here the goals are biological diversity, long-term production of high-quality timber, a reasonable economic return, and multiple use of the land. Mature trees are selectively cut, with clearcutting used only on small patches of species that benefit from it.

Figure 5-2 Building roads into inaccessible forests paves the way for timber harvesting but also to destruction and degradation.

Logging roads make timber accessible. Unhappily, that's not all. They cause erosion and sediment pollution of waterways, and they expose forests to exotic pests, diseases, and alien wildlife. Their most serious impact, however, is the chain of events they start (Figure 5-2). In many LDCs they open up once-impenetrable forests to farmers, miners, and ranchers who cut, degrade, damage, or flood large areas of trees, and to hunters who deplete wild animal species. A network of roads can lead to severe habitat fragmentation and loss of biodiversity.

Once loggers can reach a forest, the harvesting method they use depends on whether the stand is uneven- or even-aged (Figure 5-3). It also depends on the tree species being harvested, the nature of the site, and the objectives and resources of the owner. Some tree species, for example, grow best in full or moderate sunlight in large clearings. Such sun-loving species are usually harvested by shelterwood cutting, seed-tree cutting, or clear-cutting (Figure 5-3). The problem is that timber companies have a built-in economic incentive to use large-scale clear-cutting, often on species that could be harvested by less environmentally destructive methods.

In **selective cutting**, intermediate-aged or mature trees in an uneven-aged forest are cut singly or in small groups, creating gaps not much larger than those from natural treefall (Figure 5-3a). This reduces crowding, encourages the growth of younger trees, maintains an uneven-aged stand with trees of different species and sizes, and allows trees to grow back naturally. If done properly it also helps protect the site from soil erosion and wind damage. However, it's costly unless the trees removed are quite valuable; and maintaining a good mixture of tree ages, species, and sizes takes planning and skill. An unsound type of selective cutting is *high grading*, or *creaming*, which removes the most valuable trees. This practice, common in many tropical forests, ends up injuring one-third to two-thirds of the remaining trees when they are knocked over or damaged by logging equipment and when the large target trees are felled and removed.

Shelterwood cutting removes all mature trees in a series of cuttings stretched out over about 10 years (Figure 5-3b). This technique can be applied to even- or uneven-aged stands. The first cut removes most mature canopy trees, unwanted tree species, and diseased, defective, and dying trees. A second cut removes more canopy trees. A third cut removes the remaining mature trees, and the even-aged stand of young trees then grows to maturity. This method leaves a fairly natural-looking forest that can be used for a variety of purposes, and it also helps reduce soil erosion and provides good habitats for wildlife.

Seed-tree cutting harvests nearly all the stand's trees in one cutting, leaving a few uniformly distributed seed-producing trees to regenerate a new crop (Figure 5-3c). After the new trees have become established, the seed trees may be harvested.

By allowing several species to grow at once, seed-tree cutting leaves an aesthetically pleasing forest, useful for recreation, deer hunting, erosion control, and wildlife conservation. Leaving the best trees for seed can also lead to genetic improvement in the new stand.

Clear-cutting is the removal of all trees from a given area in a single cutting. The clear-cut area may be a whole stand (Figure 5-3d), a strip, or a series of patches. After all trees are cut, the site is reforested naturally from seed released by the harvest, or artificially as foresters broadcast seed over the site or plant seedlings raised in a nursery. It requires much less skill and planning than other harvesting methods and usually gives timber companies the maximum economic return. On the negative side, clear-cutting leaves ugly, unnatural forest openings (Figure 5-3d) and eliminates any potential recreational value. It also destroys wildlife habitats and thus reduces biodiversity. Furthermore, trees in stands bordering clear-cut areas are more vulnerable to windstorms, and large-scale clear-cutting on steep slopes leads to severe soil erosion, sediment water pollution, and flooding.

Q: How long will proven reserves of coal in the United States last at current consumption rates?

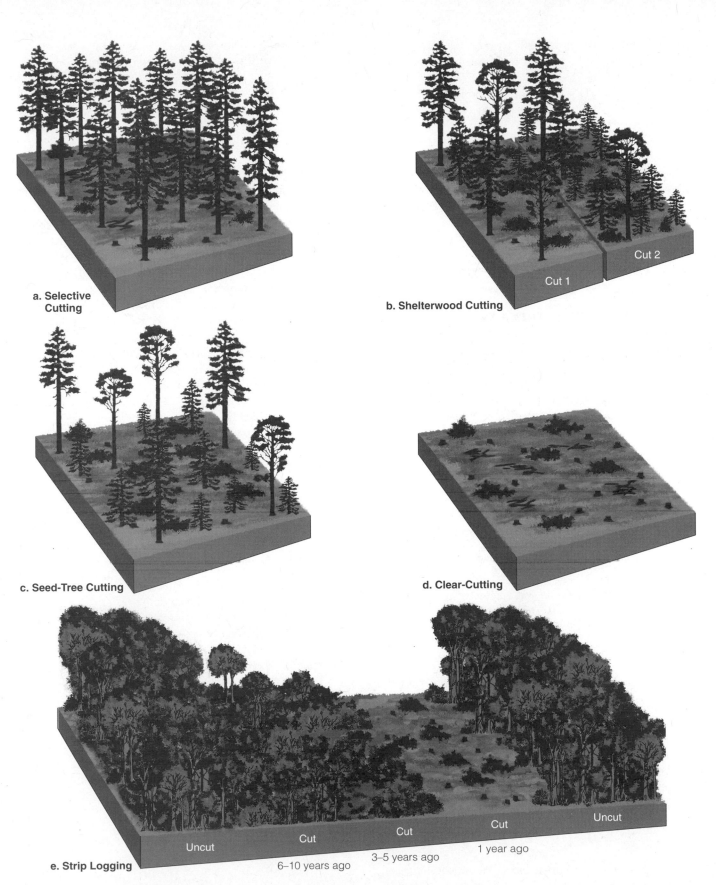

a. Selective Cutting

b. Shelterwood Cutting

Cut 1

Cut 2

c. Seed-Tree Cutting

d. Clear-Cutting

e. Strip Logging

Uncut

Cut
6–10 years ago

Cut
3–5 years ago

Cut
1 year ago

Uncut

Figure 5-3 Tree harvesting methods.

Clear-cutting—if done carefully and responsibly—is often the best way to harvest tree farms and stands of some tree species that require full or moderate sunlight for growth. However, for economic reasons, it is often done irresponsibly and used on species that don't require this method.

A variation of clear-cutting is **strip logging** (Figure 5-3e), which can allow a sustainable timber yield from forests without the widespread destruction often associated with conventional clear-cutting. A strip of trees is clear-cut along the contour of the land, with the corridor narrow enough to allow natural regeneration within a few years. After regeneration, another strip is cut above the first, and so on. This allows a forest area to be clear-cut in narrow strips over several decades with minimal damage.

SOLUTIONS: SUSTAINABLE-EARTH FORESTRY

To timber companies, sustainable forestry means getting a sustainable yield of commercial timber in as short a time as possible. This often means clearing diverse forests and replacing them with intensively managed tree farms.

To environmentalists this does not qualify as sustainable use. They call for widespread use of sustainable-Earth forestry, which recognizes that a biologically diverse forest ecosystem is the best protection against erosion, flooding, sediment water pollution, loss of biodiversity, and tree loss from fire, wind, insects, and diseases. Such sustainable-Earth forest management emphasizes:

- *Recycling more paper to reduce the demand for pulpwood*

- *Growing more timber on long rotations, generally about 100–200 years, depending on the species and the soil quality (point C, Figure 5-1)*

- *Practicing selective cutting of individual trees or small groups of most tree species (Figure 5-3a)*

- *Minimizing fragmentation of remaining larger blocks of forest*

- *Using road building and logging methods that minimize soil erosion and compaction*

- *Practicing strip logging (Figure 5-3e) instead of conventional clear-cutting and banning all clear-cutting on land that slopes more than 15–20°*

- *Leaving standing dead trees (snags) and fallen timber (boles) to maintain diverse wildlife habitats and to be recycled as nutrients (Figure 2-13)*

Sustainable-Earth forestry does not mean that tree farms or even-aged management should never be used, but it does mean that their use should be limited, especially in old-growth forests.

5-3 Forest Management in the United States

U.S. FOREST RESOURCES Though forests cover about one-third of the lower 48 states (Figure 2-27), most of their virgin forests have been cut (Figure 5-4), and what remains is threatened. U.S. forests provide habitats for more than 80% of the country's wildlife species and are a prime setting for outdoor recreation.

Nearly two-thirds of this forestland is capable of producing commercially valuable timber. Since 1950 the United States has met the demand for wood and wood products without serious depletion of its commercial forestlands.

For three centuries the United States was self-sufficient in wood. Since 1940, however, the country has been a net importer of wood, and the gap is widening even though the United States cuts more wood than any other country. The reason for this import–export gap is not higher per capita consumption of wood, which is half of what it was in 1900, but population growth, which has tripled since 1900.

MANAGING U.S. NATIONAL FORESTS About 22% of the commercial forest area in the United States is located within the 156 national forests managed by the U.S. Forest Service (Spotlight, p. 138). These forestlands serve as grazing lands for more than 3 million cattle and sheep each year, support multimillion-dollar mining operations, contain a network of roads eight times longer than the entire U.S. interstate highway system, and receive more recreational visits than any other federal public lands.

The Forest Service is required by law to manage national forests according to the principles of sustained yield and multiple use, a nearly impossible task. For example, timber company officials complain that they aren't allowed to buy and cut enough timber on public lands, especially in remaining old-growth forests in California and the Pacific Northwest (Figure 5-4).

Environmentalists, on the other hand, charge that the Forest Service has allowed timber harvesting to become the dominant use in most national forests. They point out that almost three-fourths of the Forest Service budget is devoted directly or indirectly to the sale of timber and that at current logging rates—the equivalent of about 129 football fields a day—all unprotected ancient forests on public lands in western Washington and Oregon (Figure 5-4) will be gone by the year 2023.

The agency keeps most of the money it makes on timber sales, while any losses are passed on to taxpay-

Q: What would happen if coal's harmful effects were included in its market price and government subsidies were removed?

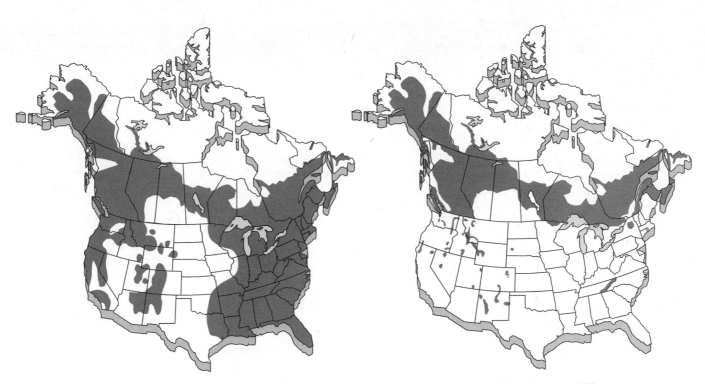

Virgin Forests, circa 1600

Virgin Forests, 1993

Figure 5-4 Vanishing old-growth forests in the United States and Canada. Since 1620, 90–95% of the virgin forests that once covered much of the lower 48 states have been cleared away. Most of the remaining old-growth forests in the lower 48 states and Alaska are on public lands. About 60% of old-growth forests in western Canada have been cleared, and much of what remains is slated for cutting. (Data from the Wilderness Society, the U.S. Forest Service, and *Atlas Historique du Canada*, Vol. 1, p. 98)

ers. Since logging increases its budget, the Forest Service has a powerful built-in incentive to encourage timber sales. Local county commissioners also exert tremendous pressure on members of Congress and Forest Service officials to keep the volume of timber cutting high because counties get 25% of the gross receipts from national forests within their boundaries.

Environmentalists and the General Accounting Office have accused the Forest Service of poor financial management of public forests. By law the Forest Service must sell timber for no less than the cost of reforesting the land it was harvested from. However, the cost of access roads is not included in this price but is provided as a subsidy to logging companies. Logging companies also get the timber itself for less than they would normally pay a private landowner.

Studies have shown that between 1978 and 1992, national forests lost at least $4.2 billion (some sources say $7 billion) from timber sales. With interest, this added at least $5.9 billion to the national debt. Timber company officials argue, however, that being able to get timber from federal lands fairly cheaply helps taxpayers by keeping lumber prices down.

CONTROVERSY OVER OLD-GROWTH DEFORESTATION To officials of timber companies the giant living trees and rotting dead trees in old-growth forests are valuable resources that should be harvested for timber, profits, and jobs, not locked up to please environmentalists. They also note that the timber industry brings millions of dollars annually into the Pacific Northwest's economy and provides jobs for about 100,000 loggers and millworkers. Timber officials claim that protecting large areas of remaining old-growth forests on public lands will cost as many as 53,000 jobs and hurt the economy of logging and milling towns throughout the Pacific Northwest; by contrast, the Wilderness Society, Forestry Policy Center, and U.S. Fish and Wildlife Service put the job loss at 9,000–34,000.

To environmentalists, America's few remaining ancient forests on public lands are a treasure whose ecological, scientific, aesthetic, and recreational values far exceed the economic value of cutting them down for short-term economic gain. The fate of these forests is a national issue because these forests are owned by all the American people, not just the timber industry

A: It would be too expensive to use and would be phased out

Multiple-Use Lands

No nation has set aside so much of its land—about 42%—for public use, enjoyment, and wildlife as the United States. Almost one-third of the country's land is managed by the federal government; 73% of it is in Alaska and another 22% in the West. The allowed uses of these public lands vary.

National Forest System These 156 forests (Figure 5-5) and 19 grasslands are managed by the Forest Service. Except for wilderness areas (15%) this land is managed using two principles: (1) The *principle of sustainable yield* states that a potentially renewable resource should not be harvested or used faster than it is replenished; (2) *the principle of multiple use* allows a variety of uses on the same land at the same time. Today national forests are used for timbering (the dominant use in most cases), mining, grazing, farming, oil and gas extraction, recreation, sport hunting, sport and commercial fishing, and conservation of watershed, soil, and wildlife resources. Off-road vehicles are usually restricted to designated routes.

National Resource Lands These grasslands, prairies, deserts, scrub forests, and other open spaces in the western states and Alaska are managed by the Bureau of Land Management under the principle of multiple use. Emphasis is on providing a secure domestic supply of energy and strategic minerals and on preserving rangelands for livestock grazing under a permit system. Some of these lands not disturbed by roads are being evaluated as wilderness areas.

Moderately Restricted-Use Lands

National Wildlife Refuges These 503 refuges (Figure 5-5) and other ranges are managed by the Fish and Wildlife Service. About 24% of this land is designated as wilderness. Most refuges protect habitats and breeding areas for waterfowl and big game to provide a harvestable supply for hunters. A few protect specific endangered species from extinction. These lands are not officially managed under the principle of multiple use. Nevertheless, sport hunting, trapping, sport and commercial fishing, oil and gas development, mining (old claims only), logging, grazing, and farming are permitted if the Department of the Interior approves such uses.

Restricted-Use Lands

National Park System These 367 units include 50 major parks (mostly in the West; see Figure 5-5) and 309 national recreation areas, monuments, memorials, battlefields, historic sites, parkways, trails, rivers, seashores, and lakeshores. All are managed by the National Park Service. Its goals are to preserve scenic and unique natural landscapes; preserve and interpret the country's historic and cultural heritage; protect wildlife habitats and wilderness areas within the parks; and provide certain types of recreation. National parks may be used only for camping, hiking, sport fishing, and boating. Motor vehicles are permitted only on roads. In national recreation areas these same activities plus sport hunting, mining, and oil and gas drilling are allowed. About 49% of the National Park System is designated as wilderness.

National Wilderness Preservation System These 474 roadless areas lie within the national parks, national wildlife refuges, and national forests. They are managed by the National Park Service, the Fish and Wildlife Service, and the Forest Service, respectively. These areas are to be preserved essentially untouched "for the use and enjoyment of the American people in such a manner as will leave them unimpaired for future use and enjoyment as wilderness." Wilderness areas are open only for recreational activities such as hiking, sport fishing, camping, nonmotorized boating, and, in some areas, sport hunting and horseback riding. Roads, logging, grazing, mining, commercial activities, and buildings are banned, except where they predate the wilderness designation. Motorized vehicles, boats, and equipment are banned except for emergencies, but aircraft may land in Alaskan wilderness.

Between 1970 and 1992 the area of land in all public-land systems except national forests increased significantly (2.7-fold in the National Park System, 3-fold in the National Wildlife Refuge System, and 9-fold in the National Wilderness Preservation System). Most of the additions, by President Carter just before he left office in 1980, are in Alaska. Since then little land has been added to these systems.

There are two major schools of thought on managing public lands. *Preservationists* seek to protect large areas from mining, timbering, and other forms of resource extraction so they can be enjoyed today and passed on unspoiled to future generations. Members of the *wise-use* school see public lands as resources to be used wisely to enhance economic growth, and to provide the greatest benefit to the greatest number of people. This should be done by managing these lands efficiently and scientifically for sustainable yield and multiple use.

Resource extractors accuse preservationists of wanting to keep us from using resources that could benefit people now. Preservationists say wise-users pay lip service to the concepts of sustainable yield and multiple use but, unless carefully regulated (which is hard to do), end up practicing unwise multiple abuse instead.

Q: How much of the world's electricity is supplied by nuclear power?

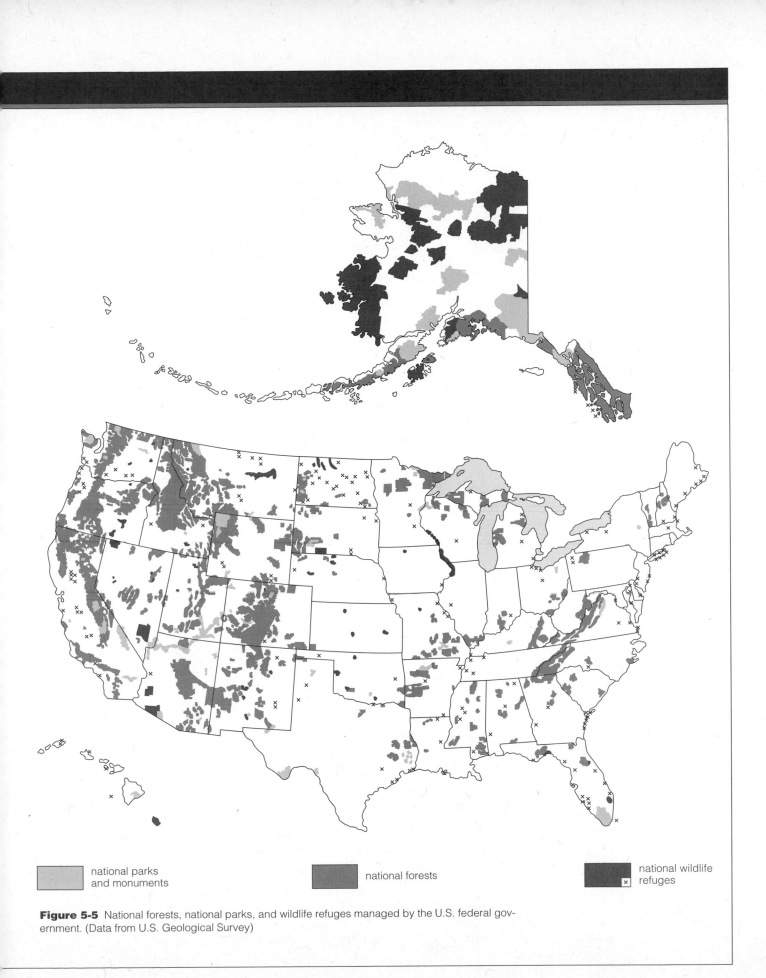

Figure 5-5 National forests, national parks, and wildlife refuges managed by the U.S. federal government. (Data from U.S. Geological Survey)

national parks and monuments

national forests

national wildlife refuges

or the residents of a region. It is a global issue because these forests are important reservoirs of irreplaceable biodiversity and because U.S. treatment of its remaining old-growth forests sets a precedent for nations it is asking to preserve their old-growth forests, wetlands, coral reefs, and other ecosystems.

Environmentalists point out that protecting old-growth forests on public lands is not the main cause of past and projected job losses in the timber industry in this region. Other factors include automation, export of raw logs overseas (depriving U.S. millworkers of jobs while providing jobs for millworkers in Japan, China, and South Korea), and timber imports from Canada.

The threatened northern spotted owl has become a symbol in the struggle between environmentalists and timber company owners over the fate of unprotected old-growth forests on public lands in the Pacific Northwest. This owl lives almost exclusively in 200-year-old Douglas fir forests in western Oregon and Washington and northern California, mostly in 17 national forests and 5 Bureau of Land Management parcels. The species is vulnerable to extinction because of its low reproductive rates and the low survival rates of juveniles through their first five years. Only 2,000–3,600 pairs remain.

In July 1990 the U.S. Fish and Wildlife Service added the spotted owl to the federal list of threatened species. This requires that its habitat be protected from logging or other practices that would decrease its chances of survival.

This decision is being vigorously fought by the timber industry. They hope to persuade Congress to revise the Endangered Species Act to allow for economic considerations. They also contend that the owls do not require old-growth forests and can adapt to younger second-growth forests.

A major problem is that the media and many politicians and citizens discuss this and other complex environmental problems on a simplistic we-versus-them basis. This disguises the fact that *the controversy over cutting of ancient forests in the Pacific Northwest isn't an owl-versus-jobs issue.* The owl and other threatened species in these forests are merely symbols of the broader clash between timber company owners who want to clear-cut most remaining old-growth stands in the national forests and environmentalists who want to protect them—or at least allow only sustainable harvesting in some areas using selective cutting.

The Endangered Species Act is the best (and only) tool environmentalists have to help them achieve this broader goal of protecting biodiversity by protecting fast-disappearing old-growth forest habitats. The truth is that both owls and humans are utterly dependent on healthy, diverse ecosystems. Timber jobs in the Northwest are disappearing for the same reasons the owls are: The ancient forests they depend on are almost gone.

Loggers, millworkers, and store owners who live in these communities are caught in the middle—pawns in a high-stakes game of corporate profit. They correctly fear for their jobs, but automation, export of raw logs mostly to Japan, and cutting of most remaining old-growth trees will also do away with their jobs.

Supporting sustainable use of public forests based on limited selective cutting, replanting and restoring cleared areas, economic diversification, and encouraging tourism are the best ways logging-based communities can remain economically and ecologically healthy.

The other part of the solution to this dilemma is to recognize that the owls, loggers, and environmentalists are not the problem. *We are all the problem.* We buy wood that is logged at such a low price that sustainable logging is not economically feasible. The marketplace is not signaling to us the real costs of destroying and degrading our forests because we don't insist that the prices of wood and wood products include their full short- and long-term environmental and social costs. Until we change the market system to include these real costs, we will continue to deplete Earth capital and eliminate potentially sustainable jobs.

SOLUTIONS: REFORMING FEDERAL FOREST MANAGEMENT Forestry experts and environmentalists have suggested several ways to reduce overexploitation of publicly owned timber resources:

- *Ban all timber cutting in national forests and fund the Forest Service completely from user fees for recreation.* The Forest Service estimates that recreational user fees would generate three times what it earns from timber sales.

- *Until a total ban is enacted, cut the present annual harvest of timber from national forests in half instead of doubling it as proposed by the timber industry.*

- *Prevent at least 50% of remaining old-growth timber in any national forest from being cut.*

- *Allow individuals, environmental organizations, or other groups to buy conservation easements that prevent harvesting of the timber on designated areas of old-growth forests on public lands.* In such *conservation-for-tax-relief swaps* purchasers would be allowed tax breaks for the funds they put up.

- *Build no more roads in national forests.*

- *Require that timber from national forests be sold at a price that includes the costs of road building, site preparation, and site regeneration and that all such sales yield a profit for taxpayers.*

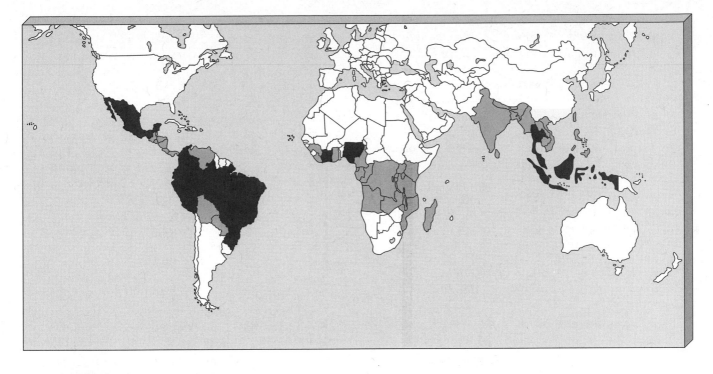

High   Moderate

Figure 5-6 Countries rapidly losing their tropical forests. (Data from UN Food and Agriculture Organization)

- *Don't use money from sales of timber in national forests to supplement the Forest Service budget, which encourages overexploitation of timber resources.*

- *Eliminate the provision that returns 25% of gross receipts from national forests to counties containing the forests or base such returns only on recreational user-fee receipts.*

- *Require use of sustainable-forestry methods (p. 136).*

- *Close loopholes in and strictly enforce the ban on exporting unprocessed logs* from the Pacific Northwest, and expand this ban to the entire United States to keep lumber mill jobs in the United States.

- *Provide dislocated timber workers and their families with financial assistance* for housing, job retraining, job searching, health insurance, and extended unemployment benefits.

- *Provide funds for extensive reforestation and restoration of denuded lands* to furnish alternative jobs for unemployed loggers and millworkers.

Timber company officials vigorously oppose most of these proposals, claiming they would cause economic disruption in their industry and in logging communities and raise the price of timber for consumers. Environmentalists argue that taxpayers are paying higher prices than they think for timber when their tax dollars are used to subsidize logging in national forests. They contend that including these and the harmful environmental costs of unsustainable timber cutting would promote more sustainable use of these resources, help sustain logging communities, and protect biodiversity. What do you think should be done?

5-4 Tropical Deforestation and the Fuelwood Crisis

SHRINKING TROPICAL FORESTS Tropical forests, which cover about 6% of Earth's land area, grow near the equator in Latin America, Africa, and Asia (Figure 2-27). They include rain forests, moist deciduous forests, dry and very dry deciduous forests, and forests on hills and mountains. About 56% of the world's tropical forests have been cleared or damaged. According to a 1993 UN Food and Agricultural Organization (FAO) report, the annual rate of loss rose by nearly 40% between 1980 and 1990 (Figure 5-6). Satellite scans and ground-level surveys indicate that these forests are vanishing at a rate of at least 154,000 square kilometers (59,000 square miles) per year—equivalent to about 34 city blocks per minute or almost two football fields per second. An equal area of these forests is damaged every year.

About 40% of this deforestation is taking place in South America (especially in the vast Amazon Basin). However, the rates of tropical deforestation in Southeast Asia and in Central America are about 2.7 times higher than in South America. Haiti has lost 98% of its original forest cover, the Philippines 97%, and Madagascar 84%.

Reforestation in the tropics scarcely deserves the name, with only 1 tree planted for every 10 trees cut. In Africa it's 1 to 29. If the current rate of loss continues, all remaining tropical forests (except for a few preserved and vulnerable patches) will be gone within 30 to 50 years, and much sooner in some areas.

Environmentalists consider what's happening to tropical forests one of the world's most serious environmental problems. These forests are homes to at least 50% (some estimate 90%) of Earth's total stock of species—most of them still unknown and unnamed.

WHY SHOULD WE CARE ABOUT TROPICAL FORESTS? The world's tropical forests touch the daily lives of everyone on Earth through the products and ecological services they provide. These forests supply half of the world's annual harvest of hardwood, hundreds of food products (including coffee, tea, cocoa, spices, nuts, chocolate, and tropical fruits), and materials such as natural latex rubber, resins, dyes, and essential oils that can be harvested sustainably. A 1988 study by a team of scientists showed that sustainable harvesting of such nonwood products as nuts, fruits, herbs, spices, oils, medicines, and latex rubber in Amazon rain forests over 50 years would generate twice as much revenue per hectare as timber production and three times as much as cattle ranching.

The active ingredients for 25% of the world's prescription drugs are substances derived from plants—most growing in tropical rain forests. Some tropical plants are used directly as medicines, especially in LDCs. However, in MDCs the medically active ingredients in such plants are identified and then synthesized using modern chemistry. This is usually cheaper and reduces the need to deplete tropical forests of such plants.

Such drugs are used in birth control pills, tranquilizers, muscle relaxers, and lifesaving drugs for treating malaria, leukemia and Hodgkin's disease, testicular and lung cancers, heart disease, high blood pressure, multiple sclerosis, venereal warts, and many other diseases. Commercial sales of these drugs account for more than $40 billion per year worldwide and $14 billion per year in the United States. Seventy percent of the 3,000 plants identified by the National Cancer Institute (NCI) as sources of cancer-fighting chemicals come from tropical forests. While you are reading this page, a plant species that could cure a type of cancer, AIDS, or some other deadly disease might be wiped out forever.

Most of the original strains of rice, wheat, and corn that supply more than half of the world's food were developed from wild tropical plants. Scientists believe that tens of thousands of strains of plants with potential value as food, including 2,450 edible fruits, await discovery in tropical forests.

Despite this immense potential, less than 1% of the estimated 125,000 flowering plant species in the world's tropical forests (and less than 3% of the world's 220,000 such species) have been examined closely for their possible use as human resources. Destroying these forests and the species they contain for short-term economic gain is like throwing away a wrapped present or burning down an ancient library before you read the books.

To most economists and investors, untouched rain forests have economic potential and need to be developed. But others believe that destruction of these reservoirs of biological and cultural diversity must be stopped. Otherwise, within a few decades we will see the premature extinction of numerous tribal cultures and millions of wild species. In addition, the Environmental Policy Institute estimates that unless the destruction of tropical forests stops, the resulting loss of water and topsoil, along with flooding, will cause as many as a billion people to starve to death during the next 30 years.

CAUSES OF TROPICAL DEFORESTATION The underlying causes of the current massive destruction and degradation of tropical forests are:

- *Population growth and poverty.* These two factors combine to drive subsistence farmers and the landless poor to tropical forests to try to grow enough food to survive.

- *Massive foreign debt and policies of governments and international development and lending agencies that encourage rapid depletion of resources to stimulate short-term economic growth.* LDCs are encouraged to borrow money from MDCs to finance economic growth. To pay the interest on their debt, these countries often sell off their forests, minerals, oil, and other resources—mostly to MDCs—at low prices dictated by the international marketplace.

The process of destroying or degrading a tropical forest begins with a road (Figure 5-2). Once the forest becomes accessible it is doomed by:

Q: What are the best ways to deal with solid waste?

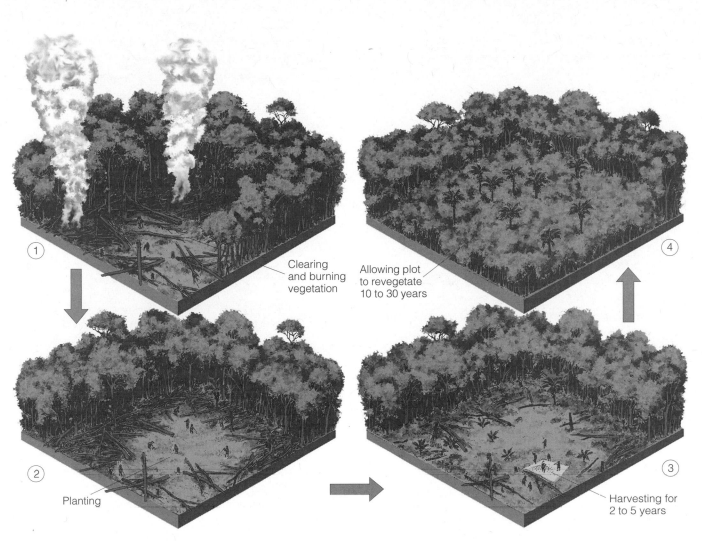

Figure 5-7 The world's first crop-growing technique may have been a combination of slash-and-burn and shifting cultivation in tropical forests. This method is sustainable if only small plots of the forest are cleared, cultivated for no more than 5 years, and then allowed to lie fallow for 10–30 years to renew soil fertility.

- *Unsustainable small-scale farming.* Colonists follow logging roads into the forest to plant crops on small cleared plots, build homes, and try to survive. With little experience, many of these newcomers cut and burn too much forest to grow crops without allowing depleted soils to recover (Figure 5-7), ultimately destroying large tracts of forest.

- *Cattle ranching.* Cattle ranches are often established on exhausted and abandoned cropland, with the ranchers often receiving government subsidies to make the ranching profitable.

- *Commercial logging.* Since 1950 the consumption of tropical lumber has risen 15-fold, with Japan now accounting for 60% of annual consumption. Other leading importers of tropical hardwoods are the United States and Great Britain. Most cleared tropical forests are not replanted, and degraded

ones are rarely restored because few, if any, of the costs of environmental degradation are included in the prices charged loggers. As tropical timber in Asia is depleted in the 1990s, cutting will shift to Latin America and Africa. The World Bank estimates that by 2000 only 10 of the 33 countries now exporting tropical timber will have any left to export. Although timber exports to MDCs contribute to tropical forest depletion and degradation, over 80% of the trees cut in LDCs are used at home.

- *Raising cash crops.* Immense plantations grow crops such as sugarcane, bananas, tea, and coffee, mostly for export to MDCs.

- *Growing of marijuana and cocaine-yielding coca.* Most of these drugs are smuggled into MDCs to supply the illegal drug trade.

- *Mining operations.* Much of the extracted minerals, such as iron ore and bauxite (aluminum ore), are exported to MDCs.

- *Oil drilling and extraction.*

- *Damming rivers and flooding large areas of forest* (Figure 4-19).

SOLUTIONS: REDUCING TROPICAL DEFORESTATION   Environmentalists have suggested a number of ways to reduce tropical deforestation:

- *Use remote-sensing satellites to find out how much of the world is covered with forest and how much has been deforested.* This could be done for about what the world spends for military purposes *every three minutes.*

- *Establish a mandatory international labeling system to identify tropical (and other) timber grown and harvested sustainably.* So far only 0.1% of the world's tropical forests are managed sustainably.

- *Reform tropical timber-cutting regulations and practices.* This would involve charging more for timber-cutting concessions, making the contracts longer (70 years) to encourage conservation and reforestation, and requiring companies to post adequate bonds for reforestation and restoration.

- *Fully fund the Rapid Assessment Program (RAP).* This program sends tropical biologists to assess the biodiversity of "hot spots"—forests and other habitats that are both rich in unique species and in imminent danger—with the goal of channeling funds and efforts toward immediate protection of these valuable ecosystems.

- *Use debt-for-nature swaps and conservation easements to encourage countries to protect areas of tropical forests or other valuable natural systems.* In a debt-for-nature swap, participating tropical countries act as custodians for protected forest reserves in return for foreign aid or debt relief (Case Study, p. 145). With conservation easements, a country, a private organization, or a group of countries compensates individual countries for protecting selected forest areas. Currently less than 5% of the world's tropical forests are part of parks and preserves, and many of these are protected only on paper.

- *Help settlers learn how to practice small-scale sustainable agriculture.*

- *Stop funding tree and crop plantations, ranches, roads, and destructive types of tourism on any land now covered by old-growth tropical forests.*

- *Concentrate farming, tree and crop plantations, and ranching activities on cleared tropical forest areas in various stages of secondary ecological succession (Figure 2-41).*

- *Set aside large protected areas for indigenous tribal peoples.* Indigenous peoples are the primary guardians and sustainable users of vast, mostly undisturbed habitats that provide much of the planet's ecosystem services important to all life. Their homelands are sanctuaries for more threatened and endangered species than all the world's official wildlife reserves. These peoples in tropical forests and other biomes, however, are being driven from their homelands by commercial resource extractors and landless peasants.

- *"Green" the multilateral development banks.* Pressure banks and international lending agencies (controlled by MDCs) not to lend money for environmentally destructive projects—especially road building (Figure 5-2)—involving tropical forests.

- *Reduce poverty and the flow of the landless poor to tropical forests by slowing population growth.*

- *Reforest and rehabilitate degraded tropical forests and watersheds.*

- *Work with local people to protect forests* (Spotlight, p. 146).

ECOLOGICAL PROTECTION IN COSTA RICA   Costa Rica, smaller in area than West Virginia, was once almost completely covered with tropical forests. Between 1963 and 1983, however, politically powerful ranching families cleared much of the country's forests to graze cattle, with most of the beef exported to the United States and western Europe. By 1983 only 17% of the country's original tropical forest remained, and soil erosion was rampant.

Despite widespread degradation tiny Costa Rica is a "superpower" of biodiversity, with an estimated 500,000 species of plants and animals. A single park in Costa Rica is home for more bird species than all of North America.

Another bright note is that in the mid-1970s Costa Rica established a system of national parks and reserves that now protects 12% of its land (6% of it in indigenous reserves), compared to only 1.8% protected in the lower 48 states of the United States. This strategy has paid off. Today revenue from tourism (almost two-thirds of it from ecotourists) is the country's largest source of outside income. Costa Rica plans to protect 17% of its land from exploitation.

THE FUELWOOD CRISIS IN LDCs   By 1985 about 1.5 billion people—almost one out of every three persons on Earth—in 63 LDCs either could not get enough fuelwood to meet their basic needs or were forced to meet their needs by consuming wood faster

Q: Where are the world's largest number of sites contaminated with radioactive materials?

Debt-for-Nature in Bolivia

In 1984 biologist Thomas Lovejoy suggested that debtor nations willing to protect part of their natural resources should be rewarded. In the **debt-for-nature swaps** Lovejoy proposed that a certain amount of foreign debt be canceled in exchange for spending a certain sum on better natural resource management. Typically, a conservation organization buys a certain amount of a country's debt from a bank at a discount rate and negotiates the swap. A government or private agency must then agree to enact and supervise the conservation program.

In 1987 Conservation International purchased $650,000 of Bolivia's $5.7-billion national debt from the Citibank affiliate in Bolivia for $100,000. In exchange for not having to pay back this part of its debt, the Bolivian government agreed to expand and protect 1.5 million hectares (3.7 million acres) of tropical forest around its existing Beni Biosphere Reserve in the Amazon Basin—containing some of the world's largest reserves of mahogany and cedar—from harmful forms of development. The government was to establish maximum legal protection for the reserve and create a $250,000 fund, with the interest to be used to manage the reserve.

The plan is supposed to be a model of how conservation of forest and wildlife resources can be compatible with sustainable economic development (Figure 5-8). Central to the plan is a virgin tropical forest to be set aside as a biological reserve. It is to be surrounded by a protective buffer of savanna used for sustainable grazing of livestock. Controlled commercial logging—as well as hunting and fishing by local natives—would be permitted in some parts of the forest but not in the mountain area above the tract, to protect the area's watershed and to prevent erosion.

As of 1993, six years after the agreement was signed, however, the Bolivian government still had not provided legal protection for the reserve. It also waited until April 1989 to contribute only $100,000 to the reserve management fund. Meanwhile, with government approval, timber companies have cut thousands of mahogany trees from the area, with most of this lumber exported to the United States. Also, the area's 5,000 native inhabitants were not consulted about the swap plan, even though they are involved in a land-ownership dispute with logging companies.

One lesson learned from this first debt-for-nature swap is that legislative and budget requirements must be met before the swap is executed. Another is that such swaps need to be carefully monitored by environmental organizations to be sure that paper proposals for sustainable development are not disguises for eventually unsustainable development.

Debt-for-nature swaps are a fine idea if carried out properly. However, they put only a small dent in the debt and environmental problems of LDCs. Critics also point out that such swaps legitimize the LDCs' $1.4 trillion debt at a time when environmentalists and debtor governments are urging that much of this debt be forgiven in return for agreements to reduce poverty, redistribute land, control population growth, and protect biodiversity and indigenous peoples in priority areas.

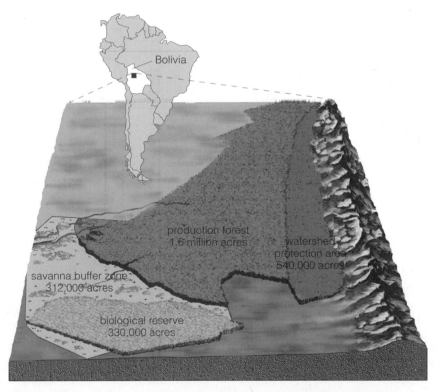

Figure 5-8 Blending economic development and conservation in a 1.5-million-hectare (3.7-million-acre) tract in Bolivia. A U.S. conservation organization arranged a debt-for-nature swap to help protect this land from destructive development.

How Farmers and Loud Monkeys Saved a Forest

It's early morning in a tropical forest in the Central American country of Belize. Suddenly, loud roars that trail off into wheezing moans—territorial calls of black howler monkeys—wake up everyone in or near the wildlife sanctuary by the Belize River. Vegetarians, these monkeys travel slowly among the treetops.

This species is the centerpiece of an experiment integrating ecology and economics by allowing local villagers to make money by helping sustain the forest and its wildlife. The project is the brainchild of American Robert Horwich. In 1985 he suggested that villagers establish a sanctuary that would benefit the local black howlers and the people. He proposed that the farmers leave thin strips of forest along the edges of their fields to provide food for the howlers, who feed on leaves, flowers, and fruits as they travel among the treetops.

To date, more than 100 farmers have done this, and the 47-square-kilometer (18-square-mile) sanctuary is now home for an estimated 1,100 black howlers. The idea has spread to seven other villages.

Now as many as 6,000 ecotourists visit the sanctuary each year to catch glimpses of its loudmouth monkeys and other wildlife. Villagers serve as tour guides, cook meals for the visitors, and lodge tourists overnight in their spare rooms.

than it was being replenished. The UN Food and Agriculture Organization projects a fuelwood crisis by the end of this century for 2.7 billion people in 77 LDCs.

Besides deforestation and accelerated soil erosion, fuelwood scarcity has other harmful effects. It places an additional burden on the poor, especially women, who must often walk long distances to gather fuel. Buying fuelwood or charcoal can take 40% of a poor family's meager income. And poor families who can't get enough fuelwood often burn dried animal dung and crop residues for cooking and heating. As a result, these natural fertilizers never reach the soil, cropland productivity is reduced, the land is degraded even more, and hunger and malnutrition increase.

LDCs can reduce the severity of the fuelwood crisis by planting more fast-growing fuelwood trees such as leucaenas and acacias, burning wood more efficiently, and switching to other fuels. Experience has

shown that planting projects are most successful when local people, especially women, are involved in their planning and implementation. Programs work best when village farmers own the land or are given ownership of any trees they grow on village land. This gives them a strong incentive to plant and protect trees for their own use and for sale.

5-5 Managing and Sustaining Rangelands

THE WORLD'S RANGELAND RESOURCES Almost half of Earth's ice-free land is **rangeland**: land that supplies forage or vegetation (grasses, grasslike plants, and shrubs) for grazing (grass-eating) and browsing (shrub-eating) animals and that is not intensively managed. Most rangelands are grasslands in areas too dry for unirrigated crops (Figure 2-27).

About 42% of the world's rangeland is used for grazing livestock. Much of the rest is too dry, cold, or remote from population centers to be grazed by large numbers of livestock animals. About 34% of the total land area of the United States is rangeland, most of it grasslands in the arid and semiarid western half of the country (Figure 2-27).

RANGELAND VEGETATION AND LIVESTOCK Most rangeland grasses have deep, complex root systems that not only anchor the plants but also sustain them through several seasons. If the leaf tip of most plants is eaten, the leaf stops growing, but the blades of rangeland grass grow from the base, not the tip. When the upper half of the shoot and blade of grass is eaten, the plant can grow back quickly. As long as only its upper half is eaten, and its lower half, or *metabolic reserve*, remains, rangeland grass is a renewable resource that can be grazed again and again. Range plants do vary in their ability to recover, however, and grazing changes the balance of plant species in grassland communities.

In addition to vast numbers of wild herbivores, the world has about 10 billion domesticated animals. About 3 billion of these are *ruminants*, mostly cattle (1.5 billion), sheep, and goats, that can digest the cellulose in grasses. Three-fourths of these forage on rangeland vegetation before being slaughtered for meat, while the rest are fattened on grain in densely populated feedlots before slaughter. Seven billion pigs, chickens, and other livestock are *nonruminants*. They cannot feed on rangeland vegetation and eat mostly cereal grains grown on cropland.

Q: Does using nuclear power add carbon dioxide to the atmosphere?

Each type of grassland has a ruminant **carrying capacity**: the maximum number of ruminants that can graze a given area without destroying the metabolic reserve needed for grass renewal. Carrying capacity is influenced by season, range conditions, climatic conditions, past grazing use, soil type, kinds of grazing animals, and amount of grazing.

Overgrazing occurs when too many animals graze too long and exceed the carrying capacity of a grassland area. It lowers the productivity of vegetation and changes the number and types of plants in an area. Large populations of wild ruminants can overgraze rangeland in prolonged dry periods, but most overgrazing is caused by excessive numbers of domestic livestock feeding too long in a particular area.

Heavy overgrazing compacts the soil, which diminishes its capacity to hold water and to regenerate itself, converts continuous grass cover into patches of grass, and thus exposes the soil to erosion, especially by wind. Overgrazing is the major cause of desertification in arid and semiarid lands (Spotlight, p. 148).

Range condition is usually classified as excellent (more than 80% of its potential forage production), good (50–80%), fair (21–49%), and poor (less than 21%). In 1990, 50% of public rangeland in the United States was rated as being in unsatisfactory (fair or poor) condition, compared with 84% in 1936. This is a considerable improvement, but there's still a long way to go.

Environmentalists point out, however, that overall estimates of rangeland condition obscure severe damage to certain heavily grazed areas, especially vital *riparian zones*. These thin strips of lush vegetation along streams help prevent floods and help keep streams from drying out during droughts by storing and releasing water slowly from spring runoff and summer storms. They also provide habitats, food, water, and shade for wildlife, acting as centers of biodiversity in the arid and semiarid western lands. Because cattle need lots of water, they will (if allowed) concentrate around riparian zones and feed there until the grass and shrubs are gone. The result: Riparian vegetation is destroyed by trampling and by overgrazing. A 1988 General Accounting Office Report concluded that "poorly managed livestock grazing is the major cause of degraded riparian habitat on federal rangelands."

MANAGING RANGELANDS The primary goal of rangeland management is to maximize livestock productivity without overgrazing rangeland vegetation. The most widely used method to prevent overgrazing is to control the *stocking rate*—the number of a particular kind of animal placed on a given area—so it doesn't exceed carrying capacity. Determining the carrying capacity of a range site is difficult and costly.

And that capacity changes because of drought, invasions by new species, and other environmental factors.

Not only the numbers, but the distribution of grazing animals over a rangeland must be controlled to prevent overgrazing. Ranchers can control distribution by fencing off damaged rangeland, rotating livestock from one grazing area to another, providing supplemental feeding at selected sites, and locating water holes and salt blocks in strategic places.

A more expensive and less widely used method of rangeland management is to suppress the growth of unwanted plants by herbicide spraying, mechanical removal, or controlled burning. A cheaper and more effective way to remove unwanted vegetation is controlled, short-term trampling by large numbers of livestock.

Growth of desirable vegetation can be increased by seeding and applying fertilizer, but this method usually costs too much. Reseeding is an excellent way to restore severely degraded rangeland, however.

Another aspect of range management for livestock is predator control. For decades hundreds of thousands of predators have been shot, trapped, and poisoned in the United States by ranchers, farmers, and federal predator control officials. Federally subsidized predator control programs reduced gray wolf and grizzly bear populations to the point where they are endangered species. Now more federal dollars are being spent by the U.S. Fish and Wildlife Service to protect and help revive them. Experience has shown that killing predators is an expensive and short-lived solution—and one that can even make matters worse.

CONTROVERSY OVER LIVESTOCK AND U.S. PUBLIC RANGELAND Some 30,000 U.S. ranchers hold what are essentially lifetime permits to graze about 4 million livestock (3 million of them cattle) on Bureau of Land Management (BLM) and National Forest Service rangelands in 16 western states. About 10% of these permits are held by small livestock operators. The other 90% belong to ranchers with large livestock operations and to corporations such as Union Oil, Getty Oil, and the Vail Ski Corporation.

Permit holders pay the federal government a grazing fee for this privilege. Since 1981 grazing fees on public rangeland have been set by Congress at only one-fourth to one-eighth the going rate for leasing comparable private land. This means that taxpayers give the 2% of U.S. ranchers with federal grazing permits subsidies amounting to about $50 million a year—the difference between the fees collected and the actual value of the grazing on this land.

The economic value of a permit is included in the overall worth of the ranches, can be used as collateral for a loan, and is usually automatically renewed every 10 years—allowing permit holders in effect to treat

Spreading Desertification

Desertification is a process whereby the productive potential of arid or semiarid land falls by 10% or more, and this drop is caused mostly by human activities. *Moderate desertification* is a 10–25% drop in productivity, and *severe desertification* is a 25–50% drop. *Very severe desertification* is a drop of 50% or more, usually creating huge gullies and sand dunes.

Desertification is a serious and growing problem in many parts of the world (Figure 5-9). The regions most affected by desertification are all cattle-producing areas. Although overgrazing by livestock is the major cause of desertification, other causes are deforestation without reforestation; surface mining without land reclamation; irrigation techniques that lead to increased erosion, salt buildup, and water-logged soil; farming on land with unsuitable terrain or soils; and soil compaction by farm machinery, cattle hoofs, and the impact of raindrops on denuded soil surfaces.

These destructive practices are linked to rapid population growth,

high human and livestock densities, poverty, and poor land management. The consequences of desertification include worsening drought, famine, declining living standards, and swelling numbers of environmental refugees whose land is too eroded to grow crops or feed livestock.

Moderate desertification can go unrecognized. For example, overgrazing has reduced the productivity of much of the grassland in the western United States. Yet most of the residents do not realize they live in a moderately desertified area.

It is estimated that 810 million hectares (2 billion acres)—an area the size of Brazil and 12 times the size of Texas—have become desertified during the past 50 years. The UN Environment Programme estimates that worldwide 33 million square kilometers (13 million square miles)—about the size of North and South America combined—are threatened by desertification. If present trends continue, desertification could threaten the livelihoods of 1.2 billion people by 2000.

Every year an estimated 60,000 square kilometers (23,000 square miles—an area the size of West Virginia) of new desert are formed, and another 210,000 square kilometers (81,000 square miles—an area the size of Kansas) lose so much soil and fertility that they are no longer worth farming or grazing.

The most effective way to slow the march of desertification is to drastically reduce overgrazing, deforestation, and the destructive forms of planting, irrigation, and mining that are to blame. In addition, reforestation programs will anchor soil and help retain water in the soil while providing fuelwood, slowing desertification, and reducing the threat of global warming.

The total cost of such prevention and rehabilitation would be about $141 billion, only 3.5 times the estimated $46 billion annual loss in agricultural productivity from desertified land. Thus, once this potential productivity is restored, the cost of the program could be recouped in 3–4 years. So far, however, only about one-tenth of the needed money had been provided.

---

federal land as part of their ranches. It's not surprising that politically influential permit holders have fought so hard to block any change in this system.

The public subsidy does not end with low grazing fees, however. When fencing, water pipelines, stock ponds, weed control, livestock predator control, planting of grass for livestock, erosion, lowered recreational values, loss of biodiversity, and other costs are factored in, it's estimated that taxpayers are providing 30,000 ranchers with an annual subsidy of about $2 billion—an average of $67,000 per rancher—to produce only 3% of the country's beef. This explains why many critics charge that the public-lands grazing programs are little more than "cowboy welfare," mostly for well-to-do ranchers.

Some environmentalists believe that all commercial grazing of livestock on public lands should be phased out over 10–15 years. They also contend that the water-poor western range is not a very good place

to raise livestock (cattle and sheep), which require a lot of water. Forage is produced at a slow rate, droughts are frequent, and animals can be grazed only part of the year.

Ranchers counter that meat produced on rangeland that is not otherwise usable for food production represents a net increase in available food. They point out that when livestock are fattened on corn and other grains, this uses land that could be producing more grains for direct human consumption. Some range scientists point out that while cattle have played a significant role in degrading western rangeland, other factors such as farming and deliberate burning are also involved.

SOLUTIONS: SUSTAINABLE MANAGEMENT OF PUBLIC RANGELAND Some environmentalists agree that with proper management ranching on western rangeland is a potentially sustainable operation.

Q: Nuclear weapons existing today could kill everyone in the world how many times?

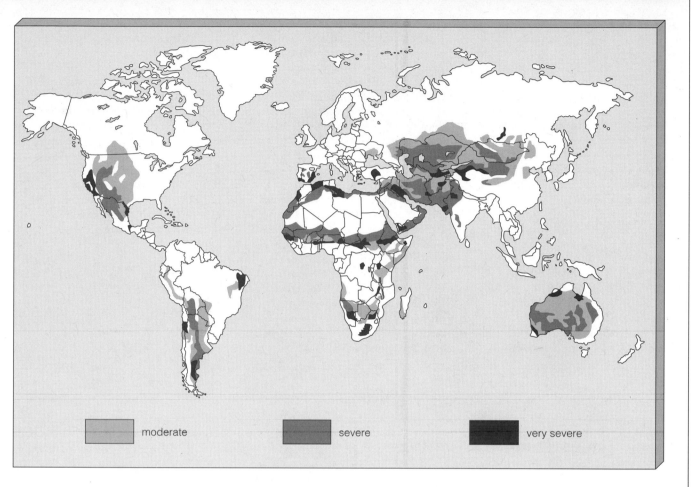

Figure 5-9 Desertification of arid and semiarid lands. (Data from UN Environment Programme and Harold E. Dregnue)

They believe that encouraging such ranching keeps much of the land from being broken up and converted to developments. To achieve this they call for curbing overgrazing on western public rangeland by:

- *Greatly reducing the number of livestock grazing on these lands.*

- *Excluding livestock grazing from riparian areas.*

- *Banning livestock grazing on poor-condition rangeland until it recovers.*

- *Greatly increasing funds for restoration of degraded rangeland.*

- *Sharply raising grazing fees to a fair market value.* In 1993 the Secretary of the Interior proposed more than doubling of grazing fees, making them about one-half the cost of grazing on private land.

- *Giving family ranchers with small ranches grazing-fee discounts.* This would help them stay in business

and keep their ranches from being converted to real estate developments. Ranchers with large operations who artificially divide their holdings to qualify would not get discounts.

- *Replacing the current noncompetitive grazing permit system with a competitive bidding system.* The current system gives ranchers with essentially lifetime permits an unfair economic advantage over ranchers who can't get such government subsidies. Competitive bidding would let free enterprise work and allow conservation and wildlife groups to obtain grazing permits and protect such lands from overgrazing.

The problem is that so far western ranchers have had enough political power to block most changes they don't like in grazing policies. A few ranchers, however, have demonstrated that rangeland can be grazed sustainably (Individuals Matter, next page).

Wyoming rancher Jack Turnell is a new breed of cowboy who gets along with environmentalists and talks about riparian ecology and biodiversity as fluently as he talks about cattle. According to Jack, "I guess I have learned how to bridge the gap between the environmentalists, the bureaucracies, and the ranching industry."

He grazes cattle on his 32,000-hectare (80,000-acre) ranch south of Cody, Wyoming, and on 16,000 hectares (40,000 acres) of Forest Service land where he has grazing rights. For the first decade after he took over the ranch he punched cows the conventional way.

This rancher disagrees with the proposals by environmentalists to raise grazing fees and even remove sheep and cattle from public rangeland. He believes that if ranchers are forced off the public range, ranches like his will be sold to developers and chopped up into vacation sites, irreversibly destroying the range for wildlife and livestock.

At the same time, he believes that ranches can be operated in more ecologically sustainable ways. To demonstrate this he began systematically rotating his cows away from the riparian areas, gave up most use of fertilizers and pesticides, and crossed his Hereford and Angus cows with a French breed that does not like to congregate around water. Most of his ranching decisions are made in consultation with range and wildlife scientists.

The results have been impressive. Riparian areas on the ranch and Forest Service land are lined with willow and other plant life, providing lush habitat for an expanding population of wildlife including antelope, deer, moose, elk, bear, and mountain lions. And Jack makes more money because the better quality grass puts more meat on his cattle. He frequently talks to cattle groups about sustainable range management; some of them think he has been chewing locoweed.

5-6 Managing and Sustaining National Parks

PARKS AROUND THE WORLD Today there are over 1,100 national parks of more than 1,000 hectares (2,500 acres) in more than 120 countries. Together they cover an area equal to that of Alaska, Texas, and California combined. This important achievement in the global conservation movement was spurred by the creation of the first public national park system in the United States in 1912.

The U.S. National Park System is dominated by 50 national parks, most of them in the West (Figure 5-5). These repositories of majestic beauty and biodiversity have been called America's crown jewels. They are supplemented by state, county, and city parks. Most state parks are located near urban areas and thus are used more heavily than national parks. Nature walks, guided tours, and other educational services by U.S. Park Service employees have given many visitors a better appreciation for and understanding of nature.

STRESSES ON PARKS Parks everywhere are under siege. In LDCs parks are often invaded by local people who desperately need wood, cropland, and other resources. Poachers kill animals to get and sell rhino horns, elephant tusks, and furs and capture valuable species for sale illegally. Park services in these countries have too little money and staff to fight these invasions, either by force or by education. Also, most of the world's national parks are too small to sustain many of their larger animal species.

Success is the biggest problem of national and state parks in the United States (and other MDCs). Annual recreational visits to National Park System units have increased more than twelvefold (and visits to state parks sevenfold) since 1950. The recreational use of state and national parks and other public lands is expected to double again between 1990 and 2020.

During the peak summer season, the most popular national and state parks are often choked with cars and trailers, and they are plagued by noise, traffic jams, litter, vandalism, poaching, deteriorating trails, polluted water, and crime. Many visitors to heavily used parks leave the city to commune with nature only to find the parks more congested, noisy, and stressful than where they came from.

Park Service rangers now spend an increasing amount of their time on law enforcement instead of on

Q: Can switching to increased use of nuclear power in the United States save much oil?

Who's Afraid of the Big Gray Wolf?

SPOTLIGHT

At one time the gray wolf ranged over most of North America. Between 1850 and 1900, 2 million wolves were shot, trapped, poisoned, and even drenched with gasoline and set afire by ranchers, hunters, and government employees. The idea was to make the West and the Great Plains safe for livestock and for big-game animals prized by hunters.

By the 1960s the gray wolf was found mostly in Alaska and Canada, with a few hundred left in Minnesota and about 50 in Montana as well. The species is now listed as endangered in all 48 lower states except Minnesota (which has 1,550–1,750 wolves), where it is listed as threatened.

Ecologists now recognize the important role these predators once played in parts of the West and the Great Plains. They culled herds of bison, elk, and mule deer, which without predators can proliferate and devastate vegetation and threaten the niches of other forms of wildlife. They killed only for food, usually taking weaker animals and thereby strengthening the genetic pool of the survivors.

In 1987 the U.S. Fish and Wildlife Service proposed that wolves be reintroduced to the Yellowstone ecosystem, which includes two national parks, seven national forests, and other federal and state land in Wyoming, Idaho, and Montana. The plan calls for introducing 10 breeding packs, each containing about 100 wolves, in three recovery areas.

The proposal to reestablish these ecological connections we eliminated brought outraged howls from ranchers who feared the wolves would attack their cattle and sheep and from hunters who were alarmed that the wolves would kill their prized big-game animals. An enraged rancher said that the idea was "like reintroducing smallpox."

An economic study estimated that restoring wolves to the Yellowstone ecosystem would bring $18 million into the local economy during the first year and about $100 million over 20 years. And Park Service officials said that they would trap or shoot any wolves roaming outside the park to feast on livestock and that ranchers would be reimbursed for lost stock from a private $100,000 fund established by Defenders of Wildlife. However, these promises fell on deaf ears, and ranchers and hunters hope to delay or defeat the plan in Congress.

The wolves may have a better chance to survive if enough of them migrate to the Yellowstone ecosystem on their own. Then, as an endangered species, they will be fully protected, at least legally. By contrast, if they are relocated to the Yellowstone ecosystem, they will be treated as an "experimental" population; then if they venture outside recovery areas, they can be killed by ranchers and hunters. Some ranchers and hunters say that, either way, they'll take care of the wolves quietly—what they call the "shoot, shovel, and shut up" solution. In 1993 a single gray wolf found in the Yellowstone ecosystem, just outside the southern boundary of Yellowstone National Park, was shot and killed. Do you think the gray wolf should be reintroduced to the Yellowstone area?

resource conservation and management; many even wear body armor. Since 1976 the number of federal park rangers—about 3,200—has not changed, while the number of visitors to park units has risen by 75 million and is expected to rise by another 162 million in the next 20 years.

Wolves (Spotlight, above), bears, and other large predators in and near various parks have all but vanished because of excessive hunting, poisoning by ranchers and federal officials, and the limited size of most parks. As a result, populations of species they once controlled have exploded, destroying vegetation and crowding out other species.

Alien species are moving into parks. Wild boars (imported to North Carolina in 1912 for hunting) are threatening vegetation in part of the Great Smoky Mountains National Park. The Brazilian pepper tree has invaded Florida's Everglades National Park.

Mountain goats in Washington's Olympic National Park trample native vegetation and accelerate erosion.

The greatest danger to many parks today, however, is from nearby human activities. Wildlife and recreational values are threatened by mining, logging, grazing, coal-burning power plants, water diversion, and urban development. Polluted air drifts hundreds of kilometers to kill trees in California's Sequoia National Park and blur the awesome vistas at Arizona's Grand Canyon. According to the National Park Service, air pollution affects scenic park views more than 90% of the time.

But that's not all. Mountains of trash wash ashore daily at Padre Island National Seashore in Texas. Water use in Las Vegas threatens to shut down geysers in the Death Valley National Monument. And unless a massive ecological restoration project works, Florida's Everglades National Park may dry up.

In a rugged mountainous region with a tropical rain forest lies a centerpiece of Costa Rica's efforts to preserve its biodiversity—the Guanacaste National Park, which has been designated an international biosphere reserve. In the park's lowlands a small, tropical seasonal forest is being restored and relinked to the rain forest on adjacent mountain slopes.

Daniel Janzen, professor of biology at the University of Pennsylvania, has helped galvanize international support and raised more than $10 million for this restoration project—the world's largest. Janzen is a leader in the growing field of rehabilitation and restoration of degraded ecosystems.

Janzen's vision is to make the nearly 40,000 people who live near the park an essential part of the restoration of the degraded forest—a concept he calls *biocultural restoration*. By actively participating in the project, local residents will reap enormous educational, economic, and environmental benefits. Local farmers have been hired to plant large areas with tree seeds and with seedlings started in Janzen's lab.

Students in grade schools, high schools, and universities study the ecology of the park in the classroom and go on annual field trips to the park itself. There are educational programs for civic groups and tourists from Costa Rica and elsewhere. These visitors and activities will stimulate the local economy. The project will also serve as a training ground in tropical forest restoration for scientists from all over the world.

Janzen recognizes that in 20 to 40 years today's children will be running the park and the local political system. If they understand the importance of their local environment, they are more likely to protect and sustain its biological resources. He understands that education, awareness, and involvement—not guards and fences—are the best ways to protect ecosystems from unsustainable use.

BETTER PARK MANAGEMENT Some park managers, especially in LDCs, are developing integrated management plans that combine conservation practices with sustainable development of the park and surrounding areas (Figure 5-8). In such a plan the inner core and especially vulnerable areas of the park are protected from development and treated as wilderness. Controlled numbers of people are allowed to use these areas only for hiking, nature study, ecological research, and other nondestructive recreational and educational activities.

In other buffer areas surrounding the core, controlled commercial logging, sustainable grazing by livestock, and sustainable hunting and fishing by local people are allowed. Money spent by park visitors adds to local income. By involving local people in developing park management plans, managers help them see the park as a vital resource they need to protect and sustain rather than ruin (Individuals Matter, above).

While integrated park management plans look good on paper, they cannot be carried out without adequate funding and the support of nearby landowners and users. Moreover, the protected inner core may be too small to sustain some of the park's larger animal species.

In the United States national parks are managed under the principle of natural regulation—as if they are wilderness ecosystems that, if left alone, will sustain themselves. Many ecologists consider this a misguided policy. Most parks are far too small to even come close to sustaining themselves, and even the biggest ones cannot be isolated from the harmful effects caused by human activities in nearby areas.

SOLUTIONS: AN AGENDA FOR U.S. NATIONAL PARKS The National Park Service has two goals that increasingly conflict: **(1)** to preserve nature in parks, and **(2)** to make nature more available to the public. The Park Service must accomplish these goals with a small budget at a time when park usage and external threats to the parks are increasing.

In 1988 the Wilderness Society and the National Parks and Conservation Association suggested a blueprint for the future of the U.S. National Park System:

- *Educate the public about the urgent need to protect, mend, and expand the system.*
- *Significantly increase the number and pay of park rangers.*
- *Acquire new parkland near threatened areas and add at least 75 new parks within the next decade.*
- *Locate most commercial park facilities (such as restaurants, hotels, and shops) outside park boundaries.*

Q: What would happen if nuclear power's harmful effects were included in its market price and government subsidies were removed?

- *Raise the fees charged to private concessionaires who operate lodging, food, and recreation services inside national parks to at least 22% of their gross receipts.* The present maximum return for taxpayers is only 5%, and the average is only 2.5% of the $1.5 billion they take in annually. Many large concessionaires have long-term contracts by which they pay the government as little as 0.75% of their gross receipts.

- *Halt concessionaire ownership of facilities in national parks, which makes buying buildings back very expensive.*

- *Wherever feasible, place visitor parking areas outside the park areas.* Use low-polluting vehicles to transport visitors to and from parking areas and within the park.

- *Greatly expand the Park Service budget for maintenance and for science and conservation programs.* The national parks face a $2-billion backlog of repairs.

- *Require the Park Service, Forest Service, and Bureau of Land Management to develop integrated management plans so activities in nearby national forests and rangelands don't degrade national parklands and wilderness areas within the parks.*

 ## 5-7 Protecting and Managing Wilderness and Marine Biodiversity

HOW MUCH SHOULD BE PROTECTED? Most wildlife biologists believe that the best way to preserve biodiversity is through a worldwide network of reserves, parks, wildlife sanctuaries, and other protected areas. According to Aldo Leopold, "a species must be saved *in many places* if it is to be saved at all."

By 1993 there were about 7,000 nature reserves, parks, and other protected areas throughout the world—occupying 4.9% of Earth's land surface. That is an important beginning, but environmentalists say that a minimum of 10% of the globe's land area is needed. Moreover, many existing reserves are too small to protect their populations of wild species and receive little actual protection.

In 1981 UNESCO proposed that at least one, and ideally five or more, *biosphere reserves* be set up in each of Earth's 193 biogeographical zones. Each reserve should be large enough to prevent gradual species loss and should be designed to combine both conservation and sustainable use of natural resources. To date more than 300 biosphere reserves have been established in 76 countries.

A well-designed biosphere reserve has three zones: **(1)** a *core area* containing an important ecosystem that has had little, if any, disturbance from human activities; **(2)** a *buffer zone*, where activities and uses are managed in ways that help protect the core; and **(3)** a second *buffer* or *transition zone*, which combines conservation and sustainable forestry, grazing, agriculture, and recreation. Buffer zones can also be used for education and research.

An international fund to help LDCs protect and manage bioregions and biosphere reserves would cost $100 million per year—about what the world spends on arms every 90 minutes. Since there won't be enough money to protect much of the world's biodiversity, environmentalists believe that efforts should be focused on the megadiversity countries (Figure 5-10). In the United States, environmentalists urge Congress to pass an Endangered Ecosystems or Biodiversity Protection Act as an important step toward preserving the country's biodiversity.

WHY PRESERVE WILDERNESS? Protecting undeveloped lands from exploitation is an important way to preserve ecological diversity. According to the U.S. Wilderness Act of 1964, **wilderness** consists of those areas "where the earth and its community of life are untrammeled by man, where man himself is a visitor who does not remain."

The Wilderness Society estimates that a wilderness area should contain at least 400,000 hectares (1 million acres). Otherwise, it can be affected by air, water, and noise pollution from nearby mining, oil and natural gas drilling, timber cutting, industry, and urban development. Environmentalists urge that remaining wilderness be protected by law everywhere, focusing first on the most endangered spots in wilderness- and species-rich countries (Figure 5-10).

We need wild places where we can experience the beauty of nature and observe natural biological diversity. We need places where we can enhance our mental and physical health by getting away from noise, stress, and large numbers of people. Wilderness preservationist John Muir advised:

Climb the mountains and get their good tidings. Nature's peace will flow into you as the sunshine into the trees. The winds will blow their freshness into you, and the storms their energy, while cares will drop off like autumn leaves.

Even those who never use the wilderness may want to know it is there, a feeling expressed by novelist Wallace Stegner:

Save a piece of country…and it does not matter in the slightest that only a few people every year will go into it. This is precisely its value…we simply need that

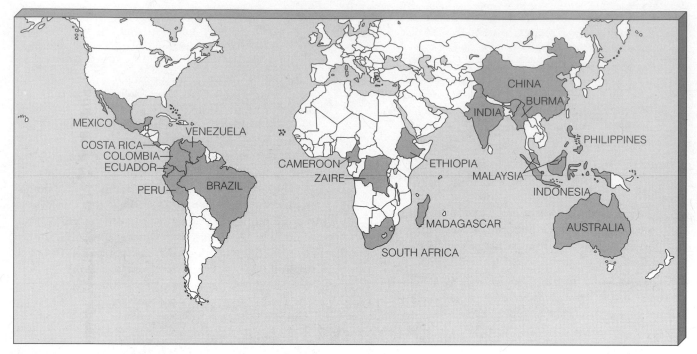

Figure 5-10 Earth's megadiversity countries. Environmentalists believe that efforts should be concentrated on preserving repositories of biodiversity in these countries. (Data from Conservation International and the World Wildlife Fund)

wild country available to us, even if we never do more than drive to its edge and look in. For it can be a means of reassuring ourselves of our sanity as creatures, a part of the geography of hope.

Wilderness areas provide recreation for growing numbers of people. Wilderness also has important ecological values. It provides undisturbed habitats for wild plants and animals, protects diverse biomes from damage, and provides a laboratory in which we can discover more about how nature works. It is a biodiversity bank and eco-insurance policy. In the words of Henry David Thoreau: "In wildness is the preservation of the world."

U.S. WILDERNESS PRESERVATION SYSTEM In the United States preservationists have been trying to keep wild areas from being developed since 1900. On the whole they have fought a losing battle. Not until 1964 did Congress pass the Wilderness Act. It allows the government to protect undeveloped tracts of public land from development as part of the National Wilderness Preservation System (Spotlight, p. 138).

Only 4% of U.S. land area is protected as wilderness, with almost three-fourths of it in Alaska. Only 1.8% of the land area of the lower 48 states is protected, most of it in the West. Of the 413 wilderness areas in the lower 48 states, only 4 are larger than 400,000 hectares. Furthermore, the present wilderness preser-

vation system includes only 81 of the country's 233 distinct ecosystems. Like the national parks, most wilderness areas in the lower 48 states are habitat islands in a sea of development.

There remain almost 40 million hectares (100 million acres) of public lands that could qualify for designation as wilderness. Environmentalists want all of this land protected as wilderness, and a vigorous effort mounted to rehabilitate other lands to enlarge existing wilderness areas. Such efforts are strongly opposed by timber, mining, ranching, energy, and other interests who want to be able to remove resources from these lands.

Wilderness recovery areas could be created by closing roads in large areas of public lands, restoring habitats, allowing natural fires to burn, and reintroducing species that have been driven from such areas. However, resource developers lobby elected officials and government agencies to build roads in national forests (and other areas being evaluated for inclusion in the wilderness system) so that they can't be designated as wilderness, and they strongly oppose the idea of wilderness recovery areas.

SOLUTIONS: WILDERNESS MANAGEMENT To protect the most popular areas from damage, wilderness managers must designate areas where camping is allowed and limit the number of people hiking or camping at any one time. Managers have increased the number of wilderness rangers to patrol vulnerable areas, and they have enlisted volunteers to pick up trash discarded by thoughtless users.

Historian and wilderness expert Roderick Nash suggests that wilderness areas be divided into three categories. The easily accessible, popular areas would be intensively managed and have trails, bridges, hikers' huts, outhouses, assigned campsites, and extensive ranger patrols. Large, remote wilderness areas would be used only by people who get a permit by demonstrating their wilderness skills. The third category—biologically unique areas—would be left undisturbed as gene pools of plant and animal species, with no human entry allowed.

PROTECTING MARINE BIODIVERSITY It is difficult to protect marine biodiversity. For one thing, shore-hugging species are adversely affected by coastal development and the accompanying massive inputs of sediment and other wastes from land. This poses a severe threat to biologically diverse and highly productive coastal ecosystems such as coral reefs, marshes, and mangrove swamps (Figure 2-32).

Protecting marine biodiversity is also difficult because much of the damage is not visible to people. In addition, the seas are viewed by many as an inexhaustible source of resources and capable of absorbing an almost infinite amount of waste and pollution. Finally, most of the world's ocean area lies outside the legal jurisdiction of countries and thus is an open-access resource subject to overexploitation because of the tragedy of the commons (Connections, p. 11).

Protecting marine biodiversity requires enacting and enforcing tough regulations to protect coral reefs, mangrove swamps, and other coastal ecosystems from unsustainable use and abuse. Also, much more effective international agreements are needed to protect biodiversity in the open seas.

Sustaining existing land and aquatic ecosystems and rehabilitating damaged ones are important tasks. This will cost a great deal of money but the long-term costs of not doing these things will be much higher.

We abuse land because we regard it as a commodity belonging to us. When we see land as a community to which we belong, we may begin to use it with love and respect.

ALDO LEOPOLD

CRITICAL THINKING

1. Should private companies cutting timber from national forests continue to be subsidized by federal payments for reforestation and for building and maintaining access roads? Explain.

2. Should all cutting on remaining old-growth forests in U.S. national forestlands be banned? Explain.

3. Explain why you agree or disagree with each of the proposals listed in Section 5-3 for reforming federal forest management in the United States.

4. What difference could the loss of essentially all the remaining virgin tropical forests and old-growth forests in North America have on your life and on the lives of your descendants?

5. Explain why you agree or disagree with each of the proposals listed in Section 5-4 concerning protection of the world's tropical forests.

6. In the name of progress, the policies of various governments are virtually eliminating the cultures of remaining hunter-gatherers and other indigenous peoples by taking over their lands. Some believe that these people should be given title to the land and minerals they and their ancestors have lived on for centuries; that they should be given a decisive voice in formulating policies about resource management in their areas; and that they should have the right to be left alone by modern civilization. We have created protected reserves for endangered wild species, so why not create reserves for these endangered human cultures? What do you think? Explain.

7. Should cattle be banned from grazing on public rangeland in the western United States? Explain.

8. Should trail bikes, dune buggies, and other ORVs be banned from public rangeland to reduce damage to vegetation and soil? Explain. Should such a ban also include national forests, national wildlife refuges, and national parks? Explain.

9. Explain why you agree or disagree with each of the proposals listed on pages 152–153 concerning the U.S. National Park System.

10. Should more wilderness areas be preserved in the United States, especially in the lower 48 states? Explain.

A: No. If everything goes right, it is not expected to become a significant producer of electricity until 2100, if then

Biodiversity: Sustaining Species

6-1 Why Preserve Wild Species?

Millions of species have vanished over Earth's long history, so why should we worry about losing a few more? Does it matter that the passenger pigeon (Case Study, p. 158), the great auk, or some unknown plant or insect in a tropical forest has become extinct mostly because of us (Figure 6-1)? Does it matter that the existence of the California condor (7 in the wild), whooping crane (142 in the wild), and hundreds of other species is threatened because of our activities? The answer is yes. There are many reasons for protecting species—each a unique and irreplaceable product of millions of years of evolution—from premature extinction.

- *Economic importance.* About 10% of the U.S. gross national product comes directly from use of wild species. Some 90% of today's food crops were domesticated from wild tropical plants. Agricultural scientists and genetic engineers will need to use existing wild plant species, most of them still unknown, to develop new crop strains, and some may become important sources of food. Wild plants and plants domesticated from wild species supply rubber, oils, dyes, fiber, paper, lumber, and other useful products. Nitrogen-fixing

microbes in the soil and root nodules supply nitrogen to grow food crops worth almost $50 billion per year worldwide ($7 billion in the U.S.). Pollination by birds and insects is essential to many food crops, including 40 U.S. crops valued at approximately $30 billion per year.

- *Medical importance.* About 75% of the world's population relies on plants or plant extracts for medicines. Prescription and nonprescription drugs worth $40 billion per year—roughly half of the medicines used in the world, and 25% of those used in the United States—have active ingredients extracted from wild species. Many animal species are used to test drugs, vaccines, chemical toxicity, and surgical procedures, and in studies of human health and disease. Under intense pressure from animal rights groups, scientists are trying to find testing methods that minimize animal suffering or, better yet, do not use animals at all. However, they warn that alternative techniques cannot replace all animal research.

- *Aesthetic and recreational importance.* Wild plants and animals are a source of beauty, wonder, joy, and recreational pleasure for many people. Wildlife tourism, sometimes called *ecotourism*, generates as much as $12 billion in revenues each year. A wildlife economist has estimated that in Kenya one male lion living to age 7 generates

Passenger pigeon

Great auk

Dodo

Bushy seaside sparrow

Aepyornis (Madagascar)

Figure 6-1 Some species that have become extinct largely because of human activities, mostly habitat loss and overhunting.

Q: What are our best energy options?

$515,000 in tourist dollars. By contrast, if killed for its skin, the lion would bring only about $1,000. Similarly, over a lifetime of 60 years a Kenyan elephant is worth close to $1 million in tourist revenue. However, care must be taken to ensure that ecotourists do not damage or disturb wildlife and ecosystems and disrupt local cultures.

- *Scientific importance.* Each species has scientific value because it can help scientists understand how life has evolved and will continue to evolve on this planet.

- *Ecological importance.* Wild species supply us and other species with food from the soil and the sea, recycle nutrients essential to agriculture, and help maintain soil fertility. They also produce oxygen and other gases in the atmosphere, moderate Earth's climate, help regulate water supplies, and store solar energy. Moreover, they detoxify poisonous substances, break down organic wastes, control potential crop pests and disease carriers, and make up a vast gene pool from which we and other species can draw.

- *Ethics.* To some people each wild species has an inherent right to exist—or to struggle to exist. According to this view, it is wrong for us to hasten the extinction of any species. Some go further and assert that each individual organism—not just each species—has a right to survive without human interference, just as each human being has the right to survive. Some people distinguish between the survival rights of plants and those of animals, mostly for practical reasons. Poet Alan Watts, for example, once said that he was a vegetarian "because cows scream louder than carrots." Other people distinguish among various types of animals. For instance, they think little about killing a fly, mosquito, cockroach, or sewer rat. Unless they are strict vegetarians, they also think little about having others kill domesticated animals in slaughterhouses to provide them with meat, leather, and other products. These same people, however, might deplore the killing of wild animals such as deer, squirrels, or rabbits.

6-2 How Species Become Depleted and Extinct

THE RISE AND FALL OF SPECIES Extinction is a natural process (Section 2-8). As the planet's surface and climate have changed over the 4.6 billion years of its existence, species have disappeared and new ones have evolved to take their places (Figure 2-38).

This rise and fall of species has not been smooth. Evidence indicates that there have been several periods when mass extinctions reduced Earth's biodiversity and other periods, called *radiations*, when the diversity of life has increased and spread because of changes in environmental conditions.

THE CURRENT EXTINCTION CRISIS: FATAL SUBTRACTION Imagine you are driving on an interstate highway at a high speed. You notice that your two passengers are passing the time unscrewing bolts, screws, and other parts of your car at random, and throwing them out the window. How long will it be before they remove enough parts to cause a crash?

This urgent question is one that we as a species should be asking ourselves. As we tinker with the only home for us and other species, we are rapidly removing parts of Earth's natural biodiversity upon which we and other species depend in ways we know little about. We are not heeding Aldo Leopold's warning: "To keep every cog and wheel is the first precaution of intelligent tinkering."

Sooner or later all species become extinct, but humans have become a primary factor in the premature extinction of more and more species as we march relentlessly across the globe (Figure 6-1). Every day at least 10 and perhaps as many as 140 species become extinct because of our activities. The loss rate may soon reach several hundred species per day.

Past mass extinctions took place slowly enough to allow new forms of life to arise as adaptations to an ever-changing world. This process started to change about 40,000 years ago when the latest version of our species came on the scene. Since agriculture began about 10,000 years ago, the extinction rates have

---

A: Improved energy efficiency and greatly increased use of renewable energy (especially solar-produced hydrogen gas) using natural gas to make the transition

The Passenger Pigeon: Gone Forever

In the early 1800s bird expert Alexander Wilson watched a single migrating flock of passenger pigeons darken the sky for over four hours. He estimated that this flock was more than 2 billion birds strong, 386 kilometers (240 miles) long, and 1.6 kilometers (1 mile) wide.

By 1914 the passenger pigeon (Figure 6-1) had disappeared forever. How could the species that was once the most common bird in North America become extinct in only a few decades?

The answer is humans. The main reasons for the extinction of this species were uncontrolled commercial hunting and loss of the bird's habitat and food supply as forests were cleared for farms and cities.

Passenger pigeons were good to eat, their feathers made good pillows, and their bones were widely used for fertilizer. They were easy to kill because they flew in gigantic flocks and nested in long, narrow colonies.

Beginning in 1858 passenger pigeon hunting became a big business. Shotguns, traps, artillery, and even dynamite were used. Birds were suffocated by burning grass or sulfur below their roosts. Live birds were used as targets in shooting galleries. In 1878 one professional pigeon trapper made $60,000 by killing 3 million birds at their nesting grounds near Petoskey, Michigan.

By the early 1880s commercial hunting had ceased because only a few thousand birds were left. At that point recovery of the species was doomed because the females laid only one egg per nest. On March 24, 1900, in Ohio a young boy shot the last known passenger pigeon in the wild. The last passenger pigeon on Earth, a hen named Martha after Martha Washington, died in the Cincinnati Zoo in 1914. Her stuffed body is now on view at the National Museum of Natural History in Washington, D.C.

soared as human settlements have expanded worldwide.

It is hard to document extinctions, since most go unrecorded. Biologists estimate that during 1993 at least 4,000 and as many as 36,000 species became extinct; the figure could reach 50,000 species per year by 2000. These scientists warn that if deforestation (especially of tropical forests), desertification, and destruction of wetlands and coral reefs continue at

their present rates, we could easily lose at least 1 million of Earth's species within the next few decades. This massive bleeding of life from the planet will rival some of the great natural mass extinctions of the past.

There are two important differences between the present mass extinction and those of the past:

- *The present extinction crisis is the first to be caused by a single species—our own.* By using 40% of Earth's terrestrial net primary productivity (Figure 2-21), we are crowding out other terrestrial species. What will happen to wildlife and the services they provide for us if our population doubles in the next 40 years and we use as much as 80% of the planet's terrestrial net primary productivity?

- *The current wildlife holocaust is taking place in only a few decades rather than over thousands to millions of years.* Such rapid extinction cannot be balanced by speciation because it takes 2,000–100,000 generations for new species to evolve.

Some analysts, however, claim that there is no extinction crisis (Spotlight, next page).

ENDANGERED AND THREATENED SPECIES

Species heading toward extinction are classified as either *endangered* or *threatened*. An **endangered species** has so few individual survivors that the species could soon become extinct over all or most of its natural range. Examples are the California condor in the United States (only 7 in the wild), the whooping crane in North America (250 left), the giant panda in central China (1,000 left), the snow leopard in central Asia (2,500 left), the black rhinoceros in Africa (4,000 left), and the rare swallowtail butterfly in Great Britain (Figure 6-2, pp. 160–161).

A **threatened species** is still abundant in its natural range but is declining in numbers and is likely to become endangered. Examples are the bald eagle, the grizzly bear, and the American alligator (Figure 6-2 and Connections, p. 35).

Some species have characteristics that make them more vulnerable than others to premature extinction (Table 6-1). Some species, such as bats, are vulnerable to extinction for a combination of reasons (Connections, p. 163).

Many wild species are not in danger of extinction, but their populations have diminished locally or regionally. Such species may be a better indicator of the condition of entire ecosystems than endangered and threatened species. They can serve as early warnings so that we can prevent species extinction rather than responding to emergencies.

Is There Really an Extinction Crisis?

E. O. Wilson and a number of other prominent biologists have warned that we are involved in a catastrophic loss of species. They expect this situation to get worse as more people consume more resources and destroy or degrade more forests and other ecosystems that are habitats for wildlife.

Some social scientists and a few biologists, however, question the idea that there is an extinction crisis. They point to several problems in estimating species loss. First, we don't know how many species there are, with estimates ranging from 5 million to 100 million. Second, it is difficult to observe species extinction, especially for species we know little, if anything, about. We know that loss and fragmentation of habitat can lead to extinction for some species, especially highly specialized ones often found in increasingly threatened habitats such as tropical forests and coral reefs. However, it is difficult to come up with a numerical relationship between habitat loss and species loss.

The annual loss of tropical forest habitat is estimated at about 1.8% per year. E. O. Wilson and several tropical biologists who have counted species in patches of tropical forest before and after destruction or degradation estimate that this 1.8% loss in habitat results in a roughly 0.5% loss of species. However, biomes vary in the number of species they contain (species diversity) and the ratio of habitat loss to species loss varies in different biomes.

Do such estimates add up to an extinction crisis? Let us assume, as Wilson and many other biologists do, that a loss of 1 million species represents an extinction crisis. If we assume a global decline in species of 0.5% per year, then we will lose 25,000 species per year if there are 5 million species; 100,000 per year if there are 20 million species; and 500,000 per year if there are 100 million species. If these assumptions are correct, then we will lose 1 million species in 40 years if there are 5 million species; in 10 years with 20 million species; and in only 2 years with 100,000 million species.

Let's assume however, that the estimate of 0.5% species loss per year is too large for the earth as a whole. If it is 0.25% per year, we will lose 1 million species in 80 years with 5 million species; in 20 years with 20 million species; and in 4 years with 100 million species. Even if we halve the estimated species loss again to 0.125% per year, we can lose 1 million species in 8 to 160 years, enough to easily qualify the situation as an extinction crisis.

The point biologists are trying to make is not that their estimates are precise. Instead, they argue that there is ample evidence we are destroying and degrading wildlife habitats at an exponentially increasing rate and that this certainly leads to a large loss of species—although the number and rate will vary in different parts of the world.

Table 6-1 Characteristics of Extinction-Prone Species

Characteristic	Examples
Low reproduction rate	Blue whale, polar bear, California condor, Andean condor, passenger pigeon, giant panda, whooping crane
Specialized feeding habits	Everglades kite (eats apple snail of southern Florida), blue whale (krill in polar upwellings), black-footed ferret (prairie dogs and pocket gophers), giant panda (bamboo), koala (certain eucalyptus leaves)
Feed at high trophic levels	Bengal tiger, bald eagle, Andean condor, timber wolf
Large size	Bengal tiger, lion, elephant, Javan rhinoceros, American bison, giant panda, grizzly bear
Limited or specialized nesting or breeding areas	Kirtland's warbler (6- to 15-year-old jack pine trees), whooping crane (marshes), orangutan (only on Sumatra and Borneo), green sea turtle (lays eggs on only a few beaches), bald eagle (prefers forested shorelines), nightingale wren (only on Barro Colorado Island, Panama)
Found in only one place or region	Woodland caribou, elephant seal, Cooke's kokio, many unique island species
Fixed migratory patterns	Blue whale, Kirtland's warbler, Bachman's warbler, whooping crane
Preys on livestock or people	Timber wolf, some crocodiles
Behavioral patterns	Passenger pigeon and white-crowned pigeon (nest in large colonies), redheaded woodpecker (flies in front of cars), Carolina parakeet (when one bird is shot, rest of flock hovers over body), Key deer (forages for cigarette butts along highways—it's a "nicotine addict")

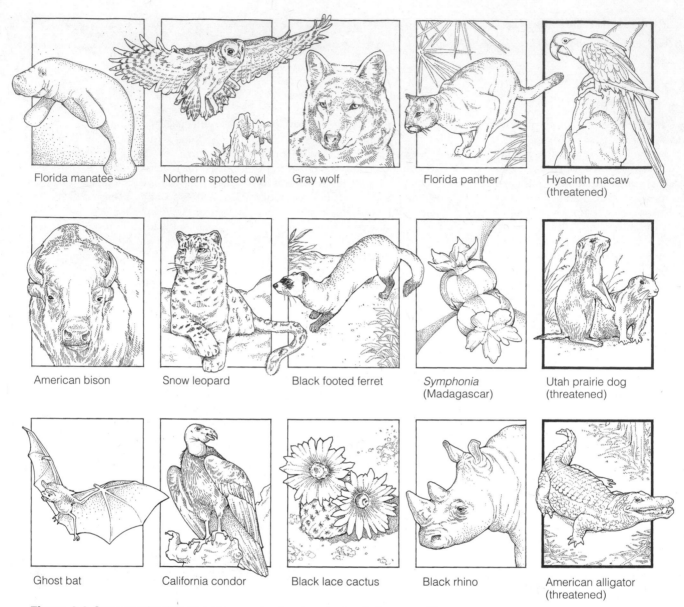

Figure 6-2 Some species that are endangered or threatened primarily because of human activities, mostly habitat loss and overhunting.

Row 1: Florida manatee · Northern spotted owl · Gray wolf · Florida panther · Hyacinth macaw (threatened)

Row 2: American bison · Snow leopard · Black footed ferret · *Symphonia* (Madagascar) · Utah prairie dog (threatened)

Row 3: Ghost bat · California condor · Black lace cactus · Black rhino · American alligator (threatened)

HABITAT LOSS AND FRAGMENTATION The underlying causes of extinction and population reduction of wildlife are human population growth (Figure 1-1) and economic systems and policies that fail to value the environment and its vital ecosystem services—and thus promote unsustainable exploitation. As our population grows, we clear, occupy, and damage more land to supply food, fuelwood, timber, and other resources.

Both affluence and poverty contribute to extinctions. Increasing affluence and economic growth lead to greater average resource use per person, which is a prime factor in taking over wildlife habitats (Figure 1-11). In LDCs the combination of rapid population growth (Figures 1-5 and 3-3) and poverty (Figure 1-6) push the poor to cut forests, grow crops on marginal land, overgraze grasslands, deplete fish species, and kill endangered animals for their valuable furs, tusks, or other parts.

Thus, the greatest threat to most wild species is losing their homes as we increasingly occupy or degrade more of the planet (Figure 6-3). Tropical deforestation (Figure 5-6) is the greatest eliminator of species, followed by destruction of coral reefs and wetlands and plowing of grasslands. In the lower 48 states 98% of the tall-grass prairies have been plowed, half of the wetlands drained, 90–95% of old-growth forests cut (Figure 5-4), and overall forest cover has been reduced by 33%. At least 500 species native to the United States have been driven to extinction, and oth-

Q: How much of all U.S. land consists of public lands?

Grizzly bear (threatened)

Arabian oryx

Bald eagle

Kirtland's warbler

African elephant

Mojave desert tortoise (threatened)

Swallowtail butterfly

Humpback chub

Golden lion tamarin

Siberian tiger

Peregrine falcon (threatened)

Giant panda

Knowlton cactus

Whooping crane

Blue whale

ers to near extinction, mostly because of habitat loss. Furthermore, much of the remaining wildlife habitat is being fragmented and polluted at an alarming rate.

Island species are especially vulnerable to extinction. The endangered *Symphonia* (Figure 6-2) clings to life on the island of Madagascar, where 90% of the original vegetation has been destroyed. Human settlements, roads (Figure 5-2), and clear-cut areas (Figure 5-3) break habitats into patches, or "habitat islands," that may be too small to support the minimum breeding populations of species. Most national parks and other protected areas are habitat islands.

Migrating species face a double habitat problem. Nearly half of the 700 U.S. bird species spend two-thirds of the year in the tropical forests of Central or South America, or the Caribbean islands, and they return to North America during the summer to breed. A U.S. Fish and Wildlife study showed that between 1978 and 1987 populations of 44 species of insect-eating, migratory songbirds in North America declined, with 20 species showing drops of 25–45%. The main culprits are logging of tropical forests in their winter habitats (Figure 5-6) and fragmentation of their summer forest habitats in North America. Three-fourths of the world's 9,000 known bird species are declining in numbers or are threatened with extinction, mostly because of habitat loss and fragmentation.

COMMERCIAL HUNTING AND POACHING Today subsistence hunting (for food) is rare because of the

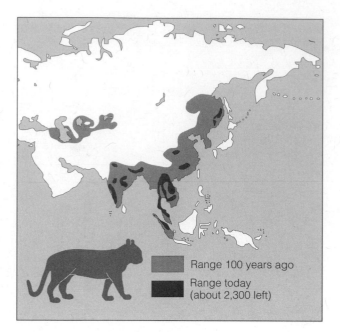

Range 100 years ago

Range today
(about 2,300 left)

Indian Tiger

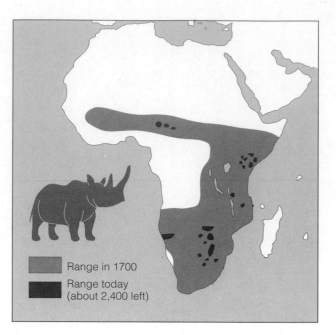

Range in 1700

Range today
(about 2,400 left)

Black Rhino

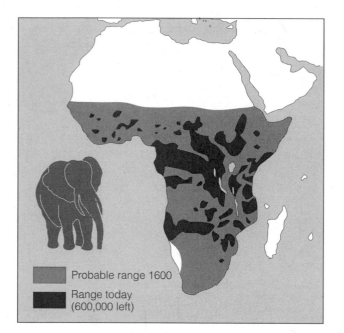

Probable range 1600

Range today
(600,000 left)

African Elephant

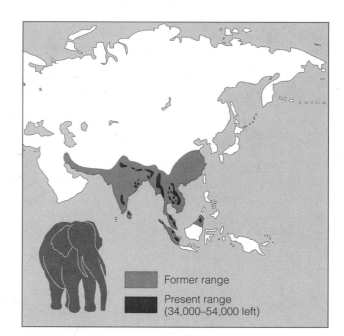

Former range

Present range
(34,000–54,000 left)

Asian or Indian Elephant

Figure 6-3 Reduction in the range of several species, mostly through a combination of habitat loss and hunting. What will happen to these and millions of other species when the global human population doubles in the next few decades? (Data from International Union for the Conservation of Nature and World Wildlife Fund)

decline in hunting-and-gathering societies. Sport hunting is closely regulated in most countries, and game species are endangered only where protective regulations do not exist or are not enforced. However, a combination of habitat loss, legal commercial hunting, and illegal commercial hunting (poaching) has driven many species, such as the American bison (Case Study, p. 164), to or over the brink of extinction (Figures 6-2 and 6-3). Bengal tigers are in trouble because a tiger fur sells for $100,000 in Tokyo. A mountain gorilla is worth $150,000; an ocelot skin $40,000; an Imperial Amazon macaw $30,000; a snow

Q: Where is most of the federally owned and managed land in the United States?

CONNECTIONS

Despite their variety (950 species) and worldwide distribution, bats have several traits that expose them to extinction from human activities. Not only do bats reproduce slowly, but many nest in huge cave colonies, where people can easily destroy them by blocking the entrances. And once the population of a bat species falls below a certain level, it may not recover because of its slow reproductive rate.

Bats play significant ecological roles and are also of great economic importance. They help control many crop-damaging insects and other pest species, such as mosquitoes and rodents. About 70% of all bat species feed on night-flying insects, making them the primary controls for such insects.

Other species of bats eat pollen; still others eat certain fruits. Because of this specialized feeding, they are the chief pollinators for certain trees, shrubs, and other plants. They also spread plants throughout tropical forests by excreting undigested seeds. If these keystone species are eliminated from an area, dependent plants would disappear. If you enjoy bananas, cashews, dates, figs, avocados, or mangos, you can thank bats. Bat research has contributed to the development of birth control and artificial insemination methods, to drug testing, studies of disease resistance and aging, vaccine production, and development of navigational aids for the blind.

People mistakenly fear bats as filthy, aggressive, rabies-carrying blood-suckers. But most bat species are harmless to people, livestock, and crops. In the United States only 10 people have died of bat-transmitted disease in four decades of record keeping. More Americans die each year from falling coconuts. Only three species of bats (none of them found in the United States) feed on blood, drawn mostly from cattle or wild animals. These bat species can be serious pests to domestic livestock but rarely affect humans.

Because of unwarranted fears of bats and misunderstanding of their vital ecological roles, several species have been driven to extinction, and others are endangered (such as the ghost bat, Figure 6-2) or threatened. We need to see bats as valuable allies—not enemies.

---

leopard skin $14,000. Rhinoceros horn sells for as much as $28,600 per kilogram.

All five species of rhinoceros are threatened with extinction because of poachers (who kill them for their horns) and loss of habitat. In Yemen, rhino horns are carved into ornate dagger handles, which sell for $500–$12,000. In China and other parts of Asia, powdered rhino horn is used for medicinal purposes and as an alleged aphrodisiac.

Trade in ivory and habitat loss have reduced African elephant numbers from 2.5 million in 1970 to 609,000 today. The 1990 international ban on the trade of ivory from African elephants has caused the bottom to drop out of the price of ivory and may help save this species, but things are not quite that simple. Increases in elephant populations in areas where their habitat has shrunk have resulted in widespread destruction of vegetation by these animals. This in turn reduces the niches available for other wild species.

Before the ban, in areas with high elephant populations, a certain number were allowed to be killed each year by local people as a source of meat and by hunters as a source of tourist income. Their ivory, sold legally, was an important source of income for local villagers and small farmers. With the ban on ivory trade, this important source of income for the poor has dried up. Some wildlife conservationists argue that people in areas where the elephant populations are not endangered should be allowed to sell ivory from culled elephants in the international marketplace. The ivory would be marked in ways to show that it was obtained legally. Proponents of this approach see this as a way to serve both local people and elephants.

As more species become endangered, the demand for them on the black market soars, hastening their extinction. Poaching of endangered or threatened species is increasing in the United States, especially in western national parks and wilderness areas covered by only 22 federal wildlife protection officers. Much of the illegal killing and trapping is done by professional poachers for Asian markets. Most poachers are not caught, and the money to be made far outweighs the risk of fines and the much smaller risk of jail.

PREDATOR AND PEST CONTROL People try to exterminate species that compete with us for food and game. For example, U.S. fruit farmers exterminated the Carolina parakeet around 1914 because it fed on fruit

CASE STUDY

In 1500, before Europeans settled North America, 60 to 125 million American bison grazed the grassy plains, prairies, and woodlands over much of the continent. A single herd might thunder past for hours. Several Native American tribes depended heavily on bison but did not deplete them, killing just enough for their food, clothing, and shelter. By 1906, however, the once-vast range of the bison had shrunk to a tiny area, and the species was driven nearly to extinction (Figure 6-4).

Figure 6-4 The range of the North American bison shrank severely between 1500 and 1906.

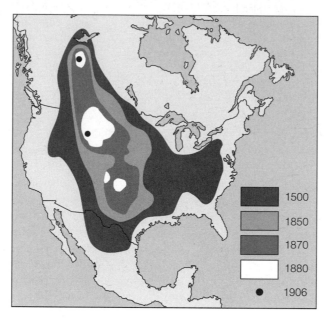

As settlers moved west after the Civil War, the sustainable balance between Native Americans and bison was upset. The Sioux, Apaches, Comanches, and other plains tribes traded bison skins to settlers for steel knives and firearms, and they began killing more bison. The most relentless slaughter, however, was caused by the intruding white settlers.

As railroads pushed westward in the late 1860s, railroad companies hired professional bison hunters—like Buffalo Bill Cody—to supply construction crews with

meat. Passengers also gunned down bison from train windows for sport, leaving the carcasses to rot. Commercial hunters shot millions of bison for their hides and tongues (considered a delicacy), leaving most of the meat to rot. "Bone pickers" collected the bleached bones that whitened the prairies and shipped them east to be ground up as fertilizer.

Farmers shot bison because they damaged crops, fences, telegraph poles, and sod houses. Ranchers killed them because they competed with cattle and sheep for grass. The U.S. Army killed bison as part of their campaign to subdue the plains tribes by killing off their primary source of food. At least 2.5 million bison perished each year between 1870 and 1875 in this form of biological warfare.

By 1892 only 85 bison were left. They were given refuge in Yellowstone National Park and protected by an 1893 law against the killing of wild animals in national parks.

In 1905, 16 people formed the American Bison Society to protect and rebuild the captive population. Soon thereafter the federal government established the National Bison Range near Missoula, Montana. Today there are an estimated 120,000 bison, about 80% of them on privately owned ranches.

---

crops. The species was easy prey because when one member of a flock was shot, the rest of the birds hovered over its body, making themselves easy targets.

As animal habitats shrink, African farmers kill large numbers of elephants to keep them from trampling and eating food crops. Ranchers, farmers, and hunters in the United States support control of species such as coyotes and wolves (Spotlight, p. 151) that can prey on livestock and species prized by game hunters. Since 1929 U.S. ranchers and government agencies have poisoned prairie dogs because horses and cattle sometimes step into the burrows and break their legs.

This poisoning has killed 99% of North America's prairie dogs (Figure 6-2). It has also nearly wiped out the endangered black-footed ferret (Figure 6-2), which preyed on the prairie dog.

PETS AND DECORATIVE PLANTS Worldwide over 5 million live wild birds are captured and sold legally each year, and 2.5 million more are captured and sold illegally. Most are sold in Europe, Japan, and the United States. Over 40 species, mostly parrots—are endangered or threatened because of this wildbird trade. Collectors of exotic birds may pay $10,000

Q: What percentage of Earth's land area is covered by tropical forests?

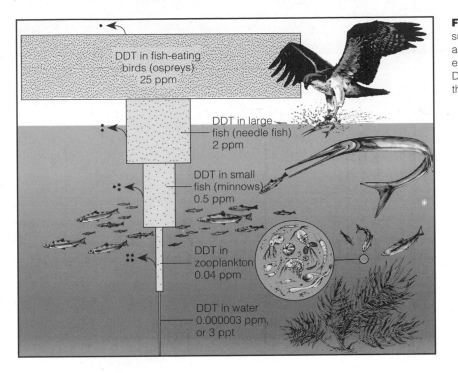

Figure 6-5 DDT concentration in the fatty tissues of organisms was biologically amplified about 10 million times in this food chain of an estuary near Long Island Sound. Dots represent DDT, and arrows show small losses of DDT through respiration and excretion.

DDT in fish-eating birds (ospreys)
25 ppm

DDT in large fish (needle fish)
2 ppm

DDT in small fish (minnows)
0.5 ppm

DDT in zooplankton
0.04 ppm

DDT in water
0.000003 ppm, or 3 ppt

for a threatened hyacinth macaw (Figure 6-2) smuggled out of Brazil. However, in its lifetime a single macaw might yield $165,000 in tourist income. For every bird that reaches a pet shop, legally or illegally, as many as 10 others die during capture or transport. A 1992 study suggested that keeping indoor pet birds for more than 10 years doubles a person's chances of getting lung cancer.

Some exotic plants, especially orchids and cacti (such as the black lace cactus, Figure 6-2), are also endangered because they are gathered, often illegally, sold to collectors, and used to decorate houses, offices, and landscapes. A collector may pay $5,000 for a single rare orchid. A single rare mature crested saguaro cactus can earn cactus rustlers as much as $15,000.

CLIMATE CHANGE AND POLLUTION A potential problem for many species is the possibility of fairly rapid (40–50 year) changes in climate accelerated by deforestation and emissions of heat-trapping gases into the atmosphere (Section 9-2). Wildlife in even the best-protected and best-managed reserves could be depleted in a few decades if such changes in climate take place as a result of projected global warming.

Another threat is toxic chemicals that degrade wildlife habitats, including wildlife refuges, and kill some plants and animals. Concentrations of slowly degradable pesticides, such as DDT, can be biologically amplified in food chains and webs (Figure 6-5). The resulting high concentrations of DDT or other slowly biodegraded, fat-soluble organic chemicals can directly kill the organisms, reduce their ability to reproduce,

or make them more vulnerable to diseases, parasites, and predators. They can also disrupt food webs.

During the 1950s and 1960s populations of ospreys, cormorants, brown pelicans, and bald eagles (Figure 6-2) plummeted. These birds feed mostly on fish at the top of aquatic food chains and webs, and thus they ingest large quantities of biologically amplified DDT in their prey. Prairie falcons, sparrow hawks, Bermuda petrels, and peregrine falcons (Figure 6-2) also died off when they ate animal prey containing DDT, such as rabbits, ground squirrels, and other crop damaging small mammals.

Research has shown that the culprit was DDE, a breakdown product of DDT, accumulating in the bodies of the affected birds. This chemical reduces the amount of calcium in the shells of their eggs. The fragile shells break, and the unborn chicks die.

Since the U.S. ban on DDT in 1972, most of these species have made a comeback. In 1980, however, DDT levels were again rising in species such as the peregrine falcon and the osprey. These species may be picking up biologically amplified DDT and other banned pesticides in Latin America, where they winter. In those countries the use of such chemicals is still legal. Illegal use of DDT and other banned pesticides in the United States may also play a role.

INTRODUCED SPECIES Travelers sometimes pick up plants and animals intentionally or accidentally, and introduce them to new geographical regions. Many of these alien species provide food, game, and aesthetic beauty, and help control pests in their new

Table 6-2 Damage Caused by Plants and Animals Imported into the United States

Name	Origin	Mode of Transport	Type of Damage
Mammals			
European wild boar	Russia	Intentionally imported (1912), escaped captivity	Destroys habitat by rooting; damages crops
Nutria (cat-sized rodent)	Argentina	Intentionally imported, escaped captivity (1940)	Alters marsh ecology; damages levees and earth dams; destroys crops
Birds			
European starling	Europe	Intentionally released (1890)	Competes with native songbirds; damages crops; transmits swine diseases; causes airport nuisance
House sparrow	England	Intentionally released by Brooklyn Institute (1853)	Damages crops; displaces native songbirds
Fish			
Carp	Germany	Intentionally released (1877)	Displaces native fish; uproots water plants; lowers waterfowl populations
Sea lamprey	North Atlantic Ocean	Entered via Welland Canal (1829)	Wiped out lake trout, lake whitefish, and sturgeon in Great Lakes
Walking catfish	Thailand	Imported into Florida	Destroys bass, bluegill, and other fish
Insects			
Argentine fire ant	Argentina	Probably entered via coffee shipments from Brazil (1918)	Damages crops; destroys native ant species
Camphor scale insect	Japan	Accidentally imported on nursery stock (1920s)	Damaged nearly 200 plant species in Louisiana, Texas, and Alabama
Japanese beetle	Japan	Accidentally imported on irises or azaleas (1911)	Defoliates more than 250 species of trees and other plants, including many of commercial importance
Plants			
Water hyacinth	Central America	Intentionally introduced (1884)	Clogs waterways; shades out other aquatic vegetation
Chestnut blight (fungus)	Asia	Accidentally imported on nursery plants (1900)	Killed nearly all eastern U.S. chestnut trees; disturbed forest ecology
Dutch elm disease (fungus)	Europe	Accidentally imported on infected elm timber used for veneers (1930)	Killed millions of elms; disturbed forest ecology

From *Biological Conservation* by David W. Ehrenfeld. Copyright © 1970 by Holt, Rinehart & Winston, Inc. Modified and reprinted by permission.

environments. Some alien species, however, have no natural predators and competitors in their new habitats, which allows them to dominate their new ecosystem and reduce the populations of many native species. Eventually such aliens can displace or wipe out native species (Table 6-2).

An example of the effects of the accidental introduction of an alien species is the fast-growing *water hyacinth* (Figure 6-6), which is native to Central and South America. In 1884 a woman took one from a New Orleans exhibition and planted it in her backyard in Florida. Within 10 years the plant, which can double its population in two weeks, had become a public menace. Unchecked by natural enemies and thriving on Florida's nutrient-rich waters, water hyacinths rapidly displaced native plants, clogging many ponds, streams, canals, and rivers, first in Florida and later in the southeastern United States.

Mechanical harvesters and herbicides have failed to keep the plant in check. Grazing Florida manatees,

Q: How much of Earth's tropical forests have been cleared or damaged?

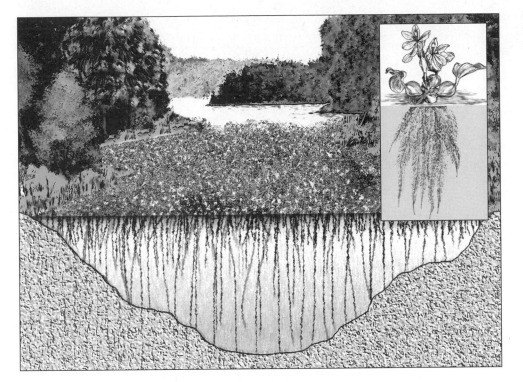

or sea cows, can control water hyacinths better than mechanical or chemical methods. However, these gentle and playful herbivores are threatened with extinction (Figure 6-2). Slashed by powerboat propellers, entangled in fishing gear—even hit on the head by oars—they reproduce too slowly to recover from these assaults and loss of habitat.

Scientists have introduced water hyacinth-eaters to help control its spread. They include a weevil from Argentina, a water snail from Puerto Rico, and the grass carp, a fish from the former Soviet Union. These species can help, but water snails and grass carp also feed on other, desirable aquatic plants.

The good news is that water hyacinths have several beneficial uses. For example, they absorb toxic chemicals in sewage treatment lagoons. They can be fermented into a biogas fuel similar to natural gas, added as a mineral and protein supplement to cattle feed, and applied to the soil as fertilizer. They can also be used to clean up polluted ponds and lakes—if their growth can be kept under control.

An example of the impact of deliberately introduced alien species on ecosystems is wild African bees, which were imported to Brazil in 1959 with the false hope that they would increase honey production. Since then these bees have moved northward into Central America and recently reached Texas. They are now heading north at 240 kilometers (150 miles) per year, though they will be stopped eventually by cold winters in the central United States. These "killer"

bees displace domestic honeybees and reduce the honey supply. Although they are not the killer bees portrayed in some horror movies, these bees are aggressive and unpredictable, and they have killed animals and even humans.

6-3 Solutions: Protecting Wild Species from Extinction

WORLD CONSERVATION STRATEGY In 1980 the International Union for Conservation of Nature and Natural Resources (IUCN), the UN Environment Programme, and the World Wildlife Fund developed the World Conservation Strategy, a long-range plan for conserving the world's biological resources. This plan was expanded in 1991. Its primary goals are to:

- Maintain essential ecological processes and life-support systems on which human survival and economic activities depend, mostly by combining wildlife conservation with sustainable development (Figure 5-8)

- Preserve species diversity and genetic diversity

- Ensure that any use of species and ecosystems is sustainable

- Minimize the depletion of nonrenewable resources
- Improve the quality of human life
- Include women and indigenous peoples in the development of conservation plans
- Monitor the sustainability of development
- Promote an ethic that includes protection of plants and animals as well as people
- Encourage recognition of the harmful environmental effects of armed conflict and economic insecurity
- Encourage rehabilitation of degraded ecosystems upon which humans depend for food and fiber

So far 40 countries have planned or established national conservation programs (the United States is not one of them). If MDCs provide enough money and scientific assistance, this conservation strategy offers hope for slowing the loss of biodiversity. Ultimately, however, no conservation strategy can protect the planet's biodiversity unless governments act to reduce poverty, control population growth, slow global warming, and reduce the destruction and degradation of tropical and old-growth forests, wetlands, and coral reefs (Chapter 5).

TREATIES AND LAWS   Several international treaties and conventions help protect endangered or threatened wild species. One of the most far-reaching is the 1975 Convention on International Trade in Endangered Species (CITES). This treaty, now signed by 119 countries, lists 675 species that cannot be commercially traded as live specimens or wildlife products because they are endangered or threatened.

However, enforcement of this treaty is spotty, convicted violators often pay only small fines, and member countries can exempt themselves from protection of any listed species. Also, much of the $5-billion-per-year illegal trade in wildlife and wildlife products goes on in countries such as Singapore that have not signed the treaty. Other centers of illegal animal trade are Argentina, Indonesia, Spain, Taiwan, and Thailand.

The United States controls imports and exports of endangered wildlife and wildlife products with two important laws. The Lacey Act of 1900 prohibits transporting live or dead wild animals or their parts across state borders without a federal permit.

The Endangered Species Act of 1973 (amended in 1982 and 1988) makes it illegal for Americans to import or trade in any product made from an endangered or threatened species unless it is used for an approved scientific purpose or to enhance the survival of the species. The act is one of the world's toughest environmental laws. It authorizes the National Marine Fisheries Service (NMFS) to identify and list endangered and threatened ocean species; the Fish and Wildlife Service (FWS) identifies and lists all other endangered and threatened species. These species cannot be hunted, killed, collected, or injured in the United States.

Any decision by either agency to list or unlist a species must be based only on biology, without economic considerations. The act also forbids federal agencies to carry out, fund, or authorize projects that would jeopardize an endangered or threatened species; or that would destroy or modify its critical habitat—the land, air, and water necessary for its survival.

Between 1970 and 1992 the number of species found only in the United States that have been placed on the official endangered and threatened list increased from 92 to 750. Also on the list are 529 species found elsewhere.

Getting listed is only half the battle. Next the FWS or the NMFS is supposed to prepare a plan to help the species recover. However, because of a lack of funds, recovery plans have been developed and approved for only about 61% of the endangered or threatened U.S. species, and half of those plans exist only on paper. Only 6 U.S. species have recovered enough to be unlisted, but 238 of the 750 listed species are stable and recovering. On the losing end, 7 listed domestic species have become extinct.

The annual federal budget for endangered species is less than what beer companies spend on two 30-second TV commercials during the Super Bowl. At this level of funding it will take up to 48 years to evaluate the almost 3,500 species (about 500 of them severely imperiled) now proposed for listing. Wildlife experts estimate that at least 400 of them will vanish while they wait, as did 34 species awaiting listing between 1980 and 1990.

The act requires that all commercial shipments of wildlife and wildlife products enter or leave the country through one of nine designated ports. Many illegal shipments slip by, however, because the 60 FWS inspectors can physically examine only about one-fourth of the 90,000 shipments that enter and leave the United States each year. Even if caught, many violators are not prosecuted, and convicted violators often pay only a small fine.

Since this act was passed there has been intense pressure by developers, logging and mining companies, and other users of land resources to allow the use of economic factors, both in evaluating species for listing and in carrying out federally funded projects that threaten the critical habitats of endangered or threatened species.

Q: At current loss rates, when will most remaining tropical forests be gone?

Environmentalists and many members of Congress, however, argue that the Endangered Species Act should be strengthened—not weakened—by:

- *Emphasizing protection of entire ecosystems to help prevent future declines in species not yet listed as threatened or endangered.*
- *Setting deadlines for development and implementation of recovery plans.*
- *Giving private landowners tax write-offs or other incentives for assisting in species recovery.*
- *Greatly increasing annual funding for endangered and threatened species from the current $55 million to $460 million—the amount needed to get the job done. This amount is about equal to what a large beer company spends each year on advertising. It amounts to spending less than $2 per year per American to help protect the entire nation's biological resources.*
- *Allowing citizens to file lawsuits immediately if an endangered species faces serious harm or extinction.*

Such proposals are vigorously opposed by those wishing to have greater access to resources on public and other lands.

WILDLIFE REFUGES   Since 1903, when President Theodore Roosevelt established the first U.S. federal wildlife refuge at Pelican Island, Florida, the National Wildlife Refuge System has grown to 503 refuges (Figure 5-5). About 85% of the area included in these refuges is in Alaska.

Over three-fourths of the refuges are wetlands for protection of migratory waterfowl. Most species on the U.S. endangered list have habitats in the refuge system, and some refuges have been set aside for specific endangered species. These have helped Florida's key deer, the brown pelican, and the trumpeter swan to recover. Environmentalists urge the establishment of more refuges for endangered plants.

Congress has not established guidelines (such as multiple use or sustained yield) for management of the National Wildlife Refuge System, as it has for other public lands (Spotlight, p. 138). As a result, the Fish and Wildlife Service has allowed many refuges to be used for hunting, fishing, trapping, timber cutting, grazing, farming, oil and gas development (Case Study, p. 170), mining, military air exercises, power and air boating, and off-road vehicles. A 1990 report by the General Accounting Office found that activities considered harmful to wildlife occur in nearly 60% of the nation's wildlife refuges.

Private groups play an important role in conserving wildlife in refuges and other protected areas. For example, since 1951 the Nature Conservancy has preserved over 1 million hectares (2.5 million acres) of forests, marshes, prairies, islands, and other areas of unique ecological or aesthetic significance in the United States.

GENE BANKS, BOTANICAL GARDENS, AND ZOOS
Botanists preserve genetic information and endangered plant species by storing their seeds in gene banks—refrigerated, low-humidity environments. Scientists urge that many more such banks be established, especially in LDCs; however, some species can't be preserved in gene banks, and maintaining the banks is very expensive.

The world's 1,500 botanical gardens and arboreta hold about 90,000 plant species. However, these sanctuaries have too little storage capacity and too little funding to preserve most of the world's rare and threatened plants.

Worldwide, 500 zoos house about 540,000 individual animals, many of them from species not threatened or endangered. Zoos and animal research centers are increasingly being used to preserve some individuals of critically endangered animal species.

Two techniques for preserving such species are egg pulling and captive breeding, with the long-term goal of reintroducing the species into protected wild habitats. *Egg pulling* involves collecting eggs laid in the wild by critically endangered bird species and hatching them in zoos or research centers. For *captive breeding* some or all individuals of a critically endangered species still in the wild are captured for breeding in captivity.

Captive breeding programs at zoos in Phoenix, San Diego, and Los Angeles saved the nearly extinct Arabian oryx (Figure 6-2). Some have been reintroduced into protected habitats in the Middle East, with the wild population now about 120. Endangered U.S. species now being bred in captivity include the California condor (Figure 6-2), the peregrine falcon (Figure 6-2), and the black-footed ferret (Figure 6-2). Endangered golden lion tamarins (Figure 6-2) bred at the National Zoo in Washington, D.C., have been released in Brazilian rain forests.

Unfortunately, keeping populations of endangered animal species in zoos and research centers is limited by lack of space and money. The captive population of each species must number 100–500 to avoid extinction through accident, disease, or loss of genetic variability through inbreeding. Moreover, caring for and breeding captive animals is very expensive. It is estimated that today's zoos and research centers have space to preserve healthy and sustainable populations of only 925 of the 2,000 large vertebrate species that could vanish from the planet. It is doubtful that the more than $6 billion needed to care for these animals for 20 years will be available.

A: 30-50 years

CASE STUDY

Should We Develop Oil and Gas in the Arctic National Wildlife Refuge?

The Arctic National Wildlife Refuge on Alaska's North Slope (Figure 6-7), which contains more than one-fifth of all the land in the U.S. wildlife refuge system, has been called the crown jewel of the system. During all or part of the year it is home for more than 160 animal species, including caribou, musk ox, snowy owls, threatened grizzly bears (Figure 6-2), arctic foxes, and migratory birds (including as many as 300,000 snow geese). It is also home for about 7,000 Inuit (Eskimos) who depend on the caribou for a large part of their diet.

Its coastal plain, the most biologically productive part of the refuge, is the only stretch of Alaska's arctic coastline not open to oil and gas

development. The big oil companies hope to change this because they believe that the area *might* contain oil and natural gas deposits. Since 1985 they have been urging Congress to open 607,000 hectares (1.5 million acres) along the coastal plain to drilling—roughly two-thirds the size of Yellowstone National Park. They argue that such exploration is needed to provide the United States with more oil and natural gas and reduce dependence on oil imports (Figure 4-31).

Environmentalists oppose this proposal and want Congress to designate the entire coastal plain as wilderness. They cite Interior Department estimates that there is only a 19% chance of finding as much oil as the United States consumes every six months. Even if the

oil does exist, environmentalists do not believe the potential degradation of any portion of this irreplaceable wilderness area would be worth it, especially considering that improvements in energy efficiency would save far more oil at a much lower cost (Section 4-2).

Officials of oil companies claim they have developed Alaska's Prudhoe Bay oil fields without significant harm to wildlife and that the area they want to open to oil and gas development is less than 1.5% of the entire coastal plain region—equivalent in size to Dulles International Airport in Washington, D.C., in an area approximately the size of South Carolina.

However, a study leaked from the Fish and Wildlife Service in 1988 revealed that oil drilling at Prudhoe Bay has caused much more air and water pollution than was anticipated before drilling began in 1972. According to this study, oil development in the coastal plain could cause the loss of 20–40% of the area's 180,000-member caribou herd, 25–50% of the remaining musk oxen, 50% or more of the wolverines, and 50% of the snow geese that live there part of the year. A 1988 EPA study also found that "violations of state and federal environmental regulations and laws are occurring at an unacceptable rate" in the Prudhoe Bay area.

Figure 6-7 Proposed oil-drilling area in Alaska's Arctic National Wildlife Refuge. (Data from U.S. Fish and Wildlife Service)

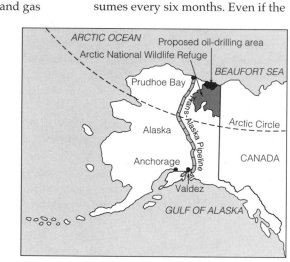

Because of limited funds and trained personnel, only a few of the world's endangered and threatened species can be saved by treaties, laws, wildlife refuges, and zoos. That means that wildlife experts must decide which species out of thousands of candidates should be saved. Many experts suggest that the limited funds for preserving threatened and endangered wildlife be concentrated on those species that **(1)** have the best chance for survival, **(2)** have the most ecological value to an ecosystem, and **(3)** are potentially useful for agriculture, medicine, or industry.

6-4 Wildlife Management

MANAGEMENT APPROACHES Wildlife management entails **(1)** manipulation of wildlife populations (especially game species) and habitats for their welfare and for human benefit, **(2)** preserving of endangered and threatened wild species, and **(3)** enforcing wildlife laws.

170

Q: What percentage of the earth's species live in tropical forests?

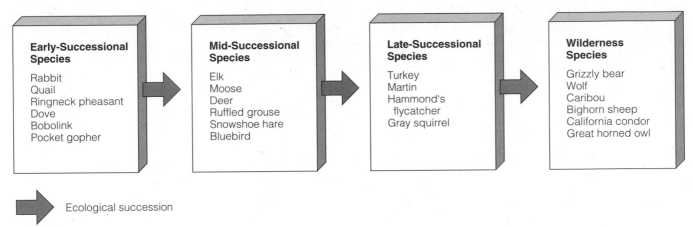

Early-Successional Species

Rabbit
Quail
Ringneck pheasant
Dove
Bobolink
Pocket gopher

Mid-Successional Species

Elk
Moose
Deer
Ruffled grouse
Snowshoe hare
Bluebird

Late-Successional Species

Turkey
Martin
Hammond's
 flycatcher
Gray squirrel

Wilderness Species

Grizzly bear
Wolf
Caribou
Bighorn sheep
California condor
Great horned owl

Ecological succession

Figure 6-8 Preferences of some wildlife species for habitats at different stages of ecological succession.

The first step in wildlife management is to decide which species are to be managed in a particular area—a source of much controversy. Ecologists stress preserving biodiversity. Wildlife conservationists are concerned about endangered species. Bird-watchers want the greatest diversity of bird species. Hunters want large populations of game species for harvest during hunting season. In the United States most wildlife management is devoted to producing surpluses of game animals and game birds.

After goals have been set, the wildlife manager must develop a management plan. Ideally the plan is based on principles of ecological succession (Figures 2-40 and 2-41), wildlife population dynamics (Figure 2-37), and an understanding of the cover, food, water, space, and other habitat requirements of each species to be managed. The manager must also take into account the number of potential hunters, their success rates, and the regulations available to prevent excessive harvesting.

This information is difficult, expensive, and time-consuming to obtain. In practice it involves much guesswork and trial and error, which is why wildlife management is as much an art as a science. Management plans must also be adapted to political pressures from conflicting groups and to budget constraints.

In the United States funds for state game management programs come from the sale of hunting and fishing licenses and from federal taxes on hunting and fishing equipment. Two-thirds of the states also have provisions on state income tax returns that allow individuals to contribute money to state wildlife programs. Only 10% of all government wildlife dollars, however, are spent to study or benefit nongame species, which make up nearly 90% of the country's wildlife species.

MANIPULATION OF VEGETATION AND WATER SUPPLIES Wildlife managers can encourage the

growth of plant species that are the preferred food and cover for a particular animal species by controlling the ecological succession of vegetation in various areas (Figure 6-8).

Various types of habitat improvement can be used to attract a desired species and encourage its population growth, including planting seeds, transplanting certain types of vegetation, building artificial nests, and deliberately setting controlled low-level ground fires to help control vegetation. Wildlife managers often create or improve ponds and lakes in wildlife refuges to provide water, food, and habitat for waterfowl and other wild animals.

POPULATION MANAGEMENT BY SPORT HUNTING Most MDCs use sport hunting laws to manage populations of game animals, although sport hunting is controversial. Licensed hunters are allowed to hunt only during certain months of the year so as to protect animals during mating season. Hunters can use only certain types of hunting equipment, such as bows and arrows, shotguns, and rifles, for a particular type of game. Limits are set on the size, number, and sex of animals that can be killed, and on the number of hunters allowed in a game refuge.

Close control of sport hunting is difficult. Accurate data on game populations may not exist and may cost too much to get. People in communities near hunting areas, who benefit from money spent by hunters, may push to have hunting quotas raised.

MANAGEMENT OF MIGRATORY WATERFOWL In North America migratory waterfowl such as ducks, geese, and swans nest in Canada during the summer. During the fall hunting season they migrate to the United States and Central America along generally fixed routes called **flyways** (Figure 6-9).

Wildlife officials manage waterfowl by regulating hunting, protecting existing habitats, and developing

A: At least 50% (some say 90%)

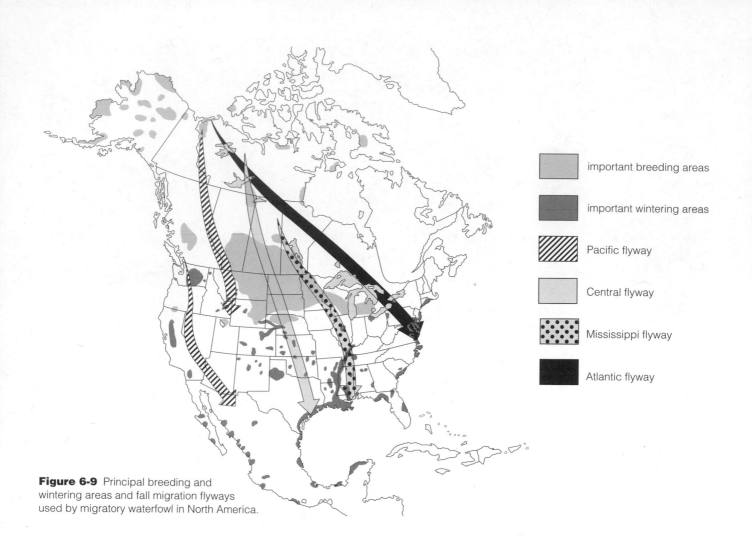

Figure 6-9 Principal breeding and wintering areas and fall migration flyways used by migratory waterfowl in North America.

Legend:
- important breeding areas
- important wintering areas
- Pacific flyway
- Central flyway
- Mississippi flyway
- Atlantic flyway

new habitats, as well as by building artificial nesting sites, ponds, and nesting islands along flyways. More than 75% of the federal wildlife refuges in the United States are wetlands used by migratory birds. Local and state agencies and private conservation groups such as Ducks Unlimited, the Audubon Society, and the Nature Conservancy have also established waterfowl refuges.

Since 1934 the Migratory Bird Hunting and Conservation Stamp Act has required waterfowl hunters to buy a duck stamp each season they hunt. Revenue from these sales goes into a fund to buy land and easements for the benefit of waterfowl.

6-5 Fishery Management

FRESHWATER FISHERY MANAGEMENT The goals of freshwater fish management are to encourage the growth of populations of desirable commercial and sport fish species and to reduce or eliminate pop-ulations of less desirable species. A number of techniques are used:

- Regulating the timing and length of fishing seasons
- Setting the size and number of fish that can be taken
- Requiring commercial fishnets to have a large enough mesh to prevent harvesting young fish
- Building reservoirs and farm ponds, and stocking them with game fish
- Fertilizing nutrient-poor lakes and ponds
- Protecting and creating spawning sites
- Protecting habitats from buildup of sediment and other forms of pollution, and removing debris
- Preventing excessive growth of aquatic plants
- Using small dams to control water flow
- Controlling predators, parasites, and diseases by improvement of habitats, breeding genetically resistant fish varieties, and using antibiotics and disinfectants

Q: What percentage of tropical forest plants have been studied for their possible use as human resources?

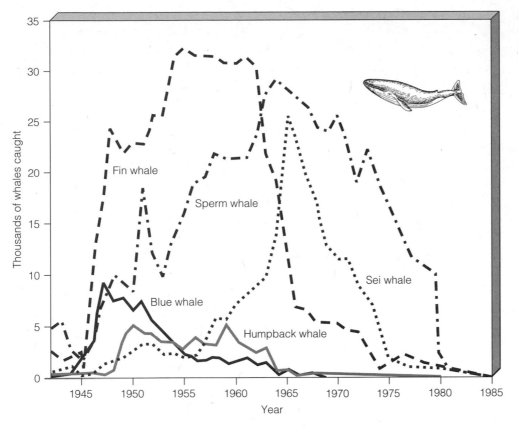

Figure 6-10 Whale harvests, showing the signs of overharvesting. (Data from International Whaling Commission)

- Using hatcheries to restock ponds, lakes, and streams with species such as trout and salmon

MARINE FISHERY MANAGEMENT   By international law the offshore fishing zone of coastal countries extends to 370 kilometers (200 nautical miles or 230 statute miles) from their shores. Foreign fishing vessels can take certain quotas of fish within such zones, called **exclusive economic zones**, only with government permission. Ocean areas beyond the legal jurisdiction of any country are known as the **high seas**. Any limits on the use of the living and mineral common-property resources in these areas are set by international maritime law and international treaties.

Managers of marine fisheries use several techniques to help prevent commercial extinction and allow depleted stocks to recover. Fishery commissions, councils, and advisory bodies with representatives from countries using a fishery can set annual quotas and establish rules for dividing the allowable catch among the participating countries. These groups may limit fishing seasons and regulate the type of fishing gear that can be used to harvest a particular species; fishing techniques such as dynamiting and poisoning, for example, are outlawed. Fishery commissions may also make it illegal to keep fish below a certain size, usually the average length of the particular fish species when it first reproduces.

As voluntary associations, however, fishery commissions don't have any legal authority to compel member states to follow their rules. Nor can they compel all countries fishing in a region to join the commission and submit to its rules. Furthermore, it is very difficult to estimate the sustainable yields of various marine species.

DECLINE OF THE WHALING INDUSTRY   *Cetaceans* are an order of mammals ranging in size from the 0.9-meter (3-foot) porpoise to the giant 15- to 30-meter (50- to 100-foot) blue whale. They can be divided into two major groups, toothed cetaceans and baleen whales.

Toothed cetaceans, such as the porpoise, sperm whale, and killer whale, bite and chew their food. They feed mostly on squid, octopus, and other marine animals. *Baleen whales*, such as the blue (Figure 6-2), gray, humpback, and finback, are filter feeders. Instead of teeth, they have several hundred horny plates made of baleen, or whalebone, which hang down from their upper jaw. These plates filter plankton, especially shrimplike krill (Figure 2-18) smaller than your thumb, from seawater. Baleen whales are the most abundant group of cetaceans.

In 1900 an estimated 4.4 million whales swam the oceans; today only about 1 million are left. Overharvesting has caused a sharp drop in the population of almost every whale species with commercial value

A: 1%

What You Can Do to Protect Wildlife Resources and Preserve Biodiversity

INDIVIDUALS MATTER

- *Improve the habitat on a patch of the earth in your immediate environment, emphasizing the promotion of biological diversity.*

- *Refuse to buy furs, ivory products, reptile-skin goods, tortoiseshell jewelry, rare orchids or cacti, coral, and endangered or threatened animal species.*

- *Leave wild animals in the wild.*

- *Reduce habitat destruction and degradation by recycling paper, cans, plastics, and other household items. Better yet, reuse items and sharply reduce your use of throwaway items.*

- *Support efforts to sharply reduce the destruction and degradation of tropical forests (Section 5-4) and old-growth forests (Section 5-3), slow projected global warming (Section 9-2), and reduce ozone depletion in the stratosphere (Section 9-3).*

- *Pressure elected officials to pass laws requiring larger fines and longer prison sentences for wildlife poachers and to provide more funds and personnel for wildlife protection.*

- *Pressure Congress to pass a national biodiversity act and to develop a national conservation program as part of the World Conservation Strategy.*

(Figure 6-10). The populations of 8 of the 11 major species of whales once hunted by the whaling industry have been reduced to commercial extinction.

A prime example is the endangered blue whale (Figure 6-2), the world's largest animal. Fully grown, it's more than 30 meters (100 feet) long—longer than three train boxcars—and weighs more than 25 elephants. The adult has a heart the size of a Volkswagen "Beetle" car, and some of its arteries are so big that a child could swim through them.

Blue whales spend about eight months of the year in Antarctic waters. There they find an abundant supply of shrimplike krill (Figure 2-18), which they filter daily by the trillions from seawater. During the winter months they migrate to warmer waters, where their young are born.

Once an estimated 200,000 blue whales roamed the Antarctic Ocean. Today the species has been hunted to near biological extinction for its oil, meat, and bone. This decline was caused by a combination of prolonged overfishing and certain natural characteristics of blue whales. Their huge size made them easy to spot. They were caught in large numbers because they grouped together in their Antarctic feeding grounds (Figure 2-18). Also, they take 25 years to mature sexually and have only one offspring every 2–5 years—a reproduction rate that makes it hard for the species to recover once its population falls to a low level.

Blue whales haven't been hunted commercially since 1964 and have been classified as an endangered species since 1975. Despite this protection some marine experts believe that too few blue whales—less than 5,000 and perhaps only 1,500–6,000—remain for the species to recover. Within a few decades the blue whale could disappear forever.

In 1946 the International Whaling Commission (IWC) was established to regulate the whaling industry. Since 1949 the IWC has set annual quotas to prevent overfishing and commercial extinction. However, these quotas often were based on inadequate scientific information or were ignored by whaling countries. Without any powers of enforcement, the IWC has been unable to stop the decline of most whale species.

In 1970 the United States stopped all commercial whaling and banned all imports of whale products, mostly because of pressure from environmentalists and the general public. Under intense pressure from environmentalists and governments of many countries, including the United States, the IWC has imposed a moratorium on commercial whaling since 1986.

The IWC, however, has allowed Japan, Norway, and Iceland to kill several hundred whales per year for "scientific" purposes. Environmentalists believe that killing whales for such purposes is a sham and that a total ban on whaling should be imposed and vigorously enforced.

In 1992 Iceland quit the IWC. And in 1993 Norway began commercial whaling again in defiance of the IWC. Japan has also threatened to resume whaling. Without continuing worldwide pressure from individuals, environmental organizations, and the U.S. government, large-scale commercial whaling may resume.

6-6 Solutions: Individual Action

We are all involved, at least indirectly, in the destruction of wildlife any time we buy or drive a car, build a house, consume almost anything, and waste electricity, paper, water, or any other resource. All those activities contribute to the destruction or degradation of wildlife habitats or to the killing of one or more individuals of some plant or animal species.

Modifying our consumption habits is a key goal in protecting wildlife, the environment, and ourselves (Individuals Matter, p. 174). This also involves supporting efforts to reduce deforestation, projected global warming, ozone depletion, population growth, and poverty—all of which threaten wildlife and our own species.

During our short time on this planet we have gained immense power over what species—including our own—live or die. We named ourselves the wise (*sapiens*) species. In the next few decades we will learn whether we are indeed a wise species with the wisdom to learn from and work with nature to protect ourselves and other species.

A greening of the human mind must precede the greening of the Earth. A green mind is one that cares, saves, and shares. These are the qualities essential for conserving biological diversity now and forever.

M. S. SWAMINATHAN

CRITICAL THINKING

1. Discuss your gut-level reaction to this statement: "It doesn't really matter that the passenger pigeon is extinct and that the blue whale, the whooping crane, the California condor, the rhinoceros, and the grizzly bear are endangered mostly because of human activities." Be honest about your reaction and give arguments for your position.

2. Make a log of your own consumption and use of food and other products for a single day. Relate your consumption to the increased destruction of wildlife and wildlife habitats in the United States, in tropical forests, and in aquatic ecosystems.

3. a. Do you accept the ethical position that each *species* has the inherent right to survive without human interference, regardless of whether it serves any useful purpose for humans? Explain.
   b. Do you believe that each *individual* of an animal species has an inherent right to survive? Explain. Would you extend such rights to individual plants and microorganisms? Explain.

4. Do you believe that the use of animals to test new drugs and vaccines and the toxicity of chemicals should be banned? Explain. What are the alternatives? Should animals be used to test cosmetics?

5. Should U.S. energy companies be allowed to drill for oil and gas in the Arctic National Wildlife Refuge? Explain.

7 Biodiversity: Sustaining Soil and Producing Food

7-1 Soil and Soil Erosion

WHAT IS SOIL?   **Soil** is a complex mixture of inorganic materials (clay, silt, pebbles, and sand), decaying organic matter, water, air, and billions of living organisms. Soil forms when life-forms decay, when solid rock weathers and crumbles, and when sediments are deposited by erosion. Unless you are a farmer, you probably think of soil as dirt—something you don't want on your hands, clothes, or carpet. Yet your life and the lives of other organisms depend on soil, especially topsoil. To a large extent all flesh is soil nutrients. Soil also provides us with wood, paper, cotton, medicines—everything we get from plants—and helps purify the water we drink. Yet since the beginning of agriculture we have abused this vital, potentially renewable resource. Entire civilizations have collapsed because they mismanaged the topsoil that supported their populations.

Mature soils are arranged in a series of zones called **soil horizons**, each with a distinct texture and composition that varies with different types of soils (Figure 7-1). A cross-sectional view of the horizons in

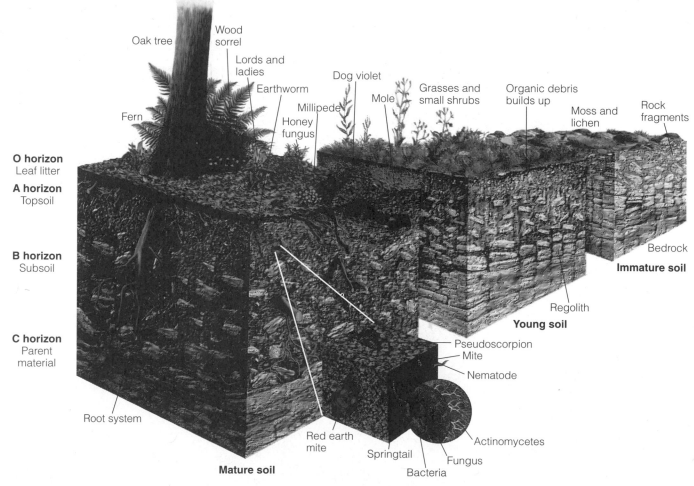

Figure 7-1 Formation and generalized profile of soils. Horizons, or layers, vary in number, composition, and thickness, depending on the type of soil. (Used by permission of Macmillan Publishing Company from Derek Elsom, *Earth*, New York: Macmillan, 1992. Copyright © 1992 by Marshall Editions Developments Limited)

Q: How many people cannot find or buy enough fuelwood to meet their basic needs?

Below that thin layer comprising the delicate
organism known as the soil is a planet as lifeless
as the moon.

G. Y. Jacks and R. O. Whyte

a soil is called a **soil profile**. Most mature soils have at least three of the possible horizons.

The top layer, the *surface-litter layer* or *O-horizon*, consists mostly of freshly fallen and partially decomposed leaves, twigs, animal waste, fungi, and other organic materials. Normally it is brown or black in color. The *topsoil layer*, or *A-horizon*, is a porous mixture of partially decomposed organic matter (humus) and some inorganic mineral particles. Usually it is darker and looser than deeper layers. The roots of most plants and most of a soil's organic matter are concentrated in these two upper layers. As long as these layers are anchored by vegetation, soil stores water and releases it in a nourishing trickle instead of a devastating flood.

The two top layers of most well-developed soils teem with bacteria, fungi, earthworms, and small insects (Figure 7-1). These layers are also home for burrowing animals such as moles and gophers. These soil-dwellers interact in complex food webs (Figure 7-2).

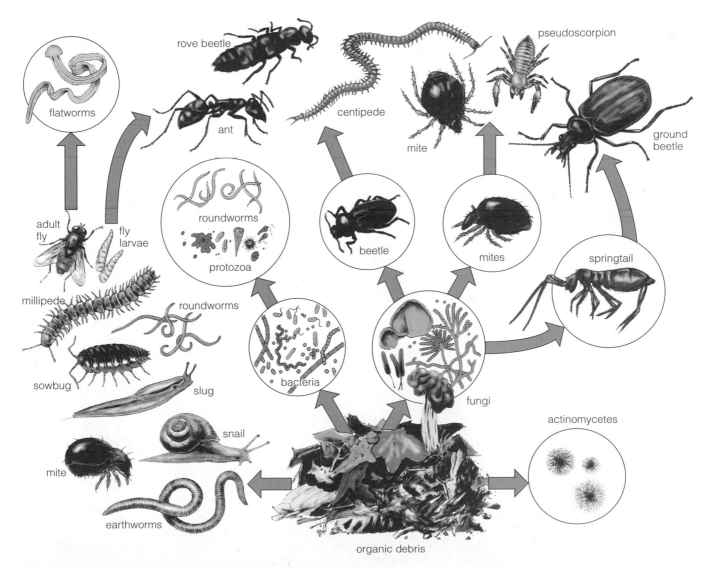

Figure 7-2 Greatly simplified food web of living organisms found in soil.

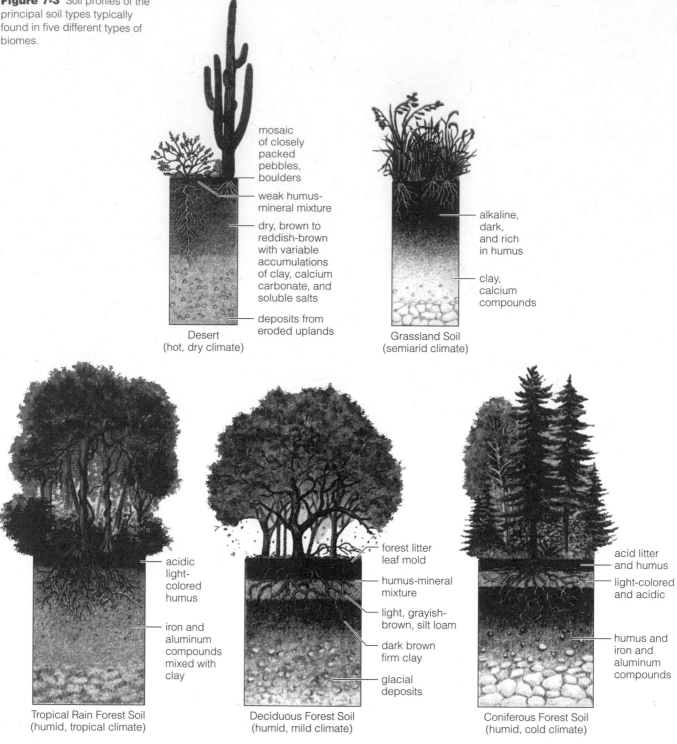

mosaic of closely packed pebbles, boulders

weak humus-mineral mixture

dry, brown to reddish-brown with variable accumulations of clay, calcium carbonate, and soluble salts

deposits from eroded uplands

Desert
(hot, dry climate)

alkaline, dark, and rich in humus

clay, calcium compounds

Grassland Soil
(semiarid climate)

acidic light-colored humus

iron and aluminum compounds mixed with clay

Tropical Rain Forest Soil
(humid, tropical climate)

forest litter leaf mold

humus-mineral mixture

light, grayish-brown, silt loam

dark brown firm clay

glacial deposits

Deciduous Forest Soil
(humid, mild climate)

acid litter and humus

light-colored and acidic

humus and iron and aluminum compounds

Coniferous Forest Soil
(humid, cold climate)

Bacteria and other decomposer microorganisms are found by the billions in every handful of topsoil. They recycle the nutrients we and other land organisms need by breaking down some of the complex organic compounds in the upper soil into simpler inorganic compounds soluble in soil water. Soil moisture carrying these dissolved nutrients is drawn up by the roots of plants and transported through stems and into leaves.

Some organic litter in the two top layers is broken down into a sticky, brown residue of partially decomposed organic material called **humus**. Because humus is only slightly soluble in water, most of it stays in the topsoil layer. A fertile soil, producing high crop yields, has a thick topsoil layer with lots of humus. Humus also helps topsoil hold water and helps keep nutrients taken up by plant roots from being carried away as rainwater percolates downward through the topsoil.

Q: By 2000 how many people may not be able to get enough fuelwood?

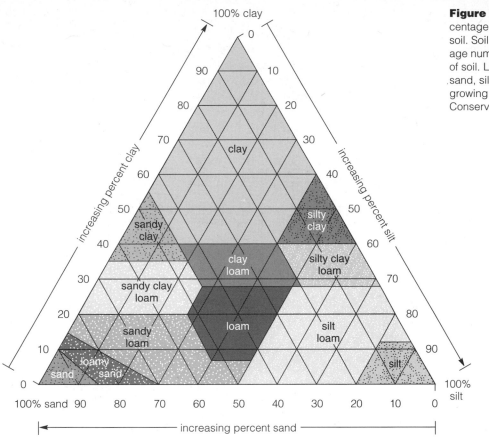

Figure 7-4 Soil texture depends on the percentages of clay, silt, and sand particles in the soil. Soil texture affects soil porosity—the average number and spacing of pores in a volume of soil. Loams—roughly equal mixtures of clay, sand, silt, and humus—are the best soils for growing most crops. (Data from Soil Conservation Service)

Color tells us a lot about how useful a soil is for growing crops. For example, dark-brown or black topsoil is nitrogen-rich and high in organic matter. Gray, bright yellow, or red topsoils are low in organic matter and will need nitrogen fertilizer to support most crops.

The *B-horizon (subsoil)* and the *C-horizon (parent material)* contain most of a soil's inorganic matter. It is mostly broken-down rock, a varying mixture of sand, silt, clay, and gravel. The C-horizon lies on a base of unweathered parent rock called bed rock.

The spaces, or pores, between the solid organic and inorganic particles in the upper and lower soil layers contain varying amounts of air (mostly nitrogen and oxygen gas) and water. Plant roots need oxygen for respiration in their cells.

Some of the rain falling on the soil percolates through the soil layers and occupies many of the pores. This downward movement of water through soil is called **infiltration**. As the water seeps down, it dissolves and picks up various soil components in upper layers and carries them to lower layers—a process called **leaching**.

Soils develop and mature slowly (Figure 7-1). Mature soils vary widely from biome to biome (Figure 2-27) in color, content, pore space, acidity (pH), and depth. Five important soil types, each with a distinct profile, are shown in Figure 7-3. Most of the world's crops are grown on soils exposed when grasslands and deciduous forests are cleared.

SOIL TEXTURE, POROSITY, AND ACIDITY   Soils vary in their content of *clay* (very fine particles), *silt* (fine particles), *sand* (medium-size particles), and *gravel* (coarse to very coarse particles). The relative amounts of the different sizes and types of mineral particles determine **soil texture**. Figure 7-4 groups soils into textural classes according to clay, silt, and sand content. Soils containing a mixture of clay, sand, silt, and humus are called **loams**.

To get an idea of a soil's texture, take a small amount of topsoil, moisten it, and rub it between your fingers and thumb. A gritty feel means that it contains a lot of sand. A sticky feel means a high clay content, and you should be able to roll it into a clump. Silt-laden soil feels smooth like flour. A loam topsoil, best suited for plant growth, has a texture between these extremes—a crumbly, spongy feeling with many of its particles clumped loosely together.

Soil texture helps determine **soil porosity**: a measure of the volume of pores or spaces per volume of soil and the average distances between those spaces. A porous soil (with many pores) can hold more water and air than a less porous soil. The average size of the

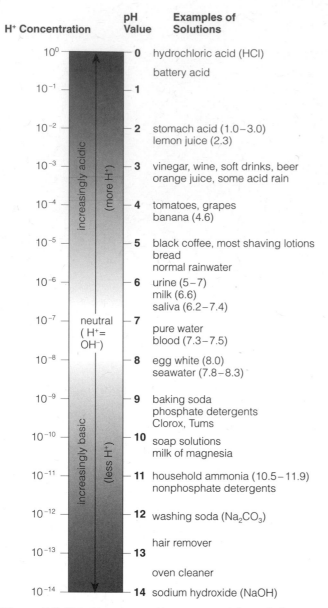

H+ Concentration	pH Value	Examples of Solutions
10^0	0	hydrochloric acid (HCl)
		battery acid
10^{-1}	1	
10^{-2}	2	stomach acid (1.0–3.0)
		lemon juice (2.3)
10^{-3}	3	vinegar, wine, soft drinks, beer orange juice, some acid rain
10^{-4}	4	tomatoes, grapes banana (4.6)
10^{-5}	5	black coffee, most shaving lotions bread normal rainwater
10^{-6}	6	urine (5–7) milk (6.6) saliva (6.2–7.4)
10^{-7}	7	pure water blood (7.3–7.5)
10^{-8}	8	egg white (8.0) seawater (7.8–8.3)
10^{-9}	9	baking soda phosphate detergents Clorox, Tums
10^{-10}	10	soap solutions milk of magnesia
10^{-11}	11	household ammonia (10.5–11.9) nonphosphate detergents
10^{-12}	12	washing soda (Na_2CO_3)
10^{-13}	13	hair remover oven cleaner
10^{-14}	14	sodium hydroxide (NaOH)

(increasingly acidic — more H^+; neutral ($H^+ = OH^-$); increasingly basic — less H^+)

Figure 7-5 The pH scale, used to measure acidity and alkalinity of water solutions. Values shown are approximate. A neutral solution has a pH of 7; one with a pH greater than 7 is basic, or alkaline; and one with a pH less than 7 is acidic. The lower the pH below 7, the more acidic the solution. Each whole-number drop in pH represents a tenfold increase in acidity.

spaces or pores in a soil determines **soil permeability**: the rate at which water and air move from upper to lower soil layers. Soil porosity is also influenced by **soil structure**: how soil particles are organized and clumped together.

Loams are the best soils for growing most crops because they hold lots of water but not too tightly for plant roots to absorb. Sandy soils are easy to work, but water flows rapidly through them. They are useful for growing irrigated crops or those with low water requirements, such as peanuts and strawberries.

The particles in clay soils are very small and easily compacted. When these soils get wet, they form large, dense clumps, explaining why wet clay can be molded into bricks and pottery. Clay soils are more porous and have a greater water-holding capacity than sandy soils, but the pore spaces are so small that these soils have a low permeability. Because little water can infiltrate to lower levels, the upper layers can easily become too waterlogged for most crops.

Acidity and basicity of substances in water solution are commonly expressed in terms of **pH** (Figure 7-5). Soils vary in acidity, and the pH of a soil influences the uptake of soil nutrients by plants. Plants vary in the pH ranges they can tolerate.

SOIL EROSION

Soil erosion is the movement of soil components, especially surface-litter and topsoil, from one place to another. The two main movers are flowing water and wind. Although wind causes some erosion, most is caused by moving water.

Some soil erosion is natural, but the roots of plants generally anchor the soil. In undisturbed vegetated ecosystems, soil is not usually lost faster than it forms. However, farming, logging, building, overgrazing by livestock, off-road vehicles, fire, and other activities that destroy plant cover leave soil vulnerable to erosion.

Losing topsoil makes a soil less fertile and less able to hold water. The resulting sediment, the largest source of water pollution, clogs irrigation ditches, boat channels, reservoirs, and lakes. Fish die. Water is cloudy and tastes bad. Flood risk increases.

Soil, especially topsoil, is classified as a potentially renewable resource because it is continuously regenerated by natural processes. However, in tropical and temperate areas it takes 200–1,000 years for 2.54 centimeters (1 inch) of new topsoil to form, depending on climate and soil type. If topsoil erodes faster than it forms on a piece of land, the soil there becomes a non-renewable resource. Annual erosion rates for farmland throughout the world are 7–100 times the natural renewal rate. Soil erosion is milder on forestland and rangeland than on cropland, but forest soil takes two to three times longer to restore itself than does cropland. Construction sites usually have the highest erosion rates by far.

Today topsoil is eroding faster than it forms on about one-third of the world's cropland. A 1992 study by the World Resources Institute found that soil on more than 12 million square kilometers (5 million square miles) of land—an area the size of China and India combined—had been seriously eroded since 1945 (Figure 7-6). The study also found that 89,000 square kilometers (34,000 square miles) of land scattered across the globe was too eroded to grow crops

Q: What percentage of the original old-growth forests in the United States have been cut?

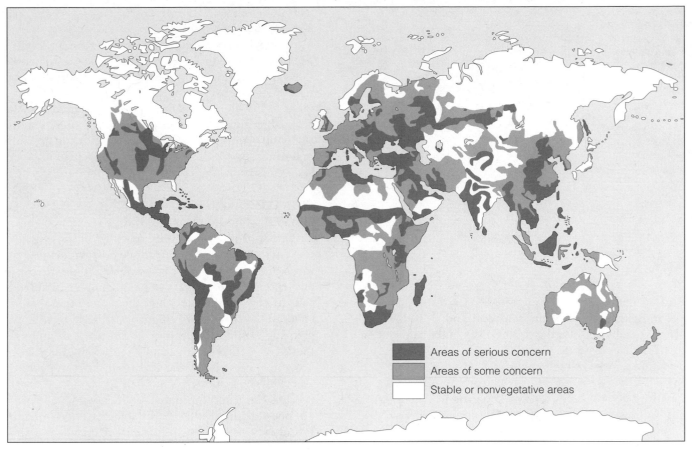

Figure 7-6 Global soil erosion. (Data from World Resources Institute)

Areas of serious concern
Areas of some concern
Stable or nonvegetative areas

anymore. Overgrazing is the worst culprit, accounting for 35% of the damage, with the heaviest losses in Africa and Australia. Deforestation causes 30% of Earth's severely eroded land and is most prevalent in Asia and South America (Figure 7-6). Unsustainable methods of farming cause 28% of such erosion, with two-thirds of the damage found in North America.

Each year we must feed 90 million more people with an estimated 24 billion metric tons (26 billion tons) less topsoil. This topsoil washing and blowing into the world's streams, lakes, and oceans each year would fill a train of freight cars long enough to encircle the planet 150 times. The situation is worsening as many farmers in LDCs plow easily erodible lands to feed themselves.

THE U.S. SITUATION In the 1930s the United States learned a harsh lesson about farming and wind erosion in the vast grasslands of the Great Plains, which stretch across 10 states, from Texas through Montana and the Dakotas. Before settlers began grazing livestock and planting crops there in the 1870s, the deep and tangled root systems of native prairie grasses (Fig-

ure 7-3) anchored the fertile topsoil firmly in place in this dry and windy region. Plowing the prairie tore up these roots, and the agricultural crops the settlers planted annually in their place had less extensive root systems.

After each harvest the land was plowed and left bare for several months, exposing it to the plains winds. Overgrazing also destroyed large expanses of grass, denuding the ground. The stage was set for severe wind erosion and crop failures, needing only a long drought to raise the curtain.

Such a drought arrived, lasting from 1926 to 1934. In the 1930s, dust clouds created by hot, dry windstorms darkened the sky at midday in some areas. Rabbits and birds choked to death on the dust. During May 1934 the entire eastern United States was blanketed with a cloud of topsoil blown off the Great Plains as far as 2,400 kilometers (1,500 miles) away. Journalists began calling the Great Plains the Dust Bowl (Figure 7-7).

Cropland equal in area to Connecticut and Maryland combined was stripped of topsoil, and an area the size of New Mexico was severely eroded. Thousands of displaced farm families from Oklahoma, Texas,

Figure 7-7
The Dust Bowl of the Great Plains, where a combination of periodic severe drought and poor soil conservation practices led to severe erosion of topsoil by wind in the 1930s.

Kansas, and other states migrated to California or to the industrial cities of the Midwest and East. Most found no jobs because the country was in the midst of the Great Depression.

In that memorable May of 1934, Hugh Bennett of the U.S. Department of Agriculture (USDA) was pleading before a congressional hearing in Washington for new programs to protect the country's topsoil. Lawmakers took action when Great Plains dust began seeping into the hearing room.

In 1935 the United States established the Soil Conservation Service (SCS) under the Department of Agriculture. With Bennett as its first head, the SCS began promoting good conservation practices, first in the Great Plains states and later in every state. Soil conservation districts were formed throughout the country, and farmers and ranchers were given technical assistance in setting up soil conservation programs. But these heroic efforts could not stop human-accelerated erosion in the Great Plains. The basic problem is that much of the region is better suited for moderate grazing than for farming. If Earth warms, the region could become even drier, and farming would have to be abandoned.

Vanishing topsoil and creeping desertification are still serious problems in parts of the United States (Figures 5-9 and 7-6). Today soil on cultivated land in the United States is eroding about 16 times faster than it can form. And erosion rates are even higher in heavily farmed regions, such as the Great Plains, which has lost one-third or more of its topsoil in the 150 years since it was first plowed. Parts of the western rangelands and the Great Plains are undergoing desertification from overcultivation, overgrazing, and depletion of groundwater used for irrigation—a new Dust Bowl waiting to happen. Some of the country's most productive agricultural lands, such as those in Iowa, have lost about half their topsoil. California's soil is eroding 80 times faster than it can be formed.

Enough topsoil erodes away each day in the United States to fill a line of dump trucks 5,600 kilometers (3,500 miles) long. About 86% of it comes from land used to graze cattle or to raise crops to feed cattle. The other 14% of eroded soil comes from land used to raise crops for human consumption. Soil expert David Pimentel estimates that the total costs of soil erosion and runoff in the United States exceed $25 billion per year—an average loss of $2.9 million per hour!

SOIL CONTAMINATION BY EXCESS SALTS AND WATER Some 18% of the world's cropland is now irrigated, producing about one-third of the world's food. Irrigated land can produce crop yields two to three times those from rain-watering, but irrigation has its downside. Irrigation water contains dissolved salts. In dry climates much of the water in this saline solution evaporates, leaving its salts, such as sodium chloride, behind in the topsoil. The accumulation of these salts, called **salinization** (Figure 7-8), stunts crop growth, lowers yields, and eventually kills crop plants and ruins the land.

It is estimated that salinization is reducing yields on one-fourth of the world's irrigated cropland. Worldwide, 50–65% of all currently irrigated cropland will probably have reduced productivity from salting by 2000.

Salts can be flushed out of soil by applying much more irrigation water than is needed for crop growth, but this practice increases pumping and crop-production costs, and it wastes enormous amounts of water. Heavily salinized soil can also be renewed by taking the land out of production for two to five years, installing an underground network of perforated drainage pipes, and flushing the soil with large quantities of low-salt water. This costly scheme, however, only slows the salt buildup; it does not stop the process. Flushing salts from the soil also makes downstream irrigation water saltier, unless the saline water can be drained into evaporation ponds rather than returned to the stream or canal. In the Indian state of Uttar Pradesh, farmers are rehabilitating salinized land by planting a salt-tolerant tree that lowers the water table by taking up water through its roots.

Another problem with irrigation in some areas is **waterlogging** (Figure 7-8). Farmers often apply heavy amounts of irrigation water to leach salts deeper into the soil. Without adequate drainage, however, water accumulates underground, gradually raising the water table. Saline water then envelops the roots of plants and kills them. Worldwide, at least one-tenth of all irrigated land suffers from waterlogging, and the problem is getting worse.

Q: How much of the U.S. Forest Service budget is devoted to timber sales?

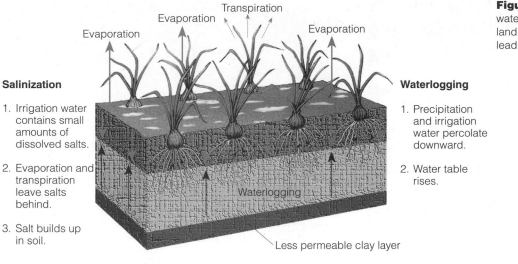

Salinization

1. Irrigation water contains small amounts of dissolved salts.

2. Evaporation and transpiration leave salts behind.

3. Salt builds up in soil.

Evaporation

Evaporation

Transpiration

Evaporation

Waterlogging

1. Precipitation and irrigation water percolate downward.

2. Water table rises.

Waterlogging

Less permeable clay layer

Figure 7-8 Salinization and waterlogging of soil on irrigated land without adequate drainage lead to decreased crop yields.

7-2 Solutions: Saving the Soil

CONSERVATION TILLAGE Soil conservation involves reducing soil erosion, preventing depletion of soil nutrients, and restoring nutrients already lost by erosion, leaching, overgrazing, and overcropping. Most methods used to control soil erosion involve keeping the soil covered with vegetation.

In **conventional-tillage farming** the land is plowed, and the soil is broken up and smoothed to make a planting surface. In areas such as the midwestern United States harsh winters prevent plowing just before the spring growing season. Thus cropfields are often plowed in the fall. This bares the soil during the winter and early spring months, leaving it vulnerable to erosion.

To reduce erosion, many U.S. farmers are using **conservation-tillage farming** (or *minimum-tillage* or *no-till farming*). The idea is to disturb the soil as little as possible in planting crops. With minimum-tillage, special tillers break up and loosen the subsurface soil without turning over the topsoil, previous crop residues, and any cover vegetation. In no-till farming special planting machines inject seeds, fertilizers, and weed-killers (herbicides) into slits made in the unplowed soil.

Besides reducing soil erosion, conservation tillage saves fuel, cuts costs, holds more water in the soil, keeps the soil from getting packed down, and allows more crops to be grown during a season (multiple cropping). Yields are at least as high as those from conventional tillage. At first, conservation tillage was thought to require more herbicides. However, a 1990 U.S. Department of Agriculture (USDA) study of maize production in the United States found no real difference in levels of herbicide use between conventional and conservation tillage systems.

Conservation tillage is now used on about one-third of U.S. croplands and is projected to be used on over half by 2000. The USDA estimates that using conservation tillage on 80% of U.S. cropland would reduce soil erosion by at least half. So far, the practice is not widely used in other parts of the world.

OTHER WAYS TO REDUCE SOIL EROSION For hundreds of years farmers have used various methods to reduce soil erosion (Figure 7-9). They include:

- **Terracing**. A steep slope is converted into a series of broad, nearly level terraces that run across the land contour with short vertical drops from one terrace to another (Figure 7-9a). Terracing retains water for crops at all levels and cuts soil erosion by controlling runoff.

- **Contour farming**. Soil erosion can be reduced 30–50% on gently sloping land by means of plowing and planting crops in rows across, rather than up and down, the sloped contour of the land (Figure 7-9b). Each row planted horizontally along the slope of the land acts as a small dam to help hold soil and slow the runoff of water.

- **Strip cropping**. A row crop like corn alternates in strips with a soil-saving cover crop, such as a grass or a grass-legume mixture, that completely covers the soil and thus reduces erosion (Figure 7-9c). The strips of cover crop trap soil that erodes from the row crop. The cover crops catch and reduce water runoff and also help prevent the spread of pests and plant diseases from one strip

a. Terracing

b. Contour Farming

c. Strip Cropping

d. Alley Cropping or Agroforestry

e. Gully Reclamation

f. Windbreaks or Shelterbelts

Figure 7-9 Soil conservation methods.

to another. In addition, they help restore soil fertility if nitrogen-fixing legumes, such as soybeans or alfalfa, are planted in some of the strips.

- **Alley cropping,** or **agroforestry.** Several crops are planted together in strips or alleys between trees and shrubs that can provide fruit and fuel-

wood (Figure 7-9d). The trees provide shade (which reduces water loss by evaporation) and help retain soil moisture and release it slowly. The hedgerow trimmings can be used as mulch (green manure) for the crops and as fodder for livestock.

Q: Between 1978 and 1992, how much money did the Forest Service lose on timber sales?

- **Gully reclamation**. Small gullies carved out of the land by erosion can be seeded with quick-growing plants such as oats, barley, and wheat for the first season, while deeper gullies can be dammed to collect silt and gradually fill in the channels (Figure 7-9e). Fast-growing shrubs, vines, and trees can also be planted to stabilize the soil, and channels can be built to divert water from the gully and prevent further erosion.

- **Windbreaks**, or **shelterbelts**. Wind erosion can be reduced by planting long rows of trees to partially block the wind (Figure 7-9f). These are especially effective if uncultivated land is kept covered with vegetation. Windbreaks also help hold soil moisture in place, supply some wood for fuel, and provide a habitat for wildlife. Unfortunately, many of the windbreaks planted in the upper Great Plains after the 1930s Dust Bowl disaster have been cut down to make way for large irrigation systems and farm machinery.

- *Land-use classification and control*. Land can be evaluated with the goal of identifying easily erodible (marginal) land that should not be planted in crops or cleared of vegetation. In the United States the Soil Conservation Service (SCS) has set up a land-use classification system. The SCS basically relies on voluntary compliance with its guidelines through almost 3,000 local and state soil- and water-conservation districts it has established, and it provides technical and economic assistance through the local district offices.

Of the world's major food-producing countries, only the United States is reducing some of its soil losses (Solutions, at right). Even so, effective soil conservation is practiced on only about half of all U.S. agricultural land and on less than half of the country's most erodible cropland.

MAINTAINING AND RESTORING SOIL

FERTILITY Fertilizers partially restore plant nutrients lost by erosion, crop harvesting and leaching. Farmers can use **organic fertilizer** from plant and animal materials and **commercial inorganic fertilizer** produced from various minerals. Three types of organic fertilizer are:

- **Animal manure**: dung and urine of cattle, horses, poultry, and other farm animals. It improves soil structure, adds organic nitrogen, and stimulates beneficial soil bacteria and fungi. Despite its effectiveness the use of animal manure in the United States has decreased, mostly because separate farms for growing crops and raising animals have replaced most mixed animal-raising

Slowing Erosion in the United States

SOLUTIONS

The 1985 Farm Act established a strategy to reduce soil erosion in the United States. In the first phase of this program farmers are given a subsidy for highly erodible land they take out of production and replant with soil-saving grass or trees for 10 years. The land in such a *conservation reserve* cannot be farmed, grazed, or cut for hay. Farmers who violate their contracts must pay back all subsidies with interest.

By 1992, more than 14 million hectares (35 million acres) of land had been placed in the conservation reserve, cutting soil erosion on U.S. cropland by almost one-third. If the program is expanded and adequately enforced, it could cut soil losses from U.S. cropland by 80%.

The second phase of the program required all farmers with highly erodible land to develop Soil Conservation Service (SCS)-approved five-year soil-conservation plans for their entire farms by the end of 1990. Farmers not implementing their plans by 1995 can lose eligibility for government subsidies and loans.

A third provision of the Farm Act authorizes the government to forgive all or part of farmers' debts to the Farmers Home Administration if they agree not to farm highly erodible cropland or wetlands for 50 years. The farmers are required to plant trees or grass on this land or to convert it back into wetlands.

In 1987, however, the SCS eased the standards that farmers' soil conservation plans must meet to keep them eligible for other subsidies. Environmentalists have also accused the SCS of laxity in enforcing the Farm Act's "swampbuster" provisions, which deny federal funds to farmers who drain or destroy wetlands on their property. Despite some weaknesses the 1985 Farm Act makes the United States the first major food-producing country to make soil conservation a national priority.

and crop-farming operations. In addition, tractors and other motorized farm machinery have replaced horses and other draft animals that naturally added manure to the soil.

- **Green manure**: fresh or growing green vegetation plowed into the soil to increase the organic matter and humus available to the next crop.

- **Compost**: a rich natural fertilizer and soil conditioner that aerates soil, improves its ability to retain water and nutrients, helps prevent erosion, and prevents nutrients from being wasted in landfills. Farmers and home owners produce it by piling up alternating layers of carbohydrate-rich plant wastes (such as grass clippings, leaves, weeds, hay, straw, and sawdust), kitchen scraps (such as vegetable remains and egg shells), animal manure, and topsoil.

Today, especially in the United States and other industrialized countries, farmers rely on *commercial inorganic fertilizers* containing nitrogen (as ammonium ions, nitrate ions, or urea), phosphorus (as phosphate ions), and potassium (as potassium ions). Other plant nutrients may also be present in low or trace amounts.

Inorganic commercial fertilizers are easily transported, stored, and applied. Worldwide, their use increased about tenfold between 1950 and 1992 but has declined slightly since 1988. Today, the additional food they help produce feeds one of every three persons in the world. Without them world food output would plummet an estimated 40%.

Commercial inorganic fertilizers have some disadvantages, however. They do not add humus to the soil. Unless animal manure and green manure are also added, the soil's content of organic matter—and thus its ability to hold water—will decrease, and the soil will become compacted and less suitable for crop growth. By decreasing the soil's porosity, inorganic fertilizers also lower the oxygen content of soil and keep added fertilizer from being taken up as efficiently. In addition, most commercial fertilizers supply only 2 or 3 of the 20-odd nutrients needed by plants.

The widespread use of commercial inorganic fertilizers, especially on sloped land near streams and lakes, causes water pollution as well. Some of the nutrients in the fertilizers are washed into nearby bodies of water, where the resulting cultural eutrophication causes algae blooms that use up dissolved oxygen depletion and kill fish. Rainwater seeping through the soil can also leach nitrates in commercial fertilizers into groundwater. Drinking water drawn from wells containing high levels of nitrate ions can be toxic, especially for infants.

Another method for conserving soil nutrients is **crop rotation**. Corn, tobacco, and cotton can deplete the topsoil of nutrients (especially nitrogen) if planted on the same land several years in a row. Farmers using crop rotation plant areas or strips with nutrient-depleting crops such as corn, tobacco, and cotton one year. The next year they plant the same areas with legumes, whose root nodules add nitrogen to the soil, or with crops such as oats, barley, rye, or sorghum. This method helps restore soil nutrients and reduces erosion by keeping the soil covered with vegetation.

Concern about soil erosion should not be limited to farmers. At least 40% of soil erosion in the United

What You Can Do to Help Protect the Soil

INDIVIDUALS MATTER

- *When building a home, save all the trees possible.* Require the contractor to disturb as little soil as possible, to set up barriers that catch any soil eroded during construction, and to save and replace any topsoil removed instead of hauling it off and selling it. Plant disturbed areas with fast-growing native ground cover (preferably not grass) immediately after construction is completed.

- *Landscape the area not used for gardening with a mix of wildflowers, herbs (for cooking and for repelling insects), low-growing ground cover, small bushes, and other forms of vegetation natural to the area.* This biologically diverse type of yard saves water, energy, and money, and it reduces infestation of mosquitoes and other damaging insects by providing a diversity of habitats for their natural predators.

- *Set up a compost bin and use it to produce mulch and soil conditioner for yard and garden plants.*

States is caused by timber cutting, overgrazing, mining, and urban development carried out without proper regard for soil conservation. Each of us has a role to play in saving soil—the base of life (Individuals Matter, above).

7-3 How Is Food Produced?

PLANTS AND ANIMALS THAT FEED THE WORLD
Global food production has increased substantially over the past two decades. However, producing food and other agricultural products by conventional means uses more soil, water, plant, animal, and energy resources—and causes more pollution and environmental damage—than any other human activity. To feed the 8.5 billion people projected by 2025, we must produce and distribute as much food during the next 30 years as was produced since agriculture began about 10,000 years ago.

Of Earth's perhaps 30,000 plants with edible parts we eat only about 30. Just 15 plants and 8 animal

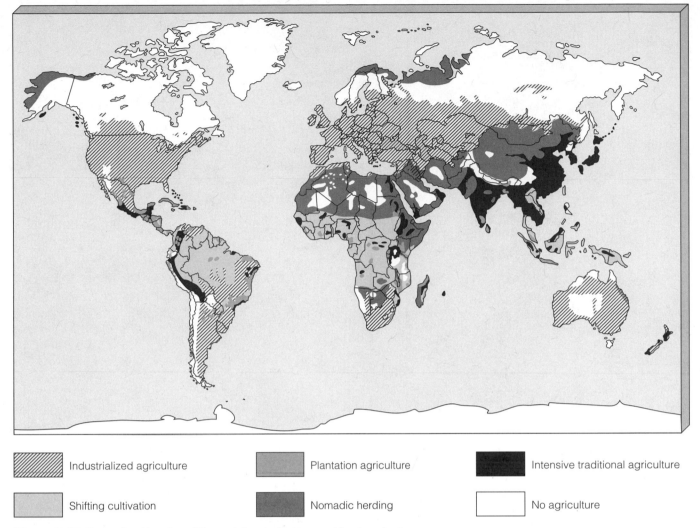

| Industrialized agriculture | Plantation agriculture | Intensive traditional agriculture |
| Shifting cultivation | Nomadic herding | No agriculture |

Figure 7-10 Generalized location of the world's principal types of food production.

species supply 90% of our food. Four crops—wheat, rice, corn, and potato—make up more of the world's total food production than all others combined.

Grain provides about half the world's calories, with two out of three people eating mainly a vegetarian diet—mostly because they can't afford meat. As incomes rise, people consume more grain indirectly in the form of meat, eggs, milk, cheese, and other products of domesticated livestock. Although only about one-third of the world's people can afford to eat meat, more than half of the world's cropland (almost two-thirds in the United States) is used to produce livestock feed to supply these individuals with meat. In addition, one-third of the world's fish catch is converted into fish meal to feed livestock consumed by meat eaters in MDCs.

TYPES OF FOOD PRODUCTION There are two major types of agricultural systems, industrialized and traditional. **Industrialized agriculture** uses large amounts of fossil-fuel energy, water, commercial fertilizers, and pesticides to produce huge quantities of one crop or animal for sale. Industrialized agriculture, practiced on about 25% of all cropland, mostly in MDCs, has spread since the mid-1960s to some LDCs (Figure 7-10). **Plantation agriculture**, a form of industrialized agriculture mostly in tropical LDCs, grows cash crops such as bananas, coffee, and cacao, mostly for sale to MDCs.

Traditional agriculture consists of two main types. **Traditional subsistence agriculture** produces enough crops or livestock for a farm family's survival and, in good years, a surplus to sell or put aside for hard times. Subsistence farmers use human labor and draft animals. Examples of this type of agriculture include shifting cultivation in tropical forests (Figure 5-7) and nomadic livestock herding. With **traditional intensive agriculture**, farmers increase their inputs of human and draft labor, fertilizer, and water to get a higher yield per area of cultivated land to produce enough

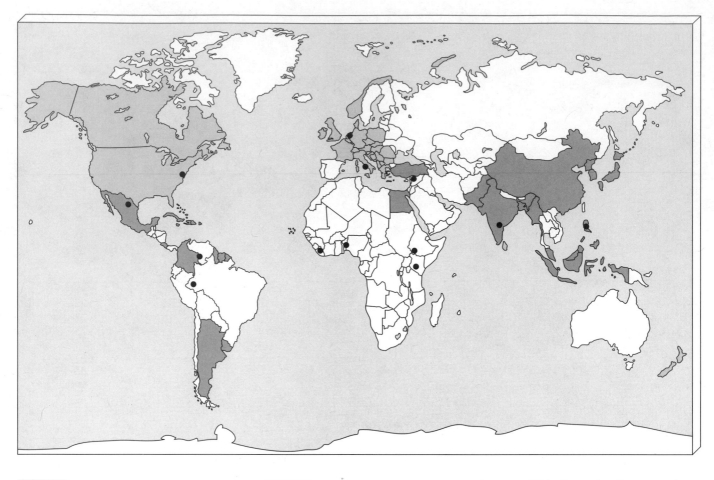

| | 1st Green Revolution (MDCs) | | 2nd Green Revolution (LDCs) | • | Major international agricultural research centers and seed banks |

Figure 7-11 Countries whose crop yields per unit of land area increased during the two green revolutions. The first took place in MDCs between 1950 and 1970, and the second since 1967 in LDCs with enough rainfall or irrigation capacity. Thirteen agricultural research centers and genetic storage banks play a key role in developing high-yield crop varieties.

food to feed their families and perhaps a surplus for sale. These forms of traditional agriculture are practiced by about 2.7 billion people—almost half the people on Earth—in LDCs.

INDUSTRIALIZED AGRICULTURE AND GREEN REVOLUTIONS Farmers can produce more either by farming more land or by getting higher yields from existing cropland. Since 1950 most of the increase in global food production has come from raising the yield per hectare, the so-called **green revolution**. This involves planting monocultures of improved plants and lavishing fertilizer, pesticides, and water on them. Between 1950 and 1970 this approach dramatically increased crop yields in most MDCs—the *first green revolution* (Figure 7-11).

Then, fast-growing dwarf varieties of rice and wheat, specially bred for tropical and subtropical climates, were introduced into several LDCs in the *sec-*

ond green revolution (Figure 7-11). With enough fertilizer, water, and pesticides, yields of these new plants can be two to five times those of traditional wheat and rice varieties. And fast growth allows farmers to grow two or even three crops a year (multiple cropping) on the same land parcel.

Nearly 90% of the increase in world grain output in the 1960s, about 70% in the 1970s, and 80% in the 1980s resulted from this second green revolution. In the 1990s at least 80% of any increase is expected to come from green-revolution techniques.

These increases depend heavily on fossil fuels to run machinery, produce and apply inorganic fertilizers and pesticides, and pump water for irrigation. All told, green-revolution agriculture now uses about 8% of the world's oil output.

These high inputs of energy, water, fertilizer, and pesticides have yielded dramatic results, but at some point additional inputs become useless because no

Q: How much of U.S. public rangeland is in unsatisfactory (fair or poor) condition?

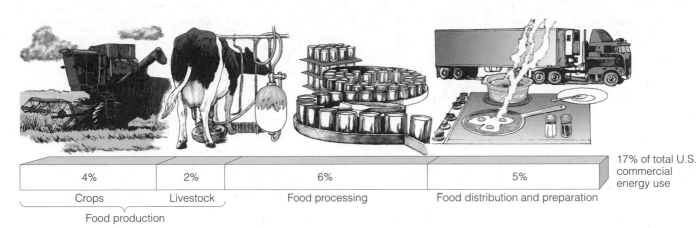

4%	2%	6%	5%
Crops	Livestock	Food processing	Food distribution and preparation

17% of total U.S. commercial energy use

Food production

Figure 7-12 Commercial energy use by the U.S. industrialized agriculture system.

more output can be squeezed from the land. In fact, yields may even start dropping because the soil erodes, loses fertility, and becomes salty and waterlogged. Aquifers can be depleted, deserts can advance, and surface and groundwater become polluted. And insect pests develop genetic resistance to pesticides.

INDUSTRIALIZED AGRICULTURE IN THE UNITED STATES
Since 1940 U.S. farmers have more than doubled crop production without cultivating more land. They have done this through industrialized agriculture, coupled with a favorable climate and some of the world's most fertile and productive soils.

Farming has become *agribusiness* as big companies and larger family-owned farms have taken control of most U.S. food production. Only 1.8% of the U.S. population lives on the country's 2.1 million farms, and only about 650,000 Americans work full-time at farming. However, about 23 million people—9% of the population—are involved in the U.S. agricultural system, from growing and processing food to distributing it and selling it at the supermarket. In terms of total annual sales, agriculture is the biggest industry in the United States—bigger than the automotive, steel, and housing industries combined. It generates about 18% of the country's GNP and 19% of all private sector jobs, employing more people than any other industry.

U.S. farmland, called the "breadbasket" of the world, produces half the world's grain exports. In 1991 one U.S. farmer fed and clothed 128 people (94 at home and 34 abroad), up from 58 persons in 1976.

The industrialization of U.S. agriculture was made possible by the availability of cheap energy. Most of this energy comes from oil, followed by natural gas used for drying and producing inorganic fertilizers. Agriculture consumes about 17% of commercial energy used in the United States each year (Figure 7-12).

Most plant crops in the United States provide more food energy than the energy used to grow them.

However, raising livestock requires much more fossil-fuel energy than the animals provide in food energy. If we include crops and livestock, U.S. farms currently use about 3 units of fossil-fuel energy to produce 1 unit of food energy. Indeed, if all people in the United States were vegetarians, the country's oil imports could be cut by 60%.

Energy efficiency is much worse if we look at the whole U.S. food system. Considering the energy used to grow, store, process, package, transport, refrigerate, and cook all plant and animal food, *an average of about 10 units of nonrenewable fossil-fuel energy are needed to put 1 unit of food energy on the table.* By comparison, every unit of energy from the human labor of subsistence farmers provides at least 1 unit of food energy and, with traditional intensive farming, up to 10 units of food energy. For example, an average piece of food eaten in the United States has traveled 2,100 kilometers (1,300 miles), with food transportation costing nearly $21 billion per year.

EXAMPLES OF TRADITIONAL AGRICULTURE
Farmers in LDCs grow about 20% of the world's food on about 75% of its cultivated land. Many traditional farmers simultaneously grow several crops on the same plot—a method called **interplanting**. This biological diversity reduces the chances of losing most or all of their year's food supply to pests, flooding, drought, or other disasters. Common interplanting strategies include

- **Polyvarietal cultivation**, in which a plot is planted with several varieties of the same crop.
- **Intercropping**, in which two or more different crops are grown at the same time on a plot—for example, a carbohydrate-rich grain that uses soil nitrogen alongside a protein-rich legume that puts it back.

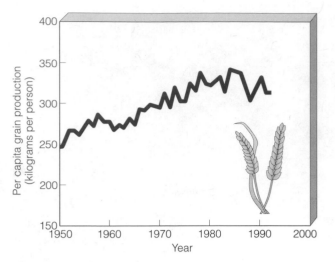

Figure 7-13 World grain production per person, 1950–92. (Data from U.S. Department of Agriculture)

■ **Agroforestry**, or **alley cropping**, a variation of intercropping in which crops and trees are planted together—for example, a grain or legume crop planted around fruit-bearing orchard trees or in rows between fast-growing trees or shrubs that can be used for fuelwood or for adding nitrogen to the soil (Figure 7-9d).

■ **Polyculture**, a more complex form of intercropping in which many different plants maturing at various times are planted together. If cultivated properly, these plots can provide food, medicines, fuel, and natural pesticides and fertilizers on a sustainable basis.

 7-4   **World Food Problems**

GOOD AND BAD NEWS ABOUT FOOD PRODUCTION   Between 1950 and 1984, world grain production (a good measure of overall food production) more than tripled, and per capita production rose by almost 50% (Figure 7-13). During the same period average food prices adjusted for inflation dropped by 25%, and the amount of food traded in the world market quadrupled.

Despite these impressive achievements in food production, population growth is outstripping food production where 2 billion people live. Global grain production increased nearly 3% per year from 1950 to the peak year of 1984. Since then, however, it has risen barely 1% per year—lower than the rate of population growth. As a result, global grain production per per-

son has declined since 1984 (Figure 7-13). Since 1978 grain production has lagged behind population growth in 69 of the 102 LDCs for which data are available. In 22 African countries per capita food production has dropped 28% since 1960 and may drop another 30% during the next 25 years. More than 100 countries now regularly import food from the United States, Canada, Australia, Argentina, western Europe, and a few other surplus producers.

NUTRITION   People who cannot grow or obtain enough food to give them 2,700 calories per day for men and 2,000 calories per day for women suffer from **undernutrition**. To maintain good health and disease resistance, however, people need not only a certain number of calories but also food with the proper amounts of protein (from animal or plant sources), carbohydrates, fats, vitamins, and minerals. People who are forced to live on a low-protein, high-starch diet of grains such as wheat, rice, or corn often suffer from **malnutrition**, or deficiencies of protein and other key nutrients. Many of the world's desperately poor people suffer from both undernutrition and malnutrition.

According to the World Health Organization, about 1.3 billion people—one out of four, and one in three children—are underfed and undernourished (a low estimate is around 0.8 billion). Each year 40 million people—half of them children under age 5—die prematurely from undernutrition, malnutrition, or normally nonfatal infections and diseases worsened by malnutrition. Some put the annual death toll at 20 million, while others say it is 60 million. With any of these estimates, we have a tragic situation.

Chronically undernourished and malnourished individuals are disease-prone and too weak to work productively or think clearly. As a result, their children are also underfed and malnourished. If these children survive to adulthood, many are locked in a tragic malnutrition-poverty cycle in which these conditions are often passed on to succeeding generations (Figure 7-14).

Each of us must have a small daily intake of vitamins that cannot be made in the human body. Although balanced diets, vitamin-fortified foods, and vitamin supplements have slashed the number of vitamin-deficiency diseases in MDCs, millions of cases occur each year in LDCs. For example, each year more than 500,000 children in LDCs are partially or totally blinded because their diet lacks vitamin A.

Other nutritional-deficiency diseases are caused by the lack of certain minerals. For example, too little iron causes anemia, which in turn causes fatigue, makes infection more likely, increases a woman's chances of dying in childbirth, and increases an infant's chances of dying from infection during its first

     Q: How much do 30,000 U.S. ranchers with permits to graze on public lands get in federal subsidies?

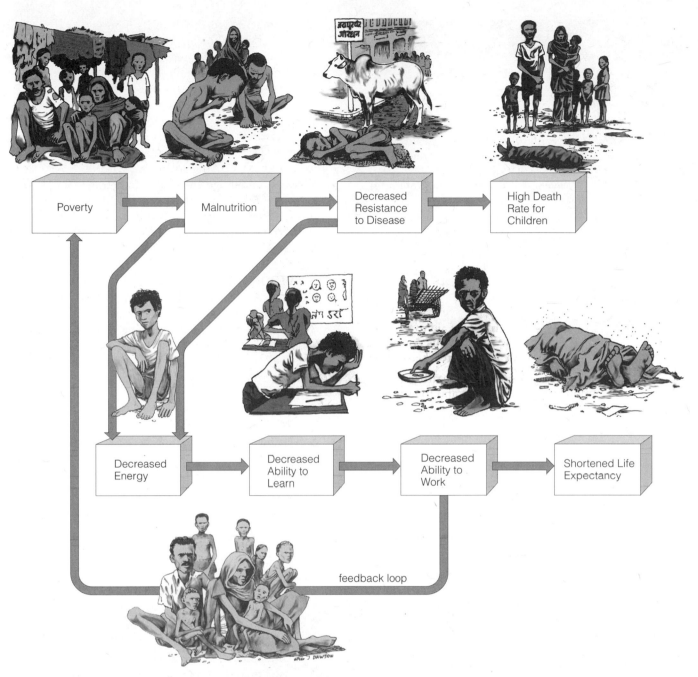

Figure 7-14 Interactions among poverty, malnutrition, and disease form a tragic cycle that tends to perpetuate such conditions in succeeding generations of families.

year of life. In tropical regions of Asia, Africa, and Latin America, iron-deficiency anemia affects about one-tenth of the men, more than half of the children, two-thirds of the pregnant women, and about half of the other women. However, children don't have to die because of malnutrition (Solutions, p. 192).

While 15% of the people in LDCs suffer from severe undernutrition and malnutrition, about 15% of the people in MDCs—including at least 34 million Americans—suffer from **overnutrition**. This is an

excessive intake of food, especially fats, that can cause obesity (excess body fat) in people who do not suffer from physiological disorders that promote obesity.

Overnutrition is associated with at least two-thirds of the deaths in the United States each year. A study of thousands of Chinese villagers indicates that the healthiest diet for humans is nearly vegetarian, with only 10–15% of calories coming from fats, in contrast to the typical meat-based diet in which 40% of the calories come from fats.

Saving Children

SOLUTIONS

Officials of the United Nations Children's Fund (UNICEF) estimate that between one-half and two-thirds of childhood deaths from nutrition-related causes could be prevented at an average annual cost of only $5–10 per child—10–19¢ per week. This life-saving program would involve the following simple measures:

- Immunizing against childhood diseases such as measles

- Encouraging breast-feeding

- Preventing dehydration from diarrhea by giving infants a solution of a fistful of sugar and a pinch of salt in a glass of water

- Preventing blindness by giving people a vitamin A capsule twice a year at a cost of about 75¢ per person

- Providing family-planning services to help mothers space births at least two years apart

- Increasing female education, with emphasis on nutrition, sterilization of drinking water, and child care

FOOD SUPPLY AND DISTRIBUTION The good news is that we produce more than enough food to meet the basic needs of every person on Earth. Indeed, if distributed equally, the grain currently produced worldwide would be enough to give 6 billion people— the projected world population for the year 1998—a meatless subsistence diet. The bad news is that food is not distributed equally among the world's people because of differences in soil, climate, political and economic power, and average income throughout the world.

By contrast, if everyone ate the diet typical of a person in an MDC, with 30–40% of the calories coming from animal products, the current world agricultural system would support only 2.5 billion people. That is less than half the present population and only one-fourth of the 10 billion people projected sometime in the next century (Figure 1-1).

Increases in global food production and food production per person often hide wide differences in food supply and quality among and within countries. For example, nearly half of India's population is too poor to buy or grow enough food to meet basic needs, and

an estimated two-thirds of its land is threatened by erosion, water shortages, and salinization. This, coupled with current population growth of 17 million per year, means that India might again suffer from famine in the 1990s and beyond.

MDCs also have pockets of poverty, hunger, and malnutrition. For example, a study by Tufts University researchers estimated that in 1991 at least 20 million people (12 million children and 8 million adults)—1 out of every 11 Americans and 1 out of 5 American children under age 18—were not getting enough food to prevent undernutrition, malnutrition, or both. This was caused mostly by cuts in food stamps and other forms of government aid since 1980 coupled with job losses.

ENVIRONMENTAL EFFECTS OF PRODUCING FOOD Agriculture—both industrialized and traditional—has a greater impact on air, soil, and water resources than any other human activity, as discussed throughout this book. These problems include

Soil Degradation

- Erosion (Figure 7-6). About 85% of U.S. topsoil loss is caused by livestock overgrazing.

- Salinization and waterlogging of heavily irrigated soils (Figure 7-8).

- Desertification caused by cultivation of marginal land with unsuitable soil or terrain, overgrazing, deforestation, and failure to use soil conservation techniques (Figure 5-9).

Water Use and Depletion

- About 69% of the water withdrawn each year is used to irrigate 18% of the world's cropland.

- Irrigation accounts for 41% of the water used in the United States each year (85% in the western United States), with at least half of this water used to irrigate crops fed to livestock and to wash manure away.

- Depletion of groundwater aquifers by withdrawals for irrigation (Figures 10-11 and 10-12).

Pollution

- Air and water pollution from extraction, processing, transportation, and combustion of fossil fuels used in industrialized agriculture (Figure 1-9).

- Air pollution from droplets of pesticides sprayed from planes or ground sprayers (Section 7-6).

- Pollution of streams, lakes, and estuaries, and killing of fish and shellfish from pesticide runoff.

Q: How much of the money taken in by private concessionaires operating in national parks is paid in user fees to the federal government?

- Pollution of groundwater caused by leaching of water-soluble pesticides, nitrates from commercial inorganic fertilizers, and salts from irrigation water.

- Overfertilization of lakes and slow-moving rivers caused by runoff of nitrates and phosphates in commercial inorganic fertilizers, livestock wastes, and food-processing wastes (Figure 10-16). Livestock in the United States produce 21 times more excrement than that produced by the country's human population. Only about half of this livestock waste is recycled to the soil as organic fertilizer.

- Sediment pollution of surface waters caused by erosion and runoff from farm fields, overgrazed rangeland, deforested land, and animal feedlots.

Biodiversity Loss

- Loss of genetic diversity in plants caused by clearing biologically diverse grasslands and forests (Sections 5-3 and 5-4) and often replacing them with monocultures.

- Endangerment and extinction of wildlife from loss of habitat when grasslands and forests are cleared and wetlands are drained for farming (Section 6-2).

Human Health Threats

- Nitrates in drinking water and pesticides in drinking water, food, and the atmosphere.

- Human and animal wastes discharged or washed into irrigation ditches and sources of drinking water (Section 10-6).

- Pesticide residues in food. Meat accounts for 55% of such residues in the U.S. diet, compared to 6% from vegetables, 4% from fruits, and 1% from grains.

7-5 Solutions to World Food Problems

INCREASING CROP YIELDS Agricultural experts expect most future increases in food production to come from increased yields per hectare on existing cropland, from improved strains of plants, and from expansion of green-revolution technology to other parts of the world. Agricultural scientists are working to create new green revolutions—or *gene revolutions*—by using genetic engineering and other forms of biotechnology (Pro/Con, p. 217). Over the next 20–40 years they hope to breed high-yield plant strains that are more resistant to insects and disease, thrive on less fertilizer, make their own nitrogen fertilizer (as do legumes), do well in slightly salty soils, withstand drought, and use solar energy more efficiently during photosynthesis. Even only occasional breakthroughs could generate enormous increases in global crop production before the middle of the next century.

However, several factors have limited the success of the green and gene revolutions so far—and may continue to do so:

- Without huge doses of fertilizer and water, most green-revolution crop varieties produce yields no higher and often lower than those from traditional strains; that is why the second green revolution has not spread to many arid and semiarid areas (Figure 7-11). Without good soil, water, and weather, new genetically engineered crop strains could fail.

- Continuing to increase inputs of fertilizer, water, and pesticides eventually produces no further increase in crop yields, as the J-shaped curve of crop productivity reaches its limits and is converted to an S-shaped curve.

- Without careful land use and environmental controls, degradation of water and soil can limit the long-term success of green and gene revolutions.

- The cost of genetically engineered crop strains is too high for most of the world's subsistence farmers in LDCs.

- The severe and increasing loss of Earth's biodiversity from deforestation, destruction and degradation of other ecosystems, and replacement of a diverse mixture of natural crop varieties with monoculture crops can limit the potential of future green and gene revolutions.

Loss of genetic diversity in plant species is a serious threat to future food production. The UN Food and Agriculture Organization estimates that by the year 2000, two-thirds of all seed planted in LDCs will be of uniform strains. This genetic uniformity increases the vulnerability of food crops to pests and diseases. This, plus widespread species extinction, severely limits the potential of future green and gene revolutions. In other words we are rapidly shrinking the world's genetic "library" just when we need it more than ever.

In the mid-1970s, for example, a valuable wild corn species was barely saved from extinction. When this strain was discovered, only a few thousand stalks

Growing Perennial Crops on the Kansas Prairie

SOLUTIONS

When you think about farms in Kansas, you probably picture endless fields of wheat or corn plowed up and planted each year. By 2040 the picture might change, thanks to pioneering work at the nonprofit Land Institute near Salina, Kansas.

The institute, founded by Wes and Dana Jackson, is experimenting with an ecological approach to agriculture on the midwestern prairie based on planting a mix of *perennial* grasses, legumes, sunflowers, and grain crops in the same field (polyculture) that don't have to be replanted each year like traditional food crops. Its goal is to raise food by mimicking many of the natural conditions of the prairie.

By eliminating yearly soil preparation and planting, perennial polyculture requires much less labor than conventional monoculture and diversified organic farms growing annual crops. Perennial polyculture rewards farmers more for their wits, creative thinking, and land care efforts, and less for routine drudgery and labor.

If the institute and similar groups doing such Earth-sustaining research succeed, within a few decades many people may be eating food made from perennials such as *Maximilian sunflower* (which produces seeds with as much protein as soybeans), *eastern gamma grass* (a relative of corn with three times as much protein as corn and twice as much as wheat), *Illinois bundleflower* (a wild nitrogen-producing legume that can enrich the soil and whose seeds may serve as livestock feed), and *giant wild rye* (once eaten by Mongols in Siberia).

survived in three tiny patches in south central Mexico that were about to be cleared by squatter cultivators and commercial loggers. This wild species is the only known perennial strain of corn. Crossbreeding it with commercial varieties could reduce the need for yearly plowing and sowing, which would reduce soil erosion, water use, and energy use. Even more important, this wild corn has a built-in genetic resistance to four of the eight major corn viruses. Furthermore, this strain grows in cooler and damper habitats than established commercial strains. Overall, the genetic benefits from this wild plant—saved from extinction mostly by luck—could total several billion dollars per year.

Wild varieties of the world's most important plants can be collected and stored in gene banks, agri-cultural research centers (Figure 7-11), and botanical gardens; however, space and money severely limit the number of species that can be preserved there. Moreover, many cannot be stored successfully in gene banks, and power failures, fires, or unintentional disposal of seeds can cause irreversible losses. Also, stored plant species stop evolving and thus are less fit for reintroduction to their native habitats, which may have changed in the meantime.

Because of these limitations, ecologists and plant scientists warn that the only effective way to preserve the genetic diversity of most plant and animal species is to protect representative ecosystems throughout the world from agriculture and other forms of development (Chapter 5).

NEW FOOD SOURCES Some analysts recommend greatly increased cultivation of various nontraditional plants to supplement or replace such staples as wheat, rice, and corn. One of many possibilities is the winged bean, a protein-rich legume now common only in New Guinea and Southeast Asia. Because of nitrogen-fixing nodules in its roots, this fast-growing plant needs little fertilizer. This plant yields so many different edible parts that some call it a "supermarket on a stalk."

Insects are also important potential sources of protein, vitamins, and minerals. In South Africa, "Mopani"—emperor moth larvae—are among several insects eaten. Kalahari Desert dwellers eat cockroaches. Lightly toasted butterflies are a favorite food in Bali. French-fried ants are sold on the streets of Bogotá, Colombia, and Malaysians love deep-fried grasshoppers. Most of these insects are 58–78% protein by weight—three to four times as rich as beef, fish, or eggs.

Scientists have identified many plants and insects that could be used as sources of food. The problem is getting farmers to cultivate such crops and convincing consumers to try new foods.

Most crops we depend on are tropical annuals. Each year the land is cleared of all vegetation, dug up, and planted with their seeds. Some plant scientists believe we should rely more on polycultures of perennial crops, which are better adapted to regional soil and climate conditions than most annuals (Solutions, at left). This would eliminate the need to till soil each year, greatly reducing use of energy. It would also save water and reduce soil erosion and sediment water pollution.

If not overharvested, certain wild animals could be an important source of food. Prolific Amazon river turtles, for example, are used as a source of protein by local people. Another delicacy is the green iguana— "the chicken of the trees." If managed properly, these large, tasty lizards yield up to 10 times as much meat

Q: How much of all U.S. land area is protected as wilderness?

as cattle on the same amount of land. In Indonesia the piglike babirusa is an important source of meat.

CULTIVATING MORE LAND Humankind grows crops on about 11% of Earth's ice-free land area and pastures livestock on nearly 25%. The rest is either covered by ice, is too dry or too wet, too hot or too cold, too steep, or has unsuitable soils.

Theoretically, the world's cropland could be more than doubled by clearing tropical forests and irrigating arid land (Figure 7-15). About 83% of the world's potential new cropland is in the remote rain forests of South America and Africa, primarily in Brazil and Zaire. Clearing rain forests to grow crops and graze livestock, however, has disastrous consequences, as discussed in Chapter 5. And in Africa, potential cropland in savanna (Figure 2-27) and other semiarid land cannot be used for farming or livestock grazing because it is infested by 22 species of the tsetse fly. Its bite can infect people with incurable sleeping sickness and transmit a fatal disease to livestock.

Researchers hope to develop new methods of intensive cultivation in tropical areas. But some scientists argue that it makes more ecological and economic sense to combine the ancient method of shifting cultivation followed by fallow periods long enough to restore soil fertility (Figure 5-7) with various forms of interplanting. Scientists also recommend plantation cultivation of rubber trees, oil palms, and banana trees, which are adapted to tropical climates and soils.

Much of the world's potentially cultivable land lies in dry areas, especially in Australia and Africa. Large-scale irrigation in these areas would be very expensive, requiring large inputs of fossil fuel to pump water long distances. Irrigation systems could deplete groundwater supplies, and the land would need constant and expensive maintenance against erosion, groundwater contamination, salinization, and waterlogging.

Thus much of the new cropland that could be developed would be marginal land requiring expensive inputs of fertilizer, water, and energy. Furthermore, these possible increases in cropland would not offset the projected loss of almost one-third of today's cultivated cropland from erosion, overgrazing, waterlogging, salinization, mining, and urbanization.

Pollution is also reducing yields on existing cropland. In the United States ozone pollution in the troposphere reduced harvests of crops by at least 5% during the 1980s. Other air pollutants, such as sulfur dioxide and nitrogen oxides, have also damaged crops. Yields of some crops and populations of marine phytoplankton that support fish and shellfish used as food have been reduced by depletion of ozone in the

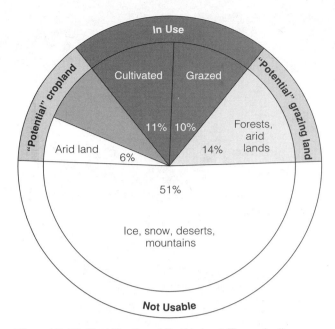

Figure 7-15 Classification of Earth's land. Theoretically we could double the amount of cropland by clearing tropical forests and irrigating arid lands. However, converting this marginal land into cropland would destroy valuable forest resources, reduce Earth's biodiversity, and cause serious environmental problems, usually without being cost-effective.

stratosphere (Section 9-3). And if the global climate changes as projected, areas where crops can be grown will shift and disrupt food production (Section 9-2).

Finally, if current population projections are accurate, the global average of 0.28 hectares (0.69 acres) of cropland per capita in 1992 is expected to decline to 0.17 hectares (0.42 acres) by 2025.

CATCHING MORE FISH Concentrations of particular aquatic species suitable for commercial harvesting in a given ocean area or inland body of water are called **fisheries.** Worldwide, people get an average of 20% of their animal protein directly from fish and shellfish, and another 5% indirectly from livestock fed with fish meal. In most Asian coastal and island regions, fish and shellfish supply 30–90% of people's animal protein.

About 86% of the annual commercial catch of fish and shellfish comes from the ocean. Ninety-nine percent of this is taken from plankton-rich waters (mostly estuaries and upwellings) within 370 kilometers (200 nautical miles) of the coast. However, this vital coastal zone is being disrupted and polluted at an alarming rate.

Various methods used to harvest commercially important marine species are shown in Figure 7-16. However, some of these methods also entrap and kill

A: 4% (only 1.8% in the lower 48 states)

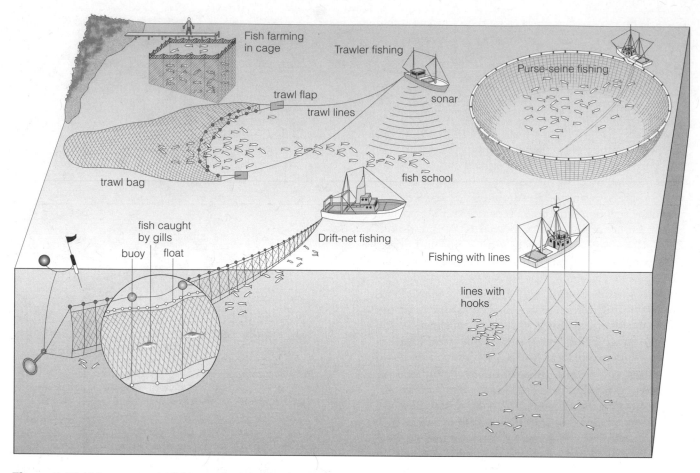

Figure 7-16 Major commercial fishing methods used to harvest or raise marine species.

large numbers of other nontarget species such as seals, dolphins, sea turtles, small whales, and other marine species. One of the greatest threats to marine biodiversity is *drift-net fishing* (Figure 7-16). These monster nets drift in the water and catch fish when their gills become entangled in the nylon mesh. Each net descends as much as 15 meters (50 feet) deep and is up to 65 kilometers (40 miles) long. Almost anything that comes in contact with these nearly invisible "curtains of death" becomes entangled. Every country that has used drift nets in its own waters has eventually banned them. In 1990 the UN General Assembly called for a moratorium of drift-net fishing in international waters after June 1992. The ban, however, has numerous loopholes, no effective mechanism for monitoring, enforcement, and punishment over the earth's vast ocean area, and compliance is voluntary.

Environmentalists believe that the only effective way to reduce drift-net fishing and tuna caught by purse-seine fishing (Figure 7-16) is to mount U.S. and global boycotts of fish caught in these ways. This tactic, led by the Earth Island Institute, caused companies selling canned tuna in the United States to stop buy-

ing tuna caught by purse-seine or drift-net methods. Consumer power works.

Between 1950 and 1989 the weight of the commercial fish catch increased more than threefold, but it has declined somewhat since 1989. Although the total fish catch has grown in most years, the per capita fish catch has declined in most years since 1970 because the human population has grown at a faster rate than the fish catch (Figure 7-17). Because of overfishing, pollution, and population growth, the world catch per person is projected to drop back to the 1960 level by 2000. The fish catch, however, could be increased by cutting waste. Currently, one-fifth of the annual catch is wasted, mainly from throwing back potentially useful fish taken along with desired species. More refrigerated storage at sea to prevent spoilage would also increase the catch.

Overfishing is taking so many fish that too little breeding stock is left to maintain numbers—that is, the sustainable yield is exceeded. Prolonged overfishing leads to **commercial extinction**: So few of a species is left that it's no longer profitable to hunt them. Fishing fleets then move to a new species or to a new region,

Q: What percentage of U.S. municipal solid waste could be recycled, composted, or reused?

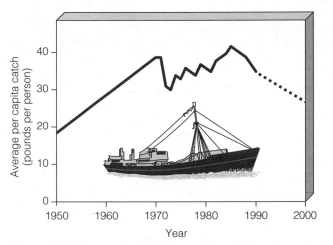

Figure 7-17 Per capita world fish catch has declined in most years since 1970 and is projected to drop further by the end of this century. (Data from United Nations and Worldwatch Institute)

hoping that the overfished species will eventually recover.

Since the early 1980s overfishing has caused declines in the yields of nearly one-third of the world's fisheries and the collapse of 42 valuable fisheries, including 42% of the species commercially fished in U.S. coastal waters.

RAISING MORE FISH: AQUACULTURE **Aquaculture**, in which fish and shellfish are raised for food, supplies about 10% of the world's commercial fish harvest. There are two basic types of aquaculture. **Fish farming** involves cultivating fish in a controlled environment, usually a pond, and harvesting them when they reach the desired size. **Fish ranching** involves holding species in captivity—usually in fenced-in areas or floating cages in coastal lagoons and estuaries—for the first few years of their lives and then harvesting the adults when they return to spawn (Figure 7-16). Ranching is useful for such species as ocean trout and salmon that spend part of their lives in the ocean and part in freshwater streams.

Species cultivated in LDCs include carp, tilapia, milkfish, clams, and oysters, which feed on phytoplankton and other aquatic plants. These are usually raised in small freshwater ponds or underwater cages. In MDCs aquaculture is used mostly to stock lakes and streams with game fish and to raise expensive fish and shellfish such as oysters, catfish, crayfish, rainbow trout, shrimp, and salmon.

Aquaculture has several advantages. First, it can produce high yields per unit of area. Second, little fuel is needed, so yields and profits are not closely tied to the price of oil, as they are in commercial marine fishing. Also, aquaculture is usually labor-intensive and can provide much-needed jobs. Experts project that freshwater and saltwater aquaculture production could be doubled during the 1990s.

There are problems, however. For one thing, large-scale aquaculture requires considerable capital and scientific knowledge, which are in short supply in LDCs. For another, scooping out huge ponds for fish and shrimp farming in some LDCs has destroyed ecologically important mangrove forests. Also, fish in aquaculture ponds can be killed by pesticide runoff from nearby croplands; and bacterial and viral infections of aquatic species can also limit yields. Finally, without adequate pollution control, waste outputs from shrimp farming and other large-scale aquaculture operations can contaminate nearby estuaries, surface water, and groundwater.

GOVERNMENT AGRICULTURAL POLICIES Agriculture is a risky business. Whether farmers have a good or a bad year is determined by factors over which they have little control—weather, crop prices, crop pests and disease, interest rates, and the global market. Because of the need for reliable food supplies despite variability, most governments provide various forms of assistance to farmers.

Governments have several choices. They can

- *Keep food prices artificially low.* This makes consumers happy but means that farmers may not be able to make a living.

- *Give farmers subsidies to keep them in business and encourage them to increase food production.* In MDCs government price supports and other subsidies for agriculture total more than $300 billion per year ($17–22 billion per year in the United States). However, if government subsidies are too generous and the weather is good, farmers may produce more food than can be sold. Food prices and profits then drop because of the surplus. Large amounts of food become available for export or food aid to LDCs, depressing world food prices. The low prices reduce the financial incentive for farmers to increase domestic food production. Moreover, the taxes citizens pay in MDCs to provide agricultural supports more than offset the lower food prices they enjoy.

- *Eliminate most or all price controls and subsidies.* This allows market competition to be the primary factor determining food prices and thus the amount of food produced.

The U.S. agricultural system produces so much food that the government pays farmers *not* to produce

A: 60–80%

Food Relief

Most people view food relief as a humanitarian effort to prevent people from dying prematurely. However, some analysts contend that giving food to starving people in countries with high population growth rates does more harm than good in the long run. By not helping people grow their own food, they argue, food relief can condemn even greater numbers to premature death in the future.

Biologist Garrett Hardin has suggested that we use the concept of *lifeboat ethics* to decide which countries get food aid. His basic premise is that there are already too many people in the lifeboat we call Earth. Thus, if food aid is given to countries that are not reducing their pop-ulations, this simply adds more people to an already-overcrowded lifeboat. Sooner or later the boat will sink and most of the passengers will drown.

Large amounts of food aid can also depress local food prices, decrease food production, and stimulate mass migration from farms to already-overburdened cities. In addition, food aid discourages the government from investing in rural agricultural development to enable the country to grow enough food for its population on a sustainable basis.

Another problem is that much food aid does not reach hunger victims. Transportation networks and storage facilities are inadequate, so that some of the food rots or is devoured by pests before it can reach the hungry. Also, typically, some of the food is stolen by officials and sold for personal profit. And some must often be given to officials as bribes for approving the unloading and transporting of the remaining food to the hungry.

Critics of food relief are not against foreign aid. Instead, they believe that such aid should be given to help countries control population growth and grow enough food to feed their population using sustainable agricultural methods (Section 7-7). Temporary food aid, they believe, should be given only when there is a complete breakdown of an area's food supply because of natural disaster. What do you think?

---

food on one-fourth of U.S. cropland, or it buys up and stores unneeded crops. Such subsidies can waste taxpayer dollars and serve as a form of welfare for wealthy farmers. In 1989, for example, nearly 60% of federal farm subsidies went to the wealthiest 25% of U.S. farms.

Some analysts call for eliminating all federal subsidies over, say, five years, and letting farmers respond to market demand. Only those who were good farmers and financial managers would be able to stay in business. However, any phaseout of farm subsidies in the United States (or in any other country) should be coupled with increased aid for the poor and the lower middle class, who would suffer the most from any increase in food prices.

Instead of eliminating all subsidies, many environmentalists believe that we should refocus them by rewarding farmers and ranchers who protect the soil, conserve water, reforest degraded land, protect and restore wetlands, and conserve wildlife. Those who didn't would receive no subsidies.

INTERNATIONAL AID Between 1945 and 1985 the United States was the world's largest donor of nonmilitary foreign aid to LDCs; since 1986 Japan has taken over that role. This aid is used mostly for agriculture and rural development, food relief, population planning, health care, and economic development.

Besides helping other countries, foreign aid stimulates economic growth and provides jobs in the donor country. For example, 70¢ of every dollar the United States gives directly to other countries is used to purchase American goods and services. Today 21 of the 50 largest buyers of U.S. farm goods are countries that once received free U.S. food. Providing food relief, however, is controversial (Pro/Con, above).

LAND REFORM An important step in reducing world hunger, malnutrition, poverty, and land degradation is land reform. This usually means giving to the landless rural poor in LDCs ownership or free use of enough government-owned land to produce their food and, ideally, enough surplus to provide some income. To date China and Taiwan have had the most successful land reform programs.

The world's most unequal land distribution is in Latin America, where 7% of the population owns 93% of the farmland. Most of this land is used for export crops such as sugar, tea, coffee, bananas, or beef, or is left idle on huge estates.

Q: How much of the world's population relies on plants or plant extracts for medicines?

7-6 Protecting Food Resources: Pesticides and Pest Control

USING PESTICIDES TO REDUCE CROP LOSSES A **pest** is any species that competes with us for food, messes up lawns, destroys wood in houses, spreads disease, or is simply a nuisance. In diverse ecosystems, populations of species—including the less than 1% we have classified as pests—are kept in control by their natural enemies (predators, parasites, and disease organisms)—another crucial type of Earth capital. When we simplify ecosystems we upset these natural checks and balances that keep any one species from taking over for very long. Then we have to figure out ways to protect our monoculture crops, tree farms, and lawns from pests that nature used to control at no charge.

Mostly we have done this by developing a variety of **pesticides** (or *biocides*): chemicals to kill organisms we consider undesirable. Common types of pesticides include **insecticides** (insect-killers), **herbicides** (weed-killers), **nematocides** (roundworm-killers), **fungicides** (fungus-killers), and **rodenticides** (rat- and mouse-killers).

Worldwide, about 2.3 million metric tons (2.5 million tons) of pesticide are used yearly—0.45 kilogram (1 pound) for each person on Earth. About 75% of these chemicals are used in MDCs, but use in LDCs is soaring. Since 1964 pesticide use in the United States has almost doubled, now exceeding 910 million kilograms (2 billion pounds) per year, or about 4 kilograms (8 pounds) per person per year—about eight times the global average. About 30% of the pesticides used in the United States are used to rid houses, gardens, lawns, parks, playing fields, swimming pools, and golf courses of unwanted pests. The average U.S. home owner applies three to six times more pesticide per hectare than do farmers. Pesticides are added to products as diverse as paints, some shampoos, carpets, mattresses, and contact lenses.

Some pesticides, called *broad-spectrum* agents, are toxic to many species. Others called *selective* or *narrow-spectrum* agents, are effective against a narrowly defined group of organisms. Pesticides vary in their *persistence*, the length of time they stay deadly and unchanged in the environment (Table 7-1).

THE CASE FOR PESTICIDES Proponents of pesticides believe that the benefits outweigh the harmful effects. They point out the following benefits:

- *Pesticides save lives.* Since 1945 DDT and other chlorinated hydrocarbon and organophosphate insecticides have probably prevented the premature deaths of at least 7 million people from insect-transmitted diseases such as malaria (carried by the *Anopheles* mosquito, Figure 8-3), bubonic plague (rat fleas), typhus (body lice and fleas), and sleeping sickness (tsetse fly).

- *They increase food supplies and lower food costs.* About 55% of the world's potential human food supply is lost to pests before (35%) or after (20%) harvest. In the United States 37% of the potential food supply is destroyed by pests before and after harvest (13% by insects, 12% by plant pathogens, and 12% by weeds). Without pesticides these losses might be worse, and food prices would rise (by 30–50% in the United States, according to pesticide company officials).

- *They increase profits for farmers.* Pesticide companies estimate that every $1 spent on pesticides leads to an increase in U.S. crop yields worth approximately $4, but this drops to about $2 if the harmful effects of pesticides are included.

- *They work faster and better than alternatives.* Pesticides can control most pests quickly and reasonably cheaply, have a long shelf life, are easily shipped and applied, and are safe when handled properly. When genetic resistance occurs, farmers can use stronger doses or switch to other pesticides.

- *The health risks of pesticides are insignificant compared with their health and other benefits.* According to Elizabeth Whelan, director of the American Council on Science and Health (ASCH), which presents the position of the pesticide industry: "The reality is that pesticides, when used in the approved regulatory manner, pose no risk to either farm workers or consumers." Pesticide proponents call the pesticide health-scare news stories distorted science and irresponsible reporting, and they point out that about 99.99% of the pesticides we eat are natural chemicals produced by plants.

- *Safer and more effective products are continually being developed.* Company scientists are developing pesticides, such as botanicals and microbotanicals (Table 7-1), that are safer to users and less damaging to the environment. Genetic engineering also holds promise (Pro/Con, p. 217). However, research and development and government-approval costs for a single pesticide have risen from $6 million in 1976 to more than $40 million today, making pesticides more costly.

Scientists continue to search for the ideal pest-killing chemical. It would

Table 7-1 Major Types of Pesticides

Type	Examples	Persistence	Biologically Amplified?
Insecticides			
Chlorinated hydrocarbons	DDT, aldrin, dieldrin, toxaphene, lindane, chlordane, methoxychlor, mirex	High (2–15 years)	Yes (Figure 6-5)
Organophosphates	malathion, parathion, diazinon, TEPP, DDVP, mevingphos	Low to moderate (1–12 weeks), but some can last several years	No
Carbamates	aldicarb, carbaryl (Sevin), propoxur, maneb, zineb	Low (days to weeks)	No
Botanicals	rotenone, pyrethrum, camphor extracted from plants, synthetic pyrethroids (variations of pyrethrum), and rotenoids (variations of rotenone)	Low (days to weeks)	No
Microbotanicals	Various bacteria, fungi, protozoans	Low (days to weeks)	No
Herbicides			
Contact chemicals	atrazine, simazine, paraquat	Low (days to weeks)	No
Systemic chemicals	2,4-D, 2,4,5-T, Silvex diruon, daminozide (Alar), alachlor (Lasso), glyphosate (Roundup)	Mostly low (days to weeks)	No
Soil sterilants	trifualin, diphenamid, dalapon, butylate	Low (days)	No
Fungicides			
Various chemicals	captan, pentachorphenol, zeneb, methyl bromide, carbon bisulfide	Mostly low (days)	No
Fumigants			
Various chemicals	carbon tetrachloride, ethylene dibromide, methyl bromide	Mostly high	Yes (for most)

- *Kill only the target pest*
- *Harm no other species*
- *Disappear or break down into something harmless after doing its job*
- *Not cause genetic resistance in target organisms*
- *Be cheaper than doing nothing*

Unfortunately, no known pesticide meets all these criteria, and most don't even come close.

THE CASE AGAINST PESTICIDES Opponents of widespread use of pesticides believe that the harmful effects outweigh the benefits. The biggest problem is the development of *genetic resistance* to pesticides by pest organisms. Insects breed rapidly and within 5–10 years (much sooner in tropical areas) develop immunity through natural selection to the chemicals we throw at them (Connections, p. 201). Just when we think we've killed them off with our arsenal of chemicals, they come back stronger than before.

Since 1950 more than 500 major insect pests have developed genetic resistance to one or more insecticides. By 2000 virtually all major insect pest species will probably show some genetic resistance. Over half of the 500-odd major weed species are resistant to one or more herbicides. Pesticide use has also led to genetic resistance in 10 species of rodents (mostly rats).

Q: How much of the medicines sold in the world have active ingredients extracted from wildlife (mostly plants)?

Because of genetic resistance, most widely used insecticides no longer protect people from insect-transmitted diseases in many parts of the world, leading to even more serious outbreaks of diseases such as malaria (Section 8-3).

Another problem is that broad-spectrum insecticides kill natural predators and parasites that may have been maintaining a pest species at a reasonable level. With natural enemies out of the way, a rapidly reproducing insect pest species can make a strong comeback within days or weeks after initially being controlled. Wiping out natural predators can also unleash new pests whose populations the predators had previously held in check.

No more than 2% (and often less than 0.1%) of the insecticides applied to crops by aerial spraying or ground spraying reach the target pests, and less than 5% of herbicides applied to crops reach the target weeds. Pesticides not reaching target pests end up in the soil, air, surface water, groundwater, bottom sediment, food, and nontarget organisms, including humans and wildlife.

During the 1950s and 1960s populations of fish-eating birds such as the osprey, brown pelican, and bald eagle (Figure 6-2) plummeted after exposure to DDT (Figure 6-5). Each year some 20% of U.S. honeybee colonies are wiped out by pesticides and another 15% are damaged, costing farmers at least $206 million per year from reduced pollination of vital crops. Pesticide runoff from cropland is a leading cause of fish kills worldwide.

Pesticides also threaten human health. The World Health Organization estimates that at least 1 million people (including 313,000 farm workers in the United States) are accidentally poisoned by pesticides each year; 4,000–20,000 of them die. At least half of them—and 90% of those killed—are farm workers in LDCs, where educational levels are low, warnings are few, and pesticide regulations are lax or nonexistent. The actual number of pesticide-related illnesses among farm workers in the United States and throughout the world is probably greatly underestimated because of poor records, lack of doctors and reporting in rural areas, and faulty diagnoses.

According to the FDA, about 1–3% of the food purchased in the United States has levels of one or more pesticides that are above the legal limit. Moreover, a 1993 study by the National Academy of Sciences concluded that the legal limits for pesticides in food may have to be reduced by up to 1,000-fold to protect children, and the study called for greatly increased research on the effects of pesticides on human health—especially that of children, who are more vulnerable to such chemicals than adults. According to the *worst-case estimate* in a 1987 study by

The Pesticide Treadmill

CONNECTIONS

When genetic resistance develops, pesticide sales representatives usually recommend more frequent applications, stronger doses, or a switch to new (usually more expensive) chemicals to keep the resistant species under control. This can put farmers on a **pesticide treadmill**, whereby they pay more and more for a pest control program that does less and less good.

A 1989 study by David Pimentel, an expert in insect ecology, based on data from more than 300 agricultural scientists and economists, concluded that

- Although the use of synthetic pesticides has increased 33-fold since 1942, the U.S. loses more of its crops to pests today (37%) than in the 1940s (31%). Losses attributed to insects almost doubled from 7% to 13% despite a tenfold increase in the use of synthetic insecticides; losses to plant diseases rose from 10% to 12%, and losses to weeds dropped from 14% to 12%.

- The estimated environmental, health, and social costs of pesticide use in the United States range from $4 billion to $10 billion per year.

- Alternative pest control practices could halve the use of chemical pesticides on 40 major crops in the United States without reducing crop yields.

- A 50% cut in pesticide use in the United States would cause retail food prices to rise by only about 0.2% but would raise average income for farmers about 9%.

the National Academy of Sciences, exposure to pesticides in food causes 4,000–20,000 cases of cancer per year in the United States. In 1987 the EPA ranked pesticide residues in foods as the third most serious environmental health threat in the United States in terms of cancer risk.

Some scientists are becoming increasingly concerned about possible genetic mutations, birth defects, nervous system disorders, and effects on the immune and endocrine systems from long-term exposure to low levels of various pesticides. Very little research has been carried out on these effects, and they are not covered adequately in pesticide health-safety laws.

According to the National Academy of Sciences, federal laws regulating the use of pesticides in the

The Circle of Poison

CONNECTIONS

Pesticide companies can make and export to other countries pesticides that have been banned or severely restricted—or never approved—in the United States. But what goes around, as they say, comes around. In what environmentalists call a *circle of poison*, residues of some of these banned or unapproved chemicals return to the United States on imported items such as coffee, cocoa, pineapples, and out-of-season melons, tomatoes, and grapes. More than one-fourth of the produce (fruits and vegetables) consumed in the United States is grown overseas.

Environmentalists have urged Congress—without success—to break this deadly circle. They believe that it is morally wrong for the United States to export pesticides known to damage human health and to allow food with residues of those pesticides to be imported for U.S. consumers.

Along Came a Spider

SOLUTIONS

In 1962 biologist Rachel Carson warned against relying on synthetic chemicals to kill insects and other species we deem pests. Chinese farmers have recently decided it's time to change strategies. Instead of spraying their rice and cotton fields with poison, they began to build little straw huts here and there around the fields in the fall.

If this sounds crazy, it was crazy like a fox. These farmers were giving aid and comfort to insects' worst enemy, one that has hunted them for millions rather than thousands of years: the spider. The little huts were for hibernating spiders. Protected from the worst of the cold, far more of them would awaken next spring. Ravenous after their winter fast, they would scuttle off into the fields to stalk their insect prey.

Even without human help the world's 30,000 known species of spiders kill far more insects every year than insecticides do. The idea of encouraging populations of spiders in fields, forests, and even houses scares most people because spiders have gotten bad press. Although a few species of spiders, such as the black widow and brown recluse, are dangerous to people, the vast majority—including the ferocious looking wolf spider—are harmless to humans. Even the giant tarantula rarely bites people, and its venom is too weak to harm us and other large mammals.

As biologist Thomas Eisner puts it, "Bugs are not going to inherit the earth. They own it now. So we might as well make peace with the landlord." As we seek new ways to coexist with the real rulers of the planet, we would do well to be sure that spiders are in our corner.

United States are inadequate and poorly enforced by both the EPA and the Food and Drug Administration (FDA). In addition to lobbying for stronger pesticide health-safety laws, many environmentalists have called for a ban on the export to other countries of pesticides banned in the United States (Connections, above).

SOLUTIONS: OTHER WAYS TO CONTROL PESTS

Chemistry is not the only answer to pests. Other strategies are:

- *Changing the type of crop planted in a field each year (crop rotation).*

- *Planting rows of hedges or trees in and around crop-fields.* These hinder insect invasions, provide habitats for their natural enemies, and also reduce erosion of soil by wind (Figure 7-9).

- *Adjusting planting times so that major insect pests either starve or get eaten by their natural predators.*

- *Growing crops in areas where their major pests do not exist.*

- *Switching from vulnerable monoculture crops to modernized versions of intercropping, agroforestry, and polyculture that use diversity to reduce losses to pests.*

- *Removing diseased or infected plants and stalks and other crop residues that harbor pests.*

- *Using plastic that can be degraded by sunlight to keep weeds from sprouting between crop rows.*

- *Using vacuum machines that gently remove harmful bugs from plants.*

- *Using crossbreeding and genetic engineering to develop food plants and animals that are genetically resistant to certain pest insects, fungi, and diseases (Pro/Con, p. 217).*

- *Using natural enemies (predators, parasites, and disease-causing bacteria and viruses).* Worldwide, more than 300 biological pest control proj-

Q: What percentage of the world's estimated plant species have been evaluated for their medical uses?

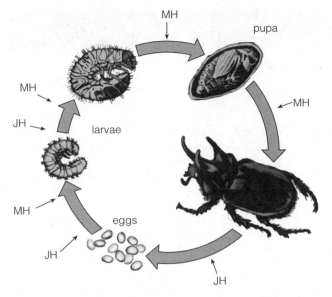

MH

pupa

MH

MH

JH

larvae

MH

eggs

JH

JH

JH

Figure 7-18 For normal growth, development, and reproduction, certain juvenile hormones (JH) and molting hormones (MH) must be present at genetically determined stages in the typical life cycle of an insect. If applied at the right time, synthetic hormones can be used to disrupt the life cycle of insect pests.

ects have been successful, especially in China (Solutions, at left). In the United States biological control has saved farmers an average of $25 for every $1 invested. However, biological agents can't always be mass-produced, and farmers find them slower to act and harder to apply than pesticides. Also, biological agents must be protected from pesticides sprayed in nearby fields.

■ *Birth control.* Males of some insect pest species (such as the screwworm fly, which can infest and kill livestock) can be lab-raised and sterilized by radiation or chemicals and then released in hordes in an infested area, to mate unsuccessfully with fertile wild females. Problems with this approach include high costs, the difficulties involved in knowing the mating times and behaviors of each target insect, and releasing enough sterile males to do the job.

■ *Insect sex attractants.* In many insect species, when a female is ready to mate she releases a minute amount of a chemical sex attractant called a *pheromone*. These pheromones, extracted from insects or synthesized in the laboratory, can be used to lure pests into traps or to attract their natural predators into cropfields (usually the more effective approach). These chemicals attract only one species, work in trace amounts, have little

chance of causing genetic resistance, and are not harmful to nontarget species. However, it is costly and time-consuming to identify, isolate, and produce the specific sex attractant for each pest or natural predator species.

■ *Insect hormones.* Each step in the insect life cycle is regulated by the timely release of juvenile hormones (JH) and molting hormones (MH) (Figure 7-18). These chemicals can be extracted from insects or synthesized in the laboratory. When applied at certain stages in an insect's life cycle, they cause the insect to die before it can reach maturity and reproduce. Insect hormones have the same advantages as sex attractants, but they take weeks to kill an insect, are often ineffective with a large infestation, sometimes break down before they can act, and are difficult and costly to produce. Also, they must be applied at exactly the right time in the target insect's life cycle, and sometimes they can affect the target's predators and other nonpest species.

■ *Zapping foods after harvest with gamma radiation.* This can extend the shelf life of some perishable foods and kill insects, parasitic worms (such as trichinae in pork), and bacteria (such as salmonellae, which infect 51,000 Americans and kill 2,000 each year). According to the FDA and the World Health Organization, over 1,000 studies show that foods exposed to low doses of gamma radiation are safe for human consumption. However, critics argue that it is too soon to see long-term effects (which might not show up for 30–40 years) and that irradiating food destroys some of its vitamins and other nutrients.

■ *Integrated Pest Management (IPM).* In this approach each crop and its pests are evaluated as an ecological system. A control program is then developed that uses a mix of cultivation, biological, and chemical methods in proper sequence and with proper timing (Solutions, p. 204).

Each of us has a role to play in reducing risks from using pesticides (Individuals Matter, p. 205).

7-7 Solutions: Sustainable Food Production

CHARACTERISTICS To many environmentalists the key to reducing world hunger, poverty, and the harmful environmental impacts of both industrialized

Is Integrated Pest Management the Wave of the Future?

SOLUTIONS

In 1986 the Indonesian government banned the use of 57 pesticides on rice and launched a nationwide program to switch to integrated pest management. The results were dramatic: Between 1987 and 1992 pesticide use dropped by 65%, rice production rose by 15%, and the country now saves about $120 million per year on pesticides—enough to cover the cost of its IPM program.

The overall aim of IPM is not eradication of pest populations but maintenance at just below economically damaging levels. Fields are carefully monitored. When a damaging level is reached, farmers first use biological and cultivation controls, including vacuuming up harmful bugs. Small amounts of insecticides (mostly botanicals or microbotanicals) are applied when absolutely necessary, and the types of chemicals are varied to slow the development of genetic resistance.

The experiences of countries such as China, Brazil, Indonesia, and the United States have shown that a

well-designed IPM program can reduce pesticide use and pest control costs by 50–90%. IPM can also reduce preharvest pest-induced crop losses by 50%, improve crop yields, reduce inputs of fertilizer and irrigation water, and slow the development of genetic resistance—because pests are zapped less often and with lower doses of pesticides. Thus IPM is an important form of pollution prevention that reduces risks to wildlife and human health.

However, IPM requires expert knowledge about each pest-crop situation, and it is slower-acting than conventional pesticides. Moreover, methods developed for a given crop in one area may not apply to another area with slightly different growing conditions. And although long-term costs are typically lower than the costs of using conventional pesticides, initial costs may be higher.

Widespread use of IPM is hindered by government subsidies of conventional chemical pesticides and by opposition of agricultural chemical companies, whose sales would drop sharply. In addition, U.S. farmers get most of their infor-

mation about pest control from pesticide salespeople and from U.S. Department of Agriculture (USDA) county farm agents, few of whom have adequate training in IPM.

Despite its potential, only about 1% of the USDA's research and education budget is spent on IPM. Environmentalists urge the USDA to promote integrated pest management by **(1)** adding a 2% sales tax on pesticides to fund IPM research and education; **(2)** setting up a federally supported demonstration IPM project on at least one farm in every county; **(3)** training USDA field personnel and county farm agents in IPM so they can help farmers use this alternative; **(4)** providing federal and state subsidies and perhaps government-backed crop-loss insurance to farmers who use IPM or other approved alternatives to pesticides; and **(5)** gradually phasing out subsidies to farmers who depend almost entirely on pesticides, once effective IPM methods have been developed for major pest species.

and traditional agriculture is to develop a variety of **sustainable-Earth agricultural systems**. This involves combining the wisdom of traditional agricultural systems with new techniques that take advantage of local climates, soils, resources, and cultural systems. Here are some general guidelines:

■ *Don't rob the soil of nutrients and waste water, and return whatever is taken from the earth.* This means minimizing soil erosion by a variety of methods (Section 7-2 and Figure 7-9), not cultivating easily erodible land, preventing livestock overgrazing, and using organic fertilizers, crop rotation, and intercropping to increase the organic content of soils. It also means not growing water-thirsty crops in arid and semiarid areas, raising water prices to encourage water conservation, and using

irrigation systems that minimize water waste, salinization, and waterlogging (Figure 10-14).

■ *Design the agricultural system to fit the environment (soil, water, climate, and pest populations) of the region.* This involves trying to learn how to work with nature in a particular place to produce food sustainably (Solutions, p. 194).

■ *Encourage systems featuring a diverse mix of crops and livestock, instead of monoculture production of a single crop or livestock type.* Emphasize increased use of polyculture and other forms of intercropping. A small but growing number of organic farmers in MDCs are returning to diversified farming.

■ *Whenever possible, rely on locally available, renewable biological resources and use them in ways that pre-*

Q: According to the EPA, how many landfills in the U.S. will eventually leak?

INDIVIDUALS MATTER

- *Give up the idea that the only good bug is a dead bug.* Recognize that insects such as spiders (Solutions, p. 202) keep most of the populations of insects we consider to be pests in control and that full-scale chemical warfare on insect pests wipes out many of our insect allies.

- *Buy organically grown produce that has not been treated with synthetic fertilizers, pesticides, or growth regulators—or grow some of your own produce this way.*

- *Don't insist on perfect-looking fruits and vegetables.* These are more likely to contain high levels of pesticide residues.

- *Get rid of most pesticide residues by carefully washing and scrubbing all fresh produce, discarding the outer leaves of lettuce and cabbage, and peeling thick-skinned fruits.*

- *Use pesticides in your home only when absolutely necessary, and use them in the smallest amount possible.*

- *Dispose of unused pesticides safely.* Contact your local health department or environmental agency for safe disposal methods.

- *Don't become obsessed with having the perfect lawn.* About 40% of U.S. lawns are treated with pesticides, typically at levels three to six times higher per acre than farmland. These chemicals can cause headaches, dizziness, nausea, and eye trouble—and more acute effects in sensitive individuals, including children who play on treated lawns and in parks. Of the 40 pesticides commonly used by the lawn-care industry, 12 are suspected human carcinogens, 10 may cause birth defects, 3 can affect reproduction, 9 can damage liver and kidneys, 20 can cause short-term nervous-system damage, and 29 cause rashes or skin disease.

- *If you hire a lawn-care company, use one that relies only on organic methods.* And get its claims in writing.

- *Urge elected officials to promote integrated pest management, strengthen pesticide laws to protect human health and the environment from the harmful effects of pesticides, and ban exports of pesticides not approved for use in the United States.*

---

serve their renewability. Examples include using organic fertilizers from animal and crop wastes (green manure and compost); planting fast-growing trees to supply fuelwood and add nitrogen to the soil; building simple devices for capturing and storing rainwater for irrigating crops; and cultivating crops adapted to local growing conditions.

- *Greatly reduce the use of fossil fuels in agriculture by using locally available renewable energy resources such as sun, wind, and flowing water (Section 4-3), and by using more organic fertilizer instead of commercial inorganic fertilizer.*

- *Emphasize biological pest control and integrated pest management (Solutions, p. 204) instead of overuse of chemical pesticides.*

- *Provide economic incentives for farmers using sustainable-Earth agricultural systems.*

- *Slow human population growth (Section 3-4).*

MAKING THE TRANSITION IN MDCs In MDCs such as the United States a shift to sustainable-Earth agriculture will not be easy. It would be opposed by agribusiness, by successful farmers with large investments in industrialized agriculture, and by specialized farmers unwilling to learn the demanding art of farming sustainably. Without proper education, it might also be resisted by consumers who might not be willing to pay higher prices for food. They are already paying these costs in the form of higher taxes and insurance and health costs, but these costs related to growing food are hidden and don't appear in market prices.

However, this shift could be brought about over 10 to 20 years by:

- *Greatly increasing government support of research and development of sustainable-Earth agricultural methods and equipment.* At present only about 1% of the Department of Agriculture's annual research budget is used for this purpose.

- *Setting up demonstration projects in each county so that farmers can see how sustainable systems work.*

- *Establishing training programs for farmers, county farm agents, and Department of Agriculture personnel in sustainable-Earth agriculture.*

What You Can Do to Promote Sustainable-Earth Agriculture

INDIVIDUALS MATTER

- *Waste less food.* An estimated 25% of all food produced in the United States is wasted. It rots in the supermarket or refrigerator, or it is scraped off the plate and into the garbage in households and restaurants.

- *Eat lower on the food chain.* This can be done by reducing or eliminating meat consumption to reduce its environmental impact.

- *Don't feed your dog or cat canned meat products.* Balanced grain pet foods are available and are better for your pet.

- *Reduce the use of pesticides on agricultural products by asking grocery stores to stock fresh produce and meat produced by organic methods.** About 0.5% of U.S. farmers grow about 3% of the country's crops using organic methods.

- *Grow some of your own food using organic farming techniques and drip irrigation to water your crops* (Figure 10-14).

---

*A *Consumer's Organic Mail-Order Directory* of farmers and wholesalers who sell organically grown food by mail can be obtained for $9.95 (plus $2.50 postage) from California Action Network, P.O. Box 464, Davis, CA 95617.

- *Think globally, eat locally.* Whenever possible eat food that is locally grown and in season. This supports your local economy, gives you more influence over how the food is grown (organic or conventional methods), saves energy from having to transport food over long distances, and reduces the use of fossil fuels and pollution. If you deal directly with local farmers, you can also save money.

- *Pressure elected officials to develop and encourage sustainable-Earth agricultural systems in the United States and throughout the world.*

- *Establishing college curricula for sustainable-Earth agriculture.*

- *Giving subsidies and tax breaks to farmers using sustainable-Earth agriculture and to agribusiness companies developing products for this type of farming.* For example, Iowa taxes fertilizers and pesticides; it then uses the revenues to support research into and development of sustainable agriculture. Minnesota provides low-interest loans for farmers engaged in sustainable agriculture. Austria, Denmark, Finland, Germany, Norway, and Sweden offer three- to five-year subsidies for farmers converting to sustainable agriculture.

- *Educating the public to understand the hidden environmental and health costs they are paying for food and gradually incorporating these costs into market prices* (Section 12-2).

Each of us has a role to play in bringing about a shift from unsustainable to sustainable agriculture at the local, national, and global levels (Individuals Matter, above).

Since 1980 global food production has barely kept ahead of population growth and has lagged behind population growth in many LDCs. Reversing this trend will require simultaneous efforts to **(1)** slow population growth (Section 3-4); **(2)** increase food production using sustainable agriculture; **(3)** rehabilitate degraded cropland, rangeland, wetlands, and coastal ecosystems; **(4)** reduce ocean pollution and overfish-

ing; and **(5)** reduce poverty which keeps people from growing or buying enough food regardless of how much is available.

At some point, either the loss of topsoil from the world's croplands will have to be checked by effective soil conservation practices, or the growth in the world's population will be checked by hunger and malnutrition.

LESTER R. BROWN

CRITICAL THINKING

1. Why should everyone, not just farmers, be concerned with soil conservation?

2. Explain how the Dust Bowl phenomenon of the 1930s could happen again. How would you try to prevent a recurrence?

3. What are the main advantages and disadvantages of commercial inorganic fertilizers? Why should both inorganic and organic fertilizers be used?

4. Summarize the advantages and limitations of each of the following proposals for increasing world food supplies and reducing hunger over the next 30 years:
   a. cultivating more land by clearing tropical forests and irrigating arid lands
   b. catching more fish in the open sea
   c. producing more fish and shellfish with aquaculture
   d. increasing the yield per area of cropland

Q: How many of Earth's species are believed to become extinct each year because of human activities?

5. Should price supports and other federal subsidies paid to U.S. farmers out of tax revenues be eliminated? Explain. Try to consult one or more farmers in answering this question.

6. Is sending food to famine victims helpful or harmful? Explain. Are there any conditions you would attach to sending such aid? Explain.

7. Should tax breaks and subsidies be used to encourage more U.S. farmers to switch to sustainable-Earth farming? Explain.

8. Environmentalists argue that because essentially all pesticides eventually fail, their use should be phased out, and farmers should be given economic incentives for switching to integrated pest management.

Explain why you agree or disagree with this proposal. How might doing this affect your lifestyle?

9. Should U.S. companies be allowed to export to other countries pesticides, medicines, and other chemicals that have been banned or severely restricted in the United States? Explain.

10. How can the use of insecticides increase the number of insect pest problems? What is the best way out of this dilemma?

A: 4,000-36,000 (11 to 99 per day)

8 Risk, Toxicology, and Human Health

8-1 Types of Hazards

HAZARDS AND RISK A **hazard** is any substance or action that can cause injury, disease, economic loss, or environmental damage—in short, a danger. **Risk** is the possibility of suffering harm from a hazard. It is expressed in terms of **probability**—a mathematical statement about how likely it is that something will happen. **Risk assessment** involves using data, assumptions, and models to estimate the probability of harm to human health or to the environment that may result from exposures to specific hazards. When we evaluate the risks we face, the key questions we need to ask are whether the risks of damage from each hazard outweigh the short- and long-term benefits, and how we can reduce the hazards and minimize the risks.

COMMON HAZARDS Here are some hazards that people face:

- *Cultural hazards.* These include unsafe living and working conditions, smoking, poor diet, drugs, drinking, driving, criminal assault, unsafe sex, and poverty (Spotlight, p. 7).

- *Chemical hazards.* These result from harmful chemicals in the air (Chapter 9), water (Chapter 10), food (Chapter 7), and soil.

- *Physical hazards.* These include ionizing radiation, noise (Figure 3-16), fires, floods, drought, tornadoes, hurricanes, landslides, earthquakes, and volcanic eruptions.

- *Biological hazards.* These are disease-causing bacteria and viruses, pollen, parasites, and animals such as pit bulls and rattlesnakes.

Most work-related illnesses and premature deaths could be prevented by stricter laws and by enforcement of existing laws governing exposure of workers to ionizing radiation and dangerous chemicals. However, political pressure by industry officials has hindered effective enforcement of these laws.

Industry representatives argue that U.S. industries have some of the world's safest workplaces and that stricter health and safety standards would cut profits and reduce competitiveness in the global marketplace. If such standards are enacted, they claim, they would have to shut down U.S. plants and move to other countries where health and safety standards—and wages—are lower.

Some environmentalists call this form of job blackmail *greenmail*. They believe that pollution taxes—and more of a company's profits—could and should be used for improving worker health and safety standards, as is done in many Japanese, Scandinavian, and German industries.

A growing number of workers are becoming involved in the environmental movement because they and their families have more to lose than most people from poorly enforced or weak environmental and occupational health and safety laws. These workers often feel they must accept high health risks to keep their jobs so they can feed themselves and their families. They and their families are the victims of greenmail.

8-2 Chemical Hazards and Toxicology

DOSE AND RESPONSE The amount of a potentially harmful substance an individual has ingested, inhaled, or absorbed through the skin is called the **dose**, and the amount of resulting health damage is called the **response**. Whether a chemical is harmful depends on (1) how big the dose is during a certain amount of time, (2) how often an exposure occurs, (3) who is exposed (adult or child, for example), and (4) how well the body's detoxification system (liver, lungs, and kidneys) works. If the body gets a large dose in a short time, its repair mechanisms can be overwhelmed. The same total dose spread out over a much longer time might cause little harm. On the other hand, some substances—such as lead—accumulate in the body so that the total dose over a long period of time can be harmful, or even fatal.

Q: How much of the hazardous waste produced in the United States is regulated by federal laws?

> *For the first time in the history of the world, every human being is now subjected to dangerous chemicals from the moment of conception until death.*
>
> RACHEL CARSON

An *acute effect* is an immediate or rapid reaction to an exposure. It can range from dizziness or a rash to death. A *chronic effect* is a long-lasting effect from exposure to a harmful substance. It can result from a single large or small dose or many doses over a long period of time. Examples include kidney and liver damage.

TYPES OF CHEMICAL HAZARDS The main types of chemical hazards are the following:

- **Toxic chemicals** are generally defined as substances fatal to over 50% of test animals at stated concentrations. Many are *neurotoxins*, which attack nerve cells. Nerve gases, potassium cyanide, heroin, chlorinated hydrocarbons (DDT, PCBs, dioxins), organophosphate pesticides (malathion, parathion), carbamate pesticides (Sevin, zineb), and various compounds of arsenic, mercury, lead, and cadmium are all neurotoxins. Most toxic chemicals are discharged into the environment by industrial and agricultural activities, but others—such as hemlock, botulinus toxin, and cobra venom—occur naturally.

- **Hazardous chemicals** are literally dangerous chemicals. They cause harm because they: are flammable or explosive; irritate or damage the skin or lungs (such as strong acidic or alkaline substances, Figure 7-5); interfere with or prevent oxygen uptake and distribution (asphyxiants such as carbon monoxide and hydrogen sulfide); or induce allergic reactions of the immune system (allergens).

- **Carcinogens** are chemicals, radiation, or viruses that cause or promote the growth of a malignant (cancerous) tumor in which certain cells multiply uncontrollably. Many cancerous tumors **metastasize**; that is, they release malignant cells that travel in body fluids to various parts of the body and start new tumors there—making treatment much more difficult. According to the World Health Organization, environmental and lifestyle factors play a key role in causing or promoting up to 80% of all cancers. Major sources of carcinogens are cigarette smoke (35–40% of cancers), diet (20–30%), occupational exposure (5–15%), and environmental pollutants (1–10%). About 10–20% of cancers are believed to be caused by inherited genetic factors or by certain viruses. Typically 10 to 40 years may elapse between the initial exposure to a carcinogen and the appearance of detectable symptoms. Healthy teenagers and young adults have trouble believing that their smoking, drinking, eating, and other lifestyle habits today could kill or harm them before they reach age 50.

- **Mutagens** are agents, such as a chemical or radiation, that cause *mutations*—changes in the DNA molecules of the genes that can be transmitted from parent to offspring. A few mutations are beneficial; some have no effect; but many are harmful.

- **Teratogens** are chemicals, radiation, or viruses that cause birth defects during the growth and development of the human embryo during pregnancy. Chemicals known to cause birth defects in laboratory animals include PCBs, thalidomide, and metals such as arsenic, cadmium, lead, and mercury.

Some people have the mistaken idea that all natural chemicals are safe and all synthetic chemicals are harmful. In fact, many synthetic chemicals are quite safe if used as intended, and a great many natural chemicals are deadly.

Avoiding or minimizing exposure to harmful or potentially harmful chemicals is not easy. According to the National Academy of Sciences, only about 10% of the 70,000 chemicals in commercial use have been thoroughly screened for toxicity, and only 2% have been adequately tested to determine whether they are carcinogens, teratogens, or mutagens. Only 2% of cosmetic ingredients, 5% of food additives, 10% of pesticides, and 18% of drugs used in medicines have been thoroughly tested. Furthermore, each year, about 1,000 new chemicals are introduced into the marketplace with little knowledge about their potentially harmful effects.

Even if we determine the biggest risks associated with a particular technology or chemical, we know

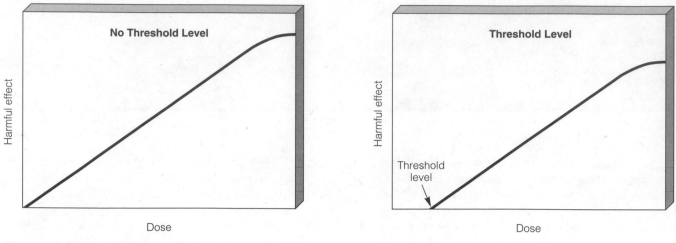

Figure 8-1 Different hypothetical dose-response curves. The curve on the left represents harmful effects that occur with increasing doses of a chemical or ionizing radiation. No dose is considered to be safe. The curve on the right shows the response from exposure to a chemical or ionizing radiation in which harmful effects appear only when the dose is above a certain threshold level. There is considerable uncertainty and controversy over which of these models applies to various harmful agents because of the difficulty in estimating the response to very low doses.

little about its possible interactions with other technologies and chemicals or about the effects of such interactions on human health and ecosystems.

Roughly one-fourth of U.S. workers risk some illness from routine exposure to one or more toxic compounds. The National Institute for Occupational Safety and Health estimates that as many as 100,000 deaths per year in the United States—at least half from cancer—are linked to workers' exposure to toxic agents. The most dangerous occupation is farming, followed by construction, mining, and factory work.

WHAT IS TOXIC? Determining the level at which a substance poses a health threat is done by laboratory investigations (*toxicology*) and by studies of human populations (*epidemiology*). Both approaches are difficult and costly, and both have certain limitations.

Toxicity is usually determined by tests on live laboratory animals (especially mice and rats); on bacteria; and on cell and tissue cultures. Tests are run to develop a **dose-response curve**, which shows the effects of various doses of a toxic agent on a group of test organisms (Figure 8-1). The results are extrapolated for low doses on the test organisms and then extrapolated to humans.

An experiment to assess acute effects often involves determining the **lethal dose**: the amount of material per unit of body weight of the test organism that kills all of the test population in a certain time. Then the dose is reduced until an exposure level is found that kills half the test population in a certain time. This is the **median lethal dose** or **LD$_{50}$**, a standard measurement in toxicity research. Using high dose levels reduces the number of test animals need-

ed, cuts the time needed to obtain results, and lowers costs. Because it is difficult to get data on responses to low doses, the results of high dose exposures are usually extrapolated to low dose levels.

There are problems with animal tests. Extrapolating test-animal data from high to low dose levels is uncertain and controversial. According to the *linear dose-response model*, any dose of ionizing radiation or of a toxic chemical is harmful; and the harm rises as the dose increases, until it reaches a saturation level (Figure 8-1, left). With the *threshold dose-response model* there is a threshold dose below which no detectable harmful effects occur, presumably because the body can repair the damage caused by low doses of some substances (Figure 8-1, right). It's very difficult, however, to establish which of these models applies at low doses.

Some scientists challenge the validity of extrapolating data from test animals to humans because human physiology and metabolism are different from those of the test animals. Others counter that such tests work fairly well, especially for revealing cancer risks when the correct experimental animal is chosen. However, animal tests take two to five years and cost $200,000–$2 million per substance. Furthermore, they are coming under increasing fire from animal rights groups. As a result, scientists are looking for substitute methods.

Also controversial are bacterial tests, as well as cell and tissue culture tests, for toxic agents. One of the most widely used bacterial tests, the Ames test, is considered an accurate predictor of whether a substance is mutagenic; it is also quick (two weeks) and cheap ($1,000 to $1,500 per substance). Some believe this test

Q: If current trends continue, what percentage of Earth's species could become extinct by 2050?

will also detect carcinogens, but the evidence for this is controversial. Cell and tissue culture tests have similar uncertainties, take several weeks to months, and cost about $18,000 per substance.

Chronic toxicity is much harder to assess than acute toxicity. The problem lies in establishing that a particular substance is responsible for chronic effects when people are exposed to hundreds, even thousands, of potentially harmful substances over a long period of time.

Another approach to testing for toxicity and determining the agents causing diseases such as cancer is *epidemiology*—an attempt to find out why some people get sick and others do not. Typically the health of people exposed to a particular toxic agent from an industrial accident—or of people working under high exposure levels, or of people in certain geographic areas—is compared with the health of people not exposed to these conditions, to see if there are statistically significant differences.

This approach also has limitations. For many toxic agents, not enough people have been exposed to high enough levels to detect statistically significant differences. Because people are exposed to many different toxic agents and disease-causing factors throughout their lives, it is often impossible to link an observed epidemiological effect with exposure to a particular toxic agent. And because epidemiology can be used only to evaluate hazards to which people have already been exposed, it is rarely useful for predicting the effects of new technologies or substances.

Thus all methods for estimating toxicity levels have serious limitations, but they are also all we have. To take this uncertainty into account and minimize harm, standards for allowed exposure to toxic substances and radiation are typically set at levels 10, 100, or even 1,000 times lower than the estimated harmful level.

This still may not be enough to protect some people, particularly those vulnerable to a particular hazard because of an allergic reaction or acute sensitivity. Ideally, all products likely to be inhaled, ingested, or absorbed would list their ingredients so that people allergic to or sensitive to certain substances could avoid exposure.

8-3 Biological Hazards: Disease in MDCs and LDCs

TYPES OF DISEASE A **transmissible disease** is caused by a living organism—often a bacterium, virus, or parasitic worm—and can be spread from one person to another. The infectious agents are spread by air, water, food, body fluids, and, in some cases, insects and other nonhuman carriers (called *vectors*). Examples are sexually transmitted diseases (Connections, p. 213), malaria, schistosomiasis, elephantiasis, sleeping sickness, and measles.

About 40% of the world's people live in malaria-prone tropical and subtropical regions (Figure 8-2). There are 200–300 million new cases each year. Some 1–2 million of these people (some estimate as many as 5 million) die each year—more than half of them children under age 5. Malaria's intermittent symptoms include fever and chills, anemia, an enlarged spleen, severe abdominal pain and headaches, extreme weakness, and greater susceptibility to other diseases.

Malaria is caused by four species of protozoa of the genus *Plasmodium*. Most cases of the disease are transmitted when an uninfected female of any one of 60 species of *Anopheles* mosquito bites an infected person, ingests blood that contains the parasite, and then bites an uninfected person. When this happens *Plasmodium* parasites move from the mosquito into the bloodstream, multiply in the liver, and then enter blood cells to continue multiplying (Figure 8-3). Malaria can also be transmitted by blood transfusions or by sharing needles. This cycle repeats itself until immunity develops, treatment is given, or the victim dies.

During the 1950s and 1960s the spread of malaria was sharply curtailed by draining swamplands and marshes, by spraying breeding areas with insecticides, and by using drugs to kill the parasites in the bloodstream.

Since 1970, however, malaria has come roaring back. Most of the malaria-carrying *Anopheles* mosquitoes have become genetically resistant to most of the insecticides used. Worse, the *Plasmodium* parasites have become genetically resistant to the common antimalarial drugs. Irrigation ditches—breeding grounds for mosquitoes—have proliferated, and malaria control budgets have been cut in the mistaken belief that the disease is under control.

Researchers are working to develop new antimalarial drugs and vaccines, and biological controls for *Anopheles* mosquitoes, but such approaches are underfunded and more difficult than originally thought. The World Health Organization estimates that only 3% of the money spent worldwide each year on biomedical research is devoted to malaria and other tropical diseases, even though more people suffer and die worldwide from these diseases than from all others combined.

Prevention offers the best approach to slowing the spread of malaria. Methods include increasing water flow in irrigation systems to prevent mosquito larvae from developing (an expensive and wasteful use of water); using mosquito nets dipped in a nontoxic insecticide (permethrin) in windows and doors of

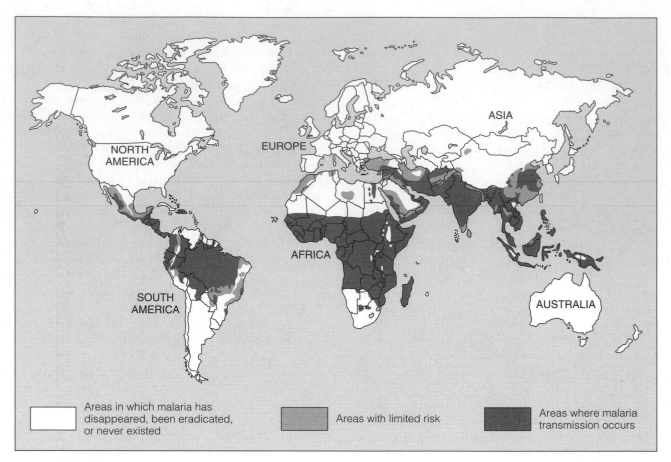

Figure 8-2 Malaria threatens about 40% of the world's population. (Data from the World Health Organization)

Areas in which malaria has disappeared, been eradicated, or never existed

Areas with limited risk

Areas where malaria transmission occurs

Figure 8-3 The life cycle of malaria.

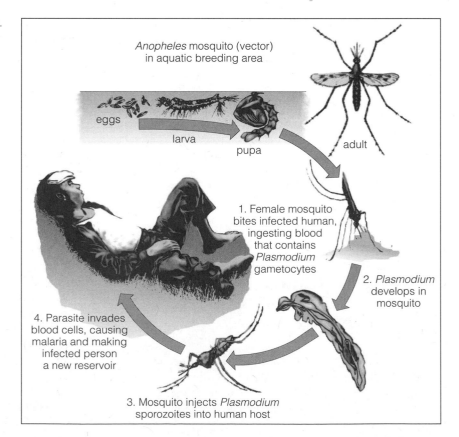

Anopheles mosquito (vector) in aquatic breeding area

eggs

larva

pupa

adult

1. Female mosquito bites infected human, ingesting blood that contains *Plasmodium* gametocytes

2. *Plasmodium* develops in mosquito

4. Parasite invades blood cells, causing malaria and making infected person a new reservoir

3. Mosquito injects *Plasmodium* sporozoites into human host

Q: What is the greatest threat to wild species?

Sexually transmitted diseases (STDs) are passed on during sexual activity. Many STDs can also be transmitted from mother to infant during birth; from one intravenous (IV) drug user to another on shared needles; and by exposure to infected blood.

Worldwide, there are about 250 million new infections and 750,000 deaths from STDs each year. By 2000 the number of deaths from STDs is expected to reach 1.5 million—an average of 4,100 per day. In the United States STDs strike about 12 million people (8 million of them under age 25) per year. The number of new reported cases of most STDs has risen every year since 1981.

Since 1981 the *acquired immune deficiency syndrome* or AIDS (which develops from the HIV virus)—a fatal disease transmitted primarily by sexual contact—has become a serious global health threat. The World Health Organization estimated that by August 1992, at least 13 million people worldwide (62% of them in sub-Saharan Africa) had been infected with the HIV virus—many of them unknowingly. By 2000, 80–120 million people are expected to be infected, with the largest proportion in Asia (42%). Heterosexual transmission accounts for about 90% of the new infections worldwide and about 6% in the United States (12% among those ages 13–24).

Within 10 years, 95% of those with the virus develop AIDS. There is as yet no cure for AIDS, although drugs may help some infected people live longer. By August 1992 an estimated 2.7 million people had AIDS (69% of them in Africa and 16% in the United States), and 2.5 million had died from the disease. By 2000 as many as 24 million people are expected to have AIDS, and the annual death toll may reach 400,000.

In the United States about 1 million people (some estimate up to 3 million) are infected with HIV, 227,000 have AIDS, and 160,000 have died from the disease. Each day about 150 Americans die from AIDS, with the disease being the sixth leading cause of death among young people ages 15–24.

---

homes; cultivating fish that feed on mosquito larvae; clearing vegetation around houses; and planting trees that soak up water in low-lying marsh areas where mosquitoes thrive.

Diseases such as cardiovascular (heart and blood vessel) disorders, most cancers, diabetes, bronchitis, emphysema, and malnutrition often have multiple (often unknown) causes. They also tend to develop slowly and progressively over time, are not caused by living organisms, and do not spread from one person to another. They are classified as **nontransmissible diseases**.

DISEASE IN LDCs   Poverty is the underlying cause of lower average life expectancy and higher infant mortality (Figure 3-7) in LDCs, as well as for poor people in MDCs. The overcrowding, unsafe drinking water, poor sanitation, and malnutrition associated with poverty increase the spread of transmissible diseases, which account for about 40% of all deaths in LDCs. The hot, wet climates of tropical and subtropical LDCs also increase the chances of infection, because disease organisms can thrive year-round.

With adequate funding, the health of people in LDCs can be improved dramatically, quickly, and cheaply by providing:

- Contraceptives (Figure 3-5), sex education, and family-planning counseling.

- Better nutrition, prenatal care, and birth assistance for pregnant women. At least 500,000 women in LDCs die each year of mostly preventable pregnancy-related causes, compared with 6,000 in MDCs.

- Better nutrition for children.

- Greatly improved postnatal care (including the promotion of breast-feeding) to reduce infant mortality.

- Immunization against tetanus, measles, diphtheria, typhoid, and tuberculosis.

- Oral rehydration for diarrhea victims (a simple solution of water, salt, and sugar).

- Antibiotics for infections.

- Clean drinking water and sanitation facilities to the one-third of the world's population that lacks them.

According to the World Health Organization, extending such primary health care to all the world's people would cost an additional $10 billion per year, a mere 4% of what the world spends every year on cigarettes or devotes every four days to military spending.

CONNECTIONS

What is roughly the size of a 30-caliber bullet, can be bought almost anywhere, and kills about 8,200 people every day? It's not AIDS, wars, or contaminated water; it's a cigarette.

Cigarette smoking is the single most preventable major cause of death and suffering among adults. Each cigarette you smoke reduces your average life span by about 10 minutes. The World Health Organization estimates that tobacco kills at least 3 million people each year from heart disease, lung cancer, other cancers, bronchitis, emphysema, and stroke. By 2050 the death toll from smoking-related diseases is projected to be 12 million annually—an average of 33,000 preventable deaths per day.

In 1992, smoking killed about 435,000 Americans—an average of 1,190 deaths per day (Figure 8-4). This death toll is equivalent to three fully loaded jumbo jets crashing every day with no survivors. Smoking kills more people each year in the United States than do all illegal drugs, alcohol, automobile accidents, suicide, and homicide combined (Figure 8-4).

Studies indicate that passive smoke (inhaled by nonsmokers) is also a killer, causing up to 40,000 premature deaths in the United States a year (3,000 of them from lung cancer), although tobacco companies dispute these findings. According to the EPA, each year secondhand smoke contributes to 150,000–300,000 respiratory infections like bronchitis and pneumonia in American children. It also triggers 8,000 to 26,000 new cases of asthma in children and aggravates symptoms in 200,000–1 million children with asthma.

Smoking costs the United States at least $65 billion per year (perhaps $95 billion) in expenses related to premature death, disability, medical treatment, increased insurance costs, and lost productivity because of illness (accounting for 19% of all absenteeism in industry). These harmful social costs amount to at least $3 per pack of cigarettes sold.

The good news is that smoking—the single greatest human health hazard—is a preventable hazard. To reduce this hazard the American Medical Association and many health experts call for:

- Banning cigarette advertising in the United States.

- Forbidding the sale of cigarettes and other tobacco products to anyone under 21, with strict penalties for violators.

- Banning all cigarette vending machines.

- Classifying nicotine as addictive and dangerous and placing its use in tobacco or other products under the jurisdiction of the Food and Drug Administration.

- Eliminating all federal subsidies to U.S. tobacco farmers and tobacco companies.

- Taxing cigarettes at about $3 a pack (instead of the current 51¢, the second lowest in the world; cigarettes are taxed at $4 per pack in Norway and at more than $3 per pack in Denmark, Canada, and Great Britain). This would discourage smoking and require people choosing to smoke to pay for the resulting harmful costs now borne by society as a whole—a *user-pays* approach. This would raise about $50 billion per year in revenue, which could be targeted to help finance a better health-care system.

- Forbidding U.S. officials to pressure other governments to import American tobacco or tobacco products. Since 1985 the federal government has threatened trade sanctions against countries that place tariffs and other restrictions on American tobacco products. Thus the U.S. government is coercing other governments into allowing imports of a hazardous (but legal) drug from America, while trying to halt the flow of illegal drugs into the United States.

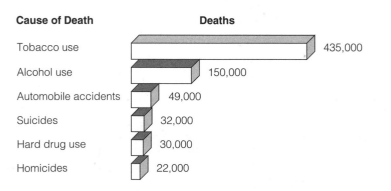

Cause of Death — **Deaths**

Tobacco use — 435,000
Alcohol use — 150,000
Automobile accidents — 49,000
Suicides — 32,000
Hard drug use — 30,000
Homicides — 22,000

Figure 8-4 Deaths in the United States from tobacco use and other causes in 1992. Smoking is by far the nation's leading cause of preventable death, causing more premature deaths each year than all the other categories in this figure combined. (Data from National Center for Health Statistics)

Q: How much of the earth's land surface has been set aside to protect wildlife?

Table 8-1 Greatest Ecological and Health Risks

High-Risk Ecological Problems

Global climate change

Stratospheric ozone depletion

Wildlife habitat alteration and destruction

Species extinction and loss of biodiversity

Medium-Risk Ecological Problems

Acid deposition

Pesticides

Airborne toxic chemicals

Toxic chemicals, nutrients, and sediment in surface waters

Low-Risk Ecological Problems

Oil spills

Groundwater pollution

Radioactive isotopes

Acid runoff to surface waters

Thermal pollution

High-Risk Human Health Problems

Indoor air pollution

Outdoor air pollution

Worker exposure to industrial or farm chemicals

Pollutants in drinking water

Pesticide residues on food

Toxic chemicals in consumer products

Data from Science Advisory Board, *Reducing Risks*, Washington, D.C., Environmental Protection Agency, 1990. Items in each category are not listed in rank order.

DISEASES IN MDCs   As a country industrializes and makes the *demographic transition* (Figure 3-21), it also makes an *epidemiological transition*, in which the infectious diseases of childhood become less important and the chronic diseases of adulthood (heart disease and stroke, cancer, and respiratory conditions) become more important in determining mortality.

Each year about 2.3 million people die in the United States: 37% from heart attacks, 22% from cancer, 7% from strokes, 5% from accidents, and the remaining 29% from a variety of causes. In the United States and other MDCs, most deaths are a result of environmental and lifestyle factors rather than infectious agents invading the body. Except for auto accidents, these deaths result from chronic diseases that take a long time to develop and have multiple causes. They are largely related to location (urban or rural), work environment, diet, smoking (Connections, p. 214), exercise, sexual habits (Connections, p. 213), and the level of use of alcohol or other harmful drugs.

Changing these harmful lifestyle factors could prevent 40–70% of all premature deaths, one-third of all cases of acute disability, and two-thirds of all cases of chronic disability. Currently about 95% of the money spent on health care in the United States is used to *treat* rather than to *prevent* disease.

8-4   Risk Analysis

ESTIMATING RISKS   Risk analysis involves identifying hazards and evaluating their associated risks (*risk assessment*); ranking risks (*comparative risk analysis*); using this and other information to determine options and make decisions about reducing or eliminating risks (*risk management*); and informing decision makers and the public about risks (*risk communication*).

Risk assessment involves determining the types of hazards involved, estimating the probability that each hazard will occur, estimating how many people are likely to be exposed to it, and how many may suffer serious harm. Probabilities based on past experience, animal and other tests, and epidemiological studies are used to estimate risks from older technologies and products. For new technologies and products, much more uncertain statistical probabilities, based on models rather than actual experience, must be calculated. Table 8-1 is an example of *comparative risk analysis*, summarizing the greatest ecological and health risks identified by a panel of scientists acting as advisers to the U.S. Environmental Protection Agency.

The more complex a technological system is and the more people that are needed to design and run it, the harder it is to calculate the risks. The overall reliability of any technological system is the product of two factors:

$$\text{system reliability (\%)} = \text{technology reliability} \times \text{human reliability} \times 100$$

With careful design, quality control, maintenance, and monitoring, a highly complex system such as a nuclear power plant or a space shuttle can achieve a high degree of technology reliability. However, human reliability is almost always much lower than technology reliability and is virtually impossible to predict; to be human is to err.

Suppose, for example, that the technology reliability of a nuclear power plant is 95% (0.95) and that the human reliability is 75% (0.75). Then the overall system reliability is only 71% ($0.95 \times 0.75 = 71\%$). Even if we could make the technology 100% reliable (1.0), the overall system reliability would still be only 75% ($1.0 \times 0.75 = 75\%$).

This crucial dependence of even the most carefully designed systems on unpredictable human reliability helps explain essentially "impossible" tragedies like Three Mile Island and Chernobyl (Connections, p. 122) nuclear power plant accidents and the explosion of the space shuttle *Challenger*.

Poor management, poor training, and poor supervision increase the chances of human errors. Maintenance workers or people who monitor warning panels in the control rooms of nuclear power plants get bored because most of the time nothing goes wrong. They may fall asleep on duty (as has happened in control rooms at several U.S. nuclear plants) or falsify maintenance records because they think the system is safe without their help. They may be distracted by personal problems or illness. And managers may order them to take shortcuts that increase short-term profits or make the managers look more productive.

One way to make a system more foolproof or "fail-safe" is to move more of the potentially fallible elements from the human side to the technical side. However, chance events such as a lightning bolt can knock out automatic control systems. And no machine or computer program can completely replace human judgment in assuring that a complex system operates properly and safely. Also, the parts in any automated control system are manufactured, assembled, tested, certified, and maintained by fallible human beings.

RISK-BENEFIT ANALYSIS AND RISK MANAGEMENT The key question is whether the estimated short- and long-term benefits of using a particular technology or product outweigh the estimated short- and long-term risks of other alternatives. One method for making such evaluations is **risk-benefit analysis**. It involves estimating the short- and long-term societal benefits and risks involved and then dividing the benefits by the risks to find a **desirability quotient**:

$$\text{desirability quotient} = \frac{\text{societal benefits}}{\text{societal risks}}$$

Assuming that benefits and risks can be calculated accurately (a big assumption), here are several possibilities:

$$\text{large desirability quotient} = \frac{\text{large societal benefits}}{\text{small societal risks}}$$

Example: *X rays*. Use of X rays (a form of ionizing radiation) to detect bone fractures and other medical problems has a large desirability quotient—provided that the dose is no larger than needed, that less harmful procedures are not available, and that doctors do not overprescribe them. Other examples in this category include mining, most dams, and airplane travel. Proponents of nuclear power plants place nuclear technology in this category.

$$\frac{\text{small desirability}}{\text{quotient}} = \frac{\text{large societal benefits}}{\text{much larger societal risks}}$$

Example: *Coal-burning power plants and nuclear power plants* (Sections 4-6 and 4-7, respectively).

$$\frac{\text{uncertain desirability}}{\text{quotient}} = \frac{\text{potentially large benefits}}{\text{unknown risks}}$$

Example: *Genetic engineering* (Pro/Con, next page). Some see biotechnology as a way to increase food supplies, degrade toxic wastes, eliminate certain genetic diseases and afflictions, and make enormous amounts of money. Others fear that, without strict controls, it could do great harm.

PROBLEMS WITH RISK ASSESSMENT Calculation of desirability quotients, as well as other ways of evaluating or expressing risk, is extremely difficult, imprecise, and controversial. Here are some of the key problems and issues.

- *Should estimates emphasize short-term risks, or should more weight be put on long-term risks*? Who decides this?

- *Should the primary goal of risk analysis be to determine how much risk is acceptable (the current approach) or to figure out how to do the least damage (a prevention approach)*?

- *Who should do a particular risk-benefit analysis or risk assessment*? Should it be the corporation or government agency that develops or manages the technology, or some independent laboratory or panel of scientists? For an outside evaluation, who chooses the people to do the study? Who pays the bill and thus can influence the outcome by denying the lab, agency, or experts future business?

- *Once a risk-assessment study is done, who reviews the results*? Is it a government agency? Independent scientists? The general public?

- *Should cumulative impacts of various risks be considered, or should risks be considered separately, as is usually done*? For example, suppose a pesticide is found to have a risk of killing one in a million people, the current EPA limit. Cumulatively, however, effects from 40 such pesticides might kill 40—or even 400—of every 1 million people. Is this acceptable (Spotlight, p. 218)?

Q: In tropical and temperate areas, how long does it take to renew 2.54 centimeters (1 inch) of topsoil?

Genetic Engineering: Savior or Monster?

"Genetic engineers" have learned how to splice genes and recombine sequences of existing DNA molecules in organisms to produce DNA with new genetic characteristics (recombinant DNA). This rapidly developing technology excites many scientists and investors. They see it as a way to increase crop and livestock yields, and also as a way to produce, patent, and sell crop varieties with greater resistance to diseases, pests, frost, and drought—and with more protein than existing varieties. They hope to create bacteria that can destroy oil spills, degrade toxic wastes, and concentrate metals found in low-grade ores, and to serve as biological "factories" for new vaccines, drugs, and therapeutic hormones. Gene therapy, proponents argue, could eliminate certain genetic diseases and other genetic afflictions.

When the U.S. Supreme Court ruled in 1980 that genetically engineered organisms could be patented, investors began pouring billions of dollars into the fledgling biotech industry, with dreams of more billions in profits. Already genetic engineering has produced a drug to reduce heart attack damage and agents to fight diabetes, hemophilia, and some forms of cancer. It has also been used to diagnose AIDS and cancer. In agriculture, gene transfer has been used to develop strawberries that resist frost, as well as smaller cows that produce more milk. Toxin-producing genes have been transferred from bacteria to plants, increasing the plants' immunity to insect attack.

Some people are worried that biotechnology may run amok. Most recognize that it is unrealistic to stop genetic engineering altogether, but they argue that it should be kept under strict control. They believe that we don't understand how nature works well enough to have unregulated control over the genetic characteristics of humans and other species.

Critics also fear that unregulated biotechnology could lead to the development of "superorganisms." For example, bacteria genetically altered to clean up ocean oil spills by degrading the oil would cause havoc if they were able to multiply rapidly and began degrading the world's remaining oil supplies. Genetically engineered organisms might also mutate, change their form and behavior, and then migrate. Unlike defective cars and other products, they couldn't be recalled.

Proponents argue that the risk of this or other biotech catastrophes is small. To have a serious effect, such organisms would have to be outstanding competitors and resistant to predation. In addition, they would have to be capable of becoming dominant in ecosystems and in the ecosphere.

Nevertheless, critics fear that the potential profits from biotechnology are so enormous that, without strict controls, greed—not ecological wisdom and restraint—will prevail. They point to the serious and widespread ecological problems when we have accidentally or deliberately introduced alien organisms into biological communities.

In 1989 a committee of prominent ecologists appointed by the Ecological Society of America warned that the ecological impacts of new combinations of genetic traits from different species would be difficult to predict. Their report called for a case-by-case review of any proposed environmental releases, as well as carefully regulated, small-scale field tests before any bioengineered organism is put into commercial use.

This controversy illustrates the difficulty of balancing the actual and potential benefits of a technology with its actual and potential risks of harm.

Some see risk analysis as a useful and much-needed tool. Others see it as a way to justify premeditated murder in the name of profit. According to hazardous-waste expert Peter Montague, "The explicit aim of risk assessment is to convince people that some number of citizens *must* be killed each year to maintain a national lifestyle based on necessities like Saran Wrap, throwaway cameras, and lawns without dandelions." Risk evaluator Mary O'Brien says "Risk assessment is industry's attempt to make the intolerable appear tolerable." Such critics accuse industries of favoring risk analysis because so little is known about health risks from pollutants and because the data that do exist are controversial. This allows risk-benefit analysis to be crafted to support almost any conclusion and then be labeled as "scientific decision making." The huge uncertainties in risk-benefit analysis also allow industries to delay regulatory decisions for decades by challenging data in the courts.

Despite the inevitable uncertainties involved, proponents argue that risk analysis is a useful way to organize available information, identify significant hazards, focus on areas that need more research, and stimulate people to make more informed decisions about health and environmental goals and priorities. However, at best, risk assessments yield only a range

The Delaney Clause

In 1958 an amendment known as the Delaney clause (after Representative James Delaney) was added to the U.S. food and drug laws. It absolutely prohibits using any additive in foods (including pesticide residues) that has been shown to cause cancer in test animals or people, with no consideration of economic or health benefits or risks. *It is one of the first examples of pollution prevention.* It is a precautionary or "better-safe-than-sorry" approach that says no deaths will be allowed because of substances added to or finding their way into foods people eat. Since 1958 the food and pesticide industries have fought hard to have this law repealed or changed to allow balancing of health and economic benefits and risks.

Despite its absolute nature, the Food and Drug Administration and the EPA have rarely used the Delaney clause to ban a food additive or pesticide that ends up as a food residue—choosing mostly to ignore or find ways around the law. This ended in 1992 when the U.S. Supreme Court ruled that food-crop residues of pesticides shown to cause cancer in test animals must be banned from use. This ruling means that the EPA would have to ban about 50 pesticides whose active ingredients have been shown to cause cancer in test animals or ask Congress to weaken the law.

Food and pesticide producers and the EPA (with the support of President Bill Clinton) want to amend the law to allow continued use of pesticides that pose a small risk, such as less than one chance of a cancer in 1 million people—the current EPA standard.

Most environmentalists believe that the Delaney clause is an excellent example of a pollution preven-tion or zero-carcinogens policy that genuinely protects the public and that should not be weakened. They argue that exposure to a cancer-causing pesticide on one crop is just one of many exposures consumers get and that the cumulative exposure to such chemicals raises the total risk considerably and should be taken into account. Several studies also indicate that permitted residues are 100–500 times what is safe for children—a position generally supported in a 1993 study by the National Academy of Sciences. Indeed, instead of revoking or weakening the Delaney clause, some health scientists believe it should be strengthened to ban substances in food that have been shown to cause mutations (mutagens), birth defects (teratogens), liver or kidney damage, or damage to the nervous, immune, or endocrine systems in test animals. What do you think?

---

of probabilities and uncertainties based on different assumptions—not the precise numbers that decision makers want.

MANAGING RISK   Once an assessment of risk is made, decisions must be made about what to do about the risk. **Risk management** includes the administrative, political, and economic actions taken to decide whether and how a particular societal risk is to be reduced to a certain level—and at what cost. Risk management involves trying to answer the following questions:

- Which of the vast number of risks facing society should be evaluated and managed with the limited funds available?

- In what sequence or priority should the risks be evaluated and managed?

- How reliable is the risk-benefit analysis or risk assessment carried out for each risk?

- How much risk is acceptable? How safe is safe enough?

- How much money will it take to reduce each risk to an acceptable level?

- How much will each risk be reduced if available funds are limited, as is usually the case?

- How will the risk management plan be communicated to the public, monitored, and enforced?

Risk managers must make difficult decisions based on inadequate and uncertain scientific data. These decisions have potentially grave consequences for human health and the environment, and they have large economic effects on industry and consumers. Each step in this process involves value judgments and trade-offs to find some reasonable compromise between conflicting political, economic, and environmental interests.

RISK PERCEPTION AND COMMUNICATION
Most of us do poorly in assessing the risks from the hazards that surround us, and we tend to be full of contradictions. For example, many people deny or shrug off the high-risk nature of activities such as motorcycling (1 death per 50 participants), smoking (1 death in 600 by age 35 for a pack-a-day smoker), a car crash (1 in 5,000 with a seat belt versus 1 in 2,500 without),

Q: Worldwide, how much topsoil is eroded each year?

parachuting (1 in 4,000), and rock climbing (1 in 5,000). Yet these same people may be terrified about the possibility of dying in a commercial airplane crash (1 in 800,000), in a train crash (1 in 20 million), from a shark attack (1 in 300 million), or from drinking water with the EPA limit of trichloroethylene (1 in 2 billion).

Being bombarded with news about people killed or harmed by various hazards distorts our sense of risk. *The real news each year is that 99% of the people on Earth didn't die.* However, that's not what we see on TV or hear about every day.

The public generally sees a technology or a product as being riskier than experts see it (Table 8-1) when:

- *It is relatively new or complex rather than familiar.* Examples might include genetic engineering or nuclear power, as opposed to dams or automobiles.

- *It is mostly involuntary instead of voluntary.* Examples might include nuclear power plants, nuclear weapons, industrial pollution, or food additives, as opposed to smoking, drinking alcohol, or driving.

- *It is viewed as unnecessary rather than as beneficial or necessary.* Examples might include CFC and hydrocarbon propellants in aerosol spray cans, or food additives used to increase sales appeal—as opposed to cars or firearms for self-defense.

- *It involves a large, well-publicized death toll from a single catastrophic accident rather than the same or even larger death toll spread out over a longer time.* Examples might include a severe nuclear power plant accident, an industrial explosion, or a plane crash, as opposed to coal-burning power plants, automobiles, smoking, or malnutrition in LDCs.

- *It involves unfair distribution of the risks.* For example, citizens are outraged when government officials decide to put a hazardous-waste landfill or incinerator in or near their neighborhood even when the decision is based on risk-benefit analysis. This is usually seen as politics, not science.

- *It is poorly communicated.* Does the decision-making agency or company seem trustworthy and concerned or dishonest, unconcerned, and arrogant (Exxon after the Valdez oil spill, the Nuclear Regulatory Agency and the nuclear industry since the Three Mile Island accident)? Does it involve the community in the decision-making process from start to finish and reveal what's going on before the real decisions are made? Does it understand, listen to, and respond to community concerns?

- *It does not involve a sincere search for and evaluation of alternatives.*

People who believe their lives and the lives of their children are being threatened because they live near an actual or proposed chemical plant, toxic-waste dump, or waste incinerator don't care that experts say the chemical is likely to kill only one in a million people in the general population. Only a few of those million people live or will live near the plant, dump, or incinerator, as they do. And that one might be their child. To them it is a personal threat, not a statistical abstraction.

Though their health needs differ drastically, the rich and the poor do have one thing in common: both die unnecessarily. The rich die of heart disease and cancer, the poor of diarrhea, pneumonia, and measles. Scientific medicine could vastly reduce the mortality caused by these illnesses. Yet, half the developing world lacks medical care of any kind.

WILLIAM U. CHANDLER

CRITICAL THINKING

1. Should standards for allowed pollution levels be set to protect the most sensitive person or only the average person in a population? Explain. Should we have zero pollution levels for all hazardous chemicals? Explain.

2. How would you go about reducing the overall threat to human health from AIDS and other STDs? What things do you do in your own life to reduce your risk of getting a sexually transmitted disease?

3. What restrictions, if any, do you believe should be placed on genetic engineering research and use? How would you enforce any restrictions?

4. Do you believe that smoking is the single greatest threat to human health? Explain why you agree or disagree.

5. Explain why you agree or disagree with each of the following proposals:
   a. All advertising of cigarettes and other tobacco products should be banned.
   b. All smoking should be banned in public buildings and commercial airplanes, buses, subways, and trains.
   c. All government subsidies to tobacco farmers and the tobacco industry should be eliminated.
   d. Cigarettes should be taxed at about $3 per pack so that U.S. smokers alone pay for the health and productivity losses now borne by society as a whole.

6. Do you believe that risk-benefit analysis should be used as the primary method to evaluate and manage risks? Explain.

7. Should the Delaney clause be left as is, strengthened to include mutagens and teratogens, revoked completely, or altered to allow risk minimization (1 cancer per million people) instead of absolute risk prevention? Explain.

A: About 23 billion metric tons (25 billion tons)—enough to fill a train of freight cars long enough to encircle the planet 150 times

9 Air, Climate, and Ozone

Atmosphere, Weather, and Climate

THE TROPOSPHERE: LIFE GIVER AND WEATHER BREEDER We live at the bottom of a "sea" of air called the **atmosphere**. This thin envelope of life-sustaining gases surrounding the earth is divided into several spherical layers characterized by abrupt changes in temperature due to differences in the absorption of incoming solar energy (Figure 9-1).

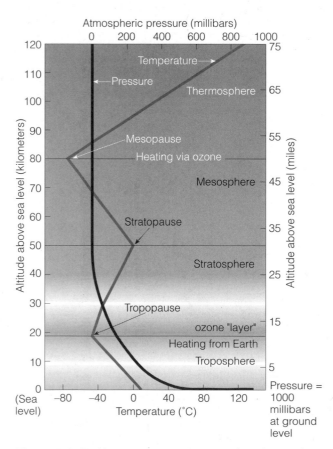

Figure 9-1 Earth's present atmosphere consists of several layers. Most ultraviolet radiation from the sun is absorbed by ozone (O_3) in the stratosphere, most of which is found in the so-called *ozone layer*, between 17 and 26 kilometers (11–16 miles) above sea level.

About 95% of the mass of Earth's air is found in the atmosphere's innermost layer, the **troposphere**, extending only about 17 kilometers (11 miles) above sea level at the equator and about 8 kilometers (5 miles) over the poles. If Earth were an apple, this lower layer, containing the air we breathe, would be no thicker than the apple's skin. This thin but nevertheless turbulent layer of rising and falling air currents and winds is the planet's weather breeder.

The composition of the atmosphere has varied considerably throughout Earth's long history. Today about 99% of the volume of clean, dry air in the troposphere consists of two gases: nitrogen (78%) and oxygen (21%). The remainder has slightly less than 1% argon (Ar), 0.036% carbon dioxide (CO_2), and trace amounts of neon (Ne), helium (He), methane (CH_4), krypton (Kr), hydrogen (H_2), xenon (Xe), and chlorofluorocarbons (CFCs, put there by human activities). Air in the troposphere also holds water vapor in amounts varying from 0.01% by volume at the frigid poles to 5% in the humid tropics.

THE STRATOSPHERE: OUR GLOBAL SUNSCREEN The atmosphere's second layer is the **stratosphere**, which extends from about 17–48 kilometers (11–30 miles) above Earth's surface (Figure 9-1). It is a much more peaceful place than the troposphere. Although the stratosphere contains less matter than the troposphere, its composition is similar, with two notable exceptions: Its volume of water vapor is about 1,000 times less and its volume of ozone (O_3) is about 1,000 times greater.

Stratospheric ozone is produced when some of the stratosphere's oxygen molecules interact with lightning and solar radiation. This thin layer of ozone keeps about 99% of the harmful ultraviolet radiation (especially ultraviolet-B, or UV-B) given off by the sun from reaching Earth's surface. This filtering action protects us from increased sunburn, skin and eye cancer, cataracts, and damage to the immune system. This global sunscreen also prevents damage to some plants, aquatic organisms, and other land animals. Furthermore, it keeps much of the oxygen in the troposphere from being converted to toxic ozone by incoming UV radiation. The trace amounts of ozone that do form in

Q: On how much of the world's cropland is soil eroding faster than it forms?

the troposphere as a component of urban smog damage plants, the respiratory systems of humans and other animals, and materials such as rubber.

Thus our good health and that of many other species depend on having enough "good" ozone in the stratosphere and as little as possible "bad" ozone in the troposphere. Unfortunately, our activities are increasing the amount of harmful ozone in the tropospheric air we must breathe and decreasing the amount of beneficial ozone in the stratosphere.

Air in the stratosphere, unlike that in the troposphere, is calm, with little vertical mixing. Pilots like to fly in this layer because it has so little turbulence and such excellent visibility (due to the almost complete absence of clouds). Flying in the stratosphere also improves fuel efficiency because the thin air offers little resistance to the forward thrust of the plane. And unlike the troposphere, temperature rises with altitude in the stratosphere until there is another reversal at the *stratopause*, which marks the end of the stratosphere and the beginning of the atmosphere's next layer (Figure 9-1).

WHAT ARE WEATHER AND CLIMATE? Every moment at any spot on Earth the troposphere has a particular set of physical properties such as temperature, pressure, humidity, precipitation, sunshine, cloud cover, and wind direction and speed. These short-term properties of the troposphere at a given place and time are what we call **weather**.

Climate is the average long-term weather of an area. It is a region's atmospheric or weather conditions, seasonal variations, and weather extremes averaged over a long period—at least 30 years. The two most important factors determining the climate of an area are temperature and precipitation (Figure 9-2).

WHAT FACTORS INFLUENCE CLIMATE? The temperature and precipitation patterns that lead to different climates are caused mostly by the way air circulates over the earth's surface. Several factors determine these patterns of global air circulation:

- *Long-term variations in the amount of solar energy striking the earth.*

- *Uneven heating of the earth's surface.* Air is heated much more at the equator, where the sun's rays strike directly throughout the year, than at the poles, where sunlight strikes at a glancing angle. These differences help explain why tropical regions near the equator are hot, polar regions are cold, and temperate regions in between generally have intermediate temperatures (Figure 9-2).

- *The tilt of the earth's axis* (an imaginary line connecting the North and South Poles). Because of this tilt various regions are tipped toward or away from the sun as the earth makes its annual revolution around the sun. This creates opposite seasons in the Northern and Southern Hemispheres.

- *Rotation of the earth.* Forces in the atmosphere created by this rotation deflect winds (moving air masses) to the right in the Northern Hemisphere and to the left in the Southern Hemisphere, in what is called the *Coriolis effect.* The result is six huge convection cells of swirling air masses—three north and three south of the equator (Figure 9-3).

- *Properties of air and water.* Cold air is denser (weighs more per unit volume) than hot air and thus tends to sink through less dense, warmer air; hot air, being less dense, tends to rise. Hot air can also hold more water vapor than cold air. When heated by the sun, ocean water evaporates and removes heat from the oceans to the atmosphere. This moist, hot air expands, becomes less dense, and rises in fairly narrow vortices that spiral upward, creating an area of low pressure at the earth's surface. As this moisture-laden air rises, it cools and releases moisture as condensation (because cold air can hold less water vapor than warm air). The heat released when water vapor condenses radiates into space. The resulting cooler, drier air becomes denser, sinks (subsides), and creates an area of high pressure. As this area flows across the earth's surface, it picks up heat and moisture and begins to rise again. The resulting small and giant convection cells circulate air, heat, and moisture both vertically and from place

A: 33%

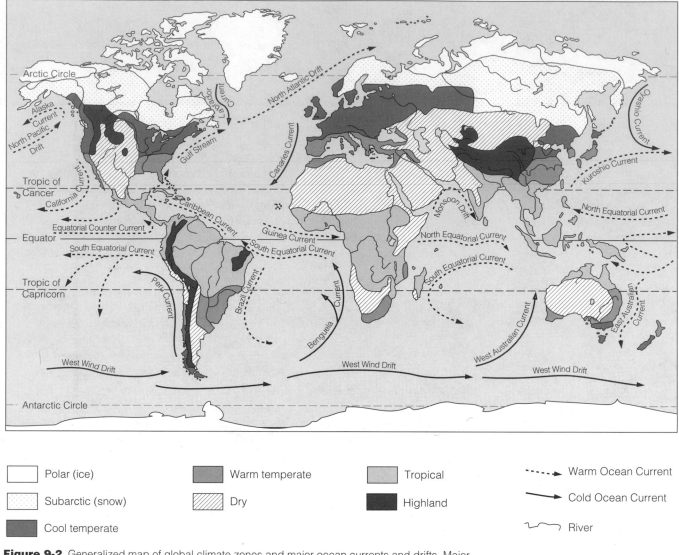

	Polar (ice)		Warm temperate		Tropical	- - - -▶ Warm Ocean Current
	Subarctic (snow)		Dry		Highland	───▶ Cold Ocean Current
	Cool temperate					～ River

Figure 9-2 Generalized map of global climate zones and major ocean currents and drifts. Major variations in climate are dictated mainly by two variables: **(1)** the temperature, with its seasonal variations, and **(2)** the quantity and distribution of precipitation.

to place in the troposphere, leading to different climates and patterns of vegetation (Figures 9-4 and 2-27).

- *Ocean currents*. The factors just listed, plus differences in water density, cause warm and cold ocean currents. These currents, along with air masses above, redistribute heat received from the sun (Figure 9-2). Ocean currents, like air currents, redistribute heat and thus influence climate and vegetation, especially near coastal areas. For example, without the warm Gulf Stream, which transports 25 times more water than all the world's rivers, the climate of northwestern Europe would be subarctic. Currents also help mix ocean waters and distribute nutrients and dissolved oxygen needed by aquatic organisms.

- *Atmospheric composition*. Small amounts of carbon dioxide and water vapor and trace amounts of ozone, methane, nitrous oxide, chlorofluorocarbons, and other gases in the troposphere play a key role in determining Earth's average temperatures and thus its climates. These gases, known as **greenhouse gases**, act somewhat like the glass panes of a greenhouse (or of a car parked in the sun with its windows rolled up): They allow light, infrared radiation, and some ultraviolet radiation from the sun (Figure 2-4) to pass through the troposphere. Earth's surface absorbs much of this solar energy and degrades it to heat, which then rises into the troposphere (Figure 2-9). Some of this heat escapes into space, and some is absorbed by molecules of greenhouse gases,

Q: How much land has become desertified during the past 50 years?

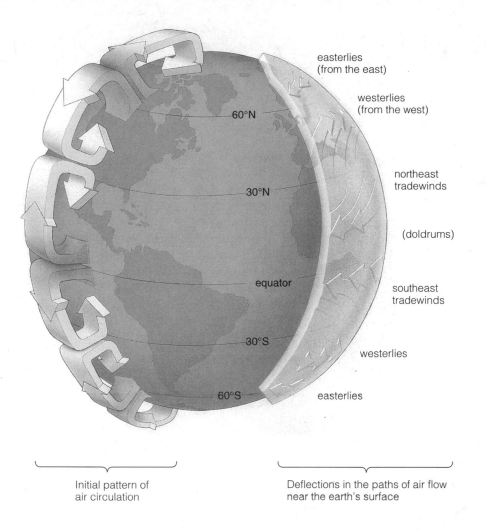

easterlies
(from the east)

westerlies
(from the west)

northeast
tradewinds

60°N

30°N

(doldrums)

equator

southeast
tradewinds

30°S

westerlies

60°S   easterlies

Initial pattern of
air circulation

Deflections in the paths of air flow
near the earth's surface

Figure 9-3 Formation of prevailing surface winds, which disrupt the general flow of air from the equator to the poles and back to the equator. As Earth rotates, its surface turns faster beneath air masses at the equator and slower beneath those at the poles. This deflects air masses moving north and south to the west or east, creating six huge convection cells in which air swirls upward and then descends toward Earth's surface at different latitudes. The direction of air movement in these cells sets up belts of prevailing winds that distribute air and moisture over Earth's surface, affecting the general types of climate found in different areas and also driving the circulation of ocean currents. (Used by permission from Cecie Starr and Ralph Taggart, *Biology: The Unity and Diversity of Life*, 6th ed., Belmont, Calif.: Wadsworth, 1992)

warming the air, and some radiates back toward the earth's surface. This trapping of heat in the troposphere is called the **greenhouse effect** (Figure 9-5). If there were no greenhouse gases, especially water vapor, Earth would be a cold and lifeless planet with an average surface temperature of –18°C (0°F) instead of its current 15°C (59°F).

| 9-2 | **Global Warming or a Lot of Hot Air?** |

SOME THINGS WE KNOW ABOUT EARTH'S CLIMATE   In 1990 and 1992 the Intergovernmental Panel on Climate Change (IPCC) published reports by several hundred leading atmospheric scientists on the best available evidence about past climate change, the greenhouse effect, and recent changes in global temperatures. According to the panel's reports and other studies, this was the current scientific consensus on these matters:

- Earth's climate is the result of complex interactions among the sun, atmosphere, oceans, land, and biosphere—interactions that we only partly understand.

- Earth's average surface temperature has fluctuated considerably over geologic time, with several ice ages covering much of the planet with thick ice during the past 800,000 years. Each glacial period lasted about 100,000 years and was followed by a warmer interglacial period of 10,000–12,500 years. As the ice melted at the end of the last ice age, average sea levels rose about 100 meters (300 feet), changing the face of the earth.

- For the past 10,000 years we have enjoyed the relative warmth of the latest interglacial period, during which mean surface temperatures have fluctuated only 0.5–1°C (0.9–1.8°F) over 100- to 200-year periods. Even these small temperature changes have led to large migrations of people. However, recent analysis of layers of ancient ice reveals that during the previous interglacial period, average temperatures varied as much as 10°C (18°F) in only a decade or two—a frightening possibility.

Figure 9-4 Global air circulation and biomes. Heat and moisture are distributed over Earth's surface by vertical convection currents that form into six large convection cells (called Hadley cells) at different latitudes. The direction of air flow and the ascent and descent of air masses in these convection cells determine Earth's general climatic zones. The uneven distribution of heat and moisture over the planet's surface leads to the forests, grasslands, and deserts that make up Earth's biomes.

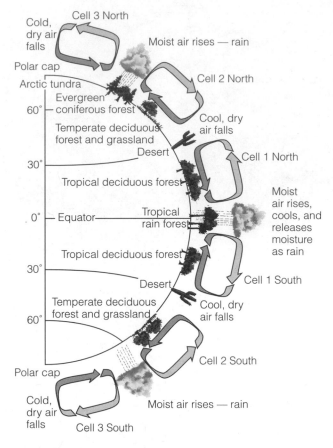

Cell 3 North
Cold, dry air falls
Moist air rises — rain
Polar cap
Arctic tundra
Cell 2 North
Evergreen coniferous forest
Cool, dry air falls
60°
Temperate deciduous forest and grassland
Desert
Cell 1 North
30°
Tropical deciduous forest
Moist air rises, cools, and releases moisture as rain
0° — Equator
Tropical rain forest
Tropical deciduous forest
Cell 1 South
30°
Desert
Cool, dry air falls
Temperate deciduous forest and grassland
60°
Cell 2 South
Polar cap
Cold, dry air falls
Moist air rises — rain
Cell 3 South

Figure 9-5 The greenhouse effect. Without the atmospheric warming provided by this effect, Earth would be a cold and mostly lifeless planet. (Used by permission from Cecie Starr and Ralph Taggart, *Biology: The Unity and Diversity of Life*, 6th ed., Belmont, Calif.: Wadsworth, 1992)

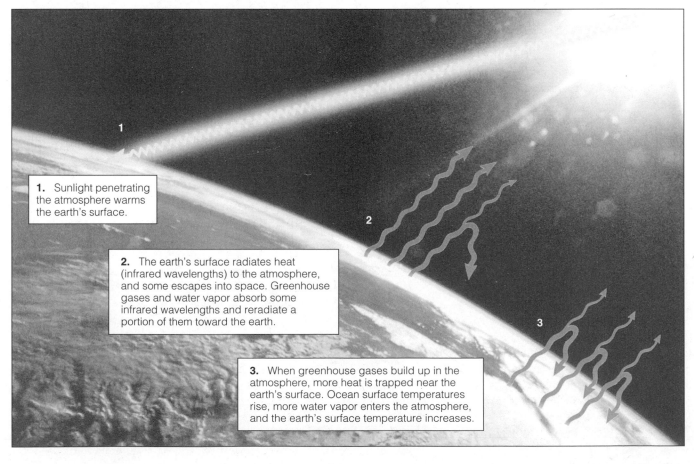

1. Sunlight penetrating the atmosphere warms the earth's surface.

2. The earth's surface radiates heat (infrared wavelengths) to the atmosphere, and some escapes into space. Greenhouse gases and water vapor absorb some infrared wavelengths and reradiate a portion of them toward the earth.

3. When greenhouse gases build up in the atmosphere, more heat is trapped near the earth's surface. Ocean surface temperatures rise, more water vapor enters the atmosphere, and the earth's surface temperature increases.

Q: What are the two most desirable ways to deal with hazardous waste?

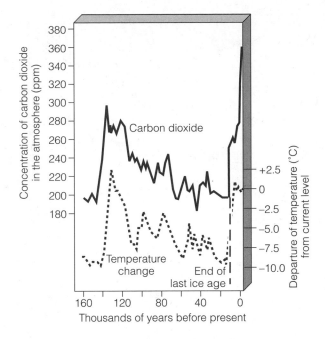

Figure 9-6 Estimated long-term variations in mean global surface temperature and average tropospheric carbon dioxide levels over the past 160,000 years. Since the last great ice age ended about 10,000 years ago, we have enjoyed a warm interglacial period. One factor in Earth's mean surface temperature is the greenhouse effect (Figure 9-5). Changes in tropospheric levels of carbon dioxide, a major greenhouse gas, correlate closely with changes in Earth's mean surface temperature and thus its climate, although other factors also influence global climate.

- Heat trapped by greenhouse gases in the atmosphere is what keeps the planet warm enough to allow us and other species to exist (Connections, p. 28).

- Over the past 160,000 years, levels of water vapor in the troposphere have remained fairly constant, while those of CO_2 have fluctuated by a factor of two. Estimated changes in the levels of tropospheric CO_2 correlate closely with estimated variations in Earth's mean surface temperature (Figure 9-6).

- Measured atmospheric levels of certain greenhouse gases—CO_2, methane, nitrous oxide, and CFCs—have risen in recent decades (Figure 9-7).

- Most of the increased levels of these greenhouse gases have been caused by human activities—burning fossil fuels, use of CFCs, agriculture, and deforestation.

- Since 1860, when measurements began, the mean global temperature has risen 0.3–0.6°C (0.5–1.1°F) (Figure 9-8).

- Eight of the 13 years from 1980 to 1992 were the hottest in the 110-year recorded history of land-surface temperature measurements, and 1990 was the hottest of all.

- So far, any temperature changes possibly caused by an enhanced greenhouse effect have been too small to exceed normal short-term swings in mean atmospheric temperature caused by volcanic eruptions, air pollution, and other climatic factors.

- Warming or cooling by more than 2°C (4°F) over a few decades would be disastrous for Earth's ecosystems and for human economic and social systems. Such rapid climate change would alter conditions faster than some species, especially plants, could adapt or migrate. It may also shift areas where people could grow food. Some areas might become uninhabitable because of drought or floods following a rise in average sea levels.

- We don't know enough about how Earth works to make accurate projections about the possible effects of our inputs of greenhouse gases on global and regional climates—and on the biosphere.

COMPUTERS AS CRYSTAL BALLS: MODELING GREENHOUSE WARMING To project the behavior of climatic and other complex systems, scientists develop mathematical models that simulate such systems and then run them on computers (Figures 3-19 and 3-20). How well the results correspond to the real world depends on the design of the model and on the accuracy of the data and assumptions used.

Current climate models generally agree on how global climate might change but disagree on changes for individual regions. Here are the main projections of the major climate models:

- Earth's mean surface temperature will rise 1.5–5.5°C (2.7–9.9°F) by 2050 if inputs of greenhouse gases continue to rise at the current rate (Figure 9-8). Even at the lower value, Earth would be warmer than it has been for 10,000 years.

- The Northern Hemisphere will warm more and faster than the Southern Hemisphere, mostly because the south has more ocean (Figure 2-31).

- Temperatures at middle and high latitudes should rise two to three times the global average, while temperatures near the equator should rise less than the global average.

- Soil will be drier in some middle latitudes, especially during summers in the Northern Hemisphere.

- More areas will have extreme heat waves and more forest and brush fires.

- The average sea level will rise 2–4 centimeters (0.8–1.6 inches) per decade.

A: Don't make them and recycle or reuse them

Figure 9-7 Increases in average concentrations of major greenhouse gases in the troposphere, mostly because of human activities. (Data from Electric Power Research Institute. Adapted and updated by permission from Cecie Starr and Ralph Taggart, *Biology: The Unity and Diversity of Life*, 6th ed., Belmont, Calif.: Wadsworth, 1992)

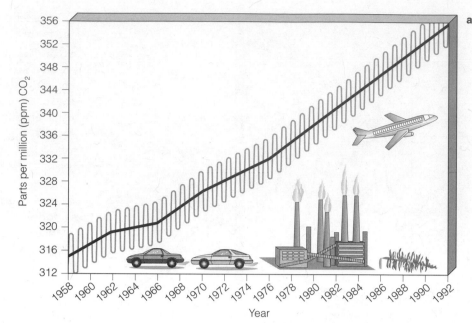

a. Carbon dioxide (CO_2) contributes about 55% to global warming from greenhouse gases produced by human activities. Industrial countries account for about 76% of annual emissions. The main sources are fossil-fuel burning (67%), and land clearing and burning (33%). CO_2 stays in the atmosphere for about 500 years.

b. Chlorofluorocarbons (CFCs) are believed to be responsible for 24% of the human contribution of greenhouse gases. They also deplete ozone in the stratosphere. The main sources are leaking air conditioners and refrigerators, evaporation of industrial solvents, production of plastic foams, and aerosol propellants. CFCs take 10–15 years to reach the stratosphere and generally trap 1,500–7,000 times as much heat per molecule as CO_2 while they are in the troposphere. This heating effect in the troposphere may be partially offset by the cooling caused when CFCs deplete ozone during their 65–110-year stay in the stratosphere.

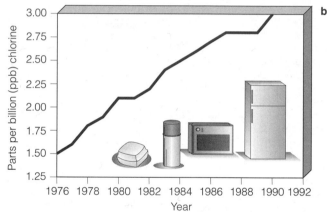

c. Methane (CH_4) accounts for about 18% of the increase in greenhouse gases. Methane is produced when bacteria break down dead organic matter in moist places that lack oxygen. These areas include swamps and other natural wetlands; rice paddies; landfills; and the intestinal tracts of cattle, sheep, and termites. Production and use of oil and natural gas—and incomplete burning of organic materials (including biomass burning in the tropics)—also are significant sources. CH_4 stays in the troposphere for 7–10 years. Each CH_4 molecule traps about 25 times as much heat as a CO_2 molecule.

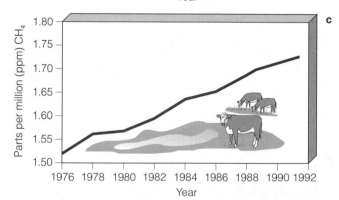

d. Nitrous oxide (N_2O) is responsible for 6% of the human input of greenhouse gases. Besides trapping heat in the troposphere, it also depletes ozone in the stratosphere. It is released from nylon production; from burning of biomass and nitrogen-rich fuels (especially coal); and from the breakdown of nitrogen fertilizers in soil, livestock wastes, and nitrate-contaminated groundwater. Its life span in the troposphere is 140–190 years, and it traps about 230 times as much heat per molecule as CO_2.

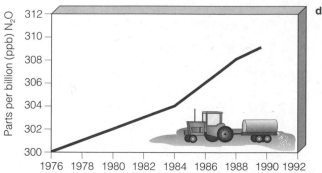

Q: What major food-producing country is doing the most to reduce soil erosion?

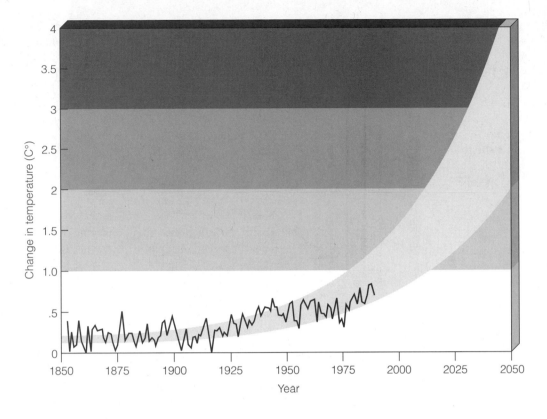

Figure 9-8 Changes in Earth's mean surface temperature between 1860 and 1990 (dark line). The upward-curving region shows global warming projected by various computer models of Earth's climate systems. Note that the computer projections *roughly* match the historically recorded change in temperature between 1860 and 1990. All current models suggest that global temperature will rise between now and 2050. Scientists admit that current models could underestimate or overestimate the amount of warming by a factor of two. (Data from National Academy of Sciences and National Center for Atmospheric Research)

A CLOUDY CRYSTAL BALL: THINGS WE DON'T KNOW

Because we have only partial knowledge about how Earth's climate system works, our models and projections are flawed, but they are all we have. Here are some factors that might dampen or amplify a rise in average atmospheric temperature, determine how fast temperatures might climb (or fall), and influence what the effects will be on various areas:

- *Changes in the amount of solar energy reaching Earth.* Solar output varies by about 0.1%—apparently in 11-year, 80-year, and other cycles—which can cause temporary warming or cooling on Earth and thus affect the projections of climate models.

- *Effect of oceans on climate.* The world's oceans could slow global warming by absorbing more heat, but this depends on how long the heat takes to reach deeper layers—something we don't know. The oceans now take up at least a third of the excess CO_2 we pump into the atmosphere, but we don't know if they can absorb more. If the oceans warm up enough, more CO_2 will bubble out of solution than dissolves (just as in a glass of ginger ale left out in the sun), amplifying and accelerating global warming. On the other hand, warmer air might speed up photosynthesis by oceanic phytoplankton, which would absorb more CO_2 from the atmosphere and slow global warming. Another possibility is that warmer air will evaporate more water from the oceans and create more clouds. Depending on their type (thick or thin) and altitude, more clouds could contribute to either warming or cooling. We don't know which type might predominate and how this would vary in different parts of the world.

- *Changes in polar ice.* The Greenland and Antarctic ice sheets act like enormous mirrors reflecting sunlight back into space. If warmer temperatures melted some of this ice and exposed darker ground or ocean that would absorb more sunlight, warming would be accelerated. Then more ice would melt, amplifying the rise in atmospheric temperature even more. On the other hand, the early stages of global warming might actually increase the amount of Earth's water stored as ice. Warmer air would carry more water vapor, which could drop more snow on some glaciers, especially the gigantic Antarctic ice sheet. If snow accumulated faster than ice was lost, the ice sheet would grow, reflect more sunlight, and help cool the atmosphere—perhaps ushering in a new ice age within a thousand years.

- *Air pollution.* Projected global warming might be offset partially by particles and droplets of various air pollutants (released by volcanic eruptions and human activities, mostly burning fossil fuels) because they reflect back some of the incoming sunlight. However, things aren't that simple. Pollutants in the lower troposphere can either warm or cool the air and surface below them, depending on the reflectivity of the underlying surface. These contradictory and patchy effects, plus improved air pollution control, make it unlikely that these air pollutants will counteract any warming very much in the next half century. Even if they did, levels of these pollutants, which already kill hundreds of thousands of people a year, and damage trees and crops, need to be reduced.

■ *Effect on photosynthesis.* Some studies suggest that more CO_2 in the atmosphere is likely to increase the rate of photosynthesis, with the increased growth of plants and other producers removing more CO_2 from the atmosphere and slowing global warming. Other studies suggest that this varies with different types of plants. Also, much of the increased plant growth could be wiped out by plant-eating insects that breed more rapidly and year-round in warmer temperatures. Again, we know little about such possibilities.

■ *Methane release.* Some scientists speculate that in a warmer world huge amounts of methane tied up in arctic tundra soils and in muds on the bottom of the Arctic Ocean might also be released if the blanket of permafrost covering tundra soils melts and the oceans warm considerably. Because methane is a potent greenhouse gas, this release could greatly amplify global warming. On the other hand, some scientists believe that bacteria in tundra soils would rapidly oxidize the escaping methane to CO_2, a less potent greenhouse gas. Again, we don't know what might happen.

Because of these and numerous other uncertainties in global climate models, projections made so far might be off by a factor of two in either direction. In other words, global warming during the next 50–100 years could be half the projected temperature increase in Figure 9-8—the best-case scenario—or double it—the worst-case scenario.

SOME POSSIBLE EFFECTS OF A WARMER WORLD

So what's the big deal? Why should we worry about a possible rise of only a few degrees in the mean surface temperature of Earth? We often have that much change between June and July, or between yesterday and today. The key point is that we are not talking about normal swings in local weather, but about a projected *global* change in average climate from a thickening blanket of greenhouse gases.

A warmer troposphere would have different consequences for different peoples and species. Some places would get drier, and some wetter. Some would get hotter and others colder. Here are some possible effects of a global warmer climate:

■ *Food production.* Food productivity could increase in some areas and drop in others. Past evidence and computer models indicate that climate belts and thus tolerance ranges of plant species (including crops) would shift northward by 100–150 kilometers (60–90 miles) or 150 meters (500 feet) vertically (Figure 2-30) for each 1°C (1.8°F) rise in the global temperature. Computer models have projected drops in the global yield of key food crops ranging from 30–70%. With current knowledge, we can't predict where changes in crop-growing capacity might occur and how long such climate changes might last before shifting again. The possible result: a changing climate with a complex and shifting set of winners and losers.

■ *Water supplies.* Lakes, streams, and aquifers in some areas that have watered ecosystems, cropfields, and cities for centuries could shrink or dry up altogether, forcing entire populations to migrate to areas with adequate water supplies—if they could. We can't say with much certainty where this might happen.

■ *Forests.* Forests in temperate and subarctic regions (Figure 9-4) would be forced to move toward the poles or to higher altitudes (Figure 2-30). However, tree species can move only through the slow growth of new trees along forest edges where their seeds fall—typically about 0.9 kilometer (0.5 mile) per year or 9 kilometers (5 miles) per decade. Thus, if climate belts moved faster than this or if migration were blocked by cities and other human barriers, entire forests of oak, beech (Figure 9-9), and other deciduous trees could die and release CO_2 as they decompose. According to Oregon State University scientists, projected drying from global warming could cause massive fires in up to 90% of North American forests, destroying wildlife habitats and injecting huge amounts of CO_2 into the atmosphere.

■ *Biodiversity.* Large-scale forest diebacks would also cause mass extinction of species that couldn't migrate to new areas. And fish would die as temperatures soared in streams and lakes, and as lowered water levels concentrated pesticides. Any shifts in regional climate would threaten many parks, wildlife reserves, wilderness areas, wetlands, and coral reefs—wiping out many current efforts to stem the loss of biodiversity.

■ *Sea level.* Water expands slightly when heated. This explains why global sea levels would rise if the oceans warmed, just as the fluid in a thermometer rises when heated. If warming at the poles caused ice sheets and glaciers to melt even partially, the global sea level would rise even more. About one-third of the world's population and more than

Q: How much of the world's irrigated cropland has reduced yields because of soil salinization?

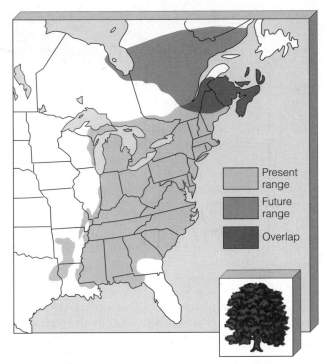

Figure 9-9 According to one projection, if CO_2 emissions doubled between 1990 and 2050, beech trees (now common throughout the eastern United States) would be able to survive only in a greatly shrunken range in northern Maine and southeastern Canada. (Data from Margaret B. Davis and Catherine Zabinski, University of Minnesota)

Present range

Future range

Overlap

one-third of the world's economic infrastructure are concentrated in coastal regions. Thus, even a moderate rise in sea level would flood low-lying areas of the world's major cities, as well as lowlands and deltas where crops are grown. It would also destroy wetlands and coral reefs and accelerate coastal erosion. One comedian jokes that she is planning to buy land in Kansas because it will probably become valuable beachfront property. Another boasts he isn't worried because he lives in a houseboat—the "Noah strategy."

■ *Weather extremes.* In a warmer world, extremes such as prolonged heat waves and droughts would become the norm in many areas. As the upper layers of seawater warmed, hurricanes and typhoons would occur more frequently and blow with much greater ferocity.

■ *Human health.* A warmer world would disrupt supplies of food and fresh water, displacing millions of people and altering disease patterns in unpredictable ways. The spread of tropical climates from the equator would bring malaria, encephalitis, yellow fever, dengue fever, and other insect-borne diseases to formerly temperate zones. Sea-level rise could spread infectious disease by flooding sewage and sanitation systems in coastal cities.

SPOTLIGHT   Denial Can Be Deadly

The denial or let's-wait-for-more-information response to possible global warming is what psychologist Robert Ornstein calls the *boiled frog syndrome*. It's like trying to alert a frog to danger as it sits in a pan of water being very slowly heated on the stove.

If the frog could talk it might say, "I'm a little warmer, but I'm doing fine." As the water gets hotter, we warn the frog that it will die, but it might reply, "The temperature has been increasing for a long time, and I'm still alive. Stop worrying."

Eventually the frog dies because it has no experience of the lethal effects of boiling water and thus cannot perceive that its situation is dangerous. Like the frog, we also face a future without precedent, and our senses are unable to pick up warnings of impending danger.

Suppose we sit like the frog, denying or not wanting to think about the possibility of climate change until Earth's mean temperature rises to the point where it exceeds normal climatic fluctuations (which some climate scientists expect to happen within the next 5–20 years). Reacting then to improve energy efficiency, replace fossil fuels with renewable energy resources, halting deforestation, and starting massive reforestation will take another 40–50 years. By then much of the damage would already have been done, and the effects would last for hundreds if not thousands of years.

On the other hand, perhaps the threat of global warming will not materialize. Should we take actions now that will cost enormous amounts of money and create political turmoil based on a cloudy crystal ball? There are no simple or easy answers.

SOLUTIONS: SLOWING GLOBAL WARMING

Some believe we should wait for more understanding and evidence before taking any serious action to deal with the possibility of global warming. However, even with better understanding, which could take decades, our knowledge will be limited because the climate system is so incredibly complex. Thus science will never be able to offer the certainty that decision makers want before making such tough decisions as phasing out fossil fuels and replacing deforestation with reforestation.

Others urge us to adopt the *precautionary principle*, the idea that when dealing with risky, unpredictable, and often irreversible environmental problems it is often wise to take action before there is enough scientific knowledge to justify it (Spotlight, above).

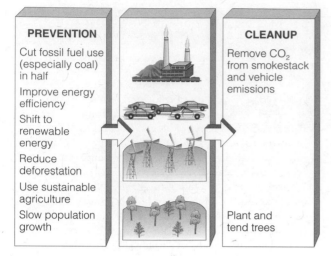

PREVENTION		CLEANUP
Cut fossil fuel use (especially coal) in half		Remove CO$_2$ from smokestack and vehicle emissions
Improve energy efficiency		
Shift to renewable energy		
Reduce deforestation		
Use sustainable agriculture		
Slow population growth		Plant and tend trees

Figure 9-10 Methods for slowing possible global warming.

The good news, according to Gus Speth, former president of the World Resources Institute, is that "even though climate change threatens to be bigger, more irreversible, and more pervasive than other environmental problems, it's also *controllable*, if we act now." According to recent studies by the National Academy of Sciences and the Congressional Office of Technology Assessment, the United States could reduce its greenhouse gas emissions by 25–35% of 1990 levels using existing technology at low or no net cost and by 48% at low-to-moderate cost.

Figure 9-10 gives various ways to slow possible global warming. Currently, none of these solutions is being vigorously pursued. The quickest, cheapest, and most effective way to reduce emissions of CO$_2$ and other air pollutants over the next two to three decades is to use energy more efficiently (Section 4-2 and Solutions, at right). According to the National Academy of Sciences, this alone could lower U.S. greenhouse gas emissions by 10–40% at no net cost to the economy. Shifting from fossil fuels to renewable *energy resources* that do not emit CO$_2$ (Section 4-3) could cut projected U.S. CO$_2$ emissions 8–15% by 2000 and virtually eliminate them by 2025.

Natural gas (Section 4-6) could be used to help make the transition to an age of energy efficiency and renewable energy. When burned, natural gas emits only half as much CO$_2$ per unit of energy as coal (Figure 4-29) and emits far smaller amounts of most other air pollutants as well. Halting deforestation (Sections 5-3 and 5-4) and switching to Earth-sustaining agriculture (Section 7-7) would reduce CO$_2$ emissions and help preserve biodiversity. Slowing population growth is also important. If we cut per capita greenhouse-gas emissions in half but world population doubles, we're back where we started.

Some analysts urge MDCs and LDCs to enter into win-win pacts to reduce the threat of global warming.

Energy Efficiency to the Rescue

SOLUTIONS

According to energy expert Amory Lovins, *the remedies for slowing global warming are things we should be doing already even if there were no threat of global warming.* He also argues that getting countries to sign treaties and agree to cut back and reallocate their use of fossil fuels in time to reduce serious environmental effects is difficult, if not almost impossible, and very costly. Climate models suggest that CO$_2$ emissions must be reduced by 80% to slow projected global warming to a safe rate. So far countries can't even agree to a 20% reduction.

According to Lovins, improving energy efficiency would be the fastest, cheapest, and surest way to slash emissions of CO$_2$ and most other air pollutants within two decades using existing technology (Section 4-2). This approach would also save the world up to $1 trillion a year in reduced energy costs—as much as the annual global military budget.

Moreover, using energy more efficiently would reduce all forms of pollution, help protect biodiversity, and forestall arguments among governments about how CO$_2$ reductions should be divided up and enforced. This approach would also make the world's supplies of fossil fuel last longer, reduce international tensions over who gets the dwindling oil supplies, and give us more time to phase in alternatives to fossil fuels.

To most environmentalists, greatly improving worldwide energy efficiency *now* is a money-saving, life-saving, Earth-saving, win-win offer that we should not refuse even if there were no possibility of climate change.

In this "let's make a deal" strategy, LDCs would agree to stop deforestation, protect biodiversity, slow population growth, enact fairer land distribution, and phase out coal burning. In return MDCs would forgive much of LDC's foreign debt and help fund the transfer of modern energy efficiency, solar energy, pollution control, pollution prevention, sustainable agriculture, and reforestation technologies to LDCs. MDCs would also agree to make substantial cuts in their use of fossil fuels, abandon ozone-depleting chemicals, greatly improve energy efficiency, stop deforestation, shift to sustainable agriculture, and slow their population growth.

Removing significant amounts of CO$_2$ from exhaust gases is currently not feasible. Available meth-

Q: What percentage of the world's irrigated cropland suffers from waterlogging?

ods can remove only about 30% of the CO_2 and would at least double the cost of electricity. Planting and tending trees is important for restoring deforested and degraded land and for reducing soil erosion, but it's only a stopgap measure for slowing CO_2 emissions. To absorb the CO_2 we put into the atmosphere, we would have to plant and tend an average of 1,000 trees per person every year. Also, if much of the newly grown forests are cleared and burned by us or by massive forest fires caused by global warming—or if much of the new forest died because of drought—most of the CO_2 removed would be released, accelerating global warming.

Some scientists have suggested various technofixes for dealing with possible global warming. These include **(1)** fertilizing the oceans with iron to stimulate the growth of marine algae, which could remove more CO_2 through photosynthesis; **(2)** covering the oceans with white Styrofoam chips to help reflect more energy away from Earth's surface; **(3)** unfurling gigantic foil-faced sun shields in space to reduce solar input; and **(4)** injecting sunlight-reflecting sulfate particulates into the stratosphere to cool Earth's surface. All of these schemes are quite expensive and would have unknown—possibly harmful —effects on the Earth's ecosystems and climate.

PREPARING FOR GLOBAL WARMING Even if we stopped adding greenhouse gases to the atmosphere now, current models project that what we have already added could warm the earth by 0.5–1.8°C (0.9–3.2°F). Some analysts suggest that we begin preparing for the long-term effects of possible global warming. Their suggestions include the following:

- *Breed food plants that need less water or can thrive in salty water.*

- *Build dikes to protect coastal areas from flooding, as the Dutch have done for centuries.*

- *Move storage tanks of hazardous materials away from coastal areas.*

- *Ban new or rebuilt construction on low-lying coastal areas.*

- *Stockpile 1–5 years' worth of key foods throughout the world as short-term insurance against disruptions in food production.*

- *Expand existing wilderness areas, parks, and wildlife refuges northward in the Northern Hemisphere and southward in the Southern Hemisphere, and create new wildlife reserves in these areas.*

- *Connect wildlife reserves with corridors that would allow mobile species to move with climate change.*

- *Waste less water (Section 10-5).*

What You Can Do to Reduce Global Warming

INDIVIDUALS MATTER

- *Reduce your use of fossil fuels.* Driving a car that gets at least 15 kilometers per liter (35 miles per gallon), joining a car pool and using mass transit, and walking or bicycling where possible will reduce your emissions of CO_2 and other air pollutants, will save energy and money, and can improve your health.

- *Use energy-efficient light bulbs (Figure 4-12), refrigerators, and other appliances.*

- *Use solar energy to heat household space or water as much as possible (Section 4-3).*

- *Cool your house by using shade trees and available breezes and by making it energy efficient.*

- *Plant and care for trees to help absorb CO_2 and to provide natural shading and cooling.*

All of the measures for slowing or responding to climate change together would cost far less than the $12 trillion we have spent since 1945 to protect us from the possibility of nuclear war. Environmentalists and most scientists see global warming as an equally serious threat. Dealing with this threat will require action at international, national, local, and individual levels (Individuals Matter, above).

9-3 Ozone Depletion: A Serious Threat or a Hoax?

THE THREAT: LETTING IN DEADLY RAYS
Thanks to the evolution of photosynthetic, oxygen-producing bacterial cells, Earth has had a stratospheric global sunscreen—the ozone layer—for the past 450 million years. However, an avalanche of evidence indicates that we are thinning this screen with our recent use of chlorine- and bromine-containing compounds.

The scientific consensus is that ozone depletion by chemicals we have released into the atmosphere is a real threat. If so, it will have serious long-term effects on human health, animal life, and the sunlight-driven producer plants that support Earth's food chains and webs. If the models of this change in the chemical makeup of the stratosphere are correct, the damage will worsen in years to come as chemicals we have already put into the atmosphere work their way up to the stratosphere and deplete ozone for decades.

CFCs: FROM DREAM CHEMICALS TO NIGHT-MARE CHEMICALS
How did we get into this mess? It started when Thomas Midgley, Jr., a General Motors chemist, discovered the first chlorofluorocarbon (CFC) in 1930, and chemists then made similar compounds to create a family of highly useful CFCs. The two most widely used are CFC-11 (trichlorofluoromethane, CCl_3F) and CFC-12 (dichlorofluoromethane, CCl_2F_2).

These amazingly useful, chemically stable, odorless, nonflammable, nontoxic, and noncorrosive compounds seemed to be dream chemicals. Cheap to make, they became popular as coolants in air conditioners and refrigerators, propellants in aerosol spray cans, cleaners for electronic parts such as computer chips, sterilants for hospital instruments, fumigants for granaries and ship cargo holds, and building blocks for the bubbles in Styrofoam used for insulation and packaging.

But it was too good to be true. In 1974 chemists Sherwood Rowland and Mario Molina made calculations indicating that CFCs were lowering the average concentration of ozone in the stratosphere and creating a global time bomb. They shocked the scientific community and the $28-billion-per-year industry making these chemicals by calling for an immediate ban of CFCs in spray cans.

Here's what Rowland and Molina found: Spray cans, discarded or leaky refrigeration and air-conditioning equipment, and the production and burning of plastic foam products release CFCs into the atmosphere. These molecules are too unreactive to be removed; and mostly through convection and random drift, they rise slowly into the stratosphere—taking 10–20 years to make the journey. There, under the influence of high-energy ultraviolet (UV) radiation, they break down and release chlorine atoms, which speed up the breakdown of ozone (O_3) into O_2 and O and cause ozone to be destroyed faster than it is formed. Each CFC molecule can last in the stratosphere for 65–110 years. During that time each chlorine atom in these molecules—like a gaseous Pac-Man—can convert as many as 100,000 molecules of O_3 to O_2. According to this hypothesis, these dream molecules have turned into a nightmare of global ozone terminators.

Although Rowland and Molina warned us of this problem in 1974, it took 15 years of interaction between the scientific and political communities before countries agreed to start slowly phasing out CFCs.* The CFC industry was a powerful, well-fund-

---

*For a fascinating account of how corporate stalling, politics, economics, and science interact, see Sharon Roan's *Ozone Crisis: The 15-Year Evolution of a Sudden Global Emergency* (New York: John Wiley, 1989).

ed adversary with a lot of profits and jobs at stake. But through 15 years of attacks Rowland and Molina held their ground, expanded their research, and relentlessly explained the meaning of their calculations to other scientists, elected officials, and the press.

CFCs are not the only ozone eaters. Here are a few others, which can release highly reactive chlorine and bromine atoms if they end up in the stratosphere and thus are exposed to intense UV radiation:

- Bromine-containing compounds called *halons* and *HBFCs* (both used in fire extinguishers) and *methyl bromide* (a widely used pesticide). Each bromine atom destroys hundreds of times more ozone molecules than does a chlorine atom.

- *Carbon tetrachloride* (a cheap, highly toxic solvent) and *methyl chloroform*, or 1,1,1-trichloroethane (used as a cleaning solvent for clothes and metals and as a propellant in more than 160 consumer products, such as correction fluid, dry-cleaning sprays, spray adhesives, and other aerosols). Substitutes are available for virtually all uses of these two chemicals.

OZONE HOLES AND OTHER SURPRISES
Each year news about ozone loss seems to get worse, and sometimes takes scientists by surprise. The first surprise came in 1985, when researchers discovered that 50% of the ozone in the upper stratosphere over the Antarctic region was being destroyed during the Antarctic spring and early summer (September–December), when sunlight returned after the dark Antarctic winter. This had not been predicted by computer models of the stratosphere. Since then this seasonal Antarctic *ozone hole*, or *ozone thinning*, has expanded in most years. In 1992 and 1993, it covered an area three times the size of the continental United States.

Measurements have shown that CFCs are the main culprits. After a weeks-long orgy of ozone depletion when sunlight returns to the Antarctic, huge clumps of ozone-depleted air flow northward and linger over parts of Australia, New Zealand, and the southern tips of South America and Africa for a few more weeks, raising UV levels in these areas by as much as 20%.

In 1988 scientists discovered that a similar but much less severe ozone thinning occurs over the North Pole during the arctic spring and early summer (February–June) with a seasonal ozone loss of 10–25%. When this mass of air breaks up each spring, clots of ozone-depleted air flow southward to linger over parts of Europe, North America, and Asia. Mostly because it flows alternately over land and water, seasonal ozone loss over the North Pole is lower than that over the South Pole.

It could get much worse. Scientists estimate that ozone losses over northern mid-latitudes will be

Q: How much of Earth's land area is suitable for cultivation?

10–30%, as ozone-destroying chemicals drift slowly into the stratosphere. In 1992 atmospheric scientists warned that if rising levels of greenhouse gases (Figure 9-7) change the climate as projected over the next 50 years, this will alter the stratosphere over the Arctic so that it will experience severe ozone thinning like that now found over Antarctica.

IS OZONE DEPLETION A HOAX? Political talk-show host Rush Limbaugh, zoologist Dixy Lee Ray, and several articles in the popular press have claimed that ozone depletion by CFCs is a hoax. The evidence for these claims comes mostly from articles and books written by S. Fred Singer (a Ph.D. physicist and climate scientist), Rogelio Maduro (who has a bachelor of science degree in geology and who is an associate editor of a science and technology magazine published by supporters of controversial politician Lyndon LaRouche), and Ralf Schauerhammer (a German writer).

Maduro and Schauerhammer claim that evidence indicates that volcanoes, seawater, and biomass burning have been releasing far more chlorine into the atmosphere than have the CFCs we have emitted. They argue that this has been going on for billions of years and the ozone layer is still here.

Scientists directly involved in ozone layer research dispute these claims, describing them as being based on selective use of out-of-date research and unwarranted extrapolation of questionable data. They point out that most chlorine from natural sources—mostly sodium chloride (NaCl) and hydrogen chloride (HCl) from the evaporation of sea spray—never makes it to the stratosphere because these compounds (unlike CFCs) are soluble in water and get washed out of the lower atmosphere by rain. If sodium chloride from sea spray were making it to the stratosphere, there should be evidence of sodium in the lower stratosphere. Measurements show that it is not there. Measurements also indicate that no more than 20% of the chlorine from biomass burning (in the form of methylchloride) is making it to the stratosphere, which is about five times less than the contribution from CFCs.

Researchers also dispute the hypothesis that large quantities of HCl are injected into the stratosphere from volcanic eruptions. Most of this water-soluble HCl is injected into the troposphere and is washed out by rain before it reaches the stratosphere. Measurements show that HCl in the stratosphere increased by less than 10% after the eruption of the Mexican volcano El Chichón in 1982 and even less from the eruption of Mt. Pinatubo in the Philippines in 1991. Singer, whose skepticism about some aspects of ozone depletion models has been cited to bolster the case of those calling the whole thing a hoax, agrees with this scientific consensus and in 1993 stated "that CFCs make the major contribution to stratospheric chlorine."

Critics of the ozone-depletion idea also point out that the expected increase in UV radiation from ozone loss in the stratosphere has not as yet been detected in urban areas in the United States and most other industrialized countries. However, it is suspected that the reason for this is that air pollution over urban areas is providing some protection from increased UV radiation at ground level—another example of connections. If such air pollution is decreased (Section 9-5) we may increase threats from increased UV radiation. However, if we don't decrease air pollution we will continue to suffer from its harmful effects (Section 9-4).

POSSIBLE CONSEQUENCES: LIFE IN THE ULTRA-VIOLET ZONE Why should we care about ozone loss? With less ozone in the stratosphere, more biologically harmful UV-B radiation will reach Earth's surface. This will give us worse sunburns, earlier wrinkles, more cataracts (a clouding of the eye lens that reduces vision and can cause blindness if not removed), and more skin cancers (Connections, p. 234). Cases of skin cancer and eye cataracts are soaring in Australia, New Zealand, South Africa, Argentina, and Chile, where the ozone layer is very thin for several months after the masses of ozone-depleted air over the South Pole drift northward. Levels of skin cancer and cataracts are also increasing rapidly in the United States (Connections, p. 234).

Other effects from increased UV exposure are (1) suppression of the human immune system, which would reduce our defenses (regardless of skin pigmentation) against a variety of infectious diseases, (2) an increase in eye-burning, highly damaging ozone and acid deposition in the troposphere (Section 9-4), (3) lower yields (about 1% for each 3% drop in stratospheric ozone) of crops such as corn, rice, soybeans, cotton, beans, peas, sorghum, and wheat, with estimated losses totaling $2.5 billion per year in the United States alone before the middle of the next century, and (4) a loss of perhaps $2 billion per year from degradation of paints, plastics, and other polymer materials in the United States alone.

In a worst-case scenario most people would have to avoid the sun altogether (see cartoon, p. 235). Even cattle could graze only at dusk. And farmers and other outdoor workers might measure their exposure to the sun in minutes.

SOLUTIONS: PROTECTING THE OZONE LAYER
The scientific consensus is that we should stop producing ozone-depleting chemicals now (global abstinence). After saying no, we will have to wait about 100 years for the ozone layer to return to 1985 levels, and another 100 to 200 years for full recovery.

A: 11%

CONNECTIONS

The Cancer You Are Most Likely to Get

Skin specialists have been warning us about the harmful effects of too much exposure to sunlight long before there was any concern about additional exposure to UV radiation from a thinning ozone layer. Years of exposure to UV ionizing radiation in sunlight is the primary cause of basal-cell and squamous-cell skin cancers, which make up 95% of all skin cancers. Typically there is a 20–30 year lag between UV exposure and development of these cancers. Caucasian children and adolescents who get only a single severe sunburn double the normal chance of getting these cancers. Some 90–95% of these types of skin cancer can be cured if detected early enough, although their removal may leave disfiguring scars. (I have had three basal-cell cancers on my face because of "catching too many rays" in my younger years. I wish I had known then what I know now.)

A third type of skin cancer, *melanoma*, spreads rapidly to other organs and kills one-fifth of its victims (most under age 40) within five years—despite surgery, chemotherapy, and radiation. Each year it kills about 100,000 people (including 6,800 Americans)—mostly Caucasians—but it can often be cured if detected early enough. Evidence suggests that people, especially Caucasians, who get three or more blistering sunburns before age 20 have five times more risk of contracting deadly malignant melanoma later in life than those who have never had severe sunburns.

In the United States melanoma cases doubled between 1980 and 1990. It is now the most prevalent type of cancer among women ages 25–29. In 1980, 1 in 250 Americans developed melanoma. By 1991 the figure was 1 in 101, and by 2000 it is projected to be 1 in 75. The EPA estimates 200,000 skin cancer deaths in the United States alone over the next 50 years.

Virtually anyone can get skin cancer, but those with fair and freckled skin, blonde or red hair, and light eye color run the highest risk. People who spend long hours in the sun or in tanning parlors multiply their chances of developing skin cancer and having wrinkled, dry skin by age 40. Nor does a dark suntan prevent skin cancer. Dark-skinned people are almost immune to sunburn but do get skin cancer, although at a rate one-tenth that of Caucasians. Outdoor workers are particularly susceptible to skin cancer on the face, neck, hands, and arms.

To protect yourself, the safest course is to stay out of the sun and say no to tanning parlors. When you are in the sun, wear tightly woven protective clothing, a wide-brimmed hat, and sunglasses that protect against UV radiation (ordinary sunglasses may actually harm your eyes by dilating your pupils so that more UV radiation strikes the retina). Unfortunately, the world's poor people can't afford such glasses. People who take antibiotics and women who take birth control pills are more susceptible to UV damage.

Apply sunscreen with a protection factor of 15 or more (25 if you have light skin) to all exposed skin, and reapply it after swimming or excessive perspiration. Children using a sunscreen with a protection factor of 15 anytime they are in the sun from birth to age 18 decrease their chance of skin cancer by 80%. Babies under a year old should not be exposed to the sun at all. Before using a particular sunscreen, run a test patch on the inside of your arm to be sure that you are not allergic to its ingredients or that it doesn't have the reverse effect and amplify sun damage (something I recently learned the hard way). If you like the bronzed look, try some of the improved creams that give you a tanned appearance without spending long hours in the sun; but again, test them for any allergic reaction first.

Get to know your moles and examine your skin surface at least once a month. The warning signs of skin cancer are a change in the size, shape, or color of a mole or wart (the major sign of malignant melanoma, which needs to be treated quickly); sudden appearance of dark spots on the skin; or a sore that keeps oozing, bleeding, and crusting over but does not heal. You should look out for precancerous growths—reddish-brown spots with a scaly crust. If you observe any of these signs, consult a doctor immediately. Are you doing all you can to protect your skin and perhaps your life from exposure to UV radiation?

Substitutes are already available for most uses of CFCs, and others are being developed (Table 9-1 and Individuals Matter, p. 236). CFCs in existing air conditioners, refrigerators, and other products must be recovered and in some cases reused until the substitutes are phased in. This will be expensive, but if ozone depletion should become more severe because of our activities, the resulting financial and health costs will be much higher.

HFCs and HCFCs may help ease the replacement of CFCs for essential uses, but models indicate that these chemicals also can deplete ozone (although at a

Q: In total sales what is the biggest industry in the United States?

Table 9-1 CFC Substitutes

Types	Pros	Cons
HCFCs (hydrochlorofluorocarbons)	Break down faster (2–20 years). Pose about 90% less danger to ozone layer. Can be used in aerosol sprays, refrigeration, air conditioning, foam, and cleaning agents.	Are greenhouse gases. Will still deplete ozone, especially if used in large quantities. Health effects largely unknown. HCFC-123 causes benign tumors in the pancreas and testes of male rats, and may be banned for use in aerosol sprays, foam, and cleaning agents. May lower energy efficiency of appliances.
HFCs (hydrofluorocarbons)	Break down faster (2–20 years). Do not contain ozone-destroying chlorine. Can be used in aerosol sprays, refrigeration, air conditioning, and foam.	Are greenhouse gases. Safety questions about flammability and toxicity still unresolved. May lower energy efficiency of appliances. Production of HFC-134a, a refrigerant substitute, yields an equal amount of methyl chloroform, a serious ozone depleter.
Hydrocarbons (such as propane and butane)	Cheap and readily available. Can be used in aerosol sprays, refrigeration, foam, and cleaning agents.	Can be flammable and poisonous. Some increase ground-level pollution.
Ammonia	Simple alternative for refrigerators; widely used before CFCs.	Toxic if inhaled. Must be handled carefully.
Water and Steam	Effective for some cleaning operations and for sterilizing medical instruments.	Creates polluted water that must be treated. Wastes water unless the used water is cleaned up and reused.
Terpenes (from the rinds of lemons and other citrus fruits)	Effective for cleaning electronic parts.	None.
Helium	Effective coolant for refrigerators, freezers, and air conditioners.	This rare gas may become scarce if use is widespread, but very little coolant is needed per appliance.

"I MISS THE OZONE LAYER...."

©1988, *Los Angeles Times* Syndicate. Reprinted with permission.

slower rate than CFCs) and should be banned no later than 2005.

CAN TECHNOFIXES SAVE US?   What about a quick fix from technology so we can keep on using CFCs? One suggestion is to collect some of the ozone-laden air at ground level over Los Angeles and other cities and ship it up to the stratosphere. Even if we knew how to do this, the Los Angeles air would dilute the stratospheric ozone concentration rather than increasing it—worsening the situation.

Two atmospheric scientists have speculated that we might inject large quantities of ethane and propane into the stratosphere, where they might react with CFCs to remove the offending chlorine atoms. They estimate this would take only 1,000 jumbo-jet flights over a critical 30-day period every year for several decades. But the scientists proposing this possibility warn that the plan could backfire, accelerate ozone depletion, and have unpredictable effects on climate.

Others have suggested using tens of thousands of lasers to blast CFCs out of the atmosphere before they can reach the stratosphere. However, the energy requirements would be enormous and expensive, and decades of research would be needed to perfect the types of lasers needed—time we don't have. Also, no one knows the possible effects on climate, birds, planes, and whatever else might be there. We need to be wary of unpredictable technofixes.

Ray Turner and His Refrigerator

Ray Turner, an aerospace manager at Hughes Aircraft in California, made an important low-tech, ozone-saving discovery by using his head—and his refrigerator. His concern for the environment led him to look for a cheap and simple substitute for the CFCs used as cleaning agents in the manufacture of most electronic circuit boards at his plant and elsewhere.

He started his search for a low-tech solution to a high-tech problem by looking in his refrigerator for a better circuit-board cleaner. He decided to put drops of various substances on a corroded penny to see whether any of them would remove the film of oxidation. Then he used his soldering gun to see if solder would stick to the cleaned surface of the penny, indicating that the film had been cleaned off.

First, he tried vinegar. No luck. Then he tried some ground-up lemon peel, also a failure. Next he tried a drop of lemon juice and watched as the solder took hold. The rest is history.

In the months that followed, Turner and a Hughes team perfected his discovery. Since it was introduced, the new cleaning technique has reduced circuit board defects by about 75% at Hughes. And Turner got a hefty bonus. Maybe you can find a solution to an environmental problem in your refrigerator.

SOME HOPEFUL PROGRESS In 1987, 24 nations meeting in Montreal developed a treaty—commonly known as the *Montreal Protocol*—to cut emissions of CFCs (but not other ozone depleters) into the atmosphere by about 35% between 1989 and 2000. In 1992, representatives of more than half the world's nations met in Copenhagen and agreed to **(1)** phase out production (except for essential uses) of CFCs, carbon tetrachloride, halons, HBFCs (halon substitutes), and chloroform by January 1, 1996; **(2)** freeze consumption of HCFCs (substitutes for CFCs that pose about 90% less danger to the ozone layer) at 1991 levels by 1996, and eliminate them by 2030; and **(3)** freeze methyl bromide production at 1991 levels by 1995.

The agreements reached so far are important examples of global cooperation. Some scientists claim that such action is premature because the models of ozone depletion and its effects are too shaky. But many scientists in this field believe that the agreements still do not go far enough fast enough. Meanwhile, individ-

What You Can Do to Help Protect the Ozone Layer

If you believe that ozone depletion is a serious threat, then here are some things you can do:

- *Don't buy products containing CFCs, carbon tetrachloride, or methyl chloroform (1,1,1-trichloroethane on most ingredient labels).*

- *Don't buy CFC-containing polystyrene foam insulation.* Types of insulation that don't contain CFCs are extended polystyrene (commonly called EPS or beadboard), fiberglass, rock wool, cellulose, and perlite.

- *Don't buy halon fire extinguishers for home use.* Instead, buy those using dry chemicals (CO₂ extinguishers release this greenhouse gas into the troposphere). If you already have a halon extinguisher, store it until a halon-reclaiming program is developed.

- *Stop using aerosol spray products, except in some necessary medical sprays.* Even those not using CFCs and HCFCs (such as Dymel) emit hydrocarbons or other propellant chemicals into the air. Use roll-on and hand-pump products instead.

- *Pressure legislators to ban all uses of CFCs, halons, methyl bromide, carbon tetrachloride, methyl chloroform by 1996 (with no loopholes), and HCFCs by 2005 instead of by 2030.*

- *Pressure legislators not to exempt the military and space programs from any phaseout of ozone-depleting chemicals.*

- *If you junk a car, refrigerator, freezer, or air conditioner, make sure the coolant is removed and kept safely for reuse or destruction.*

- *Have car and home air conditioners checked regularly for CFC leaks and repair them. If you buy a car with an air conditioner, look for one that doesn't use CFCs (available in some 1994 models).*

---

uals can play a role in reducing the threat of ozone depletion (Individuals Matter, above).

9-4 Outdoor and Indoor Air Pollution

TYPES AND SOURCES OF OUTDOOR AIR POLLUTION As clean air in the troposphere (Figure 9-1) moves across Earth's surface, it collects the products

Q: How many people on average does one U.S. farmer feed?

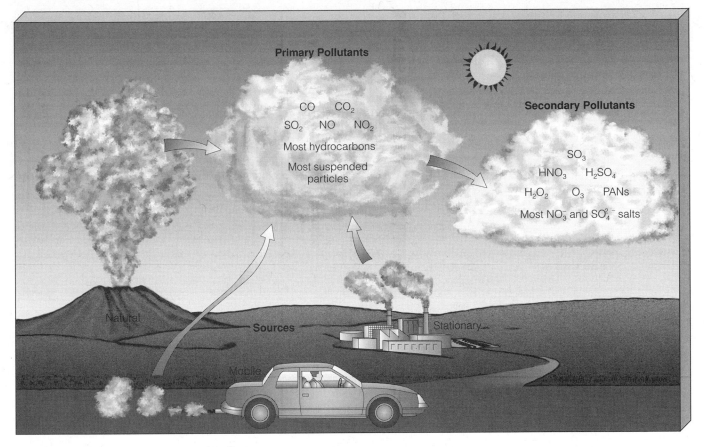

Figure 9-11 Primary and secondary air pollutants.

of natural events (volcanic eruptions and dust storms) and human activities (emissions from cars and smokestacks). These potential pollutants, called **primary pollutants**, mix with the churning air in the troposphere. Some may react with one another or with the basic components of air to form new pollutants, called **secondary pollutants** (Figure 9-11). Long-lived pollutants travel far before they return to the earth as particles, droplets, or chemicals dissolved in precipitation. Because we all must breathe air from a shared global atmospheric supply, air pollution anywhere is a potential threat elsewhere, and in some cases everywhere.

Table 9-2 lists the major classes of pollutants found in outdoor air. Outdoor pollution in industrialized countries comes mostly from five groups of primary pollutants: carbon oxides (CO and CO_2), nitrogen oxides (mostly NO and NO_2, or NO_x), sulfur oxides (SO_2 and SO_3), volatile organic compounds (mostly hydrocarbons), and suspended particles, all produced primarily by combustion of fossil fuels (Section 4-6).

In MDCs most pollutants enter the atmosphere from the burning of fossil fuels in power plants and factories (*stationary sources*) and in motor vehicles

(*mobile sources*) (Figure 9-11). In car-clogged cities like Los Angeles, São Paulo, London, and Mexico City motor vehicles are responsible for 80–88% of the air pollution.

CONNECTIONS: SMOG Photochemical smog is a mixture of primary and secondary pollutants that forms when some of the primary pollutants interact under the influence of sunlight (Figure 9-12). The resulting mix of more than 100 chemicals is dominated by ozone, a highly reactive gas that harms most living organisms.

Virtually all modern cities have photochemical smog, but it is much more common in cities with sunny, warm, dry climates and lots of motor vehicles. Los Angeles, Denver, Salt Lake City, Sydney, Mexico City, and Buenos Aires all have serious photochemical smog problems. The hotter the day, the higher the levels of ozone and other components of photochemical smog.

Thirty years ago cities like London, Chicago, and Pittsburgh burned large amounts of coal and heavy oil (which contain sulfur impurities) in power plants and factories, as well as for space heating. During winter such cities suffered from **industrial smog,** consisting

Table 9-2 Major Classes of Air Pollution

Class	Examples
Carbon oxides	Carbon monoxide (CO), carbon dioxide (CO_2)
Sulfur oxides	Sulfur dioxide (SO_2), sulfur trioxide (SO_3)
Nitrogen oxides	Nitric oxide (NO), nitrogen dioxide (NO_2), nitrous oxide (N_2O). (NO and NO_2 are often lumped together and labeled as NO_x).
Volatile organic compounds	Methane (CH_4), propane (C_3H_8), benzene (C_6H_6), chlorofluorocarbons (CFCs)
Suspended particles	Solid particles (dust, soot, asbestos, lead, nitrate and sulfate salts), liquid droplets (sulfuric acid, PCBs, dioxins, pesticides)
Photochemical oxidants	Ozone (O_3), peroxyacyl nitrates (PANs), hydrogen peroxide (H_2O_2), aldehydes
Radioactive substances	Radon-222, iodine-131, strontium-90, plutonium-239
Toxic compounds	Trace amounts of at least 600 toxic substances (many of them volatile organic compounds), 60 of them known carcinogens

mostly of a mixture of sulfur dioxide, suspended droplets of sulfuric acid (formed from some of the sulfur dioxide), and a variety of suspended solid particles (Table 9-2). Today in most parts of the world coal and heavy oil are burned only in large boilers with reasonably good pollution control or with tall smokestacks, so industrial smog, sometimes called *gray-air smog*, is rarely a problem. However, in China, Ukraine, and some eastern European countries large quantities of coal are still burned with inadequate pollution controls.

The frequency and severity of smog in an area depend on several things: the local climate and topography; the density of the population; the amount of industry; and the fuels used in industry, heating, and transportation. In areas with high average annual precipitation, rain and snow help cleanse the air of pollutants. Winds also help sweep pollutants away and bring in fresh air, but they may transfer some pollutants to distant areas (Figure 9-11).

Hills and mountains tend to reduce the flow of air in valleys below and allow pollutant levels to build up at ground level. Buildings in cities also slow wind speed and reduce dilution and removal of pollutants.

During the day the sun warms the air near the earth's surface. Normally this heated air expands and rises, carrying low-lying pollutants higher into the troposphere. Colder, denser air from surrounding high-pressure areas then sinks into the low-pressure area

created when the hot air rises (Figure 9-13). This continual mixing of the air helps keep pollutants from reaching dangerous levels near the ground.

Sometimes, however, weather conditions trap a layer of dense, cool air beneath a layer of less dense, warm air in an urban basin or valley. This is called a **temperature inversion** or a **thermal inversion** (Figure 9-13). In effect, a lid of warm air covers the region and prevents the upward-flowing air currents (that would disperse pollutants) from developing. These inversions usually last for only a few hours; but sometimes, when a high-pressure air mass stalls over an area, they last for several days. Then air pollutants at ground level build up to harmful and even lethal levels. The first U.S. air pollution disaster occurred in 1948, when fog laden with sulfur dioxide and suspended particulate matter stagnated for five days over the town of Donora in Pennsylvania's Monongahela Valley south of Pittsburgh. About 6,000 of the town's 14,000 inhabitants fell ill, and 20 of them died. This killer fog resulted from a combination of mountainous terrain surrounding the valley and stable weather conditions that trapped and concentrated deadly pollutants emitted by the community's steel mill, zinc smelter, and sulfuric acid plant. Thermal inversions also enhance the harmful effects of urban heat islands and dust domes that build up over urban areas (Figure 3-15).

A city with several million people and automobiles in an area with a sunny climate, light winds,

Q: How much of the world's cropland is used to grow livestock feed?

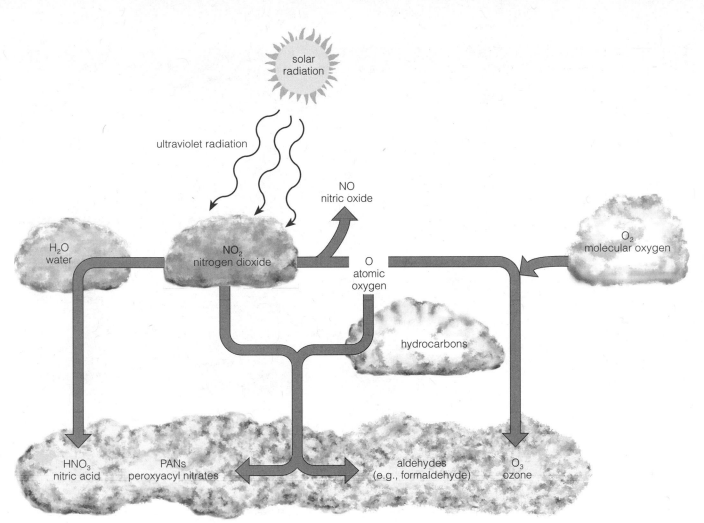

Figure 9-12 Simplified scheme of the formation of photochemical smog. The severity of smog is generally associated with atmospheric concentrations of ozone at ground level.

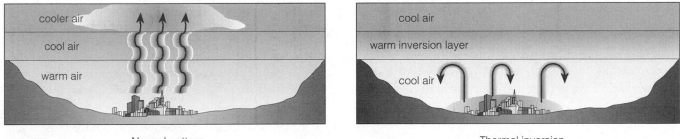

Normal pattern

Thermal inversion

Figure 9-13 Thermal inversion traps pollutants in a layer of cool air that cannot rise to carry the pollutants away.

mountains on three sides, and the ocean on the other has ideal conditions for photochemical smog worsened by frequent thermal inversions. This describes the Los Angeles basin, which has 14 million people, 10.6 million motor vehicles, thousands of factories, and thermal inversions at least half of the year. Despite having the world's toughest air pollution control program, Los

Angeles is the air pollution capital of the United States. By 2010, the Los Angeles area is expected to have 21 million people and 13 million motor vehicles.

CONNECTIONS: ACID DEPOSITION To reduce local air pollution (and meet government standards without having to add expensive air pollution control

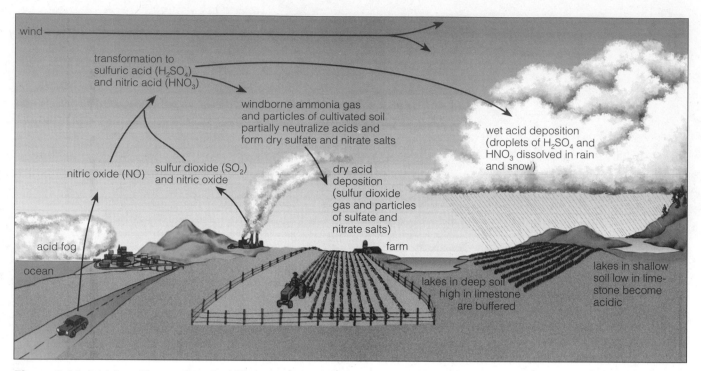

Figure 9-14 Acid deposition consists of acidified rain, snow, dust, or gas with a pH lower than 5.6. The lower the pH level, the greater the acidity of this wet and dry deposition, commonly called acid rain.

devices), coal-burning power plants, ore smelters, and industries began using tall smokestacks to spew sulfur dioxide, suspended particles, and nitrogen oxides above the inversion layer (Figure 9-13). As this practice spread in the 1960s and 1970s, pollution in downwind areas began to rise. In addition to smokestack emissions, large quantities of nitrogen oxides are also released by motor vehicles.

As sulfur dioxide and nitrogen oxides are transported as much as 1,000 kilometers (600 miles) by prevailing winds, they form secondary pollutants such as nitric acid vapor, droplets of sulfuric acid, and particles of sulfate and nitrate salts (Figure 9-14). These chemicals descend to the earth's surface in two forms: *wet* as acidic rain, snow, fog, and cloud vapor; *dry* as acidic particles. The resulting mixture is called **acid deposition**, commonly called *acid rain* (Figure 9-14). Because these acidic components remain in the atmosphere for only a few days, acid deposition occurs on a regional rather than global basis.

Acidity of substances in water is commonly expressed in terms of pH (Figure 7-5), with pH values greater than 7 being alkaline and pH values less than 7 being acidic. Natural precipitation is slightly acidic, with a pH of 5.0–5.6. However, typical rain in the eastern United States is about 10 times more acidic, with a pH of 4.3. In some areas it is 100 times more acidic, with a pH of 3—as acidic as vinegar. And some cities and mountaintops downwind from cities are bathed in acid fog as acidic as lemon juice, with a pH of 2.3—about 1,000 times the acidity of normal precipitation.

Acid deposition has a number of harmful effects, especially when the pH falls below 5.1 and below 5.5 for aquatic systems:

- It damages statues, buildings, metals, and car finishes.

- It can contaminate fish in some lakes with highly toxic methylmercury. Apparently, increased acidity of lakes converts inorganic mercury compounds in lake-bottom sediments into more toxic methylmercury, which is more soluble in the fatty tissue of animals.

- It can damage foliage and weaken trees, especially conifers such as red spruce at high elevations (bathed almost continuously in very acidic fog and clouds).

- It and other air pollutants can make trees more susceptible to stresses such as cold temperatures, diseases, insects, drought, and fungi that thrive under acidic conditions.

- It can release soluble aluminum ions from soil, which damage tree roots. When washed into lakes, the released aluminum ions also can kill many kinds of fish by clogging their gills with mucous.

Q: What are the three least desirable ways of handling hazardous waste?

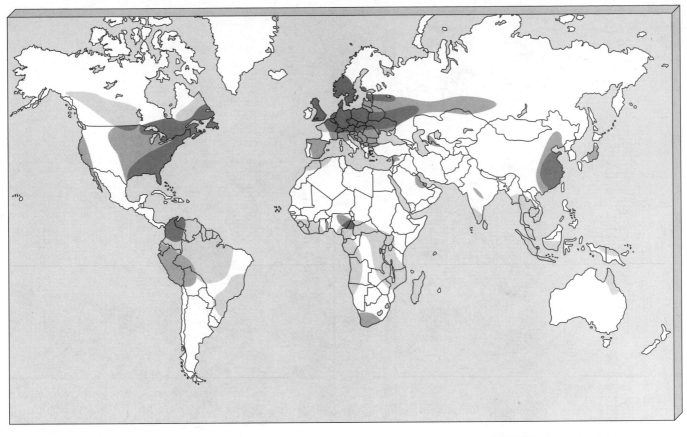

| Sensitive soils/ potential problem areas | Areas of air pollution: emissions leading to acid deposition | Present problem areas (including lakes and rivers) |

Figure 9-15 Regions where acid deposition is now a problem and regions with the potential to develop a problem. (Data from World Resource Institute and Environmental Protection Agency)

- It leads to excessive levels of nitrogen in the soil, which can overstimulate plant growth and increase depletion of other soil nutrients.

- It contributes to human respiratory diseases such as bronchitis and asthma, which can cause premature death.

Acid deposition is a serious problem (Figure 9-15) in many areas downwind from coal-burning power plants, smelters, factories, and large urban areas. A large portion of the acid-producing chemicals generated in one country may be exported to others by prevailing winds. For example, studies indicate that more than three-fourths of the acid deposition in Norway, Switzerland, Austria, Sweden, the Netherlands, and Finland is blown to those countries from industrialized areas of western and eastern Europe.

Studies also show that more than half the acid deposition in southeastern Canada and the eastern United States originates from coal- and oil-burning power plants and factories in seven states—Ohio, Indiana, Pennsylvania, Illinois, Missouri, West Virginia,

and Tennessee. In areas near and downwind from large urban areas, NO_x emissions leading to the formation of nitric acid may be the main culprit.

A large-scale, government-sponsored research study on acid deposition in the United States in the 1980s concluded that the problem was serious but not yet at a crisis stage. Representatives of coal companies, utilities, and industries burning coal and oil claim that adding expensive air pollution control equipment or burning low-sulfur coal or oil costs more than the resulting health and environmental benefits are worth. However, a 1990 study by Resources for the Future indicated that the benefits of controlling acid deposition will be worth at least $5 billion (some say $10 billion) per year, about 50% greater than the costs of controlling acid deposition.

There is some good news. A 1993 study by the U.S. Geological Survey found that the concentration of sulfate ions—a key component of acid deposition—dropped at 26 of 33 of the U.S. rainwater collection sites between 1980 and 1991. And between 1970 and 1992, emissions of sulfur dioxide in the United States

A: Incineration; burial in deep wells, ponds, pits, or landfills; ocean dumping

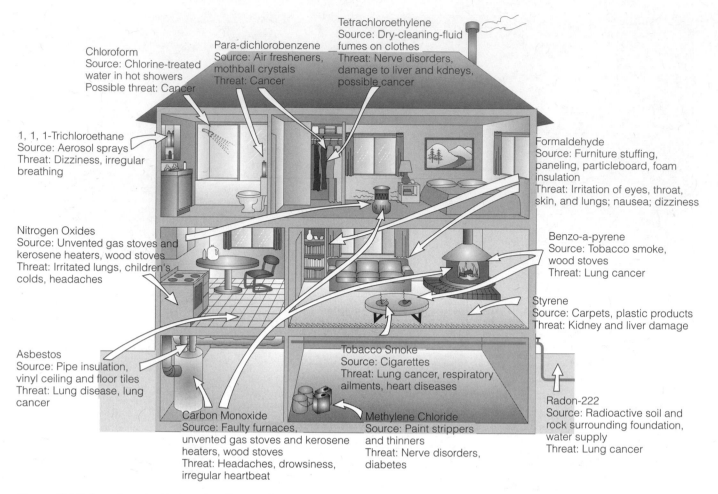

Figure 9-16 Some important indoor air pollutants. (Data from Environmental Protection Agency)

have dropped 30%. The 1990 amendments to the Clean Air Act require the nation to reduce its sulfur dioxide output by 40% of the 1980 level.

TYPES AND SOURCES OF INDOOR AIR POLLUTION If you are reading this book indoors, you may be inhaling more air pollutants with each breath than if you had been outside (Figure 9-16). The health risks from exposure to such chemicals are magnified because people spend 70–98% of their time indoors. In 1990 the EPA placed indoor air pollution at the top of the list of 18 sources of cancer risk. At greatest risk are smokers, the young, the old, the sick, pregnant women, people with breathing or heart problems, and factory workers. A 1993 study found that pollution levels inside cars can be up to 18 times higher than those outside the vehicles.

Pollutants found in buildings produce dizziness, headaches, coughing, sneezing, nausea, burning eyes, chronic fatigue, and flulike symptoms—the "sick building syndrome." According to the EPA, at least one-fifth of all U.S. buildings are considered "sick"— costing the nation $60 billion per year in absenteeism

and reduced productivity. Some indoor pollutants cause disease and premature death. According to the EPA and public health officials, cigarette smoke (Case Study, p. 214), radioactive radon-222 gas (Case Study, at right), asbestos, and formaldehyde (used in plywood, particleboard, paneling, fiberboard, and carpeting and wallpaper adhesives) are the four most dangerous indoor air pollutants.

There is intense controversy over what to do about possible exposure to tiny fibers of asbestos. Unless completely sealed within a product, asbestos easily crumbles into a dust of fibers tiny enough to become suspended in the air and to be inhaled into the lungs, where they remain for many years. Prolonged exposure to asbestos fibers can cause asbestosis (a chronic lung condition that eventually makes breathing nearly impossible), lung cancer, and mesothelioma (an inoperable cancer of the chest cavity lining). Smokers exposed to asbestos fibers have a much greater chance of dying from lung cancer than do nonsmokers exposed to such fibers.

Most of these diseases occur in people exposed for years to high levels of asbestos fibers. This group

242

Q: How many people are underfed and undernourished?

Is Your Home Contaminated with Radioactive Radon Gas?

CASE STUDY

Radon-222 is a colorless, odorless, tasteless, naturally occurring radioactive gas produced by the radioactive decay of uranium-238. Small amounts of uranium-238 are found in most soil and rock, but this isotope is much more concentrated in underground deposits of uranium, phosphate, granite, and shale.

When radon gas from such deposits seeps upward through the soil and is released outdoors, it disperses quickly in the atmosphere and decays to harmless levels. However, when the gas is drawn into buildings through cracks, drains, and hollow concrete blocks, or seeps into water in underground wells over such deposits, it can build up to high levels (Figure 9-17). Stone and other building materials obtained from radon-rich deposits can also be a source of indoor radon contamination.

Radon-222 gas quickly decays into solid particles of other radioactive elements that can be inhaled. Repeated exposure to these radioactive particles over 20–30 years can cause lung cancer, especially in smokers. According to studies by the EPA and the National Academy of Sciences, for example, 10,000–15,000 of the 130,000–140,000 new cases of lung cancer each year in the United States may be caused by prolonged exposure to radon or to radon acting together with smoking.

According to the EPA, average radon levels above 4 picocuries (one-trillionth of a curie, used to measure radioactivity) per liter of air in a closed house are considered unsafe. However, some researchers cite evidence suggesting that radon becomes dangerous only if indoor levels exceed 20 picocuries per liter—the level accepted in Canada, Sweden, and Norway.

EPA indoor radon surveys suggest that 4–5 million U.S. homes may have annual radon levels above 4 picocuries per liter of air and that 50,000–100,000 homes may have levels above 20 picocuries per liter. Unsafe levels can build up easily in a superinsulated or airtight home unless the building has an air-to-air heat exchanger to change indoor air without losing much heat. According to a 1992 EPA survey of 1,000 schools, one school in five has potentially dangerous levels of radon gas, exposing an estimated 11 million students and teachers to this health threat.

Because radon "hot spots" can occur almost anywhere, it's impossible to know which buildings have unsafe levels of radon without carrying out tests. In 1988 the EPA and the U.S. Surgeon General's Office recommended that everyone living in a detached house, a town house, or a mobile home, or on the first three floors of an apartment building test for radon.* By 1992, only 9% of U.S. households had conducted such tests (at $20–$100 per home). If testing reveals an unacceptable level, you can consult the free EPA publication *Radon Reduction Methods* for ways to reduce radon levels and health risks. Has the building where you live or work been tested for radon?

---

*For information see "Radon Detectors: How to Find Out If Your House Has a Radon Problem," *Consumer Reports*, July 1987. Ideally, radon detectors should be left in the main living area for a year.

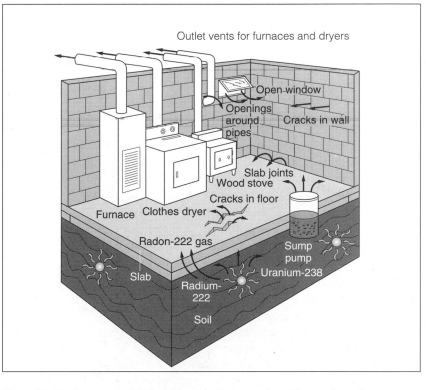

Figure 9-17 Sources and paths of entry for indoor radon-222 gas. (Data from Environmental Protection Agency)

includes asbestos miners, insulators, pipe fitters, ship-yard employees, auto mechanics (from brake linings), and workers in asbestos-producing factories. Asbestos manufacturing companies in the United States have been swamped with health claims from workers, and some have been driven into bankruptcy.

Between 1900 and 1986 asbestos was widely used in the United States. Much of it was sprayed on ceilings and walls of schools and other public and private buildings for fireproofing, soundproofing, insulation of heaters and pipes, and wall and ceiling decoration. The EPA banned those uses in 1974. In 1989 the EPA ordered a ban on almost all remaining uses of asbestos (such as brake linings, roofing shingles, and water pipes) in the United States by 1997. Representatives of the asbestos industry in the United States and Canada (which produces most of the asbestos used in the United States) challenged the ban in court, contending that with proper precautions these asbestos products can be safely used and that the costs of the ban outweigh the benefits. In 1991 a federal appeals court overturned the EPA ban. There is now general agreement that asbestos should not be removed from buildings where it has not been damaged or disturbed, but should instead be sealed or wrapped to minimize release of fibers. Improper or unnecessary removal can release more asbestos fibers than sealing off asbestos that is not crumbling.

Critics of environmentalists and excessive governmental regulation charge that much of the government-required removal of asbestos from schools and other public buildings was unnecessary and wasted billions of dollars—an example of environmental overkill.

Severe indoor air pollution, especially from particulate matter, occurs inside the dwellings of many poor rural people in LDCs. The burning of wood, dung, and crop residues in open fires or in unvented or poorly vented stoves for cooking and heating (in temperate and cold areas) exposes the people, especially women and young children, to very high levels of indoor air pollution. Partly as a result, respiratory illnesses are a major cause of death and illness in most LDCs.

DAMAGE TO HUMAN HEALTH Your respiratory system has a number of mechanisms that help protect you from air pollution. For example, hairs in your nose filter out large particles. Sticky mucus in the lining of your upper respiratory tract captures small particles and dissolves some gaseous pollutants. Sneezing and coughing expel contaminated air and mucus when your respiratory system is irritated by pollutants. Your upper respiratory tract also is lined with hundreds of thousands of tiny, mucus-coated hairlike cell structures, called cilia. They continually wave back and forth, transporting mucus and the pollutants they trap to your mouth, where they are either swallowed or expelled.

Years of smoking and exposure to air pollutants can overload or break down these natural defenses. This causes or contributes to respiratory diseases such as *lung cancer, asthma* (allergic reaction of membranes lining the bronchial tubes, causing acute shortness of breath), *chronic bronchitis* (damage to the cilia lining the bronchial tubes, causing mucus buildup, coughing, and shortness of breath), and *emphysema* (damage to air sacs leading to loss of lung elasticity and acute shortness of breath). Elderly people, infants, pregnant women, and people with heart disease, asthma, or other respiratory diseases are especially vulnerable to air pollution.

No one knows how many people die prematurely from respiratory or cardiac problems caused or aggravated by air pollution. In the United States estimates of annual deaths related to outdoor air pollution range from 7,000–180,000. If indoor air pollution is included, estimated annual deaths from air pollution in the United States range from 150,000–350,000. The wide range of estimates shows how difficult it is to get accurate information on deaths from air pollutants, mostly because of the large number of interacting factors affecting human health (Section 8-1). Millions more suffer illness and lose work time; illness effects are especially well documented for ozone. According to the EPA and the American Lung Association, air pollution costs the United States at least $150 billion annually in health care and lost work productivity, with $100 billion of that caused by indoor air pollution.

The World Health Organization estimates that worldwide about 1.3 billion people—one person in four—mostly in LDCs, live in cities where outdoor air is unhealthy to breathe (Spotlight, p. 245). The global death toll from air pollution is estimated to be at least four times the annual U.S. death toll from air pollution.

DAMAGE TO PLANTS Some gaseous pollutants—sulfur dioxide, nitrogen oxides, PANs, and especially ozone—damage leaves of crop plants and trees directly when they enter leaf pores. Spruce, fir, and other conifers, especially at high elevations, are most vulnerable to air pollution because of their long life spans and the year-round exposure of their needles to polluted air.

Prolonged exposure to high levels of multiple air pollutants can kill all trees and most other vegetation in an area. However, the effects may not be visible for several decades, when large numbers of trees suddenly begin dying off because of depletion of soil nutrients and increased susceptibility to pests, diseases, fungi, and drought. Studies indicate that this phenomenon, known as *Waldsterben* (forest death), has been a

Q: How many people die each year from hunger-related causes?

key factor in turning whole forests of spruce, fir, and beech in Europe into stump-studded meadows. A 1990 study put the cost of pollution damage to European forests at roughly $30 billion per year.

Similar diebacks in the United States have occurred, mostly on high-elevation slopes facing moving air masses (and dominated by red spruce). The most seriously affected areas are in the Appalachian Mountains. Air pollution is also implicated in the recent dieback of sugar maples in Canada and the northeastern United States.

Air pollution, mostly by ozone, also threatens some crops—especially corn, wheat, soybeans, and peanuts—and is reducing U.S. food production by 5–10%. In the United States, estimates of economic losses to agriculture as a result of air pollution range from $1.9 billion to $5.4 billion per year.

DAMAGE TO AQUATIC LIFE High acidity (low pH) can severely harm the aquatic life in freshwater lakes that have low alkaline content—or in areas where surrounding soils have little acid-neutralizing capacity. Much of the damage to aquatic life in the Northern Hemisphere is a result of *acid shock*. It is caused by the sudden runoff of large amounts of highly acidic water and toxic aluminum into lakes and streams when snow melts in the spring or when heavy rains follow a drought. The aluminum leached from the soil and lake sediment kills fish by producing mucous and clogging their gills.

At least 16,000 lakes in Norway and Sweden contain no fish, and 52,000 more have lost most of their acid-neutralizing capacity because of excess acidity. In Canada some 14,000 acidified lakes are almost fishless, and 150,000 more are in peril.

In the United States about 9,000 lakes are threatened with excess acidity, one-third of them seriously. Most are concentrated in the Northeast and the upper Midwest—especially Minnesota, Wisconsin, and the upper Great Lakes—where 80% of the lakes and streams are threatened by excess acidity. Over 200 lakes in New York's Adirondack Mountains are too acidic to support fish.

Acidified lakes can be neutralized by treating them or the surrounding soil with large amounts of limestone, but liming is an expensive and only temporary solution. Moreover, it can kill some types of plankton and aquatic plants, and it can harm wetland plants that need acidic water. It is also difficult to use correctly.

DAMAGE TO MATERIALS Each year air pollutants cause billions of dollars in damage to various materials (Table 9-3). The fallout of soot and grit on buildings, cars, and clothing requires costly cleaning. Air

The World's Most Polluted City

The air pollution capital of the world may be Cubatão, a heavily industrialized city an hour's drive south of São Paulo, Brazil. This city of 100,000 people lies in a coastal valley that has frequent thermal inversions.

Scores of factories spew thousands of tons of pollutants per day into the frequently stagnant air. More babies are born deformed in Cubatão than anywhere else in Latin America. Residents call the area "the valley of death."

In one recent year, 13,000 of the 40,000 people living in the downtown core area suffered from respiratory disease. One resident says, "On some days, if you go outside, you will vomit." The mayor refuses to live in the city.

Most residents would like to live somewhere else, but they need the jobs available in the city and cannot afford to move. The government has begun some long-overdue efforts to control air pollution, but it has a long way to go. Meanwhile, workers and their families continue to pay the price of poor health and premature death.

pollutants break down exterior paint on cars and houses, and they deteriorate roofing materials. Irreplaceable marble statues, historic buildings, and stained-glass windows throughout the world have been pitted and discolored by air pollutants. Damage to buildings in the United States from acid deposition alone is estimated at $5 billion per year.

9-5 Preventing and Controlling Air Pollution

U.S. AIR POLLUTION LEGISLATION In the United States Congress passed Clean Air Acts in 1970, 1977, and 1990, giving the federal government considerable power to control air pollution, with federal regulations enforced by each state. These laws required the EPA to establish *national ambient air quality standards (NAAQS)* for seven outdoor pollutants: suspended particulate matter, sulfur oxides, carbon monoxide, nitrogen oxides, ozone, hydrocarbons, and lead. Each

Table 9-3 Harmful Effects of Air Pollution on Materials

Material	Effects	Principal Air Pollutants
Stone and concrete	Surface erosion, discoloration, soiling	Sulfur dioxide, sulfuric acid, nitric acid, particulate matter
Metals	Corrosion, tarnishing, loss of strength	Sulfur dioxide, sulfuric acid, nitric acid, particulate matter, hydrogen sulfide
Ceramics and glass	Surface erosion	Hydrogen fluoride, particulate matter
Paints	Surface erosion, discoloration, soiling	Sulfur dioxide, hydrogen sulfide, ozone, particulate matter
Paper	Embrittlement, discoloration	Sulfur dioxide
Rubber	Cracking, loss of strength	Ozone
Leather	Surface deterioration, loss of strength	Sulfur dioxide
Textile	Deterioration, fading, soiling	Sulfur dioxide, nitrogen dioxide, ozone, particulate matter

standard specifies the maximum allowable level, averaged over a specific time period, for a certain pollutant in outdoor (ambient) air.

Since 1970 the United States has significantly reduced pollution from five of the seven major outdoor air pollutants. Emissions of nitrogen oxides have increased somewhat because of a combination of insufficient automobile emission standards and a growth in both the number of motor vehicles and the distance traveled. This has also led to increases in ozone levels in many major urban areas.

Without the Clean Air Acts, air pollution levels would be 130–315% higher today than in 1970. Even so, in 1992 at least 86 million people lived in areas that exceeded at least one air pollution standard.

A serious problem is that most U.S. air pollution control laws are based on pollution cleanup rather than pollution prevention. The only air pollutant with a sharp drop in its atmospheric level was lead, which was virtually banned in gasoline. This shows the effectiveness of the pollution prevention approach. If the current 4% annual growth in the distance that vehicles travel in the United States continues, annual emissions of nitrogen dioxide, carbon monoxide, and hydrocarbons will rise about 45% between 1995 and 2009 without stricter standards.

To help reduce SO_2 emissions, the Clean Air Act of 1990 allows utilities to buy and sell SO_2 pollution rights. With this *emissions trading policy* each utility has a specified limit on its annual SO_2 emissions. A utility that emits less SO_2 than its limit would receive pollution credits. The utility could then use its credits to avoid reductions in SO_2 emissions in some of its other facilities, bank them for future expansions, or sell them to other utilities, private citizens, or environmental groups. Instead of the government dictating how each utility should meet its emissions target, this approach lets the marketplace determine the cheapest, most efficient way to get the job done. If this market-based approach works for reducing SO_2 emissions, it could be applied to other air and water pollutants.

Some environmentalists see this as an improvement over the current regulatory approach. Others argue that it continues to set a bad example by legally sanctioning the right to pollute, especially if the annual legal pollution limits are not lowered as companies find better ways to reduce emissions. Moreover, if in trading pollution rights a *net* reduction in pollution does not result, no real progress has been achieved.

Environmentalists believe that the Clean Air Act of 1990 will further reduce air pollution in the United States. However, they point to several deficiencies in the law. These include:

- *Failing to sharply increase the fuel efficiency standards for cars and light trucks* (Figure 4-8), which would cut oil imports and air pollution more quickly and effectively than any other method and would also save consumers enormous amounts of money (Section 4-2).

- *Failing to classify the ash from municipal trash incinerators as hazardous waste*, thus encouraging incineration instead of pollution prevention as a solution to solid- and hazardous-waste reduction (Section 11-1).

- *Giving municipal trash incinerators 30-year permits*, which locks the nation into hazardous air pollution emissions and toxic waste from incinerators well into the twenty-first century and undermines pollution prevention, recycling, and reuse.

- *Setting weak standards for air pollution emissions from incinerators*, thus allowing unnecessary emissions of mercury, lead, dioxins, and other toxic pollutants.

Q: What human activity has the most harmful overall environmental impact?

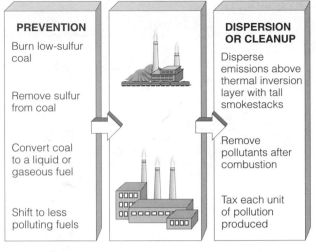

PREVENTION		DISPERSION OR CLEANUP
Burn low-sulfur coal		Disperse emissions above thermal inversion layer with tall smokestacks
Remove sulfur from coal		
Convert coal to a liquid or gaseous fuel		Remove pollutants after combustion
Shift to less polluting fuels		Tax each unit of pollution produced

Figure 9-18 Methods for reducing emissions of sulfur oxides, nitrogen oxides, and particulate matter from stationary sources such as coal-burning electric power and industrial plants.

- *Setting municipal recycling goals at a token 25% (which the law allows the EPA and states to waive) instead of an achievable 60%. This undermines recycling and reuse, and encourages reliance on burying and burning solid and hazardous wastes (Chapter 11).*

- *Doing very little to reduce emissions of carbon dioxide and other greenhouse gases (Section 9-2).*

- *Continuing to rely almost entirely on pollution cleanup rather than on pollution prevention.*

SOLUTIONS TO OUTDOOR AIR POLLUTION Figure 9-18 summarizes ways to reduce emissions of sulfur oxides, nitrogen oxides, and particulate matter from stationary sources such as electric power and industrial plants that burn coal. So far most of the emphasis has been on dispersing the pollutants with tall smokestacks or adding equipment that removes some of the pollutants after they are produced (Figure 9-19). Environmentalists call for taxes on air pollutant emissions and a shift to prevention methods.

Figure 9-20 shows ways to reduce emissions from motor vehicles. Vehicles are the primary culprit in producing photochemical smog (Figure 9-12), which contains damaging ozone (O_3). Alternative fuels were evaluated in Table 4-1 (p. 109).

Despite strict air pollution control laws, O_3 levels in the United States have been rising. Currently one of every four persons in the United States is routinely exposed to O_3 concentrations that exceed standards set under the Clean Air Act.

In 1989, California's South Coast Air Quality Management District Council proposed a drastic program to reduce O_3 and photochemical smog in the Los Angeles area. This plan would:

- *Require 10% of new cars sold in California by 2003 to emit no air pollutants.*

- *Outlaw drive-through facilities to keep vehicles from idling in lines.*

- *Substantially raise parking fees and assess high fees for families owning more than one car.*

- *Strictly control or relocate industries that release large quantities of hydrocarbons and other pollutants. These include petroleum-refining, dry-cleaning, auto-painting, printing, baking, and trash-burning plants.*

- *Find substitutes for or ban use of consumer products that release hydrocarbons. These include aerosol propellants, paints, household cleaners, and barbecue starter fluids.*

- *Eliminate gasoline-burning engines over two decades by converting trucks, buses, chain saws, outboard motors, and lawn mowers to run on electricity or on alternative fuels (Table 4-1).*

- *Require gas stations to use a hydrocarbon-vapor recovery system on gas pumps and sell alternative fuels.*

The plan may be defeated by public opinion when residents begin to feel the economic pinch from such drastic changes. Proponents argue, however, that the economic impact of not carrying out such a program will cost consumers and businesses much more. Such measures are a glimpse of what most cities will have to do as people, cars, and industries proliferate.

SOLUTIONS TO INDOOR AIR POLLUTION For many people indoor air pollution poses a greater threat to health than does outdoor air pollution. Yet the EPA spends $200 million per year trying to reduce outdoor air pollution and only $5 million a year on indoor air pollution.

To sharply reduce indoor air pollution, it's not necessary to establish mandatory indoor air quality standards and monitor the more than 100 million homes and buildings in the United States. Instead, indoor air pollution reduction can be achieved by:

- *Modifying building codes to prevent radon infiltration, or requiring use of air-to-air heat exchangers or other devices to change indoor air at regular intervals.*

- *Requiring exhaust hoods or vent pipes for appliances burning natural gas or another fossil fuel.*

- *Setting formaldehyde emission standards for building, furniture, and carpet materials.*

- *Equipping workstations with adjustable fresh air inputs (much like those for passengers on commercial aircraft).*

- *Finding substitutes for potentially harmful chemicals in aerosols, cleaning compounds, paints, and other products used indoors (Table 11-2).*

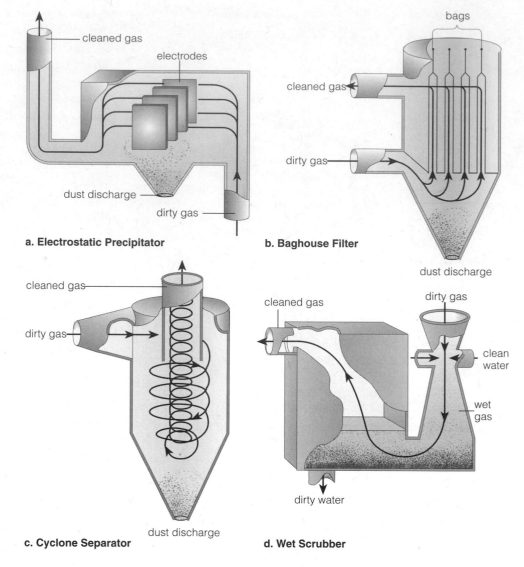

Figure 9-19 Four commonly used methods for removing particulates from the exhaust gases of electric power and industrial plants. Of these, only baghouse filters remove many of the more hazardous fine particles. Also, all produce hazardous materials that must be disposed of safely, and—except for cyclone separators—all are expensive. The wet scrubber is also used to reduce sulfur dioxide emissions.

a. Electrostatic Precipitator

b. Baghouse Filter

c. Cyclone Separator

d. Wet Scrubber

To reduce your exposure to indoor air pollutants:

- *Test for radon and take corrective measures as needed* (Case Study, p. 243).

- *Install air-to-air heat exchangers or regularly ventilate your house by opening windows.*

- *Test indoor air for formaldehyde at the beginning of the winter heating season when the house is closed up.** The cost is $200–$300.

- *Don't buy synthetic wall-to-wall carpeting, furniture, and other products containing formaldehyde, and use "low-emitting formaldehyde" or nonformaldehyde building materials.*

- *Reduce indoor levels of formaldehyde and several other toxic gases by using houseplants.* Examples are the spider or airplane plant (the most effective), golden pothos, syngonium, philodendron (especially the elephant-ear species), chrysanthemum, ligustrum, photina, variegated liriope, and Gerbera daisy. About 20 plants can help clean the air in a typical home. Plants should be potted with a mixture of soil and granular charcoal (which absorbs organic air pollutants).

- *Test your house or workplace for asbestos fiber levels if it was built before 1980.†* If airborne asbestos levels are too high, hire an independent consultant—not an asbestos-removal firm—to advise you on what

---

*To locate a testing laboratory in your area, write to Consumer Product Safety Commission, Washington, DC 20207, or call 301-492-6800.

---

†To get a free list of certified asbestos laboratories that charge $25–$50 to test a sample, send a self-addressed envelope to NIST/NVLAP, Building 411, Room A124, Gaithersburg, MD 20899, or call the EPA's Toxic Substances Control Hotline at 202-554-1404.

Q: What percentage of the crops in the United States are grown using organic methods (no pesticides or commercial fertilizers)?

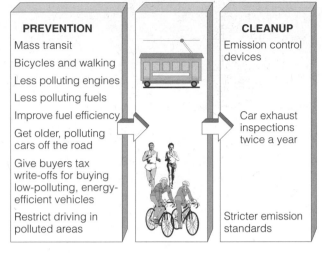

PREVENTION		CLEANUP
Mass transit		Emission control devices
Bicycles and walking		
Less polluting engines		
Less polluting fuels		
Improve fuel efficiency		Car exhaust inspections twice a year
Get older, polluting cars off the road		
Give buyers tax write-offs for buying low-polluting, energy-efficient vehicles		
Restrict driving in polluted areas		Stricter emission standards

Figure 9-20 Methods for reducing emissions from motor vehicles.

to do. (The typical charge is $500 or more, but this could save you asbestos-removal costs of $10,000–$100,000.). If asbestos fibers are not being released, asbestos-containing products can be covered or sealed. Don't buy a pre-1980 house without having its indoor air tested for asbestos.

- *Don't store gasoline, solvents, or other volatile hazardous chemicals inside a home or attached garage.*
- *Don't use commercial room deodorizers or air fresheners* (Table 11-3).
- *Don't use aerosol spray products.*
- *Don't smoke.* If you smoke, do it outside or in a closed room vented to the outside.
- *Make sure that wood-burning stoves, fireplaces, and kerosene- and gas-burning heaters are properly installed, vented, and maintained.*

CONNECTIONS: PROTECTING THE ATMOSPHERE

Environmentalists believe that protecting the commonly shared atmosphere and the health of people and other organisms will require the following significant changes throughout the world:

- *Integrate air pollution, water pollution, energy, land-use, and population regulation policies.*
- *Emphasize pollution prevention rather than pollution control.* Widespread use of solar-produced hydrogen fuel (Section 4-4) would eliminate most air pollution.
- *Improve energy efficiency* (Section 4-2).
- *Reduce use of fossil fuels, especially coal and oil* (Section 4-6).
- *Shift to renewable energy resources* (Section 4-3).
- *Emphasize distribution of low-emission and better vented cookstoves in rural areas of LDCs.*

- *Discourage automobile use* (Section 3-3).
- *Increase recycling and reuse, and reduce the production of all forms of waste* (Chapter 11).
- *Develop air quality strategies based on the air flows and pollution sources of an entire region instead of the current piecemeal, city-by-city approach.*
- *Slow population growth* (Section 3-4).
- *Include the social costs of air pollution and other forms of pollution in the market prices of goods and services* (Chapter 12).

As population and consumption rise, we can generate new air pollution faster than we can clean up the old, even in MDCs with strict air-pollution control laws. This shows the need for slowing population growth and relying on pollution prevention.

Some people have wondered whether there is intelligent life on Earth. If we can deal with the interconnected problems of possible global warming, ozone depletion, outdoor and indoor air pollution, and loss of biodiversity (Chapters 5 and 6), then the answer is a hopeful yes. Otherwise, they believe the answer is a tragic no.

The atmosphere is the key symbol of global interdependence. If we can't solve some of our problems in the face of threats to this global commons, then I can't be very optimistic about the future of the world.

MARGARET MEAD

CRITICAL THINKING

1. What consumption patterns and other features of your lifestyle directly add greenhouse gases to the atmosphere? Which, if any, of those things would you be willing to give up to slow projected global warming and reduce other forms of air pollution?

2. Explain why you agree or disagree with each of the proposals listed in Section 9-2 for
   a. slowing down emissions of greenhouse gases into the atmosphere and
   b. preparing for the effects of global warming.
   Explain your answers.
   What effects would carrying out these proposals have on your lifestyle and that of your descendants? What effects might *not* carrying out these actions have?

3. What consumption patterns and other features of your lifestyle directly and indirectly add ozone-depleting chemicals to the atmosphere? Which, if any, of those things would you be willing to give up to slow ozone depletion?

4. What topographical and climate factors either increase or help decrease air pollution in your community?

5. Should all tall smokestacks be banned? Explain.

10 Water

10-1 Water's Importance and Unique Properties

We live on the water planet. A precious film of water—most of it salt water—covers about 71% of Earth's surface (Figure 2-31). Earth's organisms are made up mostly of water. For example, a tree is about 60% water by weight, and you and most animals are about 65% water.

Fresh water is a vital resource for agriculture, manufacturing, transportation, and countless other human activities. Water also plays a key role in sculpting Earth's surface, moderating climate, and diluting pollutants.

Water has many unique—almost magical—properties. Its high boiling point and low freezing point mean that water remains a liquid in most climates on Earth. It can store a large amount of heat without a large change in temperature. This helps protect living organisms from the shock of abrupt temperature changes, it moderates Earth's climate, and it makes water an excellent coolant. Water's ability to absorb large amounts of heat as it changes into water vapor—and to release this heat as the vapor condenses back to liquid water—is a primary factor in distributing heat throughout the world (Figure 9-4). Water can also dissolve a variety of compounds. This enables it to carry dissolved nutrients throughout the tissues of living organisms, to flush waste products out of those tissues, to serve as an all-purpose cleanser, and to help remove and dilute the water-soluble wastes of civilization. However, water's superiority as a solvent also means that it is easily polluted by water-soluble wastes.

Most substances shrink when they freeze, but liquid water expands when it becomes ice. Consequently, ice has a lower density (mass per unit of volume) than liquid water. Thus ice floats on water, and bodies of water freeze from the top down instead of from the bottom up. Without this property, lakes and streams in cold climates would freeze solid, and most current forms of aquatic life would not exist.

Water—the lifeblood of the ecosphere—is truly a wondrous substance that connects us to one another, to other forms of life, and to the entire planet. Despite its importance, water is one of the most poorly managed resources on Earth. We waste it and pollute it. We also charge too little for making it available, thus encouraging even greater waste and pollution of this vital and potentially renewable resource.

10-2 Supply, Renewal, and Use of Water Resources

WORLDWIDE SUPPLY, RENEWAL, AND DISTRIBUTION Only a tiny fraction of the planet's abundant water is available to us as fresh water. About 97% is found in the oceans and is too salty for drinking, irrigation, or industry (except as a coolant).

The remaining 3% is fresh water. About 2.997% of it is locked up in ice caps or glaciers, or it is buried so deep that it costs too much to extract. Only about 0.003% of Earth's total volume of water is easily available to us as soil moisture, exploitable groundwater, water vapor, and lakes and streams. If the world's water supply were only 100 liters (26 gallons), our usable supply of fresh water would be only about 0.003 liter (one-half teaspoon).

Fortunately, this amounts to a generous supply, which is continuously collected, purified, and distributed in the *hydrologic cycle* (Figure 2-25). This natural recycling and purification process provides plenty of fresh water as long as we don't overload it with slowly degradable and nondegradable wastes or withdraw water from underground supplies faster than it is replenished. Unfortunately, we are doing both. Also, usable fresh water is unevenly distributed around the world. Differences in average annual precipitation divide the world into water "haves" and "have-nots."

As population and industrialization increase, water shortages in already water-short regions will intensify. Projected global warming (Section 9-2) also might cause changes in rainfall patterns and disrupt water supplies. No one knows what areas might be affected.

Q: How are 71% of official hazardous wastes in the United States handled?

Our liquid planet glows like a soft blue sapphire in the hard-edged darkness of space. There is nothing else like it in the solar system. It is because of water.

JOHN TODD

SURFACE WATER   The fresh water we use comes from two sources: surface water and groundwater (Figure 10-1). Precipitation that does not soak into the ground or return to the atmosphere by evaporation or transpiration is called **surface water**. It forms streams, lakes, wetlands, and artificial reservoirs.

Watersheds, also called **drainage basins**, are areas of land that drain into bodies of surface water. Water flowing off the land into these bodies is called **surface runoff**.

GROUNDWATER   Some precipitation infiltrates the ground and fills the pores in soil and rock. The subsurface area where all available soil and rock spaces are filled by water is called the **zone of saturation**, and the water in these pores is called **groundwater** (Figure 10-2). The **water table** is the upper surface of the zone of saturation. It is the fuzzy and fluctuating dividing line between saturated soil and rock (where every available pore is full), and unsaturated (but still wet) rock and soil (where the pores can absorb more water). The water table falls in dry weather and rises in wet weather. Porous, water-saturated layers of sand, gravel, or bed rock through which groundwater flows and

that can yield an economically significant amount of water are called **aquifers** (Figure 10-2).

Most aquifers are replenished naturally by precipitation, which percolates downward through soil and rock in what is called **natural recharge**. Any area of land through which water passes into an aquifer is called a **recharge area**. Groundwater moves from the recharge area through an aquifer and out to a discharge area (well, spring, lake, geyser, stream, or ocean) as part of the hydrologic cycle.

Normally, groundwater moves from points of high elevation and pressure to points of lower elevation and pressure. This movement is quite slow, typically only a meter or so (about 3 feet) per year and rarely more than 0.3 meter (1 foot) per day. Thus, most aquifers are like huge, slow-moving underground lakes.

There is 40 times as much groundwater as there is surface water. However, groundwater is unequally distributed, and only a small amount of it is economically exploitable.

If the withdrawal rate of an aquifer exceeds its natural recharge rate, the water table around the withdrawal well is lowered, creating a waterless volume

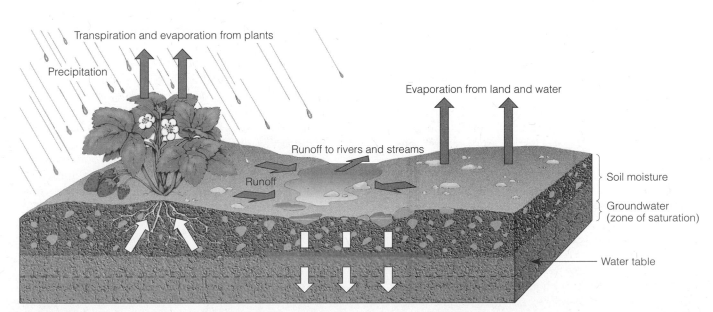

Figure 10-1 Main routes of local precipitation: surface runoff into surface waters, ground infiltration into aquifers, and evaporation and transpiration into the atmosphere.

A: Buried in deep wells, ponds, pits, or landfills (64%) and incinerated (7%)

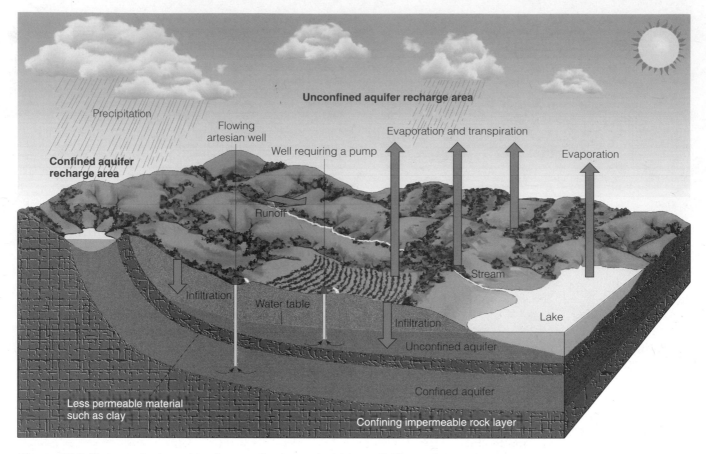

Figure 10-2 The groundwater system. An *unconfined*, or *water table*, *aquifer* forms when groundwater collects above a layer of rock or compacted clay through which water flows very slowly (low permeability). A *confined aquifer* is sandwiched between layers such as clay or shale that have low permeability. Groundwater in this type of aquifer is confined and under pressure.

known as a *cone of depression* (Figure 10-3). Any pollutant discharged onto the land above will be pulled directly into this cone and will pollute water withdrawn by the well.

Some aquifers, called *fossil aquifers*, get very little—if any—recharge. Often found deep underground, they are nonrenewable resources on a human time scale. Withdrawals from fossil aquifers amount to "water mining"—and if kept up, will deplete these ancient deposits of liquid Earth capital.

WORLD AND U.S. WATER USE Two common measures of human water use are withdrawal and consumption. **Water withdrawal** is taking water from a groundwater or surface-water source to a place of use. **Water consumption** occurs when water that has been withdrawn is not returned to the surface water or groundwater from which it came so that it may be used again in that area. This usually occurs because the water has evaporated or transpired into

the atmosphere. Worldwide, about 60% of the water withdrawn is consumed.

Since 1950 the rate of global water withdrawal has increased almost fivefold, and per capita use has trebled, largely to meet the food and other resource needs of the world's rapidly growing population. Water withdrawal rates are projected to at least double in the next two decades.

Uses of withdrawn water vary from one region to another and from one country to another (Figure 10-4). Averaged globally, about 69% of the water withdrawn each year is used to irrigate 18% of the world's cropland, much of it in the United States, the former USSR, and Mexico. A large share of irrigation water is wasted, with 70–80% of the water evaporating or seeping into the ground before reaching crops.

In the western United States irrigation accounts for about 85% of all water use, and much of this water is used inefficiently. One reason for this is that federal subsidies (mostly federally financed dams and water

Q: What percentage of the world's potential food supply is lost to pests?

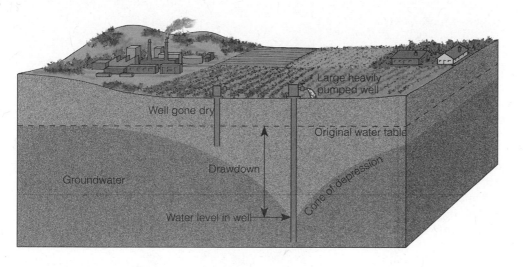

Figure 10-3 Drawdown of water table and cone of depression.

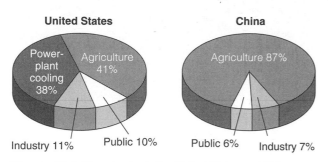

Figure 10-4 Use of water in the United States and China. (Data from Worldwatch Institute and World Resources Institute)

delivery systems) make water so cheap that Western farmers would lose money by investing in more efficient irrigation.

Worldwide, about 23% of the water withdrawn is used for energy production (oil and gas production and power-plant cooling) and industrial processing, cleaning, and removal of wastes. The amount of water U.S. industry uses each year to cool, wash, circulate, and manufacture materials is equivalent to 30% of the water in the world's streams. Agricultural and manufactured products both require large amounts of water, much of which could be used more efficiently and reused. For example, it takes 380,000 liters (100,000 gallons) to make an automobile, 3,800 liters (1,000 gallons) to produce 454 grams (1 pound) of aluminum, and 3,000 liters (800 gallons) to produce 454 grams (1 pound) of grain-fed beef in a feedlot, where large numbers of cattle are confined to a fairly small area.

Domestic and municipal use accounts for about 8% of worldwide withdrawals and about 13–16% of withdrawals in industrialized countries. As population, urbanization, and industrialization grow, the volume of wastewater needing treatment will increase enormously.

 Water Resource Problems

10-3

TOO LITTLE WATER Droughts—periods in which precipitation is much lower and evaporation is higher than normal—cause more damage and suffering worldwide than any other natural hazard. Since the 1970s drought has killed more than 24,000 people per year and created swarms of environmental refugees. At least 80 arid and semiarid countries, where nearly 40% of the world's people live, experience years-long droughts. In water-short areas many women and children must walk long distances each day, carrying heavy jars or cans, to get a meager supply of sometimes contaminated water.

Reduced precipitation, higher-than-normal temperatures, or both usually trigger a drought; rapid population growth makes it worse. Deforestation (Sections 5-3 and 5-4), overgrazing by livestock (Section 5-5), desertification (Figure 5-9), and replacing diverse natural grasslands with monoculture fields of crops also can intensify the effects of drought. Millions of poor people in LDCs have no choice but to try to survive on drought-prone land.

If global warming occurs as projected (Section 9-2), severe droughts may become more frequent in some areas of the world and jeopardize food production. Some water-starved cities may have to be abandoned. Competition between cities and farmers for scarce water is already escalating in regions such as the western United States and China.

Water will be the burning foreign policy issue for water-short countries in the 1990s and beyond. Almost 150 of the world's 214 major river systems are shared by two countries and another 50 are shared by three to ten nations. This 40% of the world's population

A: 55% (35% before harvest and 20% after harvest)

already clash over water, especially in the Middle East. The next wars in the Middle East will probably be fought over water, not oil. Most water in this dry region comes from three shared river basins: the Jordan, the Tigris-Euphrates, and the Nile (Figure 10-5).

Ethiopia, which controls the headwaters of 80% of the Nile's flow, has plans to divert more of this water; so does Sudan. This could reduce the amount of water available to water-short Egypt, whose terrain is desert except for the thin strip of irrigated cropland along the Nile and its delta. By 2025 Egypt's population is expected to double—increasing the demand for water. Its options are to go to war with Sudan and Ethiopia to obtain more water, or to slash population growth and improve irrigation efficiency.

There is also fierce competition for water among Jordan, Syria, and Israel, which get most of their water from the Jordan River basin. The 1967 Arab–Israeli war was fought in part over access to this water. Israel uses water more efficiently than any other country. Nevertheless, it is now using 95% of its renewable supply of fresh water, and the supply is projected to fall 30% short of demand by 2000 because of increased immigration. In 1991 the agriculture minister warned that Israel's water needs require that it not give up any of the territory taken from the Arabs—intensifying the Arab–Israeli conflict.

Turkey, by contrast, has abundant water and plans to build 22 dams along the upper Tigris and Euphrates and to construct pipelines to transport and sell water to parched Saudi Arabia and Kuwait—and perhaps to Syria, Israel, and Jordan. The greatest threat to Iraq is a cutoff of its water supply by Turkey and Syria. Clearly, distribution of water resources will be a key issue in any future peace talks in the volatile Middle East.

Some countries have lots of water, but the largest rivers (which carry most of the runoff) are far from agricultural and population centers where the water is needed. For example, South America has the largest annual water runoff of any continent, but 60% of the runoff flows through the Amazon River in remote areas where few people live.

Strategies for capturing some of this runoff and bringing the water to people include building dams and reservoirs and using aqueducts to transfer water to other areas. These approaches, however, are expensive and have harmful environmental impacts in addition to their benefits, as discussed in Section 10-4.

TOO MUCH WATER Some countries have enough annual precipitation but get most of it at one time of the year. In India, for example, 90% of the annual precipitation falls between June and September, the monsoon season. This downpour causes floods, waterlogs

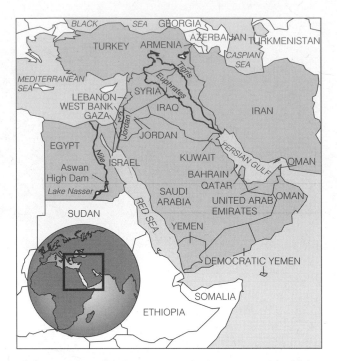

Figure 10-5 Middle Eastern countries have some of the highest population growth rates in the world. Because of their dry climate, food production depends on irrigation. In the 1990s and beyond, conflicts among countries in this region over access to water may overshadow long-standing religious and ethnic clashes, as well as disputes over ownership of oil supplies.

soils, leaches soil nutrients, and washes away topsoil and crops.

Natural flooding by streams, the most common type of flooding, is caused primarily by heavy rain or rapid melting of snow, which causes water in the stream to overflow the channel in which it normally flows and to cover the adjacent area, called a **floodplain**.

People have settled on floodplains since the beginnings of agriculture. The soil is fertile, and water is available for irrigation. Communities have access to the water for transportation of people or goods, and floodplains are flat sites useful for buildings, highways, and railroads. Prolonged rains anywhere can cause streams and lakes to overflow and flood the surrounding floodplain land, but low-lying river basins such as the Ganges River basin in India and Bangladesh are especially vulnerable. Hurricanes and typhoons can also flood low-lying coastal areas.

In the 1970s floods killed more than 4,700 people per year and caused tens of billions of dollars in property damage—a trend that continued and even worsened in the 1980s and into the 1990s—as many people in the midwestern United States learned during the great flood in the summer of 1993. In India, for example, flood losses doubled in the 1980s.

Q: What percentage of U.S. crops are lost to pests?

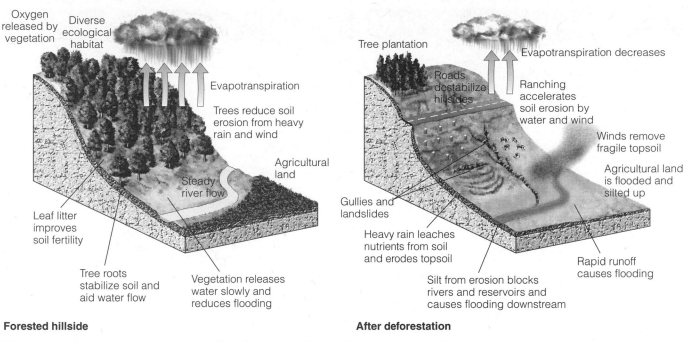

Oxygen released by vegetation

Diverse ecological habitat

Evapotranspiration

Trees reduce soil erosion from heavy rain and wind

Agricultural land

Steady river flow

Leaf litter improves soil fertility

Tree roots stabilize soil and aid water flow

Vegetation releases water slowly and reduces flooding

Forested hillside

Tree plantation

Roads destabilize hillsides

Evapotranspiration decreases

Ranching accelerates soil erosion by water and wind

Winds remove fragile topsoil

Agricultural land is flooded and silted up

Gullies and landslides

Heavy rain leaches nutrients from soil and erodes topsoil

Silt from erosion blocks rivers and reservoirs and causes flooding downstream

Rapid runoff causes flooding

After deforestation

Figure 10-6 A mountainside before and after deforestation. When a hillside or mountainside is deforested for timber and fuelwood, grazing livestock, and unsustainable farming, water from rains rushes down denuded slopes, eroding precious topsoil and flooding downstream areas. A 3,000-year-old Chinese proverb says: "To protect your rivers, protect your mountains."

Floods, like droughts, are usually called natural disasters, but human activities have contributed to the sharp rise in flood deaths and damage since the 1960s.

The main way humans increase the probability and severity of flooding is by removing vegetation—through timbering operations, overgrazing by livestock, construction, forest fires, and certain mining activities (Figure 10-6). Vegetation retards surface runoff, increasing infiltration; when the vegetation is removed by human activities or natural occurrences, precipitation reaches streams more directly, often with a large load of sediment, which increases the chance of flooding (Connections, p. 256).

Urbanization (Section 3-3) also increases flooding (even with moderate rainfall) by replacing vegetation and soil with highways, parking lots, and buildings that lead to rapid runoff of rainwater. If sea levels rise during the next century as projected, many low-lying coastal cities, wetlands, and croplands will be under water.

Ways to reduce the risks of flooding include:

■ *Deepening, widening, or straightening a section of a stream (called channelization) to allow more rapid runoff and reduce the chances of flooding.*

■ *Building artificial levees along stream banks to reduce the chances of water flowing over into nearby floodplains.*

■ *Building flood control dams across a stream to hold back and store flood water and release it more gradually.* This has benefits and drawbacks (Figure 4-19a).

■ *Floodplain management.* Data on past flood frequency and severity are used to prohibit certain types of buildings or activities in the high-risk zone, to elevate or allow only floodproof buildings on the legally defined floodplain, or to construct a floodway that allows flood water to flow through the community with minimal damage.

CONTAMINATED DRINKING WATER In many parts of the world, water quality is also degraded. Rivers in eastern Europe, Latin America, and Asia are severely polluted, as are some in MDCs. Aquifers used as sources of drinking water in many MDCs and LDCs are becoming contaminated with pesticides, fertilizers, and hazardous organic chemicals. In China, for example, 41 large cities get their drinking water from polluted groundwater.

According to the World Health Organization, 1.5 billion people don't have a safe supply of drinking water, and 1.7 billion lack adequate sanitation facilities. At least 5 million people die every year from waterborne diseases that could be prevented by clean drinking water and better sanitation. Most of the 13,700 who die each day from such diseases are children under age 5.

Bangladesh is one of the world's most densely populated countries, with 114 million people packed into an area roughly the size of Wisconsin. Women bear an average of 4.9 children, and the population could reach 211 million by 2025. Bangladesh is also one of the world's poorest countries, with an average per capita income of about $180 per year.

Most of the country consists of floodplains and shifting islands of silt formed by a delta at the mouths of three major rivers (Figure 2-35). Runoff from annual monsoon rains in the Himalaya mountains of India, Nepal, Bhutan, and China flows down the rivers through Bangladesh into the Bay of Bengal.

The people of Bangladesh are used to moderate annual flooding during the summer monsoon season, and they depend on the floodwaters to grow rice, their primary source of food. The annual deposit of Himalayan soil in the delta basin also helps maintain soil fertility.

In the past, great floods occurred every 50 years or so, but during the 1970s and 1980s they came about every 4 years. Bangladesh's flood problems begin in the Himalayan watershed. There, a combination of rapid population growth, deforestation, overgrazing, and unsustainable farming on steep, easily erodible mountain slopes has greatly diminished the ability of the soil to absorb water (Figure 10-6). Instead of being absorbed and released slowly, water from the monsoon rain runs off the denuded Himalayan foothills, carrying vital topsoil with it. This runoff, combined with heavier-than-normal monsoon rains, has caused severe flooding in Bangladesh.

In 1988, for example, a disastrous flood covered two-thirds of the country's land area for three weeks and leveled 2 million homes after the heaviest monsoon rains in 70 years. At least 2,000 people drowned, and 30 million people—1 in 4—were left homeless. At least a quarter of the country's crops were destroyed, costing at least $1.5 billion and causing thousands of people to die of starvation.

In their struggle to survive, the poor in Bangladesh have cleared many of the country's coastal mangrove forests for fuelwood and for cultivation of crops. This deforestation has led to more severe flooding because these coastal wetlands shelter the low-lying coastal areas from storm surges and cyclones with fierce winds whipping up waves as high as 9 meters (30 feet).

In 1970 as many as 1 million people drowned in one storm. Another surge killed some 140,000 people in 1991. Flood damage and deaths in areas still protected by mangrove forests are much lower than in areas where the forests have been cleared. This problem can be solved only if Bangladesh, Bhutan, China, India, and Nepal all cooperate in reforestation efforts and flood control measures, and reduce their population growth.

In 1980 the United Nations called for spending $300 billion to supply all of the world's people with clean drinking water and adequate sanitation by 1990. The $30-billion-per-year cost of this program is about what the world spends every 10 days for military purposes. Sadly, only about $1.5 billion per year was actually spent. Water pollution is discussed in more detail in Sections 10-6 and 10-7.

THE U.S. SITUATION The United States has plenty of fresh water. However, much of it is in the wrong place at the wrong time or is contaminated by agriculture and industry. From a human perspective, the eastern states usually have ample precipitation, while many of the western states have too little. In the East the largest uses for water are energy production, cooling, and manufacturing. In the West the largest use by far is irrigation.

In many parts of the eastern United States the most serious water problems are flooding, occasional shortages, and pollution. For example, 3 million residents of Long Island, New York, get their water from an aquifer that is becoming severely contaminated.

The most serious water problem in the arid and semiarid areas of the western half of the country is a shortage of runoff caused by low precipitation, high evaporation, and recurring prolonged drought. In many areas, water tables are dropping rapidly as farmers and cities deplete groundwater aquifers faster than they are recharged.

Many major urban centers, especially those in the West and Midwest, are located in areas that don't have enough water or are projected to have water shortages by 2000 (Figure 10-7). Experts project that present shortages and conflicts over water supplies will get much worse as more industries and people migrate west and compete with farmers for scarce water. These shortages could worsen even more if climate warms up as a result of an enhanced greenhouse effect (Section 9-2). Because water is such a vital resource, you might find the data in Figure 10-7 useful in deciding where to live in coming decades.

Q: Worldwide, how many people are poisoned each year by pesticides?

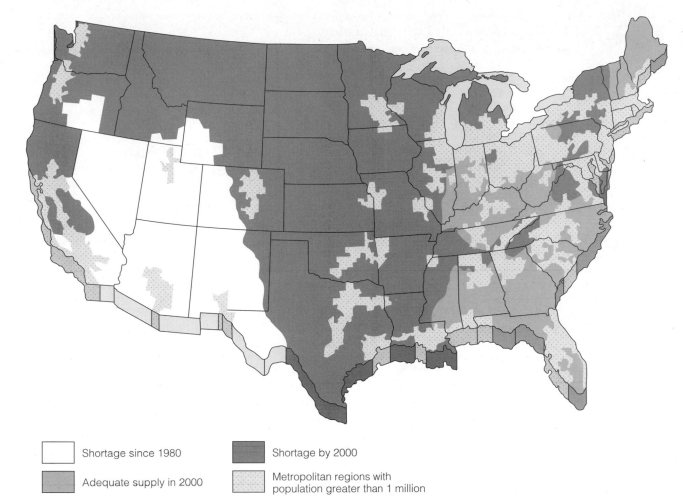

☐ Shortage since 1980	▨ Shortage by 2000
▨ Adequate supply in 2000	▨ Metropolitan regions with population greater than 1 million

Figure 10-7 Current and projected water-deficit regions in the continental United States and their proximity to metropolitan areas having populations greater than 1 million. (Data from U.S. Water Resources Council and U.S. Geological Survey)

METHODS FOR MANAGING WATER RESOURCES

One way to manage water resources is to increase the supply in a particular area by building dams and reservoirs, bringing in surface water from another area, or tapping groundwater. The other approach is to improve the efficiency of water use.

LDCs rarely have the money to develop the water storage and distribution systems needed to increase their supply. Their people must settle where the water is. In MDCs people tend to live where the climate is favorable and bring in water from another watershed.

 Solutions: Supplying More Water

CONSTRUCTING DAMS AND RESERVOIRS Rainwater and water from melting snow can be captured and stored in large reservoirs created by damming streams. This water can then be released in a controlled flow as desired to produce hydroelectric power at the dam site (Figure 4-19b), to irrigate land below the dam, to control flooding of land below the reservoir, and to provide water carried by aqueducts to towns and cities. Reservoirs are also used for recreation activities, such as swimming, fishing, and boating.

About 13.5% of the electrical power used in the United States is hydroelectric. This is a potentially renewable source of energy as long as drought or long-term changes in climate don't reduce water flow in the dam's basin. Large dams and reservoirs have benefits and drawbacks (Figure 4-19a). Building small dams, which have fewer destructive effects than large dams and reservoirs, is a useful way to trap water for irrigation.

Proposed dams in LDCs will cover vast areas and uproot millions of people. Despite protests by more than 50,000 villagers, the Indian government is going ahead with plans to build 30 large dams and thousands of smaller ones along the Namada River and 41

A: At least 1 million (with 4,000–20,000 deaths)

Water Squabbles in California

In California the basic water problem is that 75% of the population lives south of Sacramento but 75% of the rain falls north of it. The California Water Project uses a maze of giant dams, pumps, and aqueducts to transport water from water-rich northern California to heavily populated areas of the state and to arid and semiarid agricultural regions (Figure 10-8).

For decades northern and southern Californians have been feuding over how state water should be allocated under this project. Southern Californians say they need more water from the north to support Los Angeles, San Diego, and other growing urban areas, and to grow more crops. Agriculture uses 82% of the water withdrawn in California. Irrigation for just two crops, alfalfa and cotton, uses as much water as the residential needs of all 30 million Californians.

Opponents in the north say that sending more water south would degrade the Sacramento River, threaten fisheries, and reduce the flushing action that helps clean San Francisco Bay of pollutants. They also argue that much of the water already sent south is wasted and that making irrigation just 10% more efficient would provide enough water for domestic and industrial uses in southern California.

To supply agribusiness in California and other western states with cheap water, the U. S. Bureau of Reclamation has drained major rivers and lakes, and it has destroyed vast areas of wetland waterfowl habitat and salmon spawning habitat. Environmentalists believe that the federal government should not award new long-term water contracts that give many farmers and ranchers cheap, government-subsidized water for irrigating crops—especially grass for cows and "thirsty" crops such as rice, alfalfa, and cotton—that could be grown more cheaply in rain-fed areas. They also propose enacting state laws requiring cities wanting more water to pay farmers to install water-saving irrigation technology. Cities could use the water saved.

If water supplies in California were to drop sharply because of projected global warming, water delivered by the state's huge distribution system would plummet as well. Most irrigated agriculture in California would have to be abandoned, and much of the population of southern California might have to move to areas with more water. The six-year drought that northern and southern California experienced between 1986 and 1992 was a small taste of a possible future.

Groundwater is no answer. Throughout most of California it is already being withdrawn faster than it is replenished. Santa Barbara, Los Angeles, and several other southern California cities are planning experimental plants to supply fresh water by removing salt from seawater—an option five to six times more costly than state-provided water. Improving irrigation efficiency and allowing farmers to sell their water allotments are much quicker and cheaper solutions.

Figure 10-8 California Water Project and Central Arizona Project for large-scale transfer of water from one watershed to another. Arrows show general direction of water flow.

of its tributaries. These projects, however, are small compared to China's Three Gorges project—the world's largest proposed hydroelectric dam and reservoir. When completed it will create a 590-kilometer- (370-mile-) long lake on the Yangtze River. It will flood large areas of farmland and 800 existing factories and displace 1.2 million people, including two cities each containing 100,000 people.

Q: What is the most serious drawback to using chemicals to control pests (especially insects)?

Figure 10-9 Once the world's fourth largest freshwater lake, the Aral Sea has been shrinking and getting saltier since 1960 because most of the water from the rivers that replenish it has been diverted to grow cotton and food crops. As the lake shrinks, it leaves a salty desert.

WATERSHED TRANSFERS Tunnels, aqueducts, and underground pipes can transfer stream runoff collected by building dams and reservoirs from water-rich watersheds to water-poor areas. Three of the world's largest watershed transfer projects are the California Water Project (Case Study, at left), the diversion of water from rivers feeding the Aral Sea in Central Asia to irrigate cropland, and the James Bay project in Canada.

The states of Kazakhstan and Uzbekistan in the former USSR have the driest climate in Central Asia. Since 1960 enormous amounts of irrigation water have been diverted from the inland *Aral Sea*—a huge freshwater lake—and its two feeder rivers to grow cotton and food crops. The irrigation canal, the world's longest, stretches over 1,300 kilometers (800 miles).

The diversion (coupled with droughts) has caused a regional ecological disaster, described by one former USSR official as "ten times worse than the 1986 Chernobyl nuclear power plant accident" (Figure 4-36). The sea's salinity has tripled, its surface area has shrunk by 46% (Figure 10-9), and its volume has decreased 69%. The two supply rivers are mere trickles. About 30,000 square kilometers (11,600 square miles) of former lake bottom have turned into desert, and the process continues.

All the native fish are gone, devastating the area's fishing industry, which once provided work for more than 60,000 people. Two major fishing towns are now surrounded by a desert containing stranded fishing boats and rusting commercial ships. Roughly half the area's bird and mammal species have also disappeared.

Salt, dust, and dried pesticide residues have been carried as far as 300 kilometers (190 miles) away by the wind. As the salt spreads, it kills crops, trees, and wildlife, and destroys pastureland. This phenomenon has added a new term to our vocabulary of environmental ills: *salt rain*.

These changes have also affected the area's already semiarid climate. The once-huge Aral Sea acted as a thermal buffer, moderating the heat of summer and the extreme cold of winter. Now there is less rain, summers are hotter, winters are colder, and the growing season is shorter. Cotton and crop yields have dropped dramatically.

Local farmers have turned to herbicides, insecticides, and fertilizers to keep growing some crops. Many of these chemicals have percolated downward and accumulated to dangerous levels in the groundwater, from which most of the drinking water comes.

Ways to deal with this problem include **(1)** charging farmers more for irrigation water to reduce waste and encourage a shift to less water-intensive crops; **(2)** decreasing irrigation water quotas; **(3)** introducing water-saving technologies; **(4)** developing a regional integrated water management plan; **(5)** planting protective forest belts; **(6)** using underground water to supplement irrigation water and lower the water table to reduce waterlogging and salinization; **(7)** improving health services; and **(8)** slowing the area's rapid population growth (3% per year).

In 1992 Kazakhstan, Uzbekistan, Kyrgyzstan, Tadzhikistan, and Turkmenistan, which share the Aral Sea basin, signed an agreement describing how the waters of the two rivers feeding the Aral Sea should be divided, and they also created a council to manage the basin's resources. However, even with help from foreign countries, the United Nations, and agencies such as the World Bank, the money needed to save the Aral Sea may not be available.

Another major watershed transfer project is the *James Bay Project*—a $60-billion, 50-year scheme to harness the wild rivers that flow into the James and Hudson bays in Canada's Quebec province—in order to produce electric power for Canadian and U.S. consumers (Figure 10-10). If completed, it would **(1)** reverse or alter the flow of 19 giant rivers; **(2)** reshape a territory the size of France with more than 215 dams and dikes; **(3)** flood 176,000 square kilometers (68,000 square miles)—an area the size of Washington State or Germany—of boreal forest and tundra; and **(4)** displace thousands of indigenous Cree who have lived sustainably off James Bay by subsistence hunting, fishing, and trapping for 5,000 years. After 20 years and $16 billion, Phase I has been completed. The second

Figure 10-10 The James Bay Project in northern Quebec will alter or reverse the flow of 19 major rivers and flood an area the size of Washington State to produce hydropower for consumers in Quebec and the United States, especially in New York State. Phase I of this 50-year project is completed. Phase II is scheduled to begin but is being opposed by the indigenous Cree, whose ancestral hunting grounds would be flooded, and by environmentalists in Canada and the United States.

and much larger phase (Figure 10-10) is scheduled to begin soon but is being opposed in court by the Cree, whose ancestral hunting grounds would be flooded. In 1990 the federal court of Canada ordered a full environmental impact assessment for this project, including public hearings. In the summer of 1992, New York State—under intense pressure from environmentalists—canceled one of its two contracts to buy electricity produced by the James Bay Project. But the battle is not over.

TAPPING GROUNDWATER In the United States 23% of all fresh water used is groundwater. About half of the country's drinking water (96% in rural areas and 20% in urban areas) and 40% of irrigation water are pumped from aquifers.

Overuse of groundwater can cause or intensify several problems (Figure 10-11): *aquifer depletion, subsidence* (sinking of land when groundwater is withdrawn), and *intrusion of salt water into aquifers*. Groundwater can also become contaminated from industrial and agricultural activities, septic tanks, and other sources. Because groundwater is the source of about 40% of the stream flow in the United States, groundwater depletion also robs streams of water.

Currently about one-fourth of the groundwater withdrawn in the United States is not replenished. The most serious overdraft is in parts of the huge Ogallala Aquifer, extending from southern South Dakota to northwestern Texas (Case Study, p. 262). Aquifer depletion is also a serious problem in Saudi Arabia, northern China, Mexico City, Bangkok, and parts of India.

Ways to slow groundwater depletion include (1) controlling population growth, (2) not growing water-thirsty crops in dry areas, (3) developing crop strains that require less water and are more resistant to heat stress, and (4) wasting less irrigation water.

When fresh water is withdrawn from an aquifer near a coast faster than it is recharged, salt water intrudes into the aquifer (Figure 10-12). Saltwater intrusion threatens to contaminate the drinking water of many towns and cities along the Atlantic and Gulf coasts (Figure 10-11) and in the coastal areas of Israel, Syria, and the Arabian Gulf states. Another growing problem in the United States and many other MDCs is groundwater contamination (Section 10–6).

DESALINATION Desalination—the removal of dissolved salts from ocean water or brackish (slightly salty) groundwater—is another way to increase freshwater supplies. Distillation and reverse osmosis are the two most widely used methods. *Distillation* involves heating salt water until it evaporates and condenses as fresh water, leaving salts behind in solid form. In *reverse osmosis* salt water is pumped at high pressure through a thin membrane whose pores allow water molecules—but not dissolved salts—to pass through.

Currently about 7,500 desalination plants in 120 countries provide about 0.1% of the fresh water used by humans. Desalination, however, has a downside. It uses vast amounts of electricity and therefore costs three to five times more than water from conventional sources. Distributing the water from coastal desalination plants costs even more in terms of the energy needed to pump desalinated water uphill and inland. Moreover, desalination produces large quantities of brine, with high levels of salt and other minerals that must go somewhere. Dumping the concentrated brine in the ocean near the plants might seem to be the logical solution, but this would increase the salt concentration and threaten food resources in estuarine waters. And if these wastes were dumped on the land, they could contaminate groundwater and surface water.

Desalination can provide fresh water for coastal cities in arid regions, such as sparsely populated and oil-rich Saudi Arabia, where the cost of getting fresh water by any method is high. However, desalinated water will probably never be cheap enough to use for irrigating conventional crops or to meet much of the

Q: How many cancer deaths in the United States are caused by exposure to pesticide residues in foods?

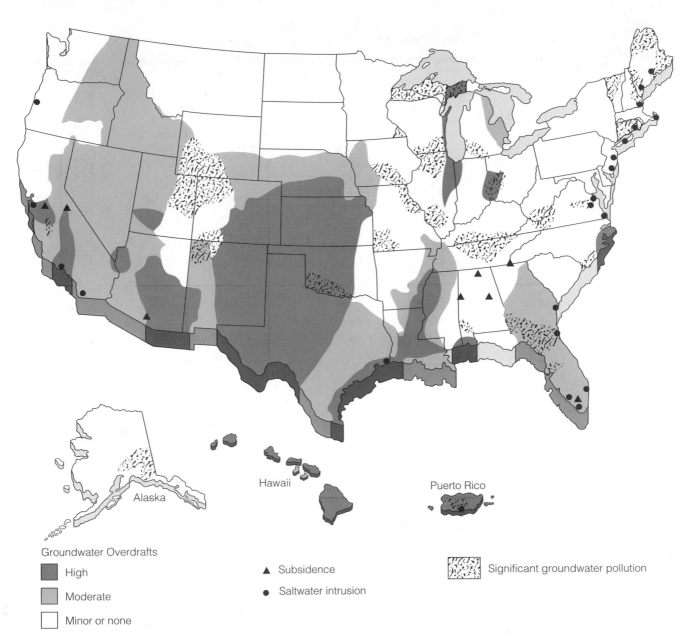

Groundwater Overdrafts

- **High** (dark)
- **Moderate** (gray)
- **Minor or none** (white)

▲ Subsidence

● Saltwater intrusion

▦ Significant groundwater pollution

Hawaii

Puerto Rico

Alaska

Figure 10-11 Areas of greatest aquifer depletion, subsidence, saltwater intrusion, and groundwater contamination in the United States. (Data from U.S. Water Resources Council and U.S. Geological Survey)

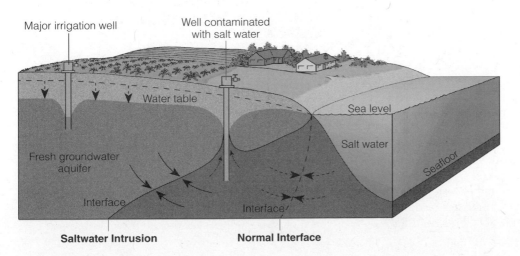

Major irrigation well

Well contaminated with salt water

Water table

Sea level

Salt water

Fresh groundwater aquifer

Seafloor

Interface

Interface

Saltwater Intrusion

Normal Interface

Figure 10-12 Saltwater intrusion along a coastal region. When the water table is lowered, the normal interface between fresh and saline groundwater moves inland (solid line).

A: 4,000–20,000 per year

Mining Water—The Shrinking Ogallala Aquifer

Water pumped from the Ogallala Aquifer (Figure 10-13)—the world's largest known aquifer—has helped transform much of a vast prairie into America's most productive farmland in an area too dry for rainfall farming. Although this aquifer is gigantic, it is essentially a nonrenewable fossil aquifer with an extremely slow recharge rate. Water is being pumped out eight times as fast as natural recharge, mostly for irrigation to supply 15% of the country's corn and wheat, 25% of its cotton, and 40% of its feedlot beef.

The withdrawal rate is 100 times the recharge rate for parts of the aquifer that lie beneath Texas, New Mexico, Oklahoma, and Colorado. At the present rate of withdrawal, water experts project that one-fourth of the aquifer's original supply will be depleted by 2020—much sooner

in areas where it is shallow. Then the area will become a desert. It will take thousands of years to replenish the aquifer. Depletion is encouraged by federal tax laws that allow farmers and ranchers to deduct the cost of drilling equipment and sinking wells.

Long before the water is gone, the high cost of pumping water from a rapidly dropping water table will force many farmers to grow water-miser crops instead of profitable but "thirsty" crops such as cotton and sugar beets. Some farmers will go out of business. If farmers in the Ogallala region con-

serve more water and switch to crops that require less water, depletion of the aquifer could be delayed.

Ogallala Aquifer

Figure 10-13 The Ogallala—the world's largest known aquifer. If the water in this aquifer were above ground, it would be enough to cover the entire lower 48 states with 0.5 meter (1.5 feet) of water. This fossil aquifer, which is renewed very slowly, is being depleted to grow crops and raise cattle.

---

world's demand for fresh water, unless efficient solar-powered methods can be developed.

CLOUD SEEDING AND TOWING ICEBERGS For years several countries, particularly the United States, have been experimenting with seeding clouds with chemicals to produce more rain over dry regions and snow over mountains. Cloud seeding involves injecting a large, suitable cloud with a powdered chemical such as silver iodide from a plane or from ground-mounted burners. Small water droplets in the cloud clump together around tiny particles of the chemical (condensation nuclei) and form drops or ice particles large enough to fall to Earth as precipitation.

Unfortunately, cloud seeding is not useful in very dry areas, where it is most needed, because rain clouds are rarely available. Furthermore, widespread cloud seeding would introduce large amounts of the cloud-seeding chemicals into soil and water systems, possibly harming people, wildlife, and agricultural productivity. A final obstacle to cloud seeding is legal disputes over the ownership of water in clouds. For example, during the 1977 drought in the western United States, the attorney general of Idaho accused officials in neighboring Washington of "cloud rustling" and threatened to file suit in federal court.

There also have been proposals to tow massive icebergs to arid coastal areas (such as Saudi Arabia and southern California) and pump the fresh water from the melting bergs ashore. However, the technology for doing this is not available, and the costs may be too high, especially for water-short LDCs.

10-5 Solutions: Using Water More Efficiently

CURBING WASTE Increasing the water supply in some areas is important, but soaring population, food needs, and industrialization, along with unpredictable shifts in water supplies, will eventually outstrip this approach. It makes much more sense economically and environmentally to use water more efficiently.

Mohamed El-Ashry of the World Resources Institute estimates that *65–70% of the water people use throughout the world is wasted through evaporation, leaks, and other losses.* The United States—the world's largest user of water—does slightly better but still wastes 50% of the water it withdraws. El-Ashry believes that it is

Q: What is the best way to control pests?

Figure 10-14 Major irrigation systems.

Gravity-Flow
(Efficiency 50% – 60%)

Water usually comes from an aqueduct system or a nearby river.

Drip Irrigation
(Efficiency 80% – 90%)

Above- or below-ground pipes or tubes deliver water to individual plant roots.

Center-Pivot
(Efficiency 70% – 80%)

Water usually pumped from underground and sprayed from mobile boom with sprinklers.

economically and technically feasible to reduce water waste to 15%, thus meeting most of the world's water needs for the foreseeable future.

Conserving water would have many other benefits. These include reducing the burden on wastewater plants and septic systems, decreasing pollution of surface water and groundwater, reducing the number of expensive dams and water-transfer projects that destroy wildlife habitats and displace people, slowing depletion of groundwater aquifers, and saving energy and money needed to supply and treat water.

A prime cause of water waste in the United States (and in most countries) is artificially low water prices. Cheap water is the only reason that farmers in Arizona and southern California can grow water-thirsty crops like alfalfa in the middle of the desert. It also enables people in Palm Springs, California, to keep their lawns and 74 golf courses green in a desert area.

Water subsidies are paid for by all taxpayers in higher taxes. Because these external costs don't show up on monthly water bills, consumers have little incentive to use less water or to install water-conserving devices and processes. Raising the price of water to reflect its true cost would be a powerful incentive for using water more efficiently.

The federal Bureau of Reclamation supplies one-fourth of the water used to irrigate land in the western United States under long-term contracts (typically 40 years) at greatly subsidized prices. During the 1990s hundreds of these long-term water contracts will come up for renewal. Sharply raising the price of federally subsidized water would encourage investments in improving water efficiency, and many of the West's water supply problems could be eased.

Another reason for the water waste in the United States is that the responsibility for water resource management in a particular watershed may be divided among many state and local governments, rather than being handled by one authority. For example, the Chicago metropolitan area has 349 water-supply systems, divided among some 2,000 local units of government over a six-county area.

In sharp contrast is the regional approach to water management used in England and Wales. The British Water Act of 1973 replaced more than 1,600 agencies with 10 regional water authorities based on natural watershed boundaries. Each water authority owns, finances, and manages all water supply and waste treatment facilities in its region. The responsibilities of each authority include water pollution control, water-based recreation, land drainage and flood control, inland navigation, and inland fisheries. Each water authority is managed by a group of elected local officials and a smaller number of officials appointed by the national government.

REDUCING IRRIGATION LOSSES Since irrigation accounts for 69% of water use and since almost two-thirds of that water is wasted, more efficient use of even a small amount of irrigation water frees water for other uses.

Most irrigation systems distribute water from a groundwater well or a surface canal by downslope or gravity flow through unlined ditches in cropfields (Figure 10-14). This method is cheap as long as farmers in water-short areas don't have to pay the real cost of making this water available. However, it delivers far more water than needed for crop growth, with only 50–60% of the water reaching crops because of evaporation, deep percolation (seepage), and runoff.

Farmers can prevent seepage by placing plastic, concrete, or tile liners in irrigation canals. Lasers can also be used as a surveying aid to help level fields so that water gets distributed more evenly. Small check dams of earth and stone can capture runoff from hillsides and channel it to fields. Holding ponds can store rainfall or capture irrigation water for recycling to crops. Reforesting watersheds also leads to a more manageable flow of irrigation water, instead of a devastating flood (Figure 10-6 and Connections, p. 256).

Many farmers served by the dwindling Ogallala Aquifer now use center-pivot sprinkler systems (Figure 10-14), with which 70–80% of the water reaches crops. Some farmers are switching to low-energy precision-application (LEPA) sprinklers. These systems bring 75-85% of the water to crops by spraying it closer to the ground and in larger droplets than does the center-pivot system. They also reduce energy use and costs by 20-30%. However, because of the high initial costs, sprinklers are used on only about 1% of the world's irrigated land.

In the 1960s, highly efficient trickle or drip irrigation systems were developed in arid Israel. A network of perforated piping, installed at or below the ground surface, releases a trickle of water close to plant roots (Figure 10-14). This minimizes evaporation and seepage, and brings 80–90% of the water to crops. These systems are expensive to install but are economically feasible for high-profit fruit, vegetable, and orchard crops and for home gardens. They would become cost-effective in most areas if water prices reflected the true cost of this resource.

Irrigation efficiency can also be improved by computer-controlled systems that monitor soil moisture and provide water only when necessary. Farmers can switch to more water-efficient, drought-resistant, and salt-tolerant crop varieties. In addition, farmers can use organic farming techniques, which produce higher crop yields per hectare and require only one-fourth of the water and commercial fertilizer of conventional farming. Since 1950 water-short Israel has used many of these techniques to slash irrigation water waste by about 84%, while irrigating 44% more land. However, as long as irrigation water is cheap and plentiful, farmers have little incentive to invest in water-saving techniques.

As fresh water becomes scarce and cities consume water once used for irrigation, carefully treated urban wastewater, which is rich in nitrate and phosphate plant nutrients—could be used for irrigation. For example, Israel now uses 35% of its municipal waste-water, mostly for irrigation, and plans to reuse 80% of this flow by 2000.

WASTING LESS WATER IN INDUSTRY Manufacturing processes can use recycled water or be redesigned to save water. Japan and Israel lead the world in conserving and recycling water in industry. For example, a paper mill in Hadera, Israel, uses one-tenth as much water as most other paper mills do. Manufacturing aluminum from recycled scrap rather than from virgin ores can reduce water needs by 97%.

In the United States industry is the largest conserver of water. However, the potential for water recycling in U.S. manufacturing has hardly been tapped because the cost of water to many industries is subsidized. A higher, more realistic price would stimulate additional water reuse and conservation in industry.

WASTING LESS WATER IN HOMES AND BUSINESSES Flushing toilets, washing hands, and bathing account for about 78% of the water used in a typical U.S. home. In the arid western United States and in dry Australia, lawn and garden watering can take 80% of a household's daily usage. Much of this water is wasted.

Green lawns in an arid or semiarid area can be replaced with vegetation adapted to a dry climate—a form of landscaping called *xeriscaping,* from the Greek word *xeros*, meaning "dry." A xeriscaped yard typically uses 30–80% less water than a conventional one.

More than half the water supply in Cairo, Lima, Mexico City, and Jakarta disappears before it can be used, mostly from leaks. Leaky pipes, water mains, toilets, bathtubs, and faucets waste 20–35% of water withdrawn from public supplies in the United States.

Many cities offer no incentive to reduce leaks and waste. In New York City, for example, 95% of the residential units don't have water meters. Users are charged flat rates, with the average family paying less than $100 a year for virtually unlimited use of high-quality water. The same is true for one-fifth of all U.S. public water systems. And many apartment dwellers have little incentive to conserve water because their water use is included in their rent.

In Boulder, Colorado, the introduction of water meters reduced water use by more than one-third. Tucson, Arizona, is a desert city that has ordinances that require conserving and reusing water. Tucson now consumes half as much water per capita as Las Vegas, a desert city where water conservation is still voluntary. There are many ways each of us can conserve water (Individuals Matter, at right).

In some parts of the United States systems can be leased that purify and completely recycle wastewater from houses, apartments, or office buildings. Such a

Q: What percentage of the USDA's research and education budget is spent on integrated pest management?

INDIVIDUALS MATTER

- For existing toilets, reduce the amount of water used per flush by putting a tall plastic container weighted with a few stones into each tank, or by buying and inserting a toilet dam.

- Install water-saving toilets that use no more than 6 liters (1.6 gallons) per flush.

- Flush toilets only when necessary. Consider using the advice found on a bathroom wall in a drought-stricken area: "If it's yellow, let it mellow—if it's brown, flush it down."

- Install water-saving showerheads and flow restrictors on all faucets.

- Check frequently for water leaks in toilets and pipes, and repair them promptly. A toilet must be leaking more than 940 liters (250 gallons) per day before you can hear the leak. To test for toilet leaks, add a water-soluble vegetable dye to the water in the tank, but don't flush. If you have a leak, some

color will show up in the bowl's water within a few minutes.

- Don't keep sink water running while brushing teeth, shaving, or washing.

- Try to wash only full loads of clothes, or fill the machine to the lowest possible level.

- When buying a new clothes washer, choose one that uses the least amount of water and fills up to different levels for loads of different sizes. Front-loading models use less water and energy than comparable top-loading models.

- Try to use an automatic dishwasher only for full loads. Also, use the short cycle and let dishes air-dry to save energy and money.

- When washing many dishes by hand, don't let the faucet run. Instead, use one filled dishpan or sink for washing and another for rinsing.

- Keep one or more large bottles of water in the refrigerator rather than

running water from the tap until it gets cold enough for drinking.

- Don't use a garbage disposal system—a large user of water. Instead, compost your food wastes.

- Wash a car from a bucket of soapy water and use the hose only for rinsing. Use a commercial car wash that recycles its water.

- Sweep walks and driveways instead of hosing them off.

- Reduce evaporation losses by watering lawns and gardens in the early morning or evening, rather than in the heat of midday or when windy.

- Use drip irrigation and mulch for gardens and flower beds. Better yet, landscape with native plants adapted to local average annual precipitation so that watering is rarely necessary.

- To irrigate plants, install a system to capture rainwater or collect, filter, and reuse normally wasted gray water from bathtubs, showers, sinks, and the clothes washer.

---

system can be installed in a small outside shed and serviced for a monthly fee about equal to that charged by most city water and sewer systems. In Tokyo all the water used in Mitsubishi's 60-story office building is purified for reuse by an automated recycling system. A New Jersey office complex cut water consumption 62% with an on-site treatment and reuse system.

A California water utility gives rebates for water-saving toilets; it also distributed some 35,000 water-saving showerheads, cutting per capita water use 40% in only one year. In 1988 Massachusetts became the first state to require that all new toilets use no more than 6 liters (1.6 gallons) per flush. Since then 14 other states have followed suit, and most have adopted water-saving standards for new faucets and showerheads.

Gray water from bathtubs, showers, bathroom sinks, and clothes washers can be collected, stored, carefully treated, and reused for irrigation and other purposes. California has become the first state to legalize reuse of gray water to irrigate landscapes. An estimated 50–75% of the water used by a typical house could be reused as gray water.

10-6 Water Pollution Problems

PRINCIPAL WATER POLLUTANTS The eight most common types of water pollutants are:

- *Disease-causing agents.* These include bacteria, viruses, protozoa, and parasitic worms that enter water from domestic sewage and animal wastes. In LDCs they are the biggest cause of sickness and death, prematurely killing an average of 25,000 people each day—half of them children under age 5. A good indicator of the quality of water for drinking or swimming is the number of colonies of *coliform bacteria* present in a 100-milli-liter (0.1-quart) sample of water. The World Health Organization recommends a coliform bacteria count of 0 colonies per 100 milliliters for drinking water, and the EPA recommends a maximum level for swimming water of 200 colonies per 100 milliliters.

- *Oxygen-demanding wastes.* These are organic wastes that can be decomposed by aerobic (oxygen-requiring) bacteria. Large populations of bacteria supported by these wastes can deplete water of dissolved oxygen, causing fish and other forms of oxygen-consuming aquatic life to die. The quantity of oxygen-demanding wastes in water can be determined by measuring the **biological oxygen demand (BOD)**: the amount of dissolved oxygen needed by aerobic decomposers to break down the organic materials in a certain volume of water over a five-day incubation period at 20°C (68°F).

- *Water-soluble inorganic chemicals.* These consist of acids, salts, and compounds of toxic metals such as mercury and lead. High levels of these chemicals can make water unfit to drink. They can also harm fish and other aquatic life, depress crop yields, and accelerate corrosion of equipment that uses water.

- *Inorganic plant nutrients*—water-soluble nitrates and phosphates that can cause excessive growth of algae and other aquatic plants, which then die and decay, depleting water of dissolved oxygen and killing fish. Excessive levels of nitrates in drinking water can reduce the oxygen-carrying capacity of the blood and can kill unborn children and infants, especially those under three months old.

- *Organic chemicals.* These include oil, gasoline, plastics, pesticides, cleaning solvents, detergents, and many other chemicals that threaten human health and harm fish and other aquatic life.

- *Sediment or suspended matter.* These are insoluble particles of soil and other solids that become suspended in water, mostly when soil is eroded from the land. By weight this is by far the biggest water pollutant. It clouds water and reduces photosynthesis. It also disrupts aquatic food webs and carries pesticides, bacteria, and other harmful substances. Sediment that settles out destroys feeding and spawning grounds of fish, and it clogs and fills lakes, artificial reservoirs, stream channels, and harbors.

- *Radioactive isotopes that are water soluble or capable of being biologically amplified to higher concentrations as they pass through food chains and webs.* Ionizing radiation from such isotopes can cause birth defects, cancer, and genetic damage.

- *Heat absorbed by water that is used to cool electric power plants.* The resulting rise in water temperature lowers dissolved oxygen content and makes aquatic organisms more vulnerable to disease, parasites, and toxic chemicals.

Total damage from water pollution in the United States is estimated to cost $20 billion per year.

POINT AND NONPOINT SOURCES **Point sources** discharge pollutants at specific locations through pipes, ditches, or sewers into bodies of surface water. Examples include factories, sewage treatment plants (which remove some but not all pollutants), active and abandoned underground mines, offshore oil wells, and oil tankers. Because point sources are at specific places (mostly in urban areas), they are fairly easy to identify, monitor, and regulate. In MDCs many industrial discharges are strictly controlled, whereas in LDCs such discharges are largely uncontrolled.

Nonpoint sources are sources that cannot be traced to any single discharge. They are usually large, poorly defined areas that pollute water by runoff, subsurface flow, and deposition from the atmosphere. Land examples include runoff of chemicals into surface water, as well as seepage into the ground from croplands, livestock feedlots, logged forests, streets, lawns, septic tanks, construction sites, parking lots, and roadways.

In the United States nonpoint pollution from agriculture—mostly in the form of sediment, inorganic fertilizer, manure, salts dissolved in irrigation water, and pesticides—is responsible for an estimated 64% of the total mass of pollutants entering streams and 57% of those entering lakes. Little progress has been made in the control of nonpoint water pollution because of the difficulty and expense of identifying and controlling discharges from so many diffuse sources.

STREAMS Flowing streams—including large ones called *rivers*—recover rapidly from degradable oxygen-demanding wastes and excess heat by a combination of dilution and bacterial decay. This recovery process works as long as streams are not overloaded with these pollutants and as long as their flow is not reduced by drought, damming, or diversion for agriculture and industry. Slowly degradable and non-degradable pollutants are not eliminated by these natural dilution and degradation processes.

This breakdown of degradable wastes by bacteria depletes dissolved oxygen, which reduces or eliminates populations of organisms with high oxygen requirements, until the stream is cleansed. The depth

Q: Worldwide, how many people die prematurely each year of causes related to smoking?

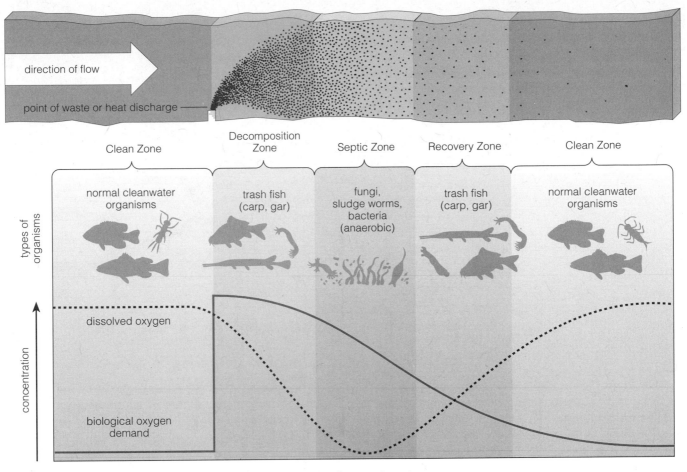

direction of flow

point of waste or heat discharge

Clean Zone · Decomposition Zone · Septic Zone · Recovery Zone · Clean Zone

types of organisms

normal cleanwater organisms

trash fish (carp, gar)

fungi, sludge worms, bacteria (anaerobic)

trash fish (carp, gar)

normal cleanwater organisms

concentration

dissolved oxygen

biological oxygen demand

time or distance downstream

Figure 10-15 The oxygen sag curve versus oxygen demand. Depending on flow rates and the amount of pollutants, streams recover from oxygen-demanding wastes and heat if they are given enough time and are not overloaded.

and width of the resulting *oxygen sag curve* (Figure 10-15) (and thus the time and distance a stream takes to recover) depend on the stream's volume, flow rate, temperature, and pH level (Figure 7-5), and on the volume of incoming degradable wastes. Similar oxygen sag curves can be plotted when heated water from power plants is discharged into streams. The types of pollutants, flow rates, dilution capacity, and recovery time vary widely with different river basins. They also vary in the three major parts of a river as it flows from its headwaters to its wider and deeper middle sections and finally to an ocean or lake (Figure 2-35).

Requiring each city to withdraw its drinking water downstream rather than upstream (as is the current practice) would dramatically improve water quality as the stream flows toward the sea. Each city would be forced to clean up its own waste outputs rather than pass them downstream. However, upstream users, who have the use of fairly clean water without high cleanup costs, fight this pollution prevention approach.

Water pollution control laws that were enacted in the 1970s have greatly increased the number and quality of wastewater treatment plants in the United States and in many other MDCs. Laws have also required industries to reduce or eliminate point source discharges into surface waters. These efforts have enabled the United States to hold the line against increased pollution of most of its streams by disease-causing agents and oxygen-demanding wastes. That is an impressive accomplishment, considering the rise in economic activity and population since the laws were passed.

One success story is the cleanup of Ohio's Cuyahoga River, which was so polluted that in 1969 it caught fire as it flowed through the city of Cleveland. That prompted city and state officials to pass laws limiting the discharge of wastes by industries into the river and sewage systems, as well as laws and funds to upgrade sewage treatment facilities. Today the river has made a comeback and is widely used by boaters and anglers.

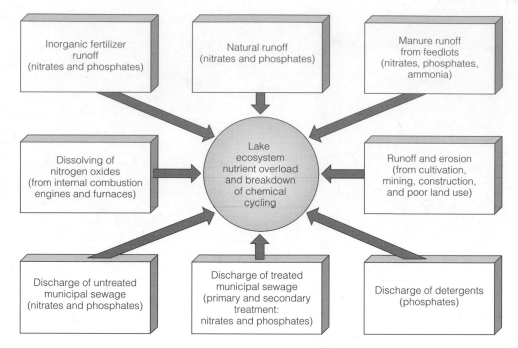

Figure 10-16 Principal sources of nutrient overload, or cultural eutrophication, in lakes, ponds, slow-flowing streams, and estuaries. The amount of nutrients from each source varies, depending on the types of human activities taking place in each airshed and watershed.

However, the truth is that we know relatively little about stream quality because water quality in 64% of U.S. stream length has not been measured. And many existing monitoring stations are not located in places designed to assess the presence or absence of pollutants from their drainage basins. Furthermore, even this limited monitoring does not measure toxics and ecological indicators of water quality.

Available data indicate that pollution of streams from huge discharges of sewage and industrial wastes is a serious and growing problem in most LDCs, where waste treatment is practically nonexistent. Numerous streams in the former USSR and in eastern European countries are severely polluted. Currently more than two-thirds of India's water resources are polluted. Of the 78 streams monitored in China, 54 are seriously polluted. In Latin America and Africa most streams passing through urban or industrial areas are severely polluted.

LAKES In lakes and reservoirs, dilution is often less effective than in streams because these bodies of water frequently contain stratified layers (Figure 2-33) that undergo little vertical mixing. Stratification also reduces levels of dissolved oxygen, especially in the bottom layer. In addition, lakes and reservoirs have little flow, further reducing dilution and replenishment of dissolved oxygen. The flushing and changing of water in lakes and large artificial reservoirs can take from 1 to 100 years, compared with several days to several weeks for streams.

Thus lakes are more vulnerable than streams to contamination by plant nutrients, oil, pesticides, and toxic substances that can destroy bottom life and kill fish. Atmospheric fallout and runoff of acids are serious problems in lakes vulnerable to acid deposition (Figure 9-14). Many toxic chemicals also enter lakes and reservoirs from the atmosphere.

Lakes receive inputs of nutrients and silt from the surrounding land basin as a result of natural erosion and runoff. Some of these lakes become more eutrophic over time (Figure 2-34), but others don't because of differences in the surrounding waterbasin. Near urban or agricultural areas the input of nutrients to a lake can be greatly accelerated by human activities, a process known as **cultural eutrophication**. It is caused mostly by nitrate- and phosphate-containing effluents from sewage treatment plants, runoff of fertilizers and animal wastes, and accelerated erosion of nutrient-rich topsoil (Figure 10-16).

During warm weather this nutrient overload produces dense growths of organisms such as algae, cyanobacteria, water hyacinths, and duckweed. Dissolved oxygen in the surface layer of water near the shore, and in the bottom layer, is depleted when large masses of algae die, fall to the bottom, and are decomposed by aerobic bacteria. This depletion can kill fish and other oxygen-consuming aquatic animals. If excess nutrients continue to flow into a lake, the bottom water becomes foul and almost devoid of animals, as anaerobic bacteria take over and produce smelly decomposition products such as hydrogen sulfide and methane.

About one-third of the 100,000 medium-to-large lakes and about 85% of the large lakes near major population centers in the United States suffer from

Q: How many Americans die because of exposure to other people's smoke (passive smoke)?

The Great Lakes: Pollution and Alien Invaders

CASE STUDY

The five interconnected Great Lakes contain at least 95% of the surface fresh water in the United States and 20% of the world's fresh surface water. The Great Lakes basin is home for about 40 million people, making up about 30% of the Canadian population and 13% of the U.S. population. About 40% of U.S. industry and half of Canadian industry are located in this watershed. Great Lakes tourism generates $16 billion annually, with $4 billion of that from sport fishing.

Despite their enormous size, these lakes are vulnerable to pollution from point and nonpoint sources because less than 1% of the water entering the Great Lakes flows out to the St. Lawrence River each year. In addition to land runoff, these lakes also receive large quantities of acids, pesticides, and other toxic chemicals by deposition from the atmosphere—often blown in from hundreds or thousands of kilometers away.

By the 1960s many areas of the Great Lakes were suffering from severe cultural eutrophication, huge fish kills, and contamination from bacteria and other wastes. The impact on Lake Erie was particular-

ly intense because it is the shallowest of the Great Lakes, it has the smallest volume of water, its drainage basin is heavily industrialized, and it has the largest human population. Many bathing beaches had to be closed, and by 1970 the lake had lost nearly all its native fish.

Since 1972 a $20-billion pollution control program, carried out jointly by Canada and the United States, has significantly decreased levels of phosphates, coliform bacteria, and many toxic industrial chemicals in the Great Lakes. Algal blooms have also decreased, dissolved oxygen levels and sport and commercial fishing have increased, and most swimming beaches have been reopened.

These improvements were brought about mainly by new or upgraded sewage treatment plants and improved treatment of industrial wastes. Also, phosphate detergents, household cleaners, and water conditioners were banned or their phosphate levels were lowered in many areas of the Great Lakes drainage basin.

The most serious pollution problem today is contamination from toxic wastes flowing into the lakes (especially Lake Erie and Lake

Ontario) from land runoff, streams, and atmospheric deposition. Toxic chemicals have contaminated many types of fish caught by anglers and depleted populations of birds, river otters, and other animals feeding on contaminated fish. A survey by Wisconsin biologists revealed that one in four fish taken from the Great Lakes is unsafe for consumption. In 1991 the U.S. government passed a law requiring accelerated cleanup of the lakes, especially of 42 toxic hot spots, and an immediate reduction in emissions of toxic air pollutants in the region. However, meeting these goals may be delayed by lack of federal and state funds.

Environmentalists call for a ban on the use of chlorine as a bleach in the pulp and paper industry around the Great Lakes; a ban on all new incinerators in the area; and an immediate ban on toxic discharge into the lakes of 70 toxic chemicals that threaten human health and wildlife.

Pollution is not the only problem. Since the 1800s the Great Lakes have been invaded by numerous alien species that have sharply reduced populations of commercial and sport fish, and caused other problems. Canals built in the early

(continued)

some degree of cultural eutrophication (Case Study, above). A quarter of China's lakes are classified as eutrophic.

The best solution to cultural eutrophication is to use prevention methods to reduce the flow of nutrients into lakes and reservoirs and pollution cleanup methods to clean up lakes suffering from excessive eutrophication. Major prevention methods include advanced waste treatment (Section 10-7), bans or limits on phosphates in household detergents and other cleaning agents, and soil conservation and land-use control to reduce nutrient runoff. Major cleanup methods are dredging bottom sediments to remove excess nutrient buildup, removing excess weeds, controlling

undesirable plant growth with herbicides and algicides, and pumping air through lakes and reservoirs to avoid oxygen depletion (an expensive and energy-intensive method).

OCEANS The oceans are the ultimate sink for much of the waste matter we produce. This is summarized in the African proverb "Water may flow in a thousand channels, but it all returns to the sea."

Oceans can dilute, disperse, and degrade large amounts of raw sewage, sewage sludge, and oil, and some types of industrial waste, especially in deep-water areas. Marine life has also proved to be more resilient than some scientists had expected, leading

1800s allowed the lakes to be invaded by the sea lamprey, a parasite that attaches itself to the body of soft-skinned fish and sucks out blood and other body fluids. Between the 1920s and the mid-1950s a combination of large populations of sea lampreys and overfishing devastated populations of sport and commercial fish. In 1954 a selective poison was found that could kill the larvae of sea lampreys. By 1962 the poison had caused a sharp drop in sea lamprey populations, and a $10-million-per-year program has kept them under control.

Since the 1980s, however, the sea lamprey has been breeding in large rivers, near the lakes, that are hard to treat with poisons. Unless other control methods are developed, the sea lamprey may again decimate populations of desirable sport and commercial fish in the Great Lakes.

In 1986 larvae of an alien species—the zebra mussel—arrived in water discharged from a European ship near Detroit. With no known natural enemies, these tiny mussels have run amok. They deplete the food supply for other lake species, clog irrigation pipes, shut down water intake systems for power plants and city water supplies, foul beaches, and grow in huge masses on boat hulls, piers, and other surfaces.

These invaders cost the Great Lakes basin at least $500 million per year, and the annual costs could reach $5 billion by 2000. The zebra mussel is expected to spread uncontrollably and dramatically alter most freshwater communities throughout the United States.

There is even worse news. In 1991 another larger and potentially more destructive species—the quagga mussel—invaded the Great Lakes, probably brought in by a Russian freighter. It can survive at greater depths and tolerate more extreme temperatures than the zebra mussel. There is concern that it may eventually colonize areas such as the Chesapeake Bay and waterways in parts of Florida.

---

them to suggest that it is generally safer to dump sewage sludge and most other hazardous wastes into the deep ocean than to bury them on land or burn them in incinerators.

Other scientists dispute this idea, pointing out that we know less about the deep ocean than we do about outer space. They add that dumping waste into the ocean would delay urgently needed pollution prevention and promote further degradation of this vital part of Earth's life-support system. Marine explorer Jacques Cousteau has warned that "the very survival of the human species depends upon the maintenance of an ocean clean and alive, spreading all around the world. The ocean is our planet's life belt."

Coastal areas—especially wetlands and estuaries, mangrove swamps, and coral reefs—bear the brunt of our enormous inputs of wastes into the ocean. This is not surprising because half the world's population lives on the coast and another quarter lives within 80 kilometers (50 miles) of the sea.

The Chesapeake Bay (Figure 10-17) is an example of an estuary in trouble because of human activities. It is the largest estuary in the United States, and one of the world's most productive. It is the largest source of oysters in the United States and the largest producer of blue crab in the world. The bay is also important for shipping, recreational boating, and sport fishing. Between 1940 and 1993 the number of people living in the Chesapeake Bay area grew from 3.7 million to 15 million and by 2000 may reach 18 million.

The estuary receives wastes from point and nonpoint sources scattered throughout a huge drainage basin that includes 9 large rivers and 141 smaller streams and creeks in parts of six states (Figure 10-17). The bay has become a huge pollution sink because it is quite shallow—with an average depth of less than 7 meters (23 feet)—and because only 1% of the waste entering it is flushed into the Atlantic Ocean.

Levels of phosphate and nitrate plant nutrients have risen sharply in many parts of the bay, causing algal blooms and oxygen depletion. Studies have shown that point sources, primarily sewage treatment plants, contribute about 60% by weight of the phosphates. Nonpoint sources, mostly runoff from urban, suburban, and agricultural land and deposition from the atmosphere, are the origin of about 60% by weight of the nitrates.

Air pollutants account for nearly 30% of the nitrogen entering the estuary. In addition, large quantities of pesticides run off cropland and urban lawns; and industries discharge large amounts of toxic wastes, often in violation of their discharge permits. Commer-

Q: What percentage of the 70,000 chemicals in commercial use have been thoroughly screened for toxicity?

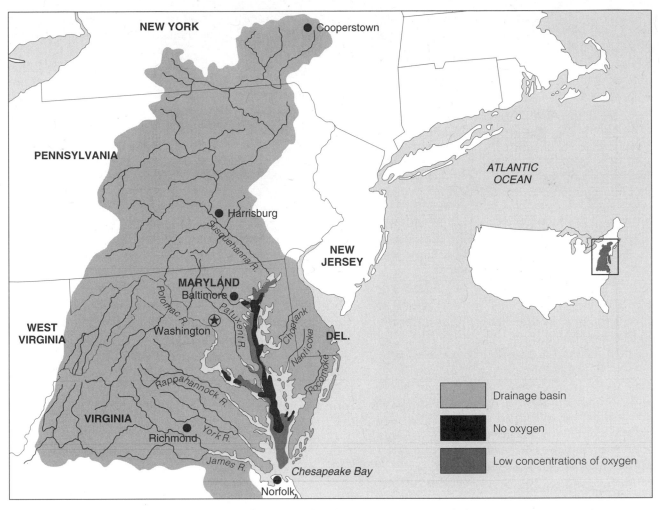

Figure 10-17 Chesapeake Bay. The largest estuary in the United States is severely degraded as a result of water pollution from point and nonpoint sources in six states, as well as from deposition of pollutants from the atmosphere.

cial harvests of oysters, crabs, and several important fish have fallen sharply since 1960 because of a combination of overfishing, pollution, and disease.

Since 1983 more than $700 million in federal and state funds have been spent on a Chesapeake Bay cleanup program that will ultimately cost several billion dollars. Since 1987 nitrogen and phosphorus from nonpoint sources dropped about 7%, but goals for the year 2000 are unlikely to be met. To add to its problems, the bay will soon be invaded by zebra mussels (Case Study, p. 269). Halting the deterioration of this vital estuary will require the prolonged, cooperative efforts of citizens, officials, and industries throughout its entire watershed, with much greater emphasis on pollution prevention.

In most coastal LDCs and in some coastal MDCs, untreated municipal sewage and industrial wastes are often dumped into the sea without treatment. In the United States about 35% of all municipal sewage ends up virtually untreated in marine waters. Most U.S. harbors and bays are badly polluted from municipal sewage, industrial wastes, and oil.

Each year fully one-third of the area of U.S. coastal waters around the lower 48 states are closed to shellfish harvesters because of pollution and habitat disruption. In 1992 there were more than 2,600 beach closings in 22 coastal states, mostly because of bacterial contamination from inadequate and overloaded sewage treatment systems. Many more would be closed if their waters were tested regularly.

Dumping of industrial waste off U.S. coasts has stopped, although it still takes place in a number of MDCs and LDCs. However, barges and ships legally dump large quantities of **dredge spoils** (materials, often laden with toxic metals, scraped from the bottoms of harbors and rivers to maintain shipping channels) off the Atlantic, Pacific, and Gulf coasts at 110 sites.

In addition, many countries, including Great Britain, dump large quantities of **sewage sludge**, a gooey mixture of toxic chemicals, infectious agents, and settled solids removed from wastewater at sewage treatment plants, into the ocean. This practice was banned in the United States as of 1992 by the Ocean Dumping Ban Act of 1988. Some elected officials and scientists oppose this ban, however, arguing that ocean disposal, especially in the deep ocean, is safer and cheaper than land dumping and incineration.

Ships also dump large amounts of their garbage at sea because it is free; the alternative is to pay $500–$1,000 per ship for garbage disposal when they dock. An international ban on such dumping would be hard to enforce. Furthermore, most ship owners would save money by dumping at sea and risking small fines if caught. Each year as many as 2 million seabirds and more than 100,000 marine mammals, including whales, seals, dolphins, sea lions, and sea turtles die when they ingest or become entangled in plastic cups, bags, six-pack yokes, broken sections of fishing nets, ropes, and other debris dumped into the sea and discarded on beaches.

Since 1985 ocean dumping of radioactive waste in the open sea beyond the limits of national jurisdiction has been banned by an international agreement. However, Great Britain and Pakistan dispose of low-level radioactive wastes in coastal areas under their jurisdiction. And in 1992 it was learned that for decades the former Soviet Union had been dumping large quantities of high- and low-level radioactive wastes into the Arctic Ocean and tributaries that flow into this ocean.

Crude petroleum (oil as it comes out of the ground) and *refined petroleum* (fuel oil, gasoline, and other processed petroleum products; Figure 4-25) are accidentally or deliberately released into the environment from a number of sources.

On March 24, 1989, the *Exxon Valdez,* a tanker more than three football fields long, went off course in a 16-kilometer-wide (10-mile) channel in Prince William Sound near Valdez, Alaska, and hit submerged rocks on a reef, creating the worst oil spill ever in U.S. waters. The rapidly spreading oil slick coated more than 1,600 kilometers (1,000 miles) of shoreline, almost the length of the shoreline between New Jersey and South Carolina. The oil killed between 300,000 and 645,000 birds (including 144 bald eagles), up to 5,500 sea otters, 30 seals, 23 whales, and unknown numbers of fish.

This multibillion-dollar accident might have been prevented if Exxon had spent $22.5 million to fit the tanker with a double hull. In the early 1970s then Interior Secretary Rogers Morton told Congress that all oil tankers using Alaskan waters would have double hulls, but under pressure from oil companies the requirement was later dropped. Today, virtually all merchant ships have double hulls—except oil tankers.

A 1992 report by Shell Petroleum indicated that 20% of the world's oil tanker fleet was suitable only for "the scrapyard."

This spill highlighted the importance of pollution prevention. Even with the best technology and fast response by well-trained people, scientists estimate that no more than 10–15% of the oil from a major spill can be recovered.

Tanker accidents and blowouts (oil escaping under high pressure from a borehole in the ocean floor) at offshore drilling rigs get most of the publicity, but more oil is released by normal operation of offshore wells, by washing tankers and releasing the oily water, and from pipeline and storage tank leaks. A 1993 Friends of the Earth study estimated that each year U.S. oil companies unnecessarily spill, leak, or waste oil equal to that held by 1,000 *Exxon Valdez* tankers, or more oil than Australia uses.

Although natural oil seeps also release large amounts of oil into the ocean at some sites, most ocean oil pollution comes from activities on land. Almost half (some experts estimate 90%) of the oil reaching the oceans is waste oil dumped onto the land or into sewers by cities, individuals, and industries. Each year oil equal to 20 times the amount spilled by the tanker *Exxon Valdez* is improperly disposed of by Americans changing their own motor oil.

Research shows that most forms of marine life recover from exposure to large amounts of crude oil within three years. However, recovery from exposure to refined oil, especially in estuaries, may take 10 years or longer. The effects of spills in cold waters (such as Alaska's Prince William Sound and Antarctic waters) and in shallow enclosed gulfs and bays (such as the Persian Gulf) generally last longer.

Oil slicks that wash onto beaches can have a serious economic impact on coastal residents, who lose income from fishing and tourist activities. Oil-polluted beaches washed by strong waves or currents are cleaned up after about a year, but beaches in sheltered areas remain contaminated for several years. Estuaries and salt marshes suffer the most damage and cannot effectively be cleaned up.

GROUNDWATER While highly visible oil spills get lots of media attention, a much greater threat to human health is the out-of-sight pollution of groundwater (Figure 10-2), which is a prime source of water for drinking and irrigation. This vital form of Earth capital is easy to deplete and pollute because it is renewed so slowly. Laws protecting groundwater are weak in the United States and nonexistent in most countries.

When groundwater becomes contaminated, it does not cleanse itself of degradable wastes, as surface water can if it is not overloaded (Figure 10-15). Because groundwater flows are slow and not turbulent, contam-

Q: Worldwide, how many people die from sexually transmitted diseases?

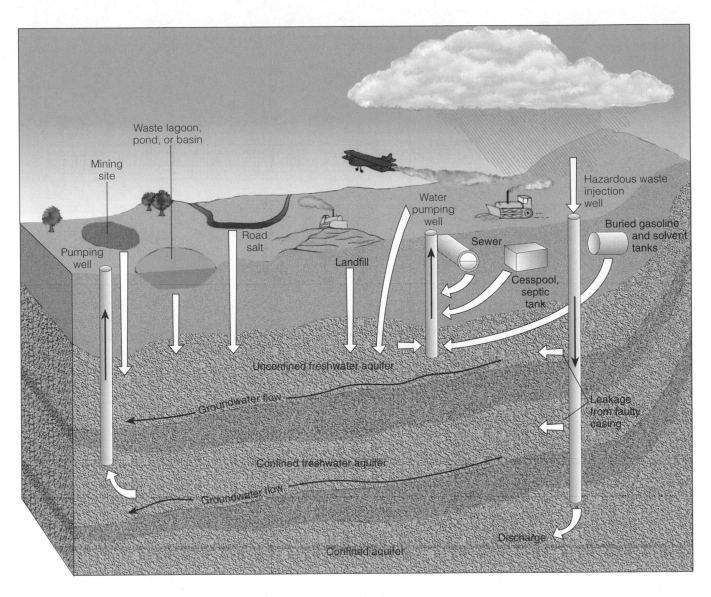

Figure 10-18 Principal sources of groundwater contamination in the United States.

inants are not effectively diluted and dispersed. Also, groundwater has fairly small populations of decomposing bacteria, and its cold temperature slows down decomposition reactions. That means it can take hundreds to thousands of years for contaminated groundwater to cleanse itself of degradable wastes, and nondegradable wastes are there permanently.

Results of limited testing of groundwater in the United States are alarming. In a 1982 survey the EPA found that 45% of the large public water systems served by groundwater were contaminated with synthetic organic chemicals that posed potential health threats. Another EPA survey in 1984 found that two-thirds of the rural household wells tested violated at least one federal health standard for drinking water, usually pesticides or nitrates from fertilizers (which cause a life-threatening blood disorder in infants dur-

ing their first year). The EPA has documented groundwater contamination by 74 pesticides in 38 states.

Crude estimates indicate that while only 2% by volume of all U.S. groundwater is contaminated, up to 25% of usable groundwater is contaminated, and in some areas, as much as 75% is contaminated. In New Jersey, for example, every major aquifer is contaminated. In California pesticides contaminate the drinking water of more than 1 million people. In Florida, where 92% of the residents rely on groundwater for drinking, over 1,000 wells have been closed.

Groundwater can be contaminated from a number of sources, including underground storage tanks, landfills, abandoned hazardous-waste dumps, deep wells used to dispose of liquid hazardous wastes, and industrial-waste storage lagoons located above or near aquifers (Figure 10-18). An EPA survey found that one-third of 26,000 industrial-waste ponds and lagoons have no liners to prevent toxic liquid wastes from seeping into aquifers. One-third of those sites are within 1.6 kilometers (1 mile) of a drinking-water well.

The EPA estimates that at least 1 million underground tanks are leaking their contents into groundwater. A slow gasoline leak of just 4 liters (1 gallon) per day can seriously contaminate the water supply for 50,000 people. Such slow leaks usually remain undetected until someone discovers that a well is contaminated.

Determining the extent of a leak can cost $25,000–$250,000. Cleanup costs from $10,000 for a small spill to $250,000 or more if the chemical reaches an aquifer. Replacing a leaking tank adds on an additional $10,000–$60,000. Legal fees and damages to injured parties can run into the millions. Stricter regulations should reduce leaks from new tanks, but they do little for the millions of older tanks that are "toxic time bombs." Some analysts call for above-ground storage of hazardous liquids so that leaks can be easily detected and collected.

10-7 Solutions: Preventing and Controlling Water Pollution

NONPOINT-SOURCE POLLUTION The leading nonpoint source of water pollution is agriculture (Section 7-4). Farmers can sharply reduce fertilizer runoff into surface waters and leaching into aquifers by not using excessive amounts of fertilizer and by using none on steeply sloped land. They can use slow-release fertilizers and alternate their plantings between row crops and soybeans or other nitrogen-fixing plants to reduce the need for fertilizer. Farmers can also be required to plant buffer zones of permanent vegetation between cultivated fields and nearby surface water.

Farmers can also reduce pesticide runoff and leaching by applying pesticides only when needed. They can reduce the need for pesticides by using biological pest control or integrated pest management (Section 7-6). Nonfarm uses of inorganic fertilizers and pesticides—on golf courses, yards, and public lands, for example—could also be sharply reduced.

Livestock growers can control runoff and infiltration of manure from feedlots and barnyards by managing animal density, planting buffers, and not locating feedlots on land that slopes toward nearby surface water. Diverting the runoff into detention basins would allow this nutrient-rich water to be pumped and applied as fertilizer to cropland or forestland.

Critical watersheds should also be reforested. Besides reducing water pollution from sediment, reforestation would reduce soil erosion and the severity of flooding (Connections, p. 256) and help slow projected global warming (Section 9-2) and loss of Earth's vital biodiversity (Chapters 5 and 6).

POINT-SOURCE POLLUTION In many LDCs and in some MDCs, sewage and waterborne industrial wastes are discharged without treatment into the nearest waterway or into wastewater lagoons. In Latin America less than 2% of urban sewage is treated. Only 15% of the urban wastewater in China receives treatment. Treatment facilities in India cover less than a third of the urban population.

In MDCs most wastes from point sources are purified to varying degrees. The Federal Water Pollution Control Act of 1972, renamed the Clean Water Act of 1977 when it was amended (along with amendments in 1981 and 1987), and the 1987 Water Quality Act form the basis of U.S. efforts to control pollution of the country's surface waters. The goal of these laws is to make all U.S. surface waters safe for fishing and swimming. Since 1972 U.S. taxpayers and the private sector have spent more than $541 billion on water pollution control—nearly all of it on end-of-pipe controls on municipal and industrial discharges from point sources mandated by these laws.

These acts require the EPA to establish *national effluent standards* and to set up a nationwide system for monitoring water quality. The effluent standards limit the amounts of certain conventional and toxic water pollutants that can be discharged into surface waters from factories, sewage treatment plants, and other point sources. Each point-source discharger must get a permit specifying the amount of each pollutant that a facility can discharge.

In rural and suburban areas with suitable soils, sewage from each house is usually discharged into a **septic tank** (Figure 10-19). About 25% of all homes in the United States are served by septic tanks.

In urban areas, most waterborne wastes from homes, businesses, factories, and storm runoff flow through a network of sewer pipes to wastewater treatment plants. Some cities have separate lines for stormwater runoff, but in 1,200 U.S. cities the lines for these two systems are combined because it is cheaper. When rains cause combined sewer systems to overflow, they discharge untreated sewage directly into surface waters.

When sewage reaches a treatment plant, it can undergo up to three levels of purification, depending on the type of plant and the degree of purity desired. **Primary sewage treatment** is a mechanical process that uses screens to filter out debris such as sticks,

Q: How many people are expected to have full-blown AIDS by 2000?

stones, and rags. Then suspended solids settle out as sludge in a settling tank (Figure 10-20).

Secondary sewage treatment is a biological process in which aerobic bacteria are used to remove up to 90% of biodegradable, oxygen-demanding organic wastes (Figure 10-20). Some plants use *trickling filters,* in which aerobic bacteria degrade sewage as it

seeps through a bed of crushed stones covered with bacteria and protozoa. Others use an *activated sludge process,* in which the sewage is pumped into a large tank and mixed for several hours with bacteria-rich sludge and air bubbles to increase degradation by microorganisms. The water then goes to a sedimentation tank, where most of the suspended solids and

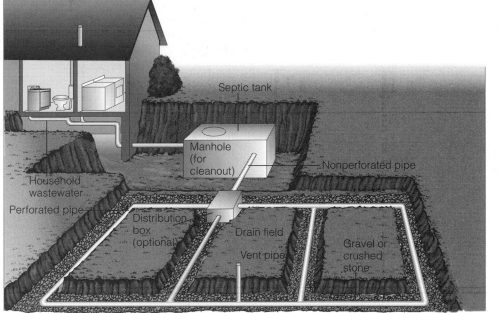

Figure 10-19 Septic tank system used for disposal of domestic sewage and wastewater in rural and suburban areas. This system traps greases and large solids and then discharges the remaining wastes over a large drainage field. As these wastes percolate downward, the soil filters out some potential pollutants, and soil bacteria decompose biodegradable materials. To be effective, septic tank systems must be properly installed in soils with adequate drainage, not placed too close together or too near well sites, and pumped out when the settling tank becomes full.

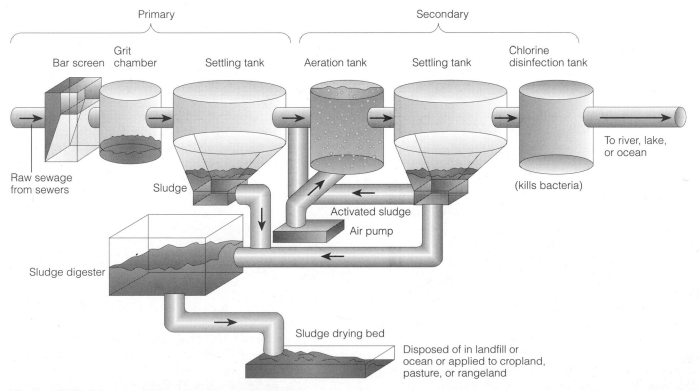

Figure 10-20 Primary and secondary sewage treatment.

microorganisms settle out as sludge. The sludge produced from either primary or secondary treatment is broken down in an anaerobic digester and incinerated, dumped in the ocean or a landfill, or applied to land as fertilizer. After secondary treatment, however, wastewater still contains about 3–5% by weight of the oxygen-demanding wastes, 3% of the suspended solids, 50% of the nitrogen (mostly as nitrates), 70% of the phosphorus (mostly as phosphates), and 30% of most toxic metal compounds and synthetic organic chemicals. Virtually none of any long-lived radioactive isotopes and persistent organic substances such as pesticides is removed.

As a result of the Clean Water Act most U.S. cities have secondary sewage treatment plants. In 1989, however, the EPA found that more than 66% of sewage treatment plants have water quality or public-health problems, and studies by the General Accounting Office have shown that most industries sometimes violate regulations. Also, 500 cities have failed to meet federal standards for sewage treatment plants, and 34 East Coast cities simply screen out large floating objects from their sewage before discharging it into coastal waters.

Advanced sewage treatment is a series of specialized chemical and physical processes that remove specific pollutants left in the water after primary and secondary treatment. Types of advanced treatment vary depending on the specific contaminants to be removed. Without advanced treatment, sewage treatment plant effluents contain enough nitrates and phosphates to contribute to accelerated eutrophication of lakes, slow-moving streams, and coastal waters (Figure 10-16). Advanced treatment is rarely used because the plants cost twice as much to build and four times as much to operate as secondary plants. However, despite the cost it is used for more than a third of the population in Finland, the former West Germany, Switzerland, and Sweden, and to a lesser degree in Denmark and Norway.

Before water is discharged after primary, secondary, or advanced (tertiary) treatment, it is bleached to remove water coloration and disinfected to kill disease-carrying bacteria and some, but not all, viruses. The usual method for doing this is *chlorination*. However, chlorine reacts with organic materials in water to form small amounts of chlorinated hydrocarbons, some of which cause cancers in test animals. Disinfectants such as ozone and ultraviolet light are being used in some places, but they cost more than chlorination.

Sewage treatment produces a toxic gooey sludge that must be disposed of or recycled as fertilizer to the land. About 54% by weight of all municipal sludge produced in the United States is applied to farmland, forests, highway medians, and degraded land as fertilizer, and 9% is composted. The rest is dumped in conventional landfills (where it can contaminate groundwater) or incinerated (which can pollute the air with traces of toxic chemicals, and the resulting toxic ash is usually buried in a landfill that will eventually leak).

Experiments show that the sludge can provide all the nitrogen and phosphorus needed to grow corn at about one-fourth the cost of using commercial inorganic fertilizer. Before it is applied to land, sewage sludge can be heated to kill harmful bacteria, as is done in Switzerland and parts of Germany; it can also be treated to remove toxic metals and organic chemicals before application, but that can be expensive. The best and cheapest solution is to prevent these toxics from reaching sewage treatment plants. However, untreated sludge can be applied to land not used for crops or livestock. Examples include forests, surface-mined land, golf courses, cemeteries, and highway medians.

It is encouraging that some communities and individuals are seeking better ways to purify contaminated water by working with nature (Solutions, p. 277).

IS YOUR WATER SAFE TO DRINK? Treatment of water for drinking by urban residents is much like wastewater treatment. Areas depending on surface water usually store it in a reservoir for several days to improve clarity and taste by allowing the dissolved oxygen content to increase and suspended matter to settle out.

The water is then pumped to a purification plant, where it is treated to meet government drinking-water standards. Usually, it is run through sand filters, then through activated charcoal, and then disinfected. In areas with very pure sources of groundwater, little, if any, treatment is necessary.

Only about 54 countries, most of them in North America and Europe, have safe drinking water. The Safe Drinking Water Act of 1974 requires the EPA to establish national drinking-water standards, called *maximum contaminant levels*, for any pollutants that "may" have adverse effects on human health. This act has helped improve drinking water in much of the United States, but there is still a long way to go. At least 700 potential pollutants are found in municipal drinking water supplies. Of the ones that have been tested, 97 cause cancers, 82 cause mutations, 28 are toxic, and 23 promote tumors in test animals.

Privately owned wells in suburban and rural areas are not required to meet federal drinking water standards. The biggest reasons are the cost of testing each well regularly (at least $1,000) and ideological opposition to mandatory testing and compliance by some home owners.

A survey by the National Wildlife Federation found that only 2% of the roughly 100,000 violations

Learning Nature's Ways to Purify Sewage

SOLUTIONS

Natural wetlands have a great—but not unlimited—capacity to cleanse. They can be used to treat urban sewage, but many have been overwhelmed by pollution or destroyed by development. An exciting low-tech, low-cost alternative to expensive waste treatment plants is to create an artificial wetland, as the residents of Arcata, California, did.

In this coastal town of 15,000, some 63 hectares (155 acres) of wetlands have been created on land that was once a dump between the town and the adjacent Humboldt Bay. The project was completed in 1974 for $3 million less than the estimated cost of a conventional treatment plant.

Here's how it works. First, sewage is held in sedimentation tanks where the solids settle out. This resulting sludge is removed and processed for use as fertilizer. The liquid is pumped into oxidation ponds, where the wastes are broken down by bacteria. After a month or so the water is released into the artificial marshes, where it is further filtered and cleansed by plants and bacteria. Although the water is clean enough to discharge directly into

the bay, state law requires that it first be chlorinated. So the town chlorinates the water and then dechlorinates it before sending it into the bay, where oyster beds thrive. Some water from the marshes is piped into the city's salmon hatchery.

The marshes and lagoons are an Audubon Society bird sanctuary and provide habitats for thousands of seabirds and marine animals. The treatment center is a city park and attracts many tourists. The town even celebrates its natural sewage-treatment system with an annual "Flush with Pride" festival. Over 150 cities and towns in the United States now use natural and artificial wetlands for treating sewage.

Can you use natural processes for treating wastewater if there isn't a wetland available or enough land to build one? According to ecologist John Todd you can—just set up a greenhouse lagoon and use sunshine the way nature does. The process begins when sewage flows into a greenhouse containing rows of large aquarium tanks covered with plants such as water hyacinths, cattails, and bulrushes. In these tanks algae and microorgan-

isms decompose wastes into nutrients absorbed by the plants. The decomposition is speeded up by sunlight streaming into the greenhouse, and toxic metals are absorbed into the tissues of trees to be transplanted outside. Then the water passes through an artificial marsh of sand, gravel, and bulrush plants that filters out algae and organic waste. Next the water flows into aquarium tanks where snails and zooplankton consume microorganisms and are themselves consumed by crayfish, tilapia, and other fish that can be eaten or sold as bait. After 10 days the now-clear water flows into a second artificial marsh for final filtering and cleansing. When working properly, such solar-aquatic treatment systems have produced water fit for drinking.

These natural alternatives to building expensive treatment plants may not solve the waste problems of large cities. But they can help and are an attractive alternative for small towns, the edges of urban areas, and rural areas.

---

of federal drinking water standards and of water-testing-and-reporting requirements (which affected 40 million people) were subject to enforcement action and fines. In 94% of the cases, people were not notified when their drinking water either was contaminated or had not been adequately tested. More money is spent on military bands each year than on the EPA's enforcement of the Safe Drinking Water Act.

Contaminated wells and concern about possible contamination of public drinking water supplies have created a boom in the number of Americans drinking bottled water at costs about 1,500 times more than that of tap water or adding water purification devices to their home systems. This has created enormous profits for both legitimate companies and con artists in these businesses. Many bottled-water drinkers are getting

ripped off. More than one-third of the bottled water comes from the same sources used to supply tap water, which is regulated much more strictly than bottled water.

To be safe, consumers should purchase bottled water only from companies that have their water frequently tested and certified, ideally by EPA-certified laboratories. Before buying bottled water the consumer should determine whether the bottler belongs to the International Bottled Water Association (IBWA) and adheres to its testing requirements. The IBWA requires its members to test for 181 contaminants, and it sends an inspector from the National Sanitation Foundation, a private lab, to bottling plants annually to check all pertinent records and make sure the plant is run cleanly.

PROTECTING COASTAL WATERS The most important suggestions for preventing excessive pollution of coastal waters and for cleaning them up include the following:

Prevention

- *Greatly reducing the discharge of toxic pollutants into coastal waters from both industrial facilities and municipal sewage treatment plants.*

- *Greatly reducing all discharges of raw sewage from sewer-line overflows by requiring separate storm and sewer lines in cities.*

- *Banning all ocean dumping of sewage sludge and hazardous dredged materials.*

- *Enacting and enforcing laws and land-use practices that sharply reduce runoff from nonpoint sources in coastal areas.*

- *Protecting sensitive marine areas from all development by designating them as ocean sanctuaries.*

- *Regulating coastal development to minimize its environmental impact, and eliminating subsidies and tax incentives that encourage harmful coastal development.*

- *Instituting a national energy policy based on energy efficiency and renewable energy resources to reduce dependence on oil (Chapter 4).*

- *Prohibiting oil drilling in ecologically sensitive offshore and near-shore areas.*

- *Collecting used oils and greases from service stations and other sources, and reprocessing them for reuse. Currently more than 90% of the used oil collected for "recycling" is burned as fuel, releasing lead, chromium, arsenic, and other pollutants into the atmosphere.*

- *Requiring all existing oil tankers to have double hulls, double bottoms, or other oil-spill prevention measures by 1998.*

- *Greatly increasing the financial liability of oil companies for cleaning up oil spills, thus encouraging pollution prevention.*

- *Routing oil tankers as far as possible from sensitive coastal areas.*

- *Having Coast Guard vessels guide tankers out of all harbors and enclosed sounds and bays.*

- *Banning the rinsing of empty oil tanker holds and the dumping of oily ballast water into the sea.*

- *Banning discharge of garbage from vessels into the sea, and levying large fines on violators.*

- *Adopting a nationwide tracking program to ensure that medical waste is safely disposed of.*

Cleanup

- *Greatly improving oil-spill cleanup capabilities. However, according to a 1990 report by the Office of Technology Assessment, there is little chance that large spills can be effectively contained or cleaned up.*

- *Upgrading all coastal sewage treatment plants to at least secondary treatment, or developing alternative methods for sewage treatment (Solutions, p. 277).*

PROTECTING GROUNDWATER Pumping polluted groundwater to the surface, cleaning it up, and returning it to the aquifer is usually prohibitively expensive—$5–$10 million or more per aquifer. Recent attempts to pump and treat contaminated aquifers show that it may take decades, even hundreds of years, of pumping before all of the contamination is forced to the surface. Thus preventing contamination is the only effective way to protect groundwater resources. Water pollution experts suggest that this could be done by:

- *Banning virtually all disposal of hazardous wastes in sanitary landfills and deep injection wells (Figure 10-18)*

- *Monitoring aquifers near existing sanitary and hazardous-waste landfills, underground tanks, and other potential sources of groundwater contamination (Figure 10-18)*

- *Controlling application of pesticides and fertilizers by farmers and home owners much more strictly*

- *Requiring that people who use private wells for drinking water have their water tested once a year*

- *Establishing pollution standards for groundwater*

- *Emphasizing aboveground storage of hazardous liquids—an in-sight-in-mind approach that allows rapid detection and collection of leaks*

SUSTAINABLE WATER USE Sustainable use of Earth's water resources involves developing an integrated approach to managing water resources and water pollution throughout each watershed. It also means reducing or eliminating water subsidies so that its market price more closely reflects water's true cost.

Once we stop overloading aquatic systems with pollutants, they recover amazingly fast. Doing this requires that we shift from pollution cleanup to pollution prevention. To make such a shift we must truly accept that the environment—air, water, soil, life—is an interconnected whole. Without an integrated approach to all forms of pollution, we will continue to shift environmental problems from one part of the

Q: Worldwide, how many people have malaria?

INDIVIDUALS MATTER

- *Use manure or compost instead of commercial inorganic fertilizers on garden and yard plants.*
- *Use biological methods or integrated pest management instead of commercial pesticides to control garden, yard, and household pests (Section 7-6).*
- *Use low-phosphate, phosphate-free, or biodegradable dishwashing liquid, laundry detergent, and shampoo.*
- *Don't use water fresheners in toilets.*
- *Use less harmful substances instead of commercial chemicals for most household cleaners (Table 11-2).*

- *Don't pour pesticides, paints, solvents, oil, or other products containing harmful chemicals down the drain or on the ground. Contact your local health department about disposal.*
- *If you get water from a private well or suspect that municipal water is contaminated, have it tested by an EPA-certified laboratory for lead, nitrates, trihalomethanes, radon, volatile organic compounds, and pesticides.*
- *Run water from taps for several minutes every morning before using the water for drinking or cooking. The water can be collected and used to water plants.*

- *If you have a septic tank, have it cleaned out every three to five years by a reputable contractor so that it won't contribute to groundwater pollution.*
- *Get to know your local bodies of water and form community watchdog groups to help monitor, protect, and restore them.*
- *Support efforts to clean up riverfronts and harbors.*

environment to another. Each of us has a role to play in reducing water waste (Individuals Matter, p. 265) and pollution (Individuals Matter, above).

It is not until the well runs dry, that we know the worth of water.

BENJAMIN FRANKLIN

CRITICAL THINKING

1. How do human activities increase the harmful effects of prolonged drought? How can these effects be reduced?

2. How do human activities contribute to flooding? How can these effects be reduced?

3. Should water's prices for all uses in the United States be raised sharply to encourage water conservation? Explain. What effects might this have on the economy, on you, on the poor, and on the environment?

4. List 10 major ways to conserve water on a personal level. Which, if any, of these practices do you now use or intend to use?

5. Why is dilution not always the solution to water pollution? Give examples and conditions for which this solution is, and is not, applicable.

6. How can a stream cleanse itself of oxygen-demanding wastes? Under what conditions will this natural cleansing system fail?

7. Should all dumping of wastes in the ocean be banned? Explain. If so, where would you put the wastes instead? What exceptions would you permit, and why?

8. Should the injection of hazardous wastes into deep-underground wells be banned? Explain. What would you do with these wastes?

11 Wastes and Resource Conservation

11-1 Wasting Resources: Solid Waste and the Throwaway Approach

SOURCES OF SOLID WASTE With only 4.7% of the world's population, the United States produces 33% of the **solid waste**: any unwanted or discarded material that is not a liquid or a gas. The United States—the world's most material nation—generates about 10 billion metric tons (11 billion tons) of solid waste per year—an average of 40 metric tons (44 tons) per person. While garbage produced directly by households and businesses is a significant problem, about 98.5% of the solid waste in the United States comes from mining, oil and natural gas production, agriculture, and industrial activities (Figure 11-1). Although individuals don't generate this waste directly, they are responsible indirectly through the products they consume.

Most mining waste is left piled near mine sites and can pollute the air, surface water, and groundwater. Although mining waste is the single largest category of U.S. solid waste, the EPA has done little to regulate its disposal, mostly because Congress has specifically exempted mining wastes from regulation as a hazardous waste. In LDCs there is even less regulation of mining procedures and wastes.

Most industrial solid waste—such as scrap metal, plastics, paper, fly ash removed by air pollution control equipment (Figure 9-19) in industrial and electrical power plants, and sludge from industrial waste treatment plants—is buried or incinerated at the plant site where it was produced.

The remaining 1.5% of solid waste produced in the United States is **municipal solid waste** from homes and businesses in or near urban areas. The estimated 178 million metric tons (196 million tons) of municipal solid waste—often referred to as garbage—produced in the United States in 1993 would fill a bumper-to-bumper convoy of garbage trucks encircling the earth almost six times. This amounts to 700 kilograms (1,540 pounds) per person annually—two to three times that in most other MDCs (except Canada) and many times that in LDCs. About 17% of these potentially usable resources is recycled or composted. The other 83% is hauled away and dumped (66%) or burned (17%) at a cost of about $30 billion per year (projected to rise to $75 billion by 2000).

Litter is also a source of solid waste. For example, helium-filled balloons are often released into the atmosphere at ball games and parties. When the helium escapes or the balloons burst, they become litter. Fish, turtles, seals, whales, and other aquatic animals die when they ingest balloons that fall into oceans and lakes. This practice also implies that it is acceptable to litter, waste helium (a scarce resource) and energy (used to separate helium from air), and kill wildlife (even if we switched to balloons that biodegraded within six weeks).

WHAT IT MEANS TO LIVE IN A THROWAWAY SOCIETY U.S. consumers throw away:

- Enough aluminum to rebuild the country's entire commercial airline fleet every three months

- Enough glass bottles to fill the two 412-meter-high (1,350-foot) towers of the New York World Trade Center every two weeks

- Enough tires each year to encircle the earth almost three times

- Enough disposable plates and cups each year to serve everyone in the world six meals

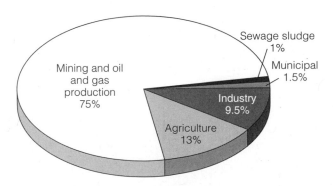

Figure 11-1 Sources of the 10 billion metric tons (11 billion tons) of solid waste produced each year in the United States. Some 65 times as much solid waste is produced by mining and industrial activities as by household garbage. (Data from Environmental Protection Agency and U.S. Bureau of Mines)

Q: How many people die from malaria each year?

Solid wastes are only raw materials we're too stupid to use.

ARTHUR C. CLARKE

- About 2 billion disposable razors, 1.6 billion throwaway ballpoint pens, and 500 million disposable cigarette lighters each year

- About 2.5 million nonreturnable plastic bottles each hour

- Some 14 billion catalogs plus 38 billion pieces of junk mail per year

And this is only part of the 1.5% of solid waste labeled as municipal in Figure 11-1.

 ## 11-2 Solutions: Reducing and Reusing Solid Waste

WHAT ARE OUR OPTIONS? There are two ways to deal with the mountains of solid waste we produce: *waste management* and *pollution (waste) prevention.* Waste management is a *throwaway* or *high-waste approach* that encourages waste production from resource use (Figures 1-9 and 2-42) and then attempts to manage the wastes in ways that will reduce environmental harm—mostly by burying them or burning them.

Sooner or later, however, even the best-designed waste incinerators release some toxic substances into the atmosphere and leave a toxic residue that must be disposed of—usually in landfill. Furthermore, even the best-designed landfills eventually leak wastes into groundwater. And eventually we run out of affordable or politically acceptable sites for landfills and incinerators.

The basic problem is that modern economic systems reward those who produce waste instead of those who try to use resources more efficiently. We give timber, mining, and energy companies tax write-offs and other subsidies to cut trees and to find and mine copper, oil, coal, and uranium. At the same time we seldom subsidize companies and businesses that recycle copper or paper, use oil or coal more efficiently, or develop renewable alternatives to fossil fuels. That tilts the economic playing field against waste prevention and in favor of waste production.

Preventing pollution and waste is a *low-waste approach* that views solid wastes as resources or wasted solids that we should be recycling, reusing, or not using in the first place (Figures 2-43 and 11-2). The low-waste approach involves teaching people to see trash cans and dumpsters as resource containers, and

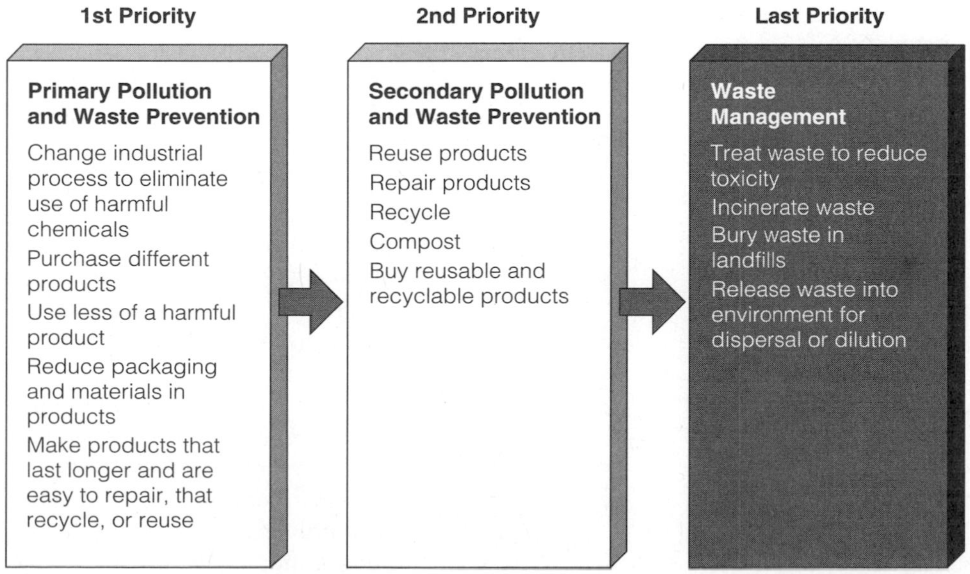

1st Priority	2nd Priority	Last Priority
Primary Pollution and Waste Prevention Change industrial process to eliminate use of harmful chemicals Purchase different products Use less of a harmful product Reduce packaging and materials in products Make products that last longer and are easy to repair, that recycle, or reuse	**Secondary Pollution and Waste Prevention** Reuse products Repair products Recycle Compost Buy reusable and recyclable products	**Waste Management** Treat waste to reduce toxicity Incinerate waste Bury waste in landfills Release waste into environment for dispersal or dilution

Figure 11-2 Priorities proposed by the National Academy of Sciences for dealing with material use and waste. So far these priorities are not being followed, with most efforts devoted to waste management (bury or burn).

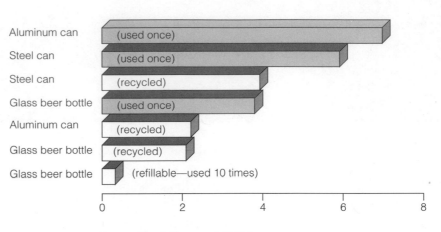

Figure 11-3 Energy used to make a 400-milliliter (12-fluid ounce) beverage container. (Data from Argonne National Laboratory)

Aluminum can (used once)
Steel can (used once)
Steel can (recycled)
Glass beer bottle (used once)
Aluminum can (recycled)
Glass beer bottle (recycled)
Glass beer bottle (refillable—used 10 times)

Energy Used (thousand BTUs)

trash as concentrated urban ore that needs to be mined for useful materials for recycling. With this approach, the economic system is used to discourage waste production and encourage waste prevention.

This prevention approach has a hierarchy of goals: **(1)** *Reduce* waste and pollution by preventing its creation; **(2)** *Reuse* as many things as possible; **(3)** *Recycle and compost* as much waste as possible; **(4)** *Incinerate or treat* waste that can't be reduced, reused, recycled, or composted; and **(5)** *Bury* what is left in state-of-the-art landfills after the first four goals have been met.

REDUCING WASTE AND POLLUTION Cutting waste and preventing pollution generally save more energy and virgin resources than recycling does, and they reduce the environmental impacts of extracting, processing, and using resources (Figure 1-9). Ways to reduce waste include:

- *Using less material per product* (lighter cars, for example).

- *Redesigning manufacturing processes to use fewer resources and produce less waste.*

- *Making products that last longer and that are easy to repair, reuse, or recycle.* Several European auto manufacturers, for example, are designing their cars for easy disassembly, reuse, and recycling of various parts, and they are trying to minimize the use of nonrecyclable or hazardous materials.

- *Cutting down on unnecessary packaging.* In the United States, packaging accounts for 50% of all paper produced, 90% of all glass, 11% of all aluminum, and 3% of all energy used. Packaging makes up about 50% by volume and 30% by weight of municipal solid waste. Nearly $1 of every $10 spent for food in the United States goes for throwaway packaging. Some U.S. manufacturers have reduced the weight of some of their packag-

ing bottles and cartons by 10–30%, but much more needs to be done.

- *Asking yourself whether you really need a particular item.*

In 1991 Germany enacted the world's toughest packaging law, designed to reduce the amount of waste being landfilled or incinerated. The goal is to recycle or reuse 65% of the nation's packaging by 1995, including 90% of metals and glass, and 80% of paper, board, and plastics. Product distributors must take back their boxes and other containers for reuse or recycling. And incineration of packaging, even if it is used to generate power, is not allowed.

REUSE: THE NEXT BEST CHOICE Reuse extends resource supplies and reduces energy use and pollution even more than recycling. A popular bumper sticker reads: "Recyclers do it more than once." A better version might be, "Recyclers do it more than once, but reusers do it the most."

One example is the refillable glass beverage bottle, which can be used 50 times or more and is the most energy-efficient beverage container on the market (Figure 11-3). Collected and filled at local bottling plants, they reduce transportation and energy costs, create local jobs, and keep more of the money people spend circulating in the local economy. Moreover, studies by Coca-Cola and PepsiCo of Canada show that 0.5-liter (16-ounce) bottles of their soft drinks cost one-third less in refillable bottles.

In 1964, 87% of beer and soda containers in the United States were refillable glass bottles, but since then most local bottling companies have been bought up or driven out of business by aluminum and large soft-drink companies, which replace the reusable bottles with throwaway aluminum cans and plastic bottles. Refillable glass bottles now make up only 11% of

Q: Are the widely used GNP and GNP per capita indicators of economic growth useful indicators of changes in life quality?

the market, and only 10 states even have returnable bottles.

Denmark has led the way by banning all beverage containers that can't be reused. To encourage use of refillable glass bottles, Ecuador has a beverage container deposit fee that is 50% higher than the cost of the drink. This has been so successful that bottles as old as 10 years continue to circulate. Sorting is not a problem because only two sizes of glass bottles are allowed. In Finland 95% of the soft drink, beer, wine, and spirits containers are refillable, and in Germany 73% are refillable.

Another reusable container is the metal or plastic lunch box that most workers and schoolchildren once used. Today many people carry their lunches in throwaway paper or plastic bags. At work people can have their own reusable glasses, cups, dishes, utensils, cloth napkins, and towels, and they can use washable cloth handkerchiefs instead of throwaway paper tissues. In Germany, outdoor festivals increasingly use washable plates, glasses, and cutlery. Plastic containers with tops are reusable for lunch items and refrigerator leftovers. They can be used in place of throwaway plastic wrap and aluminum foil (most of which is not recycled). This and most forms of reuse also save money.

Also reusable are plastic or metal garbage cans and wastebaskets, which might better be called *resource containers*. Using these containers to separate wastes for recycling and rinsing them out as needed would eliminate the need for throwaway plastic liner bags, which waste oil (because they are made from petrochemicals) and contribute to the solid waste problem and the throwaway mentality.

You've just paid for your groceries and you're offered a choice between plastic or paper bags. Which do you choose?

The answer is neither. Both are environmentally harmful, and the question of which is the more damaging has no clear-cut answer. On the one hand, plastic bags are made from nonrenewable fossil fuels, degrade slowly in landfills, and can harm wildlife if swallowed; and producing them pollutes the environment.

On the other hand, the brown paper bags in most supermarkets are made from virgin paper. Even those that supposedly contain some recycled fiber use mostly pre-consumer paper waste. Papermaking uses trees, pollutes the air and water, and releases toxic dioxins. On a weight basis, plastic bags take less energy to make and transport than paper bags, and they use less landfill space. Paper bags, however, break down faster in landfills and produce fewer toxic substances. Moreover, unlike the oil used to make plastic bags, the wood used to make paper bags is a potentially renewable resource. Also, the technology for recycling paper is more advanced than that for plastics, and recycled paper can be used in a greater variety of products.

Don't fall for labels claiming paper and plastic bags are recyclable. Just about anything is in theory recyclable. What counts is whether it is, in fact, recycled.

So don't choose between paper and plastic. Instead, bring your own *reusable* canvas or string containers when you shop for groceries or other items, or save and reuse any paper or plastic bags you get. Several of these reusable bags can be folded up and kept in a handbag, pocket, or car.

This BYOB (Bring Your Own Bag) approach eliminates the need for throwaway paper and plastic bags, both of which are environmentally harmful even if they are recycled. To encourage people to bring their own reusable bags, stores in the Netherlands charge for paper or plastic bags.

Another big solid-waste problem is created by used tires. There are now 2–3 billion used tires heaped in landfills, old mines, abandoned houses, and other dump sites throughout the United States, and the pile grows by about 250 million tires per year. Tire dumps are fire hazards and breeding grounds for mosquitoes.

Instead of being dumped, used tires can be burned to produce electricity and pulverized to make resins for products ranging from car bumpers, garbage cans, and doormats to road-building materials. If asphalt pavement were required to contain at least 20% rubber, this could create a market for 70–100 million tires per year in the United States. Discarded tires can also be reused for the foundations and walls of low-cost passive solar homes (Solutions, p. 284). And some worn-out tires have been reused to build artificial reefs to attract fish.

11-3   Solutions: Recycling Solid Waste

RECYCLING ORGANIC WASTES: COMPOSTING
Biodegradable solid waste from slaughterhouses and food-processing plants, kitchen and yard waste, manure from animal feedlots, wood, and paper soiled by food can be mixed with soil and decomposed by fungi and aerobic bacteria to produce **compost**, a sweet-smelling, dark-brown humus that is rich in organic matter and soil nutrients. It can be used as an organic soil fertilizer or conditioner, as topsoil, as a landfill cover, and as fertilizer for golf courses, parks, forests, roadway medians, and the grounds around

When is a ship not a ship? When it's an Earthship. Because then it's a passive solar house with three thick walls (made from dirt-packed used tires) partly buried in the ground, with the other wall being a slanted glass wall facing the sun to capture solar energy. Though these houses are rooted in the earth, Earthship architect Michael Reynolds sees them as vessels designed to "sail" right through good times and bad times.

Earthship houses can be cheap and can be built for as low as $2 a square meter ($20 a square foot). You could build one yourself, using things that someone else has thrown away—tires, which most tire dealers are glad to give away or even pay you to haul off, and aluminum cans.

Once the house is up, depending on the features you choose to build in, you will pay little for electricity, heating, cooling, and water-heating. You can even grow your own food in the greenhouse created by the sun-facing glass wall, which also captures solar energy for heating.

To build the walls, discarded steel-belted radial tires are filled with dirt and layered in staggered courses like bricks. Dirt (from excavated soil) is packed tight inside (usually with a sledgehammer) and between the tires to make the wall rock solid; then it's finished with a coat of plaster or adobe.

Once heated by the sun, these thick and strong walls have so much thermal mass that they stay warm for a long time, steadily radiating that warmth into the spaces they enclose. Their huge thermal mass allows them to be built in areas without enough sunlight for conventional solar homes. If, as Reynolds prefers, the whole house is partly underground on the three sides not facing the sun, an Earthship can maintain a steady mean temperature of 18–21°C (65–70°F) in such outside temperature extremes as those in Taos, New Mexico, ranging from 38°C (100°F) in summer to –34°C (–30°F) in winter.

Some of the inner walls can be built of another type of solid waste that is often thrown away—aluminum beverage cans—embedded in cement mortar. Like the tires, they are packed with dirt to provide thermal mass. To Reynolds, living in an Earthship is a great way to live more gently on the earth and also save money.

---

public buildings. All you do is create a pile of organic waste, stir it occasionally, and wait for a few months for it to rot and produce a safe, cheap fertilizer.

Compost can also be produced from giant-size piles of biodegradable solid waste in large plants or in enclosed metal containers. These approaches are used in many European countries, including the Netherlands, Germany, France, Sweden, and Italy, and in states such as Minnesota and Oregon. Odors can be controlled by enclosing the facilities and filtering the air inside, but residents near large composting plants still complain of unacceptable odors. This problem can be minimized by creating municipal compost operations near existing landfills or by using closed metal containers.

Municipal composting programs that bring in a mixed municipal solid waste (mixed garbage) and then sort and compost the organic materials usually fail. The sorting is expensive and also useless because the organic matter has already been contaminated by hazardous wastes such as household cleaners, leaking batteries, and motor oil. The result is contaminated compost that is hard to sell, and the compost piles can contaminate groundwater with toxic chemicals. Instead, communities should establish programs in which compostable organic wastes are not mixed with other solid waste and are collected in separate containers or compartmentalized garbage trucks.

Households can use backyard compost bins for food and yard wastes. Seattle, for example, promotes backyard composting by using a network of volunteer composting experts to help people get started. Apartment dwellers can compost by using indoor bins in which a special type of earthworm converts food waste into humus. By 1993, about 5% of U.S. yard waste in almost 2,300 cities was composted, with Minnesota, New Jersey, Wisconsin, and Michigan leading the way.

RECYCLING OTHER WASTES There are two types of recycling: primary and secondary. The most desirable type is *primary*, or *closed-loop, recycling*, in which products are recycled to produce new products of the same type—newspaper into newspaper and aluminum cans into aluminum cans, for example. The less desirable type is *secondary*, or *open-loop, recycling*, in which waste materials are converted into different products. This does not reduce the use of resources as much as the first type of recycling. For example, primary recycling reduces the use of virgin materials in making a product by 20–90%; secondary recycling reduces it by 25% at most.

Q: What two gases make up 99% of the volume of air in the troposphere?

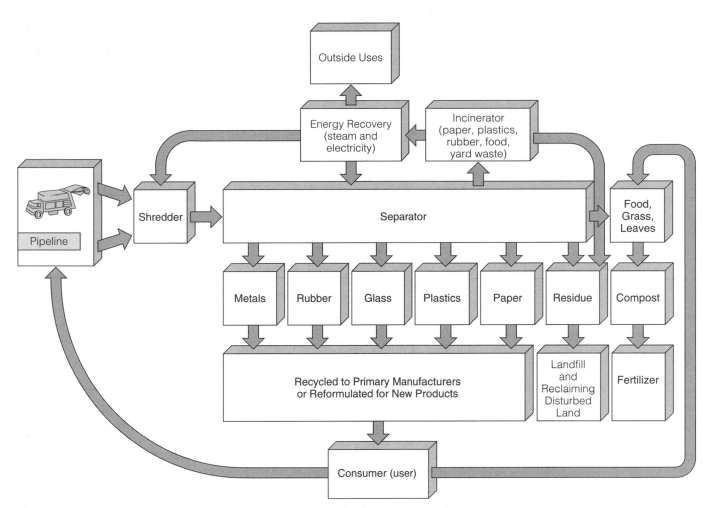

Figure 11-4 Generalized materials recovery facility used to sort mixed wastes for recycling and burning to produce energy. Because such plants depend on high volumes of trash to be economical, they discourage reuse and waste reduction.

In 1992 about 17% of municipal solid waste in the United States was recycled or composted, and a 30% recovery rate seems within reach by 2000. Japan already recycles 40% of its municipal solid waste.

Environmentalists believe we can do much better. In a recent pilot study, 100 families in East Hampton, New York, achieved an 84% recycling rate on their household trash. This shows that a 60–80% recycling and composting rate is possible. Five states—Maine, Washington, New York, California, and Iowa—plan to recycle 50% of their municipal solid waste by 2000, and New Jersey has set a 60% recycling goal. Despite such progress, more than half the states recycle less than 5% of the mass of their municipal solid waste.

CENTRALIZED RECYCLING OF MIXED WASTES
Large-scale recycling can be accomplished by collecting mixed urban waste and bringing it to centralized *materials-recovery facilities (MRFs)*. There, machines

shred and automatically separate the mixed waste to recover glass, iron, aluminum, and other valuable materials (Figure 11-4). These materials are then sold to manufacturers as raw materials, and the remaining paper, plastics, and other combustible wastes are recycled or burned. The resulting heat produces steam or electricity to run the recovery plant and for sale to nearby industries or homes.

By 1993 the United States had more than 220 materials-recovery facilities and at least 60 more in the planning stages. However, such plants are expensive to build and maintain. They also can emit toxic air pollutants and produce a toxic ash that must be disposed of safely. Furthermore, once trash is mixed it takes a lot of money and energy to separate it. To be profitable, these facilities must have a large intake of trash. Thus, their owners have a vested interest in having us produce more and more trash—the reverse of what prominent scientists say we should be doing (Figure 11-2).

SEPARATING WASTES FOR RECYCLING It makes much more sense economically and environmentally for households and businesses to separate trash into recyclable and reusable categories before it is picked up. With this approach, homes and businesses put different kinds of waste materials—usually glass, paper, metals, and plastics—into separate containers. Compartmentalized city collection trucks, private haulers, or volunteer recycling organizations pick up the segregated wastes and sell them to scrap dealers, compost plants, and manufacturers.

The source-separation approach produces little air and water pollution, reduces litter, and has low startup costs and moderate operating costs. It also saves more energy and provides more jobs for unskilled workers than centralized resource recovery plants, and it creates three to six times more jobs per unit of material than landfilling or incineration. Another advantage is that collecting aluminum, paper, glass, plastics, and other materials for recycling is an important source of income for volunteer service organizations and for many people, especially the homeless and the poor in MDCs and LDCs. In many cities in LDCs as much as 25% of the collected municipal waste is recycled by scavengers removing useful and salable materials from dump sites.

RECYCLING ALUMINUM Worldwide, the recycling rate for aluminum in 1991 was about 33% (30% in the United States). Recycling aluminum produces 95% less air pollution and 97% less water pollution, and it requires 95% less energy than mining and processing aluminum ore.

In 1992, 68% (compared to 15% in 1972) of aluminum beverage cans in the United States were recycled at more than 10,000 recycling centers set up by the aluminum industry, other private interests, and local governments. People who returned the cans got about a penny per can for their efforts, earning about $900 million. Within six weeks the average recycled aluminum can had been melted down and was back on the market as a new can. Makers of aluminum cans saved $566 million and the energy equivalent of 20 million barrels of oil. (The electricity used to produce one aluminum can from virgin ore would keep a 100-watt light bulb burning for 100 hours.)

Despite this progress, about 32% of the 92.4 billion aluminum cans produced in 1992 in the United States were still thrown away. If these cans were laid end-to-end, they would wrap around the earth more than 120 times. These discarded cans contain more aluminum than most countries use for all purposes, and each discarded aluminum can represents almost indestructible solid waste.

Recycling aluminum cans is great, but many environmentalists believe that aluminum cans could be replaced by refillable glass bottles—a switch from recycling to reuse that also creates jobs in local communities. One way to encourage this change would be to place a heavy tax on nonrefillable containers (aluminum, glass, or plastic) and no tax on reusable glass bottles. Many environmentalists also believe that unnecessary use of aluminum could be reduced by not giving the aluminum industry huge electric power subsidies, which hide the true environmental cost of using this metal. Meanwhile, they urge consumers not to buy beverages in aluminum cans and to buy reusable glass containers when they are available.

RECYCLING WASTEPAPER Overpackaging—including double packages and oversized containers—is a major contributor to paper use and waste. Junk mail also wastes enormous amounts of paper. Each year the U.S. work force throws away enough office and writing paper to build a 4-meter-high (12-foot-) wall stretching from New York City to Los Angeles. Each American throws away paper equivalent to an average of four trees per year, for a total of more than 1 billion trees.

Environmentalists estimate that at least 50% of the world's wastepaper (mostly newspapers, corrugated board and paperboard, office paper, and computer and copier paper) could be recycled by 2000. During World War II, when recycling was a national priority, the United States recycled about 45% of its wastepaper, compared to 39% in 1992 (up from 25% in 1989). Some other countries do better, including the Netherlands (53%), Japan (50%), Mexico (45%), Germany (41%), and Sweden (40%).

Recycling the Sunday newspapers in the United States would save 500,000 trees per week. Currently, only about 10% of U.S. newspapers are printed on recycled paper.

Apart from saving trees, recycling (and reusing) paper has a number of benefits. It:

- Saves energy because it takes 30–64% less energy to produce the same weight of recycled paper as to make the paper from trees.
- Reduces air pollution from pulp mills by 74–95%.
- Lowers water pollution by 35%.
- Helps prevent groundwater contamination from the toxic ink left after paper rots in landfills over a 30–60-year period.
- Conserves large quantities of water.
- Saves landfill space.

Q: What is the best way to prevent or reduce pollution?

- Creates five times more jobs than harvesting trees for pulp.
- Can save money. In 1988, for example, American Telephone and Telegraph earned more than $485,000 in revenue and saved $1.3 million in disposal costs by collecting and recycling high-grade office paper.

Separating paper from other waste materials is a key to increased recycling. Otherwise, paper becomes so contaminated that wastepaper dealers won't buy it.

In the United States tax subsidies and other financial incentives make it cheaper to make paper from trees than from recycled wastepaper—except in Florida, where virgin newsprint is taxed.

Even with the best of intentions, governments, businesses, and individuals may be fooled by claims about recycled paper products. Moreover, as usual there are trade-offs (Spotlight, at right).

RECYCLING PLASTICS Plastics are synthesized from petrochemicals (chemicals produced from oil). The plastics industry is among the leading producers of hazardous waste.

Plastics now account for about 8% by weight and 20% by volume of municipal solid wastes in the United States and about 60% of the debris found on U.S. beaches. In landfills toxic cadmium and lead compounds used as binders can leach out of plastics and ooze into groundwater and surface water. And when plastics are thrown away as litter, they can harm animals that swallow or get entangled in them. Most plastics used today are nondegradable or take 200–400 years to degrade. Even biodegradable plastics take decades to partially decompose in landfills because of a lack of oxygen and moisture.

In theory nearly all plastics could be recycled; in 1992, however, about 2.5% by weight of all plastic wastes and 5% of plastic packaging (including 14% of plastic bottles) used in the United States were recycled. Plastics are more difficult to recycle than glass or aluminum because there are so many different types of plastics. Thus for recycling to work most plastic trash must be sorted into different categories—a costly procedure.

The $140-billion-per-year U.S. plastics industry has established the Partnership for Plastics Progress (also known as P3) and the American Plastics Council, mostly to run ads promoting the value of plastics to society. Critics argue, however, that the main purpose of these organizations is to keep us buying more plastic containers, utensils, and other mostly throwaway items and to fight any laws banning or limiting the use of throwaway plastic items.

SPOTLIGHT

Recycled Paper Hype and Trade-offs

True or false: Buying recycled paper products will reduce solid waste. The answer is, not necessarily. Buying recycled paper products can save trees (grown mostly in plantations) and energy and reduce pollution, but it does not necessarily reduce solid waste. Only products made from *post-consumer waste*—intercepted on its way from consumer to the landfill—will do that.

Most recycled paper is actually made from *pre-consumer waste*—scraps and cuttings recovered from paper and printing plants. Since the paper industry has always recycled this waste, it has never contributed to landfill problems. Now this paper is labeled "recycled" as a marketing ploy, giving the false impression that people who buy such products (often at higher prices) are helping the solid-waste problem. Until government guidelines prohibit such misleading labels, we cannot expect to see much high-grade paper made from post-consumer waste. Most "recycled" paper has no more than 50% recycled fibers, with only 10% from post-consumer waste.

This book is printed on acid-free recycled paper containing the highest content of recycled fiber available (without being prohibitively expensive). We go further than simply using the best available recycled paper. Each year the publisher and I donate money both to organizations that protect existing tropical forests and also to tree-planting organizations, so that at least two trees are planted and tended for each tree used in printing this book. I also see that 50 trees are planted and tended for each tree that I use (in the form of paper) in researching and writing this book.

Environmentalists recognize the importance of plastics in many products, but many of them believe that their widespread use in throwaway beverage and food containers should be sharply reduced and replaced with less harmful and wasteful alternatives, such as reusable glass bottles.

OBSTACLES TO REUSE AND RECYCLING Several factors hinder recycling (and reuse) in the United States. One is that Americans have been conditioned by advertising and upbringing to accept a throwaway lifestyle. Another is that many of the environmental and health costs of items are not reflected in their market prices, so consumers have little incentive to recycle, reuse, or reduce their use of throwaway products.

Another serious problem is that the logging, mining, and energy industries get huge tax breaks, depletion allowances, cheap access to public lands, and other subsidies to encourage them to extract virgin resources as quickly as possible. By contrast, recycling industries get few tax breaks or other subsidies. Finally, the lack of large, steady markets for recycled materials (mostly because of a lack of tax breaks compared to virgin materials) makes recycling a risky business that attracts little investment capital.

Another problem is that some communities and businesses have leaped into recycling with little emphasis on creating a demand for recycled products. By neglecting this fundamental of economics, the supply of waste materials collected for recycling has often exceeded the demand, lowering the prices paid for such materials. To help correct this situation, in 1992 the National Recycling Coalition established a campaign to get businesses to buy recycled material and to pump up the demand for products made from recycled materials. Beginning with 25 large U.S. corporations—including McDonald's, 3M, Sears, and Coca-Cola—the coalition hopes to recruit 5,000 companies for the campaign.

Consumers also increase demand when they buy goods made from recycled materials, especially if it is based on primary recycling and is made from the highest feasible amount of post-consumer waste.

Last Resorts: Burning or Burying Solid Waste

INCINERATION In *trash-to-energy incinerators* trash is burned as a fuel to produce steam or electricity, which can be sold or used to run the incinerator. Most are *mass-burn incinerators,* which burn mixed trash without separating out hazardous materials (such as batteries) and noncombustible materials that can interfere with combustion conditions and pollute the air. Denmark and Sweden burn 50% of their solid waste to produce energy, compared with 17% in the United States.

Incinerating solid waste kills germs and reduces the volume of waste going to landfills by about 60% (not 90% as usually cited). However, incinerators are costly to build, operate, and maintain, and they create very few long-term jobs. Moreover, even with ad-

vanced air pollution control devices, incinerators release toxic substances (that can cause cancers and nervous-system disorders) into the atmosphere. And without continuous maintenance and good operator training and supervision, the air pollution control equipment on incinerators often fails, so that emission standards are exceeded.

Incinerators also produce residues of toxic *fly ash* (lightweight particles removed from smokestack emissions by air pollution control devices) and less toxic *bottom ash;* approximately 10% is fly ash, and 90% bottom ash. Usually the two types of ash are mixed and disposed of in ordinary landfills. Although the amount of material to be buried is greatly reduced, its toxicity is increased.

Newer Japanese incinerators are more strictly controlled than those built in the United States. In Japan hazardous wastes and unburnable materials that would pollute the air are removed before wastes are incinerated, which also greatly reduces the amount and toxicity of the remaining ash. This is rarely done in the United States.

Furthermore, to protect Japanese workers, bottom ash and fly ash are removed by conveyor belt and transported to carefully designed and monitored hazardous-waste landfills in sealed trucks. Before disposal the ash is often solidified in cement blocks. In the United States most ash is simply dumped into conventional landfills.

In Japan violations of air standards are punishable by large fines, plant closings, and—in some cases—jail sentences for company officials. In the United States, monitoring is not as strict, and punishment for violations is much less severe.

Japanese incinerator workers must have an engineering degree, and they spend 6-18 months learning how the incinerator works and undergo closely supervised on-site training. U.S. incinerator workers need no degrees and get far less training.

Incineration in the United States is also plagued by faulty equipment and human errors that have exposed workers and people in surrounding areas to dangerous levels of air pollution. Thanks mostly to Japanese and German technology some of the newer incinerators being built in the United States are safer.

Environmentalists have pushed Congress and the EPA to classify incinerator ash as hazardous waste, disposable only in landfills designed to handle hazardous waste, as is done in Japan. To date, however, no action has been taken, largely because waste management companies claim it would make incineration too expensive. Environmentalists counter that if the companies can't properly dispose of the toxic ash they produce, they probably shouldn't be in the incineration business.

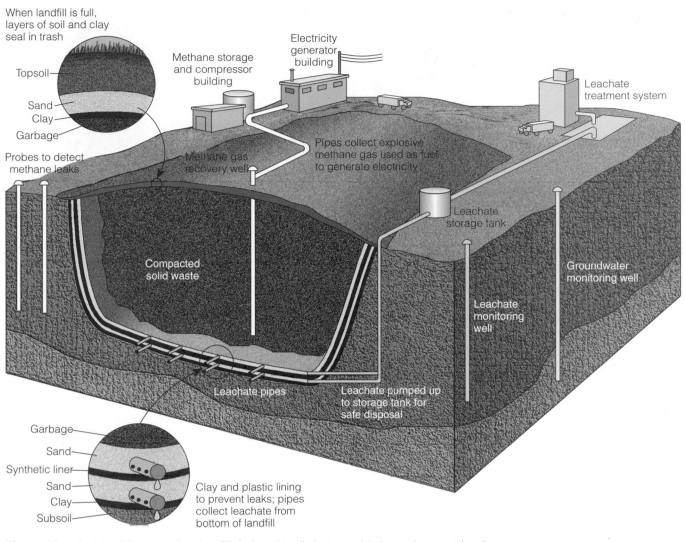

When landfill is full, layers of soil and clay seal in trash

Topsoil
Sand
Clay
Garbage

Probes to detect methane leaks

Methane storage and compressor building

Electricity generator building

Leachate treatment system

Methane gas recovery well

Pipes collect explosive methane gas used as fuel to generate electricity

Leachate storage tank

Compacted solid waste

Groundwater monitoring well

Leachate monitoring well

Leachate pipes

Leachate pumped up to storage tank for safe disposal

Garbage
Sand
Synthetic liner
Sand
Clay
Subsoil

Clay and plastic lining to prevent leaks; pipes collect leachate from bottom of landfill

Figure 11-5 A state-of-the-art sanitary landfill designed to eliminate or minimize environmental problems that plague older landfills. Only a few municipal landfills in the United States have such state-of-the-art design, and 85% of U.S. landfills are unlined. Furthermore, even state-of-the-art landfills will eventually leak, passing contamination and cleanup costs on to the next generation.

In 1993 there were 171 trash-to-energy incinerators operating in the United States. Since 1985, however, over 73 new incinerator projects have been blocked, delayed, or canceled because of public opposition and high costs—the same thing that happened to nuclear power (Section 4-7). Of the 70 plants still in the planning stage, most face stiff opposition and many may not be built, as communities discover that recycling, reuse, composting, and waste reduction are cheaper and safer alternatives that can handle 60–80% of municipal waste.

Most environmentalists oppose heavy dependence on incinerators because it encourages people to continue tossing away paper, plastics, and other burnable materials. Many existing incinerators have 20- to 30-year contracts with cities to supply them with a certain volume of trash, which makes it hard for cities to switch to large-scale recycling, composting, reuse, and

pollution prevention. In 1992, Rhode Island became the first state to ban solid-waste incineration because of its threats to the health and safety of Rhode Islanders, especially children, and its unacceptably high cost. In 1993, West Virginia enacted a similar ban.

GARBAGE GRAVEYARDS About 66% by weight of the municipal solid waste in the United States is buried in sanitary landfills, compared with 98% in Australia, 93% in Canada, 90% in Great Britain, 54% in France, 44% in Sweden, 18% in Switzerland, and 17% in Japan. A **sanitary landfill** is a garbage graveyard in which wastes are spread out in thin layers, compacted, and covered daily with a fresh layer of clay or plastic foam.

Modern state-of-the-art landfills are lined with clay and plastic before being filled with garbage (Figure 11-5). The site must be geologically suitable. The bottom is covered with an impermeable liner usually made of several layers of clay, thick plastic, and sand. This liner collects *leachate* (rainwater that is contaminated as it percolates down through the solid waste) and is supposed to keep it from leaking into groundwater. Collected leachate ("garbage juice") is pumped from the bottom of the landfill, stored in tanks, and sent either to a regular sewage treatment plant or to an on-site treatment plant. When the landfill is full, it is covered with clay, sand, gravel, and topsoil to prevent water from seeping in. Several wells are drilled around the landfill to monitor any leakage of leachate into nearby groundwater. Methane gas produced by anaerobic decomposition in the sealed landfill is collected and burned to produce steam or electricity. Since 1993, all landfills in the United States must meet such standards, forcing operators to either upgrade or close their operations.

Sanitary landfills offer certain benefits. No air-polluting open burning is allowed. Odor is seldom a problem, and rodents and insects cannot thrive. Sanitary landfills should be located so as to reduce water pollution from leaching, but that is not always done. Moreover, a sanitary landfill can be put into operation quickly, has low operating costs, and can handle a huge amount of solid waste. And after a landfill has been filled, the land can be graded, planted, and used as a park, a golf course, a ski hill, an athletic field, a wildlife area, or some other recreation area.

However, landfills also have drawbacks. While they operate they cause traffic, noise, and dust. Most also emit toxic gases. In addition, paper and other biodegradable wastes break down very slowly in today's compacted and water- and oxygen-deficient landfills. For example, newspapers dug up from some landfills are still readable after 30 or 40 years, and hot dogs, carrots, and chickens that have been dug up after 10 years have not rotted. Biodegradable plastics also take decades to decompose in landfills.

The underground anaerobic decomposition of organic wastes at landfills produces explosive methane gas, toxic hydrogen sulfide gas, and smog-forming volatile organic compounds that escape into the air. Landfills can be equipped with vent pipes to collect these gases, and the collected methane can be burned to produce steam or electricity (Figure 11-5). A single large landfill can provide enough methane to meet the energy needs of 10,000 homes. Besides saving energy, using the methane gas from all large landfills worldwide would lower atmospheric emissions of methane and help reduce projected global warming from greenhouse gases (Figures 9-7 and 9-8).

Contamination of groundwater and nearby surface water from leachate that seeps from the bottom of unlined landfills or cracks in the lining of lined land-fills is another serious problem. Only 11% of U.S. landfills collect leachate, and only 25% monitor groundwater. Even when leachate is collected it is rarely treated to render it harmless. Moreover, 86% of the landfills studied have contaminated groundwater. Once groundwater is contaminated it is extremely difficult—often impossible—to clean up. And while modern double-lined landfills (Figure 11-5) delay the release of toxic leachate into groundwater below landfills, they do not prevent it. Landfills also deprive present and future generations of valuable resources and encourage waste production instead of pollution prevention and waste reduction.

11-5 Hazardous Waste: Types and Production

WHAT IS HAZARDOUS WASTE, AND HOW MUCH IS PRODUCED? According to the Environmental Protection Agency, **hazardous waste** is any discarded material that: **(1)** contains one or more of 39 toxic, carcinogenic, mutagenic, or teratogenic compounds at levels that exceed established limits (Section 8-1); **(2)** is flammable; **(3)** is reactive or unstable enough to explode or release toxic fumes; or **(4)** is capable of corroding metal containers such as tanks, drums, and barrels.

However, this narrow official definition of hazardous wastes (mandated by Congress) does not include:

- *Radioactive wastes* (Section 4-7).

- *Hazardous and toxic materials discarded by households* (Table 11-1).

- *Mining wastes* (Figure 11-1).

- *Oil- and gas-drilling wastes,* routinely discharged into surface waters or dumped into unlined pits and landfills.

- *Liquid waste containing organic hydrocarbon compounds* (80% of all liquid hazardous waste). The EPA allows it to be burned as fuel in cement kilns and industrial furnaces with little regulation.

- *Cement kiln dust* produced when liquid hazardous wastes are burned in the kilns—a practice classified as recycling by the EPA but called dangerous "sham recycling" by environmentalists.

- *Municipal incinerator ash,* which if classified as hazardous waste would be so expensive to ship to and bury in special landfills that the whole waste incineration industry would collapse.

Q: Is there doubt about the validity of the greenhouse effect?

- *Wastes from the thousands of small businesses and factories that generate less than 100 kilograms (220 pounds) of hazardous waste per month.*

- *Waste generated by the military,* except at 116 sites so toxic that they are on the EPA's list of priority sites to be cleaned up. U.S. military installations produce more hazardous waste each year (about a ton per minute) than the top five U.S. chemical companies combined. Studies by the Department of Defense have identified over 17,482 contaminated sites at 1,855 military bases in every state.

Environmentalists call these omissions "linguistic detoxification" designed to save industries money and mislead the public. They urge that all excluded categories be designated hazardous waste—a decision that would quickly shift the emphasis from waste management and pollution control to reducing waste and preventing pollution—and save lots of money.

The EPA estimates that at least 5.5 billion metric tons (6 billion tons) of hazardous waste are produced each year in the United States—an average of 21 metric tons (23 tons) per person. However, only 6%, or 350 million metric tons (385 million tons), of the total is legally defined as hazardous waste and subject to government regulation. Thus, *94% of the country's hazardous waste is not regulated by hazardous waste laws.*

LEAD: POISONING OUR CHILDREN   One example of a toxic waste is lead. Atmospheric emissions of lead from human sources are 28 times greater than those from natural sources. And emissions of lead into the soil and aquatic ecosystems from human activities are almost three times those emitted into the atmosphere.

We take in small amounts of lead in the air we breathe, the food we eat, and the water we drink. Once lead enters the blood only about 10% is excreted. The rest is stored in the bones for decades. Even at very low levels it damages the central nervous system, especially in young children. Pregnant women can also transfer dangerous levels of lead to their unborn children.

Each year 12,000–16,000 American children (mostly poor and nonwhite) under age 9 are treated for acute lead poisoning, and about 200 die. About 30% of the survivors suffer from palsy, partial paralysis, blindness, and mental retardation.

Children under age 6 with levels greater than 10 micrograms of lead in each tenth of a liter (about half a cup) of blood are especially vulnerable. To achieve this blood level, a child would need to ingest lead equal to that in only one-third of a granule of sugar a day—something easily done by touching soil or house dust contaminated with lead and sucking the thumb. Some scientists believe that there is no minimum

Table 11-1   Common Household Toxic and Hazardous Materials

Cleaning Products

Disinfectants

Drain, toilet, and window cleaners

Oven cleaners

Bleach and ammonia

Cleaning solvents and spot removers

Septic tank cleaners

Paint and Building Products

Latex and oil-based paints

Paint thinners, solvents, and strippers

Stains, varnishes, and lacquers

Wood preservatives

Acids for etching and rust removal

Asphalt and roof tar

Gardening and Pest Control Products

Pesticide sprays and dusts

Weed killers

Ant and rodent killers

Flea powder

Automotive products

Gasoline

Used motor oil

Antifreeze

Battery acid

Solvents

Brake and transmission fluid

Rust inhibitor and rust remover

General Products

Dry cell batteries (mercury and cadmium)

Artist paints and inks

Glues and cements

Data from Science Advisory Board, *Reducing Risks*, Washington, D.C.: Environmental Protection Agency, 1990. Items in each category are not listed in rank order.

threshold for safe exposure of children and fetuses to lead.

According to a 1986 EPA study, *at least one out of six children in the United States under age 6 has unsafe blood levels of lead that may retard his or her mental, physi-*

Protecting Children from Lead Poisoning

SOLUTIONS

Ways to protect children from lead poisoning include:

- Setting lead standards to protect children and fetuses

- Requiring that all U.S. children be tested for lead by age 1, and establishing a lead-screening program to test all children under age 6

- Eliminating leaded paint and contaminated dust in housing

- Testing all community sources of drinking water, especially in schools and homes, for lead contamination, and removing the contamination or providing alternate sources of drinking water

- Banning the use of lead solder in plumbing pipes and in food cans, and removing lead from municipal drinking water systems within 7 years instead of the current 21 years

- Making sure children wash their hands thoroughly before eating

- Requiring that all ceramic ware used to cook, store, or serve food produced domestically or imported be lead-free

- Banning incineration of municipal solid waste and hazardous waste—the largest new source of lead

- Mounting a global campaign to reduce lead poisoning in LDCs

- Banning leaded gasoline throughout the world

Doing these things will cost lots of money (an estimated $50 billion in the United States). But health officials say the alternative is to keep poisoning and mentally handicapping large numbers of children.

cal, and emotional development. This epidemic affects children of every socioeconomic background, but those in poor families and minority groups suffer most.

The greatest sources of lead in the United States are:

- *Lead particles injected into the atmosphere that settle onto the soil and become outdoor or indoor dust.* Children ingest this lead as they play in contaminated soil or dust in carpeting, toys, or the floor, and then put their thumbs or hands in their mouths. The major sources of atmospheric lead particles

today are solid-waste and hazardous-waste incinerators, lead smelters, and battery manufacturing plants. Leaded gasoline, once the largest source, has been phased out, but the massive amounts of indestructible lead particles that fell out of the atmosphere for 50 years before the ban contaminate land almost everywhere. In countries that have not banned leaded gasoline, it is the largest atmospheric source of lead.

- *Interior paint in 52%, or 57 million, of the houses built before 1978, when use of lead compounds in interior and exterior paint was banned.* These houses are a major source of lead poisoning for children ages 1–3, who inhale lead dust from cracking and peeling paint or ingest it by sucking their thumbs, putting contaminated toys in their mouths, or gnawing on window sills or furniture. People living in houses or apartments built before 1980 should have samples of the paint analyzed for lead by the local health department or by a private testing laboratory (cost $100–$450).*

- *Groundwater contaminated by lead leached from landfills.* More than 3,000 sources of community drinking water are believed to be contaminated in this way.

- *Drinking water contaminated by plumbing containing lead solder.* According to the EPA nearly one in eight Americans in 819 tested communities drinks tap water containing unsafe levels of lead that is leached by acidic or soft water from solder and connectors used with copper piping in plumbing systems. Home owners with copper pipes or joints in their dwellings should have the local water department or a private laboratory (cost $20–$100) test their tap water for lead. And before buying or renting an existing house or apartment, prospective buyers or renters should have its water (that has been standing in pipes for at least 12 hours) tested for lead. In 1991 the EPA ordered removal of lead from municipal drinking water systems but gave the country's largest municipalities up to 21 years to do the job.

- *Lead solder used to seal the seams on food cans.* This applies especially to acidic foods such as tomatoes and citrus juices. This type of solder has been sharply reduced in U.S. food cans but may be found in cans of imported foods.

- *Imported cups, plates, pitchers, leaded glass crystal,*

---

*If you find lead in your home, send a postcard to U.S. Consumer Product Safety Commission, Washington, DC 20207, and ask for the free pamphlet, *What You Should Know About the Lead-Based Paint in Your Home.* Two home kits for testing paint for lead are sold by HybriVet Systems (800-262-LEAD) and Frandon Enterprises (800-359-9000).

Q: Why is there concern over a potentially enhanced greenhouse effect?

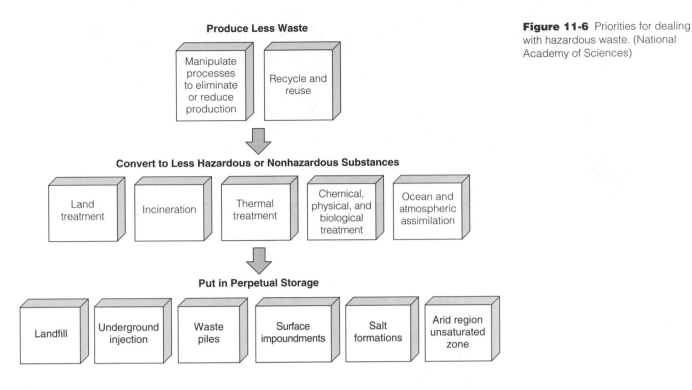

Figure 11-6 Priorities for dealing with hazardous waste. (National Academy of Sciences)

and other items used to cook, store, or serve food, espe-cially acidic foods and hot liquids and foods. *Before using such items, test them for lead content.**

- *Vegetables and fruits grown on soil contaminated by lead. This applies especially to cropland or home gardens near highways, incinerators, and smelters. Careful washing should remove at least half of this lead.*

- *Burning comic strips, Christmas wrapping paper, or painted wood, in wood stoves and fireplaces.*

According to the Centers for Disease Control and Prevention and the Department of Health and Human Services, *lead is the number one environmental health threat to children in the United States* and should be a matter of the highest priority (Solutions, p. 292).

 ### 11-6 Solutions: Dealing with Hazardous Waste

WHAT ARE OUR OPTIONS?   There are five basic options for dealing with hazardous wastes: **(1)** don't

---

*A simple home test for lead content of up to 100 items of dish-ware is available for $24.50 from Frandon Enterprises, 511 N. 48th St., Seattle, WA 98103. Commercial testing costs about $60 per item; contact American Council of Independent Laborato-ries, 1725 K Street N.W., Washington, DC 20006, (202-887-5872), for a testing lab near you.

make them in the first place (pollution prevention); **(2)** recycle or reuse them (pollution prevention if done within production processes or on site, but waste man-agement otherwise); **(3)** detoxify them; **(4)** burn them; and **(5)** hide them by putting them into a deep well, pond, pit, building, or landfill, or by dumping them in the ocean.

POLLUTION PREVENTION, RECYCLING, AND REUSE   Despite much talk about preventing pollu-tion, the order of priorities for dealing with hazardous waste in the United States is the reverse of what many prominent scientists say it should be (Figures 11-6 and 11-7). Prevention—the most desirable option—involves substituting safer chemicals, reformulating products, modifying production processes, improving operations and maintenance, and practicing closed-loop recycling and reuse of wastes on site (Solutions, p. 294).

Some people are using less hazardous (and usual-ly cheaper) cleaning products (Table 11-2) and are using pesticides and other hazardous chemicals only when absolutely necessary and in the smallest amount possible. Three inexpensive chemicals—baking soda, vinegar, and borax—can be used for most cleaning and clothes bleaching. Baking soda can also be used as a deodorant and a toothpaste.

No country has an effective pollution prevention program for hazardous waste, but countries like Den-mark, the Netherlands, Germany, and Sweden are all far ahead of the United States in this area. And in 1992

A: Because of the input of massive quantities of greenhouse gases into the atmosphere from human activities

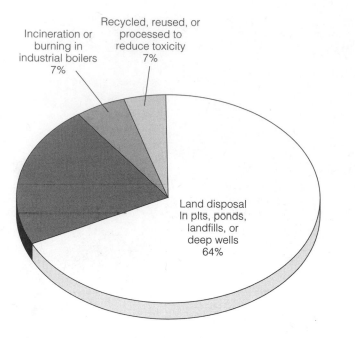

Figure 11-7 Management of hazardous waste in the United States. Even the best-designed landfills (Figure 11-5) eventually leak. Relying on landfills, deep wells, and incinerators for solid and hazardous waste disposal passes contamination and cleanup costs on to the next generation. (Data from Worldwatch Institute)

13 European nations agreed in principle to eliminate all discharges and emissions of chemicals that are toxic, persistent, or likely to bioaccumulate in food chains and webs (Figure 6-5). In short, these nations made a binding commitment to try to achieve "zero discharge" of persistent toxic substances.

Effective pollution prevention requires assuming that any waste or pollutant is potentially harmful unless shown otherwise. This *precautionary principle* is the inverse of the waste management approach, in which wastes are assumed to be benign until shown to be harmful.

After preventing pollution, the next most desirable options are recycling and reuse (Figure 11-6), currently applied to only 7% of legally regulated U.S. hazardous waste. Yet the EPA devotes less than 1% of its waste management budget to encouraging prevention, reuse, and recycling of hazardous waste.

DETOXIFICATION The next priority in hazardous-waste management is to convert any remaining waste into less hazardous or nonhazardous materials (Figure 11-6). Conversion methods include spreading biodegradable wastes on the land, using heat, chemical, or physical methods, or natural or bioengineered bacteria to break them down, and burning them on land or at sea in incinerators.

Pollution Prevention Pays

SOLUTIONS

Some U.S. firms have found that pollution prevention saves them money. In 1974 the Minnesota Mining and Manufacturing Company (3M) produced tons of hazardous waste and single-handedly accounted for 2% of all industrial emissions of air pollutants in the United States. In 1975 the company, which makes 60,000 different products in 100 manufacturing plants, began a Pollution Prevention Pays (3P) program. It redesigned equipment and processes, used fewer hazardous raw materials, identified hazardous chemical outputs and recycled or sold them as raw materials to other companies, and began making nonpolluting products.

By 1993, 3M's overall waste production was down by one-third, and emissions of air pollutants by 70%—and the company had saved over $600 million in waste disposal costs. By 2000 it plans to reduce overall generation of waste by 50% and environmental releases of hazardous and nonhazardous waste to air, water, and land by 90% of 1987 levels.

An EPA study of 28 firms engaged in waste reduction found that 54% got their investment back within a year or less and 93% got it back within three years. The key is to get everyone in the company thinking about ways to reduce waste and pollution by making it a top corporate priority. However, most firms have little incentive to reduce their output of waste because waste management costs them only about 0.1% of the total value of the products they output.

Denmark has the most comprehensive and effective hazardous-waste detoxification program. Each municipality has at least one facility that accepts paints, solvents, and other hazardous wastes from households. Toxic waste from industries is delivered to 21 transfer stations throughout the country. All waste is then transferred to a large treatment facility where about 75% of the waste is detoxified. The rest is buried in a carefully designed and monitored landfill.

Biological treatment of hazardous waste, or *bioremediation*, may be the wave of the future. In this process, bacteria secrete enzymes that break down large complex molecules into smaller molecules they can absorb. The end result is cell mass and carbon dioxide. If toxin-munching bacteria can be found or engineered for specific hazardous chemicals, these substances can be fed to them at less than half the cost

Q: What are the principal greenhouse gases?

Table 11-2 Alternatives to Some Common Household Chemicals

Chemical	Alternative	Chemical	Alternative
Deodorant	Sprinkle baking soda on a damp washcloth and wipe skin.	General surface cleaner	Mixture of vinegar, salt, and water.
Oven cleaner	Baking soda and water paste, scouring pad.	Bleach	Baking soda or borax.
Toothpaste	Baking soda.	Mildew remover	Mix ½ cup vinegar, ½ cup borax, and warm water.
Drain cleaner	Pour ½ cup salt down drain, followed by boiling water; or pour 1 handful baking soda and ½ cup white vinegar and cover tightly for one minute.	Disinfectant and general cleaner	Mix ½ cup borax in 1 gallon hot water.
Window cleaner	Add 2 teaspoons white vinegar to 1 quart warm water.	Furniture or floor polish	Mix ½ cup lemon juice and 1 cup vegetable or olive oil.
Toilet bowl, tub, and tile cleaner	Mix a paste of borax and water; rub on and let set one hour before scrubbing. Can also scrub with baking soda and a brush.	Carpet and rug shampoos	Sprinkle on cornstarch, baking soda, or borax and vacuum.
Floor cleaner	Add ½ cup vinegar to a bucket of hot water; sprinkle a sponge with borax for tough spots.	Detergents and detergent boosters	Washing soda or borax and soap powder.
Shoe polish	Polish with inside of a banana peel, then buff.	Spray starch	In a spray bottle, mix 1 tablespoon cornstarch in a pint of water.
Silver polish	Clean with baking soda and warm water.	Fabric softener	Add 1 cup white vinegar or ¼ cup baking soda to final rinse.
Air freshener	Set vinegar out in an open dish. Use an opened box of baking soda in closed areas such as refrigerators and closets. To scent the air, use pine boughs or make sachets of herbs and flowers.	Dishwasher soap	1 part borax and 1 part washing soda.
		Pesticides (indoor and outdoor)	Use natural biological controls.

of disposal in landfills, and only one-third the cost of on-site incineration. However, releasing genetically engineered microorganisms into the environment is expensive and controversial (Pro/Con, p. 217). Studies indicate that most wastes can be digested better and more cheaply by naturally occurring microbes.

INCINERATION The EPA estimates that 60% of U.S. hazardous waste could be incinerated. With proper air pollution controls and highly trained personnel, the agency considers incineration as a potentially safe, if expensive, disposal method. However, most environmentalists and some EPA scientists disagree.

Generators of hazardous waste like incinerators. Incineration generally is affordable, and anything can be burned legally. Burning gets rid of the waste and of any legal liability at the same time. Once wastes are mixed and burned it is virtually impossible to trace the resulting toxic ash or air pollution to any one customer of the incinerator company. And the EPA likes hazardous-waste incineration because it gives the appearance of solving the hazardous-waste problem in a way favored by industry.

However, after making an extensive study of hazardous-waste incineration, chemist Peter Montague, an expert in this field, has concluded that it is an out-of-control technology that should be banned. He and other environmentalists point out that all incinerators release toxic air pollution (especially small particles of metals such as lead and mercury that cannot be removed by scrubbers and other devices), create new toxic air pollutants like dioxins, and leave a highly toxic ash to be disposed of in landfills that even the EPA says will eventually leak.

Furthermore, a 1992 memo by EPA's Director of Solid Waste admitted that no U.S. hazardous-waste incinerator can destroy 99.9999% of the most hazardous chemicals, as required by law. Technically, all U.S. hazardous-waste incinerators violate federal law and should be shut down. The EPA, however, continues to allow them to operate.

Most of these pollutants move downwind from the incinerators, where people can breathe them or eat food contaminated by them. In 1993 several epidemiological studies linked respiratory and nerve-disorder problems to people working at or living near hazardous-waste

Is Deep-Well Disposal of Hazardous Waste a Good Idea?

With deep-well disposal, liquid hazardous wastes are pumped under pressure through a pipe into dry, porous geologic formations or into fracture zones of rock far beneath aquifers tapped for drinking and irrigation water (Figure 10-2). In theory these liquids soak into the porous rock material and are isolated from overlying groundwater by essentially impermeable layers of rock.

This method is simple and cheap. Also, it is less visible (because it is usually done on company land) and is less carefully regulated than other disposal methods. Its use is increasing rapidly as other methods are legally restricted or become too expensive.

If sites are chosen according to the best geological and seismic data, deep wells may be a reasonably safe way of disposing of fairly dilute solutions of organic and inorganic waste. With proper site selection and care, it may be safer than incineration. Also, if some use eventually were found for the waste, it could be pumped back to the surface.

However, the Office of Technology Assessment and many environmentalists believe that current regulations for geologic evaluation, long-term monitoring, and long-term liability if wells contaminate groundwater are inadequate and may allow injected wastes to:

- Spill or leak at the surface and leach into groundwater
- Escape into groundwater from corroded pipe casing or leaking seals in the well
- Migrate down or horizontally from the porous layer of rock, where they are transmitted to aquifers (through existing fractures or through new ones caused by earthquakes or even by stresses from the introduction of the wastes)

Until this method is more carefully evaluated and regulated, environmentalists believe that its use should not be allowed to increase.

---

incinerators. Even a videotape produced by Keep America Beautiful (the voice of the waste management industry) admits that incinerators aren't safe enough.

According to EPA hazardous-waste expert William Sanjour, EPA incinerator regulations don't work because

the regulations require no monitoring of the outside air in the vicinity of the incinerator. Because operators maintain the records, they can easily cheat. ... Government inspectors are poorly trained and have low morale and high turnover. ... Government inspectors typically work from nine to five Monday through Friday. So if there is anything particularly nasty to burn, it will be done at night or on weekends. When complaints come in ... the inspector may visit the plant but rarely finds anything. The enforcement officials tend to view the incinerator operator as their client and the public as a nuisance. ... There is no reward to inspectors for finding serious violations.

LAND DISPOSAL Most U.S. hazardous waste is disposed of by deep-well injections (Pro/Con, above), surface impoundments (Figure 10-18), and state-of-the-art landfills (Figure 11-5). Ponds, pits, or lagoons (Figure 10-18) used to store hazardous waste are supposed to be sealed with a plastic liner on the bottom.

Solid wastes settle to the bottom and accumulate, while water and other volatile compounds evaporate into the atmosphere. According to the EPA, however, 70% of these storage basins have no liners, and as many as 90% may threaten groundwater. Eventually all liners leak, and waste will percolate into groundwater. Major storms or hurricanes can cause overflows. Moreover, volatile compounds, such as hazardous organic solvents, can evaporate into the atmosphere and eventually contaminate surface water and groundwater in other locations.

About 5% of the legally regulated hazardous waste produced in the United States is concentrated, put into drums, and buried, either in one of 21 specially designed and monitored commercial hazardous waste landfills (Figure 11-5) or in one of 35 landfills run by companies to handle their own waste. Sweden goes further and buries its concentrated hazardous wastes in underground vaults (Figure 11-8). Ideally such landfills should be located in geologically and environmentally secure places, and carefully monitored for leaks.

However, both the EPA and the U.S. Office of Technology Assessment have concluded that even the best-designed landfill will eventually leak because the liners leak. They can be ripped or punctured during installation or by burrowing animals or dissolved by

Q: What are the four principal sources of human emissions of greenhouse gases?

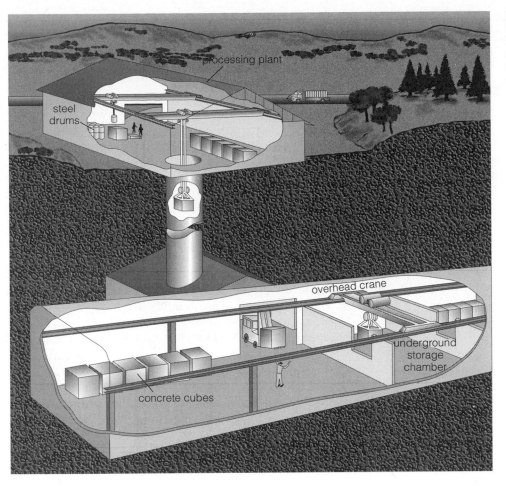

Figure 11-8 Swedish method for handling hazardous waste. Hazardous materials are placed in drums, which are embedded in concrete cubes and then stored in an underground vault.

chemical solvents. Hazardous-waste engineer Peter Montague examined four hazardous waste landfills equipped with the latest synthetic plastic liners and found they all leaked within one year.

When current and future commercial hazardous-waste landfills do leak and threaten water supplies, many of their operators will declare bankruptcy. Then the landfills will become Superfund sites, and taxpayers will pick up the tab for cleaning them up. As EPA hazardous waste expert William Sanjour points out,

> *The real cost of dumping is not borne by the producer of the waste or the disposer, but by the people whose health and property values are destroyed when the wastes migrate onto their property and by the taxpayers who pay to clean it up. ... It is better for liners to leak sooner than later, because then there will be responsible parties that they can get to clean it up. Liners don't protect communities. They protect the people who put the waste there and the politicians who let them put the waste there, because they are long since gone when the problem comes up.*

Some engineers and environmentalists have proposed storing hazardous wastes above ground in large, two-story, reinforced-concrete buildings until better technologies are developed. The first floor would contain no wastes but would have inspection walkways so people could check for leaks from above. Any leachate would be collected, treated, solidified, and returned to the storage building. Such buildings would last for many decades, perhaps as long as a century. Proponents believe that this *in-sight* approach would be a cheaper and safer disposal method than *out-of-sight* landfills or incinerators for many hazardous wastes.

There is also growing concern about accidents during some of the more than 500,000 shipments of hazardous wastes (mostly to landfills and incinerators) in the United States each year. Between 1980 and 1990, for example, there were 13,476 toxic-chemical accidents, causing 309 deaths, over 11,000 injuries, and evacuation of over 500,000 people. Few communities have the equipment and trained personnel to deal adequately with hazardous-waste spills.

A: Burning fossil fuels (57%), use of CFCs (17%), agriculture (15%), deforestation (8–30%)

11-7 Hazardous Waste Regulation in the United States

RESOURCE CONSERVATION AND RECOVERY ACT In 1976 the U.S. Congress passed the Resource Conservation and Recovery Act (RCRA, pronounced "rick-ra"), amending it in 1984. This law requires the EPA to identify hazardous wastes and set standards for their management, and it provides guidelines and financial aid for states to establish waste management programs. The law also requires all firms that store, treat, or dispose of more than 100 kilograms (220 pounds) of hazardous wastes per month to have a permit stating how such wastes are to be managed.

To reduce illegal dumping, hazardous-waste producers granted disposal permits by the EPA must use a "cradle-to-grave" system to keep track of waste transferred from point of origin to approved off-site disposal facilities. However, the EPA and state regulatory agencies do not have enough people to review the documentation of more than 750,000 hazardous-waste generators and 15,000 haulers each year, let alone detect and prosecute offenders.

If caught, violators are subject to large fines. However, many environmentalists argue that the fines are still too low—sending polluters the clear message that crime pays.

Operators of EPA-licensed hazardous-waste landfills must prevent leakage, use at least three wells to monitor the quality of groundwater around the sites, and report any contamination to the EPA. When a landfill reaches capacity and is closed, the operators must cover it with a leakproof cap and monitor the nearby groundwater for 30 years; they are financially responsible for cleanup and damages from leaks for 30 years. Environmentalists consider that provision a serious weakness in the law because leaks from most landfills may not be detected or revealed to the public until after 30 years, passing the hazards and the cleanup costs on to succeeding generations.

Recycled chemical wastes are exempted from control under RCRA. Using this loophole, the EPA (under pressure from producers and handlers of hazardous waste) allows liquid hazardous wastes to be mixed with fuel and burned in industrial boilers, industrial furnaces, and cement kilns, and calls it "recycling." Because these combustion facilities don't have to meet the permit requirements and emission standards of EPA-licensed hazardous-waste incinerators, this increasingly common practice pollutes the air with toxic metals and other hazardous chemicals. And the resulting toxic ash can be mixed with cement (which can then be used in the walls of buildings and in pipes used to deliver drinking water) instead of having to be disposed of in EPA-licensed hazardous-waste landfills. RCRA also allows hazardous wastes to be "recycled" into pesticides as "inert" ingredients.

In 1992 the EPA proposed to exempt any waste containing toxins below certain concentrations from regulation, without requiring any industry that exempted its waste to produce laboratory analyses or data to support its claim. This rule, based on EPA risk-benefit analysis (Section 8-4), would exempt up to 66% of presently defined hazardous waste from federal regulation, pollute the drinking water of at least 13,200 people getting their water from wells within 1.6 kilometers (1 mile) of landfills receiving exempt waste, and create as many as 1,681 new Superfund sites requiring expensive cleanup. According to the EPA the financial benefits to industries from this rule outweigh its estimated harmful effects.

SUPERFUND The 1980 Comprehensive Environmental Response, Compensation and Liability Act is commonly known as the Superfund program. This law (plus amendments in 1986 and 1990) established a $16.3-billion fund, financed jointly by federal and state governments and by taxes on chemical and petrochemical industries, to identify and clean up abandoned hazardous-waste dump sites and leaking underground tanks that threaten human health and the environment. The EPA is authorized to collect fines and sue the owners of abandoned sites and tanks (if they can be found and held responsible) to recover up to three times the cleanup costs.

The EPA has identified 34,000 potential hazardous-waste sites (plus 17,482 more at military bases) but has stopped looking for new ones, even though the General Accounting Office estimates that there are between 103,000 and 425,000 such sites. So far the EPA has placed more than 1,250 sites on a National Priority List for cleanup because they threaten nearby populations.

By 1993, after spending more than $12 billion, the EPA had declared only 180 sites clean or stabilized and had removed only 40 from the priority list. Only $2.4 billion was spent on site-specific activities, with the rest used for outside consultants, administration, management, and litigation. And according to a 1989 report by the Office of Technology Assessment (OTA), about 75% of the cleanups are unlikely to work over the long term.

The OTA and the Waste Management Research Institute estimate that the final list could include at least 10,000 priority sites, with cleanup costs of up to $1 trillion, not counting legal fees. Cleaning up toxic

Q: How much must global CO_2 emissions be cut by 2030 to slow projected global warming to an acceptable rate?

military dumps will cost another $100–$200 billion and take at least 30 years; and cleaning up contaminated Department of Energy sites used to make nuclear weapons will cost an additional $100–$400 billion and take 30–50 years. It is hard to imagine a more convincing reason for emphasizing pollution prevention (Figure 11-6).

Are the fears of the more than 40 million people living near identified hazardous-waste sites justified? According to a 1992 study by the National Academy of Sciences, we don't know. The study concluded that the federal government has **(1)** no comprehensive inventory of waste sites; **(2)** no program for discovering new sites; **(3)** insufficient data for determining safe exposure levels; **(4)** questionable methods for assessing the public health danger at Superfund and other hazardous-waste sites; **(5)** an inadequate system for identifying sites that require immediate action; and **(6)** did not use cost-effective methods to clean up sites.

Meanwhile, real people are living near thousands of real hazardous-waste dumps. These victims are trapped in a toxic nightmare that fills them with fear and that has made any property they own essentially worthless.

GRASS-ROOTS ACTION Studies show that incinerators, landfills, or treatment plants for hazardous wastes have traditionally been located in communities populated by African Americans, Asian Americans, Hispanics, and poor whites. Such actions have been condemned as a mixture of environmental racism and economic discrimination.

Now people of color, the poor, and middle-class whites have joined together in a loose-knit coalition known as the grass-roots movement for environmental justice. This coalition offers the following guidelines for achieving environmental justice for all:

- *Don't compromise our children's futures by cutting deals with polluters and regulators. Environmental justice should not be bought or sold.*

- *Hold polluters and elected officials who go along with them personally accountable because what they are doing is wrong.*

- *Don't fall for the argument that protesters against hazardous-waste landfills, incinerators, and injection wells are holding up progress in dealing with hazardous wastes.* Instead, recognize that the best way to deal with waste and pollution is not to produce so much of it. After that has been done we can decide what to do with what is left—a strategy supported by the National Academy of Sciences (Figure 11-6).

- *Oppose all hazardous-waste landfills, deep-disposal wells, and incinerators.* This will sharply raise the cost of dealing with hazardous materials, discourage location of such facilities in poor neighborhoods often populated by minorities, and encourage waste producers and elected officials to get serious about pollution prevention. The goal of politically powerful waste management companies is to have us produce more and more hazardous (and nonhazardous) waste so they can make higher profits.

- *Recognize that there is no such thing as "safe" disposal of hazardous waste.* Our goal should be to slash production of all waste. For especially hazardous materials the goal should be "Not in Anyone's Backyard" (NIABY) or "Not on Planet Earth" (NOPE).

- *Ban release of any toxic chemical that is persistent in any medium (water, air, sediment, soil) or that bioaccumulates in living things.* In 1992, 13 European nations agreed in principle to work toward achieving this goal.

- *Pressure elected officials to pass legislation requiring that unwanted industries and waste facilities be distributed more widely instead of being concentrated in poor and working-class neighborhoods, many populated mostly by minorities.*

- *Ban all hazardous-waste exports from one country to another* (Spotlight, p. 300).

MAKING THE TRANSITION TO A LOW-WASTE SOCIETY So far we have had our priorities for dealing with solid waste (Figure 11-2) and hazardous waste (Figure 11-6) backwards from what scientists tell us are the best ways to deal with these problems. According to this strategy, we need to replace the "two Bs" of waste management, Burn or Bury, with the "three Rs" of Earth care: Reduce (environmental maturity), Reuse (environmental middle age), Recycle (environmental adolescence). Although recycling usually saves energy and reduces pollution, it still takes energy to recycle materials (Figure 2-43).

With this new way of thinking about waste, the most important question is not: What do we do with the wastes we produce? Instead it is: How can we produce less waste and, for especially hazardous substances, no waste (Individuals Matter, p. 301)? Think of wastes as wasted resources.

Making the transition to a low-waste society will not be easy and is very controversial, but in the long run it will provide more economic and environmental benefits than not doing it. Environmentalists challenge us to set the following goals:

To save money and to escape regulations and local opposition, cities and waste disposal companies in the United States and other MDCs legally ship vast quantities of hazardous waste to other countries. Most legal U.S. exports of hazardous wastes go to Canada and Mexico, but at least nine African countries have also accepted them.

These shipments can take place without EPA approval because U.S. hazardous-waste laws allow exports for "recycling." Sometimes exported wastes labeled as materials to be recycled are dumped after reaching their destination.

U.S. companies are also exporting hazardous waste and jobs by moving highly polluting smelters and manufacturing plants to countries with weak or poorly enforced pollution control laws and with workers willing to work for lower wages under dangerous conditions. A glaring example is the growing number of U.S. and other foreign factories located along Mexico's northern border. Mexico has some strong environmental laws, but enforcement is lax. Most host countries, hungry for jobs and foreign capital, turn a blind eye to unsafe and polluting practices.

There is also a growing illegal trade in hazardous wastes across international borders. There are too few customs inspectors, and they are not trained to detect such shipments. Hazardous wastes have also been mixed with wood chips or sawdust and shipped as burnable material.

Waste disposal firms can charge high prices for picking up hazardous wastes. If they can then dispose of them—legally or illegally—at low costs, they pocket huge profits. Officials of poor LDCs find it hard to resist the income (often in the form of bribes) from receiving these wastes.

Currently at least 83 countries have banned imports of hazardous waste, and some have adopted a "return to sender" policy when illegal waste shipments are discovered. Environmentalists and some members of Congress call for the United States to ban all exports of hazardous waste (including radioactive waste). They would also ban exports of pesticides and drugs not approved for use in the United States and classify violations as criminal acts. They argue that exporting hazardous wastes to other countries (or to other states) encourages the throwaway mentality and discourages pollution prevention. Also, exports of toxic waste may come back to haunt the exporters. For instance, they may contaminate soil or fertilizer used to grow food that is imported by the exporting countries.

In 1989, 105 countries meeting in Basel, Switzerland, drew up the Basel Convention, which establishes principles to be enforced by international law that would control shipments of toxic waste across national borders. However, the United States has refused to sign the convention, and some countries and international law experts say that the pact is too vague and full of loopholes to stop the international trade in hazardous wastes.

An effective U.S. or worldwide ban on all hazardous waste exports would help but would not end illegal trade in these wastes. The potential profits are simply too great. The only real solution to the hazardous-waste problem is to stop most of it from ever being produced.

- *Cut industrial hazardous-waste production 50% over 1990 levels by 2000 and 80% by 2010.*

- *Reuse and recycle (including composting) 60% of municipal solid waste by 2000 and 80% by 2010.*

We will always produce some wastes, but we can produce much less. To prevent pollution and reduce waste, environmentalists urge us to understand and live by four key principles: **(1)** *Everything is connected;* **(2)** *there is no "away" for the wastes we produce;* **(3)** *dilution is not the solution to most pollution; and* **(4)** *the best and cheapest way to deal with waste is not to produce so much.*

The presumption should be that any waste or pollutant is potentially harmful and preventable.... With a pollution prevention strategy, human intelligence and creativity as well as science and technology can focus on preventing, eliminating, or reducing the production of all wastes and pollutants.

JOEL HIRSCHORN

CRITICAL THINKING

1. Explain why you support or oppose the following:
   a. Passing a national beverage-container deposit law
   b. Requiring that all beverage containers be reusable
   c. Requiring all households and businesses to sort recyclable materials for curbside pickup in separate containers

Q: What is the role of ozone (O_3) gas in the stratosphere?

INDIVIDUALS MATTER

- *Buy less by asking yourself if you really need a particular item.*
- *Buy things that are reusable or recyclable, and be sure to reuse and recycle them.*
- *Buy beverages in refillable glass containers instead of cans or throwaway bottles.*
- *Use plastic or metal lunch boxes and metal or plastic garbage containers without throwaway plastic liners.*
- *Carry sandwiches and store food in the refrigerator in reusable containers, instead of wrapping them in aluminum foil or plastic wrap.*
- *Use rechargeable batteries and recycle them when their useful life is over.*
- *Carry groceries and other items in a reusable basket, a canvas or string bag, or a small cart.*
- *Use sponges and washable cloth napkins, dish towels, and handkerchiefs instead of paper ones.*

- *Don't use throwaway paper and plastic plates and cups, eating utensils, and other disposable items when reusable or refillable versions are available.*
- *Buy recycled goods, especially those made by primary recycling, and then recycle them.*
- *Reduce the amount of junk mail you get.* This can be done free by writing to Mail Preference Service, Direct Marketing Association, 11 West 42nd St., P.O. Box 3681, New York, NY 10163, or by calling 212-768-7277 and asking that your name not be sold to large mailing-list companies. Of the junk mail you do receive, recycle as much of the paper as possible.
- *Buy products in concentrated form whenever possible.*
- *Choose items that have the least packaging or, better yet, no packaging ("nude products").*

- *Don't buy helium-filled balloons, and urge elected officials and school administrators to ban balloon releases except for atmospheric research and monitoring.*
- *Compost your yard and food wastes, and lobby local officials to set up a community composting program.*
- *Use pesticides and other hazardous chemicals (Table 11-1) only when absolutely necessary, and in the smallest amount possible.*
- *Use less hazardous (and usually cheaper) cleaning products (Table 11-2).*
- *Do not flush hazardous chemicals down the toilet, pour them down the drain, bury them, throw them away in the garbage, or dump them down storm drains. Consult your local health department or environmental agency for safe disposal methods.*
- *Support legislation that would encourage pollution prevention and waste reduction.*

---

d. Requiring consumers to pay for plastic or paper bags at grocery and other stores to encourage the use of reusable shopping bags

2. Keep a list for a week of the solid waste you throw away. What percentage is materials that could be recycled, reused, or burned for energy? What percentage of the items could you have done without?

3. Would you oppose locating a hazardous-waste landfill, treatment plant, deep injection well, or incinerator in your community? Explain. If you oppose these disposal facilities, how should the hazardous waste generated in your community and state be managed?

4. Give your reasons for agreeing or disagreeing with each of the following proposals for dealing with hazardous waste:
   a. Reduce the production of hazardous waste and encourage recycling and reuse of hazardous materials by levying a tax or fee on producers for each unit of waste generated.
   b. Ban all land disposal of hazardous waste to encourage recycling, reuse, and treatment and to protect groundwater from contamination.
   c. Provide low-interest loans, tax breaks, and other financial incentives to encourage industries producing hazardous waste to recycle, reuse, treat, destroy, and reduce generation of such waste.
   d. Ban the shipment of hazardous waste from the United States to any other country.
   e. Ban the shipment of hazardous waste from one state to another.

5. What changes, if any, would you be willing to make in your own lifestyle to prevent pollution and reduce waste?

---

12 Economics, Politics, and Worldviews

12-1 Economic Systems and Environmental Problems

WHAT SUPPORTS AND DRIVES ECONOMIES?
The kinds of capital used in an economy to produce material goods and services, and thus to sustain economic growth, are called **economic resources**. They fall into three groups:

1. **Earth capital** or **natural resources**: resources produced by Earth's natural processes. They include the planet's air, water, and land; nutrients and minerals in the soil and deeper in the earth's crust; wild and domesticated plants and animals (biodiversity); and nature's dilution, waste disposal, pest control, and recycling services.

2. **Manufactured capital**: items made from Earth capital. These include tools, machinery, equipment, factory buildings, and transportation and distribution facilities.

3. **Human capital**: people's physical and mental talents. Workers sell their time and talents for wages. Managers take responsibility for combining Earth capital, manufactured capital, and workers to produce an economic good. In market-based systems entrepreneurs and investors put up the monetary capital needed to produce an economic good in the hope of making a profit on their investment.

An **economy** is a system of production, distribution, and consumption of economic goods. In such a system individuals, businesses, and societies make **economic decisions** about what goods and services to produce, how to produce them, how much to produce, how to distribute them, and what to buy and sell.

TYPES OF ECONOMIC SYSTEMS There are two major types of economic systems: centrally planned and market-based.

In a **pure command economic system**, or **centrally planned economy**, all economic decisions are made by the government. This command-and-control system is based on the belief that government control and ownership of the means of production is the most efficient and equitable way to produce, use, and distribute scarce resources. The recent failure of the command-and-control economic system of the former Soviet Union and the enormous pollution and environmental degradation left behind cast serious doubts on the effectiveness of a centrally planned economy.

In a **pure market economic system**, also known as **pure capitalism**, all economic decisions are made in *markets*, where buyers (demanders) and sellers (suppliers) of economic goods freely interact without government or other interference. All economic resources are owned by private individuals and private institutions, rather than by the government. All buying and selling is based on *pure competition*, in which no seller or buyer is powerful enough to control the supply, demand, or price of a good; and all sellers and buyers have full information about and access to the market.

Economic decisions in a pure market system are governed by interactions of demand, supply, and price. Buyers want to pay as little as possible for an economic good, and sellers want to set as high a price as possible so as to maximize profit. **Market equilibrium** occurs when the quantity supplied equals the quantity demanded, and the price is no higher than buyers are willing to pay and no lower than sellers are willing to accept. Various factors can change the demand and supply of an economic good and establish a new market equilibrium.

Economists often represent pure capitalism as a circular flow of economic goods and money between households and businesses operating essentially independently of the ecosphere (Figure 12-1). By contrast, environmentalists emphasize the ultimate dependence of this or any economic system on the ecosphere (Figure 12-2).

In a pure capitalist system, a company has no legal allegiance to a particular nation, no obligation to supply any particular good or service, and no obligation to provide jobs, safe workplaces, or environmental protection. The company's only obligation is to produce the highest possible short-term economic return (profit) for the owners or stockholders whose capital the company is using to do business.

Q: How much of the stratospheric ozone over the Antarctic is destroyed from September to December each year?

When it is asked how much it will cost to protect the environment, one more question should be asked: How much will it cost our civilization if we do not?

GAYLORD NELSON

In reality, all countries have **mixed economic systems** that fall somewhere between the pure market and pure command systems. The economic systems of countries such as China and North Korea fall toward the command-and-control end of the economic spectrum, while those of countries such as the United States and Canada fall toward the market-based end of the spectrum. Most other countries fall somewhere in between.

ECONOMIC GROWTH Virtually all economies seek **economic growth**: an increase in the capacity of the economy to provide goods and services for final use.

Such growth is accomplished by maximizing the flow of matter and energy resources (throughput) by means of population growth (more consumers), more consumption per person, or both (Figures 2-42 and 12-1). Nature is seen as a "superstore" stocked with an infinite supply of goods to be used to meet the needs and ever-expanding wants of a consumer society. All economic growth is seen as good, an idea that many environmentalists and some economists challenge (Spotlight, p. 305).

GROSS NATIONAL PRODUCT: FAULTY RADAR

Economic growth is usually measured by the increase

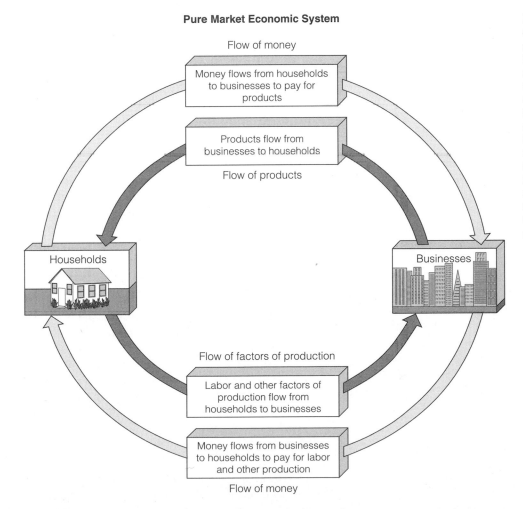

Pure Market Economic System

Flow of money

Money flows from households to businesses to pay for products

Products flow from businesses to households

Flow of products

Households

Businesses

Flow of factors of production

Labor and other factors of production flow from households to businesses

Money flows from businesses to households to pay for labor and other production

Flow of money

Figure 12-1 In a pure market economic system, economic goods and money would flow in a closed loop of households and businesses. People in households spend money to buy goods that firms produce, and firms spend money to buy factors of production (natural capital, manufactured capital, and human capital). In many economics textbooks this and other economic systems are depicted, as here, as if they were self-contained and thus not dependent on the ecosphere—a model that reinforces the idea that unlimited growth of any kind is sustainable.

A: About 50%—creating an ozone hole larger in area than the continental United States

Figure 12-2 Environmentalists see all economies as artificial subsystems dependent on resources and services provided by the sun and the ecosphere. A consumer society devoted to unlimited economic growth to satisfy ever-expanding wants assumes that ecosphere resources and services are essentially infinite or that our technological cleverness will allow us to overcome any ecosphere limits.

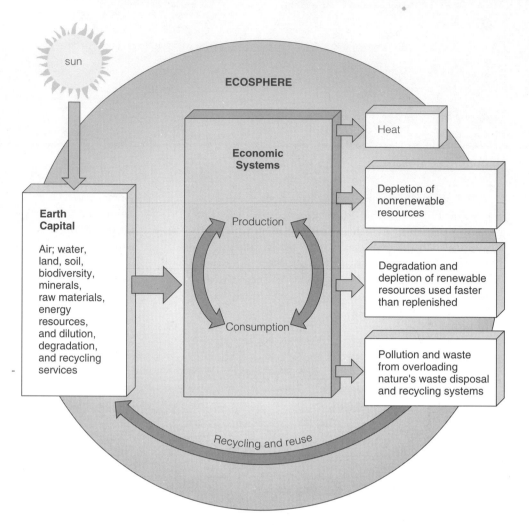

in a country's **gross national product (GNP)**: the market value in current dollars of all goods and services produced by an economy for final use during a year (an indicator introduced in the late 1940s). To get a clearer picture economists use the **real GNP**: the GNP adjusted for *inflation* (any increase in the average price level of final goods and services). And to show how the average person's slice of the economic pie is changing, economists use the **real GNP per capita**: the real GNP divided by the total population. If population expands faster than economic growth, the real GNP per capita falls.

We are urged to buy and consume more and more so that the GNP will rise, making the country and the world a better place for everyone (see cartoon). The truth is that GNP indicators were never intended to be measures of social well-being, environmental health, or even economic health because:

■ *They hide the negative impact on humans and the rest of the ecosphere of producing many goods and services.* For example, each year in the United States the estimated $150 billion in health care expenses and

other damages caused by air pollution raise the GNP and GNP per capita. So do the funeral expenses for the 150,000–350,000 Americans killed prematurely each year from air pollution in the United States. The $2.2 billion that Exxon spent partially cleaning up the oil spill from the *Exxon Valdez* tanker pushed up the GNP, as did the $1 billion spent because of the accident at the Three Mile Island nuclear power plant.

■ *They don't include depletion and degradation of natural resources or Earth capital upon which all economies ultimately depend* (Solutions, p. 5 and Figure 12-2). A country can be headed toward ecological bankruptcy—exhausting its mineral resources, eroding its soils, polluting its water, cutting down its forests, destroying its wetlands and estuaries, and depleting its wildlife and fisheries—yet have a rapidly rising GNP—at least for a while until its ecological debts come due.

■ *They hide or underestimate some positive effects on society.* For example, more energy-efficient light bulbs, appliances, and cars reduce electric and

Q: If all ozone-depleting substances were banned tomorrow, how long would it take for the ozone layer to return to 1985 levels?

To Grow or Not to Grow: Is That the Question?

In the American Northwest, the timber-based economy is in trouble, and recent efforts to save old-growth forests and the northern spotted owl (Figure 6-2) have run into an economic buzz saw. Embattled loggers and environmentalists alike have too often framed their positions in either-or terms: "Trees or jobs?" "Owls or people?" What we really need to ask is, "How can we have trees *and* jobs?" "How can we save the owls and the forests without putting people out of work?" "What happens to jobs after all the trees are cut?"

The same types of polarized positions apply to the question of economic growth in general. On one side, economists and investors argue that we must have unlimited economic growth to create jobs, satisfy people's economic needs and wants, clean up the environment, and help reduce poverty. They see the earth as an essentially unlimited source of raw materials and the environment as an infinite sink for wastes. Any resource or environmental limits can be overcome by technological innovation. To them, environmentalists put endangered species above endangered people, threaten jobs, and are against growth.

On the other hand, environmentalists and some economists argue that economic systems depend on resources and services provided by the sun and by Earth's natural processes (Figure 12-2). A healthy economy is ultimately dependent on a healthy planet. If these beliefs are correct, we must replace the economics of unlimited growth with the economics of sustainability over the next few decades.

The question then is not so much, "To grow or not to grow?" but, "How can we grow without plundering the planet?" or, "How can we grow as if Earth matters?"

Reprinted with permission of King Features Syndicate.

gasoline bills and pollution, but these register as a drop in GNP. GNP indicators also do not include the labor we put into volunteer work, the health care we give loved ones, the food we grow for ourselves, or the cooking, cleaning, and repairs we do for ourselves.

- *They tell us nothing about economic justice.* They don't tell us how resources, income, or the harmful effects of economic growth (pollution, waste dumps, land degradation) are distributed among the people in a country. UNICEF suggests that countries should be ranked not by average GNP per capita but by average income of the lowest 40% of their people.

Russell Petersen, former head of the White House Council on Environmental Quality, summed up the problem with using GNP as a guideline for progress:

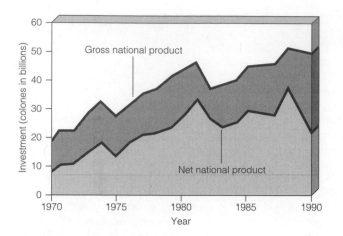

Figure 12-3 GNP and NNP for Costa Rica, 1970–90. The NNP was calculated by adjusting the GNP to include depletion of the country's forests, soils, and fisheries. If depletion of coal, mineral ores, and other nonrenewable resources had been included, Costa Rica's NNP would have grown even more slowly. (Data from World Resources Institute)

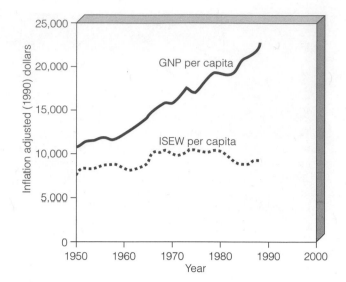

Figure 12-4 Comparison of GNP and ISEW (index of sustainable economic welfare) per person in the United States, 1950–88. After rising by 42% between 1950 and 1976, the ISEW fell 12% between 1977 and 1988. (Data from Herman E. Daly, John B. Cobb, Jr., and Clifford W. Cobb)

If we produce a million dollars worth of carcinogens, this weighs as much on the GNP scale as a million dollars worth of antibiotics. If we hire a housekeeper, this counts in the GNP, but when one's spouse manages the household, this doesn't count. Teaching counts, but learning doesn't. GNP gives no measure of the hungry, the unemployed, the sick, the ill-housed, the illiterate, the oppressed, the frightened, the unhappily employed, or those who have reached the highest level of fulfillment. Furthermore, it does not measure the waste of resources, the spending of our natural capital such as oil, or the befoulment of our life support systems.

SOLUTIONS: BETTER INDICATORS Environmentalists and some economists believe that GNP indicators should be replaced or supplemented with existing—but not widely used—indicators that measure the quality of life and our harmful impacts on the ecosphere. Here are three such indicators:

- *Net economic welfare (NEW).* This approach, developed in 1972 by economists William Nordhaus and James Tobin (and used to some extent in Japan), estimates the costs of pollution and other "negative" goods and services included in the GNP, and it subtracts them from the GNP to give the NEW. Economist David Pearce estimates that pollution and natural resource degradation subtract 1–5% from the GNP of MDCs and 5–15% for LDCs, and that in general these percentages are rising. Dividing a country's NEW by its population gives the *per capita NEW.* Since 1940 the real

NEW per capita in the United States has risen at about half the rate of the real GNP per person, and since 1968 the gap between these two indicators has been widening.

- *Net national product (NNP).* This approach, developed by economist Robert Repetto and other researchers at the World Resources Institute, includes the depletion or destruction of natural resources as a factor in GNP (Figure 12-3).

- *Index of sustainable economic welfare (ISEW).* This comprehensive indicator of well-being was developed in the 1980s by economists Herman E. Daly and John B. Cobb, Jr. It measures per capita GNP adjusted for inequalities in income distribution, depletion of nonrenewable resources, loss of wetlands, loss of farmland from soil erosion and urbanization, the cost of air and water pollution, and estimates of long-term environmental damage from ozone depletion and possible global warming. It has been falling in the United States since 1977 (Figure 12-4).

None of these new indicators is perfect, but they are much better than relying on GNP. Without such indicators we know too little about what is happening to people, the environment, and the planet's natural resource base; what needs to be done; and what types of policies work. In effect, we are trying to guide national and global economies through treacherous economic and environmental waters at ever-increasing speed using faulty radar.

Q: What does the EPA consider to be the three most dangerous indoor air pollutants in MDCs?

CONNECTIONS: INTERNAL AND EXTERNAL COSTS All economic goods and services have both internal and external costs. For example, the price you pay for a car reflects the costs of the factory, raw materials, labor, marketing, shipping, and company and dealer profits. After you buy the car, you also have to pay for gasoline, maintenance, and repair. All these direct costs, paid for by the seller and the buyer of an economic good, are called **internal costs**.

Making, distributing, and using any economic good or service also involves what economists call **externalities**. These are social costs or benefits not included in the market price of an economic good or service. For example, if a car dealer builds an aesthetically pleasing showroom and grounds, that is an **external benefit** to other people who enjoy the sight at no cost to themselves.

On the other hand, extracting and processing raw materials to make and propel cars disturbs land, pollutes the environment, reduces biodiversity, and harms people (Figure 1-9). These harmful effects are **external costs** passed on to workers, to the general public, and in some cases to future generations. Air pollution from cars also kills or weakens some types of trees, raising the price of lumber and paper. In addition, taxes may go up because the public demands that the government regulate the pollution and degradation associated with producing and operating motor vehicles.

You add to the external costs when you throw trash out of a car, drive a gas-guzzler (which adds more air pollution than a more efficient car), disconnect or don't maintain a car's air pollution control devices, drive with faulty brakes, or don't keep your motor tuned. Because these harmful costs aren't included in the market price, you don't connect them with the car or type of car you are driving. As a consumer and taxpayer, however, you pay these hidden costs sooner or later in the form of higher taxes, higher health costs, higher health insurance, and higher cleaning and maintenance bills.

These external costs also show up as environmental problems—loss of biodiversity (Chapters 5 and 6), soil erosion (Chapter 7), depletion of nonrenewable resources (Chapters 1 and 4), loss of stratospheric ozone and possible climate change (Chapter 9), air pollution (Chapter 9), water pollution (Chapter 10), and solid and hazardous waste (Chapter 11). The health (Chapter 8) and economic costs of these problems are passed on to society at large or to future generations.

To pro-growth economists, external costs are minor defects in the flow of production and consumption in a self-contained economy (Figure 12-1); they assume that these defects can be cured by the profits made from more economic growth in a free-market economy. To environmentalists and many scientists (Spotlight, p. 15) the rising number of harmful externalities is a warning sign that our economic systems are stressing the ecosphere and depleting Earth capital, and that they need to be restructured.

12-2 Solutions: Using Economics to Improve Environmental Quality

FULL-COST PRICING As long as businesses get subsidies and tax breaks for extracting and using virgin resources and are not taxed for the pollutants they produce, few will volunteer to commit economic suicide by changing. Suppose you own a company and believe it's wrong to subject your workers to hazardous conditions and to pollute the environment any more than can be handled by Earth's natural processes. If you voluntarily improve safety conditions for your workers and install pollution controls but your competitors don't, your product will cost more and you will be at a competitive disadvantage. Unless you can come up with better and more cost-effective ways to improve safety and reduce pollution, your profits will decline, and sooner or later you may go bankrupt and your employees will lose their jobs.

One way to deal with the problem of harmful external costs is for the government to add taxes, pass laws, provide subsidies, or use other strategies that force or entice producers to include all or most of this expense in the market price of economic goods. Then that price would be the **full cost** of these goods: internal costs plus its short- and long-term external costs. Full-cost pricing involves *internalizing the external costs*. This requires government action because few companies will increase their cost of doing business unless their competitors have to do it as well.

What would happen if such a policy was phased in over the next 10 to 20 years? Economic growth would be redirected. We would increase the beneficial parts of the GNP, decrease the harmful parts, increase production of beneficial goods, and raise the net economic welfare. Preventing pollution would become more profitable than cleaning it up; and waste reduction, recycling, and reuse would be more profitable than burying or burning most of the wastes we produce.

We would pay more for most things because their market prices would be closer to their true costs, but everything would be "up front." Most external costs would no longer be hidden. We would also have the information we need to make informed economic decisions (as called for by the theory behind a true

A: Cigarette smoke, radon, and formaldehyde

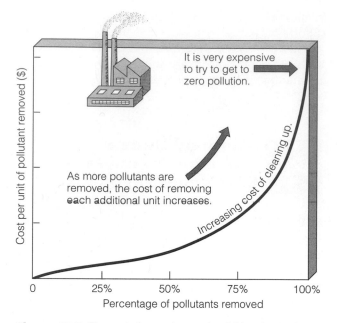

Figure 12-5 The cost of removing each additional unit of pollution rises exponentially, which explains why it is usually cheaper to prevent pollution than to clean it up.

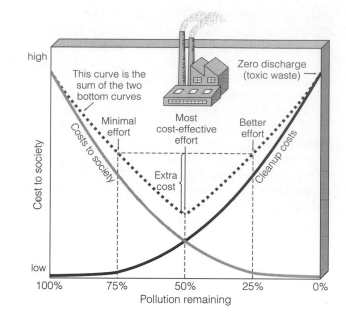

Figure 12-6 Finding the optimal level of pollution.

free-market economy) about the effects of our lifestyles on the planet's life-support systems.

Moreover, real market prices wouldn't always be higher, and some things might even cost less. Internalizing external costs encourages producers to find ways to cut costs by inventing more resource-efficient and less harmful methods of production, and to offer less harmful, Earth-sustaining (or *green*) products. Jobs would be lost in Earth-degrading businesses, but at least as many jobs—some analysts say more—could be created in Earth-sustaining businesses.

As external costs are internalized, governments must reduce income and other taxes, and withdraw subsidies once used to hide and pay for these external costs. Otherwise consumers will face higher market prices without tax relief—a policy guaranteed to fail.

Full-cost pricing makes so much sense you might be wondering why it's not more widely done. One reason is that many producers of harmful and wasteful goods fear they would have to charge so much that they couldn't stay in business or would have to give up government subsidies that have helped hide the external costs. And why should they want to change a system that's been so good to them? Another reason is that it's difficult to internalize external costs because it's not easy to put a price tag on all the harmful effects of making and using an economic good. People also disagree on the values they attach to various costs and benefits. However, making difficult choices about how resources should be used and distributed is what economics and politics are all about.

CONTROL OR PREVENTION? Shouldn't our goal be zero pollution? Ideally, yes. In the real world, not necessarily. For most pollutants, economists and some environmentalists say, the answer is no. First, nature can handle some of our wastes, as long as we don't destroy, degrade, or overload these natural processes. But toxic products that cannot be degraded by natural processes or that break down very slowly in the environment should not be produced or used (except in small amounts regulated by permits).

Second, as long as we continue to rely on pollution control we can't afford zero pollution for any but the most harmful substances. We can remove a certain percentage of the pollutants in air, water, or soil, but when we remove more, the price per unit rises sharply (Figure 12-5). Beyond a certain point, the costs will be greater than the harmful effects of pollution. As a result, some businesses could go bankrupt, and some people could lose jobs, homes, and savings. If we don't go far enough, the harmful external effects will cost more than pollution reduction.

How do we achieve this balance? Theoretically we begin by plotting a curve of the estimated economic costs of cleaning up pollution and a curve of the estimated social (external) costs of pollution. Adding the two curves together, we get a third curve showing the total costs. At the lowest point on this third curve is the balance point, called the *optimal level of pollution* (Figure 12-6).

On a graph this looks neat and simple, but environmentalists and business leaders often disagree in

Q: What is the most dangerous indoor air pollutant in LDCs?

their estimates of the harmful costs of pollution. This approach assumes that we know which substances are harmful and how much each part of the environment can handle without serious environmental harm—things we most likely will never know to the degree we need.

Some environmentalists believe that relying mostly on this regulatory, end-of-pipe approach is doomed to failure. They argue that as long as population and per capita resource use continue to rise, any gains based on pollution control will eventually be overwhelmed (Figure 1-10). Instead of spending a lot of money and time setting and enforcing standards, arguing over "optimal" levels, and cleaning up chemicals we release into the environment, they argue, we should start rewarding people for preventing pollution and penalizing those who don't.

These environmentalists also call for reversing the present assumption that a chemical or new technology is safe until it is shown to be harmful. By contrast, if a chemical or new technology were considered potentially harmful until it was shown to be safe—and if this were coupled with full-cost pricing—emphasis would shift from pollution cleanup to less costly and more effective pollution prevention.

Critics argue that this approach would wreck the economy, putting large numbers of people out of work. Proponents counter that our present course will further deplete the Earth capital upon which our economies and survival depend, eventually wrecking the environment and thus the economy, putting even more people out of work, and killing large numbers of people.

REGULATION OR MARKET FORCES? Controlling or preventing pollution and reducing resource waste require government intervention in the marketplace. This can be done either by regulation or by using market forces.

Regulation is a *command-and-control* approach that involves passing and enforcing laws that set pollution standards, establish deadlines and penalties, regulate harmful activities, ban the release of toxic chemicals into the environment, and require that certain resources be protected from use or unsustainable use.

Studies estimate that the current U.S. bill for environmental protection—over $120 billion per year—based mostly on regulation, could be cut by one-third to one-half if more effective market-based policies were used. Ways to use market forces to improve environmental quality and reduce resource waste are:

- *Providing subsidies that encourage desirable behavior.*
- *Withdrawing subsidies that encourage harmful behavior.*

- *Granting tradable pollution and resource-use rights.* This would be done by setting a total limit for a pollutant or resource use and allocating that total among manufacturers or users by permit. Permit holders not using their entire allocation could keep it as a credit against future expansion; use it in another part of their operation; or sell it to other companies. Tradable rights could also be established between countries to preserve biodiversity and to reduce emissions of greenhouse gases, ozone-destroying chemicals, lead, and other chemicals with regional or global effects.

- *Enacting green taxes.* This could include taxes on each unit of pollution discharged into the air or water, each unit of hazardous or nuclear waste produced, each unit of specified virgin resources used, each unit of pesticide used, each unit of fossil fuel used, and each unit of solid waste produced. To allow economic adjustment, such eco-taxes should be phased in over 5–10 years. At the same time, income and other taxes would be reduced so that low- and middle-income people and businesses (especially small ones that provide the most innovation and new jobs) are not penalized.

- *Charging user fees.* Users would pay fees to cover all or most costs for grazing livestock and extracting lumber and minerals from public lands, and for using water provided by government-financed projects.

- *Requiring manufacturers to post a pollution prevention bond when they open a plant, incinerator, or landfill.* After a reasonable time the deposit (with interest) would be returned *minus* estimated environmental costs.

Each of these approaches has advantages and disadvantages (Table 12-1, p. 310).

12-3 Solutions: Reducing Poverty

THE TRICKLE-DOWN APPROACH Poverty is usually defined as not being able to meet one's basic economic needs for clean air and water, food, shelter, and health care (Spotlight, p. 7). Currently, 1.2 billion people—one of every five persons on the planet—in LDCs have an annual income of less than $370 per year—roughly $1 per day—classified by the World Bank as poverty. This number is projected to rise to 1.5 billion by 2025. Poverty causes premature deaths and preventable health problems and often pushes people to make unsustainable use of potentially renewable resources in order to survive.

Table 12-1 Economic Solutions to Pollution and Resource Waste

Solution	Internalizes External Costs	Innovation	International Competitiveness	Administrative Costs	Increases Government Revenue
Regulation	Partially	Can encourage	Decreased*	High	No
Subsidies	No	Can encourage	Increased	Low	No
Withdrawing Harmful Subsidies	Yes	Can encourage	Decreased*	Low	Yes
Tradable Rights	Yes	Encourages	Decreased*	Low	Yes
Green Taxes	Yes	Encourages	Decreased*	Low	Yes
User Fees	Yes	Can encourage	Decreased*	Low	Yes
Pollution Prevention Bonds	Yes	Encourages	Decreased*	Low	No

*Unless more cost-effective and productive technologies are developed.

Most economists believe that a growing economy is the best way to help the poor. Economic growth can lead to new businesses and expansion of existing ones. This creates more jobs, enables more of the increased wealth to reach workers, and provides more tax revenues for helping the poor help themselves—the so-called *trickle-down theory.*

The facts, however, suggest either that the theory is wrong or that it has not been applied. Instead of trickling down, most of the benefits of economic growth have flowed up since 1950 to make the top fifth of the world's people much richer and the bottom fifth poorer; most of those in between have lost or gained only slightly in real income per capita (Figure 1-6).

ENCOURAGING SUSTAINABLE DEVELOPMENT
Critics of the current approach to economic development believe that dealing with the interrelated problems of poverty, environmental degradation, and population growth requires new forms of development based on Mahatma Gandhi's concept of *antyodaya*: putting the poor and their environment first, not last. They believe that more beneficial and sustainable economic development can be achieved by:

- *Protecting what works.* This involves learning where and how people are living sustainably, and not disrupting such cultures.

- *Involving local residents—including women—and private nongovernmental organizations (NGOs) in the planning and execution of all projects.* This means asking the poor what they need, giving it to them, putting them in leadership positions, and telling others about what works.

- *Making use of local wisdom, skills, and resources.* The poor generally know far more about poverty, survival, environmental sustainability, local needs, and what will work locally than do outside bureaucrats or experts.

- *Learning from other cultures about sustainable living and sharing this knowledge with people in other LDCs and in MDCs.*

WAYS TO REDUCE POVERTY Sharply reducing poverty requires governments of most LDCs to make drastic, difficult, and controversial policy changes. They include:

- *Shifting more of the national budget to aid the rural and urban poor*

- *Giving villages, villagers, and the urban poor title to common lands and to crops and trees they plant on common lands*

- *Redistributing some of the land owned by the wealthy to the poor*

- *Extending full human rights to women, with special emphasis on poor women*

Analysts urge MDCs and the rich in LDCs to help reduce poverty. Controversial ways to do this include:

- *Forgiving at least 60% of the $1.35 trillion that LDCs owe to MDCs and international lending agencies.* Some of this debt can be forgiven in exchange for agreements by the governments of LDCs to increase expenditures for rural development, family planning, health care, education, better

Q: How many people in the United States die prematurely each year because of air pollution?

land redistribution, protection of biodiversity and undeveloped areas, ecological restoration, and sustainable use of renewable resources.

■ *Increasing the nonmilitary aid to LDCs from MDCs.* This aid would go directly to the poor to help them become more self-reliant, rather than more dependent on MDCs.

■ *Shifting most international aid from large-scale to small-scale projects targeted to benefit local communities of the poor.*

■ *Requiring international lending agencies to use an environmental and social impact statement (developed by standardized guidelines) to evaluate any proposed development project.* No project should be supported unless its net environmental impact is favorable, most of its benefits go to the poorest 40% of the people affected, and the local people it affects are involved in planning and executing the project. All projects should be carefully monitored and further funding halted immediately when environmental safeguards are not followed.

■ *Lifting trade barriers that hinder the export of commodities from LDCs to MDCs.* Trade barriers in rich countries cost LDCs about $100 billion annually in lost sales and depressed prices. However, trade policies must be judged primarily on how they benefit the environment, workers, and the poorest 40% of humanity.

■ *Establishing policies that will encourage MDCs and LDCs to slow population growth and stabilize their populations as soon as possible.*

12-4 Solutions: Making the Transition to a Sustainable-Earth Economy

SUSTAINABLE-EARTH ECONOMIES: A NEW VISION What's wrong with today's economies? Most economists, business leaders, and government officials would answer, "Not much." They believe any problems caused by current market-based economic systems can be cured by further unlimited growth in an expanded global economy built around less—not more—government interference into economic matters. To them the best way to sustain the earth and its people is to free the market and let it work on a global basis.

Most environmentalists and some economists and business leaders disagree. They believe that today's economies based on depleting Earth capital and pro-

ducing huge amounts of pollution and waste (Figures 1-9 and 2-42) are unsustainable and must be converted to *sustainable-Earth economies* over the next few decades. This new vision of economics would:

■ *Change the system of economic rewards (subsidies) and penalties (taxes and regulations) in today's mixed-market economies so that the highest profits and largest source of jobs lie in Earth-sustaining economic activities.*

■ *Be guided by economic, social, and environmental indicators that distinguish between harmful and helpful forms of growth (Figures 12-3 and 12-4).*

■ *Use full-cost pricing, in which externalities are included in the market prices of all goods and services.* This would be accomplished by withdrawing Earth-degrading subsidies, adding Earth-sustaining subsidies, and using a mix of regulation, tradable pollution and resource use rights, green taxes, and user fees (Table 12-1).

■ *Slow human population growth and then gradually reduce population in all countries.*

■ *Greatly reduce poverty by meeting the basic needs of all.*

■ *Require all agencies of federal, state, and local governments to purchase products with the highest feasible percentage of post-consumer recycled materials and energy efficiency and to minimize use of disposable products.*

■ *Require all products to be audited (using standardized guidelines) for environmental impact from cradle to grave, and to carry green labels summarizing this information in easily understandable form.*

■ *Not allow the concepts of free trade and the global marketplace to restrict the freedom of any country or region to impose higher environmental, consumer, worker-safety, or resource-depletion standards than found in other countries.*

■ *Repair past damage and create jobs by using local people to replant forests and grasslands, restore soil fertility, and rehabilitate streams and wetlands.*

Even if one believes that sustainable-Earth economics is desirable, is it possible to make such a drastic change in the way people think and act? Some environmentalists, economists, and business leaders say it's not only possible but imperative and that it can be done over the next 40–50 years (the time span for the radical transformation of the current economies in most MDCs since 1950). They call for *all* government subsidies encouraging resource depletion, waste, pollution, and environmental degradation to be phased out over the next 10–20 years and replaced with taxes on such activities. During that same period, new government subsidies would be phased in for businesses built around recycling and reuse, reducing waste, preventing pollution, improving energy efficiency, and using renewable energy. Income and other taxes would be reduced to compensate for the increase in taxes leading to full-market pricing.

Economic models indicate that after this first phase is completed the entire economy would be transformed within another 30–40 years. The system for change just described is economically feasible because it represents a shift in which economic actions are rewarded (profitable) and which ones are discouraged. It doesn't go against the profit motive, but uses it to redirect the economy. Because these plans would be well publicized and would take effect over decades, businesses would have time to adjust. Because businesses go where the profits are, most of today's Earth-degrading businesses would be tomorrow's Earth-sustaining businesses—a win-win solution for business and the earth.

The problem in making this shift is not economics but politics. It involves the difficult task of convincing business leaders and elected officials to begin changing the current system of rewards and penalties that is profitable and that has given them economic and political power. This vital task requires vigorous political activity by ordinary citizens (bottom-up politics).

CONNECTIONS: JOBS AND THE ENVIRONMENT

Evidence indicates that improvements in environmental quality will not lead to a net loss of jobs. Telling workers that they must choose between their jobs and a cleaner environment is a false choice used by some business and political leaders to weaken unions, undermine improvements in worker safety and health, create fear, pit workers against environmentalists, and hide the real causes of most job losses.

Studies have shown that the major reasons for job loss in the United States are unsustainable use of potentially sustainable resources (clear-cutting old-growth forests); rapid depletion of nonrenewable resources (oil and minerals); automation; declining sales because of more efficient and innovative competitors; higher energy costs without improvements in energy efficiency (Section 4-2); cheaper labor in other countries; decline of unsustainable "sunset" industries; failure to modernize or to invest in emerging "sunrise" industries; decreased research and development by government and business; and a reduction in defense contracts. A Bureau of Labor study found that only 0.1% of the job loss in the United States in 1988, for example, was linked to environmental causes.

Jobs can be lost in any economy as businesses decline or disappear because of changes in technologies and markets and resource substitution. This can have tragic impacts on individuals and on communities dependent on sunset businesses.

The real issues are whether a country and investors are investing in new technologies and sunrise businesses (so more jobs are created than are lost), and whether people losing their jobs are retrained and helped financially until they can find new jobs.

Promoting investments in Earth-sustaining businesses will create a variety of planet-friendly jobs requiring low-, moderate-, and high-level skills. Here are some examples:

- Increasing the aluminum recycling rate to 75% would create 350,000 more jobs.

- Collecting and refilling reusable containers creates many more jobs per dollar of investment than using throwaway containers, with most of the jobs created in local communities.

- According to the Council for an Energy-Efficient Economy, improving the fuel economy of new cars in the United States to 17 kilometers per liter (40 miles per gallon) by 2000 would lead to a net gain of 70,000 jobs by spurring development of new technology and by putting more money in the hands of consumers.

- A congressional study concluded that investing $115 billion per year in solar energy and improving energy efficiency would eliminate about 1 million jobs in oil, gas, coal, and electricity production but would create 2 million new jobs. And investment of the money saved by reducing energy waste could create another 2 million jobs.

- Large numbers of jobs could also be created by establishing a national and global network of Civilian Conservation Corps supported by government funds, private enterprise, or both. They could reforest degraded areas, help restore degraded wetlands and streams, and weatherize low-income housing units.

Although a host of new jobs would be created in a sustainable-Earth economy, jobs will be lost in some industries, regions, and communities. Ways to ease the transition include (1) providing tax breaks to make it more profitable for companies to keep or hire more workers instead of replacing them with machines; (2) using incentives to encourage location of sunrise industries in hard-hit communities and helping such areas diversify their economic base; and (3) providing income and retraining assistance for workers dis-

Q: Worldwide, how many people live in cities where outdoor air is unhealthy to breathe?

Germany: Investing in the Future and the Earth

SOLUTIONS

German (and Japanese) political and business leaders see sales of environmental goods and services—already a more than $250 billion per year business—as a major source of new markets and income in the next century as environmental standards and concerns will rise everywhere.

Stricter environmental standards in Germany have paid off in a cleaner environment and the development of cutting-edge technologies that can be sold at home and abroad. In 1977 the German government started the Blue-Angel product-labeling program to inform consumers about products that cause the least environmental harm. Since 1985 a more complete cradle-to-grave environmental audit of products has been available in *Okotest* (Ecotest)—the environmental equivalent of *Consumer Reports* magazine.

The result has been a torrent of new environmentally friendly products that gives German producers a competitive edge in the rapidly growing global market for such products.

Mostly because of stricter air pollution regulations, German companies also sell the world's cleanest and most efficient gas turbines, and they have developed the world's first steel mill that uses no coal in making steel. Germany has also cut energy waste and air pollution by requiring large and medium-sized industries and utilities to use cogeneration, and Germany sells that improved technology globally.

Germany has also revolutionized the recycling business. German car companies are required to pick up and recycle all domestic cars they make. Bar-coded parts and predesigned disassembly plants can dismantle an auto for recycling in 20 minutes. Such "take-back"

requirements are being extended to almost all products to reduce use of energy and virgin raw materials. Germany plans to sell its newly developed recycling technologies to other countries. According to Carl Hahn, chairman of Volkswagen, "We must adopt the cyclical processes on which the whole of nature is based."

The German government has also supported research and development aimed at making Germany the world's leader in solar-cell technology and hydrogen fuel, which it expects will provide a rapidly increasing share of the world's energy (Section 4-4). Finally, Germany provides about $1 billion per year in green foreign aid to LDCs. Much of the aid is designed to stimulate demand for German technologies such as solar-powered lights, solar cells, and wind-powered water pumps.

---

placed from environmentally destructive businesses (a *Superfund for Workers*).

CAN WE CHANGE ECONOMIC GEARS? Critics claim that a shift toward an Earth-sustaining economy won't happen because it would be opposed by people whose subsidies were being eliminated and whose activities were being taxed. However, investors and businesspeople have just as much interest in sustaining the earth as anyone else. Forward-looking investors, corporate executives, and the governments of countries such as Japan and Germany (Solutions, above) recognize that Earth-sustaining businesses with good environmental management will prosper as the environmental revolution proceeds. They see environmental responsibility to their workers, customers, society, and the earth as part of a broadening concept of total quality. The United States invests only 4% of its GNP in future growth, compared to 8% in Germany and 16% in Japan. The environmental revolution is also an economic revolution.

12-5 Politics and U.S. Environmental Policy: Problems and Solutions

HOW GOVERNMENT WORKS IN A DEMOCRACY
Politics is the process by which individuals and groups try to influence or control the policies and actions of governments, whether local, state, national, or international. Politics is concerned with who has power over the distribution of resources and benefits—who gets what, when, and how. Thus it plays a significant role in regulating the world's economic systems, influencing economic decisions, and persuading people to work together toward common goals.

Democracy is literally government "by the people." In a *representative democracy* people govern through elected officials and representatives. In a *constitutional democracy* a constitution provides the basis of governmental authority and limits governmental power through free elections and freely expressed public opinion.

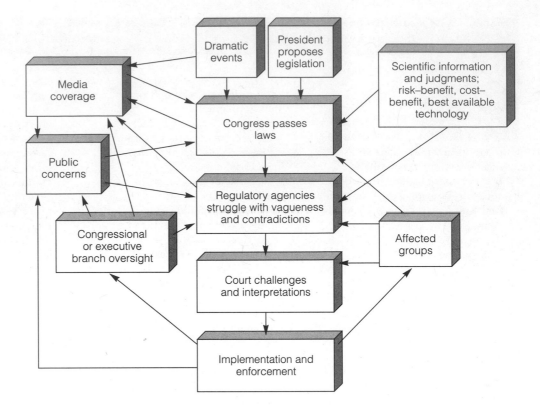

Figure 12-7 Primary forces involved in making environmental policy at the federal level in the United States.

Political systems in constitutional democracies are designed for gradual change to promote economic and political stability. Rapid change in the United States, for example, is curbed by the system of checks and balances that distribute power among the three branches of government (executive, legislative, and judicial) and among federal, state, and local governments.

Most political decisions in democracies are made by bargaining, accommodation, and compromise among leaders of competing *elites*, or power groups. The overarching goal of government by competing elites is to maintain the overall stability of the system by making only gradual change and not questioning or changing the rules of the game or the fundamental societal beliefs that gave them political or economic power.

One disadvantage of this deliberate design is that such governments mostly react to crises instead of acting to prevent them. Ralph Waldo Emerson once said, "Democracy is a raft which will never sink, but then your feet are always in the water." In other words, there is what amounts to a built-in bias against policies for protecting the environment because they often call for prevention instead of reacting to crises, require integrated planning into the future, and sometimes call for fundamental changes in societal beliefs that can threaten the power of existing elites in government and business.

Some say that we can keep on doing business and politics as usual and that no fundamental changes need to be made. Others argue the old ways of doing business and politics are so threatening to our life-support systems that we must have the wisdom and courage to reshape them into Earth-sustaining economic and political systems based on how nature works.

DEVELOPING ENVIRONMENTAL POLICY IN A DEMOCRACY Figure 12-7 summarizes the primary forces in environmental policy-making at the federal level in the United States. Similar factors are found at the state level. The first step in establishing environmental policy (or any other policy) is to persuade lawmakers that a problem exists and that the government has a responsibility to find solutions to the problem. Once over that hurdle, lawmakers try to pass laws to deal with the problem. Most environmental bills are evaluated by as many as 10 committees in both the House and the Senate. Effective proposals are often weakened by this fragmentation and by lobbying from groups opposing the law.

Even if a tough environmental law is passed, Congress must appropriate enough funds to implement and enforce it. Indeed, developing and adopting a budget for spending limited tax revenue is the most important and controversial thing members of the executive and legislative branches do. Developing a budget involves answering two key questions: **(1)** What resource use and distribution problems will be addressed? and **(2)** How much limited tax revenue will be used to address each problem?

Q: How much of Earth's enormous supply of water is available to us as usable fresh water?

Next, regulations designed to implement the law are drawn up by the appropriate government department or agency. Groups favoring or opposing the law try to influence how the regulations are written and enforced. Some of the affected parties may challenge the final regulations in court. Then the agency implements and enforces the approved regulations. Proponents or affected groups may take the agency to court for failing to implement and enforce the regulations or for enforcing them too rigidly.

Environmentalists, with backing from many other citizens and members of Congress, have pressured the U.S. Congress to enact a number of important federal environmental and resource protection laws, as discussed throughout this text and listed in Appendix 3. These laws seek to protect the environment by the following approaches:

- *Setting standards for pollution levels or limiting emissions or effluents for various classes of pollutants* (Federal Water Pollution Control Act and Clean Air Act)

- *Screening new substances for safety before they are widely used* (Toxic Substances Control Act)

- *Requiring comprehensive evaluation of the environmental impact of an activity before it is undertaken by a federal agency* (National Environmental Policy Act)

- *Setting aside or protecting various ecosystems, resources, and species from harm* (Wilderness Act and Endangered Species Act)

- *Encouraging resource conservation* (Resource Conservation and Recovery Act and National Energy Act)

Some environmental laws contain glowing rhetoric about goals but little guidance about how to meet those goals, leaving this up to regulatory agencies and the courts. In other cases the laws specify general principles for setting regulations such as the following:

- *No unreasonable risk*—for example, food regulations in the Food, Drug, and Cosmetic Act

- *No-risk*—for example, the Delaney clause, which prohibits the deliberate use of any food additive shown to cause cancer in test animals or people (Spotlight, p. 218), and the zero-discharge goals of the Safe Drinking Water Act and the Clean Water Act

- *Risk-benefit balancing* (Section 8-4)—for example, pesticide regulations

- *Standards based on best available technology*—for example, the Clean Air, Clean Water, and Safe Drinking Water acts

- *Cost-benefit balancing*—for example, the Toxic Substances Control Act and Executive Order 12291, which gives the Office of Management and Budget the power to delay indefinitely, or even veto, any federal regulation not proven to have the least cost to society

INFLUENCING PUBLIC POLICY A major theme of this book is that individuals matter. History shows that significant change comes from the bottom up, not the top down. Without grass-roots political action by millions of individual citizens and organized groups, the air you breathe and the water you drink today would be much more polluted, and much more of Earth's biodiversity would have disappeared.

There are several ways individuals can influence and change government policies in constitutional democracies:

- *Voting for candidates and ballot measures*

- *Contributing money and time to candidates running for office*

- *Lobbying, writing, or calling elected representatives asking them to pass or oppose certain laws, establish certain policies, and fund various programs*

- *Using education and persuasion*

- *Exposing fraud, waste, and illegal activities in government (whistle-blowing)*

- *Filing lawsuits*

- *Participating in grass-roots activities*

- *Using consumer buying power to help convert brown (Earth-degrading) corporations into green (Earth-sustaining) corporations*

ENVIRONMENTAL LEADERSHIP There are three types of environmental leadership:

- *Leading by example.* Individuals can use their own life and lifestyle to show others that change is possible and beneficial.

- *Working within existing economic and political systems to bring about environmental improvement, often in new, creative ways.* Individuals can influence political elites by campaigning and voting for pro-Earth candidates and by communicating with elected officials. They can also choose an environmental career.

- *Challenging the system and basic societal values and proposing and working for better solutions to environmental problems.* Leadership is more than being against something. It also involves showing people a better way to accomplish various goals.

All three types of leadership are needed to sustain the earth. Writer Kurt Vonnegut has suggested a prescription for choosing Earth-sustaining leaders:

I hope you have stopped choosing abysmally ignorant optimists for positions of leadership.... The sorts of leaders we need now are not those who promise ultimate victory over Nature, but those with the courage and intelligence to present what appear to be Nature's stern, but reasonable surrender terms:

1. *Reduce and stabilize your population.*

2. *Stop poisoning the air, the water, and the topsoil.*

3. *Stop preparing for war and start dealing with your real problems.*

4. *Teach your kids, and yourselves too, while you're at it, how to inhabit a small planet without killing it.*

5. *Stop thinking science can fix anything, if you give it a trillion dollars.*

6. *Stop thinking your grandchildren will be OK no matter how wasteful or destructive you may be, since they can go to a nice new planet on a spaceship. That is really mean and stupid.*

ENVIRONMENTAL CAREERS Besides committed Earth citizens, the environmental movement needs dedicated professionals working to help sustain the earth. You will find environmental career opportunities in a large number of fields: sustainable forestry and range management; parks and recreation; air and water quality control; solid-waste and hazardous-waste management; urban and rural land-use planning; ecological restoration; and soil, water, fishery, and wildlife conservation and management.

Environmental careers can also be found in education, planning, health and toxicology, geology, ecology, conservation biology, chemistry, climatology, population dynamics and regulation (demography), law, accounting, journalism and communication, engineering, design and architecture, energy conservation and analysis, renewable-energy technologies, hydrology, consulting, activism and lobbying, economics, diplomacy, development and marketing, and law enforcement (pollution detection and enforcement teams). You can also run for an elected office on an environmental platform.

Many employers are now scrambling for environmentally educated graduates. They are especially interested in people with scientific and engineering backgrounds and in people with double majors (business and ecology, for example) or double minors.

For details on these careers, consult the Environmental Careers Organization (formerly the CEIP Fund), *The Complete Guide to Environmental Careers* (Covelo, Calif.: Island Press, 1990); and Nicholas Basta, *The Environmental Career Guide* (New York: Wiley, 1991).

MAINSTREAM AND GRASS-ROOTS ENVIRONMENTAL GROUPS There are many types of environmental groups working at the local, state, national, and international levels (Appendix 1). These groups generally fall into two categories: mainstream and grass-roots.

Mainstream environmental groups are active mostly at the national level and to a lesser extent at the state level. Often they form coalitions to work together on issues. Mainstream groups do important work within the system and have been major forces in persuading Congress to pass environmental laws (Appendix 3). However, if they become too dependent on high salaries, large budgets, and donations from Earth-degrading businesses, they can end up spending too much time and money on fund-raising (in competition with other mainstream environmental groups). They can also have their goals corrupted by lobbyists and lose touch with ordinary people and nature.

The base of the environmental movement in the United States and in other countries consists of thousands of grass-roots groups of citizens who have organized to protect themselves from pollution and environmental damage at the local level. The motto of such groups is *think globally and act locally.* They take to the streets, forests, oceans, and other frontline sites to stop environmental abuse, make harmful activities economically unattractive, and raise public awareness of environmental abuse and the need for change.

Many local grass-roots organizations are unwilling to compromise or negotiate. Instead of dealing with environmental goals and abstractions, they are fighting perceived threats to their lives, the lives of their children and grandchildren, and the value of their property. They want pollution and environmental degradation stopped and prevented rather than merely controlled. They are inspired by the words of ecoactivist Edward Abbey: "At some point we must draw a line across the ground of our home and our being, drive a spear into the land, and say to the bulldozers, earthmovers, and corporations, 'this far and no further.'"

THE ANTI-ENVIRONMENTAL MOVEMENT Increasingly the *East–West* polarization is being replaced by a *North–South* or *Rich–Poor* clash over how Earth's limited resources and wealth should be shared and the

Q: What is the largest global use of water withdrawn from surface or groundwater sources?

related *Green–Brown* clash between proponents of conventional economics and environmental economics (Sections 12-2 and 12-4). The clash of such opposing views will dominate our political and economic lives in coming decades.

A small but growing number of U.S. political and business leaders see improving environmental quality as a way to stimulate innovation, increase profits, and create jobs while helping sustain the earth (Solutions, p. 313). However, leaders of some corporations attempt to ensure that environmental laws and regulations do little to damage corporate profit margins (a responsibility they have to shareholders) by:

- *Making donations to the election campaigns of politicians favoring their positions*

- *Putting lobbyists in Washington and in state capitals*

- *Getting industry-friendly people appointed to regulatory agencies*

- *Making donations or giving research grants to environmental organizations to influence how far they go*

- *Influencing the media by threatening to withdraw vital advertising income if those organizations probe too deeply*

- *Establishing industry-funded grass-roots groups* (Spotlight, p. 318)

- *Using the "green menace" scare tactic.* Branding environmentalists as radical, communist, anti-American terrorists who threaten jobs, the economy, national security, and traditional values—instead of people who are trying to make the planet a safer, better, and more just place to live

- *Intimidating environmental activists.* Firing or harassing whistle-blowers in industries and government service; suing individuals and environmental groups; persuading government officials to put environmental activists under surveillance and to arrest or harass them

12-6 Connections and Solutions: Global Environmental Policy

PROGRESS AT THE INTERNATIONAL LEVEL Since the United Nations Conference on the Human Environment was held in Stockholm, Sweden, in 1972, some progress has been made at addressing environmental issues at the global level. Today 115 nations have environmental protection agencies, and more than 170 international environmental treaties have been signed. These treaties cover a range of subjects including endangered species, ozone depletion, ocean pollution, global warming, biodiversity, acid deposition, preservation of Antarctica, and export of hazardous waste. The 1972 conference also created the United Nations Environment Programme (UNEP) to negotiate environmental treaties and help implement them.

THE 1992 RIO EARTH SUMMIT In June 1992 the second United Nations Conference on the Human Environment was held in Rio de Janeiro, Brazil. More than 100 heads of state, thousands of officials, and more than 1,400 accredited nongovernmental organizations (NGOs) from 178 nations met to develop plans for addressing environmental issues. The official results included:

- An Earth Charter, a nonbinding statement of broad principles for guiding global and national environmental policy

- Agenda 21, an action plan for developing the planet sustainably during the twenty-first century

- A broad statement of principles on how to protect forests

- A convention on climate change

- A convention on protecting biodiversity

- Establishment of the UN Commission on Sustainable Development, composed of high-level government representatives, to carry out and oversee implementation of these agreements

There were also failures:

- The convention on climate change lacks the targets and timetables for stabilizing carbon dioxide emissions favored by all major industrial countries except the United States (which only signed the treaty when such items were eliminated).

- The forest-protection statement was so watered down that most environmentalists consider it almost useless.

- The United States failed to sign the biodiversity treaty, which attempts to protect biodiversity and calls for rural communities and indigenous peoples in LDCs whose wildlife genetic resources were used to develop biotechnology products to receive royalties or free access to the technology. The Bush administration claimed the treaty would make the U.S. biotechnology industry less competitive and undermine the legal protection of biotechnology ideas and products. In 1993, however, the Clinton administration agreed to sign the treaty with stipulations that protected U.S. patent rights.

Browns vs. Greens: The Wise-Use Movement

Since 1988 several hundred local and regional grass-roots groups in the United States have formed a national anti-environmental coalition called the *wise-use movement*. Much of their money comes from developers and from timber, mining, oil, coal, and ranching interests.

According to one of its leaders, Ron Arnold, the goal of this movement is to "eradicate the environmental movement in the United States within a decade." According to Arnold, its specific goals are to

- *Cut all old-growth forests in the national forests and replace them with tree plantations*

- *Modify the Endangered Species Act so that economic factors override preservation of endangered and threatened species*

- *Eliminate government restrictions on wetlands development*

- *Open all public lands—including national parks and wilderness areas—to mineral and energy production*

- *Open three-fourths of the land in the National Wilderness Preservation System for mineral and energy production, off-road vehicles (ORVs), developed campsites, and commercial development*

- *Do away with the National Park Service and launch a 20-year construction program of new concessions in national parks to be run by private firms*

- *Continue mining on public lands under the provisions of the 1872 Mining Law, which allows mining interests to pay no royalties to tax-payers for hard rock minerals they remove and to buy public lands for a pittance*

- *Recognize private rights to mining claims, water, grazing permits, and timber contracts on public lands, and not raise fees for these activities*

- *Provide civil penalties against anyone who legally challenges economic action or development on federal lands*

- *Allow pro-industry (wise-use) groups or individuals to sue as "harmed parties" on behalf of industries threatened by environmentalists*

Leaders of this anti-environment movement raise funds and whip up support by branding all environmentalists as antipeople, anti-Christian, antijob, and antigrowth radical extremists who are crippling the U.S. economy, robbing landowners of the right to do what they want with their land, and trying to lock up all natural resources and remove people from all public lands in the United States. When accused of using smear tactics against environmentalists to raise money and spread the seeds of distrust, hate, and fear, Ron Arnold said, "Facts don't really matter. In politics, perception is reality."

Examples of these groups include the Center for the Defense of Free Enterprise (strategic planning, education, and implementation center for the wise use movement run by Allan Gottlieb and Ron Arnold), U.S. Council for Energy Awareness (nuclear power industry), America the Beautiful (packaging industry), Partnership for Plastics Progress (plastics industry), American Council on Science and Health (food and pesticide industries), People for the West (mining industry), Sahara Club (advocates violence against environmentalists in defense of its members' "right" to dirt bike in wilderness areas; one of its leaders tells audiences to "Throw environmentalists off the bridge. Water optional."), and Citizens for the Environment (industry-backed education group used to counter environmental ideas by using such slogans as "Recycling doesn't save forests," "Packaging prevents waste," "Toxic chemicals aren't really harmful," and "Global warming and ozone depletion are hoaxes").*

To environmentalists the well-funded, mostly industry-backed wise-use movement should be called the *earth-and-people abuse movement*. The wise-use grass-roots movement is well funded and well organized and should not be underestimated by environmentalists. However, it could have two beneficial effects on the environmental movement: **(1)** expand its membership and financial support and **(2)** force mainstream environmental organizations to work more at the grass-roots level by getting in touch with the concerns of ordinary people who are struggling to keep their jobs and who fear excessive government regulation and threats to their property values.

---

*For lists of these organizations see *The Greenpeace Guide to Anti-Environmental Organizations* (available for $7 from Odonian Press, Berkeley, CA) and *Fronting for Big Business in America* by Andy Friedman and Mark Megalli (available for $20 from Essential Information, P.O. Box 19405, Washington, DC 20036).

- Officials largely avoided addressing the issues of population and its relation to poverty and economic development, fairer distribution of Earth's wealth and income, forgiving much of the massive debt of LDCs, giving LDCs preferential access to modern environmental and energy-saving technology, creating an international tax on carbon emissions, and the environmental and economic-justice impacts of free trade.

- Countries did not commit even the minimum amount of money that conference organizers said was needed to begin implementing Agenda 21.

Q: Worldwide, how much of the water withdrawn for irrigation is wasted?

- A treaty on reversing desertification (Figure 5-9) was not developed, mainly because of opposition by the United States.

- The United States was sharply criticized for its views and lack of leadership at a time when other MDCs and LDCs desperately needed such leadership.

Does this mean that the conference was a failure? No, for two reasons. First, it gave the world a forum for talking about and seeking solutions to environmental problems. Second, paralleling the official meeting was a Global Forum that brought together more than 7,000 other nongovernmental organizations from 175 countries. These NGOs worked behind the scenes to influence official policy, formulated their own agendas for sustaining the earth and reducing poverty, learned from one another, and developed a series of new global networks, alliances, and projects. In the long run these newly formed grass-roots networks and alliances may play the greatest role in monitoring, supporting, and determining whether the commitments and plans developed by the formal conference are carried out and strengthened.

IMPROVING GLOBAL ENVIRONMENTAL PRO-TECTION Suggestions that various analysts have made for improving environmental protection at the global level include:

- *Expanding the concepts of national security and economic security to recognize that both ultimately depend on global environmental security based on sustainable use of the ecosphere* (Figure 12-2).

- *Expanding the role and budget of the United Nations Environment Programme in negotiating environmental treaties and in monitoring and overseeing their implementation.*

- *Requiring regular compliance reports from countries signing environmental treaties.*

- *Establishing an International Environmental Court to settle disputes between nations over violations of international agreements.*

- *Having heads of all countries (not just the rich countries) meet together in an Earth Summit at least every two years.*

- *Creating an Environmental Security Council as part of the United Nations.* Its mission would be to discuss environmental issues, seek solutions to environmental problems, coordinate UN responses to environmental issues, and respond to environmental emergencies.

- *Greening international lending agencies such as the World Bank and the International Monetary Fund.*

This might involve having them shift most of their investment to small-scale grass-roots projects, having local people and NGOs participate in a meaningful way in the planning and implementation of all projects, opening agency documents to public scrutiny, and requiring environmental impact assessments and monitoring for all projects.

 ## 12-7 Worldviews: A Clash of Values and Cultures

HOW SHALL WE LIVE? There are conflicting views over how serious environmental problems really are and what we should do about them. These conflicts arise mostly out of differing **worldviews**: how individuals think the world works, what they think their role in the world should be, and what they believe is right and wrong behavior (ethics). People with widely differing worldviews can take the same data and arrive at quite different conclusions because they start with entirely different assumptions. Worldviews come in many flavors, but they can be divided into two groups according to whether they put humans at the center of things or not.

HUMAN-CENTERED WORLDVIEWS Human-centered worldviews prevail in most industrial societies today. Most people in today's industrial societies have a **planetary management worldview**, which has gained wide acceptance during the past 50 years. According to this human-centered worldview, as the planet's most important and dominant species we can and should manage the planet mostly for our benefit. Other species have only *instrumental value*; that is, their value depends on whether or not they are useful to us.

These are the basic beliefs of this worldview:

- *We are the planet's most important species, and we are apart from and in charge of the rest of nature.*

- *There is always more, and it's all for us.* Earth has an essentially unlimited supply of resources, which we gain access to through use of science and technology. If we deplete a resource, we will find substitutes. If resources become scarce or substitutes can't be found, we can mine the moon, asteroids, or other planets. If we pollute an area, we can invent a technology to clean it up, dump it into space, or move into space ourselves. If we extinguish other species, we can use genetic engineering to create new and better ones.

- *All economic growth is good, more economic growth is better, and the potential for economic growth is virtually unlimitled.*
- *A healthy environment depends on a healthy economy.*
- *Our success depends on how well we can understand, control, and manage the planet for our benefit.*

There are several variations of this worldview.

- *No-problem.* There are no environmental, population, or resource problems that can't be solved by more economic growth, better management, and better technology.
- *Free-market school.* The best way to manage the planet is through a truly free-market global economy with minimal government interference. Free-market advocates would convert essentially all public property resources to private property resources and let the marketplace, governed by free-market competition (pure capitalism), decide essentially everything.
- *Responsible planetary management.* We have serious environmental, resource, and population problems that we must deal with by becoming better and more responsible planetary managers. These people follow the pragmatic principle of *enlightened self-interest*: Better Earth care is better self-care. They believe we can sustain our species by using a mixture of market-based competition and better technology, along with some government intervention to promote sustainable forms of economic growth, prevent abuse of power in the marketplace, and protect and manage public and common property resources.
- *Spaceship-Earth.* A variation of responsible planetary management in which Earth is seen as a spaceship—a complex machine that we can understand, dominate, change, and manage to prevent environmental overload and provide a good life for everyone.
- *Stewardship.* We have an ethical responsibility to be caring and responsible managers or stewards who tend the earth as if it were a garden. We can and should make the world a better place for ourselves and other species through love, care, and knowledge.

CAN WE MANAGE THE PLANET? Some people believe that ever-increasing population, production, and consumption will severely stress the natural processes that renew the air, water, and soil and that support all life and economies. They compare our pursuit of unlimited economic growth and growth in the human population to being on a treadmill that moves faster and faster. They believe that, sooner or later, we will fall off the treadmill or cause it to break down because of our limited knowledge and managerial skills compared to the incredible complexity of Earth's life-support systems.

These individuals believe that ultimately human-centered worldviews won't lead to sustainability. They argue that the unhindered free-market approach won't work because it is based on mushrooming losses of Earth capital and focused on short-term benefits regardless of the long-term harmful consequences. They agree with economist Alfred Kahn, head of the Council on Wage and Price Stability under President Carter: "No one in his or her right mind would argue that the competitive market system takes care of protecting the environment—it does not."

These critics also contend that the spaceship-Earth and stewardship versions of planetary management won't work. To them, thinking of Earth as a spaceship or a garden—simplified human constructs—that we can understand, manage, and redesign for our use with limited knowledge and only an eye blink of experience is an oversimplified and misleading way to view an incredibly complex and ever-changing planet that is the result of billions of years of evolution.

For example, we don't even know how many species live on Earth, much less what their roles are and how they interact with one another and their nonliving environment. We have only an inkling of what goes on in a handful of soil, a meadow, a patch of forest, a pond, or any other part of the earth. We are like technicians who think they can build and repair car motors after 30 seconds of training.

As biologist David Ehrenfeld puts it, "In no important instance have we been able to demonstrate comprehensive successful management of the world, nor do we understand it well enough to manage it even in theory." Environmental educator David Orr says we are losing rather than gaining the knowledge and wisdom needed to adapt creatively to continually changing environmental conditions:

> *On balance, I think, we are becoming more ignorant because we are losing cultural knowledge about how to inhabit our places on the planet sustainably, while impoverishing the genetic knowledge accumulated through millions of years of evolution.... Most research is aimed to further domination of the planet. Considerably less of it is directed at understanding the effects of domination. Less still is aimed to develop ecologically sound alternatives that enable us to live within natural limits.*

These are sobering thoughts for those who see planetary management as the solution to our problems.

Even if we had enough knowledge and wisdom to manage spaceship Earth, some critics see this as a

Q: What percentage of the world's population clash over rights to water?

threat to individual freedom. They compare the life of astronauts on spaceships with what life might be like on spaceship Earth under a comprehensive system of planetary management. The astronauts have virtually no individual freedom with virtually all of their actions dictated by a central command (ground control).

Theologian Thomas Berry calls the industrial-consumer society built upon the human-centered, technology–economic growth worldview the "supreme pathology of all history":

> We can break the mountains apart; we can drain the rivers and flood the valleys. We can turn the most luxuriant forests into throwaway paper products. We can tear apart the great grass cover of the western plains, and pour toxic chemicals into the soil and pesticides onto the fields, until the soil is dead and blows away in the wind. We can pollute the air with acids, the rivers with sewage, the seas with oil—all this in a kind of intoxication with our power for devastation.... We can invent computers capable of processing ten million calculations per second. And why? To increase the volume and speed with which we move natural resources through the consumer economy to the junk pile or the waste heap.... If, in these activities, the topography of the planet is damaged, if the environment is made inhospitable for a multitude of living species, then so be it. We are, supposedly, creating a technological wonderworld.... But our supposed progress... is bringing us to a wasteworld instead of a wonderworld.

LIFE-CENTERED WORLDVIEWS: WORKING WITH THE PLANET Critics of human-centered worldviews believe that such worldviews should be expanded to recognize *inherent* or *intrinsic value* to all forms of life (that is, value regardless of their potential or actual use to us). Proponents of such *life-centered* or *biocentric* worldviews believe that all species have an inherent right to live and flourish or at least to struggle to exist—to play their roles in evolution.

There are many biocentric or life-centered worldviews, several of them overlapping in some of their beliefs. One *biocentric* or *Earth-wisdom worldview* has the following beliefs, which are in sharp contrast to the major beliefs of human-centered worldviews:

- *Nature exists for all of Earth's species, not just for us, and we are not apart from or in charge of the rest of nature.* We need the earth, but the earth does not need us.

- *There is not always more, and it's not all for us.* Earth's limited resources should not be wasted and should be used sustainably for us and all species.

- *Some forms of economic growth are beneficial, and some are harmful.* Our goals should be to design economic and political systems that encourage Earth-sustaining forms of growth and discourage or prohibit Earth-degrading forms.

- *A healthy economy depends on a healthy environment.* Our survival, life quality, and economies are totally dependent on the rest of nature (Earth capital).

- *Our success depends on learning to cooperate with one another and with the rest of nature instead of trying to dominate and manage Earth for use by our species.* Because nature is so incredibly complex and always changing, we will never have enough information and understanding to effectively manage the planet.

People with this or other life-centered worldviews reject claims that they are antipeople or against celebrating humanity's special qualities and achievements. Rather, they call for us to expand our sense of compassion, caring, and love to individuals, species, and ecosystems—not just humans—including future generations of all forms of life. To them, recognizing the intrinsic value of all life is the best way to serve and love people.

Others say we don't need to be ecocentrists to value life. Human-centered stewardship also calls for us to value individuals, species, and ecosystems as part of our responsibility as Earth's caretakers.

Changing one's worldview is difficult and threatening. It is a cultural *mindquake* that involves questioning many of our most basic beliefs. However, once individuals change their worldviews, it no longer makes sense for them to do things in the old ways. If enough people do this, then tremendous cultural change, once considered impossible, can take place rapidly. Proponents of the Earth-wisdom and other related worldviews call for such mindquakes to become our guides for living sustainably within the next 50 years by learning how to work with the earth.

EARTH ETHICS: RESPECTING LIFE Here are some ethical guidelines various ecocentrists have proposed for helping us work with the earth:

Ecosphere and Ecosystems

- We should try to understand and cooperate with the rest of nature rather than trying to dominate and conquer it. The earth does not belong to us; we belong to the earth.

- We should work with the rest of nature to sustain the ecological integrity, biodiversity, and adaptability of Earth's life-support systems for us and other species. This requires controlling population and resource use, living off solar energy and renewable Earth income, not depleting or degrading Earth capital, and working with nature to rehabilitate or restore many of the ecosystems we have damaged.

- We have to alter nature to meet our needs or wants, but we should choose methods that do the least possible harm to us and other living things.

- Before altering nature we should carry out an Environmental Impact Analysis (EIA) and a Grandchild Impact Analysis (GIA) to help us decide whether to intervene and to discover how to inflict the minimum short- and long-term harm.

Species and Cultures

- Every species has a right to live, or at least to struggle to live, simply because it exists.

- We have the right to defend ourselves against individuals of species that do us harm and to use individuals of species to meet vital needs, but we do not have the right to cause the premature extinction of any wild species.

- The best way to protect species and individuals of species is to protect the ecosystems in which they live.

- No human culture should become extinct because of our actions.

Individual Responsibility

- We should not inflict unnecessary suffering or pain on any animal we raise or hunt for food or use for scientific or other purposes.

- We should leave wild things in the wild unless their survival depends on human protection.

- To prevent excessive deaths of people and other species, people should prevent excessive births.

- We should leave the earth in as good (or better) shape as we found it.

- We should strive to live more lightly on the earth, not because of guilt or fear, but because of a desire to make the world a better place.

- We should get to know, care about, and defend a piece of the earth.

EARTH EDUCATION: A PERSONAL VIEW Learning how to work with the earth requires a foundation of Earth education. I believe that the main goals of such an education should include the following:

- *Developing respect for all life.*

- *Understanding what we know about how the earth works and sustains itself.*

- *Understanding connections.* These include connections within nature, between people and the rest of nature, between people with different cultures and beliefs, between generations, among the problems we face, and among the solutions to these problems.

- *Understanding and evaluating one's worldview.*

- *Becoming a wisdom seeker instead of an information vessel.* We need a *wisdom revolution* that enriches our minds and lives, not an *information revolution* that clogs our brains and dims our capacity to care and share and that too often is used to dominate, deplete, and degrade the earth.

- *Learning how to evaluate and resist advertising.* Most of the $250 billion spent worldwide on advertising each year (an average of $48 per person or $448 per American) is designed to make us unhappy with what we have. As humorist Will Rogers put it, "Too many people spend money they haven't earned to buy things they don't want, to impress people they don't like." Learning how to detect psychological manipulation by analyzing TV and print ads, beginning in elementary school, is a superb way to teach critical thinking and to help us distinguish between needs and wants.

- *Learning to live sustainably in a place.* This would be a piece of Earth to which we are rooted or emotionally attached and whose sustainability and adaptability we feel driven to nurture and defend.

- *Fostering a desire to make the world a better place and to act on this desire.* As David Orr puts it, education should help students "make the leap from 'I know' to 'I care' to 'I'll do something.'"

Making Earth education the center of the learning process will not be an easy task because most teachers and members of the educational establishment are trained to think primarily in terms of disciplines, and they rigorously guard their turfs. Shifting the focus of our education system involves the following:

- *Exposing teachers, media people, and corporate and government leaders to Earth education.* This would involve the use of summer workshops, visiting teachers, team teaching, week-long retreats, and other devices.

- *Inserting examples of Earth thinking into teaching materials at all levels, beginning in kindergarten.*

- *Requiring every student graduating from high school, college, and any professional school to take one or more courses in Earth education.*

Q: How many of the world's people live in absolute poverty?

Emotional Learning: Earth Wisdom

SOLUTIONS

Formal education is important, but Aldo Leopold, Henry David Thoreau, Gary Snyder, and many others believe it's not enough. Such Earth thinkers and many religious thinkers believe that much of the essence, rhythms, and pulse of the earth within and around us must be experienced at the deepest level by our senses and feelings—our emotions.

They urge us to take the time to escape the cultural and technological "body armor" we use to insulate ourselves from wild nature and experience nature directly. They suggest that we reenchant our senses and kindle a sense of awe, wonder, and humility by standing under the stars, sitting in a forest, taking in the majesty and power of an ocean, or experiencing a stream, lake, or other part of untamed nature. We might pick up a handful of soil and try to sense the teeming microscopic life forms in it that keep us alive. We might look at a tree, a mountain, a rock, a bee and try to sense how they are a part of us, and we a part of them.

Earth thinker Michael J. Cohen suggests that each of us recognize who we really are by saying:

I am a desire for water, air, food, love, warmth, beauty, freedom, sensations, life, community, place, and spirit in the natural world. These pulsating feelings are the Planet Earth, alive and well within me. I have two mothers: my human mother and my planet mother, Earth. The planet is my womb of life.

Earth philosophers call for us to recognize that the technological cocoon we enclose ourselves in and the feeling of self-importance we hold as a species have given us a severely distorted picture of what is really important. As theologian Thomas Berry puts it:

So long as we are under the illusion that we know best what is good for the earth and for ourselves, then we will continue our present course, with its devastating consequences on the entire earth community…. We need not a human answer to an earth problem, but an Earth answer to an Earth problem…. We need only listen to what the Earth is telling us…. The time has come when we will listen, or we will die.

Experiencing nature emotionally allows us to get in touch with our deepest self, which has sensed from birth that when we destroy and degrade the natural systems that support us, we are attacking ourselves. As eco-warrior Dave Foreman puts it:

When a chain saw slices into the heartwood of a two-thousand-year old Coast Redwood, it's slicing into my guts. When a bulldozer rips through the Amazon rain forests, it's ripping into my side. When a … whaler fires an exploding harpoon into a great whale, my heart is blown to smithereens. I am the land, the land is me. Why shouldn't I be emotional, angry, passionate? Madmen and madwomen are wrecking this beautiful, blue-green, living Earth…. We must love Earth and rage against her destroyers…. The

Earth is crying. Do we hear?… We can't be perfect, but we can act.

Many psychologists believe that consciously or unconsciously we spend much of our lives in a search for roots—something to anchor us in a bewildering and frightening sea of change. As philosopher Simone Weil observed, "To be rooted is perhaps the most important and least recognized need of the human soul."

Earth philosophers say that to be rooted, each of us needs to find a *sense of place*—a stream, a mountain, a yard, a neighborhood lot, or any piece of the earth we feel truly at one with. It can be a place where we live or a place we occasionally visit and experience in our inner being. When we become part of a place, it becomes a part of us. Then we are driven to defend it from harm and to help heal its wounds.

Emotionally experiencing our connectedness with the earth leads us to recognize that the healing of the earth and the healing of the human spirit are one and the same. Earth philosophers and defenders call for us to discover and tap into the green fire that burns in our hearts and use this as a force for sustaining the earth.

Some analysts, however, consider such emotional learning to be unscientific, mystical poppycock. They believe that better scientific understanding of how the earth works is the only way to achieve sustainability. What do you think?

- *Developing and widely using measures of ecological literacy.*

- *Listening to the earth.* In 1948 Aldo Leopold said, "We can be ethical only in relation to something we can see, feel, understand, love, or otherwise have faith in." This requires experiencing the

earth with our senses and our hearts (Solutions, above).

- *Listening to children: bottom-up education.* We need to take the time to listen—truly listen—to children. Many children that I have talked with believe that much of what we are doing to the earth (and thus to them) is stupid and wrong, and they don't buy the excuses we give for not changing the way we do things.

- *Living more simply and frugally.* Although attaining happiness through material acquisition is denied by virtually every major religion and philosophy, it is preached incessantly by modern advertising. Some affluent people in MDCs, however, are adopting a lifestyle of *voluntary simplicity,* based on doing and enjoying more with less by learning to live more simply but richly. This is based on Mahatma Gandhi's *principle of enoughness:* "The earth provides enough to satisfy every person's need but not every person's greed." It means asking oneself, "How much is enough?" This is not an easy question to answer because affluent people are conditioned to want more and more, and they often think of such wants as vital needs. Voluntary simplicity by those who have more than they really need should not be confused with the *forced simplicity* of the poor, who do not have enough to meet their basic needs for food, clothing, shelter, clean water and air, and good health.

- *Avoiding common traps that lead to denial, indifference, and inaction.* These include: **(1)** *gloom-and-doom pessimism* (it's hopeless), **(2)** *blind technological optimism* (science and technofixes will always save us), **(3)** *fatalism* (we have no control over our actions and the future), **(4)** *extrapolation to infinity* ("If I can't change the entire world quickly, I won't try to change any of it."), **(5)** *paralysis-by-analysis* (searching for the perfect worldview, philosophy, solutions, and scientific information before doing anything), and **(6)** *faith in simple, easy answers.* We should be guided by philosopher and mathematician Alfred North Whitehead, who advised, "Seek simplicity and distrust it," and by writer and social critic H. L. Mencken, who warned, "For every problem there is a solution—simple, neat, and wrong."

Working with the earth requires each of us to make a personal commitment to strive to live an environmentally ethical life—not because it is mandated by law but because it is the right thing to do. It is our responsibility to ourselves, our children and grandchildren, our neighbors, and the earth.

The main ingredients of an environmental ethic are caring about the planet and all of its inhabitants, allowing unselfishness to control the immediate self-interest that harms others, and living each day so as to leave the lightest possible footprints on the planet.

ROBERT CAHN

CRITICAL THINKING

1. The primary goal of all current economic systems is to maximize growth by maximizing the production and consumption of economic goods. Do you agree with that goal? Explain. What are the alternatives?

2. Do you favor internalizing the external costs of pollution and unnecessary resource waste? Explain. How might it affect your lifestyle? Wildlife?

3. **a.** Do you believe that we should establish optimal levels or zero-discharge levels for most of the chemicals we release into the environment? Explain. What effects would adopting zero-discharge levels have on your life and lifestyle?

   b. Do you believe that all chemicals we release or propose to release into the environment should be assumed to be potentially harmful until shown to be safe? Explain. What effects would adopting this principle have on your life and lifestyle? On the national economy?

4. Do you favor making a shift to a sustainable-Earth economy? Explain. How might this affect your lifestyle? The lifestyle of any children you choose to have?

5. Do you agree or disagree with the proposals that some analysts have made for sharply reducing poverty, as listed on pages 310–311? Explain.

6. Suppose a presidential candidate ran on a platform calling for the federal government to phase in a tax on gasoline over 5–10 years to the point where gasoline would cost about $3–5 a gallon (as is the case in Japan and most western European nations). The candidate argues that this tax increase is necessary to encourage conservation of oil and gasoline, to reduce air pollution, and to enhance future economic, environmental, and military security. Some of the tax revenue would be used to provide tax relief or other aid to all people with incomes below a certain level (the poor and lower middle class), who would be hardest hit by such a consumption tax. Would you vote for this candidate who promises to triple the price of gasoline? Explain.

7. What do you believe are the greatest strengths and weaknesses of the system of government in your country related to protecting the environment and sustaining the earth? What substantial changes, if any, would you make in this system?

8. What obligations, if any, concerning the environment do you have to future generations? How many generations ahead do we have responsibilities to? List the most important environmental benefits and harmful conditions passed on to you by the previous two generations.

9. Describe your worldview. Has taking this course changed your worldview? How?

Q: Will improving environmental quality in the United States cause a net gain or a net loss of jobs?

Epilogue
Living Sustainably

If you make the world ever so little better, you will have done splendidly, and your life will have been worthwhile.

Arnold Toynbee

BECOMING EARTH CITIZENS: WORKING WITH THE EARTH In "Individuals Matter" boxes throughout this book I have listed specific actions you can take. Here are the ones I would put at the top of the list:

- *Respect all life.*

- *Learn all you can about how nature works, about how human nature and power work, and about the connections between everything.*

- *Listen to and learn from nature and from children.*

- *Evaluate the beneficial and harmful consequences of your lifestyle and profession on the earth today and in the future.*

- *Lead by example.* People are most influenced by what we do, not by what we say.

- *Tread more lightly on the earth by living more simply and frugally.* This also saves you money.

- *Do the little things based on thinking globally and acting locally.* Each small measure you take is important, sensitizes you to Earth-sustaining acts, and leads to more such acts.

- *Think and act nationally and globally.* This means targeting the big polluters (industries, industrialized agriculture, governments) and big problems (ozone depletion, biodiversity loss, possible climate change) through political action, economic boycotts, and selective consumption.

- *Get to know, care about, and defend a piece of Earth.* As poet-philosopher Gary Snyder puts it, "Find our place on the planet, dig in, and take responsibility from there."

- *Work with others to help sustain and heal the Earth, beginning in your neighborhood and community.*

- *Don't try to do everything.* Focus your energy on the few things that you feel most strongly about and that you can do something about.

- *Don't use guilt and fear to motivate other people, and don't allow other people to do this to you.* We need to nurture, reassure, understand, and love, rather than threaten, one another.

- *Have fun and take time to enjoy life.* Don't get so intense and serious that you can't laugh every day and enjoy wild nature, beauty, friendship, and love.

BRINGING ABOUT AN EARTH-WISDOM REVOLUTION We should design our lives and our societies on the basis of what we know so far about how nature sustains itself. We need a sustainable transportation, housing, and farming project in every area so people can see sustainability in action. Every country needs *thousands of points of sustainability* that are spotlighted, nurtured, and transplanted so they can grow into *millions of points of sustainability* all intertwined in a global network. These beacons of hope and change can show us how to live sustainably on this wondrous planet.

We should envision the world as made up of all kinds of matter cycles and energy flows. We should see these life-sustaining processes as a beautiful and diverse web of interrelationships—a kaleidoscope of patterns, rhythms, and connections whose very complexity and multitude of possibilities remind us that cooperation, sharing, honesty, humility, respect for all life, and love should be the guidelines for our behavior toward one another and the earth.

Where there is no dream, the people perish.

Proverbs 29:18

Publications, Environmental Organizations, and Federal and International Agencies*

PUBLICATIONS

The following publications can help you keep well informed and up to date on environmental and resource problems. Subscription prices, which tend to change, are not given.

American Biology Teacher Journal of the National Association of Biology Teachers, 11250 Roger Bacon Drive, Room 319, Reston, VA 22090

American Forests American Forestry Association, 1516 P St. NW, Washington, DC 20005

Amicus Journal Natural Resources Defense Council, 40 W. 20th St., New York, NY 10011

Annual Review of Energy Department of Energy, Forrestal Building, 1000 Independence Ave. SW, Washington, DC 20585

Audubon National Audubon Society, 950 Third Ave., New York, NY 10022

BioScience American Institute of Biological Sciences, 730 11th St. NW, Washington, DC 20001

Buzzworm: The Environmental Journal P.O. Box 6853, Syracuse, NY 13217-7930

The CoEvolution Quarterly P.O. Box 428, Sausalito, CA 94965

Conservation Biology Blackwell Scientific Publications, Inc., 52 Beacon St., Boston, MA 02108

Demographic Yearbook Department of International Economic and Social Affairs, Statistical Office, United Nations Publishing Service, United Nations, NY 10017

Earth Kalmbach Publishing Co., 21027 Crossroads Circle, Waukesha, WI 53187

Earth Island Journal Earth Island Institute, 300 Broadway, Suite 28, San Francisco, CA 94133

Earth Journal: Environmental Almanac and Resource Directory Buzzworm, Inc., 2305 Canyon Blvd., Suite 206, Boulder, CO 80302 (published annually)

Earth Work Student Conservation Association, Dept. 1PR, P.O. Box 550, Charlestown, NH 03603

The Ecologist MIT Press Journals, 55 Hayward St., Cambridge, MA 02142

Ecology Ecological Society of America, Dr. Duncan T. Patten, Center for Environmental Studies, Arizona State University, Tempe, AZ 85281

E Magazine P.O. Box 5098, Westport, CT 06881

Environment Heldref Publications, 4000 Albemarle St. NW, Washington, DC 20016

Environment Abstracts Bowker A & I Publishing, 245 W. 17th St., New York, NY 10011. In most libraries.

---

*For a more detailed list consult my longer books, *Environmental Science* and *Living in the Environment,* Belmont, Calif.: Wadsworth.

Environmental Action 6930 Carroll Park, 6th Floor, Takoma Park, MD 20912

Environmental Almanac Annual compilation by the World Resources Institute. Published by Houghton-Mifflin (Boston).

Environmental Ethics Department of Philosophy, University of North Texas, Denton, TX 76203

EPA Journal Environmental Protection Agency. Order from Government Printing Office, Washington, DC 20402.

Everyone's Backyard Citizens' Clearinghouse for Hazardous Waste, P.O. Box 926, Arlington, VA 22216

Family Planning Perspectives Planned Parenthood-World Population, 666 Fifth Ave., New York, NY 10019

Garbage: The Practical Journal for the Environment P.O. Box 56520, Boulder, CO 80321-6520

Greenpeace Magazine Greenpeace USA, 1436 U St. NW, Washington, DC 20009

In Context Box 11470, Bainbridge Island, WA 98110

International Wildlife National Wildlife Federation, 8925 Leesburg Pike, Vienna, VA 22184

Issues in Science and Technology National Academy of Sciences, 2101 Constitution Ave. NW, Washington, DC 20077-5576

Journal of Environmental Education Heldref Publications, 4000 Albemarle St. NW, Suite 504, Washington, DC 20016

National Geographic National Geographic Society, P.O. Box 2895, Washington, DC 20077-9960

National Parks and Conservation Magazine National Parks and Conservation Association, 1015 31st St. NW, Washington, DC 20007

Natural Resources Journal University of New Mexico School of Law, 1117 Stanford NE, Albuquerque, NM 87131

National Wildlife National Wildlife Federation, 1400 16th St. NW, Washington, DC 20036

Nature 711 National Press Building, Washington, DC 20045

Not Man Apart Friends of the Earth, 530 Seventh St. SE, Washington, DC 20003

Orion Nature Quarterly P.O. Box 3000, Denville, NJ 07834-9797

Planetary Citizen Stillpoint Publishing, Meetinghouse Road, Box 640, Walpole, NH 03608

Popline The Population Institute, 107 Second St. NE, Suite 207, Washington, DC 20002

Population and Vital Statistics Report United Nations Environment Programme, New York North American Office, Publication Sales Section, United Nations, New York, NY 10017

Population Bulletin Population Reference Bureau, 1875 Connecticut Ave. NW, Suite 520, Washington, DC 20009

Rachel's Hazardous Waste News Environmental Research Foundation, P.O. Box 4878, Annapolis, MD 21403

Rainforest News P.O. Box 140681, Coral Gables, FL 33115

Real World: The Voice of Ecopolitics 91 Nuns Moor Road, Newcastle upon Tyne, NE4 9BA, United Kingdom

Renewable Energy News Solar Vision, Inc., 7 Church Hill, Harrisville, NH 03450

Renewable Resources 5430 Grosvenor Lane, Bethesda, MD 20814

Rocky Mountain Institute Newsletter 1739 Snowmass Creek Rd., Snowmass, CO 81654

Science American Association for the Advancement of Science, 1333 H St. NW, Washington, DC 20005

Science News Science Service, Inc., 1719 N St. NW, Washington, DC 20036

Scientific American 415 Madison Ave., New York, NY 10017

Sierra 730 Polk St., San Francisco, CA 94108

Solar Age Solar Vision, Inc., 7 Church Hill, Harrisville, NH 03450

State of the World Worldwatch Institute, 1776 Massachusetts Ave. NW, Washington, DC 20036 (published annually)

Statistical Yearbook Department of International Economic and Social Affairs, Statistical Office, United Nations Publishing Service, United Nations, New York, NY 10017

Technology Review Room E219-430, Massachusetts Institute of Technology, Cambridge, MA 02139

The Trumpeter Journal of Ecosophy P.O. Box 5883 St. B, Victoria, B.C., Canada V8R 6S8

Wild Earth Cenozoic Society, Inc., P.O. Box 455, Richmond, VT 05477

Wilderness The Wilderness Society, 1400 I St. NW, 10th Floor, Washington, DC 20005

Wildlife Conservation New York Zoological Society, 185th St. and Southern Boulevard, Bronx, NY 10460

World Rainforest Report Rainforest Action Network, 300 Broadway, Suite 298, San Francisco, CA 94133

World Resources World Resources Institute, 1735 New York Ave. NW, Washington, DC 20006 (published every two years)

World Watch Worldwatch Institute, 1776 Massachusetts Ave. NW, Washington, DC 20036

Worldwatch Papers Worldwatch Institute, 1776 Massachusetts Ave. NW, Washington, DC 20036

Yearbook of World Energy Statistics Department of International Economic and Social Affairs, Statistical Office, United Nations Publishing Service, United Nations, New York, NY 10017

ENVIRONMENTAL AND RESOURCE ORGANIZATIONS

For a more detailed list of national, state, and local organizations, see *Conservation Directory* (published annually by the National Wildlife Federation, 1400 16th St. NW, Washington, DC 20036); *Your Resource Guide to Environmental Organizations* (Irvine, CA: Smiling Dolphin Press, 1991); *National Environmental Organizations* (published annually by US Environmental Directories, Inc., P.O. Box 65156, St. Paul, MN 55165); and *World Directory of Environmental Organizations* (published by the California Institute of Public Affairs, P.O. Box 10, Claremont, CA 91711).

American Council for an Energy Efficient Economy 1001 Connecticut Ave. NW, Suite 535, Washington, DC 20013

American Forestry Association 1516 P St. NW, Washington, DC 20005

American Humane Society 9725 E. Hampden Ave., Denver, CO 80231

American Institute of Biological Sciences, Inc. 730 11th St. NW, Washington, DC 20001

American Solar Energy Society 2400 Central Ave., Suite 6, Boulder, CO 80301

American Water Resources Association 5410 Grosvenor Lane, Suite 220, Bethesda, MD 20814

American Wind Energy Association 777 North Capitol St. NE, Suite 805, Washington, DC 20002

Carrying Capacity 1325 G St. NW, Washington, DC 20005

Center for Conservation Biology Department of Biological Sciences, Stanford University, Stanford, CA 94305

Center for Marine Conservation 1725 DeSales St. NW, Suite 500, Washington, DC 20036

Center for Plant Conservation P.O. Box 299, St. Louis, MO 63166

Center for Science in the Public Interest 1875 Connecticut Ave. NW, Suite 300, Washington, DC 20009

Citizens' Clearinghouse for Hazardous Waste P.O. Box 6806, Falls Church, VA 22040

Clean Water Action 1320 18th St. NW, Washington, DC 20036

Coastal Society 5410 Grosvenor Lane, Suite 110, Bethesda, MD 20814

Conservation Foundation 1250 24th St. NW, Suite 500, Washington, DC 20037

Council for Economic Priorities 30 Irving Pl., New York, NY 10003

Cousteau Society 930 W. 21st St., Norfolk, VA 23517

Cultural Survival 11 Divinity Ave., Cambridge, MA 02138

Defenders of Wildlife 1244 19th St. NW, Washington, DC 20036

Ducks Unlimited One Waterfowl Way, Long Grove, IL 60047

Earth First! 305 N. Sixth St., Madison, WI 53704

Earth Island Institute 300 Broadway, Suite 28, San Francisco, CA 94133

Elmwood Institute P.O. Box 5805, Berkeley, CA 94705

Energy Conservation Coalition 1525 New Hampshire Ave. NW, Washington, DC 20036

Environmental Action, Inc. 6930 Carroll Park, Suite 600, Takoma Park, MD 20912

Environmental Defense Fund, Inc. 257 Park Ave. South, New York, NY 10010

Environmental Law Institute 1616 P St. NW, Suite 200, Washington, DC 20036

Environmental Policy Institute 218 D St. SE, Washington, DC 20003

Friends of Animals 11 W. 60th St., New York, NY 10023

Friends of the Earth 218 D St. SE, Washington, DC 20003

Friends of Trees P.O. Box 1466, Chelan, WA 98816

Global Greenhouse Network 1130 17th St. NW, Suite 530, Washington, DC 20036

Global Tomorrow Coalition 1325 G St. NW, Suite 1010, Washington, DC 20005

Greenpeace, Canada 427 Bloor St., West Toronto, Ontario M5S 1X7

Greenpeace, USA, Inc. 1436 U St. NW, Washington, DC 20009

Green Seal 1733 Connecticut Ave., NW, Washington, DC 20009

Institute for Alternative Agriculture 9200 Edmonston Rd., Suite 117, Greenbelt, MD 20770

Institute for Earth Education P.O. Box 288, Warrenville, IL 60555

Institute for Local Self-Reliance 2425 18th St. NW, Washington, DC 20009

International Institute for Energy Conservation 420 C St., NE, Washington, DC 20002

International Planned Parenthood Federation 105 Madison Ave., 7th Floor, New York, NY 10016

Izaak Walton League of America 1401 Wilson Blvd., Level B, Arlington, VA 22209

League of Conservation Voters 1707 L St. NW, Suite 550, Washington, DC 20036

League of Women Voters of the U.S. 1730 M St. NW, Washington, DC 20036

National Audubon Society 950 Third Ave., New York, NY 10022

National Center for Urban Environmental Studies 516 North Charles St., Suite 501, Baltimore, MD 21201

National Clean Air Coalition 801 Pennsylvania Ave. SE, Washington, DC 20003

National Coalition Against the Misuse of Pesticides 701 E St. SE, Suite 200, Washington, DC 20001

National Coalition for Marine Conservation P.O. Box 23298, Savannah, GA 31403

National Environmental Health Association 720 S. Colorado Blvd., South Tower, Suite 970, Denver, CO 80222

National Geographic Society 17th and M Sts. NW, Washington, DC 20036

National Park Foundation P.O. Box 57473, Washington, DC 20037

National Parks and Conservation Association 1776 Massachusetts Ave. NW, Suite 200, Washington, DC 20036

National Recreation and Park Association 2775 S. Quincy St., Suite 300, Arlington, VA 22206

National Recycling Coalition 1101 30th St. NW, Suite 304, Washington, DC 20007

National Wildlife Federation 1400 16th St. NW, Washington, DC 20036

Natural Resources Defense Council 40 W. 20th St., New York, NY 10011, and 1350 New York Ave. NW, Suite 300, Washington, DC 20005

Nature Conservancy 1814 N. Lynn St., Arlington, VA 22209

New Alchemy Institute 237 Hatchville Rd., East Falmouth, MA 02536

Pesticide Action Network 965 Mission St., No. 514, San Francisco, CA 94103

Physicians for Social Responsibility 639 Massachusetts Ave., Cambridge, MA 02139

Planet/Drum Foundation P.O. Box 31251, San Francisco, CA 94131

Planned Parenthood Federation of America 810 Seventh Ave., New York, NY 10019

Population Crisis Committee 1120 19th St. NW, Washington, DC 20036-3605

Population Institute 110 Maryland Ave. NE, Suite 207, Washington, DC 20002

Population Reference Bureau 1875 Connecticut Ave. NW, Suite 520, Washington, DC 20009-5728

Public Citizen 215 Pennsylvania Ave. SE, Washington, DC 20003

Rachel Carson Council 8940 Jones Mill Rd., Chevy Chase, MD 20815

Rainforest Action Network 3450 Sansome St., Suite 700, San Francisco, CA 94111

Rainforest Alliance 270 Lafayette St., Suite 512, New York, NY 10012

Renew America 1400 16th St. NW, Suite 710, Washington, DC 20036

Resources for the Future 1616 P St. NW, Washington, DC 20036

Rocky Mountain Institute 1739 Snowmass Creek Rd., Snowmass, CO 81654

Rodale Institute 222 Main St., Emmaus, PA 18098

Save the Whales, Inc. P.O. Box 2397, 1426 Main St., Unit E, Venice, CA 90291

Scientists' Institute for Public Information 355 Lexington Ave., New York, NY 10017

Sea Shepherd Conservation Society 1314 2nd St., Santa Monica, CA 90401

Sierra Club 730 Polk St., San Francisco, CA 94109 and 408 C St. NE, Washington, DC 20002

Smithsonian Institution 1000 Jefferson Dr. SW, Washington, DC 20560

Society for Conservation Biology Department of Wildlife Ecology, University of Wisconsin, Madison, WI 53706

Soil and Water Conservation Society 7515 NE Ankeny Rd., Ankeny, IA 50021

Student Conservation Association, Inc. P.O. Box 550, Charlestown, NH 03603

Student Environmental Action Coalition (SEAC) 217 A Carolina Union, University of North Carolina, Chapel Hill, NC 27599

Survival International 2121 Decatur Place NW, Washington, DC 20008

Treepeople 12601 Mulholland Dr., Beverly Hills, CA 90210

Union of Concerned Scientists 26 Church St., Cambridge, MA 02238

U.S. Public Interest Research Group 215 Pennsylvania Ave. SE, Washington, DC 20003

Water Pollution Control Federation 601 Wythe St., Alexandria, VA 22314

The Wilderness Society 900 17th St. NW, Washington, DC 20006

Wildlife Conservation International (WCI) New York Zoological Society, 185th St. and Southern Blvd., Bronx, NY 10460

Wildlife Society 5410 Grosvenor Lane, Bethesda, MD 20814

Work on Waste 82 Judson St., Canton, NY 13617

World Resources Institute 1709 New York Ave. NW, 7th Floor, Washington, DC 20006

Worldwatch Institute 1776 Massachusetts Ave. NW, Washington, DC 20036

World Wildlife Fund 1250 24th St. NW, Suite 500, Washington, DC 20037

Zero Population Growth 1400 16th St. NW, Suite 320, Washington, DC 20036

ADDRESSES OF FEDERAL AND INTERNATIONAL AGENCIES

Agency for International Development State Building, 320 21st St. NW, Washington, DC 20523

Bureau of Land Management U.S. Department of the Interior, 18th and C Sts., Room 3619, Washington, DC 20240

Bureau of Mines 2401 E St. NW, Washington, DC 20241

Bureau of Reclamation Washington, DC 20240

Conservation and Renewable Energy Inquiry and Referral Service P.O. Box 8900, Silver Spring, MD 20907, (800) 523-2929

Department of Agriculture 14th St. and Jefferson Dr. SW, Washington, DC 20250

Department of Commerce 14th St. between Constitution Ave. and E St. NW, Washington, DC 20230

Department of Energy Forrestal Building, 1000 Independence Ave. SW, Washington, DC 20585

Department of Health and Human Services 200 Independence Ave. SW, Washington, DC 20585

Department of Housing and Urban Development 451 Seventh St. SW, Washington, DC 20410

Department of the Interior 18th and C Sts. NW, Washington, DC 20240

Department of Transportation 400 Seventh St. SW, Washington, DC 20590

Environmental Protection Agency 401 M St. SW, Washington, DC 20460

Fish and Wildlife Service Department of the Interior, 18th and C Sts. NW, Washington, DC 20240

Food and Agriculture Organization (FAO) of the United Nations 101 22nd St. NW, Suite 300, Washington, DC 20437

Food and Drug Administration Department of Health and Human Services, 5600 Fishers Lane, Rockville, MD 20852

Forest Service P.O. Box 96090, Washington, DC 20013

Government Printing Office Washington, DC 20402

International Whaling Commission The Red House, 135 Station Rd., Histon, Cambridge CB4 4NP England 02203 3971

National Center for Atmospheric Research P.O. Box 3000, Boulder, CO 80307

National Marine Fisheries Service U.S. Dept. of Commerce, NOAA, 1335 East-West Highway, Silver Spring, MD 20910

National Oceanic and Atmospheric Administration Rockville, MD 20852

National Park Service Department of the Interior, P.O. Box 37127, Washington, DC 20013

National Renewable Energy Laboratory 1617 Cole Blvd., Golden, CO 80401

National Science Foundation 1800 G St. NW, Washington, DC 20550

National Solar Heating and Cooling Information Center P.O. Box 1607, Rockville, MD 20850

Nuclear Regulatory Commission 1717 H St. NW, Washington, DC 20555

Occupational Safety and Health Administration Department of Labor, 200 Constitution Ave. NW, Washington, DC 20210

Office of Ocean and Coastal Resource Management 1825 Connecticut Ave., Suite 700, Washington, DC 20235

Office of Surface Mining Reclamation and Enforcement 1951 Constitution Ave. NW, Washington, DC 20240

Office of Technology Assessment U.S. Congress, 600 Pennsylvania Ave. SW, Washington, DC 20510

Organization for Economic Cooperation and Development (U.S. Office) 2001 L St. NW, Suite 700, Washington, DC 20036

Soil Conservation Service P.O. Box 2890, Washington, DC 20013

United Nations 1 United Nations Plaza, New York, NY 10017

United Nations Environment Programme Regional North American Office, United Nations Room DC2-0803, New York, NY 10017, and 1889 F St. NW, Washington, DC 20006

U.S. Geological Survey 12201 Sunrise Valley Dr., Reston, VA 22092

World Bank 1818 H St. NW, Washington, DC 20433

Units of Measurement

LENGTH

Metric

1 kilometer (km) = 1,000 meters (m)
1 meter (m) = 100 centimeters (cm)
1 meter (m) = 1,000 millimeters (mm)
1 centimeter (cm) = 0.01 meter (m)
1 millimeter (mm) = 0.001 meter (m)

English

1 foot (ft) = 12 inches (in)
1 yard (yd) = 3 feet (ft)
1 mile (mi) = 5,280 feet (ft)
1 nautical mile = 1.15 miles (mi)

Metric-English

1 kilometer (km) = 0.621 mile (mi)
1 meter (m) = 39.4 inches (in)
1 inch (in) = 2.54 centimeters (cm)
1 foot (ft) = 0.305 meter (m)
1 yard (yd) = 0.914 meter (m)
1 nautical mile = 1.85 kilometers (km)

AREA

Metric

1 square kilometer (km^2) = 1,000,000 square meters (m^2)
1 square meter (m^2) = 1,000,000 square millimeters (mm^2)
1 hectare (ha) = 10,000 square meters (m^2)
1 hectare (ha) = 0.01 square kilometer (km^2)

English

1 square foot (ft^2) = 144 square inches (in^2)
1 square yard (yd^2) = 9 square feet (ft^2)
1 square mile (mi^2) = 27,880,000 square feet (ft^2)
1 acre (ac) = 43,560 square feet (ft^2)

Metric-English

1 hectare (ha) = 2.471 acres (ac)
1 square kilometer (km^2) = 0.386 square mile (mi^2)
1 square meter (m^2) = 1.196 square yards (yd^2)
1 square meter (m^2) = 10.76 square feet (ft^2)
1 square centimeter (cm^2) = 0.155 square inch (in^2)

VOLUME

Metric

1 cubic kilometer (km^3) = 1,000,000,000 cubic meters (m^3)
1 cubic meter (m^3) = 1,000,000 cubic centimeters (cm^3)
1 liter (L) = 1,000 milliliters (mL) = 1,000 cubic centimeters (cm^3)
1 milliliter (mL) = 0.001 liter (L)
1 milliliter (mL) = 1 cubic centimeter (cm^3)

English

1 gallon (gal) = 4 quarts (qt)
1 quart (qt) = 2 pints (pt)

Metric-English

1 liter (L) = 0.265 gallon (gal)
1 liter (L) = 1.06 quarts (qt)
1 liter (L) = 0.0353 cubic foot (ft^3)
1 cubic meter (m^3) = 35.3 cubic feet (ft^3)
1 cubic meter (m^3) = 1.30 cubic yard (yd^3)
1 cubic kilometer (km^3) = 0.24 cubic mile (mi^3)
1 barrel (bbl) = 159 liters (L)
1 barrel (bbl) = 42 U.S. gallons (gal)

MASS

Metric

1 kilogram (kg) = 1,000 grams (g)
1 gram (g) = 1,000 milligrams (mg)
1 gram (g) = 1,000,000 micrograms (µg)
1 milligram (mg) = 0.001 gram (g)
1 microgram (µg) = 0.000001 gram (g)
1 metric ton (mt) = 1,000 kilograms (kg)

English

1 ton (t) = 2,000 pounds (lb)
1 pound (lb) = 16 ounces (oz)

Metric-English

1 metric ton (mt) = 2,200 pounds (lb) = 1.1 tons (t)
1 kilogram (kg) = 2.20 pounds (lb)
1 pound (lb) = 454 grams (g)
1 gram (g) = 0.035 ounce (oz)

ENERGY AND POWER

Metric

1 kilojoule (kJ) = 1,000 joules (J)
1 kilocalorie (kcal) = 1,000 calories (cal)
1 calorie (cal) = 4.184 joules (J)

Metric-English

1 kilojoule (kJ) = 0.949 British thermal unit (Btu)
1 kilojoule (kJ) = 0.000278 kilowatt-hour (kW-h)
1 kilocalorie (kcal) = 3.97 British thermal units (Btu)
1 kilocalorie (kcal) = 0.00116 kilowatt-hour (kW-h)
1 kilowatt-hour (kW-h) = 860 kilocalories (kcal)
1 kilowatt-hour (kW-h) = 3,400 British thermal units (Btu)
1 quad (Q) = 1,050,000,000,000,000 kilojoules (kJ)
1 quad (Q) = 2,930,000,000,000 kilowatt-hours (kW-h)

TEMPERATURE CONVERSIONS

Fahrenheit (°F) to Celsius (°C): $°C = \dfrac{(°F - 32.0)}{1.80}$

Celsius (°C) to Fahrenheit (°F): $°F = (°C \times 1.80) + 32.0$

Major U.S. Resource Conservation and Environmental Legislation

GENERAL

National Environmental Policy Act of 1969 (NEPA)
International Environmental Protection Act of 1983

ENERGY

National Energy Act of 1978, 1980
National Appliance Energy Conservation Act of 1987
Energy Policy Act of 1992

WATER QUALITY

Water Quality Act of 1965
Water Resources Planning Act of 1965
Federal Water Pollution Control Acts of 1965, 1972
Ocean Dumping Act of 1972
Safe Drinking Water Act of 1974, 1984
Water Resources Development Act of 1986
Clean Water Act of 1977, 1987
Ocean Dumping Ban Act of 1988

AIR QUALITY

Clean Air Act of 1963, 1965, 1970, 1977, 1990
Pollution Prevention Act of 1990

NOISE CONTROL

Noise Control Act of 1965
Quiet Communities Act of 1978

RESOURCES AND SOLID WASTE MANAGEMENT

Solid Waste Disposal Act of 1965
Resource Recovery Act of 1970
Resource Conservation and Recovery Act of 1976
Marine Plastic Pollution Research and Control Act of 1987

TOXIC SUBSTANCES

Hazardous Materials Transportation Act of 1975
Toxic Substances Control Act of 1976
Resource Conservation and Recovery Act of 1976
Comprehensive Environmental Response, Compensation, and Liability (Superfund) Act of 1980, 1986
Nuclear Waste Policy Act of 1982

PESTICIDES

Federal Insecticide, Fungicide, and Rodenticide Control Act of 1972, 1988

WILDLIFE CONSERVATION

Lacey Act of 1900
Migratory Bird Treaty Act of 1918
Migratory Bird Conservation Act of 1929
Migratory Bird Hunting Stamp Act of 1934
Pittman-Robertson Act of 1937
Anadromous Fish Conservation Act of 1965
Fur Seal Act of 1966
National Wildlife Refuge System Act of 1966, 1976, 1978
Species Conservation Act of 1966, 1969
Marine Mammal Protection Act of 1972
Marine Protection, Research, and Sanctuaries Act of 1972
Endangered Species Act of 1973, 1982, 1985, 1988
Fishery Conservation and Management Act of 1976, 1978, 1982
Whale Conservation and Protection Study Act of 1976
Fish and Wildlife Improvement Act of 1978
Fish and Wildlife Conservation Act of 1980 (Nongame Act)

LAND USE AND CONSERVATION

Taylor Grazing Act of 1934
Wilderness Act of 1964
Multiple Use Sustained Yield Act of 1968
Wild and Scenic Rivers Act of 1968
National Trails System Act of 1968
National Coastal Zone Management Act of 1972, 1980
Forest Reserves Management Act of 1974, 1976
Forest and Rangeland Renewable Resources Act of 1974, 1978
Federal Land Policy and Management Act of 1976
National Forest Management Act of 1976
Soil and Water Conservation Act of 1977
Surface Mining Control and Reclamation Act of 1977
Antarctic Conservation Act of 1978
Endangered American Wilderness Act of 1978
Alaskan National Interests Lands Conservation Act of 1980
Coastal Barrier Resources Act of 1982
Food Security Act of 1985

Further Readings

GENERAL SOURCES OF ENVIRON-MENTAL INFORMATION*

Ashworth, William. 1991. *The Encyclopedia of Environmental Studies*. New York: Facts on File.

Brown, Lester R., et al. Annual. *State of the World*. New York: W. W. Norton.

———. Annual. *Vital Signs*. New York: W. W. Norton.

Buzzworm Magazine Editors. Annual. *Earth Journal: Environmental Almanac and Resource Directory*. Boulder, Colo.: Buzzworm Books.

Population Reference Bureau. Annual. *World Population Data Sheet*. Washington, D.C.: Population Reference Bureau.

Rittner, Don. 1992. *Ecolinking: Everyone's Guide to Online Environmental Information*. Berkeley, Calif.: Peachpit Press.

United Nations. Annual. *Demographic Yearbook*. New York: United Nations.

United Nations Environment Programme (UNEP). Annual. *State of the Environment*. New York: UNEP.

United Nations Population Fund. Annual. *The State of World Population*. New York: United Nations Population Fund.

U.S. Bureau of the Census. Annual. *Statistical Abstract of the United States*. Washington, D.C.: U.S. Bureau of the Census.

World Health Organization (WHO). Annual. *World Health Statistics*. Geneva, Switzerland: WHO.

World Resources Institute. Annual. *The Information Please Environmental Almanac*. Boston: Houghton Mifflin.

World Resources Institute and International Institute for Environment and Development. Published every two years. *World Resources*. New York: Basic Books.

CHAPTER 1   ENVIRONMENTAL PROBLEMS AND THEIR CAUSES

Cameron, Eugene N. 1986. *At the Crossroads—The Mineral Problems of the United States*. New York: John Wiley.

Catton, William R. 1980. *Overshoot: The Ecological Basis of Revolutionary Change*. Urbana: University of Illinois Press.

Commoner, Barry. 1990. *Making Peace with the Planet*. New York: Pantheon.

Dorr, Ann. 1984. *Minerals—Foundations of Society*. Montgomery County, Md.: League of Women Voters of Montgomery County Maryland.

*For a more detailed list consult my longer books, *Environmental Science* and *Living in the Environment*, Belmont, Calif.: Wadsworth.

Ehrlich, Paul R., and Anne H. Ehrlich. 1990. *The Population Explosion*. New York: Doubleday.

———. 1991. *Healing the Planet*. Reading, Mass.: Addison-Wesley.

Global Tomorrow Coalition. 1990. *The Global Ecology Handbook: What You Can Do About the Environmental Crisis*. Boston: Beacon Press.

Hardin, Garrett. 1993. *Living Within Limits: Ecology, Economics, and Population Taboos*. New York: Oxford University Press.

Meadows, Donella H., et al. 1992. *Beyond the Limits: Confronting Global Collapse, Envisioning a Sustainable Future*. Post Mills, Vt.: Chelsea Green.

Myers, Norman. 1990. *The Gaia Atlas of Future Worlds*. New York: Anchor/Doubleday.

Myers, Norman, ed. 1993. *Gaia: An Atlas of Planet Management*. Garden City, N.Y.: Anchor Press/Doubleday.

Ray, Dixy Lee, and Lou Gusso. 1993. *Environmental Overkill: Whatever Happened to Common Sense?* Washington, D.C.: Regnery Gateway.

Young, John E.. 1992. *Mining the Earth*. Washington, D.C.: Worldwatch Institute.

Youngquist, Walter. 1990. *Mineral Resources and the Destinies of Nations*. Portland, Oreg.: National Book.

CHAPTER 2   MATTER, ENERGY, AND ECOLOGY: CONNECTIONS IN NATURE

Akin, Wallace E. 1991. *Global Patterns: Climate, Vegetation, and Soils*. Norman, Okla.: University of Oklahoma Press.

Attenborough, David, et al. 1989. *The Atlas of the Living World*. Boston: Houghton-Mifflin.

Brewer, R. 1993. *The Science of Ecology*. 2d ed. Philadelphia, Pa.: Saunders.

Ehrlich, Anne H., and Paul R. Ehrlich. 1987. *Earth*. New York: Franklin Watts.

Elsom, Derek. 1992. *Earth: The Making, Shaping, and Working of a Planet*. New York: Macmillan.

Fumento, Michael. 1993. *Science Under Siege: Balancing Technology and Environment*. New York: William Morrow.

Goldsmith, Edward, et al. 1990. *Imperiled Planet: Restoring Our Endangered Ecosystems*. Cambridge, Mass.: MIT Press.

Meadows, Donella H., et al. 1992. *Beyond the Limits: Confronting Global Collapse, Envisioning a Sustainable Future*. Post Mills, Vt.: Chelsea Green.

Nisbet, E. G. 1991. *Living Earth*. San Francisco: HarperCollins.

Odum, Eugene P. 1993. *Ecology and Our Endangered Life-Support Systems*. 2d ed. Sunderland, Mass.: Sinauer.

Rickleffs, Robert E. 1990. *Ecology*. 3d ed. San Francisco: W. H. Freeman.

Rifkin, Jeremy. 1989. *Entropy: Into the Greenhouse World: A New World View*. New York: Bantam.

Smith, Robert L. 1990. *Elements of Ecology*. 4th ed. San Francisco: Harper & Row.

Starr, Cecie, and Ralph Taggart. 1992. *Biology: The Unity and Diversity of Life*. 6th ed. Belmont, Calif.: Wadsworth.

Tudge, Colin. 1988. *The Environment of Life*. New York: Oxford University Press.

Wilson, E. O. 1992. *The Diversity of Life*. Cambridge, Mass.: Harvard University Press.

CHAPTER 3   THE HUMAN POP-ULATION: GROWTH, URBAN-IZATION, AND REGULATION

Bouvier, Leon F. 1992. *Peaceful Invasions: Immigration and Changing America*. Lantham, Md.: University Press of America.

Bouvier, Leon F., and Carol J. De Vita. 1991. "The Baby Boom—Entering Midlife." *Population Bulletin*, vol. 6, no. 3, 1–35.

Brown, Lester R., and Jodi Jacobson. 1987. *The Future of Urbanization: Facing the Ecological and Economic Restraints*. Washington, D.C.: Worldwatch Institute.

Donaldson, Peter J., and Amy Ong Tsui. 1990. "The International Family Planning Movement." *Population Bulletin*, vol. 43, no. 3, 1–42.

Ehrlich, Paul R., and Anne H. Ehrlich. 1990. *The Population Explosion*. New York: Doubleday.

Formos, Werner. 1987. *Gaining People, Losing Ground: A Blueprint for Stabilizing World Population*. Washington, D.C.: Population Institute.

Gordon, Deborah. 1991. *Steering a New Course: Transportation, Energy, and the Environment*. Covelo, Calif.: Island Press.

Grant, Lindsey. 1992. *Elephants and Volkswagens: Facing the Tough Questions About Our Overcrowded Country*. New York: W. H. Freeman.

Hardin, Garrett. 1993. *Living Within Limits: Ecology, Economics, and Population Taboos*. New York: Oxford University Press.

Harrison, Paul. 1992. *The Third Revolution: Environment, Population, and a Sustainable World*. New York: I. B. Tauris.

Hart, John. 1992. *Saving Cities, Saving Money: Environmental Strategies That Work*. Washington, D.C.: Resource Renewal Institute.

Hartmann, Betsy. 1987. *Reproductive Rights and Wrongs: The Global Politics of Population Control and Contraceptive Choice.* San Francisco: Harper & Row.

Haupt, Arthur, and Thomas T. Kane. 1985. *The Population Handbook: International.* 2d ed. Washington, D.C.: Population Reference Bureau.

Heathcote, Willimas. 1991. *Autogeddon.* London: Jonathan Cape.

Jacobson, Jodi. 1991. *Women's Reproductive Health: The Silent Emergency.* Washington, D.C.: Worldwatch Institute.

Lowe, Marcia D. 1991. *Shaping Cities: The Environmental and Human Dimensions.* Washington, D.C.: Worldwatch Institute.

———. 1993. "Rediscovering Rail." In Lester R. Brown et al. *State of the World 1993.* New York: Norton, 120–38.

MacKenzie, James J., et al. 1992. *The Going Rate: What It Really Costs to Drive.* Washington, D.C.: World Resources Institute.

Makower, Joel. 1992. *The Green Commuter.* Washington, D.C.: National Press.

Mantrell, Michael L., et al. 1989. *Creating Successful Communities: A Guidebook to Growth Management Strategies.* Covelo, Calif.: Island Press.

McHarg, Ian L. 1969. *Design with Nature.* Garden City, N.Y.: Natural History Press.

Morris, David. 1982. *Energy and the Transformation of Urban America.* San Francisco: Sierra Club Books.

Nadis, Steve, and James J. MacKenzie. 1993. *Car Trouble.* Boston: Beacon Press.

Nafis, Sadik, ed. 1991. *Population Policies and Programmes: Lessons Learned from Two Decades of Experience.* New York: United Nations Population Fund.

Population Reference Bureau. 1990. *World Population: Fundamentals of Growth.* Washington, D.C.: Population Reference Bureau.

———. Annual. *World Population Data Sheet.* Washington, D.C.: Population Reference Bureau.

Register, Richard. 1992. *Ecocities.* Berkeley, Calif.: North Atlantic Books.

Renner, Michael. 1988. *Rethinking the Role of the Automobile.* Washington, D.C.: Worldwatch Institute.

Simon, Julian L. 1989. *Population Matters: People, Resources, Environment, and Immigration.* New Brunswick, N.J.: Transaction.

Thornton, Richard D. 1991. "Why the U.S. Needs a MAGLEV System." *Technology Review,* April, 31–42.

Tien, H. Yuan, et al. 1992. "China's Demographic Dilemmas." *Population Bulletin,* vol. 47, no. 1, 1–44.

Todd, John, and George Tukel. 1990. *Reinhabiting Cities and Towns: Designing for Sustainability.* San Francisco: Planet/Drum Foundation.

Todd, John, and Nancy Jack Todd. 1993. *From Ecocities to Living Machines: Precepts for Sustainable Technologies.* Berkeley, Calif.: North Atlantic Books.

United Nations. 1991. *Consequences of Rapid Population Growth in Developing Countries.* New York: United Nations.

———. 1992. *Long-Range World Population Projections: Two Centuries of Population Growth, 1950–2150.* New York: United Nations.

van der Ryn, Sin, and Peter Calthorpe. 1986. *Sustainable Communities: A New Design Synthesis for Cities, Suburbs, and Towns.* San Francisco: Sierra Club Books.

Walter, Bob, et al., eds. 1992. *Sustainable Cities: Concepts and Strategies for Eco-City Development.* Los Angeles, Calif.: Eco-Home Media.

CHAPTER 4 ENERGY

Ahearne, John F. 1993. "The Future of Nuclear Power." *American Scientist,* vol. 81, 24–35.

American Council for an Energy Efficient Economy. 1988. *Energy Efficiency: A New Agenda.* Washington, D.C.: American Council for an Energy Efficient Economy.

Blackburn, John O. 1987. *The Renewable Energy Alternative: How the United States and the World Can Prosper Without Nuclear Energy or Coal.* Durham, N.C.: Duke University Press.

Brower, Michael. 1992. *Cool Energy: Renewable Solution to Environmental Problems.* 2d ed. Cambridge, Mass.: MIT Press.

Chernousenko, Vladimir M. 1991. *Chernobyl: Insight from the Inside.* New York: Springer-Verlag.

Cohen, Bernard L. 1990. *The Nuclear Energy Option: An Alternative for the 90s.* New York: Plenum.

Echeverria, John, et al. 1989. *Rivers at Risk: The Concerned Citizen's Guide to Hydropower.* Covelo, Calif.: Island Press.

Flavin, Christopher. 1987. *Reassessing Nuclear Power: The Fallout from Chernobyl.* Washington, D.C.: Worldwatch Institute.

———. 1992. "Building a Bridge to Sustainable Energy." In Lester Brown et al. *State of the World 1992.* New York: Norton, 27–55.

Gever, John, et al. 1991. *Beyond Oil: The Threat to Food and Fuel in Coming Decades.* Boulder: University of Colorado Press.

Goldenberg, Jose, et al. 1988. *Energy for a Sustainable World.* New York: John Wiley.

Johansson, Thomas B., et al., eds. 1992. *Renewable Energy: Sources for Fuels and Electricity.* Covelo, Calif.: Island Press.

Lenssen, Nicholas. 1991. *Nuclear Waste: The Problem That Won't Go Away.* Washington, D.C.: Worldwatch Institute.

Lovins, Amory B. 1977. *Soft Energy Paths.* Cambridge, Mass.: Ballinger.

Lovins, Amory B., and L. Hunter Lovins. 1986. *Energy Unbound: Your Invitation to Energy Abundance.* San Francisco: Sierra Club Books.

Mackenzie, James L. 1993. *Electric and Hydrogen Vehicles: Transportation Technologies for the Twenty-first Century.* Washington, D.C.: World Resources Institute.

McKeown, Walter. 1991. *Death of the Oil Age and the Birth of Hydrogen America.* San Francisco: Wild Bamboo Press.

Office of Technology Assessment. 1992a. *Building Energy Efficiency.* Washington, D.C.: Government Printing Office.

———. 1992b. *Fueling Development: Energy Technologies for Developing Countries.* Washington, D.C.: Government Printing Office.

Oppenheimer, Ernest J. 1990. *Natural Gas, the Best Energy Choice.* New York: Pen & Podium.

Pollock, Cynthia. 1986. *Decommissioning: Nuclear Power's Missing Link.* Washington, D.C.: Worldwatch Institute.

Read, Piers Paul. 1993. *Ablaze: The Story of Chernobyl.* New York: Random House.

Real Goods Trading Corporation. Annual. *Alternative Energy Sourcebook.* Ukiah, Calif.: Real Goods Trading Corporation.

Schobert, Harold H. 1987. *Coal: The Energy Source of the Past and Future.* Washington, D.C.: American Chemical Society.

Starr, Chauncey, et al. 1992. "Energy Sources: A Realistic Outlook." *Science,* vol. 256, 981–86.

Vale, Brenda, and Robert Vale. 1991. *Green Architecture.* Boston: Little, Brown.

Wilson, Alex. 1992. *Consumer Guide to Home Energy Savings.* Washington, D.C.: American Council for an Energy Efficient Economy.

Winteringham, F. P. W. 1991. *Energy Use and the Environment.* Boca Raton, Fla.: Lewis.

Zweibel, Ken. 1990. *Harnessing Solar Power: The Challenge of Photovoltaics.* New York: Plenum.

CHAPTER 5 BIODIVERSITY: SUSTAINING ECOSYSTEMS

Burger, Julina. 1990. *The Gaia Atlas of First Peoples.* New York: Anchor Books.

Caufield, Catherine. 1985. *In the Rainforest.* New York: Alfred A. Knopf.

Chagnon, Napoleon A. 1992. *Yanomamo: The Last Days of Eden.* New York: Harcourt Brace Jovanovich.

Chase, Alston. 1986. *Playing God in Yellowstone: The Destruction of America's First National Park.* New York: Atlantic Monthly Press.

Collins, Mark, ed. 1990. *The Last Rainforests: A World Conservation Atlas.* Emmaus, Pa.: Rodale Press.

Dietrich, William. 1992. *The Final Forest.* New York: Simon & Schuster.

Durning, Alan Thein. 1992. *Guardians of the Land: Indigenous Peoples and the Health of the Earth.* Washington, D.C.: Worldwatch Institute.

Ervin, Keith. 1989. *Fragile Majesty: The Battle for North America's Last Great Forest.* Seattle: The Mountaineers.

Foreman, Dave, and Howie Wolke. 1989. *The Big Outside.* Tucson: Ned Ludd Books.

Fritz, Edward. 1983. *Sterile Forest: The Case Against Clearcutting.* Austin, Tex.: Eakin Press.

Frome, Michael. 1992. *Regreening the National Parks.* Tucson: University of Arizona Press.

Goodland, Robert, ed. 1990. *Race to Save the Tropics: Ecology and Economics for a Sustainable Future.* Covelo, Calif.: Island Press.

Head, Suzanne, and Robert Heinzman. 1990. *Lessons of the Rainforest.* San Francisco: Sierra Club Books.

Hendee, John, et al. 1991. *Principles of Wilderness Management.* Golden, Colo.: Fulcrum.

Hess, Karl, Jr. 1992. *Visions Upon the Land: Man and Nature on the Western Range.* Covelo, Calif.: Island Press.

Jacobs, Lynn. 1992. *Waste of the West: Public Lands Ranching.* Tucson, Ariz.: Lynn Jacobs.

Kelly, David, and Gary Braasch. 1988. *Secrets of the Old Growth Forest.* Salt Lake City: Peregrine Smith.

Lansky, Mitch. 1992. *Beyond the Beauty Strip: Saving What's Left of Our Forests.* Gardiner, Maine: Tilbury House.

Leopold, Aldo. 1949. *A Sand County Almanac.* New York: Oxford University Press.

Maser, Chris. 1989. *Forest Primeval.* San Francisco: Sierra Club Books.

Maybury-Lewis, David. 1992. *Millennium: Tribal Wisdom and the Modern World.* New York: Viking.

Miller, Kenton, and Laura Tangley. 1991. *Trees of Life: Protecting Tropical Forests and Their Biological Wealth.* Boston, Mass.: Beacon Press.

Myers, Norman. 1984. *The Primary Source: Tropical Forests and Our Future.* New York: W. W. Norton.

Naar, Jon, and Alex J. Naar. 1993. *This Land Is Your Land: A Guide to North America's Endangered Ecosystems.* New York: Harper.

Nash, Roderick. 1982. *Wilderness and the American Mind,* 3d ed. New Haven, Conn.: Yale University Press.

National Park Service. 1992. *National Parks for the 21st Century.* Washington, D.C.: National Park Service.

Norse, Elliot A. 1990. *Ancient Forests of the Pacific Northwest.* Covelo, Calif.: Island Press.

Oelschlager, Max. 1991. *The Idea of Wilderness from Prehistory to the Age of Ecology.* New Haven, Conn.: Yale University Press.

Office of Technology Assessment. 1992. *Combined Summaries: Technologies to Sustain Tropical Forest Resources and Biological Diversity.* Washington, D.C.: Office of Technology Assessment.

O'Toole, Randal. 1987. *Reforming the Forest Service.* Covelo, Calif.: Island Press.

Pimentel, David, et al. 1992. "Conserving Biological Diversity in Agricultural/Forestry Systems." *BioScience,* vol. 42, no. 5, 354–62.

Primack, Richard B. 1993. *Essentials of Conservation Biology.* Sunderland, Mass.: Sinauer.

Robinson, Gordon. 1987. *The Forest and the Trees: A Guide to Excellent Forestry.* Covelo, Calif.: Island Press.

Runte, Alfred. 1990. *Yosemite: The Embattled Wilderness.* Lincoln: University of Nebraska Press.

———. 1991. *Public Lands, Public Heritage: The National Forest Idea.* Niwot, Colo.: Roberts Rinehart.

Ryan, John C. 1992. *Life Support: Conserving Biological Diversity.* Washington, D.C.: Worldwatch Institute.

Tobin, Richard J. 1990. *The Expendable Future: U.S. Politics and the Protection of Biodiversity.* Durham, N.C.: Duke University Press.

Trexler, Mark C., and Christine Rogers. 1993. *Keeping It Green: Using Tropical Forestry to Mitigate Global Warming.* Washington, D.C.: World Resources Institute.

Wilderness Society. 1988. *Ancient Forests: A Threatened Heritage.* Washington, D.C.: The Wilderness Society.

Wilson, E. O. 1992. *The Diversity of Life.* Cambridge, Mass.: Harvard University Press.

Wilson, E. O., ed. 1988. *Biodiversity.* Washington, D.C.: National Academy Press.

World Resources Institute (WRI), The World Conservation Union (IUCN), and United Nations Development Programme. 1992. *Global Biodiversity Strategy.* Washington, D.C.: World Resources Institute.

CHAPTER 6 BIODIVERSITY: SUSTAINING SPECIES

Ackerman, Diane. 1991. *The Moon by Whalelight.* New York: Random House.

Cox, George W. 1993. *Conservation Ecology.* Dubuque, Iowa: Wm. C. Brown.

DiSilvestro, Roger L. 1990. *Fight for Survival.* New York: John Wiley.

———. 1992. *Rebirth of Nature.* New York: John Wiley.

Durrell, Lee. 1986. *State of the Ark: An Atlas of Conservation in Action.* New York: Doubleday.

Ehrlich, Paul, and Anne Ehrlich. 1981. *Extinction.* New York: Random House.

Eldredge, Niles. 1991. *The Miner's Canary.* New York: Prentice Hall.

Grumbine, R. Edward. 1992. *Ghost Bears: Exploring the Biodiversity Crisis.* Covelo, Calif.: Island Press.

Hargrove, Eugene C. 1992. *The Animal Rights/Environmental Ethics Debate.* Ithaca: State University of New York.

Jasper, James M., and Dorothy Nelkin. 1992. *The Animal Rights Crusade: The Growth of a Moral Protest.* New York: Macmillan.

Kohm, Kathryn A., ed. 1990. *Balancing on the Brink of Extinction: The Endangered Species Act and Lessons for the Future.* Covelo, Calif.: Island Press.

Livingston, John A. 1981. *The Fallacy of Wildlife Conservation.* Toronto: McClelland and Stewart.

Luoma, Jon. 1987. *A Crowded Ark: The Role of Zoos in Wildlife Conservation.* Boston: Houghton Mifflin.

Mathiessen, Peter. 1992. *Shadows of Africa.* New York: Frank Abrams.

Miller, Kenton R. 1993. *Balancing the Scales: Managing Biodiversity at the Bioregional Level.* Washington, D.C.: World Resources Institute.

Nash, Roderick F. 1988. *The Rights of Nature: A History of Environmental Ethics.* Madison: University of Wisconsin Press.

National Wildlife Federation. 1987. *The Arctic National Wildlife Refuge Coastal Plain: A Perspective for the Future.* Washington, D.C.: National Wildlife Federation.

Owens, Delia, and Mark Owens. 1992. *The Eye of the Elephant: An Epic Adventure in the African Wilderness.* Boston, Mass.: Houghton Mifflin.

Passmore, John. 1974. *Man's Responsibility for Nature.* New York: Charles Scribner's.

Primack, Richard B. 1993. *Essentials of Conservation Biology.* Sunderland, Mass.: Sinauer.

Reisner, Marc. 1991. *Game Wars: The Undercover Pursuit of Wildlife Poachers.* New York: Viking.

Rolston, Holmes, III. 1988. *Environmental Ethics: Duties to and Values in the Natural World.* Philadelphia: Temple University Press.

Soulé, Michael E. 1986. *Conservation Biology: Science of Scarcity and Diversity.* Sunderland, Mass.: Sinauer.

Tudge, Colin. 1988. *The Environment of Life.* New York: Oxford University Press.

———. 1992. *Last Animals at the Zoo: How Mass Extinction Can be Stopped.* Covelo, Calif.: Island Press.

Tuttle, Merlin D. 1988. *America's Neighborhood Bats: Understanding and Learning to Live in Harmony with Them.* Austin: University of Texas Press.

Whelan, Tensie, ed. 1991. *Nature Tourism: Managing for the Environment.* Covelo, Calif.: Island Press.

Wilson, E. O. 1992. *The Diversity of Life.* Cambridge, Mass.: Harvard University Press.

Wolf, Edward C. 1987. *On the Brink of Extinction: Conserving the Diversity of Life.* Washington, D.C.: Worldwatch Institute.

World Wildlife Fund. 1992. *The Official World Wildlife Fund Guide to Endangered Species of North America.* Washington, D.C.: Beacham.

CHAPTER 7 BIODIVERSITY: SUSTAINING SOIL AND PRODUCING FOOD

Aliteri, Miguel A., and Susanna B. Hecht. 1990. *Agroecology and Small Farm Development.* New York: CRC Press.

Bardach, John. 1988. "Aquaculture: Moving from Craft to Industry." *Environment,* vol. 30, no. 2, 7–40.

Bartholomew, Mel. 1987. *Square Foot Gardening.* Emmaus, Pa.: Rodale Press.

Berstein, Henry, et al., eds. 1990. *The Food Question: Profits Versus People.* East Haven, Conn.: Earthscan.

Briggs, Shirley, and the Rachel Carson Council. 1992. *Basic Guide to Pesticides: Their Characteristics and Hazards.* Washington, D.C.: Taylor & Francis.

Brown, Lester R., and John E. Young. 1990. "Feeding the World in the Nineties." In Lester Brown et al. *State of the World 1990.* Washington, D.C.: Worldwatch Institute, 59–78.

Campbell, Stu. 1990. *Let It Rot: The Gardener's Guide to Composting.* Pownal, Vt.: Storey Communications.

Carson, Rachel. 1962. *Silent Spring.* Boston: Houghton Mifflin.

Coleman, Elliot. 1992. *The New Organic Grower's Four-Season Harvest.* Post Mills, Vt.: Chelsea Green.

Donahue, Roy, et al. 1990. *Soils and Their Management.* 5th ed. Petaluma, Calif.: Inter Print.

Dregnue, Harold E. 1985. "Aridity and Land Degradation." *Environment,* vol. 27, no. 8, 33–39.

Dunning, Alan B., and Holly W. Brough. 1991. *Taking Stock: Animal Farming and the Environment.* Washington, D.C.: Worldwatch Institute.

Edwards, Clive A., et al., eds. 1990. *Sustainable Agricultural Systems.* Ankeny, Iowa: Soil and Water Conservation Society.

Foster, Phillips. 1992. *The World Food Problem.* Boulder, Colo.: Rienner.

Fowler, Cary, and Pat Mooney. 1990. *Shattering: Food, Politics, and the Loss of Genetic Diversity.* Tucson: University of Arizona Press.

Friends of the Earth. 1990. *How to Get Your Lawn and Garden Off Drugs.* Ottawa, Ontario: Friends of the Earth.

Fukuoka, Masanobu. 1985. *The Natural Way of Farming: The Theory and Practice of Green Philosophy.* New York: Japan Publications.

Gips, Terry. 1987. *Breaking the Pesticide Habit.* Minneapolis: IASA.

Gordon, R. Conway, and Edward R. Barbier. 1990. *After the Green Revolution: Sustainable Agriculture for Development.* East Haven, Conn.: Earthscan.

Grainger, Alan. 1990. *The Threatening Desert: Controlling Desertification.* East Haven, Conn.: Earthscan.

Hendry, Peter. 1988. "Food and Population: Beyond Five Billion." *Population Bulletin,* April, 1–55.

Heylin, Michael, ed. 1991. "Pesticides: Costs Versus Benefits." *Chemistry & Engineering News,* 7 January, 27–56.

Hunger Project. 1985. *Ending Hunger: An Idea Whose Time Has Come.* New York: Praeger.

Hynes, Patricia. 1989. *The Recurring Silent Spring*. New York: Pergamon Press.

Jackson, Wes. 1986. *The Unsettling of America*. San Francisco: Sierra Club Books.

Jacobson, Michael, et al. 1991. *Safe Food: Eating Wisely in a Risky World*. Washington, D.C.: Planet Earth Press.

Kourik, Robert. 1990. "Combating Household Pests Without Chemical Warfare." *Garbage*, March/April, 22–29.

Landau, Matthew. 1992. *Introduction to Aquaculture*. New York: Wiley.

League of Women Voters. 1991. *U.S. Farm Policy: Who Benefits? Who Pays? Who Decides?* Washington, D.C.: League of Women Voters.

Little, Charles E. 1987. *Green Fields Forever: The Conservation Tillage Revolution in America*. Covelo, Calif.: Island Press.

Mainguet, Monique. 1991. *Desertification: Natural Background and Human Mismanagement*. New York: Springer-Verlag.

Marquardt, Sandra. 1989. *Exporting Banned Pesticides: Fueling the Circle of Poison*. Washington, D.C.: Greenpeace.

McGoodwin, Russell. 1990. *Crisis in the World's Fisheries: People, Problems, and Politics*. Stanford, Calif.: Stanford University Press.

Mollison, Bill. 1990. *Permaculture: A Practical Guide for a Sustainable Future*. Covelo, Calif.: Island Press.

National Academy of Sciences. 1989. *Alternative Agriculture*. Washington, D.C.: National Academy Press.

———. 1992. *Marine Aquaculture: Opportunities for Growth*. Washington, D.C.: National Academy Press.

Paddock, Joe, et al. 1987. *Soil and Survival: Land Stewardship and the Future of American Agriculture*. San Francisco: Sierra Club Books.

Pimentel, David, and Carl W. Hall. 1989. *Food and Natural Resources*. San Diego: Academic Press.

Pimentel, David, et al. 1992. "Environmental and Economic Cost of Pesticide Use." *BioScience*, vol. 42, no. 10, 750–60.

Rifkin, Jeremy. 1992. *Beyond Beef: The Rise and Fall of the Cattle Culture*. New York: Dutton.

Ritchie, Mark. 1990. "GATT, Agriculture, and the Environment." *The Ecologist*, vol. 20, no. 6, 214–20.

Robbins, John. 1987. *Diet for a New America*. Walpole, N.H.: Stillpoint Publishing.

Shiva, Vandana. 1991. *The Violence of the Green Revolution*. Atlantic Highlands, N.J.: Zed Books.

Soil and Water Conservation Society. 1990. *Sustainable Agricultural Systems*. Ankeny, Iowa: Soil and Water Conservation Society.

Soule, Judith D., and Jon Piper. 1992. *Farming in Nature's Image: An Ecological Approach to Agriculture*. Covelo, Calif.: Island Press.

Todd, Nancy J., and John Todd. 1984. *Bioshelters, Ocean Arks, City Farming: Ecology as a Basis for Design*. San Francisco: Sierra Club Books.

Van den Bosch, Robert. 1978. *The Pesticide Conspiracy*. New York: Doubleday.

Whelan, Elizabeth M., and Frederick J. Stare. 1983. *The 100% Natural, Purely Organic, Cholesterol-Free, Megavitamin, Low-Carbohydrate Nutrition Hoax*. New York: Atheneum.

Wolf, Edward C. 1986. *Beyond the Green Revolution: New Approaches for Third World Agriculture*. Washington, D.C.: Worldwatch Institute.

Yepsen, Roger B., Jr. 1987. *The Encyclopedia of Natural Insect and Pest Control*. Emmaus, Pa.: Rodale Press.

CHAPTER 8   RISK, TOXICOLOGY, AND HUMAN HEALTH

Ames, Bruce N., et al. 1987. "Ranking Possible Carcinogenic Hazards." *Science*, vol. 236, 271–79.

Aral, Sevgi O., and King K. Holmes. 1991. "Sexually Transmitted Diseases in the AIDS Era." *Scientific American*, vol. 264, no. 2, 62–69.

Clarke, Lee. 1989. *Acceptable Risk? Making Decisions in a Toxic Environment*. Berkeley and Los Angeles: University of California Press.

Cohen, Mark N. 1989. *Health and the Rise of Civilization*. New Haven, Conn.: Yale University Press.

Crone, Hugh D. 1986. *Chemicals and Society*. New York: Cambridge University Press.

Desowitz, Robert S. 1991. *The Malaria Capers: More Tales of Parasites and People, Research, and Reality*. New York: Norton.

Douglas, Mary, and Aaron Wildavsky. 1982. *Risk and Culture*. Berkeley: University of California Press.

Efron, Edith. 1984. *The Apocalyptics: Cancer and the Big Lie*. New York: Simon & Schuster.

Environmental Protection Agency. 1987. *Unfinished Business: A Comparative Assessment of Environmental Problems*. Washington, D.C.: Environmental Protection Agency.

Fischoff, Baruch, et al. 1984. *Acceptable Risk: Science and Determination of Safety*. New York: Cambridge University Press.

Foster, Kenneth R., et al., eds. 1993. *Phantom Risk: Scientific Inference and Law*. Cambridge, Mass.: MIT Press.

Fox, Michael W. 1992. *Superpigs and Wondercorn: The Brave New World of Biotechnology and Where It All May Lead*. New York: Lyons & Burford.

Freudenburg, William R. 1988. "Perceived Risk, Real Risk: Social Science and the Art of Probabilistic Risk Assessment." *Science*, vol. 242, 44–49.

Hall, Ross Hume. 1990. *Health and the Global Environment*. Cambridge, Mass.: Basil Blackwell.

Harris, John. 1992. *Wonderwoman and Superman: The Ethics of Human Biotechnology*. New York: Oxford University Press.

Harte, John, et al. 1992. *Toxics A to Z: A Guide to Everyday Pollution Hazards*. Berkeley: University of California Press.

Hunter, Linda Mason. 1989. *The Healthy House: An Attic-to-Basement Guide to Toxin-Free Living*. Emmaus, Pa.: Rodale Press.

Imperato, P. J., and Greg Mitchell. 1985. *Acceptable Risks*. New York: Viking Press.

Kamarin, M. A. 1988. *Toxicology: A Primer on Toxicology Principles and Applications*. Boca Raton, Fla.: Lewis.

Lewis, H. W. 1990. *Technological Risk*. New York: W. W. Norton.

Moeller, Dade W. 1992. *Environmental Health*. Cambridge, Mass.: Harvard University Press.

National Academy of Sciences. 1991. *Malaria: Obstacles and Opportunities*. Washington, D.C.: National Academy Press.

———. 1992. *Eat for Life: The Food and Nutrition Board's Guide to Reducing Your Risk of Chronic Disease*. Washington, D.C.: National Academy Press.

Nelkin, M. M., and M. S. Brown. 1984. *Workers at Risk: Voices from the Workplace*. Chicago: University of Chicago Press.

Ottoboni, M. Alice. 1991. *The Dose Makes the Poison: A Plain-Language Guide to Toxicology*. 2d ed. New York: Van Nostrand Reinhold.

Piller, Charles. 1991. *The Fail-Safe Society*. New York: Basic Books.

Rifkin, Jeremy. 1983. *Algeny*. New York: Viking/Penguin.

Rodricks, Joseph V. 1992. *Calculated Risks: The Toxicity and Human Health Risks of Chemicals in the Environment*. New York: Cambridge University Press.

Russell, Dick, et al. 1992. *Inconclusive by Design: Waste, Fraud, and Abuse in Federal Environmental Health Research*. Boston: Environmental Health Network.

Shrader-Frechette, K. S. 1991. *Risk and Rationality*. Berkeley: University of California Press.

U.S. Department of Health and Human Services. 1988. *The Surgeon General's Report on Nutrition and Health*. Washington, D.C.: Government Printing Office.

———. Annual. *The Health Consequences of Smoking*. Rockville, Md.: U.S. Department of Health and Human Services.

Wilson, Richard, and E. A. C. Crouch. 1987. "Risk Assessment and Comparisons: An Introduction." *Science*, vol. 236, 267–70.

CHAPTER 9   AIR, CLIMATE, AND OZONE

Ausubel, Jesse H. 1991. "A Second Look at the Impacts of Climate Change." *American Scientist*, vol. 79, 210–21.

Balling, Robert C., Jr. 1992. *The Heated Debate: Greenhouse Predictions Versus Climate Reality*. San Francisco: Pacific Research Institute for Public Policy.

Barry, R. C., and J. Chorley. 1987. *Atmosphere, Weather, and Climate*. 5th ed. London: Meuthen.

Bates, Albert K. 1990. *Climate in Crisis: The Greenhouse Effect and What We Can Do*. Summertown, Tenn.: Book Publishing Company.

Bloch, Ben, and Harold Lyons. 1993. *Apocalypse Not: Science, Economics, and Environmentalism*. Washington, D.C.: Cato Institute.

Borman, F. H. 1985. "Air Pollution and Forests: An Ecosystem Perspective." *BioScience*, vol. 35, no. 7, 434–41.

Bridgman, Howard. 1991. *Global Air Pollution: Problems for the 1990s*. New York: Belhaven Press.

Brookins, Douglas G. 1990. *The Indoor Radon Problem*. Irvington, N.Y.: Columbia University Press.

Broome, John. 1992. *Counting the Cost of Global Warming*. Isle of Harris, UK: White Horse Press.

Bryner, Gary. 1992. *Blue Skies, Green Politics: The Clean Air Act of 1990*. Washington, D.C.: Congressional Quarterly Press.

Coffel, Steve, and Karyn Feiden. 1991. *Indoor Pollution*. New York: Random House.

Council for Agricultural Science and Technology. 1992. *Preparing U.S. Agriculture for Global Climate Change*. Ames, Iowa: Council for Agricultural Science and Technology.

Dotto, Lydia. 1990. *Thinking the Unthinkable: Civilization and Rapid Climate Change*. Waterloo, Ontario: Wilfrid Lanier University Press.

Edgerton, Lynne T. 1990. *The Rising Tide: Global Warming and World Sea Levels.* Covelo, Calif.: Island Press.

Elson, Derek. 1987. *Atmospheric Pollution: Causes, Effects, and Control Policies.* Cambridge, Mass.: Basil Blackwell.

Environmental Protection Agency. 1989. *Policy Options for Stabilizing Global Climate.* Washington, D.C.: EPA.

Fisher, David E. 1990. *Fire and Ice: The Greenhouse Effect, Ozone Depletion, and Nuclear Winter.* San Francisco: Harper & Row.

Fishman, Albert, and Robert Kalish. 1990. *Global Alert: The Ozone Pollution Crisis.* New York: Plenum.

Flavin, Christopher. 1989. *Slowing Global Warming: A Worldwide Strategy.* Washington, D.C.: Worldwatch Institute.

French, Hilary F. 1990. *Clearing the Air: A Global Agenda.* Washington, D.C.: Worldwatch Institute.

Gates, David M. 1993. *Climate Change and Its Biological Consequences.* Sunderland, Mass.: Sinauer.

Greenhouse Crisis Foundation. 1990. *The Greenhouse Crisis: 101 Ways to Save the Earth.* Washington, D.C.: Greenhouse Crisis Foundation.

Hileman, Bette. 1992. "Web of Interactions Makes It Difficult to Untangle Global Warming Data." *Chemistry & Engineering News,* 27 April, 7–19.

Intergovernmental Panel on Climate Change (IPCC). 1990. *Climate Change: The IPCC Assessment.* New York: Cambridge University Press.

————. 1992. *The Supplementary Report to the IPCC Scientific Assessment.* New York: Cambridge University Press.

Jones, Philip D., and Tom M. L. Wiglet. 1990. "Global Warming Trends." *Scientific American,* August, 84–91.

Karplus, Walter J. 1992. *The Heavens are Falling: The Scientific Prediction of Catastrophes in Our Time.* New York: Plenum.

Lovins, Amory B., et al. 1989. *Least-Cost Energy: Solving the CO$_2$ Problem.* 2d ed. Andover, Mass.: Brick House.

Lyman, Francesca, et al. 1990. *The Greenhouse Trap: What We're Doing to the Atmosphere and How We Can Slow Global Warming.* Washington, D.C.: World Resources Institute.

MacKenzie, James J., and Mohamed T. El-Ashry. 1990. *Air Pollution's Toll on Forests and Crops.* New Haven, Conn.: Yale University Press.

Makhijani, Arjun, et al. 1992. *Saving Our Skins: The Causes and Consequences of Ozone Layer Depletion and Policies for its Restoration and Protection.* Takoma Park, Md.: Institute for Energy and Environmental Research.

Manne, Alan S., and Richard G. Richels. 1992. *Buying Greenhouse Insurance: The Economic Costs of CO$_2$ Emission Limits.* Cambridge, Mass.: MIT Press.

Mathews, Jessica Tuchman, ed. 1991. *Greenhouse Warming: Negotiating a Global Regime.* Washington, D.C.: World Resources Institute.

McKibben, Bill. 1989. *The End of Nature.* New York: Random House.

Mello, Robert A. 1987. *Last Stand of the Red Spruce.* Covelo, Calif.: Island Press.

Mintzer, Irving, and William R. Moomaw. 1991. *Escaping the Heat Trap: Probing the Prospects for a Stable Environment.* Washington, D.C.: World Resources Institute.

Mintzer, Irving, et al. 1990. *Protecting the Ozone Shield: Strategies for Phasing Out CFCs During the 1990s.* Washington, D.C.: World Resources Institute.

Mohnen, Volker A. 1988. "The Challenge of Acid Rain." *Scientific American,* vol. 259, no. 2, 30–38.

National Academy of Sciences. 1990a. *Confronting Climate Change.* Washington, D.C.: National Academy Press.

————. 1990b. *Sea Level Change.* Washington, D.C.: National Academy Press.

————. 1992. *Global Environmental Change.* Washington, D.C.: National Academy Press.

National Audubon Society. 1990. *CO$_2$ Diet for a Greenhouse Planet: A Citizen's Guide to Slowing Global Warming.* New York: National Audubon Society.

Nero, Anthony V. 1992. "A National Strategy for Indoor Radon." *Issues in Science and Technology,* Fall, 33–40.

Office of Technology Assessment. 1985. *Acid Rain and Transported Air Pollutants: Implications for Public Policy.* New York: Unipub.

————. 1989. *Catching Our Breath: Next Steps for Reducing Urban Ozone.* Washington, D.C.: Government Printing Office.

————. 1991. *Changing by Degrees: Steps to Reduce Greenhouse Gases.* Washington, D.C.: Government Printing Office.

Oppenheimer, Michael, and Robert H. Boyle. 1990. *Dead Heat: The Race Against the Greenhouse Effect.* New York: Basic Books.

Parry, Martin. 1990. *Climate Change and World Agriculture.* London: Earthscan.

Pawlick, Thomas. 1986. *A Killing Rain: The Global Threat of Acid Precipitation.* San Francisco: Sierra Club Books.

Peters, Robert L., and Thomas E. Lovejoy. 1992. *Global Warming and Biological Diversity.* New Haven, Conn.: Yale University Press.

Ray, Dixy Lee, and Lou Guzzo. 1993. *Environmental Overkill: Whatever Happened to Common Sense?* Washington, D.C.: Regnery Gateway.

Regens, James L., and Robert W. Rycroft. 1988. *The Acid Rain Controversy.* Pittsburgh: University of Pittsburgh Press.

Revkin, Andrew. 1992. *Global Warming: Understanding the Forecast.* New York: Abbeville Press.

Roan, Sharon L. 1989. *Ozone Crisis: The 15-Year Evolution of a Sudden Global Emergency.* New York: John Wiley.

Rowland, F. Sherwood. 1989. "Chlorofluorocarbons and the Depletion of Stratospheric Ozone." *American Scientist,* vol. 77, 36–45.

Rubin, G., et al. 1992. "Realistic Mitigation Options for Global Warming." *Science,* vol. 257, 148–49, 26–66.

Schneider, Stephen H. 1987. "Climate Modeling." *Scientific American,* vol. 256, no. 5, 72–80.

————. 1989. *Global Warming: Are We Entering the Greenhouse Century?* New York: Random House.

Shea, Cynthia Pollack. 1988. *Protecting Life on Earth: Steps to Save the Ozone Layer.* Washington, D.C.: Worldwatch Institute.

Smith, William H. 1991. "Air Pollution and Forest Damage." *Chemistry and Engineering News,* 11 November, 30–43.

Weiner, Jonathan. 1990. *The Next One Hundred Years: Shaping the Fate of Our Living Earth.* New York: Bantam Books.

White, Robert M. 1990. "The Great Climate Debate." *Scientific American,* July, 36–43.

Young, Louise B. 1990. *Sowing the Wind: Reflections on Earth's Atmosphere.* Englewood Cliffs, N.J.: Prentice Hall.

CHAPTER 10   WATER

Allaby, Michael. 1992. *Water: Its Global Nature.* New York: Facts on File.

Anderson, T. L. 1986. *Water Rights: Scarce Resource Allocation, Bureaucracy, and the Environment.* San Francisco: Pacific Institute for Public Policy.

Ashworth, William. 1982. *Nor Any Drop to Drink.* New York: Summit Books.

————. 1986. *The Late, Great Lakes: An Environmental History.* New York: Alfred A. Knopf.

Boon, P. J., et al., eds. 1992. *River Conservation and Management.* New York: John Wiley.

Borgese, Elisabeth Mann. 1986. *The Future of the Oceans.* New York: Harvest House.

Center for Marine Conservation. 1989. *The Exxon Valdez Oil Spill: A Management Analysis.* Washington, D.C.: Center for Marine Conservation.

Clarke, Robin. 1993. *Water: The International Crisis.* Cambridge, Mass.: MIT Press.

Edmonson, W. T. 1991. *The Uses of Ecology: Lake Washington and Beyond.* Seattle: University of Washington Press.

Environmental Protection Agency. 1990. *Citizen's Guide to Ground-Water Protection.* Washington, D.C.: Environmental Protection Agency.

Falkenmark, Malin, and Carl Widstand. 1992. "Population and Water Resources: A Delicate Balance." *Population Bulletin,* vol. 47, no. 3, 1–36.

Feldman, David Lewis. 1991. *Water Resources Management: In Search of an Environmental Ethic.* Baltimore, Md.: Johns Hopkins University Press.

Gray, N, F, 1992, *Biology of Wastewater Treatment.* New York: Oxford University Press.

Hansen, Nancy R., et al. 1988. *Controlling Nonpoint-Source Water Pollution.* New York: National Audubon Society and The Conservation Society.

Hitteman, Bette. 1988. "The Great Lakes Cleanup Effort." *Chemistry & Engineering News,* 8 February, 22–39.

Horton, Tom, and William Eichbaum. 1991. *Turning the Tide: Saving the Chesapeake Bay.* Covelo, Calif.: Island Press.

Hundley, Norris, Jr. 1992. *The Great Thirst: Californians and Water, 1770s–1990s.* Berkeley: University of California Press.

Ingram, Colin. 1991. *The Drinking Water Book.* Berkeley, Calif.: Ten Speed Press.

Irwin, Frances H. 1989. "Integrated Pollution Control." *International Environmental Affairs,* vol. 1, no. 4, 255–74.

Ives, J. D., and B. Messeric. 1989. *The Himalayan Dilemma: Reconciling Development and Conservation.* London: Routledge.

Jefferies, Michael, and Derek Mills. 1991. *Freshwater Ecology: Principles and Applications.* New York: Belhaven Press.

Keeble, John. 1991. *Out of the Channel: The Exxon Valdez Oil Spill in Prince William Sound.* San Francisco: HarperCollins.

King, Jonathan. 1985. *Troubled Water: The Poisoning of America's Drinking Water.* Emmaus, Pa.: Rodale Press.

Knopman, Debra S., and Richard A. Smith. 1993. "20 Years of the Clean Water Act." *Environment,* vol. 35, no. 1, 17–20, 34–41.

Kotlyakov, V. M. 1991. "The Aral Sea Basin: A Critical Environmental Zone." *Environment,* vol. 33, no. 1, 4–9, 36–39.

Kourik, Robert. 1988. *Gray Water Use in the Landscape.* Santa Rosa, Calif.: Edible Publications.

———. 1992. *Drip Irrigation.* Santa Rosa, Calif.: Edible Publications.

Marquardt, Sandra, et al. 1989. *Bottled Water: Sparkling Hype at a Premium Price.* Washington, D.C.: Environmental Policy Institute.

Marx, Wesley. 1991. *The Frail Ocean: A Blueprint for Change in the 1990s and Beyond.* San Francisco: Sierra Club Books.

Mason, C. F. 1991. *Biology of Freshwater Pollution.* 2d ed. New York: John Wiley.

McCutcheon, Sean. 1992. *Electric Rivers: The Story of the James River Project.* New York: Paul & Co.

Naiman, Robert J., ed. 1992. *Watershed Management: Balancing Sustainability and Environmental Change.* New York: Springer-Verlag.

National Academy of Sciences. 1992. *Water Transfers in the West: Efficiency, Equity, and the Environment.* Washington, D.C.: National Academy Press.

Patrick, Ruth, et al. 1992. *Surface Water Quality: Have the Laws Been Successful?* Princeton, N.J.: Princeton University Press.

Patrick, Ruth, E. Ford, and J. Quarles, eds. 1987. *Groundwater Contamination in the United States.* Philadelphia: University of Pennsylvania Press.

Pearce, Fred. 1992. *The Dammed: Rivers, Dams, and the Coming World Water Crisis.* London: Bodley Head.

Postel, Sandra. 1992. *The Last Oasis: Facing Water Scarcity.* New York: W. W. Norton.

Reisner, Marc. 1986. *Cadillac Desert: The American West and Its Disappearing Water.* New York: Viking Press.

Reisner, Marc, and Sara Bates. 1990. *Overtapped Oasis: Reform or Revolution for Western Water.* Covelo, Calif.: Island Press.

Sierra Club Defense Fund. 1989. *The Poisoned Well: New Strategies for Groundwater Protection.* Covelo, Calif.: Island Press.

Starr, Joyce R. 1991. "Water Wars." *Foreign Policy,* Spring, 12–45.

Worster, Donald. 1985. *Rivers of Empire: Water, Aridity, and the Growth of the American West.* New York: Pantheon.

Zwingle, Erla. 1993. "Ogallala Aquifer: Wellspring of the High Plains." *National Geographic,* March, 80–107.

CHAPTER 11 WASTES AND RESOURCE CONSERVATION

Allen, Robert. 1992. *Waste Not, Want Not.* London: Earthscan.

Bullard, Robert D. 1990. *Dumping in Dixie: Race, Class, and Environmental Quality.* Boulder, Colo.: Westview Press.

Carless, Jennifer. 1992. *Taking Out the Trash: A No-Nonsense Guide to Recycling.* Covelo, Calif.: Island Press.

Centers for Disease Control and Prevention. 1991. *Preventing Lead Poisoning in Young Children.* Atlanta, Ga.: Centers for Disease Control and Prevention.

Chepesiuk, Ron. 1991. "From Ash to Cash: The International Trade in Toxic Waste." *E Magazine,* July/August, 31–63.

Clarke, Marjorie J., et al. 1991. *Burning Garbage in the U.S.: Practice vs. State of the Art.* New York: Inform.

Cohen, Gary, and John O'Connor. 1990. *Fighting Toxics: A Manual for Protecting Family, Community, and Workplace.* Covelo, Calif.: Island Press.

Commoner, Barry. 1990. *Making Peace with the Planet.* New York: Pantheon.

Connett, Paul H. 1992. "The Disposable Society." In F. H. Bormann and Stephen R. Kellert, eds. *Ecology, Economics, Ethics.* New Haven, Conn.: Yale University Press, 99–122.

Denison, Richard A., and John Ruston. 1990. *Recycling and Incineration: Evaluating the Choices.* Covelo, Calif.: Island Press.

Durning, Alan Thein. 1992. *How Much Is Enough? The Consumer Society and the Future of the Earth.* New York: Norton.

Earth Works Group. 1990. *The Recycler's Handbook: Simple Things You Can Do.* Berkeley: Earth Works Press.

Environment Canada. 1990. *Reduction and Reuse: The First 2 Rs of Waste Management.* Ottawa: Environment Canada.

Gibbs, Lois, and Will Collette. 1987. *Solid Waste Action Project Guidebook.* Arlington, Va.: Citizen's Clearinghouse for Hazardous Waste.

Gordon, Ben, and Peter Montague. 1989. *Zero Discharge: A Citizen's Toxic Waste Manual.* Washington, D.C.: Greenpeace.

Gourlay, K. A. 1992. *World of Waste: Dilemmas of Industrial Development.* Atlantic Heights, N.J.: Zed Books.

Harte, John, et al. 1991. *Toxics A to Z: A Guide to Everyday Pollution Hazards.* Berkeley: University of California Press.

Hershkowitz, Allen, and Eugene Salermi. 1987. *Garbage Management in Japan: Leading the Way.* New York: Inform.

Institute for Local Self-Reliance. 1990. *Proven Profits from Pollution Prevention.* Washington, D.C.: Institute for Local Self-Reliance.

Kharbanda, O. P., and E. A. Stallworthy. 1990. *Waste Management: Toward a Sustainable Society.* New York: Auburn House.

Lappé, Marc. 1991. *Chemical Deception: The Toxic Threat to Health and Environment.* San Francisco: Sierra Club Books.

Lester, Stephen, and Brian Lipsett. 1989. *Track Record of the Hazardous Waste Incineration Industry.* Arlington, Va.: Citizen's Clearinghouse for Hazardous Waste.

Lipsett, B., and D. Farrell. 1990. *Solid Waste Incineration Status Report.* Arlington, Va.: Citizen's Clearinghouse for Hazardous Waste.

Minnesota Mining and Manufacturing. 1988. *Low- or Non-Pollution Technology Through Pollution Prevention.* St. Paul, Minn.: 3M Company.

Moyers, Bill. 1990. *Global Dumping Ground: The International Traffic in Hazardous Waste.* Cabin John, Md.: Seven Locks Press.

National Toxics Campaign Fund. 1991. *The U.S. Military's Toxic Legacy: America's Worst Environmental Enemy.* Boston, Mass.: National Toxics Campaign Fund.

Newsday. 1989. *Rush to Burn: Solving America's Garbage Crisis?* Covelo, Calif.: Island Press.

Office of Technology Assessment. 1987a. *From Pollution to Prevention: A Progress Report on Waste Reduction.* Washington, D.C.: Government Printing Office.

———. 1987b. *Marine Minerals: Exploring Our New Ocean Frontier.* Washington, D.C.: Government Printing Office.

Ortbal, John. 1991. *Buy Recycled! Your Practical Guide to the Environmentally Responsible Office.* Chicago: Services Marketing Group.

Platt, Brenda, et al. 1991. *Beyond 40 Percent: Record-Setting Recycling and Composting Programs.* Covelo, Calif.: Island Press.

Pollack, Cynthia. 1987. *Mining Urban Wastes: The Potential for Recycling.* Washington, D.C.: Worldwatch Institute.

Rathje, William, and Cullen Murphy. 1992. *Rubbish! The Archaeology of Garbage: What Our Garbage Tells Us About Ourselves.* San Francisco: HarperCollins.

Reynolds, Michael. 1990–91. *Earthship.* Vols. I and II. Taos, N.M.: Solar Survival Architecture.

Shulman, Seth. 1992. *The Threat at Home: Confronting the Toxic Legacy of the U.S. Military.* Boston: Beacon Press.

Theodore, Louis, and Young C. McGuinn. 1992. *Pollution Prevention.* New York: Van Nostrand Reinhold.

Water Pollution Control Federation. 1989. *Household Hazardous Waste: What You Should and Shouldn't Do.* Alexandria, Va.: Water Pollution Control Federation.

Wolf, Nancy, and Ellen Feldman. 1990. *Plastics: America's Packaging Dilemma.* Covelo, Calif.: Island Press.

Young, John E. 1991. *Discarding the Throwaway Society.* Washington, D.C.: Worldwatch Institute.

———. 1992. "Aluminum's Real Tab." *World Watch,* March/April, 26–34.

CHAPTER 12 ECONOMICS, POLITICS, AND WORLDVIEWS

Anderson, Terry, and Donald Leal. 1990. *Free Market Environmentalism.* San Francisco: Pacific Research Institute for Public Policy.

Anderson, Victor. 1991. *Alternative Economic Indicators.* New York: Routledge.

Andruss, Van, et al. 1990. *Home! A Bioregional Reader.* Philadelphia, Penn.: New Society.

Atkinson, Adrian. 1991. *Principles of Political Ecology.* London: Belhaven Press.

Basta, Nicholas. 1991. *The Environmental Career Guide: Job Opportunities with the Earth in Mind.* New York: Wiley.

Berle, Gustav. 1991. *The Green Entrepreneur.* New York: McGraw Hill.

Berry, Thomas. 1988. *The Dream of the Earth.* San Francisco: Sierra Club Books.

Borman, F. H., and Stephen R. Kellert, eds. 1992. *Ecology, Economics, Ethics.* New Haven, Conn.: Yale University Press.

Bowden, Elbert V. 1990. *Principles of Economics: Theory, Problems, Policies.* 5th ed. Cincinnati: South-Western.

Brown, Lester R., et al. 1991. *Saving the Planet: How to Shape an Environmentally Sustainable Global Economy*. New York: Norton.

Brundtland, G. H., et al. 1987. *Our Common Future: World Commission on Environment and Development*. New York: Oxford University Press.

Cairncross, Frances. 1992. *Costing the Earth*. Boston, Mass.: Harvard Business School.

Caldwell, Lynton K. 1990. *International Environmental Policy*. 2d ed. Durham, N.C.: Duke University Press.

Chiras, Daniel D. 1992. *Lessons from Nature: Learning to Live Sustainably on the Earth*. Covelo, Calif.: Island Press.

Clark, Mary E. 1989. *Adriadne's Thread: The Search for New Models of Thinking*. New York: St. Martin's Press.

Cohen, Michael J. 1988. *How Nature Works: Regenerating Kinship with Planet Earth*. Walpole, N.H.: Stillpoint.

Constanza, Robert, ed. 1992. *Ecological Economics: The Science and Management of Sustainability*. New York: Columbia University Press.

Constanza, Robert, and Herman E. Daly. 1992. "Natural Capital and Sustainable Development." *Conservation Biology*, vol. 6, no. 1, 37–46.

Daly, Herman E. 1991. *Steady-State Economics*. 2d ed. Covelo, Calif.: Island Press.

Daly, Herman E., and John B. Cobb, Jr. 1989. *For the Common Good: Redirecting the Economy Toward Community, the Environment, and a Sustainable Future*. Boston: Beacon Press.

Daly, Herman E., and Kenneth W. Townsend, eds. 1993. *Valuing the Earth: Economics, Ecology, Ethics*. Cambridge, Mass.: MIT Press.

Desjardins, Joseph R. 1993. *Environmental Ethics*. Belmont, Calif.: Wadsworth.

Devall, Bill, and George Sessions. 1985. *Deep Ecology: Living as if Nature Mattered*. Salt Lake City: Gibbs M. Smith.

Durning, Alan T. 1989. *Poverty and the Environment: Reversing the Downward Spiral*. Washington, D.C.: Worldwatch Institute.

———. 1992. *How Much Is Enough? The Consumer Society and the Earth*. New York: Norton.

Ehrenfeld, David. 1993. *Beginning Again: People and Nature in the New Millennium*. New York: Oxford University Press.

Ehrlich, Paul R., and Anne H. Ehrlich. 1991. *Healing the Planet*. Reading, Mass.: Addison-Wesley.

Environmental Careers Organization. 1993. *The New Complete Guide to Environmental Careers*. Covelo, Calif.: Island Press.

Flavin, Christopher, and John E. Young. 1993. "Shaping the Next Industrial Revolution." In Lester R. Brown et al. *State of the World 1993*. New York: Norton, 180–99.

Foreman, Dave. 1990. *Confessions of an Eco-Warrior*. New York: Crown.

French, Hilary E. 1992. *After the Earth Summit: The Future of Environmental Governance*. Washington, D.C.: Worldwatch Institute.

———. 1993. "Reconciling Trade and Environment." In Lester R. Brown et al. *State of the World 1993*. New York: Norton, 158–79.

Garbarino, James. 1992. *Toward a Sustainable Society: An Economic, Social and Environmental Agenda for Our Children's Future*. Chicago, Ill.: Noble.

Gore, Al. 1992. *Earth in the Balance: Ecology and the Human Spirit*. Boston, Mass.: Houghton Mifflin.

Greenpeace. 1993. *The Greenpeace Guide to Anti-Environmental Organizations*. Berkeley, Calif.: Odinan Press.

Greider, William. 1992. *Who Will Tell the People? The Betrayal of American Democracy*. New York: Simon & Schuster.

Hardin, Garrett. 1986. *Filters Against Folly*. New York: Penguin.

Henderson, Hazel. 1991. *Paradigms in Progress: Life Beyond Economics*. Chicago: Knowledge Systems.

Kazis, Richard, and Richard L. Grossman. 1991. *Fear at Work: Job Blackmail, Labor, and the Environment*. Philadelphia, Penn.: New Society.

Kennedy, Paul. 1993. *Preparing for the Twenty-First Century*. New York: Random House.

Lamay, Craig L., and Everette E. Dennis, eds. 1991. *Media and the Environment*. Covelo, Calif.: Island Press.

Landy, Marc K., et al. 1990. *The Environmental Protection Agency: Asking the Wrong Questions*. New York: Oxford University Press.

Leopold, Aldo. 1949. *A Sand County Almanac*. New York: Oxford University Press.

Mathews, Jessica Tuchman, ed. 1989. "Redefining Security." *Foreign Affairs*, Spring, 162–77.

Matre, Steve Van. 1990. *Earth Education*. Warrenville, Ill.: The Institute for Earth Education.

Meadows, Donella H. 1991. *Global Citizen*. Covelo, Calif.: Island Press.

Mikesell, Raymond F., and Lawrence F. Williams. 1992. *International Banks and the Environment*. San Francisco: Sierra Club Books.

Milbrath, Lester W. 1989. *Envisioning a Sustainable Society*. Albany: State University of New York Press.

Naess, Arne. 1989. *Ecology, Community, and Lifestyle*. New York: Cambridge University Press.

Norton, Bryan G. 1991. *Toward Unity Among Environmentalists*. New York: Oxford University Press.

Norwood, Vera. 1993. *Made from his Earth: American Women and Nature*. Chapel Hill, N.C.: University of North Carolina Press.

Ophuls, William, and A. Stephen Boyan, Jr. 1992. *Ecology and the Politics of Scarcity Revisited: The Unravelling of the American Dream*. San Francisco: W. H. Freeman.

Orr, David. 1992. *Ecological Literacy*. Ithaca: State University of New York Press.

Paepke, C. Owen. 1993. *The Evolution of Progress: The End of Economic Growth and the Beginning of Human Transformation*. New York: Random House.

Pearce, David, et al. 1991. *Blueprint 2: Greening the World Economy*. East Haven, Conn.: Earthscan.

Ramphal, Shridath. 1992. *Our Country, the Planet: Forging a Partnership for Survival*. Washington, D.C.: Island Press.

Renner, Michael. 1989. *National Security: The Economic and Environmental Dimensions*. Washington, D.C.: Worldwatch Institute.

———. 1991. *Jobs in a Sustainable Economy*. Washington, D.C.: Worldwatch Institute.

Repetto, Robert. 1992. "Accounting for Environ-

Repetto, Robert. 1992. "Accounting for Environmental Assets." *Scientific American*, June, 94–100.

Repetto, Robert, et al. 1992. *Green Fees: How a Tax Shift Can Work for the Environment and the Economy*. Washington, D.C.: World Resources Institute.

Rolston, Holmes, III. 1988. *Environmental Ethics: Duties to and Values in the Natural World*. Philadelphia: Temple University Press.

Rosenbaum, Walter A. 1990. *Environment, Politics, and Policy*. 2d ed. Washington, D.C.: Congressional Quarterly.

Roszak, Theodore. 1992. *The Voice of the Earth*. New York: Simon & Schuster.

Sale, Kirkpatrick. 1990. *Conquest of Paradise*. New York: Alfred A. Knopf.

Sanjor, William. 1992. *Why the EPA Is Like It Is and What Can Be Done About It*. Washington, D.C.: Environmental Research Foundation.

Schmidheiny, Stephan. 1992. *Changing Course: A Global Business Perspective on Development and the Environment*. Cambridge, Mass.: MIT Press.

Schumacher, E. F. 1973. *Small Is Beautiful: Economics As If the Earth Mattered*. San Francisco: Harper & Row.

Shabecoff, Philip. 1993. *A Fierce Green Fire: The American Environmental Movement*. New York: Hill & Wang.

Shiva, Vandana. 1989. *Staying Alive: Women, Ecology, and Development*. London: Zed.

Stead, W. Edward, and John Garner Stead. 1992. *Management for a Small Planet*. New York: Sage.

Stone, Christopher. 1993. *The Gnat Is Older than Man: Global Environment and Human Agenda*. Princeton, N.J.: Princeton University Press.

Swimme, Brian, and Thomas Berry. 1992. *The Universe Story: From the Primordial Flaring Forth to the Ecozoic Era*. San Francisco, Calif.: HarperCollins.

Taylor, Ann. 1992. *A Practical Politics of the Environment*. New York: Routledge.

Taylor, Paul W. 1986. *Respect For Nature: A Theory of Environmental Ethics*. Princeton, N.J.: Princeton University Press.

Thomas, Lewis. 1992. *The Fragile Species*. New York: Scribner's (Macmillan).

Tietenberg, Tom. 1992. *Environmental and Resource Economics*. 3d ed. Glenview, Ill.: Scott, Foresman.

Ward, Barbara. 1979. *Progress for a Small Planet*. New York: W. W. Norton.

Warner, David J. 1992. *Environmental Careers: A Practical Guide to Opportunities in the 1990s*. Boca Raton, Fla.: Lewis.

World Resources Institute. 1993. *A New Generation of Environmental Leadership: Action for the Environment and the Economy*. Washington, D.C.: World Resources Institute.

Glossary

abiotic   Nonliving. Compare *biotic*.

acclimation   Adjustment to slowly changing new conditions. Compare *threshold effect*.

acid deposition   The falling of acids and acid-forming compounds from the atmosphere to Earth's surface. Acid deposition is commonly known as *acid rain*, a term that refers only to wet deposition of droplets of acids and acid-forming compounds.

acid solution   Any water solution that has more hydrogen ions (H^+) than hydroxide ions (OH^-); any water solution with a pH less than 7. Compare *basic solution, neutral solution*.

active solar heating system   System that uses solar collectors to capture energy from the sun and store it as heat for heating space and water. A liquid or air pumped through the collectors transfers the captured heat to a storage system such as an insulated water tank or rock bed. Pumps or fans then distribute the stored heat or hot water throughout a dwelling as needed. Compare *passive solar heating system*.

adaptation   Any genetically controlled structural, physiological, or behavioral characteristic that enhances members of a population's chances of surviving and reproducing in its environment. It usually results from a beneficial mutation. See *biological evolution, differential reproduction, mutation, natural selection*.

adaptive radiation   Period of time during which numerous new species evolve to fill vacant and new ecological niches in changed environments, usually after a period of mass extinction.

advanced sewage treatment   Specialized chemical and physical processes that reduce the amount of specific pollutants left in wastewater after primary and secondary sewage treatment. This type of treatment is usually expensive. See *primary sewage treatment, secondary sewage treatment*.

aerobic respiration   Complex process that occurs in the cells of most living organisms in which nutrient organic molecules such as glucose ($C_6H_{12}O_6$) combine with oxygen (O_2) and produce carbon dioxide (CO_2),water (H_2O), and energy. Compare *photosynthesis*.

age structure   Percentage of the population (or the number of people of each sex) at each age level in a population.

agroforestry   Planting trees and crops together.

air pollution   One or more chemicals in high enough concentrations in the air to harm humans, other animals, vegetation, or materials. Excess heat or noise can also be considered as forms of air pollution. Such chemicals or physical conditions are called air pollutants. See *primary pollutant, secondary pollutant*.

alien species   See *immigrant species*.

alley cropping   Planting of crops in strips with rows of trees or shrubs on each side.

alpha particle   Positively charged matter, consisting of two neutrons and two protons, that is emitted as a form of radioactivity from the nuclei of some radioisotopes. See *beta particle, gamma rays*.

altitude   Height above sea level. Compare *latitude*.

ancient forest   See *old-growth forest*.

animal manure   Dung and urine of animals that can be used as a form of organic fertilizer. Compare *green manure*.

animals (animalia)   Eukaryotic, multicelled organisms such as sponges, jellyfishes, arthropods (insects, shrimp, lobsters), mollusks (snails, clams, oysters, octopuses), fish, amphibians (frogs, toads, salamanders), reptiles (turtles, lizards, alligators, crocodiles, snakes), birds, mammals (kangaroos, bats, cats, rabbits, elephants, whales, porpoises, monkeys, apes, humans). See *carnivore, herbivore, omnivore*.

aquaculture   Growing and harvesting of fish and shellfish for human use in freshwater ponds, irrigation ditches, and lakes, or in cages or fenced-in areas of coastal lagoons and estuaries. See *fish farming, fish ranching*.

aquatic   Pertaining to water. Compare *terrestrial*.

aquifer   Porous, water-saturated layers of sand, gravel, or bed rock that can yield an economically significant amount of water. See *confined aquifer, unconfined aquifer*.

arable land   Land that can be cultivated to grow crops.

arid   Dry. A desert or other area with an arid climate has little precipitation.

atmosphere   The whole mass of air surrounding the earth. See *stratosphere, troposphere*.

atomic number   Number of protons in the nucleus of an atom. Compare *mass number*.

atoms   Minute units made of subatomic particles that are the basic building blocks of all chemical elements and thus all matter; the smallest unit of an element that can exist and still have the unique characteristics of that element. Compare *ion, molecule*.

autotroph   See *producer*.

bacteria   Prokaryotic, one-celled organisms. Some transmit diseases. Most act as decomposers and get the nutrients they need by breaking down complex organic compounds in the tissues of living or dead organisms into simpler inorganic nutrient compounds.

barrier islands   Long, thin, low, offshore islands of sediment that generally run parallel to the shore along some coasts.

basic solution   Water solution with more hydroxide ions (OH^-) than hydrogen ions (H^+); water solution with a pH greater than 7. Compare *acid solution, neutral solution*.

beta particle   Swiftly moving electron emitted by the nucleus of a radioactive isotope. See *alpha particle, gamma rays*.

bioaccumulation   The retention or accumulation of nonbiodegradable or slowly biodegradable chemicals in the body, often in a particular part of the body. Compare *biological amplification*.

biodegradable pollutant   Material that can be broken down into simpler substances (elements and compounds) by bacteria or other decomposers. Paper and most organic wastes such as animal manure are biodegradable but can take decades to biodegrade in modern landfills. Compare *degradable pollutant, nondegradable pollutant, slowly degradable pollutant*.

biodiversity   See *biological diversity*.

biofuel   Gas or liquid fuel (such as ethyl alcohol) made from plant material (biomass).

biogeochemical cycle   Natural processes that recycle nutrients in various chemical forms from the nonliving environment to living organisms, and then back to the nonliving environment. Examples include the carbon, oxygen, nitrogen, phosphorus, and hydrologic cycles.

biological amplification   Increase in concentration of DDT, PCBs, and other slowly degradable, fat-soluble chemicals in organisms at successively higher trophic levels of a food chain or web. See *bioaccumulation*.

biological community   See *community*.

biological diversity   Variety of different species (*species diversity*), genetic variability among individuals within each species (*genetic diversity*), and variety of ecosystems (*ecological diversity*).

biological evolution   Change in the genetic makeup of a population of a species in successive generations. Note that populations—not individuals—evolve. See *adaptation, differential reproduction, natural selection, theory of evolution*.

biological oxygen demand (BOD)   Amount of dissolved oxygen needed by aerobic decomposers to break down the organic materials in a given volume of water at a certain temperature over a specified time period.

biological pest control   Control of pest populations by natural predators, parasites, or disease-causing bacteria and viruses (pathogens).

biomass   Organic matter produced by plants and other photosynthetic producers; total dry weight of all living organisms that can be supported at each trophic level in a food chain or web; dry weight of all organic matter in plants and animals in an ecosystem; plant materials and animal wastes used as fuel.

biome   Terrestrial regions inhabited by certain types of life, especially vegetation. Examples include various types of deserts, grasslands, and forests.

bioregion   A unique life-place with its own soils, landforms, watersheds, climates, native plants and animals, and many other distinct natural characteristics.

biosphere   Zone of Earth where life is found. It consists of parts of the atmosphere (the troposphere), hydrosphere (mostly surface water and groundwater), and lithosphere (mostly soil and surface rocks and sediments on the bottoms of oceans and other bodies of water) where life is found. It is also called the *ecosphere*.

biotic   Living. Living organisms make up the biotic parts of ecosystems. Compare *abiotic*.

biotic potential   Maximum rate at which the population of a given species can increase when there are no limits of any sort on its rate of growth. See *environmental resistance*.

birth rate   See *crude birth rate*.

bitumen   Gooey, black, high-sulfur, heavy oil extracted from tar sand and then upgraded to synthetic fuel oil. See *tar sand*.

breeder nuclear fission reactor   Nuclear fission reactor that produces more nuclear fuel than it consumes, by converting nonfissionable uranium-238 into fissionable plutonium-239.

calorie   Unit of energy; amount of energy needed to raise the temperature of 1 gram of water 1°C. See *kilocalorie*.

cancer   Group of more than 120 different diseases—one for each type of cell in the human body. Each type of cancer produces a tumor in which cells multiply uncontrollably and invade surrounding tissue.

capital goods   See *manufactured capital*.

capitalism   See *pure market economic system*.

carbon cycle   Cyclic movement of carbon in different chemical forms from the environment to organisms, and then back to the environment.

carcinogen   Chemicals, ionizing radiation, and viruses that cause or promote the growth of cancer. See *cancer, mutagen, teratogen*.

carnivore   Animal that feeds on other animals. Compare *herbivore, omnivore*.

carrying capacity (K)   Maximum population of a particular species that a given habitat can support over a given period of time. See *consumption overpopulation, people overpopulation*.

cell   Smallest living unit of an organism. Each cell is encased in an outer membrane or wall and contains genetic material (DNA) and other parts to perform its life function. Organisms such as bacteria consist of only one cell, but most of the organisms we are familiar with contain many cells. See *eukaryotic cell, prokaryotic cell*.

centrally planned economy   See *pure command economic system*.

CFCs   See *chlorofluorocarbons*.

chain reaction   Multiple nuclear fissions taking place within a certain mass of a fissionable isotope that release an enormous amount of energy in a short time.

chemical   One of the millions of different elements and compounds found naturally and synthesized by humans. See *compound, element*.

chemical change   Interaction between chemicals in which there is a change in the chemical composition of the elements or compounds involved. Compare *physical change*.

chemical formula   Shorthand way to show the number of atoms (or ions) in the basic structural unit of a compound. Examples are H_2O, $NaCl$, and $C_6H_{12}O_6$.

chemical reaction   See *chemical change*.

chemosynthesis   Process in which certain organisms (mostly specialized bacteria) extract inorganic compounds from their environment and convert them into organic nutrient compounds without the presence of sunlight. Compare *photosynthesis*.

chlorinated hydrocarbon   Organic compound made up of atoms of carbon, hydrogen, and chlorine. Examples include DDT and PCBs.

chlorofluorocarbons (CFCs)   Organic compounds made up of atoms of carbon, chlorine, and fluorine. An example is Freon-12 (CCl_2F_2), used as a refrigerant in refrigerators and air conditioners and in making plastics such as Styrofoam. Gaseous CFCs can deplete the ozone layer when they slowly rise into the stratosphere and their chlorine atoms react with ozone molecules.

chromosome   A grouping of various genes and associated proteins in plant and animal cells that carry certain types of genetic information. See *genes*.

clear-cutting   Method of timber harvesting in which all trees in a forested area are removed in a single cutting. Compare *seed-tree cutting, selective cutting, shelterwood cutting, strip logging*.

climate   General pattern of atmospheric or weather conditions, seasonal variations, and weather extremes in a region over a long period—at least 30 years; average weather of an area. Compare *weather*.

climax community   See *mature community*.

coal   Solid, combustible mixture of organic compounds, with 30%–98% carbon by weight, mixed with varying amounts of water and small amounts of sulfur and nitrogen. It is formed in several stages as the remains of plants are subjected to heat and pressure over millions of years.

coal gasification   Conversion of solid coal to synthetic natural gas (SNG).

coal liquefaction   Conversion of solid coal to a liquid hydrocarbon fuel such as synthetic gasoline or methanol.

coastal wetland   Land along a coastline, extending inland from an estuary that is covered with salt water all or part of the year. Examples are marshes, bays, lagoons, tidal flats, and mangrove swamps. Compare *inland wetland*.

coastal zone   Relatively warm, nutrient-rich, shallow part of the ocean that extends from the high-tide mark on land to the edge of a shelflike extension of continental land masses known as the continental shelf. Compare *open sea*.

coevolution   Evolution when two or more species interact and exert selective pressures on each other that can cause each species to undergo various adaptations. See *evolution, natural selection*.

cogeneration   Production of two useful forms of energy, such as high-temperature heat or steam and electricity, from the same fuel source.

commensalism   An interaction between organisms of different species in which one type of organism benefits, while the other type is neither helped nor harmed to any great degree. Compare *mutualism*.

commercial extinction   Depletion of the population of a wild species used as a resource to a level where it is no longer profitable to harvest the species.

commercial inorganic fertilizer   Commercially prepared mixtures of plant nutrients such as nitrates, phosphates, and potassium applied to the soil to restore fertility and increase crop yields. Compare *organic fertilizer*.

common-property resource   Resource that people are normally free to use; each user can deplete or degrade the available supply. Most are potentially renewable and are owned by no one. Examples include clean air, fish in parts of the ocean not under the control of a coastal country, migratory birds, gases of the lower atmosphere, and the ozone content of the upper atmosphere. See *tragedy of the commons*. Compare *private-property resource, public-land resources*.

community   Populations of all species living and interacting in an area at a particular time.

community development   See *ecological succession*.

competition   Two or more individual organisms of a single species (*intraspecific competition*) or two or more individuals of different species (*interspecific competition*) attempting to use the same scarce resources in the same ecosystem.

competitive exclusion principle   Inability of any two species to occupy exactly the same fundamental niche indefinitely in a habitat where there is not enough of a particular resource to meet the needs of both species. See *ecological niche, fundamental niche, realized niche*.

compost   Partially decomposed organic plant and animal matter that can be used as a soil conditioner or fertilizer.

compound   Combination of atoms, or oppositely charged ions, of two or more different elements held together by attractive forces called chemical bonds. Compare *element*.

concentration   Amount of a chemical in a particular volume or weight of air, water, soil, or other medium.

confined aquifer   Aquifer between two layers of relatively impermeable Earth materials, such as clay or shale. Compare *unconfined aquifer*.

coniferous trees   Cone-bearing trees, mostly evergreens, that have needle-shaped or scalelike leaves and that produce wood known commercially as softwood. Compare *deciduous plants*.

conservation-tillage farming   Crop cultivation in which the soil is disturbed little (minimum-tillage farming) or not at all (no-till farming) to reduce soil erosion, lower labor costs, and save energy. Compare *conventional-tillage farming*.

consumer   Organism that cannot synthesize the organic nutrients it needs and gets its organic nutrients by feeding on the tissues of producers or of other consumers; generally divided into *primary consumers* (herbivores), *secondary consumers* (carnivores), *tertiary (higher-level) consumers, omnivores,* and *detritivores* (decomposers and detritus feeders). In economics, one who uses economic goods.

consumption overpopulation   Situation in which people in the world or in a geographic region use resources at such a high rate and without sufficient pollution prevention and control that significant pollution, resource depletion, and environmental degradation occur. Compare *people overpopulation*.

continental shelf   Submerged part of a continent.

contour farming   Plowing and planting across the changing slope of land, rather than in straight lines, to help retain water and reduce soil erosion.

contraceptive   Physical, chemical, or biological method used to prevent pregnancy.

conventional-tillage farming   Making a planting surface by plowing land, breaking up the exposed soil, and then smoothing the surface. Compare *conservation-tillage farming*.

coral reef   Formation produced by massive colonies containing billions of tiny coral animals, called polyps, which secrete a stony substance (calcium carbonate) around themselves for protection. When the corals die, their empty outer skeletons form layers that cause the reef to grow. They are found in the coastal zones of warm tropical and subtropical oceans.

core   Inner zone of the earth. It consists of a solid inner core and a liquid outer core. Compare *crust, mantle*.

critical mass   Amount of fissionable nuclei needed to sustain a nuclear fission chain reaction.

crop rotation   Planting a field, or an area of a field, with different crops from year to year to reduce depletion of soil nutrients. A plant such as corn, tobacco, or cotton, which removes large amounts of nitrogen from the soil, is planted one year. The next year a legume such as soybeans, which add nitrogen to the soil, is planted.

crude birth rate   Annual number of live births per 1,000 persons in the population of a geographical area at the midpoint of a given year. Compare *crude death rate*.

crude death rate   Annual number of deaths per 1,000 persons in the population of a geographical area at the midpoint of a given year. Compare *crude birth rate*.

crude oil   Gooey liquid consisting mostly of hydrocarbon compounds and small amounts of compounds containing oxygen, sulfur, and nitrogen. Extracted from underground accumulations, it is sent to oil refineries, where it is converted to heating oil, diesel fuel, gasoline, tar, and other materials.

crust   Solid outer zone of the earth. It consists of oceanic crust and continental crust. Compare *core, mantle*.

cultural eutrophication   Overnourishment of aquatic ecosystems with plant nutrients (mostly nitrates and phosphates) because of human activities such as agriculture, urbanization, and discharges from industrial plants and sewage treatment plants. See *eutrophication*.

cyanobacteria   Single-celled, prokaryotic, microscopic organisms. Before being reclassified as monera, they were called blue-green algae.

DDT   Dichlorodiphenyltrichloroethane, a chlorinated hydrocarbon that has been widely used as a pesticide but is now banned in some countries.

death rate   See *crude death rate*.

debt-for-nature swap   Agreement in which a certain amount of foreign debt is canceled in exchange for local currency investments that will improve natural resource management or protect certain areas from harmful development in the debtor country.

deciduous plants   Trees, such as oaks and maples, and other plants that survive during dry seasons or cold seasons by shedding their leaves. Compare *coniferous trees, succulent plants*.

decomposer   Organism that digests parts of dead organisms and cast-off fragments and wastes of living organisms by breaking down the complex organic molecules in those materials into simpler inorganic compounds and then absorbing the soluble nutrients. Most of these chemicals are returned to the soil and water for reuse by producers. Decomposers consist of various bacteria and fungi. Compare *consumer, detritivore, producer*.

deforestation   Removal of trees from a forested area without adequate replanting.

degradable pollutant   Potentially polluting chemical that is broken down completely or reduced to acceptable levels by natural physical, chemical, and biological processes. Compare *biodegradable pollutant, nondegradable pollutant, slowly degradable pollutant*.

degree of urbanization   Percentage of the population in the world, or a country, living in areas with a population of more than 2,500 people (higher in some countries). Compare *urban growth*.

democracy   Government "by the people" through their elected officials and appointed representatives. In a constitutional democracy, a constitution provides the basis of governmental authority and puts restraints on governmental power through free elections and freely expressed public opinion.

demographic transition   Hypothesis that countries, as they become industrialized, have declines in death rates followed by declines in birth rates.

demography   Study of characteristics and changes in the size and structure of the human population in the world or other geographical area.

depletion time   How long it takes to use a certain fraction—usually 80%—of the known or estimated supply of a nonrenewable resource at an assumed rate of use. Finding and extracting the remaining 20% usually costs more than it is worth.

desalination   Purification of salt water or brackish (slightly salty) water by removing dissolved salts.

desert   Biome where evaporation exceeds precipitation and the average amount of precipitation is less than 25 centimeters (10 inches) per year. Such areas have little vegetation or have widely spaced, mostly low vegetation. Compare *forest, grassland*.

desertification   Conversion of rangeland, rainfed cropland, or irrigated cropland to desertlike land, with a drop in agricultural productivity of 10% or more. Usually caused by a combination of overgrazing, soil erosion, prolonged drought, and climate change.

desirability quotient   A number expressing the results of risk-benefit analysis by dividing the estimate of the benefits to society of using a particular product or technology by its estimated risks. See *risk-benefit analysis*.

detritivore   Consumer organism that feeds on detritus, parts of dead organisms and cast-off fragments and wastes of living organisms. The two principal types are *detritus feeders* and *decomposers*.

detritus   Parts of dead organisms and cast-off fragments and wastes of living organisms.

detritus feeder   Organism that extracts nutrients from fragments of dead organisms and cast-off parts and organic wastes of living organisms. Examples include earthworms, termites, and crabs. Compare *decomposer*.

deuterium (D: hydrogen-2)   Isotope of the element hydrogen, with a nucleus containing one proton and one neutron, and a mass number of 2. Compare *tritium*.

dieback   Sharp reduction in the population of a species when its numbers exceed the carrying capacity of its habitat. See *carrying capacity, consumption overpopulation, overshoot, people overpopulation*.

differential reproduction   Ability of individuals with adaptive genetic traits to produce more living offspring than individuals without such traits. See *natural selection*.

dioxins   Family of 75 different chlorinated hydrocarbon compounds formed as by-products in chemical reactions involving chlorine and hydrocarbons, usually at high temperatures.

dissolved oxygen (DO) content   Amount of oxygen gas (O_2) dissolved in a given volume of water at a particular temperature and pressure, often expressed as a concentration in parts of oxygen per million parts of water.

DNA (deoxyribonucleic acid)   Large molecules in the cells of organisms; carries genetic information in living organisms.

dose   The amount of a potentially harmful substance an individual ingests, inhales, or absorbs through the skin. Compare *response*. See *dose-response curve, lethal dose, median lethal dose*.

dose-response curve   Plot of data showing effects of various doses of a toxic agent on a group of test organisms. See *dose, lethal dose, median lethal dose, response*.

doubling time   The time it takes (usually in years) for the quantity of something growing exponentially to double. It can be calculated by dividing the annual percentage growth rate into 70. See *rule of 70*.

drainage basin   See *watershed*.

dredge spoils   Materials scraped from the bottoms of harbors and streams to maintain shipping channels. They are often contaminated with high levels of toxic substances that have settled out of the water. See *dredging*.

dredging   Type of surface mining in which chain buckets and draglines scrape up sand, gravel, and other surface deposits covered with water. It is also used to remove sediment from streams and harbors to maintain shipping channels. See *dredge spoils*.

drift-net fishing   Catching fish in huge nets that drift in the water.

drought   Condition in which an area does not get enough water because of lower than normal precipitation, higher than normal temperatures that increase evaporation, or both.

dust dome   Dome of heated air that surrounds an urban area and traps and keeps pollutants, especially suspended particulate matter. See *urban heat island*.

dust plume   Elongation of a dust dome by winds that can spread a city's pollutants hundreds of kilometers downwind.

Earth capital   Earth's natural resources and processes that sustain us and other species.

Earth-wisdom worldview   See *sustainable-Earth worldview*.

ecological diversity   The variety of forests, deserts, grasslands, oceans, streams, lakes, and other biological communities interacting with one another and with their nonliving environment. See *biological diversity*. Compare *genetic diversity, species diversity*.

ecological niche   Total way of life or role of a species in an ecosystem. Includes all physical, chemical, and biological conditions a species needs to live and reproduce in an ecosystem. See *fundamental niche, realized niche*.

ecological succession   Process in which communities of plant and animal species in a particular area are replaced over time by a series of different and usually more complex communities. See *primary succession, secondary succession*.

ecology   Study of the interactions of living organisms with one another and with their nonliving environment of matter and energy; study of the structure and functions of nature.

economic decision   Deciding what goods and services to produce, how to produce them, how much to produce, and how to distribute them to people.

economic depletion   Exhaustion of 80% of the estimated supply of a nonrenewable resource. Finding, extracting, and processing the remaining 20% usually costs more than it is worth; may also apply to the depletion of a potentially renewable resource, such as a species of fish or trees.

economic growth   Increase in the real value of all final goods and services produced by an economy; an increase in real GNP.

economic resources   Natural resources, capital goods, and labor used in an economy to produce material goods and services. See *Earth capital, human capital, manufactured capital.*

economics   Study of how individuals and groups make decisions about what to do with economic resources to meet their needs and wants.

economic system   Method that a group of people uses to choose *what* goods and services to produce, *how* to produce them, *how much* to produce, and *how to distribute* them to people. See *mixed economic system, pure command economic system, pure market economic system.*

economy   System of production, distribution, and consumption of economic goods.

ecosphere   Earth's collection of living organisms (found in the biosphere) interacting with one another and their nonliving environment (energy and matter) throughout the world; all of Earth's ecosystems. See *biosphere.*

ecosystem   Community of different species interacting with one another and with the chemical and physical factors making up the nonliving environment.

efficiency   Measure of how much output of energy or how much of a product is produced by a certain input of energy, materials, or labor. See *energy efficiency.*

electromagnetic radiation   Forms of kinetic energy traveling as electromagnetic waves. Examples include radio waves, TV waves, microwaves, infrared radiation, visible light, ultraviolet radiation, X rays, and gamma rays.

electron (e)   Tiny particle moving around outside the nucleus of an atom. Each electron has one unit of negative charge (–) and almost no mass.

element   Chemical, such as hydrogen (H), iron (Fe), sodium (Na), carbon (C), nitrogen (N), or oxygen (O), whose distinctly different atoms serve as the basic building blocks of all matter. There are 92 naturally occurring elements; another 15 have been created in laboratories. Two or more elements combine to form compounds that make up most of the world's matter. Compare *compound.*

emigration   Migration of people out of one country or area to take up permanent residence in another country or area. Compare *immigration.*

endangered species   Wild species with so few individual survivors that the species could soon become extinct in all or most of its natural range. Compare *threatened species.*

energy   Capacity to do work by performing mechanical, physical, chemical, or electrical tasks or to cause a heat transfer between two objects at different temperatures.

energy conservation   Reduction or elimination of unnecessary energy use and waste. See *energy efficiency.*

energy efficiency   Percentage of the total energy input that does useful work and is not converted into low-quality, usually useless, heat in an energy conversion system or process. See *energy quality, net useful energy.*

energy quality   Ability of a form of energy to do useful work. High-temperature heat and the chemical energy in fossil fuels and nuclear fuels are concentrated high-quality energy. Low-quality energy such as low-temperature heat is dispersed or diluted and cannot do much useful work. See *high-quality energy, low-quality energy.*

environment   All external conditions and factors, living and nonliving (chemicals and energy), that affect an organism or other specified system during its lifetime.

environmental degradation   Depletion or destruction of a potentially renewable resource such as soil, grassland, forest, or wildlife by using it at a faster rate than it is naturally replenished. If such use continues, the resource can become nonrenewable on a human time scale or nonexistent (extinct). See *sustainable yield.*

environmental resistance   All the factors jointly acting to limit the growth of a population. See *biotic potential, limiting factor.*

Environmental Revolution   See *sustainable-Earth Revolution.*

environmental science   Study of how we and other species interact with one another and with the nonliving environment of matter and energy. It is a holistic science that uses and integrates knowledge from physics, chemistry, biology (especially ecology), geology, geography, resource technology and engineering, resource conservation and management, demography (the study of population dynamics), economics, politics, and ethics.

environmental unsustainability   See *overpopulation.*

EPA   Environmental Protection Agency; responsible for managing federal efforts in the United States to control air and water pollution, reduce radiation and pesticide hazards, conduct environmental research, and regulate disposal of solid and hazardous waste.

epidemiology   Study of the patterns of disease or other harmful effects from toxic exposure within defined groups of people to find out why some people get sick and some do not.

epiphytes   Plants that use their roots to attach themselves to branches high in trees, especially in tropical forests.

erosion   Process or group of processes by which earth materials, loose or consolidated, are dissolved, loosened, and worn away, and removed from one place and deposited in another. See *weathering.*

estuary   Partially enclosed coastal area at the mouth of a river where its fresh water, carrying fertile silt and runoff from the land, mixes with salty seawater.

ethics   What we believe to be right or wrong behavior.

eukaryotic cell   Cell containing a *nucleus*, a region of genetic material surrounded by a membrane. Membranes also enclose several of the other internal parts found in a eukaryotic cell. Compare *prokaryotic cell.*

eutrophication   Physical, chemical, and biological changes that take place after a lake, an estuary, or a slow-flowing stream receives inputs of plant nutrients—mostly nitrates and phosphates—from natural erosion and runoff from the surrounding land basin. See *cultural eutrophication.*

eutrophic lake   Lake with a large or excessive supply of plant nutrients—mostly nitrates and phosphates. Compare *mesotrophic lake, oligotrophic lake.*

evaporation   Physical change in which a liquid changes into a vapor or gas.

even-aged management   Method of forest management in which trees, usually of a single species in a given stand, are maintained at about the same age and size, and are harvested all at once so a new stand may grow. Compare *uneven-aged management.*

even-aged stand   Forest area where all trees are about the same age. Usually, such stands contain trees of only one or two species. See *even-aged management, tree farm.* Compare *uneven-aged management, uneven-aged stand.*

evergreen plants   Plants that keep some of their leaves or needles throughout the year. Examples include ferns and cone-bearing trees (conifers) such as firs, spruces, pines, redwoods, and sequoias. Compare *deciduous plants, succulent plants.*

evolution   Term normally refers to biological evolution. See *biological evolution.*

exclusive economic zone   Zone extending outward for 370 kilometers (200 nautical miles or 230 statute miles) from the shores of coastal countries. Under international law each coastal country has legal rights over all marine fishery resources and ocean mineral resources in this zone. Compare *high seas.*

exhaustible resource   See *nonrenewable resource.*

exponential growth   Growth in which some quantity, such as population size or economic output, increases by a fixed percentage of the whole in a given time period; when the increase in quantity over time is plotted, this type of growth yields a J-shaped curve. Compare *linear growth.*

external benefit   Beneficial social effect of producing and using an economic good that is not included in the market price of the good. Compare *external cost, full cost, internal cost.*

external cost   Harmful social effect of producing and using an economic good that is not included in the market price of the good. Compare *external benefit, full cost, internal cost.*

externalities   Social benefits ("goods") and social costs ("bads") not included in the market price of an economic good. See *external benefit, external cost.* Compare *full cost, internal cost.*

extinction   Complete disappearance of a species from the earth. This happens when a species cannot adapt and successfully reproduce under new environmental conditions or when it evolves into one or more new species. Compare *speciation.* See *endangered species, threatened species.*

family planning   Providing information, clinical services, and contraceptives to help individuals or couples choose the number and spacing of children.

famine   Widespread malnutrition and starvation in a particular area because of a shortage of food, usually caused by a drought, war, flood, earthquake, or other catastrophic event that disrupts food production and distribution.

feedlot   Confined outdoor or indoor space used to raise hundreds to thousands of domesticated livestock. Compare *rangeland.*

fertilizer   Substance that adds inorganic or organic plant nutrients to soil and improves its ability to grow crops, trees, or other vegetation. See *commercial inorganic fertilizer, organic fertilizer.*

first law of energy   See *first law of thermodynamics.*

first law of human ecology   We can never do merely one thing. Any intrusion into nature has numerous effects, many of which are unpredictable.

first law of thermodynamics (energy)   In any physical or chemical change, no detectable amount of energy is created or destroyed, but in these processes energy can be changed from one form to another. You can't get more energy out of something than you put in; in terms of energy quantity, you can't get something for nothing (there is no free lunch).This law does not apply to nuclear changes, in which energy can be produced from small amounts of matter. See *second law of thermodynamics*.

fishery Concentrations of particular aquatic species suitable for commercial harvesting in a given ocean area or inland body of water.

fish farming Form of aquaculture in which fish are cultivated in a controlled pond or other environment and harvested when they reach the desired size. See *fish ranching*.

fish ranching Form of aquaculture in which members of a fish species such as salmon are held in captivity for the first few years of their lives, released, and then harvested as adults when they return from the ocean to their freshwater birthplace to spawn. See *fish farming*.

fissionable isotope Isotope that can split apart when hit by a neutron at the right speed and thus undergo nuclear fission. Examples include uranium-235 and plutonium-239.

floodplain Flat valley floor next to a stream channel. For legal purposes, the term is often applied to any low area that has the potential for flooding, including certain coastal areas.

flyway Generally fixed route along which waterfowl migrate from one area to another at certain seasons of the year.

food chain Series of organisms, each eating or decomposing the preceding one. Compare *food web*.

food web Complex network of many interconnected food chains and feeding relationships. Compare *food chain*.

forest Biome with enough average annual precipitation (at least 76 centimeters, or 30 inches) to support growth of various species of trees and smaller forms of vegetation. Compare *desert, grassland*.

fossil fuel Products of partial or complete decomposition of plants and animals that occur as crude oil, coal, natural gas, or heavy oils as a result of exposure to heat and pressure in the earth's crust over millions of years. See *coal, crude oil, natural gas*.

Freons See *chlorofluorocarbons*.

full cost Cost of a good when its internal costs and its short- and long-term external costs are included in its market price. Compare *external cost, internal cost*.

fundamental niche The full potential range of the physical, chemical, and biological factors a species can use, if there is no competition from other species. See *ecological niche*. Compare *realized niche*.

fungi Eukaryotic, mostly multicelled organisms such as mushrooms, molds, and yeasts. As decomposers, they get the nutrients they need by secreting enzymes that break down the organic matter in the tissue of other living or dead organisms. Then they absorb the resulting nutrients.

fungicide Chemical that kills fungi.

gamma rays A form of ionizing, electromagnetic radiation with a high energy content emitted by some radioisotopes. They readily penetrate body tissues.

gasohol Vehicle fuel consisting of a mixture of gasoline and ethyl or methyl alcohol—typically 10–23% ethanol or methanol by volume.

gene mutation See *mutation*.

gene pool The sum total of all the genes found in the individuals of a population of a particular species.

generalist species Species with a broad ecological niche. They can live in many different places, eat a variety of foods, and tolerate a wide range of environmental conditions. Examples include flies, cockroaches, mice, rats, and human beings. Compare *specialist species*.

genes Segments of various DNA molecules found in chromosomes that impart certain inheritable traits in organisms.

genetic adaptation Changes in the genetic makeup of organisms of a species that allow the species to reproduce and gain a competitive advantage under changed environmental conditions. See *differential reproduction, evolution, natural selection*.

genetic diversity Variability in the genetic makeup among individuals within a single species. See *biodiversity*. Compare *ecological diversity, species diversity*.

geothermal energy Heat transferred from the earth's underground concentrations of dry steam (steam with no water droplets), wet steam (a mixture of steam and water droplets), or hot water trapped in fractured or porous rock.

GNP See *gross national product*.

GNP per capita Annual gross national product (GNP) of a country divided by its total population. See *gross national product, real GNP per capita*.

grassland Biome found in regions where moderate annual average precipitation (25–76 centimeters, or 10–30 inches) is enough to support the growth of grass and small plants, but not enough to support large stands of trees. Compare *desert, forest*.

greenhouse effect A natural effect that traps heat in the lower atmosphere (troposphere) near the earth's surface. Some of the heat flowing back toward space from Earth's surface is absorbed by water vapor, carbon dioxide, ozone, and several other gases in the atmosphere, and then radiated back toward the earth's surface. If the atmospheric concentrations of these greenhouse gases rise, the average temperature of the lower atmosphere will gradually increase.

greenhouse gases Gases in Earth's lower atmosphere (troposphere) that cause the greenhouse effect. Examples include carbon dioxide, chlorofluorocarbons, ozone, methane, water vapor, and nitrous oxide.

green manure Freshly cut or still-growing green vegetation that is plowed into the soil to increase the organic matter and humus available to support crop growth. Compare *animal manure*.

green revolution Popular term for the introduction of scientifically bred or selected varieties of grain (rice, wheat, maize) that, with high enough inputs of fertilizer and water, can greatly increase crop yields.

gross national product (GNP) Total market value in current dollars of all goods and services produced by an economy for final use during a year. Compare *GNP per capita, real NEW per capita, real GNP, real GNP per capita*.

gross primary productivity The rate at which an ecosystem's producers capture and store a given amount of chemical energy as biomass in a given length of time. Compare *net primary productivity*.

groundwater Water that sinks into the soil and is stored in slowly flowing and slowly renewed underground reservoirs called aquifers; underground water in the zone of saturation, below the water table. See *confined aquifer, unconfined aquifer*. Compare *runoff, surface water*.

growth rate (r) Increase in the size of a population per unit of time (such as a year).

gully reclamation Restoring land suffering from gully erosion by seeding gullies with quick-growing plants, building small dams to collect silt and gradually fill in the channels, and building channels to divert water away from the gully.

habitat Place or type of place where an organism or a population of organisms lives. Compare *ecological niche*.

hazard Something that can cause injury, disease, economic loss, or environmental damage.

hazardous chemical Chemical that can cause harm because it is flammable or explosive, or that can irritate or damage the skin or lungs (such as strong acidic or alkaline substances) or cause allergic reactions of the immune system (allergens). See *toxic chemical*.

hazardous waste Any solid, liquid, or containerized gas that can catch fire easily, is corrosive to skin tissue or metals, is unstable and can explode or release toxic fumes, or has harmful concentrations of one or more toxic materials that can leach out. See *toxic waste*.

heat island See *urban heat island*.

herbicide Chemical that kills a plant or inhibits its growth.

herbivore Plant-eating organism. Examples include deer, sheep, grasshoppers, and zooplankton. Compare *carnivore, omnivore*.

heterotroph See *consumer*.

high-quality energy Energy that is organized or concentrated (low entropy) and has great ability to perform useful work. Examples include high-temperature heat and the energy in electricity, coal, oil, gasoline, sunlight, and nuclei of uranium-235. Compare *low-quality energy*.

high-quality matter Matter that is organized and contains a high concentration of a useful resource. Compare *low-quality matter*.

high seas Ocean areas beyond the legal jurisdiction of any country—beyond the exclusive economic zone. Compare *exclusive economic zone*.

high-waste society See *throwaway society*.

host Plant or animal upon which a parasite feeds.

human capital Physical and mental talents of people used to produce, distribute, and sell an economic good. Compare *Earth capital, manufactured capital*.

humification Process in which organic matter in the upper soil layers is reduced to finely divided pieces of humus or partially decomposed organic matter.

humus Slightly soluble residue of undigested or partially decomposed organic material in topsoil. This material helps retain water and water-soluble nutrients, which can be taken up by plant roots. See *humification*.

hunter-gatherers People who get their food by gathering edible wild plants and other materials and by hunting wild animals and fish.

hydrocarbon Organic compound of hydrogen and carbon atoms.

hydroelectric power plant Structure in which the energy of falling or flowing water spins a turbine generator to produce electricity.

hydrologic cycle Biogeochemical cycle that collects, purifies, and distributes the earth's fixed supply of water from the environment to living organisms, and then back to the environment.

hydropower Electrical energy produced by falling or flowing water. See *hydroelectric power plant*.

hydrosphere Earth's liquid water (oceans, lakes and other bodies of surface water, and underground water), Earth's frozen water (polar ice caps, floating ice caps, and ice in soil known as permafrost), and small amounts of water vapor in the atmosphere.

identified resources Deposits of a particular mineral-bearing material of which the location, quantity, and quality are known or have been estimated from direct geological evidence and measurements. Compare *undiscovered resources*.

igneous rock Rock formed when molten rock material (magma) wells up from Earth's interior, cools, and solidifies into rock masses. Compare *metamorphic rock, sedimentary rock*. See *rock cycle*.

immature community Community at an early stage of ecological succession. It usually has a low number of species and ecological niches, and cannot capture and use energy or cycle critical nutrients as efficiently as more complex, mature ecosystems. Compare *mature community*.

immigrant species Species that migrate into an ecosystem or that are deliberately or accidentally introduced into an ecosystem by humans. Some of these species are beneficial, while others can take over and eliminate many native species. Compare *indicator species, keystone species, native species*.

immigration Migration of people into a country or area to take up permanent residence. Compare *emigration*.

indicator species Species that serve as early warnings that a community or an ecosystem is being degraded. Compare *immigrant species, keystone species, native species*.

industrialized agriculture Using large inputs of energy from fossil fuels (especially oil and natural gas), water, fertilizer, and pesticides to produce large quantities of crops and livestock for domestic and foreign sale. Compare *subsistence farming*.

industrial smog Type of air pollution consisting mostly of a mixture of sulfur dioxide, suspended droplets of sulfuric acid formed from some of the sulfur dioxide, and a variety of suspended solid particles. Compare *photochemical smog*.

infant mortality rate Number of babies per 1,000 born each year that die before their first birthday.

infiltration Downward movement of water through soil.

inland wetland Land away from the coast, (excluding streams and lakes), such as a swamp, marsh, or bog, that is covered all or part of the year with fresh water. Compare *coastal wetland*.

inorganic fertilizer See *commercial inorganic fertilizer*.

input pollution control See *pollution prevention*.

insecticide Chemical that kills insects.

integrated pest management (IPM) Combined use of biological, chemical, and cultivation methods in proper sequence and timing to keep the size of a pest population below the size that causes economically unacceptable loss of a crop or livestock animal.

intercropping Growing two or more different crops at the same time on a plot. For example, a carbohydrate-rich grain that depletes soil nitrogen and a protein-rich legume that adds nitrogen to the soil may be intercropped. Compare *monoculture, polyculture, polyvarietal cultivation*.

intermediate goods See *manufactured capital*.

internal cost Direct cost paid by the producer and the buyer of an economic good. Compare *external cost*.

interplanting Simultaneously growing a variety of crops on the same plot. See *agroforestry, intercropping, polyculture, polyvarietal cultivation*.

interspecific competition Members of two or more species trying to use the same limited resources in an ecosystem. See *competition, competitive exclusion principle, intraspecific competition*.

intraspecific competition Two or more individual organisms of a single species trying to use the same limited resources in an ecosystem. See *competition, interspecific competition*.

inversion See *thermal inversion*.

invertebrates Animals that have no backbones. Compare *vertebrates*.

ion Atom or group of atoms with one or more positive (+) or negative (−) electrical charges. Compare *atoms, molecule*.

isotopes Two or more forms of a chemical element that have the same number of protons but different mass numbers due to different numbers of neutrons in their nuclei.

J-shaped curve Curve with a shape similar to that of the letter J; represents exponential growth.

kerogen Solid, waxy mixture of hydrocarbons found in oil shale rock. When the rock is heated to high temperatures, the kerogen is vaporized. The vapor is condensed, purified, and then sent to a refinery where gasoline, heating oil, and other products are produced. See *oil shale, shale oil*.

keystone species Species that play roles affecting many other organisms in an ecosystem. Compare *immigrant species, indicator species, native species*.

kilocalorie (kcal) Unit of energy equal to 1,000 calories. See *calorie*.

kilowatt (kw) Unit of electrical power equal to 1,000 watts. See *watt*.

kinetic energy Energy that matter has because of its motion and mass. Compare *potential energy*.

labor See *human capital*.

lake Large natural body of standing fresh water formed when water from precipitation, land runoff, or groundwater flow fills a depression in the earth created by glaciation, earth movement, volcanic activity, or a giant meteorite. See *eutrophic lake, mesotrophic lake, oligotrophic lake*.

landfill See *sanitary landfill*.

land-use planning Process for deciding the best present and future use of each parcel of land in an area.

latitude Distance from the equator. Compare *altitude*.

law of conservation of energy See *first law of thermodynamics*.

law of conservation of matter In any physical or chemical change, matter is neither created nor destroyed, but merely changed from one form to another; in physical and chemical changes, existing atoms are rearranged into either different spatial patterns (physical changes) or different combinations (chemical changes).

law of pollution prevention If you don't put something into the environment, it isn't there.

law of tolerance The existence, abundance, and distribution of a species in an ecosystem are determined by whether the levels of one or more physical or chemical factors fall within the range tolerated by the species. See *threshold effect*.

LD$_{50}$ See *median lethal dose*.

LDC See *less developed country*.

leaching Process in which various chemicals in upper layers of soil are dissolved and carried to lower layers and, in some cases, to groundwater.

less developed country (LDC) Country that has low to moderate industrialization and low to moderate GNP per capita. Most are located in Africa, Asia, and Latin America. Compare *more developed country*.

lethal dose Amount of a toxic material per unit of body weight of the test animals that kills all of the test population in a certain time. See *median lethal dose*.

life-cycle cost Initial cost plus lifetime operating costs of an economic good.

life expectancy Average number of years a newborn infant can be expected to live.

limiting factor Single factor that limits the growth, abundance, or distribution of the population of a species in an ecosystem. See *limiting factor principle*.

limiting factor principle Too much or too little of any abiotic factor can limit or prevent growth of a population of a species in an ecosystem, even if all other factors are at or near the optimum range of tolerance for the species.

linear growth Growth in which a quantity increases by some fixed amount during each unit of time. Compare *exponential growth*.

liquefied natural gas (LNG) Natural gas converted to liquid form by cooling to a very low temperature.

liquefied petroleum gas (LPG) Mixture of liquefied propane and butane gas removed from natural gas.

lithosphere Outer shell of the earth, composed of the crust and the rigid, outermost part of the mantle; material found in Earth's plates. See *crust, mantle*.

loams Soils containing a mixture of clay, sand, silt, and humus. Good for growing most crops.

low-quality energy Energy that is disorganized or dispersed and that has little ability to do useful work. An example is low-temperature heat. Compare *high-quality energy*.

low-quality matter Matter that is disorganized, is diluted or dispersed, or contains a low concentration of a useful resource. Compare *high-quality matter*.

low-waste society See *sustainable-Earth*.

LPG See *liquefied petroleum gas*.

magma Molten rock below the earth's surface.

malnutrition Faulty nutrition. Caused by a diet that does not supply an individual with enough proteins, essential fats, vitamins, minerals, and other nutrients needed for good health. Compare *overnutrition, undernutrition*.

mantle Zone of the earth's interior between its core and its crust. Compare *core, crust*. See *lithosphere*.

manufactured capital Manufactured items made from Earth capital and used to produce and distribute economic goods and services bought by consumers. These include tools, machinery, equipment, factory buildings, and transportation and distribution facilities. Compare *Earth capital, human capital*.

manure See *animal manure, green manure*.

market equilibrium State in which sellers and buyers of an economic good agree on the quantity to be produced and the price to be paid.

mass The amount of material in an object.

mass extinction A catastrophic, widespread—often global—event in which major groups of species are wiped out over a relatively short time compared to normal (background) extinctions.

mass number Sum of the number of neutrons and the number of protons in the nucleus of an atom. It gives the approximate mass of that atom. Compare *atomic number*.

mass transit Buses, trains, trolleys, and other forms of transportation that carry large numbers of people.

matter Anything that has mass (the amount of material in an object) and takes up space. On Earth, where gravity is present, we weigh an object to determine its mass.

matter quality Measure of how useful a matter resource is based on its availability and concentration. See *high-quality matter, low-quality matter*.

matter-recycling society Society that emphasizes recycling the maximum amount of all resources that can be recycled. The goal is to allow economic growth to continue without depleting matter resources and without producing excessive pollution and environmental degradation. Compare *sustainable-Earth society, throwaway society*.

mature community Fairly stable, self-sustaining community in an advanced stage of ecological succession; usually has a diverse array of species and ecological niches; captures and uses energy and cycles critical chemicals more efficiently than simpler, immature communities. Compare *immature community* .

maximum sustainable yield See *sustainable yield*.

MDC See *more developed country*.

median lethal dose (LD$_{50}$) Amount of a toxic material per unit of body weight of test animals that kills half the test population in a certain time. Compare *lethal dose*.

meltdown The melting of the core of a nuclear reactor.

mesotrophic lake Lake with a moderate supply of plant nutrients. Compare *eutrophic lake, oligotrophic lake*.

metabolic reserve Lower half of rangeland grass plants; can grow back as long as it is not consumed by herbivores.

metamorphic rock Rock produced when a pre-existing rock is subjected to high temperatures (which may cause it to melt partially), high pressures, chemically active fluids, or a combination of these agents. Compare *igneous rock, sedimentary rock*. See *rock cycle*.

metastasis Spread of malignant (cancerous) cells from a cancer to other parts of the body.

mineral Any naturally occurring inorganic substance found in the earth's crust as a crystalline solid. See *mineral resource*.

mineral resource Concentration of naturally occurring solid, liquid, or gaseous material, in or on the earth's crust, in such form and amount that its extraction and conversion into useful materials or items is currently or potentially profitable. Mineral resources are classified as metallic (such as iron and tin ores) or nonmetallic (such as fossil fuels, sand, and salt).

minimum-tillage farming See *conservation-tillage farming*.

mixed economic system Economic system that falls somewhere between pure market and pure command economic systems. Virtually all of the world's economic systems are in this category, with some closer to a pure market system and some closer to a pure command system. Compare *pure command economic system, pure market economic system*.

mixture Combination of one or more elements and compounds.

model See *scientific model*.

molecule Combination of two or more atoms of the same chemical element (such as O$_2$) or different chemical elements (such as H$_2$O) held together by chemical bonds.

monera See *bacteria, cyanobacteria*

monoculture Cultivation of a single crop, usually on a large area of land. Compare *polyculture*.

more developed country (MDC) Country that is highly industrialized and has a high GNP per capita. Compare *less developed country*.

multiple use Principle of managing public land, such as a national forest, so it is used for a variety of purposes, such as timbering, mining, recreation, grazing, wildlife preservation, and soil and water conservation. See *sustainable yield*.

municipal solid waste Solid materials discarded by homes and businesses in or near urban areas. See *solid waste*.

mutagen Chemical, or form of ionizing radiation, that causes heritable changes in the DNA molecules in the genes found in chromosomes (mutations). See *carcinogen, mutation, teratogen*.

mutation A random change in DNA molecules making up genes that can yield changes in anatomy, physiology, or behavior in offspring. See *mutagen*.

mutualism Type of species interaction in which both participating species generally benefit. Compare *commensalism*.

native species Species that normally live and thrive in a particular ecosystem. Compare *immigrant species, indicator species, keystone species*.

natural gas Underground deposits of gases consisting of 50–90% by weight methane gas (CH$_4$) and small amounts of heavier gaseous hydrocarbon compounds such as propane (C$_3$H$_8$) and butane (C$_4$H$_{10}$).

natural hazard Event that destroys or damages wildlife habitats, kills or harms humans and damages property. Examples include earthquakes, volcanoes, floods, and mass wasting.

natural radioactive decay Nuclear change in which unstable nuclei of atoms spontaneously shoot out particles (usually alpha or beta particles), energy (gamma rays), or both at a fixed rate.

natural recharge Natural replenishment of an aquifer by precipitation, which percolates downward through soil and rock. See *recharge area*.

natural resource capital See *Earth capital*.

natural resources Area of the earth's solid surface, nutrients and minerals in the soil and deeper layers of the earth's crust, water, wild and domesticated plants and animals, air, and other resources produced by the earth's natural processes. Compare *human capital, manufactured capital*. See *Earth capital*.

natural selection Process by which a particular beneficial gene or set of beneficial genes is reproduced more than others in a population through adaptation and differential reproduction. It is the major mechanism leading to biological evolution. See *adaptation, biological evolution, differential reproduction, mutation*.

nematocide Chemical that kills nematodes (roundworms).

net economic welfare (NEW) Measure of annual change in quality of life in a country. It is obtained by subtracting the value of all final products and services that decrease the quality of life from a country's GNP. See *NEW per capita*.

net energy See *net useful energy*.

net primary productivity Rate at which all the plants in an ecosystem produce net useful chemical energy; equal to the difference between the rate at which the plants in an ecosystem produce useful chemical energy (primary productivity) and the rate at which they use some of that energy through cellular respiration. Compare *primary productivity*.

net useful energy Total amount of useful energy available from an energy resource or energy system over its lifetime minus the amount of energy used (the first energy law), automatically wasted (the second energy law), and unnecessarily wasted in finding, processing, concentrating, and transporting it to users.

neutral solution Water solution containing an equal number of hydrogen ions (H$^+$) and hydroxide ions (OH$^-$); water solution with a pH of 7. Compare *acid solution, basic solution*.

neutron (n) Elementary particle in the nuclei of all atoms (except hydrogen-1). It has a relative mass of 1 and no electric charge.

NEW See *net economic welfare*.

NEW per capita Annual net economic welfare (NEW) of a country divided by its total population. See *net economic welfare, real NEW per capita*.

niche See *ecological niche*.

nitrogen cycle Cyclic movement of nitrogen in different chemical forms from the environment to organisms, and then back to the environment.

nitrogen fixation Conversion of atmospheric nitrogen gas into forms useful to plants, by lightning, bacteria, and cyanobacteria; part of the nitrogen cycle.

noise pollution Any unwanted, disturbing, or harmful sound that impairs or interferes with hearing, causes stress, hampers concentration and work efficiency, or causes accidents.

nondegradable pollutant Material that is not broken down by natural processes. Examples include the toxic elements lead and mercury. Compare *biodegradable pollutant, degradable pollutant, slowly degradable pollutant*.

nonpersistent pollutant See *degradable pollutant*.

nonpoint source Large or dispersed land areas such as crop fields, streets, and lawns that discharge pollutants into the environment over a large area. Compare *point source*.

nonrenewable resource Resource that exists in a fixed amount (stock) in various places in the earth's crust and has the potential for renewal only by geological, physical, and chemical processes taking place over hundreds of millions to billions of years. Examples include copper, aluminum, coal, and oil. We classify these resources as exhaustible because we are extracting and using them at a much faster rate than the geological time scale on which they were formed. Compare *potentially renewable resource*.

nontransmissible disease A disease that is not caused by living organisms and that does not spread from one person to another. Examples are most cancer, diabetes, cardiovascular disease, and malnutrition. Compare *transmissible disease*.

no-till farming See *conservation-tillage farming*.

nuclear energy Energy released when atomic nuclei undergo a nuclear reaction such as the spontaneous emission of radioactivity, nuclear fission, or nuclear fusion.

nuclear fission Nuclear change in which the nuclei of certain isotopes with large mass numbers (such as uranium-235 and plutonium-239) are split apart into lighter nuclei when struck by a neutron. This process releases more neutrons and a large amount of energy. Compare *nuclear fusion*.

nuclear fusion Nuclear change in which two nuclei of isotopes of elements with a low mass number (such as hydrogen-2 and hydrogen-3) are forced together at extremely high temperatures until they fuse to form a heavier nucleus (such as helium-4). This process releases a large amount of energy. Compare *nuclear fission*.

nucleus Extremely tiny center of an atom, making up most of the atom's mass. It contains one or more positively charged protons and one or more neutrons with no electrical charge (except for a hydrogen-1 atom, which has one proton and no neutrons in its nucleus).

nutrient Any food or element an organism must take in to live, grow, or reproduce.

nutrient cycle See *biogeochemical cycle*.

oil See *crude oil*.

oil shale Fine-grained rock containing varying amounts of kerogen, a solid, waxy mixture of hydrocarbon compounds. Heating the rock to high temperatures converts the kerogen into a vapor that can be condensed to form a slow-flowing heavy oil called shale oil. See *kerogen, shale oil*.

old-growth forest Virgin and old, second-growth forests containing trees that are often hundreds, sometimes thousands, of years old. Examples include forests of Douglas fir, western hemlock, giant sequoia, and coastal redwoods in the western United States. Compare *second-growth forest, tree farm*.

oligotrophic lake Lake with a low supply of plant nutrients. Compare *eutrophic lake, mesotrophic lake*.

omnivore Animal organism that can use both plants and other animals as food sources. Examples include pigs, rats, cockroaches, and people. Compare *carnivore, herbivore*.

open sea The part of an ocean that is beyond the continental shelf. Compare *coastal zone*.

optimum yield Amount of fish (or other potentially renewable resource) that can be economically harvested on a sustainable basis; usually less than the sustainable yield. See *sustainable yield*.

ore Part of a metal-yielding material that can be economically and legally extracted at a given time. An ore typically contains two parts: the ore mineral, which contains the desired metal, and waste mineral material (gangue).

organic farming Producing crops and livestock naturally by using organic fertilizer (manure, legumes, compost) and natural pest control (bugs that eat harmful bugs, plants that repel bugs, and environmental controls such as crop rotation) instead of using commercial inorganic fertilizers and synthetic pesticides and herbicides.

organic fertilizer Organic material such as animal manure, green manure, and compost, applied to cropland as a source of plant nutrients. Compare *commercial inorganic fertilizer*.

organism Any form of life.

other resources Identified and unidentified resources not classified as reserves.

output pollution control See *pollution cleanup*.

overburden Layer of soil and rock overlying a mineral deposit; removed during surface mining.

overconsumption Situation where some people consume much more than they need at the expense of those who cannot meet their basic needs and at the expense of Earth's present and future life-support systems.

overfishing Harvesting so many fish of a species, especially immature fish, that there is not enough breeding stock left to replenish the species; so it is not profitable to harvest them.

overgrazing Destruction of vegetation when too many grazing animals feed too long and exceed the carrying capacity of a rangeland area.

overnutrition Diet so high in calories, saturated (animal) fats, salt, sugar, and processed foods, and so low in vegetables and fruits that the consumer runs high risks of diabetes, hypertension, heart disease, and other health hazards. Compare *malnutrition, undernutrition*.

overpopulation State in which there are more people than can live on Earth or in a geographic region in comfort, happiness, and health and still leave the planet or region a fit place for future generations. It is a result of growing numbers of people, growing affluence (resource consumption), or both. See *carrying capacity, consumption overpopulation, dieback, overshoot, people overpopulation*.

overshoot Condition in which population size of a species temporarily exceed the carrying capacity of its habitat. This leads to a sharp reduction in its population. See *carrying capacity, consumption overpopulation, dieback, people overpopulation*.

oxygen cycle Cyclic movement of oxygen in different chemical forms from the environment to organisms, and then back to the environment.

oxygen-demanding wastes Organic materials that are usually biodegraded by aerobic (oxygen-consuming) bacteria, if there is enough dissolved oxygen in the water. See *biological oxygen demand*.

ozone layer Layer of gaseous ozone (O_3) in the stratosphere that protects life on Earth by filtering out harmful ultraviolet radiation from the sun.

PANs Peroxyacyl nitrates—a group of chemicals found in photochemical smog.

parasite Consumer organism that lives on or in and feeds on a living plant or animal, known as the host, over an extended period of time. The parasite draws nourishment from and gradually weakens its host, which may or may not kill the host.

particulate matter Solid particles or liquid droplets suspended or carried in the air.

parts per billion (ppb) Number of parts of a chemical found in one billion parts of a particular gas, liquid, or solid.

parts per million (ppm) Number of parts of a chemical found in one million parts of a particular gas, liquid, or solid.

passive solar heating system System that captures sunlight directly within a structure and converts it into low-temperature heat for heating space or water for domestic use without the use of mechanical devices. Compare *active solar heating system*.

pathogen Organism that produces disease.

PCBs See *polychlorinated biphenyls*.

people overpopulation Situation in which there are more people in the world or a geographic region than available supplies of food, water, and other vital resources can support. It can also occur where the rate of population growth so exceeds the rate of economic growth, or the distribution of wealth is so inequitable, that a number of people are too poor to grow or buy enough food, fuel, and other important resources. Compare *consumption overpopulation*.

per capita GNP See *GNP per capita*.

per capita NEW See *NEW per capita*.

per capita real NEW See *real NEW per capita*.

permafrost Permanently frozen underground layers of soil in tundra.

permeability The degree to which underground rock and soil pores are interconnected with each other and thus a measure of the degree to which water can flow freely from one pore to another. Compare *porosity*.

persistent pollutant See *slowly degradable pollutant*.

pest Unwanted organism that directly or indirectly interferes with human activities.

pesticide Any chemical designed to kill or inhibit the growth of an organism that people consider to be undesirable. See *fungicide, herbicide, insecticide*.

pesticide treadmill Situation in which the cost of using pesticides increases while their effectiveness decreases, mostly because the pest species develop genetic resistance to the pesticides.

petrochemicals Chemicals obtained by refining (distilling) crude oil and used as raw materials in the manufacture of most industrial chemicals, fertilizers, pesticides, plastics, synthetic fibers, paints, medicines, and many other products.

petroleum See *crude oil*.

pH Numeric value that indicates the relative acidity or alkalinity of a substance on a scale of 0 to 14, with the neutral point at 7. Acid solutions have pH values lower than 7, and basic or alkaline solutions have pH values greater than 7.

phosphorus cycle Cyclic movement of phosphorus in different chemical forms from the environment to organisms, and then back to the environment.

photochemical smog Complex mixture of air pollutants produced in the lower atmosphere by the reaction of hydrocarbons and nitrogen oxides under the influence of sunlight. Especially harmful components include ozone, peroxyacyl nitrates (PANs), and various aldehydes. Compare *industrial smog*.

photosynthesis Complex process that takes place in cells of green plants. Radiant energy from the sun is used to combine carbon dioxide (CO_2) and water (H_2O) to produce oxygen (O_2) and carbohydrates (such as glucose, $C_6H_{12}O_6$), and other nutrient molecules. Compare *aerobic respiration, chemosynthesis*.

photovoltaic cell (solar cell) Device in which radiant (solar) energy is converted directly into electrical energy.

physical change Process that alters one or more physical properties of an element or a compound without altering its chemical composition. Examples include changing the size and shape of a sample of matter (crushing ice and cutting aluminum foil) and changing a sample of matter from one physical state to another (boiling and freezing water). Compare *chemical change*.

phytoplankton Small, drifting plants, mostly algae and bacteria, found in aquatic ecosystems. Compare *plankton, zooplankton*.

pioneer community First integrated set of plants, animals, and decomposers found in an area undergoing primary ecological succession. See *immature community, mature community*.

pioneer species First hardy species, often microbes, mosses, and lichens, that begin colonizing a site as the first stage of ecological succession. See *ecological succession, pioneer community*.

planetary management worldview Belief that Earth is a place of unlimited resources that we can manage for our use. Any type of resource conservation that hampers short-term economic growth is unnecessary because if we pollute or deplete resources in one area, we will find substitutes; control the pollution through technology; and (if necessary) get resources from the moon and asteroids in the "new frontier" of space. See *spaceship-Earth worldview*. Compare *sustainable-Earth worldview*.

plankton Small plant organisms (phytoplankton) and animal organisms (zooplankton) that float in aquatic ecosystems.

plantation agriculture Growing specialized crops such as bananas, coffee, and cacao in tropical LDCs, primarily for sale to MDCs.

plants (plantae) Eukaryotic, mostly multicelled organisms such as algae (red, blue, and green), mosses, ferns, flowers, cacti, grasses, beans, wheat, rice, and trees. These organisms use photosynthesis to produce organic nutrients for themselves and for other organisms feeding on them. Water and other inorganic nutrients are obtained from the soil for terrestrial plants and from the water for aquatic plants.

poaching Illegal commercial hunting or fishing.

point source A single identifiable source that discharges pollutants into the environment. Examples are the smokestack of a power plant or an industrial plant, the drainpipe of a meat-packing plant, the chimney of a house, or the exhaust pipe of an automobile. Compare *nonpoint source*.

politics Process through which individuals and groups try to influence or control the policies and actions of governments that affect the local, state, national, and international communities.

pollution An undesirable change in the physical, chemical, or biological characteristics of air, water, soil, or food that can adversely affect the health, survival, or activities of humans or other living organisms.

pollution cleanup Device or process that removes or reduces the level of a pollutant after it has been produced or has entered the environment. Examples include automobile emission-control devices and sewage treatment plants. Compare *pollution prevention*.

pollution prevention Device or process that prevents a potential pollutant from forming or from entering the environment or that sharply reduces the amounts entering the environment. Compare *pollution cleanup*.

polychlorinated biphenyls (PCBs) Group of 209 different toxic, oily, synthetic chlorinated hydrocarbon compounds that can be biologically amplified in food chains and webs.

polyculture Complex form of intercropping in which a large number of different plants maturing at different times are planted together. See *intercropping*. Compare *monoculture, polyvarietal cultivation*.

polyvarietal cultivation Planting a plot of land with several varieties of the same crop. Compare *intercropping, monoculture, polyculture*.

population Group of individual organisms of the same species living within a particular area.

population crash Large number of deaths over a fairly short time, brought about when the number of individuals in a population is too large to be supported by available environmental resources.

population density Number of organisms in a particular population found in a specified area.

population dispersion General pattern in which the members of a population are arranged throughout its habitat.

population distribution Variation of population density over a particular geographical area. For example, a country has a high population density in its urban areas and a much lower population density in rural areas.

population dynamics Major abiotic and biotic factors that tend to increase or decrease the population size and the age and sex composition of species.

population size Number of individuals making up a population's gene pool.

porosity The pores (cracks and spaces) in rocks or soil, or the percentage of the rock's or soil's volume not occupied by the rock or soil itself. Compare *permeability*.

potential energy Energy stored in an object because of its position or the position of its parts. Compare *kinetic energy*.

potentially renewable resource Resource that theoretically can last indefinitely without reducing the available supply because it is replaced more rapidly through natural processes than are nonrenewable resources or because it is essentially inexhaustible (solar energy). Examples include trees in forests, grasses in grasslands, wild animals, fresh surface water in lakes and streams, most groundwater, fresh air, and fertile soil. If such a resource is used faster than it is replenished, it can be depleted and converted into a nonrenewable resource. Compare *nonrenewable resource*. See *environmental degradation*.

poverty Inability to meet basic needs for food, clothing, and shelter.

ppb See *parts per billion*.

ppm See *parts per million*.

precipitation Water in the form of rain, sleet, hail, and snow that falls from the atmosphere onto the land and bodies of water.

predation Situation in which an organism of one species (the predator) captures and feeds on parts or all of an organism of another species (the prey).

predator Organism that captures and feeds on parts or all of an organism of another species (the prey).

predator–prey relationship Interaction between two organisms of different species in which one organism (the predator) captures and feeds on parts or all of another organism (the prey).

prey Organism that is captured and serves as a source of food for an organism of another species (the predator).

primary consumer Organism that feeds directly on all or part of plants (*herbivore*) or other producers. Compare *detritivore, omnivore, secondary consumer*.

primary pollutant Chemical that has been added directly to the air by natural events or human activities and occurs in a harmful concentration. Compare *secondary pollutant*.

primary productivity See *gross primary productivity*. Compare *net primary productivity*.

primary sewage treatment Mechanical treatment of sewage in which large solids are filtered out by screens and suspended solids settle out as sludge in a sedimentation tank. Compare *advanced sewage treatment, secondary sewage treatment*.

primary succession Sequential development of communities in a bare area that has never been occupied by a community of organisms. Compare *secondary succession*.

prime reproductive age Years between ages 20 and 29, during which most women have most of their children. Compare *reproductive age*.

principle of connectedness Everything is connected to and intermingled with everything else; we are all in it together.

principle of multiple use See *multiple use*.

private-property resource Resource owned by an individual or a group of individuals other than the government. Compare *common-property resource, public-property resource*.

probability A mathematical statement about how likely it is that something will happen.

producer Organism that uses solar energy (green plant) or chemical energy (some bacteria) to manufacture the organic compounds it needs as nutrients from simple inorganic compounds obtained from its environment. Compare *consumer, decomposer*.

prokaryotic cell Cell that doesn't have a distinct nucleus. Other internal parts are also not enclosed by membranes. Compare *eukaryotic cell*.

protists (protista) Eukaryotic, mostly single-celled organisms such as diatoms, amoebas, some algae (golden brown and yellow-green), protozoans, and slime molds. Some protists produce their own organic nutrients through photosynthesis. Others are decomposers, and some feed on bacteria, other protists, or cells of multicellular organisms.

proton (p) Positively charged particle in the nuclei of all atoms. Each proton has a relative mass of 1 and a single positive charge.

public-property resource Land that is owned jointly by all citizens, but is managed for them by an agency of the local, state, or federal government. Examples include state and national parks, forests, wildlife refuges, and wilderness areas. Compare *common-property resource, private-property resource*.

pure capitalism See *pure market economic system*.

pure command economic system System in which all economic decisions are made by the government or some other central authority. Compare *mixed economic system, pure market economic system*.

pure market economic system System in which all economic decisions are made in the market, where buyers and sellers of economic goods freely interact, with no government or other interference. Compare *mixed economic system, pure command economic system*.

pyramid of energy flow Diagram representing the flow of energy through each trophic level in a food chain or food web. With each energy transfer, only a small part (typically 10%) of the usable energy entering one trophic level is transferred to the organisms at the next trophic level.

radiation Fast-moving particles (particulate radiation) or waves of energy (electromagnetic radiation).

radioactive decay Change of a radioisotope to a different isotope by the emission of radioactivity.

radioactive isotope See *radioisotope*.

radioactive waste Radioactive waste products of nuclear power plants, research, medicine, weapons production, or other processes involving nuclear reactions. See *radioactivity*.

radioactivity Nuclear change in which unstable nuclei of atoms spontaneously shoot out "chunks" of mass, energy, or both, at a fixed rate. The three principal types of radioactivity are gamma rays and fast-moving alpha particles and beta particles.

radioisotope   Isotope of an atom that spontaneously emits one or more types of radioactivity (alpha particles, beta particles, gamma rays).

rangeland   Land that supplies forage or vegetation (grasses, grasslike plants, and shrubs) for grazing and browsing animals and that is not intensively managed. Compare *feedlot*.

range of tolerance   Range of chemical and physical conditions that must be maintained for populations of a particular species to stay alive and grow, develop, and function normally. See *law of tolerance*.

real GNP   Gross national product adjusted for inflation. Compare *GNP per capita, gross national product, real GNP per capita*.

real GNP per capita   Per capita GNP adjusted for inflation. See *GNP per capita*.

realized niche   Parts of the fundamental niche of a species that are actually used by that species. See *ecological niche, fundamental niche*.

real NEW per capita   Per capita NEW adjusted for inflation. See *net economic welfare, NEW per capita*.

recharge area   Any area of land allowing water to pass through it and into an aquifer. See *aquifer, natural recharge*.

recycling   Collecting and reprocessing a resource so it can be made into new products. An example is collecting aluminum cans, melting them down, and using the aluminum to make new cans or other aluminum products. Compare *reuse*.

reforestation   Renewal of trees and other types of vegetation on land where trees have been removed; can be done naturally by seeds from nearby trees or artificially by planting seeds or seedlings.

renewable resource   See *potentially renewable resource*.

replacement-level fertility   Number of children a couple must have to replace themselves. The average for a country or the world is usually slightly higher than 2 children per couple (2.1 in the United States and 2.5 in some LDCs) because some children die before reaching their reproductive years. See *total fertility rate*.

reproduction   Production of offspring by one or more parents.

reproductive age   Ages 15 to 44, when most women have all their children. Compare *prime reproductive age*.

reproductive isolation   Long-term geographic separation of members of a particular sexually reproducing species.

reserves   Resources that have been identified and from which a usable mineral can be extracted profitably at present prices with current mining technology. See *identified resources, undiscovered resources*.

resource   Anything obtained from the living and nonliving environment to meet human needs and wants. It can also be applied to other species.

resource partitioning   Process of dividing up resources in an ecosystem so species with similar requirements (overlapping ecological niches) use the same scarce resources at different times, in different ways, or in different places. See *ecological niche, fundamental niche, realized niche*.

resource recovery   Salvaging usable metals, paper, and glass from solid waste and selling them to manufacturing industries for recycling or reuse.

respiration   See *aerobic respiration*.

response   The amount of health damage caused by exposure to a certain dose of a harmful substance or form of radiation. See *dose, dose-response curve, lethal dose, median lethal dose*.

reuse   To use a product over and over again in the same form. An example is collecting, washing, and refilling glass beverage bottles. Compare *recycling*.

riparian zones   Thin strips and patches of vegetation that surround streams. They are very important habitats and resources for wildlife.

risk   The probability that something undesirable will happen from deliberate or accidental exposure to a hazard. See *risk assessment, risk-benefit analysis, risk management*.

risk analysis   Identifying hazards, evaluating the nature and severity of risks (*risk assessment*), using this and other information to determine options and make decisions about reducing or eliminating risks (*risk management*), and communicating information about risks to decision makers and the public (*risk communication*).

risk assessment   Process of gathering data and making assumptions to estimate short- and long-term harmful effects on human health or the environment from exposure to hazards associated with the use of a particular product or technology. See *risk, risk-benefit analysis*.

risk-benefit analysis   Estimate of the short- and long-term risks and benefits of using a particular product or technology. See *desirability quotient, risk*.

risk communication   Communicating information about risks to decision makers and the public. See *risk, risk analysis, risk-benefit analysis*.

risk management   Using risk assessment and other information to determine options and make decisions about reducing or eliminating risks. See *risk, risk analysis, risk-benefit analysis, risk communication*.

rock   Any material that makes up a large, natural, continuous part of Earth's crust. See *mineral*.

rock cycle   Largest and slowest of the earth's cycles, consisting of geologic, physical, and chemical processes that form and modify rocks and soil in the earth's crust over millions of years.

rodenticide   Chemical that kills rodents.

rule of 70   Doubling time = 70/percentage growth rate. See *doubling time, exponential growth*.

runoff   Fresh water from precipitation and melting ice that flows on the earth's surface into nearby streams, lakes, wetlands, and reservoirs. See *surface runoff, surface water*. Compare *groundwater*.

rural area   Geographical area in the United States with a population of less than 2,500 people per unit of area. The number of people used in this definition may vary in different countries. Compare *urban area*.

salinity   Amount of various salts dissolved in a given volume of water.

salinization   Accumulation of salts in soil that can eventually make the soil unable to support plant growth.

saltwater intrusion   Movement of salt water into freshwater aquifers in coastal and inland areas as groundwater is withdrawn faster than it is recharged by precipitation.

sanitary landfill   Waste disposal site on land in which waste is spread in thin layers, compacted, and covered with a fresh layer of clay or plastic foam each day.

scavenger   Organism that feeds on dead organisms that either were killed by other organisms or

died naturally. Examples include vultures, flies, and crows. Compare *detritivore*.

science   Attempts to discover order in nature and then use that knowledge to make predictions about what will happen in nature. See *scientific data, scientific hypothesis, scientific law, scientific methods, scientific model, scientific theory*.

scientific data   Facts obtained by making observations and measurements. Compare *scientific hypothesis, scientific law, scientific model, scientific theory*.

scientific hypothesis   An educated guess that attempts to explain a scientific law or certain scientific observations. Compare *scientific data, scientific law, scientific model, scientific theory*.

scientific law   Summary of what scientists find happening in nature over and over in the same way. See *first law of thermodynamics, second law of thermodynamics, law of conservation of matter*. Compare *scientific data, scientific hypothesis, scientific model, scientific theory*.

scientific methods   The ways scientists gather data and formulate and test scientific laws and theories. See *scientific data, scientific hypothesis, scientific law, scientific model, scientific theory*.

scientific model   A simulation of complex processes and systems. Many are mathematical models that are run and tested using computers.

scientific theory   A well-tested and widely accepted scientific hypothesis. Compare *scientific data, scientific hypothesis, scientific model, scientific law*.

secondary consumer   Organism that feeds only on primary consumers. Most secondary consumers are animals, but some are plants. Compare *detritivore, omnivore, primary consumer*.

secondary pollutant   Harmful chemical formed in the atmosphere when a primary air pollutant reacts with normal air components or with other air pollutants. Compare *primary pollutant*.

secondary sewage treatment   Second step in most waste treatment systems, in which aerobic bacteria break down up to 90% of degradable, oxygen-demanding organic wastes in wastewater; usually done by bringing sewage and bacteria together in trickling filters or in the activated sludge process. Compare *advanced sewage treatment, primary sewage treatment*.

secondary succession   Sequential development of communities in an area in which natural vegetation has been removed or destroyed but the soil is not destroyed. Compare *primary succession*.

second-growth forest   Stands of trees resulting from secondary ecological succession. Compare *ancient forest, old-growth forest, tree farm*.

second law of energy   See *second law of thermodynamics*.

second law of thermodynamics   In any conversion of heat energy to useful work, some of the initial energy input is always degraded to a lower-quality, more dispersed, less useful energy—usually low-temperature heat that flows into the environment; you can't break even in terms of energy quality. See *first law of thermodynamics*.

sedimentary rock   Rock that forms from the accumulated products of erosion and in some cases from the compacted shells, skeletons, and other remains of dead organisms. Compare *igneous rock, metamorphic rock*. See *rock cycle*.

seed-tree cutting   Removal of nearly all trees on a site in one cutting, with a few seed-producing trees left uniformly distributed to regenerate the forest. Compare *clear-cutting, selective cutting, shelterwood cutting, strip logging*.

selective cutting Cutting of intermediate-aged, mature, or diseased trees in an uneven-aged forest stand, either singly or in small groups. This encourages the growth of younger trees and maintains an uneven-aged stand. Compare *clear-cutting, seed-tree cutting, shelterwood cutting, strip logging.*

septic tank Underground tank for treatment of wastewater from a home in rural and suburban areas. Bacteria in the tank decompose organic wastes, and the sludge settles to the bottom of the tank. The effluent flows out of the tank into the ground through a field of drain pipes.

sewage sludge Gooey mixture of toxic chemicals, infectious agents, and settled solids removed from wastewater at sewage treatment plants.

shale oil Slow-flowing, dark brown, heavy oil obtained when kerogen in oil shale is vaporized at high temperatures and then condensed. Shale oil can be refined to yield gasoline, heating oil, and other petroleum products. See *kerogen, oil shale.*

shelterbelt See *windbreak.*

shelterwood cutting Removal of mature, marketable trees in an area in a series of partial cuttings to allow regeneration of a new stand under the partial shade of older trees, which are later removed. Typically, this is done by making two or three cuts over a decade. Compare *clear-cutting, seed-tree cutting, selective cutting, strip logging.*

shifting cultivation Clearing a plot of ground in a forest, especially in tropical areas, and planting crops on it for a few years (typically two to five years) until the soil is depleted of nutrients or until the plot has been invaded by a dense growth of vegetation from the surrounding forest. Then a new plot is cleared and the process is repeated. The abandoned plot cannot sustain crop growth for 10–30 years. See *slash-and-burn cultivation.*

slash-and-burn cultivation Cutting down trees and other vegetation in a patch of forest, leaving the cut vegetation on the ground to dry, and then burning it. The ashes that are left add nutrients to the nutrient-poor soils found in most tropical forest areas. Crops are planted between tree stumps. Plots must be abandoned after a few years (typically two to five years) because of loss of soil fertility or invasion of vegetation from the surrounding forest. See *shifting cultivation.*

slowly degradable pollutant Material that is slowly broken down into simpler chemicals or reduced to acceptable levels by natural physical, chemical, and biological processes. Compare *biodegradable pollutant, degradable pollutant, nondegradable pollutant.*

sludge See *sewage sludge.*

smelting Process in which a desired metal is separated from the other elements in an ore mineral.

smog Originally a combination of smoke and fog, but now used to describe other mixtures of pollutants in the atmosphere. See *industrial smog, photochemical smog.*

soil Complex mixture of inorganic minerals (clay, silt, pebbles, and sand), decaying organic matter, water, air, and living organisms.

soil conservation Methods used to reduce soil erosion, to prevent depletion of soil nutrients, and to restore nutrients already lost by erosion, leaching, and excessive crop harvesting.

soil erosion Movement of soil components, especially topsoil, from one place to another, usually by exposure to wind, flowing water, or both. This natural process can be greatly accelerated by human activities that remove vegetation from soil.

soil horizons Horizontal zones that make up a particular mature soil. Each horizon has a distinct texture and composition that varies with different types of soils.

soil permeability Rate at which water and air move from upper to lower soil layers.

soil porosity See *porosity.*

soil profile Cross-sectional view of the horizons in a soil.

soil structure How the particles that make up a soil are organized and clumped together. See *soil permeability, soil texture.*

soil texture Relative amounts of the different types and sizes of mineral particles in a sample of soil.

soil water Underground water that partially fills pores between soil particles and rocks within the upper soil and rock layers of the earth's crust, above the water table. Compare *groundwater.*

solar capital Solar energy from the sun reaching Earth. Compare *Earth capital.*

solar cell See *photovoltaic cell.*

solar collector Device for collecting radiant energy from the sun and converting it into heat. See *active solar heating system, passive solar heating system.*

solar energy Direct radiant energy from the sun and a number of indirect forms of energy produced by the direct input. Principal indirect forms of solar energy include wind, falling and flowing water (hydropower), and biomass (solar energy converted into chemical energy stored in the chemical bonds of organic compounds in trees and other plants).

solar pond Fairly small body of fresh water or salt water from which stored solar energy can be extracted, because of the temperature difference between the hot surface layer exposed to the sun during daylight and the cooler layer beneath it.

solid waste Any unwanted or discarded material that is not a liquid or a gas. See *municipal solid waste.*

spaceship-Earth worldview Earth as a spaceship—a machine that we can understand, control, and change at will by using advanced technology. See *planetary management worldview.* Compare *sustainable-Earth worldview.*

specialist species Species with a narrow ecological niche. They may be able to live in only one type of habitat, tolerate only a narrow range of climatic and other environmental conditions, or use only one or a few types of food. Compare *generalist species.*

speciation Formation of two species from one species as a result of divergent natural selection in response to changes in environmental conditions; usually takes thousands of years. Compare *extinction.*

species Group of organisms that resemble one another in appearance, behavior, chemical makeup and processes, and genetic structure. Organisms that reproduce sexually are classified as members of the same species only if they can actually or potentially interbreed with one another and produce fertile offspring.

species diversity Number of different species and their relative abundances in a given area. See *biological diversity.* Compare *ecological diversity, genetic diversity.*

spoils Unwanted rock and other waste materials produced when a material is removed from the earth's surface or subsurface by mining, dredging, quarrying, or excavation.

S-shaped curve Leveling off of an exponential, J-shaped curve when a rapidly growing population exceeds the carrying capacity of its environment and ceases to grow in numbers. See *overshoot, population crash.*

stewardship View that because of our superior intellect and power or because of our religious beliefs we have an ethical responsibility to manage and care for domesticated plants and animals as well as for the rest of nature. Compare *planetary management worldview, sustainable-Earth worldview.*

stratosphere Second layer of the atmosphere, extending from about 17 to 48 kilometers (11 to 30 miles) above the earth's surface. It contains small amounts of gaseous ozone (O_3), which filters out about 99% of the incoming harmful ultraviolet (UV) radiation emitted by the sun. Compare *troposphere.*

stream Flowing body of surface water. Examples include creeks and rivers.

strip cropping Planting regular crops and close-growing plants, such as hay or nitrogen-fixing legumes, in alternating rows or bands to help reduce depletion of soil nutrients.

strip logging A variation of clear-cutting in which a strip of trees is clear-cut along the contour of the land, with the corridor narrow enough to allow natural regeneration within a few years. After regeneration another strip is cut above the first, and so on. Compare *clear-cutting, seed-tree cutting, selective cutting, shelterwood cutting.*

strip mining Form of surface mining in which bulldozers, power shovels, or stripping wheels remove large chunks of the earth's surface in strips. See *surface mining.* Compare *subsurface mining.*

subatomic particles Extremely small particles—electrons, protons, and neutrons—that make up the internal structure of atoms.

subsidence Slow or rapid sinking down of part of the earth's crust that is not slope related.

subsistence farming Supplementing solar energy with energy from human labor and draft animals to produce enough food to feed oneself and family members; in good years there may be enough food left over to sell or put aside for hard times. Compare *industrialized agriculture.*

subsurface mining Extraction of a metal ore or fuel resource such as coal from a deep underground deposit. Compare *surface mining.*

succession See *ecological succession.*

succulent plants Plants, such as desert cacti, that survive in dry climates by having no leaves, thus reducing the loss of scarce water. They store water and use sunlight to produce the food they need in the thick fleshy tissue of their green stems and branches. Compare *deciduous plants, evergreen plants.*

superinsulated house House that is heavily insulated and extremely airtight. Typically, active or passive solar collectors are used to heat water and an air-to-air heat exchanger is used to prevent buildup of excessive moisture and indoor air pollutants.

surface mining Removal of soil, subsoil, and other strata, and then extracting a mineral deposit found fairly close to the earth's surface. Compare *subsurface mining.*

surface runoff Water flowing off the land into bodies of surface water.

surface water Precipitation that does not infiltrate the ground or return to the atmosphere by evaporation or transpiration. See *runoff.* Compare *groundwater.*

sustainable agriculture See *sustainable-Earth agricultural system*.

sustainable development See *sustainable economic development*.

sustainable-Earth agricultural system Method of growing crops and raising livestock based on organic fertilizers, soil conservation, water conservation, biological control of pests, and minimal use of nonrenewable fossil-fuel energy.

sustainable-Earth economy Economic system in which the number of people and the quantity of goods are maintained at some constant level. This level is ecologically sustainable over time and meets at least the basic needs of all members of the population.

Sustainable-Earth Revolution Cultural change involving halting population growth and altering lifestyles, political and economic systems, and the way we treat the environment so that we can preserve the earth for ourselves and other species, and can help heal some of the wounds we have inflicted on the earth.

sustainable-Earth society Society based on working with nature by recycling and reusing discarded matter; by preventing pollution; by conserving matter and energy resources through reducing unnecessary waste and use; by not degrading renewable resources; by building things that are easy to recycle, reuse, and repair; by not allowing population size to exceed the carrying capacity of the environment; and by preserving biodiversity. See *sustainable-Earth worldview*. Compare *matter-recycling society, planetary management worldview, throwaway society*.

sustainable-Earth worldview Belief that Earth is a place with finite room and resources, so continuing population growth, production, and consumption inevitably put severe stress on natural processes that renew and maintain the resource base of air, water, and soil. To prevent environmental overload, environmental degradation, and resource depletion, people should work with nature by controlling population growth, reducing unnecessary use and waste of matter and energy resources, and not causing the premature extinction of any other species. Compare *spaceship-Earth worldview, planetary management worldview*.

sustainable economic development Forms of economic growth and activities that do not deplete or degrade natural resources upon which present and future economic growth and life depend.

sustainable living Taking no more potentially renewable resources from the natural world than can be replenished naturally, and not overloading the capacity of the environment to cleanse and renew itself by natural processes.

sustainable society A society that manages its economic development and population growth in ways that do no irreparable environmental harm. It satisfies the needs of its people without depleting Earth capital and thus jeopardizing the prospects of future generations of people or other species.

sustainable yield (sustained yield) Highest rate at which a potentially renewable resource can be used without reducing its available supply throughout the world or in a particular area. See *environmental degradation*.

symbiotic relationship Species interaction in which two kinds of organisms live together in an intimate association, with members of one or both species benefiting from the association. See *commensalism, mutualism*.

synfuels Synthetic gaseous and liquid fuels produced from solid coal or sources other than natural gas or crude oil.

synthetic natural gas (SNG) Gaseous fuel containing mostly methane produced from solid coal.

tailings Rock and other waste materials removed as impurities when waste mineral material is separated from the metal in an ore.

tar sand Deposit of a mixture of clay, sand, water, and varying amounts of a tarlike heavy oil known as bitumen. Bitumen can be extracted from tar sand by heating. It is then purified and upgraded to synthetic crude oil. See *bitumen*.

technology Creation of new products and processes that are supposed to improve our survival, comfort, and quality of life. Compare *science*.

temperature inversion See *thermal inversion*.

teratogen Chemical, ionizing agent, or virus that causes birth defects. See *carcinogen, mutagen*.

terracing Planting crops on a long, steep slope that has been converted into a series of broad, nearly level terraces with short vertical drops that run along the contour of the land to retain water and reduce soil erosion.

terrestrial Pertaining to land. Compare *aquatic*.

tertiary (higher-level) consumers Animals that feed on animal-eating animals. They feed at high trophic levels in food chains and webs. Examples include hawks, lions, bass, and sharks. Compare *detritivore, primary consumer, secondary consumer*.

tertiary sewage treatment See *advanced sewage treatment*.

theory of evolution Widely accepted idea that all life forms developed from earlier forms of life. Although this theory conflicts with the creation stories of most religions, it is the way biologists explain how life has changed over the past 3.6–3.8 billion years and why it is so diverse today.

thermal inversion Layer of dense, cool air trapped under a layer of less dense warm air. This prevents upward-flowing air currents from developing. In a prolonged inversion, air pollution in the trapped layer may build up to harmful levels.

threatened species Wild species that is still abundant in its natural range but is likely to become endangered because of a decline in numbers. Compare *endangered species*.

threshold effect The harmful or fatal effect of a small change in environmental conditions that exceeds the limit of tolerance of an organism or population of a species. See *law of tolerance*.

throwaway society The situation in most advanced industrialized countries, in which ever-increasing economic growth is sustained by maximizing the rate at which matter and energy resources are used, with little emphasis on pollution prevention, recycling, reuse, reduction of unnecessary waste, and other forms of resource conservation. Compare *matter-recycling society, sustainable-Earth society*.

total fertility rate (TFR) Estimate of the average number of children that will be born alive to a woman during her lifetime if she passes through all her childbearing years (ages 15–44) conforming to age-specific fertility rates of a given year. In simpler terms, it is an estimate of the average number of children a woman will have during her childbearing years.

totally planned economy See *pure command economic system*.

toxic chemical Chemical that is fatal to humans in low doses, or fatal to over 50% of test animals at stated concentrations. Most are neurotoxins, which attack nerve cells. See *carcinogen, hazardous chemical, mutagen, teratogen*.

toxic waste Form of hazardous waste that causes death or serious injury (such as burns, respiratory diseases, cancers, or genetic mutations). See *hazardous waste*.

traditional intensive agriculture Producing enough food for a farm family's survival and perhaps a surplus that can be sold. This type of agriculture requires higher inputs of labor, fertilizer, and water than traditional subsistence agriculture. See *traditional subsistence agriculture*.

traditional subsistence agriculture Production of enough crops or livestock for a farm family's survival and, in good years, a surplus to sell or put aside for hard times. Compare *traditional intensive agriculture*.

tragedy of the commons Depletion or degradation of a resource to which people have free and unmanaged access. An example is the depletion of commercially desirable species of fish in the open ocean beyond areas controlled by coastal countries. See *common-property resource*.

transmissible disease A disease that is caused by living organisms such as bacteria, viruses, and parasitic worms, and that is conveyed from one person to another through the air, or water, in food or body fluids, or in some cases by insects or other organisms. Compare *nontransmissible disease*.

transpiration Process in which water is absorbed by the root systems of plants, moves up through the plants, passes through pores (stomata) in their leaves or other parts, and then evaporates into the atmosphere as water vapor.

tree farm Site planted with one or only a few tree species in an even-aged stand. When the stand matures, it is usually harvested by clear-cutting and then replanted. Normally used to grow rapidly growing tree species for fuelwood, timber, or pulpwood. See *even-aged management*. Compare *old-growth forest, second-growth forest, uneven-aged management, uneven-aged stand*.

tritium (T, hydrogen-3) Isotope of hydrogen with a nucleus containing one proton and two neutrons, thus having a mass number of 3. Compare *deuterium*.

trophic level All organisms that are the same number of energy transfers away from the original source of energy (for example, sunlight) that enters an ecosystem. For example, all producers belong to the first trophic level, and all herbivores belong to the second trophic level in a food chain or a food web.

troposphere Innermost layer of the atmosphere. It contains about 75% of the mass of Earth's air and extends about 17 kilometers (11 miles) above sea level. Compare *stratosphere*.

true cost See *full cost*.

unconfined aquifer Collection of groundwater above a layer of Earth material (usually rock or clay) through which water flows very slowly (low permeability). Compare *confined aquifer*.

undernutrition Consuming insufficient food to meet one's minimum daily energy requirement, for a long enough time to cause harmful effects. Compare *malnutrition, overnutrition*.

undiscovered resources Potential supplies of a particular mineral resource, believed to exist because of geologic knowledge and theory, though specific locations, quality, and amounts are unknown. Compare *identified resources, reserves*.

uneven-aged management Method of forest management in which trees of different species in a given stand are maintained at many ages and sizes to permit continuous natural regeneration. Compare *even-aged management*.

uneven-aged stand Stand of trees in which there are considerable differences in the ages of individual trees. Usually, such stands have a variety of tree species. See *uneven-aged management*. Compare *even-aged stand, tree farm*.

upwelling Movement of nutrient-rich bottom water to the ocean's surface. This can occur far from shore but usually occurs along certain steep coastal areas where the surface layer of ocean water is pushed away from shore and replaced by cold, nutrient-rich bottom water.

urban area Geographic area with a population of 2,500 or more people. The number of people used in this definition may vary, with some countries setting the minimum number of people anywhere from 10,000 to 50,000.

urban growth Rate of growth of an urban population. Compare *degree of urbanization*.

urban heat island Buildup of heat in the atmosphere above an urban area. This heat is produced by the large concentration of cars, buildings, factories, and other heat-producing activities. See *dust dome*.

urbanization See *degree of urbanization*.

vertebrates Animals with backbones. Compare *invertebrates*.

water consumption Water that is not returned to the surface water or groundwater from which it came, mostly because of evaporation and transpiration. As a result, this water is not available for use again in the area from which it came. See *water withdrawal*.

water cycle See *hydrologic cycle*.

waterlogging Saturation of soil with irrigation water or excessive precipitation, so that the water table rises close to the surface.

water pollution Any physical or chemical change in surface water or groundwater that can harm living organisms or make water unfit for certain uses.

watershed Land area that delivers the water, sediment, and dissolved substances via small streams to a major stream (river).

water table Upper surface of the zone of saturation, in which all available pores in the soil and rock in the earth's crust are filled with water.

water withdrawal Removing water from a groundwater or surface water source and transporting it to a place of use. Compare *water consumption*.

watt Unit of power, or rate at which electrical work is done. See *kilowatt*.

weather Short-term changes in the temperature, barometric pressure, humidity, precipitation, sunshine (solar radiation), cloud cover, wind direction and speed, and other conditions in the troposphere at a given place and time. Compare *climate*.

weathering Physical and chemical processes in which solid rock exposed on the earth's surface is changed to separate solid particles and dissolved material, which can then be moved to another place as sediment. See *erosion*.

wetland Land that is covered all or part of the year with salt water or fresh water, excluding streams, lakes, and the open ocean. See *coastal wetland, inland wetland*.

wilderness Area where the earth and its community of life have not been seriously disturbed by humans and where humans are only temporary visitors.

wildlife All free, undomesticated species.

wildlife management Manipulation of populations of wild species (especially game species) and their habitats for human benefit, the welfare of other species, and the preservation of threatened and endangered wildlife species.

wildlife resources Species of wildlife that have actual or potential economic value to people.

windbreak Row of trees or hedges planted to partially block wind flow and reduce soil erosion on cultivated land.

wind farm Cluster of small to medium-sized wind turbines in a windy area to capture wind energy and convert it into electrical energy.

work What happens when a force is used to move a sample of matter over some distance or to raise its temperature. Energy is defined as the capacity to do such work.

worldview How individuals think the world works and what they think their role in the world should be. See *planetary management worldview, spaceship-Earth worldview, sustainable-Earth worldview*.

zero population growth (ZPG) State in which the birth rate (plus immigration) equals the death rate (plus emigration), so the population of a geographical area is no longer increasing.

zone of saturation Area where all available pores in soil and rock in the earth's crust are filled by water. See *water table*.

zoning Regulating how various parcels of land can be used.

zooplankton Animal plankton. Small floating herbivores that feed on plant plankton (phytoplankton). Compare *phytoplankton*.

Index

351

353